FIFTH EDITION

The Attorney-Client Privilege in Civil Litigation

Protecting and Defending Confidentiality

EDITORS
VINCENT S. WALKOWIAK
STEPHEN M. MCNABB
OSCAR REY RODRIGUEZ

TORT TRIAL & INSURANCE PRACTICE

AMERICAN BAR ASSOCIATION
Defending Liberty
Pursuing Justice

Cover design by Kelly Book/ABA Publishing.

Printed in the United States of America

15 14 13 12 11 5 4 3 2 1

Library of Congress Cataloging-in-Publication Data

The attorney-client privilege in civil litigation / Oscar Rey Rodriguez, editor.—5th ed.
p. cm.
Includes bibliographical references and index.
ISBN 978-1-61438-156-3 (alk. paper)
1. Confidential communications—Lawyers—United States. 2. Attorney and client—United States. I. Rodriguez, Oscar Rey.
KF8959.A7A935 2011
347.73'6—dc23

2011046394

Discounts are available for books ordered in bulk. Special consideration is given to state bars, CLE programs, and other bar-related organizations. Inquire at Book Publishing, ABA Publishing, American Bar Association, 321 North Clark Street, Chicago, Illinois 60654-7598.

www.ShopABA.org

SUMMARY OF CONTENTS

CONTENTS

PREFACE

This, the Fifth Edition of *The Attorney-Client Privilege in Civil Litigation*, continues the tradition of this series by introducing new and expanded coverage of the attorney-client privilege and work-product doctrine. In addition, many of the chapters continue the practice of utilizing helpful appendices of forms or other supplemental or illustrative material. The hard work of the numerous authors is reflected in each of their individual chapters.

When first published in 1989, this book was titled *The Attorney-Client Privilege under Siege*. Legislative proposals at the federal and state level to limit (or preserve) the confidentiality obligations of attorneys, and debates such as the ones over the passage and interpretation of the Sarbanes-Oxley Act, have contributed to the perception that the attorney-client privilege is, if anything, still under attack. It is, however, mounting a spirited defense. Naturally, much of this controversy is being carried out in the courts, not the legislature, as discussed in this volume. On behalf of all of the authors and my co-editors (Fulbright partners Stephen McNabb and Oscar Rey Rodriguez), I sincerely hope that this volume will contribute to a better understanding of the limits and exercise of this most important evidentiary privilege.

Vincent S. Walkowiak
Fulbright & Jaworski L.L.P.
Dallas, Texas
2011

ABOUT THE EDITORS

Vincent S. Walkowiak is recently retired from Fulbright & Jaworski L.L.P. He is currently of counsel in the Dallas office of Fulbright & Jaworski L.L.P. and, before retiring as a full-time partner, served as the co-head of the firm's product liability litigation practice group. Mr. Walkowiak has extensive experience in tort and commercial litigation, including the defense of product liability, extracontractual liability, and lender liability issues. He has represented European and Asian companies transacting business in the United States and has authored or edited more than 11 books on product liability or attorney-client privilege topics.

Mr. Walkowiak is an experienced trial attorney, having represented clients in both federal and state courts as well as in alternative dispute resolution settings, including arbitrations and mediations. In addition, he has been counsel before the U.S. Consumer Product Safety Commission, the Food and Drug Administration, and other federal and state agencies representing clients' interests in matters involving product recall issues.

Mr. Walkowiak received a B.A. in 1968 and a J.D. in 1971 from the University of Illinois.

Stephen McNabb is a partner in the Washington, D.C., office of Fulbright & Jaworski L.L.P. and is head of the firm's International Trade Practice Group. Since joining Fulbright & Jaworski in 1982, Mr. McNabb has counseled clients on compliance with international trade laws and regulations (including regulations administered by the Department of Commerce, the Department of the Treasury's Office of Foreign Assets Control, and the Department of State) and the Foreign Corrupt Practices Act. He also has represented clients in investigations and enforcement matters involving export and sanctions laws and the Foreign Corrupt Practices Act.

Mr. McNabb also is a member of the firm's White Collar Practice Group and has represented corporations and their officers, directors, and employees in other types of white collar criminal and related federal enforcement matters. He has represented clients during grand jury and congressional investigations, at trial, and before appellate courts in a wide range of criminal matters. His practice has involved counseling clients on complying with U.S. criminal laws, the organizational sentencing guidelines, and corporate prevention and detection programs.

Mr. McNabb also has extensive civil litigation experience before trial and appellate courts in such diverse fields as antitrust, employment, labor relations, torts, civil rights, and complex commercial matters. Mr. McNabb is a member of the firm's Appellate Practice Group and has argued cases in several United States courts of appeal.

Mr. McNabb is a member of the District of Columbia Bar and the American Bar Association. He is on the Advisory Board of the Corporate Counsel Institute.

Mr. McNabb received an A.B. from Harvard College in 1978 and a J.D. from the Georgetown University Law Center in 1982.

Oscar Rey Rodriguez is a litigation partner in the Dallas office of Fulbright & Jaworski L.L.P. and is a member of the Appellate Practice Group. His practice focuses on state and federal appellate and trial litigation in both tort and commercial areas. He is certified by the Texas Board of Legal Specialization in Civil Appellate Law and is the immediate past Chair of the Dallas Bar Association's Appellate Law Section. Mr. Rodriguez is an experienced appellate lawyer and has handled appeals and presented arguments in both federal and state appellate courts, including the Supreme Court of Texas.

Mr. Rodriguez is a member of the College of the State Bar of Texas, serves on the Board of Directors for the Dallas Bar Foundation, and is a Life Fellow of the Texas Bar Foundation. He is a coauthor with W. Wendell Hall, Rosemarie Kanusky, and Mark Emery of *Hall's Standards of Review in Texas*, 42 St. Mary's L.J. 3 (2010), and he is a frequent CLE presenter.

Mr. Rodriguez received his B.B.A. with highest honors from the University of Texas at El Paso in 1989 and received the "Men of Mines Award"—the university's highest award. After graduating as the valedictorian of his 1993 law school class from the Dedman School of Law at Southern Methodist University, Mr. Rodriguez served as a judicial clerk to the Supreme Court of Texas.

ABOUT THE CONTRIBUTORS

Gerardo Alcazar is a litigation associate at Robins, Kaplan, Miller & Ciresi, L.L.P. Mr. Alcazar received his B.S. from the University of Wisconsin-Milwaukee and his J.D. from the University of Wisconsin Law School. His practice focuses on property and liability insurance coverage litigation, construction litigation, and general commercial litigation. Mr. Alcazar is a member of the American Bar Association, the Hispanic National Bar Association, and the Minnesota Hispanic Bar Association.

David E. Bland is a partner at Robins, Kaplan, Miller & Ciresi, L.L.P., practicing in the firm's Los Angeles and Minneapolis offices. He received his B.A. in 1975 from the University of Minnesota and his J.D., cum laude, in 1979 from William Mitchell College of Law. His practice focuses on property and liability insurance coverage litigation, directors' and officers' coverage litigation, crime and fidelity claim evaluation and litigation, environmental litigation, construction litigation, national coordination of claim defense, drafting of policy language and endorsements to insurance policies, intellectual property litigation, and general commercial litigation. He also has an active appellate practice.

Jeffery J. Carlson received his B.A. from the University of Minnesota, where he graduated summa cum laude and was a member of Phi Beta Kappa. He earned his J.D. from the University of California, Los Angeles Law School. Mr. Carlson is the managing partner of Carlson & Messer L.L.P., a general civil litigation defense firm focusing in product liability, toxic tort litigation, professional malpractice, insurance, and employment law. Mr. Carlson has authored and coauthored many articles and lectured on numerous continuing education panels and seminars on such diverse topics as product liability law, toxic torts, trial technique, evidentiary matters, expert witnesses, and *Daubert*. He is a member of the American Bar Association, Association of Defense Trial Attorneys, Defense Research Institute (Drug & Medical Device Steering Committee), Federation of Defense and Corporate Counsel, and Product Liability Advisory Council.

Christopher Scott D'Angelo is a partner at Montgomery, McCracken, Walker & Rhoads, L.L.P., based in Philadelphia, and is Chairman of its Products Liability & Mass Torts Section and Vice Chairman of its Sports, Entertainment & Amusements Law Practice. His practice emphasizes litigation and preventive counseling in the fields of business and business torts, intellectual property, class actions, and product liability, including in his role as national counsel for several major U.S. clients and his representation of foreign concerns in the United States and U.S. concerns abroad, as well as litigation and other matters in the probate courts. Mr. D'Angelo is a member of the American Law Institute, International Association of Defense Counsel, Product Liability Advisory Council, Defense Research Institute, International Bar Association, and Federation of Defense & Corporate Counsel. He is listed in *Who's Who in America, Who's Who in American Law*, and *Who's Who in the World*, and in *The International Who's Who of Commercial Lawyers, The International Who's Who of Product Liability Lawyers*, and the *International Who's Who of Trademark Lawyers*. Mr. D'Angelo received his B.A. with distinction, and with honors in history (1975) and his J.D. (1978) from the University of Virginia.

Michael Dockterman is a partner and member of the executive committee at Wildman, Harrold, Allen & Dixon, L.L.P, a full-service law firm with one of the nation's premier litigation practices. Named by *The National Law Journal* in 2006 as one of the Top 10 "Winning Litigators" in the United States, and described by *Chambers & Partners* as a lawyer who "can see through the garbage and cut to the chase," Mr. Dockterman specializes in complex civil and criminal business litigation, and in advising clients on matters of corporate governance and compliance. He has appeared as principal trial counsel in state and federal courts in over half of the United States, and has tried both federal and state white-collar criminal cases, as well as securities, antitrust, intellectual property, environmental, contract, fraud, product liability, and amateur sports cases. Mr. Dockterman also has represented both corporate and individual interests in grand jury and other government investigations across the country involving government contracting, public corruption, securities, corporate fraud, antitrust, environmental, and other regulatory matters. Mr. Dockterman received his law degree from Duke University and his undergraduate degree from Yale University.

Arthur Garwin is ABA Professionalism Counsel and director of Publications and Conference Planning for the ABA Center for Professional Responsibility. He has served as Staff Counsel to the ABA Standing Committee on Professionalism, ABA Commission on Multidisciplinary Practice, ABA Task Force on the Model Definition of the Practice of Law, and has written numerous articles on professional responsibility, including 40 ethics columns for the *ABA Journal*. He also has served for 13 years as editor of *The Professional Lawyer*. He is the author of *The Legal Assistant's Practical Guide to Professional Responsibility* (2nd Edition) and editor of the *Annotated Model Code of Judicial Conduct* and *A Legislative History: The Development of the ABA Model Rules of Professional Conduct, 1982–2005*. Mr. Garwin has B.S. and J.D. degrees from the University of Illinois and an M.B.A. from Northwestern University. He practiced law for 15 years before coming to the ABA in 1990.

Nicole J. Highland is an associate at Vedder Price P.C. in Chicago. Ms. Highland received her B.A. with honors from the University of Illinois at Urbana-Champaign and graduated magna cum laude from Loyola University Chicago School of Law. During the year prior to joining Mayer Brown, Ms. Highland worked for the Public Defender of Cook County.

Kenneth A. Hindman is an attorney in private practice in Decatur, Georgia, and DeKalb County. His practice is concentrated on litigation of business and insurance matters, and on appellate practice. He earned a B.A. with distinction and received his J.D. from the University of Virginia, where he was an Echols Scholar and a DuPont Regional Scholar.

Scott G. Johnson is a partner in Robins, Kaplan, Miller & Ciresi, L.L.P., practicing in the firm's Los Angeles and Minneapolis offices. He received his B.S., magna cum laude, in 1982 from Winona State University and his J.D., magna cum laude, in 1986 from William Mitchell College of Law. His practice focuses primarily on property and liability insurance coverage litigation, subrogation, and general commercial litigation.

M. Colston Jones is an attorney with the firm of Protogyrou & Rigney in Norfolk, Virginia. He earned a B.A. from Haverford College and a J.D. from the Washington and Lee University School of Law.

Christina M. Jones is a senior associate at McGuireWoods L.L.P. in Richmond, Virginia, in its Product and Consumer Litigation Department. Her practice areas include defense of complex product liability cases, commercial litigation, risk management counseling, and representation at all stages before the Consumer Product Safety Commission (CPSC). She serves as national counsel and CPSC counsel to various product manufacturers and litigates cases in state and federal courts throughout the country. She earned a B.A. with distinction from the University of Virginia and earned her J.D. at the University of Virginia School of Law where she served on the *Virginia Law Review*.

Allan Kanner is the senior and founding member of Kanner & Whiteley, L.L.C. in New Orleans, where he specializes in environmental, toxic tort, insurance, class action, and complex business litigation. He is a member of the bars of Louisiana, New Jersey, New York, Pennsylvania, California, the District of Columbia, and Puerto Rico (federal). He is currently President-Elect of the Louisiana Association for Justice. Since 1990, he has been an adjunct professor of law at Tulane University Law School. In 2004, he was a visiting lecturer at the Duke Law School and Boalt Hall. Previously, he was a visiting professor at Yale Law School and the University of Texas Law School. He earned his B.A. from the University of Pennsylvania and J.D. from Harvard Law School.

Michael Knoerzer is a partner in the New York office of Clyde & Co. US L.L.P. For over 20 years, he has concentrated his practice on the litigation and arbitration of disputes of interest to insurers and reinsurers, as well as providing advice to insurers and reinsurers in noncontentious matters. Mr. Knoerzer is a frequent speaker and author on issues pertaining to excess insurance, reinsurance, and the attorney-client privilege. He has spoken at conferences conducted by ARIAS-U.S., the American Bar Association, Mealey's, the Practicing Law Institute, and the American Conference Institute. Mr. Knoerzer is a fellow of the American Bar Foundation.

Thomas J. Leach is professor of law and director of the Center for Legal Advocacy at the University of the Pacific-McGeorge School of Law in Sacramento, California, where he teaches trial advocacy. From 1978 to 1996, he was a trial attorney with the Philadelphia firm of Drinker, Biddle & Reath, practicing construction law, franchising, and product liability. Mr. Leach holds a J.D. from the University of Pennsylvania, a M.A. in teaching from Wesleyan University (1969), and a B.A. from Cornell University (1967). He has taught in numerous deposition and trial advocacy training programs for the National Institute for Trial Advocacy and currently directs its Western Deposition and Western Regional Programs.

Alan J. Martin is a partner in the Chicago office of Barnes & Thornburg L.L.P. and cochair of the firm's Property and Casualty Insurance Coverage Group. He is a member of the firm's litigation department, where he concentrates his practice on complex insurance coverage matters and commercial litigation.

Jane Thornton Mastrucci is a partner at Quintairos, Prieto, Wood & Boyer, P.A. and practices from the firm's Miami office. Her areas of practice are nursing home, hospital, insurance, and medical malpractice defense litigation. She is also one of only a handful of lawyers in Florida who specialize in nursing home administrative law. She graduated magna cum laude from the University of Notre Dame and earned a J.D. from Notre Dame Law School in 1978. She coauthored four articles with her father, John W. Thornton, Sr., and has given numerous presentations in the nursing home and healthcare fields. She is a former vice chairman of the American Bar Association's Tort Trial and Insurance Practice Section's Excess, Surplus and Reinsurance Law Committee and a member of A.I.D.A.'s Reinsurance and Insurance Arbitration Society and the Defense Research Institute.

Michael Edward McCabe, Jr. is a partner at Funk & Bolton, P.A., and concentrates his practice on civil litigation and related client counseling. He serves as counsel for both domestic and foreign clients involved in commercial litigation matters before federal and state courts and administrative agencies. Mr. McCabe received his B.S. in mechanical engineering from the University of Maryland in 1985 and his J.D., magna cum laude, from the University of Baltimore School of Law in 1992.

Demetrios G. Metropoulos is a partner at Mayer Brown L.L.P. in Chicago. His primary practice area is commercial litigation, particularly in the appellate and communications-related litigation areas. Mr. Metropoulos is ranked as a "leading lawyer" by Chambers USA. He is a graduate of Stanford Law School, where he served as a senior editor of the *Stanford Law Review* and earned membership in the Order of the Coif. Mr. Metropoulos earned his undergraduate degree from the University of Michigan. Prior to joining Mayer Brown in 1994, he worked for Coopers & Lybrand (now PricewaterhouseCoopers) and in 1993–1994 he clerked for the Honorable Joseph T. Sneed on the U.S. Court of Appeals for the Ninth Circuit.

Ann Marie Mortimer is the managing partner of the Los Angeles office of Hunton & Williams, and concentrates her practice in complex civil litigation, toxic tort, and product liability litigation. Ms. Mortimer frequently speaks on evolving issues in drug and medical device litigation, as well as litigation risk assessment and avoidance strategies. Ms. Mortimer graduated from Smith College in 1988, earned a M.Sc. from London School of Economics in 1989, and graduated from Boalt Hall in 1992.

Tibor Nagy is a partner with Susman Godfrey, L.L.P., in the firm's New York office. He earned his B.A. from Dartmouth College and his J.D. from Yale Law School in 2003. Prior to joining Susman Godfrey, Mr. Nagy was law clerk to the Honorable Melinda Harmon, U.S. District Court for the Southern District of Texas. He has authored numerous articles on trial advocacy, complex litigation, and environmental law.

Kirk A. Pasich is a partner in the Los Angeles office of Dickstein Shapiro, L.L.P. He represents insureds in complex coverage matters. He has been named by *Lawdragon* as one of the nation's 500 leading lawyers, by *Chambers USA: America's Leading Business Lawyers* as "the market leader for policyholder representation in California," and by *California Law Business* to its "Legal Dream Team" as one of California's top 25 litigators. He is the author or coauthor of several books and the author of more than 400 articles.

Cynthia Harrison Ruiz is an associate at Quintairos, Prieto, Wood & Boyer, P.A. and practices from the firm's Miami office. Her areas of practice are insurance defense litigation, medical malpractice, nursing home defense litigation, and nursing home administrative law. She graduated magna cum laude with a B.A. from the University of Colorado and earned a J.D. from the National Law Center at George Washington University. Ms. Ruiz practiced law at Spears Barnes et al. in Durham, North Carolina, for five years before relocating to Florida.

Eileen K. Sorabella is an associate in the New York office of Clyde & Co. US L.L.P. Ms. Sorabella practices in the firm's insurance and reinsurance arbitration and litigation group and focuses on the representation of clients in the life and health insurance and reinsurance industries. She has coauthored numerous articles and is a member of the New York State Bar Association and the Health Law Section of the American Bar Association.

John W. Thornton served as the Legislative and Administrative Code representative on Hospital Risk Managers' Qualifications, Rules, and Liability; acted as the legislative attorney for the Florida School Board Association; and represented the Dade County School Board. He served on the Planning Committee for the National Institute on "Reinsurance Recoverables" held in June 1988 and served on the ABA Tort Trial and Insurance Practice Section programs for more than two decades. He has spoken and written on a wide range of topics, including insurance, product liability, medical mediation and malpractice, and nursing home litigation and pre-suit procedures. He graduated magna cum laude from Notre Dame and earned a J.D. from Notre Dame Law School.

J. Tracy Walker, IV is a partner with McGuireWoods L.L.P. in Richmond, Virginia, and chairs its Product and Consumer Litigation Department. He is a graduate of the University of Virginia and Harvard Law School, and has been practicing law for over 16 years. Mr. Walker handles cases at the trial level and on appeal in state and federal courts throughout the country, and has tried cases to verdict in several states. He serves as national and regional trial counsel for various product manufacturers. Mr. Walker is a member of the Defense Research Institute.

Laurie A. Weiss is of counsel in Fulbright & Jaworski L.L.P.'s San Antonio office and has an active litigation practice. Prior to joining Fulbright & Jaworski in 1988, Ms. Weiss had a 10-year career in business, including work with a service company providing computer-based risk management information services to major U.S. corporations. She is co-head of Fulbright's E-Discovery and Information Management Group. Ms. Weiss represents clients in litigation matters and investigations involving discovery of electronically stored information and has guided clients through the meet-and-confer process and the complex process of identifying, preserving, collecting, processing, reviewing, and producing electronically stored information. Ms. Weiss received her J.D. with honors from the University of Texas School of Law.

Louis Sey Zimmerman is a partner in the Washington office of Fulbright & Jaworski L.L.P. Prior to joining the firm in 1976, he was a law clerk for U.S. District Judge Owen Cox. Mr. Zimmerman has handled a wide range of environmental and energy matters in state and federal court as well as before a variety of administrative agencies. He has spoken on a variety of energy and environmental law topics. He is a coauthor of the *Texas Environmental Law Handbook*. He graduated from Williams College and the University of Texas School of Law.

CHAPTER 1

An Overview of the Attorney-Client Privilege When the Client Is a Corporation

VINCENT S. WALKOWIAK

I. Introduction

Former Deputy Attorney General Larry D. Thompson released the "Principles of Federal Prosecution of Business Organizations"[1] (the Thompson memo) on January 23, 2003, generating a maelstrom of controversy. In the memo, Thompson instructed federal prosecutors to consider various factors when determining whether to reach a favorable plea agreement with corporations under investigation. Among those factors was a corporation's willingness to waive the attorney-client privilege and work-product doctrine protection if deemed necessary by the Justice Department. Other federal agencies followed, announcing that they too would implement similar policies. The American Bar Association and other corporate and professional groups lamented this assault on the "sanctity" of the attorney-client privilege.

Thompson's memo was the Justice Department's prevailing policy until late 2006. At that time, Deputy Attorney General Paul McNulty announced a policy change in a meeting of the Lawyers for Civil Justice. McNulty's comments were followed by the release of a highly publicized memo, "Principles of Federal Prosecution of Business Organizations," that superseded and replaced the Thompson memo.[2] Subsequent deputy attorneys general, including Mark Filip, issued similar memos, emphasizing that "waiving the attorney-client and work-product protections has never been a prerequisite . . . for a corporation to be viewed as cooperative."[3] Under Filip's leadership, the department revised its policies so that a corporation may voluntarily share information protected by the attorney-client privilege or work-product doctrine, but prosecutors may not ask for such waivers.[4]

Although significant, Thompson's memo had no effect on the substantive law of privilege; at bottom, the memo articulated a federal agency's policy regarding the circumstances under which a corporation might receive a more favorable disposition in a governmental investigation. Also, the memo was limited to attorneys representing entities being investigated for violating federal law. Far more important to the law of attorney-client privilege and work-product protection is the effect of recent legislation and court decisions interpreting the scope of these privileges and protections.

This chapter presents an overview of federal and state law regarding the attorney-client privilege as an evidentiary privilege and the procedures that relate to it, especially as they apply to communications by attorneys representing corporations. Frequently, attorney-client-privileged communications also are protected by the attorney work-product doctrine, which is a rule of civil procedure,[5] and by the attorney's ethical duty to maintain confidentiality as to information related to representation of a client.[6]

The attorney-client privilege is generally recognized as one of the oldest evidentiary privileges in Anglo-American law.[7] The intended purpose of the attorney-client privilege is to promote the free flow of information between attorneys and their clients by removing the fear that the details of their communications will be disclosed to outsiders.[8] This privilege rests on the presumption that an attorney can render accurate advice only if the client fully discloses all the relevant facts. The client is encouraged, therefore, to provide complete disclosure, even as to facts that, if disclosed, could adversely affect the client's legal position. After all, it is frequently the most harmful information that the attorney needs in order to provide the best legal advice to a client.

The attorney-client privilege can restrict or totally preclude certain communications from being discovered or admitted into evidence. For this reason, the privilege runs afoul of the general premise that every person is obligated to offer information he or she has about an issue before the courts. This general duty to disclose information is regarded as nearly sacrosanct. One important commentator on evidence, Wigmore, recognized this fact and commented as follows:

> For more than three centuries it has now been recognized as a fundamental maxim that the public (in the words sanctioned by Lord Hardwicke) has a right to every man's evidence. When we come to examine the various claims of exemption, we start with the primary assumption that there is a general duty to give what testimony one is capable of giving, and that any exemptions which may exist are distinctly exceptional, being so many derogations from a positive general rule.[9]

Nor was Professor Wigmore alone in his view that a rule that exempts some information from evidence should be narrowly construed.[10] As one court put the matter:

> [The attorney-client] privilege remains an exception to the general duty to disclose. Its benefits are all indirect and speculative; its obstruction is plain and concrete. . . . It is worth preserving for the sake of a general policy, but it is nonetheless an obstacle to the investigation of the truth. It ought to be strictly confined within the narrowest possible limits consistent with the logic of its principle.[11]

Many of the situations selected for inclusion in this chapter involve the assertion of attorney-client privilege by corporate in-house or general counsel, as well as by attorneys representing corporations. As will be discussed, the privilege presents special problems in the context of corporations, especially when asserted by in-house counsel. Although every court recognizes that in-house counsel qualify for the privilege, many courts require in-house attorneys to clear a high bar before they can successfully assert the attorney-client privilege. While this position may not be legally warranted, it is nevertheless the attitude of courts, which are typically suspicious of the role that in-house counsel play in a corporation, especially given the many nonlegal assignments that in-house lawyers perform. Further, a court's approach in resolving a corporation's attorney-client privilege issues must be considered in light of the courts' liberal interpretation of discovery rules and the narrow interpretation to which the attorney-client privilege is generally subject.

II. The Attorney-Client Privilege: First Principles

The attorney-client privilege is an evidentiary rule designed to encourage (by protecting) the free flow of information between an attorney and his or her client. The privilege is traditionally and historically a product of the common law, but it has been codified in many jurisdictions across the country. In some states, the attorney-client privilege statute merely restates the common law.[12] Other states, including Arizona and Texas, have codified the privilege in detail, specifically setting forth not only the privilege but also many of the procedural rules regarding its use.[13] Some states have also anticipated and addressed questions on how to interpret the privilege.[14]

The basic definition of the attorney-client privilege is fairly simple. Rule 503(b) of the Texas Rules of Evidence provides a good working definition of the privilege: "[a] client has a privilege to refuse to disclose and to prevent any other person from disclosing confidential communications made for the purpose of facilitating the rendition of professional legal services to the client."[15]

The assumption underlying the privilege is that our legal system is more civilized and efficient because we recognize the attorney-client privilege. Many believe that, if courts do not broadly interpret and enforce the privilege, the legal system will suffer, as clients will have to determine whether confidential disclosures to their attorney could be revealed to a party with opposing legal interests. Undoubtedly, this risk could "chill" full disclosure, causing a client to withhold important facts from the attorney. As a result, the attorney runs the risk of rendering incomplete and, perhaps, incorrect legal advice. It is believed that our adversarial legal system can encourage full disclosure only by eliminating the fear that the communication will be disclosed by the attorney and then used against the client. The attorney-client privilege helps achieve this end.

The free flow of uncensored information between an attorney and client is as important within a corporation as it is between the corporation and outside counsel. In-house counsel owe a duty to their client—the corporation. And like outside counsel, in-house counsel can perform that duty only with full knowledge of the information available to the client. It is important to understand the rationale underlying this legal doctrine, and attorneys should always argue the potential damage to the underlying policies and objectives of the attorney-client privilege when attempting to establish this privilege, regardless of the context in which the privilege is being asserted.

A. Establishing the Privilege

The attorney-client privilege attaches early in the attorney-client relationship. For example, the Rules of Evidence in Texas and Alabama define "client" as someone who consults a lawyer "*with a view* to obtaining professional legal services from [him]."[16] Once created, the privilege continues and does not end when the representation ends or the client dies.[17]

Because the privilege belongs to the client, the claim of privilege must be made by or on behalf of the client.[18] Thus, although the privilege belongs to the client, the lawyer may claim the privilege on behalf of the client and is presumed to have the authority to assert the attorney-client privilege in the absence of evidence to the contrary.[19]

In the case of a corporation, it is generally held that the privilege may only be asserted by an authorized corporate representative on behalf of the corporation.[20] Generally speaking, an attorney for the corporation is vested with presumptive authority to assert the privilege.[21] A corporation's attorney is generally in the best position to assert the privilege, whether at a deposition, when responding to written discovery, or at trial.

The attorney-client privilege, naturally, is not self-actuating, and generally a party seeking to protect privileged communication from discovery must, at some stage:

1. Affirmatively and specifically plead or assert the attorney-client privilege;
2. Produce evidence concerning the applicability of the attorney-client privilege; and
3. For written material, allow the trial court to determine whether an in camera inspection is necessary to determine if the privilege applies.

If the trial court orders an in camera inspection of the privileged communication, the party asserting the privilege should segregate and produce to the court those materials the court seeks to inspect. Failure to follow this procedure may waive any complaint of the trial court's action regarding the privilege.[22]

Thus, the party resisting discovery of material claimed to be privileged must specifically claim the privilege relied on and establish the justification for its imposition.[23] In written discovery, the discovery response must identify the privilege and identify each document to which the privilege applies. General objections will most likely not suffice. Simply listing documents under the heading "Attorney-Client/Attorney Work-Product" is generally insufficient to protect documents from discovery. A global claim that a list of documents is protected by one or more privileges is also too general to prevent their discovery. Further, merely attaching something to a privileged document does not, by itself, make the attachment privileged.[24] And while often called an absolute privilege, the attorney-client privilege is subject to exceptions.[25]

The parameters of the attorney-client privilege in federal court were fully set forth in *United States v. United Shoe Machinery Corp.*,[26] a frequently cited case from 1950, in which the court stated:

> The privilege applies only if (1) the asserted holder of the privilege is or sought to become a client; (2) the person to whom the communication was made (a) is a member of the bar of a court, or his subordinate and (b) in connection with this communication is acting as a lawyer; (3) the communication relates to a fact of which the attorney was

> informed (a) by his client (b) without the presence of strangers (c) for the purpose of securing primarily either (i) an opinion of law or (ii) legal services or (iii) assistance in some legal proceeding, and not (d) for the purpose of committing a crime or tort; and (4) the privilege has been (a) claimed and (b) not waived by the client.[27]

It is well established that the attorney-client privilege applies to the corporate client;[28] however, even this principle has not gone unchallenged. In fact, at least one court, subsequently reversed, has held that the attorney-client privilege could not be claimed by a corporation.[29] Moreover, while the procedures for asserting the attorney-client privilege are rather straightforward when applied to a client who is a natural person, they are not so simple when the client is a corporation. The most obvious difference is that the corporation speaks through the many voices of its employees, agents, and representatives. There may be so many corporate employees and agents that it is unrealistic to permit every corporate employee or agent to be able to assert the attorney-client privilege in every communication. Thus, when a corporation asserts the attorney-client privilege, there are questions about (1) which natural persons' communications are protected, (2) who within the corporation may assert the privilege, and (3) who within the corporation may waive the privilege.

Not surprisingly, there is no uniform answer to these questions, either among the states or between state and federal law. In regard to who can assert the attorney-client privilege, courts have adopted and applied two general tests: (1) the control group test and (2) the subject matter test. Determining which test applies depends on knowing a particular jurisdiction's privilege laws, which are typically found in a state's rules of evidence. Because the rule as applied may be affected by various factors, it is important for an attorney representing a corporation to understand both tests, notwithstanding the fact that few jurisdictions still follow the control group test. That said, it is not enough to know only the applicable test of a particular state because corporate litigation frequently involves parties from different states. Also, it is likely that a corporation may be sued in a state in which it is not a resident. Therefore, attorneys should be familiar with the conflicts of law rules that govern different jurisdictions because such laws could also impact the applicable privilege test.

B. Determining the Rule of Privilege: Control Group versus Subject Matter

Courts have taken two approaches in resolving attorney-client privilege issues in the context of corporations.[30] The first, or "control group test," provides that the client may be an entity and have confidential communications *only if* the corporate representative can act on the legal advice rendered or if the corporate representative has authority to obtain legal representation on behalf of the corporation.[31] This test is by far the minority rule.

The control group concept originated with *City of Philadelphia v. Westinghouse Electric Corp.*[32] In that case, defendant Westinghouse asserted the attorney-client privilege to prevent disclosure of an employee's statement to Westinghouse's general counsel. In rejecting the application of the attorney-client privilege to this communication, the court adopted the following definition of the scope of the attorney-client privilege in the corporate setting:

> [I]f the employee making the communication, of whatever rank he may be, is in a position to control or even to take a substantial part in a decision about any action which the corporation may take upon the advice of the attorney, or if he is an authorized member of a body or group which has that authority, then, in effect, he is (or personifies) the corporation when he makes his disclosure to the lawyer and the privilege would apply. In all other cases the employee would be merely giving information to the lawyer to enable the latter to advise those in the corporation having the authority to act or refrain from acting on the advice.[33]

It is obvious that the control group test is extremely narrow in defining the group of persons who may have privileged communications. Even though low-level employees frequently possess information that may be vital to addressing a corporation's legal issues, the control group test offers the protection of the attorney-client privilege *only* to communications of top management. And while the limited protection afforded by the work-product doctrine might be available for communications with counsel when litigation is anticipated, communications of a nonmanagement group employee in the absence of anticipated litigation may be unprotected. Some states, recognizing the restrictive nature of the test, have expanded the control group to include those advising top managers on legal issues.[34]

Despite the control test's limits, a minority of states continue to follow the control group test for corporations.[35] Change is constantly occurring, however, as the scope of the attorney-client privilege for corporate communications is reconsidered and more states abandon the control group test for the more liberal and realistic subject matter test.

In 1993, the Texas Supreme Court, in *National Tank Company v. Brotherton*,[36] determined the scope of a corporation's attorney-client privilege under Texas law. In a plurality opinion (which was effectively joined by all the other justices on this issue), Chief Justice Phillips wrote that Rule 503 of the then Texas Rules of Civil Evidence adopted the "control group test" by virtue of its definition of "representative of the client"—that is, "one having authority to obtain professional legal services, or to act on advice rendered pursuant thereto, on behalf of the client."[37] Thus, even if legal matters were discussed between attorneys and employees, the communications would not be considered privileged unless they were between an appropriate "control group" corporate representative and counsel. Of course, this sort of communication might be protected by the work-product doctrine if taken in anticipation of litigation. For this and other reasons, the narrow control group test was criticized and the state began to reevaluate the rule.[38]

The control group test defined the scope of the attorney-client privilege in Texas until 1998. At that time, the Texas Rules of Evidence were amended to include the subject matter test in addition to the control group test for communications by corporate employees to attorneys. In Texas, the attorney-client privilege may now be asserted on behalf of a corporation for communications by

> (A) A person having authority to obtain professional legal services, or to act on advice thereby rendered, on behalf of the client; or
> (B) Any other person who, for the purpose of effectuating legal representation for the client, makes or receives a confidential communication while acting in the scope of employment for the client.[39]

As Texas did in amending its rule for the attorney-client privilege, the Seventh Circuit Court of Appeals, some years earlier in the leading case of *Harper & Row Publishers, Inc. v. Decker*,[40] adopted the subject matter test. The Seventh Circuit recognized that an employee, while not a member of the control group, is sufficiently identified with the corporation so that the employee's communication to the corporation's attorney should be privileged when the employee makes that communication at the direction of his or her corporate supervisor.[41] However, the court imposed the additional condition that the communication between the employee and the corporation's legal counsel must be done in furtherance of the employee's official duties. As the court said, the privilege is allowed "where the subject matter upon which the attorney's advice is sought by the corporation and dealt with in the communication is the performance by the employee of the duties of his employment."[42]

While generally accepted, the principles expressed by the court in *Harper*[43] were viewed by some courts as being too broad. Thus, the court in *Diversified Industries, Inc. v. Meredith*[44] adopted what became known as the modified subject matter test. This test set forth five elements that need to be satisfied before a corporate employee's communications with counsel can be privileged:

1. The communication must be made for the purpose of securing legal advice;
2. The employee making the communication should be doing so at the direction of his corporate supervisor;
3. The employee's superior made the request for the communication in order for the corporation to secure legal advice;
4. The subject matter of the communication was within the scope of the employee's corporate duties; and

5. The communication was not disseminated beyond those persons who, because of the corporate structure, needed to know its contents.[45]

These principles ultimately gained acceptance by the U.S. Supreme Court. For instance, in *Upjohn Co. v. United States*,[46] the U.S. Supreme Court rejected the "control group" test and held that the attorney-client privilege protected communication between corporate counsel and lower-level corporate employees. This version of the "subject matter" test is employed in federal courts in nondiversity cases. In reaching its decision, the Court followed this reasoning:

> In the case of the individual client the provider of information and the person who acts on the lawyer's advice are one and the same. In the corporate context, however, it will frequently be employees beyond the control group as defined by the court below—"officers and agents . . . responsible for directing [the company's] action in response to legal advice"—who will possess the information needed by the corporation's lawyers. Middle-level—and indeed lower-level—employees can, by actions within the scope of their employment, embroil the corporation in serious legal difficulties, and it is only natural that these employees would have the relevant information needed by corporate counsel if he is adequately to advise the client with respect to such actual or potential difficulties.[47]

While the Court in *Upjohn* limited its holding to the facts before it and expressly declined to lay down a broad rule, the Court did determine the availability of the attorney-client privilege to corporations facing litigation in federal court. The holding clearly states that confidential communications by corporate employees about matters within the scope of their employment, and made for the purpose of enabling counsel to provide legal advice to the corporation, fall within the scope of the attorney-client privilege. To be sure, the Court cautioned that because the attorney-client privilege suppresses information, it could obstruct the truth-finding process; therefore, the Court said, the privilege should be narrowly construed.

Case law suggests that this perceived need for a narrow construction arises most often when a corporation seeks to invoke the privilege to protect communications of or to in-house counsel. This is primarily due to the fact that in-house counsel may play a dual role of legal advisor and business advisor. In such instances, the courts must apply a greater level of scrutiny to the contested communications to ensure that the communication occurred for legal, not business, purposes. After all, the attorney-client privilege applies only if the communication's purpose is to gain or provide legal assistance. The varied scope of responsibility of some corporate in-house attorneys suggests that courts will continue to closely analyze a corporation's claim of privilege to determine whether the communications fall outside the realm of privilege afforded to corporations.

Since *Upjohn*, the majority of states have adopted some version of the subject matter test. The subject matter test has also been cited formally by a number of states that have not adopted a specific rule.[48]

While *Upjohn* establishes that cases arising under federal law require the application of the subject matter test to corporate communications, the Federal Rules of Evidence adopt a policy consistent with the limits of federal authority in diversity cases. The Federal Rules of Evidence address this issue:

> [T]he [attorney-client] privilege of a witness [or] person . . . shall be governed by the principles of the common law as they may be interpreted by the courts of the United States in the light of reason and experience. However, in civil actions and proceedings, with respect to an element of a claim or defense as to which [s]tate law supplies the rule of decision, the privilege of a witness [or] person . . . shall be determined in accordance with [s]tate law.[49]

Therefore, in cases involving state laws, the applicable privilege rule will depend on the laws governing a particular jurisdiction. The incongruity of this principle has not been lost upon some commentators, who have pointed out that a single corporation might be involved in two cases—one based on diversity jurisdiction and the other based on federal law—in the same federal court before the same judge. In such a situation, the judge would be expected to apply *Upjohn*'s subject matter test in the case implicating federal law. In the diversity case, the judge would apply the privilege rule unique to the particular forum state, which could easily be the control group test. This incongruity, while perhaps a little far-fetched, dictates a cautionary note, and relying upon rules for traditional conflicts offers little comfort. The *Restatement (Second) of Conflicts* favors the forum's laws that will more likely hold that the communication is *unprotected* by the privilege.[50] Consequently, a jurisdiction that follows the subject matter test and the *Restatement's* view of conflicts might find itself in the awkward position of being asked to set aside its own rules regarding the attorney-client privilege and apply the control group test of another jurisdiction. This could cause a court to hold that communications typically considered privileged are no longer protected due to the imposition of a different rule. Even if this is not the result, the possibility alone suggests that a forum selection clause and choice of law clause should be a standard provision in any contract where the parties are in a position to control which standard will apply.

C. Multiple Roles of In-House Counsel

1. *In-House Counsel as Executive*

In addition to determining which laws courts will use to determine the scope of the attorney-client privilege, in-house counsel must also distinguish their role as legal advisor from that of business executive. In-house counsel must make this distinction because the attorney-client privilege extends only to communications pertaining to legal matters. The privilege does not exist for business communications.

It is presumed that communications with outside counsel are for the purpose of seeking legal advice.[51] This presumption is not given to in-house counsel because in-house counsel are perceived as being equally capable of having provided business as well as legal advice. For instance, in some corporate settings, in-house attorneys are asked only to serve as the corporation's attorney, managing litigation or otherwise performing purely legal work. In other corporations, especially those that engage a single in-house counsel, the range of responsibilities is much broader, causing in-house lawyers to provide both business and legal services to their clients.[52]

For instance, some corporate counsel have been described as the persons who advise the corporation on compliance with the myriad regulations and business practices.[53] Because of their legal training, these attorneys conduct internal investigations, chair committees, serve on the board of directors, and become de facto human resources managers, among other responsibilities. As such, these corporate attorneys may be expected to give advice of a business or legal nature, or a combination of both. The commingling of legal and business services creates problems for courts that are asked to define whether a particular communication is privileged. After all, the attorney-client privilege attaches *only* to communications between attorneys and clients made for the purpose of giving or securing legal advice. As expected, courts give increased scrutiny to corporate communications because of the broad nature of in-house counsel's responsibilities and the type of advice frequently requested of them. Basically, the courts look to whether counsel was acting in the capacity of an attorney when receiving the communication or giving the advice. If the communication of in-house counsel is made to render business advice, even to a small degree, the protection afforded by the attorney-client privilege may not be provided to that communication.

The fact that corporate counsel is an attorney does not render all communications with employees of the corporation as privileged.[54] Counsel must be acting in the capacity of an attorney when receiving or making a communication, and therefore must be communicating with the corporate employees, officers, or directors of the corporation for the purpose of formulating legal opinions or advice. The corporation, for this reason, cannot merely pass questionable documents through the legal department for review and thereby have them *declared* protected from outside scrutiny, just as it cannot provide such documents to outside counsel to protect the documents from disclosure.

Even when courts recognize that communications by corporate employees with in-house counsel are entitled to the protection of the attorney-client privilege, they seem to apply a heightened standard for determining when that privilege applies. When presented with the issue of whether the attorney-client privilege protected the communication of an in-house attorney who also served as the company's vice president, one judge concluded that the company "can shelter [in-house counsel's] advice only upon a *clear showing* that [in-house counsel] gave it in a professional legal capacity."[55] In this instance, the heightened standard that the communication be made for legal and not business reasons meant that the proponent of the privilege was required to show by affidavit the precise facts that existed to support the claim of privilege.[56]

A few precautions could assist in satisfying a court's standards. For example, in-house counsel could develop internal procedures that indicate when the in-house counsel is acting as an attorney. This will distinguish counsel's legal work, which is privileged, from the work they must perform when they are acting as an "executive" within the company. For instance, if oral communication between an employee and in-house counsel occurs for legal purposes, the in-house counsel should make sure the employee understands the purpose of such communication. If the communication is written, the document should expressly state that it is for a legal purpose and that there are no business aspects to the communications.[57] The communication should also include the other elements of the privilege. The document should state that it is requested by the employee's superior, that it is confidential, and that it is addressed to in-house counsel in the counsel's capacity as in-house counsel.

While a lawyer's membership in a particular state's bar may not be a prerequisite for asserting the attorney-client privilege, such membership is worthwhile because it supports the proposition that corporate counsel is first and foremost an attorney. The importance of this precaution is best illustrated in the context of whether internal reports and investigations are privileged. Of all the documents prepared by in-house counsel, internal reports can prove to be the most difficult to protect as privileged. Indeed, as courts continue to struggle with whether particular communications were made to corporate counsel in their business or legal capacity, the federal courts have been reluctant to protect the communications of in-house counsel who prepare client tax returns, patent viability reports, or investigative reports that are solely for internal use.[58]

The issue of corporate counsel bar membership has recently been an extremely heated topic of debate. In *Gucci America, Inc. v. Guess?, Inc.*,[59] a magistrate judge held that communications to Gucci's in-house counsel were not protected under the attorney-client privilege because its in-house counsel was not an active member of the state's bar at the time the communications were made. Nor could Gucci benefit from the privilege under the theory that it reasonably believed that in-house counsel was authorized to practice law. The court stated that a corporation must inquire into the professional licensure status of in-house counsel to ensure application of the attorney-client privilege. This decision struck a bad chord with corporations across the nation, who believed they had been burdened with the onerous task of continuously monitoring the bar status of in-house counsel.

The decision in *Gucci*, however, was short-lived; in 2011, the district court overruled the magistrate's judgment.[60] Relying on the privilege standard established by the Supreme Court in *U.S. v. United Shoe Machinery Corp.*, the district court held that Gucci's in-house counsel could receive the attorney-client privilege because he was "a member of the bar of a court." The district court went further and stated that as long as the client had a reasonable belief that it was communicating with an attorney, the attorney-client privilege would be applied to in-house counsel to protect such communications. Pursuant to this decision, corporations may continue to communicate freely with in-house lawyers without having to constantly monitor each attorney's bar membership status, so long as there is some reasonable factual basis for a belief that the lawyer is an active licensed member of a bar.

In *Simon v. G.D. Searle & Co.*,[61] the court applied Minnesota law in a diversity action regarding the attorney-client privilege.[62] In *Simon*, the defendant's risk management department developed aggregate risk statements from individual case loss information statements prepared by in-house counsel. The district court held that the individual case loss materials were privileged on the basis that Minnesota law protects statements made by a client to the attorney, as well as the attorney's advice given to the client in response to the client's inquiry.[63] An Eighth Circuit standard was next applied to the communications. This standard provided that "[w]hen a client acts on privileged information from his attorney, the results are protected from discovery to the extent that they disclose the privileged matter, directly or inferentially."[64] Ultimately the privilege claimed in *Simon* was denied in regard to the documents. The court determined that the individual figures prepared by an attorney were privileged but lost their status as privileged communications when they were given to the client and combined by the client in order to create the aggregate information. The aggregate figures were not direct compilations of the individual figures. Rather, the individual figures were factored by variables such as inflation, and thus, were changed as to be untraceable to the privileged communication.

2. *In-House Counsel as Witness*

In-house counsel is most frequently exposed to the risk of being called as a witness when the attorney signs or verifies a pleading, responds to discovery, or signs an affidavit, although this may occur in other circumstances as well.[65] To avoid being noticed for deposition, in-house counsel should make sure that all attesting matters are performed by a corporate officer rather than in-house counsel.

Attorneys who perform corporate functions beyond representation of the corporate client invite their own depositions. Admittedly, this is unavoidable in some instances. *Johnston Development Group v. Carpenters Local Union No. 1578*[66] involved a RICO action in which plaintiff's in-house counsel also served as the corporation's vice president. In that dual capacity, she was the sole person to take notes at important meetings between the parties before the litigation began, and she was the sole witness to certain prelitigation conversations of which highly disputed accounts had been given. The court was somewhat receptive to limiting the practice of deposing opposing counsel, but it acknowledged that it was forced to allow a limited examination of the in-house counsel/ vice president because she had witnessed the crucial conversations that were in controversy in the litigation.

Again, to reduce the likelihood of in-house counsel being deposed, in-house counsel should witness or attest to as few documents or purely business transactions as possible. That is, in-house counsel should *not* sign affidavits of discovery compliance or witness transactions if a corporate official is in a position to do so. Also, in-house counsel should not get involved with the mechanics of discovery, such as searching files, because this increases the likelihood of becoming a fact witness when the scope of that discovery compliance is at issue.

3. The Shelton Doctrine: Noticing the Opposing Counsel's Deposition

The attorney is not permitted to testify (and may therefore refuse to answer questions) as to communications made to him or her by the client unless the client consents. However, the right to refuse to testify exists only if

- The holder of the privilege is a client (or a potential client);
- The person to whom the communication was made is a lawyer;
- The communication relates to a fact of which the attorney was informed
    - by the client;
    - not in the presence of strangers; and
    - for the purpose of receiving a legal service; and
- The privilege has been asserted and has not been waived by the client.[67]

Parties typically attempt to notice the deposition of opposing counsel, including in-house counsel, for several reasons. First, it can be a shortcut to information available through more traditional and legitimate methods of discovery. Second, it may create grounds for the disqualification of opposing counsel under ethical rules forbidding attorneys to serve both as advocate and witness in the same trial. Third, it may be used as an inappropriate means of harassing the opposing party.

Courts have attempted to prevent such abusive depositions. To be sure, there is no total bar to deposing in-house counsel. Some federal courts have even supported efforts to depose opposing counsel, noting that the Federal Rules of Civil Procedure permit a party to "depose any person."[68] Other courts, however, have imposed strict burdens on parties seeking to depose opposing counsel. One of the first courts to do so was the Eighth Circuit in *Shelton v. American Motors Corp.*,[69] where the court granted a protective order against the taking of the deposition of an opposing party's counsel. The court in *Shelton* determined that opposing counsel can be deposed only when a party demonstrates that (1) no other means exist to obtain the information than to depose opposing counsel, (2) the information sought is relevant and nonprivileged, and (3) the information is crucial to the preparation of the case.[70] As a practical matter, the law on this issue generally seems to follow *Shelton*, meaning that most courts will permit the deposition of opposing counsel only upon a showing of substantial need and only after alternate discovery avenues have been exhausted or proven impractical.

When the deposition of counsel has been noticed, and not quashed, in-house counsel should rely on the *Shelton* policy arguments set out below to protect privileged information:

- The deposition will inevitably hinder the attorney-client relationship and inhibit counsel's preparation of the client's case;
- It is unlikely that counsel has any more nonprivileged information than is available from other sources;
- Routine attempts to depose counsel will inevitably tie up the court's time with disputes over the scope of privilege and related matters; and
- There should be no interrogation of an attorney to impeach discovery unless prior substantial evidence shows that a significant violation of the discovery obligation has occurred.

In some instances, the need to depose opposing counsel can be obviated by stipulating that certain witnesses will not be called and that certain issues will not be raised at trial. For example, in *Perry v. Jeep Eagle Corp.*,[71] the defendants avoided the deposition of their in-house counsel by arguing that the information sought was not relevant to plaintiff's claims. The defendants also stipulated that the study about which plaintiff sought to question the attorney would not be offered in evidence during the trial. The court recognized that, where a matter is not at issue, there is no need to pursue information about the matter by deposing in-house counsel.

Another alternative to deposing counsel is a discovery conference.[72] A discovery conference allows attorneys and the court to learn why counsel intend to depose certain witnesses. The purpose is to focus the court's attention on the opponent's overall discovery plan instead of the mere discovery details. This permits the court to determine whether a party can obtain the necessary information without deposing an opposing counsel.

In federal court, as in many states, parties must meet and confer before a scheduling conference "to discuss any issues about preserving discoverable information"[73] and "any issues relating to claims of privilege or of protection as trial preparation material."[74] The parties should attempt to resolve these issues as well as discuss a procedure for handling inadvertently produced material, placing such an agreement into an order of the court.[75]

Some courts considering whether to compel counsel's deposition have required attorneys to prove that the protection of attorney-client privilege or work-product immunity is justified. For example, in *In re Shopping Carts Antitrust Litigation*,[76] the court stated that a party seeking to assert the attorney-client privilege must provide information from which the court could reasonably conclude that the communication (1) concerned the seeking of legal advice; (2) was between a client and an attorney acting *in his or her professional* capacity; (3) was related to legal matters; and (4) was and is, at the client's instance, permanently protected.[77] The court found that the defendants in the *Shopping Carts* litigation failed to meet this burden.

D. Other Types of Privilege

1. *The "Joint Defense"*

Parties represented by separate lawyers often have legal interests in common. In some situations, these parties might need to communicate with one another, for example, to discuss joint strategies of defense. As long as the communications relate to a matter of common legal interest, there should not be a waiver of the attorney-client privilege or work-product immunity.[78] This protection of shared information is known as the joint defense privilege.

While courts vary as to the elements required to support a claim of joint defense privilege, a few common requirements emerge. First, as discussed above, the parties need to have a common legal interest. Courts have different interpretations of the degree of commonality required for parties. For instance, some courts, including the Ninth Circuit, permit parties to assert the privilege based on only a common legal interest.[79] Other courts, however, such as the Third Circuit, require a common defense strategy.[80] For instance, the Third Circuit held that "[t]he joint defense privilege protects communications between an individual and an attorney for another when the communications are 'part of an on-going and joint effort to set up a common defense strategy.'"[81] Several circuit and district courts have applied similar standards.[82] Parties with adverse interests may claim joint defense privilege for communications relating to their common legal interests.[83]

Second, the parties must be engaged in litigation; however, courts disagree over the degree to which litigation must loom over the relationship. At one extreme, Uniform Rule of Evidence 502(b) limits joint defense privilege to cases in which there is a "pending action."[84] This provision has been interpreted as requiring the actual institution of legal proceedings, such that communications made in the course of prelitigation settlement efforts will be denied privilege. Most federal courts require the communication to involve a matter of common interest that either is currently the subject of litigation or may reasonably be expected or anticipated to become the subject of litigation.[85]

Third, the parties do not always need to be involved in the same litigation.[86] Fourth, even though parties might share a common interest, their communications may not be protected unless they are made in furtherance of that interest.[87] Finally, the shared interest of joint defense participants generally must be a shared legal interest rather than merely a shared commercial interest.

If two parties plan to assert the joint defense privilege, they might want to first obtain a signed writing (letter or formal agreement) indicating their intent to share information pertaining to a common legal interest. Such an agreement might specify that

- The information transmitted contains confidential, privileged attorney-client communications;
- It is being sent only to counsel for other defendants in the pending matter;
- The disclosure is only to further common defenses;
- The information will not be furnished to any other person, either through copying of the joint defense letter or through disclosure of its contents, in whole or part;
- All signatories to the document voluntarily waive on behalf of their client any actions they may have at any time against any or all signatories; and
- All parties agree that no protective orders ban disclosure of such information.

A variation of the joint defense privilege is the "pooled information" situation.[88] To assert the attorney-client privilege after "pooling information," parties should establish that they are

- Parties in the same lawsuit;
- Parties who are about to be in the same lawsuit, making the communications in anticipation of litigation; or
- Parties with common defenses against a plaintiff.

The rule does not apply to situations where there is no common interest to be promoted by a joint consultation, or where the parties meet on a purely adversarial basis. Moreover, the privilege does not apply to matters irrelevant to the pending litigation or to communications with other parties themselves.[89] The principle applies only to communications with a party's lawyer or a lawyer's representative.

2. *Self-Critical Analysis*

Another distant cousin of the attorney-client privilege is sometimes termed the "self-critical analysis" privilege. This privilege was created to prevent or limit disclosure of potentially damaging information uncovered as a result of an internal evaluation or analysis.[90] However, the continued viability of a broad self-critical analysis privilege is perhaps doubtful, partly because of the inconsistency with which courts have recognized and applied the privilege. Circuit courts of appeal have declined to recognize a privilege for self-evaluation but have noted district court and state authorities applying analogues in specialized contexts.[91]

This privilege was first explicitly recognized in *Bredice v. Doctors Hospital, Inc.*[92] and is based upon strong public policy considerations. In *Bredice*, a malpractice action, the plaintiff sought production of the minutes and reports of the defendant hospital board concerning the death of a patient. The court denied the discovery requests on the grounds that "[t]here is an overwhelming public interest in having those staff meetings held on a confidential basis so that the flow of ideas and advice can continue unimpeded."[93] The court also stated that "[t]he purpose of these staff meetings is the improvement, through self-analysis, of the efficiency of medical procedures and techniques . . . and that the value of these discussions [involving constructive criticism] would be destroyed if the meetings were opened to the discovery process."[94] This privilege for healthcare providers has been codified in some states and protects from disclosure medical committee or peer review reports of the medical staff of a healthcare facility.[95]

Since *Bredice*, however, the privilege has not been uniformly accepted nor, for the most part, categorically denied. In cases where the self-critical analysis privilege has been applied, courts require various elements to invoke the privilege.[96] First, the information sought must come from an internal investigation conducted to improve or evaluate the products or procedures of a party. Second, the party must have originally intended to keep the disputed information confidential. Third, there must be a significant public interest in maintaining the confidentiality of that information. Fourth, the information must be of a type whose flow would be curtailed if discovery were allowed.

The self-critical analysis privilege has been considered in nonmedical contexts, including product liability cases. In *Lloyd v. Cessna Aircraft Co.*,[97] plaintiff's counsel sought information regarding a "top ten list" of confidential memoranda from staff meetings "designed to review, analyze, and evaluate operations for the continued self-improvement in the quality of their respective products."[98] Cessna objected to the request, alleging that the information sought was protected under a qualified privilege.

The court, after noting that the plaintiff was not seeking actual production of the list, permitted questioning of Cessna's witness. In reaching its holding, however, the court noted that "[w]ere the government seeking herein to obtain copies of the minutes or other reports of the actual discussions of Cessna's 'top ten' meetings, this Court might be inclined to follow the principles enunciated in the afore cited [self-critical analysis] cases; under such circumstances the Court would feel obligated to apply a balancing approach before allowing the wholesale disclosure of the specific details of any such meetings."[99]

In *Bradley v. Melroe Co.*,[100] the court limited the discovery of in-house investigative files of previous accidents to the factual data contained in those files. Applying a standard similar to the one required under the work-product rule, the court held that the defendant manufacturer could redact all mental impressions, opinions, evaluations, recommendations, and theories of counsel. In reaching its holding, the court noted that "in many instances, and it certainly appears to be so in this case, manufacturers study reports of accidents involving their products for the purpose of ascertaining if preventive measures can be taken to avoid future accidents."[101] The court went on to say:

> In such cases, courts have recognized a privilege of self-critical analysis precluding the discovery of impressions, opinions, and evaluations but allowing the discovery of factual data. The reasoning behind this approach is that the ultimate benefit to others from this critical analysis of the product or event far outweighs any benefits from disclosure.[102]

The U.S. Supreme Court has never recognized the self-critical analysis privilege, and historically it has been very reluctant to expand common law testimonial privileges.[103] In *University of Pennsylvania v. EEOC*, the Court reasoned that it should not adopt a privilege "where it appears that Congress has considered the relevant competing concerns but has not provided the privilege itself."[104]

Further, no circuit court of appeals has recognized the privilege; numerous courts, in fact, have refused to apply it. Most recently, the Third Circuit Court of Appeals has declined to apply the privilege in a case involving the production of an accident investigation report.[105] While the court acknowledged the policy considerations behind the privilege, it was not persuaded that they warranted the application of the privilege, "especially in light of the liberal scope of discovery afforded litigants under Rule 26, and the view that evidentiary privileges are disfavored as inconsistent with the broad scope of discovery."[106]

E. Losing the Attorney-Client Privilege

Although the rules of the privilege are relatively easy to state, their implementation is multifaceted and sometimes extremely complex. It is especially important, therefore, for attorneys to understand the privilege rules because certain threshold or procedural mistakes can lead to loss or waiver of the privilege. For instance, when assertion of the attorney-client privilege is rejected, often the statements or disclosure in question was, ab initio, beyond the scope of the privilege (that is, the communication was not between an attorney, acting as attorney, and his or her client).

In addition, the privilege is potentially waived by failing to assert it when a question about a confidential communication is asked and answered. Thus, in *West v. Solito*,[107] the court stated that neither a motion in limine nor an objection at trial would prevent the admission into evidence of privileged information that was disclosed without objection in a deposition. The court held that even though the trial court ordered that privilege objections be reserved for trial, "once the matter has been disclosed, it cannot be retracted or otherwise protected."[108] Therefore, an attorney whose client is asked for privileged information in a deposition or a trial must object and instruct the client not to answer in order to protect the privilege. If privileged documents have been produced, the attorney must attempt to regain custody of those privileged documents.[109]

In the ever-growing age of technology, lawyers are faced with new challenges in protecting the attorney-client privilege. With the rise of e-mail as the primary method of communication in the workplace, the risks of inadvertent disclosure of the attorney-client privilege have also risen. Additionally, the boom in social media as an everyday means of communication has placed more pressure on attorneys to monitor and advise their clients about the perils of disclosing otherwise privileged communications.

1. *Waiving the Privilege*

As noted earlier, in order to preserve the attorney-client privilege, not only must the privilege be claimed, but it must also be established that the privilege has not been waived.[110] In many instances, however, the issue for the attorney representing the corporation is not whether to waive the privilege but rather who can waive it.

It has been held that an employee whose communications have been claimed as privileged under the attorney-client privilege on behalf of the corporation may waive that privilege.[111] Most courts, however, follow the principles of the *Restatement (Third) of the Law Governing Lawyers*,[112] which provides that only an authorized agent of the corporation may waive the privilege of the corporation. Accordingly, it is the general rule that a corporation's privileged communication cannot be waived by the unauthorized disclosure by either a current or former employee. Corporate counsel should, of course, be proactive rather than reactive in this area. Rarely does privileged information disclosed by a current or former corporate employee in an unauthorized fashion have a positive consequence, regardless of whether a court subsequently declares the waiver as ineffective. The attorney should, therefore, instruct employees with whom he or she communicates that the communication is confidential. In addition, in-house counsel should note the possibility of a waiver occurring at an employee's deposition. When corporate employees are being deposed, the corporate attorney should be prepared to object and instruct the employee (or former employee) not to answer a question that calls for the disclosure of privileged attorney-client communications. If necessary, the attorney should terminate the deposition, seek a protective order from the court,[113] or contact the court for instructions on how to protect the privileged information. Failure to take these measures may be construed by the court as waiver of the privilege.[114]

2. *Waiver by Selective and Inadvertent Disclosure*

One of the ways a party can waive its privilege is by voluntary disclosure. Rule 511 of the Texas Rules of Evidence is representative of the "voluntary disclosure" doctrine. According to Texas Rule of Evidence 511, a party waives the privilege if "the person or a predecessor of the person while holder of the privilege voluntarily discloses or consents to disclosure of any significant part of the privileged matter unless such disclosure itself is privileged."

For example, in *Axelson, Inc. v. McIlhaney*,[115] a Texas court found that a company waived the attorney-client privilege concerning information relating to the company's internal investigation of kickbacks to its employees. The information from the company's investigation was at issue in a federal trial initiated by the company, and the information was revealed to federal law enforcement agencies as well as a national publication.

In another case, *United States v. Ruehle*,[116] the Ninth Circuit determined that statements made by a corporation's chief financial officer (CFO) to in-house counsel were not privileged because the CFO understood that in-house counsel would disclose the information to third-party auditors conducting an internal investigation of corporate stock-granting practices. Because the CFO repeatedly admitted that he knew his statements to in-house counsel would be conveyed to the auditors, he had no expectation of confidentiality, and therefore, the attorney-client privilege did not apply.

Some of the more frequently encountered "high-risk" areas for waiving the privilege by selective disclosure of information may occur in the following situations:

- Response to a government investigation[117]
- Information supplied to a government agency
- Insurance renewals
- Auditor or accountant inquiry
- Public financial disclosure documents (Securities and Exchange Commission [SEC] forms)
- Any disclosure to third parties not working under the attorney or at the attorney's direction, or for nonlegal purposes

In addition to making a voluntary disclosure, parties can waive the privilege inadvertently. For instance, on some occasions, particularly in large document productions, a party will inadvertently produce privileged documents to the opposing party. In such situations, the question is whether the inadvertent production constitutes "voluntary disclosure" and therefore waives the privilege of all communications relating to the subject matter of the disclosed documents.

The Texas Supreme Court first addressed this issue in *Granada Corp. v. First Court of Appeals*.[118] The court reasoned that, depending upon the facts, an inadvertent production of a privileged document could be either "voluntary" or "involuntary." Only a voluntary production would constitute a waiver of the privilege. In *Granada*, the court held that the producing party carries the burden of showing specific circumstances confirming the involuntary nature of an inadvertent disclosure of a privileged document.[119] The court identified the following factors as relevant to whether a particular inadvertent disclosure is "voluntary" and therefore results in waiver:

- whether "precautionary measures" were taken ("efforts reasonably calculated to prevent the disclosure");
- whether there was "delay in rectifying the error";
- the "extent of any inadvertent disclosure"; and
- the "scope of discovery."[120]

A few years after the Texas Supreme Court distinguished "voluntary" from "involuntary" disclosure in *Granada*, the Texas Legislature adopted a rule simplifying the procedures for recovering inadvertently produced privileged materials. The Texas Rules of Civil Procedure now provide that

> A party who produces material or information without intending to waive a claim of privilege does not waive that claim under these rules or the Rules of evidence if—within ten days or a shorter time ordered by the court, after the producing party actually discovers that such production was made—the producing party amends the response, identifying the material or information produced and stating the privilege asserted. If the producing party thus amends the response to assert a privilege, the requesting party must promptly return the specified material or information and any copies pending any ruling by the court denying the privilege.[121]

Until a few years ago, there was no comparable procedure under the Federal Rules of Civil Procedure. With the following observation, the Civil Rules Advisory Committee began its discussion of the need for a simplified procedure for handling inadvertent production: "[e]ver since the [Advisory] Committee began its intensive examination of discovery in 1996, a frequent complaint has been the expense and delay that accompany privilege review."[122]

Charged with proposing amendments to the Federal Rules of Civil Procedure, the committee further acknowledged that the federal procedures for dealing with inadvertent disclosure of privileged material lacked uniformity and insufficiently addressed discovery of electronic communications. To remedy this problem, the committee adopted procedures similar to those established in Texas.

The new federal procedures were implemented under, inter alia, Rule 26(b)(5)(B) of the Federal Rules of Civil Procedure, providing that when material "subject to a claim of privilege or of protection as trial preparation material" is produced, the producing party shall give notice to the party who received the material.[123] The notice shall be in writing unless the circumstances preclude written notice, such as when the production is at a deposition. The notice should state the basis for the claim of privilege. The "[receiving] party must promptly return, sequester, or destroy the specified information and any copies it has . . . and [may] not use or disclose the information until the claim is resolved."[124] If the receiving party disclosed the information before the claim of privilege, it must also take reasonable steps to retrieve the information. The receiving party need do nothing further, but it can present the information to the court for determination of whether the claim of privilege is valid, and the producing party must preserve the information until that determination is made. It is significant to note that while the Texas and Federal Rules establish a procedure for the return of certain materials, neither address the appropriate standard courts should use in determining whether an inadvertent production constituted a waiver of privilege.

The Federal Rules of Evidence were amended in September 2008 to also address inadvertent disclosure issues. Under the new Federal Rule of Evidence 502, an inadvertent disclosure does not waive the privilege if three standards are satisfied: "1) the disclosure is inadvertent; 2) the holder of the privilege . . . took reasonable steps to prevent disclosure; and 3) the holder [of the privilege] promptly took reasonable steps to rectify the [mistaken disclosure], including, (if applicable) following Federal Rule of Civil Procedure 26(b)(5)(B)."[125] Additionally, the new rule contemplates that litigants may enter Privilege Disclosure Agreements.[126] Also, when federal courts enter Privilege Disclosure Orders consistent with these agreements or enter a Privilege Disclosure Order in the absence of such an agreement, Rule 502(d) provides that the order is enforceable in subsequent federal and state court proceedings.[127] Further, subdivision (c) of Rule 502 addresses the effect in federal court of privilege disclosures that occur in state court.[128]

To be sure, Federal Rule of Evidence 502 does not make any substantive changes to the attorney-client privilege or work-product doctrine.[129] Rather, the primary purpose of the new rule is to reduce the costs associated with the production of documents in discovery. As a few commentators have said, the new rule "aims to reduce the time and effort lawyers spend screening documents before producing them by limiting the risk that disclosure of documents or information protected by the attorney-client privilege or work-product doctrine will result in broad waiver of that protection."[130] Rule 502 achieves this in several ways. For one, the rule limits the situations where an inadvertent disclosure constitutes waiver. Also, the rule limits the extent of a waiver, providing that when a waiver occurs, it does not automatically extend beyond the communications or information actually disclosed.[131]

A recent decision from a federal district court in Maine provides an example of how courts approach inadvertent disclosure claims in light of recent developments in the Federal Rules. In *Ergo Licensing, LLC v. Carefusion 303, Inc.*,[132] the district court heard a discovery dispute involving 31 pages included in the production of a 540-page document by the plaintiff. The plaintiff and defendant disagreed as to whether a waiver of the attorney-client privilege had occurred by the inadvertent disclosure of the 31 pages. The court relied on the following three-factor test to answer this question: "1) the disclosure must be inadvertent; 2) the holder of the privilege took reasonable steps to prevent the disclosure; and 3) the holder promptly took steps to rectify the error."[133]

In regard to the first prong, the court quickly decided that the plaintiff did inadvertently disclose the 31 pages. The second and third prongs were not as easy to determine. To help its analysis, the court expanded the last two elements into the following factors: (1) the reasonableness of the precautions taken to prevent inadvertent disclosure in view of the extent of the document production; (2) the number of inadvertent disclosures; (3) the extent of the disclosure; (4) any delay and measures taken to rectify the disclosure; and

(5) whether the overriding interests of justice would or would not be served by relieving the party of its errors.[134] After considering these factors, the court concluded that the inadvertent disclosure did not constitute a waiver of the attorney-client privilege.[135]

In light of this case law, the attorney responsible for a large document production should create a plan (preferably reduced to writing) for the production of documents that will minimize the chances of an inadvertent production of a privileged document. Also, an attorney who discovers that he or she has inadvertently produced a privileged document should immediately master the governing procedures and, if necessary, file any appropriate motion with the court (for example, a Motion to Compel Return of Privileged Documents Inadvertently Produced). The attorney should then become familiar with the burdens of proof expected by courts dealing with inadvertent disclosure issues (*see Granada* and *Ergo Licensing* for examples). Further, the attorney should assemble, by affidavit, the evidence needed to sustain that burden, file the affidavits in a timely manner, and have the motion set for hearing.

Moreover, it is important to note that written client communications may also lose the protection of the attorney-client privilege if they are used at trial or in a deposition to refresh the witness's recollection.[136] The Federal Rules of Evidence provide that "if a witness uses a writing to refresh memory . . . for the purpose of testifying . . . an adverse party is entitled to have the writing produced at the hearing."[137] Accordingly, if the attorney uses an otherwise privileged document to refresh his or her client's memory on the witness stand, or in preparation for a deposition, waiver has occurred.[138] Courts typically consider the work-product doctrine to be inadequate protection from disclosure when work-product documents have been used to prepare a witness for depositions.[139] Some courts have even found that the use of work-product materials for deposition purposes is an automatic waiver of the protection, meaning that a party requesting disclosure does not have to show a substantial need or undue hardship.[140] Also, privileged material used by a testifying expert to formulate an opinion generally must also be produced upon request by opposing counsel.[141]

3. *Protecting the Privilege in Today's Technological Age*

As technology evolves and the market is flooded with new means of communication—e-mail, texting, blogs, instant messaging, Facebook, MySpace, Twitter—the potential for both clients and attorneys to waive protections for attorney-client-privileged communications increases.

Two recent cases demonstrate that although e-mail has been a dominant mode of communication between attorneys and clients for the past decade, new issues concerning e-mailed communications and waiver of attorney-client privilege continue to emerge. For instance, in an attempt to efficiently keep clients informed, some lawyers blind-copy ("bcc") their clients when sending e-mails to opposing counsel. A federal court recently confirmed that this method of communication can be very risky and can result in the loss of the attorney-client privilege. In *Charm v. Kohn*,[142] Kohn's counsel sent an e-mail to opposing counsel and blind-copied Kohn. Kohn responded to the e-mail by inadvertently using the "Reply All" button, thereby sending his response, intended only for his attorney, to opposing counsel as well. Kohn's counsel immediately caught the error and requested opposing counsel to delete the message, which opposing counsel refused to do. When opposing counsel submitted the e-mail as an exhibit to a motion, Kohn moved to strike on the basis that the communication was protected by the attorney-client privilege. In determining whether the privilege survived Kohn's inadvertent disclosure, the court weighed several factors: whether Kohn and his counsel had taken reasonable steps to preserve the confidentiality of the communication, whether the action of "bcc-ing" the client gave rise to a foreseeable risk that he would respond as he did, and whether the delay in asking the court for relief suggested waiver of the privilege. Although the court ultimately held that the privilege was not waived, it warned the parties *and others* that "[r]eply all is risky. So is bcc. Further carelessness may compel a finding of waiver." This decision instructs lawyers to "advise client to be careful" and "avoid practices that exacerbate risks."[143] Instead of bcc-ing clients, a better method is to forward clients any e-mails to opposing counsel, thereby eliminating the risk that a reply to the e-mail will be sent to third parties.

Another attorney-client privilege issue that has seen recent litigation is whether e-mails regarding action against the employer and sent between client and attorney on the client's employer's computer are protected by the attorney-client privilege. The 2010 case of *Holmes v. Petrovich Development Co.*[144] held that e-mails sent by an employee to her attorney regarding possible legal action against her employer were not subject to attorney-client privilege because the employee used her work computer even though she knew that the company's policy prohibited the use of company e-mail for personal reasons. Almost every employer that has a policy on use of company computers and e-mail has substantively similar warnings, even if they are never enforced. The holding itself may not come as a surprise to most attorneys because the law in many jurisdictions states that employees have no reasonable expectation of privacy when using their employer's electronic resources. Nonetheless, even if they are aware of the general rule, clients may not consider that an employer might be able to read e-mail sent to an attorney. While this approach is not the controlling law in all jurisdictions,[145] it is an important reminder that attorneys must remain mindful of the risk, even if their clients are not.

An even more recent technological trend that poses great threat to the preservation of the attorney-client privilege is the boom in social media, as both a personal and business tool. In *McMillen v. Hummingbird Speedway, Inc.*,[146] the plaintiff was rear-ended in a stock car accident and claimed significant personal injury, including loss of health, strength, and the ability to enjoy certain pleasures of life. The court compelled the plaintiff to provide his Facebook and MySpace information to defense counsel after defendants reviewed the public portion of plaintiff's Facebook account and discovered comments about his vacations and attendance at the Daytona 500 race. The court reasoned that "[w]hen a user communicates through Facebook or MySpace . . . he or she understands and tacitly submits to the possibility that a third-party recipient, i.e., one or more site operators, will also be receiving his or her messages and may further disclose them if the operator deems disclosure to be appropriate. The fact is wholly incommensurate with a claim of confidentiality. Accordingly, McMillen cannot successfully maintain that the element of confidentiality protects his Facebook and MySpace accounts from discovery."[147]

It is especially difficult in the corporate context for lawyers to monitor and protect against a client's unintentional disclosure of attorney-client-privileged communications via social media outlets. Managers, supervisors, or employees who disclose work-related issues in status updates, chats, or blogs run the risk of waiving the privilege, thereby forcing a company to produce documents it ordinarily would have the right to withhold in litigation. It is therefore essential that in-house counsel ensure that corporate personnel understand the implications of discussing work-related issues online. An additional concern for in-house counsel is the risk that a company will waive attorney-client privilege by posting statements on its website. Nowadays, it is often part of a company's business strategy to post statements on its website to keep the public informed on various activities and to ensure continued public confidence in the company's products and services. However, if the company discloses too much (or too often), it could risk waiving privilege protections.[148]

4. *Offensive Use of the Privilege*

The "offensive use" doctrine applies when privileged material is used as a "sword" rather than as a "shield."[149] For example, if the client claims that "my former attorney didn't tell me I had a claim until the statute of limitations had expired," then the former attorney may be deposed on this topic to prevent "manifest unfairness."[150] Whether the client was aware of a fact is now relevant and relates to the heart of the claim. For this reason, if there is information that would reveal that a fact was made known to the client by the attorney, then the adversary may discover this information. The assertion of the attorney-client privilege in this setting goes well beyond the intended purposes of the attorney-client privilege, and, consequently, the privilege is unavailable to protect this type of communication. The pursuit of this type of claim is analogous to an unintentional waiver, making otherwise protected discussions and conversations discoverable.

5. *The "Good Cause" Exception*

The "good cause" exception is invoked when concerns of countervailing policy dictate that the attorney-client privilege or the work-product doctrine should be ignored. In shareholder suits, for example, courts have sometimes reasoned that the corporate attorney's true client is the shareholder and, accordingly, that communications with corporate executives cannot be privileged when the substance of the conversation is at issue. Such an analysis puts in peril many communications between in-house counsel and corporate executives because a privilege-negating shareholder suit is always possible. But one state has held that in the case of closely held corporations, the attorney's duty is owed to the corporation itself, and not to the shareholders or directors.[151] Suffice it to say, this is a dynamic area.

Some courts attribute the "good cause" exception to the Fifth Circuit's *Garner v. Wolfinbarger*[152] decision. In *Garner*, the court held that when a corporation is sued by its stockholders, the availability of the corporation's attorney-client privilege is subject to the right of the stockholders to show cause why the corporation should not be allowed to invoke the privilege.[153] The court reasoned that although the attorney-client privilege is important in the corporate context, management owes a duty to the corporation's stockholders, and this duty should be considered by the court in determining the applicability of the privilege. Toward that end, the court concluded, when breaches of duty occur, the privilege should not be allowed if the stockholders can demonstrate why the privilege should not be allowed.[154]

It is important to note that in a subsequent case, the Fifth Circuit determined that the good cause exception does not apply to work-product claims. In *In re International Systems & Controls Corp.*,[155] the court held that the *Garner* rationale was premised upon a "mutuality of interest" between shareholders and management that does not exist for work-product items prepared in anticipation of litigation by the shareholders.

That said, a leading case where the "good cause" waiver was *almost* successfully argued by a party seeking the discovery of privileged documents is *Sporck v. Peil*.[156] In *Sporck*, the court denied the plaintiff's motion to compel the production of documents that the defendant acknowledged had been provided to him by his attorney in preparation for his deposition. The defendant claimed that the selection of documents was protected from disclosure by the work-product doctrine, a less restrictive rule against nondisclosure than the attorney-client privilege. Stressing that defendant's counsel had culled the selected documents from the documents produced by defendants, the court found that the process of sifting relevant documents from the mass of produced documents was protected as attorney work product: "[w]e believe that the selection and compilation of documents by counsel in this case in preparation for pretrial discovery falls within the highly-protected category of opinion work product. . . . Rule 26(b)(3) placed an obligation on the trial court to protect against unjustified disclosure of defense counsel's selection process."[157] Notably, the court engaged in an analysis to determine whether there was "good cause" to compel production or whether the attorney-client privilege and work-product doctrine protection should be respected.

F. Distinguishing the Attorney Work-Product Doctrine from the Attorney-Client Privilege

1. The Attorney Work-Product Doctrine

The attorney work-product doctrine, which is codified in Federal Rule of Civil Procedure 26(b)(3), provides a qualified protection to materials prepared by a party's counsel or other representative in anticipation of litigation.[158] This doctrine is important in the American legal system because it helps to ensure that attorneys are able to "work with a certain degree of privacy, free from unnecessary intrusion by opposing parties and their counsel."[159] As the Supreme Court explained in *Hickman v. Taylor* in 1947, without the work-product doctrine, "the effect on the legal profession would be demoralizing. And the interests of the clients and the cause of justice would be poorly served."[160] The Court cautioned that absent work-product protections, an attorney's thought process and preparation for trial would be stifled, causing "inefficiency" and "unfairness."[161]

The attorney-client privilege should be distinguished from the attorney work-product doctrine. Work-product immunity, which may be asserted by either the lawyer or the client, is unlike attorney-client privilege, which "belongs" to the client.[162] Also, "the work-product doctrine is distinct from and broader than the attorney-client privilege"[163] in that it covers all material prepared in anticipation of litigation; it is not limited to communications between attorney and client.[164] This greater scope is, however, met by a concomitant reduction in the strength of protection offered by the *doctrine*, as compared to the *privilege*. For instance, the attorney-client privilege covers communications made by the client to the attorney or communications by the attorney to the client that incorporate or are based on a client's communications. Once properly invoked, the attorney-client privilege is virtually inviolate. The attorney work-product doctrine, on the other hand, is a qualified protection that can be overcome by showing "substantial need" and "undue hardship."[165] The party claiming work-product protections has the burden of establishing that the doctrine applies. Once that protection has been demonstrated, the burden of showing "substantial need" and "undue hardship" falls on the party seeking production.

As noted earlier, an attorney's work product is protected because it would be patently unfair and contrary to the adversarial nature of the U.S. legal system to permit discovery of materials containing an attorney's mental impressions, conclusions, opinions, or legal theories that have been created in preparation for trial.[166] For material to be considered prepared in anticipation of litigation, the prospect of litigation must be identifiable even if the litigation has yet to commence.[167] Thus, a party may not simply claim that materials have been prepared in anticipation of litigation. Rather, a party asserting attorney work-product protection may also be required to actually prove this claim.[168]

Work-product materials include a variety of information. They can include legal memoranda, impressions of witness statements, documents collected by counsel to provide an understanding of the claims or defenses, memoranda or reports from outside consultants, statistical data compiled electronically as a result of (or to evaluate) a claim or lawsuit, and the identity of confidential consultants. Federal Rule of Civil Procedure 26(b)(3) protects not only materials prepared by lawyers, but also materials, mental impressions, or opinions of other representatives concerning the litigation, including consultants and the system specialist who may have designed a computer litigation support system.[169] Not surprisingly, items otherwise considered privileged or protected under the work-product rule might lose that status by being sent to testifying experts to review.[170] It is also critical to note that documents that are merely kept in the ordinary course of business will not be protected, even though they are stored in a computerized litigation support system.[171]

2. *Limits of the Work-Product Doctrine*

The attorney work-product doctrine is a qualified protection. In fact, Rule 26(b)(3) of the Federal Rules of Civil Procedure provides specific exceptions to the general prohibition against discovery of documents and tangible things "prepared in anticipation of litigation or for trial by or for another party or its representative."[172] For instance, information prepared in anticipation of litigation can be discovered if the party seeking discovery shows "substantial need" and is unable to obtain such information by other means without "undue hardship."[173] In determining whether the requisite showing has been made, courts will consider various factors, including the importance of the information sought and the availability of, and difficulty in, obtaining such information from alternative sources.[174]

However, even if the party requesting work-product information can show a substantial need or undue hardship, Federal Rule of Civil Procedure 26(b)(3) limits discovery of the lawyer's mental impressions and opinions concerning the litigation.[175] Courts generally classify this type of information as "opinion work product."[176] As some commentators point out, a few courts have determined that the privilege afforded to opinion work product is absolute and that a showing of necessity cannot overcome the protection.[177] Other courts have held that opinion work product can be discovered, but only in rare and extraordinary circumstances.[178] In *Holmgren v. State Farm Mutual Auto Insurance Co.*,[179] the Ninth Circuit determined that discovery of opinion work product is permissible when mental impressions are at issue in the case and the need for the material is compelling.

3. *Asserting the Work-Product Doctrine in Successive Litigation*

As noted in the above-quoted portion of Rule 26, some items protected by work-product immunity can be discoverable if the discovering party makes a sufficient showing of substantial need and undue hardship. It is unwise to assume that this showing will be more difficult for a plaintiff in an already closed case. Indeed, because of the passage of time, the work-product-protected data held by corporate counsel may be the only source of pertinent information available to the plaintiff, and therefore, a court may find that the substantial need or undue hardship test is met.

The case of *Shelton v. American Motors Corp.*[180] provides insight on this matter. In that case, plaintiffs filed notices to take the depositions of several individuals, including Rita Burns, a staff attorney for American Motors Corporation. Burns was the supervising in-house counsel on certain Jeep "rollover" cases. She was deposed, but she refused to answer many questions on the basis of work-product and attorney-client privilege. These questions primarily involved the existence or nonexistence of various documents regarding the model Jeep involved in the case at hand. The work-product privilege was for materials prepared "in anticipation" of previous litigation. Burns's standard reply was as follows:

> Any information I have concerning documents which might possibly be responsive to your question, I've acquired solely through my capacity as an attorney for American Motors in my efforts to find information which would assist me in defending the company in litigation, and therefore, I decline to respond to the question.[181]

In its opinion, the lower court noted that the mere fact that documents or knowledge of documents came to an attorney while acting for a client was not sufficient to invoke the attorney-client privilege.[182] In addition, the court held that the work-product doctrine from past cases did not protect discovery of the existence or nonexistence of documents.[183] Ultimately, the district court entered a default judgment against American Motors Corporation as a sanction for Burns's repeated refusals to answer the deposition questions.

The limited issue on appeal to the Eighth Circuit was whether a deponent's mere acknowledgment of the existence of corporate documents was protected by the work-product or attorney-client privileges. The Eighth Circuit reversed the district court's judgment, holding that Burns's acknowledgment of the existence of certain documents would reveal her mental impressions, which are protected as work product.[184] In the course of its opinion, the Eighth Circuit acknowledged that the boundaries of discovery had expanded and that the practice of taking the depositions of opposing counsel was becoming increasingly popular.[185] The court stressed, however, that opposing counsel's depositions should be taken only when the party seeking to take the deposition can show that "1) no other means exist to obtain the information than to depose opposing counsel . . . ; 2) the information sought is relevant and not privileged; and 3) the information is crucial to the preparation of the case." The *Shelton* court concluded that the facts in the case did not present these "limited circumstances."[186]

III. Conclusion and Practical Tips

The attorney-client privilege is a cornerstone of the American legal system. Although deeply rooted in our nation's history, the privilege is continuously being shaped as courts interpret it and apply it to new and evolving circumstances—especially in the context of corporations. By carefully preparing and adhering to the rules that define and set the parameters of the attorney-client privilege, lawyers working for corporations can effectively use the privilege to better serve their clients.

In sum, attorneys representing corporations should consider the following tips when performing tasks involving the creation of confidential documents or conversations. In general, counsel should periodically conjure up the mental image of an adversarial proceeding in which they are attempting to establish the attorney-client privilege against an aggressive opponent. This will inevitably result in counsel paying closer attention to the formalities necessary to help preserve the privilege. In addition to the principles articulated earlier in this chapter, the attorney should consistently and judiciously follow the formalities associated with the privilege. Toward that end, they should

- Follow or refer to the *Upjohn* factors in letters and memoranda;
- Mark all appropriate documents as "privileged" and "prepared as confidential communications at request of counsel";
- Ensure that memos seeking information identify counsel by title as "counsel" and in legal opinions state that they are "in my opinion as counsel"; and
- Keep circulation and distribution of *legal* memos severely limited to "control group" personnel.

Thus, in order to maintain the attorney-client privilege, a company should specify on reports prepared by employees that the report was prepared for counsel regarding legal services. Also, the signature of counsel and statements that the report is to be confidential will help enhance the likelihood that the document is protected. In the realm of privilege and protection from waiver, it is truly the case that an ounce of prevention is worth a pound of cure.

Notes

1. Memorandum from Larry D. Thompson, Deputy Attorney General, to Heads of Department Components and United States Attorneys (Jan. 20, 2003), http://federalevidence.com/pdf/2008/06-June/Thompson2003PrincipFederalProsec.pdf. *See* appendix 1-1.
2. Memorandum from Paul McNulty, Deputy Attorney General, to Heads of Department Components and United States Attorneys (Dec. 12, 2006), http://www.justice.gov/dag/speeches/2006/mcnulty_memo.pdf. *See* appendix 1-2.
3. Memorandum from Mark Filip, Deputy Attorney General, to Heads of Department Components and United States Attorneys (Aug. 28, 2008), http://federalevidence.com/pdf/Corp_Prosec/Filip.Memorandum.2008.pdf. *See* appendix 1-3.
4. *See also* appendix 1-3.
5. *See, e.g.*, Fed. R. Civ. P. 26(b)(3).
6. *See, e.g.*, Model Rules of Prof'l Conduct R. 1.6 cmt [3].
7. *See* Annesley v. Anglesea, 17 How. St. Tr. 1139 (1743); Hunt v. Blackburn, 128 U.S. 464 (1888).
8. *See, e.g.*, Commodity Futures Trading Comm. v. Weintraub, 471 U.S. 343, 348 (1985); State *ex rel.* Romley v. Superior Court, 181 Ariz. 378, 891 P.2d 246 (Ariz. App. 1995); West v. Solito, 563 S.W.2d 240, 245 (Tex. 1978).
9. 8 J.H. Wigmore, Wigmore on Evidence § 2192 (3d ed.).

10. Fisher v. United States, 425 U.S. 391, 403 (1976) (stating that "since the privilege has the effect of withholding relevant information from the fact finder, it applies only where necessary to achieve its purpose").
11. Nat'l Labor Relations Bd. v. Harvey, 349 F.2d 900, 907 (4th Cir. 1965).
12. *See* COLO. REV. STAT. § 13-90-107(V)(b) (2003); GA. CODE ANN. § 24-9-24 (2002); NEV. REV. STAT. ANN. § 49.095 (2003); TENN. CODE ANN. § 22-3-105 (2003).
13. *See, e.g.*, ARIZ. REV. STAT. § 12-2234; TEX. R. EVID. 503.
14. Lawyers should educate themselves in the rules of unfamiliar jurisdictions in which they are handling matters. Even what many consider basic attorney-client privilege principles can differ between jurisdictions. For example, in 2011, a Pennsylvania court clarified the scope of the state's attorney-client statute: "[w]e hold that, in Pennsylvania, the attorney-client privilege operates in a two-way fashion to protect confidential client-to-attorney or attorney-to-client communications made for the purpose of obtaining or providing professional legal advice." Gillard v. AIG Ins. Co., 2011 LEXIS 393 (Pa. Feb. 23, 2011). Prior to this ruling, Pennsylvania common law inconsistently interpreted the attorney-client privilege statute; some courts narrowly read the statute to limit the privilege to client-to-lawyers communications only. *Id.*
15. TEX. R. EVID. 503(b)(1).
16. *See* TEX. R. EVID. 503(a)(1) (emphasis added); ALA. R. EVID. 502(a)(1) (emphasis added). *See also* State v. Tally, 102 Ala. 25, 15 So. 722 (1894).
17. It has been held that the privilege remains after the death of the client. Wesp v. Everson, 33 P.3d 191 (Colo. 2001); *In re* Busse's Estate, 332 Ill. App. 258, 75 N.E.2d 36 (Ill. App. 1947); Eloise Bauer & Assocs. v. Elec. Realty Assocs., 621 S.W.2d 200, 204 (Tex. Civ. App.–Texarkana 1981, writ ref'd n.r.e.).
18. *See In re* Grand Jury Subpoena Duces Tecum, 391 F. Supp. 1029, 1034 (S.D.N.Y. 1975) (defendant need not be present for counsel to assert the privilege); Sikes v. Segers, 266 Ark. 654, 587 S.W.2d 554 (1979); West v. Solito, 563 S.W.2d 240 (Tex. 1978).
19. *See, e.g.*, ALA. R. EVID. 502(c). *See also* TEX. R. EVID. 503(c) ("The person who was the lawyer or the lawyer's representative at the time of the communication is presumed to have authority to claim the privilege but only on behalf of the client."). This point was also made in Cole v. Gabriel, 822 S.W.2d 296 (Tex. App.–Fort Worth 1991 orig. proceeding) in a slightly different way when it was held that a lawyer had no standing to assert the attorney-client privilege in his individual capacity. *See also* Fisher v. United States, 425 U.S. 391 (1976); Klitzman, Klitzman & Gallagher v. Krut, 744 F.2d 955 (3d Cir. 1984).
20. *In re* Grand Jury Proceedings, 469 F.3d 24 (1st Cir. 2006) (holding that the CEO of a corporation could not intervene in a proceeding to prevent counsel for the corporation from testifying to a conversation between the CEO and counsel in his personal capacity (absent evidence the counsel represented him in his personal capacity as well as the corporation)). In a context similar to that of the corporate world, it was held that White House lawyers could not claim that their conversations with the First Lady were privileged from disclosure in an investigation in which the President and First Lady were being investigated because the attorneys represented the White House and not the First Lady or the President. *In re* Grand Jury Subpoena Duces Tecum, 112 F.3d 910 (8th Cir. 1997). *See also In re* Grand Jury Investigation, 599 F.2d 1224 (3d Cir. 1979).

21. *See, e.g.*, TEX. R. EVID. 503(c) ("The person who was the lawyer or the lawyer's representative at the time of the communication is presumed to have authority to claim the privilege but only on behalf of the client.").
22. *See* People v. Agado, 964 P.2d 565 (Colo. App. 1998); Cacamo v. Liberty Mut. Fire Ins. Co., 798 So. 2d 1210 (La. App. 2001); Loftin v. Martin, 776 S.W.2d 145 (Tex. 1989); Weisel Enters., Inc. v. Curry, 718 S.W.2d 56 (Tex. 1986) (per curiam).
23. Maura Strassberg, *Privilege Can Be Abused: Exploring the Ethical Obligations to Avoid Frivolous Claims of Attorney-Client Privilege*, 37 SETON HALL L. REV. 413 (2007) (noting that the privilege should not be frivolously claimed).
24. *In re* Human Tissue Prods. Liab. Litig., 255 F.R.D. 151 (D.N.J. 2008), *appeal denied, judgment aff'd*, Civ. No. 06-135, 2009 WL 1097671 (D.N.J. 2009).
25. A number of jurisdictions have patterned their codification of the rules of privilege after the Supreme Court draft that was ultimately not accepted by Congress in enacting the Federal Rules of Evidence but was substantially included in the 1974 Uniform Rules of Evidence. *See* Edward J. Imwinkelried, *Draft Article V of the Federal Rules of Evidence on Privileges, One of the Most Influential Pieces of Legislation Never Enacted: The Strength of the Ingroup Loyalty of the Federal Judiciary*, 28 ALA. L. REV. 41 (2006). Thus, the Texas Rules of Evidence set forth the following categories of situations in which the attorney-client privilege may not be claimed:

> (1) Furtherance of crime or fraud. If the services of the lawyer were sought or obtained to enable or aid anyone to commit or plan to commit what the client knew or reasonably should have known to be a crime or fraud;
> (2) Claimants through same deceased client. As to a communication relevant to an issue between parties who claim through the same deceased client, regardless of whether the claims are by testate or intestate succession or by inter vivos transactions;
> (3) Breach of duty by a lawyer or client. As to a communication relevant to an issue of breach of duty by a lawyer to the client or by a client to the lawyer;
> (4) Document attested by a lawyer. As to a communication relevant to an issue concerning an attested document to which the lawyer is an attesting witness; or
> (5) Joint clients. As to a communication relevant to a matter of common interest between or among two or more clients if the communication was made by any of them to a lawyer retained or consulted in common, when offered in an action between or among any of the clients.

TEX. R. EVID. 503(d). *See also* KY. R. EVID. 403(d); LA. CODE EVID. art. 506(c); Florida sets forth the following situations in which the privilege does not apply:

> (a) The services of the lawyer were sought or obtained to enable or aid anyone to commit or plan to commit what the client knew was a crime or fraud.
> (b) A communication is relevant to an issue between parties who claim through the same deceased client.
> (c) A communication is relevant to an issue of breach of duty by the lawyer to the client or by the client to the lawyer, arising from the lawyer–client relationship.

(d) A communication is relevant to an issue concerning the intention or competence of a client executing an attested document to which the lawyer is an attesting witness, or concerning the execution or attestation of the document.

(e) A communication is relevant to a matter of common interest between two or more clients, or their successors in interest, if the communication was made by them to a lawyer retained or consulted in common when offered in a civil action between the clients or their successors in interest.

FLA. STAT. § 90.502(4) (2003). It has likewise been held that statutory construction of a sunshine law preempts assertion of the attorney-client privilege in circumstances where it could otherwise have been asserted. State *ex rel.* Reno v. Neu, 434 So. 2d 1035 (Fla. Ct. App. 1983); McKay v. Bd. of Cnty. Comm'rs, 103 Nev. 490, 746 P.2d 124 (1987). *But see* Dodson v. Floyd, 529 F. Supp. 1056 (N.D. Ga. 1981).

26. 89 F. Supp. 357 (D. Mass. 1950).
27. *Id.* at 358–59.
28. *See, e.g.*, United States v. Louisville & Nashville R.R. Co., 236 U.S. 318 (1915); A. v. Dist. Court, 191 Colo. 10, 550 P.2d 315 (1976); Marriott Corp. v. Am. Acad. of Psychotherapists, Inc., 157 Ga. App. 497, 277 S.E.2d 785 (1981); Kahl v. Minn. Wood Specialty, Inc., 277 N.W.2d 395 (Minn. 1979). *See generally* Alexander C. Black, Annotation, *What Corporate Communications Are Entitled to Attorney-Client Privilege—Modern Cases*, 27 A.L.R. 5th 76 (1995).
29. *See* Radiant Burners, Inc. v. Am. Gas Ass'n, 207 F. Supp. 771 (N.D. Ill. 1962), *rev'd*, 320 F.2d 314 (7th Cir. 1963).
30. Because of ambiguities surrounding choice of law issues, if the stricter "control group" test is followed then the communication will always qualify for protection if it involves only control group personnel.
31. The "control group test" is discussed in *In re* Grand Jury Investigation, 599 F.2d 1224 (3d Cir. 1978).
32. 210 F. Supp. 483 (E.D. Pa. 1962); Hercules, Inc. v. Exxon Corp., 434 F. Supp. 136 (D. Del. 1977).
33. *City of Phila.*, 210 F. Supp. at 485.
34. Consolidation Coal Co. v. Bucyrus-Erie Co., 89 Ill. App. 2d 103, 432 N.E.2d 250 (1982).
35. *See, e.g.*,

Alaska	ALASKA R. EVID. 503(a)(2)
Hawaii	HAW. R. EVID. 503(a)(2)
Illinois	Consolidation Coal Co. v. Bucyrus-Erie Co., 89 Ill. App. 2d 103, 432 N.E.2d 250 (1982)
Maine	ME. R. EVID. 502(a)(2)
New Hampshire	N.H. R. EVID. 502(a)(2)
Oklahoma	12 OKLA. STAT. § 2502(A)(4) (2003)

See generally Brian Hamilton, *Conflict, Disparity, and Indecision: The Unsettled Corporate Attorney-Client Privilege*, 1997 ANN. SURV. AM. L. 629; Note, *Attorney-Client Privilege for Corporate Clients: The Control Group Test*, 84 HARV. L. REV. 424 (1970).

36. 851 S.W.2d 193 (Tex. 1993).
37. *Id.* at 197 (quoting then-prevailing TEX. R. CIV. EVID. 503(a)(2)).

38. *See, e.g.*, Cullen M. Godfrey, *The Revised Attorney-Client Privilege for Texas*, 30 Tex. Tech. L. Rev. 139 (1999).
39. Tex. R. Evid. 503(a)(2).
40. 423 F.2d 487 (7th Cir. 1970) (per curiam), *aff'd*, 400 U.S. 348 (1971).
41. *Id.* at 491–92.
42. *Id.*
43. *Id.* at 489.
44. 572 F.2d 596 (8th Cir. 1977).
45. *Id.* at 609.
46. 449 U.S. 383 (1981).
47. *Id.* at 391. *See also* So. Bell Tel. & Tel. Co. v. Deason, 632 So. 2d 1377 (Fla. 1994).
48. *See, e.g.*,

Alabama	Ala. R. Evid. 502(a)(2)
Arizona	Ariz. Rev. Stat. § 12-2234 (2003)
Arkansas	Courteau v. St. Paul Fire & Marine Ins. Co., 307 Ark. 513, 821 S.W.2d 45 (1991)
California	D.I. Chadbourne, Inc. v. Superior Court, 60 Cal. 2d 723, 36 Cal. Rptr. 468 (1964)
Colorado	Denver Post Corp. v. Univ. of Colo., 739 P.2d 874 (Colo. App. 1987)
Connecticut	Shew v. Freedom of Info. Comm'n, 245 Conn. 149, 714 A.2d 664 (1998)
Florida	So. Bell Tel. & Tel. Co. v. Deason, 632 So. 2d 1377 (Fla. 1994)
Georgia	Marriott Corp. v. Am. Acad. of Psychotherapists, Inc., 157 Ga. App. 497, 277 S.E.2d 785 (1981)
Kentucky	Ky. R. Evid. 503(a)(2)
Louisiana	La. Code Evid. art. 506(A)(2)
Massachusetts	Nat'l Employment Serv. Corp. v. Liberty Mut. Ins. Co., 1994 Westlaw 878920 (Mass. Sup. Ct. 1994)
Michigan	Fruehauf Trailer Corp. v. Hagelthorn, 208 Mich. App. 447, 528 N.W.2d 778, *appeal denied*, 543 N.W.2d 314 (Mich. 1995)
Mississippi	Miss. R. Evid. 502(a)(2)
Missouri	Delaporte v. Robey Bldg. Supply, Inc., 812 S.W.2d 526 (Mo. App. 1991)
Nevada	Wardleigh v. Second Judicial Dist. Ct., 111 Nev. 345, 891 P.2d 1180 (1995)
North Dakota	N.D. R. Evid. 502(a)(2)
Oregon	Or. Rev. Stat. 40.225, Rule 503(1)(d) (2001)
Tennessee	Union Planters Nat'l Bank v. ABC Records, Inc., 82 F.R.D. 472 (W.D. Tenn. 1979) (predicting Tennessee would adopt the subject matter test by construing Tenn. Code Ann. § 29-305)
Texas	Tex. R. Evid. 503(a)(2)
Utah	Utah R. Evid. 504(a)(4)
Vermont	Baisley v. Missiquoi Cemetery Ass'n, 167 Vt. 473, 708 A.2d 924 (1998)

49. Fed. R. Evid. 501.
50. Restatement (Second) of Conflicts § 139. *See also* Atl. Coast Line R.R. v. Daugherty, 111 Ga. App. 144, 141 S.E.2d 112 (1965), for the proposition that the privilege should be narrowly construed to permit liberal discovery.
51. Diversified Indus., Inc. v. Meredith, 572 F.2d 596, 610 (8th Cir. 1977).
52. *See, e.g., In re* Sealed Case, 737 F.2d 94, 99 (D.C. Cir. 1984); McCaugherty v. Siffermann, 132 F.R.D. 234 (N.D. Cal. 1990). *See generally* Grace M. Giesel, *The Legal Advice Requirement of the Attorney-Client Privilege: A Special Problem for In-House Counsel & Outside Attorneys Representing Corporations*, 48 Mercer L. Rev. 1169 (1997).
53. *See* Upjohn Co. v. United States, 449 U.S. 383 (1981).
54. This statement presupposes that corporate counsel will be an attorney admitted to the bar of a state, not necessarily the bar of the state in which the corporation is located in order to assert the privilege. *See* Paper Converting Mach. Co. v. FMC Corp., 215 F. Supp. 249 (E.D. Wis. 1963); Ga.-Pac. Plywood Co. v. U.S. Plywood Corp., 18 F.R.D. 463 (S.D.N.Y. 1956). Failure to be a member of the bar may be fatal to the claim of privilege. It has been held that communications with an unlicensed in-house counsel are not privileged. Fin. Techs. Int'l, Inc. v. Smith, 247 F. Supp. 2d 397 (S.D.N.Y. 2002). *But see* Hawes v. State, 88 Ala. 37, 7 So. 302 (1889).
55. *In re* Sealed Case, 737 F.2d at 99.
56. *See* N.C. Elec. Membership Corp. v. Carolina Power & Light Co., 110 F.R.D. 511 (M.D.N.C. 1986); Borase v. M/A Comm. Inc. 171 F.R.D. 10 (D. Mass. 1997). *See generally* So. Bell Tel. & Tel. Co. v. Deason, 632 So. 2d 1377 (Fla. 1994) for the proposition that the attorney-client privilege will be subject to a higher level of scrutiny when asserted by a corporation.
57. Malco Mfg. Co. v. Elco Corp., 45 F.R.D. 24 (D. Minn. 1968).
58. This doctrine that the communication must be for legal advice is long standing, even in the noncorporate context. *See, e.g.,* State v. Marshall, 8 Ala. 302 (1845). *See* G&S Invs. v. Belman, 145 Ariz. 258, 700 P.2d 1358 (Ariz. App. 1984); Spence v. State, 252 Ga. 338, 313 S.E.2d 475 (1984). *See also* Colton v. United States, 306 F.2d 633 (2d Cir. 1962); United States v. Lawless, 709 F.2d 485 (7th Cir. 1983); Munoz v. State Farm Mut. Auto Ins. Co., 968 P.2d 126 (Colo. App. 1998). *See also* United States v. Textron, Inc. & Subsidiaries, 577 F.3d 21 (1st Cir. 2009) (holding that attorney work-product doctrine did not shield work papers from Internal Revenue Service (IRS) summons), *cert. denied*, No. 09-750, 2010 WL 2025148 (May 24, 2010).
59. 09 Civ. 4373, 2010 U.S. Dist. LEXIS 34834 (S.D.N.Y. Apr. 8, 2010).
60. Gucci Am., Inc. v. Guess?, Inc., 09 Civ. 4373, 2011 U.S. Dist. LEXIS 15 (S.D.N.Y. Jan. 3, 2011).
61. 816 F.2d 397 (8th Cir. 1987).
62 Fed. R. Evid. 501.
63. *Simon*, 816 F.2d 397 at 402 n.4.
64. *Id.* at 403 n.6.
65. *See* Tex. R. Evid. 503(d)(4).
66. 130 F.R.D. 348 (D.N.J. 1990).
67. *United Shoe Mach. Corp.*, 89 F. Supp. at 358–59.
68. *See* Phillips v. Indianapolis Life Ins. Co., No. 1:06-cv-1544-WTL-JMS, 2009 WL 1564384, at *3 (S.D. Ind. 2009). *See also* Fed. R. Civ. P. 30(a)(1).

69. 805 F.2d 1323 (8th Cir. 1986). Not all courts agree with *Shelton*. *See, e.g.*, Phillips v. Indianapolis Life Ins. Co., No. 1:06-cv-1544-WTL-JMS, 2009 WL 1564384 (S.D. Ind. June 3, 2009).
70. *Id.* at 1327.
71. 126 F.R.D. 542 (S.D. Ind. 1989).
72. Rule 26(f)(4) of the Federal Rules of Civil Procedure requires a conference to discuss such matters.
73. FED. R. CIV. P. 26(f)(1)–(2).
74. FED. R. CIV. P. 26(f)(3)(D).
75. *Id.*
76. 95 F.R.D. 299 (S.D.N.Y. 1982).
77. *Id.* at 305–06 (emphasis added).
78. *See* Jerome G. Snider & Howard A. Ellins, CORPORATE PRIVILEGES AND CONFIDENTIAL INFORMATION § 4.02 (2009); Susan Rushing, Note, *Separating the Joint Defense Doctrine from the Attorney-Client Privilege*, 68 TEX. L. REV. 1273 (1990).
79. United States v. Austin, 416 F.3d 1016, 1021 (9th Cir. 2005) (holding that privilege can apply where parties decide on and undertake a joint defense effort or strategy).
80. *Id.*; for an extensive discussion of the competing views, see also United States v. Weissman, No. S1 94 CR. 760 CSH, 1996 WL 737042, at *7–9 (S.D.N.Y. 1996).
81. *In re* Bevill, Bresler & Schulman Asset Mgmt. Corp., 805 F.2d 120, 126 (3d Cir. 1986) (quoting Eisenberg v. Gagnon, 766 F.2d 770, 787 (3d Cir. 1985)).
82. *See* Snider & Ellins, *supra* note 78.
83. *Id.*
84. U.L.A. UNIF. R. EVID. 502(b)(iii): "A client has a privilege to refuse to disclose and to prevent any other person from disclosing a confidential communication made for the purpose of facilitating the rendition of professional legal services to the client . . . (iii) by the client or a representative of the client or the client's lawyer or a representative of the lawyer to a lawyer or a representative of a lawyer representing another party in a pending action and concerning a matter of common interest therein."
85. *See, e.g.*, Bos. Auction Co. v. W. Farm Credit Bank, 925 F. Supp. 1478, 1482–1483 (D. Haw. 1996) ("'[P]ending action' requires the institution of legal proceedings and does not include pre-litigation settlement efforts.").
86. *See, e.g.*, Dexia Credit Local v. Rogan, 2004 U.S. Dist. LEXIS 25635, at *13 (N.D. Ill. Dec. 20, 2004) (refusing to limit common interest rule to parties perfectly aligned on same side of single litigation; rather require demonstration of "actual cooperation toward a common legal goal with respect to the document they seek to withhold").
87. *See* Snider & Ellins, *supra* note 78.
88. *See* Ryals v. Canales, 767 S.W.2d 226, 228 (Tex. App–Dall. 1989, orig. proceeding) (citing H. WENDORF & D. SCHLUETER, TEXAS RULES OF EVIDENCE MANUAL 601–02 (2d ed. 1988)).
89. TEX. R. EVID. 503(b)(1) provides:

> "A client has a privilege to refuse to disclose and to prevent any other person from disclosing confidential communications made for the purpose of facilitating the rendition of professional legal services to the client [and made:] . . . (C) [by him or his representative or his lawyer] or a

representative of the lawyer, to a lawyer or a representative of a lawyer representing another party in a pending action and concerning a matter of common interest therein."

90. John F. Birmingham, Jr. & Jennifer L. Neumann, *Preserving the Attorney-Client Privilege in the Employment Environment*, 88 MICH. B.J. 36, 39 (2009).
91. Alaska Pen. Fund v. Pharmacia Corp., 554 F.3d 342, 351 n.12 (3d Cir. 2009) ("The self-critical analysis privilege has never been recognized by this Court and we see no reason to recognize it now."); *In re* Qwest Commc'ns Int'l Inc. Sec. Litig., 450 F.3d 1179, 1198 n.8 (10th Cir. 2006) (noting "a privilege for reports required to be made by law, which has been adopted by only a small minority of states") (citations omitted); *In re* Kaiser Alum. & Chem. Co., 214 F.3d 586, 593 (5th Cir. 2000) ("We need not decide whether a self-evaluation privilege should ever be recognized. We decline to recognize such a privilege in the circumstances presented, namely a case where a government agency seeks pre-accident documents."); Dowling v. Am. Haw. Cruises, Inc., 971 F.2d 423, 427 (9th Cir. 1992) (holding that "voluntary routine pre-accident safety reviews are not protected by a privilege of self-critical analysis"); Coates v. Johnson & Johnson, 756 F.2d 524, 551–52 (7th Cir. 1985) (noting lower court decisions applying a self-critical analysis privilege to an employer's affirmative action plans).
92. 50 F.R.D. 249 (D.D.C. 1970). *See also* 4 JAMES W. MOORE, MOORE'S FEDERAL PRACTICE ¶ 26.22(2) at 1287 (2d ed. 1969).
93. *Bredice*, 50 F.R.D. 249 at 251.
94. *Id.* at 250.
95. In Texas, the Occupations Code protects from disclosure the evaluation of a medical review or peer review committee. TEX. OCC. CODE § 160.007(e) (2004). The Medical Committee records and proceedings of a medical organization are also privileged (excluding business records). TEX. HEALTH & SAFETY CODE § 161.032 (2010). *See In re* Univ. of Tex. Health Ctr., 33 S.W.3d 822 (Tex. 2000); Brownwood Reg'l Hosp. v. 11th Ct. App., 927 S.W.2d 24 (Tex. 1996); Irving Healthcare Sys. v. Brooks, 927 S.W.2d 12 (Tex. 1996); Mem'l Hosp. v. McCown, 927 S.W.2d 1 (Tex. 1996). *See generally* Gail N. Friend, Jennifer L. Rangel & Madison Finch, *The New Rules of Show & Tell: Identifying and Protecting the Peer Review and Medical Committee Privileges*, 49 BAYLOR L. REV. 607 (1997).
96. *See* Brem v. DeCarlo, 162 F.R.D. 94, 101 (D. Md. 1995); Nicole Wolfe Stout, *Privileges & Immunities Available for Self-Critical Analysis & Reporting: Legal, Practical, & Ethical Considerations*, 69 J. AIR L. & COM. 561, 568–71 (2004).
97. 74 F.R.D. 518, 518–22 (E.D. Tenn. 1977).
98. *Id.* at 520.
99. *Id.* at 522.
100. 141 F.R.D. 1 (D.D.C. 1992).
101. *Id.* at 2–3.
102. *Id.*
103. *See, e.g.*, Univ. of Penn. v. EEOC, 493 U.S. 182, 189 (1990) (declining to recognize peer review materials privilege); United States v. Gillock, 445 U.S. 360, 373 (1980) (declining to create a state legislator privilege); Branzburg v. Hayes, 408 U.S. 665, 706 (1972) (declining to recognize a privilege allowing newsmen to avoid testifying about confidential sources and suggesting that the creation of such a privilege is best left to the legislature).

104. *Univ. of Penn.*, 493 U.S. at 189.
105. Slaughter v. Nat'l R.R. Passenger Corp., Civil Action No. 10-4203 (E.D. Penn. Mar. 4, 2011).
106. *Id.* (citing Herbert v. Lando, 441 U.S. 153, 175 (1979)).
107. 563 S.W.2d 240 (Tex. 1978).
108. *Id.* at 245.
109. *See, e.g.*, FED. R. EVID. 502.
110. *See generally* Kenneth S. Brown & Daniel J. Capra, *Getting Control of Waiver of Privilege in the Federal Courts: A Proposal for a Federal Rule of Evidence* 502, 58 S.C. L. REV. 211 (2006).
111. Jonathan Corp. v. Prime Comp., Inc., 114 F.R.D. 693 (E.D. Va. 1987).
112. RESTATEMENT (THIRD) OF THE LAW GOVERNING LAWYERS § 78 (2000).
113. *E.g.*, FED. R. CIV. P. 26(c).
114. Perrignon v. Bergen Brunswig Corp., 77 F.R.D. 455 (N.D. Cal. 1978).
115. 755 S.W.2d 170 (Tex. App–Amarillo 1988, orig. proceeding).
116. 583 F.3d 600 (9th Cir. 2009).
117. *See* United States v. Reyes, 239 F.R.D. 591 (N.D. Cal. 2006) (finding that voluntary disclosure to a federal investigative agency effected a waiver of the attorney-client privilege and work-product protection for the materials produced as to other litigants).
118. 844 S.W.2d 223 (Tex. 1992) (orig. proceeding).
119. *Id.* at 226.
120. *Id.* at 226–27. *See* Abamar Hous. & Dev. v. Lisa Daly Lady Decor, 698 So. 2d 276 (Fla. App. 1997), *rev. denied*, 704 So. 2d 520 (Fla. 1997).
121. TEX. R. CIV. P. 193.3(d).
122. Report of the Civil Rules Advisory Committee (May 27, 2005).
123. FED. R. CIV. P. 26(b)(5)(B).
124. *Id.*
125. *See* FED. R. EVID. 502(b). *See also* Paula Schaefer, *The Future of Inadvertent Disclosure: The Lingering Need to Revise Professional Conduct Rules*, 69 MD. L. REV. 195, 217–18 (2010).
126. *See* FED. R. EVID. 502(e); FED. R. CIV. P. 26(f); Schaefer, *supra* note 125.
127. *See* FED. R. EVID. 502(d).
128. *See* FED. R. EVID. 502(c).
129. STEVEN GOODE & OLIN GUY WELLBORN III, COURT ROOM EVIDENCE HANDBOOK, 2009–2010 STUDENT EDITION 133 (Thomson Reuters 2009).
130. *Id.*
131. *See id.*
132. 263 F.R.D. 40 (D. Me. 2009).
133. *Id.* at 46.
134. *Id.*
135. *Id.* at 47.
136. FED. R. EVID. 612.
137. *Id.*
138. *See, e.g.*, Hannan v. St. Joseph's Hosp. & Med. Ctr., 318 N.J. Super. 22, 722 A.2d 971 (1999).
139. *See* FED. R. EVID. 612. *See generally* Shipes v. BIC Corp., 154 F.R.D. 301 (M.D. Ga. 1994); Nutramax Lab., Inc. v. Twin Lab., Inc., 183 F.R.D. 458 (D. Md. 1998); Margaret Hall Found, Inc. v. Strong, 121 F.R.D. 141 (D. Mass. 1988); Redvanly v.

NYNEX Corp., 152 F.R.D. 460 (S.D.N.Y. 1993); Begner v. State Ethics Comm'n, 552 S.E.2d 431 (Ga. Ct. App. 2001).

140. *See* Berkey Photo, Inc. v. Eastman Kodak Co., 74 F.R.D. 613, 617 (S.D.N.Y. 1977) (Although the court did not order disclosure in *Berkey*, it stated, "To put the point succinctly, there will be hereafter powerful reasons to hold that materials considered work product should be withheld from prospective witnesses if they are to be withheld from opposing parties.").
141. *See In re* Christus Spohn Hosp. Kleberg, 222 S.W.3d 434 (Tex. 2007). *See also* Fed. R. Civ. P. 26(a)(2)(B).
142. 08-2789-BLS2, 2010 Mass. Super. LEXIS 276 (Mass. Super. Ct. Sept. 30, 2010).
143. *Id.* at *5.
144. 119 Cal. Rptr. 3d 878 (2011).
145. *See* Stengart v. Loving Care Agency Inc., 990 A.2d 650 (N.J. 2010) (holding that communications between attorney and client sent on employer's computer were privileged because employer's policy was ambiguous and did not clearly permit employer to access otherwise protected attorney-client communications).
146. 2010 Pa. Dist. & Cnty. Dec. LEXIS 270 (Pa. Dist. & Cnty. Sept. 9, 2010).
147. *Id.* at *9.
148. *See* Kintera, Inc. v. Convio, Inc., 219 F.R.D. 503 (S.D. Cal. 2003).
149. Allstate Ins. Co. v. Levesque, 263 F.R.D. 663, 667 (M.D. Fla. 2010); *see* GAB Bus. Servs., Inc. v. Syndicate, 809 F.2d 755 (11th Cir. 1987); HSH Nordbank AG N.Y. Branch v. Swerdlow, 259 F.R.D. 64, 74 (S.D.N.Y. 2009) (holding that in an order to prevent the attorney-client privilege from at once being used as a shield and a sword, the "at issue" doctrine precludes a party from disclosing only self-serving communications while barring discovery of other communications that an adversary could use to challenge the truth of the claim).
150. *See* Conkling v. Turner, 883 F.2d 431 (5th Cir. 1989).
151. *See* Mich. State Bar Comm. on Prof'l & Judicial Ethics, Op. CI-1178 (Jan. 18, 1988).
152. 430 F.2d 1093 (5th Cir. 1970). *See also* Lefkowitz v. Duquesne Light Co., CIV. A. Nos. 86-1046 and 86-2085, 1988 WL 169273 (W.D. Pa. 1988).
153. *Id.* at 1103–04.
154. *Id. But see* Shrivani v. Capital Invest. Corp., Inc., 112 F.R.D. 389 (D. Conn. 1986) (in which the court rejected the reasoning of *Garner*).
155. 693 F.2d 1235 (5th Cir. 1982).
156. 759 F.2d 312 (3d Cir. 1985).
157. *Id.* at 316.
158. *See, e.g., Upjohn*, 449 U.S. 383 (1976). *See also* Edward Brodsky & M. Patricia Adamski, *Law of Corporate Officers and Directors: Rights and Liabilities*, LCODR § 10:20 (2009).
159. Hickman v. Taylor, 329 U.S. 495, 510 (1947).
160. *Id.* at 511.
161. *Id.*
162. *In re* ANR Advance Transp. Co., Inc., 302 B.R. 607, 616–17 (E.D. Wis. 2003).
163. United States v. Nobles, 422 U.S. 225, 238 n.11 (1975); Sajda v. Brewton, 265 F.R.D. 334, 339 (N.D. Ind. 2009).
164. *In re* Sealed Case, 676 F.2d 793, 808 (D.C. Cir. 1982).
165. *Nobles*, 422 U.S. at 237–38.
166. *See Hickman*, 329 U.S. at 511.

167. *See* Toledo Edison Co. v. G.A. Techs., Inc. Torrey Pines Tech. Div., 847 F.2d 335, 339–40 (6th Cir. 1988) (stating that a party need only show anticipation of litigation, and need not establish the identities, positions, and responsibilities of the persons creating the materials with respect to the litigation expected). *See also* Simon v. G.D. Searle & Co., 816 F.2d 397, 401 (8th Cir. 1987) (holding that risk management and aggregate records were discoverable because they were not prepared in anticipation of any particular litigation).
168. *See* Resolution Trust Corp. v. Diamond, 773 F. Supp. 597, 603 (S.D.N.Y. 1991).
169. Fed. R. Civ. P. 26(b)(3)(B).
170. *See* Gray v. Dist. Ct., 884 P.2d 286 (Colo. 1994).
171. Goosman v. A. Duie Pyle, Inc., 320 F.2d 45 (4th Cir. 1963); Tayler v. Travelers Ins. Co., 183 F.R.D. 67 (N.D.N.Y. 1998).
172. Fed. R. Civ. P. 26(b)(3)(A).
173. *See* Fed. R. Civ. P. 26(b)(3)(A)(ii); Tex. R. Civ. P. 192.5(b)(2).
174. *See Hickman*, 329 U.S. at 511.
175. Fed. R. Civ. P. 26(b)(3)(B).
176. *See* Edward Brodsky & M. Patricia Adamski, *Law of Corporate Officers and Directors: Rights and Liabilities*, LCODR § 10:20 (2009).
177. *Id.*; *In re Allen*, 106 F.3d 582 (4th Cir. 1997) (holding that opinion work product is immune from discovery).
178. *See In re* Cendant Corp. Sec. Litig., 343 F.3d 658, 663 (3d Cir. 2003) (holding that opinion work product receives greater protection than ordinary work product and is discoverable only upon a showing of rare and exceptional circumstances).
179. 976 F.2d 573, 577 (9th Cir. 1992).
180. 805 F.2d 1323 (8th Cir. 1986).
181. *Id.* at 1325.
182. *Id.* at 1326.
183. *Id.* at 1329.
184. *Id.* at 1326.
185. *Id.* at 1327.
186. *Id.* at 1327–28.

APPENDIX 1-1

Memoranda to Accompany "Principles of Federal Prosecution of Business Organizations"

U.S. Department of Justice

Office of the Deputy Attorney General

The Deputy Attorney General

Washington, D.C. 20530
January 20, 2003

MEMORANDUM

TO: Heads of Department Components
United States Attorneys

FROM: Larry D. Thompson
Deputy Attorney General

SUBJECT: Principles of Federal Prosecution of Business Organizations

As the Corporate Fraud Task Force has advanced in its mission, we have confronted certain issues in the principles for the federal prosecution of business organizations that require revision in order to enhance our efforts against corporate fraud. While it will be a minority of cases in which a corporation or partnership is itself subjected to criminal charges, prosecutors and investigators in every matter involving business crimes must assess the merits of seeking the conviction of the business entity itself.

Attached to this memorandum are a revised set of principles to guide Department prosecutors as they make the decision whether to seek charges against a business organization. These revisions draw heavily on the combined efforts of the Corporate Fraud Task Force and the Attorney General's Advisory Committee to put the results of more than three years of experience with the principles into practice.

The main focus of the revisions is increased emphasis on and scrutiny of the authenticity of a corporation's cooperation. Too often business organizations, while purporting to cooperate with a Department investigation, in fact take steps to impede the quick and effective exposure of the complete scope of wrongdoing under investigation. The revisions make clear that such conduct should weigh in favor of a corporate prosecution. The revisions also address the efficacy of the corporate governance mechanisms in place within a corporation, to ensure that these measures are truly effective rather than mere paper programs.

Further experience with these principles may lead to additional adjustments. I look forward to hearing comments about their operation in practice. Please forward any comments to Christopher Wray, the Principal Associate Deputy Attorney General, or to Andrew Hruska, my Senior Counsel.

Federal Prosecution of Business Organizations[1]

I. Charging a Corporation: General

A. *General Principle:* Corporations should not be treated leniently because of their artificial nature nor should they be subject to harsher treatment. Vigorous enforcement of the criminal laws against corporate wrongdoers, where appropriate, results in great benefits for law enforcement and the public, particularly in the area of white collar crime. Indicting corporations for wrongdoing enables the government to address and be a force for positive change of corporate culture, alter corporate behavior, and prevent, discover, and punish white collar crime.

B. *Comment:* In all cases involving corporate wrongdoing, prosecutors should consider the factors discussed herein. First and foremost, prosecutors should be aware of the important public benefits that may flow from indicting a corporation in appropriate cases. For instance, corporations are likely to take immediate remedial steps when one is indicted for criminal conduct that is pervasive throughout a particular industry, and thus an indictment often provides a unique opportunity for deterrence on a massive scale. In addition, a corporate indictment may result in specific deterrence by changing the culture of the indicted corporation and the behavior of its employees. Finally, certain

1. While these guidelines refer to corporations, they apply to the consideration of the prosecution of all types of business organizations, including partnerships, sole proprietorships, government entities, and unincorporated associations.

crimes that carry with them a substantial risk of great public harm, e.g., environmental crimes or financial frauds, are by their nature most likely to be committed by businesses, and there may, therefore, be a substantial federal interest in indicting the corporation.

Charging a corporation, however, does not mean that individual directors, officers, employees, or shareholders should not also be charged. Prosecution of a corporation is not a substitute for the prosecution of criminally culpable individuals within or without the corporation. Because a corporation can act only through individuals, imposition of individual criminal liability may provide the strongest deterrent against future corporate wrongdoing. Only rarely should provable individual culpability not be pursued, even in the face of offers of corporate guilty pleas.

Corporations are "legal persons," capable of suing and being sued, and capable of committing crimes. Under the doctrine of *respondeat superior*, a corporation may be held criminally liable for the illegal acts of its directors, officers, employees, and agents. To hold a corporation liable for these actions, the government must establish that the corporate agent's actions (i) were within the scope of his duties and (ii) were intended, at least in part, to benefit the corporation. In all cases involving wrongdoing by corporate agents, prosecutors should consider the corporation, as well as the responsible individuals, as potential criminal targets.

Agents, however, may act for mixed reasons—both for self-aggrandizement (both direct and indirect) and for the benefit of the corporation, and a corporation may be held liable as long as one motivation of its agent is to benefit the corporation. In *United States v. Automated Medical Laboratories*, 770 F.2d 399 (4th Cir. 1985), the court affirmed the corporation's conviction for the actions of a subsidiary's employee despite its claim that the employee was acting for his own benefit, namely his "ambitious nature and his desire to ascend the corporate ladder." The court stated, "*Partucci* was clearly acting in part to benefit AML since his advancement within the corporation depended on AML's well-being and its lack of difficulties with the FDA." Similarly, in *United States v. Cincotta*, 689 F.2d 238, 241–42 (1st Cir. 1982), the court held, "criminal liability may be imposed on the corporation only where the agent is acting within the scope of his employment. That, in turn, requires that the agent be performing acts of the kind which he is authorized to perform, and those acts must be motivated—at least in part—by an intent to benefit the corporation." Applying this test, the court upheld the corporation's conviction, notwithstanding the substantial personal benefit reaped by its miscreant agents, because the fraudulent scheme required money to pass through the corporation's treasury and the fraudulently obtained goods were resold to the corporation's customers in the corporation's name. As the court concluded, "Mystic—not the individual defendants—was making money by selling oil that it had not paid for."

Moreover, the corporation need not even necessarily profit from its agent's actions for it to be held liable. *In Automated Medical Laboratories*, the Fourth Circuit stated:

> [B]enefit is not a "touchstone of criminal corporate liability; benefit at best is an evidential, not an operative, fact." Thus, whether the agent's actions ultimately redounded to the benefit of the corporation is less significant than whether the agent acted with the intent to benefit the corporation. The basic purpose of requiring that an agent have acted with the intent to benefit the corporation, however, is to insulate the corporation from criminal liability for actions of its agents which be inimical to the interests of the corporation or which may have been undertaken solely to advance the interests of that agent or of a party other than the corporation.

770 F.2d at 407 (emphasis added; quoting *Old Monastery Co. v. United States,* 147 F.2d 905, 908 (4th Cir. 1945), *cert. denied,* 326 U.S. 734 (1945)).

II. Charging a Corporation: Factors to Be Considered

A. *General Principle:* Generally, prosecutors should apply the same factors in determining whether to charge a corporation as they do with respect to individuals. *See* USAM § 9-27.220, *et seq*. Thus, the prosecutor should weigh all of the factors normally considered in the sound exercise of prosecutorial judgment: the sufficiency of the evidence; the likelihood of success at trial; the probable deterrent, rehabilitative, and other consequences of conviction; and the adequacy of noncriminal approaches. *See id.* However, due to the nature of the corporate "person," some additional factors are present. In conducting an investigation, determining whether to bring charges, and negotiating plea agreements, prosecutors should consider the following factors in reaching a decision as to the proper treatment of a corporate target:

1. the nature and seriousness of the offense, including the risk of harm to the public, and applicable policies and priorities, if any, governing the prosecution of corporations for particular categories of crime (*see* section III, *infra);*
2. the pervasiveness of wrongdoing within the corporation, including the complicity in, or condonation of, the wrongdoing by corporate management (*see* section IV, *infra);*
3. the corporation's history of similar conduct, including prior criminal, civil, and regulatory enforcement actions against it (*see* section V, *infra);*
4. the corporation's timely and voluntary disclosure of wrongdoing and its willingness to cooperate in the investigation of its agents, including, if necessary, the waiver of corporate attorney-client and work product protection (*see* section VI, *infra);*
5. the existence and adequacy of the corporation's compliance program (*see* section VII, *infra);*
6. the corporation's remedial actions, including any efforts to implement an effective corporate compliance program or to improve an existing

one, to replace responsible management, to discipline or terminate wrongdoers, to pay restitution, and to cooperate with the relevant government agencies (*see* section VIII, *infra);*

7. collateral consequences, including disproportionate harm to shareholders, pension holders and employees not proven personally culpable and impact on the public arising from the prosecution (*see* section IX, *infra);* and
8. the adequacy of the prosecution of individuals responsible for the corporation's malfeasance;
9. the adequacy of remedies such as civil or regulatory enforcement actions (*see* section X, *infra).*

B. *Comment:* As with the factors relevant to charging natural persons, the foregoing factors are intended to provide guidance rather than to mandate a particular result. The factors listed in this section are intended to be illustrative of those that should be considered and not a complete or exhaustive list.

Some or all of these factors may or may not apply to specific cases, and in some cases one factor may override all others. The nature and seriousness of the offense may be such as to warrant prosecution regardless of the other factors. Further, national law enforcement policies in various enforcement areas may require that more or less weight be given to certain of these factors than to others.

In making a decision to charge a corporation, the prosecutor generally has wide latitude in determining when, whom, how, and even whether to prosecute for violations of Federal criminal law. In exercising that discretion, prosecutors should consider the following general statements of principles that summarize appropriate considerations to be weighed and desirable practices to be followed in discharging their prosecutorial responsibilities. In doing so, prosecutors should ensure that the general purposes of the criminal law—assurance of warranted punishment, deterrence of further criminal conduct, protection of the public from dangerous and fraudulent conduct, rehabilitation of offenders, and restitution for victims and affected communities—are adequately met, taking into account the special nature of the corporate "person."

III. Charging a Corporation: Special Policy Concerns

A. *General Principle:* The nature and seriousness of the crime, including the risk of harm to the public from the criminal conduct, are obviously primary factors in determining whether to charge a corporation. In addition, corporate conduct, particularly that of national and multi-national corporations, necessarily intersects with federal economic, taxation, and criminal law enforcement policies. In applying these principles, prosecutors must consider the practices and policies of the appropriate Division of the Department, and must comply with those policies to the extent required.

B. *Comment:* In determining whether to charge a corporation, prosecutors should take into account federal law enforcement priorities as discussed above.

See USAM § 9-27-230. In addition, however, prosecutors must be aware of the specific policy goals and incentive programs established by the respective Divisions and regulatory agencies. Thus, whereas natural persons may be given incremental degrees of credit (ranging from immunity to lesser charges to sentencing considerations) for turning themselves in, making statements against their penal interest, and cooperating in the government's investigation of their own and others' wrongdoing, the same approach may not be appropriate in all circumstances with respect to corporations. As an example, it is entirely proper in many investigations for a prosecutor to consider the corporation's pre-indictment conduct, e.g., voluntary disclosure, cooperation, remediation or restitution, in determining whether to seek an indictment. However, this would not necessarily be appropriate in an antitrust investigation, in which antitrust violations, by definition, go to the heart of the corporation's business and for which the Antitrust Division has therefore established a firm policy, understood in the business community, that credit should not be given at the charging stage for a compliance program and that amnesty is available only to the first corporation to make full disclosure to the government. As another example, the Tax Division has a strong preference for prosecuting responsible individuals, rather than entities, for corporate tax offenses. Thus, in determining whether or not to charge a corporation, prosecutors should consult with the Criminal, Antitrust, Tax, and Environmental and Natural Resources Divisions, if appropriate or required.

IV. Charging a Corporation: Pervasiveness of Wrongdoing Within the Corporation

A. *General Principle:* A corporation can only act through natural persons, and it is therefore held responsible for the acts of such persons fairly attributable to it. Charging a corporation for even minor misconduct may be appropriate where the wrongdoing was pervasive and was undertaken by a large number of employees or by all the employees in a particular role within the corporation, *e.g.*, salesmen or procurement officers, or was condoned by upper management. On the other hand, in certain limited circumstances, it may not be appropriate to impose liability upon a corporation, particularly one with a compliance program in place, under a strict *respondeat superior* theory for the single isolated act of a rogue employee. There is, of course, a wide spectrum between these two extremes, and a prosecutor should exercise sound discretion in evaluating the pervasiveness of wrongdoing within a corporation.

B. *Comment:* Of these factors, the most important is the role of management. Although acts of even low-level employees may result in criminal liability, a corporation is directed by its management and management is responsible for a corporate culture in which criminal conduct is either discouraged or tacitly encouraged. As stated in commentary to the Sentencing Guidelines:

> Pervasiveness [is] case specific and [will] depend on the number, and degree of responsibility, of individuals [with] substantial authority

> . . . who participated in, condoned, or were willfully ignorant of the offense. Fewer individuals need to be involved for a finding of pervasiveness if those individuals exercised a relatively high degree of authority. Pervasiveness can occur either within an organization as a whole or within a unit of an organization.

USSG § 8C2.5, comment. (n. 4).

V. Charging a Corporation: The Corporation's Past History

A. *General Principle:* Prosecutors may consider a corporation's history of similar conduct, including prior criminal, civil, and regulatory enforcement actions against it, in determining whether to bring criminal charges.

B. *Comment:* A corporation, like a natural person, is expected to learn from its mistakes. A history of similar conduct may be probative of a corporate culture that encouraged, or at least condoned, such conduct, regardless of any compliance programs. Criminal prosecution of a corporation may be particularly appropriate where the corporation previously had been subject to non-criminal guidance, warnings, or sanctions, or previous criminal charges, and yet it either had not taken adequate action to prevent future unlawful conduct or had continued to engage in the conduct in spite of the warnings or enforcement actions taken against it. In making this determination, the corporate structure itself, *e.g.*, subsidiaries or operating divisions, should be ignored, and enforcement actions taken against the corporation or any of its divisions, subsidiaries, and affiliates should be considered. *See* USSG § 8C2.5(c) & comment. (n.6).

VI. Charging a Corporation: Cooperation and Voluntary Disclosure

A. *General Principle:* In determining whether to charge a corporation, that corporation's timely and voluntary disclosure of wrongdoing and its willingness to cooperate with the government's investigation may be relevant factors. In gauging the extent of the corporation's cooperation, the prosecutor may consider the corporation's willingness to identify the culprits within the corporation, including senior executives; to make witnesses available; to disclose the complete results of its internal investigation; and to waive attorney-client and work product protection.

B. *Comment:* In investigating wrongdoing by or within a corporation, a prosecutor is likely to encounter several obstacles resulting from the nature of the corporation itself. It will often be difficult to determine which individual took which action on behalf of the corporation. Lines of authority and responsibility may be shared among operating divisions or departments, and records and personnel may be spread throughout the United States or even among several countries. Where the criminal conduct continued over an extended period of time, the culpable or knowledgeable personnel may have been promoted, transferred, or fired, or they may have quit or retired. Accordingly, a corporation's cooperation may be critical in identifying the culprits and locating relevant evidence.

In some circumstances, therefore, granting a corporation immunity or amnesty or pretrial diversion may be considered in the course of the government's investigation. In such circumstances, prosecutors should refer to the principles governing non-prosecution agreements generally. *See* USAM § 9-27.600-650. These principles permit a non-prosecution agreement in exchange for cooperation when a corporation's "timely cooperation appears to be necessary to the public interest and other means of obtaining the desired cooperation are unavailable or would not be effective." Prosecutors should note that in the case of national or multi-national corporations, multi-district or global agreements may be necessary. Such agreements may only be entered into with the approval of each affected district or the appropriate Department official. *See* USAM § 9-27.641.

In addition, the Department, in conjunction with regulatory agencies and other executive branch departments, encourages corporations, as part of their compliance programs, to conduct internal investigations and to disclose their findings to the appropriate authorities. Some agencies, such as the SEC and the EPA, as well as the Department's Environmental and Natural Resources Division, have formal voluntary disclosure programs in which self-reporting, coupled with remediation and additional criteria, may qualify the corporation for amnesty or reduced sanctions.[2] Even in the absence of a formal program, prosecutors may consider a corporation's timely and voluntary disclosure in evaluating the adequacy of the corporation's compliance program and its management's commitment to the compliance program. However, prosecution and economic policies specific to the industry or statute may require prosecution notwithstanding a corporation's willingness to cooperate. For example, the Antitrust Division offers amnesty only to the first corporation to agree to cooperate. This creates a strong incentive for corporations participating in anti-competitive conduct to be the first to cooperate. In addition, amnesty, immunity, or reduced sanctions may not be appropriate where the corporation's business is permeated with fraud or other crimes.

One factor the prosecutor may weigh in assessing the adequacy of a corporation's cooperation is the completeness of its disclosure including, if necessary, a waiver of the attorney-client and work product protections, both with respect to its internal investigation and with respect to communications between specific officers, directors and employees and counsel. Such waivers permit the government to obtain statements of possible witnesses, subjects, and targets, without having to negotiate individual cooperation or immunity agreements. In addition, they are often critical in enabling the government to evaluate the completeness of a corporation's voluntary disclosure and cooperation.

2. In addition, the Sentencing Guidelines reward voluntary disclosure and cooperation with a reduction in the corporation's offense level. *See* USSG § 8C2.5(g).

Prosecutors may, therefore, request a waiver in appropriate circumstances.[3] The Department does not, however, consider waiver of a corporation's attorney-client and work product protection an absolute requirement, and prosecutors should consider the willingness of a corporation to waive such protection when necessary to provide timely and complete information as one factor in evaluating the corporation's cooperation.

Another factor to be weighed by the prosecutor is whether the corporation appears to be protecting its culpable employees and agents. Thus, while cases will differ depending on the circumstances, a corporation's promise of support to culpable employees and agents, either through the advancing of attorneys' fees,[4] through retaining the employees without sanction for their misconduct, or through providing information to the employees about the government's investigation pursuant to a joint defense agreement, may be considered by the prosecutor in weighing the extent and value of a corporation's cooperation. By the same token, the prosecutor should be wary of attempts to shield corporate officers and employees from liability by a willingness of the corporation to plead guilty.

Another factor to be weighed by the prosecutor is whether the corporation, while purporting to cooperate, has engaged in conduct that impedes the investigation (whether or not rising to the level of criminal obstruction). Examples of such conduct include: overly broad assertions of corporate representation of employees or former employees; inappropriate directions to employees or their counsel, such as directions not to cooperate openly and fully with the investigation including, for example, the direction to decline to be interviewed; making presentations or submissions that contain misleading assertions or omissions; incomplete or delayed production of records; and failure to promptly disclose illegal conduct known to the corporation.

Finally, a corporation's offer of cooperation does not automatically entitle it to immunity from prosecution. A corporation should not be able to escape liability merely by offering up its directors, officers, employees, or agents as in lieu of its own prosecution. Thus, a corporation's willingness to cooperate is merely one relevant factor, that needs to be considered in conjunction with the other factors, particularly those relating to the corporation's past history and the role of management in the wrongdoing.

VII. Charging a Corporation: Corporate Compliance Programs

A. *General Principle:* Compliance programs are established by corporate management to prevent and to detect misconduct and to ensure that corporate

3. This waiver should ordinarily be limited to the factual internal investigation and any contemporaneous advice given to the corporation concerning the conduct at issue. Except in unusual circumstances, prosecutors should not seek a waiver with respect to communications and work product related to advice concerning the government's criminal investigation.

4. Some states require corporations to pay the legal fees of officers under investigation prior to a formal determination of their guilt. Obviously, a corporation's compliance with governing law should not be considered a failure to cooperate.

activities are conducted in accordance with all applicable criminal and civil laws, regulations, and rules. The Department encourages such corporate self-policing, including voluntary disclosures to the government of any problems that a corporation discovers on its own. However, the existence of a compliance program is not sufficient, in and of itself, to justify not charging a corporation for criminal conduct undertaken by its officers, directors, employees, or agents. Indeed, the commission of such crimes in the face of a compliance program may suggest that the corporate management is not adequately enforcing its program. In addition, the nature of some crimes, *e.g.*, antitrust violations, may be such that national law enforcement policies mandate prosecutions of corporations notwithstanding the existence of a compliance program.

B. *Comment:* A corporate compliance program, even one specifically prohibiting the very conduct in question, does not absolve the corporation from criminal liability under the doctrine of *respondeat superior. See United States v. Basic Construction Co.*, 711 F.2d 570 (4th Cir. 1983) ("a corporation may be held criminally responsible for antitrust violations committed by its employees if they were acting within the scope of their authority, or apparent authority, and for the benefit of the corporation, even if . . . such acts were against corporate policy or express instructions."). In *United States v. Hilton Hotels Corp.*, 467 F.2d 1000 (9th Cir. 1972), *cert. denied*, 409 U.S. 1125 (1973), the Ninth Circuit affirmed antitrust liability based upon a purchasing agent for a single hotel threatening a single supplier with a boycott unless it paid dues to a local marketing association, even though the agent's actions were contrary to corporate policy and directly against express instructions from his superiors. The court reasoned that Congress, in enacting the Sherman Antitrust Act, "intended to impose liability upon business entities for the acts of those to whom they choose to delegate the conduct of their affairs, thus stimulating a maximum effort by owners and managers to assure adherence by such agents to the requirements of the Act."[5] It concluded that "general policy statements" and even direct instructions from the agent's superiors were not sufficient; "Appellant could not gain exculpation by issuing general instructions without undertaking to enforce those instructions by means commensurate with the obvious risks." *See also United States v. Beusch*, 596 F.2d 871, 878 (9th Cir. 1979) ("[A] corporation may be liable for the acts of its employees done contrary to express instructions and policies, but . . . the existence of such instructions and policies may be considered in determining whether the employee in fact acted to benefit

5. Although this case and *Basic Construction* are both antitrust cases, their reasoning applies to other criminal violations. In the Hilton case, for instance, the Ninth Circuit noted that Sherman Act violations are commercial offenses "usually motivated by a desire to enhance profits," thus, bringing the case within the normal rule that a "purpose to benefit the corporation is necessary to bring the agent's acts within the scope of his employment." 467 F.2d at 1006 & n.4. In addition, in *United States v. Automated Medical Laboratories*, 770 F.2d 399, 406 n.5 (4th Cir. 1985), the Fourth Circuit stated "that Basic Construction states a generally applicable rule on corporate criminal liability despite the fact that it addresses violations of the antitrust laws."

the corporation."); *United States v. American Radiator & Standard Sanitary Corp.*, 433 F.2d 174 (3rd Cir. 1970) (affirming conviction of corporation based upon its officer's participation in price-fixing scheme, despite corporation's defense that officer's conduct violated its "rigid anti-fraternization policy" against any socialization (and exchange of price information) with its competitors; "When the act of the agent is within the scope of his employment or his apparent authority, the corporation is held legally responsible for it, although what he did may be contrary to his actual instructions and may be unlawful.").

While the Department recognizes that no compliance program can ever prevent all criminal activity by a corporation's employees, the critical factors in evaluating any program are whether the program is adequately designed for maximum effectiveness in preventing and detecting wrongdoing by employees and whether corporate management is enforcing the program or is tacitly encouraging or pressuring employees to engage in misconduct to achieve business objectives. The Department has no formal guidelines for corporate compliance programs. The fundamental questions any prosecutor should ask are: "Is the corporation's compliance program well designed?" and "Does the corporation's compliance program work?" In answering these questions, the prosecutor should consider the comprehensiveness of the compliance program; the extent and pervasiveness of the criminal conduct; the number and level of the corporate employees involved; the seriousness, duration, and frequency of the misconduct; and any remedial actions taken by the corporation, including restitution, disciplinary action, and revisions to corporate compliance programs.[6] Prosecutors should also consider the promptness of any disclosure of wrongdoing to the government and the corporation's cooperation in the government's investigation. In evaluating compliance programs, prosecutors may consider whether the corporation has established corporate governance mechanisms that can effectively detect and prevent misconduct. For example, do the corporation's directors exercise independent review over proposed corporate actions rather than unquestioningly ratifying officers' recommendations; are the directors provided with information sufficient to enable the exercise of independent judgment, are internal audit functions conducted at a level sufficient to ensure their independence and accuracy and have the directors established an information and reporting system in the organization reasonable designed to provide management and the board of directors with timely and accurate information sufficient to allow them to reach an informed decision regarding the organization's compliance with the law. *In re: Caremark*, 698 A.2d 959 (Del. Ct. Chan. 1996).

Prosecutors should therefore attempt to determine whether a corporation's compliance program is merely a "paper program" or whether it was designed and implemented in an effective manner. In addition, prosecutors should

6. For a detailed review of these and other factors concerning corporate compliance programs, see United States Sentencing Commission, GUIDELINES MANUAL, § 8A1.2, comment. (n.3(k)) (Nov. 1997). *See* also USSG § 8C2.5(f).

determine whether the corporation has provided for a staff sufficient to audit, document, analyze, and utilize the results of the corporation's compliance efforts. In addition, prosecutors should determine whether the corporation's employees are adequately informed about the compliance program and are convinced of the corporation's commitment to it. This will enable the prosecutor to make an informed decision as to whether the corporation has adopted and implemented a truly effective compliance program that, when consistent with other federal law enforcement policies, may result in a decision to charge only the corporation's employees and agents.

Compliance programs should be designed to detect the particular types of misconduct most likely to occur in a particular corporation's line of business. Many corporations operate in complex regulatory environments outside the normal experience of criminal prosecutors. Accordingly, prosecutors should consult with relevant federal and state agencies with the expertise to evaluate the adequacy of a program's design and implementation. For instance, state and federal banking, insurance, and medical boards, the Department of Defense, the Department of Health and Human Services, the Environmental Protection Agency, and the Securities and Exchange Commission have considerable experience with compliance programs and can be very helpful to a prosecutor in evaluating such programs. In addition, the Fraud Section of the Criminal Division, the Commercial Litigation Branch of the Civil Division, and the Environmental Crimes Section of the Environment and Natural Resources Division can assist U.S. Attorneys' Offices in finding the appropriate agency office and in providing copies of compliance programs that were developed in previous cases.

VIII. Charging a Corporation: Restitution and Remediation

A. *General Principle:* Although neither a corporation nor an individual target may avoid prosecution merely by paying a sum of money, a prosecutor may consider the corporation's willingness to make restitution and steps already taken to do so. A prosecutor may also consider other remedial actions, such as implementing an effective corporate compliance program, improving an existing compliance program, and disciplining wrongdoers, in determining whether to charge the corporation.

B. *Comment:* In determining whether or not a corporation should be prosecuted, a prosecutor may consider whether meaningful remedial measures have been taken, including employee discipline and full restitution.[7] A corporation's response to misconduct says much about its willingness to ensure that such misconduct does not recur. Thus, corporations that fully recognize the seriousness of their misconduct and accept responsibility for it should be taking steps to implement the personnel, operational, and organizational changes

7. For example, the Antitrust Division's amnesty policy requires that "[w]here possible, the corporation [make] restitution to injured parties. . . ."

necessary to establish an awareness among employees that criminal conduct will not be tolerated. Among the factors prosecutors should consider and weigh are whether the corporation appropriately disciplined the wrongdoers and disclosed information concerning their illegal conduct to the government.

Employee discipline is a difficult task for many corporations because of the human element involved and sometimes because of the seniority of the employees concerned. While corporations need to be fair to their employees, they must also be unequivocally committed, at all levels of the corporation, to the highest standards of legal and ethical behavior. Effective internal discipline can be a powerful deterrent against improper behavior by a corporation's employees. In evaluating a corporation's response to wrongdoing, prosecutors may evaluate the willingness of the corporation to discipline culpable employees of all ranks and the adequacy of the discipline imposed. The prosecutor should be satisfied that the corporation's focus is on the integrity and credibility of its remedial and disciplinary measures rather than on the protection of the wrongdoers.

In addition to employee discipline, two other factors used in evaluating a corporation's remedial efforts are restitution and reform. As with natural persons, the decision whether or not to prosecute should not depend upon the target's ability to pay restitution. A corporation's efforts to pay restitution even in advance of any court order is, however, evidence of its "acceptance of responsibility" and, consistent with the practices and policies of the appropriate Division of the Department entrusted with enforcing specific criminal laws, may be considered in determining whether to bring criminal charges. Similarly, although the inadequacy of a corporate compliance program is a factor to consider when deciding whether to charge a corporation, that corporation's quick recognition of the flaws in the program and its efforts to improve the program are also factors to consider.

IX. Charging a Corporation: Collateral Consequences

A. *General Principle:* Prosecutors may consider the collateral consequences of a corporate criminal conviction in determining whether to charge the corporation with a criminal offense.

B. *Comment:* One of the factors in determining whether to charge a natural person or a corporation is whether the likely punishment is appropriate given the nature and seriousness of the crime. In the corporate context, prosecutors may take into account the possibly substantial consequences to a corporation's officers, directors, employees, and shareholders, many of whom may, depending on the size and nature (e.g., publicly vs. closely held) of the corporation and their role in its operations, have played no role in the criminal conduct, have been completely unaware of it, or have been wholly unable to prevent it. Prosecutors should also be aware of non-penal sanctions that may accompany a criminal charge, such as potential suspension or debarment from eligibility for government contracts or federal funded programs such as health care.

Whether or not such non-penal sanctions are appropriate or required in a particular case is the responsibility of the relevant agency, a decision that will be made based on the applicable statutes, regulations, and policies.

Virtually every conviction of a corporation, like virtually every conviction of an individual, will have an impact on innocent third parties, and the mere existence of such an effect is not sufficient to preclude prosecution of the corporation. Therefore, in evaluating the severity of collateral consequences, various factors already discussed, such as the pervasiveness of the criminal conduct and the adequacy of the corporation's compliance programs, should be considered in determining the weight to be given to this factor. For instance, the balance may tip in favor of prosecuting corporations in situations where the scope of the misconduct in a case is widespread and sustained within a corporate division (or spread throughout pockets of the corporate organization). In such cases, the possible unfairness of visiting punishment for the corporation's crimes upon shareholders may be of much less concern where those shareholders have substantially profited, even unknowingly, from widespread or pervasive criminal activity. Similarly, where the top layers of the corporation's management or the shareholders of a closely-held corporation were engaged in or aware of the wrongdoing and the conduct at issue was accepted as a way of doing business for an extended period, debarment may be deemed not collateral, but a direct and entirely appropriate consequence of the corporation's wrongdoing.

The appropriateness of considering such collateral consequences and the weight to be given them may depend on the special policy concerns discussed in section III, *supra*.

X. Charging a Corporation: Non-Criminal Alternatives

A. *General Principle:* Although non-criminal alternatives to prosecution often exist, prosecutors may consider whether such sanctions would adequately deter, punish, and rehabilitate a corporation that has engaged in wrongful conduct. In evaluating the adequacy of non-criminal alternatives to prosecution, *e.g.*, civil or regulatory enforcement actions, the prosecutor may consider all relevant factors, including:

1. the sanctions available under the alternative means of disposition;
2. the likelihood that an effective sanction will be imposed; and
3. the effect of non-criminal disposition on Federal law enforcement interests.

B. *Comment:* The primary goals of criminal law are deterrence, punishment, and rehabilitation. Non-criminal sanctions may not be an appropriate response to an egregious violation, a pattern of wrongdoing, or a history of non-criminal sanctions without proper remediation. In other cases, however, these goals may be satisfied without the necessity of instituting criminal proceedings. In determining whether federal criminal charges are appropriate, the prosecutor should consider the same factors (modified appropriately for the regulatory context) considered when determining whether to leave prosecution of a natural person to another jurisdiction or to seek non-criminal alternatives to prosecution. These factors include: the strength of the regulatory authority's interest; the regulatory authority's ability and willingness to take effective enforcement action; the probable sanction if the regulatory authority's enforcement action is upheld; and the effect of a non-criminal disposition on Federal law enforcement interests. *See* USAM §§ 9-27.240, 9-27.250.

XI. Charging a Corporation: Selecting Charges

A. *General Principle:* Once a prosecutor has decided to charge a corporation, the prosecutor should charge, or should recommend that the grand jury charge, the most serious offense that is consistent with the nature of the defendant's conduct and that is likely to result in a sustainable conviction.

B. *Comment:* Once the decision to charge is made, the same rules as govern charging natural persons apply. These rules require "a faithful and honest application of the Sentencing Guidelines" and an "individualized assessment of the extent to which particular charges fit the specific circumstances of the case, are consistent with the purposes of the Federal criminal code, and maximize the impact of Federal resources on crime." *See* USAM § 9-27.300. In making this determination, "it is appropriate that the attorney for the government consider, *inter alia,* such factors as the sentencing guideline range yielded by the charge, whether the penalty yielded by such sentencing range . . . is proportional to the seriousness of the defendant's conduct, and whether the charge achieves such purposes of the criminal law as punishment, protection of the public, specific and general deterrence, and rehabilitation." *See* Attorney General's Memorandum, dated October 12, 1993.

XII. Plea Agreements with Corporations

A. *General Principle:* In negotiating plea agreements with corporations, prosecutors should seek a plea to the most serious, readily provable offense charged. In addition, the terms of the plea agreement should contain appropriate provisions to ensure punishment, deterrence, rehabilitation, and compliance with the plea agreement in the corporate context. Although special circumstances may mandate a different conclusion, prosecutors generally should not agree to accept a corporate guilty plea in exchange for non-prosecution or dismissal of charges against individual officers and employees.

B. *Comment:* Prosecutors may enter into plea agreements with corporations for the same reasons and under the same constraints as apply to plea agreements with natural persons. *See* USAM §§ 9-27.400–500. This means, inter alia, that the corporation should be required to plead guilty to the most serious, readily provable offense charged. As is the case with individuals, the attorney making this determination should do so "on the basis of an individualized assessment of the extent to which particular charges fit the specific circumstances of the case, are consistent with the purposes of the federal criminal code, and maximize the impact of federal resources on crime. In making this determination, the attorney for the government considers, inter alia, such factors as the sentencing guideline range yielded by the charge, whether the penalty yielded by such sentencing range . . . is proportional to the seriousness of the defendant's conduct, and whether the charge achieves such purposes of the criminal law as punishment, protection of the public, specific and general deterrence, and rehabilitation." See Attorney General's Memorandum, dated October 12, 1993. In addition, any negotiated departures from the Sentencing Guidelines must be justifiable under the Guidelines and must be disclosed to the sentencing court. A corporation should be made to realize that pleading guilty to criminal charges constitutes an admission of guilt and not merely a resolution of an inconvenient distraction from its business. As with natural persons, pleas should be structured so that the corporation may not later "proclaim lack of culpability or even complete innocence." *See* USAM §§ 9-27.420(b)(4), 9-27.440, 9-27.500. Thus, for instance, there should be placed upon the record a sufficient factual basis for the plea to prevent later corporate assertions of innocence.

A corporate plea agreement should also contain provisions that recognize the nature of the corporate "person" and ensure that the principles of punishment, deterrence, and rehabilitation are met. In the corporate context, punishment and deterrence are generally accomplished by substantial fines, mandatory restitution, and institution of appropriate compliance measures, including, if necessary, continued judicial oversight or the use of special masters. *See* USSG §§ 8B1.1, 8C2.1, *et seq*. In addition, where the corporation is a government contractor, permanent or temporary debarment may be appropriate. Where the corporation was engaged in government contracting fraud, a prosecutor may not negotiate away an agency's right to debar or to list the corporate defendant.

In negotiating a plea agreement, prosecutors should also consider the deterrent value of prosecutions of individuals within the corporation. Therefore, one factor that a prosecutor may consider in determining whether to enter into a plea agreement is whether the corporation is seeking immunity for its employees and officers or whether the corporation is willing to cooperate in the investigation of culpable individuals. Prosecutors should rarely negotiate away individual criminal liability in a corporate plea.

Rehabilitation, of course, requires that the corporation undertake to be law-abiding in the future. It is, therefore, appropriate to require the corporation, as a condition of probation, to implement a compliance program or to reform an existing one. As discussed above, prosecutors may consult with the appropriate state and federal agencies and components of the Justice Department to ensure that a proposed compliance program is adequate and meets industry standards and best practices. *See* section VII, *supra*.

In plea agreements in which the corporation agrees to cooperate, the prosecutor should ensure that the cooperation is complete and truthful. To do so, the prosecutor may request that the corporation waive attorney-client and work product protection, make employees and agents available for debriefing, disclose the results of its internal investigation, file appropriate certified financial statements, agree to governmental or third-party audits, and take whatever other steps are necessary to ensure that the full scope of the corporate wrongdoing is disclosed and that the responsible culprits are identified and, if appropriate, prosecuted. *See* generally section VIII, *supra.*

APPENDIX I-2

U.S. Department of Justice

Office of the Deputy Attorney General

The Deputy Attorney General *Washington, D.C. 20530*

MEMORANDUM

TO: Heads of Department Components
United States Attorneys

FROM: Paul J. McNulty
Deputy Attorney General

SUBJECT: Principles of Federal Prosecution of Business Organizations

The Department experienced unprecedented success in prosecuting corporate fraud during the last four years. We have aggressively rooted out corruption in financial markets and corporate board rooms across the country. Federal prosecutors should be justifiably proud that the information used by our nation's financial markets is more reliable, our retirement plans are more secure, and the investing public is better protected as a result of our efforts. The most significant result of this enforcement initiative is that corporations increasingly recognize the need for self-policing, self-reporting, and cooperation with law enforcement. Through their self-regulation efforts, fraud undoubtedly is being prevented, sparing shareholders from the financial harm accompanying corporate corruption. The Department must continue to encourage these efforts.

Though much has been accomplished, the work of protecting the integrity of the marketplace continues. As we press forward in our enforcement duties, it is appropriate that we consider carefully proposals which could make our efforts more effective. I remain convinced that the fundamental principles that have guided our enforcement practices are sound. In particular, our corporate charging principles are not only familiar, but they are welcomed by most corporations in our country because good corporate leadership shares many of our goals. Like federal prosecutors, corporate leaders must take action to protect shareholders, preserve corporate value, and promote honesty and fair dealing with the investing public.

We have heard from responsible corporate officials recently about the challenges they face in discharging their duties to the corporation while responding in a meaningful way to a government investigation. Many of those associated with the corporate legal community have expressed concern that our practices may be discouraging full and candid communications between corporate employees and legal counsel. To the extent this is happening, it was never the intention of the Department for our corporate charging principles to cause such a result.

Therefore, I have decided to adjust certain aspects of our policy in ways that will further promote public confidence in the Department, encourage corporate fraud prevention efforts, and clarify our goals without sacrificing our ability to prosecute these important eases effectively. The new language expands upon the Department's long-standing policies concerning how we evaluate the authenticity of a corporation's cooperation with a government investigation,

This memorandum supersedes and replaces guidance contained in the Memorandum from Deputy Attorney General Larry D. Thompson entitled Principles of Federal Prosecution of Business Organizations (January 20, 2003) (the "Thompson Memorandum") and the Memorandum from the Acting Deputy Attorney General Robert D. McCallum, Jr. entitled Waiver of Corporate Attorney-Client and Work Product Protections (October 21, 2005) (the "McCallum Memorandum").

U.S. Department of Justice

Office of the Deputy Attorney General

The Deputy Attorney General *Washington, D.C. 20530*

MEMORANDUM

TO:	Heads of Department Components United States Attorneys
FROM:	Paul J. McNulty Deputy Attorney General
SUBJECT:	Principles of Federal Prosecution of Business Organizations

Federal Prosecution of Business Organizations[1]

1. Duties of the Federal Prosecutor; Duties of Corporate Leaders

The prosecution of corporate crime is a high priority for the Department of Justice. By investigating wrongdoing and bringing charges for criminal conduct, the Department plays an important role in protecting investors and ensuring public confidence in business entities and in the investment markets in which those entities participate. In this respect, federal prosecutors and corporate leaders share a common goal. Directors and officers owe a fiduciary duty to a corporation's shareholders, the corporation's true owners, and they owe duties of honest dealing to the investing public in connection with the corporation's regulatory filings and public statements. The faithful execution of these duties by corporate leadership serves the same values in promoting public trust and confidence that our criminal prosecutions are designed to serve.

A prosecutor's duty to enforce the law requires the investigation and prosecution of criminal wrongdoing if it is discovered. In carrying out this mission with the diligence and resolve necessary to vindicate the important public interests discussed above, prosecutors should be mindful of the common cause we share with responsible corporate leaders. Prosecutors should also be mindful that confidence in the Department is affected both by the results we achieve and by the real and perceived ways in which we achieve them. Thus, the manner in which we do our job as prosecutors—the professionalism we

1. While these guidelines refer to corporations, they apply to the consideration of the prosecution of all types of business organizations, including partnerships, sole proprietorships, government entities, and unincorporated associations.

demonstrate, our resourcefulness in seeking information, and our willingness to secure the facts in a manner that encourages corporate compliance and self-regulation—impacts public perception of our mission. Federal prosecutors recognize that they must maintain public confidence in the way in which they exercise their charging discretion, and that professionalism and civility have always played an important part in putting these principles into action.

II. Charging a Corporation: General Principles

A. *General Principle:* Corporations should not be treated leniently because of their artificial nature nor should they be subject to harsher treatment. Vigorous enforcement of the criminal laws against corporate wrongdoers, where appropriate, results in great benefits for law enforcement and the public, particularly in the area of white collar crime. Indicting corporations for wrongdoing enables the government to address and be a force for positive change of corporate culture, alter corporate behavior, and prevent, discover, and punish white collar crime.

B. *Comment:* In all cases involving corporate wrongdoing, prosecutors should consider the factors discussed herein. First and foremost, prosecutors should be aware of the important public benefits that may flow from indicting a corporation in appropriate cases. For instance, corporations are likely to take immediate remedial steps when one is indicted for criminal conduct that is pervasive throughout a particular industry, and thus an indictment often provides a unique opportunity for deterrence on a massive scale. In addition, a corporate indictment may result in specific deterrence by changing the culture of the indicted corporation and the behavior of its employees. Finally, certain crimes that carry with them a substantial risk of great public harm, e.g., environmental crimes or financial frauds, are by their nature most likely to be committed by businesses, and there may, therefore, be a substantial federal interest in indicting the corporation.

Charging a corporation, however, does not mean that individual directors, officers, employees, or shareholders should not also be charged. Prosecution of a corporation is not a substitute for the prosecution of criminally culpable individuals within or without the corporation. Because a corporation can act only through individuals, imposition of individual criminal liability may provide the strongest deterrent against future corporate wrongdoing. Only rarely should provable individual culpability not be pursued, even in the face of an offer of a corporate guilty plea or some other disposition of the charges against the corporation.

Corporations are "legal persons," capable of suing and being sued, and capable of committing crimes. Under the doctrine of *respondeat superior,* a corporation may be held criminally liable for the illegal acts of its directors, officers, employees, and agents. To hold a corporation liable for these actions, the government must establish that the corporate agent's actions (I) were within the scope of his duties and (II) were intended, at least in part, to benefit the corporation. In all cases involving wrongdoing by corporate agents, prosecutors should consider the corporation, as well as the responsible individuals, as potential criminal targets.

Agents, however, may act for mixed reasons—both for self-aggrandizement (both direct and indirect) and for the benefit of the corporation, and a corporation may be held liable as long as one motivation of its agent is to benefit the corporation. *See United States v. Potter*, 463 F.3d 9, 25 (1st Cir. 2006) (stating that the test to determine whether an agent is acting within the scope of employment is whether the agent is performing acts of the kind which he is authorized to perform, and those acts are motivated—at least in part—by an intent to benefit the corporation). In *United States v. Automated Medical Laboratories*, 770 F.2d 399 (4th Cir. 1985), the Fourth Circuit affirmed a corporation's conviction for the actions of a subsidiary's employee despite its claim that the employee was acting for his own benefit, namely his "ambitious nature and his desire to ascend the corporate ladder." The court stated, "*Partucci* was clearly acting in part to benefit AML since his advancement within the corporation depended on AML's well-being and its lack of difficulties with the FDA." Furthermore, in *United States v. Sun-Diamond Growers of California*, 138 F.3d 961, 969–70 (D.C. Cir. 1998), *aff'd on other grounds*, 526 U.S. 398 (1999), the D.C. Circuit rejected a corporation's argument that it should not be held criminally liable for the actions of its vice-president since the vice-president's "scheme was designed to—and did in fact—defraud [the corporation], not benefit it." According to the court, the fact that the vice-president deceived the corporation and used its money to contribute illegally to a congressional campaign did not preclude a valid finding that he acted to benefit the corporation. Part of the vice-president's job was to cultivate the corporation's relationship with the congressional candidate's brother, the Secretary of Agriculture. Therefore, the court held, the jury was entitled to conclude that the vice-president had acted with an intent, "however befuddled," to further the interests of his employer. *See also United States v. Cincotta*, 689 F.2d 238, 241–42 (1st Cir. 1982) (upholding a corporation's conviction, notwithstanding the substantial personal benefit reaped by its miscreant agents, because the fraudulent scheme required money to pass through the corporation's treasury and the fraudulently obtained goods were resold to the corporation's customers in the corporation's name).

Moreover, the corporation need not even necessarily profit from its agent's actions for it to be held liable. In *Automated Medical Laboratories*, the Fourth Circuit stated:

> [B]enefit is not a "touchstone of criminal corporate liability; benefit at best is an evidential, not an operative, fact." Thus, whether the agent's actions ultimately redounded to the benefit of the corporation is less significant than whether the agent acted with the intent to benefit the corporation. The basic purpose of requiring that an agent have acted

> with the intent to benefit the corporation, however, is to insulate the corporation from criminal liability for actions of its agents which *may* be inimical to the interests of the corporation or which may have been undertaken solely to advance the interests of that agent or of a party other than the corporation.

770 F.2d at 407 (emphasis added; *quoting Old Monastery Co. v. United States,* 147 F.2d 905, 908 (4th Cir. 1945), *cert. denied,* 326 U.S. 734 (1945)).

III. Charging a Corporation: Factors to Be Considered

A. *General Principle:* Generally, prosecutors apply the same factors in determining whether to charge a corporation as they do with respect to individuals. *See* USAM § 9-27.220, *et seq.* Thus, the prosecutor must weigh all of the factors normally considered in the sound exercise of prosecutorial judgment: the sufficiency of the evidence; the likelihood of success at trial; the probable deterrent, rehabilitative, and other consequences of conviction; and the adequacy of noncriminal approaches. *See id.* However, due to the nature of the corporate "person," some additional factors are present. In conducting an investigation, determining whether to bring charges, and negotiating plea agreements, prosecutors must consider the following factors in reaching a decision as to the proper treatment of a corporate target:

1. the nature and seriousness of the offense, including the risk of harm to the public, and applicable policies and priorities, if any, governing the prosecution of corporations for particular categories of crime (*see* section IV, *infra*);
2. the pervasiveness of wrongdoing within the corporation, including the complicity in, or condonation of, the wrongdoing by corporate management (*see* section V, *infra*);
3. the corporation's history of similar conduct, including prior criminal, civil, and regulatory enforcement actions against it (see section VI, *infra*);
4. the corporation's timely and voluntary disclosure of wrongdoing and its willingness to cooperate in the investigation of its agents (*see* section VII, *infra*);
5. the existence and adequacy of the corporation's *pre-existing* compliance program (*see* section VIII *infra*);
6. the corporation's remedial actions, including any efforts to implement an effective corporate compliance program or to improve an existing one, to replace responsible management, to discipline or terminate wrongdoers, to pay restitution, and to cooperate with the relevant government agencies (*see* section IX, *infra);*
7. collateral consequences, including disproportionate harm to shareholders, pension holders and employees not proven personally culpable and impact on the public arising from the prosecution (*see* section X, *infra*);

8. the adequacy of the prosecution of individuals responsible for the corporation's malfeasance; and
9. the adequacy of remedies such as civil or regulatory enforcement actions (*see* section XI, *infra*).

B. *Comment:* In determining whether to charge a corporation, the foregoing factors must be considered. The factors listed in this section are intended to be illustrative of those that should be considered and not a complete or exhaustive list. Some or all of these factors may or may not apply to specific cases, and in some cases one factor may override all others. For example, the nature and seriousness of the offense may be such as to warrant prosecution regardless of the other factors. In most cases, however, no single factor will be dispositive. Further, national law enforcement policies in various enforcement areas may require that more or less weight be given to certain of these factors than to others. Of course, prosecutors must exercise their judgment in applying and balancing these factors and this process does not mandate a particular result.

In making a decision to charge a corporation, the prosecutor generally has wide latitude in determining when, whom, how, and even whether to prosecute for violations of federal criminal law. In exercising that discretion, prosecutors should consider the following general statements of principles that summarize appropriate considerations to be weighed and desirable practices to be followed in discharging their prosecutorial responsibilities. In doing so, prosecutors should ensure that the general purposes of the criminal law—assurance of warranted punishment, deterrence of further criminal conduct, protection of the public from dangerous and fraudulent conduct, rehabilitation of offenders, and restitution for victims and affected communities—are adequately met, taking into account the special nature of the corporate "person."

IV. Charging a Corporation: Special Policy Concerns

A. *General Principle:* The nature and seriousness of the crime, including the risk of harm to the public from the criminal conduct, are obviously primary factors in determining whether to charge a corporation. In addition, corporate conduct, particularly that of national and multi-national corporations, necessarily intersects with federal economic, taxation, and criminal law enforcement policies. In applying these principles, prosecutors must consider the practices and policies of the appropriate Division of the Department, and must comply with those policies to the extent required.

B. *Comment:* In determining whether to charge a corporation, prosecutors should take into account federal law enforcement priorities as discussed above. *See* USAM § 9-27-230. In addition, however, prosecutors must be aware of the specific policy goals and incentive programs established by the respective Divisions and regulatory agencies. Thus, whereas natural persons may be given incremental degrees of credit (ranging from immunity to lesser charges to sentencing considerations) for turning themselves in, making statements against their penal interest, and cooperating in the government's investigation of their own and others' wrongdoing, the same approach may not be appropriate in all circumstances with respect to corporations. As an example, it is entirely proper in many investigations for a prosecutor to consider the corporation's pre-indictment conduct, e.g. voluntary disclosure, cooperation, remediation or restitution, in determining whether to seek an indictment. However, this would not necessarily be appropriate in an antitrust investigation, in which antitrust violations, by definition, go to the heart of the corporation's business and for which the Antitrust Division has therefore established a firm policy, understood in the business community, that credit should not be given at the charging stage for a compliance program and that amnesty is available only to the first corporation to make full disclosure to the government. As another example, the Tax Division has a strong preference for prosecuting responsible individuals, rather than entities, for corporate tax offenses. Thus, in determining whether or not to charge a corporation, prosecutors must consult with the Criminal, Antitrust, Tax, and Environmental and Natural Resources Divisions, if appropriate or required.

V. Charging a Corporation: Pervasiveness of Wrongdoing Within the Corporation

A. *General Principle:* A corporation can only act through natural persons, and it is therefore held responsible for the acts of such persons fairly attributable to it. Charging a corporation for even minor misconduct may be appropriate where the wrongdoing was pervasive and was undertaken by a large number of employees or by all the employees in a particular role within the corporation, *e.g.*, salesmen or procurement officers, or was condoned by upper management. On the other hand, in certain limited circumstances, it may not be appropriate to impose liability upon a corporation, particularly one with a compliance program in place, under a strict *respondeat superior* theory for the single isolated act of a rogue employee. There is, of course, a wide spectrum between these two extremes, and a prosecutor should exercise sound discretion in evaluating the pervasiveness of wrongdoing within a corporation.

B. *Comment:* Of these factors, the most important is the role of management. Although acts of even low-level employees may result in criminal liability, a corporation is directed by its management and management is responsible for a corporate culture in which criminal conduct is either discouraged or tacitly encouraged. As stated in commentary to the Sentencing Guidelines:

> Pervasiveness [is] case specific and [will] depend on the number, and degree of responsibility, of individuals [with] substantial authority . . . who participated in, condoned, or were willfully ignorant of the offense. Fewer individuals need to be involved for a finding of per-

vasiveness if those individuals exercised a relatively high degree of authority. Pervasiveness can occur either within an organization as a whole or within a unit of an organization.
See USSG § 8C2.5, comment. (n. 4).

VI. Charging a Corporation: The Corporation's Past History

A. *General Principle:* Prosecutors may consider a corporation's history of similar conduct, including prior criminal, civil, and regulatory enforcement actions against it, in determining whether to bring criminal charges.

B. *Comment:* A corporation, like a natural person, is expected to learn from its mistakes. A history of similar conduct may be probative of a corporate culture that encouraged, or at least condoned, such conduct, regardless of any compliance programs. Criminal prosecution of a corporation may be particularly appropriate where the corporation previously had been subject to non-criminal guidance, warnings, or sanctions, or previous criminal charges, and it either had not taken adequate action to prevent future unlawful conduct or had continued to engage in the conduct in spite of the warnings or enforcement actions taken against it. In making this determination, the corporate structure itself, *e.g.*, subsidiaries or operating divisions, should be ignored, and enforcement actions taken against the corporation or any of its divisions, subsidiaries, and affiliates should be considered. *See* USSG § 8C2.5(c) & comment. (n.6).

VII. Charging a Corporation: The Value of Cooperation

A. *General Principle:* In determining whether to charge a corporation, that corporation's timely and voluntary disclosure of wrongdoing and its cooperation with the government's investigation may be relevant factors. In gauging the extent of the corporation's cooperation, the prosecutor may consider, among other things, whether the corporation made a voluntary and timely disclosure, and the corporation's willingness to provide relevant evidence and to identify the culprits within the corporation, including senior executives.

B. *Comment:* In investigating wrongdoing by or within a corporation, a prosecutor is likely to encounter several obstacles resulting from the nature of the corporation itself. It will often be difficult to determine which individual took which action on behalf of the corporation. Lines of authority and responsibility may be shared among operating divisions or departments, and records and personnel may be spread throughout the United States or even among several countries. Where the criminal conduct continued over an extended period of time, the culpable or knowledgeable personnel may have been promoted, transferred, or fired, or they may have quit or retired. Accordingly, a corporation's cooperation may be critical in identifying the culprits and locating relevant evidence. Relevant considerations in determining whether a corporation has cooperated are set forth below.

1. *Qualifying for Immunity, Amnesty or Pretrial Diversion*

In some circumstances, granting a corporation immunity or amnesty or pretrial diversion may be considered in the course of the government's investigation. In such circumstances, prosecutors should refer to the principles governing non-prosecution agreements generally. *See* USAM § 9-27.600–650. These principles permit a non-prosecution agreement in exchange for cooperation when a corporation's "timely cooperation appears to be necessary to the public interest and other means of obtaining the desired cooperation are unavailable or would not be effective." Prosecutors should note that in the ease of national or multi-national corporations, multi-district or global agreements may be necessary. Such agreements may only be entered into with the approval of each affected district or the appropriate Department official. *See* USAM § 9-27.641.

In addition, the Department, in conjunction with regulatory agencies and other executive branch departments, encourages corporations, as part of their compliance programs, to conduct internal investigations and to disclose their findings to the appropriate authorities. Some agencies, such as the Securities and Exchange Commission and the Environmental Protection Agency, as well as the Department's Environmental and Natural Resources Division, have formal voluntary disclosure programs in which self-reporting, coupled with remediation and additional criteria, may qualify the corporation for amnesty or reduced sanctions. Even in the absence of a formal program, prosecutors may consider a corporation's timely and voluntary disclosure in evaluating the adequacy of the corporation's compliance program and its management's commitment to the compliance program. However, prosecution and economic policies specific to the industry or statute may require prosecution notwithstanding a corporation's willingness to cooperate. For example, the Antitrust Division offers amnesty only to the first corporation to agree to cooperate. This creates a strong incentive for corporations participating in anti-competitive conduct to be the first to cooperate. In addition, amnesty, immunity, or reduced sanctions may not be appropriate where the corporation's business is permeated with fraud or other crimes.

2. *Waiving Attorney-Client and Work Product Protections*[2]

The attorney-client and work product protections serve an extremely important function in the U.S. legal system. The attorney-client privilege is one of the oldest and most sacrosanct privileges under U.S. law. *See Upjohn v. United States*, 449 U.S. 383, 389 (1976). As the Supreme Court has stated, "its purpose is to encourage full and frank communication between attorneys and their clients and thereby promote broader public interests in the observance of

2. The Sentencing Guidelines reward voluntary disclosure and cooperation with a reduction in the corporation's offense level. *See* USSG § 8C2.5(g). The reference to consideration of a corporation's waiver of attorney-client and work product protections in reducing a corporation's culpability score in Application Note 12, was deleted effective November 1, 2006. *See* USSG § 8C2.5(g), comment. (n.12).

law and administration of justice." *Id.* The work product doctrine also serves similarly important interests.

Waiver of attorney-client and work product protections is not a prerequisite to a finding that a company has cooperated in the government's investigation. However, a company's disclosure of privileged information may permit the government to expedite its investigation. In addition, the disclosure of privileged information may be critical in enabling the government to evaluate the accuracy and completeness of the company's voluntary disclosure.

Prosecutors may only request waiver of attorney-client or work product protections when there is a legitimate need for the privileged information to fulfill their law enforcement obligations. A legitimate need for the information is not established by concluding it is merely desirable or convenient to obtain privileged information. The test requires a careful balancing of important policy considerations underlying the attorney-client privilege and work product doctrine and the law enforcement needs of the government's investigation.

Whether there is a legitimate need depends upon:

1. the likelihood and degree to which the privileged information will benefit the government's investigation;
2. whether the information sought can be obtained in a timely and complete fashion by using alternative means that do not require waiver;
3. the completeness of the voluntary disclosure already provided; and
4. the collateral consequences to a corporation of a waiver.

If a legitimate need exists, prosecutors should seek the least intrusive waiver necessary to conduct a complete and thorough investigation, and should follow a step-by-step approach to requesting information. Prosecutors should first request purely factual information, which may or may not be privileged, relating to the underlying misconduct ("Category I"). Examples of Category I information could include, without limitation, copies of key documents, witness statements, or purely factual interview memoranda regarding the underlying misconduct, organization charts created by company counsel, factual chronologies, factual summaries, or reports (or portions thereof) containing investigative facts documented by counsel.

Before requesting that a corporation waive the attorney-client or work product protections for Category 1 information, prosecutors must obtain written authorization from the United States Attorney who must provide a copy of the request to, and consult with, the Assistant Attorney General for the Criminal Division before granting or denying the request. A prosecutor's request to the United States Attorney for authorization to seek a waiver must set forth law enforcement's legitimate need for the information and identify the scope of the waiver sought. A copy of each waiver request and authorization for Category I information must be maintained in the files of the United States Attorney. If the request is authorized, the United States Attorney must communicate the request in writing to the corporation.

A corporation's response to the government's request for waiver of privilege for Category I information may be considered in determining whether a corporation has cooperated in the government's investigation.

Only if the purely tactual information provides an incomplete basis to conduct a thorough investigation should prosecutors then request that the corporation provide attorney-client communications or non-factual attorney work product ("Category II"). This information includes legal advice given to the corporation before, during, and after the underlying misconduct occurred.

This category of privileged information might include the production of attorney notes, memoranda or reports (or portions thereof) containing counsel's mental impressions and conclusions, legal determinations reached as a result of an internal investigation, or legal advice given to the corporation.

Prosecutors are cautioned that Category II information should only be sought in rare circumstances.

Before requesting that a corporation waive the attorney-client or work product protections for Category II information, the United States Attorney must obtain written authorization from the Deputy Attorney General. A United States Attorney's request for authorization to seek a waiver must set forth law enforcement's legitimate need for the information and identify the scope of the waiver sought. A copy of each waiver request and authorization for Category II information must be maintained in the files of the Deputy Attorney General. If the request is authorized, the United States Attorney must communicate the request in writing to the corporation.

If a corporation declines to provide a waiver for Category II information after a written request from the United States Attorney, prosecutors must not consider this declination against the corporation in making a charging decision. Prosecutors may always favorably consider a corporation's acquiescence to the government's waiver request in determining whether a corporation has cooperated in the government's investigation.

Requests for Category II information requiring the approval of the Deputy Attorney General do not include:

1. legal advice contemporaneous to the underlying misconduct when the corporation or one of its employees is relying upon an advice-of-counsel defense; and
2. legal advice or communications in furtherance of a crime or fraud, coming within the crime-fraud exception to the attorney-client privilege.

In these two instances, prosecutors should follow the authorization process established for requesting waiver for Category I information.

For federal prosecutors in litigating Divisions within Main Justice, waiver requests for Category I information must be submitted for approval to the Assistant Attorney General of the Division and waiver requests for Category II information must be submitted by the Assistant Attorney General for approval to the Deputy Attorney General. If the request is authorized, the

Assistant Attorney General must communicate the request in writing to the corporation.

Federal prosecutors are not required to obtain authorization if the corporation voluntarily offers privileged documents without a request by the government. However, voluntary waivers must be reported to the United States Attorney or the Assistant Attorney General in the Division where the case originated. A record of these reports must be maintained in the files of that office.

3. Shielding Culpable Employees and Agents

Another factor to be weighed by the prosecutor is whether the corporation appears to be protecting its culpable employees and agents. Thus, while cases will differ depending on the circumstances, a corporation's promise of support to culpable employees and agents, *e.g.*, through retaining the employees without sanction for their misconduct or through providing information to the employees about the government's investigation pursuant to a joint defense agreement, may be considered by the prosecutor in weighing the extent and value of a corporation's cooperation.

Prosecutors generally should not take into account whether a corporation is advancing attorneys' fees to employees or agents under investigation and indictment. Many state indemnification statutes grant corporations the power to advance the legal fees of officers under investigation prior to a formal determination of guilt. As a consequence, many corporations enter into contractual obligations to advance attorneys' fees through provisions contained in their corporate charters, bylaws or employment agreements. Therefore, a corporation's compliance with governing state law and its contractual obligations cannot be considered a failure to cooperate.[3] This prohibition is not meant to prevent a prosecutor from asking questions about an attorney's representation of a corporation or its employees.[4]

4. Obstructing the Investigation

Another factor to be weighed by the prosecutor is whether the corporation, while purporting to cooperate, has engaged in conduct intended to impede the investigation (whether or not rising to the level of criminal obstruction).

3. In extremely rare cases, the advancement of attorneys' fees may be taken into account when the totality of the circumstances show that it was intended to impede a criminal investigation. In these cases, fee advancement is considered with many other telling facts to make a determination that the corporation is acting improperly to shield itself and its culpable employees from government scrutiny. *See discussion in* Brief of Appellant-United States, *United States v. Smith and Watson*, No. 06-3999-cr (2d Cir. Nov. 6, 2006). Where these circumstances exist, approval must be obtained from the Deputy Attorney General before prosecutors may consider this factor in their charging decisions. Prosecutors should follow the authorization process established for waiver requests of Category II information (*see* section VII-2, *infra*).

4. Routine questions regarding the representation status of a corporation and its employees, including how and by whom attorneys' fees are paid, frequently arise in the course of an investigation. They may be necessary to assess other issues, such as conflict-of-interest. Such questions are appropriate and this guidance is not intended to prohibit such inquiry.

Examples of such conduct include: overly broad assertions of corporate representation of employees or former employees; overly broad or frivolous assertions of privilege to withhold the disclosure of relevant, non-privileged documents; inappropriate directions to employees or their counsel, such as directions not to cooperate openly and fully with the investigation including, for example, the direction to decline to be interviewed; making presentations or submissions that contain misleading assertions or omissions; incomplete or delayed production of records; and failure to promptly disclose illegal conduct known to the corporation.

5. *Offering Cooperation: No Entitlement to Immunity*

Finally, a corporation's offer of cooperation does not automatically entitle it to immunity from prosecution. A corporation should not be able to escape liability merely by offering up its directors, officers, employees, or agents as in lieu of its own prosecution. Thus, a corporation's willingness to cooperate is merely one relevant factor, that needs to be considered in conjunction with the other factors, particularly those relating to the corporation's past history and the role of management in the wrongdoing.

VIII. Charging a Corporation: Corporate Compliance Programs

A. *General Principle:* Compliance programs are established by corporate management to prevent and to detect misconduct and to ensure that corporate activities are conducted in accordance with all applicable criminal and civil laws, regulations, and rules. The Department encourages such corporate self-policing, including voluntary disclosures to the government of any problems that a corporation discovers on its own. However, the existence of a compliance program is not sufficient, in and of itself, to justify not charging a corporation for criminal conduct undertaken by its officers, directors, employees, or agents. Indeed, the commission of such crimes in the face of a compliance program may suggest that the corporate management is not adequately enforcing its program. In addition, the nature of some crimes, *e.g.*, antitrust violations, may be such that national law enforcement policies mandate prosecutions of corporations notwithstanding the existence of a compliance program.

B. *Comment:* A corporate compliance program, even one specifically prohibiting the very conduct in question, does not absolve the corporation from criminal liability under the doctrine of *respondeat superior*. *See United States v. Basic Construction Co.*, 711 F.2d 570 (4th Cir. 1983) ("[A] corporation may be held criminally responsible for antitrust violations committed by its employees if they were acting within the scope of their authority, or apparent authority, and for the benefit of the corporation, even if . . . such acts were against corporate policy or express instructions."). [As explained in *United States v. Potter*, 463 F.3d 9 (1st Cir. 2006),] a corporation cannot "avoid liability by adopting abstract rules" that forbid its agents from engaging in illegal acts; "even a specific directive to an agent or employee or honest efforts to police such rules do not automatically free the company for the wrongful acts of agents." Similarly, in *United States v. Hilton Hotels Corp.*, 467 F.2d 1000 (9th Cir. 1972), *cert. denied*, 409 U.S. 1125 (1973), the Ninth Circuit affirmed antitrust liability based upon a purchasing agent for a single hotel threatening a single supplier with a boycott unless it paid dues to a local marketing association, even though the agent's actions were contrary to corporate policy and directly against express instructions from his superiors. The court reasoned that Congress, in enacting the Sherman Antitrust Act, "intended to impose liability upon business entities for the acts of those to whom they choose to delegate the conduct of their affairs, thus stimulating a maximum effort by owners and managers to assure adherence by such agents to the requirements of the Act."[5] It concluded that "general policy statements" and even direct instructions from the agent's superiors were not sufficient; "Appellant could not gain exculpation by issuing general instructions without undertaking to enforce those instructions by means commensurate with the obvious risks." *See also United States v. Beusch*, 596 F.2d 871, 878 (9th Cir. 1979) ("[A] corporation may be liable for the acts of its employees done contrary to express instructions and policies, but . . . the existence of such instructions and policies may be considered in determining whether the employee in fact acted to benefit the corporation."); *United States v. American Radiator & Standard Sanitary Corp.*, 433 F.2d 174 (3rd Cir. 1970) (affirming conviction of corporation based upon its officer's participation in price-fixing scheme, despite corporation's defense that officer's conduct violated its "rigid anti-fraternization policy" against any socialization (and exchange of price information) with its competitors; "When the act of the agent is within the scope of his employment or his apparent authority, the corporation is held legally responsible for it, although what he did may be contrary to his actual instructions and may be unlawful.").

While the Department recognizes that no compliance program can ever prevent all criminal activity by a corporation's employees, the critical factors in evaluating any program are whether the program is adequately designed for maximum effectiveness in preventing and detecting wrongdoing by employees and whether corporate management is enforcing the program or is tacitly encouraging or pressuring employees to engage in misconduct to achieve business objectives. The Department has no formal guidelines for corporate compliance programs. The fundamental questions any prosecutor should ask are: "Is the corporation's compliance program well designed?" and "Does the corporation's compliance program work?" In answering these questions, the prosecutor should consider the comprehensiveness of the compliance program;

---

5. Although this case and *Basic Construction* are both antitrust cases, their reasoning applies to other criminal violations. In the *Hilton* case, for instance, the Ninth Circuit noted that Sherman Act violations are commercial offenses "usually motivated by a desire to enhance profits," thus, bringing the case within the normal rule that a "purpose to benefit the corporation is necessary to bring the agent's acts within the scope of his employment." 467 F.2d at 1006 & n4. In addition, in *United States v. Automated Medical Laboratories*, 770 F.2d 399, 406 n.5 (4th Cir. 1985), the Fourth Circuit stated "that Basic Construction states a generally applicable rule on corporate criminal liability despite the fact that it addresses violations of the antitrust laws."

the extent and pervasiveness of the criminal conduct; the number and level of the corporate employees involved; the seriousness, duration, and frequency of the misconduct; and any remedial actions taken by the corporation, including restitution, disciplinary action, and revisions to corporate compliance programs.[6] Prosecutors should also consider the promptness of any disclosure of wrongdoing to the government and the corporation's cooperation in the government's investigation. In evaluating compliance programs, prosecutors may consider whether the corporation has established corporate governance mechanisms that can effectively detect and prevent misconduct. For example, do the corporation's directors exercise independent review over proposed corporate actions rather than unquestioningly ratifying officers' recommendations; are the directors provided with information sufficient to enable the exercise of independent judgment, are internal audit functions conducted at a level sufficient to ensure their independence and accuracy and have the directors established an information and reporting system in the organization reasonably designed to provide management and the board of directors with timely and accurate information sufficient to allow them to reach an informed decision regarding the organization's compliance with the law. *In re: Caremark*, 698 A.2d 959 (Del Ct. Chan. 1996).

Prosecutors should therefore attempt to determine whether a corporation's compliance program is merely a "paper program" or whether it was designed and implemented in an effective manner. In addition, prosecutors should determine whether the corporation has provided for a staff sufficient to audit, document, analyze, and utilize the results of the corporation's compliance efforts. In addition, prosecutors should determine whether the corporation's employees are adequately informed about the compliance program and are convinced of the corporation's commitment to it. This will enable the prosecutor to make an informed decision as to whether the corporation has adopted and implemented a truly effective compliance program that, when consistent with other federal law enforcement policies, may result in a decision to charge only the corporation's employees and agents.

Compliance programs should be designed to detect the particular types of misconduct most likely to occur in a particular corporation's line of business. Many corporations operate in complex regulatory environments outside the normal experience of criminal prosecutors. Accordingly, prosecutors should consult with relevant federal and state agencies with the expertise to evaluate the adequacy of a program's design and implementation. For instance, state and federal banking, insurance, and medical boards, the Department of Defense, the Department of Health and Human Services, the Environmental Protection Agency, and the Securities and Exchange Commission have considerable experience with compliance programs and can be very helpful to a prosecutor in evaluating such programs. In addition, the Fraud Section of the

---

6. For a detailed review of these and other factors concerning corporate compliance programs, *see* USSG § 8B2.1.

Criminal Division, the Commercial Litigation Branch of the Civil Division, and the Environmental Crimes Section of the Environment and Natural Resources Division can assist U.S. Attorneys' Offices in finding the appropriate agency office and in providing copies of compliance programs that were developed in previous cases.

IX. Charging a Corporation: Restitution and Remediation

A. *General Principle:* Although neither a corporation nor an individual target may avoid prosecution merely by paying a sum of money, a prosecutor may consider the corporation's willingness to make restitution and steps already taken to do so. A prosecutor may also consider other remedial actions, such as implementing an effective corporate compliance program, improving an existing compliance program, and disciplining wrongdoers, in determining whether to charge the corporation,

B. *Comment:* In determining whether or not a corporation should be prosecuted, a prosecutor may consider whether meaningful remedial measures have been taken, including employee discipline and full restitution. A corporation's response to misconduct says much about its willingness to ensure that such misconduct does not recur. Thus, corporations that fully recognize the seriousness of their misconduct and accept responsibility for it should be taking steps to implement the personnel, operational, and organizational changes necessary to establish an awareness among employees that criminal conduct will not be tolerated. Among the factors prosecutors should consider and weigh are whether the corporation appropriately disciplined the wrongdoers and disclosed information concerning their illegal conduct to the government.

Employee discipline is a difficult task for many corporations because of the human element involved and sometimes because of the seniority of the employees concerned. While corporations need to be fair to their employees, they must also be unequivocally committed, at all levels of the corporation, to the highest standards of legal and ethical behavior. Effective internal discipline can be a powerful deterrent against improper behavior by a corporation's employees. In evaluating a corporation's response to wrongdoing, prosecutors may evaluate the willingness of the corporation to discipline culpable employees of all ranks and the adequacy of the discipline imposed. The prosecutor should be satisfied that the corporation's focus is on the integrity and credibility of its remedial and disciplinary measures rather than on the protection of the wrongdoers.

In addition to employee discipline, two other factors used in evaluating a corporation's remedial efforts are restitution and reform. As with natural persons, the decision whether or not to prosecute should not depend upon the target's ability to pay restitution. A corporation's efforts to pay restitution even in advance of any court order is, however, evidence of its "acceptance of responsibility" and, consistent with the practices and policies of the appropriate Division of the Department entrusted with enforcing specific criminal laws, may be considered in determining whether to bring criminal charges. Similarly, although the inadequacy of a corporate compliance program is a factor to consider when deciding whether to charge a corporation, that corporation's quick recognition of the flaws in the program and its efforts to improve the program are also factors to consider.

X. Charging a Corporation: Collateral Consequences

A. *General Principle:* Prosecutors may consider the collateral consequences of a corporate criminal conviction in determining whether to charge the corporation with a criminal offense.

B. *Comment:* One of the factors in determining whether to charge a natural person or a corporation is whether the likely punishment is appropriate given the nature and seriousness of the crime. In the corporate context, prosecutors may take into account the possibly substantial consequences to a corporation's officers, directors, employees, and shareholders, many of whom may, depending on the size and nature (*e.g.*, publicly vs. closely held) of the corporation and their role in its operations, have played no role in the criminal conduct, have been completely unaware of it, or have been wholly unable to prevent it. Prosecutors should also be aware of non-penal sanctions that may accompany a criminal charge, such as potential suspension or debarment from eligibility for government contracts or federal funded programs such as health care. Whether or not such non-penal sanctions are appropriate or required in a particular case is the responsibility of the relevant agency, a decision that will be made based on the applicable statutes, regulations, and policies.

Virtually every conviction of a corporation, like virtually every conviction of an individual, will have an impact on innocent third parties, and the mere existence of such an effect is not sufficient to preclude prosecution of the corporation. Therefore, in evaluating the severity of collateral consequences, various factors already discussed, such as the pervasiveness of the criminal conduct and the adequacy of the corporation's compliance programs, should be considered in determining the weight to be given to this factor. For instance, the balance may tip in favor of prosecuting corporations in situations where the scope of the misconduct in a case is widespread and sustained within a corporate division (or spread throughout pockets of the corporate organization). In such cases, the possible unfairness of visiting punishment for the corporation's crimes upon shareholders may be of much less concern where those shareholders have substantially profited, even unknowingly, from widespread or pervasive criminal activity.

Similarly, where the top layers of the corporation's management or the shareholders of a closely-held corporation were engaged in or aware of the wrongdoing and the conduct at issue was accepted as a way of doing business for an extended period, debarment may be deemed not collateral, but a direct and entirely appropriate consequence of the corporation's wrongdoing.

The appropriateness of considering such collateral consequences and the weight to be given them may depend on the special policy concerns discussed in section III, *supra.*

XI. Charging a Corporation: Non-Criminal Alternatives

A. *General Principle:* Non-criminal alternatives to prosecution often exist and prosecutors may consider whether such sanctions would adequately deter, punish, and rehabilitate a corporation that has engaged in wrongful conduct. In evaluating the adequacy of non-criminal alternatives to prosecution, *e.g.*, civil or regulatory enforcement actions, the prosecutor may consider all relevant factors, including:

1. the sanctions available under the alternative means of disposition;
2. the likelihood that an effective sanction will be imposed; and
3. the effect of non-criminal disposition on federal law enforcement interests.

B. *Comment:* The primary goals of criminal law are deterrence, punishment, and rehabilitation. Non-criminal sanctions may not be an appropriate response to an egregious violation, a pattern of wrongdoing, or a history of non-criminal sanctions without proper remediation. In other cases, however, these goals may be satisfied without the necessity of instituting criminal proceedings. In determining whether federal criminal charges are appropriate, the prosecutor should consider the same factors (modified appropriately for the regulatory context) considered when determining whether to leave prosecution of a natural person to another jurisdiction or to seek non-criminal alternatives to prosecution. These factors include: the strength of the regulatory authority's interest; the regulatory authority's ability and willingness to take effective enforcement action; the probable sanction if the regulatory authority's enforcement action is upheld; and the effect of a non-criminal disposition on federal law enforcement interests. *See* USAM §§ 9-27.240, 9-27.250.

XII. Charging a Corporation: Selecting Charges

A. *General Principle:* Once a prosecutor has decided to charge a corporation, the prosecutor should charge, or should recommend that the grand jury charge, the most serious offense that is consistent with the nature of the defendant's conduct and that is likely to result in a sustainable conviction.

B. *Comment:* Once the decision to charge is made, the same rules as govern charging natural persons apply. These rules require "a faithful and honest application of the Sentencing Guidelines" and an "individualized assessment of the extent to which particular charges fit the specific circumstances of the case, are consistent with the purposes of the federal criminal code, and maximize the impact of federal resources on crime." *See* USAM § 9-27300. In making this determination, "it is appropriate that the attorney for the government consider, inter alia, such factors as the sentencing guideline range yielded by the charge, whether the penalty yielded by such sentencing range . . . is proportional to the seriousness of the defendant's conduct, and whether the charge achieves such purposes of the criminal law as punishment, protection of the public, specific and general deterrence, and rehabilitation." *See* Attorney General's Memorandum, dated October 12, 1993.

XIII. Plea Agreements with Corporations

A. *General Principle:* In negotiating plea agreements with corporations, prosecutors should seek a plea to the most serious, readily provable offense charged. In addition, the terms of the plea agreement should contain appropriate provisions to ensure punishment, deterrence, rehabilitation, and compliance with the plea agreement in the corporate context. Although special circumstances may mandate a different conclusion, prosecutors generally should not agree to accept a corporate guilty plea in exchange for non-prosecution or dismissal of charges against individual officers and employees.

B. *Comment:* Prosecutors may enter into plea agreements with corporations for the same reasons and under the same constraints as apply to plea agreements with natural persons. *See* USAM §§ 9-27.400–500. This means, *inter alia,* that the corporation should be required to plead guilty to the most serious, readily provable offense charged. As is the case with individuals, the attorney making this determination should do so "on the basis of an individualized assessment of the extent to which particular charges fit the specific circumstances of the case, are consistent with the purposes of the federal criminal code, and maximize the impact of federal resources on crime. In making this determination, the attorney for the government considers, *inter alia,* such factors as the sentencing guideline range yielded by the charge, whether the penalty yielded by such sentencing range . . . is proportional to the seriousness of the defendant's conduct, and whether the charge achieves such purposes of the criminal law as punishment, protection of the public, specific and general deterrence, and rehabilitation." *See* Attorney General's Memorandum, dated October 12, 1993. In addition, any negotiated departures from the Sentencing Guidelines must be justifiable under the Guidelines and must be disclosed to the sentencing court. A corporation should be made to realize that pleading guilty to criminal charges constitutes an admission of guilt and not merely a resolution of an inconvenient distraction from its business. As with natural persons, pleas should be structured so that the corporation may not later "proclaim lack of culpability or even complete innocence." *See* USAM §§ 9-27.420(b)(4), 9-27.440, 9-27.500. Thus, for instance, there should be placed upon the record a sufficient factual basis for the plea to prevent later corporate assertions of innocence.

A corporate plea agreement should also contain provisions that recognize the nature of the corporate "person" and ensure that the principles of punishment, deterrence, and rehabilitation are met. In the corporate context, punishment and deterrence are generally accomplished by substantial fines, mandatory restitution, and institution of appropriate compliance measures, including, if necessary, continued judicial oversight or the use of special masters. *See* USSG §§ 8B1.1, 8C2.1, *et seq.* In addition, where the corporation is a government contractor, permanent or temporary debarment may be appropriate. Where the corporation was engaged in government contracting fraud, a prosecutor may not negotiate away an agency's right to debar or to list the corporate defendant.

In negotiating a plea agreement, prosecutors should also consider the deterrent value of prosecutions of individuals within the corporation. Therefore, one factor that a prosecutor may consider in determining whether to enter into a plea agreement is whether the corporation is seeking immunity for its employees and officers or whether the corporation is willing to cooperate in the investigation of culpable individuals. Prosecutors should rarely negotiate away individual criminal liability in a corporate plea.

Rehabilitation, of course, requires that the corporation undertake to be law-abiding in the future. It is, therefore, appropriate to require the corporation, as a condition of probation, to implement a compliance program or to reform an existing one. As discussed above, prosecutors may consult with the appropriate state and federal agencies and components of the Justice Department to ensure that a proposed compliance program is adequate and meets industry standards and best practices. *See* section VIII, *supra.*

In plea agreements in which the corporation agrees to cooperate, the prosecutor should ensure that the cooperation is complete and truthful. To do so, the prosecutor may request that the corporation waive attorney-client and work product protection, make employees and agents available for debriefing, disclose the results of its internal investigation, file appropriate certified financial statements, agree to governmental or third-party audits, and take whatever other steps are necessary to ensure that the full scope of the corporate wrongdoing is disclosed and that the responsible culprits are identified and, if appropriate, prosecuted. *See generally* section VII, *supra.*

This memorandum provides only internal Department of Justice guidance. It is not intended to, does not, and may not be relied upon to create any rights, substantive or procedural, enforceable at law by any party in any matter civil or criminal. Nor are any limitations hereby placed on otherwise lawful litigative prerogatives of the Department of Justice.

APPENDIX 1-3

U.S. Department of Justice

Office of the Deputy Attorney General

Washington, D.C. 20530
August 28, 2008

MEMORANDUM

TO: Heads of Department Components
United States Attorneys

FROM: Mark Filip
Deputy Attorney General

SUBJECT: Principles of Federal Prosecution of Business Organizations

Attached to this memorandum is a revision of the Principles of Federal Prosecution of Business Organizations, previously issued by Deputy Attorney General Paul McNulty in December 2006. The revised Principles will be set forth for the first time in the *United States Attorneys' Manual,* and will be binding on all federal prosecutors within the Department of Justice. The revised Principles will be effective immediately, on a prospective basis.

The Department of Justice, through the Deputy Attorney General's Office, has undertaken periodic revision of its policies concerning factors to consider in the prosecution of business organizations. Such revisions should not be understood as criticism of prosecutors who applied the prior policies diligently and in good faith, but rather as an effort to refine the Department's policy guidance in light of lessons learned from the Department's prosecutions as well as comments from other actors within the criminal justice system, the judiciary, and the broader legal community. As explained further below, the principal revisions to the Principles concern what measures a business entity must take to qualify for the long-recognized "cooperation" mitigating factor, as well as how payment of attorneys' fees by a business organization for its officers or employees, or participation in a joint defense or similar agreement, will be considered in the prosecutive analysis. Much of the remainder of the Principles is unchanged.

General policy guidance is, of course, important. So too is thorough training and supervision, which the Department will provide to ensure compliance with these revised Principles. But there is no substitute for the application of considered judgment by line prosecutors and United States Attorneys throughout the Nation, and by their counterparts at Main Justice in Washington, D.C. The Department and Nation are best served when federal prosecutors thoughtfully and fairly consider these Principles and apply them consistent with our concurrent mandates: (1) to aggressively enforce the law; (2) to respect the rights of criminal defendants and others involved in the criminal justice process; and (3) to promote fair outcomes for the American people.

Thank you to the many leaders of the Department who participated in the dialogue that led to these revisions. This was truly a collective effort, which is why these Principles should not bear the name of any particular individual at the Department, as prior iterations sometimes became known. In addition, that earlier practice has drawn criticism from some quarters for implying that Department policy is subject to revision with every changing of the guard. Accordingly, these Principles please should henceforth be referred to as the Department's "Principles of Federal Prosecution of Business Organizations," or the "Corporate Prosecution Principles," or by the relevant section of the United States Attorneys' Manual, as other sections typically are.

Title 9, Chapter 9-28.000

Principles of Federal Prosecution of Business Organizations

1. While these guidelines refer to corporations, they apply to the consideration of the prosecution of all types of business organizations, including partnerships, sole proprietorships, government entities, and unincorporated associations.

The prosecution of corporate crime is a high priority for the Department of Justice. By investigating allegations of wrongdoing and by bringing charges where appropriate for criminal misconduct, the Department promotes critical public interests. These interests include, to take just a few examples: (1) protecting the integrity of our free economic and capital markets; (2) protecting consumers, investors, and business entities that compete only through lawful means; and (3) protecting the American people from misconduct that would violate criminal laws safeguarding the environment.

In this regard, federal prosecutors and corporate leaders typically share common goals. For example, directors and officers owe a fiduciary duty to a corporation's shareholders, the corporation's true owners, and they owe duties of honest dealing to the investing public in connection with the corporation's regulatory filings and public statements. The faithful execution of these duties by corporate leadership serves the same values in promoting public trust and confidence that our criminal cases are designed to serve.

A prosecutor's duty to enforce the law requires the investigation and prosecution of criminal wrongdoing if it is discovered. In carrying out this mission with the diligence and resolve necessary to vindicate the important public interests discussed above, prosecutors should be mindful of the common cause we share with responsible corporate leaders. Prosecutors should also be mindful that confidence in the Department is affected both by the results we achieve and by the real and perceived ways in which we achieve them. Thus, the manner in which we do our job as prosecutors—including the professionalism we demonstrate, our willingness to secure the facts in a manner that encourages corporate compliance and self-regulation, and also our appreciation that corporate prosecutions can potentially harm blameless investors, employees, and others—affects public perception of our mission. Federal prosecutors recognize that they must maintain public confidence in the way in which they exercise their charging discretion. This endeavor requires the thoughtful analysis of all facts and circumstances presented in a given case. As always, professionalism and civility play an important part in the Department's discharge of its responsibilities in all areas, including the area of corporate investigations and prosecutions.

9-28.200 General Considerations of Corporate Liability

A. *General Principle:* Corporations should not be treated leniently because of their artificial nature nor should they be subject to harsher treatment. Vigorous enforcement of the criminal laws against corporate wrongdoers, where appropriate, results in great benefits for law enforcement and the public, particularly in the area of white collar crime. Indicting corporations for wrongdoing enables the government to be a force for positive change of corporate culture, and a force to prevent, discover, and punish serious crimes.

B. *Comment:* In all cases involving corporate wrongdoing, prosecutors should consider the factors discussed further below. In doing so, prosecutors should be aware of the public benefits that can flow from indicting a corporation in appropriate cases. For instance, corporations are likely to take immediate remedial steps when one is indicted for criminal misconduct that is pervasive throughout a particular industry, and thus an indictment can provide a unique opportunity for deterrence on a broad scale. In addition, a corporate indictment may result in specific deterrence by changing the culture of the indicted corporation and the behavior of its employees. Finally, certain crimes that carry with them a substantial risk of great public harm—*e.g.*, environmental crimes or sweeping financial frauds—may be committed by a business entity, and there may therefore be a substantial federal interest in indicting a corporation under such circumstances.

In certain instances, it may be appropriate, upon consideration of the factors set forth herein, to resolve a corporate criminal case by means other than indictment. Non-prosecution and deferred prosecution agreements, for example, occupy an important middle ground between declining prosecution and obtaining the conviction of a corporation. These agreements are discussed further in Section X, *infra*. Likewise, civil and regulatory alternatives may be appropriate in certain cases, as discussed in Section XI, *infra*.

Where a decision is made to charge a corporation, it does not necessarily follow that individual directors, officers, employees, or shareholders should not also be charged. Prosecution of a corporation is not a substitute for the prosecution of criminally culpable individuals within or without the corporation. Because a corporation can act only through individuals, imposition of individual criminal liability may provide the strongest deterrent against future corporate wrongdoing. Only rarely should provable individual culpability not be pursued, particularly if it relates to high-level corporate officers, even in the face of an offer of a corporate guilty plea or some other disposition of the charges against the corporation.

Corporations are "legal persons," capable of suing and being sued, and capable of committing crimes. Under the doctrine of *respondeat superior*, a corporation may be held criminally liable for the illegal acts of its directors, officers, employees, and agents. To hold a corporation liable for these actions, the government must establish that the corporate agent's actions (i) were within the scope of his duties and (ii) were intended, at least in part, to benefit the corporation. In all cases involving wrongdoing by corporate agents, prosecutors should not limit their focus solely to individuals or the corporation, but should consider both as potential targets.

Agents may act for mixed reasons—both for self-aggrandizement (both direct and indirect) and for the benefit of the corporation, and a corporation may be held liable as long as one motivation of its agent is to benefit the corporation. *See United States v. Potter,* 463 F.3d 9, 25 (1st Cir. 2006) (stating that the test to determine whether an agent is acting within the scope of employment is "whether the agent is performing acts of the kind which he is authorized to perform, and those acts are motivated, at least in part, by an intent to benefit the corporation."). In *United States v. Automated Medical Laboratories, Inc.,* 770 F.2d 399 (4th Cir. 1985), for example, the Fourth Circuit affirmed a corporation's conviction for the actions of a subsidiary's employee despite the corporation's claim that the employee was acting for his own benefit, namely his "ambitious nature and his desire to ascend the corporate ladder." *Id.* at 407. The court stated, "Partucci was clearly acting in part to benefit AML since his advancement within the corporation depended on AML's well-being and its lack of difficulties with the FDA." *Id.; see also United States v. Cincotta,* 689 F.2d 238, 241–42 (1st Cir. 1982) (upholding a corporation's conviction, notwithstanding the substantial personal benefit reaped by its miscreant agents, because the fraudulent scheme required money to pass through the corporation's treasury and the fraudulently obtained goods were resold to the corporation's customers in the corporation's name).

Moreover, the corporation need not even necessarily profit from its agent's actions for it to be held liable. In *Automated Medical Laboratories,* the Fourth Circuit stated:

> [B]enefit is not a "touchstone of criminal corporate liability; benefit at best is an evidential, not an operative, fact." Thus, whether the agent's actions ultimately redounded to the benefit of the corporation is less significant than whether the agent acted with the intent to benefit the corporation. The basic purpose of requiring that an agent have acted with the intent to benefit the corporation, however, is to insulate the corporation from criminal liability for actions of its agents which may be *inimical* to the interests of the corporation or which may have been undertaken solely to advance the interests of that agent or of a party other than the corporation.

770 F.2d at 407 (internal citation omitted) (quoting *Old Monastery Co.* v. *United States,* 147 F.2d 905, 908 (4th Cir. 1945)).

9-28.300 Factors to Be Considered

A. *General Principle:* Generally, prosecutors apply the same factors in determining whether to charge a corporation as they do with respect to individuals.

See USAM § 9-27.220, *et seq*. Thus, the prosecutor must weigh all of the factors normally considered in the sound exercise of prosecutorial judgment: the sufficiency of the evidence; the likelihood of success at trial; the probable deterrent, rehabilitative, and other consequences of conviction; and the adequacy of noncriminal approaches. *See id.* However, due to the nature of the corporate "person," some additional factors are present. In conducting an investigation, determining whether to bring charges, and negotiating plea or other agreements, prosecutors should consider the following factors in reaching a decision as to the proper treatment of a corporate target:

1. the nature and seriousness of the offense, including the risk of harm to the public, and applicable policies and priorities, if any, governing the prosecution of corporations for particular categories of crime (*see infra* section IV);
2. the pervasiveness of wrongdoing within the corporation, including the complicity in, or the condoning of, the wrongdoing by corporate management (*see infra* section V);
3. the corporation's history of similar misconduct, including prior criminal, civil, and regulatory enforcement actions against it (*see infra* section VI);
4. the corporation's timely and voluntary disclosure of wrongdoing and its willingness to cooperate in the investigation of its agents (*see infra* section VII);
5. the existence and effectiveness of the corporation's pre-existing compliance program (*see infra* section VIII);
6. the corporation's remedial actions, including any efforts to implement an effective corporate compliance program or to improve an existing one, to replace responsible management, to discipline or terminate wrongdoers, to pay restitution, and to cooperate with the relevant government agencies (*see infra* section IX);
7. collateral consequences, including whether there is disproportionate harm to shareholders, pension holders, employees, and others not proven personally culpable, as well as impact on the public arising from the prosecution (*see infra* section X);
8. the adequacy of the prosecution of individuals responsible for the corporation's malfeasance; and
9. the adequacy of remedies such as civil or regulatory enforcement actions (*see infra* section XI).

B. *Comment:* The factors listed in this section are intended to be illustrative of those that should be evaluated and are not an exhaustive list of potentially relevant considerations. Some of these factors may not apply to specific cases, and in some cases one factor may override all others. For example, the nature and seriousness of the offense may be such as to warrant prosecution regardless of the other factors. In most cases, however, no single factor will be dispositive.

In addition, national law enforcement policies in various enforcement areas may require that more or less weight be given to certain of these factors than to others. Of course, prosecutors must exercise their thoughtful and pragmatic judgment in applying and balancing these factors, so as to achieve a fair and just outcome and promote respect for the law.

In making a decision to charge a corporation, the prosecutor generally has substantial latitude in determining when, whom, how, and even whether to prosecute for violations of federal criminal law. In exercising that discretion, prosecutors should consider the following statements of principles that summarize the considerations they should weigh and the practices they should follow in discharging their prosecutorial responsibilities. In doing so, prosecutors should ensure that the general purposes of the criminal law—assurance of warranted punishment, deterrence of further criminal conduct, protection of the public from dangerous and fraudulent conduct, rehabilitation of offenders, and restitution for victims and affected communities—are adequately met, taking into account the special nature of the corporate "person."

9-28.400 Special Policy Concerns

A. *General Principle:* The nature and seriousness of the crime, including the risk of harm to the public from the criminal misconduct, are obviously primary factors in determining whether to charge a corporation. In addition, corporate conduct, particularly that of national and multi-national corporations, necessarily intersects with federal economic, tax, and criminal law enforcement policies. In applying these Principles, prosecutors must consider the practices and policies of the appropriate Division of the Department, and must comply with those policies to the extent required by the facts presented.

B. *Comment:* In determining whether to charge a corporation, prosecutors should take into account federal law enforcement priorities as discussed above. *See* USAM § 9-27-230. In addition, however, prosecutors must be aware of the specific policy goals and incentive programs established by the respective Divisions and regulatory agencies. Thus, whereas natural persons may be given incremental degrees of credit (ranging from immunity to lesser charges to sentencing considerations) for turning themselves in, making statements against their penal interest, and cooperating in the government's investigation of their own and others' wrongdoing, the same approach may not be appropriate in all circumstances with respect to corporations. As an example, it is entirely proper in many investigations for a prosecutor to consider the corporation's pre-indictment conduct, *e.g.*, voluntary disclosure, cooperation, remediation or restitution, in determining whether to seek an indictment. However, this would not necessarily be appropriate in an antitrust investigation, in which antitrust violations, by definition, go to the heart of the corporation's business. With this in mind, the Antitrust Division has established a firm policy, understood in the business community, that credit should not be given at the charging stage for a compliance program and that amnesty is available only to the first corporation to make full disclosure to the government. As another example, the Tax Division has a strong preference for prosecuting responsible individuals, rather than entities, for corporate tax offenses. Thus, in determining whether or not to charge a corporation, prosecutors must consult with the Criminal, Antitrust, Tax, Environmental and Natural Resources, and National Security Divisions, as appropriate.

9-28.500 Pervasiveness of Wrongdoing Within the Corporation

A. *General Principle:* A corporation can only act through natural persons, and it is therefore held responsible for the acts of such persons fairly attributable to it. Charging a corporation for even minor misconduct may be appropriate where the wrongdoing was pervasive and was undertaken by a large number of employees, or by all the employees in a particular role within the corporation, or was condoned by upper management. On the other hand, it may not be appropriate to impose liability upon a corporation, particularly one with a robust compliance program in place, under a strict *respondeat superior* theory for the single isolated act of a rogue employee. There is, of course, a wide spectrum between these two extremes, and a prosecutor should exercise sound discretion in evaluating the pervasiveness of wrongdoing within a corporation.

B. *Comment:* Of these factors, the most important is the role and conduct of management. Although acts of even low-level employees may result in criminal liability, a corporation is directed by its management and management is responsible for a corporate culture in which criminal conduct is either discouraged or tacitly encouraged. As stated in commentary to the Sentencing Guidelines:

> Pervasiveness [is] case specific and [will] depend on the number, and degree of responsibility, of individuals [with] substantial authority . . . who participated in, condoned, or were willfully ignorant of the offense. Fewer individuals need to be involved for a finding of pervasiveness if those individuals exercised a relatively high degree of authority. Pervasiveness can occur either within an organization as a whole or within a unit of an organization.

USSG § 8C2.5, cmt. (n. 4).

9-28.600 The Corporation's Past History

A. *General Principle:* Prosecutors may consider a corporation's history of similar conduct, including prior criminal, civil, and regulatory enforcement actions against it, in determining whether to bring criminal charges and how best to resolve cases.

B. *Comment:* A corporation, like a natural person, is expected to learn from its mistakes. A history of similar misconduct may be probative of a corporate culture that encouraged, or at least condoned, such misdeeds, regardless of any compliance programs. Criminal prosecution of a corporation may be particularly appropriate where the corporation previously had been subject to non-criminal guidance, warnings, or sanctions, or previous criminal charges, and it either had not taken adequate action to prevent future unlawful conduct or had continued to engage in the misconduct in spite of the warnings or enforcement actions taken against it. The corporate structure itself (e.g., the creation or existence of subsidiaries or operating divisions) is not dispositive in this analysis, and enforcement actions taken against the corporation or any of its divisions, subsidiaries, and affiliates may be considered, if germane. *See* USSG § 8C2.5(c), cmt. (n. 6).

9-28.700 The Value of Cooperation

A. *General Principle:* In determining whether to charge a corporation and how to resolve corporate criminal cases, the corporation's timely and voluntary disclosure of wrongdoing and its cooperation with the government's investigation may be relevant factors. In gauging the extent of the corporation's cooperation, the prosecutor may consider, among other things, whether the corporation made a voluntary and timely disclosure, and the corporation's willingness to provide relevant information and evidence and identify relevant actors within and outside the corporation, including senior executives.

Cooperation is a potential mitigating factor, by which a corporation—just like any other subject of a criminal investigation—can gain credit in a case that otherwise is appropriate for indictment and prosecution. Of course, the decision not to cooperate by a corporation (or individual) is not itself evidence of misconduct, at least where the lack of cooperation does not involve criminal misconduct or demonstrate consciousness of guilt (*e.g.*, suborning perjury or false statements, or refusing to comply with lawful discovery requests). Thus, failure to cooperate, in and of itself, does not support or require the filing of charges with respect to a corporation any more than with respect to an individual.

B. *Comment:* In investigating wrongdoing by or within a corporation, a prosecutor is likely to encounter several obstacles resulting from the nature of the corporation itself. It will often be difficult to determine which individual took which action on behalf of the corporation. Lines of authority and responsibility may be shared among operating divisions or departments, and records and personnel may be spread throughout the United States or even among several countries. Where the criminal conduct continued over an extended period of time, the culpable or knowledgeable personnel may have been promoted, transferred, or fired, or they may have quit or retired. Accordingly, a corporation's cooperation may be critical in identifying potentially relevant actors and locating relevant evidence, among other things, and in doing so expeditiously.

This dynamic—*i.e.*, the difficulty of determining what happened, where the evidence is, and which individuals took or promoted putatively illegal corporate actions—can have negative consequences for both the government and the corporation that is the subject or target of a government investigation. More specifically, because of corporate attribution principles concerning actions of corporate officers and employees (*see, e.g., supra* section II), uncertainty about exactly who authorized or directed apparent corporate misconduct can inure to the detriment of a corporation. For example, it may not matter under the law which of several possible executives or leaders in a chain of command approved of or authorized criminal conduct; however, that information if known might bear on the propriety of a particular disposition short of indictment of the corporation. It may not be in the interest of a corporation or the government for a charging decision to be made in the absence of such information, which might occur if, for example, a statute of limitations were relevant and authorization by any one of the officials were enough to justify a charge under the law. Moreover, and at a minimum, a protracted government investigation of such an issue could, as a collateral consequence, disrupt the corporation's business operations or even depress its stock price.

For these reasons and more, cooperation can be a favorable course for both the government and the corporation. Cooperation benefits the government—and ultimately shareholders, employees, and other often blameless victims—by allowing prosecutors and federal agents, for example, to avoid protracted delays, which compromise their ability to quickly uncover and address the full extent of widespread corporate crimes. With cooperation by the corporation, the government may be able to reduce tangible losses, limit damage to reputation, and preserve assets for restitution. At the same time, cooperation may benefit the corporation by enabling the government to focus its investigative resources in a manner that will not unduly disrupt the corporation's legitimate business operations. In addition, and critically, cooperation may benefit the corporation by presenting it with the opportunity to earn credit for its efforts.

9-28.710 Attorney-Client and Work Product Protections

The attorney-client privilege and the attorney work product protection serve an extremely important function in the American legal system. The attorney-client privilege is one of the oldest and most sacrosanct privileges under the law. *See Upjohn v. United States*, 449 U.S. 383, 389 (1981). As the Supreme Court has stated, "[i]ts purpose is to encourage full and frank communication between attorneys and their clients and thereby promote broader public interests in the observance of law and administration of justice." *Id.* The value of promoting a corporation's ability to seek frank and comprehensive legal advice is particularly important in the contemporary global business environment, where corporations often face complex and dynamic legal and regulatory obligations imposed by the federal government and also by states and foreign governments. The work product doctrine serves similarly important goals.

For these reasons, waiving the attorney-client and work product protections has never been a prerequisite under the Department's prosecution guidelines for a corporation to be viewed as cooperative. Nonetheless, a wide range of commentators and members of the American legal community and criminal justice system have asserted that the Department's policies have been used, either wittingly or unwittingly, to coerce business entities into waiving attorney-client privilege and work-product protection. Everyone agrees that a corporation may freely waive its own privileges if it chooses to do so; indeed, such waivers occur routinely when corporations are victimized by their employees or others, conduct an internal investigation, and then disclose the details of the investigation to law enforcement officials in an effort to seek prosecution of the offenders. However, the contention, from a broad array of voices, is that the Department's position on attorney-client privilege and work product protection waivers has promoted an environment in which those protections are being unfairly eroded to the detriment of all.

The Department understands that the attorney-client privilege and attorney work product protection are essential and long-recognized components of the American legal system. What the government seeks and needs to advance its legitimate (indeed, essential) law enforcement mission is not waiver of those protections, but rather the facts known to the corporation about the putative criminal misconduct under review. In addition, while a corporation remains free to convey non-factual or "core" attorney-client communications or work product—if and only if the corporation voluntarily chooses to do so—prosecutors should not ask for such waivers and are directed not to do so. The critical factor is whether the corporation has provided the facts about the events, as explained further herein.

9-28.720 Cooperation: Disclosing the Relevant Facts

Eligibility for cooperation credit is not predicated upon the waiver of attorney-client privilege or work product protection. Instead, the sort of cooperation that is most valuable to resolving allegations of misconduct by a corporation and its officers, directors, employees, or agents is disclosure of the relevant *facts* concerning such misconduct. In this regard, the analysis parallels that for a non-corporate defendant, where cooperation typically requires disclosure of relevant factual knowledge and not of discussions between an individual and his attorneys.

Thus, when the government investigates potential corporate wrongdoing, it seeks the relevant facts. For example, how and when did the alleged misconduct occur? Who promoted or approved it? Who was responsible for committing it? In this respect, the investigation of a corporation differs little from the investigation of an individual. In both cases, the government needs to know the facts to achieve a just and fair outcome. The party under investigation may choose to cooperate by disclosing the facts, and the government may give credit for the party's disclosures. If a corporation wishes to receive credit for such cooperation, which then can be considered with all other cooperative efforts and circumstances in evaluating how fairly to proceed, then the corporation, like any person, must disclose the relevant facts of which it has knowledge.[2]

(a) Disclosing the Relevant Facts—Facts Gathered Through Internal Investigation

Individuals and corporations often obtain knowledge of facts in different ways. An individual knows the facts of his or others' misconduct through his own experience and perceptions. A corporation is an artificial construct that cannot, by definition, have personal knowledge of the facts. Some of those facts may be reflected in documentary or electronic media like emails, transaction or accounting documents, and other records. Often, the corporation gathers facts through an internal investigation. Exactly how and by whom the facts are gathered is for the corporation to decide. Many corporations choose to collect information about potential misconduct through lawyers, a process that may confer attorney-client privilege or attorney work product protection on at least some of the information collected. Other corporations may choose a method of fact-gathering that does not have that effect—for example, having employee or other witness statements collected after interviews by non-attorney personnel.

Whichever process the corporation selects, the government's key measure of cooperation must remain the same as it does for an individual: has the party timely disclosed the relevant facts about the putative misconduct? That is the operative question in assigning cooperation credit for the disclosure of information—*not* whether the corporation discloses attorney-client or work product materials. Accordingly, a corporation should receive the same credit for disclosing facts contained in materials that are not protected by the attorney-client privilege or attorney work product as it would for disclosing identical facts contained in materials that are so protected.[3] On this point the Report of

2. There are other dimensions of cooperation beyond the mere disclosure of facts, of course. These can include, for example, providing non-privileged documents and other evidence, making witnesses available for interviews, and assisting in the interpretation of complex business records. This section of the Principles focuses solely on the disclosure of facts and the privilege issues that may be implicated thereby.

3. By way of example, corporate personnel are typically interviewed during an internal investigation. If the interviews are conducted by counsel for the corporation, certain notes and memoranda generated from the interviews may be subject, at least in part, to the protections of attorney-client privilege and/or attorney work product. To receive cooperation credit for providing factual information, the corporation need not produce, and prosecutors may not request, protected notes or memoranda generated by the lawyers' interviews. To earn such credit, however, the corporation does need to produce, and prosecutors may request, relevant factual information—including relevant factual information acquired through those interviews, unless the identical information has otherwise been provided—as well as relevant non-privileged evidence such as accounting and business records and emails between non-attorney employees or agents.

the House Judiciary Committee, submitted in connection with the attorney-client privilege bill passed by the House of Representatives (H.R. 3013), comports with the approach required here:

> [A]n . . . attorney of the United States may base cooperation credit on the facts that are disclosed, but is prohibited from basing cooperation credit upon whether or not the materials are protected by attorney-client privilege or attorney work product. As a result, an entity that voluntarily discloses should receive the same amount of cooperation credit for disclosing facts that happen to be contained in materials not protected by attorney-client privilege or attorney work product as it would receive for disclosing identical facts that are contained in materials protected by attorney-client privilege or attorney work product. There should be no differentials in an assessment of cooperation (i.e., neither a credit nor a penalty) based upon whether or not the materials disclosed are protected by attorney-client privilege or attorney work product.

H.R. Rep. No. 110-445 at 4 (2007).

In short, so long as the corporation timely discloses relevant facts about the putative misconduct, the corporation may receive due credit for such cooperation, regardless of whether it chooses to waive privilege or work product protection in the process.[4] Likewise, a corporation that does not disclose the relevant facts about the alleged misconduct—for whatever reason—typically should not be entitled to receive credit for cooperation.

Two final and related points bear noting about the disclosure of facts, although they should be obvious. First, the government cannot compel, and the corporation has no obligation to make, such disclosures (although the government can obviously compel the disclosure of certain records and witness testimony through subpoenas). Second, a corporation's failure to provide relevant information does not mean the corporation will be indicted. It simply means that the corporation will not be entitled to mitigating credit for that cooperation. Whether the corporation faces charges will turn, as it does in any case, on the sufficiency of the evidence, the likelihood of success at trial, and all of the other factors identified in Section III above. If there is insufficient evidence to warrant indictment, after appropriate investigation has been completed, or if the other factors weigh against indictment, then the corporation should not be indicted, irrespective of whether it has earned cooperation credit. The converse is also true: The government may charge even the most cooperative corporation pursuant to these Principles if, in weighing and balancing the factors described herein, the prosecutor determines that a charge is required in the interests of justice. Put differently, even the most sincere and thorough effort

4. In assessing the timeliness of a corporation's disclosures, prosecutors should apply a standard of reasonableness in light of the totality of circumstances.

to cooperate cannot necessarily absolve a corporation that has, for example, engaged in an egregious, orchestrated, and widespread fraud. Cooperation is a relevant potential mitigating factor, but it alone is not dispositive.

(b) Legal Advice and Attorney Work Product

Separate from (and usually preceding) the fact-gathering process in an internal investigation, a corporation, through its officers, employees, directors, or others, may have consulted with corporate counsel regarding or in a manner that concerns the legal implications of the putative misconduct at issue. Communications of this sort, which are both independent of the fact-gathering component of an internal investigation and made for the purpose of seeking or dispensing legal advice, lie at the core of the attorney-client privilege. Such communications can naturally have a salutary effect on corporate behavior—facilitating, for example, a corporation's effort to comply with complex and evolving legal and regulatory regimes.[5] Except as noted in subparagraphs (b)(i) and (b)(ii) below, a corporation need not disclose and prosecutors may not request the disclosure of such communications as a condition for the corporation's eligibility to receive cooperation credit.

Likewise, non-factual or core attorney work product—for example, an attorney's mental impressions or legal theories—lies at the core of the attorney work product doctrine. A corporation need not disclose, and prosecutors may not request, the disclosure of such attorney work product as a condition for the corporation's eligibility to receive cooperation credit.

(i) Advice of Counsel Defense in the Instant Context

Occasionally a corporation or one of its employees may assert an advice-of-counsel defense, based upon communications with in-house or outside counsel that took place prior to or contemporaneously with the underlying conduct at issue. In such situations, the defendant must tender a legitimate factual basis to support the assertion of the advice-of-counsel defense. *See, e.g., Pitt v. Dist. of Columbia*, 491 F.3d 494, 504–05 (D.C. Cir. 2007); *United States v. Wenger*, 427 F.3d 840, 853–54 (10th Cir. 2005); *United States v. Cheek*, 3 F.3d 1057, 1061–62 (7th Cir. 1993). The Department cannot fairly be asked to discharge its responsibility to the public to investigate alleged corporate crime, or to temper what would otherwise be the appropriate course of prosecutive action, by simply accepting on faith an otherwise unproven assertion that an attorney—perhaps even an unnamed attorney—approved potentially unlawful practices. Accordingly,

5. These privileged communications are not necessarily limited to those that occur contemporaneously with the underlying misconduct. They would include, for instance, legal advice provided by corporate counsel in an internal investigation report. Again, the key measure of cooperation is the disclosure of factual information known to the corporation, not the disclosure of legal advice or theories rendered in connection with the conduct at issue (subject to the two exceptions noted in Section VII(2)(b)(i-ii)).

where an advice-of-counsel defense has been asserted, prosecutors may ask for the disclosure of the communications allegedly supporting it.

(ii) Communications in Furtherance of a Crime or Fraud

Communications between a corporation (through its officers, employees, directors, or agents) and corporate counsel that are made in furtherance of a crime or fraud are, under settled precedent, outside the scope and protection of the attorney-client privilege. *See United States v. Zolin*, 491 U.S. 554, 563 (1989); *United States v. BDO Seidman, LLP*, 492 F.3d 806, 818 (7th Cir. 2007). As a result, the Department may properly request such communications if they in fact exist.

9-28.730 Obstructing the Investigation

Another factor to be weighed by the prosecutor is whether the corporation has engaged in conduct intended to impede the investigation. Examples of such conduct could include: inappropriate directions to employees or their counsel, such as directions not to be truthful or to conceal relevant facts; making representations or submissions that contain misleading assertions or material omissions; and incomplete or delayed production of records.

In evaluating cooperation, however, prosecutors should not take into account whether a corporation is advancing or reimbursing attorneys' fees or providing counsel to employees, officers, or directors under investigation or indictment. Likewise, prosecutors may not request that a corporation refrain from taking such action. This prohibition is not meant to prevent a prosecutor from asking questions about an attorney's representation of a corporation or its employees, officers, or directors, where otherwise appropriate under the law.[6] Neither is it intended to limit the otherwise applicable reach of criminal obstruction of justice statutes such as 18 U.S.C. § 1503. If the payment of attorney fees were used in a manner that would otherwise constitute criminal obstruction of justice—for example, if fees were advanced on the condition that an employee adhere to a version of the facts that the corporation and the employee knew to be false—these Principles would not (and could not) render inapplicable such criminal prohibitions.

Similarly, the mere participation by a corporation in a joint defense agreement does not render the corporation ineligible to receive cooperation credit, and prosecutors may not request that a corporation refrain from entering into such agreements. Of course, the corporation may wish to avoid putting itself in the position of being disabled, by virtue of a particular joint defense or similar agreement, from providing some relevant facts to the government and

6. Routine questions regarding the representation status of a corporation and its employees, including how and by whom attorneys' fees are paid, sometimes arise in the course of an investigation under certain circumstances—to take one example, to assess conflict-of-interest issues. Such questions can be appropriate and this guidance is not intended to prohibit such limited inquiries.

thereby limiting its ability to seek such cooperation credit. Such might be the case if the corporation gathers facts from employees who have entered into a joint defense agreement with the corporation, and who may later seek to prevent the corporation from disclosing the facts it has acquired. Corporations may wish to address this situation by crafting or participating in joint defense agreements, to the extent they choose to enter them, that provide such flexibility as they deem appropriate.

Finally, it may on occasion be appropriate for the government to consider whether the corporation has shared with others sensitive information about the investigation that the government provided to the corporation. In appropriate situations, as it does with individuals, the government may properly request that, if a corporation wishes to receive credit for cooperation, the information provided by the government to the corporation not be transmitted to others—for example, where the disclosure of such information could lead to flight by individual subjects, destruction of evidence, or dissipation or concealment of assets.

9-28.740 Offering Cooperation: No Entitlement to Immunity

A corporation's offer of cooperation or cooperation itself does not automatically entitle it to immunity from prosecution or a favorable resolution of its case. A corporation should not be able to escape liability merely by offering up its directors, officers, employees, or agents. Thus, a corporation's willingness to cooperate is not determinative; that factor, while relevant, needs to be considered in conjunction with all other factors.

9-28.750 Qualifying for Immunity, Amnesty, or Reduced Sanctions Through Voluntary Disclosures

In conjunction with regulatory agencies and other executive branch departments, the Department encourages corporations, as part of their compliance programs, to conduct internal investigations and to disclose the relevant facts to the appropriate authorities. Some agencies, such as the Securities and Exchange Commission and the Environmental Protection Agency, as well as the Department's Environmental and Natural Resources Division, have formal voluntary disclosure programs in which self-reporting, coupled with remediation and additional criteria, may qualify the corporation for amnesty or reduced sanctions. Even in the absence of a formal program, prosecutors may consider a corporation's timely and voluntary disclosure in evaluating the adequacy of the corporation's compliance program and its management's commitment to the compliance program. However, prosecution and economic policies specific to the industry or statute may require prosecution notwithstanding a corporation's willingness to cooperate. For example, the Antitrust Division has a policy of offering amnesty only to the first corporation to agree to cooperate. Moreover, amnesty, immunity, or reduced sanctions may not be appropriate where the corporation's business is permeated with fraud or other crimes.

9-28.760 Oversight Concerning Demands for Waivers of Attorney-Client Privilege or Work Product Protection by Corporations Contrary to This Policy

The Department underscores its commitment to attorney practices that are consistent with Department policies like those set forth herein concerning cooperation credit and due respect for the attorney-client privilege and work product protection. Counsel for corporations who believe that prosecutors are violating such guidance are encouraged to raise their concerns with supervisors, including the appropriate United States Attorney or Assistant Attorney General. Like any other allegation of attorney misconduct, such allegations are subject to potential investigation through established mechanisms.

9-28.800 Corporate Compliance Programs

A. *General Principle:* Compliance programs are established by corporate management to prevent and detect misconduct and to ensure that corporate activities are conducted in accordance with applicable criminal and civil laws, regulations, and rules. The Department encourages such corporate self-policing, including voluntary disclosures to the government of any problems that a corporation discovers on its own. However, the existence of a compliance program is not sufficient, in and of itself, to justify not charging a corporation for criminal misconduct undertaken by its officers, directors, employees, or agents. In addition, the nature of some crimes, *e.g.*, antitrust violations, may be such that national law enforcement policies mandate prosecutions of corporations notwithstanding the existence of a compliance program.

B. *Comment:* The existence of a corporate compliance program, even one that specifically prohibited the very conduct in question, does not absolve the corporation from criminal liability under the doctrine of *respondeat superior*. *See United States v. Basic Constr. Co.*, 711 F.2d 570, 573 (4th Cir. 1983) ("[A] corporation may be held criminally responsible for antitrust violations committed by its employees if they were acting within the scope of their authority, or apparent authority, and for the benefit of the corporation, even if . . . such acts were against corporate policy or express instructions."). As explained in *United States v. Potter*, 463 F.3d 9 (1st Cir. 2006), a corporation cannot "avoid liability by adopting abstract rules" that forbid its agents from engaging in illegal acts, because "[e]ven a specific directive to an agent or employee or honest efforts to police such rules do not automatically free the company for the wrongful acts of agents." *Id.* at 25–26. *See also United States v. Hilton Hotels Corp.*, 467 F.2d 1000, 1007 (9th Cir. 1972) (noting that a corporation "could not gain exculpation by issuing general instructions without undertaking to enforce those instructions by means commensurate with the obvious risks"); *United States v. Beusch*, 596 F.2d 871, 878 (9th Cir. 1979) ("[A] corporation may be liable for acts of its employees done contrary to express instructions and policies, but . . . the existence of such instructions and policies may be considered in determining whether the employee in fact acted to benefit the corporation.").

While the Department recognizes that no compliance program can ever prevent all criminal activity by a corporation's employees, the critical factors in evaluating any program are whether the program is adequately designed for maximum effectiveness in preventing and detecting wrongdoing by employees and whether corporate management is enforcing the program or is tacitly encouraging or pressuring employees to engage in misconduct to achieve business objectives. The Department has no formulaic requirements regarding corporate compliance programs. The fundamental questions any prosecutor should ask are: Is the corporation's compliance program well designed? Is the program being applied earnestly and in good faith? Does the corporation's compliance program work? In answering these questions, the prosecutor should consider the comprehensiveness of the compliance program; the extent and pervasiveness of the criminal misconduct; the number and level of the corporate employees involved; the seriousness, duration, and frequency of the misconduct; and any remedial actions taken by the corporation, including, for example, disciplinary action against past violators uncovered by the prior compliance program, and revisions to corporate compliance programs in light of lessons learned.[7] Prosecutors should also consider the promptness of any disclosure of wrongdoing to the government. In evaluating compliance programs, prosecutors may consider whether the corporation has established corporate governance mechanisms that can effectively detect and prevent misconduct. For example, do the corporation's directors exercise independent review over proposed corporate actions rather than unquestioningly ratifying officers' recommendations; are internal audit functions conducted at a level sufficient to ensure their independence and accuracy; and have the directors established an information and reporting system in the organization reasonably designed to provide management and directors with timely and accurate information sufficient to allow them to reach an informed decision regarding the organization's compliance with the law. *See, e.g., In re Caremark Int'l Inc. Derivative Litig.*, 698 A.2d 959, 968–70 (Del. Ch. 1996).

Prosecutors should therefore attempt to determine whether a corporation's compliance program is merely a "paper program" or whether it was designed, implemented, reviewed, and revised, as appropriate, in an effective manner. In addition, prosecutors should determine whether the corporation has provided for a staff sufficient to audit, document, analyze, and utilize the results of the corporation's compliance efforts. Prosecutors also should determine whether the corporation's employees are adequately informed about the compliance program and are convinced of the corporation's commitment to it. This will enable the prosecutor to make an informed decision as to whether the corporation has adopted and implemented a truly effective compliance program that,

---

7. For a detailed review of these and other factors concerning corporate compliance programs, *see* USSG § 8B2.1.

when consistent with other federal law enforcement policies, may result in a decision to charge only the corporation's employees and agents or to mitigate charges or sanctions against the corporation.

Compliance programs should be designed to detect the particular types of misconduct most likely to occur in a particular corporation's line of business. Many corporations operate in complex regulatory environments outside the normal experience of criminal prosecutors. Accordingly, prosecutors should consult with relevant federal and state agencies with the expertise to evaluate the adequacy of a program's design and implementation. For instance, state and federal banking, insurance, and medical boards, the Department of Defense, the Department of Health and Human Services, the Environmental Protection Agency, and the Securities and Exchange Commission have considerable experience with compliance programs and can be helpful to a prosecutor in evaluating such programs. In addition, the Fraud Section of the Criminal Division, the Commercial Litigation Branch of the Civil Division, and the Environmental Crimes Section of the Environment and Natural Resources Division can assist United States Attorneys' Offices in finding the appropriate agency office(s) for such consultation.

9-28.900 Restitution and Remediation

A. *General Principle:* Although neither a corporation nor an individual target may avoid prosecution merely by paying a sum of money, a prosecutor may consider the corporation's willingness to make restitution and steps already taken to do so. A prosecutor may also consider other remedial actions, such as improving an existing compliance program or disciplining wrongdoers, in determining whether to charge the corporation and how to resolve corporate criminal cases.

B. *Comment:* In determining whether or not to prosecute a corporation, the government may consider whether the corporation has taken meaningful remedial measures. A corporation's response to misconduct says much about its willingness to ensure that such misconduct does not recur. Thus, corporations that fully recognize the seriousness of their misconduct and accept responsibility for it should be taking steps to implement the personnel, operational, and organizational changes necessary to establish an awareness among employees that criminal conduct will not be tolerated.

Among the factors prosecutors should consider and weigh are whether the corporation appropriately disciplined wrongdoers, once those employees are identified by the corporation as culpable for the misconduct. Employee discipline is a difficult task for many corporations because of the human element involved and sometimes because of the seniority of the employees concerned. Although corporations need to be fair to their employees, they must also be committed, at all levels of the corporation, to the highest standards of legal and ethical behavior. Effective internal discipline can be a powerful deterrent against improper behavior by a corporation's employees. Prosecutors should be satisfied that the corporation's focus is on the integrity and credibility of its remedial and disciplinary measures rather than on the protection of the wrongdoers.

In addition to employee discipline, two other factors used in evaluating a corporation's remedial efforts are restitution and reform. As with natural persons, the decision whether or not to prosecute should not depend upon the target's ability to pay restitution. A corporation's efforts to pay restitution even in advance of any court order is, however, evidence of its acceptance of responsibility and, consistent with the practices and policies of the appropriate Division of the Department entrusted with enforcing specific criminal laws, may be considered in determining whether to bring criminal charges. Similarly, although the inadequacy of a corporate compliance program is a factor to consider when deciding whether to charge a corporation, that corporation's quick recognition of the flaws in the program and its efforts to improve the program are also factors to consider as to appropriate disposition of a case.

9-28.1000 Collateral Consequences

A. *General Principle:* Prosecutors may consider the collateral consequences of a corporate criminal conviction or indictment in determining whether to charge the corporation with a criminal offense and how to resolve corporate criminal cases.

B. *Comment:* One of the factors in determining whether to charge a natural person or a corporation is whether the likely punishment is appropriate given the nature and seriousness of the crime. In the corporate context, prosecutors may take into account the possibly substantial consequences to a corporation's employees, investors, pensioners, and customers, many of whom may, depending on the size and nature of the corporation and their role in its operations, have played no role in the criminal conduct, have been unaware of it, or have been unable to prevent it. Prosecutors should also be aware of non-penal sanctions that may accompany a criminal charge, such as potential suspension or debarment from eligibility for government contracts or federally funded programs such as health care programs. Determining whether or not such non-penal sanctions are appropriate or required in a particular case is the responsibility of the relevant agency, and is a decision that will be made based on the applicable statutes, regulations, and policies.

Virtually every conviction of a corporation, like virtually every conviction of an individual, will have an impact on innocent third parties, and the mere existence of such an effect is not sufficient to preclude prosecution of the corporation. Therefore, in evaluating the relevance of collateral consequences, various factors already discussed, such as the pervasiveness of the criminal conduct and the adequacy of the corporation's compliance programs, should be considered in determining the weight to be given to this factor. For instance, the balance may tip in favor of prosecuting corporations in situations where the scope of the misconduct in a case is widespread and sustained within a corporate division (or spread throughout pockets of the corporate organization). In such cases, the possible unfairness of visiting punishment for the corporation's crimes upon shareholders may be of much less concern where those shareholders have substantially profited, even unknowingly, from widespread or pervasive criminal activity. Similarly, where the top layers of the corporation's management or the shareholders of a closely-held corporation were engaged in or aware of the wrongdoing, and the conduct at issue was accepted as a way of doing business for an extended period, debarment may be deemed not collateral, but a direct and entirely appropriate consequence of the corporation's wrongdoing.

On the other hand, where the collateral consequences of a corporate conviction for innocent third parties would be significant, it may be appropriate to consider a non-prosecution or deferred prosecution agreement with conditions designed, among other things, to promote compliance with applicable law and to prevent recidivism. Such agreements are a third option, besides a criminal indictment, on the one hand, and a declination, on the other. Declining prosecution may allow a corporate criminal to escape without consequences. Obtaining a conviction may produce a result that seriously harms innocent third parties who played no role in the criminal conduct. Under appropriate circumstances, a deferred prosecution or non-prosecution agreement can help restore the integrity of a company's operations and preserve the financial viability of a corporation that has engaged in criminal conduct, while preserving the government's ability to prosecute a recalcitrant corporation that materially breaches the agreement. Such agreements achieve other important objectives as well, like prompt restitution for victims.[8] Ultimately, the appropriateness of a criminal charge against a corporation, or some lesser alternative, must be evaluated in a pragmatic and reasoned way that produces a fair outcome, taking into consideration, among other things, the Department's need to promote and ensure respect for the law.

9-28.1100 Other Civil or Regulatory Alternatives

A. *General Principle:* Non-criminal alternatives to prosecution often exist and prosecutors may consider whether such sanctions would adequately deter, punish, and rehabilitate a corporation that has engaged in wrongful conduct. In evaluating the adequacy of non-criminal alternatives to prosecution—*e.g.*, civil or regulatory enforcement actions—the prosecutor may consider all relevant factors, including:

1. the sanctions available under the alternative means of disposition;
2. the likelihood that an effective sanction will be imposed; and
3. the effect of non-criminal disposition on federal law enforcement interests.

8. Prosecutors should note that in the case of national or multi-national corporations, multi-district or global agreements may be necessary. Such agreements may only be entered into with the approval of each affected district or the appropriate Department official. *See id.* § 9-27.641.

B. *Comment:* The primary goals of criminal law are deterrence, punishment, and rehabilitation. Non-criminal sanctions may not be an appropriate response to a serious violation, a pattern of wrongdoing, or prior non-criminal sanctions without proper remediation. In other cases, however, these goals may be satisfied through civil or regulatory actions. In determining whether a federal criminal resolution is appropriate, the prosecutor should consider the same factors (modified appropriately for the regulatory context) considered when determining whether to leave prosecution of a natural person to another jurisdiction or to seek non-criminal alternatives to prosecution. These factors include: the strength of the regulatory authority's interest; the regulatory authority's ability and willingness to take effective enforcement action; the probable sanction if the regulatory authority's enforcement action is upheld; and the effect of a non-criminal disposition on federal law enforcement interests. *See* USAM §§ 9-27.240, 9-27.250.

9-28.1200 Selecting Charges

A. *General Principle:* Once a prosecutor has decided to charge a corporation, the prosecutor at least presumptively should charge, or should recommend that the grand jury charge, the most serious offense that is consistent with the nature of the defendant's misconduct and that is likely to result in a sustainable conviction.

B. *Comment:* Once the decision to charge is made, the same rules as govern charging natural persons apply. These rules require "a faithful and honest application of the Sentencing Guidelines" and an "individualized assessment of the extent to which particular charges fit the specific circumstances of the case, are consistent with the purposes of the Federal criminal code, and maximize the impact of Federal resources on crime." *See* USAM § 9-27.300. In making this determination, "it is appropriate that the attorney for the government consider, *inter alia,* such factors as the [advisory] sentencing guideline range yielded by the charge, whether the penalty yielded by such sentencing range . . . is proportional to the seriousness of the defendant's conduct, and whether the charge achieves such purposes of the criminal law as punishment, protection of the public, specific and general deterrence, and rehabilitation." *Id.*

9-28.1300 Plea Agreements with Corporations

A. *General Principle:* In negotiating plea agreements with corporations, as with individuals, prosecutors should generally seek a plea to the most serious, readily provable offense charged. In addition, the terms of the plea agreement should contain appropriate provisions to ensure punishment, deterrence, rehabilitation, and compliance with the plea agreement in the corporate context. Although special circumstances may mandate a different conclusion, prosecutors generally should not agree to accept a corporate guilty plea in exchange for non-prosecution or dismissal of charges against individual officers and employees.

B. *Comment:* Prosecutors may enter into plea agreements with corporations for the same reasons and under the same constraints as apply to plea agreements with natural persons. *See* USAM §§ 9-27.400–530. This means, inter alia, that the corporation should generally be required to plead guilty to the most serious, readily provable offense charged. In addition, any negotiated departures or recommended variances from the advisory Sentencing Guidelines must be justifiable under the Guidelines or 18 U.S.C. § 3553 and must be disclosed to the sentencing court. A corporation should be made to realize that pleading guilty to criminal charges constitutes an admission of guilt and not merely a resolution of an inconvenient distraction from its business. As with natural persons, pleas should be structured so that the corporation may not later "proclaim lack of culpability or even complete innocence." *See* USAM §§ 9-27.420(b)(4), 9-27.440, 9-27.500. Thus, for instance, there should be placed upon the record a sufficient factual basis for the plea to prevent later corporate assertions of innocence.

A corporate plea agreement should also contain provisions that recognize the nature of the corporate "person" and that ensure that the principles of punishment, deterrence, and rehabilitation are met. In the corporate context, punishment and deterrence are generally accomplished by substantial fines, mandatory restitution, and institution of appropriate compliance measures, including, if necessary, continued judicial oversight or the use of special masters or corporate monitors. *See* USSG §§ 8B1.1, 8C2.1, *et seq*. In addition, where the corporation is a government contractor, permanent or temporary debarment may be appropriate. Where the corporation was engaged in fraud against the government (e.g., contracting fraud), a prosecutor may not negotiate away an agency's right to debar or delist the corporate defendant.

In negotiating a plea agreement, prosecutors should also consider the deterrent value of prosecutions of individuals within the corporation. Therefore, one factor that a prosecutor may consider in determining whether to enter into a plea agreement is whether the corporation is seeking immunity for its employees and officers or whether the corporation is willing to cooperate in the investigation of culpable individuals as outlined herein. Prosecutors should rarely negotiate away individual criminal liability in a corporate plea.

Rehabilitation, of course, requires that the corporation undertake to be law-abiding in the future. It is, therefore, appropriate to require the corporation, as a condition of probation, to implement a compliance program or to reform an existing one. As discussed above, prosecutors may consult with the appropriate state and federal agencies and components of the Justice Department to ensure that a proposed compliance program is adequate and meets industry standards and best practices. *See supra* section VIII.

In plea agreements in which the corporation agrees to cooperate, the prosecutor should ensure that the cooperation is entirely truthful. To do so, the prosecutor may request that the corporation make appropriate disclosures of relevant factual information and documents, make employees and agents available for debriefing, file appropriate certified financial statements, agree to governmental or third-party audits, and take whatever other steps are necessary to ensure that the full scope of the corporate wrongdoing is disclosed and that the responsible personnel are identified and, if appropriate, prosecuted. *See generally supra* section VII. In taking such steps, Department prosecutors should recognize that attorney-client communications are often essential to a corporation's efforts to comply with complex regulatory and legal regimes, and that, as discussed at length above, cooperation is not measured by the waiver of attorney-client privilege and work product protection, but rather is measured by the disclosure of facts and other considerations identified herein such as making witnesses available for interviews and assisting in the interpretation of complex documents or business records.

These Principles provide only internal Department of Justice guidance. They are not intended to, do not, and may not be relied upon to create any rights, substantive or procedural, enforceable at law by any party in any matter civil or criminal. Nor are any limitations hereby placed on otherwise lawful litigative prerogatives of the Department of Justice.

CHAPTER 2

The Attorney-Client Privilege: A Practical Guide for Corporate Counsel

MICHAEL A. KNOERZER
EILEEN K. SORABELLA

I. Introduction

If you are reading this, you are probably in-house counsel for a corporate enterprise. Do you assume that what you write and say is protected by the attorney-client privilege? Are you sure? How much of what you communicate to your corporate client would be protected by the attorney-client privilege if scrutinized by a court in a discovery battle? What will the consequences be for your corporate client (and for you) if these communications are deemed not to be privileged?

If you are not a little bit scared, you don't know the law. The goal of this guide is not to scare you, but to give comfort by laying out a number of basic guidelines that at least give you a start toward protecting your communications. Obviously, no writing can take the place of legal advice and common sense. These guidelines are not a substitute for sound legal advice when acting under duress, such as upon the service of a subpoena. By following the steps set out below, however, a corporation will be able to improve the chances that its assertion of attorney-client privilege is upheld.

II. Protecting the Attorney-Client Communication Privilege: A Step-by-Step Guide for In-House Counsel

A. Step 1: Know the Elements of the Attorney-Client Privilege

Knowing the elements of the attorney-client privilege is the first step toward successfully asserting it. Countless authorities have defined the attorney-client privilege, but none have improved upon the definition written in 1950 by the U.S. District Court of Massachusetts in *United States v. United Shoe Machinery Corp.*, declaring that the attorney-client privilege applies only if

> (1) the asserted holder of the privilege is or sought to become a client; (2) the person to whom the communication was made (a) is a member of the bar of a court, or his subordinate and (b) in connection with this communication is acting as a lawyer, (3) the communication relates to a fact of which the attorney was informed (a) by his client (b) without the presence of strangers (c) for the purpose of securing primarily either (i) an opinion on law or (ii) legal services or (iii) assistance in some legal proceeding, and not (d) for the purpose of committing a crime or tort; and (4) the privilege has been (a) claimed and (b) not waived, by the client.[1]

As comprehensive as this definition is, be aware that the elements of attorney-client privilege vary slightly from jurisdiction to jurisdiction. Take the time to review the applicable standards in the jurisdiction in which you practice. Also, keep in mind that it is not just the general counsel who might be making privileged communications; all attorneys in the corporation must know the elements of the attorney-client privilege.

B. Step 2: Attorney, Know Thyself

1. What Titles Do You Have? What Responsibilities Do You Have? Under Which Title or Responsibility Are You Working at Any Given Time?

Most corporate counsel have more than one title: they possess not only a purely legal title such as "Associate General Counsel" but also a nonlegal title such as "Assistant Vice President." The presence of a nonlegal title on a communication written by corporate counsel can have unintended consequences. Courts may take note of the presence of the attorney's nonlegal title on a communication as evidence that the communication was not made strictly for the purpose of conveying legal advice.

It is impractical to suggest that corporate counsel not maintain any nonlegal title within a corporation, although for purposes of maintaining the attorney-client privilege, that suggestion would be ideal. A more practical approach is to use only the legal title when issuing communications that are intended to be privileged.

A more radical approach, but one that has been adopted by many insurers and reinsurers (which, owing to their business of adjusting claims, have even more complex questions regarding the privilege), is to entirely separate the general counsel's office from other parts of the corporation's functions, such as the claims department. In this way, a corporation can better control the extent to which its counsel are working in nonlegal, and therefore nonprivileged, capacities.

2. Maintain an Active Bar Membership

An essential element of the attorney-client communication privilege is that the communication must be made to an attorney (or to narrowly defined personnel closely associated with an attorney). Are you an attorney? You have a diploma from law school, you passed the bar, and you've been admitted to the bar. Sounds like you are an attorney, doesn't it? Maybe not. Are you admitted in the jurisdiction in which you are practicing? Are you a member of the bar in that jurisdiction? If not, your status as an attorney may be called into question. A recent case addressed this issue, resulting in some anxious moments for the company and disaster for the in-house counsel.

The case in question is *Gucci America, Inc. v. Guess?, Inc.* (*Gucci II*), which involved an in-house lawyer for Gucci who had voluntarily changed his bar status to "inactive" several years earlier. Based on the fact that the lawyer was inactive, a federal magistrate judge ruled that the attorney was not "actually authorized to engage in the practice of law."[2] The magistrate judge reasoned that to be an attorney, it is necessary to be an active member of the bar.

On review, the district court judge set aside the magistrate judge's ruling. In reviewing the magistrate judge's order, the court found this conclusion to be "contrary to law," explaining that in order for the privilege to apply, *United Shoe* requires only that the person be a "member of the bar of a court."[3] The attorney was technically still a member of the bar of a federal court in California and a member of the California state bar—albeit an inactive member.[4] Moreover, the attorney held the position of legal director, and every *legal* communication between him and the client was "clearly intended" to be a protected attorney-client communication.[5] The court concluded that "Gucci should not be penalized because its attorney, a member of the bar in two jurisdictions, may not have been 'authorized to practice law' based on his 'inactive' status as a member of the California bar."[6]

The court also addressed the "reasonable belief" exception, which provides that "[e]ven if the communications at issue were not made to an attorney, the privilege may be successfully claimed if the client reasonably believed that the person to whom the communications were made was in fact an attorney."[7] The magistrate judge had determined that Gucci could not rely on the reasonable belief exception because it had not exercised "due diligence" to confirm whether the legal director was authorized to practice law.[8] A number of courts have applied the privilege when the person to whom the communication was made was not a member of any bar, so long as the client reasonably believed it was communicating with an attorney.[9] The court noted that there was no precedent to suggest that the "reasonable expectation" exception imposed a "due diligence" requirement on corporations, as opposed to individuals, and concluded:

> [A]ny other result would place an unfair and potentially disruptive burden on corporate entities. To require businesses to continually check whether their in-house counsel have maintained active membership in bar associations before confiding in them simply does not make sense. While an attorney has an obligation to ensure that he is properly practicing law—and faces the specter of disciplinary action if he engages in unauthorized practice—the sins of the attorney must not be visited on the client so long as the client has acted reasonably in its belief that counsel is, in fact, an attorney.[10]

Although Gucci ultimately was successful in preserving its privileged materials, it spent significant time and resources to achieve that result, and the lawyer was terminated from his position in the process. It seems advisable that in-house counsel, as a "best practice," maintain an active bar membership, completing the necessary continuing legal education and registration requirements.

C. Step 3: Know Your Audience

Every communication involves two sides: the sender and the receiver. A corporate counsel, by sending an otherwise privileged communication as an attorney, has only solved half of the equation. The other half of the equation is to solve who is the appropriate recipient of the communication. There exist inconsistencies among jurisdictions with regard to who is the proper recipient of a privileged communication. Corporate counsel would be well served to be aware of the different approaches taken by different courts.

The most narrow standard is known as the control group test, under which counsel are permitted to have privileged communications with persons with the power to act on any legal advice given.[11] The control group test has been criticized and discredited because it does not reflect the reality of the world in which the in-house attorney operates. Counsel are often required to meet with various employees within the corporation to receive the information necessary to render comprehensive legal advice. Most courts, recognizing this reality, have adopted a broader test that permits corporate counsel to acquire information from nonmanagement personnel without destroying the privileged nature of the communication.

There are limits, however. When holding meetings involving both legal and nonlegal matters, consider who should attend the meeting and whether certain individuals should attend only parts of the meeting.[12] When circulating privileged memoranda, limit circulation to only the necessary individuals to help to protect the privilege.[13] Include an instruction in the communication that further circulation is prohibited.

D. Step 4: Pay Heed to "Optics": Ensure That Your Communication Has All the Earmarks of a Communication Intended to Be Privileged

A document that is merely labeled as confidential does not "magically become so."[14] Courts will not allow "a corporation . . . to insulate its files from discovery simply by sending a 'cc' to in-house counsel."[15]

Nonetheless, experience teaches that optics matter, not only to prove intent to make a document privileged, but also to prove intent not to waive the privilege. If a magistrate judge or special master is called upon to review hundreds of documents for privilege, it does not take much imagination to see that certain routine practices, used when appropriate, will aid the reviewer:

- Use only your legal title.
- On each page, have a footer that says "Attorney-client privileged communication and attorney work product."
- Include at the outset of the communication a statement to the effect that the communication is "in response to a request for legal advice."
- Nonattorneys should include in their communication a statement to the effect that the communication is "a request for legal advice."
- Limit the communication to strictly legal matters.
- When communicating by e-mail, be mindful of the recipients you include; the fewer, the better. Always think twice before hitting the "reply all" button.
- Do not reply to an e-mail concerning business matters with an e-mail containing legal advice; instead, start a new string.
- If you intend a communication to be privileged, include an admonition that it should not be forwarded internally without your approval and should *never* be forwarded to someone outside the corporation.

This is especially important for e-mail communications because they are so easily disseminated.

- Advise your client to avoid mass e-mails mixing legal and nonlegal recipients. Instead, if the client requires input from counsel, the client should send a separate e-mail to the legal department.
- Retain a copy of the communication in the legal department in a file (electronic or paper) that is limited to privileged documents. Inadvertent waiver occurs because privileged and nonprivileged documents are sometimes mixed and then produced together.

Creating a separate filing system for confidential communications demonstrates corporate counsel's desire to keep the information confidential[16] and also provides a clear indication that the communication was not made in the course of counsel's daily business activities.

Counsel should be careful not to overuse or abuse the first four of these techniques. Experience also teaches that, if counsel routinely label all documents as "confidential" or "privileged," regardless of substance, the designation loses significance and a court will be unlikely to pay it much heed.[17] As always, the communication must be for the purpose of obtaining or providing legal advice that only a lawyer can provide.[18]

E. Step 5: Candidly Identify Nonprivileged Communications and Keep Them Separate

There is sometimes, within a corporation, an insufficient appreciation for the difference between "confidential business communications" and "attorney-client-privileged communications." Many experienced attorneys (either in-house or outside counsel) have been confronted with the uncomfortable position of being asked to be present during a nonprivileged business discussion because the client hopes that the lawyer's presence will cloak the communications in privilege. Many lawyers find themselves copied on purely business-related e-mails, perhaps in the hope that sensitive business information can be transmogrified into privileged communications.

More frequently, corporate counsel are invited to become involved in business communications simply because their business advice is valued. It is impossible and impractical for counsel to avoid these business matters. However, certain steps should be taken so that later there is no confusion as to when counsel were acting in a legal capacity and when counsel were acting in a business capacity:

- When asked to take on a nonlegal project, corporate counsel should remind the client that communications related to the project will not be shielded from discovery by the attorney-client privilege.
- Use your business title, not your legal title, on any written communication.

- State at the outset of the communication that it is understood not to be a privileged communication. (This may seem overly cautious, but it enhances your credibility when you state that a communication without that warning is, indeed, intended to be privileged.)
- Limit the communication to strictly business matters.
- Advise your client to separate communications to you concerning business matters from requests for legal advice.
- File the business communication separate and apart from privileged communications. Consider keeping a paper copy of the communication (if any) outside of the legal department.

Corporate counsel may consider drafting separate e-mails or memoranda for legal and nonlegal issues and advice. If legal and business advice must be conveyed in the same communication, it may be useful to address these issues in separate sections of the document so that privileged legal communications may be easily redacted later on, if necessary. Although the inclusion of nonlegal advice is not necessarily fatal to the privilege, corporate counsel should be mindful that most courts applying the privilege require the communication to be of a "predominantly legal" character. [19] Most importantly, corporate counsel should not assume that blending business and legal advice in the same communication will extend the cover of privilege to the nonlegal aspects of the communication.

Be aware that, even when you are cautious and informed, the rules can change under your feet.

F. Step 6: Know the Difference between Legal Work and Business Tasks

Of all the "nettlesome questions" presented by the application of the attorney-client privilege to corporate lawyers, none has caused more ink to be spilled than the issue of whether the corporate attorney is rendering legal advice or business advice. "The cornerstone of the [attorney-client] privilege has always rested on the notion that the communication must be for the purpose of securing or rendering legal advice."[20] If the attorney is simply asked to give business advice, and not legal advice, all or part of the communication between the attorney and the client may not be protected.[21] "Although on occasion seamlessly intertwined, there is nevertheless a sharp distinction between legal and business advice; the privilege protects only the former, and not the latter."[22]

1. *What Is "Legal Advice"?*

In order to successfully assert that the attorney-client privilege applies to its communications, the corporation must make a clear showing that in-house counsel's advice was given in a legal capacity[23] and is primarily of a legal character.[24] A communication is "primarily legal" if the corporation can show that it "would not have been made but for the [corporation]'s need for legal advice or services."[25] "[T]he critical inquiry is whether, viewing the lawyer's communication in its full content and context, it was made in order to render legal advice or services to the client."[26] Courts have recognized that "[t]he overlap between 'business' advice and 'legal' advice requires a pragmatic approach"[27] and, therefore, "[t]he mere fact that business advice is given or solicited does not . . . automatically render the privilege lost: where the advice given is predominantly legal, as opposed to business, in nature the privilege will still attach."[28]

A court examining the distinction between legal services and nonlegal services will consider "whether a non-lawyer could do the task or rather whether the task was a 'lawyer-related task.'"[29] Recognized "lawyer-related tasks" include "applying law to a set of facts; reviewing client conduct based upon the effective laws or regulations; [and] advising the client about status or trends in the law."[30] The fact that a communication refers to nonlegal matters does not, in and of itself, forfeit a privilege that otherwise properly applies.[31] Courts have recognized that an in-house counsel's memorandum is privileged if it "concerns legal rights and obligations and where it evidences other professional skills such as a lawyer's judgment and recommended legal strategies."[32]

Thus the role of the attorney is "not restricted to citing cases and espousing legal theories."[33] If a communication reflects professional skills, "such as a lawyer's judgment and recommended legal strategies,"[34] it need not demonstrate precise legal research. Advice to a client "is an amalgamation of education, knowledge, experience and legal wisdom which counsel may draw upon to give a frank and unconstrained opinion. That is the essence of effective legal representation."[35]

2. *What Is "Business Advice"?*

Many communications between attorneys and their corporate clients are not privileged, such as advice to a client regarding the date of trial,[36] information provided to an attorney for the purpose of preparing a tax return,[37] and communications arising out of an investigation undertaken for the purpose of making business recommendations to the corporation.[38] The exclusion of the privilege hinges on the principle that, for the attorney-client privilege to apply, the "confidential communication must be for the *primary* purpose of soliciting legal, rather than business, advice."[39] Discoverable documents have been held to include "draft by-laws, promissory notes, security agreements, incorporation documents, partnership documents and tax information. These documents are business related and do not contain personal legal advice."[40]

As previously outlined, courts have held that if an attorney is performing the work of a nonlawyer, the privilege will not apply unless there is a significant legal element involved. If a task could have been "readily performed by a non-lawyer—as when facts are gathered for business decisions," the privilege will not apply.[41]

For example, in *Western Trails, Inc. v. Camp Coast to Coast, Inc.*,[42] the U.S. District Court for the District of Columbia held that documents relating to the development, formulation, and application of a company's membership sales policy were not protected by the privilege, even though they were prepared by an attorney. The court determined that any businessman could easily have performed the services he conducted and no legal advice was required. The court considered, but did not find decisive, the fact that the attorney had "expressly noted in one document addressing the proposed [policy] that he had conducted no legal research concerning alternative formulations of the [policy] suggested by him."[43] The court explained that the absence of any apparent legal research in an attorney's communication is not fatal as long as the communication reflects the attorney's professional skills and judgment.[44]

Further, a corporation cannot use counsel to shield otherwise unprivileged information by simply forwarding it to an attorney, copying counsel on an e-mail, or having an attorney conduct an investigation.[45] Particularly with respect to insurance claims, courts often dismiss privilege claims that involve lawyers acting in an investigative role.[46]

3. *Specific Tasks: Privileged or Not?*

Counsel may be surprised to learn that many tasks may seem to be of a strictly legal nature (contract negotiation, for example), but in fact are not. This section addresses several specific tasks that corporate counsel are frequently asked to undertake and explores how courts have applied the privilege in each context.

a. Contract Drafting, Review, and Negotiation

The line between legal advice and business advice is perhaps at its haziest when in-house counsel are involved in negotiating contracts. For example, in *Note Funding Corp. v. Bobian Investment Co., N.V.*,[47] the plaintiff sought discovery of communications regarding business negotiations and analyses that were "handled in whole or part" by the attorneys for the corporation. Considering whether the attorney-client privilege applies when an attorney is engaged in negotiations on behalf of the corporation, the court noted that

> Assessment of this argument requires the court to tread an occasionally blurry line. In pursuing large and complex financial transactions, commercial entities often seek the assistance of attorneys who are well equipped both by training and by experience to assess the risks and advantages in alternative business strategies. When providing this assistance, counsel are not limited to offering their client purely abstract advice as to the rules of law that may apply to their situation. Of necessity, counsel will often be required to assess specific tactics in putting together transactions or shaping the terms of commercial agreements, and their evaluation of alternative approaches may well take into account not only the potential impact of applicable legal norms, but also the commercial needs of their client and the financial benefits or risks of these alternative strategies.[48]

The court stated that the "fact that an attorney's advice encompasses commercial as well as legal considerations does not vitiate the privilege."[49] According to the court, the key distinction is "whether the attorney's performance depends principally on his knowledge of or application of legal requirements or principles, rather than his expertise in matters of commercial practice."[50]

A similar result was reached in *Diversey U.S. Holdings, Inc. v. Sara Lee Corp.*[51] Sara Lee's counsel participated in the negotiation of a contract implementing an agreement reached by officers of the two corporations. The U.S. District Court for the Northern District of Illinois held that "[d]rafting legal documents is a core activity of lawyers, and obtaining information and feedback from clients is a necessary part of the process."[52] The communications in question were found to be privileged because "the gathering of information by an attorney from the client . . . enable[d] the attorney to provide competent legal services—in this case, the drafting of a contract."[53]

In *Georgia-Pacific Corp. v. GAF Roofing Manufacturing Corp.*,[54] the U.S. District Court for the Southern District of New York found that an attorney negotiating a contract was acting in a business capacity.[55] GAF's in-house environmental attorney had acted as its negotiator with respect to environmental provisions in an asset purchase agreement between Georgia-Pacific and GAF. After GAF terminated the agreement because of concerns about environmental risks, Georgia-Pacific commenced a breach of contract action and sought to depose the GAF attorney. The court determined that GAF's in-house environmental attorney acted "[a]s a negotiator on behalf of management"[56] and found that the documents in question were not privileged.

Similarly, *Cooper-Rutter Associates, Inc. v. Anchor National Life Insurance Co.*[57] concerned two handwritten memoranda that were "prepared by an individual who was both in-house counsel and corporate secretary to one of the defendants."[58] The court found that the documents "concern[ed] both the business and legal aspects of the defendants' ongoing negotiations with the plaintiff" regarding the business transaction out of which the lawsuit arose.[59] Based on this finding, New York's Appellate Division, Second Department, ruled that "the documents were not primarily of legal character, but expressed substantial non-legal concerns," and therefore were not privileged.[60] Interestingly, it seems the court did not protect from discovery the portions of the memoranda that did contain legal advice.

b. Regulatory Compliance and Filings

Corporate counsel who are responsible for their client's regulatory compliance and filings should be aware that courts will closely examine their communications in this regard to determine if those communications are made for the purpose of obtaining legal advice.

In *In re Vioxx Products Liability Litigation*, Merck & Co. sought to protect over 60,000 documents, many of which were e-mails, under a "pervasive regulation" theory. Merck argued that "because the drug industry is so extensively regulated by the FDA, virtually everything a member of the industry does carries potential legal problems vis-à-vis government regulators."[61] The court acknowledged that "services that initially appear to be non-legal in nature . . . could, in fact, be legal advice in the context of the drug industry." The court, however, rejected Merck's pervasive regulation theory:

> Accepting such a theory would effectively immunize most of the industry's internal communications because most drug companies are probably structured like Merck where virtually every communication leaving the company has to go through the legal department for review, comment and approval. The fact that the industry is so heavily regulated does not justify dispensing with each company's burden of persuasion on the elements of attorney-client privilege.[62]

The court required Merck to establish, on a document-by-document basis, that the *primary purpose* of each communication was to request or provide legal advice in order for the privilege to apply.

The U.S. District Court for the Middle District of Florida followed *Vioxx* in *In re Seroquel Products Liability Litigation*. The *Seroquel* court dismissed most of AstraZeneca's privilege claims, rejecting the "pervasive regulation" theory argued by the drug company:

> This argument goes way too far. Almost any act by a business (or an individual for that matter) carries the potential for running afoul of some law or regulation or giving rise to a civil action. The pharmaceutical industry is subject to more regulation and more complex regulation than some other industries (though less than some others). The fact of extensive or pervasive regulation does not make the everyday business activities legally privileged from discovery. Routine inclusion of attorneys in the corporate effort of creating marketing and scientific documents does not support the inference that the underlying communications were created and transmitted primarily to obtain legal advice as is required to justify a privilege.[63]

In *Washington v. American Tobacco Co.*,[64] RJR Tobacco Company attempted to assert the attorney-client privilege with respect to meeting minutes drafted on behalf of in-house counsel to "enable counsel to review the proceedings and ensure compliance with various regulatory schemes."[65] While the court held that two sentences in particular "would reveal the substance of RJR's inquiry, thereby chilling a client's willingness to place its legal problems before counsel,"[66] it refused to apply the privilege to the document as a whole. The court explained:

> RJR has offered no evidence . . . to support its assertion that in-house counsel reviewed these minutes to monitor the industry's regulatory compliance. Even if the court accepted such an unsubstantiated claim,

the document itself does not reflect or contain a request for legal advice on such matters, nor does it suggest that a review by counsel is expected.[67]

A similar approach was taken in *United States v. Northrop Grumman Corp.*,[68] but it yielded different results. Northrop asserted the attorney-client privilege with respect to a regulatory compliance review that "was undertaken by its legal department in anticipation of a wide-scale government audit as a way to gauge Northrop's regulatory compliance and potential liability."[69] The court held that the privilege applied because the communication in question was primarily legal in nature, explaining that an attorney's regulatory monitoring would be reviewed under the same standard as any other attorney task.

Courts are unlikely to find the privilege to protect communications regarding documents that are ultimately disclosed publicly, such as filings with the Securities and Exchange Commission.[70] In *In re Grand Jury Proceedings*,[71] the U.S. Court of Appeals for the Fourth Circuit addressed the application of the privilege where corporate counsel assist in the preparation of a public filing. The court found that "[i]f a client communicates information to his attorney with the understanding that the information will be revealed to others, that information as well as 'the details underlying the data which was to be published' will not enjoy the privilege."[72] The intention of disclosure was a key factor in determining whether the privilege attached. The court did state, however, that "the attorney-client privilege does protect communications made between attorney and client when the client is only considering publication of a disclosure document and is seeking legal advice regarding that possibility."[73]

c. Intellectual Property Protection

Courts examining the attorney-client privilege in the context of the protection and enforcement of intellectual property frequently address whether the privilege applies to documents that are prepared for public disclosure. Courts have split on the issue of how complex technical information further complicates the application of the privilege.[74] One line of cases has held that any expectation of confidentiality is precluded because the applying party owes a duty of full disclosure to the Patent and Trademark Office.[75] However, more courts have adopted the view announced in *Knogo Corp. v. United States*[76] that "the successful assertion of the attorney-client privilege can exist in regard to communications which are primarily technical expositions."[77]

In *Knogo*, the Court of Claims Trial Division explained the difficulty of applying the general principles of the attorney-client privilege to the patent application process, but it found that the expectation of confidentiality made it only reasonable that communications made to counsel leading up to a patent application would be covered by the privilege.[78] The U.S. District Court for the Northern District of California took a similar approach in *Advanced Cardiovascular Systems, Inc. v. C.R. Bard, Inc.*[79] The defendant moved to compel disclosure of communications between inventors and their patent counsel and to compel certain testimony. The court rejected an earlier decision[80] that reasoned that "the attorney-client privilege should not attach, presumptively, to private communications from inventor to lawyer that consist primarily of technical information related to an anticipated patent application."[81] The court explained that counsel brings to the patent application process "an understanding of (among other things) the criteria used by the PTO in deciding whether to issue patents and of the legal principles or considerations that come into play when parties seek to enforce a patent against an alleged infringer or to challenge a patent's validity."[82]

d. Employment and Labor Law and Policy

Corporate counsel are routinely called upon to advise their client with respect to employment policies and decisions, but some of these activities may subject an attorney's communications to disclosure. In *Neuder v. Battelle Pacific Northwest National Laboratory*,[83] the plaintiff alleged wrongful termination and sought production of documents from the company's Personnel Action Review Committee (PARC), which made the termination decision. The company asserted that the documents were privileged based on the participation of in-house counsel as a member of the committee. The U.S. District Court for the District of Columbia found that the primary purpose of the committee was to render a business decision—the decision to terminate. The court explained that "when a committee inquires about the legal implications of a proposed decision to terminate an employee, the business purpose of the decision predominates over the legal issues being discussed."[84]

e. Risk Management

Courts have refused to recognize the privilege in situations where communications are made for the purpose of risk management alone. In *Fine v. Facet Aerospace*,[85] a flight instructor alleged that the crash was caused by water in the fuel system and brought claims against the plane's manufacturer for negligence and strict products liability. The manufacturer asserted attorney-client privilege with respect to a report concerning the company's exposure to litigation due to fuel contamination. The manufacturer's in-house counsel averred that he had provided privileged documents that had been incorporated into the risk management report, which was drafted by the engineering department. The court held that "[w]hile one goal of such an analysis is . . . to reduce costs associated with litigation, a myriad of business interests motivate a manufacturer to enhance the safety of its product."[86] The court found that risk management documents did not serve a primarily legal function and accordingly the privilege did not attach.

f. Real Estate

An attorney's participation in a real estate transaction will not, in itself, shield communications from disclosure under the privilege.[87] Unless the party attempting to assert the privilege can show that counsel were actively involved in rendering legal services, the privilege will not apply to communications surrounding real estate transactions. In *In re Arnold & McDowell*,[88] the court held that where an attorney acted merely as the preparer of documents, the privilege would not apply:

> [The] documents in question were prepared by the petitioner and pertain only to the effectuation of the real estate transaction itself. The communications that go into the drawing of these documents, including information as to the location and value of the property, are not the kind of communications that can be termed "confidential" within the context of the attorney-client relationship. In preparing these documents, the petitioner simply requested that information necessary to complete the requested transaction. Since the petitioner acted only as a scrivener in preparing the documents, the confidentiality inherent in an attorney-client relationship was never established as to that information provided for use in the documents.[89]

Similarly, in *Pollock v. United States*,[90] the U.S. Court of Appeals for the Fifth Circuit was unable to recognize a significant element of legal advice within communications between an attorney and his client concerning a real estate transaction. The court stated that "[w]here the attorney is a mere scrivener or the transaction involves a simple transfer of title to real estate and there is no consultation for legal advice, it has been held that communications to an attorney are not privileged."[91]

g. Communication by E-mail

A court considering a challenge to a corporation's assertion of privilege over e-mail communications is likely to examine those communications closely to ensure that they are worthy of the protections of the privilege. Of course, e-mail communications are subject to the same standards as any other communication, but e-mails present unique challenges regarding the application of the privilege.

In *Vioxx*, many of the documents in question were internal e-mails that were widely disseminated within the company, addressed to multiple lawyers and nonlawyers. Merck argued that the "pervasive regulation" it faces requires Merck employees to send these mass e-mails in a "collaborative effort to accomplish a legally sufficient draft."[92] The court rejected Merck's argument, explaining:

> The structure of Merck's enterprise, with its legal department having such broad powers, and the manner in which it circulates documents has consequences that Merck must live with relative to its burden of persuasion when privilege is asserted. When, for example, Merck simultaneously sends communications to both lawyers and nonlawyers, it usually cannot claim that the primary purpose of the com-

> munication was for legal advice or assistance because the communication served both business and legal purposes.[93]

The *Vioxx* court suggested that if Merck blind-copied its attorneys—or, better yet, sent them entirely separate e-mails attaching the same materials sent to the business teams—then the single communication sent to counsel would be privileged even if it otherwise served mixed purposes.[94]

In *Rowe v. E.I. DuPont de Nemours & Co.*,[95] plaintiffs relied on *Vioxx* to challenge the privilege asserted by a corporation over certain e-mails between its employees and its in-house counsel. The plaintiffs argued that because the e-mails were sent primarily to nonlawyers, they were not privileged. The court rejected this assertion, explaining that the nature of the communication, rather than the ratio of lawyers to nonlawyers involved, controls the determination:

> The Court rejects [the] argument that because the e-mails . . . were sent primarily to non-lawyers, they could not have predominantly served a legal purpose and therefore are not attorney-client privileged. The Court in *In re Vioxx* noted that e-mails from in-house counsel could be attorney-client privileged—even if sent to non-lawyer employees—as long as the e-mails were sent for the purpose of circulating legal advice "to those within the corporate structure who needed the advice in order to fulfill their corporate responsibilities," or to "inform those recipients of the nature of the legal advice being sought[.]" Thus, in deciding whether the attorney-client privilege attaches to an e-mail from in-house counsel, the court's inquiry should not focus on whether the recipients of the e-mail are lawyers; rather, the court must determine whether the primary purpose and content of the e-mail is predominantly legal.[96]

The take-away for corporate counsel is this: regardless of the method of communication, reviewing courts will require a party claiming the attorney-client privilege to prove that the elements of the attorney-client privilege exist. E-mails receive no special treatment and, indeed, may raise more questions if they are sent to lawyers and nonlawyers simultaneously. To maximize the likelihood of protecting privileged e-mails, take the same precautions you would when writing a letter or a memo.

h. Joint Representation of Parent Companies and Subsidiaries

In *Teleglobe Communications Corp. v. BCE, Inc. (In re Teleglobe Communications Corp.)*, the Third Circuit addressed the application of the privilege in the context of a dispute between parent company Bell Canada Enterprises (BCE) and its bankrupt subsidiary, Teleglobe. Prior to Teleglobe's bankruptcy, BCE and Teleglobe were serviced by a centralized legal department. As Teleglobe began experiencing financial difficulties, the legal department worked with both BCE and Teleglobe to examine Teleglobe's options—an endeavor the companies dubbed "Project X." BCE also hired outside lawyers to work on Project X, and those lawyers passed privileged communications to BCE through the in-house legal department. Ultimately, BCE decided to cut off funding for Teleglobe, which filed for bankruptcy.[97] In bankruptcy, the Teleglobe debtors brought suit against BCE for breach of fiduciary duty and other claims.[98] On the basis of privilege, BCE withheld communications with its in-house lawyers concerning "Project X."[99] Teleglobe challenged BCE's assertion of the privilege, claiming that the in-house lawyers represented the entire corporate family and contending that it had equal access to the communications in question.

The Third Circuit explained that the joint-client privilege, and not the common interest privilege, controlled the analysis.[100] The court said that where, as here, a parent and one or more of its subsidiaries have a common interest and are represented by an in-house legal department, they are "joint clients" for the purpose of in-house counsel's representation.[101] While a lawyer may represent more than one client at a time, the court admonished that the lawyer has an ethical obligation to end the joint representation as soon as the clients' interests begin to diverge.[102] The court recognized the unique difficulties faced by in-house counsel in representing multiple entities within a corporate family, and it counseled:

> In sum, in-house counsel have available numerous means to protect a parent company's privilege. By taking care not to begin joint representations except when necessary, to limit the scope of joint representations, and seasonably to separate counsel on matters in which subsidiaries are adverse to the parent, in-house counsel can maintain sufficient control over the parent's privileged communications.[103]

Ultimately, the Third Circuit upheld BCE's assertion of the privilege and remanded to the trial court. The Third Circuit instructed that because waiver of the joint client privilege requires waiver from all clients, Teleglobe could not unilaterally waive the privilege.[104]

i. Representation of Client in Privilege-Hostile Jurisdictions

As noted above, the elements of the attorney-client privilege vary slightly from jurisdiction to jurisdiction. This chapter does not address those variations. However, we are compelled to note two recent decisions—one in Pennsylvania and one in the European Union—that impose severe limitations on the existence of the privilege.

In January 2010, the Pennsylvania Supreme Court issued an evenly split opinion in *Nationwide Mutual Insurance Co. v. Fleming*.[105] The court's even split left standing the earlier decision of the Superior Court, which interpreted the state's attorney-client privilege statute to mean that the privilege only applies to communications made by a client to an attorney, *and not to communications made by an attorney to the client*.[106] The Superior Court determined that, under the statute, communications from an attorney to his or her client were only privileged to "the extent that they reveal confidential communications previously made by the client to counsel for the purpose of obtaining legal advice."[107] Although *Nationwide* concerned communications by in-house counsel, the statute and the rule seemingly apply equally to communications by in-house and outside counsel. The Pennsylvania Supreme Court agreed to hear the issue again in a separate case, *Gillard v. AIG Insurance Co.*[108] In a detailed and careful opinion released on February 23, 2011, the Supreme Court of Pennsylvania finally settled the issue and rejected the "one-way street" paradigm some lower courts had applied and instead endorsed the mainstream rule—"[i]n Pennsylvania, the attorney-client privilege operates in a two-way fashion to protect confidential client-to-attorney or attorney-to-client communications made for the purpose of obtaining or providing professional legal advice.[109]

In September 2010, the European Court of Justice (ECJ), the European Union's (EU) highest court, caught the attention of in-house counsel around the world when it ruled that, at least in the context of competition investigations, communications between in-house counsel and their corporate employers do not enjoy the protection of the attorney-client privilege, which is called the "legal professional privilege" in the EU.

In *Akzo Nobel Chemicals Ltd. & Akcros Chemicals Ltd. v. Commission*, the Dutch chemical company sought protection for documents seized by investigators in a competition inquiry, including communications between Akzo's in-house counsel and the company's general manager. The ECJ rejected Akzo's efforts to protect these documents from disclosure, reasoning that the employment relationship between an in-house attorney and the corporation prevents the attorney from having the "independence" necessary for privileged communications to take place. The court said that "[i]t follows, both from the in-house lawyer's economic dependence and the close ties with his employer, that he does not enjoy the level of professional independence comparable to that of an external lawyer."[110] The ECJ rejected the argument that in-house counsel are bound by the same professional and ethical obligations to which external lawyers are bound. The privilege continues to apply to communications between external counsel and their corporate clients.

While the ECJ's *Akzo* decision is consistent with a 1982 ECJ decision, many in the EU legal community were hopeful that the *Akzo* court would take the opportunity to reconsider the standard. For now, however, corporations subject to the laws of the EU should involve external counsel in all legal communications pertaining to competition matters in order to protect legal communications from disclosure.

j. Communication with the Board of Directors

Corporate counsel are often called upon to advise the client's board of directors and, in some instances, are asked to participate as a member of the board. Of course, as with all other communications between attorneys and their corporate clients, only communications with the board members that request or render legal advice will be protected by the privilege, and the rest is subject to disclosure.[111] Although corporate counsel are frequently tasked with drafting board meeting minutes, those minutes will not be privileged unless it can be demonstrated that communications during the meeting were made for the purpose of obtaining or rendering legal advice.[112]

The challenge may be greatest for the attorney who also serves as a director. Noting the precariousness of this position, "the comment to Model Rule 1.7 advises that before accepting a position on the board of directors of a client, a lawyer should consider whether working in the dual role will compromise the lawyer's independent professional judgment."[113] Both the attorney and client must also understand that "by assuming this dual function . . . the corporation's assertion of the attorney-client privilege may be subject to stricter scrutiny."[114]

This greater level of scrutiny has implications with respect to documents provided to the attorney-director for review. In *United States v. International Business Machines Corp.*,[115] IBM claimed that "in a situation where several persons, including a lawyer, are asked for advice upon a particular course of conduct, the communication, *as far as the lawyer is concerned*, is one seeking legal advice, and thus *his* response would be privileged."[116] The court rejected this claim, holding instead that if a document was prepared for review by both legal and nonlegal personnel, "it cannot be said that the primary purpose of the document [was] to secure legal advice,"[117] and therefore was not privileged.[118]

k. Common Interest Privilege

Corporations often enter into common interest agreements—that is, agreements memorializing and setting forth the contours of a purported common interest—in the belief that doing so will allow a corporation to share privileged information with third parties while shielding that privileged information from prying eyes without the risk of waiver. Unfortunately, misunderstanding about common interest agreements abounds, and they may not offer the scope of protection that parties expect they will receive when they enter into those agreements.

The common interest doctrine is an exception to the rule that no privilege attaches to attorney-client communications made in the presence of a third party.[119] To invoke the common interest doctrine, a party must establish (1) that the communication was made by separate parties in the course of a matter of common interest; (2) that the communication was made to further that effort; and (3) that the privilege has not otherwise been waived.[120] In its most common formulation, a common interest exists if (1) the nature of both parties' interests are identical, not similar; (2) the nature of the common interest is legal, not solely commercial; and (3) the communication was shared with the attorney of the member of the community of interest.[121]

Naturally, merely entering into a common interest agreement cannot transform a shared business interest into a shared legal interest, nor can a common interest turn nonprivileged information into privileged information.[122] Accordingly, it is imperative that counsel fully assess the relationship between the parties, the circumstances surrounding the agreement, and the information to be shared prior to disclosing information to another party. Parties sharing information pursuant to a common interest agreement where no legally sufficient common interest exists risk being deemed to have waived the attorney-client privilege as to those documents. Further, it is worth noting that it is uncertain that entering into a common interest agreement can protect information against use in later adversarial proceedings among the parties, even if the agreement attempts to limit such use.[123]

The common interest doctrine is of particular interest to insurers and their insureds, as they often find themselves sharing information for the purposes of litigating potentially covered claims. While the analysis is quite fact-intensive, parties should proceed with extreme caution. Many courts have failed to find that an insured and insurer are subject to the common interest doctrine, particularly where the insurer is not providing a defense for the insured.[124] For instance, in *Imperial Corp. of America v. Alshuler*, the court held that an insured had waived privilege by sharing with its insurer an analysis of its liability exposure, even though a joint defense agreement was in effect between the corporate defendant and the directors and officers (and had been agreed to by the insurer).[125] In finding that there could be no reasonable expectation that the substance of the communication would remain confidential, the court stated that

> [a]ny other result would be an overly broad use of the joint defense privilege. Were the court to accept the directors' and officers' interpretation of the joint defense privilege, any time two or more contractually related entities disclosed confidential information to each other during normal business transactions, the privilege would not be waived unless the parties became directly adverse to each other in subsequent litigation. That is, a mere contractual relationship would allow entities to exchange privileged information for any reason, at any time, without third parties ever being allowed access to the information. Obviously, this is not a logical result.[126]

Counsel operating under a common interest agreement should be cautious when communicating and sharing information among parties. Even if the communication relates to a common purpose, that communication will be discoverable if it is deemed to be business-related rather than legal in nature.

l. Litigation Holds

Several recent court decisions[127] have underscored the importance of issuing a litigation hold in the face of an impending dispute. A corporation that fails to take steps to preserve its files, whether of the electronic or old-fashioned paper variety, risks being sanctioned for spoliation in an ensuing litigation.[128] (A piece of advice: If your company does not already have policies and practices in place to preserve documents and electronic data when a dispute arises, it should implement such policies and practices without delay.)

The task of drafting and distributing litigation holds often falls to in-house counsel, who should be aware that the privilege is not iron-clad as it applies to these communications. "As a general matter hold letters are not discoverable, particularly when a party has made an adequate showing that the letters include material protected under attorney-client privilege or the work-product doctrine."[129] Even though the communication itself might be privileged, however, an adversary is "entitled to know which categories of . . . information employees were instructed to preserve and collect, and what specific actions they were instructed to undertake to that end."[130] In *In re eBay Seller Antitrust Litigation*, the court recognized the privileged nature of counsel's litigation hold directive, but refused to preclude plaintiffs from asking eBay witnesses about the steps eBay took to preserve documents. The court reasoned that "[a]lthough plaintiffs may not be entitled to probe into what exactly eBay's employees were told by its attorneys, they are certainly entitled to know what eBay's employees are doing with respect to collecting and preserving [electronically stored information]."[131]

Moreover, if spoliation occurs, the "prevailing view" is that counsel's litigation hold notices are discoverable.[132] For example, in *Major Tours, Inc. v. Colorel*, the court determined that there had been a preliminary showing of spoliation of evidence and, as a result, ordered the production of defendant's litigation hold letters. Counsel are well advised to monitor closely the preservation of evidence.

III. Conclusion

In a time when in-house counsel's roles and responsibilities are many and the corporate assertion of privilege is viewed with skepticism by courts and commentators, corporate counsel may begin to wonder whether any of their communications with their client will enjoy the protection of the attorney-client privilege. However, by understanding the privilege and the way courts apply it, in-house counsel can take steps to enhance the likelihood that a reviewing court will recognize privileged communications and protect them from disclosure.

Notes

1. United States v. United Shoe Mach. Corp., 89 F. Supp. 357, 358–59 (D. Mass. 1950); *see also In re* Pfohl Bros. Landfill Litig., 1997 U.S. Dist. LEXIS 10709, at *18–19 (W.D.N.Y. Mar. 14, 1997); *accord* United States v. White, 950 F.2d 426, 430 (7th Cir. 1991); Am. Standard, Inc. v. Pfizer, Inc., 828 F.2d 734 (Fed. Cir. 1987); Robert Bosch LLC v. Pylon Mfg. Corp., 263 F.R.D. 142, 144 (D. Del. 2009); Jones v. Murphy, 256 F.R.D. 510, 512 (D. Md. 2008).
2. Gucci Am., Inc. v. Guess?, Inc. (*Gucci II*), No. 09 Civ. 4373, 2010 WL 2720079, at *5 (S.D.N.Y. June 29, 2010).
3. *Id.* at *13–14.
4. *Id.* at *10–11.

5. *Id.* at *14.
6. *Id.*
7. *Id.* at *7.
8. *Id.* at *8.
9. *Id.* at *17.
10. *Id.* at *24.
11. Thomas W. Hyland & Molly Hood Craig, *Attorney-Client Privilege and Word Product Doctrine in the Corporate Setting*, 62 Def. Couns. J. 558 (1995).
12. *Id.* at 562.
13. *Id.*
14. Reich v. Hercules, Inc., 857 F. Supp. 367, 372 (D.N.J. 1994).
15. U.S. Postal Serv. v. Phelps Dodge Ref. Corp., 852 F. Supp. 156, 163–64 (E.D.N.Y. 1994).
16. Hyland & Craig at 562.
17. *Id.*
18. ABB Kent-Taylor, Inc. v. Stallings & Co., 172 F.R.D. 53, 57 (W.D.N.Y. 1996).
19. *Id.*
20. First Fed. Sav. Bank of Hegewisch v. United States, 55 Fed. Cl. 263, 267 (Ct. Fed. Cl. 2003).
21. *See* Boca Investerings P'ship v. United States, 31 F. Supp. 2d 9 (D.D.C. 1998) (holding that communications made by and to in-house counsel by a corporate client seeking and obtaining legal advice are protected by the attorney-client privilege, but communications made by and to in-house counsel with respect to business matters, management decisions, or business advice are not); Hardy v. N.Y. News, Inc., 114 F.R.D. 633 (S.D.N.Y. 1987) (holding that communication with in-house attorney was not privileged because the attorney was not acting in the role of attorney but in the role of director of employee or labor relations); Note Funding Corp. v. Bobian Inv. Co., No. 93 Civ. 7427 (DAB), 1995 WL 662402, at *5 (S.D.N.Y. Nov. 9, 1995); People v. Belge, 59 A.D.2d 307, 309, 399 N.Y.S.2d 539, 540 (4th Dep't 1977).
22. First Fed. Sav. Bank of Hegewisch v. United States, 55 Fed. Cl. at 268.
23. *See In re* Grand Jury Subpoena, 599 F.2d 504, 510 (2d Cir. 1979).
24. Rossi v. Blue Cross & Blue Shield of Greater N.Y., 73 N.Y.2d 588.
25. First Chi. Int'l v. United Exch. Co., 125 F.R.D. 55, 57 (S.D.N.Y. 1989).
26. Spectrum Sys. Int'l Corp. v. Chem. Bank, 78 N.Y.2d 371, 379 (Ct. App. 1991); Allied Irish Banks, P.L.C. v. Bank of Am., N.A., 252 F.R.D. 163, 168 (S.D.N.Y. 2008).
27. ABB Kent-Taylor, Inc. v. Stallings & Co., 172 F.R.D. 53, 55 (W.D.N.Y. 1996).
28. *Id.* (quoting United States v. Davis, 131 F.R.D. 391, 401 (S.D.N.Y. 1990)); *see also In re* Currency Conversion Fee Antitrust Litig., MDL No. 1409, M 21-95, 2002 U.S. Dist. LEXIS 21196, at *6 (S.D.N.Y. Nov. 4, 2002) (finding document entitled to attorney-client privilege even if some portion could be considered business advice where the document predominantly provided legal advice).
29. Nat'l Empl. Serv. Corp. v. Liberty Mut. Ins. Co., No. 93-2528-G, 1994 WL 878920 (Mass. Super. Dec. 12, 1994).
30. *Id.* at *2.
31. *Spectrum*, 78 N.Y.2d at 380; *Rossi*, 73 N.Y.2d at 594.
32. *Rossi*, 73 N.Y.2d at 594.
33. *ABB Kent-Taylor*, 172 F.R.D. at 56.

34. *Id.* at 57 (citation omitted).
35. *Id.*
36. United States v. Uptain, 552 F.2d 1108, 1109 (5th Cir. 1977).
37. *In re* Grand Jury Investigation, 842 F.2d 1223, 1224–25 (11th Cir. 1987).
38. Diversified Indus., Inc. v. Meredith, 572 F.2d 596, 603 (8th Cir. 1977).
39. N.C. Elec. Membership Corp. v. Carolina Power & Light Co., 110 F.R.D. 511, 514 (M.D.N.C. 1986) (emphasis added).
40. Montgomery v. Leftwich, Moore & Douglas, 161 F.R.D. 224, 227 (D.D.C. 1995).
41. Sackman v. Liggett Group, Inc., 920 F. Supp. 357 (E.D.N.Y. 1996).
42. W. Trails, Inc. v. Camp Coast to Coast, Inc., 139 F.R.D. 4 (D.D.C. 1991).
43. *Id.* at 11.
44. *Id. See also* Bank Hapoalim, B.M. v. Am. Home Assur. Co., No. 92 Civ. 3561 (KMW), 1994 WL 119575 (S.D.N.Y. Apr. 6, 1994); *Spectrum*, 78 N.Y.2d at 380.
45. *Spectrum*, 78 N.Y.2d at 379 (holding that "an investigative report does not become privileged merely because it was sent to an attorney. Nor is such a report privileged merely because an investigation was conducted by an attorney."); *In re* Human Tissue Prods. Liab. Litig., Civ. No. 06-135, 2009 WL 1097671, at *2 (D.N.J. Apr. 23, 2009).
46. *See* OneBeacon Ins. Co. v. Forman Int'l, Ltd., No. 04 Civ. 2271 (RWS), 2006 WL 3771010, at *5 (S.D.N.Y. Dec. 15, 2006); *see also* Brooklyn Union Gas Co. v. Am. Home Assur. Co., 803 N.Y.S.2d 532 (N.Y. App. Div. 1st Dep't 2005); Tudor Ins. Co. v. McKenna Assocs., No. 01 Civ. 0115 (DAB) (JCF), 2003 WL 21488058 (S.D.N.Y. June 25, 2003).
47. Note Funding Corp. v. Bobian Inv. Co., No. 93 Civ. 7427, 1995 WL 662402 (S.D.N.Y. Nov. 9, 1995).
48. *Id.* at *2.
49. *Id.* at *3.
50. *Id.* at *3.
51. Diversey U.S. Holdings, Inc. v. Sara Lee Corp., No. 91 C 6234, 1994 WL 71462 (N.D. Ill. Mar. 3, 1994).
52. *Id.* at 1.
53. *Id.*
54. Ga.-Pac. Corp. v. GAF Roofing Mfg. Corp., No. 93 Civ. 5125 (RPP), 1996 U.S. Dist. LEXIS 671 (S.D.N.Y. Jan. 24, 1996).
55. *Id.*
56. *Id.* at 12.
57. Cooper-Rutter Assocs., Inc. v. Anchor Nat'l Life Ins. Co., 168 A.D.2d 663 (2d Dep't 1990).
58. *Id.* at 663.
59. *Id.*
60. *Id.*
61. *In re* Vioxx Prods. Liab. Litig., 501 F. Supp. 789, 800 (E.D. La. 2007).
62. *Id.* at 801.
63. *In re* Seroquel Prods. Liab. Litig., No. 6:06-md-1769-Orl-22DAB, 2008 U.S. Dist. LEXIS 39467, at *104–05 (M.D. Fla. May 7, 2008).
64. Washington v. Am. Tobacco Co., No. 96-2-15056-8 SEA, 1997 WL 728262 (Wash. Super. Nov. 21, 1997).
65. *Id.* at *14.
66. *Id.* at *3.

67. *Id.* at *14.
68. United States v. Northrop Grumman Corp., No. 89 C 6111, 2002 WL 31478259 (N.D. Ill. Nov. 5, 2002).
69. *Id.* at *1.
70. Freeport-McMoRan Sulphur LLC v. Mike Mullen Energy Equip. Res., Inc., No. Civ. A. 03-1496, 2004 WL 1488665 (E.D. La. June 30, 2004); *see also In re* Grand Jury Proceedings, 33 F.3d 342 (4th Cir. 1994).
71. 33 F.3d 342 (4th Cir. 1994).
72. *Id.* at 354 (quoting *In re* Grand Jury 83-2 John Doe No. 462 (Under Seal), 748 F.2d 875 (4th Cir. 1984)).
73. *Id.*
74. *Compare* Jack Winter, Inc. v. Koratron Co., 54 F.R.D. 44 (N.D. Cal. 1971), *with* Knogo Corp. v. United States, 213 U.S.P.Q. 936 (Ct. Cl. Trial Div. 1980). *See also* Probert v. Clorox Corp., 258 F.R.D. 491, 497–98 (D. Utah 2009) (comparing *Winter* and *Knogo*).
75. *Jack Winter*, 54 F.R.D. 44; Hercules Inc. v. Exxon Corp., 434 F. Supp. 136 (D. Del. 1977).
76. Knogo Corp. v. United States, No. 194-79, 1980 U.S. Ct. Cl. LEXIS 1262 (Ct. Cl. Feb. 16, 1980).
77. *Id.* at 10.
78. *Id.* at 4.
79. Advanced Cardiovascular Sys., Inc. v. C.R. Bard, Inc., 144 F.R.D. 372 (N.D. Cal. 1992).
80. Hewlett-Packard Co. v. Bausch & Lomb, Inc., 116 F.R.D. 533 (N.D. Cal. 1987).
81. *Advanced Cardiovascular Sys.*, 144 F.R.D. at 374 (reversing paradigm established in *Jack Winter*).
82. *Id.* at 375.
83. Neuder v. Battelle Pac. Nw. Nat'l Lab., 194 F.R.D. 289 (D.D.C. 2000).
84. *Id.* at 293 (quoting Marten v. Yellow Freight Sys., Inc., No. 96-2013-GTV, 1998 U.S. Dist. LEXIS 1249, at *8 (D. Kan. Jan. 13, 1998)); *see also* Hardy v. N.Y. News, Inc., 114 F.R.D. 633 (S.D.N.Y. 1987); Lindley v. Life Investors Ins. Co. of Am., 267 F.R.D. 382, 391 (N.D. Okla. 2010); *but see* Schmidt v. Levi Strauss & Co., No. C04-01026, 2007 U.S. Dist. LEXIS 14537 (N.D. Cal. Feb. 13, 2007).
85. Fine v. Facet Aerospace Prods. Co., 133 F.R.D. 439 (S.D.N.Y. 1990).
86. *Id.* at 444.
87. *In re* Arnold & McDowell, 566 F. Supp. 752 (D. Minn. 1983); Pollock v. United States, 202 F.2d 281 (5th Cir. 1953).
88. *In re Arnold*, 566 F. Supp. 752.
89. *Id.* at 755.
90. 202 F.2d 281 (5th Cir. 1953).
91. *Id.* at 286.
92. *In re* Vioxx Prods. Liab. Litig., 501 F. Supp. 789, 803 (E.D. La. 2007).
93. *Id.* at 805.
94. *Id.*
95. No. 06-1810-RMB-AMD, 2008 U.S. Dist. LEXIS 81053 (D.N.J. Sept. 30, 2008).
96. *Id.* at *41–42 (quoting *Vioxx*, 501 F. Supp. at 811–12).
97. *See generally* Teleglobe Commc'ns Corp. v. BCE, Inc. (*In re* Teleglobe Commc'ns Corp.), 493 F.3d 345, 353–54 (3d Cir. 2007).
98. *See id.* at 354.

99. *See id.*
100. *Id.* at 362.
101. *Id.*
102. *Id.* at 368.
103. *Id.* at 374.
104. *Id.* at 379–80.
105. 992 A.2d 65 (Pa. 2010).
106. *See* Nationwide Mut. Ins. Co. v. Fleming *(Nationwide I)*, 924 A.2d 1259 (Pa. Super. Ct. 2007).
107. *Nationwide I*, 924 A.2d at 1269.
108. 990 A.2d 1147 (Pa. 2010) (granting petition for appeal from Gillard v. AIG Ins. Co., 947 A.2d 836 (Pa. Super. Ct., 2008)).
109. Gillard v. AIG Ins. Co., No. 10 EAP 2010, 2011 WL 650552, at *11 (Pa. Feb. 23, 2011) (footnote omitted).
110. Case C-550/07P, Akzo Nobel Chemicals Ltd. & Akcros Chemicals Ltd. v. Commission, 2007 E.C.R. 11-03532 at 3549 ¶ 49.
111. N. Pacifica, LLC v. City of Pacifica, 274 F. Supp. 2d 1118, 1128–29 (N.D. Cal. 2003).
112. *In re* Ford Motor Co., 110 F.3d 954, 965–66 (3d Cir. 1997).
113. E. Norman Veasey & Christine T. DiGuglielmo, *The Tensions, Stresses, and Professional Responsibilities of the Lawyer for the Corporation*, 62 Bus. Law. 1 (2006).
114. *Id.* (quoting Marc I. Steinberg, *The Role of Inside Counsel in the 1990s: A View from Outside*, 49 SMU L. Rev. 483, 494 (1996)).
115. United States. v. Int'l Bus. Machs. Corp., 66 F.R.D. 206 (S.D.N.Y. 1974).
116. *Id.* at 212–13.
117. *Id.* Preferred Care Partners Holding Corp. v. Humana, Inc., 258 F.R.D. 684, 689 (S.D. Fla. 2009).
118. *Id.; see also In re* Vioxx Prods. Liab. Litig., 501 F. Supp. 2d 789, 805 (E.D. La. 2007).
119. United States v. BDO Seidman, LLP, 492 F.3d 806, 815 (7th Cir. 2007).
120. *In re* Leslie Controls, Inc., 437 B.R. 493, 497 (Bankr. D. Del. 2010).
121. Carl Zeiss Vision Int'l v. Signet Armorlite, Inc., Civil No. 07-cv-0894-DMS (POR), 2009 U.S. Dist. LEXIS 111877, at *24 (S.D. Cal. Dec. 1, 2009) (citing Teleglobe Commc'ns Corp. v. BCE, Inc. (*In re* Teleglobe Commc'ns Corp.), 493 F.3d 345, 364–65 (3d Cir. 2007)).
122. *See* Doctor's Assocs. v. QIP Holder LLC, 3:06CV01710 (VLB), 2009 U.S. Dist. LEXIS 55270, at *11 (D. Conn. Feb. 26, 2009) ("Just because there is an agreed common interest . . . does not make a communication or document privileged. That doctrine only eliminates waiver."); Allied Irish Banks, p.l.c. v. Bank of Am., N.A., 252 F.R.D. 163, 171 (S.D.N.Y. 2008) ("Before a communication can be protected under the common interest rule, the communication must meet the elements of the attorney-client privilege . . . [C]ase law has repeatedly held that communications regarding business matters—even where litigation is pending or imminent—do not qualify for protection from discovery under the common interest rule" (internal citation omitted)).
123. There is very little case law guidance on this issue, but at least one court, in the bankruptcy context, has declined to enforce this type of agreement as contrary to bankruptcy public policy. *In re* Ginn-LA St. Lucie Ltd. v. Ginn-LA Quail W. Ltd., 439 B.R. 801 (Bankr. S.D. Fla. 2010). The Restatement (Third) of the Law Governing Lawyers suggests that such agreements may be enforceable, but it

admits that "no authority has been found for dealing with the enforceability of agreements among members of a common-interest arrangement that the privilege shall be preserved, even in subsequent adverse proceedings between them." § 76, cmt. f (2000); *see also id.* at § 75, cmt. d ("[n]o direct authority has been found for giving effect to agreements among co-clients that the privilege shall be preserved in subsequent adverse proceedings between them").

124. *See* N. River Ins. Co. v. Columbia Cas. Co., 90 Civ. 2518 (MJL), 1995 U.S. Dist. LEXIS 53 (S.D.N.Y. Jan. 5, 1995); *see also* Cont'l Cas. Co. v. St. Paul Surplus Lines Ins. Co., 265 F.R.D. 510 (E.D. Cal. 2010); Remington Arms Co. v. Liberty Mut. Ins. Co., 142 F.R.D. 408 (D. Del. 1992); Bituminous Cas. Corp. v. Tonka Corp., 140 F.R.D. 381 (D. Minn. 1992); Metro. Life Ins. Co. v. Aetna Cas. & Sur. Co., 249 Conn. 36, 730 A.2d 51 (Conn. 1999); Am. Re-Ins. Co. v. U.S. F.&G. Co., 40 A.D.3d 486, 837 N.Y.S.2d 616 (N.Y. App. Div. 2007).
125. 167 F.R.D. 447 (S.D. Cal. 1995).
126. *Id.* at 456.
127. *See, e.g.*, Zubulake v. UBS Warburg LLC, 229 F.R.D. 422, 431 (S.D.N.Y. 2004).
128. *See id.* at 432.
129. Major Tours, Inc. v. Colorel, No. 05-3091, 2009 U.S. Dist. LEXIS 68128, at *6 (D.N.J. Aug. 4, 2009); *see also* Muro v. Target Corp., 250 F.R.D. 350, 360 (N.D. Ill. 2007).
130. *See Major Tours*, 2009 U.S. Dist. LEXIS 68128, at *7.
131. *In re* eBay Seller Antitrust Litig., No. 07-01882, 2007 U.S. Dist. LEXIS 75498, at *7–8 (N.D. Cal. Oct. 2, 2007).
132. *Major Tours*, 2009 U.S. Dist. LEXIS 68128, at *7–8.

CHAPTER 3

Perspectives on the Attorney-Client Privilege and the Work-Product Doctrine

ALLAN KANNER
TIBOR NAGY

I. Introduction

Privileges limit the obligations of a party or nonparty to produce otherwise proper discovery. Two of the oldest and most universally accepted privileges are the attorney-client privilege and the work-product doctrine. Historically, these privileges have reflected a balance between the goal of full disclosure at trial[1] and the facilitation of our adversary system of justice, in particular the need for unfettered communication with counsel and the protection of attorney work product.

As times change, however, greater importance is being placed on judicial management, particularly in complex cases. Concerns about efficiency and fair results have led courts to seek the truth as directly as possible, pushing the discovery-privilege balance toward greater disclosure. The balance has been further pushed by increasing efforts by industry to involve attorneys in managing risk,[2] on the one hand, and by government to regulate with greater disclosure and reporting requirements, on the other.[3] Cultural aversion to lawyer secrecy and lawyer complicity in client wrongdoing no doubt has also had an impact.[4] This essay explores the changes driven by these phenomena. We focus on three particular privilege contexts: (1) the evolving role of corporate counsel and changing conceptions of secrecy; (2) the use of the crime-fraud exception to the attorney-client privilege and work-product doctrine; and (3) attorney contact with former corporate employees. In each context, new problems have pushed courts to seek answers by falling back on the policy underlying the privileges, which, in turn, has led to a trend of greater disclosure in discovery.

II. The Attorney-Client Privilege and the Work-Product Doctrine

Privileges exist to promote social policy. If the privilege is abused, there ceases to be a justification for it.[5] The modern justification for the husband-wife privilege, for example, "is its perceived role in fostering the harmony and sanctity of the marriage relationship."[6] If, however, this justification does not actually apply in a given case—if, for example, the marriage is a sham or the contested testimony concerns spousal abuse—the privilege gives way, "in the light of reason and experience," to the general rule of full disclosure.[7]

Similarly, the attorney-client privilege and the work-product doctrine are not absolute privileges. Unlike the husband-wife privilege or the physician-patient privilege, the attorney-client privilege and the work-product doctrine serve the specific purpose of facilitating the proper functioning of our civil and criminal justice systems, and not some purpose independent of the law. Thus, when applying either the attorney-client privilege or the work-product doctrine would not actually further the legitimate ends of our justice system, courts should and have recognized exceptions.

A. The Attorney-Client Privilege

A classic statement of the reason for the attorney-client privilege appears in *Swidler & Berlin v. United States*:

> The attorney-client privilege is one of the oldest recognized privileges for confidential communications. The privilege is intended to encour-

age "full and frank communications between attorneys and their clients and thereby promote broader public interests in the observance of law and the administration of justice."[8]

Given this purpose, the primary factual question relative to the application of the attorney-client privilege is, why did the attorney and client communicate? Generally, if the communication was the result of the client's lawfully seeking and the attorney's lawfully rendering legal services, the privilege applies. If, however, the communication was the result of the client's seeking to conceal a past crime or to perpetrate a future one, protecting the confidentiality of the communication no longer serves the purpose of the attorney-client privilege and the privilege does not apply.[9] Other exceptions to the privilege have been similarly developed by the courts in a purposive fashion.[10]

In keeping with this purposive approach, the party asserting the attorney-client privilege has the burden of proving its existence; blanket claims of privilege will not suffice.[11] The elements of the privilege under federal law are as follows:

(1) the asserted holder of the privilege is or sought to become a client; and
(2) the person to whom the communication was made
  (a) is a member of a bar or a court, or his agent/subordinate, and
  (b) in connection with this communication is acting as a lawyer or assisting communication between the attorney and client; and
(3) the communication relates to a fact of which the attorney was informed
  (a) by his client, and
  (b) without the presence of strangers, and
  (c) for the purpose of securing primarily either
    (i) an opinion on law or
    (ii) legal services or
    (iii) assistance in some legal proceeding, and
    (iv) not for the purpose of committing a crime or tort; and
(4) the privilege has been
  (a) claimed and
  (b) not waived by the client[12]

As these elements make clear, the attorney-client privilege applies not only to statements made to the attorney, but also to statements made to the attorney's agents in the course of the representation.[13] If the privilege applies, furthermore, the communications are rendered *inadmissible*, and not simply undiscoverable.[14]

The traditional rule regarding the privilege when the client is a corporation was stated in *Philadelphia v. Westinghouse Electric Corp.*: an employee's statement to corporate counsel is not privileged unless the employee "is in a position to control or even to take a substantial part in a decision about any action which the corporation may take upon the advice of an attorney, or he is an authorized member of a body or group which has that authority."[15] In *Upjohn v. United States*, the Supreme Court rejected this so-called control group test and held that the attorney-client privilege could apply to lower-level employees.[16] The attorney-client privilege belongs to the client, however, and the corporate attorney-client privilege is no different: it can be asserted or waived only by an authorized corporate representative.[17] It therefore also extends to communications with former employees.[18]

The attorney-client privilege may not apply when the client puts an otherwise protected communication "at issue." One version of the "at issue" exception, enunciated in *Hearn v. Rhay*, states that a party may be deemed to have waived the privilege where

(1) assertion of privilege was a result of some affirmative act, such as filing suit;
(2) through this affirmative act, the asserting party put protected information at issue by making it relevant to the case; and
(3) application of privilege would deny opposing party access to information vital to its defense.[19]

Thus, under this version of the exception, the mere placing of a party's state of mind at issue in litigation results in waiver. For example, prison officials who raise the affirmative defense of immunity waive the attorney-client privilege with respect to communications bearing on their knowledge of prisoners' constitutional rights.[20] Another version of the "at issue" exception requires a showing of overt and explicit reliance on the advice of counsel to trigger waiver. Thus, for example, an insured consumer product manufacturer does not necessarily waive the attorney-client privilege with respect to advice from its counsel simply by bringing a declaratory action for coverage, even though its state of mind is in issue and the contested communications are highly relevant.[21]

However, while *Hearn* is widely considered the controlling test regarding the "at issue" exception, it has come under recent criticism. The Second Circuit in *In re County of Erie* recently criticized *Hearn*'s rationale that an assertion of privilege by one who pleads a claim or affirmative defense "puts the protected information at issue by making it relevant to the case," because in the Second Circuit's view, "privileged information may be in some sense *relevant* in any lawsuit."[22] Instead, the Second Circuit in *County of Erie* held that "a party must *rely* on privileged advice from his counsel to make his claim or defense."[23]

B. The Work-Product Doctrine

The work-product doctrine affords protection to materials prepared by an attorney or her agent in anticipation of litigation or for use in trial.[24] It is therefore distinct from and broader than the attorney-client privilege. In the civil context, the doctrine is codified in Federal Rule of Civil Procedure 26(b)(3), which provides that "the court shall protect against disclosure of the mental impressions, conclusions, opinions, or legal theories of an attorney or other representative of a party concerning the litigation."

In contrast to the confidentiality rationale underlying the attorney-client privilege, the work-product doctrine is based primarily on an antifreeloader principle. The Advisory Committee for the 1970 amendments to Rule 26(b), for example, noted that each side to litigation "should be encouraged to prepare independently" and that "one side should not automatically have the benefit of the detailed preparatory work of the other side."[25] As one court has put it, "[t]he immunity for this class of document is little more than an 'anti-freeloader' rule designed to prohibit one adverse party from riding to court on the enterprise of the other."[26] One way to think of the distinction between the two privileges is to consider the following. If the attorney-client privilege applies, the relevant information is rendered *inadmissible*, in keeping with the need to preserve the confidentiality of attorney-client communications. If, on the other hand, the work-product doctrine and not the attorney-client privilege applies, the relevant information is not necessarily inadmissible at all; indeed, it may be centrally relevant and very much admissible at trial. It would, however, generally not be subject to *discovery*. The adverse party would have to do its own work to obtain the information.

Furthermore, in order to be protected by the work-product doctrine, the documents or items must have been prepared "in anticipation of litigation or for trial."[27] Where documents are prepared with more than one purpose in mind, it will be considered work product only if "the primary motivating purpose" behind its preparation was "to aid in possible future litigation."[28] Controversy arises when the privilege is invoked for something done, arguably, in anticipation of litigation and not involving the skills of an attorney preparing for trial. For example, many businesses are increasingly subject to government reporting requirements, or routinely receive reports in the course of business.[29] These matters almost certainly are not privileged, despite the fact that in-house counsel are typically involved.[30] Likewise, the fact that a corporation sought an expert's opinion about the safety of a device does not in itself make that opinion work product. If the opinion was obtained prior to any particular litigation being anticipated, the work-product objection is not proper.

An early recognition of this is found in *Moran v. Pittsburgh-Des Moines Steel Co.*,[31] a wrongful death action arising out of the explosion of a liquefied gas tank constructed by defendants. The plaintiff in that case encountered objections when her attorney tried, during a deposition, to probe the thought processes of the employee responsible for the final approval of the design and materials used in building the tank. Overruling these objections, the court stressed that this expert was not someone specially retained to form an opinion on a given set of facts, but rather was the one "who decided all matters for the adverse party in the creation of the object from which the cause of action arises."[32] In the setting of this lawsuit, the expert's opinion was actually an ingredient of the events giving rise to the litigation.

> Although the answers to these [deposition] questions will carry the opinion of the witness, it will amount to a statement of facts as to why certain things were done, or not done, by the defendants. Unless this information is made available, and this is the one person who knows, a full and complete picture will not be presented when consideration is given as to whether negligence or lack of care existed in the construction of said tank.[33]

Material that is prepared, or knowledge that is obtained as part of any organization's normal course of business, is not work product because it cannot be said to have been prepared "primarily" to aid in possible future litigation.[34] The work-product objection is not proper, and should not be asserted, where the discovery requested asks for underlying factual information in defendant's possession.[35]

III. Investigations by In-House and Outside Counsel

The growing practice of risk management and the increasingly important role of counsel in the everyday life of corporations in highly regulated industries appear to blur the already vague conception of what it means to say something is being done "in anticipation of trial." Some defendants are attempting to argue that the product of such self-analysis—which has been called the "Pinto privilege," since it would protect documents akin to those in the famous *Pinto* case—should be privileged in order to encourage such socially beneficial contemplation. This increased reliance upon the services of in-house counsel has caused courts to reevaluate the scope of the attorney-client and work-product privileges in this area. Initially, it is recognized that no legal difference exists between the application of these privileges to in-house and outside counsel.[36] Nevertheless, as the tasks of in-house counsel grow more diversified, parties seeking full disclosure of the allegedly protected information have sought to distinguish the applicability of the privileges to the various roles played by counsel. At one extreme, for example, is the in-house litigator who is doing a job not unlike his or her outside colleague, such as trial preparation in a matter in litigation. At the other extreme is the individual who has a law degree but is essentially doing a business job that could be accomplished by an MBA graduate. Clearly, communications with the in-house litigator are easily evaluated under the traditional attorney-client privilege. Similarly, the business work of a corporate employee who happens to have a law degree is easily determined not to be privileged. The difficult question is, how, if at all, should the attorney-client privilege apply when the employee's role is part lawyer, part business executive?

The traditional law-business dichotomy has eroded substantially in regulated fields. For example, a business team in a regulated telecommunications company may include a lawyer who is giving strategic advice one moment and legal advice the next. Similarly, an attorney may be in the environmental department of a manufacturing concern as part of a compliance team as opposed to the general counsel's office. Is such an attorney an environmental professional or counselor, or both? The process has come to be much less formal than the traditional image of getting an opinion from counsel.

A. The Changing Role of In-House Counsel

The role of in-house counsel is undergoing a radical transformation that warrants reexamination of certain traditional ideas about the proper application of the attorney-client privilege. In short, the factual underpinnings of *Upjohn Co. v. United States*[37] may no longer exist in all cases. Consider, for example, the roles played by Stephen D. Ramsey, an attorney who is employed as vice president of corporate environmental programs for General Electric. Ramsey is not only an attorney, but also both the most knowledgeable person at GE regarding the company's environmental hazardous substances and cleanup policies and the head of GE personnel responsible for executing those policies. In May 1990, *The American Lawyer* interviewed GE's general counsel, Benjamin Heinman, who said that he lured Ramsey in house for what he described as "not just a legal job. . . . He'll be running a whole environmental area." *The American Lawyer* also interviewed Ramsey himself and reported that his job entailed

> creating, developing, and managing environmental programs. He'll oversee 30 people, including engineers, technicians, and ten lawyers. "I'll be ensuring that GE *at a corporate and business level* is doing everything they can to comply with existing laws and governmental regulations and [where possible] *to go beyond that*," adds Ramsey.
>
> * * *
>
> Ramsey says he plans to help craft policies to govern waste management and pollutant levels at GE's numerous facilities abroad.[38]

In fact, GE's own press release of April 3, 1990, quoted GE chairman John F. Welch, Jr. as saying "Steve Ramsey's strong environmental background and proven track record will be extremely valuable in leading an environmental effort that *will involve all employees at every level of the company*." The press release also said: "He will be responsible for ensuring consistent state-of-the-art environmental practices across the company's 13 key businesses in both the U.S. and abroad and for public policy issues involving the environment."[39]

Ramsey's job, and those of an increasing number of executives, clearly involve an intimately interwoven set of issues. In some cases, it is possible to distinguish an in-house counsel's attorney responsibilities from his or her business or administrative ones. For example, in *United States v. Lipshy*,[40] the defendant Lipshy was both senior vice president and acting general counsel of the Zale Corporation. In response to allegations of misconduct made by a previous officer of Zale, the corporation requested Lipshy to serve as counsel to an ad hoc committee formed to investigate the allegations. In this capacity, Lipshy conducted interviews of company officers and employees. The court noted that although Lipshy signed the investigative report he submitted to Zale's Board of Directors as "Senior Vice President," such a title was not descriptive of his function in conducting the examination. Rather, the court analyzed Lipshy's investigation in the context in which it was performed—for the "purpose of obtaining information needed to advise the Committee in the legal implication of charges of misconduct"—and found it to be privileged.[41]

Nevertheless, courts have experienced some difficulty in determining whether communications sought to be shielded by the privilege involve business or legal advice. The task becomes particularly problematic when business and legal considerations are intertwined. While this factor will not destroy the privilege, commingling of legal and business advice provokes closer scrutiny of the communications. For example, in *SCM Corporation v. Xerox Corp.*,[42] the chief executive officer and president of Xerox Corporation, in response to questions concerning the business reasons for granting or refusing to grant licenses, testified that the reasons were so intertwined with legal advice that he could not answer without disclosing privileged communications. This tactic did not thwart the court's inquiry, however. While recognizing that the "mere mention" of business considerations was not sufficient to compel disclosure of otherwise privileged communications, the court noted that when the ultimate decisions required exercise of business judgment, the "relevant nonlegal considerations incidental to the formulation of legal advice were business reasons and not privileged."[43] The court reasoned that such considerations

> are like any other business evaluations and motivations and do not enjoy protection because they are alluded to by conscientious counsel. To protect the business components in the decisional process would be a distortion of the privilege. The attorney-client privilege was not intended to encourage businessmen to discuss basic reasons for a particular course of action.[44]

Because the witness could not isolate the separate business and legal aspects, he was ordered to answer the objectionable questions in an affidavit to be submitted for in camera inspection, and he was further ordered to describe in the affidavit his decision-making process in order to enable the court to determine whether the business considerations were incidental to the legal consultation. Thus, although business interests might be influenced by legal considerations, the business concerns were subject to disclosure, even though the legal advice from counsel was protected.

Not all courts have required the production of mixed legal and business communications, however. In *Sealy Mattress Co. of N.J., Inc. v. Sealy, Inc.*,[45] defendants sought the return of a letter authored by counsel for defendant and inadvertently produced during expedited discovery. The court, while recognizing plaintiff's claim that the letter contained business advice that was not privileged, nonetheless stated:

> [T]he January 6, 1987 letter contains an admixture of business and legal advice that is not readily divisible into separate categories. Indeed, any effort to parse the advice which is "legal" from that which is "business" would be hazardous at best. Accordingly, the letter must be treated as one to which the privilege would attach, subject, of course, to any exceptions to the attorney-client privilege that may apply.[46]

Thus, while the entire document would not be within the scope of the attorney-client privilege under *SCM Corp.* because it contained a mixture of business and legal advice, it would be within the attorney-client privilege under *Ohio-Sealy*.

B. The Use of Outside Counsel in Internal Investigations

One way to increase the likelihood that communications conveyed during an internal investigation will be protected by the attorney-client privilege is to use outside counsel. *Diversified Industries, Inc. v. Meredith*[47] illustrates the point. In that case the court upheld a corporation's claim of privilege for a report by outside counsel who had been retained to investigate bribery charges. The report of the investigation, which was based on interviews of employees and an analysis of data compiled by an accounting firm, evaluated the corporation's conduct and issued recommendations.

The court first noted that the fact that the matter was referred by the corporation to a law firm was *prima facie evidence* for the purpose of obtaining legal advice, "absent a clear showing to the contrary."[48] The court noted that the mandate of the firm was to conduct a full "professional investigation."[49] For example, the firm was authorized to interview any employee of the corporation who might have knowledge of the facts. "Perhaps most importantly, it was given the authority to analyze the accounting data, to evaluate and draw conclusions as to the propriety of past actions and to make recommendations for possible future courses of action."[50] The court also noted that, although "[a]ccountants could have been hired by Diversified to audit the books and lay investigators could have been employed to interview employees . . . neither could have had the training, skills and background necessary to make the independent analysis and recommendations which the Board felt was essential to the future welfare of the corporation."[51]

For the purpose of planning such investigations, furthermore, the dissent in this case is instructive. The dissent focused on the minutes of board meetings at which the law firm was hired as an investigator, not as a legal counsel, and the fact that the report consisted primarily of a description of the investigation. It was also noted that the "recommendations could have been made by any firm of private investigators, or by accountants, or by bankers, or, for that matter, by any person possessing ordinary common sense and business prudence."[52]

Thus, courts are likely to examine whether the information sought and acted upon by counsel involved the application of law to facts or the rendering of an opinion of law in response to the client's legal inquiries. While there is formally no legal distinction between in-house and outside counsel for the purpose of the attorney-client privilege, the activities of in-house counsel will probably be subjected to closer scrutiny. Accordingly, where in-house counsel performs all or part of the investigation or the preparation of the report, care should be taken to substantiate that he is acting in a legal, rather than business, capacity. If outside counsel are retained, it should be made clear that *legal* services are an integral part of their duties.

C. Changing Conceptions of Secrecy

Although courts have traditionally espoused doctrines averse to secrecy,[53] recent trends have increased this aversion and have led to the creation of new rules governing confidentiality and the lawyer-client relationship. For example, in *Pansy v. Borough of Stroudsburg*, the Third Circuit held that local newspapers had standing to intervene and challenge a confidentiality order entered by the district court in facilitating a settlement in an employment discrimination suit.[54] After commenting on "the widespread and increasing use by district courts of confidentiality orders to facilitate settlements, and the consequential sacrifice of public access to the information deemed confidential by such orders,"[55] the court held that the district court had abused its discretion in granting and maintaining the order of confidentiality:

> [S]imply because courts have the power to grant orders of confidentiality does not mean that such orders may be granted arbitrarily. Disturbingly, some courts routinely sign orders which contain confidentiality clauses without considering the propriety of such orders, or the countervailing public interests which are sacrificed by the orders. Because defendants request orders of confidentiality as a condition of settlement, courts are willing to grant these requests in an effort to facilitate settlement without sufficiently inquiring into the potential public interest in obtaining information concerning the settlement agreement.[56]

Every circuit court that has considered the question has come to the conclusion that nonparties may permissively intervene for the purpose of challenging confidentiality orders.[57] Furthermore, the indiscriminate issuance of confidentiality orders and the resulting secrecy of information generated through judicial proceedings have become increasingly disfavored in the courts.[58]

The recent wave of corporate scandals and the resulting backlash have added to this antisecrecy trend, and it is now clear that new rules are likely to govern the confidentiality of communications between attorneys and clients. In 2003, the American Bar Association voted to adopt amendments to its Model Rules of Professional Conduct, including amendments to Model Rule 1.6, Confidentiality of Information, and Model Rule 1.13, Organization as Client.[59] As amended, Rule 1.6 permits an attorney to release information to enable affected persons or authorities "to prevent the client from committing a crime or fraud that is reasonably certain to result in substantial injury to the financial interests or property of another and in furtherance of which the client has used or is using the lawyer's services." Previously the rule allowed lawyers to reveal information related to the representation of a client only if such a disclosure was believed necessary to prevent "reasonably certain death or substantial bodily harm." The amended rule thus brings lawyers' duty of confidentiality into conformance with the prevailing scope of the attorney-client privilege.[60]

Model Rule 1.13, which governs attorneys' duties of confidentiality with respect to organizational clients, now provides that if a lawyer representing a corporation or other organization "knows" that a corporate officer or employee is engaged in a violation of law that is likely to result in "substantial injury" to the organization, "then the lawyer shall proceed as is reasonably necessary in the best interest of the organization." In addition, unless the lawyer "reasonably believes that it is not necessary in the best interest of the organization to do so, the lawyer shall refer the matter to higher authority in the organization, including, if warranted by the circumstances, to the highest authority that can act on behalf of the organization as determined by applicable law."

Amended Model Rule 1.13(c) further provides that if internal up-the-ladder reporting fails to elicit an appropriate response to the violation, "then the lawyer may reveal information relating to the representation whether or not Rule 1.6 permits such disclosure, but only if and to the extent the lawyer reasonably believes necessary to prevent substantial injury to the organization." The new rule thus allows disclosure of confidential information to *outsiders* in appropriate circumstances. The old rule allowed lawyers to resign from the representation, but stopped short of allowing them to report the wrongdoing to outsiders. Significantly, Rule 1.13(d) makes clear that permission to report wrongdoing outside the organization does not apply when a lawyer has been engaged by the organization to investigate an alleged violation of law or to defend an organization or corporate officer accused of violating the law.

Although the practical effect of the amendments is yet to be seen,[61] they clearly respond to the increasing aversion to lawyer secrecy and perceived complicity in corporate client wrongdoing. Courts applying rules modeled after Rule 1.13(d), centrally important to internal investigations, are likely to have to confront the issues raised earlier in this part.

IV. The Crime-Fraud Exception

Regardless of whether in-house or outside counsel are involved, there has been a pronounced trend toward utilizing an exception to the attorney-client privilege and the work-product doctrine that is recognized both under federal law and in all 50 states: the crime-fraud exception. The crime-fraud exception has played a critical role in tobacco litigation,[62] and, in the wake of an atmosphere of corporate scandals, the doctrine was recently given new force in the amendments to the Model Rules of Professional Conduct discussed above.[63] Perhaps most significantly, courts have increasingly adopted evidentiary standards that give more meaningful effect to this exception to the attorney-client privilege.

A. Origin and Purpose

It has often been noted that the attorney-client privilege is the oldest and most universally accepted privilege recognized by the common law.[64] The crime-fraud exception, in turn, is perhaps the oldest and most universally accepted exception to the privilege. Wigmore's treatise begins its discussion of the crime-fraud exception with the following:

> It has been agreed from the beginning that the privilege cannot avail to protect the client in concerting with the attorney a crime or other evil enterprise. This is for the logically sufficient reason that no such enterprise falls within the just scope of the relation between adviser and client.[65]

The purpose of the crime-fraud exception, then, is straightforward: clients should not be able to use legal advice to perpetrate or plan unlawful activity and then use the privilege as a shield from disclosure.[66] In the words of the leading Supreme Court opinion, "the purpose of the crime-fraud exception [is] to assure that the 'seal of secrecy' between lawyer and client does not extend to communications made for the purpose of getting advice for the commission of a fraud or crime."[67]

B. Scope of the Exception

While the purpose of the exception is straightforward, its precise scope is not. As a general rule, otherwise privileged communications are not protected if they are meant to further future or ongoing criminal or fraudulent conduct, including other wrongful conduct such as intentional torts.[68] There are, furthermore, several well-established principles regarding the exception's application. Communications regarding *past* crime or fraud are within the attorney-client privilege.[69] The attorney-client privilege, furthermore, "is strongest where a client seeks counsel's advice to determine the legality of conduct before taking action."[70] When, however, a client seeks advice for the purpose of furthering a *present* or *future* crime or fraud, or for the purpose of *concealing* a past crime or fraud, the exception applies and the communications are not privileged.[71] Finally, it is well established that the attorney's innocence is irrelevant when applying the crime-fraud exception. The focus is on the client's conduct and intentions.[72]

A significant difference, however, can be found among jurisdictions as to what conduct falls within the exception. Several courts have adopted a strict, technical version of the exception: the conduct in question must satisfy statutorily or judicially recognized elements of a particular crime or fraud.[73] Under this view, for example, a client who sought advice for the purpose of engaging in "inequitable conduct" in the course of prosecuting a patent application—which, under the substantive patent law, would mean the client forfeits the right to enforce the patent—would still receive the benefit of the attorney-client privilege, so long as the conduct did not meet all of the technical elements of common law fraud (for example, the privilege challenger can prove *scienter* but cannot prove reliance by the Patent and Trademark Office).[74]

Most courts today, however, apply a broader view of the crime-fraud exception.[75] Thus, in these jurisdictions, legal advice sought with fraudulent intent does not receive the benefit of the attorney-client privilege, regardless of whether the client happens to succeed in inducing reliance. In the patent application scenario discussed above, for example, the party who had engaged in inequitable conduct before the Patent and Trademark Office would not receive the benefit of the privilege, even if the privilege challenger could not prove reliance.

Similarly, the existence of potential defenses to criminal or tortious conduct does not necessarily preclude application of the crime-fraud exception, as illustrated by a 2000 decision from the Fifth Circuit.[76] In *In re Grand Jury Subpoena* the government argued that certain documents, which had been inadvertently disclosed, revealed that the defendant corporation had used its counsel to help it conceal the extent of its noncompliance with environmental regulations from state and federal regulators. In response, the corporation argued that the existence of potential defenses to the alleged violations precluded application of the crime-fraud exception to its claim of attorney-client privilege.[77] After considering both claims, Judge Robert Parker noted:

> While the targets of this investigation may have valid defenses that preclude indictment or conviction for fraud or criminal environmental violations, the existence of a potential defense does not mean that the district court reversibly erred. . . . [A]ppellants' argument that they complied with one potentially valid interpretation of the regulations does not speak to whether the Government made out a prima facie case of fraud. . . . Therefore, we find no error in the district court's denial of Appellants' motion to quash subpoenas.[78]

This broader view of the crime-fraud exception is much more consistent with the policies on which the attorney-client privilege is based. As the Supreme Court has noted: "The attorney-client privilege is not without its costs. Since the privilege has the effect of withholding relevant information from the fact-finder, it applies only where necessary to achieve its purpose."[79] The scope of the attorney-client privilege, then, is not appropriately determined by technicalities but by considerations of substantive justice. Courts should not limit the exception to conduct that consists of statutorily or judicially defined elements of a particular crime or fraud. While such formal, legal notice of wrongful conduct is relevant to whether conduct can be held criminal, it plainly goes beyond what is required to achieve the purpose of the attorney-client privilege.

C. Evidentiary Standards

Another question that courts must confront in applying the crime-fraud exception is what evidentiary standards should be used. While courts have not adopted a single, definitive procedure for making crime-fraud exception determinations, there appears to be a well-established consensus that the parties seeking discovery need only meet a burden of making out a prima facie case of the underlying crime or fraud. Several courts, however, have adopted a rule that requires parties to show by a preponderance of the evidence that the exception applies. The policies underlying the crime-fraud exception and the leading case law strongly suggest that the preponderance standard is the wrong rule and should not be followed.

In the federal courts, any consideration of the proper procedure for determining whether the crime-fraud exception applies must begin with *Zolin v. United States.*[80] Prior to the Supreme Court's opinion in *Zolin*, there was considerable controversy among the circuits about what evidence courts could consider in making a crime-fraud exception determination. The rule finally established in *Zolin* was clear: courts could consider "any relevant evidence, lawfully obtained, that has not been adjudicated to be privileged."[81] This, of course, includes the contested communications themselves, which are often the best evidence of their own true nature. Thus *Zolin* clearly established the propriety of in camera review of allegedly privileged communications.[82] Furthermore, the *Zolin* court specified that the party contesting the claim of privilege "must present evidence sufficient to support a reasonable belief that *in camera* review may yield evidence that establishes the exception's applicability."[83] Once this showing is made, however, the contested communications themselves "may provide the evidentiary basis for the ultimate showing that the crime-fraud exception applies."[84] That is, the court held that independent evidence of the crime or fraud was not required to apply the exception.

While *Zolin* established the requirement for obtaining in camera review of contested communications, it did not resolve the question of ultimate burden of proof, and different standards have emerged in the courts.[85] The most troubling of these standards holds that the party contesting the privilege must establish by a preponderance of the evidence that the crime-fraud exception applies. For example, in *Laser Industries, Ltd. v. Reliant Technologies, Inc.*, the district court recognized that the question of the burden of proof to be applied in making a crime-fraud exception determination "remains open."[86] The court, in a lengthy opinion that ruminates on the policies underlying the attorney-client privilege and the crime-fraud exception, held that in addition to the initial evidentiary showing described in *Zolin*, the party contesting the privilege should bear the ultimate burden of proof on the issue, that burden being a preponderance of the evidence.[87] This was the right decision, according to the court, for two reasons. First, placing the burden of proof on the alleged privilege holder would "impose unjustifiable burdens on courts," since shifting the burden of persuasion would make "the temptation to initiate such challenges

. . . considerable."[88] Second, this latter rule would "jeopardize" the attorney-client privilege because "counsel might feel pressured to disclose considerable information about those communications and the circumstances in which they were made in order to reduce the likelihood that the court would not find their explanations satisfactory."[89]

The *Laser Industries* court is wrong on both points. First, it is not at all clear that parties who have a good-faith belief that the crime-fraud exception applies will not, even if they bear the ultimate burden of proof, move ahead with their prima facie showing and request for in camera inspection under *Zolin*—at the very least they would be bringing the issue to the court's attention. Second, far from jeopardizing the attorney-client privilege, placing the burden of persuasion on the alleged privilege holder ensures that the privilege is not abused. This is so for at least two reasons. First, the general rule is and always has been that the party claiming the privilege has the burden of proving its existence.[90] That burden should include persuading the court that, after an opponent has made a prima facie showing of crime or fraud, the attorney-client communications were not made for unlawful purposes. Second, from a truth-seeking perspective it is plainly more efficient to place the burden of persuasion on the alleged privilege holder, since that party (1) has superior information on the nature of the communications and (2) is asking the court to prevent disclosure of relevant evidence precisely because of its nature. Finally, there is no merit to the *Laser Industries* court's concern that "counsel might feel pressured to disclose considerable information" about the communications: if the party seeking discovery can make the prima facie showing under *Zolin*, the alleged privilege holder is already required to disclose the most confidential information to the court—the statements themselves.

A better approach, and one much more consistent with the policies behind the attorney-client privilege and the crime-fraud exception, is the procedure used by the court in *Gutter v. E.I. DuPont de Nemours*.[91] In *Gutter*, a securities class action, the court held that the plaintiffs had established a prima facie case of fraud and then addressed the question of the appropriate burden of proof. After recognizing that "many courts have struggled with questions such as . . . the ultimate burden of proof,"[92] the court concluded that the appropriate procedure is as follows:

> [T]he party opposing the privilege on the crime-fraud exception has the initial burden of producing evidence which, if unexplained, would be *prima facie* proof of the existence of the exception. The burden of persuasion then shifts to the party asserting the privilege to give a reasonable explanation of its conduct.[93]

As discussed above, placing the burden of persuasion on the party claiming the privilege is more consistent with the truth-seeking function of the civil justice system. If the contested communications in *Gutter* really deserved the "seal of secrecy" of the attorney-client privilege, the defendants were clearly in the better position to so convince the court. Furthermore, as the *Gutter* court noted, the rule it adopted was "consistent with the general rule that the burden of proof to establish the existence of the attorney-client privilege rests on the party who claims the privilege."[94] In other words, the *Gutter* rule and not the rule in *Laser Industries* works to preserve the policy underlying the attorney-client privilege.

D. Building a Crime-Fraud Exception Argument in Mass Disaster Cases

As discussed above, the party seeking disclosure bears at least the burden of establishing a prima facie case that the crime-fraud exception applies. Because this entails demonstrating that communications or work product that has not even been disclosed was used for a particular purpose, the burden can be a difficult one, and the type of evidence that can be used is of particular interest. This is particularly so in the mass disaster context, where defendants' incentives to engage in cover-ups involving counsel, and to ensure that these cover-ups never come to light, are particularly high.

Perhaps the leading opinion on this issue is *In re A.H. Robins Co., Inc., "Dalkon Shield" IUD Products Liability Litigation*.[95] During the multidistrict litigation involving A.H. Robins's infamous intrauterine device, plaintiffs' counsel moved to compel production of five memoranda, known as the "Burke memoranda," that Robins claimed were protected by both the attorney-client privilege and the work-product doctrine. The "Burke memoranda" were drafted by Robins's attorneys, addressed to regional and district managers and sales representatives, and signed by one of Robins's vice presidents and, in one case, its general counsel. Robins claimed that all five memoranda requested information needed by counsel to defend it in litigation. Plaintiffs' counsel argued that the crime-fraud exception should be applied to Robins's claims of attorney-client privilege and work-product doctrine protection. In writing the order ultimately compelling production, Judge Theis noted: "The focal issue is whether the record reflects sufficient evidence to invoke the crime or fraud exception. The court does not offer any opinion as to the truth of the facts asserted in the pleadings. At this juncture, the court is concerned solely with applying the known facts to the plaintiffs' burden of establishing only a prima facie showing of crime or fraud."[96] The court applied Kansas law on the crime-fraud exception, which did not allow using the contested documents themselves as evidence that the exception should apply. The court was thus concerned solely with independent evidence of crime or fraud.

Plaintiffs sought first to establish that Robins had engaged in the fraud of misrepresenting the safety of its products to consumers and second to establish that Robins had used its counsel in furtherance of that fraud. The single most comprehensive piece of evidence offered by the plaintiffs was the report issued by the special masters who had been appointed to monitor and assist with discovery in related Dalkon litigation in the District of Minnesota. The masters had examined over 15,000 pages of documents that had been produced for in camera inspection. Over Robins's objections, Judge Theis took judicial notice of the report's conclusions, including the masters' determination that Robins had knowingly misrepresented the safety of its product and that a prima facie case of fraud had been established. As to the involvement of Robins's counsel, the masters reasoned as follows:

> Plaintiffs maintain that the ongoing scheme to misrepresent to the public the nature and efficacy of the Dalkon Shield was perpetuated in a cover up phase at the direction of William A. Forest, Jr., Secretary and General Counsel. It is clear from the various depositions and exhibits that the legal department was closely involved in questions of labeling, marketing, product characteristics, and dealings with the FDA, as well as litigation about the Dalkon Shield. Thus, it is a reasonable inference that corporate counsel was aware of the facts giving rise to the ongoing fraudulent scheme discussed above.[97]

The second piece of evidence, relied upon both in the masters' report and independently by Judge Theis, was Robins's conduct in other Dalkon Shield cases. The masters, for example, pointed to the decision in *Harre v. A.H. Robins*, in which the Eleventh Circuit concluded that a Robins expert witness had committed perjury with the complicity of counsel.[98] The masters stated, "We obviously do not rely on these decisions for our factual determinations in this matter, but they do tend to corroborate our finding of at least a prima facie case of a massive fraudulent scheme perpetrated on the public with the knowing assistance of members of the professional bar."[99] Similarly, Judge Theis concluded that

> Although Robins complains about the use of other proceedings as evidence of crime or fraud in the instant case, the court finds Robins [sic] procedural conduct in other cases to be relevant to the present motion. When the issue is whether Robins perpetrated a massive fraud to deceive the public, the cases across the country cannot be viewed as discrete and isolated instances.[100]

Accordingly, the court reviewed several cases from around the country in which plaintiffs had requested the same "secret" documents relating to Robins's testing of its product. The cases revealed a pattern of settling cases to avoid production of the documents; engaging in stalling tactics, including motions for reconsideration, motions for stay pending appeal, and petitions for writ of mandamus; and refusing outright to comply with orders for production. Judge Theis stated:

> While the court recognizes that Robins has an absolute duty to protect its client's interests, and although the various steps of defense may appear innocuous in isolation, when viewed collectively and in tan-

> dem with the evidence contained in the Masters' Report, the repeated delays and instances of nonproduction provide support for the application of the crime or fraud exception.[101]

Proceedings in other cases thus formed a critical part of the plaintiffs' prima facie case that the crime-fraud exception should apply, and there is no doubt that they heavily if not decisively influenced Judge Theis's ruling. A favorable report by a special master is obviously good evidence to have in making out a case for applying the crime-fraud exception. Plaintiffs' counsel, however, should also be sure to monitor and record the relevant activity of defendants' attorneys in other cases. To that end, litigation groups could prove especially helpful in winning the crime-fraud exception argument in mass disaster cases.

V. Communications with Former Employees

Modern courts have generally forbidden attorneys from communicating with represented persons outside the presence of their counsel. An issue that has received recent attention is how this general rule applies in the context of ex parte contact with a corporation's former employees. The rule most courts apply to this issue is Rule 4.2 of the ABA Model Rules of Professional Conduct:

> In representing a client, a lawyer shall not communicate about the subject of the representation with a person the lawyer knows to be represented by another lawyer in the matter, unless the lawyer has the consent of the other lawyer or is authorized to do so by a law or a court order.[102]

As is readily apparent, Rule 4.2 was created to protect the attorney-client relationship and privileged information which stems therefrom.[103] Comment 7 provides that consent from the organization's lawyer is not necessary to communicate with a former constituent of the organization, and a majority of courts have held that Rule 4.2 does not generally prohibit this type of contact. Where, however, privileged or otherwise confidential information is clearly implicated, courts have held that the rule bars ex parte contact with former employees. The extent to which such contact is barred, and the specific scenarios that trigger the bar, differ widely among the states.[104] Generally, typical scenarios in which ex parte contact would be barred include those in which the former employee had been in a managerial position or belonged to the control group during his employment; where the former employee had participated in the litigation or was otherwise exposed to relevant privileged or confidential information; or where the former employee's acts or omissions could be imputed to the organization for liability purposes.

One case that squarely addresses the issue of ex parte contacts with former employees and the application of Rule 4.2 is *In re Shell Oil Refinery*.[105] The case involved a plaintiff attorney's ex parte contact with an employee of Shell. In addition to providing general information, the employee secreted proprietary documents from Shell and gave them to the attorney.

In issuing a protective order prohibiting the plaintiff attorney from using documents obtained outside normal discovery channels and prohibiting further ex parte contact with this employee, the court noted the three categories of persons enumerated in the comment to Model Rule 4.2 that an attorney should treat as "parties" for the purpose of the rule:

1. persons with managerial responsibility;
2. any other person whose acts or omissions concerning the subject of the representation may be imputed to the organization for liability purposes; or,
3. whose statements may constitute admissions on the part of the organization.[106]

The court further stated that "[i]nformal interviews with employees of a corporate party can in certain circumstances be entirely appropriate. For example, under Rule 4.2 a low level employee whose conduct or scope of employment was not involved in the disputed events could be interviewed *ex parte* by adverse counsel." The court noted that if the communication had merely been an interview with the employee, the question would focus on whether or not the communication was with a "party."

Subsequent to the order issued above, Shell discovered the name of the employee who had secreted the information and thus terminated his employment. The court then amended the order to prohibit any ex parte communication with the now ex-employee, stating that the order should apply to him regardless of his status because although he presumably no longer had access to Shell documents, he was still able to convey proprietary information to the attorney.

The *Shell Oil* court's amendment to its ex parte communication order is indicative of courts' concern with preventing "disclosure of privileged information by the former employee."[107] Courts generally reason that because "[a] ny privilege existing between the former employee and the organization's counsel belongs to the organization, [the privilege] can only be waived by the organization."[108] That is, the attorney-client privilege operates to prevent disclosure of privileged information by former employees, and courts prohibit ex parte contacts with former employees to serve that end.[109] Whether or not the former employee possesses privileged material, however, is dealt with on a case-by-case basis.[110] If there is no risk of inappropriate disclosure or if the former employee can longer bind the corporation, ex parte contact with the former employee should not be prohibited.

In *Wright ex rel. Wright v. Group Health Hospital*, for example, the Washington Supreme Court held that since the former employees could no longer bind the corporation, they were entirely outside the restrictions on ex parte contact imposed by the state's version of Model Rule 4.2.[111] In *Wright* an injured child and his parents had sued a hospital and doctor, alleging that they committed malpractice in the mother's labor and delivery of the child. The family's lawyer asked for and received a list of nurses involved in caring for the mother, but counsel for the hospital advised the family's lawyer that he considered the nurses to be his clients and that the family's lawyer was to make no efforts to contact them. The family's lawyer disagreed and moved for a protective order confirming his right to conduct ex parte interviews of current and former employees as long as they were not managerial. Reversing a trial court order denying the motion, the Washington Supreme Court noted that the family's lawyer intended to interview nurses who, unlike the doctor, were not formally parties to the pending litigation, even though they were or had been employees of a party. The court observed that the issue presented a policy conflict between the need of the adverse attorney for information that might be in the corporation's exclusive possession but too expensive or impractical to obtain through formal discovery and the need of the corporation to protect itself. After reviewing a range of decisions on the topic, the court concluded that the best test was one that interpreted "party" to mean those employees with legal authority to speak for and bind the corporation. The court stated that, because former employees cannot possibly speak for a corporation, the general rule against ex parte contacts with represented parties did not apply to them.

Where the relevant concern for the organization is not that its former employees' statements can be imputed to it but rather the disclosure of information protected by the attorney-client privilege, courts have to balance the need for informal discovery in the civil justice system against the risk of violating the attorney-client privilege. In *G-I Holdings, Inc. v. Baron & Budd*, for example, the plaintiff, a holding company for former asbestos manufacturers, brought a civil RICO suit against a leading asbestos plaintiffs' law firm.[112] The holding company hired investigators to conduct ex parte interviews with the law firm's current and former employees, including paralegals and word processors. The law firm sought a protective order from the court, claiming that the interviews threatened to invade the attorney-client privilege between the firm and its clients. The court noted that

> It is consistent with time-honored and decision-honored principles that counsel for all parties have a right to interview an adverse party's witnesses (the witness willing) in private, without the presence or consent of opposing counsel and without a transcript being made. This principle applies to former employees of an adverse party. Indeed, *ex parte* interviews with such persons have been recognized as having an important role in information gathering in that former employees often have emotional or economic ties to their former employer and would sometimes be reluctant to come forward with potentially damaging information if they could only do so in the presence of the corporation's attorney.[113]

The court thus recognized both the legitimacy and the importance of ex parte contacts with former employees. Nevertheless, the court also recognized the countervailing interests:

> However, former employees who possess knowledge regarding privileged communications do present a "distinct problem" where *ex parte* interviews are concerned. One aspect of this problem is that, where the former employee is a lay person, it is unrealistic to think that he will know what information or communications are privileged, so that even where disclosure of such matters is not intended it may well occur inadvertently.[114]

The court then balanced the hardships and concluded that a protective order was required. Two factors were particularly significant: the former employees had been "extensively" exposed to privileged information; and "the investigators are themselves lay persons and, thus, are in little better position than the interviewees to assess whether privileged material is being disclosed."[115] Finally, the court considered the appropriate nature and scope of the protective order. It concluded that the parties had a choice: (1) no ex parte interviews could take place, and instead notice would have to be given to the defendant law firm, so that its counsel could be present during the interviews; or (2) the interviews would take place before a special master, who would monitor the interviews with respect to the issue of privilege.[116]

The *G-I Holdings* court thus gave adequate consideration to the concerns on both sides of the ex parte contacts dispute. The opinion illustrates two important points that must be considered when conducting ex parte interviews. First, interviews conducted by laypersons such as investigators are likely to be seen as posing a greater threat to privileged communications than those conducted by counsel. Second, courts are not likely to find the use of form questions or form warnings during such interviews to be adequate protection of privileged communications, particularly when the former employees are laypeople.[117] When ex parte interviews with former employees are necessary, attorneys should conduct the interviews themselves whenever possible. Furthermore, because former employees are often laypeople, adequate precautions must be taken to protect privileged information. Rather than using form questions, counsel should identify easily discernible *topics* and determine whether discussion of these topics threatens the asserted privilege. If not, ex parte interviews limited to these topics are entirely appropriate.

VI. Conclusion

In the landmark case of *United States v. Nixon*, the Supreme Court stated that "exceptions to the demand for every man's evidence are not lightly created nor expansively construed, for they are in derogation of the search for truth."[118] The attorney-client privilege and the work-product doctrine are two well-established exceptions to the demand for every man's evidence, exceptions considered essential to the proper functioning of our legal system. As our society changes, however, our legal system and the values that shape it change as well. Courts have reexamined the roles played by corporate attorneys, the propriety of keeping information generated through judicial proceedings secret, and the proper procedure for determining whether attorney-client communications occurred in furtherance of a crime or fraud. As this essay has shown, courts have typically dealt with these issues by taking a purposive approach to the attorney-client privilege and the work-product doctrine. The conclusions they have reached indicate a trend toward greater disclosure and toward narrowing the exceptions to the demand for every man's evidence.

Notes

1. Stated another way, the emphasis is on avoiding trial by ambush. *E.g.*, Herbert v. Lando, 441 U.S. 153, 177 (1979) ("the deposition-discovery rules are to be accorded a broad and liberal treatment to effect their purpose of adequately informing the litigants in civil trials").
2. *See, e.g.*, D.M. Osborne, *The Sidley-Heineman Connection*, AM. LAWYER (May 1990), discussed *infra.*
3. *See generally* Lance Cole, *Revoking Our Privileges: Federal Law Enforcement's Multi-Front Assault on the Attorney-Client Privilege (And Why It Is Misguided)*, 48 VILL. L. REV. 469 (2003).
4. *See, e.g.*, Seth Stern, *Attorneys Face New Rules on Secrets*, CHRISTIAN SCI. MONITOR, Aug. 13, 2003, http://www.csmonitor.com/2003/0813/p02s01-usju.html.
5. 8 J.H. WIGMORE, WIGMORE ON EVIDENCE § 2298, at 5777 (McNaughton rev. 1961) ("[I]t is difficult to see how . . . the law can protect a deliberate plan to defy the law and oust another person of his rights whatever the precise nature of those rights might be.").
6. Trammel v. United States, 445 U.S. 40, 44 (1980).
7. FED. R. EVID. 501.
8. 524 U.S. 399 (1998).
9. *See infra* discussion of the crime-fraud exception in section IV.
10. *See, e.g.*, Trammel v. United States, 445 U.S. 40, 44 (1980) (discussing development of spousal privilege).
11. United States v. Munoz, 233 F.3d 1117, 1128 (9th Cir. 2000); United States v. Graf, 610 F.3d 1148 (9th Cir. 2010).
12. Rhone-Poulenc Rorer, Inc. v. Home Indem. Co., 32 F.3d 851, 862 (3d Cir. 1994); Sullivan v. Warminster Tp., 2011 WL 780543 (E.D. Pa. Mar. 4, 2011).
13. *Id.; see also* Advanced Tech. Assoc., Inc. v. Herley Indus., Inc., 1996 WL 711018, at *5 (E.D. Pa. 1996); United States v. Kovel, 296 F.2d 918 (2d Cir. 1961) (communications to accountant that enabled attorney to prepare defense in tax fraud case were protected by privilege).
14. In contrast, if a communication is protected by the work-product doctrine, it is not necessarily inadmissible, but rather is rendered generally undiscoverable. *See infra* discussion in section II.B.
15. Philadelphia v. Westinghouse Elec. Corp., 210 F. Supp. 483, 485 (E.D. Pa. 1962).
16. Upjohn v. United States, 449 U.S. 383 (1981).

17. Commodity Futures Trading Comm'n v. Weintraub, 471 U.S. 343, 348 (1985).
18. Union Pac. R.R. Co. v. Mower, 219 F.3d 1069, 1072 n.2 (9th Cir. 2000); *see also infra* discussion of communications with former employees in section V.
19. Hearn v. Rhay, 68 F.R.D. 574, 581 (E.D. Wash. 1975).
20. *Id.*
21. Rhone-Poulenc Rorer Inc. v. Home Indem. Co., 32 F.3d 851 (3d Cir. 1994) (requiring overt and explicit reliance on advice of counsel to trigger waiver).
22. 546 F.3d 222, 229 (2d Cir. 2008).
23. *Id.; see also* Aristocrat Leisure Ltd. v. Deutsche Bank Trust Co. Ams., 2009 WL 3111766 (S.D.N.Y. 2009).
24. Hickman v. Taylor, 329 U.S. 495 (1947).
25. Fed. R. Civ. P. 26, advisory committee's note to 1970 Amendment, *reprinted in* 48 F.R.D. 487, 501 (1970).
26. Nat'l Union Fire Ins. v. Murray Sheet Metal, 967 F.2d 980, 985 (4th Cir. 1992).
27. A main feature of the 1970 amendments to the Federal Rules of Civil Procedure was the inclusion of explicit regulations where disclosures of work product are involved. Rule 26(b)(3) provides that even though "documents and tangible things" may be "otherwise discoverable" in that they are "relevant to the subject matter," where they were "prepared in anticipation of litigation or for trial," then discovery may be obtained "only upon a showing that the party seeking discovery has substantial need of the materials in the preparation of the party's case and that the party is unable without undue hardship to obtain the substantial equivalent of the materials by other means." Rule 26(b)(3) eschews the phrase "work product" and uses somewhat different phraseology in its description of the showing that must be made to obtain discovery in this area. The Federal Rule extends its protection to the product of the preparation activities not only of the party but also to any representative of the party, such as "[the party's] attorney, consultant, surety, indemnitor, insurer, or agent."
28. *See* Binks Mfg. Co. v. Nat'l Presto Indus., Inc., 709 F.2d 1109, 1119 (7th Cir. 1983); *In re* Leslie Fay Cos. Sec. Litig., 161 F.R.D. 274 (S.D.N.Y. 1995) (foreseeing litigation and conducting an internal investigation does not automatically qualify the investigative materials as work product), citing 8 Charles A. Wright, *et al.*, Federal Practice and Procedure § 2024 (2d ed. 1994).
29. *E.g.*, Allan Kanner, *Superfund and the Future of Toxic Tort Litigation*, 2 Toxics L. Rep. (BNA) 671 (Nov. 11, 1987).
30. *E.g.*, Nat'l Union Fire Ins. Co. v. Murray Sheet Metal Co., 967 F.2d 980, 984 (4th Cir. 1992); *see also* Burden-Meeks v. Welch, 319 F.3d 897, 899 (7th Cir. 2003) ("Federal law extends the privilege to communications about legal subjects, and it is hard to see why a business evaluation meets that description. Hiring lawyers to do consultants' work does not bring a privilege into play.").
31. Moran v. Pittsburgh-Des Moines Steel Co., 6 F.R.D. 594 (W.D. Pa. 1947).
32. *Id.*
33. *Id.* at 596.
34. *See* Fed. R. Civ. P. 26(b)(4); *see also In re* United Telecomm., Inc., 151 F.R.D. 127 (D. Kan. 1993); Am. Bankers Ins. Co. v. Colo. Flying Acad., 97 F.R.D. 515, 517 (D. Colo. 1983); Fine v. Bellefonte Underwriters Ins. Co., 91 F.R.D. 420, 423 (S.D.N.Y. 1981); APL Corp. v. Aetna Cas. & Sur. Co., 91 F.R.D. 10, 13 (D. Md. 1980).
35. *See* Hickman v. Taylor, 329 U.S. 495, 508–509 (1947). To some extent, counsel on both sides must have an appreciation of an organization's business, including

applicable regulations and regulatory schemes, in order to deal effectively with work-product concerns.

36. *See* United States v. Davis, 131 F.R.D. 391 (S.D.N.Y. 1990).
37. 449 U.S. 383 (1981).
38. Osborne, *supra* note 2, at 8 (emphasis added).
39. *Id.* (emphasis added).
40. United States v. Lipshy, 492 F. Supp. 35 (N.D. Tex. 1979).
41. *Id.*
42. SCM Corp. v. Xerox Corp., 70 F.R.D. 508 (D. Conn. 1976).
43. *Id.* at 517. *See also Davis*, 131 F.R.D. 391 (the mere fact that business advice is given or solicited does not automatically render the privilege lost; where the advice is prominently legal, as opposed to business in nature, the privilege will still attach).
44. *Id.* (citations omitted).
45. Sealy Mattress Co. of N.J., Inc., v. Sealy, Inc., 1987 WL 12500, slip op. (Del. Ch. 1987).
46 *Id.* at *3.
47. Diversified Indus., Inc. v. Meredith, 572 F.2d 596 (8th Cir. 1978) (en banc).
48. *Id.* at 610.
49. *Id.* at 609.
50. *Id.* at 610.
51. *Id.*
52. *Id.* at 615.
53. *See, e.g.*, United States v. Nixon, 418 U.S. 683, 710 (1974) ("[E]xceptions to the demand for every man's evidence are not lightly created nor expansively construed, for they are in derogation of the search for truth."); Littlejohn v. Bic Corp., 851 F.2d 673 (newspaper's "motions for intervention and access were based, in part, on the public's common law right of access to judicial proceedings and records. The existence of such a right is beyond dispute.").
54. 23 F.3d 772 (3d Cir. 1994).
55. *Id.* at 775.
56. *Id.* at 785–86.
57. E.E.O.C. v. Nat'l Children's Ctr., Inc., 146 F.3d 1042, 1045 (D.C. Cir. 1998); *but see* Bond v. Utreras, 585 F.3d 1061 (7th Cir. 2009) (holding that when a third party seeks intervention under Rule 24(b) to challenge a protective order in a case or controversy that is "no longer live," the intervenor must meet Article III standing requirements in addition to those of Rule 24(b) for permissive intervention).
58. *Id.*; *see also* Ford v. City of Huntsville, 242 F.3d 235 (5th Cir. 2001) (district court abused its discretion in entering confidentiality order without adequately identifying compelling reason for it); *In re* Enron Corp. Sec., Derivative & "ERISA" Litig., 229 F.R.D. 126 (S.D. Tex. 2005) (citing E.E.O.C. flexible standard); San Jose Mercury News v. U.S. Dist. Ct.–N. Dist., 187 F.3d 1096, 1103 (9th Cir. 1999) ("the fruits of pretrial discovery are, in the absence of a court order to the contrary, presumptively public" and where the district court "entered a blanket stipulated protective order pursuant to Rule 26(c)[,] [s]uch blanket orders are inherently subject to challenge and modification, as the party resisting disclosure generally has not made a particularized showing of good cause with respect to any individual document").
59. *See generally* ABA Section of Business Law eSource (Aug. 2003), http://www.abanet.org/buslaw/newsletter/0015/.

60. *See infra* discussion of the crime-fraud exception to the attorney-client privilege, which holds that otherwise privileged communications are not protected if they are meant to further future or ongoing criminal or fraudulent conduct, including other wrongful conduct such as intentional torts.
61. *See generally* David Lew, *Revised Model Rule 1.6: What Effect Will the New Rule Have on Practicing Attorneys?*, 18 GEO. J. LEGAL ETHICS 881 (2004) (practical impact of these rules will not be known for some time).
62. *See generally* Ronald Motley & Tucker Player, *Issues in "Crime-Fraud" Practice and Procedure: The Tobacco Litigation Experience*, 49 S.C. L. REV. 187 (1998); and Christine Hatfield, Comment, *The Privilege Doctrines—Are They Just Another Discovery Tool Utilized by the Tobacco Industry to Conceal Damaging Information?*, 16 PACE L. REV. 525 (1996).
63. *See* MODEL RULES OF PROF'L CONDUCT R. 1.13 & 1.6 (as amended).
64. Upjohn Co. v. United States, 449 U.S. 383, 389 (1981).
65. 8 J.H. WIGMORE, WIGMORE ON EVIDENCE § 2298 (John T. McNaughton rev. 1961).
66. The same rationale applies to the work-product doctrine. *See, e.g., In re* Int'l Sys. & Controls Corp. Sec. Litig., 693 F.2d 1235, 1242 (5th Cir. 1982).
67. United States v. Zolin, 491 U.S. 554, 563 (1989) (citations omitted).
68. *In re* Grand Jury Subpoena, 223 F.3d 213, 217 (3d Cir. 2000); *In re* Sealed Case, 754 F.2d 395, 399 (D.C. Cir. 1985).
69. Zolin v. United States, 491 U.S. 554, 562 (1989).
70. United States v. Jacobs, 117 F.3d 82, 88 (2d Cir. 1997).
71. *In re Sealed Case*, 754 F.2d 395, 399 (D.C. Cir. 1985); *In re* John Doe Corp., 675 F.2d 482, 491 (2d Cir. 1982).
72. *In re* BankAmerica Corp. Sec. Litig., 270 F.3d 639, 642 (8th Cir. 2001); United States v. Chen, 99 F.3d 1495, 1504 (9th Cir. 1996); *In re* Grand Jury Proceedings v. (Under Seal), 102 F.3d 748, 750–51 (4th Cir. 1996); *In re* Grand Jury Proceedings, 680 F.2d 1026, 1028 (5th Cir. 1982).
73. *See, e.g.*, Union Carbide Corp. v. Dow Chem. Co., 619 F. Supp. 1036, 1051 (D. Del. 1985); Research Corp. v. Gourmet's Delight Mushroom Co., 560 F. Supp. 811, 820 (E.D. Pa. 1983).
74. Laser Indus., Ltd. v. Reliant Techs., Inc., 167 F.R.D. 417, 423 (N.D. Cal. 1996).
75. *See, e.g., In re Sealed Case*, 754 F.2d 395, 399 (D.C. Cir. 1985) (extending the exception to "crime, fraud or other misconduct"); Cooksey v. Hilton Int'l Co., 863 F. Supp. 150, 151 (S.D.N.Y. 1994) (applying the exception to "intentional torts moored in fraud"); Volcanic Gardens Mgmt. Co. v. Paxson, 847 S.W.2d 343, 347 (Tex. Ct. App. 1993) (refusing to limit the application of the exception only in cases of common law or criminal fraud).
76. *In re* Grand Jury Subpoena, 220 F.3d 406 (5th Cir. 2000).
77. *Id.* at 410.
78. *Id.*
79. United States v. Zolin, 491 U.S. 554, 562 (1989) (citations omitted).
80. *Zolin*, 491 U.S. 554.
81. *Id.* at 575.
82. *See, e.g., In re* BankAmerica Corp. Sec. Litig., 270 F.3d 639, 644 (8th Cir. 2001) ("We have found no case in which this court affirmed an order to produce documents under the crime-fraud exception where the district court did not first review the documents in camera.").
83. 491 U.S. at 574–75.

84. *Id.* at 574 n.12.
85. *See, e.g.*, United States v. Jacobs, 117 F.3d 82, 87 (2d Cir. 1997) (parties must "demonstrate that there is a factual basis for a showing of probable cause to believe that crime or fraud has been committed and that the communications in question were in furtherance of the fraud or crime," after which decision regarding exception is left to discretion of the trial court); *In re* Sealed Case, 107 F.3d 46, 50 (D.C. Cir. 1997) (party "offers evidence that if believed by the trier of fact would establish the elements of an ongoing or imminent crime or fraud," then decision is left to trial court's discretion); United States v. Martin, 278 F.3d 988, 1001 (9th Cir. 2001) (parties "must present the district court with sufficient evidence to make its prima facie case . . . [and] must persuade the court to find that the communications with the lawyer were in furtherance of an intended or present illegality and that there is some relationship between the communications and the illegality").
86. 167 F.R.D. 417, 432 (N.D. Cal. 1996).
87. *Id.* at 433.
88. *Id.*
89. *Id.*
90. *See* United States v. Rodriguez, 948 F.2d 914, 916 (5th Cir. 1991).
91. 124 F. Supp. 2d 1291 (S.D. Fla. 2000).
92. *Id.* at 1305. The court cited as an example but did not discuss *Laser Industries.*
93. *Id.* at 1307.
94. *Id.*
95. 107 F.R.D. 2 (MDL No. 211) (D. Kan. 1985).
96. *Id.* at *9.
97. *Id.* at *11.
98. *See* 750 F.2d 1501 (11th. Cir. 1985).
99. 107 F.R.D. at *11.
100. *Id.* at 13.
101. *Id.* at 14.
102. Most states have adopted the Model Rule or the functional equivalent. *See generally* Benjamin J. Vernia, *Right of Attorney to Conduct Ex Parte Interviews with Former Corporate Employees*, 57 A.L.R. 5th 633 (1998).
103. Dubois v. Gradco Sys., Inc., 136 F.R.D. 341, 344 (D. Conn. 1991) (citing G. HAZARD & W. HODES, THE LAW OF LAWYERING: A HANDBOOK ON THE MODEL RULES OF PROFESSIONAL CONDUCT 436 (1988 Supp.)).
104. *See* Benjamin J. Vernia, *Right of Attorney to Conduct Ex Parte Interviews with Former Corporate Employees*, 57 A.L.R. 5th 633 §§ 3 & 5 (1998).
105. 143 F.R.D. 105 (E.D. La. 1992).
106. *Id.* at 107–108 (The language of the comment has changed since 1992, when the opinion was written.).
107. Cram v. Lamson & Sessions Co. Carlon Div., 148 F.R.D. 259, 261 (S.D. Iowa 1993); Polycast Tech. Corp. v. Uniroyal, Inc., 129 F.R.D. 621 (S.D.N.Y. 1990).
108. Sequa Corp. v. Lititech, Inc., 807 F. Supp. 653, 668 (D. Colo. 1992); *Cram,* 148 F.R.D. at 266.
109. Valassis v. Samelson, 143 F.R.D. 118, 124 (E.D. Mich. 1992).
110. *Polycast*, 129 F.R.D. at 628; Browning v. AT&T Paradyne, 838 F. Supp. 1564, 1567 (M.D. Fla. 1993).
111. 691 P.2d 564 (Wash. 1984).

112. 199 F.R.D. 529 (S.D.N.Y. 2001).
113. *Id.* at 533 (citing *Polycast*, 129 F.R.D. 621 (S.D.N.Y. 1990)).
114. *Id.*
115. *Id.* at 535.
116. *Id.* at 536.
117. *See, e.g.*, Benjamin J. Vernia, *Right of Attorney to Conduct Ex Parte Interviews with Former Corporate Employees*, 57 A.L.R. 5th 633 (1998) (suggesting that attorneys should "establish a script of statements and questions to be followed in all initial contacts with former employees").
118. United States v. Nixon, 418 U.S. 683, 710 (1974).

CHAPTER 4

Confidentiality and Its Relationship to the Attorney-Client Privilege

ARTHUR GARWIN

I. Introduction

Confidentiality and attorney-client privilege are related but distinct concepts that are frequently confused. The attorney-client privilege applies "in judicial and other proceedings in which a lawyer may be called as a witness or otherwise required to produce evidence concerning a client."[1] This privilege "protects against compelled disclosure of a relatively narrow category of communications between lawyer and client."[2] Compelled disclosure might occur in a deposition, for example, or in response to a subpoena. If a lawyer is asked a question in a deposition or at a trial that arguably calls for an answer containing privileged information, the lawyer is obligated to refuse to answer (unless the client agrees to waive the privilege), and force a ruling by the court. If the court agrees that the testimony would be privileged, the court will sustain the objection and effectively order the lawyer not to answer.

Confidentiality is a principle of legal ethics that governs whether a lawyer may reveal information related to a client representation. Confidentiality rules are not limited to judicial or other proceedings, but rather apply in all representational contexts.[3] In addition, confidentiality applies to all information related to a representation,[4] whatever its source, and not merely to client communications.[5] The exceptions are drawn narrowly and the scope of confidentiality is applied expansively.[6] Since confidentiality is an ethics rule, the ramification of a breach by the lawyer of the lawyer's duty of confidentiality is a possible disciplinary action and sanction against the lawyer.

Everything that is privileged is also protected by the confidentiality principle but the converse is not true.[7] The confidentiality rule covers far more than communications between a client and a lawyer. Not everything that is protected by the confidentiality rule is protected by the attorney-client privilege. And the duty to maintain confidentiality does not expand the scope of the privilege.[8] "Attorney-client privilege has numerous exceptions, which courts apply liberally. Much of what would be confidential ultimately proves to be subject to discovery or production in court."[9]

Moreover, the privilege protects only the communications themselves, not underlying facts, the disclosure of which may be compelled from those who communicated them to the attorney.[10] Thus, the other side can ask your client: "Is X true," and demand an answer (in a formal proceeding), unless something like the Fifth Amendment applies. But it cannot ask the client: "Did you tell your lawyer whether X is true?" Furthermore, as explained in the example in the following excerpt, even a lawyer could be compelled to testify about the facts if he or she gained knowledge of them without a communication from the client:

> The distinction between information about a client and communication about that information leads to a further distinction between observations and communicative acts. For example, a lawyer's observations about a client's physical condition are not privileged, even though the lawyer presumably would not have been in a position to make the observations absent a relationship of confidentiality and trust. At the same time, and conversely, a genuine communication from a client to a lawyer retains its privileged character, even if it is made demonstratively, through body language or gestures, rather than with words. Thus, as explained in illustrations accompanying Restatement of the Law Governing Lawyers § 69, Comment *e*, if a client—in response to his attorney's question—silently rolls up his sleeve to reveal a tattoo, the lawyer could not be compelled to testify about the tattoo. But the

opposite would be true if the same client visited his lawyer's office wearing a short-sleeve shirt, and the lawyer noticed the tattoo.[11]

II. Model Rule 1.6—Confidentiality of Information

The Model Rules of Professional Conduct were adopted by the American Bar Association in 1983, replacing the Model Code of Professional Responsibility. Since that time almost every state has adopted the Model Rules format and Model Rule 1.6 or some modified version of it. Model Rule 1.6, as originally adopted, contained only two exceptions: current (b)(5) and a less permissive version of (b)(1). In 2002, the ABA added current (b)(4) and (b)(6). Then, in 2003, the ABA added (b)(2) and (b)(3) (see further discussion about the context of these additions at section II.D.2, Crime-Fraud Exception, *infra*). Over half the states have adopted some version of paragraphs (b)(2) and (b)(3).[12]

ABA Model Rule 1.6: Confidentiality of Information

(a) A lawyer shall not reveal information relating to the representation of a client unless the client gives informed consent, the disclosure is impliedly authorized in order to carry out the representation or the disclosure is permitted by paragraph (b).

(b) A lawyer may reveal information relating to the representation of a client to the extent the lawyer reasonably believes necessary:

- (1) to prevent reasonably certain death or substantial bodily harm;
- (2) to prevent the client from committing a crime or fraud that is reasonably certain to result in substantial injury to the financial interests or property of another and in furtherance of which the client has used or is using the lawyer's services;
- (3) to prevent, mitigate or rectify substantial injury to the financial interests or property of another that is reasonably certain to result or has resulted from the client's commission of a crime or fraud in furtherance of which the client has used the lawyer's services;
- (4) to secure legal advice about the lawyer's compliance with these Rules;
- (5) to establish a claim or defense on behalf of the lawyer in a controversy between the lawyer and the client, to establish a defense to a criminal charge or civil claim against the lawyer based upon conduct in which the client was involved, or to respond to allegations in any proceeding concerning the lawyer's representation of the client; or
- (6) to comply with other law or a court order.

In general, as discussed above, a lawyer has a duty to keep confidential information relating to the representation of a client. However, this duty is subject to several exceptions. In the case of each exception, the disclosure is permitted only to the extent the lawyer reasonably believes necessary.

A. Public Information

The *Restatement of the Law Governing Lawyers* states, "The law generally provides that a client communication cannot become public and still remain protected by the attorney-client privilege. . . . The scant case authority is divided on the question whether the definition of confidential client information includes publicly available information. . . ."[13] Rule 1.6 is silent on the subject of previously disclosed information, but *Lawyer Law: Comparing the ABA Model Rules of Professional Conduct with the ALI Restatement (Third) of the Law Governing Lawyers* states, "Unlike the rules relating to attorney-client privilege and work-product protection, failure to protect confidential client information adequately does not make the information less confidential. The lawyer's obligation to protect the information continues even after its initial disclosure."[14]

This question of confidentiality of public information is particularly relevant in the context of the conflicts rules, where, for example, information protected by Model Rule 1.6 figures in the equation of whether a duty to a former client under Model Rule 1.9(b) prohibits representation.[15] In discussing disqualification of lawyers due to conflicts with duties owed to former clients, the Comment to Model Rule 1.9 states: "Information that has been disclosed to the public or to other parties adverse to the former client ordinarily will not be disqualifying."[16] As expressed by the *Restatement*:

> The absence of a similarly limiting provision in ABA Model Rule 1.8(b), which applies to ongoing representations, is not inconsistent. Any such lawyer use would be impermissible on the broad ground (see ABA Model Rule 1.7) that a lawyer may not use even publicly known information to the detriment of a current client, whether to further a personal interest of the lawyer or to further the interest of another client. Revealing client information adversely in a way that is gratuitous or negligent would violate the duty to take all reasonably available steps to advance the client's lawful objectives.[17]

However, this conclusion derives from the duty of loyalty, not confidentiality.[18] Model Rule 1.6 does not put generally known information outside the boundaries of confidentiality. Though the duty that would be violated would be that of loyalty to the client, rather than confidentiality, the result is the same and the duties are inextricably bound in this context. However, Hazard, Hodes, and Jarvis, in *The Law of Lawyering*, criticize what they perceive to be the too-broad nature of the confidentiality rule in regard to public information:

> [R]ead literally and in isolation, the rule is so stringent as to approach the unworkable and the unrealistic. . . . [It] does not exclude information "relating to a client" that happens to be in the public domain or

> generally known. Thus, unless this commonsense limitation is read in to Rule 1.6(a), a lawyer could be disciplined merely for writing about a client's case, revealing only material that was in the trial transcript or other public documents.
>
> . . . [T]he overinclusion of too much material within the universe of protected confidential information can have awkward consequences. If a lawyer is charged with disclosing information that is technically protected by Rule 1.6, but would not be protected under a sensible reading of the rule, there will be inevitable pressure to force the situation into one of the other recognized exceptions to reach the proper result. Over the long run, this could harm the basically well-balanced regime of limited and narrow exceptions.[19]

B. Paragraph (a) Impliedly Authorized Disclosures

Model Rule 1.6(a) specifically permits disclosure of client information when "impliedly authorized in order to carry out the representation." Comment [5] to the Rule and ABA Formal Opinion 08-453 make it clear that disclosures between lawyers within a firm are impliedly authorized.[20] The Comment also states that "[e]xcept to the extent that the client's instructions or special circumstances limit that authority . . . a lawyer may be "impliedly authorized" to admit a fact that cannot properly be disputed or to make a disclosure that facilitates a satisfactory conclusion to a matter."[21] Thus, for example, the District of Columbia Bar Legal Ethics Committee has stated that an attorney may disclose confidential information of a deceased client if "the attorney has reasonable grounds for believing that release of the information is impliedly authorized in furthering the interests of the former client in settling her estate."[22] The ABA Standing Committee on Ethics and Professional Responsibility has said that a lawyer hired by an insurance company to defend an insured "may disclose the insured's confidential information . . . to the insurer if the lawyer reasonably believes that doing so will advance the interests of the insured" and will not "affect a material interest of the insured adversely."[23] On the other hand, the Committee also has stated that "[a] lawyer should not, absent informed client consent, reveal to a judge the limits of the lawyer's settlement authority or the lawyer's advice to the client regarding settlement."[24]

C. Authorized Disclosures

As paragraph (a) of the Rule indicates, if disclosure is not impliedly authorized or otherwise permitted by the Rule's exceptions (see below), then client consent is required. That consent must be informed, which means that "the lawyer has communicated adequate information and explanation about the material risks of and reasonably available alternatives to the proposed course of conduct."[25]

What is adequate information and explanation in the context of Rule 1.6? "[R]elevant issues include whether disclosure could result in waiver of the attorney-client privilege, or in further dissemination or use of the information."[26]

D. Paragraph (b) Exceptions

1. Physical Harm

Paragraph (b)(1) was amended in February 2002, pursuant to the Report with Recommendation of the Commission on Evaluation of the Rules of Professional Conduct. (Ethics 2000 Commission). Prior to the amendment, the rule permitted disclosure "to prevent the client from committing a criminal act that the lawyer believes is likely to result in imminent death or substantial bodily harm." The exception was broadened in three ways. First, the word "imminent" was replaced with "reasonably certain." Thus, "the exception now authorizes disclosure to prevent serious physical harm that may occur at a later date."[27] For example, "a lawyer who knows that a client has accidentally discharged toxic waste into a town's water supply may reveal this information to the authorities if there is a present and substantial risk that a person who drinks the water will contract a life-threatening or debilitating disease and the lawyer's disclosure is necessary to eliminate the threat or reduce the number of victims."[28]

Second, there is no longer a requirement that the client be the one who will cause this level of harm. It could be the client's uncle or business partner whom the client would prefer to protect. Third, the criminal-act requirement was removed.

The hypothetical often used to illustrate perceived problems related to this exception prior to the 2003 rule change was derived from the case of *Spaulding v. Zimmerman*.[29]

> In that celebrated case, lawyers were defending the driver in a civil suit arising out of a serious automobile accident. The defendant's doctor examined the plaintiff and discovered a life-threatening aortic aneurysm that was probably—but not certainly—caused by the accident. The plaintiff's own doctor had not discovered the aneurysm, and plaintiff's lawyers had (mistakenly) not requested the defense team's medical reports. A settlement agreement was worked out and approved by the court, while the plaintiff and his lawyers were still in the dark about plaintiff's true medical condition.
>
> * * * *
>
> No confidentiality issue was presented in the actual case, because the lawyers unilaterally decided *not* to disclose, but it is certainly possible that even if the clients had been told about the aneurysm, they would have embargoed the information. In that event, the ultimate question would have to be faced: would the lawyers have discretion to disclose against the wishes of their clients in this extraordinary circumstance, or would they be *prohibited* by the rules of ethics from doing what is morally right?[30]

Under the current rule, the lawyers would have the discretion to disclose.

2. Crime-Fraud Exception

Paragraphs (b)(2) and (b)(3) of Model Rule 1.6 were adopted by the ABA House of Delegates and added to the rule in August 2003 pursuant to the Report with Recommendation of the ABA Task Force on Corporate Responsibility.[31] These changes, which were driven by the "issues relating to corporate responsibility arising out of the unexpected and traumatic bankruptcy of Enron and other Enron-like situations,"[32] were consistent with the existing rules in many states.

Paragraph (b)(2) addresses preventing a client's action that is going to cause harm, whereas paragraph (b)(3) addresses preventing, mitigating, or rectifying harm resulting from an action by the client that has already occurred. In both instances, the exception applies only when the lawyer's services have been or are being used in furtherance of the crime or fraud. So, if a client merely tells his lawyer that he is about to commit a crime or fraud (presumably one that would not result in reasonably certain death or substantial bodily harm and thus be covered under paragraph (b)(1)), paragraph (b)(2) does not provide a vehicle for the lawyer to reveal that confidential information. Likewise, if the client "confesses" to the lawyer about a completed crime or fraud, the lawyer cannot reveal information in order to prevent, rectify, or mitigate the financial harm if the lawyer's services have not be used in furtherance thereof.

While these exceptions are discretionary in form, it is possible that lawyers will convert "may reveal" into "must reveal" to avoid getting sued or prosecuted later themselves. In addition, Model Rule 4.1(b) provides that "in the course of representing a client a lawyer shall not knowingly fail to disclose a material fact when disclosure is necessary to avoid assisting a criminal or fraudulent act by a client, unless disclosure is prohibited by Rule 1.6." Thus, if it is permissive to reveal under Rule 1.6, it becomes mandatory under Rule 4.1 if the information to be revealed is material and the disclosure is necessary to avoid assisting the client's criminal or fraudulent act. This assumes, of course, that the lawyer's participation was "innocent," because otherwise the lawyer would have been an accessory to the crime or fraud and would have violated Rule 1.2(d) (which states that "a lawyer shall not counsel a client to engage, or assist a client, in conduct that the lawyer knows is criminal or fraudulent") at the time the lawyer provided the services, and violated Rule 1.16(a) by not withdrawing.

The crime-fraud exception to the confidentiality rule is similar to, but not the same as the crime-fraud exception to the attorney-client privilege. The confidentiality exception

> applies only when the likelihood of financial loss is great and the lawyer reasonably believes that use or revelation is necessary to prevent the crime or fraud or to prevent, rectify, or mitigate the loss it causes. . . . In contrast, the crime-fraud exception to the attorney-client privilege . . . applies without regard to the consequences of the intended act so long as the act itself is a crime or fraud. That exception to the attorney-client privilege applies only when a client consults a lawyer with intention to obtain assistance to commit a crime or fraud or so

> uses the lawyer's services, whereas the [confidentiality exception] applies regardless of the client's intention at the time of consultation. . . . Finally, [the confidentiality exception] is limited to client acts in which a lawyer's services are employed; the crime-fraud exception [to the attorney-client privilege] applies whether or not the lawyer's services are so employed. Due to the several differences . . . a finding that a lawyer permissibly used or disclosed confidential client information . . . and a determination whether [the exception to the attorney-client privilege] applies must be made independently.[33]

Two examples from the *Restatement of the Law Governing Lawyers* illustrate how these exceptions operate.

In the first instance, a lawyer prepares an opinion letter on behalf of a client. The lawyer later receives information that gives him reason to believe that the transaction for which he wrote the letter was criminal or fraudulent, a fact that the lawyer did not know at the time he wrote the letter. Because the lawyer's services were used, the lawyer has discretion to disclose the information in order to prevent, mitigate, or rectify any substantial injury to the financial interests or property of another that is reasonably certain to result or has resulted from the transaction.[34]

In the second instance, a client seeks assistance from a lawyer in defending against charges by a regulatory agency of participation in a scheme to defraud. The loss to the victim has already occurred. Though the lawyer comes to believe that the client's acts were fraudulent and caused the harm, she does not have discretion to disclose the client's confidential information because her services were not used in furtherance of the fraud.[35]

3. *Ethics Advice*

Paragraph (b)(4) of Model Rule 1.6 was added in February 2002 pursuant to the Report with Recommendation of the Ethics 2000 Commission. "Although disclosure to secure ethics advice will '[i]n most situations' be impliedly authorized, Rule 1.6(b)(4) permits disclosure even without implicit authorization[36] 'because of the importance of a lawyer's compliance with the Rules of Professional Conduct.'"[37] "Moreover, clients are adequately protected by the requirement that such disclosures be made only when protected by the attorney-client evidentiary privilege."[38] This is so because the person consulted will also be a lawyer, who will establish a new attorney-client privilege with the inquiring lawyer. The second lawyer also will be subject to a new confidentiality obligation vis-à-vis the inquiring lawyer under Rule 1.6.

The following illustration from *The Law of Lawyering* provides a good example of how this exception operates.

> Lawyer L is representing a client in a difficult matter involving novel and complex legal issues. Opposing counsel has also threatened—informally so far—to move to disqualify L, claiming that L violated

> the rules of professional conduct. L retains another lawyer to provide himself with legal advice about handling the legal issues in the underlying case. Shortly thereafter, L informally consults [a professional responsibility] expert . . . about the ethical issues that have arisen.
> * * * *
>
> The disclosures L must make to the consulting lawyer are in furtherance of the main representation, and are accordingly "impliedly authorized" under Rule 1.6(a), even when the consultation is not revealed to the client. . . .
>
> The analysis does not change merely because the consultation with the legal ethics expert is an informal one. The law professor probably needs to be given some client information in order to be able to respond properly, and the law professor—being a lawyer as well—must also abide by normal confidentiality and conflict of interest rules. The consultation and attendant disclosures are again "impliedly authorized" in the sense of Rule 1.6(a), because disqualification of L would adversely affect the client. However, out of an abundance of caution, L should reveal only such details as are necessary to a full understanding of the issues involved. L should not reveal the identity of his client unless it is germane.[39]

The ABA Standing Committee on Ethics and Professional Responsibility has suggested that the exception provided by paragraph (b)(4) provides a basis for the revelation of confidential information to an intermediary lawyer for the purpose of determining what conflicts may exist when lawyers change firms.[40] The Opinion, however, does not require the use of an intermediary lawyer when checking for conflicts between the incoming lawyer and the new firm. The Committee allows that the situation does not really fit into any of the Rule's exceptions, but that "[b]ecause conflicts information is needed to detect and resolve conflicts of interest when lawyers move between firms, as a general matter and subject to [certain] limitations . . . , disclosure of conflicts information otherwise protected by Rule 1.6 should be considered permissible as necessary to comply with the Rules."[41]

4. *Claim or Defense*

Paragraph (b)(5) contains the only exception to the Rule that has not been either added or amended since the original adoption of the Rule in 1983 (although it has been renumbered).[42] Perhaps the most common use of this exception is to allow a lawyer to reveal confidential information to collect a fee.[43] However, "[t]his right to use confidences . . . does not create a right to blackmail the client. The lawyer may not state to the client: 'Pay the fee or I will reveal to your employer your income tax problems.' The lawyer may only exercise the right to reveal client information to the extent that it is reasonably *necessary* to establish or collect the fee. There must not be any extortion or unnecessary disclosure."[44]

The exception also applies to other kinds of claims. For example, the ABA Standing Committee on Ethics and Professional Responsibility has concluded "that a retaliatory discharge or similar claim by a former in-house lawyer against her employer is a 'claim' under Rule 1.6 (b)."[45]

The self-defense portion of the exception permits disclosure to defend claims brought against the lawyer by clients or third parties, "for example, a person claiming to have been defrauded by the lawyer and client acting together. The lawyer's right to respond arises when an assertion of such complicity has been made. Paragraph (b)(5) does not require the lawyer to await the commencement of an action or proceeding that charges such complicity, so that the defense may be established by responding directly to a third party who has made such an assertion."[46]

5. Other Law or Court Order

Paragraph (b)(6) was added in February 2002 pursuant to the Report with Recommendation of the Ethics 2000 Commission. It distinguished the prior position as follows:

> Prior to the amendment, the Rule did not address whether lawyers are permitted or required to disclose information when such disclosure is required by other law or a court order. Former Comment [20], however, stated that a lawyer must comply with the final orders of a court or other tribunal requiring the lawyer to give information about the client, and former Comment [21] referred to other law that may supersede Rule 1.6. The Commission recommended that the text of Rule 1.6 be amended explicitly to permit, but not require, disclosure to comply with law or court orders. No change in substance was intended. See also Comments [12] and [13].[47]

However, similar to the crime-fraud exceptions above, this exception, while discretionary in form, in practice converts "may reveal" into "must reveal" because of the "other law" or "court order" that applies. For example, in the case of a court order, the conversion may take place as follows. Someone demands that a lawyer provide information about a client. The lawyer's first response, instinctually, is: "Sorry, it's privileged." Only after a court rules that there is no privilege does the lawyer retreat to: "Okay, but it's still confidential." However, then the court says: "Fine. It may be confidential, so you can't reveal the information to your wife or your golfing buddies—but I'm ordering you to answer anyway, because we're in court, and in court only the evidence rules apply. And by the way, even though it's confidential, there's an exception that allows you to disclose in situations just like this one." Then the lawyer says (to himself): "I think that 'may disclose' just turned into 'must disclose,' because the judge is going to hold me in contempt if I don't comply. And I won't get into trouble with the lawyer disciplinary authorities if I do testify, because of the permission given me under the court order exception to the confidentiality rule."

E. Other Laws

The Annotated Model Rules of Professional Conduct provides the following examples of this exception:

> [T]he Internal Revenue Code, 26 U.S.C. § 6050, . . . compels lawyers to disclose, through IRS Form 8300, the identities of clients and the amounts and payment dates of all cash fees in excess of $10,000.
>
> * * * *
>
> The issue also arises in connection with statutes requiring that child abuse be reported. *See, e.g.*, N.Y. City Ethics Op. 1997-2 (1997) (lawyer employed by social service agency may disclose information relating to abuse of minor client to social service agency if required by law).[48]

And even though the other law may require disclosure, the lawyer "must discuss the matter with the client to the extent required by Rule 1.4."[49]

F. Court Orders

The Annotated Model Rules of Professional Conduct set the parameter within which an attorney must disclose client information as follows:

> Although a determination of whether a lawyer must reveal client information in an adversarial proceeding will turn on rules of evidence rather than rules of ethics, the lawyer's ethical duty of confidentiality governs important aspects of the lawyer's response to a demand for information.[50]

The Rules go on to state:

> Absent informed consent of the client to do otherwise, the lawyer should assert on behalf of the client all nonfrivolous claims that the order is not authorized by law or that the information sought is protected against disclosure by the attorney-client privilege or other applicable law.[51]

However, the scope of the protection offered by the attorney-client privilege is not increased by application of the duty of confidentiality, which will thus not provide a reason for noncompliance with a court order.[52] Nevertheless, "[i]f the lawyer is ordered to disclose the information, the lawyer's ethical obligation is to disclose no more than the court requires."[53]

Legal Ethics: The Lawyer's Deskbook on Professional Responsibility provides an example of how the limitation upon this exception might work in practice. In the course of representing a client regarding a business proposal, a lawyer uncovers information from third parties that relates to the representation. Pursuant to a criminal investigation, a court later orders the lawyer to reveal this information to a grand jury on the grounds that it is not protected by the evidentiary privilege, having not been the result of a communication between the client and the lawyer. The lawyer obeys the court order. Later, reporters ask him whether he complied. He answers: "Yes." Then they ask him what he said to the grand jury. If the lawyer tells them, the lawyer will commit a disciplinary violation by revealing information relating to the representation that remains protected by the confidentiality rule.[54]

Notes

1. Model Rules of Prof'l Conduct R. 1.6 cmt. [3] (2009).
2. Thomas D. Morgan, Lawyer Law, Comparing the ABA Model Rules of Professional Conduct with the ALI Restatement (Third) of the Law Governing Lawyers 243 (2005).
3. *See* X Corp. v. Doe, 805 F. Supp. 1298 (E.D. Va. 1992) (Whereas "the attorney client-privilege is . . . applied in the litigation context by judges, not lawyers, for the purpose of deciding whether to compel the disclosure of putatively privileged material . . . the . . . standard for disclosure of confidential information is one that is applied in the first instance by lawyers, not judges, as they struggle with the decision whether voluntarily to disclose certain confidential information they believe reflects an ongoing or future fraud. Judges apply the . . . standard in the second instance only to review post hoc whether a voluntary disclosure was ethically appropriate or, as here, to decide whether to enjoin a potential voluntary disclosure. . . ."). *See also* Fred C. Zacharias, *Harmonizing Privilege and Confidentiality*, 41 S. Tex. L. Rev. 69 (Winter 1999) (discussing why confidentiality rules developed so broadly); Fred C. Zacharias, *Rethinking Confidentiality*, 74 Iowa L. Rev. 351 (1989) (discussing why the client protective basis for this broad development may be misplaced).
4. "Neither Model Rules 1.6's prohibition against revealing 'information relating to the representation of a client' nor Model Code DR 4-101's protection of client confidences or secrets makes any exception for information that has been previously disclosed or is publicly available." Laws. Man. on Prof. Conduct (ABA/BNA) 55:310 (Sept. 21, 2005) [hereinafter Laws. Man.]. The choice of the word "confidence" to represent "privilege," in this context adds to the confusion between the concepts. *See also* Fred C. Zacharias, *The Fallacy That Attorney-Client Privilege Has Been Eroded: Ramifications and Lessons for the Bar*, Prof. Law., 1999 Symposium Issue 39.
5. *See* Model Rule 1.6, *infra*. *See also* Restatement (Third) of the Law Governing Lawyers § 59 (2000) [hereinafter Restatement]. The attorney-client privilege and the rule of confidentiality also apply to prospective clients. *See* Model Rule 1.18(b) (regarding confidentiality and prospective clients) and Restatement § 70 (2000) (regarding the attorney-client privilege and prospective clients). For

purposes of this discussion, references will be made only to current or former clients.

6. Zacharias, *Harmonizing Privilege and Confidentiality*, *supra* note 3. *See also* RESTATEMENT, *supra* note 5, § 59 cmt. b (2000) ("The expansive definition of client information not protected by the attorney-client privilege that nonetheless a lawyer is obliged to keep confidential comes primarily from the law of agency and rules of professional regulation.") and RONALD D. ROTUNDA & JOHN S. DZIENKOWSKI, LEGAL ETHICS: THE LAWYER'S DESKBOOK ON PROFESSIONAL RESPONSIBILITY § 1.6-1 (2010–2011) (The attorney is the agent of her client, who is the principal. Under a general rule of agency law, the agent must neither use nor disclose information confidentially given to him by the principal or acquired by him during the course of or on account of his agency. . . . Restatement of the Law of Agency, Second, § 395.).
7. "The confidentiality rule . . . applies not only to matters communicated in confidence by the client but also to all information relating to the representation, whatever its source." MODEL RULES OF PROF'L CONDUCT R. 1.6 cmt. [3] (2009). *See also* Laws. Man., *supra* note 4, at 55:305 *et seq.* (comparing the protection afforded under the ethics rules with that under afforded by the attorney-client privilege in regard to client identity; client's whereabouts; financial, billing and fee data; and publicly available or previously disclosed information).
8. Adams v. Franklin, 924 A.2d 993 (D.C. 2007).
9. Zacharias, *Harmonizing Privilege and Confidentiality*, *supra* note 3. ("[A]ttorney-client privilege rules are products of lawsuits. Courts and legislators make the rules. Whoever adopts the rules initially, it is judges who interpret them and flesh them out. Because privilege applies only when one client attempts to prevent the other side's access to potentially probative evidence in litigation, courts implementing privilege are cognizant of secrecy's negative attributes. Thus, judges tend to interpret attorney-client privilege narrowly.").
10. *See* Upjohn Co. v. United States, 449 U.S. 383, 395 (1981).
11. GEOFFREY C. HAZARD, JR., W. WILLIAM HODES & PETER R. JARVIS, THE LAW OF LAWYERING § 9.7, at 9-27 (3d ed. 2010) (endnote omitted).
12. *See* ABA, CPR Policy Implementation Comm., Variations of the ABA Model Rules of Professional Conduct, Rule 1.6 (Oct. 21, 2010), http://www.americanbar.org/groups/professional_responsibility/policy/rule_charts.html.
13. RESTATEMENT, *supra* note 5, § 59 cmt. d (2000).
14. MORGAN, *supra* note 2, at 293. *See also* BENNETT, COHEN & WHITTAKER, ANNOTATED MODEL RULES OF PROF'L CONDUCT, at 97–98 (7th ed. 2011).
15. MODEL RULES OF PROF'L CONDUCT R. 1.9 (2009):
    (b) A lawyer shall not knowingly represent a person in the same or a substantially related matter in which a firm with which the lawyer formerly was associated had previously represented a client
        (1) whose interests are materially adverse to that person; and
        (2) about whom the lawyer had acquired information protected by Rules 1.6 and 1.9(c) that is material to the matter;
16. MODEL RULES OF PROF'L CONDUCT R. 1.9 cmt. [3] (2009).
17. RESTATEMENT, *supra* note 5, § 59 cmt. d (2000) (citations omitted).
18. "Loyalty and independent judgment are essential elements in the lawyer's relationship to a client." MODEL RULES OF PROF'L CONDUCT R. 1.7 cmt. [1] (2009).
19. HAZARD, HODES & JARVIS, *supra* note 11, § 9.15, at 9-60 (endnotes omitted).

20. Of course, disclosure may not be made to a lawyer in the firm who has been screened from participation in the matter because of a conflict.
21. Model Rules of Prof'l Conduct R. 1.6 cmt. [5] (2009).
22. D.C. Ethics Op. 324 (2004). *See also* Haw. Ethics Op. 38 (1999); Kan. Ethics Op. 01-01 (2001).
23. ABA Formal Ethics Op. 01-421 (2001). *See generally* Restatement, *supra* note 5, § 61 (2000) (permitting disclosure that advances client's interests). *See also* ABA Informal Ethics Op. 86-1518 (1986) (interpreting exception for disclosures impliedly authorized as permitting lawyer to disclose to opposing counsel, without client consultation, inadvertent omission of contract provision).
24. ABA Formal Ethics Op. 93-370 (1993).
25. Model Rules of Prof'l Conduct R. 1.0(e) (2009).
26. Bennett, Cohen & Whittaker, *supra* note 14, at 99.
27. *Id.* at 101.
28. Model Rules of Prof'l Conduct R. 1.6 cmt [6] (2009).
29. Spaulding v. Zimmerman, 116 N.W.2d 704 (Minn. 1962).
30. Hazard, Hodes & Jarvis, *supra* note 11, § 9.20, at 9-81 to 9-83 (endnote omitted). For a thorough examination of this case, including interviews with some of the historical characters, see Roger Cramton & Lori Knowles, *Professional Secrecy and Its Exceptions:* Spaulding v. Zimmerman *Revisited*, 83 Minn. L. Rev. 63 (1998),.
31. *See* ABA, Ctr. for Prof'l Responsibility, Model Rules of Professional Conduct, http://www.americanbar.org/groups/professional_responsibility/publications/model_rules_of_professional_conduct.html. The ABA House of Delegates had previously rejected the same recommendation made by the Ethics 2000 Commission two years earlier.
32. *Id.* (quoting Robert Hirshon, President of the American Bar Association, Charge to ABA Task Force on Corporate Responsibility, Mar. 28, 2002).
33. Restatement, *supra* note 5, § 67, at 507.
34. *Id.* at 508.
35. *Id.* at 508–09.
36. See discussion *supra* regarding impliedly authorized disclosure.
37. Bennett, Cohen & Whittaker, *supra* note 14, at 104 (quoting Model Rules of Prof'l Conduct R. 1.6 cmt. [9] (2007)).
38. ABA, Ctr. for Prof'l Responsibility, Model Rule 1.6: Reporter's Explanation of Changes, http://www.americanbar.org/groups/professional_responsibility/policy/ethics_2000_commission/e2k_rule16rem.html.
39. Hazard, Hodes & Jarvis, *supra* note 11, § 9.17, at 9-70, 9-71.
40. ABA Standing Comm. on Ethics and Prof'l Responsibility, Formal Op. 09-455 (2009).
41. *Id.* at 3.
42. *See* ABA, A Legislative History: The Development of the ABA Model Rules of Professional Conduct, 1982–2005, at 99–141 (2006).
43. "This aspect of the rule expresses the principle that the beneficiary of a fiduciary relationship may not exploit it to the detriment of the fiduciary." Model Rules of Prof'l Conduct R. 1.6 cmt. [11] (2009).
44. Rotunda & Dzienkowski, *supra* note 6, § 1.6-12(c) (footnote omitted).
45. ABA Standing Comm. on Ethics and Prof'l Responsibility, Formal Op. 01-424 (2001). "Whether, and to what extent, former in-house counsel may sue their

former employers for employment-related matters varies among jurisdictions, and has changed over time. Historically some Model Code jurisdictions had not permitted such actions unless they could be maintained without violating client confidences." Bennett, Cohen & Whittaker, *supra* note 14, at 109.

46. Model Rules of Prof'l Conduct R. 1.6 cmt. [10] (2009). *See also* Hazard, Hodes & Jarvis, *supra* note 11, § 9.23, *Disclosure of Client Confidences as a Matter of Preemptive Self-Defense.*
47. ABA, Ctr. for Prof'l Responsibility, Model Rule 1.6: Reporter's Explanation of Changes, http://www.americanbar.org/groups/professional_responsibility/policy/ethics_2000_commission/e2k_rule16rem.html.
48. Bennett, Cohen & Whittaker, *supra* note 14, at 112.
49. Model Rules of Prof'l Conduct R. 1.6 cmt. [12] (2009).
50. Bennett, Cohen & Whittaker, *supra* note 14, at 96.
51. Model Rules of Prof'l Conduct R. 1.6 cmt. [13] (2009).
52. Adams v. Franklin, 924 A.2d 993 (D.C. 2007).
53. Bennett, Cohen & Whittaker, *supra* note 14, at 94 (citing Ariz. Ethics Op. 2000-11 (2000) (lawyer called as witness in legal proceeding must invoke attorney-client privilege regarding communication with client *and* Rule 1.6 concerning all other information relating to representation, but lawyer must comply with final order of court in matter); R.I. Ethics Op. 2000-8 (2000) (lawyer questioned at deposition about matters relating to representation of deceased client is required by Rule 1.6 to invoke lawyer-client privilege, ethical duty of confidentiality, and, if applicable, work-product doctrine; lawyer must comply with final orders of court requiring disclosure)).
54. Rotunda & Dzienkowski, *supra* note 6, § 1.6-1.

CHAPTER 5

Preserving Candor between Lawyers and Clients: The Hidden Danger from Exceptions to the Attorney-Client Privilege

KENNETH A. HINDMAN
M. COLSTON JONES*

* This chapter is an outgrowth of chapters published in earlier editions of this book: Hindman & Burke, *The Attorney-Client Privilege in the "Bad Faith" Case: Does It Still Protect Anything?*, *in* THE ATTORNEY-CLIENT PRIVILEGE UNDER SIEGE (ABA 1989); Burke & Hindman, *The Attorney-Client Privilege in the "Bad Faith" Case: Does It Still Protect Anything?*, *in* ATTORNEY-CLIENT PRIVILEGE IN CIVIL LITIGATION (2d ed., ABA 1997), and Hindman & Wagner, *Preserving Candor: The Hidden Danger from "Exceptions" to the Attorney-Client Privilege*, *in* ATTORNEY-CLIENT PRIVILEGE IN CIVIL LITIGATION (3d ed., ABA 2005) and (4th ed., ABA 2009).

I. *What Lawyers and Clients Understand About the Attorney-Client Privilege, and What It Means to Them*

Most lawyers believe that their communications to their clients, and those from their clients to them, are protected from disclosure by the attorney-client privilege, with only very limited exceptions.[1] It is also almost certain that clients generally rarely worry about the possibility that their communications might not be covered by the privilege because of the subject being discussed or the type of work to be performed by the lawyer. Their conception of the attorney-client privilege would probably resemble the type of privilege described by the Supreme Court of Missouri:

> When a client goes to an attorney and asks him to represent him on a claim which he believes he has against someone or which is being asserted against him, even if he as yet has no knowledge or information about the claim, subsequent communications by the attorney to the client should be privileged. Some of the advice given by the attorney may be based on information obtained from sources other than the client. Some of what the attorney says will not actually be advice as to a course of conduct to be followed. Part may be an analysis of what is known to date of the situation. Part may be a discussion of additional avenues to be pursued. Part may be keeping the client advised of things done or opinions formed to date. All of these communications, not just the advice, are essential elements of attorney-client consultation. All should be protected.[2]

This chapter suggests, however, that lawyers and clients who hold to this traditional view of the attorney-client privilege are likely to be mistaken, in that their communications are almost certain to be at some risk of disclosure, even if those communications are kept strictly confidential.[3]

There is a real danger that expansion of the exceptions to the attorney-client privilege will destroy the basic understanding between lawyers and clients that their communications are confidential. Further, expansion of these exceptions and the resultant loss of trust between lawyers and clients could well destroy the ability of lawyers to assess the merits of their clients' cases based upon full information. In turn, lawyers would thereby lose their ability to resolve their clients' matters informally, which would cause grave harm to the legal system as a whole. To avoid these serious consequences, the courts should construe exceptions to the attorney-client privilege narrowly; but should punish severely those who attempt to manipulate the attorney-client privilege to conceal evidence.

II. *The Unspoken Understanding between Lawyers and Clients*

As the U.S. Supreme Court has recognized, clients tell their lawyers things about which they are ashamed, embarrassed, or fearful.[4] Clients do not typically know exactly what information is legally pertinent, and they therefore disclose a range of information that, in many cases, they earnestly desire to keep private.[5] It is common sense that if clients believed that lawyers would be forced to disclose what clients said to them, candid attorney-client communications would cease.[6] This is perhaps more clearly the case with individual clients than with corporate/business clients, but it is true in both settings.

For example, lawyers who have practiced in Europe, where there is often no privilege, have reported that the absence of the privilege had an inhibiting effect on communications; while oral communications continued to be candid to some extent, written communications became sanitized, and much more circumspect, against the possibility of their being disclosed.[7] The effect of such loss of candor is not only that clients will not tell their lawyers the (potentially embarrassing or dangerous) truth, but also that lawyers will no longer give clients clear, unequivocal advice.[8]

Only by free communication with the client can a lawyer assess the merits of the client's position, talk frankly with the opposing party or lawyer, and reach a fair resolution of the client's problem. This is the process by which nearly all cases are resolved. A lawyer who does not know the truth cannot discuss cases frankly enough to resolve them. Similarly, if lawyers cannot give their clients advice clearly and confidentially, the process will not work, because clients will not understand proposed resolutions and the reasons for them, and will therefore be unlikely to agree to those resolutions.

III. The Source of the Danger: Substantive Law

The danger to the attorney-client privilege arises from the modern trend to base some types of liability on the opposing party's state of mind, the reasonableness of the opposing party's actions, or similar subjective considerations. That is, liability in such cases is based not only on whether a party adhered to a standard of conduct, or fulfilled the terms of a contract, but also on *how* the party did so. Once a party's state of mind is placed at issue, it is easy to argue that what the party told his or her lawyer, and any advice the party received from the lawyer, are relevant evidence.

There are many different contexts in which the law now allows liability to be based on intent or state of mind: the most obvious are claims against insurers based on allegations of bad faith. Liability under state abusive litigation statutes and under Federal Rule 11 also turns, at least in part, on whether the defending party had a good-faith basis for its actions.

There is no way to avoid the conflict between claims of "need for" discovery of attorney-client communications in such cases, and the normal assumption that such communications are privileged.[9] The substantive law has jumped ahead of clear thinking about its effect on the privilege, so that determining when and to what extent bad-faith claims[10] affect the attorney-client privilege has become wildly unpredictable and uncertain.

IV. The Source of the Danger: Procedural and Process Considerations

The proliferation of substantive bad-faith claims has coincided with acceptance by some courts and scholars of the "Wigmore view" of a tightly restricted attorney-client privilege. In that view:

> Its benefits are all indirect and speculative; its obstruction is plain and concrete. . . . It is worth preserving for the sake of a general policy, but it is nonetheless an obstacle to the investigation of the truth. It ought to be strictly confined within the narrowest possible limits consistent with the logic of its principle.[11]

That is, the privilege is a necessary evil, to be restricted to its narrowest bounds. Therefore, under the Wigmore view, (1) the privilege is the exception rather than the rule; and (2) exceptions to the privilege are to be interpreted broadly. This point of view is contrary to the traditional view, and to the expectations of most attorneys and their clients.[12]

Courts attempting to apply a restricted privilege have created a bewildering group of criteria and explanations for how and when the privilege applies; for example:

- "[T]he Court should recognize a privilege only where the *injury* that would inure to the relation by the disclosure of the communications [is] *greater than the benefit* thereby gained for a correct disposal of litigation."[13]
- "[C]ommunications [made by attorneys] are shielded only if they rest on confidential information obtained from the client. . . . The attorney-client privilege, therefore, does not protect an attorney's opinion or advice, but only the secrecy of the underlying facts obtained from the client."[14]
- "[T]he privilege should attach only where extending its protection would foster more forthright and complete communication between the attorney and her client about the client's legal dilemma."[15]
- "The information-holder's motive for the communication, to the extent that it can be discerned from the document, thus is an important consideration. If the information-holder will communicate with the attorney even if the privilege does not exist, or if a nonlegal objective is sufficient to stimulate communication with the attorney, then there is no reason for the privilege to attach."[16]

Formulations of the privilege such as these make it difficult for lawyers and clients "to predict with some degree of certainty whether particular discussions will be protected," as the U.S. Supreme Court has said that they should be able to do.[17] The Court's concern was that "an uncertain privilege, or one that purports to be certain but results in widely varying applications by the Courts, is little better than no privilege at all."[18]

The problem of uncertainty has been made worse by the willingness of some courts to remove the privilege from otherwise protected communications, based on bad-faith allegations in later litigation. Attorneys and their clients cannot anticipate whether a court will determine after the fact that a confidential communication has become "at issue."[19]

Removing the privilege because a communication is at issue makes application of the privilege uncertain because the communication is placed at issue by allegations made by the opposing party, rather than by any action of the privilege holder. Some courts recognized early on that allowing privileges to be waived because of the other party's allegations would quickly make any privilege useless. For example, the Texas Supreme Court accurately observed that:

> [I]f a plaintiff attempting to prove the validity of a claim against an insurer could obtain the insurer's investigative files merely by alleging the insurer acted in bad faith, all insurance claims would contain such allegations.[20]

One Arizona federal court held that attorney-client communications were placed at issue by a counterclaim contending that the plaintiff filed suit on patents it knew were invalid.[21] Other courts have held that the privilege is lost where a party responds to an allegation of knowingly wrongful action by explaining why it believed that its actions were justified.[22] The court held that the defending party could avoid losing the privilege by simply denying allegations of wrongdoing, but would lose the privilege if it "advances its own interpretation of the law as a defense."[23] The defending party disavowed any reliance on advice of its counsel, stating that it was relying on the objective merits of its legal position, but it was held nevertheless to have "thrust" its lawyer's knowledge into the litigation and to have waived the privilege.[24] Not surprisingly, this holding was criticized as introducing "intolerable uncertainty into the question whether attorneys and their clients can regard communications as privileged."[25]

While a few courts have refused to allow such after-the-fact privilege determinations,[26] many more appear willing to permit them, creating real practical problems for attorneys and clients, and ignoring the U.S. Supreme Court's admonition that:

> Balancing *ex post* the importance of the information against client interest . . . introduces substantial uncertainty into the privilege's application. For just that reason, we have rejected use of a balancing test in defining the contours of the privilege.[27]

Loose and undefined standards make the privilege uncertain not only for attorneys and clients; these standards also create problems for the courts. As one federal district court judge observed:

> Lawyers love to know the secret communications between opposing parties and their counsel. And some lawyers love to strike fear into hearts of opponents by attempting to discover those communications. Motions to penetrate clearly applicable privileges can be tools for harassment. . . . The looser the standard [for the privilege], the greater the risk that it will be abused for such tactical purposes. . . . If . . . relatively soft showings were sufficient both to generate substantial adversarial proceedings and to shift the risk of nonpersuasion to the holder of the privilege, the temptation to initiate such challenges would be considerable. . . . Using a less substantial, poorly defined, and only vaguely understood standard also makes rulings on challenges to the privilege less predictable. When the rulings are less predictable, the incentives to launch challenges increase—as do the burdens on the courts.[28]

The problems caused by this lack of standards can be seen in the way exceptions to the privilege are applied.

V. How Restricting the Scope of the Privilege Expands Exceptions to the Privilege

Three general types of exceptions to the privilege have developed: (1) the exception for nonlegal work performed by a lawyer; (2) the at issue/bad faith exception and (3) the crime-fraud exception. Restricting the scope of the privilege and qualifying its applicability makes each type of exception broader and more difficult to apply, and creates conflicts with the traditional practices of attorneys and clients.

A. Exception for "Nonlegal" Work

This exception removes the privilege from work that, although performed by lawyer, is not viewed as legal work. That means either that (1) the work is seen as not involving "lawyering" skills (i.e., not applying legal principles to solving a problem) or (2) the work is of the type that would otherwise be classified as "legal," but the privilege is removed because the lawyer's work is part of the normal course of business of his client.

Removing the privilege under this type of exception necessarily conflicts with the desire of clients to hire lawyers to perform a variety of tasks, some of which could very well be performed by nonlawyers. For example, some courts have denied the privilege where lawyers performed fact investigations for their clients.[29]

As the U.S. Supreme Court recognized in *Upjohn*, however: "The first step in the resolution of any legal problem is ascertaining the factual background, and sifting through the facts with an eye to the legally relevant."[30] The Supreme Court's reasoning has been followed in many cases, acknowledging that clients often want to have a lawyer investigate a matter, regardless of whether a nonlawyer could also do so. As one federal circuit court observed, if a party simply needed a lay investigator to collect and summarize information, it could have used its own staff and avoided the expense of hiring counsel; however, "clients often do retain lawyers to perform investigative work because they want the benefit of a lawyer's expertise and judgment"; in that particular case, the court emphasized that "[the lawyer's] interview memoranda evidenced that her understanding of the underlying *legal* issues dictated the direction of the interviews."[31]

The privilege applies in such a traditional view simply because the lawyer's work "pertains to a matter on which the attorney was consulted for his professional advice."[32]

Other courts have denied protection to a lawyer's work that, from the client's point of view, was done pursuant to a request for legal advice, because the work was characterized as part of the client's "normal course of business."[33] In some cases, the courts make rough assumptions as to whether lawyers' work is protected, based more on whether the lawyers were outside or in-house counsel, or on their positions in the client's business organization, than on the specifics of their clients' requests for legal assistance.[34]

In some cases, a lawyer's work is seen as part of the normal course of business of his client because the lawyer actually makes management decisions, or performs work that is required of the client by law or by contract. Removing the privilege in such situations likely does not conflict with most clients' concept of the privilege, since the lawyer in that type of setting is participating in a business decision or transaction, rather than acting as an advisor to the client.[35]

Even determining whether a lawyer is performing "business" or "legal" work creates practical problems for the courts. In any such case, applying the exception requires the type of fact-based analysis performed by the district court in the *ChevronTexaco* case, where the court determined:

> These communications were not made primarily, if at all, for the purpose of seeking legal advice. The contents of these communications are purely financial. They reflect factual information used to implement the transaction.[36]

Obviously, coming to such a conclusion required that the court read the documents involved in detail, and determine where each fit into the overall series of events. If nothing else, the court's conclusion that the contents of the particular set of e-mails at issue was "purely financial" shows that the court read the entire set of documents.

B. "Bad Faith"/"At Issue" Exception

Clients can avoid losing the privilege under the nonlawyer-work exception by having their lawyers act as advisors, rather than as participants, or by being prepared to present independent evidence as to a matter investigated by lawyers. Most clients, the authors believe, would readily accept that a lawyer's participation in the actual events at issue (e.g., having voted to terminate an employee in a wrongful discharge case) means that the lawyer's work would not be privileged. Clients would probably also accept that, for example, they could not legitimately refuse to disclose facts discovered by a lawyer on the grounds of privilege.

Clients understand that the lawyer's role is to be outside the client's decisions, and that such separation is necessary for the client to preserve the right to consider the lawyer's advice privileged. That conception of the roles of attorneys and clients worked well enough when the operative facts of cases were what the client did, and when the client's actions alone determined whether the client had met the terms of a contract or committed a tort. Under this earlier view of things, whether the client had received legal advice was beside the point; the content of that advice was certainly beside the point.

As discussed above, however, the advent of bad-faith causes of action has led to placing the decision-making process behind any client action at issue. The bad-faith causes of action that underlie the exception are now part of our substantive law, and will remain so. The courts have struggled to allow the privilege to coexist with them, without being destroyed by them, but the inherent nature of bad-faith claims makes that difficult.

A bad-faith case is resolved under legal principles such as "whether an insurer has acted in bad faith towards its insured depends on the reasonableness of its conduct . . . [and] whether the insurer knew that its conduct was unreasonable"; a finding of bad faith "is predicated precisely on the *manner* in which [defendant] reached its decision."[37]

Such a determination requires inquiries into "any investigations conducted by the [defendant], the information available to the company at the time its decision was made, and the manner in which the company arrived at its decision, including reliance on advice of counsel."[38] That is, the operative facts in a bad-faith case include all steps the client took to reach the decision in question.[39]

In turn, the courts have held that "bad faith actions . . . can only be proved by showing exactly how the company processed the claim, how thoroughly it was considered and why the company took the action it did."[40] From that, it followed that documents held by the accused party were freely discoverable.[41] Some courts have dismissed out of hand claims of privilege in bad faith cases, even where part of the materials in question were attorney-client letters: "the time-worn claims of . . . attorney-client privilege cannot be invoked to the [defendant's] benefit where the only issue in the case is whether the company breached its duty of good faith in processing the insured's claim."[42]

A client may carefully use his lawyer as an advisor rather than a participant in the client's decisions, but the lawyer's advice may nevertheless be put at issue by bad-faith allegations. In bad-faith situations, the lawyer's advice becomes as much of an issue as the client's decision in the underlying dispute. In fact, the underlying dispute (breach of contract, commission of a tort) may become irrelevant, because the client may be held independently liable for the breach of an implied covenant of good faith and fair dealing[43] or an abusive litigation statute.

By placing virtually any attorney-client communication at risk of disclosure on bad-faith grounds, however, the courts have made it risky for clients to consult attorneys when they fear that they may be "doing wrong." Those, of course, are the very situations in which clients are most likely to consult lawyers. One of the principal bases for the U.S. Supreme Court's approval of a broad corporate attorney-client privilege in *Upjohn* was the following:

> The narrow scope given the attorney-client privilege by the court below not only makes it difficult for corporate attorneys to formulate sound advice when their client is faced with a specific legal problem, but also threatens the valuable efforts of corporate counsel to ensure their client's compliance with the law.[44]

That is, if clients are afraid to disclose their concerns about the lawfulness of their planned actions, lawyers cannot fulfill their roles as counselors, to guide their clients' actions to conform to the law.

Even if the bad-faith exception does not negate the privilege entirely, the uncertainty about when exceptions to the privilege might apply will have that effect. This consequence can be avoided (1) if the courts recognize that clients have the right to be advised by lawyers; and (2) if lawyers and clients recognize that the substantive law now requires that they carefully consider how lawyers are used, in light of potential bad-faith liability.

In dealing with this problem, the courts have acknowledged that "it would be a rare confidential communication that would not satisfy the relevancy test."[45] Also, attorney-client communications have "pragmatic importance," but if the privilege could be abrogated on that ground, "the privilege would have little meaning."[46]

Avoiding the loss of the privilege requires that the courts restrict the situations in which an opposing party can force abrogation of the privilege by way of its allegations against the privilege holder. For example, the advice of counsel is not necessarily "interjected into" a case by a responding party's denial of allegations, where the responding party may have had legal advice regarding those allegations.[47]

Courts also should be wary of allowing essentially legal arguments to form the basis for waiver of the privilege (e.g., they should determine the legitimacy of legal positions on the merits of those positions, rather than allowing discovery of attorney opinions as to the strength of those positions.)

Lawyers and clients in this era, however, must recognize that the decision-making process of the client may be placed at issue with respect to any action the client takes. Clients, therefore, cannot ignore the fact that *they* must be able to explain the bases for their decisions, since the substantive law has made those relevant to liability.

Clients must therefore either participate themselves in work such as investigations undertaken by lawyers, or must have an independent basis (aside from advice, facts, or conclusions conveyed by a lawyer) for any decisions that rest on information provided by lawyers. This approach would not allow clients simply to turn matters over to lawyers, then sign off on the recommended course of action; clients must become more personally involved in those matters. Only by truly being able to provide evidence as to how and why decisions were reached can clients expect the courts to uphold the privilege for lawyers' advice. That is, the reasoning behind decisions must be the client's rather than the lawyer's.

If clients do not accept this responsibility, they will likely have to choose between having a lawyer with knowledge of the decision-making process testify, or being precluded from offering evidence to explain conduct, particularly where only the lawyer can give the explanation, but the information has not been produced on grounds of privilege.[48]

Courts thus must respect the legitimacy of clients' consultation with lawyers, and refrain from ordering disclosure of such communications on the basis of simple allegations of bad faith. These considerations also have caused increasing and similar problems for the courts in interpreting the crime-fraud exception to the privilege.

C. "Crime Fraud" Exception

The crime-fraud exception developed to prevent clients from profiting from abuse of the attorney-client relationship. For example, one court found evidence of "an ongoing or imminent crime or fraud" in a " pervasive and systematic scheme to destroy or alter subpoenaed evidence," coupled with "routinely perjured testimony" by the party's archivist, "all with the knowledge and participation of [party's] legal department."[49] In another case, the exception applied where fiduciaries accused of creating false financial statements sought legal assistance in rescinding a sale "for their own personal benefit," in conflict with the interests of the company's shareholders.[50]

The exception, however, has increasingly been applied not in cases of real abuse, but to simple allegations of tort. At the same time, the showing required to invoke the exception has become increasingly minimal.

Without much apparent hesitation, some courts have leaped from applying the exception to cases of crime or fraud to allegations of tortious conduct. As one court put it: "We are convinced that the consideration underlying the firmly established denial of the privilege for communications and furtherance of crime or fraud . . . is equally compelling with regard to communications in furtherance of the intentional tort [emotional distress] of which plaintiffs herein complain."[51]

The crime-fraud exception has become increasingly difficult to apply consistently because the showing required to invoke the exception has decreased, even as the breadth of its coverage has increased. For example, one court held that the "prima facie case" required to defeat the privilege consisted of "requiring that the evidence in favor of [the] proposition be sufficient to support a finding in its favor, if all of the evidence to the contrary be disregarded."[52] In other words, the privilege could be done away with by meeting the motion to dismiss standard, without necessarily proving any facts, and without considering any evidence to the contrary. Another court required only that there be a showing of "some foundation in fact" to constitute a prima facie case to abrogate the privilege.[53]

With "tort" or "bad faith" becoming a common adjunct to any litigation, the danger is apparent that even minimal accusations of such conduct will abrogate the privilege on crime-fraud grounds.[54]

The courts have therefore been forced to confront the danger that this exception, like the bad-faith exception, will destroy the ability of clients to consult attorneys about potentially problematic conduct. As one court put it:

> Good-faith consultations with attorneys by clients who are uncertain about the legal implications of a proposed course of conduct are entitled to the privilege, even if that action should later be held improper.[55]

Similarly,

> If legal advice loses its privileged status merely because the opponent claims that the advice was sought to conceal a fraud, the privilege quickly evaporates. If that were the law, few clients would dare talk to lawyers, because the privilege would disappear the moment their opponent charged a cover-up.[56]

In order to preserve the predominant place of the privilege in relation to the crime-fraud exception, the courts should return to applying the exception only to cases to which it clearly applies. For example, most jurisdictions require that fraud be pleaded "with specificity." The courts should refuse to apply the exception when a proponent has not set out the level of factual support required under such pleading rules.[57]

Similarly, the courts should reject attempts to use tort allegations as crimes or frauds; for example, a defendant's delays in responding to a plaintiff's insurance claim, and other investigatory activity, cannot legitimately be described as crimes.[58] Another court explained the "fundamental differences between fraud and bad faith" as follows:

> Bad faith denial of insurance means simply that the insurer breached an implied contractual agreement. . . . This need not implicate false or misleading statements by the insurer. For example, an insurer may act in bad faith if it simply denies coverage without any explanation. The gravamen of fraud, however, is falsity. . . .[59]

The court went on to point out that "even courts that find bad faith within the crime-fraud exception have difficulty equating bad faith with fraud.

Ultimately, these courts simply make a policy decision that bad faith should not be protected by the lawyer-client privilege."[60]

Other courts have refused to draw strained inferences of criminal or fraudulent conduct as bases for invoking the exception (e.g., court refused to infer that legal advice was sought in order to further illegal conduct from fact that client discussed campaign finance laws with counsel, then "within weeks" violated those laws).[61] Some courts have required more-convincing circumstantial evidence to support the exception (e.g., client knew when he consulted attorney that his intended conduct was unlawful, because he had surreptitiously created corporations to receive funds from his employer, he immediately received "substantial funds" following initial payments by his employer, and he had agreed in writing to abide by his employer's policy against self-dealing).[62]

Judicial self-restraint of this type is especially necessary to avoid overburdening the courts with fact-intensive privilege determinations.

VI. Why the Courts Are Not the Answer

Reported cases increasingly reveal that proponents of the exceptions discussed above believe that the courts can ensure that the exceptions are applied fairly and consistently. This position was notably adopted by the U.S. Supreme Court in the recent case of *Mohawk Industries, Inc. v. Carpenter*.[63] In *Mohawk*, the Supreme Court held that decisions concerning claims of attorney-client privilege are not reviewable by federal appellate courts under the collateral order doctrine; instead, a party wishing to appeal such a decision will generally not be permitted to do so until the conclusion of the litigation. In reaching this decision, the Supreme Court reasoned that "[m]ost district court rulings on these matters [involving the attorney-client privilege] involve the routine application of settled legal principles."[64] The Supreme Court further noted that such decisions "are unlikely to be reversed on appeal, particularly when they rest on factual determinations for which appellate deference is the norm."[65]

Proponents of the exceptions appear also to believe that, upon a minimal showing that an exception may apply to a group of documents, they should be able to have a court physically review the documents in camera. Advocates of in camera inspections rarely, however, acknowledge the degree to which such inspections interfere with the normal work of the courts.

In the law review article *The Corporate Attorney-Client Privilege: A Study of the Participants*, several magistrates and judges "volunteered that when corporate parties were involved," in camera reviews could be "time consuming, tedious, or unpleasant task[s] to be avoided whenever possible."[66] One federal magistrate commented, along the same lines:

> The larger the volume of documents reviewed *in camera*, the greater the potential harm to the privilege and the greater burden on the courts. These kinds of burdens consume finite judicial resources. . . .

> In other words, large-scale inspections of the kind that would be involved here impose real and substantial costs on the administration of justice.[67]

In addition, it is difficult for judges to conduct such reviews during the pretrial discovery stage of cases (when, however, most such reviews appear to occur). Most judges have no reason to learn the details of a case at the discovery stage; that usually occurs, at the earliest, when a motion for summary judgment is filed. Not surprisingly, one magistrate commented that "it is especially difficult during the early stages of pretrial discovery to know whether particular facts are even relevant to the litigation."[68]

Perhaps because they dislike conducting in camera reviews themselves, judges often delegate those reviews to their law clerks. The clerks, however, are often less capable than the parties or the judge of competently resolving such disputes, since they typically lack trial or general practice experience.[69]

The burden that in camera inspections impose on the courts is made worse by the fact that, under the current very loose and unspecific standards for applying the privilege, such inspections may routinely be required. That is so because under many newer formulations of the privilege, it is not possible to determine whether a communication is privileged based only on the fact that it is an attorney-client communication. Rather, the context of the communication and the intent of the parties may have to be ascertained. Under such standards, there are few obvious answers to questions of privilege.

Loose and vague standards also virtually ensure that when a court conducts an in camera review, the court will have to read each document in full, and analyze it in reference both to other documents reviewed, and to several external factors.

The need for in camera reviews whenever a party argues that the privilege should not apply, and the depth of treatment required in any review can easily be seen, where the decision as to whether the privilege applies must turn on factors such as:

- The degree of injury that disclosure would cause to the attorney-client relationship;[70]
- Whether a communication "rests on" or "discloses" client confidences;[71]
- The effect that upholding the privilege would have on fostering "more forthright and complete communication" between lawyer and client;[72]
- Whether a "nonlegal objective" would have been sufficient to stimulate communication with the lawyer.[73]

Especially considering the increasing caseloads and cuts in resources that confront almost all courts, it is absolutely unrealistic to expect the courts to give in camera reviews the time and attention their theoretical purpose would require.

Perhaps the worst aspect of emphasizing the courts' role in resolving privilege questions is that emphasis is thereby drawn away from attorney-client relationships outside litigation; it is there that the most serious harm from the expansion of the exceptions will occur.

VII. Why Litigation-Based Rules Should Not Define the Privilege

Those favoring the expansion of exceptions to the attorney-client privilege are concerned with what evidence will be available in discovery or admissible at trial. They argue that putting all relevant evidence before the fact-finder will increase the likelihood of a just result. The authors believe, however, that defining the scope of the privilege and its exceptions according to such litigation-based considerations is both shortsighted and foolish.

While litigated cases make up an insignificant fraction of all matters about which clients consult attorneys, virtually no attention has been given to the effect that litigation-based rules would have on the vast majority of nonlitigated matters. Even established commentators attempting to explain the privilege as it exists today seem to be blind to the importance of keeping attorney-client communications outside of litigation confidential, arguing that it is evidentiary disclosure that clients fear. It is obvious, however, from the discussion above that a qualified, uncertain privilege, subject to exceptions, would have the general effect of frightening clients away from consulting lawyers.

In reaching its decision in *Mohawk*, the Supreme Court acknowledged that the possibility of disclosure of attorney-client communications can have a chilling effect on the frankness of those communications. The Supreme Court, however, reasoned that the unavailability of an interlocutory appeal to vindicate a claim of privilege would not result in a "discernible chill" because "in deciding how freely to speak, clients and counsel are unlikely to focus on the remote prospect of an erroneous disclosure order, let alone the timing of a possible appeal."[74] The Supreme Court also noted that under current law, "clients and counsel must account for the possibility that they will later be required by law to disclose their communications for a variety of reasons—for example, because they misjudged the scope of the privilege, because they waived the privilege, or because their communications fell within the privilege's crime-fraud exception."[75]

The *Mohawk* Court expressed a willingness to accept an abrogation of candid communication between attorneys and clients as a necessary cost of the exceptions to the privilege. This cost is necessarily increased, however, by vaguely defined exceptions to the privilege. The primary reason that vaguely defined exceptions are dangerous to the legal system is that they could well make the overall legal system unworkable in the interest of satisfying largely theoretical concerns of academics and of the parties in a tiny number of cases in litigation. Anyone who considers this an overstatement of the problem should examine the specific justifications advanced for restricting the privilege, and particularly the factual assumptions made by their authors. Such published contentions[76] include (1) that clients are unwilling to be candid with their lawyers unless they are aware that there is a likelihood of litigation;[77] (2) that the functioning of the legal profession would not be affected if there were no absolute non-litigation-related privilege;[78] (3) that there is no persuasive empirical evidence that functioning attorney-client relationships would be destroyed if non-litigation-related communications were revealed in litigation, and that the only clients who would be deterred by the possibility of such disclosures are those who are "extra-cautious and concerned about the prospect of litigation";[79] (4) that even if imposing a requirement that communications be litigation-related in order to be privileged did affect how clients behaved toward their lawyers, such a limitation would still be justified, because it would aid the litigation process, and the privilege itself has a litigation-based rationale;[80] and (5) that a justification of the privilege based on its effect on the courts would automatically be stronger than one "framed in terms of benefit to professional relationships entirely extrinsic to the judicial process."[81]

Full disclosure of the facts probably does increase the likelihood of a just result in any given case, but the legal system should be more concerned with whether full information is conveyed by clients to their lawyers in everyday consultations, rather than with whether such information is presented in court.

In the authors' experience, virtually all cases that pass through our legal system are resolved by lawyers; the number of matters adjudicated in courts is minuscule by comparison. It is clear that lawyers have to know the facts from their clients, warts and all.[82] Lawyers resolve cases by making judgments about the merits and equities of their clients' cases, talking frankly with opposing lawyers to find a fair resolution of the problem, and convincing their clients that the recommended resolution should be accepted. Each stage of the process requires that the lawyer and client know all of the facts, and be able to speak frankly to each other. For example, one way for lawyers to establish trust in negotiations is to acknowledge the weaknesses in their clients' cases. Lawyers also must be able to convey to their clients conclusions that the clients may not want to hear, such as that a seemingly unsatisfactory settlement is fair, given the deficiencies in the client's case.[83]

The process described occurs constantly; in some cases the lawyer may even advise a client not to pursue a matter at all, based on the client's frank disclosures. That, too, is a "resolution" of a case.

It seems clear that if the process described becomes impossible because clients are afraid that their communications will be disclosed, the legal system will quickly become overloaded as many cases that otherwise would be quickly resolved instead proceed to litigation. It is also possible that clients will resolve matters without any attorney involvement. On the other hand, if the privilege were circumscribed as suggested, the effect on the legal system as a whole would be negligible.

VIII. Conclusion

The authors believe that, in their efforts to manipulate the attorney-client privilege in discovery and evidentiary matters, courts and commentators have lost sight of the larger picture. Proposals to restrict the privilege to litigation-related communications dismiss the importance of the confidentiality of attorneys' consultative communications to clients. Furthermore, these proposals ignore the damage caused by disclosures of attorney-client communications, and the effect that the absence of a privilege would have on the ability of lawyers to handle most cases. These attitudes reflect a profound ignorance of how clients in the real world think. It is difficult to understand how anyone with even slight exposure to the way that lawyers resolve problems in the real world could take the position that removing the privilege for nonlitigation communications could be justified in light of its inevitable effect. Once the privilege becomes doubtful or uncertain, the potential for harm to the legal system as a whole is quite real.

Such harm is particularly hard to justify where the attempt to expand the use of privileged material in court is both impractical and unlikely, in any event, to yield evidence of any real importance.

Ultimately, preserving the privilege requires that the system as a whole trusts lawyers not to abuse the privilege.[84] Some abuse would undoubtedly occur under the scheme for the privilege recommended in this chapter; it would be naive to pretend otherwise after the revelations of lawyer misconduct in the Enron debacle, for example.[85]

There is no doubt, however, that a certain number of lawyers who want to abuse the privilege will get away with it, simply because there is no way to know what occurs in the course of the millions of attorney-client communications that occur every day. This will be so no matter how severe the rules regarding exceptions to the privilege become, simply because only a minor fraction of any abuses will come to light.

Furthermore, as the U.S. Supreme Court has observed in *Upjohn*, denying disclosure of privileged documents "puts the adversary in no worse position than if the communications had never taken place."[86] Correspondingly, if the exceptions overcome the privilege, written attorney-client communications will simply cease to exist.[87] Moreover, the judges in the *St. John's Law Review* study found that the privileged information at issue in litigated cases only rarely turned out to be "necessary" (i.e., crucial or highly significant) to proving a claim or a defense.[88]

The courts do, however, have a significant responsibility in preserving the privilege. While it is clear to the authors that the courts cannot, and should not, monitor the relations between lawyers and clients in general, they should vigorously impose sanctions against lawyers and clients who set up systems to abuse the privilege. Published examples include (1) an insurer that retained a particular law firm "as a matter of course" to investigate all claims over $25,000 (thereby attempting to make its whole investigation "privileged");[89] (2) an insurer that, upon realizing its policies did not contain exclusions barring serious environmental claims, "referred" all such claims to a law firm, bypassing its own adjusters and conducting no adjustment activities, in an effort to preclude discovery;[90] and (3) a hospital that signed up a hospital employee who witnessed an accident as an "individual client," interviewed the "client," then refused to allow the "client" to see a summary of his interview when he was unable, at his deposition two years later, to recall the events surrounding the accident.[91]

The authors believe that the courts are well able to recognize such tactics, and that they have the ability to determine if this type of abuse is occurring (e.g., by questioning the attorneys and clients involved in camera). Behavior such as that mentioned makes it appear to the public that the privilege is simply another means of hiding information; it should therefore be punished with severity, in order to preserve public support for the privilege and its many other benefits.

The general public's ability in the future to consult lawyers confidentially, without fear that those discussions will be disclosed, and the enormously beneficial practical consequences that flow from that ability, will be damaged, unless the courts are mindful of the danger posed by expanding exceptions to the attorney-client privilege.

Notes

1. Such as where objective behavior shows that no effort was made to keep communications confidential; e.g., publishing advice in newsletter. S. Guar. Ins. Co. v. Ash, 383 S.E.2d 579, 583–84 (Ga. App. 1989) (conducting conference in presence of a third party, sending attorney-client letter to third party).
2. State *ex rel.* Great Am. Ins. Co. v. Smith, 574 S.W.2d 379, 384–85 (Mo. 1978) (footnotes omitted).
3. *See, e.g.*, State Farm Mut. Auto. Ins. Co. v. Lee, 13 P.3d 1169, 1176 n.4 (Ariz. 2000) (Even conduct that in no way "evinces" an intention to waive the privilege may nevertheless cause a waiver "when the conduct . . . places the claimant in such a position, with reference to the evidence, that it would be unfair and inconsistent to permit the retention of the privilege[.]") (quoting 8 J.H. Wigmore, Wigmore on Evidence § 2388, at 855). *Compare* Sayre Enters., Inc. v. Allstate Ins. Co., 2006 WL 3613286, at *4, *5 (W.D. Va. 2006) (rejecting *Lee* analysis, and noting that under Virginia law privilege is not abrogated "even for the purpose of administering justice"), *with* Roehrs v. Minn. Life Ins. Co., 228 F.R.D. 642, 646 (D. Ariz. 2005) (following *Lee* where adjustors relied in part on advice of counsel).
4. Swidler & Berlin v. United States, 524 U.S. 399, 407–08 (1998).
5. *Id.* at 407–08 (attorneys act as counselors on personal and family matters; "confidences about family matters or financial problems must be revealed. . . . The same is true of owners of small businesses . . .)."
6. *See generally* Vincent C. Alexander, *The Corporate Attorney-Client Privilege: A Study of the Participants*, 63 St. John's L. Rev. 191, 269 n.247 (1989) (suggesting that even if clients do not know the exact terms of the privilege, they would surely know it if there were no privilege).
7. *Id.* at 255 (speculating that oral communications are affected less because there is no written evidence of their content).
8. *Id.* at 274 (the danger of such sanitized advice is that "instead of condemning proposed illegal conduct in no uncertain terms, the lawyer's legal opinion

might be framed in an ambiguous manner, perhaps leading the client to take action that would violate the law or result in litigation").

9. *Compare Great Am.*, 574 S.W.2d at 383 (noting Dean Wigmore's emphasis on the fundamental societal need to have all evidence having a rational probative value placed before the trier of fact in a lawsuit), *with* Wesp v. Everson, 33 P.3d 191, 197 (Colo. 2001) ("Because the attorney-client privilege may frustrate the fact-finding process, it exists in constant tension with the judicial system's truth-seeking goals. However, that tension is the price that society must pay for the availability of justice to every citizen, which is the value that the privilege is designed to ensure.") (citations and internal punctuation omitted). *See also In re* Schafer, 66 P.3d 1036, 1041 (Wash. 2003) ("The attorney-client privilege is pivotal in the orderly administration of the legal system, which is the cornerstone of a just society. The reasoning is tripartite: to maintain the adversarial system, parties must utilize lawyers to resolve disputes; lawyers must know all the relevant facts to advocate effectively; and clients will not confide in lawyers and provide them with the necessary information unless the client knows what he says will remain confidential[.]").
10. "Bad faith" is a term of art encompassing the types of cases mentioned above.
11. Coleman v. Am. Broad. Cos., 106 F.R.D. 201, 205 n.2 (D.D.C. 1985).
12. *Great Am.*, 574 S.W.2d at 383 (noting that some commentators "view confidentiality of communications between attorney and client as the more fundamental policy, to which disclosure is the exception").
13. Dinkins v. State of Ohio, 116 F.R.D. 270, 272–73 (N.D. Ohio 1987) (case involving a claimed investigatory privilege) (emphasis in original) (internal punctuation omitted).
14. Alexander v. FBI, 193 F.R.D. 1, 5 (D.D.C. 2000) (internal punctuation omitted). *See also* Loftis v. Amica Mut. Ins. Co., 175 F.R.D. 5, 7, 10 (D. Conn. 1997) (attorney letter containing legal advice on exposure to bad-faith claim was not within privilege because it did not disclose any client confidences).
15. United States v. ChevronTexaco Corp., 241 F. Supp. 2d 1065, 1070 (N.D. Cal. 2002) (emphasis omitted).
16. Robinson v. Tex. Auto. Dealers Ass'n, 214 F.R.D. 432, 439–40 (E.D. Tex. 2003) (internal quotation marks omitted), *rev'd on other grounds, In re* Tex. Auto. Dealers Ass'n, 2003 WL 21911333 (5th Cir. 2003).
17. Upjohn Co. v. United States, 449 U.S. 383, 393 (1981).
18. *Id.* at 393; *see also* Samaritan Found. v. Goodfarb, 862 P.2d 870, 879 (Ariz. 1993) ("[A]n uncertain privilege has the potential of achieving the worst possible result: it could harm the truth seeking process without a corresponding increase in candor. . . . [A] narrow but absolute privilege is preferable to a broad but amorphous one.").
19. As they can more likely anticipate the loss of the privilege if they do not keep communications confidential, or if they discuss an ongoing crime or fraud.
20. Md. Am. Gen. Ins. Co. v. Blackmon, 639 S.W.2d 455, 458 (Tex. 1982) (case involving the work-product privilege); *see also* Sayre Enters., Inc. v. Allstate Ins. Co., 2006 WL 3613286, at *5 (W.D. Va. 2006); Genentech, Inc. v. Insmed Inc., 234 F.R.D. 667, 670 (N.D. Cal. 2006) ("The danger, if the implied waiver doctrine is not applied cautiously, is that the party asserting waiver could unilaterally effect that waiver through its pleading strategy.").
21. Kockums Indus. Ltd. v. Salem Equip., Inc., 561 F. Supp. 168, 172 (D. Or. 1983).

22. State Farm Mut. Auto. Ins. Co. v. Lee, 13 P.3d 1169, 1175 (Ariz. 2000).
23. *Id.* at 1178, 1179.
24. *Id.* at 1180, 1184.
25. *Id.* at 1186 (McGregor, J., dissenting).
26. *See, e.g.*, Dixie Mill Supply Co., Inc. v. Cont'l Cas. Co., 168 F.R.D. 554, 556–57 (E.D. La. 1996) ("[Plaintiff] insists that defendants have affirmatively placed at issue their state of mind and their knowledge of Louisiana law, which must have come from their attorneys, by asserting that they acted in good faith in compliance with the insurance policies and their legal obligations. . . . Such a rule would permit a plaintiff to force a defendant to abrogate its privileges simply by asserting in the complaint that the defendant acted in bad faith, which the defendant then denies and says that, to the contrary, it acted in good faith. . . . [A]ttorney advice is not in issue because it is relevant, and does not necessarily become an issue merely because the attorney's advice might affect the client's state of mind in a relevant manner." (internal quotation marks omitted)).
27. Swidler & Berlin v. United States, 524 U.S. 399, 409 (1998) (citing Upjohn Co. v. United States, 449 U.S. 383, 393 (1981).).
28. Laser Indus., Ltd. v. Reliant Techs., Inc., 167 F.R.D. 417, 424, 433, 441 (N.D. Cal. 1996) (applying crime-fraud exception to privilege).
29. *See, e.g.*, Nat'l Farmers Union Prop. & Cas. Co. v. Dist. Court, 718 P.2d 1044, 1049 (Colo. 1986) (en banc) (denying privilege for portion of attorney's memorandum summarizing "the results of a factual investigation").
30. *Upjohn*, 449 U.S. at 390–91.
31. *In re* Allen, 106 F.3d 582, 602 n.19, 604, 605 (4th Cir. 1997); *see also* Dunn v. State Farm Fire & Cas. Co., 122 F.R.D. 507, 509 (N.D. Miss. 1988), *aff'd*, 927 F.2d 869 (5th Cir. 1991) (a lawyer brings to bear the "training, skills, and background necessary to make the professional independent analysis and legal recommendations sought by [the client]"); *see also* Lipton Realty, Inc. v. St. Louis Hous. Auth., 705 S.W.2d 565, 570 (Mo. Ct. App. 1986) (lawyer's letter to client, detailing his on-site observations of condition of buildings and recommending settlement negotiations, was privileged); Grace M. Geisel, *The Legal Advice Requirement of the Attorney-Client Privilege: A Special Problem for In-House Counsel and Outside Attorneys Representing Corporations*, 48 MERCER L. REV. 1169, 1195, 1201 (Spring 1997) (advocating approach under which assistance given by attorney in a corporate setting, which included questions of commercial strategy and tactics, was held privileged, because advice was given in a context where "the attorney is presenting the issues and analyzing the choices on the basis of his legal expertise and with an obvious eye to the constraints imposed by applicable law," since this was part of service expected from modern lawyers); Amy L. Weiss, *In-House Counsel Beware: Wearing the Business Hat Could Mean Losing the Privilege*, 11 GEO. J. LEGAL ETHICS 393, 404–05 (Winter 1998) (endorsing approach of *S. Bell Tel. & Tel. Co. v. Deason*, 632 So. 2d 1377 (Fla. 1994): question is not whether communications were made to obtain legal advice, but rather whether they were made in the course of seeking legal services; this takes modern corporate context, in which attorneys use their professional training to perform a myriad of legal services other than rendering legal advice, into account).
32. *Lipton*, 705 S.W.2d at 570.
33. Some courts have held that certain types of tasks, even if performed by lawyers, are not within the privilege; e.g., preparing tax returns is viewed as primarily

an accounting function, even though it may require some knowledge of law. *See* United States v. Davis, 636 F.2d 1028, 1043 (5th Cir. 1981). *But see* United States v. Textron Inc. & Subsidiaries, 2007 WL 2458325, at *6 (D.R.I. 2007) (attorney's advice on tax consequences of transaction was rooted in law; tax planning and advice on statutory interpretation or case law are lawyer's work; tax accrual worksheets sought by IRS were privileged because they contained lawyer's opinions on areas in which the law was uncertain, along with his evaluation of client's chances of prevailing in later litigation).

34. *See, e.g.*, United States v. ChevronTexaco Corp., 241 F. Supp. 2d 1065, 1076 (N.D. Cal. 2002) (communications between a corporation and its outside legal counsel are presumed to be made in order to seek legal advice, but that presumption does not extend to communications with in-house counsel); *see also, e.g.*, Boca Investerings P'ship v. United States, 31 F. Supp. 2d 9, 12 (D.D.C. 1998) ("One important indicator of whether a lawyer is involved in giving legal advice . . . is his or her place in the corporation's organizational chart." There is a presumption that a lawyer in the legal department is giving legal advice, but an opposite presumption where a lawyer "works for the Financial Group or some other seemingly management or business side of the house."); Alison M. Hill, *A Problem of Privilege: In-House Counsel and the Attorney-Client Privilege in the United States and the European Community*, 27 CASE W. RES. J. INT'L L. 145, 146 & n.6, 147, 164 n.92 (Winter 1995) (describing a 1982 European Court of Justice decision that lawyers employed by corporations would no longer be covered by the attorney-client privilege because their "independence" had thereby been compromised). *Cf.* Elizabeth G. Thornburgh, *Sanctifying Secrecy: The Mythology of the Corporate Attorney-Client Privilege*, 69 NOTRE DAME L. REV. 157, 159 (1993) (arguing that "[O]nly elimination of the corporate attorney-client privilege can free the court system from the distortion and expense that was created by expanding the privilege to include corporate secrets.").
35. *See, e.g.*, City of Elmira v. Larry Walter, Inc., 453 N.Y.S.2d 259, 260 (N.Y. App. Div. 1982) (lawyer also made business decision responding to request that surety complete construction project); Marten v. Yellow Freight Sys., Inc., 1998 WL 13244, at *9 (D. Kan. 1998) (lawyer who was required to serve on "employment review committee" and who voted to terminate employee); Mission Nat'l Ins. Co. v. Lilly, 112 F.R.D. 160, 164 (D. Minn. 1986) (factual investigation by lawyers that was required by terms of insurance policy); Sanders v. Ala. State Bar, 161 F.R.D. 470, 473 (M.D. Ala. 1995) (recommendation by Bar counsel not privileged because investigating complaints and making recommendations was normal business of Bar).
36. *ChevronTexaco*, 241 F. Supp. 2d at 1078.
37. Deese v. State Farm Mut. Auto. Ins. Co., 838 P.2d 1265, 1268, 1270 (Ariz. 1992).
38. *In re* Bergeson, 112 F.R.D. 692, 697 (D. Mont. 1986).
39. *See City of Elmira*, 453 N.Y.S.2d at 260.
40. Brown v. Superior Court, 670 P.2d 725, 734 (Ariz. 1983) (en banc) (construing work-product privilege).
41. *Id.* at 734.
42. Silva v. Fire Ins. Exch., 112 F.R.D. 699, 700 (D. Mont. 1986).
43. *Deese*, 838 P.2d at 1270 ("absence of a breach of an express term of the policy is not fatal to a bad faith claim where the plaintiff can prove a breach of the implied covenant of good faith and fair dealing").

44. Upjohn Co. v. United States, 449 U.S. 383, 392 (1981). The authors suggest that the Supreme Court's statements apply with even greater force to the behavior of individual clients and the benefit of their lawyers' actions.
45. Dontzin v. Myer, 694 A.2d 264, 268 (N.J. Super. App. Div. 1997).
46. Twin City Fire Ins. Co. v. Burke, 63 P.3d 282, 287 (Ariz. 2003) (en banc).
47. *Id.* at 286. Note, however, that the conduct of the defendant in this case was not directly at issue.
48. *See, e.g.*, United Techs. Corp. v. Am. Home Assurance Co., 118 F. Supp. 2d 174, 178 n.2 (D. Conn. 2000) (where discovery concerning communications with lawyers assigned to handle claims was withheld as privileged, "there could be no explanatory testimony from those attorneys to dispel the clear negative inferences that no good faith claims settlement practice was underway").
49. *In re* Sealed Case, 754 F.2d 395, 399, 400 (D.C. Cir. 1985).
50. *In re* Diasonics Sec. Litig., 110 F.R.D. 570, 575 (D. Colo. 1986).
51. Diamond v. Stratton, 95 F.R.D. 503, 505 (S.D.N.Y. 1982); *see* Coleman v. Am. Broad. Cos., 106 F.R.D. 201, 207 (D.D.C. 1985) (listing other decisions applying the exception to tort allegations).
52. United Servs. Auto. Ass'n v. Werley, 526 P.2d 28, 32 n.15 (Alaska 1974); *cf.* Laser Indus., Ltd. v. Reliant Techs., Inc., 167 F.R.D. 417, 425 (N.D. Cal. 1996) (courts would reason unreliably if they were permitted to consider only the evidence of the party trying to penetrate the privilege, without regard to the opposing party's evidence).
53. Caldwell v. Dist. Court, 644 P.2d 26, 32 (Colo. 1982). *See also* Koch v. Specialized Care Servs., Inc., 437 F. Supp. 2d 362, 373 (D. Md. 2005) (exception can apply even if proponent does not plead a specific crime or cause of action in fraud).
54. *See* State *ex rel.* Allstate Ins. Co. v. Madden, 601 S.E.2d 25, 45 (W. Va. 2004) (Albright, J., dissenting) (Intent requirement for crime-fraud exception "bears emphasis in light of the fact that there appears to be a concerted attempt underway to use the crime-fraud exception to gain access to the insurance claims file . . . or what is referred to by lawyers in bad-faith litigation as the 'ticket to the gold mine.'").
55. State *ex rel.* N. Pac. Lumber Co. v. Unis, 579 P.2d 1291, 1295 (Or. 1978) (*quoted in Caldwell*, 644 P.2d at 32).
56. Nesse v. Pittman, 202 F.R.D. 344, 351 (D.D.C. 2001).
57. *See Madden*, 601 S.E.2d at 48 (Maynard, C.J., dissenting) (Since cause of action for fraud requires proof by clear and convincing evidence, insofar as the misdeed upon which a party bases his or her assertion of the crime-fraud exception also consists of fraudulent conduct, then the proper quantum of proof likewise would be clear and convincing evidence.).
58. Ferrara & DiMercurio, Inc. v. St. Paul Mercury Ins. Co., 173 F.R.D. 7, 12 (D. Mass. 1997).
59. Freedom Trust v. Chubb Group of Ins. Cos., 38 F. Supp. 2d 1170, 1172–73 (C.D. Cal. 1999); *Madden*, 601 S.E.2d at 43 (most significant and troubling flaw in decision allowing discovery is that majority overlooked that bad faith and civil fraud are not synonymous legal concepts).
60. *Freedom Trust*, 38 F. Supp. 2d at 1173 n.3 (citing *Werley*, 526 P.2d 28, as an example of such a court). *See also* Koch v. Specialized Care Servs., Inc., 437 F. Supp. 2d 362, 373, 375 (D. Md. 2005) (Evidence codes and cases are divided on extending the crime-fraud exception to wrongs that, although criminal or fraudulent,

"have hallmarks of clear illegality, and the threat of serious harm." Argues that exception should be expanded because "legislatures classify illegal acts as crimes or frauds for purposes and policies different from those defining the privilege." Court from this leaped to conclusion that "limiting the exception to crimes and frauds produces an exception narrower than principle and policy would otherwise indicate"; endorses view that "any distinction between crimes and frauds and other wrongdoings" is an "overly crude boundary.").

61. *In re* Sealed Case, 107 F.3d 46, 50 (D.C. Cir. 1997).
62. United States v. Skeddle, 989 F. Supp. 890, 901–02 (N.D. Ohio 1997). *See also In re* Economou, 362 B.R. 893, 898 (Bankr. N.D. Ill. 2007) (prima facie case showed that client had transferred property while mortgage was in default, and that attorney assisted client in scheme by preparing documents to implement transfers.)
63. Mohawk Indus., Inc. v. Carpenter, 130 S. Ct. 599 (2009).
64. *Id.* at 607.
65. *Id.* at 607.
66. Alexander, *supra* note 6, at 256–57 (internal quotation marks omitted).
67. Laser Indus., Ltd. v. Reliant Techs., Inc., 167 F.R.D. 417, 421 (N.D. Cal. 1996); *see also* United Investors Life Ins. v. Nationwide Life Ins., 233 F.R.D. 483, 486 (N.D. Miss. 2006) ("This court will not grant an *in camera* inspection where, as here, there are potentially hundreds, perhaps thousands, of documents which would require review.")
68. Alexander, *supra* note 6, at 260; *see also Laser*, 167 F.R.D. at 436 ("judges should exercise considerable caution when they are pressed during the discovery stage of complex litigation to find that a showing of crime or fraud that is sufficient to justify penetrating the privilege has been made").
69. Discussions with several colleagues who served as judicial clerks revealed that they uniformly found conducting in camera document reviews extremely difficult and time-consuming, for the reasons stated.
70. *See ChevronTexaco*, 241 F. Supp. 2d 1065.
71. *See Robinson*, 214 F.R.D. 432.
72. *See* Upjohn Co. v. United States, 449 U.S. 383 (1981).
73. *See id.* at 393; *see also* Samaritan Found. v. Goodfarb, 862 P.2d 870, 879 (Ariz. 1993).
74. Mohawk Indus., Inc. v. Carpenter, 130 S. Ct. 599, 607 (2009).
75. *Id.*
76. Norman Abrams, *Unpacking the Power of an Ante-Litigation Limitation on Consultation-for-Advice/Treatment Evidentiary Privileges*, 21 QUINNIPIAC L. REV. 1089 (2003).
77. *Id.* at 1100.
78. *Id.* at 1112–13.
79. *Id.*
80. *Id.* at 1114 n.46.
81. *Id.* at 1114–15.
82. *See* Alexander, *supra* note 6, at 396 n.733 (one in-house lawyer "said that the principal value of the attorney-client privilege . . . is the protection it offers to 'the mistakes, speculations, opinions, theories, ideas, and inferences' that clients communicate to lawyers").
83. *See, e.g.*, State *ex rel.* U.S. Fid. & Guar. Co. v. Mont. Second Judicial Dist. Court, 783 P.2d 911, 915–16 (Mont. 1989) (privilege "allows for an honest, careful and

prompt analysis by qualified persons. . . . The free flow of information between attorney and client equally benefits the claimant because it is this kind of communication which results in the settlement of most insurance claims.").

84. As one judge put it: "If the majority does not believe that corporations can be trusted with a meaningful attorney-client privilege, they should say so and attempt to justify such a conclusion." *Samaritan Found.*, 844 P.2d at 614 (Voss, P.J., dissenting), *rev'd*, 862 P.2d 870.
85. The authors suggest that the risk of harm from abuse of the privilege may be lessened by the fact that areas where such conduct might affect large numbers of people are often strictly regulated outside the court system (e.g., Securities and Exchange Commission, Sarbanes-Oxley Act).
86. Upjohn Co. v. United States, 449 U.S. 383, 395 (1981).
87. *See supra* notes 8 and 9.
88. Alexander, *supra* note 6, at 259 n.190.
89. Mission Nat'l Ins. Co. v. Lilly, 112 F.R.D. 160, 162 (D. Minn. 1986).
90. United Techs. Corp. v. Am. Home Assurance Co., 118 F. Supp. 2d 174, 176 (D. Conn. 2000).
91. *Samaritan Found.*, 862 P.2d at 873, 880.

CHAPTER 6

Protection of Attorney-Client Privilege and Work Product in the Electronic Disclosure Era

LAURIE A. WEISS

I. Introduction: Attorney-Client Privilege and Work-Product Doctrine under Strain

The attorney-client privilege has long been one of the most important evidentiary privileges available to lawyers and clients.[1] The privilege and the work-product doctrine[2] are designed to encourage free and open discussion between counsel and clients. In today's electronic age, even small and midsize companies generate large volumes and a wide variety of electronically stored information (ESI). Litigation often involves review and production of tens or hundreds of thousands of electronic documents. For both inside and outside counsel, preserving a claim of privilege is a difficult issue.

II. Challenge of the Information Age: Increasing Data Volumes and Rising Costs of Attorney Review

Attorney review of client documents to avoid inadvertent production of privileged information traditionally has been part of the litigation discovery process. Massive proliferation of ESI, however, has caused privilege review to become an increasingly daunting and expensive task. Conducting a page-by-page privilege review in today's e-world is time-consuming and burdensome, and the costs can be astronomical. As a result, there is growing pressure in some cases to produce large volumes of data without prior attorney review. Further, even when a diligent privilege review is conducted, large volumes of data and the complex variety of ESI make it more probable that privileged documents will be missed during review and inadvertently produced.

The high cost of privilege review is confirmed by corporate counsel who responded to Fulbright & Jaworski L.L.P.'s Fourth Annual Litigation Trends Survey, released October 2007.[3] The survey is the largest of its kind, with over 300 general counsel or heads of litigation responding in 2007. More than a quarter of the respondents estimated that at least one-fifth of their annual litigation expense went toward a preproduction privilege review, including the 16 percent of respondents for whom it represented at least 30 percent of litigation spending. Even among smaller companies, 30 percent said the preproduction process accounted for a fifth or more of overall litigation costs. For billion-dollar firms, it was 33 percent of annual spending. One $1 billion-plus respondent stated it had spent over $3 million on preproduction privilege review in a single matter. Further, 17 percent of responding U.S. companies and 40 percent of U.K. companies reported that they had waived attorney-client privilege as a result of inadvertent production of ESI.

III. Scope of the Problem: Proliferation of Electronically Stored Information

A terabyte of information is not infrequently the relevant unit of measure in large civil litigation or government investigations today. A terabyte is 1,000 gigabytes, or 1 million megabytes. Depending on the type of data, a terabyte of information may fill 50,000 to 75,000 pages of paper.[4] To understand the scope of these figures, a terabyte of printed paper pages would produce a stack approximately equal to the height of 58 Empire State buildings.[5]

Page-by-page privilege review is a time-consuming process. An average electronic document contains five to eight pages.[6] A skilled attorney using available technology may attain an average review rate of 100 documents per hour. If that attorney works 2,000 hours a year, it could take five years to review one million documents.

Discovery on such a scale is not atypical today, and U.S. courts are grappling every day with the new reality. In *Rowe Entertainment, Inc. v. William Morris Agency*,[7] four defendants moved for a protective order relieving them of the obligation of producing e-mail in response to the plaintiff's extensive discovery requests. Each defendant submitted an estimate of the total cost of producing and reviewing the requested e-mails for discovery. The results were alarming. The four defendants calculated costs of $9,750,000, $290,110, $515,000, and $403,000 to produce and review the e-mails requested by plaintiff.[8] The defendants additionally noted that it would take a number of years to respond to plaintiff's electronic-discovery requests.[9]

The court in *Hopson v. Mayor of Baltimore*[10] analyzed the costs associated with digital discovery. The court found that considerable costs associated with the discovery process must be borne even before lawyers begin the job of privilege review.[11] To help meet their clients' needs, lawyers will often engage consultants to help manage electronic discovery (e-discovery) and assist in the tasks of seeking and responding to discovery requests, preserving electronic documents, and producing them in proper form for litigation. According to the *Hopson* court, "Some consultants are nothing short of giddy in their projections of the expected fees to be earned from these services."[12] A 2005 Socha-Gelbmann Electronic Discovery Survey, which analyzed commercial e-discovery data revenues, indicated that revenues for 2005 were nearly $1.3 billion.[13] The survey projected that the commercial e-discovery market would grow 37 percent from 2005 to 2006, 37 percent from 2006 to 2007, and 29 percent from 2007 to 2008.[14] At this rate of increase, it is apparent that the costs will become unbearable unless some change is effected.

IV. Government Investigations: Requests for Limited Disclosure and "Selective Waiver" by Federal, State, and Local Regulatory Authorities

A separate challenge to preservation of privileged electronic data exists in the context of government investigations. Corporations since the mid-1990s have been and continue to be asked to waive the corporate attorney-client privilege and provide full disclosure to government investigators of otherwise privileged communications. The government's interest is in maximizing the effectiveness and efficiency of government investigations. Privileged communications frequently provide the roadmap to corporate problems and actions taken in response. Corporations have an interest both in (1) protecting the confidentiality of communications with, and advice given by, their counsel and (2) being viewed as fully cooperative with government investigators. Corporations struggle to balance these competing interests, and the dilemma is made worse by the fact that in some jurisdictions, even limited disclosure of privileged communications in the context of a government investigation may effect a waiver as to other parties.[15]

V. Uncertainty Regarding Court's Response to Waiver Arguments

In certain jurisdictions, the inadvertent disclosure or selective waiver of a privileged document will effect a waiver of the attorney-client privilege or the work-product protection with respect to that document, and may even effect a waiver of privilege with respect to the entire subject matter addressed by the document. Even in more forgiving jurisdictions, the inadvertent disclosure of a privileged document will result in waiver if the court concludes that privilege review was not conducted with sufficient care.

VI. Judicial Approaches to Waiver

As outlined in the table, U.S. courts generally adhere to three different approaches when considering whether the inadvertent production of a privileged document will effect a waiver of privilege over the document itself and over the subject matter addressed by the document. A jurisdiction's approach to privilege waiver is determined by substantive law. Although procedural mechanisms may exist to effect a return of inadvertently disclosed privileged documents, the effect of the inadvertent disclosure is determined by substantive law of the jurisdiction.

A small number of courts take a *lenient* approach, holding that inadvertent disclosure of a privileged document does not effect waiver of privilege with respect to that particular document and, perforce, cannot effect a broad subject matter waiver.

The majority of courts adhere to a *middle ground* approach, holding that inadvertent disclosure of a privileged document may effect waiver of privilege with respect to that document. Courts in these jurisdictions will consider such

JURISDICTIONAL APPROACHES TO PRIVILEGE WAIVER

		Jurisdictions Following Approach	
Approach	**Description of Approach**	**Federal**	**State**[16]
Lenient[17]	Inadvertent disclosure does not effect waiver.	3rd Circuit[18] 7th Circuit (district courts) 8th Circuit 11th Circuit (some district courts)	California Georgia (lower courts) Louisiana (lower courts) Illinois (lower courts) Maine Texas[19]
Middle[20]	Inadvertent disclosure may effect waiver; extent of waiver is within court's discretion.	2nd Circuit 3rd Circuit 4th Circuit (district courts) 5th Circuit 6th Circuit 9th Circuit 10th Circuit (district courts) 11th Circuit (some district courts)	Colorado Connecticut Delaware (lower courts) Florida (lower courts) Hawaii Indiana (lower courts) Maryland Massachusetts Michigan (lower courts) Missouri New Jersey (lower courts) New Mexico New York North Dakota Ohio (lower courts) Oregon (lower courts) Pennsylvania (lower courts) Utah Washington W. Virginia (lower courts)
Strict[21]	Inadvertent disclosure effects waiver as to document and subject matter.	1st Circuit D.C. Circuit Federal Circuit	

factors as the reasonableness of precautions taken to prevent disclosure, the time taken to rectify error, and fairness to the parties to determine whether privilege was waived. The extent of waiver, if found, is left to the court's discretion, but is often limited to the document that had been inadvertently disclosed.

Finally, a minority of courts take a *strict* approach, holding that inadvertent disclosure of a privileged document constitutes waiver of privilege with respect to that particular document and also with respect to the entire subject matter addressed by the document.

VII. Federal Rules of Civil Procedure

A. Rule 26(b)(5)

The e-discovery amendments to the Federal Rules of Civil Procedure recognize that where massive generation of electronic information occurs daily at major companies and where large volumes of documents are produced in litigation, there will inevitably be inadvertent production of privileged or protected documents. "Blunders are inevitable," in the words of the Civil Rules Advisory Committee.[22] By design, Rule 26(b)(5) focuses on procedures for the assertion of privilege protection, instead of focusing on the substantive law of privilege: "Rule 26(b)(5)(B) does not address whether the privilege or protection that is asserted after production was waived by the production. The courts have developed principles to determine whether, and under what circumstances, waiver results from inadvertent production of privileged or protected information."[23] The Advisory Committee Note for Rule 26(b)(5) recognizes that the proliferation of ESI warrants procedural changes to help manage the burdens of a privilege review: "When the review is of [ESI], the risk of waiver, and the time and effort required to avoid it, can increase substantially because of the volume of [ESI] and the difficulty in ensuring that all information to be produced has in fact been reviewed."[24] As amended, Rule 26(b)(5) provides procedures for both the producing party and the requesting party to use when faced with a privilege review.

When information is produced that is "subject to a claim of privilege or of protection as trial-preparation material," the producing party making the claim should give written notice to the receiving party (or parties) as soon as possible, in order to preserve the underlying substantive claim that the producing party acted diligently.[25] The written notice should state the basis for the claim.[26] Operation of the rule is mandatory as against the receiving party: "After being notified, a party must promptly return, sequester, or destroy the specified information and any copies it has and may not use or disclose the information until the claim is resolved."[27] In addition to returning, sequestering, or destroying the information, the receiving party must retrieve it from third parties.[28] A receiving party is not obliged to do anything further: "A receiving party may promptly present the information to the court under seal for a determination of the claim."[29] Preservation of the disputed item by the producing party pending resolution of the claim is mandatory: "The producing party must preserve the information until the claim is resolved."[30]

B. Rule 26(f) and Rule 16(b)

The Advisory Committee Note for Rule 26(b)(5) asserts that the rule operates

> in tandem with Rule 26(f), which is amended to direct the parties to discuss privilege issues in preparing their discovery plan, and which,

with amended Rule 16(b), allows the parties to ask the court to include in an order any agreements the parties reach regarding issues of privilege or trial-preparation material protection.[31]

At a Rule 26(f) "meet and confer" conference, the parties are directed to discuss "any issues relating to claims of privilege or of protection as trial-preparation material, including—if the parties agree on a procedure to assert such claims after production—whether to ask the court to include their agreement in an order."[32] The Court's Rule 16(b) Scheduling Order may now include "any agreements the parties reach [e.g., any clawback or quick-peek agreements] for asserting claims of privilege or of protection as trial-preparation material after production."[33] Meet-and-confer agreements and Rule 16(b) Orders may be evaluated by a court when determining whether waiver has occurred.[34] Further, "[s]uch agreements and orders ordinarily control if they adopt procedures different from those in Rule 26(b)(5)(B)."[35] The December 1, 2006, amendments brought early, focused attention to ESI issues, including the increased burdens associated with a privilege review in today's e-world.

VIII. Clawback Agreements

In a clawback agreement, the producing and receiving parties agree to return inadvertently produced privileged or protected information upon prompt demand by the producing party.[36] The use of such an agreement is often discussed at the Rule 26(f) meet-and-confer, and a clawback can be incorporated into the Rule 16(b) Scheduling Order. The Rule 26(f) Advisory Committee Note endorses clawback agreements in appropriate cases: "[T]hese agreements . . . can facilitate prompt and economical discovery by reducing delay before the discovering party obtains access to documents, and by reducing the cost and burden of review by the producing party."[37] A clawback agreement can especially benefit parties involved with high volume productions; however, the agreement should not be used to justify a less stringent privilege review. Further, a clawback agreement should incorporate any local jurisdictional requirements. For example, Texas Rule of Civil Procedure 193.3(d) requires the producing party to take certain actions within 10 days of discovering an inadvertent production of privileged or protected material:[38] such a requirement should be met by the terms of a clawback agreement.

While clawbacks may aid the discovery process when faced with the review and production of gigabytes of ESI, such agreements are far from risk-free."[39] Clawbacks do not bind third parties, who may argue that the production of privileged or protected material waived the privilege as to them.[40] Additionally, clawbacks are not recognized in all jurisdictions, such as jurisdictions that follow the strict approach to privilege waiver. Therefore, it is important, especially in the jurisdictions that follow the middle ground or the strict approach to inadvertent waiver, to incorporate clawbacks into applicable scheduling or discovery orders. If the court orders the production of a document, the producing party's argument against voluntary waiver of applicable privileges is stronger when a clawback is incorporated into a scheduling or discovery order.[41]

IX. Quick-Peek Agreements

Under a quick-peek agreement, the producing party provides unreviewed materials for initial examination without waiving any privilege protection.[42] The requesting party designates documents it wishes to have actually produced, which becomes the Rule 34 request.[43] The responding (producing) party then screens only the designated documents, asserting privilege claims as provided in Rule 26(b)(5)(A).[44] Quick peeks are mentioned in the Rule 26(f) Advisory Committee Note as a method to help "minimize [the] costs and delays" when trying to "minimize the risk of waiver."[45] As is the case with clawbacks, quick-peek agreements may benefit parties involved with a high-volume review of ESI; however, such agreements have many drawbacks, as well.

The *Sedona Principles* identify five main drawbacks of quick-peek agreements: (1) voluntarily allowing an adversary to see privileged information is inconsistent with the protections and tenets of privilege law; (2) quick-peek agreements may not be enforceable against third parties; (3) voluntarily entering into quick peeks may violate counsel's ethical duty to protect a client's secrets and confidences; (4) disclosure of privileged information can adversely affect a client's interest since the "genie cannot be put back in the lamp"; and (5) privacy rights of employees and nonparties may be violated with a voluntary quick-peek production.[46] Quick-peek agreements should not replace an organized and thorough privilege review. The *Sedona Principles* suggest that in the limited situations a quick-peek order may be in the parties' best interests, the court should enter an order that

> (1) indicates that the court is compelling the manner of productions; (2) states such production does not result in an express or implied waiver of any privilege or protection for the produced documents or any other documents; (3) directs that the reviewing party cannot discuss the contents of the documents or take any notes during the review process; (4) permits the reviewing party to select those document that it believes are relevant to the case; and (5) orders that for each selected document, the producing party either (a) produces the selected document, (b) places the selected document on a privilege log, or (c) places the selected document on a non-responsive log.[47]

Due to a balancing of the benefits and drawbacks, the use of quick-peek agreements has become much less common than the use of clawback agreements. At least some privileged information can be initially withheld under a clawback agreement, which is not the case with a quick-peek agreement.

X. Federal Rule of Evidence 502

Rule of Evidence 502, entitled Attorney-Client Privilege and Work Product Limitations on Waiver, was enacted by Congress in 2008 and signed into law on September 18, 2008.

A. History of Rule 502

The purpose of Rule of Evidence 502 is to unify judicial review of inadvertent disclosure of privileged information.[48] Rule 502 is the result of a January 2006 request by F. James Sensenbrenner, Jr., Chair of the U.S. House of Representatives Committee on the Judiciary. Rep. Sensenbrenner expressed concerns about lack of clarity on "forfeiture of privileges" and urged the Judicial Conference to adopt a rule that would protect against the forfeiture of privilege where a disclosure is the result of an innocent mistake; permit parties and courts to protect against the consequences of waiver by permitting disclosures of privileged information between the parties to a litigation; and allow persons and entities to cooperate with the government agencies by turning over privileged information without waiving all privileges as to other parties in subsequent litigation.[49] Rule 502 attempts to resolve longstanding disputes in the courts about the effect of certain disclosures of communications or information protected by the attorney-client privilege or as work product and to provide more uniform standards under which parties can determine whether certain disclosures will result in waiver.

The task of drafting a proposed rule was referred to the Advisory Committee on Evidence Rules, and the first draft in early 2006 was the subject of hearings at Fordham University in April 2006.[50] The initial draft presented for public comment included nonwaiver provisions for inadvertent disclosures and selective waivers in the context of government investigations.[51] A revised rule was released for public comment in August 2006. The public comment period ended in February 2007.

B. September 2007 Version of Rule 502 as Submitted to Congress

As a result of public comment, a number of modifications were made to proposed Rule 502. The Advisory Committee issued its revised proposed Rule 502 in April 2007, and on May 15, 2007, the Advisory Committee issued a recommendation that proposed Rule 502 be approved by the Standing Committee and sent to Congress.[52] The revised proposed Rule was approved by the Standing Committee and the Judicial Conference, and the Judicial Conference submitted the proposed Rule 502 to Congress by letter dated September 26, 2007, from Judge Lee. H. Rosenthal, Chair of the Committee on Rules of Practice and Procedure.[53]

In its submittal letter, the Judicial Conference noted that the proposal was being submitted directly to Congress because of the limitations on the rule-making function of the federal courts in matters dealing with evidentiary privilege. Unlike all other federal rules of procedure prescribed under the Rules Enabling Act, those rules governing evidentiary privilege must be approved by an Act of Congress, 28 U.S.C. § 2074(b).[54]

Under Rule 502, disclosure of privileged or protected material in a federal proceeding or to a federal office or agency operates as waiver "to an undisclosed communication or information in a federal or state proceeding only if: (1) the waiver is intentional; (2) the disclosed and undisclosed communications or information concern the same subject matter; and (3) [the communications] ought in fairness [be] considered together."[55] The disclosure of privileged material would not effect waiver of privilege in another federal or state proceeding if: "(1) the disclosure is inadvertent; (2) the holder of the privilege or protection took reasonable steps to prevent disclosure; and (3) the holder [of the privilege] promptly took reasonable steps to rectify the error, including (if applicable) following Fed. R. Civ. P. 26(b)(5)(B)."[56] Additionally, if a disclosure is made in a state court proceeding and is not the subject of a state court order concerning waiver, then waiver will not be found in a federal proceeding if "the disclosure: (1) would not be a waiver under this rule if it had been made in a federal proceeding; or (2) is not a waiver under the law of the state where the disclosure occurred."[57]

Rule 502 establishes the validity of nonwaiver agreements as between parties to litigation, and the Rule states that such agreements are binding on third parties if the agreement is incorporated into a court order.[58] Further, the proposed Advisory Committee Note to the Rule states:

> The rule makes no attempt to alter federal or state law on whether a communication or information is protected under the attorney-client privilege or work-product immunity as an initial matter. . . . The rule governs only certain waivers by disclosure. Other common-law waiver doctrines may result in a finding of waiver even where there is no disclosure of privileged information or work product. . . . The rule is not intended to displace or modify federal common law concerning waiver of privilege or work product where no disclosure has been made.[59]

C. Rule 502 as Enacted

Rule 502 provides that a waiver "extends to an undisclosed communication or information in a federal or state proceeding only if (1) the waiver is intentional; (2) the disclosed and undisclosed communications or information concern the same subject matter; and (3) they ought in fairness to be considered together."[60] Moreover, the Rule specifically addresses privilege waiver stemming from an inadvertent disclosure, stating that a "disclosure does not operate as a waiver in a federal or state proceeding if: (1) the disclosure is inadvertent; (2) the holder of the privilege or protection took reasonable steps to prevent disclosure; and (3) the holder promptly took reasonable steps to rectify the error, including (if applicable) following Fed. R. Civ. P. 26(b)(5)(B)."[61]

D. Limitations of Rule 502

Rule 502 leaves several issues unresolved. First, revised Rule 502 does not apply to a disclosure made in a state proceeding when the disclosed communication or information is subsequently offered in another state proceeding ("state to state" problem). Revised Rule 502 does govern state courts with regard to the effect of disclosures initially made in federal court proceedings, meaning that a state court may not find a waiver when Rule 502 would not and the disclosure is initially made at the federal level. Second, revised Rule 502 does not incorporate provisions dealing with "selective waiver"; thus, disclosure of protected communications or information to the government waives the protection only selectively, to the government, and not to any other person or entity. The selective-waiver provision "proved to be very controversial."[62] The Advisory Committee received several comments expressing concern that the selective-waiver provision would add to the "culture of waiver" that has been created by government agencies' and regulatory entities' belief that it is appropriate to expect investigated corporations to disclose protected information and waive privilege protections.[63]

E. Developing Case Law Interpreting Rule 502

As a practical matter, although Rule 502 is intended to reduce the cost of litigation, especially with regard to electronic discovery, parties may continue to engage in costly document review for fear of not satisfying the "reasonable steps" requirement.

A number of courts have applied Rule 502 to determine whether or not privilege has been waived through inadvertent production. The inquiry is highly case-specific. The following sections identify factors considered by the courts in determining whether "reasonable steps were taken to prevent inadvertent production."

1. *Factors Supporting Nonwaiver*

- Inadvertent production was due to a technology or vendor problem or error.[64]
- Process included attorney or experienced paralegal review, volume of inadvertently produced documents was low, and counsel took prompt measures to rectify inadvertent disclosure (e.g., prompt request for return of documents, objection to use at deposition).[65]
- Volume of documents produced was high and number of inadvertently produced documents was relatively low, privilege issues were complicated by number of law firms implicated in correspondence, and process included attorney review by associates supervised by senior associates.[66]
- Process included use of key-word searching and manual review, and counsel took immediate action pursuant to parties' clawback agreement.[67]

- Inadvertent production included inadvertently unredacted portions of partially redacted document, but volume of mistaken redaction was low and counsel took prompt action to rectify error upon discovery.[68]

2. *Factors That May Indicate Waiver*

- Failure to establish nature of privilege claims or precautions taken to prevent disclosure resulted in finding that production was not "inadvertent."[69]
- Defendants did not indicate methodology used to review documents for privilege or explain why efforts were reasonable, and thus failed to meet burden of proving nonwaiver.[70]
- Defendants failed to adequately establish reasonable measures taken to prevent disclosure of documents, object to use of documents at deposition, request return of documents, or otherwise rectify error following discovery.[71]
- Electronic documents at issue were produced on other occasions.[72]
- Privileged communications were forwarded vie e-mail to third party.[73]
- Electronic documents were produced without clawback agreement or prior review because of technical difficulties opening files.[74]
- Privileged materials were stored on computer of third-party business partner, where business relationship soured and privilege holder failed to take prompt action to protect privileged materials.[75]
- Seller of commercial facility disclosed privileged e-mail to third-party buyer through decision to temporarily continue providing e-mail services to seller's former employees who became buyer's employees.[76]
- Defendants failed to review process and recheck subsequent electronic productions to prevent further inadvertent production of privileged documents after notice of prior inadvertent production.[77]

XI. Practice Considerations for Preserving Privileges

Rule 502 limits the circumstances in which inadvertent disclosure of privileged information may result in a waiver, as well as the scope of a potential waiver. However, the Rule contemplates that the parties take reasonable steps to avoid inadvertent disclosure and preserve privilege.

Large volume alone should not cause counsel to avoid privilege reviews. Processes and procedures can be developed to manage seemingly daunting privilege reviews in an efficient and cost effective manner. In appropriate circumstances, the following practical suggestions may help organize and manage the privilege review process.

A. Meet-and-Confer Process

One way in which parties can assert greater control of e-discovery costs is by adding e-discovery topics and privilege-review issues to the Rule 26(f) meet-and-confer sessions that must occur "as soon as practicable" in federal actions. The meet-and-confer process can be effective in limiting the data universe and establishing time frames for privilege review. Agreements of the parties can help to limit the universe of potentially discoverable documents, thereby reducing the burden of document review and the concomitant risk of inadvertent disclosure of privileged information. Counsel operating in strict jurisdictions should, during their meet-and-confer sessions, attempt to agree upon adequate time periods for discovery, including privilege review.

B. Nonwaiver Agreements to Minimize Damage

Rule 502 encourages parties to make agreements, such as clawbacks, regarding waivers. Although clawbacks do not bind third parties under Rule 26, Rule 502 makes clawback agreements binding on third parties if the agreement is incorporated in a court order.[78] Moreover, a clawback agreement indicates to the court that a litigating party has taken "reasonable steps" to prevent disclosure. Some courts have found that parties waived their privilege with respect to inadvertently disclosed documents when they failed to vigorously pursue a clawback agreement, particularly when coupled with inadequate quality assurance processes and inability to articulate a reasonable methodology to prevent disclosure.[79] Thus, Rule 502 creates added incentive to incorporate a clawback agreement into a court order.

C. Defensible Processes for Privilege Review and Recovery of Inadvertently Produced Documents

Counsel in all jurisdictions should develop and document reasonable precautions to ensure that privileged material is not inadvertently produced. Counsel operating in courts that adhere to the middle ground approach or in federal litigation subject to Rule 502 should seek prompt return of any inadvertently produced documents and be prepared to prove that all reasonable precautions were taken during the privilege review. A reasonable privilege-review process may include use of specialized e-discovery counsel or consultants, review platforms and electronic review tools, emerging search and retrieval technologies, or technology-assisted methods for categorizing and analyzing groups of documents. Use of available technology and methods, coupled with strategic human review, can help minimize the risk of waiver.

Victor Stanley Inc. v. Creative Pipe Inc.[80] demonstrates that a party implementing a technology-assisted methodology to search for relevant or privileged/protected documents must test its reliability for quality assurance.[81] Sampling the body of data that does not come up in the search helps ensure that the search and retrieval software and review methodology are not missing potentially privileged information. Parties subject to an e-discovery request involving large data volumes must carefully design technology-assisted methods to identify relevant or privileged information and speed document review. Selection of appropriate search methodologies, implementation of adequate processes for quality assurance, and ability to articulate and defend the methodology are critical to the producing party's defense of process and avoidance of inadvertent privilege waiver.[82] The party developing and testing the methodology must be prepared to explain to the court the rationale for the methods chosen and the quality assurance processes implemented.[83]

D. Adequate Privilege Log

Preparation of a defensible privilege log is important in privilege. Privilege logs listing tens of thousands of individual electronic documents likely will not be reviewed by a court, and the risk of privilege waiver may be heightened. Consider preparing privilege logs of electronic documents by category and sorting the privilege log into categories from which a court could choose to review a representative sample. Defining relevant categories of documents will depend on the matters at issue and the document set. Examples of defensible categories may include, among others, legal department communications regarding draft agreements or contracts; in-house legal department advice to business units and other departments; communications with outside counsel seeking or providing legal advice; and communications regarding internal investigations subject to attorney-client or work-product privilege.

XII. Conclusion

The primary purpose for protection of attorney-client privilege and work product is to promote full and frank communications between attorneys and their clients. ESI is being created at ever-increasing rates. The amount of potentially relevant information subject to a privilege review in any one litigation matter will continue to increase. Increasing data volumes, coupled with increased complexity of ESI, increase the risk of privilege waiver resulting from mistakes in review and inadvertent production of ESI. Rule of Evidence 502 will help mitigate the risk of privilege waiver by limiting the circumstances in which inadvertent disclosure will result in waiver. Risk of waiver can be further minimized with a combination of solid processes, technology tools, strategic agreements, and human review tailored to the circumstances of the case, the number and type of privileged documents, and privilege review itself.

Notes

1. *See, e.g.*, Upjohn Co v. United States, 449 U.S. 383, 389–93 (1981) (discussing importance of the attorney-client privilege).
2. *See, e.g.*, Hickman v. Taylor, 329 U.S. 495, 500 (1947) (discussing need to protect attorney work product).
3. Fulbright & Jaworski L.L.P., Fourth Annual Litigation Trends Survey, http://www.fulbright.com.
4. Hon. Ronald J. Hedges, Discovery of Digital Information (2d ed. 2006), http://www.cgocouncil.com/resources/hedges_edition2.pdf (discussion of storage capacity).

5. Empire State Building: Official Internet Site, Facts & Trivia, http://www.esbnyc.com (height of Empire State Building); Forensic Consulting Solutions, LLC, Frequently Asked Questions, http://www.aboutfcs.com/ (paper and electronic equivalents). For those with an interest in such matters, the next measures of data storage beyond the terabyte are the petabyte (1,000 terabytes) and the exabyte (1,000 petabytes). It has been estimated that five exabytes could contain all the words ever spoken by human beings. *See, e.g.*, Sch. of Info. & Mgmt. Sys., Univ. of Cal. at Berkeley, How Much Information? 2003, http://www2.sims.berkeley.edu/research/projects/how-much-info-2003/execsum.htm.
6. Setec Investigations, How Many Pages per Gigabyte and Megabyte?, http://www.setecinvestigations.com/resources/techhints/techhint1.php.
7. Rowe Ent., Inc. v. William Morris Agency, 205 F.R.D. 421 (S.D.N.Y. 2002) (*questioned in* Zubulake v. UBS Warburg, LLC (*Zubulake III*), 216 F.R.D. 280, 284 (S.D.N.Y. 2003)). The eight-factor test for cost shifting formulated by U.S. Magistrate Judge Francis in *Rowe* was questioned and modified by Judge Scheindlin in *Zubulake III*.
8. *Rowe*, 205 F.R.D. at 425–26. *See also* Medtronic Sofamor Danek, Inc. v. Michelson, 229 F.R.D. 550, 557–58 (W.D. Tenn. 2003) (noting that Medtronic estimated that its privilege-review costs would be between $16.5 million and $70 million); Toshiba Am. Elec. Components, Inc. v. Superior Court, 21 Cal. Rptr. 3d 532, 535 (Cal. Ct. App. 2004) ("Complete processing of all tapes, which would include analyzing the data contained in the tapes, identifying and restoring files, searching the restored files for responsive items, and producing the specified data, would cost between $1.5 and $1.9 million.").
9. While the *Rowe* court did shift some of the discovery costs to the plaintiff, it ultimately held that the costs associated with privilege review were to fall on the defendants' shoulders. 205 F.R.D. at 425–26. Other courts have also followed the trend of refusing to shift costs associated with privilege review to the requesting party. *See, e.g., Zubulake III*, 216 F.R.D. 280. Ironically, after three years of discovery, the *Rowe* court granted each of the three nonsettling defendants' motions for summary judgment. Thus while the defendants may have ultimately escaped liability in the case, they still bore the substantial costs of privilege review.
10. Hopson v. Mayor of Balt., 232 F.R.D. 228 (D. Md. 2005).
11. *Id.* at 239.
12. *Id.*
13. George Socha & Thomas Gelbmann, *Fourth Socha-Gelbmann Report Sees Growth in EDD's Future*, L. Tech. News, Aug. 2, 2006, http://www.law.com/jsp/legaltechnology/PubArticleFriendlyLT.jsp?id=1154423138895.
14. *Id.*
15. *See, e.g., In re* Columbia/HCA Healthcare Corp. Billing Practice Litig., 293 F.3d 289, 314 (6th Cir. 2002) (Boggs, J., dissenting) ("the public interest in easing government investigations counsels against holding the attorney-work-product privilege waived when the holder of the privilege discloses privileged information to the government . . . a limited disclosure pursuant to a government agency's investigatory request ought not waive the privileges as to all other parties").
16. Some states do not yet have published decisions indicating their position on the issue of inadvertent disclosure and waiver of privilege. Case law is developing in all jurisdictions, and it is important to conduct current research of the

substantive law in relevant jurisdictions when making decisions or providing client advice.

17. Notable examples are *Eisenberg v. Gagnon*, 766 F.2d 770 (3d Cir. 1985) (holding that in order for there to be waiver of attorney-client privilege, the waiver must be knowing), and *Corey v. Norman, Hanson & DeTroy*, 742 A.2d 933 (Me. 1999) ("A truly inadvertent disclosure cannot and does not constitute a waiver of the attorney-client privilege.").
18. The United States Court of Appeals for the Third Circuit adopts the lenient approach for attorney-client privilege and the middle ground approach for work-product privilege. *See In re* Grand Jury, 138 F.3d 978 (3d Cir. 1998).
19. Texas Rule of Civil Procedure 193.3, a procedural rule, provides that privilege is not waived upon inadvertent production if the producing party amends its response, identifies the material or information produced, and states the asserted privilege within 10 days after discovery of the inadvertent production is made. *See* Tex. R. Civ. P. 193.3.
20. Notable examples are *In re* Grand Jury Proceedings, 219 F.3d 175 (2d Cir. 2000) (noting the use of the middle ground approach in the Circuit and stating, "Further, when waiver occurs as a result of inadvertent disclosure, courts have limited the scope of that waiver based on the circumstances involved and overall fairness."), and State *ex. rel.* Allstate Insurance Co. v. Gaughan, 508 S.E.2d 75 (W. Va. 1998) ("We, too, believe that the . . . 'middle test' strikes the proper balance in determining on a case-by-case basis whether or not the inadvertent disclosure of attorney-client privileged communication constitutes a waiver of the privilege.").
21. Notable examples are Texaco Puerto Rico, Inc. v. Dep't of Consumer Affairs, 60 F.3d 867 (1st Cir. 1995) ("it is apodictic that inadvertent disclosure may work a waiver of privilege"), and Carter v. Gibbs, 909 F.2d 1450 (Fed. Cir. 1990) ("It is irrelevant whether the attachment was inadvertent. . . . Voluntary disclosure of attorney work product to an adversary in the litigation for which the attorney produced that information defeats the policy underlying the privilege . . . . Granting the motion would do no more than seal the bag from which the cat has already escaped.").
22. *Hobson*, 232 F.R.D. at 233 (citing Advisory Comm. on the Fed. Rules of Civil Procedure, Report to the Standing Committee on the Rules of Practice and Procedure, Judicial Conference of the United States 52 (Sept. 2005)).
23. Fed. R. Civ. P. 26(b)(5) advisory committee's note.
24. *Id.*
25. Fed. R. Civ. P. 26(b)(5).
26. *Id.*
27. *Id.*
28. *Id.*
29. *Id.*
30. *Id.*
31. Fed. R. Civ. P. 26(b)(5) advisory committee's note.
32. Fed. R. Civ. P. 26(f)(4).
33. Fed. R. Civ. P. 16(b)(6).
34. Fed. R. Civ. P. 26(b)(5) advisory committee's note.
35. *Id.*
36. Fed. R. Civ. P. 26(f) advisory committee's note.

37. *Id.*
38. Tex. R. Civ. P. 193.3(d).
39. *See* Hopson v. Mayor of Balt., 232 F.R.D. 228, 235 (D. Md. 2005).
40. *See id.*
41. *See id.* at 238 ("[I]t is essential to the success of this approach in avoiding waiver that the production of inadvertently produced privileged electronic data must be at the compulsion of the court, rather than solely by the voluntary act of the producing party.").
42. Fed. R. Civ. P. 26(f) advisory committee's note.
43. *Id.*
44. *Id.*
45. *Id.*
46. The Sedona Principles: Best Practices, Recommendations & Principles for Addressing Electronic Document Discovery (The Sedona Conference Working Group Series, 2d ed. 2007), cmt. 10.d.
47. *Id.*
48. Prior to the enactment of Rule 502, a federal court's approach to privilege waiver was determined by the substantive law of the jurisdiction, which in diversity cases included state law. However, under Rule 502, courts should apply federal privilege law rather than the substantive law of the jurisdiction. Rule 502 states, "Notwithstanding Rule 501, this rule applies even if State law provides the rule of decision." *See* Fed. R. Evid. 502(f).
49. Letter from Hon. F. James Sensenbrenner, Jr., Chair of the U.S. Cong. Comm. on the Judiciary, to Leonidas Ralph Mecham, Dir. of the Admin. Office of the U.S. Courts (Jan. 23, 2006).
50. A. Prasad & V. Meyers, *Practical Implications of Proposed Rule 502*, 8 Sedona Conf. J. 133, 135 (Fall 2007).
51. *Id.* at 136.
52. Report of the Advisory Comm. on Evidence Rules (May 15, 2007), http://www.uscourts.gov/rules/jc09-2007/App_C_EV_JC_Report_051507.pdf.
53. *See* Comm. on Rules of Practice & Procedure, Judicial Conference of United States, U.S. Judicial Conference's Letter to Congress on Evidence Rule 502 (Sept. 26, 2007), and accompanying Proposed Amendment to the Federal Rule of Evidence 502, Attorney-Client Privilege and Work Product; Limitations on Waiver (Sept. 2007).
54. U.S. Judicial Conference's Letter to Congress on Evidence Rule 502, *supra* note 49.
55. Proposed Amendment to the Federal Rule of Evidence 502, *supra* note 49.
56. *Id.*
57. *Id.*
58. *Id.*
59. *Id.* (internal citations omitted).
60. Fed. R. Evid. 502(a).
61. Fed. R. Evid. 502(b).
62. U.S. Judicial Conference's Letter to Congress on Evidence Rule 502, *supra* note 49.
63. Prasad & Meyers, *supra* note 50, at 139–40.
64. *See, e.g.*, Alcon Mfg., Ltd. v. Apotex, Inc., 2008 WL 5070465 (S.D. Ind. Nov. 26, 2008) ("electronic break error" caused inadvertent production and plaintiff

acted promptly to seek return of document upon discovery); Heriot v. Byrne, 2009 WL 742769 (N.D. Ill. Mar. 20, 2009) (inadvertent production was due to vendor's mistake, and where counsel took prompt action to seek return upon discovering disclosure, court adopted test combining prior case law and Rule 502 to find no waiver); Multiquip, Inc. v. Water Mgmt. Sys., LLC, 2009 WL 4261214 (D. Idaho Nov. 23, 2009) (as a result of autofill e-mail function, defendant mistakenly sent privileged communication to third party who forwarded to opposing counsel; court found defendant's reliance on "system that had worked in a particular way in the past" was reasonable); Olem Shoe Corp. v. Wash. Shoe Co., 2010 WL 3981694 (S.D. Fla. Oct. 8, 2010) (no waiver where commercial copy service inadvertently disclosed privileged materials despite clear instructions to copy service and clear marking of documents as privileged).

65. *See, e.g.*, Am. Coal Sales Co. v. Nova Scotia Power, Inc., 2009 WL 467576 (S.D. Ohio Feb. 23, 2009); Clubcom, LLC v. Captive Media, Inc., 2009 WL 1885712 (W.D. Pa. June 30, 2009); Coburn Group, LLC v. Whitecap Advisors, LLC, 640 F. Supp. 2d 1032 (N.D. Ill. 2009); Ergo Licensing, LLC v. Carefusion 303, Inc., 263 F.R.D. 40 (D. Me. 2009); Fuller v. Interview, Inc., 2009 WL 3241542 (S.D.N.Y. Sept. 30, 2009); Jeanes-Kemp, LLC v. Johnson Controls, Inc., 2010 WL 3522028 (S.D. Miss. Sept. 1, 2010); Kumar v. Hilton Hotels Corp., 2009 WL 1683479 (W.D. Tenn. June 16, 2009).
66. *See, e.g.*, Bd. of Trs. Sheet Metal Workers Nat'l Pension Fund v. Palladium Equity Partners, LLC, 2010 WL 2787434 (E.D. Mich. July 14, 2010).
67. *See, e.g.*, Kandel v. Brother Int'l Corp., 683 F. Supp. 2d 1076 (C.D. Cal. 2010).
68. King Pharm. Inc. v. Purdue Pharma L.P., 2010 WL 2243872 (W.D. Va. June 2, 2010).
69. Callan v. Christian Audigier, Inc., 263 F.R.D. 564 (C.D. Cal. 2009).
70. Amobi v. D.C. Dep't of Corr., 262 F.R.D. 45 (D.D.C. 2009 (authored by Magistrate Judge Facciola and containing analysis of waiver pursuant to Rule 502); Smith v. Life Investors Inc., 2009 WL 2045197 (W.D. Pa. July 9, 2009) (where defendant performed electronic search without plaintiff's input and refused to produce search terms, defendant failed to demonstrate that methodology was reasonable under Federal Rule of Civil Procedure 26(b)(5)).
71. *See, e.g.*, Eden Isle Marina, Inc. v. United States, 89 Fed. Cl. 480 (Fed. Cl. Aug. 28, 2009) (detailed discovery opinion and analysis of Rule 402); N. Am. Rescue Prods., Inc. v. Bound Tree Med., LLC, 2010 WL 1873291 (S.D. Ohio May 10, 2010).
72. *Eden Isle Marina*, 89 Fed. Cl. 480.
73. Great Am. Ins. Co. v. Liberty Surplus Ins. Co., 2009 WL 3052680 (N.D. Cal. Sept. 18, 2009) (rejecting reliance on Federal Rule of Civil Procedure 26(b)(5)(b)).
74. Info. Global Solutions (MI), Inc. v. St. Paul Fire & Marine Ins. Co., 2009 WL 2390174 (N.D. Cal. Aug. 3, 2009).
75. Alpert v. Riley, 2010 WL 1556566 (S.D. Tex. Apr. 19, 2010).
76. Soc'y of Prof'l Eng'g Employees in Aerospace, IFPTE Local 2001 v. Boeing Co., 2010 WL 1141269 (D. Kan. Mar. 22, 2010).
77. United States v. Sensient Colors, Inc., 2009 WL 2905474 (D.N.J. Sept. 9, 2009).
78. Specifically, Rule 502(e) states, "An agreement on the effect of disclosure in a Federal proceeding is binding only on the parties to the agreement, unless it is incorporated into a court order." FED. R. EVID. 502(e).
79. Victor Stanley, Inc. v. Creative Pipe, Inc., 250 F.R.D. 251, 255 (D. Md. 2008) (noting that the defendants abandoned efforts to obtain a clawback agreement and

did not apply adequate quality assurance processes to the use of key search terms and finding that defendants waived privilege with respect to 165 electronic documents they inadvertently disclosed during discovery).

80. 250 F.R.D. 251 (D. Md. 2008).
81. *Id.* at 261 (explaining that although key word searching is recognized as a means of winnowing relevant documents from a large repository, the producing party must use sampling and other quality assurance technologies to effect a complete and reasonable search).
82. *Id.* at 262 ("Use of search and information retrieval methodology, for the purpose of identifying and withholding privileged or work-product protected information from production, requires the utmost care in selecting methodology that is appropriate for the task because the consequence of failing to do so, as in this case, may be the disclosure of privileged/protected information to an adverse party, resulting in a determination by the court that the privilege/protection has been waived.").
83. *Id.* at 262 (stating that the party selecting the methodology must be prepared to explain the rationale for the methods chosen to the court).

CHAPTER 7

Communications between Attorneys and Putative Class Members

ALLAN KANNER
TIBOR NAGY

I. Introduction

The traditional view of disputes in our legal system is that they are discrete events. A stockbroker defrauded an investor. A phone company breached its contract with a customer. A boss fired a worker. The resulting lawsuit in any of these cases was traditionally a one-on-one fight, what Professor Chayes has referred to as the "bipolar mode" of litigation.[1]

Today we might look for patterns or group wrongs in those same events. For example, in the "boss firing a worker" hypothetical we may look, in appropriate circumstances, for patterns of discrimination or harassment. Group litigation, in particular the use of class actions, has emerged as a superior alternative to the traditional bipolar suit in many areas of the law. This changing conception about the nature and role of litigation in addressing root causes, moreover, has materially altered our view of how an attorney can and should communicate with potential clients. The civil rights and labor movements in particular taught us that it is not only proper but often desirable for an informed lawyer to share information with lay people, including potential clients, about their rights. This recognition of the need for the targeted dissemination of information has moved into other substantive areas in which systemic wrongs occur, and traditional restraints on lawyer advertising and solicitation have accordingly weakened.

In this chapter we examine the modern case law governing attorney contact with potential clients in the class-action setting. Section II examines the rules restricting communications between lawyers and nonclients generally, in particular the rules against solicitation and contact with represented parties, and discusses how these rules apply in the class-action setting. The traditional model of no-comment rules is examined, as is the modern framework that replaced that model with the Supreme Court's decision in *Gulf Oil Co. v. Bernard*.[2] In section III we examine communications between class counsel and putative class members in the three stages of a class action: (1) precertification; (2) postcertification but before the end of the opt-out period; and (3) postcertification, post-opt-out period. Particular attention is given to when such communications may be prohibited and when courts will conclude that an attorney-client relationship exists between class counsel and putative class members. Section IV examines how the involvement of an organization that putative class members belong to, for example a labor union, affects the analyses discussed in section III. Finally, section V discusses communications with putative class members in opt-*in* class actions, such as cases brought under the Fair Labor Standards Act.[3]

II. Communications with Nonclients Generally

A. Rules against Solicitation, Contact with Represented Parties, and Misleading Statements

When dealing with nonclients, lawyers must observe the various rules that govern communications with potential clients and opposing parties. The most important rules with respect to potential clients are states' ethical rules against solicitation. Most states have rules that prohibit in-person and direct telephone solicitation, as well as restrictions on solicitation and advertisements by mail.

The goal of such rules is to avoid exploitation of potential clients, especially those in vulnerable situations, and to prevent activities that would undermine the public view of the profession. Model Rule 7.3, which is representative of the rules actually adopted in most jurisdictions, states the following:

> (a) A lawyer shall not by in-person, live telephone or real-time electronic contact solicit professional employment from a prospective client when a significant motive for the lawyer's doing so is the lawyer's pecuniary gain, unless the person contacted:
> (1) is a lawyer; or
> (2) has a family, close personal, or prior professional relationship with the lawyer.
>
> (b) A lawyer shall not solicit professional employment from a prospective client by written, recorded or electronic communication or by in-person, telephone or real-time electronic contact even when not otherwise prohibited by paragraph (a), if:
> (1) the prospective client has made known to the lawyer a desire not to be solicited by the lawyer; or
> (2) the solicitation involves coercion, duress or harassment.[4]

Although there is undoubtedly a right to communicate with nonclients, rules such as these must be strictly followed. That said, abuses likely occur at country clubs and in hospitals every day.

With respect to communications with opposing parties, the most important rules are those barring contacts with parties represented by counsel. Model Rule 4.2 is followed in most jurisdictions:

> In representing a client, a lawyer shall not communicate about the subject of the representation with a person the lawyer knows to be represented by another lawyer in the matter, unless the lawyer has the consent of the other lawyer or is authorized to do so by law or a court order.[5]

The rule is meant to prevent undue influence by lawyers on opposing parties.[6] When the opposing party is a corporation, the rule generally applies to management and to any other employees who may have privileged information. In the corporate context, the rule may also apply to former employees.[7]

Both solicitation rules and rules against contact with represented parties of course apply to class actions. In the class-action context, however, these rules can be more difficult to interpret and apply, for at least two major reasons. First, many class actions are about matters in the public interest and so raise First Amendment issues. Second, courts have been somewhat sloppy in describing the status of putative class actions prior to their actual certification. Thus, in the early stages of a class action, for example, the precise status of putative class members is often unclear. During the precertification and opt-out periods it can be difficult to determine whether putative class members are actual or potential clients, or whether they are represented parties or nonparties. Plaintiff's counsel, wanting to disseminate information or conduct discovery related to certification, may risk charges of solicitation, especially with respect to class members who have retained other counsel. Defense counsel, wanting to settle claims or investigate the scope of liability, may risk violating Model Rule 4.2. Furthermore, because class actions have a public law aspect to them and because the stakes involved are often very high, courts have been particularly sensitive to the potential for misleading and self-serving communications by both plaintiffs' and defense counsel. Plaintiff's counsel, for example, might attempt to "drum up" litigation, or convey a misleading sense of urgency about joining a class.[8] Defense counsel, on the other hand, might mislead class members into opting out, or might otherwise misrepresent class members' rights.[9]

B. The Traditional Model: No-Comment Local Rules

To deal with the problem of communications with putative class members, many courts, following the first edition of the *Manual for Complex Litigation*, initially adopted a prophylactic approach in which the district court adopted a "no comment" local rule or individual judges issued gag orders.[10] Many federal district courts, for example, had local rules that stated something like the following:

> In every case sought to be maintained by any party as a class action, all parties thereto and their counsel are hereby forbidden, directly or indirectly, orally or in writing, to communicate concerning such actions with any potential or actual class member, not a formal party to the case, without approval by the Court.[11]

The same result, in jurisdictions that did not have a no-comment local rule, was often achieved by individual judges' use of blanket protective orders.[12]

No-comment rules have numerous flaws. As an initial matter, they are overly broad prior restraints on speech that almost certainly violate attorneys' First Amendment rights.[13] In addition, the rules often operate to harm the interests of putative class members, preventing them from obtaining much-needed legal advice and hindering the efficient operation of group litigation. In the late 1970s, as class actions became increasingly common, courts began to recognize the problems posed by no-comment rules.[14] In 1981, in *Gulf Oil Co. v. Bernard*,[15] the Supreme Court struck down the use of such rules in the federal courts.

In April 1976, Gulf Oil Company and the Equal Employment Opportunity Commission (EEOC) entered into a conciliation agreement involving alleged discrimination against black and female employees at the company's Port Arthur, Texas, refinery. Gulf agreed to cease various allegedly discriminatory practices, to undertake an affirmative-action program covering hiring and promotion, and to offer back pay to alleged victims of discrimination based on a set formula. Gulf began to send notices to the 643 employees eligible for back pay, stating the exact amount available to each person in return for execution within 30 days of a full release of all discrimination claims dating from the relevant time period.

Shortly thereafter, a class action was filed on behalf of all current and former African-American employees, alleging racial discrimination in employment and seeking injunctive, declaratory, and monetary relief. Gulf promptly filed a motion for an order limiting communications by parties and their counsel with potential class members. An accompanying brief described the EEOC conciliation agreement, asserting that 452 of the 643 employees entitled to back pay under that agreement had signed releases and been paid by the time the class action was filed. Furthermore, Gulf claimed that one of the attorneys for the class had recently attended a meeting of 75 class members, where he had discussed the case and recommended that the employees not sign the releases sent under the conciliation agreement. The attorney allegedly advised employees to return checks they already had received, since they could receive at least double the amounts involved through the class action. The district court, without making any findings of fact, entered a temporary order prohibiting all communications concerning the case from parties or their counsel to potential or actual class members. The court later issued a modified order that imposed a complete ban on all communications concerning the class action between parties or their counsel and any actual or potential class member who was not a formal party, without the court's prior approval. The modified order exempted communications from Gulf describing the EEOC conciliation agreement and making settlement offers to class members. On appeal from a subsequent final order, respondents argued that the limitations on communications imposed by the district court were beyond the power granted the court in Federal Rule of Civil Procedure 23(d) and were unconstitutional under the First Amendment. A divided panel of the Fifth Circuit affirmed the district court, but on rehearing en banc that decision was reversed and the district court order was held to be an unconstitutional prior restraint on expression.[16]

The Supreme Court affirmed, though limited its decision to a holding that the district court abused its discretion under Rule 23(d). The Court agreed that "[b]ecause of the potential for abuse, a district court has both the duty and the broad authority to exercise control over a class action and to enter appropriate orders governing the conduct of counsel and parties."[17] Nevertheless, district courts' discretion is "not unlimited." The Court, in a passage that is particularly helpful for determining the scope of district courts' authority to limit communications between class counsel and putative class members, stated the following:

> The order interfered with their efforts to inform potential class members of the existence of this lawsuit, and may have been particularly injurious—not only to respondents but to the class as a whole—

> because the employees at that time were being pressed to decide whether to accept a backpay offer from Gulf that required them to sign a full release of all liability for discriminatory acts. In addition, the order made it more difficult for respondents, as the class representatives, to obtain information about the merits of the case from the persons they sought to represent.
>
> Because of these potential problems, an order limiting communications between parties and potential class members should be based on a clear record and specific findings that reflect a weighing of the need for a limitation and the potential interference with the rights of the parties. Only such a determination can ensure that the court is furthering, rather than hindering, the policies embodied in the Federal Rules of Civil Procedure, especially Rule 23. In addition, such a weighing—identifying the potential abuses being addressed—should result in a carefully drawn order that limits speech as little as possible, consistent with the rights of the parties under the circumstances.[18]

The Court therefore held that blanket prohibitions on communications with potential class members exceeded district courts' authority under Rule 23. No longer could unfounded protective orders, like the one in *Gulf Oil*, and "no comment" local rules, like those found in many districts at the time, be used to manage communications with class members. Notably, the Court also identified particular communications between class counsel and putative class members that *were* appropriate in the precertification setting: informing potential class members of the existence of the lawsuit; advising them to obtain legal advice before signing releases with the defendant; and generally "obtain[ing] information about the merits of the case."[19] The Court thus recognized the fundamental importance of precertification communications with putative class members.

C. The Modern Model: Case Management

Blanket restraints on communications with putative class members are therefore no longer tolerated by most federal courts.[20] In the federal system, *Gulf Oil* makes clear that such restraints violate Rule 23. In state courts, such restraints not only violate public policy and the efficient administration of group litigation, but also are probably unconstitutional.[21]

The void left by the erosion of no-comment rules, however, has not been filled by a new, coherent model of how courts should govern communications with putative class members. Instead, courts and leading authorities continue to disagree about what types of communications are appropriate in different circumstances.[22] In a sense this, and not some particular set of rules, is what the *Gulf Oil* court envisioned: decisions to restrict communications between attorneys and putative class members are supposed to be fact-specific, case-by-case determinations. Although more flexible, this new model is often hard to navigate, and a consideration of what courts typically do in generally applicable situations is therefore useful.

III. Communications with Putative Class Members

Three situations applicable to all class actions are the stages of the certification process: (1) precertification; (2) the opt-out period (i.e., postcertification but before the end of the opt-out period); and (3) postcertification and post-opt-out period. The extent to which a party may communicate directly with potential class members is determined, in large part, by which stage the class action has reached. We consider each stage in turn.

A. Precertification

In a traditional lawsuit, when an attorney files a complaint on a client's behalf, the existence of an attorney-client relationship is unquestioned. In a class action, the same is true of class counsel and the class representatives. There is, however, no such clarity with respect to the relationship between class counsel and unnamed class members. The majority view in the federal courts is that an attorney-client relationship does not exist between class counsel and putative class members until the district court certifies the class.[23] In state courts the predominant view is less clear, with one authority suggesting that an attorney-client relationship is created "as of the time the complaint is filed with the court,"[24] while many states' courts seems to disagree.[25] Whatever court one is in, it is clear that even if no formal attorney-client relationship exists between class counsel and putative class members, unnamed members of the class are *not* mere third parties to the litigation. Instead, they have a unique status in the case that warrants careful treatment by plaintiffs' and defense counsel alike. In this regard, while defendants' attorneys may communicate with potential class members in the "ordinary course of business," they may not give "false, misleading, or intimidating information, conceal material information, or attempt to influence the decision about whether to request exclusion from a (certified) class."[26] Newberg opines that defense counsel can communicate with putative class members "only in the ordinary course of business" and only if "they do not infringe on what some courts have characterized as the *constructive attorney-client relationship* that exists between counsel for class representatives and the members of the class."[27] The key variable is likely to be the nature and purpose of the subject communication.

As a general rule, then, both plaintiffs' and defense counsel are free to communicate with putative class members prior to certification, but these communications are limited. Class counsel are typically free to provide additional information, respond to inquiries, and seek information needed to represent the class.[28] Defense counsel are typically free to make communications in the ordinary course of business and to discuss settlement offers with individual class members, though they must take care not to give false or misleading information or attempt to influence class members in making their decision whether to remain in the class.[29] As the cases discussed below illustrate, however, because of the contentiousness of class-action litigation—as well as the fact that a number of courts still have no-comment local rules—precertification communications with putative class members often end up being governed by a court order.

1. Jackson v. Motel 6 Multipurpose, Inc. *and* Abdallah v. Coca-Cola Co. In *Jackson v. Motel 6 Multipurpose, Inc.*, the Eleventh Circuit granted a writ of mandamus vacating a district court's order allowing certain communications between plaintiffs' counsel and putative class members.[30] Two class actions, later consolidated, had been filed against Motel 6, alleging racial discrimination against employees and customers. Because the district court had a no-comment local rule,[31] plaintiffs' counsel moved for an order allowing relief from the rule, and specifically requesting that they be allowed to do the following:

- establish a toll-free number to which potential class members may call;
- publish notices of the ongoing litigation in publications nationwide and solicit information about potential class members and their alleged experiences with discrimination at Motel 6 motels;
- respond to requests for information from those who respond to the advertisements or call the toll-free number;
- distribute mass mailings to Motel 6 employees soliciting information regarding the plaintiffs' allegations of discrimination at Motel 6 motels; and
- further communicate ex parte with any "persons who may have knowledge of" the alleged discrimination, except for current Motel 6 management or supervisory employees.[32]

The district court, which had not yet ruled on the motions for class certification, granted the order.

By the time Motel 6's second petition for mandamus was heard, the district court had certified one of the classes, the *Jackson* class, and referred the certification decision of the other class, the *Petaccia* class, to the magistrate. The Eleventh Circuit held that the *Jackson* class was erroneously certified and concluded that "the communications order was an abuse of discretion from the beginning." In a less than convincing opinion, the court focused on the fact that the district court entered the communications order long before it ruled on certification and on the danger to Motel 6's reputation in concluding that the order was an abuse of discretion:

> The communications order was entered months prior to any decision regarding whether either of the two proposed classes would in fact be certified. While we cannot say that orders authorizing communication

> with potential class members may never precede class certification, district courts must strive to avoid authorizing injurious class communications that might later prove unnecessary. An order authorizing class communications prior to class certification is likely to be an abuse of discretion when (1) the communication authorized by the order is widespread and clearly injurious and (2) a certification decision is not imminent or it is unlikely that a class will in fact be certified. In such circumstances, the danger of abuse that always attends class communications—the possibility that plaintiffs might use widespread publication of their claims, disguised as class communications, to coerce defendants into settlement—is not outweighed by any need for immediate communications.
>
> The advertisements and mass mailings allowed by the order at issue in the instant petition are nationwide in scope and are surely causing serious and irreparable harm to Motel 6's reputation and to its relationship with its employees. . . . Moreover, the order was entered almost six months prior to the court's decision to certify the *Jackson* class and to refer the *Petaccia* plaintiffs' motion for class certification to a magistrate judge.[33]

The court did make an exception for the mass mailings:

> We note, however, that insofar as the district court's February 21 order authorizes the *Petaccia* plaintiffs to conduct mass mailings to Motel 6 employees, it authorizes inquiries and communications that would be allowable as a normal discovery matter, whether the *Petaccia* class is certified or not.[34]

The *Motel 6* decision is likely wrongly decided for two reasons. First, and most importantly, it adopts precisely the posture of ruling on communications orders struck down in *Gulf Oil*: communications between class counsel and putative class members were *presumed* inappropriate unless class counsel could make a showing otherwise. Indeed, the district court's local rule, the lawfulness of which the Eleventh Circuit did not directly address, said exactly that.[35] *Gulf Oil,* however, makes clear that communications between class counsel and putative class members, at least with respect to district courts' authority to interfere with such communications under Rule 23(d), are presumptively valid. District courts should not *authorize* communications prior to certification but rather, based on specific facts in the record, should only *limit* them, and should do that in as narrowly tailored a manner as possible.

Second, it is error to assume, as the Eleventh Circuit clearly did, that an "order authorizing class communications prior to class certification is likely to be an abuse of discretion when . . . a certification decision is not imminent or it is unlikely that a class will in fact be certified."[36] *Gulf Oil* makes clear that the imminence of a district court's decision on certification is not nearly as significant as the *Motel 6* court suggests. Not only had the district court in *Gulf Oil not* ruled on certification, it had initially dismissed the plaintiffs' complaint as untimely.[37] The Supreme Court, in an opinion that was explicitly meant to "determine the scope of a district court's authority to limit communications from named plaintiffs and their counsel to prospective class members,"[38] said *nothing* about the imminence of a decision on certification. Moreover, the Court's conclusion that the no-comment order in the *Gulf Oil* case was improper was specifically based on reasons that make clear that the imminence of a decision on certification is irrelevant:

> The order interfered with their efforts to inform potential class members of the existence of this lawsuit, and may have been particularly injurious—not only to respondents but to the class as a whole—because the employees at that time were being pressed to decide whether to accept a backpay offer from Gulf that required them to sign a full release of all liability for discriminatory acts. In addition, the order made it more difficult for respondents, as the class representatives, to obtain information about the merits of the case from the persons they sought to represent.[39]

Both informing putative class members of the existence of a class action and obtaining information about the merits of the case from them—communications that are indisputably legitimate under *Gulf Oil*—frequently and often necessarily occur long before the district courts' decision on certification.[40]

Despite its flaws, class counsel must be familiar with *Motel 6* in order to meet defense counsel's likely reliance on it. For example, in *Abdallah v. Coca-Cola Co.*,[41] a widely publicized case filed shortly after *Motel 6*, defendants relied centrally on *Motel 6* in seeking an order to limit class counsel's contact with putative class members. A racial discrimination class action was filed on behalf of employees of Coca-Cola, and, again because of a no-comment local rule in the district court, plaintiffs' counsel moved for an order allowing certain communications. Relying specifically on *Motel 6* and the fact that "the certification decision will not be made at any time in the near future," the district court limited class counsel's ability to communicate with putative class members to responding to unsolicited inquiries. According to the court, "[s]uch communications, when initiated by potential class members and not Plaintiffs' counsel, are neither widespread nor injurious." Because of the *Motel 6* "widespread and injurious" standard, however, the court ordered plaintiffs' counsel to remove the class-action complaint from a website on which it had been posted subsequent to the filing of the suit.[42]

Notably, the *Abdallah* court made two rulings that were not based on *Motel 6*. Because of the "inherent danger" that communications by an employer could "deter potential class members from participating in the suit," the court prohibited Coca-Cola "from discussing this lawsuit directly with potential class members, except to the extent it needs to speak with managerial employees to investigate the acts, omissions, and statements they committed that may expose Coca-Cola to liability in this action."[43] Furthermore, the court denied Coca-Cola's request that plaintiffs' counsel be prohibited from contacting employees "deemed to be represented by the Company's counsel," which the company claimed included (1) supervisory and managerial employees; (2) any employees whose acts or admissions could be attributed to Coca-Cola; (3) employees involved in defending the action; and (4) those likely to have privileged information. Though it recognized that the state's ethical rules prohibited ex parte contacts with opposing parties, the court concluded that "upper level employees of Coca-Cola have a right to bring a discrimination claim against their employer. Therefore, to the extent that these employees wish to pursue employment claims against Coca-Cola, they may communicate freely with Plaintiffs and their counsel."[44]

2. Hammond v. City of Junction City

The *Abdallah* court's decision to allow employees "deemed to be represented by the Company's counsel" to contact and communicate freely with class plaintiffs and their counsel is undoubtedly correct under the Model Rules. There is no question, in short, that employees have a right to sue their employer, and that in doing so they can retain and communicate with their own counsel. It is worth noting, however, that courts sometimes rely on the principle that no attorney-client relationship exists between class counsel and putative class members until a class is certified to erroneously conclude that class counsel should not be allowed to engage in precertification, ex parte communications with managerial employees who are potential class members, even if the communication relates solely to the development of the class action and does not implicate the corporation's privileged information. This was precisely the court's ruling in *Hammond v. City of Junction City*,[45] in which the district court held that class counsel's contact with the defendant's director of human relations was not only not privileged, since it occurred before certification and therefore before there was an attorney-client relationship, but also violated the ethical prohibition against contacting a party represented by counsel. To avoid such a restraint on precertification communications with putative class members, counsel (1) should emphasize that *Gulf Oil* makes clear that precertification contacts with putative class members are perfectly appropriate and are often essential to the development of a class action,[46] and (2) should directly address any concerns regarding privileged information that corporate employees may have and take specific precautions with respect to such information during any ex parte contacts.[47]

B. The Opt-Out Period

Once a class has been certified, most courts hold that the rules governing communications apply as though each class member is a client of class counsel.[48] Under those rules, in particular Model Rule 4.2, defendants and their counsel ordinarily may communicate with class members or putative class members only through class counsel for plaintiffs.[49] This is so even in opt-out class actions, where many putative class members may elect to opt out before the end of the opt-out period.[50] Thus attorneys other than class counsel, in particular defense counsel and objectors, must take care not to engage in inappropriate communications with the class.[51] Recent court decisions balance the need to monitor the notice process with safeguarding the ability of parties to communicate.[52] The authority of the court also includes the power to invalidate opt outs procured through fraud, duress, or other improper conduct.[53]

1. Kleiner v. First National Bank of Atlanta

The classic case concerning inappropriate communications by defense counsel at this stage of a class action is *Kleiner v. First National Bank of Atlanta.*[54] *Kleiner* involved what Judge Vance called "a ground-breaking class action against the First National Bank of Atlanta . . . sounding in fraud, RICO and breach of contract."[55] Several weeks after the trial judge certified the class under Rule 23(b)(3), but before the end of the opt-out period, defense counsel sought to obtain discovery from a number of putative class members. Class counsel moved for a protective order, arguing that discovery and unilateral contacts by the bank before the close of the exclusion period would intimidate potential class members and discourage them from participating in the suit. The court granted the order prohibiting the bank's requested discovery, but specifically took the broader question of unsupervised contacts between the bank and class members under advisement pending further briefing.

Several weeks later the bank "seized upon the idea of soliciting class exclusion requests as a means to reducing its potential liability and quelling the adverse publicity the lawsuit had spawned."[56] Furthermore, defense counsel decided that phone calls would be better than letters, given the danger that people would disregard letters as more "junk mail." Because the putative class consisted of bank customers, the bank had access to class members' contact information, and indeed its loan officers had developed relationships with many of the potential plaintiffs. The bank officers were told to "do the best selling job they had ever done," and the telephone campaign soliciting opt-outs took place, not coincidentally, during the district judge's two-week vacation. The campaign proved very successful: the bank's officers obtained opt-out commitments from 2,800 of the 3,000 putative class members contacted, representing a sum total of $694,997,218 in past or present loans. The district judge, however, was not pleased. Upon returning from her vacation, she held a hearing on the matter and declared the solicitation scheme illegal under Model Rule 4.2 and the district court's local rule banning solicitation of opt-outs. Defense counsel was held to have knowingly participated in the scheme and to have given legal advice in bad faith. He was sanctioned $50,000; was ordered to pay, along with his firm and the bank, all legal fees associated with the hearing and costs for curative notice; and was disqualified from further representation in the case. As a final measure, the district court ruled that the exclusion requests would be voidable following entry of judgment.

The Fifth Circuit affirmed the district court's ruling that the solicitation scheme violated Model Rule 4.2, and further held that the scheme violated the court's protective order.[57] Thus, even though the opt-out period had not ended and many of the bank's customers may very well have elected to opt out, the court of appeals confirmed that class counsel and the putative class members should be treated as though they had an attorney-client relationship. In a cogent discussion of the proper role of trial judges in policing communications with putative class members, Judge Vance went on to discuss the authority of district courts to ban opt-out solicitations under Rule 23. Addressing solicitation requests generally, the court stated:

> When confronted with claims pressed by a plaintiff class, it is obviously in defendants' interest to diminish the size of the class and thus the range of potential liability by soliciting exclusion requests. Such conduct reduces the effectiveness of the 23(b)(3) class action for no reason except to undermine the purposes of the rule. A unilateral communications scheme, moreover, is rife with potential for coercion. If the class and the class opponent are involved in an ongoing business relationship, communications from the class opponent to the class may be coercive. . . . Unsupervised, unilateral communications with the plaintiff class sabotage the goal of informed consent by urging exclusion on the basis of a one-sided presentation of the facts, without opportunity for rebuttal. The damage from misstatements could well be irreparable.[58]

With respect to the specific solicitation scheme in *Kleiner*, the court stated:

> In view of the tension between the preference for class adjudication and the individual autonomy afforded by exclusion, it is critical that the class receive accurate and impartial information regarding the status, purposes and effects of the class action. . . . In this case, the carefully constructed edifice of check and countercheck, notice and reply, was obliterated when the telephones were lifted from their cradles. The Bank's actions obstructed the district court in the discharge of its duty to "protect both the absent class and the integrity of the judicial process by monitoring the actions before it." The Bank's subterfuge and subversion constituted an intolerable affront to the authority of the district court to police class member contacts. Accordingly, we hold that the trial court had ample discretion under Rules 23(b)(3) and 23(d) to prohibit the Bank's overtures.[59]

The *Kleiner* court went beyond its holding that an attorney-client relationship exists between class counsel and putative class members after certification and emphasized that "it is critical that the class receive accurate and impartial information." Although mindful of *Gulf Oil*, *Kleiner* firmly establishes "the authority of the district court to police class member contacts" when misleading information or other improper influence on putative class members is threatened.

2. Georgine v. Amchem Products, Inc.

As *Kleiner* illustrated, class counsel and putative class members are generally held to have an attorney-client relationship during the opt-out period, despite the fact that a number of potential class members may elect to opt out. Typically, then, inappropriate communications with putative class members are not likely to come from class counsel during the opt-out period—though they may, as in *Kleiner*, come from defense counsel. One source of potential communications problems, however, is objectors. After a class has been certified and, as is typically the case, a settlement has been proposed, objecting counsel have a strong incentive to encourage putative class members to opt out. A leading case illustrating this problem is *Georgine v. Amchem Products, Inc.*[60]

In *Georgine*, a massive class of asbestos-exposure victims had been certified by the district court.[61] During the opt-out period, dozens of objectors began a campaign of soliciting opt-outs, primarily through the mass-mailing of letters to putative class members. These letters reached over 650,000 potential class members, 236,323 of whom ultimately elected to opt out of the class settlement. Class counsel and the defendants (the "settling parties") in the case filed a joint motion requesting that the court remedy the adverse effects of the opt-out solicitation campaign. In particular, the settling parties sought (1) the negation of all exclusion requests; (2) the creation of a second notice and opt-out period for class members who timely requested exclusion from the class; and (3) the issuance of an injunction requiring that all communications by asbestos plaintiffs' attorneys that concern the class action or settlement bear a "Disclosure Statement."[62]

The court began its analysis by discussing the harm caused by misleading communications to putative class members, and by examining the allegedly misleading communications sent by the objectors:

> Misleading communications to class members concerning litigation pose a serious threat to the fairness of the litigation process, the adequacy of representation and the administration of justice generally. . . . Here, I find that unilateral communications with class members by various attorneys were misleading and made it unlikely that class members, who received these communications or were informed of their contents, made an informed choice to exclude themselves from the class. . . . Many of the letters and advertisements were misleading because they (1) made statements regarding the terms of the settlement that created false impressions about the effect of the settlement on the recipient, e.g., the false statement that opting out is the only way to secure future compensation; asbestos companies can back out of the settlement at any time; and (2) did not reveal the personal interests

> of the drafters of the letters and advertisements. Moreover, because these communications contained only one-sided attacks on the terms of the settlement without any discussion of the settlement benefits or the existence of the Court-approved notice materials, the effect of the misleading aspects of the communications was compounded.[63]

The court then discussed several of the most misleading of the objectors' letters. The single most misleading letter, according to the court, was a mailing sent by the law firm of Baron & Budd. This letter stated that "[t]he only way to protect your rights to future compensation is to sign the enclosed 'opt out' form immediately" and that "[i]f you do not send in this form immediately, YOU WILL LOSE VALUABLE RIGHTS IN THE EVENT YOU DEVELOP AN ASBESTOS-RELATED DISEASE IN THE FUTURE."[64] Although it was true that some of the recipients of the letter might not have qualified for compensation under the terms of the settlement, the court concluded that "the letter creates the impression to all readers, both those who will be eligible to receive compensation in the future and those who will not, that the only way to obtain future compensation is to sign the enclosed opt-out form. That simply is incorrect."[65] Furthermore, the court criticized the letter for failing to explain any of the benefits of the settlement and for "encourag[ing] recipients to make decisions to opt out of the class without the benefit of the Court-approved notice materials."[66] Finally, the court observed that "the most disturbing aspect of the letter is that it fails to mention that Baron & Budd represents class members who are objecting to the settlement and, therefore, are not neutral observers." After examining numerous similar communications, the court granted the settling parties' request for the negation of all exclusion requests and the creation of a second notice and opt-out period.

Georgine illustrates a principled, well-reasoned application of *Gulf Oil*. The court engaged in a thorough review of the record, and decided upon a remedy specifically tailored to remedy the identified harm caused by the misleading communications. Although recognizing the inherent bias on the part of objectors, the court did not attempt to impose any blanket restriction on their communication with putative class members. Indeed, the court seemed legitimately open to the use of forthright communications by objectors: "[T]his Court encourages the free flow of ideas relating to the advantages and disadvantages of the settlement, in order to evaluate the relative merits of conflicting arguments."[67] It is worth noting that of all the misleading characteristics of the contested letters, the one that bothered the court the most was the failure of the objectors to identify their biases: "In the instant case, because none of the communications at issue revealed to the recipient that the drafter had a financial motive to obtain additional opt-outs, the recipient was not on notice to closely scrutinize the substance of the communications."[68] While objections to proposed settlements are sometimes in the best interests of the class, objectors have no legitimate reason to hide their financial interest in soliciting class members' opt-outs. Courts can and most likely will use their "broad authority to exercise control over a class action" to remedy the effects of any misleading communications.

C. Postcertification, Post-Opt-Out Period

Once a class has been certified and the opt-out period has closed, it is clear that an attorney-client relationship exists between class counsel and all class members who have not opted out.[69] Thus, subject to the requirement of court approval for settlement or dismissal of the suit, class counsel can freely communicate with class members. Moreover, in keeping with the rule against communications with represented parties, defense counsel are barred from communicating with class members, other than through class counsel.[70]

IV. The Role of Class Members' Organizations

An advocacy group and its agents, such as a union concerned about workplace health hazards, have broad First Amendment rights of speech and association that include the right to help their members protect themselves through the legal system,[71] to hire attorneys to act as personal counsel for members,[72] and to advise injured members to seek legal advice and even refer them to specific outside attorneys for assistance in personal injury litigation.[73] In *United Transportation Union v. State Bar of Michigan*, for example, the Supreme Court held that a state court injunction restraining a railroad union from giving or furnishing legal advice to its members or their families violated the First Amendment.[74] The Court, reflecting on the line of cases that required this result, stated the following:

> In the context of this case we deal with a cooperative union of workers seeking to assist its members in effectively asserting claims under the [Federal Employer's Liability Act]. But the principle here involved cannot be limited to the facts of this case. At issue is the basic right to group legal action, a right first asserted in this Court by an association of Negroes seeking the protection of freedoms guaranteed by the Constitution. The common thread running through our decisions in *NAACP v. Button, Trainmen,* and *United Mine Workers* is that collective activity undertaken to obtain meaningful access to the courts is a fundamental right within the protection of the First Amendment. However, that right would be a hollow promise if courts could deny associations of workers or others the means of enabling their members to meet the costs of legal representation.[75]

An association, therefore, has a well-established First Amendment right to communicate with its members for the purpose of providing or aiding in the provision of legal aid. This interest intersects with the law regarding communications with putative class members when an association is a named party and class representative in a class action in which its members are putative class members. For example, a union and several workers may bring suit on behalf of all members of the union.[76] Similarly, a civil rights group[77] or a state optometric association[78] might seek to bring class actions on behalf of their members. In these scenarios, does the *United Transportation Union* line of cases give the association—either directly or through class counsel—a broader right to communicate with putative class members than would be the case for ordinary, individual class representatives?

In theory, it seems the answer to this question is no. This is not, however, because associations do not have broad First Amendment rights to communicate with their members, but rather because *Gulf Oil* makes clear that ordinary, individual class representatives and their class counsel have broad rights to communicate with putative class members, too: "[A]n order limiting communications between parties and potential class members should be based on a clear record and specific findings that reflect a weighing of the need for a limitation and the potential interference with the rights of the parties."[79] However, as we have seen, federal courts have not uniformly applied the *Gulf Oil* standard, and in those situations the fact that an association is a class representative can provide a second basis for challenging a restraint on communications with putative class members. Although there appear to be no published cases dealing with this precise issue, the First Amendment rights of associations and their members under the *United Transportation Union* line of cases is well established, and courts that have certified class actions with associations as class representatives have recognized that the associations (typically unions or civil rights groups) would use their greater, collective resources to furnish legal services to their members.[80] Unfettered communications with the associations' members, therefore, is arguably implicit.

V. Opt-In Class Actions

Section 216(b) of the Fair Labor Standards Act[81] (FLSA) provides a private right of action for employees to recover unpaid minimum wages and overtime compensation; to redress retaliatory discharges; and to enforce the terms of the Age Discrimination in Employment Act (ADEA). Actions under section 216(b) can be brought individually or as collective actions. Unlike modern class actions, however, section 216(b) actions operate as "spurious" or "opt in" class actions: "No employee shall be a party plaintiff to any such action unless he gives his consent in writing to become such a party and such consent is filed in the court in which such action is brought."[82] The role of notice in these opt-in actions, therefore, is different and arguably even more important than notice in opt-out actions: without notice of the suit and of one's right to opt in, a potential plaintiff literally *cannot* participate in the litigation.

While individual notice is required in opt-out class actions under Rule 23, the federal courts were long divided on the issue of whether a district court even had the authority to facilitate the joinder of section 216(b) class members by approving the sending of notice in opt-in actions brought under FLSA. Some courts held that notice of a proposed action under section 216(b) was neither required nor authorized, and that a district court lacked authority to direct notice to potential class members.[83] Other courts held that such notice was improper solicitation of litigation.[84] On the other hand, several courts concluded that the right to bring a representative action carried with it the right to notify those persons whom the plaintiff wished to represent, and thus approved notification of potential class members.[85]

The split in the lower courts was resolved by the Supreme Court in *Hoffman La-Roche Inc. v. Sperling*,[86] an action brought under ADEA in which plaintiffs sought court-approved notice under section 216(b). Stressing the "wisdom and necessity" of "judicial intervention in the management of litigation" and noting that the rationale of *Gulf Oil* applied in section 216(b) actions, the Court held that "district courts have *discretion*, in appropriate cases, to implement 29 U.S.C. § 216(b) . . . by facilitating notice to potential plaintiffs."[87] Such court-facilitated notice can, for example, serve "the legitimate goal of avoiding a multiplicity of duplicative suits and setting cutoff dates to expedite disposition of the action."[88]

The Court in *Hoffman*, however, specifically refused to examine the details of the notice at issue in the case, and emphasized that it was "confirm[ing] the existence of the trial court's discretion, not the details of its exercise."[89] Furthermore, the Court stated, "We do not address any conflicts between court-authorized notice and communications with potential plaintiffs by counsel."[90] Thus, the Court specifically left open the possibility that a district court could refuse to approve or otherwise facilitate notice to potential plaintiffs in a section 216(b) action, and that notice would have to be accomplished by "communications with potential plaintiffs by counsel" that did not involve the court.[91]

Several pre-*Hoffman* opinions that refused to issue or allow notice under section 216(b) illustrate how courts conceive of the nature and scope of these direct communications between class counsel and potential plaintiffs. In *Dolan v. Project Construction Corp.*,[92] for example, the Court of Appeals for the Tenth Circuit affirmed an order of the district court refusing to issue court-approved notice under section 216(b) and, further, granting a protective order with respect to discovery plaintiffs had sought in order to learn the names and addresses of potential plaintiffs. Although it concluded that court-approved notice was inappropriate, the *Dolan* court expected that plaintiffs' counsel would seek out and contact potential plaintiffs on their own:

> However, recent United States Supreme Court cases regarding legal communication dictate the allowance of a level of reasonable communication by the plaintiff and counsel with those parties he can discover without judicial assistance. . . . Additionally, "an order limiting communications between parties and potential class members should be based on a clear record and specific findings that reflect a weighing of the need for a limitation and the potential interference with the rights

> of the parties." Although *Gulf Oil* is a case involving a Rule 23 action, the principle of law is applicable to all representative actions.[93]

Thus, under *Dolan*, even if a district court refuses to facilitate notice under section 216(b), it should not interfere with plaintiffs' attorneys' attempts to inform potential class members of the suit, unless such interference is consistent with *Gulf Oil*.

The Seventh Circuit, in another pre-*Hoffman* case, took a different approach. In *Woods v. New York Life Insurance*,[94] the court held that district courts could review and approve communications between section 216(b) plaintiffs and potential class members but could not send out notice that was on judicial letterhead or that was signed by a judicial officer. The court addressed the concern, shared by many plaintiffs' attorneys bringing actions under section 216(b), that the judicial imprimatur on the notice was necessary in order to avoid potential solicitation complaints under state law:

> At oral argument the plaintiffs' counsel stated that he wanted the imprimatur in order to shield himself from a possible complaint under state law that he was trying to stir up litigation; but if the notice is approved by a federal court under the authority that we hold it has by virtue of section 16(b) of the Fair Labor Standards Act, any effort by the state to punish the lawyer who mails the notice would violate the supremacy clause of the United States Constitution. It is the court's order, not its letterhead or its clerk's signature, that provides the lawyer with immunity from a state's efforts to prevent communications authorized by section 16(b). Indeed the order may be unnecessary; section 16(b) of its own force may preempt state laws that operate to prevent the representative plaintiff or his counsel from communicating with other (actual or potential) class members; such laws could even raise First Amendment problems.[95]

Notably, however, the *Woods* court did *not* believe that class counsel could freely contact potential plaintiffs, even if the content of the communications was perfectly appropriate. Instead, the court envisioned the following procedure, at least in section 216(b) actions:

> Before this suit was filed, Woods had sent invitations to other members of the class to join with him, and New York Life does not challenge his right to do this. After suit was filed, however, we do not think it would have been proper for Woods or his counsel to have sent out such invitations without first communicating to the defendant's counsel his intention to do so, so that the defendant's counsel would have an opportunity to verify the accuracy of the notice and, if he wished, to move for an order amending the notice or limiting its distribution in an appropriate manner. We cannot find any express basis

> in rule or statute for inferring either the duty of the plaintiff's counsel to notify the defendant's counsel in this manner or the power of the district court to regulate the content and distribution of the notice to potential class members; but we think both the duty and the power may fairly be inferred from section 16(b) itself and from Rule 83 of the Federal Rules of Civil Procedure, which provides that "in all cases not provided for by rule, the district courts may regulate their practice in any manner not inconsistent with" the Federal Rules. Once a section 16(b) action is commenced, the defendant has a vital interest in, and the court a managerial responsibility regarding, the joinder of additional parties plaintiff, and these concerns support the modest duty and power that we infer.[96]

While the *Woods* court recognized the right of class counsel to communicate with potential class members, as well as the potential "First Amendment problems" with state laws interfering with such communications, the court invented a procedure under section 216(b) that, in effect, requires class counsel to obtain approval by either defense counsel or the court before sending out notice to potential class members. Such a requirement is arguably inconsistent with *Gulf Oil*, which the Supreme Court has explicitly held applies to actions under section 216(b).[97]

Finally, in *Goerke v. Commercial Contractors & Supply Co.*,[98] the district court for the Northern District of Georgia adopted the reasoning of the Tenth Circuit in *Dolan* in holding that it had no power under FLSA to authorize notice to potential class members. Because plaintiffs' counsel, like the plaintiffs' attorneys in *Wood*, expressed concern about violating the rules of the State Bar of Georgia, the court specifically addressed the alternative to court-approved notice under section 216(b):

> The denial of this motion, however, does not preclude the plaintiff engaging in protected communication with other potential plaintiffs who can be discovered without intervention by the court. . . . As the Supreme Court has held in *Gulf Oil Company vs. Bernard*, an order limiting communications between parties and potential class members "should be based on a clear record and specific findings that reflect a weighing of the need for limitation and the potential interference with the rights of the parties." There is no question that *Bernard* dealt with a Rule 23 class action, and was based upon the standards of the *Federal Rules of Civil Procedure*. However . . . the rationale behind *Bernard* was equally applicable to a representative action under 216(b). Thus, although this court has found that it has no power to approve and authorize the dissemination of a notice to potential class members, there are forms of protected communication in which plaintiff's counsel can engage with potential class members. As regards plain-

> tiff's fears, expressed in the brief in support of this motion, plaintiff need only make certain that any communications in which he engages are directed toward the provision of *notice*, rather than toward active solicitation of individuals to join in the present litigation.[99]

Thus, the *Goerke* court specifically held that in the absence of court-approved notice, class counsel in a section 216(b) action could communicate with potential class members and such communications would be governed by the principles set forth in *Gulf Oil*. Numerous courts have since reached the same conclusion, holding that the standard set forth in *Gulf Oil* applies to collective actions under § 216(b).[100]

VI. Conclusion

As the Supreme Court made clear in *Gulf Oil*, communications between class counsel and putative class members are critical to the prosecution of class actions. Thus, while district courts have broad authority to police these communications, their decision to do so must be based on a clear record and specific findings that reflect a weighing of the need for the limitation and the potential for interference with the rights of the parties. Only such a determination, as the Court itself has stated, "can ensure that the [district] court is furthering, rather than hindering, the policies embodied in the Federal Rules of Civil Procedure, especially Rule 23."[101] Furthermore, the analysis in *Gulf Oil* applies with, if anything, even more force in the other class-action contexts discussed in this chapter. When a union or civil rights group is a named plaintiff in a class action, for example, the groups' First Amendment rights to communicate with and provide legal assistance to their members provides an additional argument against interference with class counsel's contacts with the putative class. In opt-in class actions under FLSA, furthermore, it is now clear that district courts have the authority to issue notice to putative class members. The fact that class members will not be able to participate in the suit unless they affirmatively opt in strongly suggests that courts should approve and issue notice. At the very least, they should not hinder class counsel from communicating with putative class members.

Notes

1. Abram Chayes, *The Role of the Judge in Public Law Litigation*, 89 Harv. L. Rev. 1281 (1976) (nature of dispute affects procedure); *see also* David Rosenberg, *The Causal Connection in Mass Exposure Cases: A "Public Law" Vision of the Tort System*, 97 Harv. L. Rev. 851 (1984) (role of class action).
2. 452 U.S. 89 (1981).
3. 29 U.S.C. §§ 201 *et seq.*
4. Model Rules of Prof'l Conduct R. 7.3 (2002).

5. MODEL RULES OF PROF'L CONDUCT R. 4.2 (2002).
6. Dubois v. Gradco Sys., Inc., 136 F.R.D. 341, 344 (D. Conn. 1991) (citing G. HAZARD & W. HODES, THE LAW OF LAWYERING: A HANDBOOK ON THE MODEL RULES OF PROFESSIONAL CONDUCT 436 (1988 Supp.)).
7. *See* chapter 3, Perspectives on the Attorney-Client Privilege and Work-Product Doctrine, sections II.A & V.
8. *See, e.g., In re* McKesson HBOC, Inc. Sec. Litig., 126 F. Supp. 2d 1239, 1245 (N.D. Cal. 2000) (counsel's solicitations to potential class members improper because they communicated "a gratuitous sense of urgency").
9. *See, e.g.,* Kleiner v. First Nat'l Bank of Atlanta, 751 F.2d 1193 (5th Cir. 1985) (affirming imposition of substantial sanctions upon defense counsel who had participated in campaign of seeking opt-outs from putative class members).
10. Pamela Mathy, *The Validity of Class Action No Comment Rules,* 13 RUTGERS L.J. 285, 285 (1982); *see also* Gulf Oil Co. v. Bernard, 619 F.2d 459, 464 n.3 (5th Cir. 1980) (en banc) (noting that both the 1973 and 1977 editions of the *Manual for Complex Litigation* advocated this approach).
11. Middle Dist. Fla. Local Rule 4.04(e) (no longer in effect).
12. *See, e.g.,* Gulf Oil Co. v. Bernard, 452 U.S. 89 (1981).
13. Gulf Oil Co. v. Bernard, 619 F.2d 459 (5th Cir. 1980) (en banc).
14. *See, e.g.,* Rodgers v. U.S. Steel Corp., 508 F.2d 152 (3d Cir. 1975); *Gulf Oil,* 619 F.2d 459.
15. *Gulf Oil,* 452 U.S. 89.
16. *Gulf Oil,* 619 F.2d 459.
17. *Gulf Oil,* 452 U.S. at 100.
18. *Id.* at 101–02.
19. *Id.* at 101.
20. *See, e.g.,* Gates v. Cook, 234 F.3d 221, 227 (5th Cir. 2000); Wiginton v. Ellis, 2003 WL 22232907, at *3, slip op. (N.D. Ill., Sept. 16, 2003). However, some federal district courts, notably the Northern District of Georgia, still have no-comment local rules. *See infra* discussion of Abdallah v. Coca-Cola Co., 186 F.R.D. 672 (N.D. Ga. 1999).
21. *Gulf Oil,* 619 F.2d 459.
22. *See* MANUAL FOR COMPLEX LITIGATION § 21.12 ("Rule 23(d) authorizes the court to regulate communications with potential class members, even before certification. Such regulations, however, could implicate the First Amendment. . . . Most judges are reluctant to restrict communications between the parties or their counsel and potential class members, except when necessary to prevent serious misconduct."). *Compare, e.g.,* THOMAS A. DICKERSON, CLASS ACTIONS: THE LAW OF 50 STATES § 4.06[2], at 4-57 (2001) ("The members of the purported class on whose behalf a class action is instituted are deemed represented by counsel for the class representatives as of the time the complaint is filed with the court."), *with* Atari, Inc. v. Super. Ct., 212 Cal. Rptr. 773, 776 (Ct. App. 1985) ("We cannot accept the suggestion that a potential (but as yet unapproached) class member should be deemed 'a party . . . represented by counsel' even before the class is certified. . . .").
23. MANUAL FOR COMPLEX LITIGATION § 21.33 (describing how attorney-client relationship is formed after class certification).
24. THOMAS A. DICKERSON, CLASS ACTIONS: THE LAW OF 50 STATES § 4.06[2], at 4-57 (2001) ("The members of the purported class on whose behalf a class action is

instituted are deemed represented by counsel for the class representatives as of the time the complaint is filed with the court.").

25. *See, e.g., Atari*, 212 Cal. Rptr. at 776 ("We cannot accept the suggestion that a potential (but as yet unapproached) class member should be deemed 'a party . . . represented by counsel' even before the class is certified. . . ."); Lewis v. Bayer AG, 2002 WL 1472339 (Pa. Com. Pl., June 12, 2002) (holding, without addressing question of whether putative class members were deemed represented by class counsel prior to certification, that defendant was allowed to contact putative class members regarding adverse drug reactions).
26. Manual for Complex Litigation § 21.12.
27. 3 Herbert Newberg & Alba Conte, Newberg on Class Actions 3d § 15.14, at 15-41 (1992).
28. *See Gulf Oil*, 452 U.S. 89; Oppenheimer Fund, Inc., v. Sanders, 437 U.S. 340, 354 n.20 (1978); *see also* Manual for Complex Litigation § 21.12.
29. *See* Kleiner v. First Nat'l Bank of Atlanta, 751 F.2d 1193 (5th Cir. 1985); Turner v. Bernstein, 768 A.2d 24 (Del. Ch. 2000); Belt v. Emcare Inc., 299 F. Supp. 2d 664 (E.D. Tex. 2003); *see also* Manual for Complex Litigation § 21.12.
30. 130 F.3d 999 (11th Cir. 1997).
31. Middle Dist. Fla. Local Rule 4.04(e) (no longer in effect) ("In every case sought to be maintained by any party as a class action, all parties thereto and their counsel are hereby forbidden, directly or indirectly, orally or in writing, to communicate concerning such actions with any potential or actual class member, not a formal party to the case, without approval by the Court.").
32. *Jackson*, 130 F.3d at 1002.
33. *Id.* at 1004.
34. *Id.* at 1008 n.19.
35. *See* Middle Dist. Fla. Local Rule 4.04(e), *supra* note 31.
36. *Jackson*, 130 F.3d 1004.
37. Gulf Oil Co. v. Bernard, 452 U.S. 89, 97 n.8 (1981).
38. *Id.* at 91.
39. *Id.* at 101.
40. *See also* Friedman v. Intervet, Inc., 2010 WL 3087432, at *5–7 (N.D. Ohio 2010). The court in *Friedman* rejected a defendant's argument against an order requiring it to inform any prospective class members that it contacted of the existence of pending litigation. The defendant had invoked *Motel 6*, arguing in part that ultimate class certification was unlikely and therefore limitations on the defendants' communications would be unnecessary. The court, however, ruled that it must balance "concern for unnecessary limitations on defendant's communications against the purposes of Rule 23 and class actions," where unlimited contacts by the defendants could "allow them to reduce their potential liability by encouraging potential class members not to join the litigation." *Id.* at *5–7.
41. 186 F.R.D. 672 (N.D. Ga. 1999).
42. *Id.* at 678.
43. *Id.* at 679.
44. *Id.* at 677. *See also* Spratley v. State Farm Mut. Auto. Ins. Co., 78 P.3d 603, 609 (Utah 2003) (holding that attorneys who resigned from State Farm claiming that demands of their jobs would force them to violate attorney ethics rules could, in suit for constructive discharge and retaliation, disclose privileged

and confidential information to the extent "reasonably necessary to establish their claim against State Farm").

45. 2002 WL 169370, No 00-2146 (D. Kan. Jan. 23, 2002).
46. *See supra* text accompanying note 40.
47. *See, e.g.*, Benjamin J. Vernia, *Right of Attorney to Conduct Ex Parte Interviews with Former Corporate Employees*, 57 A.L.R. 5th 633 (1998) (suggesting that attorneys should "establish a script of statements and questions to be followed in all initial contacts with former employees").
48. *See* MANUAL FOR COMPLEX LITIGATION § 21.33 ("Once a class has been certified, the rules governing communications apply as though each class member is a client of the class counsel.").
49. *But see* Roberts v. Weim, 130 F.R.D. 416 (N.D. Cal 1988) (denying plaintiff's request for an order requiring prior approval of any communications by defense counsel to putative class members during opt-out period).
50. Newberg suggests the possibility of a less absolute view, premised on the likelihood that at least some putative class members will opt out of the litigation after certification and before the exclusion period expires. *See* 3 NEWBERG & CONTE, *supra* note 27, § 15.15, at 15-43 to 15-44 (1992). Under that view, postcertification communications may still be permissible (albeit potentially hazardous if the court disagrees) on grounds that the putative class member being communicated with retains an independent right to make his or her own decisions until the end of the exclusion period.
51. *See* Clincy v. Galardi S. Enters., Inc., 2010 WL 966639 (N.D. Ga. 2010) (requiring that following conditional class certification, any further written communication by defendant employer to potential opt-in plaintiffs must contain court-prescribed rider acknowledging unlawfulness of attempts by defendant to discourage participation in suit, and further allowing plaintiffs' counsel to contact such potential opt-in class members to discuss action).
52. *See In re* Cmty. Bank of N. Va. & Guar. Nat'l Bank of Tallahassee Second Mortgage Loan Litig., 418 F.3d 277, 310 (3d Cir. 2005) ("Because the advantage of class action litigation comes at the cost of binding absent class members through the res judicata effect of litigation over which they lack control, the district courts must closely monitor the notice process and take steps to safeguard class members from 'unauthorized [and] misleading communications from the parties or their counsel.'") (quoting Erhardt v. Prudential Group, Inc., 629 F.2d 843, 846 (2d Cir. 1980)). *But see* Cox Nuclear Med. v. Gold Cup Coffee Servs., Inc., 214 F.R.D. 696 (S.D. Ala. 2003); McLaughlin v. Liberty Mut. Ins. Co., 224 F.R.D. 295 (D. Mass. 2004) (court improperly restrained communication absent finding of abuse).
53. *See, e.g.*, Wang v. Chinese Daily News, Inc., 2010 WL 3733568 (9th Cir. 2010).
54. 751 F.2d 1193 (5th Cir. 1985).
55. *Id.* at 1196.
56. *Id.* at 1197.
57. *Id.* at 1200 n.15.
58. *Id.* at 1202–03.
59. *Id.* at 1203.
60. 160 F.R.D. 478 (E.D. Pa. 1995). Another potential source of trouble is competing counsel in securities class actions. *See In re* Worldcom, Inc. Sec. Litig., 2003 WL 22701241 (S.D.N.Y. Nov. 17, 2003) (discussing misleading letters sent by securities class action firm to absent class members and ordering curative notice).

61. For an extensive discussion of the history of this litigation, *see* Georgine v. Amchem Prods., Inc., 157 F.R.D. 246, 257–61 (E.D. Pa. 1994).
62. *Amchem Prods.*, 160 F.R.D. at 489. Notably, the settling parties elected not to seek an order banning all potentially misleading communications by objectors with putative class members during the second opt-out period. Class counsel specifically informed the court that while they supported the inclusion of a disclosure statement on all future communications, they could not support "any order that would restrain attorney-client communications in any manner." *Id.* at n.11.
63. *Id.* at 490.
64. *Id.* at 491.
65. *Id.*
66. *Id.* at 490.
67. *Id.* at 495.
68. *Id.* at 496.
69. *See* 3 NEWBERG & CONTE, *supra* note 27, § 15.18, at 15-49.
70. *See also* Williams v. Quinn, 2010 WL 3021576 (N.D. Ill. 2010) (holding that after certification, counsel representing class objectors were barred from initiating contact with additional class members without first seeking permission of the class members' representative counsel).
71. Mozzochi v. Borden, 959 F.2d 1174, 1180 (2d Cir. 1992); NAACP v. Button, 371 U.S. 415, 432–33 (1963) (enforcement of barratry statute may be invalid if it prohibits privileged exercise of first amendment rights "whether or not . . . the petitioner has engaged in privileged conduct"); United States v. Spock, 416 F.2d 165 (1st Cir. 1969) (conspiracy law held not enforceable against protected advocacy of opposition to Vietnam War).
72. United Mine Workers v. Ill. Bar Ass'n, 389 U.S. 217, 221–22 (1967).
73. Bhd. of R.R. Trainmen v. Virginia *ex rel.* Va. State Bar, 377 U.S. 1 (1964). *See also United Mine Workers*, 389 U.S. at 223–25 (governmental interference violates associational rights, as well as First and Fourteenth Amendment concerns, even if it is justified by a legitimate objective, such as the avoidance of conflicts of interest in attorney-client relationships, unless government shows that a serious impairment of the objective would clearly occur absent the challenged interference, and that no less-intrusive regulation could prevent such impairment).
74. United Transp. Union v. State Bar of Mich., 401 U.S. 576 (1971).
75. *Id.* at 585–86.
76. *See, e.g.*, Int'l Woodworkers of Am. v. Ga.-Pac. Corp., 568 F.2d 64, 67 (8th Cir. 1977); Soc. Servs. Union, Local 535 v. Cnty. of Santa Clara, 609 F.2d 944 (9th Cir. 1979); Nat'l Assoc. of Letter Carriers v. U.S. Civil Serv. Comm., 346 F. Supp. 578 (D.D.C. 1972), *rev'd on other grounds*, 413 U.S. 548 (1972); Glass, Molders, Pottery Plastics, & Allied Workers Int'l Union v. Wickes Cos., Inc., No. L-06023-88 (Sup. Ct., Camden Cty., N.J., Feb. 24, 1992).
77. Hispanics United of DuPage Cnty. v. Vill. of Addison, Ill., 160 F.R.D. 681 (N.D. Ill. 1995); Alliance to End Repression v. Rochford, 565 F.2d 975 (7th Cir. 1977); League of United Latin Am. Citizens v. Salinas Fire Dep't, 88 F.R.D. 533, 543 (N.D. Cal. 1980); Women's Comm. for Equal Employment Opportunity v. Nat'l Broad. Co., 71 F.R.D. 666 (S.D.N.Y. 1976).
78. Ala. Optometric Ass'n v. Ala. State Bd. of Health, 379 F. Supp. 1332 (M.D. Ala. 1974).

79. Gulf Oil Co. v. Bernard, 452 U.S. 89, 102 (1981).
80. *Soc. Servs. Union, Local 535*, 609 F.2d at 946 ("It is now clear that unions may maintain actions under Title VII on behalf of their members. Indeed, policy considerations weigh strongly in favor of affording standing to unions which file suit to end discriminatory employment practices. The financial backing and legal expertise that unions can provide would materially advance the type of private enforcement essential to the effectiveness of Title VII."); *League of United Latin Am. Citizens*, 88 F.R.D. at 543 ("Organizations dedicated to the eradication of prejudice and bias and to the promotion of equal opportunity for their members are . . . [even] more suited to class representation than the union [in *Soc. Servs. Union*]."); Int'l Woodworkers of Am. v. Chesapeake Bay Plywood Corp., 659 F.2d 1259, 1268 (4th Cir. 1981) ("[T]he Union, as a class representative with standing under Article III to raise its members' claims, is seeking to redress injuries suffered by its members. Here it acts merely as a conduit for the vindication of its members' rights to be free of discrimination in their employment.").
81. 29 U.S.C. §§ 201 *et seq.*
82. *Id.* at 216(b).
83. *See* Baker v. Michie Co., 93 F.R.D. 494 (W.D. Va. 1982); McKenna v. Champion Int'l Corp., 747 F.2d 1211 (8th Cir. 1984).
84. *Baker*, 93 F.R.D. 494; Roshto v. Chrysler Corp., 67 F.R.D. 28 (E.D. La 1975).
85. Braunstein v. E. Photographic Labs., Inc., 600 F.2d 335 (2d Cir. 1978); Woods v. N.Y. Life Ins. Co., 686 F.2d 578 (7th Cir. 1982); Riojas v. Seal Produce, Inc., 82 F.R.D. 613 (S.D. Tex. 1979).
86. Hoffman La-Roche Inc. v. Sperling, 493 U.S. 165 (1989).
87. *Id.* at 169 (emphasis added).
88. *Id.* at 172; *see also* Whalen v. United States, 85 Fed. Cl. 380, 388 (Fed. Cl. 2009) (holding that exercise of court discretion in facilitating notice to avoid multiplicity of duplicative suits and to set cutoff dates was appropriate in collective action such as one under Fair Labor Standards Act).
89. *Id.* at 171.
90. *Id.* at 171 n.2.
91. *Id.*
92. 725 F.2d 1263 (10th Cir. 1984).
93. *Id.* at 1269.
94. 686 F.2d 578 (7th Cir. 1982).
95. *Id.* at 581.
96. *Id.* at 580.
97. Hoffman La-Roche Inc. v. Sperling, 493 U.S. 165, 171 (1989).
98. 600 F. Supp. 1155 (N.D. Ga. 1984).
99. *Id.* at 1161 (citations omitted).
100. *See, e.g.*, Howard v. Securitas Sec. Servs., USA Inc., 630 F. Supp. 2d 905, 909 (N.D. Ill. 2009); Maddox v. Knowledge Learning Corp., 499 F. Supp. 2d 1338, 1343 (N.D. Ga. 2007); Parks v. Eastwood Ins. Servs., Inc., 235 F. Supp. 2d 1082, 1085 (C.D. Cal. 2002); Belt v. Emcare, Inc., 299 F. Supp. 2d 664, 667–68 (E.D. Tex. 2003); Jones v. Casey's Gen. Stores, 517 F. Supp. 2d 1080, 1086 (S.D. Iowa 2007).
101. Gulf Oil Co. v. Bernard, 452 U.S. 89, 101–02 (1981).

CHAPTER 8

Communications between Related Corporations and the Attorney-Client Privilege

VINCENT S. WALKOWIAK

I. Direct Communications between a Parent Corporation and Its Subsidiary

The purpose of the attorney-client privilege is to promote complete disclosure between attorney and client by protecting confidential communications between them.[1] However, the privilege "will not conceal everything said and done in connection with an attorney's legal representation of a client in a matter."[2] The privilege applies only if (1) the asserted holder of the privilege is or sought to become a client; (2) the person to whom the communication was made is an attorney; and (3) the communication relates to a fact of which the attorney was informed by his client in confidence for the purpose of securing legal advice.[3] The privilege shields communications by the client to the attorney or the attorney to the client.[4] The privilege does not apply if it has been waived,[5] if the legal advice is sought for the purpose of committing fraud or a crime,[6] or if it falls under any of the exceptions to which the privilege is subject.[7]

Communications exchanged between related or similarly interested corporations have in some instances been held protected by the attorney-client privilege.[8] Courts have reached this conclusion by applying one of three tests: (1) the "common ownership" test illustrated in *United States v. United Shoe Machinery Corp.*;[9] (2) the "community of interest" test illustrated in *Duplan v. Deering*;[10] and (3) the "joint defense" test illustrated in *Weil Ceramics & Glass, Inc. v. Work*.[11]

II. The "Common Ownership" Test

In the leading case of *United Shoe* from 1950,[12] the court held that the "client" for purposes of the attorney-client privilege was the parent corporation and all of its affiliates and subsidiaries. In *United Shoe*, all of the corporations used the same in-house and outside counsel, which simplified the matter of privilege for the court. It becomes more difficult for the court to determine the limits of the attorney-client privilege when the parent and its subsidiaries and/or affiliates share confidential communications but have different in-house legal staffs or employ different counsel.

United Shoe was followed in 1980 by the court in *American Telephone & Telegraph (AT&T)*,[13] a complex antitrust action where the court approved and adopted substantive and procedural guidelines relating to the law of privilege and its application to related corporations. The *AT&T* court, citing the Supreme Court's opinion in *United Shoe*, directed that the attorney-client privilege applied to communications between AT&T and its wholly owned subsidiaries, considered collectively.[14] However, the court in *AT&T* did not indicate whether the parent and its subsidiaries employed different counsel.

When companies are under common ownership but retain separate counsel, they can share communications and still be protected by the attorney-client privilege,[15] where, inter alia, courts have applied the community-of-interest test, discussed next, to determine whether specific communications are protected.[16]

III. The "Community of Interest" Test

In the 1974 case *Duplan*,[17] the court applied the community-of-interest test and addressed whether communications between a parent and subsidiary were privileged when those entities did not employ a common attorney. In *Duplan*, a patent-antitrust case, the court held that there was a sufficient community of interest between a French corporation, which was a patent owner, and some of its subsidiaries for the attorney-client privilege to apply to communications made to or received by them.[18] In order for the privilege to apply, however, the common interest must be an identical legal interest.[19] As the court stated: "The key consideration is that the nature of the interest be identical, not similar, and be legal, not solely commercial."[20] The court continued:

> Although an interest of a third party corporation from a commercial standpoint would not establish a sufficient community of interest, the fact that the communications are among formally different corporate entities *which are under common ownership* or control leads this court to treat such inter-related corporate communications in the same manner as intra-corporate communications. . . . Thus, if a corporation with a legal interest in an attorney-client communication relays it to another related corporation, the attorney-client privilege is not thereby waived. If the communications were relayed to an unrelated third-party corporation, the privilege would be waived.[21]

Thus, the privilege was sustained between the parent and its subsidiaries because of their community of interest, even though the parent and subsidiary corporations each employed their own separate attorneys.[22]

In *Scott Paper Co. v. Ceilcote Co.*,[23] an employee of defendant Ceilcote sent a letter to its parent corporation's in-house counsel, and plaintiff sought discovery of the letter. The court applied Maine's Rule of Evidence 502(b), which provided:

> A client has a privilege to refuse to disclose and to prevent any other person from disclosing confidential communications made for the purpose of facilitating the rendition of professional legal services *to the client between himself or his representative* and his lawyer or his lawyer's representative.[24]

Holding that the letter at issue was written by a "representative" of the client, contained information regarding the subject matter of the litigation, and requested legal advice, the court concluded that the letter was protected by the attorney-client privilege.

The court in *Roberts v. Carrier Corp.*[25] adopted the community-of-interest test first articulated in *Duplan* and extended it to apply to communications between related subsidiaries. In *Roberts*, the plaintiff brought suit for injuries suffered in a house fire allegedly caused by a Carrier-manufactured furnace. The plaintiff sought discovery pertaining to a valve that was manufactured by the Essex Group. The Essex Group, Carrier, and Hamilton were all wholly owned subsidiaries of United Technologies. The Essex Group claimed that the information that the plaintiff sought concerning the valve was in Hamilton's possession. Specifically, the plaintiff sought to discover "all communications and/or agreements between Carrier and Hamilton concerning this lawsuit, whether written or not."[26] Hamilton and Carrier objected to the request on the basis of attorney-client privilege and the work-product doctrine.

The court found that existing case law dealing with communications between a parent and a subsidiary "suggests that the privilege can extend further."[27] Accordingly, the court held that the two related subsidiaries, Carrier and Hamilton, had an identical legal interest based on the defense of the claim alleging malfunction of the valve, which established a sufficient community of interest to uphold the privilege. The court stated:

> While Hamilton is not a party to the Texas lawsuit, and thus technically is not defending a claim against it, it nevertheless has a significant interest in the outcome of [plaintiff's] case, given that it is now responsible (within the United Technologies family) for [the valve]. The legal consequences of this case will have an impact on other present or potential litigation involving [the valve], an impact to be directly felt by Hamilton. Thus, a concerted effort with Carrier is in Hamilton's immediate and long range interest. Within the confines of this case, the identity of interest arises out of the valve itself and the defense of the claim involving it. Thus, inter-related-corporate communications, as the *Duplan* court describes them, between Hamilton and Carrier do not waive the attorney-client privilege that each enjoys in consulting with its attorneys because of their relationship via United Technologies and the identical legal interest shared in defending a claim involving [the valve].[28]

Other courts have also found communications between related corporations to be protected by the attorney-client privilege. For instance, in *Insurance Co. of North America v. Superior Court*, a California appellate court addressing the issue of whether direct communications between subsidiaries and their parent are protected by the attorney-client privilege concluded that the privilege applies by reasoning that the communication was in furtherance of the subsidiary's interest.[29] In this case, GAF, an asbestos manufacturer, brought suit against INA Corporation, the parent holding company, and its wholly owned subsidiaries, Insurance Company of North America (Subsidiary One) and INA (Subsidiary Two). Subsidiary Two was GAF's products liability insurer. In order to investigate the extent of coverage of Subsidiary Two's products liability insurance policies with respect to asbestos-related claims against its insureds, Subsidiary Two hired outside counsel. Outside counsel met with officers of Subsidiary Two to discuss these matters, and GAF sought to discover the memoranda, notes, and conversations connected with this meeting. Subsidiary Two asserted that the attorney-client privilege rendered such materials confidential. GAF responded by asserting that the privilege was inapplicable due to the presence at the meeting of the vice-president of the parent and the president of Subsidiary One.

The court examined California Evidence Code section 952, which defined a confidential communications as follows:

> [I]nformation transmitted between a client and his lawyer in the course of that relationship and in confidence by a means which, so far as the client is aware, discloses the information to no third persons other than those who are present to further the interest of the client in the consultation or those to whom disclosure is reasonably necessary for the transmission of the information to the accomplishment of the purpose for which the lawyer is consulted, and includes a legal opinion formed and the advice given by the lawyer in the course of that relationship.[30]

The court then concluded that the officers were not outsiders at the meeting, as the vice president of the parent was acting in the capacity of legal consultant and adviser to Subsidiary Two, and the president of Subsidiary One was a part-time expert consultant and adviser on reserve policies and sound actuarial practices.[31] Finding these functions necessary to further the interests of the client, Subsidiary Two, the court concluded that the communications were entitled to the protection afforded by the attorney-client privilege.

Addressing the general question of whether under California law an officer or employee of a holding or related company can exchange otherwise protected communications with a wholly owned subsidiary or affiliate without destroying the confidentiality of the attorney-client communication, the court stated:

> The key concept here is need to know. While involvement of an unnecessary third person in attorney-client communications destroys confidentiality, involvement of third persons to whom disclosure is reasonably necessary to further the purpose of the legal consultation preserves confidentiality of communication. . . . INA was not a solitary island in a remote ocean but a member of large archipelago of wholly-owned subsidiaries located in INA Corporation's inland sea. Basic policy and direction on critical problems would ultimately be determined by the parent company. As the court observed in *Duplan Corporation v. Deering Milliken*, 397 F. Supp. 1146, 1164 (D.S.C. 1975): "The chain of command in military, business, government, and private societies is an accepted pattern of modern civilization." Such being the case, simultaneous delivery of legal advice to a subsidiary client and a controlling parent company, a delivery which facilitates speedy and accurate determination of business policy by the parent, furthers the interest of the client in the consultation.[32]

Moreover, the court asserted that the protection provided by the attorney-client privilege is not limited to instances where a subsidiary's attorney-client consultation is attended by the president of the holding company, but

> applies equally to other representatives of the holding company and its affiliates who are present for good business reasons to further the

> interest of the client. *Absent some conflict of interest or some evidence of antagonism among entities*, disclosure of counsel's legal opinion to holding company and affiliated company officers and employees who need to know this information in order to properly perform their duties is a disclosure which is reasonably necessary to accomplish the purpose for which counsel have been consulted. Hence it is privileged.[33]

IV. The "Joint Defense" Test

Communications between corporations may also be protected by the attorney-client privilege under the theory that they are conducting a "joint defense" (also known as the "common defense" theory). This defense protects confidential communications between codefendants (or potential codefendants) and jointly retained counsel against disclosure from third parties.[34] Waiver of the privilege requires consent of all codefendants except as between litigation adversaries.[35]

For example, in *Weil*,[36] commonly owned subsidiaries were shielded by the attorney-client privilege because they were codefendants. *Weil* involved three related corporations: Lladro, S.A., which manufactured porcelain products; Disenos Artisticos E Industriales, S.A. (DAISA), which designed the products; and Weil Ceramics & Glass, Inc., which distributed the products. All three corporations were wholly owned by Sodigei, which in turn was owned by the Lladro brothers. DAISA filed suit against Karen-Leslie Co. and two of its affiliates. Karen-Leslie was a company engaged in the acquisition and sale of hard goods, including these products. The suit charged copyright infringement. Weil also filed suit against the same defendants claiming trademark violations. The defendants then interposed a counterclaim claiming that all three corporations violated antitrust laws.

In the course of discovery, DAISA and Weil refused to produce a number of documents asserting the attorney-client privilege and the work-product doctrine to correspondence between the attorneys for Lladro and DAISA, and DAISA and Weil. The court sustained the application of the attorney-client privilege to the exchange of information between the attorneys for the subsidiaries on three separate grounds, applying all three tests discussed in this chapter. First, the court found that the joint-defense rule was applicable because all three of the corporations were named as codefendants and coconspirators. The joint-defense rule, according to the court, allowed counsel for codefendants to share privileged information without fear of waiver. Second, the court found that all three corporations satisfied the community-of-interest rule articulated in *Duplan*.[37] Finally, the court, citing *United Shoe*, sustained the claim of privilege on the ground that the corporations were commonly owned and thus should be considered a single client for attorney-client privilege purposes.

Where the original communication would have been protected by the attorney-client privilege but for the waiver implied by the sharing of information with an unrelated corporation, the joint-defense theory has prevented waiver of privilege.[38] In *Transmirra Products Corp. v. Monsanto Chemical Co.*,[39] a patent infringement case, communications between the attorneys for corporations who were sued by a common plaintiff were at issue. Addressing the attorney-client privilege, the court stated: "[P]ersons represented by different attorneys but conducting a joint defense may pool information without waiving [the attorney-client] privilege."[40] In undertaking to apply the attorney-client privilege to these communications, the court cited with approval to *Schmitt v. Emory*,[41] in which the joint-defense privilege was previously recognized.

In *Schmitt* the court had held that:

> Where an attorney furnished a copy of a document entrusted to him by his client to an attorney who is engaged in maintaining substantially the same cause on behalf of other parties in the same litigation, without an express understanding that the recipient shall not communicate the contents thereof to others, the communication is made not for the purpose of allowing unlimited publication and use, but in confidence, for the limited and restricted purpose to assist in asserting their common claims. The copy is given and accepted under the privilege between the attorney furnishing it and his client. For the occasion, the recipient of the copy stands under the same restraints arising from the privileged character of the document as the counsel who furnished it, and consequently he has no right, and cannot be compelled to produce or disclose its contents.[42]

Transmirra applied the work-product doctrine to the communication in order to determine if the communication was privileged, because the defendant did not raise the attorney-client privilege as a basis for the confidentiality of the document. However, the reasoning employed in *Transmirra* has been applied to cases dealing with the attorney-client privilege as well. For example, in *In re Grand Jury Subpoena Duces Tecum dated Nov. 16, 1974*,[43] the discoverability of certain notations and memoranda recording interviews and discussions between independently represented defendants in a securities fraud action were involved. The court held that the documents memorializing the meetings between prospective codefendants were protected by the attorney-client privilege because the defendants were participants in a common defense.[44] Moreover, the court rejected the contention that in order to establish the defense of a joint defense the statement needed to be made by an interested party in the presence of his own attorney.[45]

Similarly, in *Continental Oil Co. v. United States*,[46] memoranda exchanged between two unrelated corporations were held to be protected by the attorney-client privilege based on the joint-defense doctrine. The corporations, Standard Oil and Continental Oil, had interviewed their own employees in connection with a grand jury proceeding. The parties exchanged memoranda recording these interviews "in order to apprise each other as to the nature and scope of the inquiry proceeding before the Grand Jury."[47] Upholding the defendants' assertion of privilege, the court noted that it was irrelevant that an indictment had not yet been returned and that the parties were not yet actual joint defendants.[48]

Not all communications made between corporations asserting a common defense will be protected by the attorney-client privilege.[49] For example, in *Magna Leasing, Inc. v. Staten Island Mall*,[50] the plaintiff sought discovery of a settlement agreement between the defendant and a third party, Chase Manhattan Mortgage and Realty Trust. The court rejected the defendant's claim that a settlement agreement was privileged because it contained communications concerning joint defenses. The court emphasized that the communications at issue must relate to the joint defense:

> Communications among the attorneys for co-defendants are privileged only *if the communications are designed to further a joint or common defense. . . .*
>
> In the instant case, the settlement agreement insofar as we have ordered disclosure, relates merely to the transfer of assets between defendants and Chase. The relevant portions embody no communications concerning the manner or substance of parties' joint or common defense of the actions brought by the other tenants.[51]

Thus, according to the court, in order to claim the protection of the attorney-client privilege the documents must relate to the joint defense.

V. Summary of the Three Tests

In short, the attorney-client privilege may be asserted by a corporation when it shares otherwise confidential communications with another corporation if (1) the corporations are considered a "single client" because of their common ownership; (2) the corporations share an identical legal interest in the litigation (community of interest); or (3) the corporations are codefendants or potential codefendants (joint defense).

VI. The Work-Product Doctrine as It Applies to Communications between Related Corporations

The Supreme Court has recognized qualified protection for materials prepared by an attorney acting for his client in anticipation of litigation.[52] This privilege has been extended to include the work of agents of the attorney.[53] Documents protected by the work-product doctrine are generally discoverable only upon a showing of substantial need and that the party seeking the information is unable, without undue hardship, to obtain the substantial equivalent of the materials by other means.[54] There is generally no work-product protection for documents that were prepared in the regular course of business prior to the onset of litigation[55] or for other nonlitigation purposes.[56] The protection for work done in anticipation of litigation applies even if the litigation never actually takes place.[57]

The work-product doctrine covers oral communications as well as tangible materials such as documents.[58] As the court in *Transmirra* stated: "There should be no essential difference between an exchange of written legal memoranda among attorneys and one of ideas and opinions developed during conversations or conferences."[59]

The issue of whether the work-product doctrine attaches to communications between related corporations is important because the work-product doctrine is broader than the attorney-client privilege. Moreover, any waiver of attorney-client privilege does not affect the protection granted to an attorney's work product.[60]

In *Duplan*,[61] the court held that the work-product privilege may attach to joint consultations between a parent and subsidiary if the communications were for purposes of gathering evidence during preparation for litigation:[62] "The sharing of information between counsel for parties having common interests does not destroy the work product privilege during the course of litigation."[63]

Similarly, other cases involving nonrelated corporations have found the work-product privilege applies to shared information when the corporations have a community of interest in potential or actual litigation. For instance, in *Transmirra*,[64] discussed previously, the plaintiff sought discovery of information regarding legal assistance rendered to a third party whom the plaintiff had previously charged with infringement of the same patent. Holding that the communications between the former defendant and the present defendant were protected by the work-product doctrine, the court relied on the community of interest between the two defendants in the litigation.

> One could not deny the advantages of, and even the necessity for, an exchange or pooling of information between attorneys representing parties sharing such a common interest in litigation, actual or prospective.[65]

Similarly, in *Burlington Industries v. Exxon Corp.*,[66] the court held that the exchange of information between joint licensees that have a mutual interest in a patent action is protected by the work-product doctrine:

> Upon a proper showing of the existence of such joint licensing program, documents prepared by attorneys in anticipation of litigation involving their clients, and exchanged in confidence between attorneys representing the joint licensors, will not lose the protection of the work product doctrine.[67]

The court stated that the party with whom the claimant of the privilege shares a community of interest need not be a party to the litigation.[68]

In addition to documents and communications exchanged between related corporations, interviews of potential witnesses conducted by counsel for a parent corporation when the subsidiary is being sued should also be protected, as it is clear that interviews of witnesses in anticipation of litigation are entitled to the protection of the privilege.[69] In jurisdictions that recognize that the work-product doctrine protects witness statements, the reasoning of *Duplan*[70] may apply. Under *Duplan*, the exchange of information between counsel for parties entitled to assert a common work-product doctrine will apply to a corporation's interviews of witnesses connected with the litigation. Caution is the key word here, however, as a number of jurisdictions have specifically made witnesses' statements discoverable and in some instances have excluded witness statements from the protection afforded by the work-product doctrine.[71] Thus even though it was a witness statement that gave rise to the recognition of the attorney work-product doctrine, witness statements are no longer protected from disclosure in Texas and states that follow a similar rule.

Thus, it has generally been held that the work-product doctrine will protect communications between related corporations that share a community of interest in litigation.

VII. Degree of Ownership Required for "Common Ownership" to Apply

Most of the cases that have held the attorney-client privilege or work-product doctrine applicable to communications between parents and subsidiaries have not discussed the effect of the extent of the parent's stock ownership.[72] However, in *AT&T*,[73] the court addressed the issue of whether the percentage of ownership of the subsidiary should affect whether a parent and its subsidiaries are treated as a single client for purposes of the attorney-client privilege. The *AT&T* court held that only the parent's wholly owned subsidiaries and majority-owned subsidiaries should be considered a single client for attorney-client privilege purposes. The court excluded minority-owned companies from the rule explaining:

> The cases referring to parent, subsidiary, and affiliate corporations in regard to the attorney-client privilege simply reach the conclusion that there was a single client without examining this question. Perhaps the conclusion to be reached may well depend on where one begins. If analysis begins with the proposition that corporations under unified control are "one" even though comprised of components held in varying degrees of ownership, then a minority-owned company can be assimilated to one in which substantial, although not majority, ownership is held. On the other hand, if analysis begins with the proposition that formerly distinct corporations are separate persons except as specific legal purpose warrants treating them as one, then a different conclusion is reached.[74]

The court rejected the prospect that minority-owned subsidiaries and their parents could be considered a "single client" within the attorney-client privilege because a minority-owned company is a distinct corporation with independent stockholders. However, the court stated that "we found no cases in which there was a consideration of the degree of ownership required to give rise to the parent, subsidiary, or affiliate relationship."[75]

VIII. Control of Privilege before and after Sale of Related Corporation

When a parent corporation sells a subsidiary, an issue is raised as to which corporation now controls the attorney-client privilege as to communications between the two entities before the sale. Generally, when control of a corporation passes, the authority to assert or waive attorney-client privilege passes as well.[76]

In *Commodity Futures Trading Commission v. Weintraub*,[77] the Supreme Court recognized that new managers of a corporation may waive the attorney-client privilege as to communications by former officers and directors. In *Weintraub*, the Supreme Court held that the trustee of a corporation in bankruptcy has the power to waive the debtor corporation's attorney-client privilege with respect to communications that occurred before the filing for bankruptcy. The Court noted that for solvent corporations, the power to waive the privilege is exercised by officers and directors consistently with their fiduciary duty to act in the best interest of the corporation.[78] The Court further stated:

> When control of a corporation passes to new management, the authority to assert and waive the corporation's attorney-client privilege passes as well. New management installed as a result of a takeover, merger, loss of confidence by shareholders, or simply normal succession, may waive the attorney-client privilege with respect to communications made by former officers and directors. Displaced managers may not assert the privilege over the wishes of current managers.[79]

Lower courts applying this rule hold that the new managers control the attorney-client privilege even as to communications that former, now displaced, managers may have made to counsel concerning subjects within the scope of the former managers' corporate duties.[80]

The reasoning in *Weintraub* has been extended to cases involving the sale of a subsidiary.[81] The court in *In re Sealed Case*[82] addressed the issue of who controls the attorney-client privilege of a corporate subsidiary after it is sold with respect to confidential communications between the subsidiary and parent prior to the sale. In *Sealed Case*, the parent corporation sold all of the stock of the subsidiary corporation to the purchaser. After the sale, the purchaser filed a securities fraud lawsuit against the parent seller. The purchaser moved to compel production of certain documents that the parent corporation claimed were privileged as attorney-client communications. The subsidiary (now controlled by the purchaser) waived its attorney-client privilege in favor of the purchaser. The documents at issue fell into two categories: (1) memoranda between subsidiary officers and employees and in-house counsel in the parent's legal department who handled legal matters for both the parent and the subsidiary, and (2) documents relating to a lawsuit in which subsidiary and seller were both defendants and represented by the same counsel.

As to the first set of documents, the court relied on the principle stated in *Weintraub*, "that a normal consequence of a succession of corporate management, with or without a change in ownership, is that the new management has the authority to assert or waive the corporation's privilege based on their determination of the best interests of the corporation."[83] Thus, the court concluded that the parties to a subsidiary divestiture by sale of stock should be treated as having contracted on the assumption that after the sale, the management of the divested corporation will control its attorney-client privilege. It ordered the documents produced. However, the court noted that the parties are free to vary this rule by agreement. Moreover, the court opined in dicta that confidentiality can be protected by employing separate counsel for the subsidiary.

As to the second set of documents, the court concluded that the privilege that attached to the joint-defense material could not be waived by the subsidiary in favor of the subsidiary's purchaser without the parent seller's consent. Where the subsidiary seeks access of joint-defense material "for the benefit of its new owner particularly where its new owner is a litigation adversary of its former parent, the argument for applying the special waiver rule of the joint defense cases is strong."[84]

In *Medcom Holding Co. v. Baxter Travenol Laboratories, Inc.*,[85] the court adopted reasoning similar to that in *Sealed Case*, holding that an acquiring company controlled the subsidiary's attorney-client privilege with respect to communications between the subsidiary and the former parent occurring prior to, and relating to, the sale of the subsidiary. In *Medcom*, Baxter, the parent, sold Medcom, Inc., its subsidiary, to Medcom Holding. Medcom Holding sought to compel production of communications between officers and employees of Medcom, Inc. and attorneys in Baxter's legal department that related to the sale of Medcom, Inc. Baxter's in-house counsel handled matters for both Baxter and its subsidiaries. Affirming the lower court's determination that parties who negotiate a corporate acquisition should expect that the privilege of the acquired corporation are incidents of the sale, the court stated:

> In issue here . . . is Medcom, Inc.'s right to control its own privilege rights after divestiture from Baxter. Although both Medcom, Inc. and Baxter are entitled to assert the attorney-client privilege with respect to communications made on their behalf, either may waive it. A client may waive a privilege by voluntary disclosure to a third party; the disclosure breaches the confidentiality of the attorney-client relationship and, therefore, waives the privilege. Medcom, Inc. has elected

> to voluntarily disclose the privileged information to its current sole shareholder Medcom Holding; this waives the privilege.[86]

Like *Sealed Case, Medcom* also involved confidential communications between the former parent and its former subsidiary as codefendants. Similarly, the *Medcom* court held that the subsidiary, Medcom, Inc., could not unilaterally waive its joint-defense privilege in favor of Medcom Holding, its purchaser.

New management may not control the attorney-client privilege with respect to communications between a subsidiary's officers and its own independent counsel where these communications were a violation of the fiduciary duty owed to the parent.[87] Thus, in *In re Diasonics Securities Litigation,*[88] the court held that after divestiture of a subsidiary, the attorney-client privilege remained with the parent. However, *Diasonics* involved unique facts. In that case, Diasonics acquired Fischer Corp. Two stockholders of Fischer continued in their capacity as officers of the subsidiary and additionally became officers of Diasonics.

Thereafter these officers sought rescission of the acquisition and, after rescission, they resigned their positions with the parent. Subsequently, Diasonics was sued by its stockholders, who claimed misrepresentations in connection with a public offering of Diasonics common stock. Plaintiffs sought discovery of documents regarding the Fischer transaction. Fischer claimed that the attorney-client privilege protected notes made by the officers during their employment by both Diasonics and Fischer concerning their consultations with an attorney regarding the possible rescission.

Rejecting this contention, the court held that the officers had breached their fiduciary duty to the shareholders of Diasonics and thus could not raise the privilege:

> The attorney-client communications were made when the two individuals had a fiduciary responsibility to the board of directors and shareholders of Diasonics and not to the presently existing board and shareholders of Fischer, therefore, if any right exists in corporation to raise the attorney-client privilege, it remained with Diasonics and with Fischer after it had separated from Diasonics.[89]

Diasonics was distinguished by both the *Sealed Case* court and the *Medcom* court because it involved breach of fiduciary duty and fraud. As the *Diasonics* court itself stated: "[A] fiduciary cannot hide behind the attorney-client privilege to avoid discovery of his wrongdoing."[90]

Unlike a sale of stock, the right to assert the attorney-client privilege does not always pass upon a sale of assets of a corporation.[91] Often the determination turns on whether all the assets, or merely a portion of the assets, were transferred.[92] In *Sobol v. E.P. Dutton, Inc.,*[93] plaintiff sued defendant Dutton for breach of contract. Dutton had purchased the rights to plaintiff's book from

Nelson. Plaintiff sought discovery of correspondence between employees of Nelson and Nelson's outside counsel. Dutton averred that the attorney-client privilege that attached to these communications passed to Dutton when Dutton purchased the rights from Nelson. Distinguishing *Weintraub*, the court pointed out that Dutton was not the new management of Nelson. Holding that the right to assert the attorney-client privilege was unavailable, the court stated:

> Neither *Weintraub* nor any other case cited by Dutton holds that the attorney-client privilege is an incident of the sale of a portion of tangible assets of a corporation and is transferred upon sale. *Dutton did not purchase all of Nelson, but only a portion of its assets.* Dutton and Nelson engaged in an ordinary commercial transaction in which Dutton purchased contractual rights previously assigned to Nelson by the plaintiff. *This transaction has nothing to do with the attorney-client relationship between Nelson and its counsel.*[94]

The 2004 case *Soverain Software LLC v. Gap, Inc.* described the rule in these terms:

> Whether the attorney-client relationship transfers to new owners [of a client's assets] turns on the practical consequences rather than the formalities of the particular transaction. . . . If the practical consequences of the transaction result in the transfer of control of the business and the continuation of the business under new management, the authority to assert or waive an attorney-client privilege will follow as well.[95]

Absent a transfer of control, the assignor is usually able to retain rights to assert the privilege in matters dealing with the assigned assets.[96] For example, in *NL Industries, Inc. v. Koomey, Inc.*,[97] the original owner of a patent transferred and assigned the patent to another company. The court held that the transfer did not result in a transfer of the attorney-client privilege with respect to communications between the original patent owner and its counsel, and the court refused to allow the transferee to waive the privilege for the original owner.[98]

IX. Conclusion

Otherwise-protected communications shared between corporations have been held to be protected by the attorney-client privilege under three tests: (1) corporations that are under common ownership constitute a single client for purposes of the attorney-client privilege; (2) corporations that share a community of interest do not waive privilege by sharing information relating to the exact same legal interest; and (3) corporations that are engaged in a joint defense to litigation, or certain anticipated litigation, do not waive privilege by sharing information related to their joint defense. Similarly, communications that constitute work product may remain protected by the qualified privilege despite the fact that they were shared with a related corporation if the corporations share a community of interest.

Additionally, when a parent corporation and subsidiary share otherwise protected attorney-client communications, and the parent later sells the subsidiary, the courts have held that the attorney-client privilege is controlled by the subsidiary's new management. When only assets are transferred, control of the privilege depends on the level of control exerted by the assignee.

Notes

1. 8 J.H. Wigmore, Wigmore on Evidence § 2291 (1961).
2. *In re* Fischel, 557 F.2d 209, 212 (9th Cir. 1977).
3. United States v. United Shoe Mach. Corp., 89 F. Supp. 357, 358 (D. Mass. 1950) (disapproved on other grounds in Sperry v. Florida, 373 U.S. 379 (1963)).
4. *See* Ga.-Pac. Plywood Co. v. U.S. Plywood Corp., 18 F.R.D. 463 (S.D.N.Y. 1956) ("Since communications by the attorney to the client might reveal the substance of a client's communication they are also within the privilege").
5. *See United Shoe*, 89 F. Supp. 357.
6. *See id.* at 358.
7. For example, Texas has codified the exceptions for the attorney-client privilege in Texas Rule of Evidence 503(d) as follows:

   (d) Exceptions. There is no privilege under this rule:

   (1) *Furtherance of crime or fraud.* If the services of the lawyer were sought or obtained to enable or aid anyone to commit or plan to commit what the client knew or reasonably should have known to be a crime or fraud;

   (2) *Claimants through same deceased client.* As to a communication relevant to an issue between parties who claim through the same deceased client, regardless of whether the claims are by testate or intestate succession or by inter vivos transactions;

   (3) *Breach of duty by a lawyer or client.* As to a communication relevant to an issue of breach of duty by a lawyer to the client or by a client to the lawyer;

   (4) *Document attested by a lawyer.* As to a communication relevant to an issue concerning an attested document to which the lawyer is an attesting witness; or

   (5) *Joint clients.* As to a communication relevant to a matter of common interest between or among two or more clients if the communication was made by any of them to a lawyer retained or consulted in common, when offered in an action between or among any of the clients.

   Tex. R. Evid. 503(d).

8. *See, e.g.*, United States v. Am. Tel. & Tel. Co., 86 F.R.D. 603, 616–18 (D.D.C. 1979); *In re* Sealed Case, 120 F.R.D. 66, 70 (N.D. Ill. 1988) (legal advice provided jointly to multiple corporate clients is generally privileged against third parties).
9. *United Shoe*, 89 F. Supp. at 358.

10. Duplan v. Deering, 397 F. Supp. 1146, 1184–85 (D.S.C. 1974) (criticized on other grounds by Fed. Deposit Ins. Corp. v. Marine Midland Realty Credit, 138 F.R.D. 479 (E.D. Va. 1991)).
11. Weil Ceramics & Glass, Inc. v. Work, 110 F.R.D. 500 (E.D.N.Y. 1986).
12. *United Shoe*, 89 F. Supp. at 359. *See also In re* Teleglobe Commc'ns Corp., 493 F.3d 345, 370 (3d Cir. 2007).
13. *Am. Tel. & Tel. Co.*, 86 F.R.D. at 616.
14. *United Shoe*, 89 F. Supp. 357; *Am. Tel. & Tel. Co.*, 86 F.R.D. at 616.
15. *See* Bowne, Inc. v. AmBase Corp., 150 F.R.D. 465 (S.D.N.Y. 1993) (court refused to apply the attorney-client privilege to communications between a parent and subsidiary because they failed to show common legal representation or a common legal interest); Music Sales Corp. v. Morris, 52 U.S.P.Q.2d 1852 (S.D.N.Y. 1999).
16. *See, e.g.*, *Weil*, 110 F.R.D. 500; *Bowne*, 150 F.R.D. 465.
17. Duplan v. Deering, 397 F. Supp. 1146, 1184–85 (D.S.C. 1974).
18. *Id.*
19. *Duplan*, 397 F. Supp. 1146.
20. *Id.* at 1172. *See also* Bank Brussels Lambert v. Credit Lyonnais, 160 F.R.D. 437 (S.D.N.Y. 1995). *But see* Bagley v. TRW, Inc., 204 F.R.D. 170 (C.D. Cal. 2001).
21. *Duplan*, 397 F. Supp. at 1172 (emphasis added). *See also* Shamis v. Ambassador Factors Corp., 34 F. Supp. 2d 879 (S.D.N.Y. 1999) (no privilege for unrelated third-party corporation).
22. *See also* Conagra, Inc. v. Sammons, 40 Fed. R. Serv. 2d 1328 (D. Minn. 1984) (applying Montana law). *But see* Adams v. Teck Cominco Alaska, Inc., 232 F.R.D. 341 (D. Alaska 2005).
23. Scott Paper Co. v. Ceilcote Co., 103 F.R.D. 591, 597 (D. Me. 1984). *But see* Maine v. U.S. Dep't of Interior, 298 F.3d 60, 67 (1st Cir. 2002).
24. *Scott Paper*, 103 F.R.D. at 597 (emphasis added).
25. Roberts v. Carrier Corp., 107 F.R.D. 678, 687–88 (N.D. Ind. 1985) (applying Indiana law).
26. *Id.* at 681.
27. *Id.* at 688.
28. *Id.* at 688.
29. Ins. Co. of N. Am. v. Superior Court, 166 Cal. Rptr. 880 (Cal. Ct. App. 1980).
30. *Id.* at 883.
31. *Id.* at 884.
32. *Id.* at 886.
33. *Id.* at 887 (emphasis added). *See also* George v. Siemens Indus. Automation, 182 F.R.D. 134 (D. N.J. 1998) (privilege applies to corporations with similar legal interests); Bank Brussels Lambert v. Credit Lyonnais, 160 F.R.D. 437 (S.D.N.Y. 1995) (same).
34. *In re* Grand Jury Subpoena Duces Tecum Dated Nov. 16, 1974, 406 F. Supp. 381 (S.D.N.Y. 1975).
35. *See* Medcom Holding v. Baxter Travenol Labs., Inc., 689 F. Supp. 841, 845 (N.D. Ill. 1988); Duplan v. Deering, 397 F. Supp. 1146, 1191 (D.S.C. 1974).
36. Weil Ceramics & Glass, Inc. v. Work, 110 F.R.D. 500 (E.D.N.Y. 1986).
37. *Duplan*, 397 F. Supp. 1146.
38. *See, e.g.*, Cont'l Oil Co. v. United States, 330 F.2d 347 (9th Cir. 1964); Transmirra Prods. Corp. v. Monsanto Chem. Co., 26 F.R.D. 572 (S.D.N.Y. 1960).

39. *Transmirra*, 26 F.R.D. 572.
40. *Id.* at 576.
41. Schmitt v. Emory, 2 N.W.2d 413, 414 (Minn. 1942), *overruled on other grounds by* Leer v. Chi. Ry. Co., 308 N.W.2d 305 (Minn. 1981) (privilege sustained where joint interest in excluding particular evidence was present).
42. *Schmitt*, 2 N.W.2d at 417.
43. *In re* Grand Jury Subpoena, 406 F. Supp. 381.
44. *Id.* at 391.
45. *Id.* at 391. *But see* Schachar v. Am. Acad. of Ophthalmology, Inc., 106 F.R.D. 193 (N.D. Ill. 1985) (attorney must be a party to the communication for privilege to attach).
46. Cont'l Oil Co. v. United States, 330 F.2d 347 (9th Cir. 1964).
47. *Id.* at 348.
48. *Id.* at 350.
49. *See, e.g.*, Adams v. Teck Cominco Alaska, Inc., 232 F.R.D. 341 (D. Alaska 2005).
50. Magna Leasing, Inc. v. Staten Island Mall, 76 F.R.D. 559 (S.D.N.Y. 1977).
51. *Id.* at 564 (emphasis added).
52. Hickman v. Taylor, 329 U.S. 495 (1947) (superseded by statute as stated in Hawkins v. Dist. Ct. of Fourth Judicial Dist., 638 P.2d 1372 (Colo. 1982)).
53. United States v. Nobles, 422 U.S. 225 (1975). *But see* State v. Riddle, 8 P.3d 980, 987 (Or. 2000) (noting that the *Nobles* decision is not binding in state jurisdictions). *See generally* Annot., 35 A.L.R.3d 412 (1971).
54. *See* Fed. R. Civ. P. 26(b)(3). *See also In re* Joint E. & S. Dist. Asbestos Litig., 119 F.R.D. 4 (E.D.N.Y. 1988) (product book, containing photographs of asbestos products, that constituted attorney work product was discoverable upon showing of substantial need).
55. *See, e.g.*, Hardy v. N.Y. News, Inc., 114 F.R.D. 633 (S.D.N.Y. 1987) (fact that documents prepared for business purpose were also determined to be of potential use in pending litigation does not turn those documents into attorney work product).
56. *See* United States v. El Paso Co., 682 F.2d 530, 542 (5th Cir. 1982), *cert. denied*, 466 U.S. 944 (1984) (materials assembled pursuant to public requirements unrelated to litigation are not protected by work-product doctrine qualified immunity). *But see* United States v. Adlman, 134 F.3d 1194, 1198 (2d Cir. 1998) (refusing to adopt the Fifth Circuit standard for the Second Circuit, stating that "[t]he *El Paso* requirement that the document be prepared to aid in litigation. . . . is at odds with the text and the policies of [Rule 26(b)(3)]").
57. *See, e.g.*, *In re* Fin. Corp. of Am., 119 B.R. 728 (Bankr. C.D. Cal. 1990); *In re* Fed. Copper of Tenn., Inc., 19 B.R. 177 (Bankr. M.D. Tenn. 1982).
58. Delco Wire & Cable, Inc. v. Weinberger, 109 F.R.D. 680, 691 (E.D. Pa. 1986) (principles announced in *Hickman* concerning attorney work product protects, although the federal rule applies only to tangible items).
59. Transmirra Prods. Corp. v. Monsanto Chem. Co., 26 F.R.D. 572, 579 (S.D.N.Y. 1960). *See also In re* Grand Jury Subpoena Dated Nov. 8, 1979, 622 F.2d 933 (6th Cir. 1980) (work product consists of tangible and intangible material).
60. *See Transmirra*, 26 F.R.D. at 578.
61. Duplan v. Deering, 397 F. Supp. 1146, 1172 (D.S.C. 1974).
62. "Preparation for litigation" can have a broad meaning. For example, in *In re Fin. Corp. of Am.*, 119 B.R. 728 (Bankr. C.D. Cal. 1990), the attorney work-product

doctrine protected documents prepared by parent and subsidiary corporations in anticipation of litigation with a trustee of the parent from discovery by the trustee, despite the fact that no litigation had commenced at the time the work was done.

63. *Duplan*, 397 F. Supp. at 1172. *See also* United States v. Am. Tel. & Tel. Co., 86 F.R.D. 603, 634 (D.D.C. 1979) (a party does not lose the trial preparation material privilege by disclosing material to a person aligned in interest against a common adversary).
64. *Transmirra*, 26 F.R.D. 572.
65. *Id.* at 579.
66. Burlington Indus. v. Exxon Corp., 65 F.R.D. 26, 45 (D. Md. 1974). *But see In re* Grand Jury Subpoena, 220 F.R.D. 130, 148 (D. Mass. 2004) (adopting looser sliding scale standard of Third and Fifth Circuits for "anticipation of litigation" as discussed in United States v. El Paso Co., 682 F.2d 530 (5th Cir. 1982)).
67. *Burlington Indus.*, 65 F.R.D. at 45.
68. *Id.* at 43. *See also* Stanley Works v. Haeger Potteries, Inc., 35 F.R.D. 551, 555 (N.D. Ill. 1964) ("Where attorneys for parties having a mutual interest in litigation exchange their work product, it remains protected by a qualified privilege.").
69. Hickman v. Taylor, 329 U.S. 495, 505 (1947) (superseded by rule as stated in Krueger v. State Farm Fire & Cas. Co., C0-94-557, 1994 WL 440258 (Minn. Ct. App. Aug. 16, 1994) ("The prohibition against disclosure of an attorney's 'mental impressions, conclusions, opinions, or legal theories' comes from the United States Supreme Court's decision in *Hickman*. . . . Minnesota follows the *Hickman* holding."). *See also* Schuler v. United States, 113 F.R.D. 518 (W.D. Mich. 1986).
70. Duplan v. Deering, 397 F. Supp. 1146 (D.S.C. 1974).
71. The Texas Rules of Civil Procedure define the permissible scope of discovery regarding witness statements in the following manner:

    > A party may obtain discovery of the statement of any person with knowledge of relevant facts—a "witness statement"—regardless of when the statement was made.

    Tex. R. Civ. P. 192.3(h). Addressing specifically the possible assertion of the work-product doctrine to attempt to exclude such statements, the rules state:

    > Even if made or prepared in anticipation of litigation or for trial, the following is not work product protected from discovery:
    > (1) information discoverable under Rule 192.3 concerning experts, trial witness, witness statements and contentions.

    Tex. R. Civ. P. 192.5(c). *See In re* Team Transp., Inc., 996 S.W.2d 256 (Tex. App. 14th 1999, no pet.), in which an employee who had witnessed an accident had sent a letter to the insurance carrier for her employer describing the accident. The letter was discoverable. *Id.* at 259. *See also In re* Jimenez, 4 S.W.3d 894 (Tex. App. 1st 1999, no pet.); *In re* W & G Trucking, Inc., 990 S.W.2d 473 (Tex. App. 9th 1999, no pet.). However, while witness statements are not protected, notes taken during a conversation or interview with a witness are defined as not being a witness statement and consequently may be privileged. Tex. R. Civ. P. 192.3. An attorney may still interview a witness and preserve the notes that are taken under the attorney work-product doctrine, but if they attempt to memorialize these comments by having the witness sign a statement, or transcribe those notes in virtually any manner, that transcription may represent a statement of the witness and be discoverable.

Statements of witnesses may still be privileged if they are attorney-client privileged statements. *See* Tex. R. Civ. P. 192, cmt. 9; *In re* Fontenot, 13 S.W.3d 111 (Tex. App. 2d 2000, no pet.).

72. *See, e.g., Duplan*, 397 F. Supp. at 1184–85 (emphasizing that community of interest between the corporations must be legal, not commercial); United States v. United Shoe Mach. Corp., 89 F. Supp. 357, 359 (D. Mass. 1950) (court relied upon fact that the corporations all used same counsel and their legal affairs were closely related); Ins. Co. of N. Am. v. Superior Court, 166 Cal. Rptr. 880 (although subsidiaries were wholly owned by parent, court did not rely on this fact in its reasoning).
73. United States v. Am. Tel. & Tel. Co., 86 F.R.D. 603, 616–17 (D.D.C. 1979).
74. *Id.*
75. *Id.*
76. *In re* Hechinger Inv. Co. of Del., 285 B.R. 601 (D. Del. 2002); 28 A.L.R.5th 1 (1995). The same view is supported by Uniform Rule of Evidence 502(c) (1974 & 1986), which states that the successor of a corporation is entitled to claim the corporation's attorney-client privilege, even if the corporation is no longer in existence. *See also* MacKenzie-Childs LLC v. MacKenzie-Childs, 262 F.R.D. 241 (W.D.N.Y. 2009).
77. Commodity Futures Trading Comm'n v. Weintraub, 471 U.S. 343 (1985).
78. *See* Rialto v. U.S. Dep't of Def., 492 F. Supp. 2d 1193, 1197 (C.D. Cal. 2007) (interpreting California Corporations Code section 2010 to mean that "a dissolved corporation is not entitled to assert the attorney-client privilege"); Lopes v. Vieira, 688 F. Supp. 2d 1050, 1061 (E.D. Cal. 2010) ("a corporation dissolved pursuant to California law may not invoke or waive the attorney-client privilege even when it must defend itself as a party to litigation").
79. *Weintraub*, 471 U.S. at 378.
80. *MacKenzie-Childs*, 262 F.R.D. 241.
81. *See* O'Leary v. Purcell Co., 108 F.R.D. 641, 644 (M.D.N.C. 1985) (surviving corporation from a merger has standing to assert attorney-client privilege with respect to documents produced by merged subsidiary); Polycast Tech. Corp. v. Uniroyal, Inc. 125 F.R.D. 47 (S.D.N.Y. 1989) (holding that purchaser of all stock of subsidiary corporation had right to waive attorney-client privilege for communications between subsidiary and counsel that took place before the sale).
82. *In re* Sealed Case, 120 F.R.D. 66 (N.D. Ill. 1988). *Cf.* Bank Brussels Lambert v. Credit Lyonnais, 160 F.R.D. 437 (S.D.N.Y. 1995).
83. 120 F.R.D. at 70.
84. *Id.* at 72.
85. Medcom Holding Co. v. Baxter Travenol Labs., Inc., 689 F. Supp. 841 (N.D. Ill. 1988). *But see In re* Santa Fe Trail Transp. Co., 121 B.R. 794 (Bankr. N.D. Ill. 1990) (distinguishing case from *Medcom*, holding no privilege available because no one in the parent's legal department intended the privilege to exist between the parent and subsidiary).
86. *Medcom*, 689 F. Supp. at 844 (citations omitted).
87. *See In re* Diasonics Sec. Litig., 110 F.R.D. 570 (D. Colo. 1986).
88. *Id.*
89. *Id.* at 574.

90. *Id.* at 576.
91. *See* Rialto v. U.S. Dep't of Def., 492 F. Supp. 2d 1193 (C.D. Cal. 2007); *In re* Crescent Beach Inn, 37 B.R. 894 (Bankr. D. Me. 1984); 28 A.L.R.5th 1 (1995) (under certain circumstances, the assignee of all or most of a corporation's assets could assert the corporation's attorney-client privilege).
92. *See generally* 28 A.L.R.5th 1 (1995).
93. Sobol v. E.P. Dutton, Inc., 112 F.R.D. 99 (S.D.N.Y. 1986). *See also* Fed. Deposit Ins. Corp. v. McAtee, 124 F.R.D. 662 (D. Kan. 1988); NCL Corp. v. Lone Star Bldg. Ctrs., Inc. 144 B.R. 170 (S.D. Fla. 1992).
94. *Sobol*, 112 F.R.D. at 103 (emphasis added).
95. Soverain Software LLC v. Gap, Inc., 340 F. Supp. 2d 760, 763 (internal citations omitted).
96. 28 A.L.R.5th 1, 6. *See also* Cont'l Coatings Corp. v. Metco, Inc., 50 F.R.D. 382 (N.D. Ill. 1970).
97. NL Indus., Inc. v. Koomey, Inc., 647 F. Supp. 936 (S.D. Tex. 1984).
98. *Id.*

CHAPTER 9

Federal Courts' Application of the Work-Product Doctrine to Nonparties

CHRISTINA M. JONES
J. TRACY WALKER, IV*

I. Introduction

Companies and businesses subject to frequent litigation often employ claims management practices that include lawyer-directed investigations and early claim evaluations. A company may use such tools to facilitate the early resolution of claims, or, when resolution is not possible, to prepare for litigation. Subject to certain limitations, if litigation against the company does ensue, the materials created by the company or its agents in reasonable anticipation of litigation are protected from disclosure by Federal Rule of Civil Procedure 26(b)(3), commonly referred to as the work-product doctrine. This doctrine traces its roots to *Hickman v. Taylor*.[1]

The basic elements of the work-product doctrine are explored in depth in other chapters. This chapter explores the applicability of the doctrine in situations where (1) the entity creating the materials is not named a party in the

* The authors are grateful to Joseph E. Blackburn III for his considerable research assistance.

litigation in which discovery is sought, and (2) the entity creating the materials is a party, but the materials at issue were created in connection with a matter other than that giving rise to the litigation. In other words, what happens if a company investigating a claim is not sued, but others are, and the materials gathered by the company in anticipation of litigation are requested by one of the parties? What happens if the company is not sued, but the materials it gathered in anticipation of litigation are later requested in other litigation against the company?

Federal courts are divided on these questions. The courts disagree as to both the availability and the scope of the work-product protection afforded to nonparties. Some courts interpret Rule 26(b)(3) very strictly, applying its protections only to the party litigants before it in a particular action, whereas other courts take a much broader view and grant work-product protection without regard to party status, as long as the materials at issue were gathered in reasonable anticipation of litigation.

This chapter explores the history of the work-product doctrine and the divergent lines of reasoning used by federal courts applying the protection to nonparties, and it provides guidance to practitioners wishing to assert or overcome the work-product doctrine on behalf of a nonparty.[2]

II. Origin of the Work-Product Doctrine and Underlying Policy

The scope and rationale of the work-product doctrine was first articulated by the U.S. Supreme Court in *Hickman v. Taylor*,[3] in which the Court considered whether memoranda, statements, and mental impressions of an attorney acting on behalf of his client in anticipation of litigation were discoverable by opposing counsel when not otherwise covered by the attorney-client privilege. In determining that the materials were not discoverable, the Court determined that neither Rule 26 nor any other rule applicable at the time contemplated production.[4]

> That is not because the subject matter is privileged or irrelevant, as those concepts are used in these rules. Here is simply an attempt, without purported necessity or justification, to secure written statements, private memoranda and personal recollections prepared or formed by an adverse party's counsel in the course of his legal duties. As such, it falls outside the arena of discovery and contravenes the public policy underlying the orderly prosecution and defense of legal claims. Not even the most liberal of discovery theories can justify unwarranted inquiries into the files and mental impressions of an attorney.[5]

The Court justified its holding on policy reasons including the potential for attorneys to refrain from writing down their findings or impressions and recognizing that "inefficiency, unfairness and sharp practices would inevitably develop in the giving of legal advice and preparation of cases for trial."[6] Absent the protection, the effect on practitioners would be "demoralizing."[7]

Thus, *Hickman* recognized a qualified protection for work-product materials created by adverse parties' attorneys that might be overcome upon a showing of necessity and an inability to otherwise obtain the information or materials sought.[8] The *Hickman* decision did not squarely address application of the work-product protection to nonparties, and the few courts that addressed the issue in that era reached differing conclusions.[9]

The work-product doctrine was later codified in Rule 26(b)(3) as follows:

> Ordinarily, a party may not discover documents and tangible things that are prepared in anticipation of litigation or for trial by or for any other party or its representative, (including the other party's attorney, consultant, surety, indemnitor, insurer or agent.) But, subject to Rule 26(b)(4), those materials may be discovered if:
> (i) they are otherwise discoverable under Rule 26(b)(1); and
> (ii) the party shows that it has substantial need for the materials to prepare its case and cannot, without undue hardship, obtain their substantial equivalent by other means.[10]

As codified, the text of Rule 26(b)(3) limits work-product protection[11] to "a party or its representative," and courts within most of the federal circuits have held that the rule's work-product protections apply *only* to parties to the litigation in which the discovery is sought. These decisions have strictly interpreted the literal text of Rule 26(b)(3), which prevents discovery of documents "prepared in anticipation of litigation or for trial *by or for another party* or its representative." Such decisions, however, often run counter to the policy rationale for the doctrine articulated in *Hickman*, which focused on the purpose for which materials are prepared rather than the party status of the preparer. Not surprisingly, then, many federal courts have, in appropriate circumstances, extended work-product protection to persons not party to the litigation in which the discovery arose.[12]

The case law within and between the circuits is inconsistent. However, courts appear to take three general approaches, either (1) narrowly limiting the doctrine to parties to the specific litigation in which discovery is sought per the literal text of Rule 26(b)(3); (2) liberally applying the doctrine to nonparties able to satisfy the *Hickman* criteria; or (3) acknowledging the text of Rule 26 as applying only to parties but relying on case law precedent and/or policy reasons to either extend or deny work-product protection on a case-by-case basis. Cases employing each of these lines of reasoning are addressed next.

III. Decisions Narrowly Interpreting Rule 26(b)(3) or Otherwise Denying Work-Product Protection to Nonparties

Numerous courts, including several circuit courts, have narrowly interpreted the scope of the work-product doctrine to limit its protections to the literal terms of Rule 26(b)(3), refusing to protect nonparty materials from discovery, even when they were initially made in reasonable anticipation of litigation. For example, the Ninth Circuit, in *In re California Public Utilities Commission*,[13] strictly limited work-product protection to parties. The court found that "although some courts have extended the work product privilege outside the literal bounds of the rule, . . . the rule, on its face, limits its protection to one who is a party (or a party's representative) to the litigation in which discovery is sought."[14] Similarly, the Eleventh Circuit concluded in *Tambourine Comercio Internacional v. Solowsky* that the work-product doctrine does not apply to a nonparty.[15] The court cited with approval Wright and Miller's statement in *Federal Practice & Procedure* § 2024 that "documents prepared for one who is not a party to the present suit are wholly unprotected by Rule 26(b)(3) even though the person may be a party to a closely related lawsuit in which he will be disadvantaged if he must disclose in the present suit."[16] The Eleventh Circuit acknowledged that its interpretation of the rule "is somewhat unsettling" but determined that it must nevertheless "abide by the plain text and meaning of the Rule."[17]

Many federal district courts have likewise concluded that based on the plain language of Rule 26(b)(3), nonparties are not afforded the protection of the work-product doctrine. For example, in the highly publicized case of *Ramsey v. NYP Holdings, Inc.*,[18] the Ramseys, on behalf of their son, brought a libel action against NYP Holdings, publisher of the *New York Post*, for an article that suggested their son was involved in the death of the couple's daughter, JonBenét Ramsey. NYP sought discovery of documents generated by an investigation sponsored by the Ramseys relating to the death of their daughter, over which the Ramseys sought to assert work-product protection.[19] The court rejected the work-product doctrine because the Ramseys were not parties to the litigation, only representatives of their minor son.[20] The court strictly construed Rule 26(b)(3) and noted that "documents prepared by one who is not a party to the present suit are wholly unprotected by Rule 26(b)(3) even though the person may be a party to a closely related lawsuit in which he will be disadvantaged if he must disclose in the present suit."[21] While the court noted that there is the potential harm of allowing a party to poach from the work of another lawyer and his client, "the potential harm of treating Rule 26(b)(3) as inapplicable to non-party witnesses is far less acute than the adverse effect of compelling disclosure of work product between adversary parties."[22]

The strict limitation of the work-product doctrine to parties and their representatives has led to the incongruous result that materials prepared by an insurer for its insureds that have been sued are protected, while materials prepared for a noninsured for the same incident are not protected. For example, in *Kirschbaum v. WRGSB Associates*,[23] defendants moved to quash a subpoena issued to nonparty Travelers Insurance, which insured both BR Management, a nonparty, and the named defendants. The court held that the plaintiff was entitled to documents prepared on behalf of Travelers' nonparty insured, but it was not entitled to the documents prepared for the named defendants.[24]

Perhaps even more incongruous is the instance of a former party who, when dismissed, is deemed to no longer enjoy the protection, even where the litigation remains ongoing against other parties. This situation arose in *Collins v. Mullins*,[25] where plaintiff Collins filed suit against a sheriff and his deputy alleging that he was physically assaulted by the deputy. After the sheriff was voluntarily dismissed as a party, but before the dismissal order was finalized, Collins moved to compel production of his internal investigation files.[26] The sheriff argued that because a final order had not been entered, he was technically still a party, and the work-product doctrine was therefore applicable. When the court later entered a final order dismissing the sheriff, it granted Collins' motion to compel production of the investigation files on the grounds that the information was now sought from a nonparty.[27]

Courts refusing to extend the doctrine to nonparties frequently cite the nonparty's lack of direct financial interest in the subject litigation. For example, in *Polycast Technology Corp. v. Uniroyal, Inc.*,[28] Polycast alleged that Uniroyal provided misleading financial information in its sale of a subsidiary. Deloitte & Touche, an accounting firm involved in the transaction and subsequently retained as Polycast's independent auditor, sought to withhold production of certain documents on the grounds that they were subject to the work-product doctrine.[29] The court found that the work-product doctrine applies only to (1) documents or tangible things, (2) prepared in anticipation of litigation, (3) by or for a party or by or for a party's representative.[30] Because Deloitte & Touche was not a party, the work-product doctrine was not applicable.[31] While the court noted that courts have at times extended the doctrine to those "interested" in the action, it found that Deloitte & Touche was not legally aligned with any party and had no interest in the outcome.[32] Despite recognizing the potential danger that a litigant might circumvent the rule by first obtaining documents from a nonparty and then add it as a party, the court concluded that "speculation as to such tactics does not justify ignoring the explicit requirements of Rule 26(b)(3)."[33] Similarly, in *Bunting v. Gainsville Machine Co.*,[34] plaintiff sued the defendant for negligent installation of machinery, which resulted in a workplace injury. The defendant subpoenaed documents from the plaintiff's employer's insurance company, Liberty Mutual.[35] The district court denied a motion for a protective order, finding that Liberty Mutual was not afforded the protection of Rule 26(b)(3) because it was not a party to the litigation.[36] While the court noted that Liberty Mutual, after having paid plaintiff, had an interest in the plaintiff recovering, the interest was too remote, and "it would be stretching too far the language of Rule 26(b)(3) and the reason underlying it to accord plaintiffs the protection which they seek against the disclosure of the documents in the possession of Liberty Mutual."[37]

Perhaps the most restrictive application of the protection is by courts that refuse to afford the protection to nonparties even when they are involved or potentially involved in closely related litigation. An example of this approach is the Sixth Circuit's decision in *Arkwright Mutual Insurance Co. v. National Union Fire Insurance Co.*[38] After a fire broke out in GE's facilities where Murray Sheet Metal employees were performing welding work, Murray Sheet Metal immediately began an internal investigation, recognizing the possibility of being involved in future litigation relating to the fire.[39] Murray's insurance carrier, Erie, hired UBA Fire Investigators to investigate and hired attorneys to represent Murray.[40] Subsequently, GE's insurer, Arkwright, sued its reinsurer, National Fire. National Fire then subpoenaed the investigative documents prepared by Murray Sheet Metal and UBA.[41] The Sixth Circuit, enforcing a literal reading of Rule 26(b)(3), determined that none of the documents created by Murray, Erie, or UBA was protected by the work-product doctrine because none of the three entities was a party to the litigation.[42] As the court explained, the plain meaning of legislation should be conclusive, and the language of Rule 26(b)(3) stating "by or for a party" clearly restricted its application to parties.[43]

Similarly, in *Smith v. Fifthian*,[44] the court entertained a motion to compel production of documents from a nonparty. The documents contained statements made by nonparties to the lawsuit who were parties in a related state court action.[45] The court concluded that the work-product doctrine was not applicable, as it applies only to documents prepared by or for a party.[46] The court explained that "federal courts have repeatedly held that a non-party witness may not invoke work product protection to preclude production of material prepared by or for that witness, even if created in anticipation of the witness's own pending or anticipated litigation."[47]

One court, citing the Sixth Circuit's opinion in *Arkwright*, surprisingly held that even where an insurance company was involved in one of several consolidated actions arising from an explosion, it must nonetheless produce its investigative files to a requesting entity involved in a related consolidated case to which the insurance company was not a party.[48] The court explicitly rejected the proposition that being a party to a consolidated action closely related and arising out of the same accident was sufficient to trigger Rule 26(b)(3)'s protections.[49]

Finally, even in instances where courts consider extending the doctrine to nonparties, they sometimes decline to do so if the underlying purposes of the doctrine are not furthered. For example, in *Gonzalez v. New York*,[50] the court noted that work-product doctrine is potentially broader than the literal terms of Rule 26(b)(3), and that the "purpose of the work product doctrine is to create a 'zone of privacy' that allows an attorney to prepare for litigation 'free from unnecessary intrusion by his adversaries.'"[51] The court recognized that the doctrine should be applied where disclosure would (1) alter attorney behavior, (2) reward sloth, or (3) interfere with ongoing litigation.[52] Because none of these purposes was implicated, the doctrine did not apply.[53]

IV. Decisions Granting Work-Product Protection to Nonparties

Despite the numerous decisions strictly limiting work-product protection, many courts have interpreted Rule 26(b)(3) more broadly, finding that the rule only partially codifies the common law work-product doctrine established in *Hickman v. Taylor*.[54] The following discussion highlights the differing decisions rendered within various federal circuits.

In a thorough and well-reasoned opinion, the Eastern District of Pennsylvania in *In re Student Finance Corp.*[55] extended work-product protection to nonparties, finding that Rule 26(b)(3) is only a "partial codification" of the work-product privilege. The decision presents a strong and coherent argument supporting a court's authority to provide such protection to nonparties. The court began its analysis by examining the *Hickman* decision, and reasoned that the purpose of the doctrine is to "protect the ability of an attorney to perform his necessary duties for his clients . . . [which makes it essential] that a lawyer work with a certain degree of privacy, free from unnecessary intrusion by opposing parties and their counsel."[56] The court recognized that *Hickman* did not address whether the doctrine was limited solely to parties, but found from *Hickman*'s sweeping language that it arguably includes third parties.[57] It explicitly noted that "while courts are not in complete agreement as to the application of work product to non-parties, federal courts have consistently extended the protection to oral statements, despite Rule 26(b)(3)'s language limiting it to "documents or tangible things."[58] As such, the court concluded that the nonparties in this case could assert work-product privilege, finding that Rule 26(b)(3) only "partially" codified the privilege and left "room for the privilege to be asserted outside its terms in appropriate cases."[59] The court had authority to extend the work-product privilege beyond the express terms of the rule's language through three methods: (1) Rule 45, which allows a court to quash a subpoena if it requires disclosure of "privileged or other protected matter";[60] (2) Rule 26(c), which authorizes protective orders;[61] and (3) *Hickman*, which provides authority to protect work product outside the terms of Rule 26(b)(3).[62] In summary, the court found that "nothing in the test of [Rule 26] or its history, or in the relevant advisory committee notes, suggests that it was intended to foreclose the application of the attorney work product privilege outside its terms in appropriate cases."[63]

Numerous courts have followed the reasoning of *In re Student Finance Corp.* For example, in *Carnes v. Crete Carrier Corp.*,[64] a wrongful-death action, defendant sought to compel production of documents from nonparty UPS. UPS produced some documents relating to the accident that killed Robert Carnes, but withheld others on the grounds of work-product privilege.[65] The court noted that some courts have strictly construed the language of Rule 26(b)(3) to limit the work-product doctrine to parties, while others have provided broader application to nonparties.[66] In concluding that UPS could assert work-product protection, it "agree[d] with the reasoning set out in *In re Student Fin. Corp.* Although the text of Rule 26(b)(3) appears to limit work product to parties, Rule 26(c), Rule 45, and *Hickman* suggest that the scope of protection should extend to a nonparty such as UPS under the facts of this case. Even courts that strictly applied the text of Rule 26(b)(3) to deny work product protection noted the possibility of or granted protective orders for the same information."[67] The court explained that because UPS may be a party to litigation at some point in the future, requiring production would be "unduly burdensome and therefore, unjust."[68]

Other courts extending the protection to nonparties have recognized the potential prejudice to a nonparty where it is involved in related litigation. For example, in *800 Front Street Corp. v. Travelers Property Casualty Co.*,[69] the plaintiff, 800 Front Street Corp., sought funds from its insurance carrier after a boiler failed and caused damage to its property.[70] A group of nonparties, "the Liquidators," purchased the personal property located at the premises after the damage occurred.[71] The Liquidators hired experts from Exponent to investigate the failed boiler, and defendant Travelers sought the Exponent report, claiming there was no work-product protection because the Liquidators and Exponent were not parties to the litigation.[72] Notably, the Liquidators were separately pursing a claim under the Travelers policy, and the court recognized the claims were likely to be consolidated.[73] Despite a recent Southern District of New York decision holding that work-product protection is not afforded to a nonparty "even if the non-party is itself a party to a closely related lawsuit in which he will be disadvantaged if he must disclose in the instant suit," this court extended the protection to the nonparty.[74] The court distinguished *Ricoh* in that the nonparty there did not have an adequate interest in the litigation.[75] Here, because it was expected that the Liquidators' case would be consolidated in the near future, the court treated the Liquidators as parties to the present lawsuit.[76]

The Third Circuit Court of Appeals employed similar reasoning in *In re Grand Jury Proceedings*,[77] where it concluded that documents prepared for an administrative proceeding before the Environmental Protection Agency were privileged under the work-product doctrine because they concerned the same matters that gave rise to the subject grand jury investigation. The court cited the temporal connection between the two proceedings with the matters proceeding at the same time.[78] As such, the court concluded that the documents were privileged "even though they may not have been prepared specifically in connection with the grand jury investigations."[79]

Still other courts have extended the protection even further to nonparties who are not presently involved in litigation but whose involvement is reasonably foreseeable. For example, in *Basinger v. Glacier Carriers, Inc.*,[80] plaintiff's decedent's estate sought the investigative file compiled by Remco, the insurer of nonparty Maple Pot Restaurant. Maple Pot allegedly served the decedent alcohol prior to the accident, and Remco conducted the subsequent investigation analyzing the merits of a potential claim against the restaurant.[81] Despite neither Remco nor Maple Pot being a party to the instant action, the court granted them work-product protection concluding they would likely eventually be joined as third-party defendants.[82] The court concluded that "certainly, if a party to litigation is partially protected by Rule 26(b)(3) from having to disclose certain information to an opposing party, it is unduly 'burdensome' and therefore, unjust, to require a non-party to deliver the same kind of information to a party who may subsequently join the non-party in the litigation."[83]

V. *Advice for Practitioners*

Practitioners seeking to assert or overcome the work-product protection on behalf of nonparties should first consult the applicable rules and case law of jurisdictions where litigation may be filed or where discovery may be sought. Where there is doubt about the scope or application of the privilege, attorneys should advise consultants and others to refrain from drafting sensitive or potentially discoverable documents prior to the formal initiation of litigation. Certainly, irrespective of the scope of the protection, measures to ensure confidentiality and prevent disclosure to adversaries should be maintained.

When seeking to assert the protection on behalf of a nonparty, attorneys should cite the policy reasoning of *Hickman* and the importance of allowing a "zone of privacy" for materials created in reasonable anticipation of litigation, even if no such litigation actually develops. The importance of unfettered claim investigation and analysis without the specter of disclosure later should be a central emphasis, along with the policy issues implicated by allowing other parties to purloin or piggyback on the work and diligence of entities that are successfully able to avoid litigation. Practitioners also might emphasize that Rule 26(b)(3) itself attaches to materials created in "anticipation of litigation." Accordingly, the protections begin to attach before a lawsuit is filed and before "parties" exist, so that the doctrine should logically apply in the same fashion to entities who are similarly situated but are not later named in a lawsuit.[84] In addition, numerous cases support the notion that Rule 26(b)(3) only partially codifies the common law work-product doctrine, which has been extended to protect intangible work product and the work of nonparties.

Where a nonparty remains subject to potential litigation as a third-party defendant or where there is a potential for separate but closely related litigation, courts should be made aware of the potential for gamesmanship whereby other parties purposefully decline to name an entity in one lawsuit, serve discovery seeking all of that nonparty's work product, and then later name that party in the lawsuit or in a separate lawsuit, effectively eviscerating the protections that the entity would have otherwise enjoyed and using its diligent work against it.

Finally, even in jurisdictions that strictly limit application of Rule 26(b)(3) to parties, nonparties may still seek a protective order under Rule 45 or may rely on the court's powers under Rule 26(c) to limit the scope of discovery. For example, where production of work-product materials by a nonparty is compelled, the confidentiality of those materials can be maintained through an appropriately drafted protective order that strictly limits distribution of the documents to attorneys or experts involved in the subject litigation, bars use or reference to those documents in any other cases, and requires return of all such documents at the conclusion of the case in which production is compelled.

VI. Conclusion

While the work-product protection is nearly universally recognized and afforded to parties to litigation, its application to nonparties remains an unsettled issue in many jurisdictions. Courts within and across different federal circuits have reached differing conclusions as to whether, and under what circumstances, the protection applies to nonparties. Absent further direction from the U.S. Supreme Court or a revision to the Federal Rules, it is unlikely that the apparent divergent views will be definitively reconciled. Accordingly, at the outset of any claim investigation, practitioners should carefully review the relevant case law in the jurisdictions in which discovery is likely to be sought and should advise their clients and consultants accordingly. In the face of negative case law, attorneys seeking to assert the protection under Rule 26(b)(3) should acknowledge the division of authority and emphasize the policy reasons underlying a liberal application of the doctrine. Otherwise, attorneys may rely on broader availability of protective orders under Rule 25 and other sections of Rule 26.

Notes

1. 329 U.S. 495 (1947).
2. Some of the cases cited in this chapter have been subsequently discussed, disagreed with, appealed, overturned, or have subsequent history not referenced herein. Cases cited herein are intended to provide an overview of various lines of reasoning and applications of the privilege but should not be viewed as providing the current state of the law in any given jurisdiction.
3. 329 U.S. 495 (1947).
4. *Id.* at 510.
5. *Id.*
6. *Id.* at 511.
7. *Id.*
8. *Id.* Case law addressing the requisite showing to overcome the work-product protection on the basis of necessity or undue hardship is outside the scope of this chapter.
9. *Compare* Shepherd v. Castle, 20 F.R.D. 184, 187 (W.D. Mo. 1957) (refusing to extend protection to nonparty), *with* Republic Gear Co. v. Borg-Warner Corp., 381 F.2d 551, 557–58 (2d Cir. 1967) (applying protection to third-party materials created in anticipation of separate but related litigation).
10. Fed. R. Civ. P. 26(b)(3).
11. Notably, Rule 26(b)(3) actually expanded the work-product doctrine beyond lawyer-created materials to include materials created by any party's "representative."
12. Preliminary research revealed reported cases affording work-product protection to nonparties within all but the First, Fifth, and D.C. Circuits.
13. 892 F.2d 778, 781 (9th Cir. 1989).
14. *Id.* at 781.
15. 312 F. App'x 263, 284 (11th Cir. 2009).
16. *Id.* at 284.
17. *Id.* 284–85.
18. 2002 U.S. Dist. LEXIS 11728 (S.D.N.Y. June 26, 2008).
19. *Id.* at *1–2.
20. *Id.* at *25.
21. *Id.* at *19 (quoting Wright & Marcus, Federal Practice and Procedure: Civil § 2024, at 354–56 (2d ed. 1994)).

22. *Id.* at 22–23; *accord* Johnson v. Standex Int'l Corp., 153 F.R.D. 80 (E.D. Va. 1994) (denying work-product protection to employer whose files related to workplace accident were subpoenaed by defendant machine manufacturer, because employer was not a party and therefore Rule 26(b)(3) was inapplicable); *see generally* Howell v. New York, 2007 U.S. Dist. LEXIS 71063 (E.D.N.Y. Sept. 25, 2007) (in dicta expressing doubts about the potential applicability of the doctrine to a nonparty district attorney's files). Additional cases in which federal district courts refused to extend the work-product protection to nonparties include Hernandez v. Longini, 1997 U.S. Dist. LEXIS 18679, at *6 (N.D. Ill. Nov. 12, 1997) (weight of authority dictated that work-product protection did not apply to nonparties and considerations supporting the doctrine such as protecting the more diligent attorney were not implicated because the prior criminal case had been closed); Ostrowski v. Holem, 2003 U.S. Dist. LEXIS 794, at *13 (N.D. Ill. Jan. 21, 2003) (work-product protection inapplicable to nonparty state's attorney); *Cook v. Chicago*, 2010 U.S. Dist. LEXIS 7031, at *3 (N.D. Ill. Jan 26, 2010) ("a non-party may not assert the work-product doctrine to protect its files or documents."); Schultz v. Talley, 152 F.R.D. 181, 184 (W.D. Mo. 1993) (protection inapplicable to nonparty assistant attorney general's investigative file from prior criminal investigation); Klein v. Jefferson Parish Sch. Bd., 2003 U.S. Dist. LEXIS 6514, at *10 (E.D. La. Apr. 10, 2003) (quoting *Schultz*); Prucha v. M&N Modern Hydraulic Press Co., 76 F.R.D. 207 (W.D. Wis. 1977); Hawkins v. South Plains Int'l Trucks, Inc., 139 F.R.D. 682 (D. Colo. 1991); *In re Polypropylene Carpet Antitrust Litig.*, 181 F.R.D. 680, 683 (N.D. Ga. 1998); Doubleday v. Ruh, 149 F.R.D. 601, 604 (E.D. Cal. 1993); Loustalet v. Refco, Inc., 154 F.R.D. 243, 245 (C.D. Cal. 1993); and United States v. Graham, 555 F. Supp. 2d 1046, 1048 (N.D. Cal. 2008).
23. 1998 U.S. Dist. LEXIS 8860 (E.D. Pa. June 17, 1998).
24. *Id.* at *3.
25. 170 F.R.D. 132 (W.D. Va. 1996). The temporal scope of the work-product doctrine is generally outside the scope of this chapter. However, a situation where numerous entities investigate an incident simultaneously and create work product in anticipation of litigation that never ensues is arguably distinguishable from situations where work product is created in one matter that eventually concludes and those materials are then later sought in an another matter. For example, decisions ordering production in civil cases of now-concluded criminal investigation files may be distinguishable from instances where accidents or incidents are investigated simultaneously by many entities and their production is sought in later litigation involving different parties but related matters.
26. *Id.* at 2.
27. *Id.* at 136.
28. 1990 U.S. Dist. LEXIS 12444 (S.D.N.Y. Sept. 20, 1990).
29. *Id.* at *1.
30. *Id.* at *3.
31. *Id.*
32. *Id.*
33. *Id.* at *5.
34. 53 F.R.D. 594 (D. Del. 1971).
35. *Id.* at 595.
36. *Id.*

37. *Id.* at 595; *accord* Ricoh Co. v. Aeroflex Inc., 219 F.R.D. 66, 67–70 (S.D.N.Y. 2003).
38. 1994 U.S. App. LEXIS 3828 (Feb. 25, 1994).
39. *Id.* at *2.
40. *Id.*
41. *Id.* at *4.
42. *Id.* at *14.
43. *Id.* at *12.
44. 2006 U.S. Dist. LEXIS 11964 (W.D. La. Mar. 2, 2006).
45. *Id.* at *2–3.
46. *Id.* at *3.
47. *Id.*; *accord* Rickman v. Deere & Co., 154 F.R.D. 137, 138 (E.D. Va. 1993); *aff'd*, 36 F.3d 1093 (4th Cir. 1994) (Workers' compensation insurer for plaintiff's employer conducted an investigation regarding its possible subrogation rights against Deere & Co.; defendant sought production of the insurer's investigation report, and the court compelled discovery holding that because the insurer was the carrier for plaintiff's employer, not the plaintiff, it was not a representative of a party. While the reports were prepared in anticipation of subrogation litigation, they did not "fall within the literal terms of Rule 26(b)(3) for the purposes of this action."). However, courts refusing to extend the work-product protection to nonparties who are or were involved in related litigation seem to run contrary to the U.S. Supreme Court's dicta in *Fed. Trade Comm. v. Grolier Inc.*, 462 U.S. 19, 25 wherein the Court noted that neither Rule 26(b)(3) nor the Advisory Committee's comments address the temporal scope of the work-product protection. Nonetheless, the literal terms of the rule protect materials prepared for by or for a party to *any* litigation. *Id.* While this case does not address the instance of a nonparty uninvolved in any litigation whatsoever, it does suggest that a party involved in some capacity in any litigation enjoys the work-product protection, even in related cases to which it is not a party.
48. Bryant v. Ferrellgas, Inc., 2008 U.S. Dist. LEXIS 47148 (E.D. Mich. June 17, 2008).
49. *Id.* at *4. The court did not address or discuss the potential for gamesmanship that might encourage purposefully filing separate cases against various parties in order to evade Rule 26(b)(3)'s protections and then using those materials against the producing party in the separately filed litigation.
50. 2009 U.S. Dist. LEXIS 64835 (E.D.N.Y. July 28, 2009).
51. *Id.* at *10 (quoting United States v. Adlman, 134 F.3d 1194, 1196 (2d Cir. 1998).
52. *Id.*
53. *Id.*; *accord* Abdell v. New York, 2006 U.S. Dist. LEXIS 66114 (S.D.N.Y. Sept. 14, 2006); Fortunati v. Campagne, 2009 U.S. Dist. LEXIS 10729 (D. Vt. Feb. 12, 2009) (same); Haus v. New York, 2006 U.S. Dist. LEXIS 85225 (S.D.N.Y. Nov. 16, 2006) (same); *see generally* Carter v. Philadelphia, 2000 U.S. Dist. LEXIS 6658, at *3–4 (E.D. Pa. May 5, 2000) (allowing production, because materials prepared for a prior criminal prosecution presented no danger that the plaintiff would benefit from the work of his adversaries).
54. Numerous cases have recognized that Rule 26(b)(3) only partially codified the *Hickman* doctrine. *E.g.*, Sporck v. Peil, 759 F.2d 312 (3d Cir. 1985). While these cases generally do not address application to nonparties, they do affirm that the work-product protection at common law is broader than the literal confines of Rule 26(b)(3).
55. 2006 U.S. Dist. LEXIS 86603 (Nov. 29, 2006).

56. *Id.* at *17.
57. *Id.* at *18.
58. *Id.* at *21. The extent of protection afforded to intangible work product is outside the scope of this chapter, but can have important consequences on the discoverability of an investigator's actions, mental impressions, and so on. For an example of these consequences, see *Bross v. Chevron U.S.A. Inc.*, No. Civ. A. 06-1523, 2009 U.S. Dist. LEXIS 25391, at *4–5, *18, *19 (W.D. La. Mar. 25, 2009).
59. 2006 U.S. Dist. LEXIS 86603, at *31–32.
60. Federal Rule of Civil Procedure 45(c)(3–4) provides in pertinent part that a subpoena may be quashed or modified when it "requires disclosure of privileged or other protected matter, if no exception or waiver applies; or (iv) subjects *a person* to undue burden" (emphasis added).
61. Federal Rule of Civil Procedure 26(c)(1) provides in pertinent part, "[a] party *or any person from whom discovery is sought* may move for a protective order in the court where the action is pending" (emphasis added). The Rule expressly allows a court to forbid inquiry into certain matters or to limit the scope of disclosure or discovery. *Id.* at 26(c)(1)(D). *See also* Ready v. Grafton Ferry Boat Co., 2009 U.S. Dist. LEXIS 94099, at *5 (S.D. Ill. Oct. 8, 2009) (noting that even where Rule 26(b)(3) is inapplicable to nonparties, courts "can continue to arrive at sensible decisions by the issuance of a protective order under Rule 26(c)"); S.F. Bay Area Transit Dist. v. Spencer, 2006 U.S. Dist. LEXIS 73140, at *8 (N.D. Ca. Sept. 25, 2006) (noting Ninth Circuit precedent limiting Rule 26(b)(3) protections to parties but recognizing the alternate method of a protective order under Rule 26(c) to limit discovery on a nonparty); Asarco, LLC v. Ams. Mining Corp., 2007 U.S. Dist. LEXIS 84604, at *2, *18 (D. Idaho Nov. 15, 2007) (recognizing split of authority under Rule 26(b)(3) and declining to adopt a position in lieu of employing the protections under Rule 26(c) for a protective order and Rule 45 to quash subpoenas).
62. 2006 U.S. Dist. LEXIS 86603, at *33–34.
63. *Id.* at *32.
64. 244 F.R.D. 694, 696 (N.D. Ga. 2007).
65. *Id.*
66. *Id.* at 697–98.
67. *Id.* at 699.
68. *Id.*
69. 2006 U.S. Dist. LEXIS 84160 (E.D.N.Y. Nov. 17, 2006).
70. *Id.* at *2.
71. *Id.* at *3.
72. *Id.* at *9.
73. *Id.* at *3 n.1.
74. *Id.* at 9–10 (quoting Ricoh Co. v. Aeroflex, Inc., 219 F.R.D. 66 (S.D.N.Y. 2003)).
75. *Id.* at 10.
76. *Id.*
77. 604 F.2d 798 (3d Cir. 1979).
78. *Id.* at 803.
79. *Id. See also* United States v. Skeddle, 989 F. Supp. 912, 914–15 (N.D. Ohio 1997) (although entity was not a party, it was in an adversarial position and failure to extend the protection would jeopardize the nonparty's ability to fairly assert its rights in civil suits to resume after conclusion of the instant case). The *Skeddle*

court implicitly rejected the Sixth Circuit's decision in *Arkwright Mut. Ins. Co. v. Nat'l Union Fire Ins. Co.*, 1994 U.S. App. LEXIS 3828 (6th Cir. Feb. 25, 1994), in criminal contexts.

80. 107 F.R.D. 771 (M.D. Pa. 1985).
81. *Id.* at 772.
82. *Id.*
83. *Id.*; *accord* Arkwright Mut. Ins. Co. v. Nat'l Union Fire Ins. Co., 771 F. Supp. 149, 151 (S.D. W. Va. 1991) (affording the protection to a nonparty and holding that the "privilege applies as long as the document is prepared in contemplation of some particular litigation . . . [and] the probability of such future litigation [is] substantial."); *but see* Collins v. Mullins, 170 F.R.D. 132 (W.D. Va. 1996) (holding that work-product protection was inapplicable to a former party who had been dismissed from the case and referring to the *Arkwright* decision as an "aberration")). For additional cases extending the work-product protection to nonparties, see *Jean v. New York*, 2010 U.S. Dist. LEXIS 2282 (E.D.N.Y. Jan. 12, 2010) (because the district attorney, a nonparty, had a continuing interest in the matters, this was a sufficient basis to extend the protection), and *Wilson v. New York*, 2009 U.S. Dist. LEXIS 69015 (E.D.N.Y. Jan 20, 2009).
84. A similar line of reasoning would apply to protect entities that enter into joint-defense agreements but are not later named as parties.

CHAPTER 10

Applying the Attorney-Client Privilege to Investigations Involving Attorneys: What Is Fair Game in Discovery?

DAVID E. BLAND
SCOTT G. JOHNSON

I. Introduction

A typical law firm currently takes on far more duties than its traditional role of providing solely legal advice. Indeed, in an effort to achieve the "full service" that many of its clients desire, lawyers and their employees often find themselves rendering investigative, as well as legal, assistance in a myriad of different factual settings. Examples include an investigation of potential medical malpractice on behalf of a hospital,[1] an investigation into allegations of sexual molestation by an elementary school teacher,[2] an investigation of sexual discrimination complaints on behalf of an employer,[3] an investigation on behalf of a factory owner of an explosion that killed and injured several on-site contractors,[4] an investigation into the back-dating of stock options,[5] an investigation of potential arson on behalf of a property insurance carrier,[6] an investigation into possible trademark infringement by a competitor,[7]an investigation of potential fraud and other improprieties on behalf of a bank,[8] an investigation on behalf of a multinational corporation of questionable payments to a foreign governmental official to secure government business,[9] an investigation into allegations that laboratory managers impeded a separate internal ethics investigation,[10] and an investigation into the insurance aspects surrounding the World Trade Center attack.[11] Attorneys then communicate the results of their investigations to their clients.[12]

When the client's adversary seeks discovery of the communications between the client and the attorney investigator in subsequent litigation, a dispute often arises as to what documents or information must be produced. The attorney-client privilege generally protects only those communications between attorney and client where the attorney is acting in his or her capacity as an attorney and not in some other capacity. The attorney-client privilege similarly applies only to those communications between attorneys and clients made for the purpose of obtaining or giving legal advice.[13]

Whether the attorney-client privilege shields production of the documents and information relating to an attorney's investigation turns in the first instance on whether the attorney was acting in his or her capacity as an attorney and, if so, whether the attorney-client communication containing the results of the investigation was made with the purpose of giving legal advice. The scope of the attorney-client privilege also may depend upon whether the client is a corporation or an individual and whether the attorney's advice is based on information from nonclients. The work-product doctrine also may protect written documents containing the attorney's investigative results if the investigation was performed "in anticipation of litigation." This chapter addresses these issues as well as others that arise as a result of an attorney's investigation.

II. The Attorney-Client Privilege Defined

The attorney-client privilege is the "oldest of the privileges for confidential communications known to the common law," dating back to the days of Elizabethan England.[14] Its purpose is to "encourage full and frank communication between attorneys and their clients and thereby promote broader public interests in the observance of law and administration of justice."[15] Thus, it affords complete protection from disclosure to confidential communications between attorney and client, but is subject to several exceptions.[16] The "attorney-client privilege protects both the confidential giving of professional advice by an attorney acting in the capacity of a legal advisor to those who can act on it, as well as the giving of information to the lawyer to enable counsel to give sound and informed advice."[17] But since the privilege hinders full discovery of the truth, it is oftentimes narrowly construed.[18]

The following criteria, set forth in Professor Wigmore's treatise on evidence,[19] are typical of the requirements most jurisdictions have established to determine whether the attorney-client privilege applies: (1) Where legal advice of any kind is sought (2) from a professional legal adviser in his capacity as such, (3) the communications relating to that purpose, (4) made in confidence (5) by the client, (6) are at his instance permanently protected (7) from disclosure by himself or by the legal adviser, (8) except the protection be waived.[20]

While the attorney-client privilege protects the disclosure of confidential information communicated between a client and an attorney for the purpose of obtaining or giving legal advice or assistance,[21] the attorney-client privilege does not prevent the disclosure of facts, documents, or other matters not privileged.[22] Thus, during discovery, a client must disclose the facts of which he is aware, whether or not the client disclosed them to the attorney, but neither the client nor the attorney can be questioned about whether those facts were disclosed and what advice was given.[23] Similarly, documents supplied to an attorney are not protected from disclosure in discovery, but whether or not they were provided to the attorney is a privileged matter.[24] Documents created by virtue of the attorney-client relationship may be protected from disclosure by the work-product doctrine.[25]

The attorney-client privilege applies not only to communications made directly to attorneys, but also to communications made to the subordinates or employees of attorneys, such as investigators, paralegals, law clerks, secretaries, or other persons acting as agents of the attorney.[26] Thus, statements made by the client to a private investigator employed by the client's attorney are protected by the attorney-client privilege to the same extent as if made directly to the attorney.[27]

III. Is the Attorney Investigator Acting in the Capacity of an Attorney?

The attorney-client privilege attaches only to communications made by or to an attorney acting in his or her "capacity as such."[28] Thus, the first issue addressed is whether an attorney hired to conduct an investigation is acting in his or her capacity as an attorney. Generally, an attorney is acting in the capacity of an attorney when he or she is being consulted by a client for the purpose of obtaining legal services or advice.[29] The privilege will not apply to attorney-client communications in cases where the client hires the attorney for business or personal advice or to perform the work of a nonlawyer.[30] Many courts dealing with attorney investigations, however, have had great difficulty in drawing the line between attorneys who are rendering legal advice and those who are merely performing the ordinary business of claims investigation for their clients.[31]

The disagreement among legal scholars highlights how important the resolution of this question is. Indeed, Charles Wright and Kenneth Graham express the view that "no privilege applies where the lawyer's primary function is as a detective. Where the lawyer is retained for the purposes of litigation, the privilege should apply only where the investigation is one that cannot be carried out by non-lawyer investigators[.]"[32] But even Wright and Graham openly acknowledge their disagreement on the issue.[33] This position was roundly criticized by the Ninth Circuit Court of Appeals in *United States v. Rowe*,[34] and, as set forth in more detail below, appears to be the minority view. On the other hand, the American Law Institute favors the broad approach that protects all communications from lawyer to client.[35] The Institute favors the broad approach because it "avoids difficult questions in determining whether a lawyer's communication itself discloses a client communication."[36]

A. Attorney Investigator Acting in Capacity of Attorney

The New York Court of Appeals provided an excellent analysis of the "acting as such" requirement in *Spectrum Systems International Corp. v. Chemical Bank*.[37] There, Chemical Bank retained a law firm to "perform an investigation and render legal advice to Chemical regarding possible fraud by its employees and outside vendors, and to counsel Chemical with respect to litigation options."[38] The law firm interviewed Chemical's employees, a former Chemical officer, and representatives of Spectrum itself.[39] The law firm then prepared a report of the results of its investigation. The "Spectrum" section of the report consisted of a three-page narrative describing the problem and the facts, and a final paragraph containing the firm's opinion as to the possible claims, an estimate of Chemical's damages, the weaknesses of such a claim, and the firm's view that there was insufficient proof to establish particular matters described in the letter.[40] After Spectrum sued Chemical and learned about the report, Spectrum requested it in discovery. Chemical moved for a protective order. The trial court, without ever viewing the documents, ordered the documents produced.[41]

On appeal, the appellate division modified the order, requiring the trial court to conduct an in camera inspection to determine materiality and necessity.[42] The appellate division, having itself reviewed the documents, concluded that the documents were not privileged because, as the purpose of the investigation was to obtain business, rather than legal, advice, Chemical had not met its burden of proving that the investigation was done by lawyers acting as lawyers:

> The communications pertain to an investigation of the plaintiff corporation and its employees, and suggest corruption prevention measures to be employed in the future. The records do not focus on any imminent litigation, nor on the parties' legal rights or obligations. There is no indication that legal research was performed in order to reach any conclusion with regard to the parties' legal positions. The outside law firm's final report, instead, reveals that meetings were to be held at some future date to discuss the course of action to be taken.
>
> The information requested was assembled to aid defendant in the operation of its business and as such, is not exempt from disclosure. . . . [D]efendant's own affirmation attests to the fact that the material was not prepared primarily for litigation and that, in fact, there were other motivating forces behind its preparation.[43]

The appellate division, nonetheless, granted leave to appeal to the court of appeals, certifying one question—was its order properly made?[44]

The court of appeals answered this question in the negative.[45] Unlike the appellate division, the court of appeals found that the purpose of the attorney's investigation was to render legal advice to the client:

> [T]he privilege is not narrowly confined to the repetition of confidences that were supplied to the lawyer by the client. That cramped view of the attorney-client privilege is at odds with the underlying policy of encouraging open communication; it poses inordinate practical difficulties in making surgical separations so as not to risk revealing client confidences; and it denies that an attorney can have *any* role in fact-gathering incident to the rendition of legal advice and services. The memorandum in *Rossi* included the lawyer's conversations with plaintiff's counsel and with third parties, as well as the lawyer's opinion and advice. Yet we determined, from reviewing the full content and context of the communication, that its purpose was to convey legal advice to the client, and we held the entire document exempt from discovery. We reach the same conclusion here.
>
> [A]n investigative report does not become privileged merely because it was sent to an attorney. Nor is such a report privileged merely because an investigation was conducted by an attorney; a lawyer's communication is not cloaked with privilege when the lawyer is

> hired for business or personal advice, or to do the work of a non-lawyer. Yet it is also the case that, while information received from third persons may not itself be privileged, a lawyer's communication to a client that includes such information in its legal analysis and advice may stand on different footing. The critical inquiry is whether, viewing the lawyer's communication in its full content and context, it was made in order to render legal advice or services to the client.[46]
>
> Here we conclude that the facts were selected and presented in the [law firm's] report as the foundation for the law firm's advice, and that the communication was primarily and predominantly of a legal character.[47]

The court rejected any requirements that litigation be contemplated or that the attorney's investigative report contain legal research in order to be privileged:

> The prospect of litigation may be relevant to the subject of work product and trial preparation materials, but the attorney-client privilege is not tied to the contemplation of litigation. . . .
>
> * * * *
>
> Similarly, the absence of legal research in an attorney's communication is not determinative of privilege, so long as the communication reflects the attorney's professional skills and judgments. Legal advice may be grounded in experience as well as research.[48]

More recently, in *Sandra T.E. v. South Berwyn School District 100*,[49] the Seventh Circuit Court of Appeals was called upon to analyze this issue in the context of claims of sexual molestation against an elementary school teacher and his school district employer.[50] Sidley Austin LLP was hired by the school board to conduct an investigation and to provide legal advice to the district.[51] Sidley and the school board entered into a written retention agreement.[52] The board sent a letter to all parents advising them of Sidley's retention.[53] Sidley interviewed both current and former employees of the district and some third-party witnesses.[54] None of the interviews was recorded; the Sidley attorneys took notes during the interviews and later drafted memoranda summarizing them.[55] Sidley provided the school board with a written executive summary as well as an oral report of the legal advice it was retained to provide.[56]

The victims and their families sued the school district in January 2005.[57] Plaintiffs first sought production of the Sidley materials from a Sidley partner by way of a deposition subpoena with an accompanying request for documents.[58] Sidley turned over more than 1,000 pages of documents but withheld the witness interview summaries and other internal legal memoranda.[59] Plaintiffs moved to compel the school district to turn over the materials, and the trial court so ordered, finding that Sidley was hired as an "investigator, not as an attorney."[60] When plaintiffs found out that these materials were in Sidley's possession, and not in the school district's, plaintiffs subpoenaed Sidley directly.[61] When Sidley continued to assert a privilege claim, plaintiffs sought an order compelling Sidley to produce the documents.[62] The trial court, reiterating the view that Sidley was an investigator, not an attorney, ordered production, and Sidley appealed.[63]

The Seventh Circuit reversed, concluding that Sidley was acting as an attorney while investigating the details of the allegations of sexual molestation.[64] The appellate court concluded that the trial court erred by not considering the engagement letter:

> The engagement letter spells out that the Board retained Sidley to provide legal services in connection with developing the School Board's response to [teacher]'s sexual abuse of his students. Sidley's investigation of the factual circumstances surrounding the abuse was an integral part of the package of legal services for which it was hired and a necessary prerequisite to the provision of legal advice about how the District should respond. . . . [T]he conduct of Sidley attorneys during the investigation confirms that they were acting in their capacity as attorneys. During the confidential interviews with school-district employees, the attorneys provided so-called "*Upjohn* warnings" emphasizing that Sidley represented the School Board and not the employee and that the School Board had control over whether the conversations remained privileged. No third parties attended the interviews, the School Board received [Sidley]'s report of the firm's findings during an executive session not open to the public, and the written executive summary that Sidley turned over to the Board was marked "Privileged and Confidential," "Attorney-Client Communication," and "Attorney Work Product."[65]

The court reached a similar conclusion in *Leucadia, Inc. v. Reliance Insurance Co.*,[66] where a subsidiary retained outside counsel to draft a company policy on conflicts of interest and to thereafter investigate past conduct to determine whether it complied with the newly drafted policy. Leucadia then filed suit under a bond issued by Reliance, and Reliance sought production of the outside counsel's 65-page report analyzing a series of past transactions on the basis that the information was gathered as part of a factual investigation, not for the rendition of legal services.[67] The court rejected this argument, holding: "Here counsel were engaged to determine whether plaintiff had legally enforceable rights against its employees or its insurer, and the privilege extends to factual matter given to counsel to enable them to render such an opinion."[68]

Courts in other cases have also found that an attorney investigator was acting in his or her capacity as an attorney. For example, in *State ex rel. U.S. Fidelity & Guaranty Co. v. Canady*[69] and *Dunn v. State Farm Fire & Casualty Co.*,[70] the courts concluded that an attorney retained by the insurer to investigate a suspicious fire was acting as an attorney, not an investigator, and his reports to the insurer were protected communications.[71] Similarly, in *In re State Commission of Investigation Subpoena No. 5441*,[72] the court found that an attorney hired by a school board association was acting in the capacity of a lawyer during his investigation of alleged improprieties in an investment program run by an insurance group of which the school board association was a member.[73] In *Bross v. Chevron U.S.A. Inc.*,[74] the court found that a root cause analysis report, prepared following the death of an oil worker by nonlawyers at the direction of a lawyer, was privileged because the investigators were directed by and reported only to counsel.[75] Also, in *Carte Blanche (Singapore) PTE, Ltd. v. Diners Club International, Inc.*,[76] the court found that an attorney investigating a proposed transaction in connection with an existing franchise agreement acted in his capacity as a lawyer in doing so.[77] Finally, the Fourth Circuit, in *In re Allen*, held that an attorney hired to investigate possible document mismanagement and breaches of confidentiality in an Attorney General's office was acting in her capacity as an attorney and that reports relating to her investigation were privileged because they were connected to the furnishing of legal advice.[78]

A seemingly contrary result was reached by the Missouri Court of Appeals in *Crow v. Crawford & Co.*[79] At issue there was a set of notes taken by an employee of the defendant, which was hired by a self-insured company as a third-party administrator for its workers' compensation claims.[80] The notes were apparently made during the employee's investigation into plaintiff's workers' compensation claim.[81] Even though the note-taker was not an attorney or an employee of an attorney,[82] the appellate court upheld the trial court's conclusion that the notes were protected by the attorney-client privilege.[83] The appellate court reasoned: "Documents prepared by an agent or employee at the employer's direction for the purpose of obtaining advice of counsel or for use in prospective or pending litigation are encompassed by the attorney-client privilege."[84]

B. Attorney Investigator Not Acting in Capacity of Attorney

Courts have not permitted clients to cloak a routine business investigation with attorney-client privilege protection simply by retaining an attorney to conduct that investigation.[85] Most of these cases have arisen in the context of an insurance company client where the courts have found that the attorney's investigation was part of the insurer's ordinary business of claims investigation.[86]

Mission National Insurance Co. v. Lilly[87] is a good example. There, Mission insured a nightclub in northern Minnesota that was destroyed by fire. Because Mission retained the Cozen & O'Connor law firm "as a matter of course to conduct its claims adjustment investigations in a geographic area including Minnesota for all claims exceeding $25,000,"[88] the Cozen firm investigated the loss and corresponded with Mission. After Mission sued for declaratory relief, the insured sought production of Mission's claim file, including correspondence from Cozen's office.[89] The court concluded that the Cozen firm was not acting as counsel, but was performing a business function of Mission, thereby rendering the results of Cozen's investigation discoverable:

> It is not the precepts of law that give rise to the difficulty in this case; instead, the difficulty exists because of plaintiffs [sic] decision, immediately upon receiving notice of the fire, to employ attorneys to fulfill its ordinary business function of claims investigation. Counsel for plaintiff agrees that Cozen & O'Connor was the only party responsible for performing that pure, ordinary business function. . . .
>
> * * * *
>
> To the extent that Cozen & O'Connor acted as claims adjusters, then, their work-product, communications to client, and impressions about the facts will be treated herein as the ordinary business of plaintiff, outside the scope of the asserted privileges. This approach results in the majority of the file being discoverable.[90]

A similar result was reached in *St. Paul Reinsurance Co. v. Commercial Financial Corp.*[91] There, St. Paul Reinsurance Co. and Zurich Reinsurance (London) Ltd. provided employment practice liability coverage to Commercial Financial Corp. (CFC).[92] The insurers filed a declaratory judgment action, claiming that CFC made material misrepresentations in its application for coverage.[93] On that basis, they denied CFC's claims for coverage of employment discrimination claims by employees and sought rescission of the policy. CFC filed a counterclaim arguing that the insurers acted in bad faith by denying the claims.[94] To support its defense and counterclaims, CFC sought discovery of certain claim investigations undertaken by the insurers, which the insurers attempted to shield on the grounds of attorney-client privilege.[95]

The insurers had hired an attorney to conduct an investigation into CFC's claims. CFC argued that the insurers had an existing obligation in the ordinary course of business to investigate and adjust CFC's claims; thus, the insurers could not shield the claims investigation documents produced by the attorney under the attorney-client privilege.[96] The insurers responded that the documents generated after they began to consider rescission of the policy were privileged, since, at that point, they ceased to be normal business functions.[97]

The court agreed with CFC, rejecting the insurers' argument that the claims investigation files should be shielded from discovery because they were prepared by an attorney.[98] Specifically, the court held that even when the insurers and their attorney began to consider rescission on the grounds of nondisclosure, that consideration was part of the investigation of the availability of coverage, and, therefore, part of an insurer's normal business processes.[99]

While *Lilly* and *St. Paul Reinsurance* present fairly clear examples of an attorney performing an investigation that is part of the client's ordinary business, *National Farmers Union Property & Casualty Co. v. District Court*[100] demonstrates that the line between an ordinary business investigation and an investigation to provide legal advice is not always clear.

In *National Farmers Union*, the court held that communications between the attorneys and their insurance company client that described a factual investigation were not protected by the attorney-client privilege. National Farmers Union (NFU) provided lease guaranty insurance to its insured, Tenneco, whereby NFU guaranteed payment of rents that came due under a sublease during the policy period in the event of a default. Following a default on the sublease payments, Tenneco made a claim under the NFU policy.[101] NFU referred the matter to its general counsel, who in turn contacted outside counsel to investigate whether the claim was covered under the policy. Outside counsel submitted a lengthy memorandum to NFU's general counsel relating the results of the investigation.[102] NFU subsequently denied Tenneco's claim. Tenneco sued and later filed a motion to compel production of certain documents, including the memorandum from the outside counsel to NFU's general counsel. Following in camera review, the trial court ruled that the first 27 pages of the memorandum were discoverable as ordinary business records.[103]

On appeal, NFU argued that the memorandum was prepared by outside counsel in response to a request for legal advice relating to an investigation of the origination of the policy and the validity of the claim. The Colorado Supreme Court, however, rejected this argument. First, the court reasoned that the attorneys interviewed various officers and employees to determine the factual circumstances concerning the issuance of the policy and were acting more in the role of claims investigators than legal counsel for NFU. Second, the court reasoned that the dominant purpose of the interviews was to provide NFU with the factual circumstances underlying the issuance of the policy. Third, the court noted that there was no showing that the persons interviewed by the attorneys were ever informed that the attorneys were acting as company counsel or that the purpose of the investigation was to allow the company to obtain legal advice. Finally, the court stated that there was no indication that the employees were ever told that the investigation was confidential.[104] The court held that the attorney-client privilege did not protect the first 27 pages of the memorandum because the information was not legal advice but the result of a factual investigation relating to the issuance of the policy.[105] The remainder of the memorandum contained legal conclusions and was not discoverable.[106]

In his dissent, Justice Rovira focused on the role of the attorneys hired by NFU, noting that upon receiving the insured's demand for payment, NFU referred the matter to its general counsel, who, in turn, retained outside attorneys to investigate the circumstances under which the policy was issued and determine whether the insured's claim should be denied.[107] The outside attorneys then initiated the investigation and submitted a memorandum to NFU, which provided information concerning the facts and circumstances surrounding the issuance of the policy and counsel's recommendation regarding whether the insured's claim should be paid.[108] The dissent concluded: "Where, as here, the client seeks the assistance of counsel to determine the operative facts and obtain legal advice based on those facts, I would, consistent with the purposes of the privilege, protect the memorandum against compelled disclosure."[109]

In essence, the Colorado Supreme Court relied on the premise that the attorneys hired by NFU were not acting as attorneys, but rather were acting in another capacity—as claims investigators. *National Farmers Union*, however, appears wrongly decided. The court failed to focus on the real reason the attorneys were retained—to render an opinion concerning whether the insured's claims should be denied. The attorneys had to investigate the facts to determine the circumstances under which the policy was issued before they could render their opinion on the denial of the claim. The attorneys were not acting as claims investigators, but rather as attorneys hired to investigate the factual circumstances and render a legal opinion accordingly.[110]

Investigations conducted by attorneys hired by insureds may also be discoverable, as illustrated by *SR International Business Insurance Co. v. World Trade Center Properties LLC*,[111] which arose out of the September 11, 2001, attack on the World Trade Center. There, a lender for World Trade Center leaseholders retained an insurance advisor in July 2001 to help determine the amount of insurance coverage that the leaseholders should obtain.[112] After the September 11 attack, the lender's employees and the insurance advisor conducted an investigation to gather information regarding the available insurance.[113] In the subsequent suit by the leaseholders for insurance coverage, SR International moved for an order compelling production of the documents resulting from the post–September 11 investigation.[114] The lender, however, claimed that the information-gathering activities were protected by the attorney-client privilege, since the employees of the insurance advisor were acting as litigation consultants to the lender's in-house counsel in the investigation following the September 11 attack.[115]

The U.S. District Court for the Southern District of New York held that the communications with investors after the terrorist attack were performed in the normal course of business and therefore were not protected.[116] The court found that the purpose of the investor meetings was to provide information in response to the investors' inquiries and not to provide legal advice. The court also found that notes documenting facts were not protected because the attorney-client privilege does not protect underlying facts.[117] The court did find, however, that some meetings between the lenders' employees and the lender's in-house counsel were privileged, since those communications sought legal advice.[118]

C. Summary

The *Spectrum Systems*, *South Berwyn School District*, and *Leucadia* cases illustrate that the communications between attorney and client relating to the attorney's investigation will be protected by the attorney-client privilege as long as the attorney is acting in his or her capacity as an attorney. The *National Farmers Union*, *Lilly*, *St. Paul Reinsurance*, and *SR International* cases, however, demonstrate that not all attorneys conducting investigations on behalf of clients are acting in the capacity of an attorney. Where, as in *Lilly*, *St. Paul Reinsurance*, and *SR International*, the attorney is performing an investigation that can be generally considered part of the client's ordinary business practices, a client cannot shield the results of that investigation simply by having an attorney conduct the investigation. *National Farmers Union* illustrates that the line between an ordinary business investigation and an investigation for purposes of obtaining legal advice is not always clear. To obtain attorney-client privilege protection of attorney-client investigative communications, the party seeking to invoke the privilege must carry the burden of establishing that the attorney's investigation was conducted to render legal advice to the client. *Spectrum Systems* correctly notes that the prospect of litigation is irrelevant to a determination of whether the client is seeking legal advice and that an attorney-investigator is acting in the capacity of an attorney where the attorney's report integrates the factual results of the investigation with the attorney's assessment of the client's legal position or options.

IV. Special Problems Facing Corporations That Retain Counsel to Investigate

Corporations face a special problem when they hire attorneys to investigate and provide legal advice: Which employees can the attorney talk to and keep the communications within the attorney-client privilege? The first case to establish guidelines in these situations was *City of Philadelphia v. Westinghouse Electric Corp.*[119] The court there determined that those employees in the "control group" would be covered by the privilege.[120] The control group included only those members of senior management who may be in a position to control or take action on the advice of the attorney.[121] While some courts followed the control group approach,[122] other courts developed a "subject matter" test, which required application of several factors to determine if the subject matter of an attorney-client communication was privileged.[123]

A. Supreme Court Rejects Control Group Test

In *Upjohn Co. v. United States*,[124] the Supreme Court directly addressed a factual situation where an attorney conducted an investigation and interviewed numerous corporate employees, many of whom were not within the control group. In *Upjohn*, the attorney's investigation commenced after independent accountants conducting an audit of one of Upjohn's foreign subsidiaries discovered that improper payments had been made to foreign government officials in order to secure government business. After the accountants informed Upjohn's general counsel, Gerard Thomas, of the bribes, Thomas consulted with outside counsel and decided to enlist the aid of outside counsel in investigating the questionable payments.[125] Outside counsel prepared a letter containing a questionnaire that was sent by Upjohn's chairman to various Upjohn employees, including those outside the control group. The letter, which included an admonition that the investigation was "highly confidential," specified that the purpose of the investigation was to determine the nature and magnitude of any payments made by Upjohn to any foreign government officials, and stated that management needed full information concerning any such payments.[126] The responses were sent directly to Thomas. Thomas and outside counsel also interviewed the recipients of the questionnaires and 33 other Upjohn employees and took notes during these interviews.[127]

The Internal Revenue Service thereafter began an investigation to determine the tax consequences of the alleged payments after receiving a report about them from Upjohn.[128] In the course of the investigation, the Internal Revenue Service subpoenaed all of Thomas's investigative files, including the questionnaires, memoranda, and notes of the interviews. After Upjohn refused to produce the questionnaires and notes, the IRS sought enforcement from the district court, which ordered their production. The Third Circuit upheld this decision.[129]

On further appeal, the Supreme Court held that the communications made by the employees (and the responses to the questionnaires) were protected by the attorney-client privilege.[130] The Court rejected the application of the control group test because it discouraged the communication of relevant information by the client's employees to the attorneys seeking to render legal advice to the corporation.[131] The Court recognized that because lower-echelon corporate employees often embroil a corporation in serious legal difficulties, these employees often have the only relevant information needed by counsel to render legal advice to the corporation. If the communications with these employees are not privileged, the Court reasoned that the attorney faced a "Hobson's choice"—interview employees without the protection of the attorney-client privilege or forgo those interviews and render advice to the corporation based on incomplete information.[132] Because the control group test too narrowly protected what the Court believed was privileged information, the Court rejected it in favor of the subject matter approach.[133]

Upjohn, which arose from an IRS investigation, addressed the federal common law attorney-client privilege[134] and, thus, is not binding on state courts[135] or on federal courts in diversity cases.[136] Some state courts have followed the *Upjohn* approach,[137] while others have modified the *Upjohn* test. For example, in *Southern Bell Telephone & Telegraph Co. v. Deason*,[138] the Florida Supreme Court had to determine the extent of the attorney-client privilege when a regulated utility with a duty to disclose investigates its own conduct through counsel.[139] The Florida Public Services Commission (PSC) argued that because Southern Bell was regulated by state statute, the *Upjohn* rule did not apply, and the information it sought was not protected by the attorney-client privilege.[140] The court first rejected the control group test because it failed to recognize the "crucial role [that] middle and lower-level employees play in the corporation's activities."[141] The court then rejected the PSC's argument that the rules of privilege should be applied differently because Southern Bell was a regulated industry.[142] The court adopted the subject matter test,[143] relying principally on the rule developed in *Harper & Row Publishers, Inc. v. Decker*[144] as modified by *Diversified Industries, Inc. v. Meredith*.[145] The court then applied the rule it had announced to the information Southern Bell claimed was privileged, allowing the PSC to discover some of it, and protecting some from discovery.[146]

B. The Control Group Theory Remains Viable in Illinois

Even in light of *Upjohn*, the control group theory continues to be applied in at least one jurisdiction. In *Consolidation Coal Co. v. Bucyrus-Erie Co.*,[147] the Illinois Supreme Court rejected the *Upjohn* approach in favor of the control group test.[148] The court reasoned that the control group test struck a reasonable balance between protecting corporate decision makers' consultations with counsel and minimizing the amount of factual information that is immune from discovery.[149] Under this theory, however, communications to and from the person whose conduct gave rise to the potential corporate liability are protected, whether or not that person is part of the control group.[150]

Indeed, until a subsequent change in a state rule of evidence, the Texas Supreme Court also continued to endorse the control group approach. In *National Tank Co. v. Brotherton*,[151] the court interpreted its rule of evidence as adopting the control group test and refused to protect the statements taken by National's risk control coordinator—on behalf of National's general counsel—under the attorney-client privilege.[152] The court ruled that the employees the coordinator interviewed were not "representatives" of National for the purposes of the Texas rule, and therefore, communications from those employees were not privileged.[153] Even though the employees "may have been speaking with management's blessing," the court held, they had not been authorized to seek legal advice on National's behalf, and thus fell outside the group of employees whose communications with counsel would be privileged.[154]

In 1998, the Texas Legislature revised the applicable rule of evidence, thereby replacing the "control group" test previously used and analyzed in *National Tank*.[155] Subsequent Texas appellate court decisions have interpreted the revision to adopt the broader subject-matter test, finding privilege if "the employee makes the communication at the direction of his superiors in the corporation and where the subject matter upon which the attorney's advice is sought by the corporation and dealt with in the communication is the performance by the employee of the duties of his employment."[156]

C. Arizona Adopts a Third Approach

In *Samaritan Foundation v. Goodfarb*,[157] the Arizona Supreme Court rejected both the control group test and the subject matter test in favor of the "functional approach." In *Samaritan*, a child's heart stopped during surgery and the hospital's lawyer investigated the incident. The lawyer directed a nurse paralegal to interview three nurses and a scrub technician who were present during the surgery. The paralegal summarized the interviews in a memorandum that she submitted to the hospital's corporate counsel.[158]

The child sued, and when the employees were unable to remember during their depositions what happened in the operating room, she sought production of the summaries prepared by the paralegal.[159] The trial court rejected the hospital's argument that the summaries were protected by the attorney-client privilege, but gave them limited protection under the work-product doctrine.[160] The hospital appealed, and the appellate court upheld the trial court's ruling, adopting a modified form of the control group test for application of the attorney-client privilege.[161] The appellate court found that the requisite showing of need for the information had been made and upheld the trial court's decision that the summaries were discoverable.[162]

The Arizona Supreme Court rejected the court of appeals' "qualified privilege" approach,[163] opting instead for the "functional approach," which focuses on the relationship between the communicator and the need for legal services.[164] The court rejected both *Upjohn*'s subject matter test and the control group test for the same reason—both would protect communications made by employees of a corporation in their capacity as witnesses to an event in which they were uninvolved from a liability perspective.[165] In the court's view, any privilege that attaches to communications between corporate employees and the corporation's attorneys must protect the legitimate needs of the corporation to obtain legal advice, yet not be so broad as to encompass statements made by mere witnesses to an event.[166] The court held that:

> [W]here someone other than the employee initiates the communication, a factual communication by a corporate employee to corporate counsel is within the corporation's privilege if it concerns the employee's own conduct within the scope of his or her employment and is made to assist the lawyer in assessing or responding to the legal consequences of that conduct for the corporate client. This excludes from the privilege communications from those who, but for their status as officers, agents or employees, are witnesses.[167]

Because the statements of the employees in this case were not of the kind described, the court ruled that the paralegal's summaries were discoverable.[168]

In response to the *Samaritan* decision, the Arizona legislature enacted section 12-2234 of the Arizona Statutes,[169] which modifies the *Samaritan* decision and codifies the attorney-client privilege applicable not just to corporations, but to all business entities.[170] This statute protects communications with any employee of an entity and counsel if the communication is either (1) for the purpose of providing legal advice to the entity or (2) for the purpose of obtaining information in order to provide such advice.[171] The statute also provides that the employee is not relieved of a duty to disclose facts by virtue of the statute.[172] Accordingly, the witness statements the court viewed as not privileged in *Samaritan* would have been privileged under the statute.

It should be noted, however, that section 12-2234 of the Arizona Statutes applies only in the *civil* context. In *Roman Catholic Diocese v. Superior Court*,[173] the Arizona Court of Appeals rejected the plaintiff's contention that Arizona Statute section 13-4062(2), the codification of the attorney-client privilege in criminal cases, should be interpreted in a manner similar to its revised civil counterpart.[174] The court observed that the civil and criminal attorney-client statutes were very similar when *Samaritan* was decided.[175] After the *Samaritan* decision, the legislature amended the civil attorney-client privilege statute in an effort to broaden the privilege afforded to corporations in civil cases.[176] The Arizona Legislature, however, did *not* modify the criminal attorney-client privilege statute—and without such a modification, the court declined to extend the civil privilege to criminal cases.[177]

D. Summary

As the foregoing cases demonstrate, the fact that a lawyer investigates in her capacity as a lawyer for a corporate client does not necessarily mean that the communications to or from that lawyer will be protected. In those jurisdictions that follow *Upjohn*, an attorney can be more confident that the communications with the client's employees will be protected. In a control group jurisdiction, the communications will not be protected by the attorney-client privilege unless the communicator or recipient of the communication from the attorney is within the narrowly defined control group or is the person whose conduct gave rise to the potential liability. In states that follow Arizona's functional approach, communications to or from an employee whose conduct may give rise to liability of the corporation are protected; communications to or from mere witnesses to an event are not.

V. Information from Nonclients: Is It Protected?

Another issue that arises in cases where attorneys conduct investigations is the scope of protection for information supplied by nonclients. Indeed, in some investigations, much of the information will be supplied by nonclients. The attorney transmits the information to his or her client, and it forms the basis of counsel's legal advice and recommendations.

A. Application of the Attorney-Client Privilege

Under Professor Wigmore's approach, the attorney-client privilege does not apply if the attorney's legal advice to the client is based on information obtained from third parties.[178] This rule, if accurately stated, directly affects communications between attorneys and clients in a variety of contexts.[179] In fact, many courts hold that there is no attorney-client privilege for documents relating to factual information obtained from nonclient sources.[180]

The court in *United States v. United Shoe Machinery Corp.*[181] followed the Wigmore approach. There, the government brought a civil antitrust action against United Shoe and sought to introduce numerous exhibits that United claimed were attorney-client privileged.[182] The first category of exhibits included letters to or from outside attorneys.[183] At the time of the communications, "each of the law partnerships was counsel for United, its subsidiaries and affiliates."[184] The court found that the privilege did not apply when the legal advice is based on "facts disclosed to the attorney by a person outside the organization of defendant and its affiliates."[185]

United Shoe is not simply an archaic decision with no recent support. Its support, however, appears limited to the federal courts. In *Merrin Jewelry Co. v. St. Paul Fire & Marine Insurance Co.*,[186] the court held that the report of an attorney hired by St. Paul to conduct an examination under oath in response to a theft claim was not privileged because it was based on information obtained from a nonclient during the examination.[187] Similarly, in *J.P. Foley & Co. v. Vanderbilt*,[188] the court ordered production of communications from attorney to client because they were based on information from third parties.[189]

While not going as far as *United Shoe*, other courts have ordered parties to produce facts that the party's attorney discovered from nonclient sources. In *Carte Blanche (Singapore) PTE, Ltd. v. Diners Club International, Inc.*,[190] for example, the court ordered the client to produce its attorney's letter containing the results of an investigation from various nonclient sources.[191] Similarly, in *Allen v. West Point-Pepperell, Inc.*,[192] the court found that "plaintiffs and [counsel] must disclose to defendants all facts of which they were aware at all times relevant to this action, whether or not those facts were communicated by plaintiffs to [counsel] and whether or not those facts were learned by plaintiffs from [counsel],"[193] but all written communications between plaintiffs and counsel were deemed privileged and not discoverable.[194] And more recently, the court in the patent case *Martin Marietta Materials, Inc. v. Bedford Reinforced Plastics, Inc.*,[195] deemed communications between plaintiffs' attorneys and outside counsel regarding prior art privileged, but not the underlying communications to the inventor.[196] Similarly, a Louisiana federal court allowed the deposition of nonlawyer investigators to proceed, even though it found that the written report prepared by the proposed deponents was privileged.[197]

In contrast, the Missouri Supreme Court considered and rejected the Wigmore approach in *State ex rel. Great American Insurance Co. v. Smith*.[198] There, Great American insured Cannova, who reported a fire loss and made claim for the damage. Great American hired an attorney, Risjord, to investigate the loss. At the conclusion of Risjord's investigation, Great American denied Cannova's claim on the grounds of arson, and Cannova sued.[199] Great American's claim files were produced, except for three letters from Risjord to Great American, which Great American claimed were privileged.[200] After the trial court ordered production of the letters, Great American sought prohibition, and the supreme court ordered the trial court to conduct an in camera review of the letters pursuant to the direction set forth in the opinion, which approximated the Wigmore approach.[201] The trial court reviewed the letters in camera and again ordered their production.[202]

Great American appealed again, and this time the supreme court rejected the Wigmore approach it had adopted in the earlier decision and reversed the trial court's order.[203] The court's rationale is instructive. First, the court determined that Wigmore's view was a narrow one, directed toward limiting the scope of protected information.[204] The court found that society's interests were better served by protecting communication between attorney and client beyond that suggested by Wigmore.[205] Second, the court found that the rule proposed by the American Law Institute[206] better reflected the reality of an attorney-client relationship today.[207] The court then adopted a two-part test to determine whether the privilege applies:

> There is no question but that the three letters Risjord wrote to relators pertained to these matters in which he had been employed. Risjord so stated and the court's findings as set out in the letter of April 21, 1977, so show. If this were not so, we would direct the court to conduct a hearing and examine representatives of relators or Risjord or both to determine whether at the time the letters were written, the relation of attorney and client regarding the insurance claims existed, and whether the letters pertained to the matters for which Risjord had been employed. If either answer were in the negative, the privilege would not apply.[208]

When comparing the Wigmore view to that of the court in *Great American*, the better-reasoned view is that of the Missouri Supreme Court, keeping in mind the scope of the privilege—communications are protected, but facts are not.[209] The *Great American* court emphasized the protective scope of the attorney-client privilege as it applies to investigative reports:

> When a client goes to an attorney and asks him to represent him on a claim which he believes he has against someone or which is being asserted against him, even if he as yet has no knowledge or information about the claim, subsequent communications by the attorney to the client should be privileged. Some of the advice given by the attorney may be based on information obtained from sources other than the client. Some of what the attorney says will not actually be advice as to a course of conduct to be followed. Part may be analysis of what is known to date of the situation. Part may be a discussion of additional avenues to be pursued. Part may be keeping the client advised of things done or opinions formed to date. All of these communications, not just the advice, are essential elements of attorney-client consultation. All should be protected.[210]

But the court also distinguishes information that is not protected by the attorney-client privilege and, thus, is discoverable:

> This does not mean that discoverable factual information can be made privileged by being recited by the attorney or the client in their confidential communications. Only the actual attorney-client communications are privileged. . . . If [the investigative report documents

prepared by investigators who were hired by the attorney or client] had been attached to or discussed in the letters from Risjord to relators [client], the fact that the attorney's letters would be privileged would not cause the GAB reports or the FBI letter to become protected by the attorney-client privilege.[211]

B. Are Former Employees Clients or Third Parties?

One question left open in *Upjohn* is whether communications with a corporation's former employees are protected by the attorney-client privilege.[212] Because this issue had not been addressed in the courts below, the *Upjohn* Court declined to opine on it.[213]

But in *In re Coordinated Pretrial Proceedings*,[214] the Ninth Circuit applied the *Upjohn* rule in the context of former employees. The trial court disqualified defense counsel from representing present employees (other than corporate executives) and former employees in discovery depositions[215] because the court wanted to allow the plaintiffs to inquire fully into the communications made at "orientation" sessions between the witnesses and defense counsel.[216] On appeal, the court applied the principles of *Upjohn*, which had been decided after the trial court ruled, and concluded that the trial court's ruling would have been different.[217] The court concluded that the *Upjohn* rationale applied with equal force to former employees:

> Although *Upjohn* was specifically limited to current employees, the same rationale applies to the ex-employees (and current employees) involved in this case. Former employees, as well as current employees, may possess the relevant information needed by corporate counsel to advise the client with respect to actual or potential difficulties. Again, the attorney-client privilege is served by the certainty that conversations between the attorney and client will remain privileged after the employee leaves.[218]

Other federal and state courts have reached the same conclusion.[219] Furthermore, the Fourth Circuit noted, in *In re Allen*,[220] that courts that have declined to apply the attorney-client privilege to communications between the client's attorney and former employees have done so because they were following state law or because the former employee was not an employee when the relevant conduct occurred.[221]

Waiver, however, does not occur when an attorney shares privileged materials with a consultant hired by the client, as *In re Bieter* illustrates.[222] There, a land developer hired an independent contractor, Klohs, to provide advice and guidance as to commercial and retail development in Minnesota.[223] The consultant worked with the architects, consultants, and the developer's counsel, and also appeared at public hearings about the proposed development on behalf of the developer.[224] After a lawsuit was filed by the developer against a Minnesota city, the consultant attended meetings with the developer and its attorney.[225] In an affidavit filed in the trial court, the developer's attorney indicated that he viewed the consultant as one of the developer's representatives.[226] After the trial court allowed discovery of the communications with the consultant, the developer sought a writ of mandamus overturning the trial court's ruling.[227]

The court of appeals reversed the trial court, holding that communications with the consultant were privileged.[228] The court first relied on Supreme Court Standard 503(b),[229] even though the proposed rule was never made a part of the Federal Rules of Evidence by Congress, because it states the federal common law applicable to RICO actions.[230] Finding no cases directly on point, the court next relied on a post-*Upjohn* law review article[231] that set forth five principles to guide courts in deciding these issues.[232] The court found that third principle—the "information-giver must be an employee, agent, or independent contractor with a significant relationship to the corporation and the corporation's involvement in the transaction that is the subject of legal services"—applied directly to the facts before it[233] and chose to adopt it in reversing the trial court's decision.[234]

C. What Must Be Disclosed?

Even if attorney-client privileged communications contain discoverable factual information, it does not necessarily mean that communications containing those facts "are fair game in discovery."[235] Some courts hold that the written communications do not have to be produced, but rather the client must, in either depositions or interrogatory responses, disclose the discoverable factual information.[236] Other courts require the written communication to be produced with the exception of any redacted portions relating to legal advice.[237]

If the Court's admonition in *Upjohn* that the protection of the attorney-client privilege applies only to communications and not facts is correct, then the obvious answer is that the communication should never be produced, but the party must always provide requested information in response to interrogatories or in depositions. The *Upjohn* Court clearly stated that the witnesses interviewed by counsel could be deposed and had to answer questions; what the government could not obtain were the questionnaires those witnesses filled out. In *Samaritan*, for example, the hospital should have disclosed all of the *facts* the nurses knew in response to well-crafted interrogatories, even when the nurses could not recall those facts in their depositions.

VI. Additional Attorney-Client Privilege Issues

A. Who Is the Client?

In some cases, an attorney may actually have two clients, even though only one client is or will be named as a party in litigation. An attorney representing both the insurer and the insured in a subrogation suit and an attorney representing a liability insurer and the insured in a casualty defense matter are just two examples.[238] The attorney-client privilege should apply whether or not the person asserting the privilege is named as a party. In *United Coal Cos. v. Powell Construction Co.*,[239] for example, the court held that communications between United Coal's property insurance carrier and an attorney it retained to file a subrogation action on its behalf but in the name of the insured, which also retained the attorney to recover its uninsured loss, were privileged.[240]

Other courts, however, have taken a more restrictive view. In *Sterling Drilling Co. v. Spector*,[241] the court found that an attorney hired by an insured's insurer to defend the insured in subsequent litigation represented only the insurer. *Sterling Drilling* involved the death of a worker in an industrial accident. The employer's insurer hired an attorney to conduct an investigation into the insured's punitive damages exposure and to provide legal advice regarding those damages.[242] While the *Sterling* court implicitly found that the insurer shared an attorney-client privilege with the investigating attorney, the court refused to extend this protection to the employer because there was "no evidence that [the investigating attorney] had any real contact with [the employer] concerning the conduct of the investigation including the taking of the statements."[243]

B. When Is the Client a Client?

The attorney-client privilege also applies to communications between an attorney and a prospective client.[244] The privilege will be inapplicable, however, where there is no clear prospective attorney-client relationship[245] as the case *Poluch v. American Fan Co.*[246] illustrates. There, Poluch was injured at work, and his employer's workers' compensation carrier retained Creative Services, an investigative agency, to determine the nature and extent of Poluch's injuries and the potential financial exposure of the workers' compensation carrier.[247] Poluch hired her own attorney to pursue legal action against the manufacturer of the equipment allegedly responsible for Poluch's injury. After Creative Services completed its investigation, but before Poluch initiated a products liability action against the manufacturer, Poluch's attorney was also retained by the workers' compensation carrier to represent its subrogated interest. The workers' compensation carrier then turned over the entire workers' compensation file to Poluch's attorney.[248]

In discovery, the manufacturer requested production of the entire workers' compensation file. Poluch turned over certain portions of the file but withheld the investigation report. Poluch's counsel argued that the workers' compensation carrier was always in some sense "a de facto client."[249] Poluch's attorney argued that the prospect of subrogation was a matter always considered by the insurer, and, therefore, the information obtained by the carrier's investigator was protected by the attorney-client privilege or the work-product doctrine.[250] The court disagreed, holding that no attorney-client relationship existed between Poluch's attorney and the workers' compensation carrier at the time of the investigation, and, therefore, the attorney-client privilege did not apply.[251]

The court also found that the work-product doctrine did not apply because of the lack of an attorney-client relationship at the time of the investigation.[252]

Three recent cases have analyzed the attorney-client privilege as it applies to situations involving prospective clients. In a case involving a dispute surrounding a tax strategy, *Diversified Group, Inc. v. Daugerdas*,[253] the U.S. District Court for the Southern District of New York held that communications predating the attorney engagement agreement were not privileged because there was no indication that the client intended to obtain legal advice from the communication. In fact, the court stated that there was "strong proof" that the client sought business, not legal, advice from the attorney.[254] Although the communications here did not fall within the purview of a prospective attorney-client relationship, the court noted that "[c]ommunications with an attorney that predate formal retention may be privileged 'if the party divulging [the] confidences and secrets to [the] attorney believes that he is approaching the attorney in a professional capacity with the intent to secure legal advice.'"[255]

The court in *Auscape International v. National Geographic Society*[256] focused on letters sent to prospective class action participants. There, the court held that the letters were not privileged, even if the sending of the letters was intended to further the interests of existing clients, because they constituted a form of "direct mail advertising."[257] The court analogized the letters to radio commercials advising potential plaintiffs that they may have a claim for asbestos exposure.[258] Advertising by direct mail should not be considered privileged while advertising by radio is not privileged, the court reasoned. Application of the privilege in this context, the court said, "would take the attorney-client privilege to a galaxy far, far away from its roots and one that it is unnecessary to visit."[259]

By contrast, the court in *Barton v. U.S. District Court for the Central District of California*[260] determined that a law firm's Internet questionnaires regarding an antidepressant drug *were* protected by the attorney-client privilege, even if those filling out the questionnaires were not ultimately retained by the law firm. In *Barton*, the law firm for the plaintiffs in a class action suit maintained what it called an "initial contact" questionnaire for those affected by the antidepressant Paxil.[261] The questionnaire asked for extensive information about the use of the drug and its symptoms, but later required the person filling out the form to acknowledge—by checking a "yes" box—that the questionnaire did not "constitute a request for legal advice," and did not form an attorney-client relationship.[262]

The manufacturer sought disclosure of the four named plaintiffs' questionnaires, arguing that the disclaimer waived any potential privilege.[263] The district court agreed, concluding that, due to the plaintiffs' having checked the "yes" box, the communications were not "confidential."[264] It therefore ordered the communications to be produced.[265]

The Ninth Circuit, granting the plaintiffs' writ of mandamus, vacated the district court's order.[266] Applying California law, the court noted that the attorney-client privilege extends beyond the relationship between a client and a retained attorney:

> Prospective clients' communications with a view to obtaining legal services are plainly covered by the attorney-client privilege under California law, regardless of whether they have retained the lawyer, and regardless of whether they ever retain the lawyer. . . . "[T]he fiduciary relationship existing between lawyer and client extends to preliminary consultation by a prospective client with a view to retention of the lawyer, although actual employment does not result."[267]

C. Has the Privilege Been Waived?

The attorney-client privilege is, of course, waived when the communications have been revealed to third parties.[268] Courts have developed a limited exception to this rule where the parties have a common legal interest.[269] This exception has come to be known as the "joint defense" or "common interest" privilege, and can apply to both cooperating plaintiffs and cooperating witnesses.[270] Generally, to establish the existence of this privilege, the party asserting the privilege must show that (1) the communications were made in the course of a joint litigation effort, (2) the statements were designed to further the effort, and (3) the privilege has not otherwise been waived.[271] Courts analyze several factors when determining whether parties qualify for the joint-defense or common-interest privilege, such as the method of payment, allocation of decision-making roles, requests for advice, presence at meetings, and frequency and content of correspondence.[272]

In *Broessel v. Triad Guaranty Insurance Corp.*,[273] the U.S. District Court for the Western District of Kentucky identified three different situations where the common-interest or joint-defense privilege applies. First, the court noted that privilege can extend to a single attorney representing multiple clients in the same matter.[274] Second, the privilege may apply to multiple parties with separate counsel if these parties share a common defense.[275] Third, the court noted, the common interest is deemed sufficient to preclude waiver "when two or more clients share a common legal *or commercial interest* and, therefore, share legal advice with respect to that common interest."[276] In the third of these situations, even "communications made years before" litigation may still be deemed privileged under certain circumstances.[277] For example, because the parties in *Broessel* had created a trade organization and were involved in legislative and regulatory matters, they were deemed to have a "common legal interest" and certain communications between them were therefore privileged.[278]

In cases involving an attorney's investigation, the attorney-client privilege can be waived when the substance of the attorney's investigation has been placed "at issue"—as a defense or claim—in litigation. Under the at-issue doctrine, a party may be deemed to have waived the privilege where:

> (1) assertion of the privilege was a result of some affirmative act, such as filing suit, by the asserting party; (2) through this affirmative act, the asserting party put the protected information at issue by making

> it relevant to the case; and (3) application of the privilege would have denied the opposing party access to information vital to his defense.[279]

Courts have narrowly construed the at-issue waiver, limiting it to situations where the party puts the contents of an attorney-client communication at issue by asserting a claim or defense it intends to prove through disclosure of that communication.[280] For example, in *Harding v. Dana Transport, Inc.*,[281] the defendant hired outside counsel to perform an investigation after two employees filed an administrative complaint for sexual harassment. In defense of the administrative action, Dana asserted that it had "fully investigated" plaintiffs' complaint and "found that there is no supporting evidence" that the acts complained of occurred.[282] In a later Title VII proceeding in federal court, the defendant sought to introduce evidence of the investigation as a defense to the plaintiffs' claim, because proof of "sufficiently effective" procedures for investigating and remediating alleged discrimination is a valid defense.[283] At the same time, however, Dana resisted attempts by plaintiffs' counsel to inquire into the substance of the investigation by invoking the attorney-client privilege.[284] The court found that the defendant had waived the privilege by raising the investigation as a defense to the plaintiffs' Title VII and New Jersey state claims.[285] The court's rationale, in part, was that "[w]ithout such information, the plaintiffs cannot determine the seriousness of Dana's investigation into the plaintiffs' allegations of sexual harassment."[286] Because "the investigation, itself, provides a defense to liability," plaintiffs must be permitted to probe the substance of the investigation, not merely the fact that it occurred.[287] Other jurisdictions faced with similar situations have adopted the *Harding* rationale.[288]

Similarly, the New Mexico Court of Appeals, in *Gingrich v. Sandia Corp.*,[289] found that defendant waived the privilege that would have protected disclosure of an investigative report by (1) disclosing it to persons outside the scope of the attorney-client privilege, and (2) directly relying on it in an effort to defeat plaintiff's claims.[290] The court upheld the trial court's ruling, and also upheld the trial court's decision that waiver constituted a subject-matter waiver requiring the production of all communications in the subject.[291]

The Connecticut Supreme Court, in *Metropolitan Life Insurance Co. v. Aetna Casualty & Surety Co.*,[292] established limits on the at-issue doctrine. In *Metropolitan Life*, the insured, who sued the excess liability insurer to recover the cost of settling asbestos tort cases after the insurer refused to defend the insured, sought to prevent disclosure of documents containing communications with other attorneys regarding the settlement of the tort cases.[293] The court held that the documents were protected by the attorney-client privilege. Although the insured's senior officials had relied on counsel's advice to settle the asbestos tort actions, the insured was not relying on those privileged communications to prove the reasonableness of the settlements.[294] The court stated the following:

> Merely because the communications are relevant does not place them at issue. . . . If admitting that one relied on legal advice in making a

> decision put the communications relating to the advice at issue, such advice would be at issue whenever the legal decision was litigated. If that were true, the at issue doctrine would severely erode the attorney-client privilege and undermine the public policy considerations upon which it is based.[295]

VII. Work-Product Issues

Even if attorney-client communications from attorney to client reflecting factual information or information received from nonclients are not protected by the attorney-client privilege, the work-product doctrine may preclude discovery in some cases. Work-product issues arise frequently in litigation involving insurance investigations.[296]

The work-product doctrine was first recognized by the U.S. Supreme Court in *Hickman v. Taylor*.[297] In *Hickman*, the Court addressed the discoverability of statements taken by a lawyer representing a tugboat company. The statements had been taken from several witnesses to a tugboat accident that killed five crew members and were recorded in memoranda prepared by the attorney.[298] The Court held that the attorney-client privilege was inapplicable, but it also held that the memoranda were not discoverable based on an immunity for materials prepared by attorneys in anticipation of litigation.[299] The Court indicated that the statements might be discoverable upon a sufficient showing of need, but that it would be nearly impossible to discover information containing the attorney's mental impressions.[300]

The *Hickman* decision was essentially codified in a 1970 amendment to Rule 26 of the Federal Rules of Civil Procedure.[301] Rule 26(b)(3) of the Federal Rules of Civil Procedure protects from disclosure documents and materials otherwise discoverable that were prepared in anticipation of litigation or for trial by or for another party or by or for the other party's representative, including an attorney, consultant, insurer, or agent, except upon a showing that the party seeking discovery has substantial need for the materials in the preparation of its case and is unable, without undue hardship, to obtain the substantial equivalent of the materials by other means.[302] Rule 26(b)(3), however, provides virtually absolute protection to work-product materials that contain the mental impressions, conclusions, opinions, or legal theories of an attorney or other representative of a party concerning the litigation.[303] The reasoning behind the nearly unconditional protection of opinion work product was described by the Fourth Circuit, in *Chaudhry v. Gallerizzo*:[304]

> "[C]ourts should proceed cautiously when requested to adopt a rule that would have an inhibitive effect on an attorney's freedom to express and record his mental impressions and opinions without fear of having these impressions and opinions used against the client." As a result, "opinion work product enjoys a nearly absolute

> immunity and can be discovered only in very rare and extraordinary circumstances."[305]

Most states have similar, if not identical, rules providing strong protection to work-product materials.[306]

Assuming the documents are relevant, courts generally use a two-step analysis to determine whether the work-product doctrine provides protection to the disclosure of the documents: Were they compiled in anticipation of litigation or trial, and if so, has the party seeking discovery shown substantial need and undue hardship?[307]

A. In Anticipation of Litigation

The first step in the analysis—whether the document was prepared "in anticipation of litigation"—is the one most often addressed by the courts. This issue arises most often because the line between documents prepared in the ordinary course of business and those prepared in anticipation of litigation is not always clear. Generally, courts ask not whether litigation was a certainty but rather whether the document was prepared "with an eye toward litigation."[308]

Courts have taken differing views as to the meaning of the phrase "in anticipation of litigation." For example, the Fifth Circuit requires that a document be prepared "primarily to assist in litigation" for work-product protection to apply. In *United States v. Davis*,[309] the Fifth Circuit held that documents prepared in conjunction with a tax return were not protected by the work-product doctrine. In so holding, the court held that work-product protection applies to a document only if the "primary motivating purpose behind the creation of the document was to aid in possible future litigation."[310] Thus, under the Fifth Circuit's standard, a document is protected by the work-product doctrine only if the party invoking the doctrine establishes that the document was created *primarily* to assist in possible future litigation; if the document was created primarily to aid in a business decision and secondarily to aid in future litigation, the document is not protected by the work-product doctrine.

Indeed, the U.S. District Court for the District of Maryland appears to have taken an even stricter stance on work product. In *Neuberger Berman Real Estate Income Fund, Inc. v. Lola Brown Trust No. 1B*,[311] the court remarked, "The fact that defendant anticipated litigation with plaintiffs does not make all documents thereafter 'generated by or for its attorneys subject to work product immunity.'"[312] Instead, the court held, a party claiming such immunity must establish an underlying "nexus" between the preparation of the document and the *specific* litigation.[313] If a party cannot establish such a nexus, the court held, the privilege "generally does not apply."[314]

More recently, the Sixth Circuit Court of Appeals, in *In re Professionals Direct Insurance Co.*,[315] held that the work-product protection applied to documents prepared in anticipation of litigation even if the document also serves an ordinary business purpose.[316] The party claiming that a document is protected must show that the anticipated litigation was the "driving force" behind the preparation of the document.[317]

Notwithstanding the restrictive language of *Davis* and *Neuberger*, the more common standard for defining "in anticipation of litigation" is set out in the Second Circuit's decision in *United States v. Adlman*.[318] There, an aerospace manufacturer considered merging with its subsidiaries. The merger was designed to produce a loss and corresponding tax refund; therefore, the manufacturer expected an IRS challenge that would result in litigation. Litigation with the IRS did ensue, and the IRS moved to compel production of a legal memorandum prepared by the manufacturer's accountant/lawyer.[319]

The *Adlman* court framed the issue as follows: "[W]hether Rule 26(b)(3) is inapplicable to a litigation analysis prepared by a party or its representative in order to inform a business decision which turns on the party's assessment of the likely outcome of litigation expected to result from the transaction."[320] Use of the "primary motivating purpose" test that was endorsed by the Fifth Circuit would not protect the present document, the court reasoned, because the document's primary purpose was to "inform a business decision," not to aid in possible future litigation.[321] This scenario forced the court to undertake a critical analysis of the "primary motivating purpose" test, since, in the *Adlman* court's opinion, use of the "primary motivating purpose" test would impede business transactions and access to information needed to make sound decisions. Furthermore, the use of the "primary motivating purpose" test in these circumstances would offend the very purpose of the work-product doctrine and leave no "zone of privacy" for companies to obtain an assessment of how litigation may affect their business decisions.[322]

Based on the foregoing analysis, the *Adlman* court adopted a "because of" standard—a document prepared "because of" anticipated litigation will be protected by the work-product doctrine:

> A document created because of anticipated litigation, which tends to reveal mental impressions, conclusions, opinions, or theories concerning the litigation, does not lose work-product protection merely because it is intended to assist in the making of a business decision influenced by the likely outcome of the anticipated litigation. Where a document was created because of anticipated litigation, and would not have been prepared in substantially similar form but for the prospect of litigation, it falls within Rule 26(b)(3).[323]

In *Jumpsport, Inc. v. Jumpking, Inc.*,[324] the U.S. District Court for the Northern District of California promulgated a third standard for determining whether a document is prepared "in anticipation of litigation." There, the court concluded that deciding whether a document was prepared in anticipation of litigation requires a two-prong test. The first prong considers "whether the party trying to invoke work product protection has shown that the prospect of litigation was a substantial factor in the mix of considerations, purposes, or forces that led to the preparation of the document."[325] If this prong is satisfied, the court must ask a second question: whether denying protection to the document would harm the policy objectives underlying the work-product doctrine (or, conversely, whether granting work-product protection would advance the policy objectives surrounding the work-product doctrine).[326] A document is granted protection only if it meets both requirements, which the document at issue in *Jumpsport*—a draft report prepared by an accounting and consulting firm that contained a description of the U.S. economy and the sporting goods market, a company overview, a valuation of invested capital and intellectual property, and a valuation synthesis and conclusion—did not.[327]

No matter which test the court employs, the "in anticipation of litigation" requirement does not include documents prepared merely to avoid litigation. As the court in *In re Grand Jury Proceedings* stated, "[T]o find that 'avoidance of litigation' without more constitutes 'in anticipation of litigation' would 'represent an insurmountable barrier to normal discovery' and could subsume all compliance activities by a company as protected from discovery."[328] Because of the divergent views as to what constitutes "in anticipation of litigation," courts have looked at whether an attorney's investigation was conducted in the ordinary course of business or whether it was conducted in anticipation of litigation on a case-by-case basis. For example, in *Ryall v. Appleton Electric Co.*,[329] the court found that notes of interviews by the client's chief employment counsel in a sexual harassment investigation commenced in response to contact by an employee's attorney, which indicated that litigation was imminent, were protected by the work-product doctrine.[330] Similarly, in *Arkwright Mutual Insurance Co. v. National Union Fire Insurance Co.*,[331] the court determined that a subrogation investigation undertaken by counsel for a property insurer was not within the normal business activities of the insurer and was therefore protected by the work-product doctrine.[332] In contrast, the court in *In re Leslie Fay Cos., Inc. Securities Litigation*[333] held that the work-product doctrine did not protect documents relating to an attorney's investigation of a client's publicly alleged accounting irregularities.[334] The investigation was conducted primarily for business purposes because the client used the investigation results to make decisions on firing responsible personnel; to implement a new financial structure, organization, and internal control systems; and to reassure creditors and lenders that the culpable parties and suspect internal policies "were being vigorously sought and rooted out."[335] Finally, in *City of Springfield v. Rexnord Corp.*, the court held that documents that might have been prepared in anticipation of possible litigation with the Massachusetts Department of Environmental Quality Engineering were not protected by the work-product doctrine, since they were prepared primarily for media inquiries and represented the corporation's public statements.[336]

B. Substantial Need

The final step in the analysis is determining whether materials and documents prepared in anticipation of litigation may still be discoverable because the requesting party can establish that it has a substantial need for the materials and is unable, without undue hardship, to obtain the substantial equivalent of the materials by other means.[337] Courts generally find such a need where a witness, for example, is unavailable or hostile, or has difficulty recalling information previously given to an attorney.[338] Some courts also find such a need when bad-faith allegations are made.[339] While factual materials may be discovered upon a showing of "substantial need," the attorney's mental impressions, conclusions, opinions, or legal theories are not discoverable.[340]

C. Witness Statements

The most frequently litigated issue is whether statements from nonclients are afforded protection by the work-product doctrine. Some courts hold that the statements are not protected at all, some hold the statements are "core" work product,[341] while others resolve the issue under the substantial need concept. The following cases are representative of the means by which courts resolve this issue.

A recent California Court of Appeal case, *Coito v. Superior Court*,[342] falls into the first category. There, the 13-year-old son of plaintiff drowned in a river in Modesto.[343] The possibly criminal conduct of several other juveniles present at the site led the California Bureau of Investigation to take recorded statements from four of them.[344] After plaintiff sued the state and the City of Modesto, the state used its interviews as a basis for questioning one of the juveniles in depositions.[345] Plaintiff then requested all the statements, and the state refused, claiming the statements were protected by the attorney-client privilege and were also attorney work product.[346] The trial court upheld the state's position as to all of the statements except the one the state used to question the deponent.[347]

On appeal, the court of appeal looked at the codification of the work-product privilege[348] and prior decisions by the California courts[349] in ultimately concluding that the statements were not protected.[350] The court summarily rejected the trial court's reliance on *Nacht & Lewis Architects, Inc. v. Superior Court*[351] and rejected the state's argument that the questions asked of the witnesses revealed the mental impressions of the attorney.[352] The dissenting judge agreed with the majority that the witness statements were not "absolute work product" under California law,[353] but contended that they may be "qualified work product."[354] The dissenter would have remanded the case to the trial court for a determination of the qualified work product issue.[355]

Soter v. Cowles Publishing Co.[356] is representative of the cases that protect witness statements taken by lawyers as core work product. There, a nine-year-old student with a peanut allergy ultimately died after ingesting a peanut-butter cookie on a school field trip.[357] The school district, through its insurance carrier,[358] undertook an investigation of the circumstances surrounding the death and, when sued by the child's parents, resolved the case through mediation.[359] Thereafter, a reporter for a Seattle newspaper filed a request for the school district's investigation files under Washington's Public Records Act.[360] The school district produced all the records except for 75 documents it claimed were protected from disclosure.[361] The trial court agreed with the district, as did the court of appeals.[362]

The Washington Supreme Court thoroughly analyzed the issue and affirmed the appellate court.[363] The court concluded that counsel's notes of interviews with school district employees were protected by the attorney-client privilege.[364] Notes of interviews with parent chaperones and other students constituted attorney opinion work product, and were protected from disclosure on that basis.[365] The court stated: " [A]ll of the notes taken by attorneys or other members of a legal team when interviewing witnesses constitute opinion work product that will be revealed only in rare circumstances, for example, where the attorney's mental impressions are at issue or where there are issues of attorney crime or fraud."[366]

Bickler v. Senior Lifestyle Corp.[367] is representative of those cases that look at the issue of substantial need in determining whether witness statements are discoverable. There, plaintiff was injured in a collision with another resident and sued the care facility for negligence.[368] Shortly after the incident, the care facility conducted an investigation at the direction of in-house counsel.[369] Eighteen employees were interviewed as a part of the investigation, and each provided a written statement.[370] After litigation was commenced, plaintiff sought production of the statements.[371] The court concluded that the statements were not protected by the attorney-client privilege[372] and went on to consider whether they constituted work product.[373] The court determined that the documents were not routine business documents, but were, in fact, documents created in anticipation of litigation.[374] The court next considered plaintiff's claim of substantial need and concluded that one statement should be produced because the witness, when deposed, had some loss of memory.[375] The court concluded that plaintiff had failed to prove substantial need for the remaining statements.[376]

A recent decision in a criminal case highlights how the work-product doctrine is applied to attorney investigations.[377] The United States brought an action against baseball great Roger Clemens for various crimes arising out of his testimony before Congress during its investigation of steroid use in professional baseball.[378] The Commissioner of Baseball retained former senator George Mitchell to investigate the steroid use claims for him, and provide him with recommendations.[379] Mitchell in turn retained DLA Piper as his counsel.[380] During the course of its work, DLA Piper interviewed many witnesses, and thereafter prepared detailed memoranda of the interviews.[381] Clemens subpoenaed DLA Piper, seeking production of three of DLA Piper's notes of interviews taken in connection with the preparation of the Mitchell Report.[382] DLA Piper moved to quash the subpoena, arguing that the requested information was opinion work product protected from disclosure to Clemens.[383] The court held a hearing during which the involved DLA Piper attorneys testified, and the court also reviewed the disputed documents in camera.[384]

The court first acknowledged that the rules set forth by the Supreme Court in *Hickman v. Taylor*[385] applied in criminal cases as well as in civil cases.[386] DLA Piper urged the court to quash the subpoena, arguing that the interview summaries were opinion work product afforded almost complete protection from discovery.[387] The court focused on the nature of the interview summaries to determine whether they were opinion work product or fact work product.[388] After reviewing the documents themselves, the court heard testimony from the DLA Piper attorneys that conducted the interviews to learn more about the preparation of the summaries to help it determine whether they were fact or opinion work product.[389] After reviewing the documents themselves, as well as the testimony of DLA Piper attorneys, the court concluded that the documents were fact work product, and, for the most part, discoverable.[390]

This case is interesting for two reasons. First, the court noted that the work-product doctrine applies to materials prepared for litigation,[391] but chose to apply it in this context where the interviews were done simply to provide legal advice to the Commissioner of Baseball outside the context of any litigation. Second, and perhaps more important, the court cited to and discussed *Upjohn Co. v. United States*,[392] but never discussed or applied that portion of the *Upjohn* decision that the attorney-client privilege protected the investigation done by the Upjohn attorneys.[393] The question that remained undecided in *Upjohn* was whether the attorney-client privilege applied to the interviews of ex-employees.[394] To the extent the interviews in *Clemens* were conducted for the purpose of providing legal advice to the Commissioner of Baseball, it is at least arguable that the summaries were not discoverable because they were protected by the attorney-client privilege.

D. Summary

In sum, an attorney cannot ensure that the results of an investigation will be protected by the work-product doctrine. An attorney, however, can take steps to help establish that investigation materials were prepared in anticipation of litigation. For example, an attorney can, upon receiving a request to evaluate and investigate on behalf of a client, send a confirming letter to the client, noting that the attorney is investigating and evaluating the matter in anticipation of litigation and specifying the precise claims the attorney "anticipates." An attorney can make sure not to perform a task that the client would perform as a regular part of its business if it had not hired the attorney, especially if the client is an insurance company. A lawyer can also make sure that any related claims are considered to protect the work product of all of those involved. A lawyer should determine the law applicable to statements from nonclients before deciding whether to take them and how to record them. Finally, while the work-product doctrine may shield *documents* from discovery, most courts hold that an opposing party can, by interrogatories or by deposition, discover factual information learned during an investigation.[395]

VIII. Conclusion

The attorney who conducts a factual investigation for the purpose of providing legal advice to a client should be able to communicate those facts to the client within the purview of the attorney-client privilege. This is clearly the majority rule, but it has not garnered a universal following. An attorney undertaking an investigation for a corporation may not be able to speak with employees at every level within the company under the cloak of the privilege, although the majority rule protects communications by corporate employees with knowledge no matter what position they hold in the company. The better-reasoned rule protects communications with third parties, at least where such facts were necessary to the rendering of the requested legal advice. Again, this rule is not universally followed. Even in those jurisdictions that may not recognize a privilege as to third-party facts, absent extraordinary circumstances, the work-product doctrine often shields the communications from discovery.

Attorney-Client Privilege Practice Pointers

Who Is the "Attorney"?

- Attorneys acting in the capacity of attorneys are allowed to claim privilege. *See* Spectrum Sys. Int'l Corp. v. Chem. Bank, 581 N.E.2d 1055 (N.Y. 1991) (attorneys retained to conduct investigation in order to render legal advice); Leucadia, Inc. v. Reliance Ins. Co., 101 F.R.D. 674 (S.D.N.Y. 1983) (same).
- Attorneys acting in other capacities, however, are not allowed to claim privilege. *See* St. Paul Reinsurance Co. v. Commercial Fin. Corp., 197 F.R.D. 620 (N.D. Iowa 2000) (attorney retained to conduct investigation of loss); Mission Nat'l Ins. Co. v. Lilly, 112 F.R.D. 160 (D. Minn. 1986) (same).
- Employees and subordinates of attorneys are included in the privilege. *See* NXIVM Corp. v. O'Hara, 241 F.R.D. 109, 138 (N.D.N.Y. 2007); Broessel v. Triad Guar. Ins. Corp., 238 F.R.D. 215, 218–19 (W.D. Ky. 2006).

Who Is the "Client"?

Corporations

- In federal courts, as well as most state courts, some form of the "subject matter" test is used, in which attorney-client privilege applies to employees of corporations if (1) the employee makes the communications at the direction of the employee's superior; and (2) the subject matter upon which the attorney's advice is sought by the corporation and dealt with in the communication is the performance by the employee of the duties of his or her employment. *See* Upjohn Co. v. United States, 449 U.S. 383 (1981); Lexington Pub. Library v. Clark, 90 S.W.3d 53, 59 (Ky. 2002); Wardleigh v. Dist. Court, 891 P.2d 1180 (Nev. 1995).
- In some jurisdictions, the "control group" test applies, in which only communications with those who actually control the corporation or normally advise those in control are privileged. Consolidation Coal Co. v. Bucyrus-Erie Co., 432 N.E.2d 250 (Ill. 1982).
- In Arizona, the courts have adopted the "functional approach" in civil cases, which focuses on the relationship between the communicator and the need for legal services. Samaritan Found. v. Goodfarb, 862 P.2d 870 (Ariz. 1993).

Insurers

- In many cases where the insured was hired to represent both the insured and the insurer, the attorney-client privilege generally extends to communications between the attorney and both clients. *See, e.g.*, Port Auth. of N.Y. v. Arcadian Corp., Civ. No. 96-1635, 1996 U.S. Dist. LEXIS 22038 (D.N.J. Sept. 30, 1996) (holding that an attorney who represents an insurer in a subrogation action also owes a fiduciary duty to the insured); Doctors' Co. Ins. Servs. v. Superior Court, 275 Cal. Rptr. 674, 680–81 (Cal. Ct. App. 1990) (holding that an attorney employed by an insurance company to defend an action against an insured represents both the insurer and the insured).

- In some jurisdictions, however, the attorney-client privilege extends only to communications between the attorney and the insured, even when the insurer hires the attorney. *See* Sterling Drilling Co. v. Spector, 761 S.W.2d 74 (Tex. App. 1988).

Prospective Clients

- In general, communications with prospective clients are privileged if such communications are made for the purpose of obtaining legal advice. This remains true even if the attorney is not ultimately retained. *See* Bennett Silvershein Assoc. v. Furman, 776 F. Supp. 800 (S.D.N.Y. 1991).
- If the communications are not made for the purposes of obtaining legal advice, the communications are not privileged. Diversified Group, Inc. v. Daugerdas, 304 F. Supp. 2d 507 (S.D.N.Y. 2003).
- Mass mailings to potential clients are also not considered privileged. Auscape Int'l v. Nat'l Geographic Soc'y, No. 02 Civ. 6441 (LAK), 2002 WL 31250727 (S.D.N.Y. Oct. 8, 2002).

Joint-Defense Agreements

- Parties with a common interest may maintain the attorney-client privilege under certain circumstances if the parties are cooperating in litigation. *See, e.g.*, Loustalet v. Refco, Inc., 154 F.R.D. 243, 247 (C.D. Cal. 1993); United States v. Evans, 113 F.3d 1457, 1467 (7th Cir. 1997) (quoting United States v. Schwimmer, 892 F.2d 237, 243–44 (2d Cir. 1989)).

What Information Is Protected?

Communications involving Information from Nonclients

- Under Professor Wigmore's approach, the attorney-client privilege does not apply if the legal advice to the client is based on information obtained from third parties. United States v. United Shoe Mach. Corp., 89 F. Supp. 357 (D. Mass. 1950); Merrin Jewelry Co. v. St. Paul Fire & Marine Ins. Co., 49 F.R.D. 54 (S.D.N.Y. 1970).
- Other courts have been less restrictive on the privilege, holding that though the *underlying facts* communicated from third parties may not be privileged, the actual communications between the attorney and client *are* privileged. State *ex rel.* Great Am. Ins. Co. v. Smith, 574 S.W.2d 379 (Mo. 1978), *overruling on later appeal*, 563 S.W.2d 62 (Mo. 1978). *See also* Soter v. Cowles Publ'g Co., 174 P.2d 60 (Wash. 2007), *aff'g* 130 P.3d. 840 (Wash. App. 2006).

Does the Work-Product Doctrine Apply?

State or Federal Court

- The Federal Rules of Civil Procedure apply to all cases filed in federal courts, and Rule 26 determines the extent of the work-product protection afforded documents prepared in anticipation of litigation. Hickman v. Taylor, 329 U.S. 495 (1947).
- State court rules can vary from those applied in the federal courts. *See, e.g.*, Coito v. Superior Court, 106 Cal. Rptr. 3d 342 (Cal. Ct. App. 2010), *review granted and opinion superseded*, 232 P.3d 97 (Cal. 2010).
- One of the most frequently litigated issue involving work-product claims are statements taken from third-party witnesses. Before such statements are taken, a careful review of the applicable state or federal decisions should be undertaken to maximize the protection to be given to such statements.

Notes

1. Samaritan Found. v. Goodfarb, 862 P.2d 870 (Ariz. 1993); Hyams v. Evanston Hosp., 587 N.E.2d 1127 (Ill. App. Ct. 1992).
2. Sandra T.E. v. S. Berwyn Sch. Dist. 100, 600 F.3d 612 (7th Cir. 2010).
3. Harding v. Dana Transp. Inc., 914 F. Supp. 1084 (D.N.J. 1996).
4. Nat'l Tank Co. v. Brotherton, 851 S.W.2d 193 (Tex. 1993).
5. United States v. Ruehle, 583 F.3d 600 (9th Cir. 2009).
6. Dunn v. State Farm Fire & Cas. Co., 927 F.2d 869 (5th Cir. 1991); Burr v. United Farm Bureau Mut. Ins. Co., 560 N.E.2d 1250 (Ind. Ct. App. 1990); State *ex rel.* U.S. Fid. & Guar. Co. v. Canady, 460 S.E.2d 677 (W. Va. 1995).
7. Gucci Am. Inc. v. Guess?, Inc., 271 F.R.D. 58 (S.D.N.Y. 2010).
8. Spectrum Sys. Int'l Corp. v. Chem. Bank, 581 N.E.2d 1055 (N.Y. 1991).
9. Upjohn Co. v. United States, 449 U.S. 383 (1981).
10. Gingrich v. Sancia Corp., 165 P.2d 1135 (N.M. Ct. App. 2007).
11. SR Int'l Bus. Ins. Co. v. World Trade Ctr. Props. LLC, No. 01 Civ. 9291 (JSM), 2002 U.S. Dist. LEXIS 11949 (S.D.N.Y. July 3, 2002).
12. *See In re* Allen, 106 F.3d 582, 602 (4th Cir. 1997) (noting that "[c]ourts have consistently recognized that investigation may be an important part of an attorney's legal services to a client").
13. *See infra* section III.
14. *Upjohn*, 449 U.S. at 389; *see also* 8 James H. Wigmore, Evidence in Trials at Common Law § 2290, at 542 (John T. McNaughton rev. ed. 1961 & Supp. 1996).
15. *Upjohn*, 449 U.S. at 389.
16. For example, Ohio courts have recognized a "bad faith" exception to the general rule. *See* Garg v. State Auto. Mut. Ins. Co., 800 N.E.2d 757, 761 (Ohio Ct. App. 2003) (holding that the attorney-client privilege did not protect materials in a claims file created prior to the denial of the claim that would provide insight into whether the insurer acted in bad faith in handling the insured's claims); Boone v. Vanliner Ins. Co., 744 N.E.2d 154, 158 (Ohio 2001) (holding that "in an action alleging bad faith denial of insurance coverage, the insured is entitled to discover claims file materials containing attorney-client communications related to the issue of coverage that were created prior to the denial of coverage"); Moskovitz v. Mt. Sinai Med. Ctr., 635 N.E.2d 331, 349 (Ohio 1994) ("[D]ocuments and other things showing the lack of a good faith effort to settle by a party or the attorneys acting on his or her behalf are wholly unworthy of the protections afforded by any claimed privilege.").

    A similar exception to the general rule, the "crime fraud" exception, applies if the client communicates with its attorney to obtain advice or assistance while committing what the client knows is a crime or fraud. *E.g.*, Nationwide Mut. Ins. Co. v. Fleming, 924 A.2d 1259, 1265 (Pa. Super. Ct. 2007); *In re* Gen. Agents Ins. Co. of Am., Inc., 224 S.W.3d 806, 818–19 (Tex. Ct. App. 2007); Ginsburg v. Pachter, 893 So. 2d 586, 588 (Fla. Dist. Ct. App. 2004).
17. PSE Consulting, Inc. v. Frank Mercede & Sons, Inc., 838 A.2d 135, 167 (Conn. 2004) (internal quotation marks and citing references omitted); *see, e.g.*, *In re* EchoStar Commc'ns Corp., 448 F.3d 1294, 1300–01 (Fed. Cir. 2006); Chaudhry v. Gallerizzo, 174 F.3d 394, 402 (4th Cir. 1999); *In re* Lindsey, 158 F.3d 1263, 1267 (D.C. Cir. 1998); United States v. Chen, 99 F.3d 1495, 1501 (9th Cir. 1996); United States v. Textron Inc., 507 F. Supp. 2d 138, 146 (D.R.I. 2007); Evans v. United

Servs. Auto. Ass'n, 541 S.E.2d 782, 790 (N.C. Ct. App. 2001); *In re* Ford Motor Co., 988 S.W.2d 714, 718 (Tex. 1998). *See also* WIGMORE, *supra* note 14, § 2320, at 628 ("That the *attorney's communications to* the client are also within the privilege was always assumed in the earlier cases, and has seldom been brought into question.") (footnotes omitted.) *But see* Nationwide Mut. Ins. Co. v. Fleming, 924 A.2d 1259, 1264 (Pa. Super. Ct. 2007), *aff'd by an equally divided court*, 992 A.2d 65 (Pa. 2010) (holding that "the privilege protects confidential communications from an attorney to his or her client only to the extent that such communications contain and would thus reveal confidential communications from the client"); *see also* Harrisburg Auth. v. CIT Capital USA, Inc., 716 F. Supp. 2d 380, n.11 (M.D. Pa. 2010) (noting that the supreme court's decision in *Nationwide* did not decide whether the attorney-client privilege applies to communications from attorneys to clients).

18. *See, e.g., In re* Grand Jury Subpoena, 204 F.3d 516, 519–20 (4th Cir. 2000); Hicks v. Bush, 452 F. Supp. 2d 88, 100 (D.D.C. 2006).
19. WIGMORE, *supra* note 14, § 2292, at 554.
20. United States v. United Shoe Mach. Corp., 89 F. Supp. 357, 358–59 (D. Mass. 1950). *See, e.g.*, Cavallaro v. United States, 284 F.3d 236, 245 (1st Cir. 2002); United States v. Martin, 278 F.3d 998, 999 (9th Cir. 2002); United States v. Int'l Bhd. of Teamsters, 119 F.3d 210, 214 (2d Cir. 1997); *In re* Miller, 584 S.E.2d 772, 786 (N.C. 1994); People v. Simms, 736 N.E.2d 1092, 1117 (Ill. 2000).
21. *See generally* KENNETH S. BROUN, MCCORMICK ON EVIDENCE §§ 87–97 (6th ed. 2006); WIGMORE, *supra* note 14, §§ 2290–2329. *See, e.g.*, Allied Irish Banks v. Bank of Am., N.A., 240 F.R.D. 96, 103 (S.D.N.Y. 2007); Evans v. Atwood, 177 F.R.D. 1, 3 (D.D.C. 1997); Schenet v. Anderson, 678 F. Supp. 1280, 1281 (E.D. Mich. 1988); Potts v. Allis-Chalmers Corp., 118 F.R.D. 597, 602 (N.D. Ind. 1987); Henson v. Wyeth Lab., Inc. 118 F.R.D. 584, 587 (W.D. Va. 1987).
22. Upjohn Co. v. United States, 449 U.S. 383, 395–96 (1981). Quoting from Philadelphia v. Westinghouse Elec. Corp., 205 F. Supp. 830, 831 (E.D. Pa. 1962), the Court stated:

    > [The] protection of the privilege extends only to *communications* and not facts. A fact is one thing and a communication concerning that fact is an entirely different thing. The client cannot be compelled to answer the question, "What did you say or write to the attorney?" but may not refuse to disclose any relevant fact within his knowledge merely because he incorporated a statement of such fact into his communication to his attorney.

    Id. (emphasis added by *Upjohn* Court); *see also* Resolution Trust Corp. v. Dabney, 73 F.3d 262, 266 (10th Cir. 1995); Dunkin' Donuts Inc. v. Mary's Donuts, Inc., 206 F.R.D. 518, 520–21 (S.D. Fla. 2002); Onwuka v. Fed. Express Corp., 178 F.R.D. 508, 515 (D. Minn. 1997); Phillips Elecs. N. Am. Corp. v. Universal Elecs. Inc., 892 F. Supp. 108, 110 (D. Del. 1995); Swarthmore Radiation Oncology, Inc. v. Lapes, 155 F.R.D. 90, 92 (E.D. Pa. 1994). *See generally* Wigmore, *supra* note 14, §§ 2306–2311.
23. *See, e.g.*, Kan. Wastewater, Inc. v. Alliant Techsystems, Inc., 217 F.R.D. 525, 528–29 (D. Kan. 2003).
24. *See, e.g.*, Sneider v. Kimberly-Clark Corp., 91 F.R.D. 1, 4 (N.D. Ill. 1980); *In re* Ampicillin Antitrust Litig., 81 F.R.D. 377, 385 n.9 (D.D.C. 1978).
25. *See infra* notes 296–376 and accompanying text.

26. *See* NXIVM Corp. v. O'Hara, 241 F.R.D. 109, 138 (N.D.N.Y. 2007); Broessel v. Triad Guar. Ins. Corp., 238 F.R.D. 215, 218–19 (W.D. Ky. 2006). *But see* Reed Dairy Farm v. Consumers Power Co., 576 N.W.2d 709 (Mich. Ct. App. 1998) (holding that the attorney-client privilege did not attach to attorney's paralegal, because, even though an employee of the attorney, he was not acting as an agent of the attorney, and the information sought was not the type that the attorney-client privilege was designed to protect).
27. Sanchez v. Matta, 229 F.R.D. 649, 660 (D.N.M. 2004); Clark v. City of Munster, 115 F.R.D. 609, 613 (N.D. Ind. 1987); Am. Nat'l Watermattress Corp. v. Manville, 642 P.2d 1330, 1333–34 (Alaska 1982). It makes no difference whether the investigator is an employee of the attorney or is hired by the attorney to conduct the investigation.
28. *See supra* note 14 and accompanying text.
29. *See* Westinghouse Elec. Corp. v. Kerr-McGee Corp., 580 F.2d 1311, 1319–20 (7th Cir. 1978), *cert. denied*, 439 U.S. 955 (1978); Henson v. Wyeth Lab., Inc., 118 F.R.D. 584, 587 (W.D. Va. 1987); Heathcoat v. Santa Fe Int'l Corp., 532 F. Supp. 961, 964 (E.D. Ark. 1982); *see also* United States *ex rel.* Fago v. M & T Mortgage Corp., 238 F.R.D. 3, 10–11 (D.D.C. 2006) (holding that communications with counsel concerning legal advice were protected by attorney-client privilege, but communications made by and to the same lawyer with respect to business matters were not protected by privilege).
30. *See, e.g.*, *Westinghouse*, 580 F.2d at 1320; NXIVM Corp. v. O'Hara, 241 F.R.D. 109, 130 (N.D.N.Y. 2007) (holding that communication with lawyer who was "coordinating media, public relations, lobbying, and other non-legal services" were not privileged); *see also* Smithkline Beecham Corp. v. Apotex Corp., 194 F.R.D. 624 (N.D. Ill. 2000) (holding that attorney-authored meeting agendas were not protected by the attorney-client privilege in patent infringement suit, since it was unlikely that legal advice was involved); *Henson*, 118 F.R.D. at 587. *See generally* WIGMORE, *supra* note 14, §§ 2296–2299.
31. *See, e.g.*, St. Paul Reinsurance Co. v. Commercial Fin. Corp., 197 F.R.D. 620, 641–42 (N.D. Iowa 2000); Goodyear Tire & Rubber Co. v. Chiles Power Supply, Inc., 190 F.R.D. 532, 535 (S.D. Ind. 1999) (noting that there is no bright-line rule for courts deciding whether an attorney is acting in his or her capacity as such).
32. 24 C. WRIGHT & K. GRAHAM, FEDERAL PRACTICE AND PROCEDURE § 5478, at 229 (1986 & Supp 2009).
33. *See id* at n.178.

    The senior author does not fully agree with the statement in the text. He agrees with the distinction adopted by the cases cited at notes 174 [Diamond v. City of Mobile, 86 F.R.D. 324, 328 (N.D. Ala. 1978)] and 175 [*In re* LTV Securities Litigation, 89 F.R.D. 595, 600-01 (N.D. Tex. 1981)] above, that there is no privilege if the lawyer is purely an investigator but that investigative work is "professional legal services" if it is incidental to the rendering of legal advice.

34. 96 F.3d 1294, 1296 n.1 (9th Cir. 1996). *See also* State *ex rel.* Toledo Blade Co. v. Toledo-Lucas Cnty. Port Auth., 905 N.E.2d 1221 (Ohio 2009) (specifically rejecting Wright and Graham's approach).
35. RESTATEMENT (THIRD) OF THE LAW GOVERNING LAWYERS § 69 (1998 & Supp. 2010).
36. *Id.* at cmt. i, illus. 7.

37. 581 N.E.2d 1055 (N.Y. 1991).
38. *Id.* at 1058.
39. *Id.*
40. *Id.*
41. *Id.* at 1059.
42. Spectrum Sys. Int'l Corp. v. Chem. Bank, 558 N.Y.S.2d 486 (N.Y. App. Div. 1990), *modified*, 581 N.E.2d 1055 (N.Y. 1991).
43. *Id.* at 488.
44. *Spectrum Sys.*, 581 N.E.2d at 1059.
45. *Id.* at 1059, 1062.
46. *Id.* at 1060–61 (citations omitted).
47. *Id.*
48. *Id.* at 1061–62.
49. 600 F.3d 612 (7th Cir. 2010).
50. The teacher ultimately confessed to the crimes he was charged with and received a sentence of 20 years. *Id.* at 615.
51. *Id.* at 616 ("The School Board wanted Sidley to review the criminal charges filed against [teacher], investigate the actions of school administrators in response to the allegations of sexual abuse, examine whether any district employees had failed to comply with district policies or federal or state law, and analyze the effectiveness of the District's existing compliance procedures.").
52. *Id.*
53. *Id.*
54. *Id.*
55. *Id.*
56. *Id.*
57. *Id.*
58. *Id.*
59. *Id.* at 616–17.
60. *Id.*
61. *Id.*
62. *Id.*
63. *Id.*
64. *Id.* at 618–21.
65. *Id.* at 620; *see also* Gingrich v. Sandia Corp., 165 P.2d 1135, 1139 (N.M. Ct. App. 2007).
66. 101 F.R.D. 674 (S.D.N.Y. 1983).
67. *Id.* at 676–77.
68. *Id.* at 678; *see also* State v. von Bulow, 475 A.2d 995, 1005 (R.I. 1984) (finding that an attorney hired to investigate the circumstances surrounding Martha von Bulow's comatose condition was acting as an attorney during his investigation).
69. 460 S.E.2d 677 (W. Va. 1995).
70. 927 F.2d 869 (5th Cir. 1991). *Accord* Hawes v. Langston, 853 So. 2d 1237, 1244 (Miss. 2003) ("the privilege relates to and covers *all information* regarding the client received by the attorney in his professional capacity and in the course of his representation of the client).
71. *Id.* at 875 ("The privilege is not waived if the attorneys perform investigative tasks provided that these investigative tasks are related to the rendition of legal services."); *Canady*, 460 S.E.2d at 689–90, 692. Because of the absence of crucial factual findings, however, the *Canady* court remanded the issue to the

trial court for further consideration in light of the court's opinion. The *Canady* court also refused, however, to "adopt a *per se* rule making ordinary investigative employees, who hold licenses to practice law, attorneys for purposes of the attorney-client privilege." *Id.* at 690. In the insurance industry context, such a decision "would shield from discovery documents that otherwise would not be entitled to any protection if written by an employee who holds no law license but who performs the same investigation and duties." *Id.*

72. 544 A.2d 893 (N.J. Super. Ct. App. Div. 1988).
73. *Id.* at 895.
74. No. 06-1523, 2009 WL 854446 (E.D. La. Mar. 25, 2009).
75. *Id.* at *1–2, *4.
76. 130 F.R.D. 28 (S.D.N.Y. 1990).
77. *Id.* at 31–32.
78. 106 F.3d 582, 602–03 (4th Cir. 1997).
79. 259 S.W.2d 104 (Mo. Ct. App. 2008).
80. *Id.* at 111.
81. *Id.* at 111–12, 122.
82. *Id.* at 122.
83. *Id.*
84. *Id.*
85. *See, e.g.*, Griffith v. Davis, 161 F.R.D. 687, 697 (C.D. Cal. 1995) ("defendant . . . cannot prevent disclosure of an administrative investigation by having its litigation counsel (or an agent of its litigation counsel) conduct that investigation").
86. St. Paul Reinsurance Co., Ltd. v. Commercial Fin. Corp., 197 F.R.D. 620, 642 (N.D. Iowa 2000) (holding that communications to attorney acting as a claims investigator were not protected by attorney-client privilege); Bertalo's Rest. Inc. v. Exch. Ins. Co., 658 N.Y.S.2d 656, 659 (N.Y. App. Div. 1997). California has recognized the importance of files created in the investigation of a claim filed by an insured by promulgating regulations that require insurance companies to investigate every filed claim and maintain claims files containing all documents, notes, and work papers relevant to each claim. *See* 2,002 Ranch, L.L.C. v. Superior Court, No. D042323, 2003 Cal. App. LEXIS 1804, at *37–38 (Cal. Ct. App. Dec. 5, 2003) (citing Cal. Code Regs. tit. 10, § 2695.5, subdiv. (e)(3) & § 2695.3, subdivs. (a) & (b)). *2,002 Ranch* noted, however, that the entirety of the claims file is not discoverable—attorney-client protected communications are exempt from discovery. *See id.* at *39.
87. 112 F.R.D. 160 (D. Minn. 1986).
88. *Id.* at 162.
89. *Id.* at 162–63.
90. *Id.* at 163. The court also relied on the fact that Mission retained other counsel to handle the lawsuit that Lilly filed. *Id.*
91. 197 F.R.D. 620 (N.D. Iowa 2000).
92. *Id.* at 623.
93. *Id.*
94. *Id.* at 624.
95. *Id.* at 626.
96. *Id.*
97. *Id.* at 637.
98. *Id.* at 641.

99. *Id.* at 638.
100. 718 P.2d 1044 (Colo. 1986). *Accord* Compton v. Safeway, Inc., 169 P.3d 135 (Colo. 2007). *But see* Bonnano v. Quizno's Franchise Co. LLC, No. 06-cv-02358-WYD-KLM, 2008 WL 1801173, at *3 (D. Colo. Apr. 18, 2008) (finding investigating attorney was acting in legal capacity and results of investigation therefore protected).
101. *Id.* at 1046.
102. There is no indication that the key factor here was that the investigative work was performed by outside counsel and not in-house counsel.
103. 718 P.2d at 1046, 1048.
104. *Id.* at 1049.
105. *Id.*
106. *Id.*
107. *Id.* at 1050 (Rovira, J., dissenting).
108. *Id.*
109. *Id.*
110. *National Farmers Union* has been criticized by commentators. *See* Kenneth A. Hindman & Paul W. Burke, *A Frightening Discovery*, Brief, Spring 1988, at 18. Notwithstanding this criticism, *National Farmers Union* remains good law in Colorado. *See* Markwest Hydrocarbon, Inc. v. Liberty Mut. Ins. Co., No. 05-cv-1948, 2007 WL 1106105 (D. Colo. Apr 12, 2007).
111. No. 01 Civ. 9291 (JSM), 2002 U.S. Dist. LEXIS 11949 (S.D.N.Y. July 3, 2002).
112. *Id.* at *2.
113. *Id.*
114. *Id.* at *1.
115. *Id.* at *2–3.
116. *Id.* at *13.
117. *Id.* at *12.
118. *Id.*
119. 210 F. Supp. 483 (E.D. Pa. 1962), *mandamus denied sub nom.* Gen. Elec. Co. v. Kirkpatrick, 312 F.2d 742 (3d Cir. 1962), *cert. denied*, 372 U.S. 943 (1963).
120. *Id.* at 485.
121. *Id. See generally In re* Grand Jury Investigation, 599 F.2d 1224 (3d Cir. 1979) (adopting control group approach).
122. *See, e.g.*, Natta v. Hogan, 392 F.2d 686 (10th Cir. 1968).
123. Diversified Indus., Inc. v. Meredith, 572 F.2d 596 (8th Cir. 1977) (en banc); Harper & Row Publishers, Inc. v. Decker, 423 F.2d 487 (7th Cir. 1970), *aff'd per curiam without opinion by an equally divided Court*, 400 U.S. 348 (1971). In *Harper & Row*, the court held that employee communications are privileged when (1) the employee makes the communications at the direction of the employee's superior and (2) the subject matter upon which the attorney's advice is sought by the corporation and dealt with in the communication is the performance by the employee of the duties of his or her employment. *Harper & Row*, 423 F.2d at 491–92. *Meredith* expanded the second *Harper & Row* factor and added three additional factors:

    (1) The communication was made for the purpose of securing legal advice; (2) the employee making the communication did so at the direction of his corporate superior; (3) the superior made the request so the corporation

> could secure legal advice; (4) the subject matter of the communication is within the scope of the employee's corporate duties; and (5) the communication is not disseminated beyond those persons who, because of the corporate structure, need to know its contents.

Meredith, 572 F.2d at 609.

124. 449 U.S. 383 (1981).
125. *Id.* at 386.
126. *Id.* at 387.
127. *Id.*
128. *Id.* Upjohn simultaneously sent the report to the SEC and to the IRS.
129. United States v. Upjohn Co., 600 F.2d 1223 (6th Cir. 1979), *rev'd*, 449 U.S. 383 (1981).
130. *Upjohn*, 449 U.S. at 390–91. Because the Court viewed investigative activities as a necessary predicate to the rendering of legal advice, the Court determined that the activities of Thomas and outside counsel were done in the capacity of lawyers:

> The communications at issue were made by Upjohn employees to counsel for Upjohn acting as such, at the direction of corporate superiors in order to secure legal advice from counsel. As the magistrate found, "Mr. Thomas consulted with the Chairman of the Board and outside counsel and thereafter conducted a factual investigation to determine the nature and extent of the questionable payments and to be in a position to give legal advice to the company with respect to the payments." . . . Information, not available from upper-echelon management, was needed to supply a basis for legal advice concerning compliance with securities and tax laws, foreign laws, currency regulations, duties to shareholders, and potential litigation in each of these areas.

Id. at 394.

131. *Id.* at 392.
132. *Id.* at 391–92. The Court quoted in part from *Diversified Indus., Inc. v. Meredith*, 572 F.2d 596 (8th Cir. 1978), which highlighted the scope of the "Hobson's choice" inherent in adopting the subject-matter test.
133. *Upjohn*, 449 U.S. at 397.
134. Some courts have applied *Upjohn* to cases interpreting ethical rules barring ex parte contact with represented parties when the party is an organization, of which a detailed discussion is outside the scope of this chapter. *See* Palmer v. Pioneer Inn Assocs., Ltd., 59 P.3d 1237 (Nev. 2002) (the no-contact rule restricts contact with only those employees whose actions are legally binding on the organization); *see also* Snider v. Superior Court, 7 Cal. Rptr. 3d 119 (Cal. Ct. App. 2003) (citing *Upjohn* and *Palmer* in support of its rejection of the control group test for determining whether a witness was a party under the no-contact rule). *But see* Capital Cities/ABC, Inc., 52 Fair Empl. Prac. Cas. (BNA) 1842 (S.D.N.Y. 1990) (holding that the *Upjohn* decision should not be extended to ex parte contact cases).
135. FED. R. EVID. 501 ("[I]n civil actions and proceedings, with respect to an element of a claim or defense as to which State law supplies the rule of decision, the privilege of a witness, person, government, State, or political subdivision

thereof shall be determined in accordance with State law."); *see, e.g.*, Samaritan Found. v. Goodfarb, 862 P.2d 870, 873–76 (Ariz. 1993); Consolidation Coal Co. v. Bucyrus-Erie Co., 432 N.E.2d 250, 254–57 (Ill. 1982).

136. Under the Federal Rules of Evidence, *Upjohn* will govern in any case in federal court where there is federal question jurisdiction, but state law will control in those federal cases where there is diversity jurisdiction. *See* FED. R. EVID. 501; *see, e.g.*, Nakajima v. Gen. Motors Corp., 857 F. Supp. 100, 104 (D.D.C. 1994); Barrett Indus. Trucks, Inc. v. Old Republic Ins. Co., 129 F.R.D. 515, 516–17 (N.D. Ill. 1990); Command Transp., Inc. v. Y.S. Line (USA) Corp., 116 F.R.D. 94, 95, 97 n.10 (D. Mass. 1987).
137. *See, e.g.*, Lexington Pub. Library v. Clark, 90 S.W.3d 53, 59 (Ky. 2002); Wardleigh v. Dist. Court, 891 P.2d 1180 (Nev. 1995).
138. 632 So. 2d 1377 (Fla. 1994).
139. *Id.* at 1379–80, 1384–89. The court identified a number of different kinds of information claimed to be privileged, including audits, interviews between security personnel and employees, notes of interviews of employees by counsel, and statistical analyses. *Id.*
140. *Id.* at 1381–82.
141. *Id.* at 1381. The court explained:

> Although upper-echelon management may be responsible for making decisions on behalf of the corporation, the noncontrol-group employees are frequently the ones responsible for implementing those decisions. Thus, an attorney representing the corporation is charged with gathering facts from employees with information relevant to the corporation's legal problems, regardless of their rank.

Id.

142. *Id.* at 1382.
143. *Id.* at 1383. Under the *Southern Bell* test, a corporation's communications with counsel are protected by the attorney-client privilege if (1) the communication would not have been made but for the contemplation of legal services; (2) the employee making the communication was directed to do so by his or her corporate superior; (3) the superior made the request of the employee as part of the corporation's efforts to secure legal services or advice; (4) the content of the communication relates to the legal services being rendered to the corporation, and the subject matter is within the scope of the employee's duties at the corporation, and (5) the communication is not disseminated beyond those persons, who, because of the corporation's structure, need to know its contents. *Id.*; *see also* Tyne v. Time Warner Ent. Co., 212 F.R.D. 596 (M.D. Fla. 2002) (noting that Florida has rejected the control group test in favor of the subject matter test).
144. 423 F.2d 487 (7th Cir. 1970), *aff'd per curiam without opinion by an equally divided Court*, 400 U.S. 348 (1971).
145. 572 F.2d 596 (8th Cir. 1977). The *Harper & Row/Meredith* subject matter test can be found *supra* at note 123.
146. 632 So. 2d at 1384–89.
147. 432 N.E.2d 250 (Ill. 1982).
148. *Id.* at 256–57. There, Bucyrus-Erie's counsel conducted an investigation into the failure of equipment manufactured by Bucyrus-Erie that damaged Consolida-

tion's coal mine. *Id.* at 251. At issue were Bucyrus-Erie's attorney's notes and a metallurgical report of a Bucyrus-Erie employee. *Id.* The notes in question were made by in-house counsel of interviews with numerous Bucyrus-Erie employees. *Id.* The report was described as a notebook containing objective information, mathematical computations, formulae, tables, charts, drawings, photographs, industry specifications, and handwritten notes. *Id.* at 254. The trial court rejected Bucyrus-Erie's objections to discovery of these documents, and the court of appeals essentially affirmed the trial court's decision. *Id.* at 253–54. *See also* Equity Residential v. Kendall Risk Mgmt., Inc., 246 F.R.D. 557 (N.D. Ill. 2007) (noting Illinois's continuing application of control-group test, but choosing to apply Connecticut law to attorney-client communications that occurred in Connecticut).

149. *Id.* at 257. The court defined a member of the control group as one "whose advisory role to top management in a particular area is such that a decision would not normally be made without his advice or opinion, and whose opinion in fact forms the basis of any final decision by those with actual authority." *Id.* at 258. If the individual merely supplies information to those on whom top management relies, that individual is not within the control group. *Id.* Because Sailors was not in the control group, his report was not protected. *Id.*

150. Golminas v. Fred Teitelbaum Constr. Co., 251 N.E.2d 314 (Ill. App. Ct. 1969). The court stated the following:

> [T]he principle underlying the attorney-client privilege would demand that an employee's communications should be privileged when the employee of the defendant corporation is also a defendant or is a person who may be charged with liability and makes statements regarding facts with which he or his employer may be charged, which statements are given or delivered to the attorney who represents either or both of them.

Id. at 318.

151. 851 S.W.2d 193 (Tex. 1993).

152. At the time, the applicable Texas rule provided privilege to representatives of the client "having authority to obtain professional legal services, or to act on advice rendered pursuant thereto, on behalf of the client." *Nat'l Tank*, 851 S.W.2d at 197 (citing Tex. R. Civ. Evid. 503(a)(2)).

153. *Nat'l Tank*, 851 S.W.2d at 197.

154. *Id.* at 199.

155. *See In re* Monsanto Co., 998 S.W.2d 917 (Tex. Ct. App. 1999).

156. *Id.* at 922.

157. 862 P.2d 870 (Ariz. 1993).

158. *Id.* at 873.

159. *Id.*

160. *Id.* The trial court ordered in camera inspection of the documents, and all protected information would be redacted before the summaries—the "functional equivalent of a witness statement"—were turned over to plaintiffs. *See* Samaritan Found. v. Superior Court, 844 P.2d 593, 596 (Ariz. Ct. App. 1992), *vacated in part*, 862 P.2d 870 (Ariz. 1993).

161. *Samaritan*, 844 P.2d at 605. The traditional control group test was modified by the court in these respects: (1) management must direct a corporate employee to communicate in confidence with the corporation's legal staff about mat-

ters within the scope of the employment; (2) no requirement of "anticipation of litigation" applies; (3) the qualified privilege can be overcome in the same way as the work-product doctrine—proof of substantial need and the inability to obtain the substantial equivalent by other means; and (4) the party seeking discovery must show that its substantial need outweighs the corporation's interest in maintaining confidentiality. *Id.* at 605–06.

162. *Id.* at 607.
163. The court noted that a qualified privilege "is an uncertain privilege, and an uncertain privilege is tantamount to no privilege at all." *Id.* at 879.
164. *Id.*
165. *Id.*
166. *Id.* In a recent decision, the Arizona Supreme Court determined that the attorney-client privilege for such communications also extends to government entities. State *ex rel.* Thomas v. Schneider, 130 P.3d 991, 995 (Ariz. 2006).
167. *Samaritan*, 862 P.2d at 880.
168. *Id.* at 880–81. The court commented on one other fact that appears to have had some impact on the court's decision. At the time of the interviews, each of the witnesses signed a form consenting to representation by Samaritan if a claim was filed against her. *Samaritan*, 844 P.2d at 596. The supreme court viewed this as an "acknowledgment that the corporation was not satisfied that the employee statements were within the corporation's privilege. . . . [I]t is difficult to see what these forms intended to accomplish other than to silence the employees by shielding their communications in the cloak of the attorney-client privilege." *Samaritan*, 862 P.2d at 880–81.

    In a case of first impression, the Iowa Supreme Court was called upon to decide the scope of the attorney-client privilege in the corporate context. Keefe v. Bernard, 774 N.W.2d 663 (Iowa 2009). The court, rejecting the control-group test, chose to adopt the standard set forth in *Samaritan*. *Id.* at 672.
169. ARIZ. REV. STAT. ANN. § 12-2234 (2006). For a review of the legislative history and a commentary on the statute generally, see W. Todd Coleman, Note, *Arizona's Attorney-Client Communications Privilege for Corporations*, 27 ARIZ. ST. L.J. 335 (1995). The author concludes that the legislative history suggests that the statute was intended to be a codification of *Upjohn*. *See id.* at 351–53.
170. ARIZ. REV. STAT. ANN. § 12-2234(B) (2006). The statute applies to an employee of a "corporation, governmental entity, partnership, business, association or other similar entity or an employer." *Id.*
171. *Id.* § 12-2234(B.1), (B.2).
172. *Id.* § 12-2234(C).
173. 62 P.3d 970 (Ariz. Ct. App. 2003).
174. *Id.* at 972.
175. *Id.* at 971.
176. *Id.*
177. *Id.* at 975.
178. WIGMORE, *supra* note 14, § 2320, at 628. Professor Wigmore states: "That the *attorney's communications* to the client are also within the privilege was always assumed in the earlier cases and has seldom been brought into question." *Id.* The supporting footnote cites to one early case, *United States v. United Shoe Mach. Corp.*, 89 F. Supp. 357 (D. Mass. 1950), for the proposition that legal advice based on information from third parties is not privileged.

179. The rule would not protect communications in virtually every area of litigation, for it is truly the rare case that does not involve facts obtained from non-client third parties.
180. *See, e.g.*, Dombrowski v. Bell Atl. Corp., 128 F. Supp. 2d 216, 219 (E.D. Pa. 2000); Standard Chartered Bank PLC v. Ayala Int'l Holdings (U.S.) Inc., 111 F.R.D. 76, 80 (S.D.N.Y. 1986); *see also* Kenford Co. v. Cnty. of Erie, 390 N.Y.S.2d 715, 719 (N.Y. App. Div. 1977) ("[I]n this respect, the attorney serves as a fact-gathering agent for the client.").
181. 89 F. Supp. 357 (D. Mass. 1950).
182. Defendant produced these documents to the government in response to a subpoena subject to agreement from the government that all privilege objections would be preserved and were not waived. *Id.* at 359. This fact was not raised by the court as a factor in its decision. *Id.*
183. *Id.* It is not clear who within the company communicated with outside counsel, but this fact is unimportant to the result ultimately reached.
184. *Id.*
185. *Id.*
186. 49 F.R.D. 54 (S.D.N.Y. 1970).
187. *Id.* at 57. The court held that because the policy allowed the examination under oath to be conducted by "any person" designated by the insurer, the fact that the insurer chose an attorney should not allow the insurer to protect the attorney's report. *Id.* After in camera review, the court commented: "The [in camera] study discloses that the report consists almost *in toto* of an analysis of the sworn testimony such as 'any person' (lawyer or not) might have made. The facts are summarized; credibility is appraised; inferences are proposed—all tasks we entrust daily to lay jurors." *Id.* This kind of information would likely be protected from discovery by Federal Rule of Civil Procedure 26(b)(3) as the "mental impressions, conclusions, [or] opinions" of an attorney or other representative of a party. *See infra* notes 301–302 and accompanying text.
188. 65 F.R.D. 523 (S.D.N.Y. 1974).
189. *Id.* at 526.
190. 130 F.R.D. 28 (S.D.N.Y. 1990).
191. *Id.* at 33. The magistrate judge reviewed the attorney's letter in camera and "found them to be communicating factual information, not legal advice." *Id.* The Magistrate Judge ordered the letter to be produced, with the exception of redacted portions relating to legal advice. The district court upheld the Magistrate Judge's ruling. *Id.*
192. 848 F. Supp. 423 (S.D.N.Y. 1994).
193. *Id.* at 428.
194. *Id.*
195. 227 F.R.D. 382, 394–95 (W.D. Pa. 2005).
196. *Id.* at 394–95.
197. Bross v. Chevron U.S.A. Inc., No. 06-1523, 2009 WL 854446, at *6 (W.D. La. Mar. 25, 2009) ("Neither [proposed deponent] nor the other team members are attorneys, and statements made to them by witnesses, statements made by team members to witnesses or to each other, are not privileged.")
198. 574 S.W.2d 379 (Mo. 1978), *overruling on later appeal*, 563 S.W.2d 62 (Mo. 1978).
199. *Id.* at 380.
200. *Id.* at 380–81.

201. *Id.*
202. *Id.* at 382.
203. *Id.*
204. *Id.* at 382–83. The court found the Wigmore approach would protect only (1) advice from the lawyer concerning a communication from a client, (2) anything the lawyer said that could be an admission of the client, and (3) anything the lawyer said that would lead to an inference about what the client may have said to the lawyer. The court found this insufficient "to accomplish the objective for which the privilege was created and now exists." *Id.* at 384.
205. *Id.* at 383.
206. *Id.* at 384 (citing ALI Model Code of Evidence, Rule 209(d) (1942), which defines a "confidential communication between client and lawyer" as "information transmitted by a voluntary act of disclosure between a client and his lawyer in confidence"; this definition includes information transmitted voluntarily by any means).
207. *Id.* at 383. The court stated:

    > The nature and complexity of our present system of justice and the relationships among people and between the people and their government make the preservation and protection of the attorney-client privilege even more essential. If this is to be accomplished, when one undertakes to confer in confidence with an attorney whom he employs in connection with a particular matter at hand, it is vital that all of what the client says to the lawyer and what the lawyer says to the client to be treated as confidential and protected by the attorney-client privilege. This is what the client expects.

    Id.
208. *Id.* at 386.
209. *Id.* at 385.
210. *Id.* at 384–85 (footnotes omitted).
211. *Id.* at 385; *see also* Allied Irish Banks v. Bank of Am., N.A., 240 F.R.D. 96 (S.D.N.Y. 2007) (holding that attorney-client privilege did not apply to drafts of investigative report prepared by attorney for independent banking expert, memos of attorney's investigation interviews, and reports of attorney communications with plaintiff bank's board of directors, as there was no showing that the documents were primarily or predominantly of legal character); *In re* Bd. of Registration for the Healing Arts v. Spinden, 798 S.W.2d 472, 476 (Mo. Ct. App. 1990) (holding that investigative reports prepared by state medical board investigators acting at direction of board's general counsel were discoverable by doctor in administrative action). In *Rossi v. Blue Cross & Blue Shield of Greater New York*, 540 N.E.2d 703 (N.Y. 1989), in-house counsel wrote a memorandum to Blue Cross's medical director, describing the results of an investigation counsel had undertaken, including conversations with plaintiff's attorney, conversations with the Food and Drug Administration, an analysis of a Blue Cross reimbursement policy, and his opinion and advice regarding a form used to reject certain kinds of medical charges. *Id.* at 704. The court decided that the entire memorandum was protected by the attorney-client privilege, stating:

    > So long as the communication is primarily or predominately of a legal character, the privilege is not lost merely by reason of the fact that it also

> refers to certain non-legal matters. Indeed, the nature of a lawyer's role is such that legal advice may often include reference to other relevant considerations. Here, it is plain from the content and context of the communication that it was for the purpose of facilitating the lawyer's rendition of legal advice to his client.

Id. at 706 (citations omitted).

212. The *Upjohn* court noted that seven of the 86 employees interviewed by counsel had terminated their employment by the time they were interviewed. Upjohn Co. v. United States, 449 U.S. 383, 394 n.3 (1981).
213. In a concurring opinion, Chief Justice Burger suggested that the *Upjohn* rule should apply to communications otherwise falling within the framework of *Upjohn. See id.* at 402–03.
214. 658 F.2d 1355 (9th Cir. 1981), *cert. denied*, 455 U.S. 990 (1982).
215. *Id.* at 1356.
216. *Id.* at 1359.
217. *Id.* at 1361.
218. *Id.* at 1361 n.7 (citations omitted). This opinion remains as recognized authority in the Ninth Circuit. *See* United States v. Chen, 99 F.3d 1495, 1502 (9th Cir. 1996).
219. *See, e.g.*, Guillen v. City of Chicago, 956 F. Supp. 1416, 1425 (N.D. Ill. 1997); Command Transp., Inc. v. Y.S. Line (USA) Corp., 116 F.R.D. 94, 96–97 (D. Mass. 1987); Porter v. Arco Metals Co., 642 F. Supp. 1116, 1118 (D. Mont. 1986); Denver Post Corp. v. Univ. of Colo., 739 P.2d 874, 880 (Colo. Ct. App. 1987). *But see* Infosystems, Inc. v. Ceridian Corp., 197 F.R.D. 303, 305–06 (E.D. Mich. 2000) (holding that no privilege can attach to communications with former employees absent special circumstances). For cases reaching similar conclusions, but in different contexts, see *Peralta v. Cendant Corp.*, 190 F.R.D. 38 (D. Conn. 1999) (holding that the attorney-client privilege attaches to communications with former employees only if the communications relate to knowledge obtained during employment or the communications were held with the employee prior to termination and were privileged at that time); *Camden v. State*, 910 F. Supp. 1115 (D. Md. 1996); and *Fruehauf Trailer Corp. v. Hagelthorn*, 528 N.W.2d 778 (Mich. Ct. App. 1995).
220. 106 F.3d 582 (4th Cir. 1997).
221. *Id.* at 606 (citing Nakajima v. Gen. Motors Corp., 857 F. Supp. 100, 104 (D.D.C. 1994) (D.C. law); Barrett Indus. Trucks v. Old Republic Ins. Co., 129 F.R.D. 515, 517–18 (N.D. Ill. 1990) (Illinois law); Connolly Data Sys. v. Victor Techs., 114 F.R.D. 89, 93–94 (S.D. Cal. 1987) (California law)).
222. 16 F.3d 929 (8th Cir. 1994).
223. *Id.* at 934.
224. *Id.*
225. *Id.*
226. *Id.*
227. *Id.* at 930.
228. *Id.* at 941.
229. *Id.* at 935. Supreme Court Standard 503(b) provides as follows:

> A client has a privilege to refuse to disclose and to prevent any other person from disclosing confidential communications made for the purpose of facilitating the rendition of professional legal services to the client, (1)

> between himself or his representatives and his lawyer or his lawyer's representative, or (2) between his lawyer and his lawyer's representatives, or (3) by him or his lawyer to a lawyer representing another in a matter of common interest, or (4) between representatives of the client or between the client and a representative of the client, or (5) between lawyers representing the client.

3 Jack B. Weinstein & Margaret A. Berger, Weinstein's Federal Evidence § 503.01 (Joseph M. McLaughlin ed., 2d ed. 2010).

230. *See, e.g.*, United States v. Spector, 793 F.2d 932, 938 (8th Cir. 1986) (citation omitted), *cert. denied*, 479 U.S. 1031 (1987); United States v. (Under Seal), 748 F.2d 871, 874 n.5 (4th Cir. 1984) (Supreme Court Standard 503 "provides a comprehensive guide to the federal common law of attorney-client privilege").
231. John E. Sexton, *A Post-*Upjohn *Consideration of the Corporate Attorney-Client Privilege*, 57 N.Y.U. L. Rev. 443, 498 (1982).
232. 16 F.3d at 936.
233. *Id.* at 937.
234. *Id.* at 940. The court stated: "Klohs is, for purposes of the privilege, the functional equivalent of Bieter's employee, and the communications in question fell within the scope of his duties, were made at the behest of his superior, and were made for the purpose of seeking legal advice for Bieter." *Accord* United States v. Graf, 610 F.3d 1148 (9th Cir. 2010); Hope for Families & Cmty. Serv., Inc. v. Warren, No. 3:06-CV-1113-WKW, 2009 WL 1066525 (M.D. Ala. Apr. 21, 2009); Every Penny Counts, Inc. v. Am. Express Co., No. 8:07-cv-1255-T-26MAP, 2008 WL 2074407 (M.D. Fla. May 15, 2008); Am. Mfrs. Mut. Ins. Co. v. Payton Lane Nursing Home, Inc., No. CV 05-5155(SJF)(AKT), 2008 WL 5231831 (E.D.N.Y. Dec. 11, 2008); Davis v. City of Seattle, No. C06-1659Z, 2007 WL 4166154 (W.D. Wash. Nov. 20, 2007); Alliance Constr. Solutions Inc. v. Dep't of Corr., 54 P.3d 861 (Colo. 2002). *See also* Fed. Trade Comm'n v. GlaxoSmithKline, 294 F.3d 141, 147–48 (D.C. Cir. 2002); Elec. Workers Local No. 26 Pension Trust Fund v. Trust Fund Advisors, Inc., 266 F.R.D. 1 (D.D.C. 2010).
235. Documents in a party's counsel's files are within the scope of documents that must be produced in response to a discovery request directed to that party. Rule 34 of the Federal Rules of Civil Procedure, for example, requires parties to produce requested documents that are within their possession, custody, or control. *See* Fed. R. Civ. P. 34. "Control" is broadly construed to mean not only physical possession but the legal or practical right to obtain them from another source on demand. *See, e.g.*, Golden Trade v. Lee Apparel Co., 143 F.R.D. 514, 525 (S.D.N.Y. 1992); M.L.C., Inc. v. N. Am. Philips Corp., 109 F.R.D. 134, 136 (S.D.N.Y. 1986). Thus, "documents in the possession of a party's counsel are deemed within the control of the party, regardless of the origin of the documents." Arkwright Mut. Ins. Co. v. Nat'l Union Fire Ins. Co., No. 90 Civ. 7811, 1994 WL 510043, at *3 (S.D.N.Y. Sept. 16, 1994); *see also* Hanson v. Gartland S.S. Co., 34 F.R.D. 493, 496 (N.D. Ohio 1964).
236. *See, e.g.*, Arkwright Mut. Ins. Co. v. Nat'l Union Fire Ins. Co., No. 90 Civ. 7811, 1994 WL 510043 (S.D.N.Y. Sept. 16, 1994). In *Arkwright*, National Union sought production of documents in the possession of Arkwright's counsel in prior litigation and in possession of counsel hired by Arkwright to conduct a subrogation investigation. National Union argued that some of the claimed attorney-client privileged documents lost their privilege because they contain dis-

coverable factual information. The court rejected National Union's argument, noting "[t]hat principle simply means that Arkwright must, in either depositions or interrogatory responses, disclose relevant facts if National Union inquires, not that any privileged communications containing facts are fair game in discovery." *Id.* at *8. *See also* Bovis Lend Lease, LMB, Inc. v. Seasons Contracting Corp., 2002 WL 31729693, at *18 (S.D.N.Y. Dec. 5, 2002).

237. *See, e.g.*, Carte Blanche (Singapore) PTE, Ltd. v. Diners Club Int'l, Inc., 130 F.R.D. 28, 31 (S.D.N.Y. 1990) (information the court called "factual" obtained from third parties must be disclosed).

238. *See, e.g.*, Port Auth. of N.Y. v. Arcadian Corp., Civ. No. 96-1635, 1996 U.S. Dist. LEXIS 22038 (D.N.J. Sept. 30, 1996) (holding that an attorney who represents an insurer in a subrogation action also owes a fiduciary duty to the insured); Doctors' Co. Ins. Servs. v. Superior Court, 275 Cal. Rptr. 674, 680–81 (Cal. Ct. App. 1990) (holding that an attorney employed by an insurance company to defend an action against an insured represents both the insurer and the insured). *But see* Pine Island Farmers Coop. v. Erstad & Riemer, P.A., 649 N.W.2d 444 (Minn. 2002) (holding that defense counsel did not represent both the insured and the insurer in an action brought against the insured, because defense counsel did not consult with or obtain the express consent of the insured to engage in the dual representation).

239. 839 F.2d 958 (3d Cir. 1988).

240. *Id.* at 965. In this case, United Coal Cos. owned a coal mine and processing plant, and operated an aerial tramway to transport coal refuse from one of its processing facilities. *Id.* at 960. United sustained a loss when a haul rope broke, causing 62 cars on the aerial tramway to fall to the ground. United's property insurers paid United $1.5 million, thereby becoming subrogated to United's rights against the manufacturer and installer. *Id.* The subrogation receipts authorized the insurers to sue in United's name. The insurers retained attorneys to pursue subrogation. United also retained the same attorneys to recover its uninsured loss. The attorneys filed suit in United's name against the manufacturer and installer for the entire loss, including United's uninsured loss. *Id.* During the course of discovery, defendants filed discovery requests seeking the production of two letters from the attorneys to the property insurers. *Id.* at 961. United withheld these documents from production as privileged, and defendants moved to compel. *Id.* at 960–61. The trial court granted the motion to compel because the insurers were not named plaintiffs in the action. The reported colloquy between the court and counsel for the plaintiff is instructive:

> COUNSEL: Your Honor, I think the problem is the insurance companies are our clients. You know, if I could just have a moment to address this.
>
> THE COURT: Not according to the caption of the case.
>
> COUNSEL: They may not be named plaintiffs. They are our clients. We were retained by them. They have an interest in this action.
>
> THE COURT: If those documents are not in the hands of these defendants by Monday at noon, this case will be dismissed.
>
> *Id.* at 964.

On appeal, the Third Circuit, recognizing the true nature of a subrogation action, determined that the trial court had erred:

It is undisputed that the correspondence in issue is between attorneys and insurance companies which retained them to prosecute this action.

Where, as here, an attorney represents two clients, the privilege applies to those clients as against a common adversary. . . . Thus the district court committed legal error when it ruled that the non-party status of the insurers was dispositive on their claim of attorney client privilege. They were clients, and no more was required to support their assertion of the privilege.

Id. at 965.

241. 761 S.W.2d 74 (Tex. App. 1988).

242. *Id.* at 76.

243. *Id.* In many jurisdictions, communications made by an insured to his liability insurance company, concerning an event that may be made the basis of a claim against him covered by the policy, is a privileged attorney-client communication if the policy requires the liability insurer to defend the insured through its attorney and the communication is intended for the information or assistance of the attorney hired by the liability insurer to defend the insured. *See, e.g.*, State Farm Fire & Cas. Co. v. Superior Court, 254 Cal. Rptr. 543 (Cal. Ct. App. 1988); Hyams v. Evanston Hosp., 587 N.E.2d 1127 (Ill. App. Ct. 1992). Other courts have explicitly refused to apply the attorney-client privilege to insured-insurer communications. *See, e.g.*, Linde Thomson Langworthy Kohn & Van Dyke v. Resolution Trust Corp., 5 F.3d 1508, 1515 (D.C. Cir. 1993); Nationwide Mut. Fire Ins. Co. v. Bourlon, 617 S.E.2d 40, 47 (N.C. Ct. App. 2005).

244. *In re* Bevill, Bresler & Schulman Asset Mgmt. Corp., 805 F.2d 120, 124 n.1 (3d Cir. 1986); Moore v. Tri-City Hosp. Auth., 118 F.R.D. 646, 648 (N.D. Ga. 1988); Am. Nat'l Watermattress Corp. v. Manville, 642 P.2d 1330, 1333 (Alaska 1982); Nat'l W. Life Ins. Co. v. Walters, 216 So. 2d 485, 486 (Fla. Dist. Ct. App. 1968).

245. Potential clients are increasingly requesting that firms engage in competitive interviewing processes in which a client (usually a large corporation) interviews several different law firms for the same assignment. Participating in such a process can raise several ethical issues, including the creation of an attorney-client relationship between the law firm and the prospective client even when the law firm did not intend such a relationship to exist, the concomitant creation of a duty to maintain confidences of that "client," and disqualification of the firm from representing another party in the same or a substantially related matter, even though the law firm was not retained. *See, e.g.*, B.F. Goodrich Co. v. Formosa Plastics Corp., 638 F. Supp. 1050 (S.D. Tex. 1986) (holding that no attorney-client relationship had been created during one-day interview, because firm had not actually received confidential information); Bridge Prods., Inc. v. Quantum Chem. Corp., 20 Envtl. L. Rep. (Envtl. L. Inst.) 20,940 (N.D. Ill. Apr. 27, 1990) (disqualifying firm based on a prior interview attended by the corporation's CEO, its general counsel, and two lawyers from the firm, since the corporation had shared confidences with the firm and had reasonably believed that the firm was acting as its attorney); Kenneth D. Agran, *The Treacherous Path to the Diamond-Studded Tiara: Ethical Dilemmas in Legal Beauty Contests*, 9 GEO. J. LEGAL ETHICS 1307 (1996) (recommending presumption of lawyer-client relationship in initial consultation, rebuttable only by written waiver from prospective client); Debra Bassett Perschbacher & Rex R. Perschbacher, *Enter at Your Own Risk: The Initial Consultation & Conflicts of Interest*, 3 GEO. J. LEGAL ETHICS 689, 704–05 (1990) (arguing that the lawyer

must make it clear to the prospective client that no attorney-client relationship is being created by the consultation).

246. 119 F.R.D. 621 (D. Mass. 1988).
247. *Id.* at 622.
248. *Id.*
249. *Id.*
250. *Id.* at 621–22.
251. *Id.* at 622.
252. *Id.*
253. Diversified Group, Inc. v. Daugerdas, 304 F. Supp. 2d 507 (S.D.N.Y. 2003).
254. *Id.* at 513. The Maryland courts, however, have noted that even communications with business rather than litigation counsel may be cloaked by attorney-client privilege if litigation counsel instructs that such communications remain confidential. *E.g.*, Devetter v. Alex. Brown Mgmt. Servs., Inc., No. 24-C-03-007514, 2006 WL 1314014 (Md. Cir. Ct. Mar. 22, 2006). In *Devetter*, the trial court determined that communications to litigation counsel through its business counsel could remain confidential under the "intermediary doctrine":

    > The "critical factor" in determining whether the doctrine applies is whether the communications are made in confidence for the purpose of obtaining legal advice from the lawyer. In the instant case, it is undisputed that the representatives of Ballentine Finn were instructed by Plaintiffs to treat their communications as strictly confidential. Indeed, they were not to communicate with anyone other than Plaintiffs and their counsel.

    Id. at *8 (citations omitted). Under such circumstances, even law firms providing primarily business advice may enjoy some protection through attorney-client privilege. *Id.*
255. *Diversified Group*, 304 F. Supp. 2d at 513 (quoting Bennett Silvershein Assoc. v. Furman, 776 F. Supp. 800, 803 (S.D.N.Y. 1991) (internal quotation marks and citation omitted)).
256. No. 02 Civ. 6441 (LAK), 2002 WL 31250727 (S.D.N.Y. Oct. 8, 2002).
257. *Id.* at *1.
258. *Id.*
259. *Id.*
260. 410 F.3d 1104, 1110–12 (9th Cir. 2005).
261. *Id.* at 1107.
262. *Id.* The law firm required this acknowledgment because it did not want the thousands of responses it received to create attorney-client relationships, thus "leav[ing] itself open to suits for malpractice for those who answered." *Id.*
263. *Id.* at 1110.
264. *Id.* at 1108.
265. *Id.*
266. *Id.* at 1106.
267. *Id.* at 1111 (quoting Beery v. State Bar of Cal., 739 P.2d 1289, 1293 (Cal. 1987). *But see* Castaneda v. Burger King Corp., No. C 08-4262 WHA (JL), 2009 WL 2382688, at *6 (N.D. Cal. July 31, 2009) (holding that communications *Barton* found privileged did not mean there was an attorney-client relationship between putative class members and class counsel).
268. *See, e.g.*, *In re* Subpoenas Duces Tecum, 738 F.2d 1367, 1369 (D.C. Cir. 1984); *In re* Grand Jury Proceedings, 727 F.2d 1352, 1356 (4th Cir. 1984). As a gen-

eral rule, only the client, and not its counsel, may waive the attorney-client privilege. *See, e.g.*, United States v. AT&T, 642 F.2d 1285, 1299 (D.C. Cir. 1980); Carte Blanche (Singapore) PTE, Ltd. v. Diners Club Int'l, Inc., 130 F.R.D. 28, 31 (S.D.N.Y. 1990); Leibel v. Gen. Motors Corp., 646 N.W.2d 179, 185 (Mich. Ct. App. 2002) ("The attorney-client privilege is personal to the client, and only the client can waive it."). However, the attorney may waive the attorney-client privilege on behalf of his client where the client voluntarily discloses or voluntarily consents to disclosure of the privileged communication. *See, e.g.*, Perrignon v. Bergen Brunswig Corp., 77 F.R.D. 455, 460 (N.D. Cal. 1978).

269. *See, e.g.*, *In re* Grand Jury Subpoenas, 902 F.2d 244, 248–49 (4th Cir. 1990); Waller v. Fin. Corp. of Am., 828 F.2d 579, 583 n.7 (9th Cir. 1987); *In re* Bevill, Bresler & Schulman Asset Mgmt. Corp., 805 F.2d 120, 126 (3d Cir. 1986); Weil Ceramics & Glass, Inc. v. Work, 110 F.R.D. 500, 502–03 (E.D.N.Y. 1986); *In re* Bairnco Corp. Sec. Litig., 148 F.R.D. 91, 102 (S.D.N.Y. 1993).
270. *See, e.g.*, Loustalet v. Refco, Inc., 154 F.R.D. 243, 247 (C.D. Cal. 1993); United States v. Evans, 113 F.3d 1457, 1467 (7th Cir. 1997) (quoting United States v. Schwimmer, 892 F.2d 237, 243–44 (2d Cir. 1989)).
271. *In re* Bevill, Bresler & Schulman Asset Mgmt. Corp., 805 F.2d 120, 126 (3d Cir. 1986); Intex Recreation Corp. v. Team Worldwide Corp., 471 F. Supp. 2d 11, 16 (D.D.C. 2007).
272. FDIC v. Ogden Corp., 202 F.3d 454, 461 (1st Cir. 2000) (citing McMorgan & Co. v. First Cal. Mortgage Co., 931 F. Supp. 699, 702 (N.D. Cal. 1996).
273. 238 F.R.D. 215 (W.D. Ky. 2006).
274. *Id.* at 219.
275. *Id.* at 219–20.
276. *Id.* at 220 (emphasis added).
277. *Id.*
278. *Id.*
279. Hearn v. Rhay, 68 F.R.D. 574, 581 (E.D. Wash. 1975). Many courts applying the at-issue waiver follow *Hearn*'s three-factor test. *See, e.g.*, Conkling v. Turner, 883 F.2d 431, 434 (5th Cir. 1989) (citing cases); Remington Arms Co. v. Liberty Mut. Ins. Co., 142 F.R.D. 408, 413 (D. Del. 1992); Williams v. Sprint/United Mgmt. Co., 464 F. Supp. 2d 1100, 1104 (D. Kan. 2006). Other courts follow a variation of *Hearn*'s three-factor test. *See, e.g.*, Koppers Co. v. Aetna Cas. & Sur. Co., 847 F. Supp. 360, 363 (W.D. Pa. 1994). In *Koppers*, for example, the court adopted the first two *Hearn* factors but replaced the third factor with a balancing test—"the likelihood of chilling the type of ordinarily-privileged communication is outweighed by the unfairness to the seeking party if privilege is found." *Id.* at 363–64.
280. *See, e.g.*, N. River Ins. Co. v. Phila. Reinsurance Corp., 797 F. Supp. 363, 370 (D.N.J. 1992); Fox v. Cal. Sierra Fin. Serv., 120 F.R.D. 520 (N.D. Cal. 1988); Metro. Life Ins. Co. v. Aetna Cas. & Sur. Co., 730 A.2d 51, 60 (Conn. 1999).
281. 914 F. Supp. 1084 (D.N.J. 1996).
282. *Id.* at 1093.
283. *Id.* at 1094.
284. *Id.* at 1088.
285. *Id.* at 1091–92.
286. *Id.* at 1094.
287. *Id.* at 1096.
288. *See, e.g.*, EEOC v. WRS Infrastructure & Env't., Inc., No. 09 C 4272, 2010 WL 2604747, at *3 (N.D. Ill. June 23, 2010); Reitz v. City of Mt. Juliet, 680 F. Supp.

2d 888, 892–93 (M.D., Tenn. 2010); EEOC v. Outback Steakhouse of Fla., Inc., 251 F.R.D. 603, 611–12 (D. Colo. 2008); Carpenter v. Mohawk Indus. Inc., No. 4:07-CV-0049-HLM, 2007 WL 5971741 (N.D. Ga. Oct. 1, 2007); Walker v. Cnty. of Contra Costa, 227 F.R.D. 529, 533 (N.D. Cal. 2005).

289. 165 P.2d 1135 (N.M. Ct. App. 2007).
290. *Id.* at 1139.
291. *Id.* at 1142.
292. 730 A.2d 51 (Conn. 1999).
293. *Id.* at 53.
294. *Id.* at 61.
295. *Id.*
296. *See, e.g.*, St. Paul Reinsurance Co. v. Commercial Fin. Corp., 197 F.R.D. 620, 630 (N.D. Iowa 2000) ("Numerous courts have noted the difficulty of determining the scope of work product privilege as it applies to insurance claims files or records from an insurer's investigation of an insured's claim. . . ."); Goodyear Tire & Rubber Co. v. Chiles Power Supply, Inc., 190 F.R.D. 532, 535 (S.D. Ind. 1999) ("Because an insurer's business is to investigate claims that may or may not result in litigation, application of the work product privilege to insurance claims investigations has been frequently litigated."); Ex parte Nationwide Mut. Fire Ins. Co., 898 So. 2d 720, 722–24 (Ala. 2004).
297. 329 U.S. 495 (1947).
298. *Id.* at 498.
299. *Id.* at 510.
300. *Id.* at 509–12.
301. Fed. R. Civ. P. 26 advisory committee's note.
302. Fed. R. Civ. P. 26(b)(3).
303. Upjohn Co. v. United States, 449 U.S. 383, 397–402 (1981). While the Court stopped short of adopting an absolute rule because the issue had not been directly decided below, the Court held that the notes prepared by the attorneys during conversations were likely not discoverable. *Id.* at 401–02. The Court stated:

> [S]uch work product [the notes] cannot be disclosed simply on a showing of substantial need and inability to obtain the equivalent without undue hardship.
>
> While we are not prepared at this juncture to say that such material is always protected by the work product rule, we think a far stronger showing of necessity and unavailability by other means than was made by the Government or applied by the Magistrate in this case would be necessary to compel disclosure.

Id.

304. 174 F.3d 394 (4th Cir. 1999).
305. *Id.* at 403 (quoting *In re* Grand Jury Proceedings, 33 F.3d 342, 348 (4th Cir. 1994)) (internal citations omitted); *see also* Conn. Indem. Co. v. Carrier Haulers, Inc., 197 F.R.D. 564, 570 (W.D.N.C. 2000) ("The work product privilege is intended to prevent a litigant from taking a free ride on the research and thinking of his opponent's lawyer and to avoid the resulting deterrent to a lawyer's committing his thoughts to paper.").
306. *See, e.g.*, Ariz. R. Civ. P. 26(b)(3) (West 2010); Cal. Civ. Proc. Code §§ 2018.010–.080 (West 2010); Mich. Ct. R. 2.302(B)(3) (West 2010); Minn. R. Civ. P. 26.02(3) (West 2010).

307. Taroli v. Gen. Elec. Co., 114 F.R.D. 97, 98 (N.D. Ind. 1987), *aff'd*, 840 F.2d 920 (7th Cir. 1988); State Farm Fire & Cas. Co. v. Perrigan, 102 F.R.D. 235, 237 (W.D. Va. 1984).
308. Hickman v. Taylor, 329 U.S. 495, 511 (1947). *Compare* United States v. Adlman, 68 F.3d 1495 (2d Cir. 1995) (holding that the work-product protection can apply even when the event giving rise to the litigation has not yet occurred), *and* A. Michael's Piano, Inc. v. Fed. Trade Comm'n, 18 F.3d 138, 146 (2d Cir. 1994) (holding that documents prepared during close out of an investigation by employees who believed litigation would never occur are protected), *with* Binks Mfg. Co. v. Nat'l Presto Indus., Inc., 709 F.2d 1109, 1120 (7th Cir. 1983) (holding that an investigation performed while settlement discussions were ongoing was not in anticipation of litigation).
309. 636 F.2d 1028 (5th Cir. 1981).
310. *Id.* at 1040.
311. 230 F.R.D. 398 (D. Md. 2005) (citing Burton v. B.J. Reynolds Tobacco Co., 170 F.R.D. 481, 485 (D. Kan. 1997)).
312. *Neuberger*, 230 F.R.D. at 418.
313. *Id.*
314. *Id.*
315. 578 F.3d 432 (6th Cir. 2009).
316. *Id.* at 439. The court ultimately found that the burden had not been met and that the documents were discoverable. *Id.* at 443.
317. *Id.* (relying on United States v. Roxworthy, 457 F.3d 590, 594 (6th Cir. 2006)). *Accord* United States v. Deloitte LLP, 610 F.3d 129, 136 (D.D.C. 2010); Sandra T.E. v. S. Berwyn Sch. Dist. 100, 600 F.3d 612, 622 (7th Cir. 2010); *In re* Grand Jury Subpoena, 357 F.3d 900, 907 (9th Cir. 2004); PepsiCo, Inc. v. Baird, Kurtz & Dobson LLP, 305 F.3d 813, 817 (8th Cir. 2002); Maine v. U.S. Dep't of the Interior, 298 F.3d 60, 68 (1st Cir. 2002); Montgomery Cnty. v. Microvote Corp., 175 F.3d 296, 305 (3d Cir. 1999); United States v. Adlman, 134 F.3d 1194, 1195 (2d Cir. 1998); Nat'l Union Fire Ins. Co. v. Murray Sheet Metal Co., 967 F.2d 980, 984 (4th Cir. 1992). The Fifth Circuit, however, requires that anticipation of litigation be the "primary motivating purpose" behind the document's creation. United States v. El Paso Co., 682 F.2d 530, 542 (5th Cir. 1982).
318. 134 F.3d 1194 (2d Cir. 1998).
319. *Id.* at 1195.
320. *Id.* at 1197.
321. *Id.* at 1198.
322. *Id.* at 1201–02.
323. *Id.* at 1195; *see also* Lawrence E. Jaffe Pension Plan v. Household Int'l, Inc., 237 F.R.D. 176, 181 (N.D. Ill. 2006) ("[requiring that] the primary motivating purpose for creating the document must be to 'aid in litigation' is overly narrow and contrary to the principles underlying the work product doctrine.").
324. 213 F.R.D. 329 (N.D. Cal. 2003).
325. *Id.* at 330–31.
326. *Id.* at 331.
327. *Id.*
328. *In re* Grand Jury Proceedings, 2001 WL 1167497, at *52 (S.D.N.Y. Oct. 3, 2001) (quoting *In re* William L. Derienzo, 96 Civ. 01186, 1998 WL 283201, at *5 (Bankr. M.D. Pa. Apr. 28, 1998)).
329. 153 F.R.D. 660 (D. Colo. 1994).

330. *Id.* at 662–63; *see also In re* Grand Jury Subpoena, 599 F.2d 504, 511 (2d Cir. 1979) (holding that questionnaire prepared and sent by attorney to 71 employees of corporate client and the employees' replies and memoranda containing results of interviews with 39 of the employees were prepared in anticipation of litigation).
331. No. 90 Civ. 7811, 1994 WL 510043 (S.D.N.Y. Sept. 16, 1994).
332. *Id.* at *9. Because insurers investigate claims in the ordinary course of business, courts have struggled to apply the work-product doctrine in insurance cases. There appear to be three different approaches to the question of whether documents compiled by an attorney or insurer after an insurance loss have been prepared in anticipation of litigation.

    The first approach generally denies protection to insurance reports prepared after a loss that may generate a potential claim. *See, e.g.*, Thomas Organ Co. v. Jadranska Slobodna Plovidba, 54 F.R.D. 367, 374 (N.D. Ill. 1972).

    The second view provides the work-product protection to documents if they were generated after a loss that likely will be litigated. *See, e.g.*, Basinger v. Glacial Carriers, Inc., 107 F.R.D. 771, 773–74 (M.D. Pa. 1985).

    The final approach is a case-by-case analysis that considers the unique factual context of the given factual situation. This is the approach taken by most courts today. *See, e.g.*, McNulty v. Bally's Park Place, Inc., 120 F.R.D. 27 (E.D. Pa. 1988) (statement taken by insurance adjuster from witness at the request of insured's legal department was prepared in anticipation of litigation but statement was discoverable because of substantial need of plaintiff in view of fact that witness was the only eyewitness to the incident in question, and was not located); Taroli v. Gen. Elec. Co., 114 F.R.D. 97 (N.D. Ind. 1987) (defendant failed to demonstrate that its investigation following injury caused by explosion of fluorescent light bulb manufactured by defendant was conducted in anticipation of litigation, even where defendant received subrogation notice from plaintiff's workers' compensation carrier); W. Nat'l. Bank of Denver v. Emp'rs Ins. of Wausau, 109 F.R.D. 55 (D. Colo. 1985) (holding that investigation by law firm hired by liability insurer was not work product, but rather the investigative file of the insurer prepared in the ordinary course of business); State Farm Fire & Cas. Co. v. Perrigan, 102 F.R.D. 235 (W.D. Va. 1984) (investigative report prepared by independent investigator hired by insurer was not work product but rather prepared during the ordinary course of investigating a fire); Fine v. Bellefonte Underwriters Ins. Co., 91 F.R.D. 420 (S.D.N.Y. 1981) (holding that investigation by insurer was routine investigation of possibly resistible claim and reports generated during such investigation held discoverable).
333. 161 F.R.D. 274 (S.D.N.Y. 1995).
334. *Id.* at 280–81.
335. *Id.*; *see also* Phillips Elecs. N. Am. Corp. v. Universal Elecs. Inc., 892 F. Supp. 108, 110 (D. Del. 1995) (documents relating to patent infringement investigations, tests and analyses performed by plaintiff's employees for its in-house counsel were prepared in the ordinary course of business).
336. 196 F.R.D. 7 (D. Mass. 2000).
337. Miller v. Holzmann, 238 F.R.D. 30, 33 (D.D.C. 2006) (holding that defendant had substantial need for disclosure of plaintiff's selection of approximately 20,000 documents to scan; the action was an extremely complex case with many parties, the action had been in litigation for over 10 years and was procedurally

in midst of expedited discovery schedule that involved numerous depositions and review of thousands of documents, and disclosure would accelerate the progress of the litigation).

338. EEOC v. Int'l Profit Assocs., Inc., 206 F.R.D. 215, 221 (N.D. Ill. 2002); McNulty v. Bally's Park Place, Inc., 120 F.R.D. 27, 30 (E.D. Pa. 1988); Long's Drug Stores v. Howe, 657 P.2d 412, 417 (Ariz. 1983). *But see* Duffy v. Wilson, 289 S.W.2d 555, 559 (Ky. 2009) (holding that witness statements taken shortly after the death of a high school football player immediately after practice were not discoverable (1) because plaintiff had not taken the deposition of those interviewed by the school district and (2) "witness's memory only fades to a certain extent over a period of time.") The dissenting justice stated: "[C]ommon sense dictates that the written statements taken from witnesses within two weeks of this tragedy, and those taken six months later, cannot be the 'substantial equivalent' in quality or veracity." *Id.* at 561.
339. *See, e.g.*, Brown v. Superior Court, 670 P.2d 725 (Ariz. 1983) (complete file of insurer subject to discovery on ground that substantial equivalent not obtainable; no attorney-client privilege asserted). *But see* Aetna Cas. & Sur. Co. v. Superior Court, 200 Cal. Rptr. 471 (Cal. Ct. App. 1984) (communications between attorney and insurer not discoverable in bad-faith action when insurer's representatives can articulate insurer's reasons for denying claim).
340. Fed. R. Civ. P. 26(b)(3); Upjohn Co. v. United States, 449 U.S. 383 (1981); *In re* Leslie Fay Cos. Sec. Litig., 161 F.R.D. 274, 279 (S.D.N.Y. 1995). The U.S. Supreme Court has said that "[a]t its core, the work-product doctrine shelters the mental processes of the attorney, providing a privileged area within which he can analyze and prepare his client's case." United States v. Nobles, 422 U.S. 225, 238 (1975).
341. "Core" work product is work product containing "mental impressions, conclusions, opinions, or legal theories of a party's attorney or other representative concerning the litigation." *See* Fed. R. Civ. P. 26(b)(3)(B).
342. 106 Cal. Rptr. 3d 342 (Cal. Ct. App. 2010), *review granted and opinion superseded*, 232 P.3d 97 (Cal. 2010). The supreme court's grant of review does not specify the issues to be reviewed. Even though the grant of review supersedes the cited opinion, it is instructive nonetheless.
343. *Id.* at 344–45.
344. *Id.* at 345.
345. *Id.*
346. *Id.* at 345–46.
347. *Id.* at 346. The trial court relied on *Nacht & Lewis Architects, Inc. v. Superior Court*, 54 Cal. Rptr. 2d 575 (Cal. Ct. App. 1996) in reaching its decision that the witness statements were automatically "absolute work product" because the statements were taken by an investigator given a list of questions by an attorney. California distinguishes between "absolute work product" and "qualified work product." Absolute work product is defined in California Civil Procedure Code section 2018.030(a) (West 2010) as "[a] writing that reflects an attorney's impressions, conclusions, opinions, or legal research or theories" and "is not discoverable under any circumstances." Qualified work product is defined in section 2018.030(b) as "[t]he work product of an attorney, other than a writing described in subdivision (a)" and "is not discoverable unless the court determines that denial of discovery will unfairly prejudice the party

seeking discovery in preparing that party's claim or defense or will result in an injustice."

348. Cal. Civ. Proc. Code §§ 2018.010–2018.080
349. *Id.* at 348–51.
350. *Id.* at 351. The court relied on *Greyhound Corp. v. Superior Court*, 364 P.2d 266 (Cal. 1961), and *Beesley v. Superior Court*, 373 P.2d 454 (Cal. 1962), both of which allowed discovery of percipient witness statements. Both cases were decided before the adoption of the Civil Discovery Act. *Contra* Mitchell Eng'g v. City of San Francisco, No. C 08-04022 SI, 2010 WL 1853493 (N.D. Cal. May 6, 2010) (decided under federal law).
351. 54 Cal. Rptr. 2d 575 (Cal. Ct. App. 1996).
352. *Id.* at 351–52.
353. *Id.* at 356–59.
354. *Id.* at 359–62.
355. *Id.* at 362.
356. 174 P.2d 60 (Wash. 2007), *aff'g* 130 P.3d 840 (Wash. App. 2006).
357. *Id.* at 64–66.
358. *Id.* at 65.
359. *Id.* at 66.
360. *Id.* at 64. *See* Wash. Rev. Code § 42.56 (2010).
361. *Id.*
362. *Id.* at 68.
363. *Id.* at 69–78.
364. *Id.* at 76–77.
365. *Id.* at 75.
366. *Id.* at 75; *see also* Zawadzki v. Cmty. Hosp. Ass'n, No 09-cv-01682-LTB-MEH, 09-cv-02450-CMA, 2010 WL 3085719 (D. Colo. Aug. 6, 2010).
367. 266 F.R.D. 379 (D. Ariz. 2010).
368. *Id.* at 381.
369. *Id.*
370. *Id.*
371. *Id.*
372. *Id.* at 381–82.
373. *Id.* at 382–83.
374. *Id.* at 383.
375. *Id.* at 384–85.
376. *Id.* at 385.
377. United States v. Clemens, Crim. Action No. 10-223 (RBW) (D.D.C. June 21, 2011).
378. *Id.* slip op. at 1.
379. *Id.* at 2–3.
380. *Id.*
381. *Id.* at 9.
382. *Id.* at 1. The subpoena sought production of the statements of Jose Canseco, Brian McNamee, and Kirk Radomski.
383. *Id.* at 1–2.
384. *Id.* at 4–8.
385. 329 U.S. 495 (1947).
386. United States v. Clemens, slip op. at 11 (relying on United States v. Nobles, 422 U.S. 225, 238 (1975)).

387. *Id.* at 10.
388. *Id.* at 28–37.
389. *Id.* at 7–10.
390. *Id.* at 37–38. The opinion is silent as to what the court would have done had it found that the interviews were opinion work product.
391. *Id.* at 26 n.17 ("It is not perfectly clear what the Circuit meant when it held that facts elicited in a 'litigation-related investigation' are necessarily reflective of an attorney's focus, and that facts garnered from a more generalized inquiry are not entitled to 'opinion' work-product protection.").
392. 449 U.S. 383 (1981).
393. *Clemens*, slip op. at 16–17.
394. *Compare Upjohn*, 449 U.S. 383, 394 n.3 (remanding the issue of discoverability of the ex-employee interviews), *with id.* at 402–03 (Burger, C.J., concurring) (urging adoption of "bright line" rule protecting the ex-employee interviews that relate to the past employment if requested by management).
395. *See, e.g.*, Raso v. CMC Equip. Rental, Inc., 154 F.R.D. 126, 128 (E.D. Pa. 1994); Eoppolo v. Nat'l R.R. Passenger Corp., 108 F.R.D. 292, 294 (E.D. Pa. 1985).

CHAPTER 11

Protecting the Attorney-Client Privilege during an Internal Investigation

MICHAEL DOCKTERMAN*

* The author gratefully acknowledges the invaluable contributions of Chung-Han Lee and Tracy Hannan in the research and drafting of this chapter.

I. Introduction

When a corporation[1] faces legal exposure arising from the conduct of its affairs, it turns to its lawyers for help. Such corporate internal investigations have been conducted in a wide variety of circumstances ranging from derivative demands to employee misconduct to litigation. Since 2004, the Federal Sentencing Guidelines have required a corporation to have an effective program to aid in detecting criminal conduct as well as to demonstrate a commitment to ethical conduct and compliance with the law. Even if the potential exposure is not criminal in nature, the corporation may want to assess the exposure to provide appropriate guidance for the "governing authority" and "high-level personnel" of the corporation, as those terms are defined in chapter 8 of the Sentencing Guidelines.[2] Amendments to the Guidelines, effective in November 2010, focus sharply on the obligation to act on misconduct discovered during the course of an investigation.[3] In order to provide advice, counsel may conduct an internal investigation into the facts and circumstances giving rise to the exposure. The investigation often is undertaken in anticipation of litigation, but there are instances in which the investigation is intended to develop recommendations for new business practices rather than to assess or avoid liability. At the outset of each investigation, counsel and the client must take appropriate steps to protect a privileged investigation from disclosure, both to ensure a candid assessment of the exposure and to promote pointed advice on how to address that exposure.[4] The primary protection for the confidentiality of the investigation arises from the attorney-client privilege accorded to communications relative to seeking and providing legal advice and from the exemption from discovery for the attorney's work product.

This chapter provides practical advice on how to create and protect the attorney-client privilege, maintain the protections of the work-product doctrine, and plan for the unwanted disclosure of the fruits of an investigation, when performing an internal investigation for a corporation or other private entity. The chapter begins with a short discussion of the legal bases for assertion of the attorney-client privilege in the context of corporate investigations, then discusses generally the tools, strategies, and precautions that in-house counsel and outside attorneys can employ to ensure that the attorney-client privilege is maintained and not inadvertently or mistakenly waived. The chapter takes the same approach to preservation of attorney work product. Finally, the chapter considers how to preserve the privilege and the exemption during internal disclosure, disclosure to those with a common interest, disclosure to other nonadversarial parties like witnesses and internal auditors, and disclosure to consulting experts.

II. Attorney-Client Privilege

A. Elements of the Privilege

The attorney-client privilege is recognized in all the states and in the federal courts. As covered in more detail in chapter 1, the basic elements of the attorney-client privilege are (1) a client; (2) a lawyer or the lawyer's subordinate; (3) retention of the lawyer to provide legal advice; (4) a confidential communication between the client and the lawyer within the scope of the retention and not for the commission of a crime or tort; and (5) an intent that the communication remain confidential. The definitions of "client" and "communication," and the scope of a permissible "retention," vary among the states and between state and federal law. It therefore is important to consider which state's law is likely to govern questions of privilege and work product, and to design the group of people within the corporation who constitute the "client" to fit within the law of the governing state. While challenges to the confidentiality of the investigation can come from private parties in any state, or from state or federal authorities in multiple locations, the best place to start is with the law where the corporation is organized.

B. Identifying the "Client"

Once the lawyer has decided which law to follow, he or she must advise the client how to constitute itself under the governing state law. In an internal corporate investigation, the client is the corporation itself. The privilege belongs solely to the corporation, and only the corporation has the authority to assert and to waive the privilege. Who has that authority and how it is exercised depends on who speaks for the corporation in the investigation.[5] The individual requesting advice may be the chief executive officer, chief financial officer, or another member of senior management; the director of compliance or internal audit; the director of human resources; internal counsel; the board of directors; or a board committee. The corporate personnel generally fall within the Sentencing Guidelines' definition of "high-level personnel," while the board members are part of the "governing authority" assumed to be overseeing, rather than acting for, the corporation.[6] In some investigations, however, the board supplants management for purposes of the investigation.[7] Each type of client requires a different reporting relationship, and each is constituted as the "client" in a different way. In every instance, the client should be documented and a discrete reporting relationship established from the attorney to the client.

The lawyers asked to provide the advice, and sometimes the clients receiving the advice, often need technical assistance to allow them to understand the issues. Technical help may be drawn from internal resources or from outside consultants. Some internal technical people may be enlisted onto the investigation team and become part of the client, while other internal technical people may provide limited information and not fall within the ambit of "client." Just as it is important to document the former as part of the client, it is prudent to define the limited role to be played by those people within the corporation or retained as special consultants who are charged with receiving the confidential information so they may provide their technical assistance within the protection of the privilege.

The Supreme Court's decision in *Upjohn Co. v. United States*[8] remains the leading case on the scope of the attorney-client privilege protecting communications about internal corporate investigations. Prior to *Upjohn*, courts employed two different tests to determine whether a communication with a lawyer was protected by the privilege. Some used a control group test, which required that the person making the communication be "in a position to control or even to take a substantial part in a decision about any action which the corporation may take upon the advice of the attorney."[9] Other courts used a subject matter test, which looked to whether (1) the employee making the communications did so at the direction of his or her superiors in the corporation, and (2) the subject matter upon which the attorney's advice was sought fell within the scope of the employee's duties.

In *Upjohn*, the Supreme Court rejected a strict control group test in favor of determining the applicability of the attorney-client privilege on a case-by-case basis. The Court held that "the privilege exists to protect not only the giving of professional advice to those who can act on it but also the giving of information to the lawyer to enable him to give sound and informed advice. The first step in the resolution of any legal problem is ascertaining the factual background and sifting through the facts with an eye to the legally relevant."[10] While the protection is not a blanket spread over all communications between a lawyer and client to facilitate the advice,

> as a general rule, a communication is privileged at least when, as here, an employee or former employee speaks at the direction of the management with an attorney regarding conduct or proposed conduct within the scope of employment. The attorney must be one authorized by management to inquire into the subject and must be seeking information to assist counsel in performing any of the following functions: (a) evaluating whether the employee's conduct has bound or would bind the corporation; (b) assessing the legal consequences, if any, of that conduct; or (c) formulating appropriate legal responses to actions that have been or may be taken by others with regard to that conduct.[11]

While state courts following *Upjohn* have differed in their definitions of "control group" and on the authority that the control group may delegate, there is general agreement that corporate task forces can be formed to undertake and to receive the fruits of an investigation. The manner in which the group is constituted, and the way in which it seeks advice, are described in greater detail in chapter 1.

C. What Is Protected?

Once the client has been identified, courts generally have enforced the attorney-client privilege where the matters discussed with counsel fall within the client's corporate duties. Assuming that the prerequisites to establish the privilege have been met, the general rule is that only communications are protected; the underlying facts themselves are not protected from disclosure simply because they were contained in a communication. In other words, the request for advice and the facts on which advice is sought, as well as the advice and the facts and legal arguments supporting the advice, are privileged; that clients asked the lawyers to consider facts or documents, discussed the issues, and considered the lawyers' advice cannot be discovered in the absence of the crime-fraud exception to the privilege.[12] But the underlying information contained in the communication likely exists in its native form, before it was gathered for or by the lawyers in connection with the investigation. The information in its native form may be discovered independently, and the fact that it was discussed with lawyers does not prevent it from being disclosed if it is separately requested.

To preserve the privilege when information is gathered from corporate files, the documents requested and relied upon should be copied and stamped as part of the investigation file. The copies are privileged because they are the things on which advice is sought or the bases on which advice is given. The originals (or other copies) of the documents, however, do not become privileged simply because they have been reviewed during the investigation. The better practice is not to mark originals, so that if there is ever a subsequent request for the documents, they will not reflect that they were gathered and reviewed by counsel. If this protocol is followed, the communication of advice based on counsel's investigation should remain absolutely protected.

The same theory governs witness interviews but, in practice, the problem is trickier. Employees should be told that they are being interviewed in connection with the investigation, that the matter is confidential, and that they are not to discuss the interview with anyone. They also should be told that the investigation is privileged, that the privilege belongs to the corporation, and that they are not authorized to waive the privilege (unless, of course, they are part of the client for the investigation, in which case they must be admonished that the interview is not to be disclosed until a formal decision has been made whether to waive the privilege). In order to protect the information, courts have required a showing that the control group expressly asked lower-level employees to communicate with counsel so that counsel could provide a legal opinion. Absent such an express request, there is no guarantee that communications from lower-level employees will be protected.[13] The employees should be told to contact the interviewers (or someone else charged for this purpose) in the event a third party tries to talk to them about the subject matter of the investigation. The information the employees provide should be kept separate from information gathered from them for other purposes—for example, to document business practices for auditing of human resource files—and they should be told not to refer to the interview when providing similar information to others for business purposes. Interview notes should be kept separate from personnel dossiers or other employee files within the corporation. The fruits of the interviews should be treated exactly like the documents gathered for the investigation. If this protocol is followed, the communication of legal advice on the witnesses' information should be absolutely protected by the privilege.

D. Asking for Legal Advice

Although an implicit request for a legal opinion is usually sufficient to preserve the privilege, it is better for the client to make an explicit request. In fact, some courts have required a written request for legal advice for the privilege to attach.[14] The advice being sought must be "legal" in nature and not just business advice.[15] The purpose of the engagement must be "legal" and not merely "investigative" in nature, which underscores the importance of the engagement letter in articulating the legal focus of the investigation.[16] If the communications are being treated as privileged, they must be kept confidential and restricted to the client or those assisting the client in the investigation. If the communications are made in the presence of or disseminated to third parties, they will lose their privileged status and no longer be protected or confidential. If the communications are used to make business decisions, they similarly will lose their privileged status.

The safest course to preserve the privilege is for the client to ask for advice in writing—commonly known as an *Upjohn* letter. For example, if the CEO wants to know the extent of the corporation's exposure as a result of discussions among national sales managers at industry gatherings, the CEO should send a formal memorandum to the general counsel asking for advice on the corporation's potential legal liability arising from certain activities of its salespeople and their competitors. The letter should request advice in contemplation of litigation and should direct that any activities undertaken to provide the advice, including the use of internal resources or outside consultants, be kept confidential. The letter should direct that the requested legal advice be provided only to the CEO or to those designated to act for the corporation in this context. The general counsel, in turn, should either task in-house lawyers or engage outside counsel to conduct an internal investigation to allow the general counsel to advise the CEO on the matter; the request should also be in writing. The same rule applies if the request is generated by the internal counsel. The formal engagement document should state that any investigation is to be conducted under the attorney-client privilege and that the dissemination of information concerning the investigation should be limited to those few people tasked to assist in the process. Copies of a sample *Upjohn* internal request and an internal memorandum authorizing the investigation are attached as appendix 13-1 and appendix 13-2.

If the corporation does not have internal counsel, the engagement letter from outside counsel should confirm the request for legal advice in the same manner as an *Upjohn* letter and should set out the terms of outside counsel's engagement. In a similar vein, if the advice is sought, and the investigation is authorized, by the board of directors or a committee of the board, communications must be restricted to the board or its committee. At least one influential state court has held that a committee of the board—formed to conduct an internal investigation into options backdating—waived the attorney-client privilege over its outside counsel's report when the report was shared with the entire board of directors.[17] The board or committee may direct that one of its members act as a liaison, or that outside counsel communicate through the general counsel on behalf of the board, to provide the advice. The lines of communication protected by the privilege should be set out in the *Upjohn* letter, the engagement letter, or both, taking care that the language in the documents describing the line of communication is consistent.

E. Preserving the Privilege When Establishing the Investigation Team

Once the client has been defined and the questions on which the corporation seeks advice have been delineated, the investigation team must be formed. If the entire team will consist of outside lawyers, outside counsel should document its team appropriately. If any internal resources will be used in the investigation, those lawyers and support staff (including technical help) working on the investigation should be told that they are working on a privileged and confidential task and that they may not disseminate information about the investigation. The delegation of authority should be reduced to writing; a form of internal authorization is attached as appendix 13-3.

Internal resources fall into two broad categories: those on the investigation team who will actually conduct the investigation, and those who are brought in for strictly defined tasks such as document collection and creation of summaries on which the investigation team will rely. Those who are incorporated into the investigation team should be treated in the same manner as paraprofessionals or outside consultants: they should be informed about the nature of the investigation and the privilege under which it has been undertaken and instructed that they do not have the authority to waive the privilege or to disclose anything about the investigation. They should be told to keep their work product confidential and separate from their other assignments. If they routinely bill their time to charge numbers, they should be given a separate charge number for hours spent on the investigation. Their work product should be segregated from other files and labeled separately, and those support personnel assigned to help with the investigation should be instructed to maintain the documents separately from ordinary working files, and those documents are best kept under lock and key. Just as outside consultants engaged to assist on technical or support matters should be given a separate document reflecting the special nature of the work and instructing them to maintain its confidentiality, those internal nonlawyers asked to join the investigation team should treat the investigation as a separate task that has a defined beginning and end.

The second group of internal resources on which the corporation may draw are those who are proficient in separable tasks necessary to complete the investigation. In a defense industry internal investigation into mischarging, for example, pricing information may require internal resources to gather and analyze the pricing data. If the corporation chooses someone from the accounting department who routinely analyzes such information for government audits, the employee must be instructed not to use the information gathered for the investigation for any other business purpose. This instruction is critical because it usually means that the employee will have to do nearly the same task twice: once within the ambit of the privileged investigation and once within the cycle of the employee's regular duties. Yet if information gathered for the investigation is incorporated into an audit report sent to the government, the instructions given to the employee by counsel and the information gathered by that employee may become discoverable; worse, the privilege may be deemed waived. As with those employees who are on the investigation team, the employees in this second group should be told to keep their work confidential and separate from their other assignments. If the employees routinely bill their time to charge numbers, they should be given a separate charge number for hours spent on these tasks. Their analyses and supporting documentation should be segregated from other files, labeled separately, and kept under lock and key.

F. Identifying Information Subject to the Privilege

As noted above, to preserve the privilege when information is gathered from corporate files, the documents requested and relied upon should be copied, with the copies given document control numbers and then stamped with the legend "Privileged and Confidential—Attorney Work Product" (or something similar) as part of the investigation file. If the documents are gathered electronically, the same process should be followed on any discs or servers on which the documents are stored. Any new documents created for the investigation should be authored by lawyers on the investigation team or by support personnel working at the attorneys' specific direction. If employees who are not otherwise involved in the investigation are asked to create summaries, analyses, or spreadsheets of information, they should be told that the document is being created for an internal investigation and that they are not authorized to discuss the project with anyone outside the investigation team. Similarly, members of the investigation team should be instructed not to provide any unnecessary details of the investigation to employees outside the team who assist in such limited tasks. There is a legitimate temptation to provide more information in order to give "context" to the employees and to obtain a more useful product from their work; but the safer course is to be as circumspect as circumstances will allow.

Just as the documents upon which the investigation results are premised should be marked as privileged and confidential, all communications from the client providing information, and all advice from the lawyers communicated to the client, should bear a similar legend designating them as privileged and confidential. The advice also constitutes counsel's work product; but if it is communicated to the client it generally is the client's to disclose, although counsel's permission must be sought before the work-product exemption is waived.

G. Expecting to Waive the Privilege

There are many reasons, ranging from leniency under the Sentencing Guidelines to restoration of the corporate image, that a client may decide to waive the attorney-client privilege. Federal agencies call for disclosure under a wide variety of programs, including the Department of Defense Office of Inspector General's Voluntary Disclosure Program, the Department of Health and Human Services Office of Inspector General's Self-Disclosure Protocol, the Antitrust Division's Corporate Leniency Program, or a Wells Submission to the Securities and Exchange Commission. The investigation report may be shared in these circumstances pursuant to a nonwaiver stipulation or agreement to attempt to maintain the privilege, but increasingly courts have held that such voluntary disclosures to government agencies can result in a broad waiver of all attorney-client (and work product) protection when private litigants seek discovery of the report in litigation.[18] The current version of the Department of Justice's *Principles of Federal Prosecution of Business Organizations*—known as the Filip Memorandum[19]—avows that the Justice Department respects the attorney-client privilege and counsel's work product and will not request a waiver of either, but will insist upon production of "factual information." In the government's formulation, "a corporation need not disclose, and prosecutors may not request, the disclosure of such attorney work product as a condition for the corporation's eligibility to receive cooperation credit,"[20] but a corporation that does not find a way to "disclose the relevant facts about the alleged misconduct—for whatever reason—typically should not be entitled to receive credit for cooperation."[21] The example provided in the Filip Memorandum starkly frames the problem:

> By way of example, corporate personnel are typically interviewed during an internal investigation. If the interviews are conducted by counsel for the corporation, certain notes and memoranda generated from the interviews may be subject, at least in part, to the protections of attorney-client privilege and/or attorney work product. To receive cooperation credit for providing factual information, the corporation need not produce, and prosecutors may not request, protected notes or memoranda generated by the lawyers' interviews. To earn such credit, however, the corporation does need to produce, and prosecutors may request, relevant factual information—including relevant factual information acquired through those interviews, unless the identical information has otherwise been provided—as well as relevant non-privileged evidence such as accounting and business records and emails between non-attorney employees or agents.[22]

The corporation's decision whether to disclose is always complicated. Against the prospect of disclosure, the investigation must be conducted in light of the possibility that the client will waive its privilege over the facts found and the advice sought and communicated.

In litigation, a court may find that the information gathered in an investigation must be disclosed in discovery over the objection of the corporation and the authority (whether management, the board, or a board committee) directing the actions of the corporation. In 2009, the Supreme Court resolved a split in the circuits and held that a judicial decision to compel disclosure of information is not immediately appealable, and therefore warned that "clients and counsel must account for the possibility that they will later be required by law to disclose their communications for a variety of reasons—for example, because they misjudged the scope of the privilege, because they waived the privilege, or because their communications fell within the privilege's crime-fraud exception."[23]

Similarly, some courts have found that reference to the results of an internal investigation to explain corporate action also can warrant disclosure of the investigative materials themselves.[24] The better rule, recently articulated by the Second Circuit, is that "a party must *rely* on privileged advice from his counsel to make his claim or defense" to effect a waiver of the privilege.[25] In some circuits, including the Second Circuit, such orders may be tested immediately by writ of mandamus, while in other Circuits a party must subject itself to criminal contempt to test an order of disclosure before trial. The reasons for determining questions of privilege before trial were fully vetted by the Supreme Court in *Mohawk Industries, Inc. v. Carpenter*,[26] but did not persuade the Court to allow prejudgment appellate review of orders disclosing privileged material, requiring counsel to consider unwanted disclosure as an ever-present eventuality.

Preparation of the investigation materials with disclosure in mind is a good idea in all cases. Even if there is no immediate demand for the investigation materials, disclosure does not have to come in immediate response to government requests, press of publicity, or reliance on counsel's advice as a defense. Even if no court orders that materials be disclosed while the investigation is fresh, the privilege, as well as the corporation's interest in maintaining the privilege, can erode over time.[27] All documents should be gathered and all advice created with the potential for disclosure in mind, no matter how sensitive or "privileged" the matters covered in the communication may be.

III. Work-Product Doctrine

Distinct from privileged communications, the work-product doctrine protects the theories, analysis, and mental impressions of counsel working to advise a client in anticipation of litigation. The exemption from discovery accorded attorney work product is broader than the attorney-client privilege but less absolute; the exemption applies only to materials prepared in anticipation of litigation and does not protect the materials if the work product is the only place where information resides.[28] The work-product exemption belongs to the attorney, a principle that applies even when the work product is physically in the hands of the client, but that has been eroded by recent decisions extending the power to waive the exemption to the client as well as counsel.[29] The work-product doctrine arises from a complex of interrelated interests, ranging from the client's desire to obtain good legal advice undistorted by mechanisms to avoid discovery, to the concerns of attorneys whose clients' aims have diverged from those of their counsel. The boundaries of the exemption are necessarily fluid and must be determined on a case-by-case basis.

Hickman v. Taylor[30] remains the leading case on the work-product doctrine and the protections accorded attorney work product. Generally, material that has been created by counsel in anticipation of litigation is protected from disclosure in discovery. The exemption from discovery is qualified, however, in that the adversary may obtain the information by showing sufficient need for the material and a lack of other sources for the information contained in the material. *Hickman* also recognized that the attorney's thinking—theories, analysis, mental impressions, beliefs, concerns, or questions—lies at the heart of the adversary system, and privacy is essential for the attorney's thinking.[31] The Court drew a distinction, therefore, between the factual information in counsel's materials and the evaluative aspects of those materials.[32] For this reason, the work-product doctrine affords the greatest, if not absolute, protection for material that would reveal counsel's theories, analysis, mental impressions, or beliefs. Facts incorporated in the work product, however, may be obtained upon a showing of substantial need.[33]

The work-product exemption has been incorporated in part into the Federal Rules of Civil Procedure, the Federal Rules of Criminal Procedure, and many corresponding state rules. Federal Rule of Civil Procedure 26(b)(3) distinguishes between "ordinary work product," which includes factual exhibits (including documents) prepared for litigation, and "opinion work product," which includes the mental impressions, conclusions, opinions, or legal theories of any attorney or other representative of a party concerning the litigation. This distinction is similar to the differences between opinion "core attorney work product" and the "factual information" that the Department of Justice may consider when assessing a corporation's cooperation under the Filip Memorandum, with the greater protection accorded an attorney's opinions. Ordinary work product generally can be discovered upon a showing of substantial need and undue hardship, while opinion work product is rarely, if ever, discoverable. In a different formulation, Federal Rule of Criminal Procedure 16(b)(2)(A) exempts "reports, memoranda, or other documents made by the defendant, or the defendant's attorney or agent, during the case's investigation or defense." On its face, Rule 16(b)(2)(A) does not distinguish between the two types of work product. These rules, however, only provide a statutory basis for invoking exemptions from pretrial discovery. They do not provide guidance for defining the work product or for assessing evidentiary issues following production.

The exemption from discovery extends beyond pretrial proceedings to grand jury investigations,[34] administrative inquiries,[35] and arbitrations.[36] The starting point for analyzing the exemption remains, for each invocation of the doctrine, the Supreme Court's analysis in *Hickman*. Although ordinary work product can be obtained upon a showing of substantial need and inability to obtain the factual information without undue hardship, opinion work product generally will withstand all but "extraordinary justification."[37] Unlike the attorney-client privilege, the exemption applies to many things that are not communications or advice. For example, the collection of a specific group of documents by counsel to support an internal investigation is protected on the theory that the selection reveals the attorney's thought process.[38] That protection, however, affords little solace if the client has waived its attorney-client privilege and provided counsel's investigation report to the government in an effort to demonstrate corporate cooperation during preindictment discussions, notwithstanding counsel's separate work product interest. As a practical matter, notwithstanding the attorney's legal right to assert the exemption, it is the rare lawyer who declines consent to disclosure of an investigation report when the client has waived the attorney-client privilege and has asked the lawyer to waive the work-product exemption.

A. Elements of the Work-Product Doctrine

In classic formulation, the work-product doctrine exempts from discovery documents and tangible things (1) otherwise discoverable; (2) prepared in anticipation of litigation or for trial; (3) by counsel or counsel's representatives or for another party or that party's representative. In the context of an internal investigation, it is useful to begin with the premise that the investigation has been undertaken by counsel for the purpose of analyzing the issues on which advice has been sought. The premise is founded in the fundamental fact that upon receiving the engagement, the attorney has formulated an investigation plan in anticipation of litigation and directed its implementation in order to form the opinions necessary to provide the client with the requested advice. Those documents selected for review, those persons chosen for interview, and those issues researched or analyzed all reflect the attorney's theories of the case and thought processes in formulating opinions. If nonattorneys are engaged to assist in the process, the attorney specifies the scope of their work and incorporates their work product into the attorney's own. Upon that premise, the entire investigation constitutes counsel's work product.

The challenge is to document the steps taken in an investigation and the materials created by the investigation team as being solely within the work-product exemption. To fall within the protections of the work-product doctrine, the materials generated during the internal investigation must be created in a way that reflects their exempt status. Documents created by the investigation team should be crafted as reflections on materials reviewed. Information gleaned from interviews and analyses of research should be addressed to the investigation topic and not be developed for later use in a business context. The databases, indices, and abstracts of documents, and even the selection of particular supporting documents, that are created as part of the investigation will be protected only if they may reveal the direction of an attorney's thinking regarding the case; if the documents also are designed for business use, for example, internal financial audits or personnel decisions, they will lose their exempt status. Specifically, document summaries and interview notes that reflect impressions of, or place values on, information gleaned from the investigation are generally protected by the work-product doctrine because they reflect the attorney's thought processes. If, on the other hand, they reflect the work of support personnel and are intended to summarize business information for other uses as well as to aid the investigation team, they will not be exempt. In the same vein, the mere fact that someone prepared an analysis for ordinary business purposes that subsequently is relied upon by the attorney to provide advice does not transmute the analysis into work product.

As with privileged documents, those materials created or selected by counsel as part of the investigation process that counsel wishes to exempt from discovery should be stamped "Privileged and Confidential—Attorney Work Product" (or something similar) and incorporated into the investigation file. The copies placed in the investigation file are exempt because they reflect the formulation of legal advice or the bases on which advice is given. The copies should be given document control numbers as well as a legend. As with documents subject to the attorney-client privilege, the originals (or other copies) of the documents do not become exempt simply because they were reviewed during the investigation. The better practice, therefore, is not to mark the original documents the attorneys review so that if there is ever a subsequent request for those documents, the originals will not reflect that they were gathered and reviewed by counsel.

Those working on the project should follow the same rules for preserving the confidentiality of exempt documents that they follow for privileged documents, as set out above. The information that employees provide should be kept separate from information provided by them for other purposes. Interview notes should be kept separate from personnel dossiers or other employee files within the corporation. The fruits of any interviews should be treated exactly like the documents gathered for the investigation. Indeed, some courts have allowed the work-product doctrine to protect the names and addresses of witnesses who were interviewed in preparation for litigation if the appropriate confidential restrictions are placed on the interview lists and the interviews are limited to the investigative purpose.

B. Preserving the Exemption

The rules for preserving the work-product exemption are virtually identical to those governing preservation of the attorney-client privilege. As with privileged information, the attorney's work product should not be shared outside the investigation team. If employees who are not otherwise involved in the investigation are asked to create summaries, analyses, or spreadsheets of information, they should be told that the documents are being created for an internal investigation. They should be told that they are not authorized to discuss the work product with anyone outside the investigation team. Similarly, members of the investigation team should be instructed not to provide any unnecessary details of the investigation to anyone outside the investigation team.

Since an element of the doctrine is that the materials "otherwise discoverable" were prepared "in anticipation of litigation," they must be treated by the lawyers in that way. Even if no litigation has actually been threatened, either the initiating memorandum for the investigation or the summaries created at each phase of the investigation should relate to the anticipated litigation. Otherwise, the investigation team is subject to the argument that the threat of litigation was not perceived as real or imminent. One way to document the threat of litigation is to create a file memorandum to catalog the array of potential claims and claimants the client must consider. Another link to anticipated litigation is postponement of routine destruction of the original documents either considered in the investigation or implicated in the claims through a "discovery hold" until the statute of limitations on the anticipated claims has expired.

C. Expecting to Waive the Exemption

Because it is impossible to predict the circumstances in which production of work product will be sought, the fruits of the investigation should be created with an eye toward the ultimate production of ordinary work product. Some of the work product created in every internal investigation contains "factual information" that will be treated as ordinary work product and subject to production if it is not otherwise easily available. Whether it is considered "factual information" as opposed to "core attorney work product" under the Filip Memorandum, "ordinary work product" under Rule 26(b)(3), or otherwise sought as the only material available to the opponent that contains the relevant facts, the factual information in the attorney's work product is at greater risk of production than opinion work product. This poses the question whether the work product itself should be segregated into two parts, one of which is expected to be produced and one of which will be guarded as pure opinion.

Some lawyers try to overlay factual information with attorney opinions in order to shield the information from discovery, even though the intermediate remedy of redaction is almost always available. In the context of most discovery requests for investigation files, however, this is not necessary. The discovery request may be cloaked in a variety of guises, but at its essence the propounder wants a copy of the materials (or at least the ordinary work product) in the internal investigation file. The safer practice, therefore, is to keep only copies of materials considered by the investigation team in the investigative files as work product. The originals of those documents and other tangible things can be preserved in their native form for discovery in the ordinary course of subsequent litigation without revealing how they were chosen, analyzed, and folded into the attorney's theories of the case. If the client can argue that all of the underlying documents and other materials on which counsel relied during the internal investigation have otherwise been made available for production in response to other discovery requests, the party propounding the discovery is deprived of the hardship argument at the heart of most successful efforts to overcome the exemption.

Opinion work product, on the other hand, should be drafted so that its nature is apparent on its face and therefore deserving of greater protection. Memoranda knitting together the facts developed by the investigation team are the essence of the way that lawyers act within our system of jurisprudence to promote justice and to protect their clients' interests.[39] The fact that the memoranda analyze theories that an opponent has not considered underscores why such opinion work product deserves to be exempt from discovery. Similarly, the investigation team's impressions of witnesses, of the import of documents, or of the strengths and weaknesses of a case reflect counsel's thinking in a way that is at the heart of the adversary system. Production of such opinion work product would undermine the adversary process as well as work a hardship on the litigant whose lawyer's innermost thoughts are laid bare. These policy considerations have been found compelling when work product is sought. So long as the opinion work-product documents are not the only place where critical factual information resides, the opinion work product should remain inviolate.

Witness interviews present a similar, although more complicated, challenge. Those persons interviewed during the course of an investigation may be recorded or their statements taken down. If formal statements are taken, they should be treated as if they will be produced despite valid objections that the names of the witnesses and the questions asked of them reveal the investigation team's thought processes. The investigation team may consider taking no formal statements and creating all interview notes in an evaluative way, but if a witness dies or is absent from the jurisdiction at the time of the discovery request, the evaluative notes may become the only source of that witness's information and therefore subject to the "extraordinary justification" argument discussed above. Alternatively, the interview team might consider conducting successive interviews, with the notes of a preliminary interview treated as opinion work product while a succeeding formal statement is treated as ordinary work product. Irrespective of the method chosen, the distinction between ordinary and opinion work product should be paramount in the minds of the investigation team.

In determining whether such distinctions will be honored, the investigation team should consider how its materials will be viewed in camera when a court is deciding whether to allow discovery of the work product. If the fruits of the investigation reflect only opinion work product, the investigation team has made it hard for the court to accommodate the discovery request and may have put the entire investigation file at greater risk of in camera review. On the other hand, if the work-product materials are all factual, it is more likely they will not be exempt from discovery. Similarly, if the materials have been shared outside the investigation team or used for any other purpose, the fact that they were created during the investigation will not protect them from production.

IV. Preserving the Privilege and the Exemption

When the fruits of an investigation are shared, counsel must consider how to preserve both the privilege and the exemption over the investigative materials. The results of a corporate investigation might be shared, for example, with lawyers for individual employees or for other corporate subjects of a governmental inquiry. As noted above, an investigation report might be shared with a government agency under a stipulation of nondisclosure as part of a corporation's cooperation with that inquiry. Internally, a corporation may wish to share the results of an internal investigation to address problems discovered during the investigation. In each instance, sharing the information gathered or the advice given can lead to waiver of the privilege or the exemption.

As the pretrial discovery rules imply, the materials generated during an investigation and even the opinions formed by counsel and communicated to the client may be sought in civil, criminal, and administrative litigation. If the privileged materials have been shared outside the control group within the corporation, or if the exempt materials have been disclosed outside the investigation team to anyone other than the client or co-counsel with a common interest, the propounder of the discovery request will argue that the confidentiality of the materials has been waived and the materials (or the information in the materials) should be produced. The first question in these circumstances, of course, is whether the propounder of the request knows that an internal investigation has been conducted. Sometimes, the fact of the investigation—although not its fruits—has been made public by the client. In other instances, the fact of the investigation has been leaked through witnesses or through unauthorized disclosures by persons who did not have the authority to waive either the privilege or the exemption. And sometimes the client has made the report public but still seeks to protect the supporting files on which the report was based.[40]

It also is important to consider both the purpose and the terms of the interview before the necessary sharing of information with interviewees and their counsel. Many lawyers give each witness an *Upjohn* or corporate *Miranda* warning to make clear that they do not represent the witness, that the fruits of the interview are privileged to the corporation and not to the witness, and that the witness may want to consult with her own attorney. But the giving of such warnings does not, of itself, protect the corporation against a charge that the witness has rights in the information provided, especially if the same lawyers have jointly represented the witness and the corporation in other litigation.[41] This evolving area of the law affects disciplinary actions taken against an employee based on statements made in the interview, the company's use of information when dealing with the government, and questions that may arise under policies of insurance for directors, officers, and the corporation itself. To resolve such questions may prompt the company to consider disclosure of some or all of the investigation report under joint defense, common interest, or other shared privileges, but each such disclosure multiplies the likelihood that the privilege and the exemption will be deemed waived.

In these circumstances, how does counsel protect the internal investigation when its fruits have been requested in discovery? The preceding sections contain several suggestions for preserving the underlying information in native form to make it available for discovery independent of the investigation; for preserving the analysis of witness interviews independently; for segregating investigation files to preserve their privilege and exemption; for segregating ordinary from opinion work product; and for safeguarding the bases for and provision of advice. But the critical exercise is how *not* to waive the privilege or the exemption inadvertently when sharing the information within a permitted group outside the investigation team or the client, while still demonstrating that the privilege and exemption should be honored.

The issue has received significant attention in the *Principles of Federal Prosecution of Business Organizations* as those principles have evolved. Congress has considered legislation aimed expressly at preserving the privilege and the exemption.[42] When the Standing Committee on Rules of Practice and Procedure of the Judicial Conference of the United States proposed new Federal Rule of Evidence 502, it included provisions to limit waivers of the attorney-client privilege and the work-product exemption.[43] As detailed in the Evidence Rules Advisory Committee's report, the risk of subject matter waiver of both the privilege and the exemption led to a variety of proposals to deal with inadvertent waiver, selective waiver, and the enforceability of confidentiality orders in the courts and before government agencies. None of these resolved the problem, leading to the intermediate position taken in the rule.

Two of the general principles on which all members of the Advisory Committee agreed are instructive. First, a subject matter waiver should be found only when privilege or work product already has been disclosed and a further disclosure "ought in fairness" be required to protect against a misrepresentation that might arise from the previous disclosure. Second, an inadvertent disclosure should not constitute a waiver if the holder of the privilege or exemption took reasonable precautions to prevent disclosure and, further, took reasonably prompt measures to rectify the error once the holder knew or should have known of the disclosure. With those principles in mind, it is useful to consider some of the common situations where disclosure of the fruits of an investigation can lead to a finding that the privilege and the exemption have been waived.

Although this chapter treats disclosure of privileged and exempt materials together, it is important to analyze the actual materials disclosed independently. First, the privilege belongs to the client while the exemption generally protects a lawyer's mental impressions and work product.[44] Waiver of the privilege ordinarily will lead to disclosure of the advice given by counsel, but it does not necessarily expose the attorney's underlying analysis or opinions.[45] Second, while the privilege generally is deemed waived whenever the attorney-client communication has been disclosed to someone outside the attorney-client relationship, the work-product exemption is considered to be waived only when the work product is disclosed to an adversary.[46] Third, the inadvertent-waiver cases distinguish between the privilege and the exemption,[47] and that distinction must be considered for both intentional and inadvertent waiver. The safest course is never to share privileged communications with anyone outside the client group; if information is to be shared with others, it should be created for that purpose and the work-product doctrine used as the basis for maintaining the exemption of the original work product from discovery.

A. Internal Disclosure

Once a corporation has made the significant investment required to conduct a proper internal investigation, it may want to apply the lessons learned from the investigation to improve its controls, modify its processes, defend a shareholder or derivative lawsuit, or change its personnel wholly apart from the investigation itself. It is hard to argue with any corporate inclination to improve, but by sharing the fruits of an investigation internally—outside the control group and the investigation team—the corporation runs the risk of waiving both its privilege over the advice and the lawyer's work-product protection for mental impressions and analysis. Some attorneys adopt a "just wait until the time is right" attitude toward internal disclosure, counseling the client to address the issues when the investigation has ended and litigation over the underlying subject matter has terminated. But this attitude may be inconsistent with the corporate mandate to "fix the problems" and also may run counter to a prosecutor's assessment of the client's good faith in deterring unlawful conduct.

If the client wants to use the fruits of the internal investigation for multiple purposes, it must accept the fact that all uses of the fruits of the investigation beyond the investigative purpose and the defined client open the door to the waiver of the privilege and the exemption.[48] There are, however, some ways in which the knowledge gained from the investigation can be put to other uses without creating undue risk of disclosure. The members of the "client," for example, can direct corrective measures through their subordinates without sharing the actual fruits of the investigation. General counsel can advise senior managers whose operations have been touched by the investigation on areas of improvement without reference to the investigation. Project teams can be tasked to take a second look at areas within the corporation with the directive that they assess weaknesses and suggest improvements independent of anything done by the investigation team.

If these steps are taken by the corporation, a few fundamental operating rules should be observed to preserve the privilege and the exemption. First, the corrective actions must not be grounded in the investigation. Second, privileged communications generated during the investigation should not be disclosed, summarized, or referenced outside the control group. Third, work product generated for the investigation should not be shared outside the investigation team. Having offered this suggestion, however, it may be unrealistic to expect that no materials will be shown to others internally; and if they are disclosed outside the investigation team, great care should be taken to imbue the work product with indicia of a confidentiality created for a special, not a general, business purpose. Fourth, corrective actions should be documented and based on independent assessments by people charged with making the changes, for example, internal auditors who propose new controls in areas where the investigation team has identified weaknesses in the control system. Finally, throughout the process, the fruits of the investigation should remain segregated, and copies should not be filed with the corporation's regular business records.

B. Disclosure to a Party with a Common Interest

During the course of government investigations, it is common for corporate counsel to share the results of internal investigations with lawyers for other companies under government scrutiny or with the lawyers for some of the employees whose conduct is at the heart of the investigation. The vehicle by which counsel share such information is often a joint-defense agreement, either oral or written, by which the attorneys agree to treat the information they share as joint work product. The basis for work-product protection of the shared information is the common-interest doctrine.[49] The common-interest doctrine does not extend the protection of the attorney-client privilege unless the parties share a legal interest, so privileged materials should not be shared with lawyers for other companies or individuals. But the common-interest doctrine can allow work product to be shared among counsel with a common interest, or to be given to outside consultants like accountants or crisis management advisors engaged to address a common problem, without waiving the exemption. Attorneys who receive work-product information within a joint defense may then share the information with their clients as a component of the privileged advice they provide.

Attorneys differ on whether a written joint-defense agreement is preferable to an oral agreement to preserve the privilege. The arguments on both sides of the question are sound, but a written agreement defining the common interest, confirming the confidentiality of the information shared, and setting the bounds for further disclosure establishes a written record on which a court may rely to preserve the exemption. The nondisclosure provisions of the joint-defense agreement receive treatment similar to the nondisclosure stipulations made with government agencies and occasionally can be more effective against third parties who seek the information for wholly unrelated reasons. For example, courts have held that neither party to a joint-defense agreement may waive the exemption without the other's consent.[50] Nondisclosure stipulations with a government agency to prevent subsequent disclosure of work product provided pursuant to the stipulation are not always so effective.

To guard against inadvertent or unwanted waiver of privileged or exempt materials in this context, the following steps should be taken: First, no privileged materials should ever be shared outside the client group. Second, if the work product of an investigation is to be shared with counsel for parties with a common interest, the information should be shared orally by attorneys for one of the parties with attorneys for one or more of the other parties. Third, a file memorandum should be created by each side memorializing the information shared and the circumstances under which it was shared, including explicit reference to the common interest and the specific agreement not to disclose the information outside the joint-defense group without permission of the sharing parties. Fourth, if actual documents are shared, they should be given control numbers and the numbers recorded in a cover letter or file memorandum reflecting what was provided. Fifth, the cover letter or file memorandum should reference the common interest and the specific agreement not to share the documents outside the joint-defense group without permission of the sharing parties. Finally, information gleaned by counsel through such sharing arrangements should be communicated to their respective clients in a privileged communication memorialized in an attorney's file memorandum.[51]

C. Disclosure to a Nonadversary Third Party

The two most common nonadversarial recipients of information from an internal investigation who are not themselves engaged in the investigation are third-party witnesses and the corporation's auditors. In almost all cases, the witness will not be a member of the "client" group, and if he or she is told matters covered by the attorney-client privilege, it is arguable that the privilege has been waived. Unless the witness is a former employee or agent still bound by a separate duty to follow the corporation's instructions, or engaged as a consultant to the investigation team, the third-party witness cannot be told that the work product shared in an interview must be kept confidential. The same rules hold true for the corporation's independent auditors, and while the accountants may want to keep the information confidential, they may not be allowed to if a court compels their response to a subpoena.[52]

In the case of third-party witnesses, the mere disclosure of work product does not waive the exemption. But when questioned at a deposition, there is no doctrine witnesses can invoke that precludes disclosure of the questions they were asked or the materials they were shown during the prior interview. Similarly, when the attorney who conducted the interview invokes the work-product exemption to preclude production of the documents shown to the witnesses, that attorney invites both the argument that work product was waived as to those documents that were no longer in native form (e.g., summaries or spreadsheets created by counsel but shown to the witnesses) and the argument that the materials shown to the witnesses caused them to shade their testimony and therefore are subject to production to test their credibility.[53] The better practice, therefore, is to assume that any materials generated during an investigation that are shared with a third-party witness will come to light in discovery.

Disclosure may or may not be sought by the independent auditor to the corporation, but following Sarbanes-Oxley the likelihood that the accountants will want to see the report is high. In this context, if the accountants are acting solely as the independent auditors of the corporation and not as consultants either to the corporation or to the investigation team, disclosure creates a serious risk of waiver of the work-product exemption because the accountants' duties also run to the shareholders and the investing public, not just to the corporation. Both because the common interest shared by investigating lawyers and the auditors is limited and because other interests arising from the auditor's duty of public disclosure conflict with the lawyer's expectation of confidentiality at the heart of the common-interest doctrine, the investigation team's expectation of continued confidentiality for the shared work product should be low if the auditor's request is based on its obligation to attest to management's preparation of the corporate books.

The auditors have a valid interest in knowing the subject matter of the investigation and whether any liabilities assessed by the investigation team are material to the corporation. Materiality is not determined solely by the amount at risk but also by reflection on management's credibility. These considerations highlight the divergent interests of the lawyers and the accountants when independent auditors ask to see either the investigation report or the underlying materials on which the report is based. Lawyers are bound to say relatively little by the ABA Statement of Policy Regarding Lawyers' Responses to Auditors' Requests for Information (December, 1975). The auditors, for their part, have their own duty to discover fraud and assess the integrity of management, and must inquire under the AICPA Statement of Financial Accounting Standards No. 5[54] and possibly other reporting standards. For companies that must report publicly, the problem is acute because the corporation rarely wants to risk a dispute with its auditors over a matter that, if disclosed to the auditors, would not be deemed by them to be material. But sharing the results of an internal investigation with the corporation's public accountants, like sharing those results with the SEC or with a stock exchange, is a virtual guarantee that the attorney-client privilege will have been waived,[55] putting corresponding pressure on the work-product exemption from discovery. The better rule, adopted by the D.C. Circuit in 2010, is that sharing the results does not necessarily waive the work-product exemption, but it will likely trigger an inquiry into the circumstances of disclosure and prompt at least an in camera review of the report and some evidence justifying both the application of the exemption to the work product and its nondisclosure.[56]

The law in this area is still developing and there is no clear guidance on how to proceed. At least one court has upheld the exemption on the theory that a "business and its auditor can and should be aligned insofar as they both seek to prevent, detect and root out corporate fraud."[57] But the Supreme Court's language in *United States v. Arthur Young & Co.*,[58] that the auditor's "'public watchdog' function demands that the accountant maintain total independence from the client at all times and requires complete fidelity to the public trust," can be at odds with investigating counsel's efforts to control the circumstances of disclosure. When the auditors want to know what has been investigated, some lawyers agree to discuss the issues generally with the auditors and then guard carefully against disclosing anything the lawyers would not say publicly. Other lawyers counsel their clients to make a separate disclosure of the underlying issue directly to the auditors and then invite the auditors to conduct their own investigation within the context of their audit. Still others follow the precept that if management has deemed the matter immaterial, irrelevant to the integrity of the company's finances, and otherwise outside the regular audit program, there is no need to disclose the matter separately to the auditors. If the auditors ask to see the fruits of an internal investigation or to discuss counsel's advice as part of an audit, however, counsel should treat whatever is said to the auditors as if it were neither privileged nor exempt and should guard carefully against making statements that might be construed as waivers relating to the entire subject matter of the investigation.

D. Disclosure to a Consultant or Expert

Disclosure to a consulting expert, or to a consultant engaged to assist on technical matters in the investigation, whether or not an "expert" in the field, should not disturb either the privilege or the exemption if the engagement is properly documented. But once the fruits of an investigation are given to an expert whose testimony is envisioned, the protections afforded by the privilege and the exemption are lost, and there is a real risk that the privilege and the exemption will be waived. The basis for disclosure lies in the language of Federal Rule of Civil Procedure 26(a)(2)(B), which requires production of all "data or other information considered by the witness in forming the opinions." The same rule holds true when a witness will testify in a criminal trial, although the timing of production differs.[59] Although some litigants have attempted to avoid the rule by asserting that the expert did not "rely upon" the investigative materials when forming an opinion, the better rule is to withhold privileged or exempt material from a testifying expert to protect the privilege and the exemption.

The rule is murkier when the consulting expert actually prepares a portion of the work product. While these questions have arisen primarily in the context of tax disputes when a corporation engages counsel and consultants to prepare tax analyses that may lead to a challenge by the IRS to the tax treatment of certain assets or liabilities, the cases may apply as well to the work product of any investigation where the company is motivated by both a business purpose and a realistic fear of litigation over the issue. Different circuits have adopted different tests for protecting such materials. The First Circuit, for example, while articulating a "because of" rationale, actually follows a narrow "prepared for" test to determine whether the materials were prepared exclusively in anticipation of litigation, finding that if the corporation may also have had other business purposes for the work, the work product falls outside the exemption.[60] The Fifth Circuit has adopted a "primary purpose" test similar to that employed by the First Circuit to determine whether the preparation of the documents was primarily motivated to assist in future litigation.[61] The Second

Circuit, in contrast, applies a broader "because of" test, protecting the work product created when both litigation anticipation and a business purpose coexist.[62] The D.C. Circuit,[63] Third Circuit,[64] Fourth Circuit,[65] Sixth Circuit,[66] Eighth Circuit,[67] and Ninth Circuit[68] all appear to be in accord with the Second Circuit. The Seventh Circuit has long followed its own, similar, approach.[69] These cases, however, are intensely fact-driven and do not provide a uniform rule. There is, therefore, room for government agencies and private parties to seek production of investigative materials when the materials prepared by consultants, while an integral part of the investigation, also are used by the corporation for other purposes.

There also are reasons to share investigative materials with nontestifying experts after the investigation has been concluded. Such disclosures are treated differently under Federal Rule of Civil Procedure 26(b)(4)(B). But although providing the fruits of an investigation to a consulting expert may be protected as falling within counsel's work product, the only sound analytical justification for providing the consultant with privileged communications is if the consultant's opinion is sought on the meaning of something within that privileged communication to enable counsel to give advice on the communication. In that limited circumstance, the consultant is acting as an extension of the attorney in providing legal advice, which allows preservation of the privilege as well as the exemption.[70] As a general rule, however, giving a consulting expert a privileged communication in later litigation constitutes a waiver of the privilege.

Notes

1. Analytically, there is little distinction among the collective entities—corporation (whether or not for profit), partnership, limited liability company, or joint venture—in this context. The chapter therefore speaks in terms of corporate internal investigations but applies to collective entities generally.
2. U.S. Sentencing Guidelines Manual § 8A1.2 cmt. n.3, § 8B2.1 cmt. n.1.
3. U.S. Sentencing Guidelines Manual § 8B2.1(b)(4) cmt. n.6 (as amended), § 8C2.5 cmt. n.11 (as amended).
4. Some courts have restricted the privilege to legal advice sought in anticipation of litigation as an additional safeguard against blanket invocation of the privilege in response to discovery. See chapter 1 for a discussion of this issue. This chapter assumes that the prerequisites for assertion of the privilege have been met and concentrates on preservation of the privilege against inadvertent waiver by inadequate safeguards or undue disclosure of the fruits of the investigation.
5. As covered in more detail in chapter 1, there often is a conflict between the interests of the corporate client and the officers, employees, and agents of the corporation. Counsel for the corporation must be particularly sensitive to this potential conflict for a number of reasons, including the possible disqualification of corporate counsel for undertaking multiple representations that later conflict. Even when the conflict issues have been resolved, the corporation can act only through its officers, employees, and agents. Because both privileged and nonprivileged communications take place through these actors, there are

rules governing when a communication is privileged and when it is not, and when a corporate officer, employee, or agent may disclose information from interviews or from a report. The rules that those entrusted with the role of "client" must follow to preserve the confidentiality of the investigation should be articulated both at the outset of the investigation and periodically throughout the investigation as a reminder to all involved in the investigation. The issue may be complicated further by decisions that suggest there is a distinction between the corporation and the board of directors or a board committee as a matter of state law. But these cases miss the point: the corporation is the client, yet the management structure of the corporation may be supplanted by the board or a special committee when doubt has been cast on management. Any conflict arises from a temporary withdrawal of corporate authority from the officers or the entire board, not from any new client relationship.

6. U.S. Sentencing Guidelines Manual § 8A1.2 cmt. n.3; § 8B2.1 cmt. n.1.
7. See chapter 10 for a discussion of the role of the board or special committee in these circumstances.
8. 449 U.S. 383 (1981).
9. *Id.* at 390 (quoting Philadelphia v. Westinghouse Elec. Corp., 210 F. Supp. 483, 485 (E.D. Pa. 1962)).
10. *Id.* at 390–91.
11. *Id.* at 403 (Burger, J., concurring).
12. *See* chapter 3 for a discussion of the crime-fraud exception.
13. *Cf.* Indep. Petrochemical Corp. v. Aetna Cas. & Sur. Co., 654 F. Supp. 1334, 1365 (D.D.C. 1986) ("Without showing that such communications are part of the control group's effort to secure legal advice, every memorandum and conversation between corporate employee and corporate counsel would be confidential, which would expand the privilege far beyond its bounds and unnecessarily frustrate the efforts of others to discover corporate activity.").
14. U.S. Postal Serv. v. Phelps Dodge Ref. Corp., 852 F. Supp. 156, 160 (E.D.N.Y. 1994) (noting that "house counsel have increased participation in the day-to-day operations of large corporations"; thus "if the information-holder will communicate with the attorney even if the privilege does not exist, or if a nonlegal objective is sufficient to stimulate communication with the attorney, then there is no reason for the privilege to attach") (internal citation omitted).
15. *See* Visa U.S.A., Inc. v. First Data Corp., No. C-02-1786JSW (EMC), 2004 WL 1878209, at *8 (N.D. Cal. Aug. 23, 2004) (concluding that where documents prepared with the assistance of attorneys would have been prepared in substantially identical form in making a business decision, no attorney-client or work-product protections applied).
16. Sandra T.E. v. S. Berwyn Sch. Dist. 100, 600 F.3d 612, 620–22 (7th Cir. 2010).
17. Ryan v. Gifford, 2007 WL 4259557, at *3 (Del. Ch. Nov. 30, 2007).
18. See chapter 3 for a discussion of the effect of voluntary disclosure even when protected by a confidentiality agreement.
19. The revised *Principles of Federal Prosecution of Business Organizations* are reprinted in appendix 1-3 of chapter 1.
20. *Principles of Federal Prosecution of Business Organizations* 9-28.720(b).
21. *Id.* at 9-28.720(a).
22. *Id.* at 9-28.720(a), n.3.
23. Mohawk Indus., Inc. v. Carpenter, 130 S. Ct. 599, 607 (2009).

24. *Cf.* Hearn v. Rhay, 68 F.R.D. 574, 580–81 (E.D. Wash. 1975).
25. *In re* Erie Cnty., 546 F.3d 222, 229 (2d Cir. 2008).
26. *Principles of Federal Prosecution of Business Organizations* 9-28.720(a), n.3.
27. *Cf.* Commodity Futures Trading Comm'n v. Weintraub, 471 U.S. 343, 354 (1985) (power to waive passes to trustee of bankrupt corporation); Lewis v. United States, 2004 WL 3203121, at *4 (W.D. Tenn. Dec. 7, 2004), *aff'd*, 2005 WL 1926655 (W.D. Tenn. June 20, 2005) (privilege should not apply to "dead" corporation).
28. *See generally* 8 Charles Alan Wright, Arthur R. Miller, & Richard L. Marcus, Federal Practice and Procedure § 2025 (3d ed. 2010) (discussing the use of the exemption in federal court).
29. *See, e.g.*, *In re* Grand Jury Proceedings, 43 F.3d 966, 972 (5th Cir. 1994) ("In contrast to the attorney-client privilege, the work product privilege belongs to both the client and the attorney, either one of whom may assert it. Thus, a waiver by the client of the work product privilege will not deprive the attorney of his own work product privilege, and vice versa").
30. Hickman v. Taylor, 329 U.S. 495 (1947).
31. *Id.*
32. *Id.* at 509.
33. *See* chapter 1 for a discussion of "substantial need."
34. *In re* Grand Jury Subpoena, 599 F.2d 504, 509 (2d Cir. 1979).
35. Upjohn Co. v. United States, 449 U.S. 383 (1981).
36. Samuels v. Mitchell, 155 F.R.D. 195, 200 (N.D. Cal. 1994).
37. *In re* Sealed Case, 676 F.2d 793, 810 (D.C. Cir. 1982).
38. *See* chapter 1 for a discussion of the breadth of the exemption.
39. *Hickman*, 329 U.S. at 510–11.
40. In still other circumstances, the client has made a limited disclosure to the government pursuant to a stipulation of nondisclosure to third parties. A client's agreement with a government agency that limited disclosure to that agency without waiving the privilege or the exemption is covered in chapter 11. *See, e.g.*, *In re* Cardinal Health, Inc. Sec. Litig., 2007 WL 495150 (S.D.N.Y. Jan. 26, 2007). Those instances in which a client has asserted a defense of advice of counsel based on the investigation, or where there has been an allegation of attorney malpractice in the investigation, are beyond the scope of this chapter.
41. Consider the facts summarized in *United States v. Ruehle*, 583 F.3d 600 (9th Cir. 2009), and the risks to counsel and the corporation posed by disputes over the use of interviews conducted during an investigation.
42. *See* S. 186, 110th Cong. (as introduced, Jan. 4, 2007).
43. *Report of the Advisory Committee on Evidence Rules*, May 15, 2006. The language preserving the privilege upon disclosure to a government agency was dropped from the final proposed rule.
44. *See* chapter 1 for a discussion of the difference between attorney work product and the attorney-client privilege.
45. *Cf.* Hercules, Inc. v. Exxon Corp., 434 F. Supp. 136, 156 (D. Del. 1977).
46. United States v. AT&T, 642 F.2d 1285, 1299 (D.C. Cir. 1980).
47. *E.g.*, Falise v. Am. Tobacco Co., 193 F.R.D. 73, 82–83 (E.D.N.Y. 2000).
48. *See infra* section IV.D.
49. *See* chapter 8 for a general discussion of the common interest doctrine.
50. *See* John Morrell & Co. v. Local 304A, UFCW, 913 F.2d 544, 556 (8th Cir. 1990), *cert. denied*, 500 U.S. 905 (1991).

51. *See* chapter 8 for a discussion of joint-defense agreements.
52. Another common "disclosure" that is beyond the scope of this chapter occurs when a member of the control group shares information about the investigation with a family member or a close friend (or even another lawyer, creating havoc for both the client and the new lawyer). Though the disclosure is not to an adversary, preserving arguments that the disclosure does not affect the work-product exemption, telling a family member or friend about advice received from an attorney raises questions about waiver of the attorney-client privilege.
53. *See, e.g.*, Ricoh Co. v. Aeroflex Inc., 219 F.R.D. 66, 70 (S.D.N.Y. 2003).
54. These standards are in the process of being revised and the new version of FAS 5 should be consulted.
55. United States v. AT&T, 642 F.2d 1285, 1299 (D.C. Cir. 1980).
56. United States v. Deloitte LLP, 610 F.3d 129, 139–40 (D.C. Cir. 2010).
57. Merrill Lynch & Co. v. Allegheny Energy, Inc., 229 F.R.D. 441, 448 (S.D.N.Y. 2004).
58. 465 U.S. 805, 818 (1984).
59. *See* FED R. CRIM. P. 16.
60. United States v. Textron, Inc., 577 F.3d 21, 30–31 (5th Cir. 2009) (en banc).
61. United States v. El Paso, 682 F.2d 530, 542–43 (5th Cir. 1982) (finding no work-product exemption where the "primary purpose" for tax workpapers was to bring the corporation's books into conformity with GAAP).
62. United States v. Adlman, 134 F.3d 1194, 1202 (2d Cir. 1998) (document accorded work-product protection if it can be fairly said to have been prepared or obtained "because of" the prospect of litigation regardless whether the document served a dual purpose of assisting a business decision).
63. *In re* Sealed Case, 146 F.3d 881, 883–84 (D.C. Cir. 1998).
64. Montgomery Cnty. v. MicroVote Corp., 175 F.3d 296, 305 (3d Cir. 1999).
65. Nat'l Union Fire Ins. Co. v. Murray Sheet Metal Co., 967 F.2d 980, 984 (4th Cir. 1992).
66. *In re* Prof'ls Direct Ins. Co., 578 F.3d 432, 439 (6th Cir. 2009).
67. PepsiCo, Inc. v. Baird, Kurtz & Dobson LLP, 305 F.3d 813, 817 (8th Cir. 2002).
68. *In re* Grand Jury Subpoena, 357 F.3d 900, 907–08 (9th Cir. 2004).
69. *In re* Special Sept. 1978 Grand Jury (II), 640 F.2d 49, 61 (7th Cir. 1980).
70. *United States v. Kovel*, 296 F.2d 918 (2d Cir. 1961) is the leading case on disclosure to experts who assist counsel in technical areas to enable the attorney to provide legal advice to the client.

APPENDIX 11-1

Sample *Upjohn* Letter

June 30, 2008

Portia Trant, Esq.
General Counsel
Worldwide Enterprises, Inc.
One Worldwide Place
Metropolis, Terra 12345

Dear Portia:

I request that you investigate and provide legal advice to the Company concerning certain matters that have come to our attention involving [briefly describe]. Your investigation should be conducted within the attorney-client privilege, and you should feel free to engage such professional assistance as you deem warranted. I expect you to treat the matter confidentially and to proceed expeditiously.

You should report with your advice [directly to me.] [to the Audit Committee of the Board of Directors, which will act with executive authority for the Company to avoid any appearance of bias on my part.] A resolution authorizing this line of authority is attached.

Sincerely yours,

APPENDIX 11-2

Sample Memorandum Authorizing Investigation

TO: Legal Department

FROM: Portia Trant

RE: Internal Investigation

DATE: July 1, 2010

The Legal Department has been asked to provide advice to the Company concerning [briefly describe]. I have authorized an internal investigation into the facts and circumstances giving rise to this request to enable me to advise the Company concerning its litigation exposure. I have engaged [name] and her firm as outside counsel to [assist in] [conduct] the investigation and have asked [name] to coordinate the investigation internally.

This confidential investigation will be conducted within the attorney-client privilege. The investigation materials and any report of the investigation will be counsel's work product. Please take all appropriate steps to preserve the attorney-client privilege and the work-product exemption from discovery throughout the investigation. Any decision whether to disclose confidential privileged or exempt materials will rest with me in consultation with the appropriate client.

APPENDIX 11-3

Sample Delegation of Authority

TO: Recipients

FROM: Portia Trant, General Counsel

RE: Internal Investigation

DATE: July 1, 2010

The Legal Department requires your assistance in connection with an internal investigation of [briefly describe]. We hereby request your assistance and delegate the necessary authority to you on behalf of the Legal Department to carry out various tasks that will aid us in the investigation and defense of actual or anticipated litigation. All of your projects will be directed by our counsel.

Our work is subject to the attorney-client privilege and the attorney work-product protection. Since we are engaging you to assist us, we intend that all of the activities that you undertake pursuant to this assignment will also be subject to all privileges and protections applicable to us as attorneys. We therefore ask that you communicate only with attorneys in the Legal Department or with our outside counsel about substantive issues, the results of your activities, or any questions that you might have. Similarly, you should not write any reports or commit anything to writing until you have consulted with counsel.

Kindly confirm your understanding of this Delegation of Authority by signing it and returning it to me. We appreciate your assistance in this legal matter.

/s/______________________________

Printed Name:______________________

Date: ____________________________

CHAPTER 12

Contacting Employees, Former Employees, and Other Witnesses Currently or Formerly Affiliated with the Opposing Party—Conflict between the Permissive Scope of Fact Investigation and Protection of Attorney-Client Communication*

VINCENT S. WALKOWIAK

* This chapter is an update and rewrite of Alan F. Wagner, *"Who Can I Talk To?" Scaling the Wall of the Attorney-Client Privilege in Contacting Witnesses*, *in* THE ATTORNEY-CLIENT PRIVILEGE UNDER SIEGE (2d ed.).

I. Definition of the Problem

Whether you represent the plaintiff or defendant or are in-house counsel, the proper investigation of a claim or defense inevitably involves interviewing persons with knowledge. Though no attorney would consider contacting a party without first contacting the attorney representing that party, certain potential witnesses cannot be interviewed without the permission of the opposing party. Whether a witness can be interviewed without first contacting opposing counsel becomes particularly clouded in litigation involving corporations when the potential witness is a current employee, or more typically, a former employee. This chapter addresses the problems associated with witness contact where the witness may have some current or former affiliation with an opposing party, but whose position does not clearly indicate that they are or were represented by the employer's counsel.

There are few clear solutions to this problem. The answers that the courts have provided are nearly as varied as the factual circumstances in which these issues have been presented. The courts regrettably seem to disagree on the underlying purposes of the rules involved, and their interpretations have produced widely disparate results. Few common themes or bright line tests have emerged beyond the obvious restriction against communicating directly with a represented individual, or in some instances the managerial level of a corporate party. Beyond these situations, there is little clear law for counsel to rely upon in making strategic litigation decisions that they can be confident will not be criticized later as unethical and improper.

All states have adopted ethical rules that preclude ex parte communication with parties represented by counsel.[1] Rule 4.2 of the American Bar Association Model Rules of Professional Conduct, entitled "Communication with Person Represented by Counsel," addresses the prohibition on speaking with represented persons in the following manner:

> In representing a client, a lawyer shall not communicate about the subject of the representation with a person the lawyer knows to be represented by another lawyer in the matter, unless the lawyer has the consent of the other lawyer or is authorized to do so by law or a court order.[2]

This rule is clear enough when the parties are individuals.[3] A lawyer shall not communicate with a represented party, however that communication comes about. In *Faison v. Thornton*,[4] the defendant himself contacted the plaintiffs' counsel directly, without knowledge of his attorney, and discussed the litigation with plaintiffs' counsel. In disqualifying the plaintiffs' counsel for the contact, the court noted that the rule does not permit the represented person to waive the protection of this rule and that counsel, if contacted by an adverse party, is obliged to terminate the communication and contact opposing counsel to continue any further communication with the represented party.[5] The rule is less clear when applied to a current or former employee of a corporation or other business entity and was even murkier prior to the 1995 amendment, which substituted the word "person" for "party." While courts regularly found that corporate organizations were included as parties under this rule, the principle issue in contention was and continues to be which employees or agents of that corporate organization could be approached ex parte.[6]

The ABA rules and comment are substantially similar to the rules adopted by the states.[7] In Florida, prior to the ABA's 1995 amendment, the rule was clearer and broader than the ABA counterpart. Rules such as Florida's led to the 1995 amendment to the ABA rule. The Florida rule made the obligation under the ABA rule clearer by the substitution of "person" for "party" in the definition of the prohibited communication, a change that was subsequently adopted by the ABA in 1995.[8]

Unfortunately, neither the Florida version nor the ABA amendment has removed all ambiguity. Courts have continued to struggle when determining the scope of whether a particular employee falls within the class protected by this rule of ethics.

II. Current Employees

Courts have articulated a number of tests to determine whether a current employee falls within a protected category: the control group test, the binding-admission test, the balancing test, the blanket test, the managing-speaking test, the scope-of-employment test, and the alter ego test.[9]

All of these tests recognize that there are key individuals in every corporation who cannot be contacted by an opposing party's counsel without the permission of the company's attorney. This key group includes "those top management persons who had the responsibility of making final decisions and those employees whose advisory role to top management form the basis of any final decision by top management."[10] Also included are "those employees who have the legal authority to 'bind' the corporation in a legal evidentiary sense, that is, those employees who have 'speaking authority' for the corporation."[11] An employee who serves as an internal technical expert may be neither part of the control group nor one whose conduct may establish the company's liability. Nevertheless, the public policy underlying the need to protect an in-house expert's work has been recognized. Protection has been afforded the information of such an in-house expert so that the expert's role in evaluating and improving company products can proceed without fear that such actions will later be used against the company in lawsuits by prohibiting contact of an employee who serves as a technical expert.[12] One of the broadest tests is the scope-of-employment test, which precludes ex parte interviews with current employees about "matters within the scope of the employee's employment."[13]

Combining many of the above factors, the New Jersey Supreme Court articulated the following standards of conduct under New Jersey's Professional Rule of Conduct 4.2:

> [W]e shall for the present limit the application of RPC 4.2 in the organizational context to (a) the control group, which for now, we interpret to mean those employees of the organization entrusted with the management of the case or matter in question, and (b) the employee or employees whose conduct, in and of itself, establishes the organization's liability. With respect to that latter class of employees, we interpret the RPC to require notice of rather than consent from the organization's attorney and to be in effect after filing of an indictment or civil complaint. Any deliberate delay in filing to circumvent the ethical restraints of the RPC will not be countenance. For now, these ethical restraints apply to the interview of present and former employees in the two classes.[14]

Thus, "for now" counsel would be barred from any ex parte contact with an opponent's present or former management employees who are within the "control group," but permitted, but only with notice, to pursue contacts with present employees who are not within the control group.[15]

III. Former Employees

Although there is some authority to the contrary,[16] the majority of courts have ruled that Rule 4.2 does not prohibit communication with former employees.[17] The ABA has taken this position:

> [I]t is the opinion of the Committee that a lawyer representing a client in a matter adverse to a corporate party that is represented by another lawyer may, without violating Model Rule 4.2, communication about the subject to the representation with an unrepresented former employee of the corporate party without the consent of the corporation's lawyer.[18]

Many courts agree. In *Hanntz v. Shiley, Inc., Division of Pfizer, Inc.*,[19] a product liability action involving allegedly defective artificial heart valves, the court permitted plaintiff's counsel to interview, ex parte, Pfizer employees familiar with how heart valves are handled during the manufacturing process. The court concluded that applying Rule 4.2 to former employees does not serve the rule's primary purposes of preventing a "represented party from being overwhelmed by opposing counsel in the absence of friendly counsel" and preventing "the disruption of the attorney-client relationship by opposing counsel."[20] Former employees, even managerial employees, the court held, cannot bind the corporation once their agency relationship with the corporation is terminated.[21] In addition, statements made by such employees cannot be imputed to the corporation as a party admission, as least under the Federal Rules of Evidence, because the employee is not acting within the scope of his or her employment.[22]

But contact with former employees is not without limits, as counsel learned in *Rentclub v. Transamerica Rental Finance Corp.*,[23] a federal case arising in the Middle District of Pennsylvania. In *Rentclub*, counsel for one party retained the other party's former chief financial officer as a "trial consultant." Five days after the former CFO received his fee, he executed an affidavit adverse to his former employer. This prompted a motion to disqualify the law firm for its communication with the former employee and the alleged appearance of professional impropriety.[24]

In disqualifying counsel, the trial court first held that a former employee may be considered a "party" after it reviewed the rule's comments, which defined "party" as including (1) managerial employees, (2) any other person whose acts or omissions in connection with the matter at issue may be imputed to the corporation for liability, and (3) persons whose statements constitute admissions by the corporation.[25] Noting that the first and third categories "are clearly limited to current employees," the court determined that the second category would include a former employee who possessed privileged or confidential information or materials.

> [A] former employee who is a "party" because of his position and knowledge will remain a party even after he leaves the corporation because that employee has a memory. The corporation continues to have a vital interest in the employee's knowledge of privileged information and its potential release to opposing counsel in litigation after the employee leaves.[26]

Because the former chief financial officer fell within its interpretation of the rule, the district court disqualified the firm that had retained him as a trial consultant.[27]

The same court was faced with a similar problem in *Browning v. AT&T Paradyne*.[28] In *Browning*, a supervisory employee of a corporate defendant evaluated and terminated fellow employees in a corporate reduction in force. Soon thereafter, the supervisor himself was terminated. When the terminated supervisor joined with the former employees he had helped terminate and brought an age discrimination suit, the corporate defendant moved to disqualify plaintiff's counsel for communicating with the former supervisor.

The court was unwilling to give the *Rentclub* decision such reach, noting that such a construction would place the former employee in an untenable predicament: he could not be represented by defendant's counsel because his and the company's interests were in conflict. The court found that the plaintiffs' counsel could not logically be accused of having ex parte communications with their own client.[29]

The *Rentclub* decision has not been more broadly interpreted applied within the same federal district. For example, in *Lang v. Reedy Creek Improvement District*,[30] the court refused to expand *Rentclub* and allowed counsel to conduct ex parte communications with former firefighters in their investigation of a sex discrimination suit brought by other female former fire fighters.

Recognizing that the *Rentclub* decision focused on high-level employees who were privy to privileged or confidential information, the *Lang* court found the need to weigh the conflicting needs of the parties:

> the Plaintiffs' need for informal discovery and the Defendants' need for effective legal representation and to avoid both unnecessary impediments to informal discovery and inadequate protection of corporate interests.[31]

Balancing these interests, the court noted that "[p]roof of wrongdoing, and especially of discrimination is difficult to establish and Plaintiffs must be afforded the opportunities to discover all factual information pertinent to their case."[32] The *Lang* court, however, did not give plaintiffs' counsel carte blanche to interview everyone with such information. It precluded contact with current employees. The court stated:

> [I]t would be difficult to conceive of a scenario in which Plaintiffs could contact current employees . . . without risking violation of the ethical rules. . . . Because of the increased risks of prejudice to the defendants that would arise from ex *parte* communications with current employees, the plain language of the ethical rules, and defendants' opposition to such contact, the court is unwilling to give plaintiffs the "green light for such discovery."[33]

The court set strict guidelines for the proposed contact by the plaintiffs' counsel. It required that counsel immediately identify herself as the attorney representing the plaintiff, to specify the purpose of the contact, and to advise the former employee that she need not participate in the interview. The court also cautioned counsel to avoid the disclosure of privileged materials. Plaintiffs' counsel was directed to create a list of all persons contacted and preserve all statements and notes resulting from the contacts. These lists, statements, and notes were subject to review by defense counsel to protect the attorney work-product privilege.[34]

The permissible scope of contact with former employees may not be clear within even the same jurisdiction. In *Barfuss v. Diversicare Corp. of America*[35] and *Reynoso v. Greynold's Park Manor, Inc.*,[36] two Florida state courts charted two very different paths regarding the scope of communications with former employees. In *Barfuss*, the court ruled that plaintiff's counsel was not permitted to communicate with former nursing home employees who had participated in the plaintiff's care. On the other hand, the court permitted counsel to speak with former employees who did not provide any care to the plaintiff, characterizing these employees as "merely witnesses" to the plaintiff's care, and thus, not likely to possess privileged information.[37]

The other Florida district court provided a more liberal view of the rule by permitting broader questioning of employees.[38] In *Reynoso*, the court held that Rule 4-4.2 did not prevent the plaintiff from conducting ex parte interviews—either directly or through investigators—with 60 former employees of the defendant nursing home who had formerly worked in the plaintiff's ward.[39] In doing so, the court was quick to counsel that "no inquiry can be made into any matters that are the subject of attorney/client privilege, and the requirements of Rule 4-4.3, entitled *'Dealing with Unrepresented Persons,'* must be scrupulously observed."[40] The *Reynoso* decision was followed by another Florida court in *Estate of Schwartz v. H.B.A. Management*,[41] which also permitted contact with former nursing-home employees.

The American Bar Association has issued a formal ethics opinion in agreement with the more liberal view that an attorney may speak with former employees, seemingly without regard to the position previously held by the employees:

> [A] lawyer representing a client in a matter adverse to a corporate party that is represented by another attorney may, without violating Model Rule 4.2, communicate about the subject of the representation with an unrepresented former employee of the corporate party without the consent of the corporation's lawyer.[42]

However, the ABA Opinion sounds a note of caution:

> [N]either the Rule nor its comment purports to deal with *former* employees of a corporate party. Because an organizational party (as contrasted to an individual party) necessarily acts through others, however, the concerns reflected in the Comment to Rule 4.2 may survive the termination of the employment relationship.[43]

The Florida Bar reached the same result in its analysis of the rule, finding that "former managers and other former employees are not within the scope of the rule of *ex parte* contact." As comforting as these opinions might seem, they are not binding on any court, including those courts in Florida that may be called upon to review the matter.

The court in *Lang* is not alone in permitting contact with former employees only after the establishment of a strict protocol for the contact, and providing to the opposing parties the fruits of the interviews as a condition of the sought-after ex parte communication.[44] Some courts, however, have taken a less restrictive view and permit contact with former employees unhampered by considerations other than the applicable ethical rules regulating contact with an unrepresented person. In *Rewis v. FMC Corp*,[45] the court took the least restrictive approach to the ex parte communication issue—holding that the ethical rule did not reach former employees, even former managerial employees, with whom counsel is free to communicate. Of course, the court noted that contact with former employees who were in fact represented by the company's counsel would be impermissible and proscribed inquiry into privileged matters.

A number of other courts have also given counsel permission to contact any former employee. In doing so, these courts often explain their decisions as in accord with the purpose of the rule. The rule, they say, presumes that persons contacted by counsel may be susceptible to manipulation by opposing counsel. It is designed to prevent unrepresented persons from being overwhelmed in the absence of friendly counsel and to protect the attorney-client privilege.[46]

In *Hanntz v. Shiley, Inc., Division of Pfizer, Inc.*,[47] the court acknowledged these concerns but held that they were only "remotely, if ever, implicated in the situation of a former employee" and that the ethical restrictions on communication with the unrepresented would protect against inquiry into privileged matters and other unfair tactics. While nothing in the rule or the comment limits the categories of persons with whom communication is prohibited to current employees, it is likewise true that they do not indicate that the rule reaches beyond the bounds of employment.[48]

Some courts, while permitting contact with former employees, have prohibited contact with former managerial employees whose acts are the subject of the litigation or who had some part in the alleged wrongful acts.[49]

The price for guessing wrong about how a particular judge will feel about the particular communication with former or current employees can be stiff. The question often presents itself in the context of a motion to disqualify. Counsel will find themselves fighting an ethical war on pain of disqualification. Sometimes courts impose less onerous sanctions, such as fees, the exclusion of testimony, or fines.[50]

It appears that a majority of courts interpret the rule to permit contact with former employees, although in doing so they frequently point out other ethical constraints in dealing with unrepresented persons such as impermissibly acquiring privileged information.[51] The attorney-client privilege covering a communication between a former employee and an organization's counsel "belongs to the organization, and can only be waived by the organization."[52] This remains so even after the employee has left their employment.

Thus, where a former employee has information that is protected by the corporation's attorney-client privilege, the scope of the opposing party's inquiry is severely limited and effectively makes such an employee off limits.[53] A similar caution was expressed by the court in *Dubois v. Gradco Systems, Inc.*,[54] in which the court stated, "[W]ith respect to any unrepresented former employee, plaintiff's counsel must take care not to seek to include or listen to disclosures by the former employees of any privileged attorney-client communications to which the employee was privy."[55] The court's opinion in *Rentclub*[56] is entirely consistent with this line of decisions. The ABA has taken a similar position:

> With respect to *any* unrepresented former employee, of course, the potentially-communicating adversary attorney must be careful not to seek to induce the former employee to violate the privilege attaching to attorney-client communications to the extent that his or her communications as a former employee with his or her former employer's counsel are protected by the privilege (a privilege not belonging to or for the benefit of the former employee, by the former employer). Such an attempt could violate Rule 4.4 (requiring respect for the rights of third persons).[57]

A corporation faced with the testimony of a former employee therefore has both the right and the duty to aggressively protect privileged information from disclosure, particularly when the employee is playing a role in litigation against the company. Employers can also take comfort in knowing that the adversary's attorney giving consideration to exploitation of the former employee may be given pause by the risk of violating Rule 4.4 of the Rules of Professional Conduct and the fallout from such a violation, which might include disciplinary proceedings, disqualification as counsel, or exclusion of testimony. The message in such circumstances to former employees and plaintiffs' counsel alike should be that the privilege and all communications that are encompassed by it will be maintained and defended by the corporation by whatever means are necessary.

IV. Creation of Attorney-Client Relationships with Former Employees

The attorney-client relationship cannot be created ex parte. An attorney that represents a corporation cannot unilaterally take on the representation of an employee unless that employee agrees to that representation. Nor can an employee assert that corporate counsel represents the employee when corporate counsel has agreed to represent only the corporation.

In *Brown v. St. Joseph's County*,[58] the defendant argued that plaintiff's counsel was prohibited from communicating with former employees because its insurance carrier provided coverage for current and former employees and had provided counsel to its former employees. The court, noting that the attorney-client relationship was generally determined by principles of agency and contract, held that it could not be unilaterally created without the "client's" consent and refused to permit the assertion of the privilege.[59]

V. Strategies to Prevent Access to Key People and Information

A. Identify Key People

Within a large organization, it is impossible to identify every individual who could potentially become a witness. However, the most likely candidates are those involved in policy decisions and those who are or were part of the litigation defense team. These individuals can be identified on a "short list." Management should be aware that employees in these areas possess information that could be distorted by an adversary and used against the company. With respect to such persons a conscious effort must be made, during employment and particularly at termination, to minimize the risk that they will testify against the corporation. The best way to prevent future litigation problems may be for the employee's supervisor and the company's human resources department to address any personnel problems in a timely fashion.

When the names of former employees have to be disclosed in discovery, the company or its counsel should contact them to alert them of this fact and let them know that they may be contacted by opposing counsel. Obviously, ethical considerations must be honored. Whereas current employees may be advised to refrain from giving information to another party, former employees may not. However, it is permissible to suggest to ex-employees that, in view of possible obligations arising out of the past employment, they might prefer to refer opposing counsel either to their own attorney or to the company's counsel. In any event, a serious effort should be made to build a positive relationship with the ex-employee, possibly utilizing the good offices of a present employee friendly to the former colleague.

1. *Require Confidentiality Agreements*

Confidentiality agreements can also be an effective method of protecting confidential business information and trade secrets. Although strictly speaking, written agreements are not necessary to enforce nondisclosure of trade secrets, they are evidence that the employee was aware that the company deemed the information confidential and proprietary. Courts have routinely upheld employment agreements containing noncompetition agreements and confidentiality agreements if they do not overreach.[60] As with any contract, confidentiality agreements require consideration to be enforceable. It is best to include any such agreement in the initial agreements at the beginning of employment. A confidentiality agreement signed at termination as a condition of obtaining the final paycheck may not reflect sufficient consideration and may be unenforceable.

2. *Enjoin the Former Employee*

Breach of a valid confidentiality agreement provides a legal basis to enjoin a former employee from working with opposing counsel. In *Uniroyal Goodrich Tire Co. v. Hudson*,[61] for example, the court refused to dissolve an injunction it had issued precluding William Hudson, a former Uniroyal employee, from giving expert testimony in a product liability action pending in state court in Georgia. Uniroyal successfully argued that the agreement signed by Hudson, which prohibited him from disclosing or using Uniroyal trade secrets and confidential or proprietary information, was a valid and enforceable contract and that Hudson's testimony would conflict with the secrecy agreement.

In addition, many states have common law and statutory prohibitions against the disclosure of confidential business information.[62] These prohibitions are perhaps strongest and most likely to be enforced with respect to those whose work was predominantly and intimately integrated with legal counsel.[63] Counsel should be able to enjoin a former employee in this category from consulting and testifying for parties adverse to his or her former employer.

In *American Motors Corp. v. Huffstutler*,[64] the Ohio Supreme Court reinstated AMC's permanent injunction preventing one of AMC's former employees from testifying and consulting with attorneys in product liability litigation involving AMC without AMC's consent or an order of the court. The employee, Rahn Huffstutler, had worked for AMC as an engineer. While employed by AMC, he attended law school and, after graduation, was admitted to the Ohio bar. Huffstutler subsequently became manager of a product-design study group and worked closely with both in-house and private outside counsel on product liability cases. Later, he became a technical specialist, responsible for new vehicle model and production analysis, and thereafter became AMC's manager of quality services. Huffstutler was terminated by AMC, and soon began marketing himself as an expert witness against AMC.[65] In upholding the permanent injunction, the Ohio Supreme Court wrote:

> Huffstutler was an agent of AMC Jeep's Legal Department and frequently gave legal advice and performed legal analysis; that he served from 1981 to 1982 as an important member of the products liability defense team; that he represented AMC Jeep as counsel in product liability matters and routinely consulted with AMC Jeep's legal staff and retained counsel; that he assisted AMC Jeep's legal staff in retaining expert witnesses and met with experts to prepare strategy for defense; that he recommended outside counsel; that he suggested lines of testimony and cross-examination; and that he gave generously of his engineering ,judgment and legal training to assist counsel in the preparation of defenses.[66]

The court viewed Huffstutler as, at a minimum, an agent of AMC's legal counsel and as such held him subject to all of the restrictions of the attorney-client privilege and work-product doctrine.[67] In so doing, the court also explained that "[t]he attorney-client privilege . . . protects against any dissemination of information obtained in the confidential relationship. Thus, allowing consultation and discussion (even without testifying) of privileged information would effectively emasculate the privilege."[68]

Similarly, in *Elwell v. General Motors*,[69] General Motors successfully obtained a permanent injunction precluding Ronald Elwell, a former GM engineer who worked as a member of GM's in-house litigation defense team, from

> consulting or discussing with or disclosing to any person any of General Motors Corporation's trade secrets, confidential information or matters of attorney-client work product relating in any manner to the subject matter of any products liability litigation whether already filed

> or filed in the future which Ronald Elwell received, had knowledge of, or was entrusted with during his employment with General Motors Corporation.[70]

Elwell's duties as an in-house litigation expert included, among other things, interpreting technical information made available to GM's legal staff and outside counsel; consulting with GM's engineers in connection with product liability litigation; advising GM's lawyers on strategic litigation issues and responding to counsel's inquiries before, during, and after trial; developing demonstrative evidence to be used at trial, including laboratory testing of components and crash testing of vehicles; and testifying as an expert witness for GM in cases challenging the fuel systems of GM vehicles. Elwell was also enjoined from testifying, without the prior written consent of General Motors Corporation, either upon deposition or at trial, as an expert witness, or as a witness of any kind, and from consulting with attorneys or their agents in any litigation already filed or to be filed in the future, involving General Motors Corporation as an owner, seller, manufacturer and/or designer of the product(s) in issue. The court's order, however, expressly exempted Elwell's activity in connection with the Moseley litigation, in which he had already provided deposition testimony. In so doing, the court concluded that GM had met its burden of establishing (1) that it would be irreparably harmed if Elwell disclosed privileged information in his possession; (2) that GM had no adequate remedy at law; and (3) that the public interest weighed in favor of granting the permanent injunction. *Elwell* illustrates the advisability of choosing a forum for injunction proceedings apart from the jurisdiction in which a products liability case involving the former employee is pending.

3. *Quash Third-Party Subpoenas*

Through discovery or investigation, counsel may identify a pertinent former employee who is not interested in being a turncoat. This has not deterred some counsel on occasion from noticing such an individual for a deposition and having a subpoena served to enforce the former employee's presence. The attorney may not be seeking to elicit new information to help his case, but may be attempting to put words into the witness's mouth using leading questions and documents already in his possession. The former employee could be faced with responding to questions beginning with "Isn't it true that . . ." followed by the extract sought to be memorialized by the witness's sworn testimony. Under the Federal Rules of Civil Procedure, there is a mechanism for preventing this "back door" approach.

Rule 45, which governs third-party subpoenas, enables an employee to move to quash the subpoena if it "requires disclosure of privileged or other protected matter and that no exception or waiver applies."[71] The same tactic can be taken if the subpoena "requires disclosure of a trade secret or other confidential research, development, or commercial information."[72] It would be appropriate to furnish counsel to the former employee for this purpose. Furthermore, the company itself should have standing to seek, on behalf of a former employee, an order to protect the company's rights and privileges with respect to the information sought by way of deposition pursuant to Federal Rule 45.[73]

B. Trial Strategies

1. *Move to Disqualify*

A motion to disqualify former employees and experts can be used before trial. In *Lumber & Cedar Co. v. Norton Co.*,[74] involving a product defect claim by a window manufacturer against a window sealant manufacturer, the plaintiff window manufacturer successfully moved to disqualify the defendant's expert on the ground that the expert had previously been engaged as a consulting engineer for the plaintiff. In granting this motion, the court noted that the matters involved in the pending litigation were "substantially related" to the matters worked on by the expert, in which he obtained a "basic understanding of . . . modus operandi, patterns of operation, decision-making-process and the like."[75] In some jurisdictions, a motion in limine may be the preferred vehicle to disqualify a former employee from testifying at trial, or at least to bar testimony of privileged or other confidential information.[76]

In a particularly egregious case, it may also be possible to move to disqualify the attorney or firm that improperly obtains privileged information. The oft-cited case of *Williams v. Trans World Airlines, Inc.*,[77] involving a former TWA employee who had assisted attorneys in investigating employment discrimination charges, provides a good example of a law firm being disqualified for using a former employee. In so doing, the court wrote:

> Non-lawyer personnel are widely used by lawyers to assist in rendering legal services. Paralegals, investigators, and secretaries must have ready access to client confidences in order to assist their attorney employers. If information provided by a client in confidence to an attorney for the purpose of obtaining legal advice could be used against the client because a member of the attorney's non-lawyer support staff left the attorney's employment, it would have a devastating effect both on the free flow of information between client and attorney and on the cost and quality of the legal services rendered by an attorney. Every departing secretary, investigator, or paralegal would be free to impart confidential information to the opposition without effective restraint. The only practical way to assure that this will not happen and to preserve public trust in the scrupulous administration of justice is to subject these "agents" of lawyers to the same disability lawyers have when they leave legal employment with confidential information.[78]

2. *Size Up the Hostile Ex-Employee Witness*

The ex-employee with a grudge against the former employer is an old story and probably dates back to the beginnings of master-servant relationships.

The causes are not infinite but are so numerous that there is no point in trying to list them. Events in our economy in recent years, for example, downsizing and restructuring, have the potential for creating ex-employees who feel, rightly or wrongly, that their loyalties have been betrayed. Such ex-employees may be ripe prospects for a retaliatory strike delivered by testifying against their old employer in the context of a products claim.

While one should not become lost in amateur psychological analyses of such individuals, some consideration of the background of their feelings of antagonism may be helpful in developing an approach for cross-examination. The antagonism may not be universal. The employee may have fond relationships with former coworkers and even with supervisors. With some individuals, bitter feelings may be overridden by appealing to the individual's own sense of integrity or professionalism. There may be, in many cases, the opportunity for defense counsel to induce the ex-employee to soften the effect of anticipated adverse testimony.

3. *Defuse the Former Witness at Trial*

There always will be cases in which, for whatever reason, a former employee will show up as a witness and will be permitted a great deal of freedom by the court to testify. The gravamen of the testimony of such a witness is generally not the merits of the case, but establishment of the company as a corporate rogue routinely making decisions exalting profits over safety, and systematically destroying or concealing unfavorable documents.

Any discussion of strategy on dealing with the former employee on cross-examination must start with a disclaimer: every case and every witness is different. Each lawyer will have a personal method and style that will be right for him or her. Even though we are in a highly subjective area, a few observations might be helpful. It goes without saying that once the former employee's role has been established, a searing and perhaps exhaustive deposition should be scheduled as promptly as possible. Limitations of the former employee's knowledge and role in past decisions and events can be identified. Also, concessions may be obtained, such as the former employee's observations of responsible conduct on the part of the corporation, that might undercut the theme of the rogue corporation.

As noted above, the former employee is usually but not invariably hostile. If possible, this hostility can be used to attack the credibility of the testimony. Merely establishing that the witness bears hostility against the former employer is, however, seldom enough because the jury may view the hostility as justified and not enough to discredit the former employee's testimony. Unless the circumstances giving rise to the hostility weigh heavily against the former employee, it is probably best to establish only the existence of hostility, and not attempt to establish the reason for the hostility. Once hostility has been established, the cross-examination of the former employee can set the stage for affirmative evidence presented by the company in its own case to refute the substance of the former employee's claims.

With a concerted strategy that incorporates defense witnesses and documents along with the former employee's cross-examination, the ultimate goal should be to demonstrate that the ex-employee is a bitter individual who will exaggerate his importance, fill the gaps in his firsthand knowledge with raw speculation, and take great liberties with the truth in seeking revenge on his former employer. This may not always be possible, and it never will be easy to accomplish, but it just might make the opposing counsel regret that he ever recruited the former employee.

VI. Conclusion

As discussed in this chapter, the former employee witness is not in court to testify on the merits. His or her role is to poison the atmosphere so the company will not get a fair trial. The problem this creates is not one that can be ignored. Wherever possible it should be anticipated and efforts made to minimize its insertion into litigation. Where the law permits the availability of such a witness to opposing counsel, the turncoat issue should be attacked. At trial, the problem must be addressed in opening statement and put into context right at the beginning. Once the evidence is completed, there should be no loose ends that have not been attended to either in cross-examination or in the defendant's case. If things have gone right, opposing counsel's use of the turncoat may be the most effective argument of all in demonstrating the lack of merit of the claim.

Notes

1. *See generally* Annotated Model Rules of Prof'l Conduct (7th ed. 2011).
2. Model Rules of Prof'l Conduct, R. 4.2 (2009).
3. *See generally* Stephen M. Sinaiko, *Ex Parte Communication and the Corporate Adversary: A New Approach*, 66 N.Y.U. L. Rev. 1456, 1463–75 (1991) (discussing the purposes underlying the prohibition of ex parte communication of represented parties).
4. 863 F. Supp. 1204 (D. Nev. 1993).
5. *Id.* at 1213.
6. *See generally* Jerome N. Krulewitch, *Ex Parte Communication with Corporate Parties: The Communication with One of Adverse Interest*, 82 Nw. U. L. Rev. 1274 (1988).
7. *See, e.g.*, Fla. Bar re Rules Regulating the Fla. Bar, 494 So. 2d 977, 978 (Fla. 1986).
8. Annotated Model Rules of Prof'l Conduct R. 4.2 (4th ed. 1999).
9. *See* Sinaiko, *supra* note 3, at 1482; *see also* John D. Hodson, Annotation, *Right of Attorney to Conduct Ex Parte Interviews with Corporate Party's Nonmanagement Employees*, 50 A.L.R. 4th 652, 656–57 (1985).
10. Fair Auto. Repair, Inc. v. Car-X Serv. Sys. Inc., 128 Ill. App. 3d 763, 471 N.E.2d 554, 560 (Ill. App. 1984) (articulating the control group test); Messing, Rudovsky & Waliky, P.C. v. President & Fellows of Harvard Coll., 436 Mass. 347, 764 N.E.2d 825 (2002); *see also In re* Investigation of FMC Corp., 430 F. Supp. 1108 (S.D. W. Va. 1977) (applying West Virginia law to preclude interviews of only the president, chairman of the board, and select plant managers).

11. Wright *ex rel.* Wright v. Group Health Hosp., 103 Wash. 2d 192, 691 P.2d 564, 569 (1984) (setting forth the binding admission test); *see also* Niesig v. Team I, 76 N.Y.2d 363, 558 N.E.2d 1030, 1035, 559 N.Y.S.2d 493 (1990) (precluding ex parte communication with "corporate employees whose acts or omissions in the matter under inquiry are binding on the corporation," that is, "employees with 'speaking authority' for the corporation," "employees who are so closely identified with the interests of the corporate party as to be indistinguishable from it," and those "actually effectuating the advice of counsel in the matter"; and agents of a party who can bind the party in litigation or settle controversies on its behalf); Frey v. Dep't of Health & Human Servs., 106 F.R.D. 32, 37–38 (E.D.N.Y. 1985); Chancellor v. Boeing Co., 678 F. Supp. 250 (D. Kan. 1988); State v. Ciba-Geigy Corp., 247 N.J. Super. 314, 589 A.2d 180 (N.J. 1991).
12. *See, e.g., In re* Shell Oil Refinery, 132 F.R.D. 437, 441 (E.D. La. 1990) (noting that the protection of in-house expert's work "supports improved public safety and other social benefits of self-analysis"); Hermsdorfter v. Am. Motors Corp., 96 F.R.D. 13, 15 (W.D.N.Y. 1982).
13. Mass. Bar Ass'n, Formal Op. 7, at 1 (1982).
14. *In re* Op. 668 of the Advisory Comm. on Prof'l Ethics, 134 N.J. 284, 303, 633 A.2d 959, 964 (1993).
15. *Id.*
16. A few courts have read Rule 4.2 as prohibiting ex parte communication with former employees of a corporate party "if there is the possibility of the witnesses' testimony being imputed [to the company]," Pub. Serv. Elec. & Gas Co. v. Associated Elec. & Gas Ins. Serv., Ltd., 745 F. Supp. 1037, 1042 (D.N.J. 1990), a position that effectively precludes ex parte contact with all former employees who may have any information about the events in litigation. The Ninth Circuit has rules that ex parte communication with a former employee should be prohibited because such employees "may possess the relevant information needed by corporate counsel to advise the client with respect to actual or potential difficulties. *In re* Coordinated Pretrial Proceedings in Petroleum Prods. Antitrust Litig., 658 F.2d 1355, 1361 n.7 (9th Cir. 1981) (finding that the rationale of *Upjohn* applies with equal vigor to ex-employees), *cert. denied*, 455 U.S. 990 (1982) (citation omitted). "Again, the attorney-client privilege is served by the certainty that conversations between the attorney and client will remain privileged after the employee leaves." *Id.*
17. *See, e.g.*, Sherrod v. Furniture Ctr., 769 F. Supp. 1021, 1022 (W.D. Tenn. 1991); Hanntz v. Shiley, Inc., 766 F. Supp. 258, 263 (D.N.J. 1991); Dillon Co. v. SICO Co., No. 92-1512, 1993 U.S. Dist. LEXIS 17450, at *11 (E.D. Pa. Nov. 24, 1993). In *Dillon*, the court articulated the following test to determine when Rule 4.2 should be applied to former employees:

    > [A] rational approach should be employed whereby the propriety of the ex parte contact is determined by assessing the actual likelihood of disclosure of privileged materials, not a nebulous fear that such disclosure might occur. That assessment would depend upon weighing such factors as the positions of the former employees in relation to the issues in the suit; whether they were privy to communication between the former employer and its counsel concerning the subject matter of the litigation, or otherwise; the nature of the inquiry by opposing counsel; and how much

> time had elapsed between the end of the employment relationship and the questioning by opposing counsel. When such factors point to the conclusion that there is a substantial risk of disclosure of privileged matters, as opposed to the risk of the adverse party learning information which might be damaging to the former employer's litigation position, then appropriate notice should be given to the former employees concerning the former employer and, perhaps, the former employer's counsel should be notified prior to any ex parte interview. Any question concerning the appropriateness of the adversary's decision to proceed with ex parte contact with specific former employees can be resolved by determining whether any information gathered by the opponent actually intrudes upon privileged matters. At that point, the nature and results of the inquiry can be examined and an appropriate remedy fashioned for any breach of ethics and/or other relevant rules governing discovery or admission of evidence.

Id.

18. ABA Comm. on Ethics and Prof'l Responsibility, Formal Op. 91-359 (1991). A Connecticut district court, partly relying on the ABA's formal opinion, concluded that Connecticut's analogue to Rule 4.2 does not prohibit ex parte contact with former employees. Dubois v. Gradco Sys., Inc., 136 F.R.D. 341, 345 (D. Conn. 1991). In so doing, the court reasoned that if the drafters of Model Rule 4.2 meant "other person" to include former employees, they easily could have done so explicitly. *Id.* There seems little doubt that the drafters would have been explicit had they intended, as defendants claim they did intend, to overturn the traditional view that the former employees are not encompassed within the term some "party." *In re* Domestic Air Transp. Antitrust Litig., 141 F.R.D. 556, 561 (N.D. Ga. 1992) ("Rule 4.2 does not prohibit communications with former employees of a defendant corporation as long as the former employees are not in fact represented by the corporation's attorney."). *But see* Lang v. Superior Court, 170 Ariz. 602, 826 P.2d 1228 (1992) (refusing to follow the ABA's formal opinion because former employees may be persons whose acts or omissions in connection with the matter in litigation might be imputed to the corporate defendant).
19. 766 F. Supp. 258 (D.N.J. 1991).
20. *Id.* at 265.
21. *Id.* at 266.
22. *Id.*
23. 811 F. Supp. 651 (M.D. Fla. 1992), *aff'd*, 43 F.3d 1439 (11th Cir. 1995).
24. As the *Rentclub* court noted, Florida's Code of Professional Responsibility does not note an express provision that such conduct has the appearance of impropriety, but Florida case law unquestionably retains the requirement. State Farm Mut. Auto. Co. v. K.A.W., 575 So. 2d 630, 633 (Fla. 1991) ("[E]ven the appearance of impropriety may, under the appropriate circumstances, require prompt remedial action. . . . Consequently, any doubt is to be resolved in favor of disqualification.")
25. *Rentclub*, 811 F. Supp. at 657.
26. *Id.* at 658.
27. The court seemed to be particularly troubled by the firm for having paid the witness for factual testimony and not "trial consultation." The court thus

applied a two-prong test to determine whether the appearance of impropriety warranted disqualification:

> First, although proof of actual wrongdoing is not required, there must exist a reasonable possibility that some specific identifiable impropriety did in fact occur. Second, the likelihood of public suspicion or obloquy must outweigh the social interests that will be served by the attorney's continued participation in the case."

Rentclub, 811 F. Supp. at 64 (citing Norton v. Tallahassee Mem. Hosp., 689 F.2d 938 (11th Cir. 1982)).

28. 838 F. Supp. 1564 (M.D. Fla. 1993).
29. *Id.* at 1567–68.
30. 888 F. Supp. 1143 (M.D. Fla. 1995).
31. *Id.* at 1145.
32. *Id.* at 1148.
33. *Id.*
34. *Lang*, 888 F. Supp. at 1148–49.
35. 656 So. 2d 486 (Fla. Ct. App. 1995).
36. 659 So. 2d 1156 (Fla. Ct. App. 1995).
37. *Barfuss*, 656 So. 2d at 486, *overruled by* H.B.A. Mgmt. v. Estate of Schwartz *ex rel.* Schwartz, 693 So. 2d 541 (Fla. 1997). In *H.B.A. Mgmt.*, the Florida Supreme Court did away with the distinction "between former employees who witnessed an event and those whose act or omission caused the event." 693 So. 2d at 546.
38. *See* Manor Care of Dunedin, Inc. v. Keiser, 611 So. 2d 1305 (Fla. Ct. App. 1992) (permitting contact with all former nursing-home employees).
39. 659 So. 2d at 1157–1158.
40. *Id.*
41. 673 So. 2d 116 (Fla. 4th DCA 1996).
42. ABA Comm. on Ethics and Prof'l Responsibility, Formal Op. 91-359 (1991).
43. *Id.*
44. Curley v. Cumberland Farms, Inc., 134 F.R.D. 77, 92 (D.N.J. 1991) (permitting contact with nonmanagerial, former employees); *In re* Home Shopping Network, 1989 WL 201085 (M.D. Fla. 1989); Suggs v. Capital Cities/ABC, Inc., 1990 WL 182314 (S.D.N.Y. 1990); *In re* Envtl. Ins. Declaratory Judgment Action, 252 N.J. Super. 510, 600 A.2d 165 (1993).
45. Case No. 88-47-CIV-T-10(C) (M.D. Fla. 1989).
46. Frey v. Dep't of Health & Human Servs., 106 F.R.D. 32, 34 (E.D.N.Y. 1985); Valassis v. Samelson, 143 F.R.D. 118, 120 (E.D. Mich. 1992); Curley v. Cumberland Farms, Inc., 134 F.R.D. 77, 87 (D.N.J. 1991); Sherrod v. Furniture Ctr., 769 F. Supp. 1021, 1022 (W.D. Tenn. 1991).
47. 766 F. Supp 258, 265 (D.N.J. 1991).
48. *See also* Centennial Mgmt. Servs., Inc. v. AXA Re Vie, 193 F.R.D. 671 (D. Kan. 2000) (stating that former employees who no longer have an employment relationship are not included within the meaning of the term "party" for purposes of the rule prohibiting lawyer contact with a party).
49. Chancellor v. Boeing Co., 678 F. Supp. 250 (D. Kan. 1988); Porter v. Arco Metals Div. of Atl. Richfield, 642 F. Supp. 1116, 1118 (D. Mont. 1986); Amarin Plastics, Inc., v. Md. Cup Corp., 116 F.R.D. 36, 39–40 (D. Mass. 1987); Frey v. Dep't of Health & Human Servs., 106 F.R.D. 32, 36 (E.D.N.Y. 1985); Univ. Patents, Inc., v.

Kligman, 737 F. Supp. 325, 328 (E.D. Pa. 1990); PPG Indus., Inc., v. BASF Corp., 134 F.R.D. 118, 121 (W.D. Pa. 1990); Bobele v. Superior Court, 199 Cal. App. 3d 708; 245 Cal Rptr. 144, 147 (1988).

50. Rentclub v. Transamerica Rental Fin. Corp., 811 F. Supp. 651 (M.D. Fla. 1992), *aff'd*, 43 F.3d 1439 (11th Cir. 1995); Faison v. Thornton, 863 F. Supp. 1204 (D. Nev. 1993); Cagguila v. Wythe Labs., 127 F.R.D. 653 (E.D. Pa. 1989); Univ. Patents, Inc., v. Kligman, 737 F. Supp. 325, 328 (E.D. Pa. 1990); Sheldon v. Hess, 599 F. Supp. 905 (S.D. Tex. 1984); Am. Prot. Ins. Co. v. MGM Grand Hotel, No. CV-L V-82-26 HDM (D. Nev. Mar. 13, 1986); Camden v. Maryland, No. PJM 93-1854 (D. Ma. Jan. 24, 1996); Noorily v. Thomas Betts Corp., No. 93-2227 (D.N.J. Aug. 17, 1995).
51. Cram v. Lamson & Sessions Co., 148 F.R.D. 259 (S.D. Iowa 1993); Wright v. Wright, 691 P.2d 564 (Wash. 1984); United States v. W. Elec., 1990-1 Cases (CCH) ¶68,939, 1990 WL 39129 (D.C. Cir. 1990); Siguel v. Trs. of Tufts Coll., 1990 WL 29199 (D. Mass. 1990); Niesig v. Team I, 76 N.Y.2d 363, 369, 559 N.Y.S. 493, 558 N.E.2d 1030 (1990); DiOssi v. Edison, 583 A.2d 1343, 1345 (Del. 1990); Goff v. Wheaton Indus, 145 F.R.D. 351, 356 (D.N.J. 1992); Hanntz v. Shiley, Inc., 766 F. Supp. 258 (D.N.J. 1991); Action Air Freight, Inc., v. Pilot Air Freight Corp., 769 F. Supp. 899, 904 (E.D. Pa. 1991), *appeal dismissed*, 961 F.2d 207 (3d Cir. 1992); Shearson Lehman Bros. v. Wasatch Bank, 139 F.R.D. 412, 418 (D. Utah 1991); Dubois v. Gradco Sys., Inc., 136 F.R.D. 341, 345–47 (D. Conn. 1991); Valassis v. Samelson, 143 F.R.D. 118, 120 (E.D. Mich. 1992); *In re* Domestic Air Transp. Antitrust Litig., 141 F.R.D. 556, 564 (M.D. Ga. 1992); Strawser v. Exxon, 843 P.2d 613, 621 (Wyo. 1992); State v. CIBA-GEIGY Corp., 247 N.J. Super. 314, 589 A.2d 180 (1991), McCallum v. CSX Transp., Inc., 149 F.R.D. 104, 110 (M.D. N.C. 1993); Brown v. St. Joseph's Cnty., 148 F.R.D. 246 (N.D. Ind. 1993).
52. *E.g.*, Cram v. Lamson & Sessions Co., 148 F.R.D. 259, 266 (S.D. Iowa 1993) (quoting Sequa Corp. v. Lititech, Inc., 807 F. Supp. 653, 668 (D. Colo. 1992)).
53. Thus, the court in *Breedlove v. Tele-Trip Co.*, No. 91C5702, 1992 WL 202147, at *2 (N.D. Ill. Aug. 14, 1992), concluded that no formal order barring communication with former employees who may be privy to privileged conversation or information is necessary because plaintiff's counsel, an officer of the court, is, "of course, barred from exploring these communications or other privileged matters with the witnesses").
54. 136 F.R.D. 341 (D. Conn. 1991).
55. *Id.* at 347.
56. 811 F. Supp. 651 (N.D. Fla. 1992).
57. ABA Comm. on Ethics and Prof'l Responsibility, Formal Op. 91-359 (1991).
58. 148 F. Supp. 246 (N.D. Ind. 1993).
59. *Id.* at 250; *see* United States v. Keplinger, 766 F. Supp. 678, 701–02 (7th Cir. 1985).
60. *See, e.g.*, Basicomputer Corp. v. Scott, 973 F.2d 507, 511–12 (6th Cir. 1992) (indicating that Ohio law recognizes the enforceability of nondisclosure agreements between employers and employees); Uniroyal Goodrich Tire Co. v. Hudson, No. 93-CV-74346-DI, 1994 WL 289000, at *3 (E.D. Mich. June 28, 1994) (enforcing an agreement signed by a former employee of Uniroyal prohibiting him from disclosing or using Uniroyal trade secrets and confidential or proprietary information after he left the company).
61. No. 93-CV-74346-D1, 1994 WL 289000, at *3 (E.D. Mich. June 28, 1994).
62. *See. e.g.*, Ohio Rev. Code Ann. § 1333.81 ("No employee of another, who in the course and within the scope of his employment receives any confidential matter

or information, shall knowingly, without the consent of his employer, furnish or disclose such matter or information to any person not privileged to acquire it."); Valises v. Samelson, 143 F.R.D. 118, 124 (E.D. Mich. 1992) (noting that individuals who become privy to privileged information during their employment remain precluded from disclosing that information even after they end their employment).

63. *Valises*, 143 F.R.D. at 124; Palmer v. Zobec, 144 F.R.D. 66, 67 (D. Md. 1992); Mayer v. Dell, 139 F.R.D. 1, 3 (D.D.C. 1991); Marvin Lumber & Cedar Co. v. Norton Co., 113 F.R.D. 588, 590–91 (D. Minn. 1986); Conforti & Eisele, Inc. v. Div. of Bldg. & Constr., 170 N.J. Super. 64, 405 A.2d 487, 492 (1979); United States v. Kovel, 296 F.2d 918, 921 (2d Cir. 1961); Williams v. Trans World Airlines, Inc., 588 F. Supp. 1037, 1044 (W.D. Mo. 1984).
64. 575 N.E.2d 116 (Ohio 1991).
65. *Id.* at 119.
66. *Id.* at 118.
67. *Id.* at 119.
68. *Id.* at 120–21; *see also* People v. Marcy, 91 Mich. App. 399, 283 N.W.2d 754, 757 (1979) ("Although decisions vary from one jurisdiction to another, the attorney-client privilege has been extended to cover, inter alia, an accountant, investigator, engineer . . . employed by either the client or the attorney to assist the attorney. . . ."); D. I. Chadbourne Inc. v. Superior Court, 60 Cal. 2d 723, 36 Cal. Rptr. 468, 388 P.2d 700, 709 (1964); *see generally Annotation, Persons Other than Client or Attorney Affected by, or Included within, Attorney-Client Privilege,* 96 A.L.R. 2d 125 (1964).
69. No. 91-115946NZ (Mich. Cir. Ct. 1992).
70. *Id.* at 1-2. Elwell's duties as an in-house litigation expert included, among other things, interpreting technical information made available to GM's legal staff and outside counsel; consulting with GM's engineers in connection with product liability litigation; advising GM's lawyers on strategic litigation issues and responding to counsel's inquiries before, during, and after trial; developing demonstrative evidence to be used at trial, including laboratory testing of components and crash testing of vehicles; and testifying as an expert witness for GM in cases challenging the fuel systems of GM vehicles.
71. Fed. R. Civ. P. 45(c)(3)(A)(iii).
72. Fed. R. Civ. P. 45(c)(3)(13)(i).
73. *See* David D. Siegel, *Practice Commentaries*, 28 U.S.C.A. at 391, Fed. R. Civ. P. 38 to 50, C45-22 (West 1992) (the adverse party may move to quash a nonparty subpoena "if that party has its own rights to assert in suppressing the subpoena, as where the subpoena seeks materials that would fall under one of the privileged categories (involving the party's privilege, of course)").
74. 113 F.R.D. 588 (D. Minn. 1986).
75. *Id.* at 591. Although *Marvin Lumber* involved a turncoat expert, as opposed to a turncoat employee, the case is still instructive. *See generally* Michael Hoening, *The "Turncoat" Expert*, N.Y. L.J., Sept. 9, 1991, at 3; Richard A. Saloman & Charles F. Regan, Jr., *Dealing with the Turncoat Expert*, Prod. Safety & Liab. Rep. (BNA) 644 (May 31, 1991).
76. *See* discussion of *Dillon Cos. v. SICO, supra* note 17.
77. 588 F. Supp. 1037 (W.D. Mo. 1984).

78. *Id.* at 1044. *See also* Rentclub Inc. v. Transamerica Rental Fin. Corp., 811 F. Supp. 651 (M.D. Fla. 1992) (disqualifying attorney who hired former CFO of defendant as a "trial consultant" because the former executive was privy to relevant confidential and proprietary information); Univ. Patents. Inc. v. Kligman, 737 F. Supp. 325 (E.D. Pa. 1990) (denying plaintiffs' motion for disqualification because defendant's attorneys had conducted ex parte interviews with plaintiffs' employees, but precluding the use of the information obtained from the employees (1) who were officers, directors, or managers; (2) whose acts or omissions could bind or impute liability to the plaintiffs; and (3) whose statements could be used as admissions against the plaintiffs).

CHAPTER 13

Discovery of the Nontestifying In-House Expert Assigned to Litigation

ANN MARIE MORTIMER*

* The author gratefully acknowledges the research assistance of Diana Biason, Hunton & Williams, LLP, and Joseph C. Kearfott for their thoughtful analysis of this issue in an earlier edition of this chapter.

I. Introduction

You receive an urgent call from one of your best clients. The bad news is that several months ago there was an industrial accident at its largest manufacturing facility. The good news is that nobody was hurt. The predictable news is that residents of Pleasantville, USA, in which the facility is located, just filed a class-action complaint alleging personal injuries and property diminution as a result of a "suspicious black cloud" that was released into the environment and that hung over the town for several hours immediately following the accident.

Knowing the roster of chemicals used by your client in its manufacturing process, your mind starts whirring with the list of possible personal injury allegations, including increased risk of cancer, immune suppression, various respiratory ailments, reproductive impairment, and a long list of other brain and organ damage claims. You learn that hours after the accident a number of the local residents were admitted to the hospital with a range of health complaints, fortunately none of them serious. The complaint was filed after a tense town hall meeting populated by concerned residents, disgruntled former employees of your client, and some of the area's best and brightest from the local plaintiffs bar: all the ingredients for a high-visibility lawsuit. You have been hired to defend the lawsuit.

A veteran of these type of toxic tort suits, you know that health claims based on diffuse environmental exposures to certain chemicals turn on critical expert testimony on issues including the dose and related effect of exposures to these chemicals, modeling of exposure levels, and a range of other scientific issues. You also know from experience that expert selection of both consulting and testifying experts can make the difference between success and failure. As your mind starts flipping through the names of possible experts, your client suggests you utilize in-house experts on the toxicity of the implicated chemicals and the projected plume of the cloud, not only for the sake of cost and efficiency sake, but also because of the experts' deep knowledge in these areas. You agree that the in-house experts will be specially assigned to the case for trial and will not be called as testifying experts. Despite these preliminary safeguards, alarm bells are ringing loudly and insistently in your head: What are the discovery risks for these in-house nontestifying experts, and what steps should you take up front to minimize that risk?

II. Understanding Rule 26(b)(4)(B): A Historical Perspective

When the Federal Rules of Civil Procedure were first adopted in 1938, there was no express provision governing expert testimony. For more than 30 years chaos reigned. While some courts permitted unfettered discovery of expert testimony, drawing broadly from concepts of "fairness" and the policy reason animating the discovery rules, other courts flatly rejected the notion of expert discovery, expressing concern that one side should not be assisted in "coat-tailing" on the diligence of the other party.[1] Responding to mounting inconsistencies and growing criticism of this case-by-case approach, subdivision (b)(4) of Rule 26 was added to the Federal Rules as part of the sweeping discovery reforms of 1970. According to the Advisory Committee, Rule 26(b)(4) was adopted in recognition of the growing role of experts in anticipation of and at trial, and to provide for a uniform system for discovery of expert information, or, in the words of the Advisory Committee, to deal "with discovery of information including facts and opinions obtained by a party from an expert retained by that party in relation to litigation or obtained by the expert and not yet transmitted to the party."[2] Rule 26(b)(4) was intended to provide a comprehensive framework for resolution of expert discovery issues, and it purports to be the exclusive means by which discovery can be obtained of "facts known and opinions held by experts, . . . acquired or developed in anticipation of litigation or for trial."[3]

Perhaps the most basic and significant feature of Rule 26 is that it expressly permits discovery of expert opinions, repudiating the view that expert work product was totally immune from discovery under the umbrella of either the attorney-client privilege or the work-product doctrine. On its face, Rule 26(b)(4) further drew a sharp distinction between the discoverability of testifying experts governed by Rule 26(b)(4)(A) and of nontestifying experts governed by Rule 26(b)(4)(B). Under this two-tier approach, liberal discovery of testifying experts is sanctioned under subsection (b)(4)(A), whereas discovery of nontestifying experts "who ha[ve] been retained or specially employed . . . in anticipation of litigation or preparation for trial" is allowable only "upon a showing of exceptional circumstances."[4]

Although Rule 26(b)(4)(B) creates a safe harbor from discovery whereby the facts and opinions of nontestifying specially retained or employed experts are shielded from discovery absent a showing of exceptional circumstances, the protection of the rule is by no means absolute, and therefore, at best, must be viewed as providing a qualified immunity from discovery. As one court rightly noted, "Rule 26(b)(4)(B) 'is not an impenetrable fortress against discovery and parties seeking discovery can make a showing of exceptional circumstances when there is no practicable alternative by which they can obtain information.'"[5] The creation of this qualified immunity is supported by sound policy reasons. First, the usual justification for expert discovery—to prevent trial by ambush and allow for adequate trial preparation—simply does not exist in the case of a nontestifying expert.[6] Apart from this distinction, there are other sound policy reasons in favor of liberal application of Rule 26(b)(4)(B) to nontestifying experts, including "(1) encouraging counsel to obtain the necessary expert advice without fear that the adversary may obtain such information; (2) preventing unfairness that would result from allowing an opposing party to reap the benefits from another party's efforts and expense; (3) preventing a chilling effect on experts serving as consultants if their testimony could be compelled; and (4) preventing prejudice to the retaining party if the opposing party were allowed to call at trial an expert who provided an unfavorable opinion to the party who first retained them."[7]

While the policy reasons animating adoption of the rule have stayed constant since its introduction in 1970, the text of the rule was modified in 1993, including by adding an amendment to subsection (a)(2) to require the identify of experts to be disclosed and that the disclosure be accompanied by a written report prepared and signed by the expert witness. Making explicit that this requirement extends to employee-experts, the requirements of Rule 26 applies to expert witnesses who are "retained or specially employed to provide expert testimony" and to those "whose duties as an employee of the party regularly involve giving expert testimony."[8]

Despite this clarification and the intent of the drafters to demystify the expert discovery process and impose uniformity on discovery requirements for experts, significant ambiguities remain, particularly with respect to application of the discovery rules to nontestifying in-house experts. First, and most obviously, prior to the 1993 amendments, Rule 26 did not specifically address employees or in-house experts, prompting some courts to conclude that the nontestifying employee expert could not qualify for expert status at all, and should be treated as an "ordinary witness" with no special dispensation from the usual liberal rules of discovery, limited only by the broad relevance standard of Rule 26(b)(1).[9] Reasoning that employees lacked the required objectivity to "see all sides of the issue," these courts relied heavily on the "specially employed" language in the rule to deny that an expert already employed and assigned for trial preparation could be eligible for the qualified discovery immunity afforded by Rule 26(b)(4)(B) and to conclude that in-house "experts" were not experts at all for purposes of Rule 26(b)(4)(B).[10]

Other commentators have urged that the exact opposite should apply and that nontestifying in-house experts should enjoy total immunity from any discovery, applying the same logic that shields consultants "informally consulted in preparation for trial" from all discovery.[11] The rationale for this "total protection" approach relies heavily on a strict constructionist reading of the former introductory language of Rule 26(b)(4)(B) (deleted in the 1993 amendments), which stated that discovery of experts who acquired information in anticipation of litigation or for trial "may be obtained *only* as follows."[12] Because nontestifying in-house experts may acquire information for the first time in anticipation of litigation or for preparation for trial yet they are not specifically identified in any of the rule's subsections, one may infer that no discovery of the in-house expert is permitted. This interpretation is arguably further bolstered with reference to the 1970 Advisory Committee Note, which states that because "informally consulted" experts are not expressly addressed in the rule, and the rule is intended to be comprehensive and exclusive in scope with respect to expert testimony, applying the same logic, no discovery may be had of these experts.[13] Since like informally consulted experts, nontestifying in-house experts are not expressly addressed in this subsection, a consistent interpretation would likewise immunize them from discovery.[14] To date, no federal courts have adopted this reasoning to completely shield in-house, nontestifying experts from discovery. Indeed, at least one court has been willing to encroach upon the formerly impregnable fortress of informally consulted experts by allowing discovery under Rule 45 by independent investigative methods on "informally consulted" expert witnesses.[15] Applying this same reasoning to nontestifying in-house experts, it seems doubtful that a strong argument can be made in favor of the view that nontestifying in-house experts should enjoy unqualified immunity from discovery.[16]

Although these divergent approaches to Rule 26(b)(4)(B) have prompted some commentators to conclude that there are actually three views of protection for nontestifying in-house experts under the rule—total protection, no protection, and qualified protection—since no court has either ruled that an in-house nontestifying expert is totally immune from protection or persisted with the overly restrictive "no protection" approach since the 1993 amendments, the real battleground with respect to Rule 26(b)(4)(B) appears to be how to navigate around potential discovery landmines embedded in the rule to be eligible for qualified protection under it. Although the 1993 amendments appear to resolve the issue of whether on the face in-house consultants can qualify as "experts" under the rule, many ambiguities and questions of construction remain, creating fertile opportunity for creative lawyering. For example, as for determining eligibility for the rule's qualified protection, the precise meaning of "retained or specially employed" is open to interpretation. Query, for example, if there is overlap between the in-house consultant's existing job responsibilities and the topics on which the consultant can be deemed to be "retained" or "specially employed." The phrase "in preparation for trial" also leaves room for argument. Even if the nontestifying in-house expert qualifies definitionally under Rule 26(b)(4)(B), the issue of what constitutes "exceptional circumstances" for piercing the qualified protection of the rule is also a matter of debate. The remainder of this chapter concentrates on that issue.

III. Making the Case for Qualified Protection of Nontestifying, In-House Experts under Rule 26(b)(4)(B)

For the reasons discussed above, the two extreme views that nontestifying in-house experts are either totally exempt from discovery or never eligible for the qualified protection of Rule 26(b)(4)(B) are neither satisfactory nor the apparent majority view. Instead, the prevailing view appears to be the middle ground: a regular employee can qualify for protection from discovery under Rule 26(b)(4)(B) where he is not an actor or viewer of the events giving rise to the lawsuit, and he is specially employed or assigned by a party to a particularly identified matter in anticipation of litigation or trial. For example, in *Seiffer v. Topsy's International, Inc.*, at the request of counsel, a partner of third-party defendant Touche Ross reviewed audit papers at stake in the litigation and made a report to counsel. Touche Ross resisted discovery on the grounds that the partner was an expert "specially retained or employed" within the meaning of Rule 26(b)(4)(B) and that no exceptional circumstances existed warranting departure from the rule against discovery of nontestifying experts. The court agreed, relying on four important facts: (1) the partner was not "simply a general employee" but had performed his review at counsel's request; (2) he had no prior involvement with the audits at issue in the lawsuit; (3) the analysis performed and the report prepared were specifically undertaken at the request of counsel; and (4) he was not designated as a testifying witness.[17] The court was further persuaded that the parenthetical language of the Advisory Committee Note, by strong negative implication, supported the view that "an in-house expert may be specially employed as well as an expert drawn from personnel other than the party's own."[18]

Perhaps the most thoughtful analysis of the discoverability of an in-house nontestifying expert was that done by the court in *In re Shell Oil Refinery*.[19] Much like the facts of the hypothetical in the introduction to this chapter, *Shell Oil* involved a class-action lawsuit resulting from an explosion at an oil refinery. At issue was the discoverability of the testimony of two in-house expert employees who were originally designated as testifying experts and had conducted certain tests at the direction of counsel, but were later de-designated and listed as nontestifying consultants. Having first allowed the defendant to de-designate the two employees as testifiers, the court turned to the issue of whether in-house experts could be "retained or specially employed" within the meaning of Rule 26(b)(4)(B). Ruling in the affirmative, the court reasoned:

> The Court finds that the persuasive authority favors application of Rule 24(b)(4)(B) to non-testifying in-house experts. To rule otherwise would encourage economic waste by requiring an employer to hire independent experts to obtain the protection of Rule 24(b)(4). Protection of an in-house expert's opinion's [sic] supports improved public safety and other social benefits of self-analysis. That the work of an in-house expert is used not only to defend a lawsuit but also to improve a company's operations or product design does not remove him from the parameters of Rule 26(b)(4)(B).[20]

Continuing with this economic waste policy argument, the court further reasoned that so long as the work was undertaken at the direction of counsel in anticipation of or preparation for trial, the fact that the employee was not additionally compensated for the work and still retained other outside work responsibilities did not destroy the expert's eligibility for Rule 26(b)(4)(B) protection.[21] The court's logic, though not universally accepted, passes the ultimate litmus test: common sense. Viewed from the perspective of the stated purpose of the Federal Rules of Civil Procedure—namely, to "secure the just, speedy, and inexpensive determination of every action"[22]—an approach that compels duplication of effort and expenditure of additional resources by forcing reliance on outside consultants has no obvious merit. Indeed, this result might not only stifle the type of internal self-examination that often helps effectuate positive change, but it would drive up already notoriously high litigation costs and contribute to a litigation system criticized for advantaging the economically strong. Allowing discovery of a nontestifying in-house expert's opinions would, moreover, likely chill rigorous trial preparation, both out of fear of creating unfavorable facts subject to discovery and to avoid the "free rider" problem of opening the litigation playbook to the other side and allowing the adversary to poach off the diligent party's trial preparation. For all these reasons, *Shell Oil* and its progeny represent the better view of the applicability of Rule 26(b)(4)(B) to in-house nontestifying experts.[23]

IV. Practical Challenges in Applying Rule 26(b)(4)(B) to In-House Experts

Beyond the first hurdle of convincing a court that an in-house nontestifying witness can be an "expert" within the meaning of Rule 26(b)(4)(B), the densely packed wording of this subsection is chock-full of potential traps for the unwary. Each and every clause of the subsection has meaning and imparts its own set of qualifying criteria for eligibility for the protection of 24(b)(4)(B). Common traps and concerns are discussed in this section.

A. What Does "Specially Retained" Mean in the Context of an Existing In-House Employee?

As a threshold matter, in order to be eligible for the qualified immunity of Rule 26(b)(4)(B) the in-house expert must be determined to be "specially retained" in anticipation of or for purposes of litigation. The prevailing view since *Shell Oil* seems to be that an employee can serve in the dual role of "specially retained" expert while at the same time maintaining his or her ordinary job responsibilities, so long as the would-be expert was not involved in the events that are the subject of the litigation and the expert tasks are (1) identifiable and (2) undertaken at the direction of and for report to counsel. Some courts, however, have rejected the notion that an in-house employee can qualify as an expert at all while still performing his or her regular job responsibilities, but have accepted that regular employees can under some circumstances serve as specially employed experts for purposes of Rule 26(b)(4)(B).[24] Although this appears to be a minority view, part of your risk calculus up front—taking into account the scope of the assignment, the resources of your client, the stakes of the case, and the controlling law in your jurisdiction—should be whether or not to greenlight your would-be expert to continue on his or her normal job responsibilities while serving as your specially retained or employed expert. To further bolster the argument that the in-house expert is "specially retained," the client should avoid asking the would-be expert to wear too many internal hats simultaneously. Courts have taken a dim view of attempts to designate an in-house employee both as a nontestifying expert and as a fact witness and even a Rule 30(b)(6) witness.[25] To avoid creating the appearance that the client is attempting both to benefit from the witness's "positive" testimony and to shield itself from "negative testimony," nontestifying experts should not be identified as both expert and fact witnesses. At minimum, the subject of the witness's expert testimony and factual knowledge should be sufficiently distinct as to allow a rational boundary to be drawn between the two areas of testimony.

B. What Does "In Anticipation of Litigation" Mean?

A lawyer who wishes to seek assistance from an in-house nontestifying expert without jeopardizing the protection of Rule 26(b)(4)(B) need not wait until a complaint is filed—all that is required is that the expert be consulted in "anticipation of litigation." Courts have taken a relatively liberal view of what this requirement means. While there is no requirement that a lawsuit actually be filed in order to conclude that an expert has been retained or employed in anticipation of litigation, "more than a remote possibility of litigation" is necessary.[26] Determined on a case-by-case basis, whether or not an act is taken in anticipation of litigation has, in the context of the work-product doctrine, been held to require "both a reasonable anticipation of litigation as well as a causal connection between the work and the litigation. . . . As a test for anticipation, this Court adopted the standard of the District of Columbia Circuit: '[T]he lawyer must at least have a subjective belief that litigation was a real possibility, and that belief must have been objectively reasonable.'"[27] Most courts further require that there be a plausible nexus between the work undertaken and potential litigation.[28] Where there is no evidence that the proffered expert's work or services differ in some way from his or her day to day job responsibilities, it is less likely the witness would qualify for nontestifying expert immunity.[29]

In the context of the in-house expert, this last requirement has special significance, as the expert will not be immunized from testifying about knowledge he or she obtained *prior to or unrelated to* anticipated litigation as a general employee. Even a legitimate designation of an in-house expert as specially retained in anticipation of litigation will not reach back and immunize preretention knowledge. Indeed, it has long been recognized "that one may simultaneously be a litigation expert with Rule 26(b)(4)(B) protection as to some matters and simply an unprotected actor or witness as to others."[30] In selecting your in-house expert, consider carefully and investigate diligently whether the proposed expert has any problematic preexisting knowledge and whether being designated as an in-house expert would increase the likelihood of that person becoming a discovery target, making disclosure of the preexisting knowledge more probable. You should consider all of these factors in evaluating whether the "anticipation of litigation" requirement has been satisfied in your case.

C. What Qualifies as "Exceptional Circumstances" for Purposes of Piercing the Qualified Discovery Protection of Rule 26(b)(4)(B)?

No matter how strong your argument that your in-house nontestifying expert was specially retained or employed in anticipation of litigation, discovery is still allowable in "exceptional circumstances." Although in theory the phrase itself seems pregnant with possibility, in practice courts set a high bar for circumstances in which discovery of a qualifying in-house expert can be taken. Moreover, once the champion of the privilege demonstrates that the discovery target is a qualified nontestifying expert, the burden shifts to the seeker of discovery to show that the "exceptional circumstances" requirement has been satisfied.[31] Claims of economic hardship generally fall short of the mark and tend to succeed only when there is an issue of judicial rather than litigant resources at stake.[32] Courts have required "impracticability" of the noneconomic variety; for example, where data or evidence no longer exists or has been altered or destroyed, disadvantaging one side or another.[33] The second line of cases finding "exceptional circumstances" involve those rare situations in which it is impossible or near impossible to replicate the expert discovery on a contested issue. "Under Rule 26(b)(4)(B), a party 'carries a heavy burden in demonstrating the existence of exceptional circumstances.' ... Exceptional circumstances may exist where (1) the object or condition at issue is destroyed or has deteriorated after the nontestifying expert observes it but before the moving party's expert has an opportunity to observe it; or (2) there are no other available experts in the same field or subject area."[34]

D. Who Has the Burden of Demonstrating Whether the Prerequisites of Rule 26(b)(4)(B) Have Been Met?

As might be expected, the burden is on the party seeking the protection of Rule 26(b)(4)(B) in the first instance to establish the prerequisites for its application. "[T]he party seeking protection of the opinions must establish that the expert was retained in anticipation of litigation."[35] However, once the prerequisites for protection under the rule have been established, the burden shifts to the proponent of the discovery to demonstrate that "exceptional circumstances" exist sufficient to warrant departure from discovery immunity under the rule.[36]

E. Does the Identity of a Nontestifying In-House Expert Need to Be Disclosed?

While not unanimous, the majority view is that, like the "facts and opinions" of a specially employed in-house nontestifying expert, the identity of the expert is available only upon a showing of exceptional circumstances.[37] The leading case on this point is *Ager v. Jane C. Stortmont Hospital & Training School for Nurses*,[38] in which the court, after analyzing the language and the purpose of the rule, concluded that a discovery proponent carries a "heavy burden" in seeking the identity of a nontestifying expert witness, satisfied only on a showing of exceptional circumstances. Anything else, the court concluded, would be contrary to the intent of the drafters: "In sum, we hold that the identity, and other collateral information concerning an expert who is retained or specially employed in anticipation of litigation, but not expected to be called as a witness at trial, is not discoverable except . . . upon a showing of exceptional circumstances."[39]

F. What Are the Differences between an "Informally Consulted" Expert and a Nontestifying Expert?

Although some courts rather confusingly describe Rule 26(b)(4)(B) as the "free consultation privilege"[40] on the theory that the rule creates a qualified privilege against disclosure, this should in no way be confused with the entirely separate and complete discovery bar that applies to informal consultations with experts. Before assuming that your contacts with an in-house expert are "informal" and therefore totally immune from discovery, it is important to have in mind the distinctions between an "an informally consulted expert" and a Rule 26(b)(4)(B) expert. Although there is no one uniform test applied by all courts to differentiate "informally consulted" experts from Rule 26(b)(4)(B) candidates, certain factors are routinely considered that bear mention. These include (1) the manner in which the consultation was initiated; (2) the nature, type, and extent of information provided to or determined by the expert for review; (3) the duration and the intensity of the consultative relationship; (4) whether payment was given for the consultation; and (5) whether confidentiality was a feature of the consultation.[41] Although it may appear tempting to attempt to classify all nontestifying experts as "informally consulted" for purposes of invoking a total discovery ban, it is a strategy that risks alienating the court, encouraging diminished vigilance with respect to your treatment of your nontestifying expert, artificially limiting your contact with and the usefulness of your expert, and resulting in unintended disclosures. The better approach is to weigh the factors outlined above and err on the side of caution.

V. Practice Pointers for Minimizing Discovery Risk

The 1970 adoption of Rule 26(b)(4)(B) was a quantum leap forward in imposing consistency and predictability on the rules governing expert discovery, but uncertainties and matters of discretion and interpretation still exist. Although there are no guarantees that an individual judge will prohibit discovery of your in-house nontestifying expert, certain practical steps will help reduce the risk of unintended disclosures of sensitive information. These steps include the following:

1. Formalize the consultant's role by drafting a consulting agreement that memorializes his or her specific assignment to work on the litigation under the direction of counsel. Ideally, the in-house expert will be assigned to work exclusively on the litigation during his or her tenure as an expert.
2. Be certain that the employee was not an "actor or viewer" of the events giving rise to the litigation and, if possible, do not designate the witness as a Rule 30(b)(6) or fact witness.
3. Have the employee report directly to the lawyer assigned to the litigation, undertake assignments and create written product only at the

direction of counsel, and provide results directly to counsel, not to be shared with other employees.

4. Observe boundaries between the nontestifying in-house expert and the testifying expert, because anything the testifier relies on—including the work of your nontestifying expert—becomes discoverable. Do not use the employee to ghostwrite the report of a testifying expert. It is also wise to limit contact between the testifier and nontestifier, as increased contact increases the risk of discovery of the nontestifier.
5. Have the employee segregate reports and correspondence with defense counsel in a separate file clearly distinguished from records kept in the ordinary course of business.
6. Consider providing additional compensation to the employee to bolster the argument of "special employment."
7. Analyze the risk, personally interview proposed in-house experts, and understand the full scope of their knowledge and exposure to the issues at stake in the litigation *before* engaging anyone as your nontestifying expert. Always be mindful of the risk of discovery and the qualified nature of 24(b)(4)(B) protection in every conversation and every disclosure you make to your nontestifying expert employee.
8. Make certain that your client has another witness capable of responding to a Rule 30(b)(6) request in his or her area of expertise should such a deposition be requested.

VI. Conclusion

Although in the years since the 1993 amendments we have come closer to approaching the ideal of judicial consensus on the scope and applicability of Rule 26(b)(4)(B), the law is not entirely consistent, and courts are afforded the wide discretion in ruling on these issues. The ambiguities in the rule itself urge caution and planning when considering use of an in-house nontestifying expert with the expectation that he or she will be immune from discovery with respect to litigation consultation. Following the guidelines outlined in this chapter, while not guaranteed to deliver success, should at least provide the beginnings of a plan to avoid obvious failure.

Notes

1. *See, e.g.*, United States v. Meyer, 398 F.2d 66 (9th Cir. 1968) (allowing discovery of expert appraiser's estimates of property value in condemnation action); *cf.* Am. Oil Co. v. Penn. Petro. Prod. Co., 23 F.R.D. 680 (D.R.I. 1959) (denying expert discovery).
2. Fed. R. Civ. P. 26(b)(4) advisory committee's note to 1970 Amendment.
3. This article concentrates primarily on Federal Rule of Civil Procedure 26(b)(4)(B) and the federal cases interpreting it, although many states have adopted

rules of procedure that are similar if not identical to the Federal Rules. Rule 26(b)(4) states in pertinent part:

> (4) Trial Preparation: Experts
> (A) A party may depose any person who has been identified as an expert whose opinions may be presented at trial. If a report from the expert is required under subdivision (a)(2)(B), the deposition shall not be conducted until after the report is provided.
> (B) A party may, through interrogatories or by deposition, discover facts known or opinions held by an expert who has been retained or specially employed by another party in anticipation of litigation or preparation for trial and who is not expected to be called as a witness at trial only as provided in Rule 35(b) or upon a showing of exceptional circumstances under which it is impracticable for the party seeking discovery to obtain facts or opinions on the same subject by other means.
> (C) Unless manifest injustice would result, (i) the court shall require that the party seeking discovery pay the expert a reasonable fee for time spent in responding to discovery under this subdivision; and (ii) with respect to discovery obtained under subdivision (b)(4)(B) of this rule the court shall require the party seeking discovery to pay the other party a fair portion of the fees and expenses reasonably incurred by the latter in obtaining facts and opinions from the expert.

4. Recent revisions to Rule 26(b)(4)(C), effective December 1, 2010, impose new limits on the traditionally liberal discovery standard applicable to testifying experts by providing work-product protection against discovery regarding draft expert disclosures or reports, and even communications between testifying experts and counsel, subject to three qualifications: (1) discovery will be permissible with respect to communications regarding compensation for the expert's study or testimony (Rule 26(b)(4)(C)(i)); (2) discovery is permitted to *identify* facts or data the party's attorney provided to the expert and the expert relied upon in forming the basis of his or her opinion, although communications related to the potential relevance or analysis of those facts will be protected (Rule 26(b)(4)(C)(ii)); and (3) discovery is permitted to identify any assumptions that counsel provided to the expert and the expert relied upon in forming the opinions expressed (Rule 26(b)(4)(C)(iii)).
5. Bank Brussels Lambert v. Chase Manhattan Bank, 175 F.R.D. 34 (S.D.N.Y. 1997) (quoting Hartford Fire Ins. v. Pure Air on the Lake Ltd., 154 F.R.D. 202, 207 (N.D. Ind. 1993).
6. *See, e.g.*, Mantolete v. Bolger, 96 F.R.D. 179, 181 (D. Ariz. 1982) (As distinguished from testifying experts, "[t]here is no need for comparable exchange of information regarding non-witness experts who act as consultants and advisors to counsel regarding the course litigation should take.").
7. Plymovent Corp. v. Air Techs. Solutions, Inc., 243 F.R.D. 139 (D.N.J. 2007) (citing Callaway Golf Co. v. Dunlop Slazenger Grp. Ams., Inc., 2002 WL 1906628, at *1 n.3, 2002 U.S. Dist. LEXIS 15429, at *5 n.3 (D. Del. Aug. 14, 2002).
8. Fed. R. Civ. P. 26(a)(2)(A).
9. *See. e.g.*, Va. Elec. & Power Co. v. Sun Shipbuilding & Dry Dock Co., 68 F.R.D. 397 (E.D. Va. 1975).

10. *Id.* at 407–08; *see also* Clark v. Gen. Motors Corp., 20 Fed. R. Serv. 679, 687 (D. Mass. 1975) (noting that the nontestifying in-house expert was a "regular employee" and that this fact "makes all the difference in the world," the magistrate concluded that as "regular employees" in-house experts fell outside the scope contemplated by Rule 26(b)(4)(B)); NEC Am. Inc. v. United States, 636 F. Supp. 476, 480 (C.I.T. 1986) (because expert witness was employee of plaintiff, he was not entitled to protection under Rule 26(b)(4)(B)), *aff'd*, 857 F.2d 787 (Fed. Cir. 1988), *cert. denied*, 489 U.S. 1017 (1989); Kan.-Neb. Natural Gas v. Marathon Oil Co., 109 F.R.D. 12, 16 (D. Neb. 1985) ("the use of the terms 'retained or specially employed' implies something more than simply the assignment of a current employee to a particular problem raised by current litigation").
11. *See* Comment, *Ambiguities after the 1970 Amendments to the Federal Rules of Civil Procedure Relating to Discovery of Experts and Attorney's Work Product*, 17 WAYNE L. REV. 1145, 1167 (1971).
12. FED. R. CIV. P. 26(b)(4)(B) (amended 1993) (emphasis added).
13. Advisory Comm. Note, 48 F.R.D. 487, 503 (1970).
14. *See* Comment, *supra* note 11, at 1167.
15. *See* Procter & Gamble Co. v. Haugen, 184 F.R.D. 410, 413 (D. Utah 1999).
16. Indeed, some states have expressly amended their rules to avoid this result and to protect in-house experts. James T. Hayes & Paul T. Ryder Jr., *Rule 26(b)(4)(B) of the Federal Rules of Civil Procedure: Discovery of Expert Information*, 42 U. MIAMI L. REV. 1101, n.496 (1988). Of course, research of your jurisdiction and forum's rules is the essential starting point of any analysis of these issues.
17. 69 F.R.D. 69, 72 (D. Kan. 1975).
18. *Id.* at 73 n.3; *see* Advisory Comm. Note, 48 F.R.D. at 503 ("Subdivision (b)(4)(B) deals with an expert who has been retained or specially employed by a party in anticipation of litigation or preparation for trial (thus excluding an employee who *is simply a general employee of the party not specially employed on the case*).") (emphasis added); *see also In re* Sinking Barge Ranger I, 92 F.R.D. 486, 489 n.5 (S.D. Tex. 1981) ("It may be possible for a party's regular employees to be specifically employed in anticipation of litigation or preparation for trial.") (dictum).
19. 132 F.R.D. 437 (E.D. La. 1990).
20. *Id.* at 441.
21. *Id.* It is worth noting, however, that the court later ruled that while the nontestifying experts could, absent a showing of exceptional circumstances, be shielded from discovery regarding the tests they performed at the direction of counsel in anticipation of litigation, their general knowledge of Shell's refinery operations, which they gained outside of their special litigation role, was subject to deposition discovery. This is an important reminder that Rule 26(b)(4)(B) protection extends *only* to work actually performed at the direction of counsel for purposes of the litigation and *not* to the employee's general knowledge that either predated or extends beyond the scope of the employee's litigation assignment. In other words, counsel cannot use a Rule 26(b)(4)(B) designation to cloak an employee's general knowledge obtained outside the litigation task to which the employee is assigned or to immunize percipient employee testimony.
22. FED. R. CIV. P. 1.
23. *See, e.g.*, Kiser v. Gen. Motors Corp., 2000 WL 1006239 (E.D. La. 1990) (adopting the approach of *Shell Oil* and holding that in-house nontestifying expert fell within the scope of 24(b)(4)(B) where expert was not working exclusively on

litigation and received no additional compensation for his expert work because "[expert] was not merely conducting normal business activities. He was specifically employed for litigation assistance."); Cent. Green Co. v. United States, 2003 U.S. Dist. LEXIS 26526 (E.D. Cal. Feb. 24, 2003) (following *Shell Oil* in holding that work performed for and at direction of counsel for litigation purposes is shielded by Rule 26(b)(4)(B)); California *ex rel.* Wheeler v. S. Pac. Transp. Co., 1993 U.S. Dist LEXIS 21128 (E.D. Cal. Sep. 2, 1993) (purporting to follow *Shell Oil* but rejecting notion that in-house expert could simultaneously have "dual role" of specially retained expert while still maintaining regular work responsibilities).

24. *See Wheeler*, 1993 U.S. Dist LEXIS 21128, at *14 ("The court believes that unless the employee is solely performing as an advisor to the litigation, the employee's dual use prevents his facts and opinions, and hence prepared documents reflecting the same, from being protected by work product. The party utilizing in-house experts could otherwise preclude from discovery releasable information by the simple ruse of claiming that all of the expert employees were assisting in the litigation. The key criteria in determining whether information acquired or created by employee experts is disclosable is whether the information was obtained in significant part because of an independent duty to acquire or create it.").
25. *See, e.g.*, ZCT Sys. Grp., Inc., v. Flightsafety Int'l, No. 08-CV-447, 2010 WL 1257824 (N.D. Okla. Mar. 26, 2010) (disallowing designation of same employee as a fact witness, Rule 30(b)(6) witness, and Rule 26(b)(4)(B) expert nontestifier where there was no evidence that witness had been "specially retained" as expert, no evidence that witness was acting at direction of outside counsel, and no specific designation of nature of expert testimony, and where witness was "deeply involved in the factual evidence of the case" and had been designated both as a Rule 30(b)(6) witness and as a potential witness. Animating the court's decision was a concern about the fact that the client appeared to be "cherry picking" areas of testimony to use affirmatively and other areas to shield). *But see* Sensormatic Elec. Corp. v. W.G. Sec. Prods., Inc., 2006 WL 1305166 (E.D. Tex. May 11, 2006) (allowing nontestifying expert designation for former employee who acted as a fact witness with respect to development of original patent, and expert with respect to separate area of comparison between original patent and allegedly infringing patent).
26. Bank Brussels Lambert v. Chase Manhattan Bank, 175 F.R.D. 34, ___ (S.D.N.Y. 1997) (quoting United States v. Bell, 1994 WL 665295, at *4 (N.D. Cal. Nov. 9, 1994)).
27. PolyMedica Corp. Sec. Litig., 235 F.R.D. 28, 31 (D. Mass. 2006) (citations omitted).
28. *Id.*
29. *In re* Asbestos Prods. Liab. Litig., 256 F.R.D. 151, 156 (2009).
30. Marine Petroleum Co. v. Champlin Petroleum Co., 641 F.2d 984, 992 (D.C. Cir. 1979).
31. *PolyMedica Corp.*, 235 F.R.D. at 33.
32. *Id.*
33. Examples of critical evidence destruction or alteration might include where the roof was removed in a defective roof case; a ruptured pipe replaced in a case regarding sewer spillage; and where a tissue sample had been completely used by one side's experts. *See, e.g.*, Bank Brussels Lambert v. Chase Manhattan Bank, 175 F.R.D. 34, 44–45 (S.D.N.Y. 1997) (citing cases and examples of exceptional circumstances).

34. FMC Corp. v. Vendo Co., 196 F. Supp. 2d 1023, 1046 (E.D. Cal. 2002).
35. *See, e.g.*, Shipes v. BIC Corp., 154 F.R.D. 301 (M.D. Ga. 1994) (recognizing that an in-house expert may qualify for discovery immunity under Rule 26(b)(4)(B) but denying protection where employee was designated as a "quality assurance manager" and not specially retained or employed for litigation).
36. *PolyMedica Corp.*, 235 F.R.D. at 33.
37. *See In re* Pizza Time Theatre Sec. Litig., 113 F.R.D. 94, 97–98 (N.D. Cal. 1986).
38. 622 F.2d 496 (10th Cir. 1980).
39. *Id.* at n.6.
40. *See. e.g.*, FMC Corp. v. Vendo Co., 196 F. Supp. 2d 1023, 1044 (E.D. Cal. 2002) (describing Rule 26(b)(4)(B) protection as "the free consultation privilege"); Tex. Lawyers Ins. Exch. v. Resolution Trust Corp., 822 F. Supp. 380, 382 (W.D. Tex. 1993) (referring to the "consultant witness privilege").
41. *See, e.g.*, Ager v. Jane C. Stormont Hosp. & Training Sch. for Nurses, 622 F.2d 496 (10th Cir. 1980).

CHAPTER 14

Loss of Attorney-Client Privilege through Inadvertent Disclosure of Privileged Documents

VINCENT S. WALKOWIAK
THOMAS J. LEACH

I. Introduction

Every attorney makes mistakes. Some mistakes are serious; others are not. Some mistakes are correctable; others are not. Although not every document within the attorney-client privilege has great significance, as a general matter, an attorney's inadvertent disclosure of privileged documents can have serious consequences. Thus, the issue becomes whether such a mistake is correctable or irrevocable.

The problem of inadvertent disclosure of privileged documents arises in various ways,[1] but it occurs most commonly in the context of pretrial production of documents. Reliance on the fax machine and, more significantly, e-mail has changed the landscape of pretrial production, however, and has created more concern for inadvertent disclosure and need for greater privilege review.

This point was emphasized to the Advisory Committee for the 2006 Amendments to the Federal Rules of Civil Procedure.

> Ever since the [Advisory] Committee began its intensive examination of discovery in 1996, a frequent complaint has been the expense and delay that accompany privilege review.[2]

Regardless of the manner of the inadvertent disclosure, pretrial production in document intensive litigation remains the paradigm case.

Although a unique case in many respects, *Transamerica Computer Co. v IBM Corp.*[3] illustrates the problem. IBM was a defendant in an antitrust case brought by Control Data Corporation. The district judge overseeing the litigation issued a pretrial order dramatically accelerating the document inspection that had been in progress. The court of appeals described the effect of this order as

> requir[ing] IBM to produce within a three-month period for inspection and for adversary copying approximately 17 million pages of documents. To say the least, the logistical problems confronting IBM were monumental and were exacerbated by a number of factors. For example, the documents which CDC sought to have IBM produce for inspection had not been produced during any previous litigation and they were not grouped or batched together so as to be readily accessible. Most of the documents were particularly difficult to screen for privilege, for they were letters and memoranda contained in myriad headquarters-type files randomly strewn throughout various IBM branches and divisional headquarters.[4]

IBM screened each of the 17 million pages by the discovery deadline. Although approximately 491,000 pages were withheld under a privilege claim, some 1,138 privileged documents (about 5,800 pages) were inadvertently disclosed. Because of the extraordinary circumstances involved, the court ultimately found that the privilege was not lost as a result of this inadvertent production of privileged materials.[5]

E-mail has greatly increased the number of documents that are discoverable and, consequently, necessary to review for privilege. E-mail has numerous advantages, such as cost, efficiency, speed, and versatility; and attorneys and law firms rely on this form of communication with clients and outside counsel.[6] But while paper documents can be destroyed or returned, erasing or retrieving an e-mail is altogether more difficult.[7] Even if the attorney and the client delete an e-mail message from their computers, most of the electronic information will still be stored on a back-up system file or remain on the computer hard drive.[8] Further, some courts have opined that e-mail is not secure,[9] and some commentators have compared e-mail to sending a postcard through the mail.[10]

Imagine a case where an attorney drafts a highly confidential document and wants to send it to outside co-counsel for an opinion. The attorney knows that the most efficient way to send the document is through e-mail because co-counsel can receive it and return suggestions with ease.[11] The attorney types the e-mail and hits send, but mistakenly sends it to opposing counsel rather than co-counsel.[12] The attorney may be unable to cancel the e-mail and now faces the possibility of waiver of the attorney-client privilege through this inadvertent e-mailing of the client's highly confidential document.[13] Although courts and recent rule changes have yet to comprehensively address the issue of the inadvertent disclosure of privileged information through e-mail, they have addressed inadvertent disclosure of privileged material during pretrial production and, consequently, have set important rules and revealed trends.

As of December, 2006, amendments to the Federal Rules of Civil Procedure affect procedures for asserting attorney-client privilege when privileged materials are inadvertently produced in federal court litigation. Previously, there were no established procedures for handling claims of privilege over inadvertently produced material in litigation governed by the Federal Rules of Civil Procedure. But a body of law had developed involving various procedures adopted by different circuits.

It is important to note that the rule changes did not affect the legal standards that federal courts follow in determining whether the privilege has been waived. Instead, they created procedures for bringing the issue of whether privilege had been waived to the court's attention. Although the procedural rules eliminated the automatic waiver principle by inadvertent disclosure followed by some federal circuits, they did not affect the ultimate determination.

Currently, under Rule 26(f),[14] a scheduling order may include procedures for disclosing electronically stored material and may also contain agreed-upon procedures for asserting claims of privilege or work-product doctrine protection after production. Rule 26(f) provides:

> [T]he parties must confer as soon as practicable—and in any event at least 21 days before a scheduling conference is held or a scheduling order is due under Rule 16(b) . . . [to]discuss any issues about preserving discoverable information; and develop a proposed discovery plan.. . . stat[ing] the parties' views and proposals on . . . (C) any issues about disclosure or discovery of electronically stored information, including the form or forms in which it should be produced; (D) any issues about claims of privilege or of protection as trial-preparation materials, including—if the parties agree on a procedure to assert these claims after production–whether to ask the court to include their agreement in an order. . . . [15]

The most significant change, however, is contained in Rule 26(b)(5)(B), which provides that a party who produces privileged or work-doctrine protected material may notify the recipient who must then return, sequester, or destroy the material (and any copies) until the court resolves the claim of privilege. Specifically, rule 26(b)(5)(B) states:

> *(5) Claiming Privilege or Protecting Trial-Preparation Materials.*
> . . . . (B) *Information Produced.* If information produced in discovery is subject to a claim of privilege or of protection as trial-preparation material, the party making the claim may notify any party that received the information of the claim and the basis for it. After being notified, a party must promptly return, sequester, or destroy the specified information and any copies it has; must not use or disclose the information until the claim is resolved; must take reasonable steps to retrieve the information if the party disclosed it before being notified; and may promptly present the information to the court under seal for a determination of the claim. The producing party must preserve the information until the claim is resolved.[16]

As noted above, the procedural rule does not affect the court's determination of whether there has been a waiver of the privilege but does provide that disclosure is not conclusive of waiver.

Early on, at least one state jurisdiction also amended its procedural rules to address the issue of inadvertent waiver.[17] Because of its rule-oriented approach, Texas likewise eliminated the need to review case law to determine how to assert that privileged documents had been inadvertently produced.[18] The majority of jurisdictions have not, however, taken the approach of addressing the method of preserving privilege while determining whether waiver has taken place. And neither the federal procedural changes nor the Texas rule changes address what standard the court should apply to determine if the inadvertent disclosure (or other actions) waived privilege.

Those jurisdictions that still decide the issue by case law employ three different tests to determine if the mere production of privileged documents results in a loss of the privilege. The different tests reflect a long-standing ambivalence about the attorney-client privilege and, in our view, some confusion about the concept of waiver. Accordingly, before considering the various tests, it is helpful to address the core concepts of privilege and waiver.

II. Attorney-Client Privilege and Waiver

The attorney-client privilege is the oldest of all privileges protecting confidential communications known to the common law.[19] The privilege is generally regarded as an essential component of the adversary system and thought to uphold the honor of the profession.[20] As the Supreme Court has explained:

> Its purpose is to encourage full and frank communication between attorneys and their clients and thereby promote broader public interests in the observance of law and administration of justice. The

> privilege recognizes that sound legal advice or advocacy serves public ends and that such advice or advocacy depends upon the lawyer's being fully informed by the client.[21]

In the absence of this privilege, clients would be dissuaded from seeking legal advice or hesitant to reveal adverse information that may not remain confidential.[22] Therefore, the privilege is so important that one judge has described it as "sacred."[23]

On the other hand, the adversary system is fundamentally a truth-seeking process. Because the attorney-client privilege (like all privileges) may suppress relevant information, it can hamper the search for the truth by forcing courts to exclude otherwise relevant evidence.[24] Wigmore observes that the privilege "is worth preserving for the sake of a general policy but it is nonetheless an obstacle to the investigation of the truth. It ought to be strictly confined within the narrowest possible limits consistent with the logic of its principle."[25] Or, as Professor Hazard says, though it is regarded as indispensable to the lawyer's role as advocate and counselor, "the attorney-client privilege has its victims" because it is "not only a principle of privacy, but also a device for cover-ups."[26] Reflecting this ambivalence are courts that have produced opinions adopting a liberal construction of the privilege in some cases while employing a strict one in others.[27] It is also demonstrated by the existence of several tests for determining whether the inadvertent disclosure of privileged documents results in loss of the privilege.

The loss of privilege from inadvertent production of privileged materials is almost universally regarded as a "waiver" issue.[28] Although it may be necessary to apply this label to the conclusion that the privilege has been lost (for example, to place the conclusion within the scope of the governing statutory scheme), it is dangerous to try to use the waiver concept as a means of reaching that conclusion—at least without being aware that this approach dramatically skews the analysis.[29]

"Waiver" is traditionally defined as "an intentional relinquishment or abandonment of a known right or privilege."[30] This definition makes the producing party's intention virtually conclusive of the matter regardless of whether the party took reasonable steps to preserve the privilege or even affirmatively caused the privileged communications to be disclosed.

On a more practical level, however, the demands of society require an assessment of the action or inaction in terms broader than only the actor's intent. Thus, when the conduct of the privilege-holder is objectively inconsistent with upholding the privilege, the conduct is said to result in an "implied waiver."[31] But to say there is an implied waiver despite the privilege-holder's insistence that he did not intend to waive it requires that "waiver" means something more than just the intentional relinquishment of a known right.

This apparent paradox can be resolved by undertaking a functional analysis of the waiver concept. In reality, the operative concept of waiver incorporates the reasonable expectations of society and the judicial system: a person who intends privileged matters to remain so must act accordingly. Therefore, at any stage of legal proceedings, failure to claim attorney-client privilege constitutes waiver.[32] Nevertheless, because of the inconsistent application of the waiver doctrine, it seems fair to say that "waiver" is a shorthand term used to cover several distinct situations in which courts refuse to recognize the privilege.[33] Therefore, use of the term does not advance analysis of any given privilege question. The traditional concept of waiver focuses on the intent of the privilege-holder. Although intent may be more or less important in any given case, its significance should be addressed directly—not assumed by automatic application of the waiver rubric.

The possibility of losing privilege through inadvertent disclosure is a major issue to be addressed. Regarding the loss of privilege through inadvertent disclosure, the courts do not agree on one approach to determine if the privilege is lost.[34] Instead, the answer is found on a continuum of tests.[35] The consensus, however, seems to be that the producing party has the burden of establishing that the privilege has not been lost by the production.[36] Presently, with each of the three tests, the privilege-holder could find three different results with respect to inadvertent disclosure. Therefore, the courts' failure to follow a uniform approach creates much confusion and uncertainty among lawyers who face these issues.[37]

III. The Strict Approach: Privilege Automatically Lost by Disclosure

The traditional test for determining whether production of privileged documents to a litigation adversary results in loss of the privilege is extraordinarily simple: disclosure automatically means the end of the privilege. Wigmore, the leading proponent of this "strict responsibility" test, explains that "the risk of insufficient precautions is on the client" because the attorney and client have the means to preserve the confidentiality of their communications and therefore, must bear the risk of failure.[38]

Advocates of this view stress that the privilege acts as an obstacle to discovery of the truth;[39] that disclosure of privileged materials makes it impossible to achieve the benefits of the privilege (i.e., secrecy);[40] and that "when the policy underlying the rule can no longer be served, it would amount to no more than mechanical obedience to a formula to continue to recognize it."[41]

Additionally, some courts favor the strict test because "mistake or inadvertence is, after all, merely a euphemism for negligence, and, certainly . . . one is expected to pay a price for one's negligence."[42] And one court specifically rejected the "middle ground" test because "the opinions of the courts in these cases, after a substantial amount of verbiage, can be reduced to a bottom line to the effect that the precautions were inadequate because they were not effective in preventing the disclosure of privileged documents."[43]

Another rationale for the strict approach centers on the unfairness to the party seeking to use the inadvertently disclosed communications. Once a party adopts the disclosed information into its case preparation, "fairness requires that [the] privilege cease whether [the opponent] intended the result or not."[44] In *Suburban Sew 'N Sweep. Inc. v. Swiss-Bernina., Inc.*,[45] because the information in the obtained documents formed the basis of the lawsuit, plaintiff would have been unable to proceed if it were not allowed to use the communications. The court recognized that the issue of privilege was a "close question," but ruled the communications admissible after adopting the strict approach.[46] Due to the unusual circumstances, the court was persuaded that the policy of encouraging open communication between attorneys and their clients would not be served by recognizing the privilege.[47]

Finally, some courts are attracted to the strict approach because it forces self-regulatory behavior. In *In re Sealed Case*, the court explained that the strict approach creates a strong incentive for careful document management, stating, "The courts will grant no greater protection to those who assert the privilege than their own precautions warrant."[48] If an attorney wants to keep the privilege, it is completely within the power of the attorney and the client to retain the confidentiality. "In other words, if a client wishes to preserve the privilege, it must treat the confidentiality of attorney-client communications like jewels—if not crown jewels."[49]

An attorney arguing against a claim of privilege for inadvertently disclosed documents can also invoke significant practical advantages in support of the strict responsibility test: it is exceptionally predictable and easy to apply, thus minimizing litigation and encouraging the greatest possible diligence in protecting the privilege. Moreover, although the point is often overlooked, this approach is the most consistent with the waiver rules typically applied during trial. If an attorney's client is asked a question that would invade the privilege, the attorney's failure to object in a timely fashion results in a loss of the privilege.[50] If the privilege can be lost in circumstances where a split-second decision must be made, it seems appropriate to apply at least an equally strict rule to pretrial discovery, where there is far greater opportunity and time to analyze the situation and make an informed decision regarding whether to invoke the privilege.

A good example of this rationale's application is found in *In re Grand Jury Investigation of Ocean Transportation*.[51] In this case, defendant's original counsel gave opposing counsel a group of documents marked with a "P." After review, opposing counsel asked if these specific documents were intended to be privileged. Defendant's counsel, after investigating, replied that they were not intended to be privileged. Six months later, the defendant's new counsel discovered the error. The court noted:

> Perhaps this latter rule should not be strictly applied to all cases of unknown or inadvertent disclosure; this, however, is not a case where any such exception would be appropriate. Here, the disclosure cannot be viewed as having been inadvertent in all respects. Original counsel

> knew that some papers marked "P" had been divulged. This production was brought to their attention on at least one occasion; each time, however, said counsel declined to assert the privilege.[52]

Where the question is unsettled, as it is in many jurisdictions, a party opposing a claim of privilege for inadvertently disclosed documents should consider urging the court's adoption of the strict responsibility rule.[53] But although this approach may have some appeal because it makes attorneys and clients accountable for their carelessness in handling privileged matters,[54] it has been rejected by many jurisdictions because of its pronounced inflexibility and significant intrusion on the attorney-client relationship.[55] These courts also argue that the strict approach sacrifices the value of protecting the client for the sake of predictable results.[56] Therefore, counsel should not be surprised if a court finds that "[t]he automatic waiver rule is too harsh" because it "depriv[es] the client of protection against the use of the privileged communication in court. An error quickly discovered could not be corrected under this approach once the documents had been turned over, even if the opposing party had little opportunity to view the documents."[57] Although actual cases are not decided by trends, they are often influenced by them, and "[t]he modem trend is away from the strict responsibility approach."[58]

IV. The Lenient Approach: Client's Subjective Intent to Waive

Competing with the strict responsibility test is its polar opposite—the client's subjective-intent test. Differing formulations of the test exist, but its central focus is the client's intent to waive the privilege. Put simply, the subjective-intent test holds that as long as the client did not intend to waive the privilege, the privilege remains intact despite disclosure of the client's confidences to the adversary.[59]

A client's lack of intent to preserve the privilege may be sufficient reason to hold that it has been waived, but it is difficult to see why the converse should be true. One of the few cases adopting this approach is *Mendenhall v. Barber-Greene Co.*[60] According to the *Mendenhall* court, "the better-reasoned rule is that mere inadvertent production does not waive the privilege" because "[i]nadvertent production is the antithesis" of an intentional relinquishment of a known right and, if the privilege is for the welfare of the *client*, more than the *attorney's* negligence should be required before the *client* loses the privilege.[61]

Despite the potential appeal of this test, there are very serious problems with the analysis in *Mendenhall*. First, the authorities cited as representing the "better-reasoned rule"[62] contain little analysis and all involve application of a New York statute that required a waiver to be made in open court. Commenting on *Mendenhall*, another district court observed that the cited cases have "limited precedential value."[63]

Second, *Mendenhall*'s rationale is as weak as its cited authority. As noted above, to define waiver as an intentional relinquishment of a known right is to beg the question of whether the privilege should be upheld or not. Further, the court's suggestion that a distinction should be drawn between the client and the attorney ignores the basic rule charging clients with the conduct of their lawyers.[64]

Although one court has reasoned that the *Mendenhall* approach is preferable to the strict approach when dealing with discovery situations involving the production of thousands of documents,[65] *Mendenhall* is not generally followed.[66] The primary objection to its approach is that it exalts subjective considerations over objective ones, including whether the client and the attorney have taken reasonable efforts to protect the privilege and the effects on the opposing party and the litigation process in trying to resurrect the privilege after disclosure. Additionally, the courts have opined that this approach gives little incentive for attorneys to maintain tight control over privileged documents.[67]

Like the strict responsibility test, the practical advantages of the subjective-intent test are predictability and clear application, which minimize litigation. It also "remains true to the core principle of attorney-client privilege, which is that it exists to protect the client and must be waived by the client."[68] With its focus on subjective intent, however, this approach arguably does encourage careful preservation of confidences. As a potential solution to these objections, some commentators have proposed a modified form of this test that requires both objective and subjective manifestations of intent.[69]

V. The Middle Ground: Evaluation of the Circumstances Test

Rejecting both extremes, most courts in recent years have used a balancing test to determine whether inadvertent production of privileged documents forfeits the privilege. Referred to by several different names, this approach is one "under which the courts make a decision based on an evaluation of the circumstances, rather than automatically finding a waiver or a retention of the privilege."[70] Its proponents generally agree that "[a]lthough a more difficult approach to employ, ultimately this approach is fairer to both parties and the policy of preserving the privilege for confidential communications as it focuses on the confidentiality aspect of the privilege."[71]

This middle-ground approach weighs the surrounding circumstances to determine whether production of the privileged documents should result in a loss of privilege. Under this approach, the court evaluates five factors of the inadvertent disclosure to determine if the privilege should remain intact: (1) the reasonableness of the precautions taken to prevent inadvertent disclosure; (2) the time taken to rectify the error; (3) the scope of the discovery; (4) the extent of the disclosure; and (5) the "overreaching issue of fairness."[72]

In *Lois Sportswear, U.S.A., Inc. v. Levi Strauss & Co.*, the court narrowly upheld the privilege against a demand for production after plaintiff's counsel had inadvertently been allowed to review 22 privileged documents that were mistakenly included in the 16,000 pages defendant made available.[73] Because the documents had been reviewed by but not produced to opposing counsel, the "time to rectify" factor inherently weighed in defendant's favor. The rather extensive discovery demand, the comparatively small number of privileged documents disclosed, and the fact that they had only been visually inspected all similarly weighed in defendant's favor.

Nevertheless, Levi almost lost because "[a]s to the reasonableness of the precautions, Levi only just adequately protected its privilege."[74] Criticisms of Levi's efforts included that (1) Levi apparently had no practice of designating documents as confidential at the time of origination; (2) there was no specific description of the screening instructions given by Levi's deputy general counsel to the paralegal actually doing the screening; and (3) there was no specific evidence that the procedures actually followed had screened out any privileged documents.[75]

In support of the middle of the road approach, one court has stated that this approach should be favored because, as to the consideration of fairness, it takes into account the special problems that arise during discovery.[76] Illustrating this flexibility is *Hydraflow, Inc. v. Enidine Inc.*,[77] in which plaintiff's local counsel, when delivering documents to the court for an in camera inspection, accidentally delivered copies to opposing counsel. The court emphasized that the delivery was clearly a mistake and that the overreaching issue of fairness weighed heavily in plaintiff's favor.[78] In reaching this conclusion, the court weighed the reasonableness of the precautions taken, the extent of the document production, the extent and number of inadvertent disclosures, and the promptness of measures taken to remedy the inadvertent disclosure.[79]

An extensive discussion of the law in this area is set forth in *Kanter v. Superior Court*.[80] Although the opinion in *Kanter* has been withdrawn and ordered not published in the official *California Reporter* under Rule 976 of the California Rules of Court, the court's analysis and approach to the case's difficult facts is noteworthy. In *Kanter*, defendants' counsel sent documents to a copy service with instructions to copy everything but noting that "privileged docs. (yellowed pages) are to be kept in our office." The copied documents were then returned to defendants' counsel in a single box and he forwarded them to plaintiff's attorney. The box, however, contained copies of the entire litigation file from the underlying case, including some 160 privileged documents.[81]

Approximately 15 months later, plaintiff's counsel deposed Mr. Edelstein who had been the defense lawyer in the underlying case. During the deposition, plaintiff's counsel referred to certain documents that defendants' counsel claimed were privileged and had been inadvertently produced.[82] Defendants then moved for a protective order and the return of the privileged documents while plaintiff's attorney moved to compel answers to the questions Edelstein had refused to answer regarding these documents. Ultimately, the trial court ruled for defendants, but the court of appeals issued a peremptory writ overturning the order.[83]

Kanter was a case of first impression in California. After discussing the possible approaches, the court adopted the multifactor balancing test and concluded that every factor weighed against sustaining the claim of privilege.[84] As noted, this opinion was subsequently withdrawn by the court and ordered not published by the court that rendered it.

The case law does not permit meaningful generalization on the weighing of the different factors. For example, in *Lois Sportswear*, most of the factors supported the same decision. In *Hartford Fire Ins. Co. v. Garvey*,[85] the court found a waiver where the error was rectified quickly but reasonable precaution had not been taken, the scope of discovery was limited, and disclosure was complete. In *Parkway Gallery, Inc. v. Kittinger/Pennsylvania House Group, Inc.*,[86] the court started with a presumption that disclosure equaled waiver of privilege and then reviewed the various factors. The requested discovery was extensive, but the court did not count this as favoring defendants because they were not operating under severe time constraints. Defendants also reacted quickly when the error was discovered, but the court was not convinced the screening precautions were sufficient and stressed that when disclosure is complete, a court cannot restore confidentiality but "can only attempt to restrain further erosion."[87] Given these considerations, the court observed that granting a protective order would require "a very strong showing with respect to the other factors."[88] Ultimately, the court held that the privilege was waived. Lastly, in *Gray v. Bicknell*,[89] Bicknell inadvertently disclosed two letters between him and his attorney that addressed a wide range of matters relating to the litigation. The court briefly analyzed each of the approaches and found the middle-ground test to be the best one because it struck the appropriate balance between protecting the privilege and allowing unprotected disclosure to waive the privilege where appropriate.[90] Finding no waiver of the privilege, the court noted that the litigation involved vast numbers of documents and that in the course of production, a paralegal inadvertently included the two letters.

Although the test is consistently presented as multifactor, further analysis suggests that courts concentrate primarily on two factors: the conduct of the client and lawyer claiming the privilege, and the prejudice to the recipient should the court uphold the privilege despite disclosure. Thus, "reasonable precautions" is arguably an umbrella concept that encompasses the time taken to rectify the error, the scope of discovery, and special circumstances, all of which ask the same question: Did the lawyer/client invoking the privilege act in the careful manner expected from someone truly concerned with guarding a confidence, both before and after the inadvertent disclosure?

The other overarching concept is that of fairness, which includes the extent of disclosure and special circumstances. The time taken to rectify the error must also be included in this list because it affects prejudice. Here, the basic question is: Would it be fair to require the recipient of the privileged information to expunge all knowledge of it from the litigation?[91] If parties have integrated privileged documents into their trial preparation, the efforts to "restore" the privilege may place them at a permanent disadvantage. In *Kanter*, for example, the court agreed that "given the time that the documents were in the hands of plaintiff's counsel, the information gleaned from the documents has saturated counsel's mind; thereby, presenting the old dilemma of 'unringing the bell.'"[92]

Unlike the previous two approaches, the middle-ground test is criticized for its uncertainty and the wide discretion it gives judges. Nevertheless, this approach accounts for the inevitable error in modern, extremely document-intensive litigation, but continues to treat an attorney's carelessness and negligence as an indication of waiver.[93] As the *Gray* court pointed out, the middle-ground test is the most thoughtful approach because it gives the courts broader discretion to determine whether waiver occurred through inadvertent disclosure and if so, the scope of that waiver.[94]

VI. How to Protect the Privilege: Avoiding Production and Retrieving Privileged Materials

As the preceding discussion demonstrates, inadvertent disclosure of privileged documents does not necessarily end the privilege. Nevertheless, both lawyer and client should assume that it will and plan accordingly. This will minimize the risk of inadvertent disclosure and maximize the chance that if such disclosure occurs, it will not be fatal to the privilege. With the increasing technological advances and reliance on e-mail communication, there must be greater protection of and attention to the issue of inadvertent disclosure.

Both attorney and client should make a practice of identifying privileged communications and keeping them segregated from unprivileged documents, as well as, when applicable, placing such notation in the subject line of e-mail communication. For example, many attorneys stamp or type "Privileged Attorney-Client Communication" on documents. Even if such a document is not kept apart from unprivileged communication, it will be easier to identify by anyone who screens the documents. A sophisticated client could also color-code or otherwise mark different types of communications.

When a document-production request is made, an attorney should carefully oversee the process and create a record that demonstrates the care taken to prevent disclosure of privileged documents. First, counsel should obtain from the client an estimate of how long it will take the client to compile documents and make a preliminary segregation of privileged documents. The attorney should then add the time necessary for a second review by the attorney or someone directly under the attorney's supervision. If production is demanded before this two-step review can be accomplished, counsel should attempt to obtain additional time either by agreement or by court order. If time pressure necessitates a compromise of the screening procedures, this should also be reflected in the record. Moreover, although some courts reject stipulations that production of privileged documents will not constitute a waiver of the privilege,[95] such a stipulation should still be obtained if possible. Additionally, every effort should be made to obtain a court order to the effect that inadvertent disclosure will not result in loss of the privilege.[96] With respect to e-mail communication, a confidential attorney-client privilege paragraph should also be included in all potentially protected e-mails. This paragraph may not guarantee the protection of privilege and prevent waiver,[97] but it is a necessary step in protecting one's client.

Time permitting, a two-stage screening process should be used. The lawyer should give instructions to the client in a form that can be used as a self-serving exhibit if necessary. In these instructions, the attorney should briefly explain attorney-client privilege and categorically identify materials falling (or likely to fall) within the privilege such as all correspondence to or from counsel, incident reports, and legal memoranda. Ideally, initial screening should be done by someone with legal training under the supervision of in-house counsel. As a general matter, the screener should be instructed to err on the side of privilege.

During the initial screening, separate lists of privileged and unprivileged documents should be prepared. For each document, the author(s) and recipient(s) should be identified by name and position (e.g., Jane Jones, Risk Manager, to Richard Smith, General Counsel), date, and general subject matter.

Counsel must be responsible for the next level of review. At a minimum, counsel must personally review the lists of documents. Any that appear to be wrongly categorized should be inspected by counsel. Beyond this, someone with legal training of at least that of a paralegal should completely review all documents. Again, a self-serving screening instruction should be put in writing. Uncertainty about whether a document is privileged or not must be resolved by counsel. Once all privileged documents have been identified, they should be marked as such and segregated. If copies are made, they should not be done while the unprivileged materials are copied.

All documents sent or otherwise disclosed to opposing counsel should be marked in a way that will make it possible to tell after the fact exactly what was disclosed. Counsel should also retain an exact duplicate set of anything disclosed. Immediately after disclosure, someone who has participated in the screening process should review the duplicate set to see if anything was inadvertently disclosed. Again, all of these efforts should be documented.

When production is actually made, counsel should consider sending a letter explaining that every effort has been made to produce all requested documents that are not privileged, and that if any privileged documents were produced, it was inadvertent and not intended as a waiver. Often, identification of any documents claimed to be privileged must be made.[98] The list of privileged documents informs opposing counsel that no document on the list was intended to be disclosed.

Counsel who has reason to believe privileged documents have been disclosed must immediately act to protect the privilege.[99] In jurisdictions that have an established rule for asserting the privilege after an inadvertent production, either by procedural rule or case law, those procedures should be carefully followed. But even in those jurisdictions that do not have an established procedure, some commonsense procedure should be followed. First, a demand for return of the documents must be made. Second, the attorney must file a motion for a protective order seeking return of the documents, all copies, notes, and so forth, and prohibiting any disclosure of, use of, or reference to the documents. If opposing counsel will not agree to treat the documents as privileged pending resolution of the motion, these efforts should proceed on an emergency basis.[100]

If the jurisdiction appears to follow the traditional test of automatic loss of privilege through disclosure, a full-scale attack should be mounted against this test. If the jurisdiction is not already committed to the evaluation of the circumstances approach, counsel should consider advocating the subjective-intent approach as a first line of attack. Under the evaluation of the circumstances approach, all favorable criteria should be emphasized, but particularly the efforts made to protect the privilege and the lack of prejudice to the other side.[101]

An attorney will not always succeed in curing any mistaken disclosure of privileged documents, but a careful, conscientious attorney has by far the best chance of doing so.

Notes

1. *Compare, e.g.*, Suburban Sew 'N Sweep, Inc. v. Swiss-Bernina, Inc., 91 F.R.D. 254 (N.D. Ill. 1981) (privileged documents culled from a trash container and privilege waived), *with* McCafferty's Inc. v. Bank of Glen Burnie, 179 F.R.D. 163 (D. Md. 1998) (privileged documents culled from trash container and privilege not waived). *See generally* Brian M. Smith, Note, *Be Careful How You Use It or You May Lose It: A Modern Look at Corporate Attorney-Client Privilege and the Ease of Waiver in Various Circuits*, 75 U. DET. MERCY L. REV. 389 (1998).
2. Report of the Civil Rules Advisory Comm. 54 (May 27, 2005), http://www.uscourts.gov/uscourts/RulesAndPolicies/rules/Reports/CV5-2005.pdf.
3. 573 F.2d 646 (9th Cir. 1978).
4. *Id.* at 648.
5. *Id.* at 651–52.
6. Amy M. Fulmer Stevenson, Comment, *Making a Wrong Turn on the Information Superhighway: Electronic Mail, the Attorney-Client Privilege and Inadvertent Disclosure*, 26 CAP. U. L. REV. 347, 350–51 (1997).
7. *Id.* at 351.
8. *Id.*
9. *See, e.g.*, ACLU v. Reno, 929 F. Supp. 824, 834 (E.D. Pa. 1996) ("Unlike postal mail, simple e-mail generally is not 'sealed' or secure, and can be accessed or viewed on intermediate computers between the sender and recipient (unless the message is encrypted).").
10. *See, e.g.*, Fulmer Stevenson, *supra* note 6, at 353 ("If a lawyer would not want postal workers reading a postcard containing privileged communications, that lawyer probably should not send E-mail in clear-text.").
11. *Id.* at 357.
12. *Id.*
13. *Id.*
14. The Committee on Rules of Practice and Procedure of the Judicial Conference of the United States has proposed amendments to Rule 26 regarding the disclo-

sure and discovery of expert trial witness testimony, to be effective December 1, 2010. For the text of the proposed rule, see http://www.uscourts.gov/uscourts/RulesAndPolicies/rules/Supreme%20Court%202009/CV-Clean-Rules.pdf.

15. FED. R. CIV. P. 26(f)(1), (3)(C)–(D).
16. FED. R. CIV. P. 26(b)(5)(B).
17. TEX. R. CIV. P. 193.3(d) states:

> *(d) Privilege not waived by production.* A party who produces material or information without intending to waive a claim of privilege does not waive that claim under these rules or the Rules of Evidence if—within ten days or a shorter time ordered by the court, after the producing party actually discovers that such production was made—the producing party amends the response, identifying the material or information produced and stating the privilege asserted. If the producing party thus amends the response to assert a privilege, the requesting party must promptly return the specified material or information and any copies pending any ruling by the court denying the privilege.

18. *See id.*
19. *See* 8 JOHN H. WIGMORE, EVIDENCE § 2290, at 542 (McNaughton rev. ed. 1961). For an interesting qualification of this general proposition, see Geoffrey C. Hazard, Jr., *An Historical Perspective on the Attorney-Client Privilege*, 66 CAL. L. REV. 1061 (1978).
20. Robert A. Pikowsky, *Privilege and Confidentiality of Attorney-Client Communication via Email*, 51 BAYLOR L. REV. 483, 488–89 (1999).
21. Upjohn Co. v. United States, 449 U.S. 383, 389 (1981). *See also* Trammel v. United States, 445 U.S. 40, 51 (1980) ("The lawyer-client privilege rests on the need for the advocate and counselor to know all that relates to the client's reasons for seeking representation if the professional mission is to be carried out."); Hunt v. Blackburn, 128 U.S. 464, 470 (1888) ("The rule . . . is founded upon the necessity, in the interest and administration of justice, of the aid of persons having knowledge of the law and skilled in its practice, which assistance can only be safely and readily availed of when free from the consequences or the apprehension of disclosure.").
22. Pikowsky, *supra* note 20, at 489.
23. *See* People v. Kor, 277 P.2d 94, 100 (Cal. Ct. App. 1954) (Shinn, J., concurring).
24. Pikowsky, *supra* note 20, at 489.
25. WIGMORE, *supra* note 19, § 2291, at 554.
26. Hazard, *supra* note 19, at 1062.
27. *Compare* People v. Flores, 139 Cal. Rptr. 546, 549 (Ct. App. 1977) (liberal construction), *with* Gonzales v. Mun. Court, 136 Cal. Rptr. 475, 481 (Ct. App. 1977) (strict construction).
28. *See, e.g.*, Goldsborough v. Eagle Crest Partners, Ltd., 805 P.2d 723 (1991), *aff'd*, 838 P.2d 1069 (1992). *See generally* George A. Davidson & William H. Voth, *Waiver of the Attorney-Client Privilege*, 64 OR. L. REV. 637 (1986); Wesley M. Ayres, Comment, *Attorney-Client Privilege: The Necessity of Intent to Waive the Privilege in Inadvertent Disclosure Cases*, 18 PAC. L.J. 59 (1986); James M. Grippando, *Attorney-Client Privilege: Implied Waiver through Inadvertent Disclosure of Documents*, 39 U. MIAMI L. REV. 511 (1985); Note, *Inadvertent Disclosure of Documents Subject to the Attorney-Client Privilege*, 82 MICH. L. REV. 598 (1983). *But see* TEX. R. CIV.

P. 193.3(d), cmt. 4, in which the question of whether waiver principles should apply to inadvertent disclosure is squarely addressed by rule and rejected:

> d. Rule 193.3(d) is a new provision that allows a party to assert a claim of privilege to material or information produced inadvertently without intending to waive the privilege. The provision is commonly used in complex cases to reduce costs and risks in large document productions. The focus is on the intent to waive the privilege, not the intent to produce the material or information. A party who fails to diligently screen documents before producing them does not waive a claim of privilege. This rule is thus broader than *Tex. R. Evid. 511* and overturns *Granada Corp. v. First Court of Appeals*, 844 S.W.2d 223 (Tex. 1992), to the extent the two conflict. The ten-day period (which may be shortened by the court) allowed for an amended response does not run from the production of the material or information but from the party's first awareness of the mistake. To avoid complications at trial, a party may identify prior to trial the documents intended to be offered, thereby triggering the obligation to assert any overlooked privilege under this rule. A trial court may also order this procedure.

29. This point was made by the court in Ciba-Geigy v. Sando, Ltd., 916 F. Supp. 404, 411 (D.N.J. 1995), when it stated that a waiver is a knowing and intentional act, which inadvertent disclosure is not.
30. Johnson v. Zerbst, 304 U.S. 458, 464 (1938).
31. *See, e.g.*, Lee v. State Farm Mut. Auto. Ins. Co., 249 F.R.D. 662, 682–83 (D. Colo. 2008); Chi. Title Ins. Co. v. Superior Court, 220 Cal. Rptr. 507, 512 (Ct. App. 1985).
32. Pikowsky, *supra* note 20, at 494.
33. Davidson & Voth, *supra* note 28, at 639; Pikowsky, *supra* note 20, at 494.
34. Fulmer Stevenson, *supra* note 6, at 359.
35. *Id.*
36. *See, e.g.*, Jordan v. Court of Appeals for Fourth Supreme Judicial Dist., 701 S.W.2d 644, 649 (Tex. 1985) ("If the matter for which a privilege is sought has been disclosed to a third party, thus raising the question of waiver of the privilege, the party asserting the privilege has the burden of proving that no waiver has occurred.").
37. Fulmer Stevenson, *supra* note 6, at 359–60.
38. WIGMORE, *supra* note 19, § 2325, at 633.
39. *See, e.g.*, Neuberger Berman Real Estate Fund, Inc. v. Lola Brown Trust No. 1B, 230 F.R.D. 398, 409 (D. Md. 2005) ("[B]ecause the privilege interferes with the truth seeking process and is in derogation of the public's right to every man's evidence, it is not favored by the federal courts and is to be strictly confined within the narrowest possible limits consistent with the logic of its principle." (quoting *In re* Grand Jury Proceedings, 727 F.2d 1352, 1355 (4th Cir. 1984)); Cobell v. Norton, 213 F.R.D. 16, 23 (D.C. Cir. 2003) ("[B]ecause of the privilege's adverse effect on the full disclosure of the truth, it must be narrowly construed.") (quoting *In re* Grand Jury Investigation of Ocean Transp., 604 F.2d 672, 675 (D.C. Cir. 1979)).
40. United States v. Kelsey-Hayes Wheel Co., 15 F.R.D. 461, 465 (E.D. Mich. 1954); W.R. Grace & Co. v. Pullman, Inc., 446 F. Supp. 771, 775 (W.D. Okla. 1976).
41. *Kelsey-Hayes Wheel Co.*, 15 F.R.D. at 465.
42. *In re* Standard Fin. Mgmt. Corp., 77 B.R. 324, 330 (Bankr. D. Mass. 1987).

43. Int'l Digital Sys. Corp. v. Digital Equip. Corp., 120 F.R.D. 445, 449 (D. Mass. 1988).
44. WIGMORE, *supra* note 19, § 2327, at 636.
45. 91 F.R.D. 254, 256 (N.D. Ill. 1981).
46. *Id.* at 259–60.
47. *Id.* at 260.
48. *In re* Sealed Case, 877 F.2d 976, 980 (D.C. Cir. 1989).
49. *Id.*
50. *E.g.*, Julrik Prods., Inc. v. Chester, 113 Cal. Rptr. 527, 529 (Ct. App. 1974); Mize v. Atchison., T. & S.F. Ry. Co., 120 Cal. Rptr. 787, 795 (Ct. App. 1975).
51. 604 F.2d 672 (D.C. Cir. 1979), *cert. denied*, 444 U.S. 915 (1979).
52. *Id.* at 675.
53. In its modern enlightened form, only voluntary disclosure would automatically result in loss of privilege, eliminating the extreme claim that documents lose their privilege when they are stolen. *See* Note, *supra* note 28, at 612–16 (discussing voluntary disclosure test).
54. As the court stated in *In re* Standard Fin. Mgmt. Corp.: "[M]istake or inadvertence is, after all, merely a euphemism for negligence, and certainly . . . one is expected to pay a price for one's negligence." 77 B.R. 324, 330 (Bankr. D. Mass 1987).
55. Gray v. Bicknell, 86 F.3d 1472, 1483 (8th Cir. 1996).
56. *See, e.g.*, *id.*
57. Kanter v. Superior Court, 253 Cal. Rptr. 810, 816–17 (Ct. App. 1988). Although ordered not citable and not published in the official reports, the court's rationale in *Kanter* is quite enlightening.
58. Ayres, *supra* note 28, at 74.
59. *Id.* at 81–82; *Gray*, 86 F.3d at 1483. Compare this approach with the Texas approach, which does not inquire into intent at all.
60. 531 F. Supp. 951 (N.D. Ill. 1982).
61. *Id.* at 954–55; *see also* Farm Credit Bank v. Huether, 454 N.W.2d 710, 722 (N.D. 1990) (discussing *Mendenhall*).
62. *See Mendenhall*, 531 F. Supp. at 954–55 (citing Dunn Chem. Co. v. Sybron Corp., 1975-2 Trade Cas. (CCH) ¶ 60,561, ¶ 67,463 (S.D.N.Y. 1975); Conn. Mut. Life Ins. Co. v. Shields, 18 F.R.D. 448, 451 (S.D.N.Y. 1955)).
63. *See* Hartford Fire Ins. Co. v. Garvey, 109 F.R.D. 323, 329 (N.D. Cal. 1985); *see also* Kanter v. Superior Court, 253 Cal. Rptr. 810, 814 (Ct. App. 1988).
64. *See In re* Grand Jury Investigation of Ocean Transp., 604 F.2d 672, 675 (D.C. Cir. 1979). *See generally* Carroll v. Abbott Labs., Inc., 654 P.2d 775, 777–78 (Cal. 1982).
65. Kan.-Neb. Natural Gas v. Marathon Oil, 109 F.R.D. 12, 21 (D. Neb. 1985).
66. Michigan appears to have a similar rule. *See* Sterling v. Keidan, 162 Mich. App. 88, 412 N.W.2d 255 (1987). *But see, e.g.*, *Hartford*, 109 F.R.D. at 331–32; Chubb Integrated Sys. v. Nat'l Bank of Wash., 103 F.R.D. 52, 66 (D.D.C. 1984); United States v. Willis, 565 F. Supp. 1186, 1204 (S.D. Iowa 1983); Champion Int'l Corp. v. Int'l Paper Co., 486 F. Supp. 1328, 1332 (N.D. Ga. 1980); Duplan Corp. v. Deering Milliken, Inc., 397 F. Supp. 1146, 1162 (D.S.C. 1974).
67. *E.g.*, Gray v. Bicknell, 86 F.3d 1472, 1483 (8th Cir. 1996).
68. *Id.*
69. *See, e.g.*, Note, *supra* note 28, at 610.
70. Farm Credit Bank v. Huether, 454 N.W.2d 710, 722 (N.D. 1998).
71. Kanter v. Superior Court, 253 Cal. Rptr. 810, 817 (Ct. App. 1988). One advocate of this approach even claims it "is more understandable and easier to apply

than the strict responsibility standard." Grippando, *supra* note 28, at 527. This is, however, a difficult position to sustain for a multifactor balancing test. *See* Ayres, *supra* note 28, at 79–80 (discussing problems raised by the circumstances test).

72. *Gray*, 86 F.3d at 1483–84; Alldread v. City of Grenada, 988 F.2d 1425, 1433 (5th Cir. 1993); Lois Sportswear, U.S.A. Inc. v. Levi Strauss & Co., 104 F.R.D. 103 (S.D.N.Y. 1985).
73. 104 F.R.D. 103.
74. *Id.* at 105.
75. *Id.*
76. *See Gray*, 86 F.3d at 1484 ("The middle test is best suited to achieving a fair result. It accounts for the errors that inevitably occur in modern, document-intensive litigation. . . .").
77. 145 F.R.D. 626 (W.D.N.Y. 1993).
78. *Id.* at 638. It may be surmised that the court took this view partly because the error was local counsel's, not supervising counsel's.
79. *Id.*
80. 253 Cal. Rptr. 810 (Ct. App. 1988).
81. *Id.* at 811–12.
82. *Id.* at 812.
83. *Id.* at 820.
84. *See id.* at 815–18.
85. 109 F.R.D. 323 (N.D. Cal. 1985).
86. 116 F.R.D. 46 (M.D.N.C. 1987).
87. *Id.* at 52.
88. *Id.*
89. 86 F.3d 1472, 1482 (8th Cir. 1996).
90. *Id.* at 1484.
91. *But see* United States v. Pepper's Steel & Alloys, Inc., 742 F. Supp. 641, 645 (S.D. Fla. 1990) (calling receipt of documents a "windfall").
92. Kanter v. Superior Court, 253 Cal. Rptr. 810, 820 (Ct. App. 1988). One article on the subject suggests that, as an analytical tool, estoppel may be the more appropriate rubric under which to test the correct result of one party's inadvertent production of privileged information to its opponent. *See* John T. Hundley, *"Inadvertent Waiver" of Evidentiary Privileges: Can Reformulating the Issue Lead to More Sensible Decisions?*, 19 S. ILL. U. L.J. 263 (1995). Although the notion of estoppel seems to underlie the discussions of "fairness" in many of the cases, it is also true that the opinions do not directly frame the question as one of estoppel *vel non*. When we consider that the negligence concept is used to support both the strict and middle-ground tests—under the strict test if you make the mistake you lose; under the middle-ground test you may lose, and you probably have an uphill battle to win—it seems correct to rate harm to the nonproducing party as a crucial, and perhaps the most important, factor. Given that, in normal negligence settings, even when it has been found that a duty owed has been breached no liability attaches unless harm is shown, it may be logically argued that the same standard should apply when the question is the "liability" of a negligent document producer. To be sure, it may be only the rare case in which no harm can be demonstrated, but that rarity does not render the estoppel factor inappropriate.

93. *See Gray*, 86 F.3d at 1484.
94. *Id.*
95. *See, e.g.*, Permian Corp. v. United States, 665 F.2d 1214, 1216 (D.C. Cir. 1981); Chubb Integrated Sys. v. Nat'l Bank of Wash., 103 F.R.D. 52, 67–68 (D.D.C. 1984).
96. *See* Transamerica Computer Co. v. IBM Corp., 573 F.2d 646, 649–50 (9th Cir. 1978.
97. *See, e.g.*, Data Gen. Corp. v. Grumman Sys. Support Corp., 139 F.R.D. 556, 561 (D. Mass. 1991) (finding several documents' privilege waived despite being marked "Confidential" because "merely marking the documents in such a manner does not constitute the requisite protection required").
98. *See, e.g.*, Fed. R. Civ. P. 26(b)(5).
99. Some jurisdictions dictate the time period in which the attorney has to respond to the inadvertent production. For example, in Texas, the producing party has 10 days (or a shorter period ordered by the court) to amend its production responses and assert privilege. *See* Tex. R. Civ. P. 193.3(d). The benefits of the Texas approach are obvious, however, as it does not require any evaluation of the production to determine if the waiver has occurred and a request requires return of the allegedly privileged document.
100. Although it can be argued that the party denying the claim of privilege for facially privileged materials should have the burden of proving waiver, where the documents have been produced courts typically place the burden of establishing a nonwaiver on the party claiming privilege. *See, e.g.*, Weil v. Inv./Indicators, Research & Mgmt., 647 F.2d 18, 25 (9th Cir. 1981); Kanter v. Superior Court, 253 Cal. Rptr. 810, 811 (Ct. App. 1988).
101. Counsel should also be prepared to do damage control in the event the privilege is held to be lost. Unlike the case of a voluntary waiver, courts are less inclined to hold that disclosure of some privileged documents results in a waiver with respect to all other communications on the same subject matter. *See, e.g.*, *Weil*, 647 F.2d at 25; Parkway Gallery Furniture, Inc. v. Kittinger/Pa. House Grp., Inc., 116 F.R.D. 46, 52 (M.D.N.C. 1987). Moreover, a court might be persuaded to grant a protective order and to modify trial procedures to limit the disclosure of the materials to the case in which the error occurred.

CHAPTER 15

Putting Attorneys on the Witness Stand and Their Advice at Issue: The Perils of Selective Waiver of Privilege*

ALAN J. MARTIN
DEMETRIOS G. METROPOULOS
NICOLE J. HIGHLAND

* This chapter is an update of a chapter originally co-authored by Alan J. Martin and Nancy K. Linnerooth in the 1989 edition of this publication. Veronica L. Spicer of Mayer Brown LLP co-authored a previous update to this chapter.

I. Introduction

What would possess a litigant to put his attorney on the witness stand or his advice at issue? At first glance, many tactical considerations weigh in favor of such efforts. For example, in today's environment of complex commercial litigation a litigant's attorney typically has the best command of the facts. Unlike other witnesses who may only be privy to pieces of the puzzle, the attorney is uniquely situated to be a "big picture" person as a result of having gathered and marshaled the facts.

A closely related consideration is the continuity represented by the attorney. Large companies frequently have employee turnover commensurate to their size, and large cases frequently wind their way through pretrial discovery for an extended period of time. The one constant may be the attorney.

Training can also hold a lawyer in good stead to be a witness. Attorneys tend to be authoritative and articulate speakers. Trial attorneys have years of experience presenting complex legal issues to a jury in lay terms. Knowing the goals of cross-examination, they also possess the wherewithal to anticipate and avoid pitfalls that often trap the uninitiated. As zealous advocates, attorneys can go a long way toward articulating facts in a manner consistent with the "company line."

The strategy of reliance on either the testimony or advice of counsel also comports with commercial reality. Facing an increasingly complex web of laws and regulations on the one hand, and an increasingly litigious society on the other, corporations and businesspeople have given attorneys a correspondingly greater role in everyday decision making. Should litigation nonetheless arise from those decisions, a natural response is to turn to the same attorneys, who not only have firsthand knowledge of the challenged decision but also are most familiar with the legal process.

In the insurance coverage area, the temptation to use attorney witnesses can be great. For example, a company confronted with a rash of product liability cases can be expected to turn to its trusted attorneys to handle the defense. If the number of cases is large, the resulting discovery almost certainly will touch upon the inner workings of the company. A long-standing relationship with a given law firm can go a long way toward the recognition and careful handling of sensitive areas. At the same time, a dispute may arise with the company's insurer as to coverage for costs allegedly related to the defense. Given the sensitivity of the issues and the potential for overlap, the company may determine to use the same law firm and attorneys both to defend the underlying cases and to press the insurance coverage claims. Such a strategy is not without peril, if the attorneys become needed witnesses.

Under the scenario outlined, the same law firm handling the underlying defense also advances claims for insurance coverage. As a result, the law firm is in a unique position to structure the underlying defense in a manner that affects the insurance coverage and, thereby, potentially reinforces its client's claims. Because insurance carriers and their policyholders usually make every effort to avoid trial among themselves until the underlying crisis has passed, the policyholder's attorneys can represent their client on both fronts until just before the trial of the coverage dispute. At that time, with the underlying cases all but history, the attorneys can withdraw as counsel for the insured in the coverage litigation in order to act as trial witnesses regarding the defense of the underlying cases.

Once the attorneys withdraw and are designated as witnesses, however, the question immediately becomes: "To what extent has privilege been waived?" The classic "sword and shield" scenario arises. On the one hand, the insured seeks to use the attorneys' testimony and advice regarding the structure of the underlying defense as a sword at trial while, on the other hand, it invokes the attorney-client privilege and the work-product immunity to shield previous communications regarding coverage issues. As is discussed below, the potential for waiver of privilege dramatically alters the attractiveness of an attorney as a witness—so much so that many civil litigants are unwilling to risk the consequences of such actions. While it is not completely unknown for attorneys to be called as witnesses in criminal matters, a certain number of civil cases have considered the issue as well. This case law suggests, however, that the perils are very real and that one is well advised to think carefully before reaching for this particular sword.

II. The Attorney as Witness

Those civil cases on the subject of attorney witnesses make it clear that a party who names retained counsel as a witness risks waiver of both the privilege for attorney-client communications and the work-product immunity on communications that relate to the subject of the attorney's testimony.[1] Furthermore, courts have been willing to interpret the waiver as having a long reach into otherwise privileged communications and immune documents. The subsequent sections describe this area of the law, beginning with the early cases, particularly in the patent area, and following with areas of particular concern for commercial litigators, such as work-product immunity, expert witnesses, and corporate representatives.

A. *Handgards*

A leading, early case on the issue of attorney witnesses is *Handgards, Inc. v. Johnson & Johnson*.[2] Handgards alleged that Johnson & Johnson brought a series of patent infringement suits against it in bad faith as part of a conspiracy to eliminate competition. In order to rebut assertions that its attorneys knew the patents were invalid at the time they filed suit, Johnson & Johnson planned to call as witnesses three of its lawyers, who were primarily responsible for the prior patent cases, to testify as to legal advice they gave Johnson & Johnson.

The court found that Johnson & Johnson's "deliberate injection of the advice of counsel into a case waives the attorney-client privilege as to communications and documents relating to the advice."[3] This waiver encompassed not only the advice about which the attorneys would testify, but also their entire litigation files, which the court ordered to be submitted for an in camera inspection to determine which documents fell within Handgards' production request.

B. Underlying Considerations

The reasoning of the court in *Handgards* is followed by most courts faced with similar circumstances. The main justification for finding that Johnson & Johnson waived its attorney-client privilege, according to the court, was that it would be unfair to Handgards to allow Johnson & Johnson to disclose self-serving communications at the same time that it withheld damaging ones on the same subject. Other courts have analogized such a tactic to using the privilege as both a sword and a shield. If a party uses part of privileged communications with a lawyer as a "sword" to support a position in litigation, a claim of privilege may not shield unfavorable communications on the same issue from an opponent.[4]

Necessity is another theme to which courts return in justifying a finding of waiver of the privilege. For example, in *Leybold-Heraeus Technologies, Inc. v. Midwest Instrument Co.*,[5] the court found persuasive the argument that waiver was mandated by the opposing party's need to ascertain the basis of opinions in order to effectively cross-examine two attorneys who had been designated as trial witnesses. There, as in *Handgards*, a patentee (LHT) named its attorneys as witnesses to testify as to their asserted good faith in filing suit against an alleged infringer (Minco). In an opinion adopting *Handgards*, the court found that LHT waived its privilege because of the necessity that Minco have all communications regarding the same subjects on which the attorneys would testify in order to perform an adequate cross-examination.[6]

C. Work-Product Immunity

Courts have taken pains to point out that work product has a source of immunity from discovery independent of the attorney-client privilege.[7] The attorney-client privilege is intended "to encourage full and frank communication between attorneys and their clients."[8] The work-product doctrine was developed to protect lawyers' privacy, allowing for case development without fear of adversaries later looking over their shoulder or raiding the fruits of their efforts.[9] Indeed, the "mental impressions, conclusions, opinions, or legal theories of a party's attorney"—more commonly known as "opinion" work product—enjoy heightened protection,[10] which some courts have even deemed "nearly absolute."[11] In theory, then, a waiver of the attorney-client privilege does not necessarily result in a breach of the work-product immunity.

Once a court has found that a party needs information that is in the hands of the opposing party and counsel in order to effectively cross-examine an attorney witness, the logical (and sometimes only) place to find such information is in the attorney's work product. So, with a nod to the distinctiveness of the two doctrines, courts nevertheless open discovery on work product after the client waives the attorney-client privilege by calling counsel as a witness. Thus, the court in *Handgards* ordered the attorney witnesses to produce "a wide range of materials, including all relevant records, opinion letters, interviews of witnesses, internal files, memoranda, and notes" related to the attorneys' opinions of the merits of their client's patents and the related infringement suits.[12] Similarly, in *Leybold-Heraeus*, the opposing party gained access to documents in which the attorney witnesses participated, either as authors or as recipients, and which related to the issue of their good faith in conducting the underlying patent lawsuits.[13]

D. Attorneys Testifying Outside Their Capacity as Such

1. *The Attorney as an Expert Witness*

Variations on the waiver of privilege involve the use of attorneys as "expert" witnesses. The added twist: discovery rules require an expert to disclose information considered in forming an opinion—even privileged information.[14] The question now is how much—not whether—information must be disclosed. Some courts have adopted a bright-line rule that Federal Rule of Civil Procedure 26 mandates disclosure of all information shared with a testifying expert, including an attorney's mental impressions and opinions. Other courts have ruled that "core attorney work product" is protected from discovery.[15] The principle of fundamental fairness still comes into play for many courts.[16]

Once again, the intellectual property context has provided fertile ground for these discovery disputes. This is perhaps understandable: a patent or copyright attorney often possesses an extensive and uniquely specialized technical and professional background, combined with knowledge gained through the patent or copyright application process or through trial preparation. The latter source of knowledge, however—which would otherwise be protected under the work-product doctrine—often becomes fair game when the attorney seeks to become a testifying expert. Perhaps of most concern to the litigant, the attorney expert may be required to disclose *all* information relevant to an opinion—including trial strategy as well as theories that had been *rejected*. In other words, the party seeking to offer an attorney expert must first turn over sensitive work product and legal theories, and then watch its attorney critique (or even reject) those theories on the stand.

Vaughan Furniture Co. v. Featureline Manufacturing, Inc.[17] presents a useful illustration of these concerns. The plaintiff in *Vaughan Furniture* listed one of its attorneys (who had been involved in the suit from the start) as an expert on its copyright and patent claims, but sought to withhold work-product materials documenting trial strategy discussions between the prospective expert and its other attorneys. Observing that the documents would be "necessary for appropriate cross-examination," the court curtly rejected plaintiff's work-product objections: "A party waives the opinion work product protection of its attorney by naming its attorney as an expert witness."[18]

The court then outlined the broad scope of its ruling, stating that the waiver applied "to those documents which the expert reviewed at any time and which would be relevant to the formulation of [the attorney's] expert opinion."[19] The relevant documents included those "discussing trial strategy," and included opinions "even if the opinions were rejected as a basis for the expert opinion."[20] As the court put it, "A change of opinion by the expert can be an important fact."[21] As a result, the sole limitation on disclosure would be items "completely unrelated to the subject matter of [the expert's] opinion."[22]

2. *The Attorney as a Corporate Representative*

In a related vein, attorneys who hold multiple roles in a company and then serve as the company's representative under Federal Rule of Civil Procedure 30(b)(6) may also face these issues. In *Adler v. Wallace Computer Services, Inc.*,[23] Wallace's general counsel—and vice president—served as the company's Rule 30(b)(6) representative. The court held that in this second role, of a Rule 30(b)(6) representative, the attorney waived Wallace's attorney-client privilege by answering deposition questions based on privileged information.[24] Because of those disclosures, the court granted plaintiff's motion to compel answers to questions that the attorney had declined to answer on the basis of attorney-client privilege.

However, designating in-house counsel as a 30(b)(6) representative does not always result in a waiver of privilege. The mere fact that a party designates its in-house attorney as its 30(b)(6) representative does not automatically waive privilege, and no waiver will occur so long as the designee does not reveal any privileged communications.[25] In-house counsel can safely answer purely factual questions posed that do not ask for the substance of communications between attorney and client.[26] Yet if an in-house counsel testifies to any portion of an attorney-client communication, the privilege is waived and in-house counsel cannot then refuse to fill in the remaining facts by claiming attorney-client privilege.[27] Essentially, an in-house attorney can avoid a waiver of privilege by avoiding answering any and all questions related to legal communications.

In contrast, however, portions of an in-house attorney's work product may be subject to a waiver even if there are no questions posed related to legal communications. When in-house counsel is designated to testify to factual matters, the company waives the attorney's fact work product.[28] This may be only a minor concern as fact work product is often discoverable even absent a waiver. The key inquiries for a company to make in selecting its Rule 30(b)(6) representative is whether the subject matter of the deposition, as set forth in the notice of deposition, is purely factual and, if so, whether the company is comfortable disclosing any nonopinion work product related to that subject matter.

III. Putting the Advice of Counsel at Issue

Although the emergence of attorneys as witnesses is relatively recent, courts have long found implied waivers of the attorney-client privilege where a party puts the advice of its attorney "at issue" in litigation. Yet, in recent years, courts have expanded the scope of the circumstances that constitute such a waiver to include, for example, situations in which a party puts its state of mind at issue and the court finds privileged matter to be the best evidence of the party's state of mind. Thus, in addition to the danger that the *scope* of a waiver may exceed expectations, a litigant must face the possibility that its pleadings and strategies might implicitly—even unintentionally—effect a waiver of privilege where none had been foreseen at all.

A. Criminal Cases

The theory of implied waiver of the attorney-client privilege has some of its early roots in criminal cases. The most clear-cut and uncontroversial of the decisions involve prisoners who move to set aside their convictions on the grounds that they received ineffective assistance of counsel. Courts have routinely held that this waives the attorney-client privilege.[29] In *Johnson v. Alabama*, the Eleventh Circuit held that "there should be no confusion that a habeas petitioner alleging that his counsel made unreasonable strategic decisions waives any claim of privilege over the contents of communications with counsel relevant to assessing the reasonableness of those decisions in the circumstances."[30]

In *United States v. Mierzwicki*,[31] a case more closely related to the civil context, the defendant in a prosecution for tax evasion alleged that he amended his returns on the advice of his former attorney. He was held to have waived the attorney-client privilege with respect to evidence about his former attorney's advocacy of his interest.[32]

B. Civil Cases: The General Rule

Although *Mierzwicki* is a criminal case, the holding is the same in civil cases: where a party relies on the advice of counsel as a defense, the opposing party can explore privileged matters to see if the advice was given and taken.[33]

Panter v. Marshall Field & Co. arose out of Marshall Field's successful opposition to a takeover bid. As part of that opposition, Marshall Field had filed an antitrust suit against the prospective bidder. After the takeover fizzled, certain Marshall Field shareholders filed a class action against the company, its officers, and directors (collectively, "Marshall Field"), alleging violations of the securities laws. Marshall Field sought to "rely heavily" on an "advice of counsel" defense,[34] but also claimed protection for certain documents under the attorney-client privilege and work-product doctrine.[35]

The district court first rejected Marshall Field's claim of privilege: "Where, as here, a party asserts as an essential element of his defense reliance upon the advice of counsel, we believe the party waives the attorney-client privilege with respect to all communications, whether written or oral, to or from counsel concerning the transactions for which counsel's advice was sought."[36]

The *Panter* court then turned its attention to the assertion of "work product" privilege. There, despite acknowledging (in a footnote) the different scope and purposes of the attorney-client privilege and work-product doctrine, the court reached the same conclusion:

> Whether styled as a showing of a sufficiently compelling need or as a waiver of the work-product privilege, we find that the defendants' reliance in this litigation upon the advice of counsel as a major justification for their actions . . . and as a defense to these shareholders' suits renders the advice and actions of counsel a central issue, and as such overcomes the attorneys' work-product privilege. . . .[37]

C. *Hearn* and Progeny: The "State of Mind" Exception

By pleading reliance on the advice of counsel as a defense, a party typically seeks to disprove the alleged existence of a culpable "state of mind"—whether it be the intent to commit a crime, as in *Mierzwicki*, or the existence of "bad faith" in handling an insurance claim, as in *Wender v. United Services Auto Ass'n*.[38] But, as the preceding discussion makes clear, the party that employs such a strategy risks losing the protection afforded by the attorney-client privilege and work-product doctrine.

The next logical question is whether a party can base a defense, or even an affirmative claim for relief, on its state of mind *alone*, and thus stop short of an implied privilege waiver. This is the question faced in *Hearn v. Rhay*,[39] a particularly influential case on this subject. *Hearn* helped open the floodgates of implied waiver and has been relied upon by some courts to vitiate the attorney-client privilege on even slight pretexts.

1. Hearn *and the Qualified Immunity Defense*

Hearn was a civil rights action brought against prison officials by an inmate who alleged that his confinement in a mental health unit constituted "cruel and unusual punishment" and violated his right to due process.[40] Defendants asserted the affirmative defense of "qualified immunity"—in other words, they contended that they acted in good faith, pursuant to their understanding of the law, and were therefore immune from the suit for damages.[41] The plaintiff sought discovery of all the legal advice the defendants received on the legality of his confinement in the mental health unit. The court agreed with the plaintiff's contention that the defendants waived their attorney-client privilege by asserting their qualified immunity as a defense.[42]

In an oft-quoted passage, the *Hearn* court analyzed several cases where the privilege was held to be waived, and drew the following conclusions:

> All of these established exceptions to the rules of privilege have a common denominator; in each instance, the party asserting the privilege placed information protected by it in issue through some affirmative act for his own benefit, and to allow the privilege to protect against disclosure of such information would have been *manifestly unfair* to the opposing party. The factors common to each exception may be summarized as follows: (1) assertion of the privilege was a result of some affirmative act, such as filing suit, by the asserting party; (2) through this affirmative act, the asserting party put the protected information at issue by making it relevant to the case; and (3) application of the privilege would have denied the opposing party access to information *vital* to his defense. Thus, where these three conditions exist, a court should find that the party asserting a privilege has impliedly waived it through his own affirmative conduct.[43]

The *Hearn* court found all three elements present in the case before it. Concluding that the content of the asserted privileged communications was "inextricably merged with the elements of plaintiff's case and defendants' affirmative defense," the court allowed discovery of any legal advice and confidential communications between the defendants and the state attorney general that related to the issues of malice towards the plaintiff or knowledge of plaintiff's constitutional rights.[44]

The holding in *Hearn* has considerable emotional appeal: in making his case, the plaintiff prisoner had presented substantial evidence showing that the conditions of his confinement were "deplorable" and that those conditions persisted even after the attorney general notified one of the defendants that such confinement violated plaintiff's constitutional rights.[45] In addition, the court's logic—particularly its consideration of the "manifest[] unfair[ness]" of defendants' partial disclosure and its reference to the plaintiff's "vital" need for the allegedly protected communications—parallels the "fairness" and "necessity" considerations underlying the more traditional implied waiver decisions described above.[46] Finally, even though the *Hearn* defendants neither put their attorney on the stand nor directly pleaded reliance on his advice, they did plead "state of mind" as a defense—and, as the court found, the circumstances of the case "inextricably merged" attorney-client communications with that "state of mind."[47]

As the ensuing discussion shows, subsequent decisions have applied the Hearn court's broad language, and its flexible three-part test, in a wide array of settings.[48] As a result, today's litigant must consider the risk that a proposed claim or defense might put the legal advice and work product of its attorneys "at issue."

2. The "Good Faith" Defense

"Good faith" is a common defense to numerous torts outside the civil rights context. These cases represent the simplest, and shortest, extension of *Hearn*'s reasoning. For example, in *McLaughlin v. Lunde Truck Sales, Inc.*,[49] a suit by the Department of Labor to enjoin alleged violations of federal minimum wage laws, the defendants argued that they acted in good-faith reliance on representations by Department of Labor officials, and offered an affidavit by their former attorney to support that position. The Department of Labor argued, and the court held, that the defendants waived their attorney-client privilege by asserting "good faith" and by "injecting their former counsel's affidavit in support of their good faith defense."[50]

Similarly, the defendants in *Dawson v. New York Life Insurance Co.*[51] asserted a qualified privilege to justify their allegedly defamatory speeches. "Good faith" was an element of this defense, and because the defendants had used information obtained from their attorneys to help write their speeches, the court held that any applicable privilege had been waived.[52]

In some circumstances, a careful attorney may be able to craft a good-faith defense and not waive attorney-client privilege.[53] An example of care in pleading is *Cardtoons, L.C. v. Major League Baseball Players Ass'n*.[54] In *Cardtoons*, plaintiff planned to print parody baseball cards—sparking a cease-and-desist letter from defendant. Plaintiff responded with a suit alleging a potpourri of claims, including several that required proof of defendant's intent. While the court warned that the issue of waiver could be teed up again if the defendant relied on attorney work product at trial in support of its good-faith argument, it found that the defendant's assertion of good faith, when plaintiff had the burden of proving bad faith, was insufficient in and of itself to waive the attorney-client privilege. The mere fact that privileged communications would make it easier for plaintiff to prove its case was not enough to waive defendant's attorney-client privilege.[55]

Cardtoons is distinguishable from *McLaughlin* and *Dawson* in two important ways. First, the good-faith defense in *Cardtoons* simply denied an element of plaintiff's claim. It was not an affirmative defense that was voluntarily injected into the case. In *McLaughlin*, by contrast, good faith was part of a qualified privilege defense to a defamation claim. Similarly, in *Dawson* good faith was asserted as an affirmative defense to a Fair Labor Standards Act claim. Second, the defendant in *Cardtoons* did not claim or imply that attorney work product was the primary support for its good-faith claim. Reliance on attorney work product arose only in response to plaintiff's request for admissions, depositions of defendant's attorney, and oral argument on plaintiff's motion to compel. Even then, defendant showed that the attorney work product was, at best, one factor among several and not necessary to support its case. Despite plaintiff's questions about attorney work product, the court did not consider the material "at issue" without some affirmative act or representation from defendant that it was going to rely on the substance of the material. By contrast, in *McLaughlin*, the defendant voluntarily submitted an affidavit from its counsel regarding his interpretation of events—implying that it relied upon that information in making its good-faith determination.[56] It is important to note that a party can, in essence, volunteer reliance on attorney advice when that is the only logical support for its position. For example, potentially protected information was central to supporting (and refuting) the qualified privilege claim in *Dawson*. Although defendant did not explicitly volunteer that it would rely on attorney-client information, that reliance was implied when all of the relevant deponents (defendant's employees) stated that they either (1) directly relied on attorney information to prepare allegedly defamatory statements or (2) knew of the attorney information before making such statements. Thus, while courts clearly consider whether reliance on an attorney is volunteered, a party should be careful to not implicitly "volunteer" such reliance.

3. *Equitable Estoppel*

A party may also make state of mind an issue by trying to toll a statute of limitations. Adopting the reasoning of *Hearn*, the district court in *Connell v. Bernstein-Macaulay, Inc.* found that the privilege was waived where the plaintiff buyers of securities claimed that the defendant underwriters were estopped to assert the statutory bar, as they had convinced the plaintiffs to withhold suit while they tried to save the corporation.[57] The court found that the plaintiffs had waived the privilege on the issue of whether or not they had withheld suit solely or principally because of the defendants' persuasion. In broad language, the court stated:

> [W]here a litigant seeks to avoid a statutory protection which has been established for the benefit of his adversary [by a claim of estoppel]; and where it appears that there is a good faith basis for believing that invasion of the attorney-client privilege would shed light on the validity of such claim of estoppel; the party making such assertion must be deemed to have waived the privilege.[58]

Clearly, the *Connell* court was reluctant to permit an assertion of attorney-client privilege to defeat the public policy reflected in the tolling statute. In using such broad language, however, the court ignored its implications: invasion of the attorney-client privilege would "shed light" on the validity of virtually *any* claim.[59]

Courts have also found waiver as a result of estoppel claims in other, more generic contexts. For example, when the defendant in a patent infringement action claimed that the plaintiff was estopped from enforcing its patent because of defendant's detrimental reliance on the plaintiff's previous inaction, the court in *Southwire Co. v. Essex Group Inc.* found a waiver as to any documents that tended to show the defendant had instead relied on the advice of its lawyers that the patent was invalid.[60] Although there was some objective evidence available showing reliance on inaction, the *Southwire* court found that, in fairness, the plaintiff should be permitted discovery of privileged documents to show the defendant's subjective intent.[61] The court found the claim of waiver particularly compelling in view of the defendant's reliance on the opinions of its lawyers as a defense to a different claim, that of willful infringement.[62] This alternative theory gave some credence to plaintiff's claim that the defendant relied on something other than plaintiff's inaction.

4. *Fraud*

The issue of reliance is also present in cases of alleged fraud. Accordingly, as one might expect, the issue of implied waiver has arisen as well. In *Sedco International, S.A. v. Cory*,[63] the Eighth Circuit held that an investor, by asserting fraudulent inducement, "at most, waived his right to assert the privilege to prevent disclosure of communications which might have proven he did not rely on [his opponent's] statements or that such reliance was unreasonable." However, the court refused to compel disclosure of privileged communications, finding that none of those communications could possibly show that the investor relied on anything other than the alleged misstatements.[64]

Some later opinions have followed *Sedco*'s legal conclusion, finding that allegations of fraud constitute an implied waiver of privilege.[65] Other courts have adopted *Sedco*'s factual finding that privileged matters were not relevant to the issue of reliance, and thus have allowed disclosure only from the alleged victim itself (e.g., what it knew, why it acted).[66]

5. *Contractual Intent*

State of mind issues also arise in connection with contract disputes. In many cases, one party will try to go beyond the four corners of its agreement and introduce extrinsic evidence of its underlying understanding or intent. Because attorneys often play a role in contract negotiation, their advice is arguably "intertwined" with the client's contractual intent. Thus, it should come as no surprise that several courts have found the party employing such a strategy to have waived its attorney-client privilege.[67]

Back-to-back decisions by a Massachusetts federal district court in the case of *Sax v. Sax*[68] provide a useful illustration of this principle at work. *Sax* involved a "Memorandum Agreement" between Lawrence Sax and John Sax. Both parties were represented by counsel during the lengthy negotiations that preceded the agreement. Lawrence Sax sued to enforce the agreement; John Sax alleged, among other things, that the agreement was invalid because it was vague and the parties did not have a mutual understanding of its terms.[69]

In an opinion filed March 15, 1991, the district court observed that "John Sax has raised an issue of his lack of understanding of the Memorandum Agreement in circumstances in which perhaps the only person who would have explained the agreement to him was his attorney."[70] As a result, the court held that he had implicitly waived his attorney-client privilege.[71]

Apparently believing that turnabout would be fair play, John Sax then filed a motion challenging Lawrence Sax's privilege claims. This time, the district judge ruled differently: finding that Lawrence Sax had simply sought a declaration that the agreement, as written, was valid—without relying on extrinsic evidence, his attorney's advice, or his own "state of mind"—the court upheld his privilege claims.[72]

D. Beyond "State of Mind"

As the preceding section describes, *Hearn* itself, and much of its progeny, focus on a party's allegations as to its state of mind. Yet *Hearn*'s underlying rationales—fairness and necessity—are not logically confined to state of mind issues. Thus, some decisions hold that a party loses privilege by making other factual allegations that implicitly put attorney advice or work product "at issue."

In *United States v. Exxon Corp.*,[73] the government accused Exxon of overcharging its customers. As a defense, Exxon asserted that it had relied, in good faith, on representations by the Department of Energy. The court found that Exxon had accordingly waived attorney-client privilege, reasoning that "[t]here is no other reasonable way for plaintiff to explore Exxon's corporate state of mind, a consideration now central to this suit."[74]

Thus far, then, the *Exxon* decision simply tracked previous case law in finding a waiver based on the assertion of an affirmative state of mind defense. At that point, however, the court went on to consider Exxon's motion to dismiss for lack of indispensable parties, in which Exxon alleged that it did not cause overcharges by other owners of oil interests. As with Exxon's good-faith defense, the court held that the defense of causation effected a waiver of privilege. As the court explained matters, "Whether Exxon had an overall scheme to pressure other interest owners to adopt certain pricing policies can only be effectively determined by exploring attorney-client discussions wherein such a scheme *may* have been concocted."[75]

The Delaware Supreme Court took a similar view of an insurance company's "causation" defense in *Tackett v. State Farm Fire & Casualty Insurance Co.*[76] The policyholders in *Tackett* sued State Farm for its alleged "bad faith" delay in processing a claim. State Farm, perhaps leery of the consequences of an "advice of counsel" or "good faith" defense, alleged instead that it had processed the claim in "routine" fashion, and that any delay had been caused by its policyholders' lack of cooperation. The court had no trouble finding that State Farm's allegations implicated its communications with counsel and thus waived privilege as to *any* legal advice received during the claims handling process. Observing that "[f]airness requires that assertions of fact be tested by disclosure," the court held that "where, as here, an insurer makes factual representations which implicitly rely upon legal advice as justification for nonpayment of claims, the insurer cannot shield itself from disclosure of the *complete advice of counsel* relevant to the handling of the claim."[77]

Damages claims may also put attorney advice or work product at issue. In *Rutgard v. Haynes*,[78] a legal malpractice case, the court noted that a party does not waive attorney-client privilege simply by including attorneys' fees in a damages claim. But in *Rutgard*, the plaintiff also claimed damages for a settlement negotiated by another attorney. In those circumstances, the court found that the reasonableness of the attorney's actions in negotiating the settlement was at issue and privileged information was discoverable.[79]

E. Further Extensions of the Implied Waiver Doctrine

1. *Refusal of Advice-of-Counsel Defense*

Hearn addressed the situation where a party implicitly places attorney advice at issue without affirmatively pleading an advice-of-counsel defense. Later decisions suggest that a waiver may be possible even when that party expressly *refuses* to rely on an advice-of-counsel defense. In *In re Consolidated Litigation Concerning International Harvester's Disposition of Wisconsin Steel*,[80] International Harvester (IH) sold the assets of a subsidiary to a buyer who not long thereafter filed for bankruptcy. The buyers, who had assumed responsibility for the subsidiary's pension liabilities, joined the pension guaranty company and the subsidiary's employees in an action against IH. They claimed that IH knew the buyers were doomed to fail and that the sale was merely a sham to avoid pension liabilities.[81]

IH specifically disclaimed any intention of relying on an advice-of-counsel defense. However, IH's defense position was that it acted *reasonably* on the basis of information known to it. The court said that it "would be reluctant" to grant a discovery motion if IH could present its proposed defense without disclosing any attorney-client communications. The court warned that if IH relied on any attorney-client communications to show that it acted reasonably, it would waive the privilege as to those communications and all others that pertained to the same subject matter.[82]

The Second Circuit's decision in the criminal securities-fraud case *United States v. Bilzerian*[83] takes this analysis one step further. The defendant in *Bilzerian* sought to testify that he had made a good-faith attempt to comply with the securities laws in certain investment transactions, which were later found illegal. Bilzerian did not plan to assert an advice-of-counsel defense; indeed, he did not plan to disclose the content or even the existence of any privileged communications. Nonetheless, the trial court held—and the Second Circuit agreed—that the proposed defense would result in a waiver of attorney-client privilege.[84] Citing *Hearn* and *Exxon*, the appellate court explained that Bilzerian's "good faith" testimony "would have put his knowledge of the law and the basis for his understanding of what the law required in issue," and that otherwise privileged communications "would have been directly relevant in determining the extent of his knowledge and, as a result, his intent."[85]

As previously described, decisions in the criminal arena laid some of the early foundations of the "at issue" doctrine, while civil cases like *Hearn* expanded that doctrine to create a wide-ranging state of mind exception.

Bilzerian shows that principles developed in the civil context are now, in turn, influencing decisions in criminal cases. The doctrine of implied waiver has come full circle.

2. *Pleading by Opponent*

Not only may a litigant put his own attorney's advice at issue—affirmatively or implicitly—but the *opposing* party may also place this advice at issue through its pleadings. In *Bird v. Penn Central Co.*,[86] plaintiffs sued to rescind certain insurance policies. The policyholders raised the defense of laches, claiming that the plaintiffs knew or should have known of the grounds for rescission long before they brought suit, since their counsel had investigated prior claims that the defendants had made under the policies. The court found a crucial issue to be what the plaintiffs knew or should have known, and therefore it held that the relevant work product of plaintiffs' attorneys, including legal theories and conclusions, was discoverable:

> Because the nature of [the opposing party's] defense concerns knowledge, legal theories and conclusions of plaintiffs' attorneys charged with claim investigation, such "advice of counsel" evidenced in these documents is discoverable when it is directly relevant to a possible rescission action or suggests reasons to indicate the propriety of such an action.[87]

Likewise, in *AM International, Inc. v. Eastman Kodak Co.*,[88] the court was persuaded that because Kodak alleged that AM International, Inc. (AMI) knowingly filed suit based on invalid patents, discovery from AMI was appropriate. Since this allegation put the opinions of AMI's attorneys directly at issue, and Kodak's need was "compelling," the court ordered the relevant work product produced. In a nutshell, "[a]n attorney's work product is discoverable where such information is directly at issue and the need for production is compelling."[89]

IV. Pretrial Procedure

A. General Considerations

As should be apparent, courts generally do not find it necessary to wait until a party's lawyer has actually been placed on the witness stand before allowing discovery of privileged material. To do so would defeat the purpose of discovery. Once a party indicates that counsel may testify, the opposing party is entitled to pretrial discovery of the issues related to the attorney's proposed testimony.[90]

However, the Northern District of Illinois recently challenged the seemingly intuitive notion that an opposing party need not wait until an attorney's testimony has transpired to seek discovery of privileged material related to the anticipated testimony. In *In re Application for an Order for Judicial Assistance in a Foreign Proceeding in the Labor Court of Brazil*,[91] the petitioner filed a motion to compel, seeking the disclosure of compliance forms completed by McDonald's Corporation's legal department. McDonald's had indicated that it planned to call its general counsel as a witness, and the petitioner asserted that this fact was sufficient to waive the work-product doctrine for any documents associated with McDonald's general counsel.[92] The court denied the petitioner's motion to compel, finding that waiver results only if the testimony reveals the content of privileged communications. The court reasoned that since the attorney's testimony had not yet transpired and communications had not yet been revealed, no waiver had occurred and the petitioner's claim was, at that time, merely speculative.[93] The court did not address the quandary it may face if, at trial, McDonald's general counsel does in fact reveal privileged communications on the witness stand and the opposing party does not possess the knowledge or materials that it would have otherwise obtained through the discovery process necessary to conduct a proper cross-examination.

B. Deposing Counsel

Deposing counsel, particularly trial counsel, presents a unique set of complicated issues as courts regularly recognize that such depositions provide an "opportunity for harassment; it disrupts the opposing attorney's preparation for trial, and could ultimately lead to disqualification of opposing counsel if the attorney is called as a trial witness."[94] Accordingly, courts generally disfavor attempts to depose opposing counsel and believe that they are disruptive of the adversarial process.[95] Considering this backdrop, even when privileged material is deemed discoverable, counsel may be able to avoid being deposed—if someone else can provide the requested information.

The seminal case for determining when a party can depose opposing counsel is *Shelton v. American Motors Corp.*[96] In *Shelton*, the Eighth Circuit formulated a three-part test for determining when opposing counsel may be deposed. A party must show that (1) no other means exist to obtain the information; (2) the information is relevant and nonprivileged; and (3) the information is crucial to the case.[97]

While *Shelton* is the case courts most frequently cite when faced with the question of whether to allow a deposition of opposing counsel, its circumstances are limited and it is often questioned by other courts. The Eighth Circuit limited its own *Shelton* ruling in *Pamida v. E.S. Originals, Inc.*,[98] finding the *Shelton* factors unnecessary when attorneys were to be deposed concerning their knowledge of a concluded action that was relevant to an ongoing action. Rather than protect attorneys who represent clients in two different actions when only the attorneys know certain crucial information about the prior case, the party seeking the deposition need only show either waiver of privilege or substantial need and undue hardship under Federal Rule of Civil Procedure 26(b)(3).[99] Other courts have refused to apply *Shelton* and instead require a full evaluation of the circumstances as opposed to the application of a rote test.[100] Still other courts have implemented a flexible application of the *Shelton* factors, taking additional factors into consideration.[101] These factors include

> the need to take the deposition; the lawyer's role in the underlying action and in the primary action; the risk of encountering privilege and interfering in the attorney client relationship; avoiding unnecessary expense; and the means and extent of discovery already conducted to obtain the information to be gleaned from the attorney.[102]

If an attorney witness refuses to answer questions at a deposition after a client waives the attorney-client privilege, courts are prepared to bar the attorney's testimony on any issue related to the privilege.[103] The plaintiff in *Torres v. 100 North LaSalle Partnership* intended to call as a witness her former lawyer, who claimed privilege in refusing to answer 12 questions at his deposition. The court gave the plaintiff a choice: if she allowed the deposition to be reopened and directed the lawyer to answer questions, he could testify without restriction at trial; otherwise he would be barred from testifying on any issue as to which he had asserted the privilege.[104]

C. *Northbrook v. Procter & Gamble*

Addressing discovery issues related to the waiver of the attorney-client privilege, the Northern District of Illinois rendered a series of decisions in the case of *Northbrook Excess & Surplus Insurance Co. v. Procter & Gamble Co.*[105] *Northbrook* involved a declaratory judgment action by certain excess insurers of Procter & Gamble (P&G) to determine their coverage obligations as a result of toxic shock syndrome litigation against P&G and its "Rely" tampon. On January 14, 1988, the magistrate rendered the first decision relating to attorney-client privilege and work-product immunity which, among other issues, considered the status of *in-house* P&G attorneys designated as trial witnesses. The magistrate was unequivocal in finding a complete subject matter waiver for P&G's claims of attorney-client privilege and work product:

> P&G attorneys . . . who have been designated as trial witnesses, are ordered to testify in full in deposition as to matters on which they are to testify at trial and without regard to any claim of attorney-client or work product privilege. By designating those attorneys as trial witnesses, P&G has waived both privileges, but only with respect to the subjects on which they will testify at trial.[106]

P&G did not appeal the decision to the district judge.

The parties' focus then shifted to P&G's outside counsel, Dinsmore & Shohl ("Dinsmore"). The relationship between the Dinsmore firm and P&G went back to the turn of the century, and Dinsmore had served as P&G's national coordinating counsel in the toxic shock litigation. Dinsmore also represented P&G in the insurance coverage litigation. Thus, in the early days of the coverage suit, the insurers had moved to disqualify Dinsmore on the grounds that its attorneys would be required as trial witnesses. P&G persuaded the court that, for the time being at least, Dinsmore testimony would not be required, and the district judge denied the insurers' motion without prejudice.

Just days before the close of discovery—and following close on the heels of the magistrate's January 14 ruling as to P&G's in-house attorneys—Dinsmore withdrew as trial counsel on grounds that its attorneys would testify at trial after all on the handling of the underlying Rely defense. The insurers in turn protested P&G's last-minute reversal and moved to exclude any such testimony.[107] P&G vigorously opposed the motion, criticizing the proposed exclusion as "drastic" and "potentially outcome determinative."[108] The magistrate agreed—but also allowed the insurers to reopen discovery on a limited basis.[109] In so doing, the magistrate nonetheless acknowledged that "[j]ust what additional discovery the insurers wish to undertake is not clear."[110]

With discovery reopened, the insurers played their hole card—serving a subpoena on Dinsmore that called not only for documents related to the underlying Rely defense efforts (which P&G conceded were discoverable) but for "[a]ll documents relating to the present insurance coverage dispute between [P&G] and the Insurers."[111] P&G filed for a protective order, contending that its attorneys would testify only on defense issues, not on coverage issues, and that the latter subjects remained privileged from discovery.

In an opinion dated July 8, 1988, the magistrate ruled on P&G's objections. Framing the insurers' arguments in favor of a wholesale waiver, the magistrate stated:

> The insurers argue that from the inception of the Rely litigation insurance coverage issues were inextricably intertwined with decisions by P&G and Dinsmore regarding the Rely defense effort and that Dinsmore was involved in structuring that defense effort and various defense activities for which P&G claims insurance coverage so as to give an untrue appearance that they were defense oriented. The insurers say that those expenditures and activities were not matters on which P&G initially expected insurance coverage, but their true purpose was to create an appearance which would support insurance claims rather than to conduct a reasonable and efficient defense. The insurers also maintain that they are entitled to use the involvement of Dinsmore attorneys in coverage issues to impeach the testimony of those witnesses relating to the Rely defense effort.[112]

The magistrate agreed with this assessment, noting that deposition excerpts and documents showed that from the beginning P&G and Dinsmore perceived a close relationship between insurance coverage issues and various Rely defense activities. Accordingly, he concluded that "P&G has waived its attorney client privilege as to insurance coverage questions relating to Rely defense activities."[113]

In regards to work-product immunity, the magistrate found a corresponding waiver on two grounds. First, to the extent that a showing of "compelling need" was necessary, he found that it had been made.[114] The magistrate noted that "[d]ocuments relating to Dinsmore's treatment of the insurance coverage issues in relation to its conduct of the underlying product liability litigation may bear on central issues in this case and are not available from any other source."[115] Second, he reasoned that "[w]ork product immunity may also be waived by the appearance of the attorney as a witness."[116]

The magistrate's decision left open the possibility of some limitation on the waiver if P&G could demonstrate that it completed its basic decisions relating to the conduct of Rely defense efforts at a given point in time and then subsequently focused on the prosecution of the coverage litigation.[117] The burden of establishing this limitation, however, fell squarely on P&G.[118] The magistrate also cautioned P&G—twice—that failure to provide the requested discovery would lead him to reconsider his ruling allowing Dinsmore attorneys to testify at trial.[119]

P&G appealed to the district court judge. On December 28, 1988, the district court affirmed the magistrate's ruling.[120] While reassuring P&G that the ruling did not give the insurers authority to "root around through all the Dinsmore files," the judge accepted the magistrate's central premise that privilege claims were waived "as to insurance coverage questions relating to Rely defense activities."[121]

In the court's view, because Dinsmore attorneys were supposed to testify on "what" was done to defend the Rely cases and "why," documents relevant to these considerations were discoverable even if they contained otherwise privileged information regarding policy coverage considerations.[122] As the court stressed in the closing paragraph of its opinion, "To the extent that 'what' and 'why' involve policy coverage considerations, so be it."[123]

One can only assume that when P&G first considered designating Dinsmore attorneys as witnesses in the coverage action, and then fought tooth and nail to persuade the court to go along, it did not contemplate having to produce to the insurers documents relating to that very litigation.

V. Scope of Privilege Waiver

A. Scope of Attorney-Client Privilege Waiver

Most courts agree that a waiver of attorney-client privilege, whether express or implied, extends to all communications on the applicable "subject matter" once the waiver has been established. Their application of this test, however, can be as elusive, as expansive, and as unpredictable as the concepts of "fairness" and "necessity" on which the doctrine of implied waiver rests. Furthermore, issues arise when an attorney has testified in a prior proceeding and later claims privilege on the same subject matter in a subsequent proceeding. Further still, instances where the testimony of one attorney can result in a waiver of privilege of communications that took place between the client and another attorney can further broaden the scope of the waiver of the attorney-client privilege.

1. *Subject Matter Waiver*

Variations on the determination of what is related to the same subject matter as a particular communication begin with the allocation of the initial burden of proof between the opposing parties. In some jurisdictions, the party seeking to limit the scope of a waiver faces an uphill battle. Courts generally disfavor privileges and construe them narrowly.[124] Moreover, a finding of waiver is made more likely because courts generally place the burden of establishing privilege on the claimant.[125] The party asserting the attorney-client privilege has the burden of proving not only that the communications at issue are privileged, but also that the privilege has not been waived[126] and that the scope of such waiver can be limited.[127] This does not mean, however, that the party asserting the attorney-client privilege need both make and refute the opposing party's case for waiver. As described in *First Federal Savings Bank of Hegewisch v. United States*,[128] the party asserting the privilege has the initial burden of establishing the elements of the privilege, but the burden then shifts to the party opposing the privilege to establish a prima facie case of waiver. If that case is made, the burden shifts back to the party asserting the privilege to rebut the prima facie case by demonstrating that the privilege is still viable.

The issue then becomes the scope of waiver. Since the waiver doctrine is designed to *prevent* a party from selective (and possibly distorted) disclosure of privileged communications, these courts naturally take a skeptical look at attempted subject matter limitations.[129]

Conversely, however, some decisions give priority to the interests served by the attorney-client privilege, and narrowly construe the scope of its waiver.[130] In such cases, "[i]f a discernible line exists between the information withheld and the information disclosed, the line should be maintained."[131] In justifying a narrow construction of the scope of implied waiver, the Ninth Circuit described the doctrine as "striking a bargain with the holder of the privilege by letting him know how much of the privilege he must waive in order to proceed with his claim."[132] Under this philosophy, (1) waiver should be no broader than necessary to ensure the fairness of the proceedings, (2) the holder of the privilege has the option of preserving the confidentiality of the privileged communications by abandoning his claim, and (3) the party turning over protective materials is entitled to rely on the limits of the waiver as described by the court.[133] Thus, such cases acknowledge that, in some circumstances, limits on waiver can be discerned and realistically applied. By doing so, they give the party opposing discovery more of an opportunity to lessen the scope and consequences of waiver.

Further complicating the issues is the disparity in factual situations, both in the context from which privileged communications spring and in the type and subject of the communications themselves. For obvious reasons, courts do not explain in detail the nature of documents that they find privileged. Indeed, many decisions simply record the results of a document-by-document in camera review, and thus have little general applicability.

The variations in philosophy and results continue even on appellate review.[134] Appellate courts differ in the degree of deference they are willing to give a trial judge in assessing the scope of a privilege waiver. The U.S. Court of Appeals for the D.C. Circuit, for instance, applies the deferential "abuse of discretion" standard,[135] as does the Tenth Circuit.[136] On the other hand, the Sixth Circuit uses the nondeferential "de novo" standard that generally applies to a trial court's legal conclusions.[137]

2. *Prior Proceedings*

Even if an attorney does not testify in a proceeding and advice of counsel is not at issue, an attorney's prior testimony in a different proceeding can result in a waiver of privilege. If a party calls its attorney as a fact witness in a prior proceeding, the party waives the attorney-client privilege with respect to the subject of the testimony adduced in the prior proceeding.[138] This waiver is not limited to the prior proceeding; if the same subject matter is at issue in a subsequent proceeding, the waiver remains.

3. *Multiple Attorneys*

In addition, an opposing party might also gain access to the advice and opinions of *other* attorneys consulted by that client, and to communications and analyses dated *after* the opinion on which the client relies.[139] Once again, the rationale is fairness—courts find that the jury, in assessing whether a party was "reasonable" in relying on one attorney's advice, is entitled to know if the client received overwhelming advice to the contrary from other attorneys,[140] or if the client subsequently learned that this original advice was wrong.[141]

The issues surrounding multiple attorneys arise most frequently in the context of patent litigation, wherein one attorney has offered an opinion letter and another attorney is serving as trial counsel in the subsequent infringement action. In general, courts are reluctant to extend the waiver of privilege to trial counsel. Even courts acknowledging the wide breadth of subject-matter waiver and maintaining that subject-matter waiver requires that a party disclose communications made to any and all attorneys that involve the same subject will exempt trial counsel of record from such disclosure.[142] Recognizing that some courts do, however, extend the privilege waiver to trial counsel, while others refuse to do so, and still others extend the waiver only for communications casting doubt on the opinions asserted, the court in *In re Seagate Technology, LLC*[143] found that the significantly different functions of trial counsel and opinion counsel advise against extending the waiver. Applying a standard of fairness, the court held that disclosing the opinions of opinion counsel generally does not constitute waiver of the attorney-client privilege for communications with trial counsel, except in unusual circumstances.[144] Such unusual circumstances can include (1) the client choosing to retain the same counsel that offered the advice-of-counsel opinion to litigate the matter;[145] (2) trial counsel attempting to use his or her status to "erect a barrier" to discovery;[146] or (3) counsel "play[ing] cute" by circumscribing information provided to opinion counsel and funneling it through other lawyers in the firm.[147]

B. Scope of Work-Product Waiver

Within the broad confines set by competing trial court philosophies and appellate standards regarding scope of waiver, there are specific recurring issues that warrant attention in litigation planning. For example, where a party attempts to rely on the advice or opinions of counsel, most courts find—and many litigants concede—that its opponent is entitled to discover the analyses underlying that opinion.[148] Thus, courts will freely find that the advising attorney's work product, even opinion work product, is discoverable to the broadest extent consonant with direct relevance to the proffered advice.[149]

However, the scope of the work-product waiver is not the same "subject matter" waiver as applies to the waiver of attorney-client privilege. For example, production of work product from an opinion letter does not necessarily waive all work-product protections on all documents related to the same subject, including underlying research and drafts not communicated to the client.[150] Applying such a broad subject-matter waiver would render harsh results such as a wholesale production of all work product whenever a court orders production of any work product.[151] In determining what a party must produce, courts can consider the policy, needs, any undue hardship on a party, and the benefits versus burdens of production.[152] Essentially, courts should require a "plus factor" before adopting the broadest reaches of waiver of work product.[153]

In addition, most courts will impose a temporal limitation on a waiver of work product, requiring production only of documents created before suit was filed. Because of an enhanced interest in protecting against disclosure of trial strategy, the waiver of work product will end once the lawsuit is filed.[154] However, when advice of counsel is given after litigation has begun, the waiver cannot be limited to pretrial.[155] Furthermore, if a party relying on advice of counsel changes its position from what was originally stated in the advice-of-counsel opinion, fairness dictates that the court extend the waiver post-suit.[156]

There is a split of authority on whether work product that was not shared with the client is subject to a work-product waiver. One line of cases takes an expansive view of the scope of waiver while other cases hold that the waiver does not extend to documents unless they were disclosed to the client.[157] On the one hand, the attorney's file will not always reflect whether a document was shared with the client, and the failure to share certain materials with the client may be compelling evidence against the adequacy of the advice.[158] On the other hand, there is seemingly no compelling reason why an attorney's private thoughts would be probative of the client's ability to rely on the attorney's advice.[159]

Issues regarding multiple attorneys, particularly in advice-of-counsel cases, are just as prevalent with regard to the scope of work-product waiver as they are in the context of waiver of the attorney-client privilege. Courts' reluctance to extend waiver to trial counsel operates in even greater force when it comes to opinion work product. The same rationale for limiting waiver of the attorney-client privilege with respect to trial counsel is even greater as applied to work product because of the nature of the work-product doctrine.[160] Trial counsel's mental processes are entitled to the utmost protection; thus, a waiver commensurate with the nature of that protection is appropriate.[161] However, even trial counsel's opinion work product is still subject to disclosure if the opposing party can make the appropriate showing under Rule 26(b)(3).[162]

Given the wide variety of decisions in the area of scope of waiver, the most important lesson for the litigant lies not as much in attempting to discern or construct a clear-cut legal standard, but in recognizing that there might not be one. In assessing a litigation strategy that risks a waiver of privilege, one should carefully consider the scope of that waiver, more specifically (1) whether the magistrate or judge with jurisdiction over the case takes a broad or narrow view on such issues, (2) whether the party can draw a defensible boundary on discovery, and (3) whether and how it can handle a "worst case," broad-scope waiver.

VI. Conclusion

Throughout the course of a lawsuit, attorneys and their clients are concerned about pursuing, and preserving, every available theory of defense or relief. The prevailing standards of liberal "notice" pleading and free-form discovery facilitate, and thus reinforce, such an approach. There is, however, always a danger that some theories may prove counterproductive in the context of the case as a whole.

The very real possibility that a certain theory may force its proponent's attorneys to the witness stand, or to put their advice at issue, significantly raises the stakes. As the preceding analysis makes clear, a party may studiously avoid any reliance on the advice of counsel, but still implicitly (albeit inadvertently) open the door to otherwise privileged matters. Alternatively, that party may voluntarily put its attorneys on the stand, fully expecting to waive privilege on certain communications—only to find, as in *Northbrook*, that the scope of its waiver far exceeds expectations.

True, a party may find that it has no choice but to press a certain claim and risk a "subject matter" waiver. Also, a party may find that privileged communications are, on balance, favorable or even critical to its case: the instinctive reaction to jealously guard privileged materials may not always be the right one. The important lesson is that attorney and client should anticipate the inevitable discovery battles and make an informed decision to risk or not risk a waiver of privilege—before a court, with help from the opposing party, makes that decision for them.

Notes

1. This chapter does not address the issue of waiver of the attorney-client privilege by failure to object when an opponent questions a party's attorney in the same case, Young v. Taylor, 466 F.2d 1329 (10th Cir. 1972) (failure to object

during examination of defendant attorney waived privilege as to testimony of attorney's secretary regarding privileged conversation she heard between two defendants), or in a related case, Drimmer v. Appleton, 628 F. Supp. 1249 (S.D.N.Y. 1986) (failure to object to testimony at hearing on motion in Nevada to enforce settlement agreement waived privilege in subsequent New York trial on settlement agreement), or by disclosure to a governmental agency, Westinghouse Elec. Corp. v. Republic of the Philippines, 951 F.2d 1414 (3d Cir. 1991) (by voluntarily disclosing results of outside counsel's investigation to the SEC and to the Department of Justice, client waived attorney-client privilege and work-product immunity in subsequent action brought by Philippine government).

2. 413 F. Supp. 926 (N.D. Cal. 1976).
3. *Id.* at 929.
4. Chevron Corp. v. Pennzoil Co., 974 F.2d 1156 (9th Cir. 1992); *see also* Overbaugh v. United States, 483 F. Supp. 2d 223 (N.D.N.Y. 2007); United States v. Duke Energy Corp., 208 F.R.D. 553 (M.D.N.C. 2002), *vacated on other grounds*, Envtl. Def. v. Duke Energy Corp., 549 U.S. 561 (2007); Rivera v. Kmart Corp., 190 F.R.D. 298 (D.P.R. 2000); SNK Corp. of Am. v. Atlus Dream Entm't Co., Ltd., 188 F.R.D. 566, 571, 573 (N.D. Cal. 1999).
5. 118 F.R.D. 609 (E.D. Wis. 1987).
6. *Id.* at 614. Note that just as a party can waive the attorney-client privilege by putting its lawyer on the stand, one can also waive the privilege by calling as a witness some third party, like an investigator hired by the attorney, whose communications are otherwise protected by the attorney-client privilege. *See* Clark v. City of Munster, 115 F.R.D. 609 (N.D. Ind. 1987) (if plaintiff was to call private investigators hired by attorney to assist in defense of criminal proceeding as witnesses in subsequent civil action, plaintiff would waive attorney-client privilege and would have to produce investigators' files to defendants); Brown v. Trigg, 791 F.2d 598 (7th Cir. 1986) (defendant in adult trial for felony-murder waived attorney-client privilege and work-product protection by having administrator of polygraph test testify at juvenile court waiver hearing).
7. *Handgards*, 413 F. Supp. at 929; Vilastor-Kent Theatre Corp. v. Brandt, 19 F.R.D. 522, 524 (S.D.N.Y. 1956).
8. Upjohn Co. v. United States, 449 U.S. 383, 389 (1981).
9. *See* Hickman v. Taylor, 329 U.S. 495, 510–11 (1947).
10. *See* Fed. R. Civ. P. 26(b)(3)(B).
11. *In re* Allen, 106 F.3d 582, 607 (4th Cir. 1997) (quotations and citations omitted); *but see* Rutgard v. Haynes, 185 F.R.D. 596, 601 (S.D. Cal. 1999) (opinion work product is discoverable when information is directly at issue and need is compelling).
12. 413 F. Supp. at 928.
13. 118 F.R.D. at 614.
14. *See* 1993 Comm. Notes to Fed. R. Civ. P. 26(a)(2).
15. Mfg. Admin. & Mgmt. Sys., Inc. v. ICT Grp., Inc., 212 F.R.D. 110, 114 (E.D.N.Y. 2002) (citations omitted).
16. *See In re* Pioneer Hi-Bred Int'l, Inc., 238 F.3d 1370, 1375 (Fed. Cir. 2001) ("[F]undamental fairness requires disclosure of all information supplied to a testifying expert in connection with his testimony."); *see also* Herman v. Marine Midland Bank, 207 F.R.D. 26, 29 (W.D.N.Y. 2002) ("[T]he expert disclosure requirement of Rule 26(a)(2)(B) trumps the substantial protection otherwise accorded opinion work product under Rule 26(b)(3).").

17. 156 F.R.D. 123 (M.D.N.C. 1994).
18. *Id.* at 128.
19. *Id.*
20. *Id.*
21. *Id.*
22. *Id.* at 128–29. Additional decisions in this area, which reach similar results, include *Bio-Rad Labs., Inc. v. Pharmacia, Inc.*, 130 F.R.D. 116 (N.D. Cal. 1990), and *Mushroom Assocs. v. Monterey Mushrooms, Inc.*, 25 U.S.P.Q.2d 1304 (N.D. Cal. 1992).
23. 202 F.R.D. 666 (N.D. Ga. 2001).
24. *Id.* at 674–75.
25. Sony Elecs., Inc. v. Soundview Techs., Inc., 217 F.R.D. 104 (D. Conn. 2002).
26. *Id.* at 110.
27. *Adler*, 202 F.R.D. at 675.
28. State *ex rel.* United Hosp. Ctr., Inc. v. Bedell, 484 S.E.2d 199, 216 (W. Va. 1997).
29. *See* Johnson v. Alabama, 256 F.3d 1156, 1179 (11th Cir. 2001) (state prisoner filed a federal habeas corpus petition based on, among other things, the allegedly unreasonable trial strategy selected by counsel).
30. *Id.* at 1179; *see also* United States v. Woodall, 438 F.2d 1317, 1324–25 (5th Cir. 1970) (defendant waived privilege by seeking to withdraw guilty pleas on basis that he lacked knowledge of their consequences and by filing affidavit that coercion from former counsel voided pleas). These holdings are akin to the general principle that the attorney-client privilege does not apply in a dispute between the attorney and client.
31. 500 F. Supp. 1331 (D. Md. 1980).
32. *Id.* at 1334–35.
33. *See* Panter v. Marshall Field & Co., 80 F.R.D. 718, 719–21 (N.D. Ill. 1978) (reliance on advice of counsel asserted as defense to alleged violations of securities laws); *see also* Twigg v. Pilgrim's Pride Corp., 2007 U.S. Dist. LEXIS 14669, at *24, *28 (N.D. W. Va. 2007) (advice of counsel defense asserted as a defense to an alleged violation of the Family Medical Leave Act); Minn. Specialty Crops, Inc. v. Minn. Wild Hockey Club, L.P., 210 F.R.D. 673, 675–76 (D. Minn. 2002) (advice of counsel defense adopted to trademark infringement claims); Wender v. United Servs. Auto. Ass'n, 434 A.2d 1372, 1374 (D.C. 1981) (reliance on advice of counsel asserted by insurance company to alleged bad faith failure to settle underlying lawsuit).
34. 80 F.R.D. at 720.
35. *Id.* at 719–20.
36. *Id.* at 721 (citations omitted).
37. *Id.* at 725 (footnote omitted).
38. 434 A.2d 1372 (D.C. 1981).
39. 68 F.R.D. 574 (E.D. Wash. 1975).
40. *Id.* at 577.
41. *Id.*
42. *Id.* at 581.
43. *Id.* (emphasis added).
44. *Id.* at 582–83.
45. *Id.* at 582.
46. *Id.* at 581–82.

47. *Id.*
48. *Hearn* is a middle ground between (1) the "automatic waiver" rule, which provides that "a litigant automatically waives the privilege upon assertion of a claim, counterclaim, or affirmative defense that raises as an issue a matter to which otherwise privileged material is relevant" and (2) the more deferential standard that "a litigant waives the attorney-client privilege if, and only if, the litigant directly puts the attorney's advice at issue in the litigation." Frontier Ref., Inc. v. Gorman-Rupp Co., Inc., 136 F.3d 695, 699–700 (10th Cir. 1998).
49. 714 F. Supp. 916 (N.D. Ill. 1989).
50. *Id.* at 919.
51. 901 F. Supp. 1362 (N.D. Ill. 1995).
52. *Id.* at 1367; *see also* Claffey v. River Oaks Hyundai, 486 F. Supp. 2d 776 (N.D. Ill. 2007) (holding that the attorney-client privilege may be waived when a company relies on consultations with counsel as part of its defense); *In re* Omnicom Grp., Inc. Sec. Litig., 233 F.R.D. 400 (S.D.N.Y. 2006); Roehrs v. Minn. Life Ins. Co., 228 F.R.D. 642 (D. Ariz. 2005) (requiring production of notes from the insurance adjusters to the insurer's lawyers and the lawyers' replies because the adjusters had testified that they relied on the insurer's lawyers' statements in denying the plaintiff's claims).
53. *See* United States v. Newell, 315 F.3d 510, 525 (5th Cir. 2002) (attorney-client privilege not waived when party showed that good-faith defense "was not based on advice of counsel, but rather on a simple lack of knowledge of the wrongdoing and absence of intent to participate in it").
54. 199 F.R.D. 677 (N.D. Okla. 2001).
55. *Id.* at 681–83.
56. *See* Trouble v. Wet Seal, Inc., 179 F. Supp. 2d 291, 303–04 (S.D.N.Y. 2001) (party can protect attorney-client privilege as long as it does not rely on advice of counsel for defense of good faith).
57. Connell v. Bernstein-Macaulay, Inc., 407 F. Supp. 420 (S.D.N.Y. 1976).
58. *Id.* at 423 (footnote omitted).
59. Other cases involving tolling provisions include *Conkling v. Turner*, 883 F.2d 431 (5th Cir. 1989) (by claiming that the statute was tolled until his attorney informed him of defendant's alleged fraud, plaintiff waived the privilege), Russell v. Curtin Matheson Scientific, Inc., 493 F. Supp. 456 (S.D. Tex. 1980) (by claiming that 180-day notice requirement was tolled because the Department of Labor affirmatively misled them as to that requirement, plaintiffs waived the privilege for communications that occurred more than 180 days prior to actual filing of notice), and Byers v. Burleson, 100 F.R.D. 436 (D.D.C. 1983) (by claiming that the statute was tolled while he was allegedly unaware of grounds for legal malpractice action, plaintiff waived the privilege).
60. Southwire Co. v. Essex Grp., Inc., 570 F. Supp. 643, 649–50 (N.D. Ill. 1983).
61. *Id.* at 649.
62. *Id.* at 645–46, 649–50.
63. 683 F.2d 1201, 1206 (8th Cir. 1982).
64. *Id.* at 1206–07.
65. *See, e.g.*, Sedillos v. Bd. of Educ. of Sch. Dist. No. 1, 313 F. Supp. 2d 1091 (D. Colo. 2004); Synalloy Corp. v. Gray, 142 F.R.D. 266 (D. Del. 1992); FDIC v. Wise, 139 F.R.D. 168 (D. Colo. 1991).
66. *See, e.g.*, Pippenger v. Gruppe, 883 F. Supp. 1201 (S.D. Ind. 1994).

67. *See, e.g.*, Pitney-Bowes, Inc. v. Mestre, 86 F.R.D. 444 (S.D. Fla. 1980), *aff'd on other grounds*, 701 F.2d 1365 (11th Cir. 1983); *see also* Medtronic, Inc. v. Intermedics, Inc., 162 F.R.D. 133 (D. Minn. 1995) (holding that defendant's potential use of extrinsic evidence would effect a waiver of attorney-client privilege, and giving defendant 10 days to notify plaintiff whether it would use such evidence at trial). Indeed, where the contract in question is a settlement agreement, the scope of this waiver may extend to attorney work product. *See* Coleco Indus., Inc. v. Universal City Studios, Inc., 110 F.R.D. 688, 691–92 (S.D.N.Y. 1986).
68. 136 F.R.D. 542 (D. Mass. 1991).
69. *Id.* at 543.
70. *Id.* at 544.
71. *Id.*
72. *Id.*
73. 94 F.R.D. 246 (D.D.C. 1981).
74. *Id.* at 249.
75. *Id.* (emphasis added). One commentator has described this facet of the *Exxon* decision as "outrageous." Note, *Developments in the Law—Privileged Communications*, 98 HARV. L. REV. 1450, 1642 (1985). It bears noting that, had the government instead tried to use the more traditional "crime fraud" exception to pierce privileged communications relating to Exxon's purported pricing "scheme," it would have had to make a preliminary showing that the scheme had been "concocted." *See* United States v. Zolin, 491 U.S. 554, 570–72 (1989).
76. 653 A.2d 254 (Del. 1995).
77. *Id.* at 260 (emphasis added).
78. 185 F.R.D. 596, 599 (S.D. Cal. 1999).
79. *Id.* at 599–600.
80. 666 F. Supp. 1148 (N.D. Ill. 1987).
81. *Id.* at 1150.
82. *Id.* at 1151.
83. 926 F.2d 1285 (2d Cir. 1991).
84. *Id.* at 1294. In the same vein, several litigants have tried to avoid a waiver by relying only on the fact that they *consulted* counsel, without disclosing or relying on any specific communications or opinions. For the most part, these efforts have proved unsuccessful. *See, e.g.*, Dorr-Oliver Inc. v. Fluid-Quip, Inc., 834 F. Supp. 1008, 1012 (N.D. Ill. 1993) ("Defendants cannot have it both ways; they cannot seek refuge in consultation with counsel as evidence of their good faith yet prevent [plaintiff] from discovering the contents of the communication.").
85. 926 F.2d at 1292.
86. 61 F.R.D. 43 (E.D. Pa. 1973).
87. *Id.* at 47.
88. 217 U.S.P.Q. (BNA) 1001 (N.D. Ill. 1982).
89. *Id.* at 1002.
90. *Handgards*, 413 F. Supp. at 929.
91. 244 F.R.D. 434 (N.D. Ill. 2007).
92. *Id.* at 441–42.
93. *Id.* at 442.
94. Marco Island Partners v. Oak Dev. Corp., 117 F.R.D. 418, 420 (N.D. Ill. 1987).
95. Caterpillar Inc. v. Friedmann, 164 F.R.D. 76, 78 (D. Or. 1995) (quoting *In re* Sause Bros. Ocean Towing, 144 F.R.D. 111, 116–17 (D. Or. 1991)).

96. 805 F.2d 1323, 1327 (8th Cir. 1986) (deposition only appropriate in limited circumstances; trial counsel is not "absolutely immune" from being deposed). *See* Simmons Foods, Inc. v. Willis, 191 F.R.D. 625, 630 (D. Kan. 2000) (noting that *Shelton* test is majority rule).
97. *Shelton*, 805 F.2d at 1327; *see also* Pamida, Inc. v. E.S. Originals, Inc., 281 F.3d 726, 729 (8th Cir. 2002) (applying the *Shelton* factors); Nguyen v. Excel Corp., 197 F.3d 200, 208–09 (5th Cir. 1999) (counsel deposed when executives were unable to respond to queries without stating reliance on counsel or consulting with counsel).
98. 281 F.3d 726 (8th Cir. 2002).
99. *Id.* at 730–31.
100. Taylor Mach. Works, Inc. v. Pioneer Distrib. Inc., No. 06-1126, 2006 WL 1686140 at *3–4 (C.D. Ill. 2006).
101. *See id.* at *3 (synthesizing additional factors considered by multiple courts).
102. *Id.*
103. Torres v. 100 N. LaSalle P'ship, No. 80 C 6454, 1983 U.S. Dist. LEXIS 10343 (N.D. Ill. Dec. 29, 1983). Of course, if a party refuses *all* discovery the court would likely refuse to allow the attorney to take the stand at all. *Cf.* Int'l Tel. & Tel. Corp. v. United Tel. Co. of Fla., 60 F.R.D. 177, 186 (M.D. Fla. 1973) (failure of party to allow pretrial discovery of privileged matter that party intends to introduce at trial will preclude introduction of that evidence).
104. 1983 U.S. Dist. LEXIS 10343, at *3–4.
105. No. 83 C 3150 (N.D. Ill. 1988).
106. Northbrook Excess & Surplus Ins. Co. v. Procter & Gamble Co., No. 83 C 3150, 1988 WL 5027, at *1 (N.D. Ill. Jan. 14, 1988) (citing *Handgards*, 413 F. Supp. at 926).
107. Northbrook Excess & Surplus Ins. Co. v. Procter & Gamble Co., No. 83 C 3150, 1988 WL 28753, at *1 (N.D. Ill. Mar. 21, 1988).
108. *Id.* at *2.
109. *Id.*
110. *Id.*
111. Northbrook Excess & Surplus Ins. Co. v. Procter & Gamble Co., No. 83 C 3150, 1988 WL 74462, at *1 (N.D. Ill. July 8, 1988).
112. *Id.* at *2.
113. *Id.* at *2.
114. *Id.* at *3.
115. *Id.*
116. *Id.* (citing Brown v. Trigg, 791 F.2d 598, 601 (7th Cir. 1986)).
117. *Id.* at *2.
118. *Id.*
119. *Id.* at *1, *3.
120. Northbrook Excess & Surplus Ins. Co. v. Procter & Gamble Co., 83 C 3150, 1988 WL 142218 (N.D. Ill. Dec. 28, 1988).
121. *Id.* at *2.
122. *Id.*
123. *Id.*
124. *See* Radiant Burners, Inc. v. Am. Gas Ass'n, 320 F.2d 314, 323 (7th Cir. 1963) (citing 8 J.H. WIGMORE, WIGMORE ON EVIDENCE § 2291).
125. FTC v. Shaffner, 626 F.2d 32, 37 (7th Cir. 1980); Schachar v. Am. Acad. of Ophthalmology, Inc., 106 F.R.D. 187, 191 (N.D. Ill. 1985). As always, counsel should

research the law of his or her jurisdiction. Under state law, presumptions may differ. *See* Murray v. Gemplus Int'l, S.A., 217 F.R.D. 362, 366 n.5 (E.D. Pa. 2003) ("Unlike federal common law, Pennsylvania places the burden of proof on the party which asserts that the privilege has been waived.") (quotations and citations omitted); *see also* Black v. Sw. Water Conservation Dist., 74 P.3d 462, 467 (Colo. Ct. App. 2003).

Another point to note is that there is some disagreement about the burden for proving waiver of work-product immunity. *See* SEC v. Buntrock, 217 F.R.D. 441, 447 (N.D. Ill. 2003) ("The burden is on the party asserting a waiver of work product immunity to establish the waiver."); *but see* Bank of Am., N.A. v. Terra Nova Ins. Co., 212 F.R.D. 166, 169 (S.D.N.Y. 2002) ("The party asserting the protection afforded by the work product doctrine has the burden of showing both that the protection exists and that it has not been waived.").

126. *In re* Consol. Litig. Concerning Int'l Harvester's Disposition of Wis. Steel, 666 F. Supp. 1148, 1157 (N.D. Ill. 1987).
127. *See* Fujisawa Pharm. Co., Ltd. v. Kapoor, 162 F.R.D. 539, 541 (N.D. Ill. 1995), *aff'd in part and rev'd in part, on other grounds*, 115 F.3d 1332 (7th Cir. 1997).
128. 55 Fed. Cl. 263, 267 (Fed. Cl. 2003).
129. *See* Glenmede Trust Co. v. Thompson, 56 F.3d 476, 486 (3d Cir. 1995) ("There is an inherent risk in permitting the party asserting a defense of its reliance on advice of counsel to define the parameters of the waiver of the attorney-client privilege as to that advice.").
130. *See, e.g.*, Starsight Telecast, Inc. v. Gemstar Dev. Corp., 158 F.R.D. 650, 655 (N.D. Cal. 1994).
131. *Id.* (quotation omitted).
132. Bittaker v. Woodford, 331 F.3d 715, 720 (9th Cir. 2003).
133. *Id.* at 720–21; *see also* Atl. Inv. Mgmt., LLC v. Millennium Fund I, Ltd., 212 F.R.D. 395, 398–99 (N.D. Ill. 2002) (waiver limited to communications relevant to defense based on privilege).
134. Although we do not address this issue, there was some disagreement among the circuits as to when a party can appeal a court's privilege ruling. In *United States v. Philip Morris Inc.*, 314 F.3d 612 (D.C. Cir. 2003), *abrogated in part by Mohawk Indus., Inc. v. Carpenter*, 130 S. Ct. 599 (2009), the D.C. Circuit discussed the importance of the attorney-client privilege and agreed to hear an interlocutory appeal involving the attorney-client privilege under the collateral order doctrine. Rejecting holdings from other circuits that a party could obtain effective review of an adverse privilege ruling by refusing to release material, standing in contempt, and then appealing the contempt order, the D.C. Circuit stated that it did not consider civil contempt an appealable order and that a party might decide not to risk sanctions—even to preserve a clearly meritorious privilege claim. *Id.* at 620.

    However, the Supreme Court addressed the issue of the availability of collateral appeals in the attorney-client privilege context in the case of *Mohawk Indus., Inc. v. Carpenter*. There, the Court resolved the circuit split by holding that the collateral order doctrine does not extend to disclosure orders adverse to the attorney-client privilege. 130 S. Ct. at 609.
135. *See In re* Sealed Case, 877 F.2d 976, 981 (D.C. Cir. 1989).
136. *See* Motley v. Marathon Oil Co., 71 F.3d 1547, 1550 (10th Cir. 1995).
137. *In re* Grand Jury Proceedings Oct. 12, 1995, 78 F.3d 251, 253–54 (6th Cir. 1996).

138. United States v. Titchell, 261 F.3d 348, 351–52 (3d Cir. 2001). *See also* GFI, Inc. v. Franklin Corp., 60 U.S.P.Q.2d 1141, 1143 (Fed. Cir. 2001) (party waived its attorney-client privilege by allowing its attorney to testify about privileged matters in an earlier case).
139. *See, e.g.*, Micron Separations, Inc. v. Pall Corp., 159 F.R.D. 361, 363–65 (D. Mass. 1995).
140. *See, e.g.*, SEC v. Forma, 117 F.R.D. 516, 523 n.5 (S.D.N.Y. 1987).
141. *See, e.g.*, *Micron Separations*, 159 F.R.D. at 363.
142. Chiron Corp. v. Genentech, Inc., 179 F. Supp. 2d 1182, 1186–87 (E.D. Cal. 2001).
143. 497 F.3d 1360 (Fed. Cir. 2007).
144. *Id.* at 1374–75.
145. BASF Aktiengesellschaft v. Reilly Indus., Inc., 283 F. Supp. 2d 1000, 1007 (S.D. Ind. 2003).
146. Michlin v. Canon, Inc., 208 F.R.D. 172, 174 (E.D. Mich. 2002).
147. *Id.*
148. *See* Garfinkle v. Arcata Nat'l Corp., 64 F.R.D. 688, 689 (S.D.N.Y. 1974) (holding that defendant's reliance on attorney's opinion letter entitled plaintiff to examine the surrounding circumstances: "[Plaintiff] cannot be limited to the letter itself—the finished product. He is entitled to know how the letter came into being.").
149. *Chiron*, 179 F. Supp. 2d at 1190.
150. K.W. Muth Co. v. Bing-Lear Mfg. Grp., LLC, 219 F.R.D. 554, 565–67 (E.D. Mich. 2003).
151. *Id.* at 567.
152. *Id.* at 569–70.
153. *Id.* at 576.
154. Aspex Eyewear, Inc. v. E'Lite Optik, Inc., 276 F. Supp. 2d 1084, 1095 (D. Nev. 2003).
155. *K.W. Muth Co.*, 219 F.R.D. at 574.
156. *BASF Aktiengesellschaft*, 283 F. Supp. 2d at 1006.
157. *Aspex Eyewear*, 276 F. Supp. 2d at 1091–92.
158. *Id.* at 1094.
159. *BASF Aktiengesellschaft*, 283 F. Supp. 2d at 1005 (citations omitted).
160. *In re* Seagate Tech., 497 F.3d 1360, 1375 (Fed. Cir. 2007).
161. *Id.* at 1375–76.
162. *Id.* at 1376.

CHAPTER 16

The Application of the Attorney-Client Privilege and the Work-Product Doctrine to Communications between Insureds and Insurance Carriers

KIRK A. PASICH

I. Introduction

When there has been an accident, an occurrence, a claim made, or some other event that may be covered by insurance, an insured typically communicates with its insurance carrier. This initial communication is typically followed by additional communications, by the transmittal of information, and even by the carrier interviewing employees and potential witnesses. There are often at least two purposes behind these communications. First, the insured typically communicates with its carriers so that it may obtain the benefit of the insurance coverage it purchased. This obviously includes a defense against and indemnification for any claims. Second, the carrier may want to investigate the claim and related events to determine whether the claim is covered and whether its obligations are excused because of the insured's conduct or because of an exclusion.

Upon receiving notice of an actual or potential claim, the carrier has a duty to investigate. This duty extends not only to the facts regarding the claim and the insured's potential exposure, but also to the facts that support coverage for the claim. As the California Supreme Court has explained:

> [I]t is essential that an insurer fully inquire into possible bases that might support the insured's claim. . . . [A]n insurer cannot reasonably and in good faith deny payments to its insured without thoroughly investigating the foundation for its denial.[1]

During its investigation, the carrier may create and compile various documents relating to the defense against the claim and to its coverage determination. These documents often include documents relating to the substantive merits of the claim asserted against the insured and to coverage defenses the carrier may wish to assert, such as the defense that the insured expected and intended to inflict the injury claimed by the underlying plaintiff. The investigatory documents may include witness statements, post-accident reports, assessments by claims adjusters, or advice letters from in-house or outside counsel, and communications from attorneys defending the insured against the claim.

When the insured and the insurance carrier are working together to defend a claim, neither will want their own communications or the results of the carrier's investigation revealed to third parties, the underlying claimant, or potential claimants. In this case, the attorney work-product doctrine may offer the parties some protection from disclosure.

Likewise, when the insured and an insurance carrier are embroiled in a coverage dispute, neither usually wants third parties to have access to their documents, but both want and claim a right to access the other's documents. For example, the insured often will seek to discover all information the carrier may have in its claims file in order to determine why the carrier denied coverage and if that denial was in bad faith.

In turn, the carrier may want access to documents found in the underlying defense counsel's files and to documents that might show that there is no coverage because the insured intended to inflict injury—the very documents the underlying plaintiff will want to use to establish the insured's liability. In this situation, there is a real tension between the parties' efforts to litigate their coverage dispute and the need to avoid creating the very liability for which the insured is seeking a defense from the carrier. To the extent possible, this issue should be avoided because an insurance carrier should not be able to create the very liability it is supposed to be defending its insured against by attempting to establish that it has no duty to indemnify the insured.[2]

However, regardless of how or when a coverage dispute is resolved, there frequently are questions over who has access to what information. Generally speaking, these questions include the following:

- Is information gathered by an insurance carrier in its investigation of a claim protected from discovery by a third-party claimant?
- Is information gathered by an insurance carrier in its investigation of a claim protected from discovery by the insured?
- Are the underlying defense files protected from disclosure to a carrier?
- Are communications between insurance carriers and insureds protected from disclosure to third-party claimants?

There typically is no privilege known as the "insured-carrier" privilege.[3] However, most states recognize that communications between an insured and an insurance carrier are protected by the attorney-client privilege, at least to the extent the communication relates to the defense of the claim. A minority of the states and at least some federal courts have reached a contrary conclusion, holding that such communications are *not* protected by the attorney-client privilege.[4]

II. Application of the Attorney-Client Privilege

A. The Majority View

As noted above, the majority view is that an insured's communications to its insurance carriers regarding a possible claim or other event potentially covered by insurance may be covered by the attorney-client privilege. Courts following the majority view typically hold that an insured's communications to its carriers generally are protected from disclosure by the attorney-client privilege. This means that communications about potentially covered events are protected by the privilege against disclosure to third parties, including potential claimants.[5]

This approach is premised on the theory that communications from an insured to a carrier are primarily made so that the information communicated can be relayed to the attorney retained by the carrier to defend the insured. As the Illinois Supreme Court explained in the leading decision supporting the broad approach:

> [B]y the terms of the common liability insurance contract, the insured effectively delegates to the insurer the selection of an attorney and the conduct of the defense of any civil litigation. The insured is ordinarily not represented by counsel of his own choosing either at the time of making the communication or during the course of litigation. Under such circumstances we believe that the insured may properly assume that the communication is made to the insurer as an agent for the dominant purpose of transmitting it to an attorney for the protection of the interests of the insured.[6]

Even under the majority view, not necessarily all communications to insurance-related entities are protected. For example, in *Shere v. Marshall Field & Co.*,[7] the insured's safety director prepared a claim report on a form supplied by an independent adjusting service retained by the insured and one of its carriers. When the injured claimant sought to compel production of the report in the lawsuit against the insured, the insured was ordered to produce the report. The insured's attorney was subsequently held in contempt for refusing to produce the report. The Illinois Appellate Court affirmed, stating:

> In the instant case the statement was given by the Director of Safety to Safety and Claims Service. Safety and Claims Service is an independent contractor retained by both defendant and by defendant's excess-public-liability insurer to investigate and adjust claims. However, it is not an insurer. The attorney-client privilege has never been extended to cover communications to such third parties. There was no contractual obligation on the part of Safety and Claims Service to defend as there was in the *Ryan* case, and there is no reason to assume that it was an agent for the defendant's attorneys. We therefore find no reason to extend the privilege to the instant independent investigating and adjusting service.[8]

Furthermore, even under the majority view many courts recognize that the attorney-client privilege does not apply just because there is a communication between an insured and a carrier relating to the defense against a possible claim. Many courts hold that the attorney-client privilege protects communications only if (1) the *dominant purpose* of those communications relates to the defense of the insured by counsel retained by the carrier and (2) the insured had a reasonable expectation of confidentiality.[9]

The leading decision is *Gene Compton's Corp. v. Superior Court*.[10] In this case, the California Court of Appeal considered whether the privilege attached to an accident report prepared by one of the insured's employees, which was subsequently given to the carrier and thereafter given to an attorney first appointed by the insurer *after* the time the insured gave the report to the carrier. The court noted that the evidence before it demonstrated that the communication was made for the predominant purpose of transmittal to the attorney selected to defend the insured and that the information was intended to be confidential. Based on these findings, the court held that this constituted a privileged communication, stating:

> [I]n such circumstances as are here involved the transmission of a privileged communication to the attorney through the agency of an insurance carrier does not destroy the privilege.[11]

The California Supreme Court subsequently disapproved the implication in *Gene Compton's* that communications from an insured to an insurance carrier are privileged as a matter of law.[12] However, the court approved of the "dominant purpose" test and "left intact *Gene Compton's*."[13] Hence, California law is clear that communications may be privileged if the trier of fact decides that the primary purpose for the communications was for transmittal to an attorney at some point during the course of professional employment.[14]

A similar approach was taken in *State v. Pavin*.[15] In *Pavin*, the insured was involved in an automobile accident. Ten days after the accident, he was interviewed in the hospital by an insurance adjuster, who prepared a statement. The insured refused to sign the statement, noting that his mother had been advised by an attorney that he should not do so. Subsequently, the insured was convicted of the crime of fourth-degree death by automobile. One of the key items of evidence admitted against him was the unsigned statement prepared by the insurance adjuster. On appeal, the insured argued that the statement was protected by the attorney-client privilege and had been erroneously admitted into evidence.

The New Jersey Superior Court, Appellate Division, rejected this argument. In doing so, the court considered the various approaches taken by other courts, citing to decisions in many other states. The court rejected the notion of a per se privilege, instead finding a fact-based inquiry to be the "better approach."[16] It summarized the support for that approach as follows:

> Those cases which have concluded that communications between an insured and his adjuster are not per se privileged note that an insurance carrier has the right to review and consider an insured's statement for any legitimate purpose connected with the company's business, such as coverage, cooperation, or renewal. The statement is ordinarily used by the insurer to determine whether and on what basis adjustment of the claim could be attempted. Only if adjustment is not effected and a claim is pursued, will the information be turned over to counsel for use in litigation. If the insured gives a false statement, or a statement which supplies facts regarding some other defense against

> the insurer's liability under the policy, the insurer can make use of those facts to the detriment of the insured. Thus these cases say that the relationship is not automatically comparable at all stages to that of attorney and client, since it is not at all clear that the insured's interests are being protected by the insurance carrier.[17]

With this reasoning in mind, the court considered the facts before it. The court first noted that the adjuster interviewed the insured within a few days after the accident and before any claim was filed. The court then noted that there was no evidence that the adjuster was acting on instructions of any attorney or that an attorney had even been retained by the carrier. Finally, the court noted that the insured's "expectation of privacy was non-existent" because he did not think of the adjuster as his legal adviser, refusing to sign the prepared statement on the advice of his mother's attorney.[18]

Another court employed the same methodology. In *Lectrolarm Custom Systems, Inc. v. Pelco Sales, Inc.*,[19] the court found that even when an insurance carrier has reserved its rights to deny coverage, there is a "common interest" between the insured and the carrier and that, therefore, "disclosure of privileged information by [the insured] to [the carrier] does not waive the attorney client privilege or the work product doctrine."[20] The court explained as follows:

> [T]he attorney-client privilege is not automatically waived if an otherwise privileged document is disclosed to a third party. The most common situation in which disclosure occurs without waiver is where parties have a common interest. The existence of a common defense allows the parties and counsel allied in that defense to disclose privileged information to each other without destroying the privileged nature of those communications. This "common defense doctrine" also referred to as the "joint defense privilege" expands the application of the privileges to circumstances in which parties are represented by separate counsel but engage in a common legal enterprise.[21]

The court also reasoned that "the threat of production" to a claimant of information shared between an insured and its carrier would "create[] a wedge between the insured and their insurance carrier which is not in the best interests of any of the parties in this or any other litigation."[22]

Thus, under the majority view, communications between insureds and their insurance carriers will be protected because the communications are inherently deemed to be privileged or because they were made for the dominant purpose of protecting the insured's rights, with a reasonable expectation of confidentiality, and/or regarding a subject of common interest (that is, the insured's potential exposure). Therefore, the following questions should be answered affirmatively in order for the communications to be protected from disclosure to third parties (such as governmental agencies and private claimants):

1. Was the communication made for the dominant purpose of protecting the insured's rights?
2. Was the communication made with a reasonable expectation of confidentiality?
3. Was there a "common interest" in the matter to which the communication relates?

B. The Minority View

Some courts have held that communications between insureds and carriers are not protected by the attorney-client privilege.[23] These courts base their decisions on the theory that communications between an insured and a carrier are unlike communications between a client and an attorney because an insurer may use information it obtains from an insured for purposes that are contrary to the insured's interests. As the Wisconsin Supreme Court has explained:

> When the insured makes such a statement he is ordinarily fulfilling a condition of his policy, requiring him to notify the insurer of the occurrence and circumstances of the accident and to co-operate with the insurer. If the statement be false, the insurer may use it against the insured as foundation for a claim of non-co-operation. If the statement discloses facts giving rise to some other defense against the insurer's liability under the policy, the insurer is doubtless free to make use of those facts.[24]

In *Langdon v. Champion*,[25] the Alaska Supreme Court addressed the applicability of the attorney-client privilege to information compiled in an insurer's files. The court first compared the majority and minority views:

> A shrinking majority of states prohibit discovery of statements made by an insured to his insurer. Most of these courts base their decision on provisions in the insurance policy which require the insurer to defend the insured and the insured to cooperate in the investigation.
>
> . . . .
>
> A substantial and growing minority of state courts, on the other hand, have concluded that statements made to an insurer by the insured are generally not protected by the attorney-client privilege. . . . The federal rule is likewise. . . .
>
> Courts adopting this view reason that communications between insured and insurer are not in the same class as communications between client and attorney, because the insurer may use its information for purposes inimical to the interests of the insured.[26]

The court then concluded as follows:

> We find the growing minority and federal rule most persuasive. In our opinion, the cases according protection to statements between insurers and insureds have extended the attorney-client privilege into areas in which it was never intended to apply. Moreover, the minority rule is more in line with our policy favoring liberal discovery. . . .
>
> We therefore hold that the attorney-client privilege does not extend to statements made by an insured to his insurer, except in those cases where it can be shown that the adjustor received the communication at the express direction of counsel for the insured. Only in the latter instance do we think it can fairly be said that the adjustor is acting as "one employed to assist the lawyer in the rendition of professional legal services," thus making him a "representative of the lawyer" within the meaning of [Alaska] Evidence Rule 503(a) (4).[27]

C. Witness Interviews by Carriers or Their Counsel

Even if the attorney-client privilege applies to a particular communication, another question commonly encountered is whether the privilege applies to witness interviews conducted by an insurance carrier or its counsel. As a general rule, the privilege only protects interviews with the "corporation" or certain of its employees. Interviews with nonemployee witnesses typically will *not* be protected.[28] Therefore, interviews by insurers of nonemployee witnesses will not be protected by the attorney-client privilege.

However, some courts have recognized that the privilege should apply to interviews of the insured's employees. In *D.I. Chadbourne v. Superior Court*, the California Supreme Court set forth the rules to be applied in California when an employee communicates with the employer's carrier. The applicability of the various rules turned on the status of the employee in the corporation or in the litigation.[29] According to the court, the attorney-client privilege does not apply in the following situations:

1. When an employer directs an employee, at the request of its carrier, to make a statement to the carrier to be communicated to the employer's attorney *if* the carrier has not advised the employer that the employee's statement is to be obtained and used in such a manner;[30]
2. When an employee of a defendant corporation is not a codefendant or a person who may be charged with liability, except for a situation where the employee is the natural person to be speaking for the corporation;[31]
3. When "an employee has been a witness to matters which require communication to the corporate employer's attorney, and the employee has no connection with those matters other than as a witness," even though his employer required him to make the statement;[32] and
4. When an employee "has not been expressly directed by his employer to make a statement, [and the employee] does not know that his state-

ment is sought on a confidential basis (or knowing that fact does not intend [the statement] to be confidential)."[33]

However, the *Chadbourne* court held that the privilege does apply in several situations, including

1. When an employee makes a report as part of his or her normal duties or if the employer requests a report to be made and the dominant purpose of the request is confidential transmission of the report to an attorney;[34] and
2. When an employee is a defendant in his or her own right or is a person who may be charged with liability.[35]

These guidelines make sense given that California follows the "dominant purpose" approach to applying the attorney-client privilege to insured/carrier communications.[36] They also make sense under the broader approach because they do not unnecessarily interfere with the liberal discovery policy utilized in most jurisdictions. Other courts have reached similar conclusions. For example, in *Schipp v. General Motors Corp.*,[37] the court held that an insured's recorded statement to her insurer was protected by the attorney-client privilege. The court explained:

> It should have been obvious when [the insured] gave her recorded statement that claims would be made against her and that she would call upon her insurer to defend those claims. . . . [The insured] was entitled to expect that her insurance carrier would engage a lawyer to represent her, which means that she was entitled to view her insurer as her representative for purposes of obtaining legal services. [Her] statement to her insurer was a step in the process of obtaining legal representation pursuant to the insurance contract.[38]

Many other states hold the same view.[39]

Of course, in the minority of states that do not protect insured/carrier communications with the attorney-client privilege, the privilege would not apply to witness interviews.[40]

D. The Impact of a Carrier's Reservation of Rights or Declination on the Applicability of the Attorney-Client Privilege

The impact of an insurance carrier's reservation of rights or declination on the applicability of the attorney-client privilege to an insured's communications with its carriers has seldom been addressed. However, there are decisions that provide some guidance.

In *Dixie Manufacturing Co. v. Ricks*,[41] the insured's president met with counsel employed by its carrier regarding a lawsuit brought against the insured by an employee. At trial, the attorney was permitted to testify over the insured's objection. The Georgia Supreme Court affirmed on appeal. In doing so, the court emphasized that the attorney had, before meeting with the insured, informed the insured that the carrier was not liable under its policy and that the attorney did not, and would not, represent the insured. In light of these facts, the court concluded that it did "not see how the evidence objected to can be regarded as privileged communications between an attorney and his client."[42]

In *State ex rel. L.Y. v. Davis*,[43] the carrier denied coverage for a potential claim against its insured after receiving from its insured information regarding the claim. When the claimant sued, he requested production of this information, arguing that the carrier's denial of coverage meant that there was no insured-insurer relationship with respect to this claim. The court disagreed, stating:

> If communications between insured and insurer are to be privileged only if the insurer ultimately admits coverage, there is no incentive for the insured to make full disclosure to his insurer. In fact, it may be impossible and, at best, difficult for the insurer to determine whether coverage exists without the insured making a full explanation of the circumstance surrounding the claim.[44]

Therefore, the court concluded that "claims need not actually be covered before any communications between insured and insurers are covered."[45]

Thus, it seems that at least until such time as the insurance carrier makes it clear to the insured that it will not provide a defense and will not be retaining counsel for the insured, the attorney-client privilege arguably should apply if the dominant purpose of the communications is for transmittal to an attorney. However, if the insured communicates with the carrier knowing that the carrier will not provide a defense, it seems the communications arguably would not be privileged.

As for the impact of reservations of rights, the analysis employed in *State ex rel. L.Y.* would seem to apply. With a reservation of rights, the carrier typically assumes the defense against the claim. Thus, there is no reason to treat communications from an insured relating to the defense of the claim any differently than they would be treated if the carrier assumed the defense without a reservation of rights. In fact, such a result is consistent with the *Restatement of the Law Governing Lawyers*. As noted above, the *Restatement* recognizes that communications between the defense lawyer and the carrier's representatives "should be regarded as privileged and otherwise immune from discovery by the claimant or another party to the proceeding."[46]

However, not all courts agree. For example, in *Continental Casualty Co. v. St. Paul Surplus Lines Insurance Co.*,[47] an equipment lessee's insurer sued the equipment manufacturer's insurer. Both the lessee and the manufacturer tendered their defense to the lessee's insurer. The lessee's insurer agreed to defend the lessee, but initially refused to defend the manufacturer and, in fact, paid for the lessee's cross-suit against the manufacturer. However, two years later it agreed to defend the manufacturer and paid for independent defense counsel for the manufacturer. The manufacturer's insurer did not defend either party. Its policy was subject to a self-insured retention and gave it the right, but not the duty, to defend the insured. After the lessee's insurer settled the underlying lawsuit, it sought contribution from the manufacturer's insurer. It also sought discovery of communications among the manufacturer, the manufacturer's insurer, and independent defense counsel. The court permitted the discovery. It ruled that "the privileged relationship relates only to communications between [independent defense counsel] and his client, [the manufacturer], and not to [the manufacturer's insurer]."[48] The court explained:

> [W]hile the conflict of interest is explicit between an insured and a defending insurer that reserved its rights, such a conflict is also objectively manifested between an insured and a non-defending insurer that retains its own interests in the outcome of the litigation while sitting on the sidelines.[49]

The manufacturer, its insurer, and defense counsel argued that the privilege should apply to their communications because while the insurance policy did not require that the manufacturer's insurer defend the manufacturer, it did give the insurer "the right to investigate or defend and did require [the manufacturer] to provide information to [the insurer] about the [underlying] action."[50] They also argued that

> a failure to extend the privilege to those communications "would place an insured in a position of having to choose between violating the terms of the insurance contract and opening its confidential communications to the world."[51]

The court disagreed: "In California, evidentiary privileges are statutorily created and must be strictly construed."[52] It noted that California Civil Code section 2860 protects the attorney-privilege as to communications shared with the insured's insurer when the insurer is defending the insured under a reservation of rights. However, it emphasized that any "disclosure and cooperation requirements do not require the disclosure of privileged material."[53] It then held:

> [T]he attorney-client privilege has never been extended to cover communications among an insured, defense counsel, and an insurer that is not defending its insured without reservation, let alone an insurer that is not defending its insured at all. This court does not find any justification for creating a new privilege to cover those communications.[54]

California had addressed this issue at least in part by statute. California Civil Code section 2860, which governs an insured's right to select counsel when there is a conflict of interest between insured and carrier, requires that the insured disclose to the carrier all information concerning the action except privileged materials relevant to coverage disputes.[55] Section 2860(d) provides that "[a]ny information disclosed [to the carrier] by the insured or by independent counsel is not a waiver of the privilege as to any other party."[56] Thus, in California, a carrier's declination or reservation should not affect the applicability of the attorney-client privilege.

III. Application of the Work-Product Doctrine

The work-product doctrine may offer some protection to communications between an insured and an insurance carrier and also may prevent discovery by third parties of information contained in the carrier's claims files. The purpose of the doctrine is to assure the lawyer the "opportunity to work 'with a certain degree of privacy, free from unnecessary intrusion by opposing parties and their counsel.'"[57] Under this doctrine, an attorney's mental impressions and work product, at least to the extent generated in anticipation of litigation, will be discoverable only upon a showing of "good cause."[58] "Fact" work product, which includes "non-legal opinions and thoughts about the facts [of the claim]," is discoverable upon the moving party's showing of substantial need and undue hardship. Conversely, "opinion" work product may be more difficult to discover. Opinion work product consists of the attorney's "mental impressions, conclusions, opinions or legal theories."[59] Consequently, the claims adjusters' and counsel's thoughts regarding a claim should be insulated from third-party discovery. Thus, if a claims adjuster has a law degree or if claims assessment is performed by either in-house or outside counsel, the insured and/or its insurance carriers can seek to invoke the doctrine.

The Federal Rules of Civil Procedure state that materials prepared in "anticipation of litigation" are not discoverable unless the moving party has "substantial need of the materials" and is unable "without undue hardship [to] obtain the substantial equivalent [of the materials] by other means."[60] This rule applies to documents prepared by a party's representative, including its insurer.[61] It even can extend to documents prepared by a nonlawyer.[62] Thus, if the material was not prepared in anticipation of litigation, but instead was prepared as part of the ordinary course of business, the work-product doctrine will not protect it from discovery. Whether documents have been prepared in anticipation of litigation or in the ordinary course of business will be determined on a case-by-case basis.[63] Further, many courts have held that the privilege must be asserted on a document-by-document basis, as opposed to asserting the privilege over all the materials at issue.[64]

However, there is no bright-line standard delineating the scope of the work-product doctrine. Jurisdictions following the federal rule have adopted both majority and minority views, while other jurisdictions, including California, have developed their own standards.[65] Consequently, whether the doctrine applies to protect documents from disclosure can be determined only by reference to the applicable standard in the particular jurisdiction.

A. The Majority View: Information in an Insurance Carrier's Claim Files Is Collected in the Ordinary Course of Business

If the documents at issue were not prepared or collected in anticipation of litigation, then the work-product doctrine will not apply and the documents will be discoverable upon a showing of relevance.[66]

Among the states that follow the federal rule, the majority view recognizes that a significant part of an insurance carrier's business is to investigate and assess claims. As the Colorado Supreme Court explained:

> Because a substantial part of an insurance company's business is to investigate claims made by an insured against the company or by some other party against an insured, it must be presumed that such investigations are part of the normal business activity of the company and that reports and witness' statements compiled by or on behalf of the insurer in the course of such investigations are ordinary business records as distinguished from trial preparation materials.[67]

Based on this rationale, these courts hold that unless the carrier's investigation was performed at the request of or under the direction of counsel, all materials resulting from the investigation are "conclusively presumed to have been made in the ordinary course of business and not in anticipation of litigation."[68] In fact, even if the carrier retains a law firm to perform the claims assessment, this will not necessarily protect the claims file information from discovery.[69]

However, the federal courts following the majority rule offer no clear guidelines regarding the level of certainty needed to transform investigative material from work performed in the ordinary course of business to work performed in anticipation of litigation. Some courts note that the "[m]ere likelihood of litigation in the future is insufficient for invoking the privilege. Rather, the probability of litigation must be substantial and the commencement of litigation imminent."[70] For these courts, "[t]he mere contingency that litigation may result is not determinative. . . . While litigation need not be imminent, the primary motivating purpose behind the creation of a document or investigative report must be to aid in possible future litigation."[71]

Other courts have focused not on the pendency of litigation, but rather on the document itself. "[T]he test should be whether, in light of the nature of the document and the factual situation in the particular case, the document can fairly be said to have been prepared or obtained because of the prospect of litigation."[72]

Thus, under the majority federal view, information in an insurance carrier's claim files should not be deemed to be work product unless the carrier proves, on a document-by-document basis, that the information was prepared in anticipation of litigation.

B. The Minority View: Information in an Insurance Carrier's Claim File Is Collected in Anticipation of Litigation

Under the minority view, courts accept that all insurance carrier investigations generally are undertaken in anticipation of litigation. As the Iowa Supreme Court observed:

> In our litigious society, when an insured reports to his insurer that he has been involved in an incident involving another person, the insurer can reasonably anticipate that some action will be taken by the other party. The seeds of prospective litigation have been sown, and the prudent party, anticipating this fact, will begin to prepare his case. Although a claim may be settled short of the instigation of legal action, there is an ever-present possibility of a claim's ending in litigation. The recognition of this possibility provides, in any given case, the impetus for the insurer to garner information regarding the circumstances of a claim."[73]

Based on this rationale, these courts conclude that most information in an insurance carrier's claim files is protected from discovery by the work-product doctrine.[74]

While the minority view may not permit the insured to discover certain claim documents in coverage litigation against a carrier, it does protect the insured and the carrier from being forced to disclose potentially damaging documents to an underlying claimant. Furthermore, the protection afforded under the minority view may vary, depending upon who is seeking access to the material in question. As one court explained:

> When the party seeking the work product does not have a special relationship with the insurer, different considerations may apply. For example, in investigations of an accident, because of potential claims by the third party against the insured, the possibility of litigation might arise at an earlier time. However, when the claim is made by its insured, an insurance company cannot in good faith contend that there is a reasonable possibility of litigation with respect to every claim submitted to it.[75]

In jurisdictions that follow the federal rule, but have not adopted a position on the question of whether an insurance carrier's claim files constitute "work product," the majority rule should be adopted. As the Alaska Supreme Court reasoned in rejecting the minority view:

> The minority rule, we believe, is flawed because it presumes too much. Simply because an event has occurred which may require an

> insurer to provide payments under its contract with an insured does not automatically transform an insurer's activities into preparation for litigation. An insurance company routinely investigates possible claims whether or not there is any possibility of litigation, and we do not believe that [the work-product doctrine] was intended to insulate insurers from discovery merely because they regularly deal with potential claims. The minority rule also improperly relieves insurers and their insureds of a substantial portion of the obligations of discovery imposed on parties generally. . . . Indeed, under the minority rule, hardly any document authorized by or for an insurer is discoverable without the showing of substantial need and undue hardship. . . .[76]

C. The California View

Not all jurisdictions follow the federal statute. California, for example, has a statute protecting work product from disclosure that is broader than the federal rule. In California, work product is not discoverable unless denial "will unfairly prejudice the party seeking discovery,"[77] and in no event may a "writing that reflects an attorney's impressions, conclusions, opinions, or legal research or theories" be discovered.[78]

The California rule protects work product in all legal contexts, not just work performed in anticipation of litigation.[79]

Furthermore, the policy behind the privilege in California is essentially the same as the federal policy. The privilege is intended to preserve the rights of attorneys to prepare for trial with a certain amount of privacy and to prevent attorneys from reaping the benefits of their opponents' work.[80]

D. Protection of the Work-Product Doctrine

In many insurance coverage cases, there are questions as to the timing of occurrences and the extent of any damage or injury involved. This is particularly true in environmental coverage litigation. As a result, insurance carriers often seek to discover reports by outside consultants in connection with any underlying litigation. In jurisdictions following the federal rule, the discoverability of these reports will depend upon which view of "anticipation of litigation" the jurisdiction follows. Even if such reports are "work product" in the underlying litigation, they may be discoverable in the coverage litigation. Courts differ as to whether the work-product protection lapses once litigation or anticipation of litigation has ended or whether it offers "perpetual protection," thereby preventing discovery of the material in later proceedings.[81]

1. The Limited Protection View

Some courts hold that the protection extends only to documents prepared in anticipation of the specific litigation before the court. "Thus, documents prepared for one case are freely discoverable in another case."[82]

Moreover, one court following the limited protection view has required not only that the documents be prepared in preparation for the specific action before the court but also that the parties be adversaries in order for the privilege to apply.

> Here, the sought-after materials were . . . prepared for the mutual benefit of insureds and insurers against a third-party adversary. Insurers were not the adversary from whom the attorney's trial strategies and opinions required protection. Insurers and insureds have only become adversarial since the termination of the primary litigation. While the work-product materials, had they been requested by the third-party opponent in the underlying lawsuit, would have been entitled to protection, the same protection is not warranted here.[83]

2. *The Broad Protection View*

However, both the Fourth and Eighth Circuits have held that reports prepared in previous litigation are not discoverable in the current litigation.[84] In *In re Murphy*, the court held that the work-product doctrine protects documents prepared in anticipation of unrelated, terminated litigation. The court reasoned that this protection was consistent with the purpose of the work-product doctrine as announced by the U.S. Supreme Court in *Hickman v. Taylor*,[85] which recognized the attorney's need for enough privacy to perform his duties responsibly and effectively.[86] According to the *Murphy* court,

> What is needed, if we are to remain faithful to the articulated policies of Hickman, is a perpetual protection for work product, one that extends beyond the termination of the litigation for which the documents were prepared. Any less protection would generate the very evils that the Court in Hickman attempted to avoid.[87]

California also appears to follow the Fourth and Eighth Circuit's view of broad protection.[88]

3. *The Intermediate View*

A third approach was recognized in *Levingston v. Allis-Chalmers Corp.*[89] In *Levingston*, the court held that the work-product doctrine applies only when the two suits are related.[90] Thus, to the extent that the underlying litigation and coverage litigation are deemed to be closely related—as they should be—the underlying defense files should be treated as work product and should not be discoverable in the coverage litigation.[91]

E. Waiver of the Work-Product Doctrine

Even if documents qualify as work product, the protection against discovery may be waived. However, determining when the doctrine has been waived may not be easy.

1. *Waiver under Federal Law*

Federal courts are split on what represents a waiver of the attorney work-product doctrine. The majority of federal courts hold that conduct that might constitute a waiver of the attorney-client privilege will not necessarily result in a waiver of the work-product protection. As one court stated:

> We do not consider the strict standard of waiver in the attorney-client privilege context . . . to be appropriate for work product cases. . . . The purpose of the work product doctrine is to protect information against opposing parties, rather than against all others outside a particular confidential relationship, in order to encourage effective trial preparation. . . . A disclosure made in the pursuit of such trial preparation, and not inconsistent with maintaining secrecy against opponents, should be allowed without waiver of the privilege.[92]

This led the court to conclude that "while the mere showing of a voluntary disclosure to a third person will generally suffice to show waiver of the attorney-client privilege, it should not suffice in itself for waiver of the work product privilege."[93]

In contrast, a minority of courts hold that the standard for waiver of the work-product protection is the same as the standard as waiver of the attorney-client privilege—that is, the disclosure or consent to disclosure of work-product material by the holder of the privilege waives it.[94]

Whichever standard is used to determine waiver, most federal courts agree that disclosure to an allied party will not waive the privilege.[95] As stated in *In re Crazy Eddie Securities Litigation*,[96] "Counsel may therefore share work product, including ideas, opinions, and legal theories, with those having similar interests in fully preparing litigation against a common adversary."

This should mean that when an insurance carrier is defending its insured against a "common adversary," disclosure to the insured of any information in the claims file and disclosure to the carrier of defense files should not waive the work-product protection as to third parties, including the underlying claimants.[97] When the insured and insurer are coparties, this "allied party" or "common adversary" exception to the waiver doctrine protects the insured from disclosing a claims file or insured-insurer communications to third-party claimants.

2. *Waiver under California Law*

There is no waiver provision in California Code of Civil Procedure section 2018.010 *et seq.*, the California statute stating the work-product doctrine. As a result, California courts have not reached a consensus on what standard is to be used to determine if the protection has been waived.

In *Williamson v. Superior Court*,[98] the California Supreme Court held that the fact that parties may be codefendants does not assure that they are not adversaries. The court specifically recognized that on the facts before it, the sharing of information among codefendants is not necessarily the sharing of information among allied parties. As the court noted, "Each codefendant seeks to disclaim any responsibility for the alleged injuries, and argues that if there is responsibility for the alleged injuries it is due to the failure of the other. Certainly, there exists that relationship which suggests a conflict of interest."[99]

Thus, as one commentator has suggested, *Williamson* implies that California would follow the federal minority rule and hold that disclosure to anyone, even a codefendant, could constitute waiver of the privilege.[100]

However, in *Fellows v. Superior Court*,[101] the court seemed to follow the rule followed by a majority of federal courts. In *Fellows*, the claimants had brought a bad-faith action against an insurance carrier for failure to settle their uninsured motorist claims after the issue of coverage had been resolved by an arbitrator. The carrier sought production of the files of the claimants' former attorney. The court held that although the attorney had turned the file over to the claimants, this did not constitute waiver of the work-product doctrine.[102] The court also held that initiation of a civil action by the claimants against the carrier did not waive the protection:

> [A]uthorization by the attorney to his client to waive the privilege cannot be construed as a waiver in and of itself. Nor can the action of an attorney in disclosing the contents of his file to his client be construed as a waiver by disclosure of the privileged material *since the disclosure* is not to a *disinterested person*. . . . but to the client whose interest in nondisclosure is supported by the policy reasons which underlie the creation of the privilege.[103]

Thus, *Fellows* indicates that, like the majority of federal courts, California recognizes that disclosure of work product to persons with a common interest or a common adversary should not waive the work-product privilege.

However, a different conclusion was reached in *Durkin v. Shields (In re Imperial Corp. of America)*.[104] There, the insured's defense counsel provided the directors and officers (D&O) liability insurer with letters assessing the insureds' risk in the underlying litigation and settlement demands. The underlying plaintiffs contended that these letters were not privileged or subject to work-product protection. The insureds argued that even though the D&O insurer did not have a duty to defend (it had a duty to indemnify for defense costs), it shared a "common interest" in the ultimate outcome of the lawsuit so that the privilege should attach to their communications. The court rejected this argument, even though the insurers had signed joint-defense agreements with the insureds and their codefendants. The court held as follows regarding the attorney-client privilege:

> [The insureds' defense counsel] did not have an attorney-client relationship with [the insurer]. [Defense counsel's] letters were not written by or to clients of [defense counsel] and do not reveal any directors' or

> officers' communications to [defense counsel]. The letters were written for the purpose of apprising [the insurer] of the status of the case, not for seeking or imparting legal advice. [The insurer] did not have a duty to defend the [insureds] and did not defend the [insureds], nor pay their legal expenses. Finally, [the insurer] and [the insureds] did not share common legal representation; rather, [the insurer] had separate representation.[105]

The court then held that any work-product protection had been waived by providing the letters to the insurers:

> At the time [defense counsel] sent the letter to [the claims adjuster], the [insureds] and [the insurer] were not adversaries in litigation. However, there can be no doubt that [defense counsel] was aware that when an insurer has not committed to indemnify its insured after demand has been made to do so, the possibility of a future coverage action pitting the insured against the insurer is a distinct possibility. Therefore, there can be no doubt that [defense counsel] understood that at the time the letter was sent to [the claims adjuster] and copied to [another insurer], . . . litigation between his clients and [the insurers] . . . was a very real possibility. Consequently, [defense counsel's] transmittal of the . . . letter to [the insurers] not only increased the likelihood, but virtually assured, that potential opponents in future litigation would gain access to the disputed documents as well as to [defense counsel's] opinions and thought process regarding his clients' liability.[106]

IV. Safeguards an Insured May Employ to Protect the Attorney-Client Privilege and the Work-Product Doctrine

In those jurisdictions that do not recognize the applicability of the attorney-client privilege and/or work-product doctrine to an insured's communications with its carriers, there is little an insured can do to protect communications other than to carefully screen the contents of the communications to minimize any damage should the communications be used by a claimant.

However, in jurisdictions that recognize that such communications or the information conveyed may be protected by the privilege and/or the doctrine, an insured can take steps to maximize the likely application of those protections. These steps include the following:

1. Make sure the predominant purpose of the communication relates to a defense against the claim. Because a court might conduct an in camera examination of any communications, it is probably a good idea to include appropriate language in any communication, such as

"This letter provides information that may assist the counsel retained to defend us against the claim. . . ."

2. Make sure that the communication is made with the expectation of confidentiality. It is useful in this regard to instruct (preferably in writing, to create a "paper trail") anyone communicating with insurers about claims that all communications are to be regarded as confidential and for the purpose of assisting counsel in defending against a claim.
3. Make sure that any communication is actually sent to the counsel selected to defend the insured.
4. If the carrier wants to interview the insured's employees, determine in advance the purpose of the interviews. If the purpose is to learn when, for example, the insured first knew that chemicals were leaking into groundwater, that information may relate not only to the defense against a claim but also to the carrier's determination of whether the claim is covered (e.g., was the damage "expected and intended" by the insured or was the problem a "known risk" that should have been disclosed in the policy application?). If there is more than one possible reason for the interview, a court might conclude that the dominant purpose did not relate to the defense of the claims.
5. Keep in mind that if an insured is represented by its own counsel (for example, coverage counsel) in its communications and meetings with its carriers, the appearance is created that the insured is not looking to its carrier as a legal advisor. This could lead a court to conclude that there was no attorney-client relationship between the insured and the carrier (as agent for the defense counsel ultimately selected), which means that even in jurisdictions following the most favorable approach, the attorney-client privilege might not apply to the communications.
6. Consider requesting the carrier to select counsel before there are any substantive communications or witness interviews. Then, the attorney could request the communications and interviews, which might improve the chances of the work-product doctrine being applied. Furthermore, if counsel are retained before communications, this eliminates an argument accepted by some courts in rejecting the applicability of the privilege—that counsel had not been retained at the time of the communication.
7. Carefully monitor any discussions with carriers of coverage issues. Under even the broadest views, these discussions might not be protected from discovery because they do not relate to the defense of the claim.
8. Know which jurisdiction's law will apply and what that law is with respect to an insured's communications with carriers, *before* the communications occur, if possible.

V. Conclusion

As the above demonstrates, all communications between an insured and an insurer should be carefully monitored to ensure, to the extent possible, that the protections afforded by the attorney-client privilege and the work-product doctrine will apply. To the extent there is any doubt, insureds should err on the side of caution insofar as the specifics of what is communicated to insurance carriers (but without violating the duty to cooperate imposed by most insurance policies). Of course, carriers also have reason to tread carefully in this area. After all, if a communication from an insured to a carrier turns out to be the evidence that a claimant uses to establish the insured's liability, it may be the carrier who bears the financial burden, at least to the extent of the aggregate limits of its insurance policy.

Notes

1. Egan v. Mut. of Omaha Ins. Co., 24 Cal. 3d 809, 819, 620 P.2d 141, 169 Cal. Rptr. 691 (1979), *cert. denied and appeal dismissed*, 445 U.S. 912 (1980). *See also* ALLAN D. WINDT, INSURANCE CLAIMS AND DISPUTES § 2.5, at 16–17 (5th ed. 2007) ("The implied covenant of good faith and fair dealing in the policy should necessarily require the insurer to conduct any necessary investigation in a timely fashion and to conduct a reasonable investigation before denying coverage."); Ross v. Pioneer Life Ins. Co., 2008 U.S. Dist. LEXIS 33193, at *41–42 (C.D. Cal. 2008) ("Among the most critical factors bearing on the insurer's good faith is the adequacy of its investigation of the claim. . . . An unreasonable failure to investigate amounting to such unfair dealing may be found when an insurer fails to consider, or seek to discover, evidence relevant to the issues of liability and damages. . . . ").
2. *See* Tews Funeral Home, Inc. v. Ohio Cas. Ins. Co., 832 F.2d 1037, 1046 (7th Cir. 1987) (a determination of the duty to indemnify "is premature while the underlying action is pending if the indemnity decision would require a court to adjudicate facts in the underlying dispute"); Montrose Chem. Corp. v. Superior Court, 6 Cal. 4th 287, 301, 861 P.2d 1153, 24 Cal. Rptr. 2d 467 (1993) ("To eliminate the risk of inconsistent factual determinations that could prejudice the insured, a stay of the declaratory relief action pending resolution of the third party suit is appropriate when the coverage action turns on facts to be litigated in the underlying action."); Cal-Farm Ins. Co. v. TAC Exterminators, Inc., 172 Cal. App. 3d 564, 572, 218 Cal. Rptr. 407 (1985) (when underlying action has not yet been tried, "the resolution of coverage must be determined by accepting as true all the allegations contained in the complaint in the underlying action"); *see also* Santa's Best Craft, LLC v. St. Paul Fire & Marine Ins. Co., 611 F.3d 339, 350–51 (7th Cir. 2010) ("[A]n insured is not required to apportion its liability for different claims because that would either require the coverage litigation to be a retrial of the merits of the insured's underlying lawsuit and/or would discourage settlement because the insured would essentially have to prove its own liability for the underlying conduct even if it had not made that concession

in arriving at a settlement."); Entercom Sacramento, LLC v. Am. Home Assurance Co., 2008 U.S. Dist. LEXIS 37753 (N.D. Cal. May 8, 2008) ("Stay of a declaratory relief action to determine coverage is often in order when the coverage question turns on facts to be litigated in the underlying third party action '[t] o eliminate the risk of inconsistent factual determinations that could prejudice the insured.'").

3. *See* Lectrolarm Custom Sys., Inc. v. Pelco Sales, Inc., 212 F.R.D. 567, 571 (E.D. Cal. 2002) ("Federal courts have never recognized a blanket privilege regarding insured-insurer communications."); *cf.* Mid-Century Ins. Co. v. Wheeler, 2010 U.S. Dist. LEXIS 63432, at *4–5 (W.D. Mo. June 24, 2010) (applying an insurer-insured privilege as adopted by the Missouri Supreme Court).
4. *Cf.* Cutchin v. State, 143 Md. App. 81, 90–91, 792 A.2d 359 (2002) (acknowledging two views, but noting that the decisions involved "turn on their facts and few, if any, truly stand for the proposition that all insured-liability or indemnity insurer communications are privileged, or the proposition that none are privileged").
5. *See, e.g.*, Metroflight, Inc. v. Argonaut Ins. Co., 403 F. Supp. 1195, 1197–98 (N.D. Tex. 1975) (there is a privilege for communications from insured to carrier regarding facts of claim when intended to assist counsel in defense); Bellmann v. Dist. Court, 187 Colo. 350, 531 P.2d 632 (1975), *overruled on other grounds*, Kay Labs., Inc. v. Dist. Court, 653 P.2d 721 (Colo. 1982); Grand Union Co. v. Patrick, 247 So. 2d 474 (Fla. Dist. Ct. App. 1971); People v. Ryan, 30 Ill. 2d 456, 197 N.E.2d 15 (1964); State *ex rel.* Cain v. Barker, 540 S.W.2d 50 (Mo. 1976); *see also* United States v. Hoeffner, 254 F.R.D. 302, 307 (S.D. Tex. 2008) ("Here, the Court finds the documents requested in the subpoenas seek communications that were prepared to assist with the defense of claims against Liberty Mutual, Travelers, National Casualty, Continental Casualty, and National Union's insureds. Because compliance with the subpoenas would require the disclosure of privileged and protected matter to which no exception to waiver would apply, and any disclosure would necessarily waive these privileges, the Court finds compliance would be unreasonable and oppressive under Rule 17(c)(2)."); Landmark Screens, LLC v. Morgan, Lewis & Bockius LLP, 2010 U.S. Dist. LEXIS 9435, at *13–14 (N.D. Cal. Jan. 15, 2010) (recognizing "that communications between an insured to his liability insurance company about a potential claim is treated as a privileged communication").
6. People v. Ryan, 30 Ill. 2d 456, 197 N.E.2d 15, 17 (1964). *See also* Scripps Health v. Superior Court, 109 Cal. App. 4th 529, 535, 135 Cal. Rptr. 2d 126 (2003) ("It has long been recognized that communications made by an insured to his 'liability insurance company, concerning an event which may be made the basis of a claim against him covered by the policy, is a privileged communication, as being between attorney and client, if the policy requires the company to defend him through its attorney, and the communication is intended for the information or assistance of the attorney in so defending him.'"); Bellmann v. Dist. Court, 187 Colo. 350, 531 P.2d 632, 634 (1975) ("Since control of [the insured's] defense rested entirely with [the carrier] and counsel retained by [it], we hold that the insurance investigator who took the [insured's] statement was, in effect, an agent of the attorneys for the purpose of acquiring and transmitting this information to them."); Grand Union Co. v. Patrick, 247 So. 2d 474 (Fla. Dist. Ct. App. 1971) (communication of accident report to carrier protected by

attorney-client privilege because communication was, in essence, a communication between insured and counsel to benefit the defense of the case); Braglia v. Cephus, 146 Ill. App. 3d 241, 496 N.E.2d 1171, 1176 (1986) (following *Ryan*); Martin v. Clark, 92 Ill. App. 3d 518, 415 N.E.2d 30, 32 (1980) (following *Ryan* and holding that statement given by insured to carrier "was protected by the attorney-client privilege and . . . should not have been subject to discovery"); State *ex rel.* Tillman v. Copeland, 271 S.W.3d 42, 46–47 (Mo. Ct. App. 2008) (statements made by insured to insurer were privileged where the communication was intended to assist the attorney defending the insured); Wielgus v. Ryobi Techs., Inc., 2010 U.S. Dist. LEXIS 80425, at *10–11 (N.D. Ill. Aug. 4, 2010) ("The Supreme Court of Illinois has also extended the attorney-client privilege to communications between an insured and insurer where the insurer owes an obligation to defend the insured. The rationale for the extension of the privilege is that agents of insurers serve as a communication conduit between an insured and the attorney to be retained by the insurer for the benefit of the insured and his or her defense.") (citations omitted); 81 Am. Jur. 2d *Witnesses* § 414 (2010) (Under the broad approach, the carrier "is regarded as a mere intermediate agent to transmit the communications to the attorneys of its claims department or to an eventual trial attorney if an action is brought."); 55 A.L.R.4th 336, 342 (2008). In fact, the *Restatement of the Law Governing Lawyers* recognizes this broad approach. The *Restatement* states:

> [C]ommunications between the lawyer and representatives of the insurer concerning such matters as progress reports, case evaluations, and settlement should be regarded as privileged and otherwise immune from discovery by the claimant or another party to the proceeding. Similarly, communications between counsel retained by an insurer to coordinate the efforts of multiple counsel for insureds in multiple suits and such coordinating counsel are subject to privilege.

Restatement (Third) of the Law Governing Lawyers § 134 cmt. f (2000). The *Restatement* also provides:

> The privilege applies to communications to and from the client disclosed to persons who hire the lawyer as an incident of the lawyer's engagement. Thus, the privilege covers communications by a client-insured to an insurance-company investigator who is to convey the facts to the client's lawyer designated by the insurer, as well as communications from the lawyer for the insured to the insurer in providing a progress report or discussing litigation strategy or settlement. . . .

Id. § 70 cmt. f, illus. 5.

7. 26 Ill. App. 3d 728, 327 N.E.2d 92 (1974).
8. *Id.* at 94. *See also* Restatement (Third) of the Law Governing Lawyers, § 70 cmt. f, illus. 5 (2000) (recognizing that privilege does not apply to "communications by an insured to an insurance investigator who will report to the company"). *But see* D.I. Chadbourne, Inc. v. Superior Court, 60 Cal. 2d 723, 727, 388 P.2d 700, 36 Cal. Rptr. 468 (1964) (question of fact as to whether privilege attaches when communication from insured's employee to independent contractor employed by carrier for subsequent transmittal to carrier and then to counsel selected by insurer); Gene Compton's Corp. v. Superior Court, 205 Cal.

App. 2d 365, 366, 23 Cal. Rptr. 250 (1962) (insured's communication to insurance broker for transmission to carrier privileged), disapproved on other grounds, D.I. Chadbourne, Inc. v. Superior Court, 60 Cal. 2d 723, 388 P.2d 700, 36 Cal. Rptr. 468 (1964); *In re* Tetra Techs., Inc., 2010 U.S. Dist. LEXIS 33012, at *14–15 (S.D. Tex. Apr. 5, 2010) ("Thus, to the extent the communications identified by Plaintiffs between the Defendants, the insurance brokers, and the attorneys fall within this test, or were made to facilitate the rendition of legal services and involve an attorney, the Court holds that they fall within attorney-client privilege and are not subject to discovery."); Markwest Hydrocarbon, Inc. v. Liberty Mut. Ins. Co., 2007 U.S. Dist. LEXIS 27243, at *10–12 (D. Colo. Apr. 12, 2007) (independent adjuster is an agent of an insurer and communications with the adjuster are protected by the attorney-client privilege. where elements of privilege are met).

9. *See, e.g.*, State v. Anderson, 247 Minn. 469, 78 N.W.2d 320 (1956) (statements by insured to carrier not privileged because not shown that statements made for exclusive use in insured's defense and in confidence); Jacobi v. Podevels, 23 Wis. 2d 152, 127 N.W.2d 73 (Wis. 1964) (statements by insured to insurance adjuster not privileged because no action pending or threatened and no counsel retained for insured); *see also* TIG Ins. Co. v. Firemen's Ins. Co., 2010 U.S. Dist. LEXIS 61519, at *15–16 n.5 (D.D.C. June 22, 2010) ("It is worth noting that the court does not recognize an implicit attorney-client privilege in all insured-insurer communications; instead, this privilege arises only when such communication is for the purpose of pursuing legal representation or the procurement of legal advice."); Kingsway Fin. Servs. v. PricewaterhouseCoopers LLP, 2008 U.S. Dist. LEXIS 77018 (S.D.N.Y. Oct. 2, 2008) ("Generally, the determination of whether the attorney-client privilege attaches to an insured-insurer communication turns on the nature and purpose of the communication. 'Certainly, where the insured communicates with the insurer for the express purpose of seeking legal advice with respect to a concrete claim, or for the purpose of aiding an insurer-provided attorney in preparing a specific legal case, the law would exalt form over substance if it were to deny application of the attorney-client privilege.'") (quotation omitted).
10. 205 Cal. App. 2d 365, 23 Cal. Rptr. 250 (1962).
11. *Id.* at 379.
12. *See* D.I. Chadbourne, Inc. v. Superior Court, 60 Cal. 2d 723, 731, 388 P.2d 700, 36 Cal. Rptr. 468 (1964).
13. Travelers Ins. Cos. v. Superior Court, 143 Cal. App. 3d 436, 451, 191 Cal. Rptr. 871 (1983).
14. *Id. See also* Heffron v. L.A. Transit Lines, 170 Cal. App. 2d 709, 718, 339 P.2d 567 (1959) (communication privileged "if the policy requires the company to defend [the insured] through its attorney, and the communication is intended for the information or assistance of the attorney in so defending him").
15. 202 N.J. Super. 255, 494 A.2d 834 (1985).
16. 494 A.2d at 837.
17. *Id.* at 837.
18. *Id.* at 838.
19. 212 F.R.D. 567 (E.D. Cal. 2002).
20. *Id.* at 572.
21. *Id.* (citations omitted); *see also* Kingsway Fin. Servs. v. PricewaterhouseCoopers LLP, 2008 U.S. Dist. LEXIS 77018 (S.D.N.Y. Oct. 2, 2008), at *24–25 ("[The] fact that the parties are currently adverse in a related action does not alter the fact that

[insured] and [insurer] shared a common interest at the time the communications were made.").

22. *Id.* at 573.
23. *See, e.g.*, Rogers v. Aetna Cas. & Sur. Co., 601 F.2d 840, 845 (5th Cir. 1979); Jackson v. Kroblin Refrigerated Xpress, Inc., 49 F.R.D. 134, 136–37 (N.D. W. Va. 1970); Gottlieb v. Bresler, 24 F.R.D. 371, 372 (D.D.C. 1959) ("[A] communication received by a liability insurance company from one of its insureds concerning a matter covered by the insurance policy is not a privileged communication."); Longs Drug Stores v. Howe, 134 Ariz. 424, 657 P.2d 412, 415–16 (1983); Conley v. Graybeal, 315 A.2d 609, 610 (Del. Super. Ct. 1974); DiCenzo v. Izawa, 68 Haw. 528, 723 P.2d 171, 176–78 (1986).
24. Jacobi v. Podevels, 23 Wis. 2d 152, 127 N.W.2d 73, 76 (1964).
25. 752 P.2d 999 (Alaska 1988).
26. *Id.* at 1002–03.
27. *Id.* at 1003–04.
28. *See, e.g.*, Van Alen v. Anchorage Ski Club, Inc., 536 P.2d 784, 787 (Alaska 1975) ("eyewitness" statements taken by insurers not protected by work-product doctrine); D.I. Chadbourne, Inc. v. Superior Court, 60 Cal. 2d 723, 734, 388 P.2d 700, 36 Cal. Rptr. 468 (1964) (attorney-client privilege does not attach to statement by a witness who is not an employee of the client corporation). *See also* Trade Ctr. Props., Inc. v. Superior Court, 185 Cal. App. 2d 409, 411, 8 Cal. Rptr. 345 (1960) Equity Residential v. Kendall Risk Mgmt., Inc. 246 F.R.D. 557, 567 (N.D. Ill. 2007).
29. *Chadbourne*, 60 Cal. 2d at 736–38.
30. *Id.* at 737–38 (employer's intent controls as to whether privilege applies and if carrier has not advised employer that statement will be obtained for attorney, "it cannot be said that the corporation intended the statement to be made as a confidential communication from client to attorney").
31. *Id.* at 736–37.
32. *Id.* at 737. *See also* Alpha Beta Co. v. Superior Court, 157 Cal. App. 3d 818, 827, 203 Cal. Rptr. 752 (1984) (following *Chadbourne* in holding some information obtained from an employee who had no connection with the litigation other than as a witness not privileged); *see also* Costco Wholesale Corp. v. Superior Court, 47 Cal. 4th 725, 734, 219 P.3d 736, 101 Cal. Rptr. 3d 758 (2009).
33. *Chadbourne*, 60 Cal. 2d at 737–38. *See also* Zurich Am. Ins. Co. v. Superior Court, 155 Cal. App. 4th 1485, 1497, 66 Cal. Rptr. 3d 833 (2007).
34. *Chadbourne*, 60 Cal. 2d at 737; *see also* AMCO Ins. Co. v. Madera Quality Nut LLC, 2006 WL 931437, at *9 (E.D. Cal. Apr. 11, 2006) (employee statements made as part of company's internal investigation of insurance fraud were privileged where "dominant purpose was to obtain information with the ultimate intent to provide legal advice"); Sierra Vista Hosp. v. Superior Court, 248 Cal. App. 2d 359, 365, 56 Cal. Rptr. 387 (1967) (privilege applies to report made by hospital administrator whose duties were those of a general business manager and included protection of the employer hospital from "legal action or liability").
35. *Id.* at 736.
36. *See* Scripps Health v. Superior Court, 109 Cal. App. 4th 529, 533–34, 135 Cal. Rptr. 2d 126 (2003) ("When the corporate employer has more than one purpose in requiring the report, the dominant purpose will control"; report held privileged when one purpose was quality assurance/peer review because "dominant purpose" was attorney review in anticipation of possible litigation); Costco Wholesale Corp. v. Superior Court, 47 Cal. 4th 725, 735, 219 P.3d 736,

101 Cal. Rptr. 3d 758 (2009) ("[T]he dominant-purpose test determines whether the relationship between the attorney and the corporate employee is an attorney-client relationship; if the corporation's dominant purpose in requiring the employee to make a statement is the confidential transmittal to the corporation's attorney of information emanating from the corporation, the communication is privileged.").

37. 457 F. Supp. 2d 917 (E.D. Ark. 2006).
38. *Id.* at 922–23.
39. *See id.* at 919 ("many states—in what appears to be a majority—have held, depending on varying factors, that . . . a communication [between an insurer and its insured] may be protected by the privilege"); Grewell v. State Farm Mut. Auto. Ins. Co., 102 S.W.3d 33, 36–37 (Mo. 2003) ("[B]y the terms of the common liability insurance contract, the insured effectively delegates to the insurer the selection of any attorney and the conduct of the defense of any civil litigation. . . . We believe that the same salutary reasons for the privileges exist when the communication is directly between the client and attorney. . . .").
40. *See, e.g.*, Calabro v. Stone, 225 F.R.D. 96, 99 (E.D.N.Y. 2004) ("Federal courts in the Second Circuit have not routinely shielded documents such as accident reports from discovery; rather they have required proof that the material 'is prepared exclusively and in specific response to imminent litigation. . . .' The mere contingency that litigation could result is not sufficient to trigger protection under the work product doctrine. . . . This is particularly true in the insurance context because 'the very business of the producing party is to evaluate claims that may ultimately ripen into litigation.'").
41. 153 Ga. 364, 112 S.E. 370 (1922).
42. *Id.* at 370. *See also* Cont'l Cas. Co. v. St. Paul Surplus Lines Ins. Co., 265 F.R.D. 510, 522 (E.D. Cal. 2010) (insured's communications to insurer were not privileged where insurer made clear it would not defend insured); NL Indus. v. Commercial Union Ins. Co., 144 F.R.D. 225, 231 (D.N.J. 1992) ("To permit insurers, however, unrestrained access to attorney-client communications and work product where those insurers refused to take part in litigation despite notice and an opportunity to participate would distort the 'common interest' doctrine.").
43. 723 S.W.2d 74 (Mo. Ct. App. 1986).
44. *Id.* at 75.
45. *Id.*
46. Restatement (Third) of the Law Governing Lawyers, § 134 cmt. f (2000). *See* Lectrolarm Custom Sys., Inc. v. Pelco Sales, Inc., 212 F.R.D. 567, 571–73 (E.D. Cal. 2002) (rejecting underlying plaintiff's request for production of documents from carrier even though carrier had reserved rights, noting that "common defense doctrine" preserved attorney-client privilege).
47. 265 F.R.D. 510 (E.D. Cal. 2010).
48. *Id.* at 523.
49. *Id.* at 525.
50. *Id.*
51. *Id.* at 521
52. *Id.* at 518.
53. *Id.* at 520 (citing Cal. Civ. Code § 2860(f); Assurance Co. of Am. v. Haven, 32 Cal. App. 4th 78, 90, 38 Cal. Rptr. 2d 25 (1995) ("[T]he duties specified in Civil Code section 2860 that *Cumis* counsel owes the insurer are limited to the duties to disclose, inform, consult and cooperate regarding *nonprivileged* information.")).

54. *Id*. at 525. *See also* Vt. Gas Sys. v. U.S. Fid. & Guar. Co., 1551 F.R.D. 268, 277 (D. Vt. 1993) ("The 'common interest' doctrine does not apply where there is an adversarial relationship between the insured and insurer as to whether coverage exists, the parties have never shared the same counsel or litigation strategy and the documents at issue were prepared in an atmosphere of uncertainty as to the scope of any identity of interest shared by the parties."); Heffron v. L.A. Transit Lines, 170 Cal. App. 2d 709, 718, 339 P.2d 567 (1959) (communication privilege "if the policy requires the company to defend [the insured] through its attorney, and the communication is intended for the information or assistance of the attorney in so defending him"); Sawyer v. Sw. Airlines, 2002 U.S. Dist. LEXIS 25111, at *11 (D. Kan. Dec. 23, 2002) (underlying plaintiff's motion to compel production of documents exchanged between insured and carrier denied because an insured and carrier, who had duty to defend, "have an interest in common . . . that [is] of a legal and not commercial nature").
55. Cal. Civ. Code § 2860.
56. *Id.*
57. Conn. Mut. Life Ins. Co. v. Shields, 16 F.R.D. 5, 8 (S.D.N.Y. 1954); Linde v. Arab Bank, PLC, 608 F. Supp. 2d 351, 357 (S.D.N.Y. 2009).
58. *See* Hickman v. Taylor, 329 U.S. 495, 510 (1947).
59. Fed. R. Civ. P. 26(b)(3). Duplan Corp. v. Moulinage et Retorderie de Chavanoz, 509 F.2d 730 (4th Cir. 1974), *cert. denied*, 420 U.S. 997 (1975). *See also In re* Murphy, 560 F.2d 326 (8th Cir. 1977); United States v. Deloitte LLP, 610 F.3d 129, 135 (D.C. Cir. 2010) (opinion work product is "virtually undiscoverable").
60. Fed. R. Civ. P. 26(b)(3).
61. *Id.*
62. Diversified Indus., Inc. v. Meredith, 572 F.2d 596, 603 (8th Cir. 1977); Sandra T.E. v. S. Berwyn Sch. Dist. 100, 600 F.3d 612, 622 (7th Cir. 2010); United States v. Deloitte LLP, 610 F.3d 135–35, 139–40 (D.C. Cir. 2010).
63. *See* Pete Rinaldi's Fast Foods, Inc. v. Great Am. Ins. Cos., 123 F.R.D. 198 (M.D.N.C. 1988); Upjohn Co. v. United States, 449 U.S. 383, 396–97 (1981).
64. *See, e.g.*, Auto-Owners Ins. Co. v. Totaltape, Inc., 135 F.R.D. 199, 202 (M.D. Fla. 1990) ("[t]he trend in lower federal courts is to analyze work product claims concerning insurance claims files on a case by case basis"); Burr v. United Farm Bureau Mut. Inc. Co., 560 N.E.2d 1250, 1256 (Ind. Ct. App. 1990) ("the privilege must be asserted on a document by document basis and with the utmost clarity"); AIU Ins. Co. v. TIG Ins. Co., 2008 WL 4067437, at *14 (S.D.N.Y. Aug. 28, 2008) (when determining whether insurance claims files were properly withheld, "rather than determine that the work-product doctrine applies based on a categorical presumption, the better course here is to engage in a fact-specific inquiry to determine whether each document was created in anticipation of litigation"), *order modified on reconsid.*, 2009 WL 1953039 (S.D.N.Y. Jul 08, 2009).
65. *See* BP Alaska Exploration, Inc. v. Superior Court, 199 Cal. App. 3d 1240, 1250 (1988) ("federal law is not controlling in California").
66. Thomas Organ Co. v. Jadranska Slobodna Plovidba, 54 F.R.D. 367, 370 (N.D. Ill. 1972).
67. Hawkins v. Dist. Court, 638 P.2d 1372, 1378 (Colo. 1982); Bronsink v. Allied Prop. & Cas. Ins., 2010 U.S. Dist. LEXIS 29166, at *6 (W.D. Wash. Mar. 4, 2010) ("In the insurance context, materials prepared as part of claims investigation are generally not considered work product due to the industry's need to investigate claims. Such materials are part of the ordinary course of business unless there

is a sufficiently concrete connection between the investigation and potential litigation."); *cf.* Underwriters Ins. Co. v. Atlanta Gas Light Co., 248 F.R.D. 663, 668 (N.D. Ga. 2008) ("As the federal courts have generally recognized: '[W]hen a liability insurer investigates a third party claim, the investigation is made in anticipation of claims, which, if denied, likely will lead to litigation. For this reason it is logical to conclude that, while files generated in relation to first party claims are made in the ordinary course of business and are discoverable, files generated during the investigation of third party claims are made in anticipation of litigation and are not discoverable.'").

68. Henry Enters., Inc. v. Smith, 592 P.2d 915, 920 (Kan. 1979). *Accord* Illiana Surgery & Med. Ctr. LLC v. Hartford Fire Ins. Co., 2008 U.S. Dist. LEXIS 94713 (N.D. Ind. Nov. 18, 2008) ("Claim file materials that are part of a factual evaluation or investigation into an insured's claim, if created before a final coverage decision has been made, are presumed to have been prepared in the ordinary and routine course of the insurer's business."); Harper v. Auto-Owners Ins. Co., 138 F.R.D. 655, 663 (S.D. Ind. 1991) ("[A] document or thing produced or used by an insurer to evaluate an insured's claim in order to arrive at a claims decision in the ordinary and regular course of business is not work product. . . ."); W. Nat'l Bank v. Emp'rs Ins., 109 F.R.D. 55 (D. Colo. 1985); APL Corp. v. Aetna Cas. & Sur. Co., 91 F.R.D. 10, 17 (D. Md. 1980) ("[W]hile litigation often results from an insurance company's denial of a claim, it cannot be said that any document prepared by an insurance company after such a claim has arisen is prepared in anticipation of litigation within the meaning of Rule 26(b)(3)."); Benton v. Brookfield Props. Corp., 2003 U.S. Dist. LEXIS 13020, at *7 (S.D.N.Y. July 29, 2003) ("An insurance company's decision whether to afford coverage is part of its normal business decision-making and does not constitute work-product even though the insurance company may face the prospect that if coverage is denied, the insured will commence litigation against it."); Langdon v. Champion, 752 P.2d 999, 1007 (Alaska 1988) ("An insurance company routinely investigates possible claims whether or not there is any possibility of litigation, and we do not believe that [the work-product doctrine] was intended to insulate insurers from discovery merely because they regularly deal with potential claims.").

69. *See* Mission Nat'l Ins. Co. v. Lilly, 112 F.R.D. 160 (D. Minn. 1986); Tilden-Coil Constructors, Inc. v. Landmark Am. Ins. Co., 2010 U.S. Dist. LEXIS 106369, at *4–5 (W.D. Wash. Sept. 23, 2010) (even though attorney drafted denial letter, letter was part of ordinary course of the insurer's business of claim determination); Am. Home Assurance Co. v. United States, 2009 U.S. Dist. LEXIS 93597, at *9 (D.N.J. Oct. 7, 2009) ("simple involvement of counsel in an insurer's claim investigation does not transform the investigation to one undertaken in anticipation of litigation").

70. Stauffer Chem. Co. v. Monsanto Co., 623 F. Supp 148, 152 (E.D. Mo. 1985).

71. Janicker v. George Wash. Univ., 94 F.R.D. 648, 650 (D.D.C. 1982); Schwarz & Schwarz of Va. L.L.C. v. Certain Underwriters, 2009 U.S. Dist. LEXIS 33019, at *7–8 (W.D. Va. Apr. 16, 2009) ("Thus, there is no bright-line test for when work product protection applies for insurance companies, and instead courts must undertake a case-by-case analysis. . . . 'This approach realistically recognizes that at some point an insurance company shifts its activity from the ordinary course of business to anticipation of litigation. . . .' The 'pivotal point' is when the probability of litigation becomes 'substantial and imminent,' or stated otherwise, when litigation becomes 'fairly foreseeable.'") (citation omitted).

72. *APL*, 91 F.R.D. at 15 (citation omitted). *See* Cowie v. State Farm Fire & Cas. Co., 2007 U.S. Dist. LEXIS 52117, at 4–6 (E.D. Tenn. July 17, 2007) ("The dispute in this case centers on the meaning of 'in anticipation of litigation.' This phrase, as it applies to insurance companies, presents an especially thorny problem because insurance companies, by the very nature of their business, have a duty to investigate claims.... Nevertheless, a number of courts in other jurisdictions have been faced with this particular discovery dilemma . . . and a majority of them have applied a standard based on whether the documents were prepared primarily for the purpose of adjusting the claim or primarily in anticipation of litigation. . . . To answer the question of the primary purpose of a document, the court must engage in a fact intensive analysis on a case-by-case basis."); William A. Gross Constr. Assocs. v. Am. Mfrs. Mut. Ins. Co., 262 F.R.D. 354, 360 (S.D.N.Y. 2009) ("'Where a document was created because of anticipated litigation, and would not have been prepared in substantially similar form but for the prospect of that litigation, it falls within Rule 26(b)(3).' Where the threat of litigation is accompanied by a non-litigation purpose for the generation of the documents at issue, '[w]hether there is work product protection turns on whether the material 'would have been prepared irrespective of the expected litigation. . . . '") (citations omitted); Amica Mut. Ins. Co. v. W.C. Bradley Co., 217 F.R.D. 79, 83 (D. Mass. 2003) ("Coverage investigations by insurance companies are not *per se* conducted in anticipation of litigation, and a determination as to whether documents generated during such investigations were prepared in anticipation of litigation, as opposed to in the ordinary course of business, should be made on a case-by-case basis."); Henderson v. Zurn Indus., Inc., 131 F.R.D. 560 (S.D. Ind. 1990) (same).
73. Ashmead v. Harris, 336 N.W.2d 197, 201 (Iowa 1983) (quoting Fireman's Fund Ins. Co. v. McAlpine, 391 A.2d 84, 89–90 (R.I. 1978)). *See Ex parte* Nationwide Mut. Ins. Co., 898 So. 2d 720, 723 (Ala. 2004) (individual injured in automobile accident was undergoing surgery; therefore, carrier "could have reasonably concluded that its insured would be sued"); Liberty Mut. Fire Ins. Co. v. Kaufman, 885 So. 2d 905, 910 (Fla. Ct. App. 2004) ("Generally, an insurer's claims and litigation files constitute work product and are protected from production.").
74. *See* Almaguer v. Chi., R.I. & P.R.R. Co., 55 F.R.D. 147, 148 (D. Neb. 1972).
75. Pete Rinaldi's Fast Foods, Inc. v. Great Am. Ins. Cos., 123 F.R.D. 198, 202 (M.D.N.C. 1988). *See also* Henderson v. Zurn Indus., Inc., 131 F.R.D. 560, 571 n.11 (S.D. Ind. 1990) (court acknowledged a difference between third-party claims against a carrier and direct first-party claims; "one would expect there to be more litigation on third-party claims than on direct first-party contract actions, with a resultant increased anticipation of such litigation in the third-party context"); Underwriters Ins. Co. v. Atlanta Gas Light Co., 248 F.R.D. 663, 668 (N.D. Ga. 2008) ("As the federal courts have generally recognized: '[W]hen a liability insurer investigates a third party claim, the investigation is made in anticipation of claims, which, if denied, likely will lead to litigation. For this reason it is logical to conclude that, while files generated in relation to first party claims are made in the ordinary course of business and are discoverable, files generated during the investigation of third party claims are made in anticipation of litigation and are not discoverable.'").
76. Langdon v. Champion, 752 P.2d 999, 1006–07 (Alaska 1988).
77. Cal. Civ. Proc. Code § 2018.030(b).

78. *Id.* § 2018.030(a).
79. *Id.*; Rumac, Inc. v. Bottomley, 143 Cal. App. 3d 810, 192 Cal. Rptr. 104 (1983); Laguna Beach Cnty. Water Dist. v. Superior Court, 124 Cal. App. 4th 1453, 1461, 22 Cal. Rptr. 3d 387, 393 (2004). However, like the federal rule, opinion work product also enjoys absolute immunity in California. *See* BP Alaska Exploration, Inc. v. Superior Court, 199 Cal. App. 3d 1240, 245 Cal. Rptr. 682 (1988); Rico v. Mitsubishi Motors Corp., 42 Cal. 4th 807, 171 P.3d 1092, 68 Cal. Rptr. 3d 758 (2007).
80. *See* CAL. CIV. PROC. CODE § 2018.020(a)–(b).
81. *See* Levingston v. Allis-Chalmers Corp., 109 F.R.D. 546 (S.D. Miss. 1985); Fed. Trade Comm'n v. Grolier, Inc., 462 U.S. 19 (1983).
82. *Levingston*, 109 F.R.D. at 552. *See* United States v. Int'l Bus. Machs. Corp., 66 F.R.D. 154, 178 (S.D.N.Y. 1974) (documents must be prepared in anticipation of the litigation in which special immunity accorded to such material is sought); Honeywell, Inc. v. Piper Aircraft Corp., 50 F.R.D. 117, 119 (M.D. Pa. 1970) (same); Hanover Shoe, Inc. v. United Shoe Mach. Corp., 207 F. Supp. 407, 410 (M.D. Pa. 1962) (materials must be prepared for case at bar); Wong v. Thomas, 238 F.R.D. 548, 551 (D.N.J. 2007) (prosecutors cannot assert work-product protection for criminal investigation file in subsequent civil suits).
83. Waste Mgmt., Inc. v. Int'l Surplus Lines Ins. Co., 144 Ill. 2d 178, 579 N.E.2d 322 (1991).
84. *See* Duplan Corp. v. Moulinage et Retorderie de Chavanoz, 509 F.2d 730 (4th Cir. 1974), *cert. denied*, 420 U.S. 997 (1975); *In re* Murphy, 560 F.2d 326 (8th Cir. 1977); Pamida, Inc. v. E.S. Originals, Inc., 281 F.3d 726, 731 (8th Cir. 2002).
85. 329 U.S. 495 (1947).
86. *Murphy*, 560 F.2d at 333.
87. *Id.* at 334.
88. *See* Fellows v. Superior Court, 108 Cal. App. 3d 55, 62, 166 Cal. Rptr. 274 (1980) ("[T]he attorney's work product privilege . . . survives the termination of the litigation or matter in which the work product is prepared and may be claimed in subsequent litigation—whether related or unrelated to the prior matter—to preclude disclosure of the attorney's work product."). *See also* Planalto v. Ohio Cas. Ins. Co., 256 F.R.D. 16, 19 (D. Me. 2009) (stating that "the emerging majority of courts" hold that work product extends into subsequent litigation); Jicarilla Apache Nation v. United States, 88 Fed. Cl. 1 (Fed. Cl. 2009) (following broad protection rule).
89. 109 F.R.D. 546 (S.D. Miss. 1985).
90. *Id.* at 552. *Accord* Hercules, Inc. v. Exxon Corp., 434 F. Supp. 136, 153 (D. Del. 1977) ("[T]his Court accepts the 'sounder view' that the documents prepared for one case have the same protection in a second case where the two cases are closely related in parties or subject matter."); Republic Gear Co. v. Borg-Warner Corp., 381 F.2d 551, 557 (2d Cir. 1967); Midland Inv. Co. v. Van Alstyne, Noel & Co., 59 F.R.D. 134, 138 (S.D.N.Y. 1973); Underwriters Ins. Co. v. Atlanta Gas Light Co., 248 F.R.D. 663, 668 (N.D. Ga. 2008) (insurance claims files prepared in anticipation of underlying claim were protected in bad-faith litigation; "Particularly where cases are closely related, courts have generally found that documents produced in anticipation of litigating one case remain protected in a subsequent cases if they were created by or for a party to the subsequent litigation."); La. Mun. Police Emps. Ret. Sys. v. Sealed Air Corp., 253 F.R.D. 300, 309 n.3 (D.N.J. 2008) ("work-product protection applies to documents prepared for a different case

so long as the two cases are closely related in parties or subject matter"); Cohen v. City of New York, 255 F.R.D. 110, 124 (S.D.N.Y. 2008) ("the weight of authority now clearly favors protecting work product that was generated as part of an earlier litigation at least where, as here, that litigation is related to the current suit"). *See also* Anchondo v. Anderson, Crenshaw & Assocs., L.L.C., 256 F.R.D. 661, 672 (D.N.M. 2009) (work-product protection may extend into subsequent litigation but "[i]t is unclear whether the doctrine applies only to subsequent litigation that is closely related to the earlier litigation") (citing Frontier Ref., Inc. v. Gorman-Rupp Co., Inc., 136 F.3d 695, 703 (10th Cir. 1998)).

91. *See* Special Magistrate's Report and Recommendation No. 2, *In re* Tex. E. Transmission Corp. PCB Contamination Ins. Coverage Litig., MDL Docket No. 764 (E.D. Pa. Apr. 8, 1991), *reprinted in* 5 MEALEY'S LITIG. REPORTS—INS., No. 23, § C (Apr. 16, 1991).
92. United States v. Am. Tel. & Tel. Co., 642 F.2d 1285, 1299 (D.C. Cir. 1980) (citation omitted). *See also* United States v. Deloitte LLP, 610 F.3d 129, 139–40 (D.C. Cir. 2010) ("While voluntary disclosure waives the attorney-client privilege, it does not necessarily waive work-product protection. . . . [T]he attorney-client privilege and the work-product doctrine serve different purposes: the former protects the attorney-client relationship by safeguarding confidential communications, whereas the latter promotes the adversary process by insulating an attorney's litigation preparation from discovery. Voluntary disclosure waives the attorney-client privilege because it is inconsistent with the confidential attorney-client relationship. Voluntary disclosure does not necessarily waive work-product protection, however, because it does not necessarily undercut the adversary process. Nevertheless, disclosing work product to a third party can waive protection if such disclosure, under the circumstances, is inconsistent with the maintenance of secrecy from the disclosing party's adversary. Under this standard, the voluntary disclosure of attorney work product to an adversary or a conduit to an adversary waives work-product protection for that material.") (internal citations and quotation marks omitted).
93. *Am. Tel. & Tel. Co.*, 642 F.2d at 1299 (emphasis omitted).
94. *See* D'Ippolito v. Cities Serv. Co., 39 F.R.D. 610 (S.D.N.Y. 1965).
95. Cont'l Oil Co. v. United States, 330 F.2d 347 (9th Cir. 1964); *see also* United States v. Deloitte LLP, 610 F.3d 129, 139–40 (D.C. Cir. 2010) (disclosure of work product to auditor did not waive privilege because auditor was not an adversary or a potential adversary).
96. 131 F.R.D. 374, 379 (E.D.N.Y. 1990); *see also* Am. Eagle Outfitters, Inc. v. Payless ShoeSource, Inc., 2009 WL 3786210, at *3 (E.D.N.Y. Nov. 12, 2009).
97. *See* Bovis Lend Lease, LMB, Inc. v. Seasons Contracting Corp., 2002 U.S. Dist. LEXIS 23322, at *14, 17 (S.D.N.Y. Dec. 5, 2002) ("certainly, documents created after litigation has already commenced, when the claims handlers' work has plainly shifted from investigating the initial claim to assisting in the defense of the pending litigation and evaluating litigation exposure, are likely to be covered by the work product doctrine. . . . Similarly, correspondence between an insured and its liability insurer, written 'as a consequence of pending litigation for the purpose of mounting a defense to the claim' is entitled to work product protection."); Kingsway Fin. Servs., Inc. v. PricewaterhouseCoopers LLP, 2008 WL 4452134, at *10 (S.D.N.Y. Oct. 2, 2008) ("Work-product protection may be waived by voluntary disclosure to a party outside the privileged relationship. Work-product protection, however, is only waived when the disclosure is to

an adversary or materially increases the likelihood of disclosure to an adversary. In this case, disclosure of materials to an insurer does not waive the work-product protection because such disclosure does not "materially increase the likelihood of disclosure to an adversary.") (internal citations and quotation marks omitted). *See also* Niagara Mohawk Power Corp. v. Stone & Webster Eng'g Corp., 125 F.R.D. 578, 587 (N.D.N.Y. 1989) ("sharing work product material with a friendly party does not waive the work product protection as it applies to an adverse third party"); Nidec Corp. v. Victor Co. of Japan, 2007 WL 2156256, at *1 (N.D. Cal. July 26, 2007) ("For work product, protection is waived where disclosure of the otherwise privileged documents is made to a third party, and that disclosure enables an adversary to gain access to the information.") (internal quotation marks omitted).

98. 21 Cal. 3d 829, 582 P.2d 126, 148 Cal. Rptr. 39 (1978).
99. *Id.* at 836 (quoting Gorman Rupp Indus., Inc. v. Superior Court, 20 Cal. App. 3d 28, 31, 97 Cal. Rptr. 377 (1971)).
100. *See* Greg Kopta, *Applying the Attorney-Client and Work Product Privileges to Allied Party Exchange of Information in California*, 36 UCLA L. Rev. 151, 192–93 (1988).
101. 108 Cal. App. 3d 55, 166 Cal. Rptr. 274 (1980).
102. *Id.* at 65–66; *see also, e.g.*, Laguna Beach Cnty. Water Dist. v. Superior Court, 124 Cal. App. 4th 1453, 1461, 22 Cal. Rptr. 3d 387, 393 (2004) (holding that attorney did not waive work-product protection by disclosing audit response letters containing work product to his client's auditor: "[B]ased on the contents of the letters, which contain the attorney's thoughts, impressions, and opinions, plus the purpose of the work product doctrine, and the rule that waiver occurs only when work product is disclosed to a third party who has no interest in maintaining the confidentiality . . . of a significant part of the work product, we conclude [the attorney's] audit response letters to [the auditor] remained protected work product.") (internal citations and quotation marks omitted); Meza v. H. Muehlstein & Co., 176 Cal. App. 4th 969, 981–83, 98 Cal. Rptr. 3d 422, 431–33 (2009) (holding that sharing of work product among defense counsel with a common interest did not waive work-product protections: "Under the common interest doctrine, an attorney can disclose work product to an attorney representing a separate client without waiving the attorney work-product privilege if (1) the disclosure relates to a common interest of the attorneys' respective clients; (2) the disclosing attorney has a reasonable expectation that the other attorney will preserve confidentiality; and (3) the disclosure is reasonably necessary for the accomplishment of the purpose for which the disclosing attorney was consulted. . . . California recognizes the common interest doctrine. . . . Substantial evidence supports the trial court's finding that communications among defense counsel were "reasonably necessary" for the accomplishment of the purpose for which defense counsel were retained. It is clear from the declarations submitted by defendants that defense counsel shared their confidential ideas about the case with each other in order to better prepare for trial. Accordingly, under the common interest doctrine, the attorney work product privilege was not waived.") (footnotes and internal citations and quotation marks omitted).
103. *Id.* (emphasis added).
104. 167 F.R.D. 447 (S.D. Cal. 1995).
105. *Id.* at 452–53.
106. *Id.* at 454–55.

CHAPTER 17

Attorney-Client Privilege and Work-Product Immunity in Patent Litigation

MICHAEL EDWARD MCCABE, JR.*

* The views expressed in this chapter are the personal opinions of the author alone and not those of the law firm Oblon, Spivak, McClelland, Maier & Neustadt, P.C., its attorneys, or its clients.

I. Introduction and Overview

The general legal principles governing attorney-client privilege and work-product immunity are the same in patent cases as they are in other areas of the law. Unfortunately, the applications of those known principles by district courts and administrative agencies to fact patterns that are largely unique to patent suits have resulted in decisions that are far from uniform. Since most privilege and work-product issues are, as a practical matter, resolved at the trial level without a meaningful opportunity for appellate review, litigants who seek judicial intervention to resolve issues of privilege or work product in patent cases more often than not do so without the benefit of a clear legal roadmap of appellate precedent to guide them.

This general lack of binding precedent can be viewed either as a blessing or a curse. Most issues of privilege or immunity are very fact specific, and a resourceful litigant can almost always find *some* authority, from *some* tribunal, to support a particular position they wish to take on such issues. The general lack of appellate authority regarding the many unique privilege and work-product issues that may arise during a typical patent case, coupled with the relatively high stakes of patent litigation, invariably leads to more disputes before the courts and relevant agencies over the application, limits, and scope of the attorney-client privilege and work-product doctrine.

This chapter provides an overview of the current state of the law on attorney-client privilege and work-product immunity in contested patent matters. It is not intended to address all possible issues of privilege or work product that may arise in a patent case. Rather, the discussion is focused on those particular privilege or work-product subjects that seem to come up most frequently.

Following this introduction, this chapter is organized in six sections. Section II provides an overview on the general rules of privilege and work product in patent cases. Section III addresses how communications relating to the invention process may be privileged or immune from discovery. Section IV discusses issues relating to who is an "attorney" and whether communications with patent agents (foreign or domestic) may be privileged, with specific examples of how U.S. courts have interpreted and applied the laws of a number of foreign countries in determining whether a privilege exists for such communications in the United States. Section V provides an overview of how issues of privilege and work product are decided by the International Trade Commission and the Board of Patent Appeals and Interferences. Section VI provides an analysis of the general rules concerning waiver of privilege, including the scope of waiver when the state of mind of the accused infringer is in issue. Section VII addresses privilege issues that relate to the patentee's state of mind, including how the crime-fraud exception may apply in patent cases to pierce the patentee's privilege.

II. General Rules on Privilege and Work Product in Patent Cases

The Supreme Court has observed that "[t]he attorney-client privilege is the oldest of the privileges for confidential communications known to the common law."[1] In patent cases, as in all other federal civil cases, the Federal Rules of Civil Procedure define the limits of discovery. Rule 26(b)(1) provides for relatively broad discovery of

> any nonprivileged matter that is relevant to any party's claim or defense. . . . Relevant information need not be admissible at the trial if the discovery appears reasonably calculated to lead to the discovery of admissible evidence.

It is, of course, proper to withhold from discovery in a patent case documents or testimony that are protected by the attorney-client privilege or work-product immunity. In contrast to the discovery provisions allowing for generally broad discovery, the privilege limitation usually is restricted to its narrowest bounds,[2] because an assertion of privilege is generally viewed by judges as an obstacle to the investigation of truth.[3]

A. Attorney-Client Privilege

The purpose of the attorney-client privilege is "to encourage full and frank communication between attorneys and their clients and thereby promote broader public interests in the observance of law and administration of justice."[4] That said, the privilege is not without limitations. As one circuit court observed, the attorney-client privilege is "[n]arrowly defined, riddled with exceptions, and subject to continuing criticism."[5] Furthermore, "since the privilege has the effect of withholding relevant information from the fact-finder, it applies only where necessary to achieve its purpose."[6]

To sustain a claim of attorney-client privilege in a patent case, the withheld document or communication must meet a number of requirements. The requirements articulated by the district court's decision in *United States v.*

United Shoe Machinery Corp. are often used in patent cases as the yardstick against which courts tend to measure attorney-client privilege:

> The privilege applies only if (1) the asserted holder of the privilege is or sought to become a client; (2) the person to whom the communication is made (a) is a member of the bar of a court, or his subordinate and (b) in connection with the communication is acting as a lawyer; (3) the communication related to a fact of which the attorney was informed (a) by his client (b) without the presence of strangers (c) for the purpose of securing primarily either (i) an opinion on law or (ii) or legal services or (iii) assistance in some legal proceeding, and not (d) for the purpose of committing a crime or tort; and (4) the privilege has been (a) claimed and (b) not waived by the client.[7]

One central inquiry in determining whether a communication is privileged usually is whether the "communication" at issue (whether it is conveyed orally or in a document) is one that was made by a client to an attorney for the purpose of obtaining legal advice or services.[8] In addition, confidentiality is often a critical threshold for establishing the privilege, and it is well established that "[t]he attorney-client privilege evaporates upon any voluntary disclosure of confidential information to a third party."[9] Furthermore, waiver of the attorney-client privilege will apply "to all other communications relating to the same subject matter."[10] The mere existence of an attorney-client relationship does not raise a presumption of confidentiality.[11]

The attorney-client privilege applies to communications to or from an attorney only to the extent that they reflect information obtained in confidence from the client for the purpose of obtaining legal advice, as opposed to business information.[12] Although communications between the attorney and the client may be privileged, the facts underlying those communications are not.[13] To the extent that a communication by an attorney simply reveals the contents of public information or information from a third party, it is not protected by the attorney-client privilege unless it also contains legal advice or responds to a request for advice.[14] Furthermore, simply because an attorney may have been copied on a communication does not necessarily convert that communication into a privileged communication. Legal advice must have been sought or requested for the communication to be privileged.[15]

A "general description of the work performed by an attorney is not protected by the attorney-client privilege."[16] Furthermore, "[a]cts or services performed by an attorney during the course of the representation are not within the privilege because they are not communications."[17] In addition, '"[t]he subject matter of meetings with an attorney, the persons present, the location of the meetings, or the persons arranging the meetings are not protected by the privilege.'"[18]

B. Work-Product Immunity

The work-product immunity doctrine is a related yet distinct concept from the attorney-client privilege.[19] Whereas the attorney-client privilege is designed to protect the client's expectations that their confidential communications with counsel will be insulated from discovery by outsiders, the work-product immunity doctrine is intended to protect the attorney. The work-product immunity doctrine thus protects from discovery materials developed by an attorney or on his or her behalf.[20] Not all "attorney work product" is afforded protection. To qualify under the work-product immunity doctrine, the document in question must have been "prepared in anticipation of litigation or for trial."[21]

Work product comprises the files and the mental impressions of an attorney reflected, for example, in interviews, statements, memoranda, correspondence, briefs, personal beliefs, and countless other tangible and intangible ways prepared in anticipation of litigation.[22] Work product is (1) a document or tangible thing, (2) that was prepared in anticipation of litigation, and (3) that was prepared by or for a party, or by or for his representative.[23] Documents prepared in the ordinary course of business, or for any other nonlitigation purpose, generally will not qualify as being protected from discovery by the work-product immunity doctrine.[24]

For a document to be considered work product, litigation need not have actually been commenced. All that is required is that a substantial probability of litigation existed when the document was created.[25] It is typically not required that the work-product immunity pertains only to a specific litigation.[26] Nevertheless, the mere possibility of future litigation in and of itself is usually insufficient to evoke the work-product immunity privilege.[27] The work-product assessment is a fact-specific inquiry, and in making the determination as to whether a particular document was created in anticipation of litigation or for trial, the court must look at the circumstances of each case.[28] Like the attorney-client privilege, courts strictly confine the scope of the work-product exception "within the narrowest possible limits consistent with the logic of its principle."[29]

III. Communications Relating to the Conception and Patenting of an Invention as Privileged or Work Product

Accused patent infringers invariably wish to discover documents and communications relating to the creation and patenting of the invention that is the subject of their litigation. Such communications often are relevant to a myriad of potentially important issues, such as claim interpretation, infringement, validity, and inequitable conduct. Not surprisingly, there are a number of specific types of communications that are commonly the subject of discovery requests in patent cases. Whether a privilege attaches to such communications normally depends upon (1) the timing of the communication, (2) the context and subject matter of the communication, and (3) the identities of the parties to the communication.

For example, usually the inventors or assignee will possess documents and communications relating to some technical problem that they (or their employer) wish to solve. As part of their efforts to solve that problem, the inventors may create laboratory notebooks, research memoranda, and similar types of business records documenting their work, including tests they have conducted and their findings and conclusions. Such "purely" technical documents normally will not qualify as privileged because they ordinarily do not request legal advice or services or responses to such requests.

As time goes on in the "invention" process, a question may be raised regarding whether the results of the technical work are patentable. The inventors may submit an invention disclosure or a request for authorization to file a patent application. Additionally, concerns may be raised about whether a proposed new product or design embodying the inventors' discovery might infringe on any third-party patents. The question often arises in patent cases whether, and to what extent, the substance of these various communications and associated documents are privileged. The Federal Circuit's decision in *In re Spalding Sports Worldwide, Inc.*[30] is the appropriate starting point for addressing such issues.

A. The Privilege Standard Set Forth in the *Spalding* Decision

In *Spalding*, the district court ordered a patentee to produce an internal corporate "invention record" pertaining to the invention of what eventually became the patent-in-suit, concluding that such a communication was not privileged. An invention record is a standard form "generally used by corporations as a means for inventors to disclose to the corporation's patent attorneys that an invention has been made and to initiate patent action. They are usually short documents containing space for such information as names of inventors, description and scope of invention, closest prior art, first date of conception and disclosure to others, dates of publication, etc."[31] On appeal, the Federal Circuit vacated the district court's order to produce the invention record. The appellate court held that the corporation's invention record was protected by the attorney-client privilege.

The Federal Circuit began its analysis by deciding whether it must apply regional circuit law or its own law to the privilege question. The court concluded that whether an invention record qualifies as a privileged document is a question unique to patent law because the invention record relates to an invention submitted for consideration for possible patent protection; it thus clearly implicates substantive patent law.[32] Thus freed from possibly conflicting decisions from other circuit courts, and applying its own law in this case of first impression, the Federal Circuit held that "an invention record constitutes a privileged communication, as long as it is provided to an attorney for the purpose of securing primarily a legal opinion, or legal services, or assistance in a legal proceeding."[33] The court ultimately concluded that the corporation's invention record at issue was privileged because it "was prepared and submitted primarily for the purpose of obtaining legal advice on patentability and legal services in preparing a patent application."[34]

That the invention record document included technical information did not change the privileged nature of the document. The Federal Circuit reasoned,

"The fact that much of the technical information in one form or another finds its way into the patent application, to be made public when the patent issues, should not preclude the assertion of the privilege over the communication in which that information was disclosed to the attorney."[35]

In dicta, the court addressed the so called *Jack Winter*[36] line of district court decisions, which held that the transmission of technical information to an attorney, and documents relating to patent prosecution, were not privileged because the attorney was acting merely as a "conduit" between the client and the U.S. Patent and Trademark Office (PTO).[37] The Federal Circuit distinguished *Jack Winter* and its progeny as "not deal[ing] specifically with invention records" and concluded that, in any event, it was not bound by those decisions.[38] The Federal Circuit concluded that "the better rule [regarding privilege] is the one articulated in [*Spalding*]."[39]

B. District Court Cases Applying *Spalding*

The *Spalding* case does not stand for the blanket proposition that all invention and patent prosecution-related communications are privileged. Strictly speaking, the Federal Circuit's holding was limited to invention records submitted to patent counsel for the purpose of obtaining legal advice on patentability. Nevertheless, the court's choice of law analysis, and its criticism of the "conduit" theory, fundamentally changed the privilege landscape and have resulted in a general strengthening of a patent applicant's claim to withhold as privileged a number of different types of documents and communications that are commonly created in the course of the conception, reduction to practice, and patenting of an invention.

For example, in *Martin Marietta Materials, Inc. v. Bedford Reinforced Plastics, Inc.*,[40] the district court applied *Spalding* in concluding that communications between a client and counsel regarding prior art and the duty to disclose material information to the PTO was privileged.[41] The privileged communications included "relevant technical information" that was required to "evaluate patentability and/or to prepare a patent application."[42]

Similarly, in *Innogenetics, N.V. v. Abbott Laboratories*,[43] the district court refused to limit its interpretation of the *Spalding* decision to invention disclosures. The district court held that "if it appears that a document was conveyed from [in-house patent department personnel] to one of [plaintiff's] outside patent lawyers for the purpose of obtaining legal advice concerning the preparation of the priority or patent applications at issue, or was prepared by the outside patent lawyers in response to such a request, then I will deem it privileged."[44]

In *Softview Computer Products Corp. v. Haworth, Inc.*,[45] the court observed that "[t]he *Spalding* court relied in part on *Knogo Corp. v. United States*. . . . The line of cases that follow *Knogo* stand for the proposition that the attorney-client privilege *may* attach to communications regarding patent prosecution, so long as those communications meet the other criteria of the privilege."[46] The district court in *Softview* applied the *Spalding* standard for privilege to all of the withheld documents at issue relating to the patentee's U.S. patent application.[47]

In *McCook Metals L.L.C. v. Alcoa Inc.*,[48] the district court applied *Spalding* in concluding that a variety of prosecution-related documents, including draft patent applications, invention control reports, inventor questionnaires, and a duty of disclosure reminder form, were privileged.[49] With regard to draft patent applications in particular, the district court in *McCook* acknowledged that other (pre-*Spalding*) courts had refused to extend the privilege to such documents on the ground that much of the information contained in the drafts eventually were placed in the public domain by means of a successful patent prosecution.[50] The court in *McCook* disagreed with the rationale of those contrary cases because they failed to recognize the legal importance that a first-rate patent attorney adds to the legal protection afforded the client by the proper legal draftsmanship of an airtight patent that is successfully and properly prosecuted.[51]

In *Ergo Licensing, LLC v. Carefusion*,[52] the defendant sought to compel a patentee's documents that the defendant characterized as "drafts of Patent Office forms." The district court acknowledged that "[c]ase law differs on the question of whether drafts of documents intended to be filed with a government agency, and thus intended to be public, are covered by the attorney-client privilege." The district court followed the reasoning articulated in *In re Rivastigmine Patent Litigation*,[53] a 2006 district court decision that analyzed post-*Spalding* cases and concluded that the "emerging trend" was to apply the attorney-client privilege to drafts of patent applications. The district court in *Ergo Licensing* adopted the district court's reasoning in *In re Rivastigmine* and concluded that the "draft Patent Office forms" that were in issue "are draft documents that are also covered by the attorney-client privilege."[54]

Other recent cases that have applied *Spalding* in upholding a claim of attorney-client privilege to prevent discovery of documents and communications relating to patent preparation, prosecution, or opinions include

- *Bergstrom, Inc. v. Glacier Bay, Inc.*[55]—holding that inventors' communications to attorney of prior art either before the patent application was filed or before the patent issued were privileged.
- *Carl Zeiss Vision Int'l GmbH v. Signet Armorlite, Inc.*[56]—holding that clearance opinion provided by counsel to clients was privileged under *Spalding*.
- *Joon Park v. CAS Enterprises, Inc.*[57]—holding that e-mails regarding patent prosecution as well as drafts of documents that were to be filed in the PTO were privileged under *Spalding*.
- *Probert v. Clorox Co.*[58]—granting protective order to prevent defendant from deposing plaintiff's patent counsel concerning the invention, prosecution, and interpretation of the patent-in-suit because the subjects of the deposition were likely to involve privileged communications under *Spalding*.

C. The Limits of the *Spalding* Decision

District courts have applied *Spalding* beyond invention records to a host of other communications and documents that typically are created in the course of patenting an invention, including documents that contain only technical information. Regardless of how the communication is labeled, however, it must still satisfy the other *United Shoe* requirements for the privilege to apply.[59]

Thus, even under the *Spalding* standard, the purpose of the communication must be primarily for or in connection with legal advice or legal services.[60] The invention record at issue in *Spalding* was submitted by the inventors to Spalding's corporate legal department for the purpose of making a patentability determination.[61] If an attorney is merely forwarding documents or communications between the client and a governmental agency (such as the PTO or a foreign patent office) without any request, or response to request, for legal advice or services, then a court could conclude that no privilege attaches to the substance of such communications.[62] There are no "per se" rules in determining whether a particular document constitutes a request for legal advice. In making such an assessment, courts usually look to the overall tenor of the document to determine if such a request was either expressed *or* implied.[63]

In addition, under the *Spalding* test for privilege, the attorney-client communication must still be confidential to qualify for any protection.[64] To the extent that a communication by an attorney is based on a nonconfidential source, for example, public information or information from a third party, it may not qualify as protected by the attorney-client privilege.[65]

The privilege also does not apply to documents relating primarily to business matters.[66] Whether a communication or document is "primarily" relating to business or is "primarily" relating to legal matters may not be easy to decide.[67] Furthermore, one district court, applying *Spalding*, concluded that a client's authorization to file a patent application, a memorandum of a conference with a patent examiner, a status report regarding a patent application, a memorandum regarding a patent search, and a notification that the client's patent was about to issue and instructions to mark its device with the patent number were not privileged because none of those documents contained confidential information or legal advice.[68]

Whether the results of a prior art search are privileged in the aftermath of *Spalding* still is not entirely clear. Before the Federal Circuit's decision in *Spalding*, a number of district courts had held that prior art searches and prior art studies in general were not privileged because they did not contain or reflect information obtained in confidence from the client.[69] In *Spalding*, the accused infringer similarly argued that a portion of Spalding's invention record that included a list of prior art was not privileged because that portion of the record did not request legal advice.[70] The Federal Circuit rejected this argument, finding that it was unnecessary to dissect the document to separately evaluate each of its components.[71] According to the court in *Spalding*, it is enough that the overall tenor of the document indicates that it is a request for legal advice or services.[72] Based upon the broad standard set forth in the *Spalding* decision, a document containing a prior art search would probably be considered privileged if the primary purpose of conducting the prior art search were either to evaluate patentability or to aid counsel in the preparation of a patent application.[73]

Finally, the *Spalding* decision and its choice of Federal Circuit law have no application when the communications in question are not unique to patent law, or are not affected by substantive patent law. Thus, for example, when the communication or document in question relates to patent licenses or similar types of contractual issues, the law of the regional circuit, and not the Federal Circuit, most likely will be applied in determining whether the communication is privileged.[74]

D. Patent Prosecution Documents as Work Product

In litigation, patentees sometimes assert that documents prepared in connection with patent prosecution activities are immune from discovery as attorney work-product. Some district courts have held that the work-product immunity doctrine does *not* extend to preparation for ex parte proceedings, such as patent proceedings.[75] Those courts that reject an immunity theory for prosecution documents reason that the mere fact that a document is prepared when litigation is foreseeable does not mean that the document was prepared in anticipation of litigation.[76] To qualify as work product, the document must be prepared *because of* the prospect of litigation when the preparer faces an actual claim or a potential claim following an actual event or series of events that reasonably could result in litigation.[77] Patent prosecution documents thus ordinarily cannot be protected as work product because they are not typically created in anticipation of litigation.[78]

For example, the district court in *Bristol-Myers Squibb Co. v. Rhone-Poulenc Rorer, Inc.*[79] rejected the proposition that patent prosecution documents are work product. The court reasoned that documents relating to or in furtherance of the prosecution of a patent application are not work product because the primary motivating purpose behind the performance of the work is to obtain a patent.[80] The court further held that patent prosecution documents are not created "in anticipation of or concerning litigation."[81] A patent prosecution is not adversarial, but rather proceeds ex parte.[82] Since the purpose of the work-product privilege is to protect the adversarial process,[83] normally there is no basis for extending this form of privilege to patent prosecutions.

Some district courts have extended work-product immunity to documents prepared in connection with patent prosecution activities if it is shown that the work also was performed in anticipation of litigation.[84] In *In re Minebea Corp.*,[85] for example, a patentee sought work-product protection for prosecution-related documents that were created before the patent issued. The district court upheld the immunity claim and explained:

> Generally, work performed by an attorney to prepare and prosecute a patent application does not fall within the parameters of the work-product protection . . . since the prosecution of a patent application is a non-adversarial, ex parte proceeding . . . This rule does not, however, preclude application of the work product protection to work

performed to prosecute a patent application if it was also performed in anticipation of or concerning litigation.[86]

The court in *Minebea* concluded that information pertaining to the patent prosecution was subject to work-product immunity if it was prepared on or after the date that the patentee anticipated litigation, regardless of the fact that the patent did not issue until almost one year later.[87] According to some courts, the crucial date (for applying work-product immunity) is the date upon which the party asserting the work-product doctrine anticipated litigation regarding the patent, not when the patent was actually issued.[88]

IV. Communications with Domestic and Foreign Patent Agents and Foreign Counsel as Privileged

A. Who Qualifies as an "Attorney"

It is axiomatic that for the privilege to apply there must be a communication between a client and an attorney. What does "attorney" mean, exactly, in this context? Under the often-cited test for privilege formulated in *United Shoe*, an attorney "is a member of the bar of a court" (or his or her subordinate).[89] Although this requirement seems straightforward enough, interesting things can happen if either (1) the "attorney," though licensed to practice law at some point in his or her career, is at the time of the communication on inactive status, or (2) the "attorney" is not really an attorney at all, but the client nevertheless *believes* that the supposed "attorney" is, in fact, a bar member. Both of these scenarios arose in *Gucci America, Inc. v. Guess?, Inc.*[90]

In *Gucci*, a trademark infringement case, plaintiff withheld as privileged various internal communications with its "in-house legal counsel." Apparently unbeknownst to plaintiff, the in-house counsel had voluntarily taken "inactive" status with the California state bar prior to joining the plaintiff's company, and he remained inactive throughout his tenure with the company.

Plaintiff first asserted that its in-house counsel was still an "attorney" in that he was a "member" of the California state bar, albeit an inactive one. The district court rejected this argument. The court concluded that as a matter of state law, the in-house counsel "did not possess the type of bar membership that authorized him to engage in the practice of law" and that California state law "explicitly limits the practice of law to active [bar] members."[91]

Plaintiff next argued that it should be able to avail itself of the privilege because it was not aware that its in-house counsel was, in fact, on inactive status. The court explained that "the privilege should be extended to those who make confidential communications to an individual in the genuine, but mistaken, belief that he is an attorney."[92] Nevertheless, the district court refused to apply the "mistake" exception because there was no evidence that plaintiff had ever made "any effort to ascertain his qualifications as an attorney" or had "even asked [him] for credentials proving his bar admission."[93] Accordingly, the court ordered the production of the withheld communications.

B. Communications with U.S. Patent Agents

The "attorney" requirement to the "attorney-client" privilege has a unique twist when the communication involves a registered patent agent. Registered patent agents are authorized to practice law, albeit limited to matters before the PTO.[94] U.S. registered patent agents thus may provide legal advice and services concerning patentability. They can also prepare, file, and prosecute patent applications before the PTO.

Despite these similarities with attorneys, patent agents obviously are not members of the bar of any court. The issue sometimes arises in patent cases whether communications between a client and a U.S. patent agent are protected by the attorney-client privilege. Unfortunately, "there is no consensus on whether, and to what extent, the attorney-client privilege applies to non-attorney patent agents."[95]

1. *Courts Not Recognizing U.S. Patent Agent Privilege*

It appears that the greater weight of authority strictly, and literally, interprets the "attorney" prong of the attorney-client communication requirement. The courts that have adopted this view reason that "attorney" means just that—a member of a bar of a court—and because a U.S. patent agent is not a member of the bar of any *court*, there is no patent agent-client privilege.[96]

There is one generally recognized exception to this line of cases. That is, the privilege may still apply to communications between a U.S. registered patent agent and his or her client *if* the patent agent is performing his duties under the supervision and control of an attorney—which would normally be the case when the patent agent is employed by a law firm or a corporate law department and is supervised by a bar member.[97] In such cases, the attorney-client privilege would not apply to the registered U.S. patent agent based upon his or her PTO bar membership. Rather, the privilege would apply *because of* the attorney's role in supervising or controlling the registered patent agent's activities and communications.[98] In such "supervision" cases, the attorney-client privilege applies (assuming all other elements of the test are met) to the client's communications with a U.S. registered patent agent much in the same way that it might apply to communications between a client and, for example, a paralegal, secretary, or some other nonattorney who is working under the direction and control of an attorney.[99]

2. *Courts Recognizing U.S. Patent Agent Privilege*

Despite what might be the controlling weight of authority opposing a patent agent privilege, some courts have recognized the existence of a form of attorney-client privilege for patent agents in their own right (i.e., not requiring that the individual be operating under the supervision of an attorney at law for the privilege to apply).[100] Courts that have found a privilege for U.S. patent agent-client communications frequently cite to the U.S. Supreme Court's decision in *Sperry v. Florida*,[101] a disciplinary case over whether a registered patent agent violated Florida state law by practicing law without a state law license. In concluding that the agent was permitted to practice patent law in Florida, the Supreme Court in *Sperry* explained that "[t]he preparation and prosecution of patent applications for others constitutes the practice of law."[102] The Supreme Court summarized the "attorney-like" functions of patent agents as follows:

> Such conduct inevitably requires the practitioner to consider and advise his clients as to the patentability of their inventions under the statutory criteria as well as to consider the advisability of relying upon alternative forms of protection which may be available under state law. It also involves participation in his drafting of the specification and claims of the patent application which this Court long ago noted constitute(s) one of the most difficult legal instruments to draw with accuracy. And upon rejection of the application, the practitioner may also assist in the preparation of amendments which frequently requires written argument to establish the patentability of the claimed invention under the applicable rules of law and in light of the prior art.[103]

Sperry did not involve the issue of whether a patent agent-client communication was privileged. However, a number of district courts have held that the existence of a "U.S. patent agent privilege" is simply a logical extension of the Court's reasoning in *Sperry*, which in effect treated patent agents as "quasi-attorneys" at least to the extent of their limited right to practice patent law before the PTO.

For example, in *In re Ampicillin Antitrust Litigation*,[104] the district court held that a "patent agent-client" privilege exists. The court explained as follows:

> [W]here a client, in confidence, seeks legal advice from a registered patent agent who is authorized to represent that client in an adversary process that will substantially affect the legal rights of the client, which thereby necessitates a full and free disclosure from the client to the representative so that the legal representation may be effective, the privilege will be available.[105]

3. Limits on U.S. Patent Agent Privilege

In those courts that have recognized a "U.S. patent agent-client privilege" in its own right (not dependent on supervision of a state bar member), the scope of that privilege is limited to what patent agents are licensed to do. A patent agent's registration before the PTO "does not authorize the general practice of patent law, but sanctions only the performance of those services which are reasonably necessary and incident to the preparation and prosecution of patent applications."[106] Consequently, "[n]o case provides blanket attorney-client privilege between a USPTO recognized non-lawyer patent agent and his client over all intellectual property matters."[107] In fact, those courts that have recognized a U.S. patent agent privilege have limited the scope of that privilege to encompass only those services that such agents are legally licensed to perform, that is, representation in preparing and prosecuting patent applications before the U.S. Patent Office.[108]

When a U.S. patent agent goes beyond that limited role, their "status" as a patent agent does not provide him or her with any special protections. As one district court explained:

> A patent agent's claim to attorney-client privilege has its foundations in the USPTO's limited authorization to non-lawyer patent agents to practice law. Essentially, the authorization provides the individual with the status of an attorney, but only for a limited purpose, i.e., the purpose for which the USPTO registered the non-attorney as an agent to practice before it. Thus, by definition, communications between a patent agent and a client beyond that limited purpose are not privileged.[109]

For patent agents who are not acting under the supervision and control of an attorney, this limitation on the scope of privilege makes perfect sense. This express limitation is consistent with the general rule that the attorney-client privilege does not apply to communications with an attorney who is acting in a nonlegal capacity.[110] For example, communications between a client and a U.S. patent agent concerning the licensing or enforcement of an *issued* patent ordinarily would not be covered under the patent agent privilege unless the patent agent is acting under the supervision or control of an attorney. This is because the PTO bar membership does not extend to those types of post-patent issuance services.

B. Communications with Foreign Patent Agents and Foreign Attorneys

When the communication involves a *foreign* attorney or patent agent and his or her client, the privilege analysis can get a bit more complicated. In many foreign countries, attorneys at law do not prepare or prosecute patent applications. Typically this service is provided by a patent agent. Nevertheless, it is not unusual for an individual who meets a U.S. practitioner's definition of a "patent agent" (i.e., a nonattorney technical specialist who is not a general attorney at law but who is nonetheless authorized by the law of a foreign country to prepare and prosecute patent applications before the patent office of a foreign country) to be referred to as a "patent attorney."[111] A U.S. court will thus look beyond the individual's title and should focus instead on the individual's qualifications in their home country.

That does not end the analysis. An issue that is frequently raised in U.S. patent litigation is whether communications with such foreign (i.e., non-U.S.) "patent agents" (or "patent attorneys") are privileged in a U.S. case. This can arise, for example, when a patent that is involved in a U.S. litigation has foreign counterparts, and the defendant seeks discovery of all of the foreign counterpart files.

Determining whether the attorney-client privilege applies to communications involving clients and foreign patent agents or foreign attorneys "has not always been simple or consistent."[112] Neither the Federal Circuit, nor any other circuit court, has issued to date a published decision that has discussed the scope or applicability of a foreign patent agent or foreign patent attorney privilege in U.S. litigation.

Under Federal Rule of Evidence 501, courts generally look to federal law to determine whether an evidentiary privilege may be invoked.[113] Although there are a few district courts that have refused to recognize an attorney-client privilege for foreign patent agents under *any* circumstances,[114] most federal courts that have published decisions on this issue have applied a two-step analysis.

First, the court must decide which country's law to apply. If the court determines that U.S. law applies, the court will typically apply the *United Shoe* standard (or some variation of it) and determine based on that test whether the communication with the foreign agent is privileged by those standards. If the court determines that it must apply foreign law, the court then must decide whether (1) the particular foreign law in question recognizes an evidentiary privilege for the individual patent professional (agent or attorney) in question; and (2) if the foreign law does recognize such a privilege in general, does the particular communication in question satisfy the test for privilege imposed under foreign law. If the district court concludes that an attorney-client privilege exists under the foreign country in question, and the communication meets the foreign country's test for privilege, then as a matter of comity the district court should treat the communication as privileged from disclosure in a U.S. legal proceeding.[115]

1. *Whose Law to Apply*

The "choice of law" rule that district courts have applied in their analysis of the foreign agent or foreign attorney privilege question has been determined to date by regional circuit law only and not by the Federal Circuit. As a result, there is currently no uniform set of choice of law rules that apply to patent cases considering the foreign privilege issue.

Some district courts follow the "touching base" rule.[116] The touching-base approach has been described as follows:

> [C]ommunications by a foreign client with foreign patent agents "relating to assistance in prosecuting patent applications in the United States" are governed by American privilege law whereas communications "relating to assistance in prosecuting patent applications in their own foreign country" or "rendering legal advice . . . on the patent law of their own country" are, as a matter of comity, governed by the privilege "law of the foreign country in which the patent application is filed," even if the client is a party to an American lawsuit.[117]

Those courts that apply the touching-base approach look to the foreign law of privilege only where those communications relate solely to activities outside of the United States.[118] Under this general approach, "[i]f a communication with a foreign patent agent involves a foreign patent application, then as a matter of comity, the law of that foreign country is considered regarding whether that law provides a privilege comparable to the attorney-client privilege."[119] Under a strict interpretation of the touching-base approach, however, even a minimal amount of contact with the United States would preclude the application of foreign law to the question of privilege.[120]

Some courts have criticized the touching-base approach as too rigid. Those courts have observed that under the touching-base standard, a document could touch base with the United States if it merely emanated here or if it simply mentioned a U.S. patent.[121]

Other district courts have applied a balancing test to the choice of law question.[122] Under the balancing test, the district court or other administrative fact finder attempts to ascertain which country has the dominant interest in the communication, considering such interests as the parties to and substance of the communication, the place where the relationship was centered at the time of the communication, the needs of the international system, and whether the application of foreign privilege law would be clearly inconsistent with important policies embedded in federal law.[123] Some district courts view the traditional approach as being more consistent with the *Restatement (Second) of Conflicts*.[124] The "traditional" approach has been described as looking to the law of the country that has "'the most direct and compelling interest' in whether [the] communications should remain confidential."[125]

Finally, some district courts have endorsed a combination of the touching-base and traditional tests. Under the combination approach, the district court applies a touching-base analysis to those communications that have no connection, or only an incidental connection, to the United States, and it applies the traditional approach to those communications that have more than an incidental connection to the United States.[126]

2. *Determining Privilege under Foreign Law*

If court decides that the foreign patent agent (or foreign attorney) privilege question should be decided as a matter of foreign law, the court next decides (1) whether the law of the applicable foreign country recognizes an evidentiary privilege for communications with such foreign patent attorney or agents, and (2) if the foreign law does recognize such a privilege, whether all of the requirements for asserting the privilege under the law of that foreign country have been shown by the party seeking to assert the privilege.[127] In every case, "[t]he burden is on the party asserting the privilege to provide the court with the applicable foreign law, and [to] demonstrate that the privilege applies to the documents it seeks to exclude from discovery."[128]

Some district courts have gone so far as to hold that the party seeking to establish the privileged nature of foreign patent agent communications involving multiple countries must show that the privilege is recognized "for each and every country for which it claims the privilege."[129] Normally, to meet this burden, the party asserting the privilege will need to "provide affidavits from legal experts in the laws of these countries stating the applicable law of the attorney-client privilege, and demonstrating that the law supports the privilege asserted."[130] A number of courts that have addressed this issue have also explained that the privilege for foreign patent agents, like privilege in other contexts, is "strictly construed, and all doubts should be resolved in favor of disclosure."[131]

Even if the party seeking to withhold documents or oral communications shows that patent agent communications are eligible for privilege protection under the law of the applicable nation, it must still show that each communication it has withheld satisfies the requirements of that country's privilege law. Thus, for example, some countries do not provide any protection to documents intended to be filed with the foreign patent office, or information reporting on actions taken by the foreign patent office, since that information would not be considered confidential.[132]

As a practical matter, convincing a judge whether a particular country's law recognizes an evidentiary privilege for patent agent communications can be a difficult, time consuming, and expensive task. Furthermore, as some of the cases below illustrate, the outcome of such privilege contests can be unpredictable. Indeed, in some cases district courts attempting to ascertain the law of the same foreign country have sometime reached different conclusions as to whether that country recognizes an evidentiary privilege for confidential communications with foreign patent agents/attorneys.

a. Japan

A number of district courts have considered whether Japanese law recognizes an evidentiary privilege for communications with Japanese patent agents (*benrishi*) or Japanese attorneys (*bengoshi*) that is similar to the attorney-client privilege in the United States. Prior to 1998, most of the U.S. district courts that considered this issue and had issued published decisions concluded that there was no privilege that covered communications with either a Japanese patent agent or patent attorney.[133]

In 1998, Japan amended its Code of Civil Procedure. The revised law expressly extended an evidentiary privilege both to Japanese *benrishi* and *bengoshi*.[134] The change to the Code also retroactively applied to documents that were created before the 1998 amendment, as well as to subsequent documents.[135] District courts that have since interpreted the revised law of Japan (i.e., post-1998) and that have issued published decisions have concluded that Japanese law now recognizes an evidentiary privilege for confidential communications between a client and a Japanese patent agent or attorney.[136]

For example, in *Eisai Ltd. v. Dr. Reddy's Laboratories, Inc.*,[137] the district court concluded that an attorney-client privilege exists under Japanese law because *benrishi* may refuse to testify about facts they should keep secret and the holder of documents can refuse to produce them.[138] Moreover, those district courts that have considered this issue under Japanese law have concluded that the changes made to the Code of Civil Procedure of Japan do not offend fundamental principles of American justice or public policy and that they should, therefore, be embraced as a matter of comity in a U.S. patent litigation.[139]

b. France

Whether France recognizes an attorney-client privilege for communications with French patent agents has been the subject of differing views.[140] In *Bristol-Myers Squibb Co. v. Rhone-Poulenc Rorer, Inc.*,[141] the Southern District of New York, after a thorough analysis of competing expert testimony on the issue, concluded that French law does not recognize an attorney-client privilege for patent agents.[142]

Other federal district courts, however, have found that French law does recognize an evidentiary privilege for confidential communications between a client and a French patent agent.[143] For example, in *Duplan Corp. v. Deering Milliken, Inc.*,[144] the district court held that, as a matter of French law, communications to or from French patent agents who are acting as patent counsel in France are protected from discovery in the United States by the attorney-client privilege. The district court in that case concluded that the attorney-client privilege protects communications with French patent agents who "are rendering legal advice to foreign corporate control group members, their representatives, or foreign attorneys on the patent law of their own country."[145]

In response to the *Bristol-Myers Squibb Co.* decision, the French Parliament passed Article L. 422-11, which intended to create an attorney-client privilege between "Industrial Property Attorneys" and their clients.[146] Even with this revision, however, the situation in France is complicated in part because different titles are associated with different intellectual property professionals. For example, "Industrial Property Attorneys" may act as patent agents. Thus, it would appear that Article L. 422-11 establishes an attorney-client privilege between all French patent agents and their clients.[147] However, not all French patent agents are Industrial Property Attorneys.[148] Further complicating the analysis, French patent agents licensed before 1990, when the title of Industrial Property Attorney was created, are now considered to be licensed under a "Special List."[149] In *Commissariat a L'Energie Atomique v. Samsung Elec. Co.*, the District of Delaware concluded that the provisions of Article L. 422-11 do not apply to those French patent agents practicing on the "Special List."[150]

Therefore, even following the passage of Article L. 422-11, courts are still left with the task of determining whether an evidentiary privilege attaches to communications between a French patent agent who is not an Industrial Property Attorney, and his or her clients.

c. Germany

Several district courts have issued published decisions that conclude that an evidentiary privilege applies under German law comparable to that accorded to U.S. attorneys. Those district courts have thus found that confidential communications between German patent agents and their clients are privileged.[151] At least one district court reached the opposite conclusion; however, it appears that in that one case, the patentee failed to present sufficient evidence of German law.[152]

These different results emphasize the importance of proof in establishing the existence of a foreign privilege. Normally, such proof is provided by legal expert testimony or affidavits on the substance of foreign law and whether that foreign law recognizes an evidentiary privilege for patent agent communications.[153]

d. United Kingdom

Whether communications between a British patent agent and their clients are privileged under the law of the United Kingdom has been the subject of a number of published decisions.[154] To date, those decisions uniformly have held that there is such a privilege recognized under U.K. law.

For example, in *In re Rivastigmine Patent Litigation*,[155] the patentee withheld communications between it and its U.K. law firm regarding the prosecution of a foreign counterpart patent. According to the district court, the patentee provided evidence sufficient to demonstrate that U.K. law recognizes a privilege for communications regarding patent matters between a client and a patent agent (also referred to as a patent attorney) registered in the U.K., a patent agent registered with the European Patent Office, or a partnership of patent agents and attorneys.[156] At least one district court has limited such a privilege "only to patent agent communications concerning formal patent proceedings before the appropriate British tribunals."[157]

e. South Korea

At least one district court has concluded that an evidentiary privilege can exist between a South Korean attorney and client notwithstanding the fact that South Korean law itself does not recognize an attorney-client privilege or work-product doctrine.[158] In *Astra Aktiebolag v. Andrx Pharmaceuticals, Inc.*, the court applied U.S. privilege law notwithstanding the fact that the contested communications and work product did not "touch base" with the United States.[159] The court held that the Korean communications were not discoverable because many documents would have been privileged under American law and, thus, would not have been discoverable under Korean law.[160] Because "virtually no disclosure [or discovery] is contemplated" by Korean attorneys in their practice of law, the court reasoned that comity and U.S. public policy outweighed the application of a nonexistent Korean privilege law that would have required disclosure of the communications and documentation.[161]

f. People's Republic of China

Until 1997, when the Law of the People's Republic of China on Lawyers (Lawyer's Law) became effective, the People's Republic of China did not protect the confidential information of a client. Article 33 of the Lawyer's Law states that "[a] lawyer should keep state secrets and a litigant's commercial secrets learned through conducting the business activities of a lawyer's practice, and should not disclose the privacy of litigants."[162] While this provision created something akin to an attorney-client privilege, it was without teeth. To be sure, Article 70 of the Law of Civil Procedure of the People's Republic of China (Civil Procedure Law) established an obligation upon attorneys to testify at trial if any facts are known that are relevant to the case.[163] This provision of the Civil Procedure Law, combined with the section of the Lawyer's Law that allows the court to revoke an attorney's license if facts are concealed from the court,[164] effectively prevented meaningful protection of confidential communications between attorney and client.

In 2008, however, China did an about-face. It amended the Lawyer's Law to include an affirmative duty to protect client's confidential information and added a provision to eliminate the obligation placed on attorneys to testify at trial.[165] While client-confidentiality requirements in the People's Republic of China have been strengthened, the current form of the Lawyer's Law has not explicitly established an evidentiary privilege, and case law has yet to define the types of communication or documentation, if any, that may be deemed privileged in a U.S. litigation.

g. European Patent Attorney

The European patent attorney, while not an attorney at law, provides his or her clients with patentability opinions, prepares and prosecutes patent applications, and provides opinions relating to the validity or infringement of a European patent or application. In the hopes of strengthening European patent attorneys' efforts to resist discovery of confidential client communications, the European Patent Convention was revised in December of 2007 to include an attorney-client privilege.[166] The privilege prevents any communication or document relating to the aforementioned duties of a European patent attorney from being disclosed in proceedings before the European Patent Office unless, of course, the privilege is waived by the client.[167] At least two district courts have recognized the existence of an evidentiary privilege for confidential communications between European patent attorneys and their clients.[168]

V. *Attorney-Client Privilege in Patent-Related Administrative Proceedings*

A. Section 337 Investigations before the ITC

Section 337 of the Tariff Act of 1930 (19 U.S.C. § 1337) prohibits importation of a product into the United States that infringes a valid U.S. intellectual property right.[169] If a violation of § 337 is found, the International Trade Commission (ITC) can issue an exclusion order banning the importation of the infringing product into the United States.[170]

Discovery begins shortly after the commencement of an ITC investigation and proceeds in a similar, although expedited, fashion as compared to traditional discovery practice at the district court level. Discovery disputes are governed by a set of ground rules promulgated by the administrative law judge (ALJ) presiding over the investigation. Although the ground rules applicable to any investigation are specific to the presiding ALJ, most ALJs require a "meet and confer" before a discovery-related motion is filed.[171]

A party wishing to challenge an adverse order regarding privilege must follow special interlocutory appeal rules codified in 19 C.F.R. § 210.24. In general, rulings by the ALJ may not be appealed until the ALJ issues an initial determination in the investigation.[172] However, 19 C.F.R. § 210.24(b)(2) provides that a decision relating to the designation of information as confidential may be appealed immediately with leave of the ALJ.[173] Interlocutory appeals are heard by the six-member Commission, which also reviews initial determinations made by the ALJs and issues final determinations and exclusion orders if infringement is found.

Traditional privilege rules, based upon federal common law and decisions promulgated by the ALJs and Commissioners themselves, apply during the course of discovery.[174] At least one ALJ has recognized an attorney-client privilege for communications relating to the conception and patenting of an invention.[175] With respect to patent agents, ALJ Saxon has found that "confidential communications between a patent agent and his client in connection with a patent prosecution [are privileged;] however, communications between the patent [agent] and client not related to patent prosecutions and in the realm of the general practice of law are not privileged."[176]

ALJs at the ITC have in some cases extended the attorney-client privilege to communications with foreign attorneys and foreign nonattorney patent agents in connection with confidential communications that arise out of patent drafting and prosecution.[177] However, as in district court litigations, the party asserting the privilege must first establish (1) what country's law applies; (2) whether the law of the foreign country recognizes the right of the foreign attorney, or nonattorney patent agent, to render advice "in confidence in connection with a patent application in that country"; and (3) if a foreign privilege does exist generally, whether its requirements were met in the present case.[178]

B. Interferences before the BPAI

Patent interferences are administrative proceedings conducted before the Board of Patent Appeals and Interferences (BPAI) of the PTO "to determine any question of patentability or priority of invention between two or more parties claiming the same patentable invention."[179] The administrative patent judges (APJs) of the BPAI may enter an order allowing for limited discovery in an interference.[180]

As set forth in 37 C.F.R. § 41.150, discovery as a matter of right is limited to (1) certain mandatory disclosures of "every requested patent, patent application, literature reference, and test standard mentioned in the specification of the party's involved patent or application," and (2) "any exhibit cited in a motion or in testimony."[181] Any additional discovery that a party might want to take is available only if authorized by the APJ and then only upon a showing that the "interests of justice" requires that discovery be granted.[182] Disputes may arise in an interference concerning the applicability, scope, or waiver of the attorney-client privilege.

For evidentiary matters in general, interference proceedings before the BPAI are subject to both the Federal Rules of Evidence and the regulations promulgated by the director of the PTO.[183] The decision in *Ginter v. Benson*[184] is instructive for its discussion of how the BPAI handles questions concerning the attorney-client privilege in interference proceedings.

In *Ginter*, Ginter, the junior party in the interference, relied upon testimony of a patent attorney and the named inventors regarding certain draft patent applications, the drafting process, the amount of time spent working on the drafts, and attorney bills to prove attorney diligence toward a constructive reduction to practice.[185] Benson, the senior party, was permitted by the BPAI to file a motion to compel seeking production of all drafts leading up to the filing of the patent application that was involved in the interference. Ginter opposed the motion on the grounds that its draft patent applications were privileged. Benson asserted that Ginter had waived the privilege.[186]

The first issue discussed by the BPAI in *Ginter* was choice of law. The BPAI wrote that it initially thought it should apply the choice of law rules followed by the Federal Circuit, which, in turn, "applies regional circuit law to certain non-patent 'procedural' matters, including matters related to privilege."[187] Ultimately, however, the BPAI concluded that "there is no need to engage in a choice of regional circuit law." It reasoned that because the PTO is "a creature of statute," the patent statute authorizes the director of the PTO to establish regulations, and one of those regulations includes authorization for the BPAI to permit limited discovery in interferences; the law that it should apply is "the regulations promulgated by the Director independent of where (1) a party or witness 'resides,' (2) a deposition is being taken or (3) the PTO 'resides.'"[188]

The BPAI in *Ginter* next explained that under PTO regulations governing interference proceedings, there are generally two types of discovery: "automatic discovery" and "additional discovery." The BPAI decided that within the meaning of the regulations, the discovery requests were for additional discovery. To obtain such additional discovery, the BPAI stated, it was the burden of the party seeking the discovery to demonstrate that the additional discovery "meets the 'interests of justice standard' which appears in [37 C.F.R.] § 41.150(b)(1)."[189]

The BPAI acknowledged the Federal Circuit's decision in *In re Spalding* (addressed above), but it decided that "*Spalding* is not 'controlling' because *Spalding* did not involve interpretation of discovery rules applicable to PTO proceedings with respect to draft patent applications." Nevertheless, the BPAI did consider the *Spalding* decision, and it found that *Spalding* "should be applied in determining whether it is in the 'interests of justice' to order a party to produce drafts of patent applications." Thus, following the reasoning in *Spalding* (while taking pains to state that it was not bound by that decision), the BPAI concluded that draft patent applications are generally privileged.

The BPAI in *Ginter* concluded that Benson did not demonstrate that a waiver of the privilege was within the "interests of justice." The BPAI explained that Benson "has not made out a sufficient case [for waiver of the attorney-client privilege] within the meaning of the regulations."[190] The draft patent applications in question "would appear to have limited value in helping Benson 'counter' Ginter's alleged reasonable diligence" during the relevant time frame. Thus, the BPAI held that "it has not been shown that it would be in the interests of justice to order the production of pre-31 January 1995 drafts even if those drafts were not covered by the attorney-client privilege."[191]

The BPAI's decision in *Ginter* confirmed that the attorney-client privilege does exist in interferences. The BPAI stated that "[t]here is no reason why a party in an interference should lose its attorney-client privilege just because it is before an administrative agency where discovery practice under the rules applicable to district courts are not applicable."[192] Furthermore, the BPAI interpreted the PTO's regulations "to authorize, in a proper case, issuance of an order to compel discovery of attorney-client privileged material if the privilege has been waived."[193] The BPAI concluded that questions regarding the applicability and waiver of the attorney-client privilege in interferences are resolved "on a case by case basis" according to the "interests of justice" standard, and that "decisions by district courts and courts of appeal may be helpful in resolving issues arising under our 'interests of justice' standard"—with "decisions of the Supreme Court and the Federal Circuit" being entitled to greater weight than those of other courts.[194]

VI. Waiver of Privilege or Immunity

In patent cases, a voluntary waiver with respect to one or more privileged documents reflecting communications between an attorney and the client in discussing certain subject matter generally waives the privilege as to all contemporaneous communications between that attorney and that client on that subject matter.[195] When a client voluntarily waives the privilege as to some documents that the client considers not damaging and asserts the privilege as to other documents that the client considers damaging, the client may be compelled to produce all documents relating to the matter. The rationale for this rule is that a client cannot be allowed, after disclosing as much as he pleases, to withhold the remainder. He may elect to withhold or to disclose, but after a certain point the election remains final. Voluntary disclosure of privileged communications or work product to an adversary generally waives the privilege as to other communications on the same subject.[196]

A. Waiver by Inadvertent Disclosure

The attorney-client privilege may be lost in a patent case, as in other types of cases, through an inadvertent waiver. These situations typically arise if the party seeking to maintain the privilege, (usually but not always a corporate entity) is not careful in maintaining the confidentiality of its privileged documents. In litigation, a party may also waive the privilege inadvertently such as by error resulting from a careless document production procedure.[197]

According to the Advisory Committee Notes to the 2006 revisions to Federal Rule of Civil Procedure 26(b)(5):

> The Committee has repeatedly been advised that the risk of privilege waiver, and the work necessary to avoid it, add to the costs and delay of discovery. When the review is of electronically stored information, the risk of waiver, and the time and effort required to avoid it, can increase substantially because of the volume of electronically stored information and the difficulty in ensuring that all information to be produced has in fact been reviewed.[198]

The district courts have not uniformly or consistently treated whether an inadvertent production waives the attorney-client privilege. To be sure, some district courts have held that an inadvertent production is never a waiver; some district courts have held that it is always a waiver; and still other district courts have held that it is only a waiver if, in the totality of circumstances, adequate measures were not taken to avoid the disclosure.[199] In fact, some district courts subscribe to all three views.[200]

To alleviate uncertainty and create more uniformity regarding the waiver of privilege (especially when the waiver was inadvertent), legislation was passed in 2008 that created Federal Rule of Evidence 502, Attorney-Client Privilege and Work Product; Limitations on Waiver.[201] FRE 502(a) defines the scope of a waiver of privilege or immunity insofar as it relates to other (undisclosed) communications or information as follows:

> When the disclosure [of a privileged communication or work-product material] is made in a Federal proceeding or to a Federal office or agency and waives the attorney-client privilege or work-product protection, the waiver extends to an undisclosed communication or information . . . only if:
>
> 1. the waiver is intentional;
> 2. the disclosed and undisclosed communications or information concern the same subject matter; and
> 3. they ought in fairness to be considered together.[202]

With respect to the issue of inadvertent waivers, FRE 502(b) provides that a disclosure of a privileged communication or work-product material is not a waiver if three conditions are met:

> 1. the disclosure is inadvertent;
> 2. the holder of the privilege or protection took reasonable steps to prevent disclosure; and
> 3. the holder promptly took reasonable steps to rectify the error....[203]

FRE 502(b) hopefully will serve its purpose of avoiding protracted battles over waiver in patent cases, which typically involve enormous volumes of documents. For example, in *King Pharmaceuticals, Inc. v. Purdue Pharma L.P.*,[204] a patent infringement case involving the production of millions of documents, the accused infringer asserted that four pages of a document it had produced were privileged and had been inadvertently produced. The disclosure was discovered when plaintiff's counsel used the document during a deposition. The district court agreed that the disclosure of the four pages satisfied FRE 502(b) in that it was very limited in light of the overall production, and that the accused infringer acted promptly under Federal Rule of Civil Procedure 26(b)(5)(B) to notify opposing counsel of the claim and the basis for it. Consequently, the district court ordered patentee's counsel to destroy all copies of the privileged document and not to use or disclose the privileged information.[205] Other courts in patent cases have followed FRE 502(b) in refusing to find a waiver of privilege.[206]

Most patent cases involve the entry, prior to discovery, of a protective order to protect confidential information. A patent litigant would be wise to deal with the possibility of an inadvertent production by including an inadvertent disclosure of privileged or work-product materials provision in the protective order. In fact, the protective order solution is specifically addressed in the Advisory Committee Notes to Rule 26(b)(5)(B). Furthermore, FRE 502(d) provides that a court "may order that the privilege or protection is not waived by disclosure connected with the litigation." When parties have stipulated to such a provision, and the district court has entered the parties' agreement as an order of the court, the terms of the protective order should control whether an inadvertent production waives privilege.[207]

Regardless of whether a protective order controls the issue, the burden rests on the producing party to establish that its disclosure was truly inadvertent.[208] Some district courts have required parties seeking the return of a privileged document allegedly produced inadvertently to act "timely."[209] Moreover, if the producing party is found to have engaged in purposeful or grossly negligent acts in allowing the production of privileged documents, the district court might very well conclude that their production was not "inadvertent."[210] Indeed, some district courts have also refused to order the return of a privileged document if it was produced because of a mistake of counsel or counsel's exercise of poor judgment, concluding that such conduct was "advertent" and not "inadvertent."[211]

B. Waiver by Accused Infringer's Reliance on Advice of Counsel

Patent infringement is a strict liability tort, and thus the accused infringer's state of mind is not relevant to establishing liability. There are two notable exceptions to this general rule.

The first exception is when the patentee alleges that the infringement (whether direct or indirect) was willful. Complaints for patent infringement commonly include an allegation of willfulness along with a plea for enhanced damages and attorneys' fees.[212] Where an accused infringer is alleged to have acted willfully, evidence that the accused infringer relied upon competent legal advice could be relevant to whether or not the accused party acted willfully.

The second exception is when the claim is for actively inducing infringement under 35 U.S.C. § 271(b). In 2008, the Federal Circuit clarified that inducement requires that the alleged infringer knowingly induced the acts of another that directly infringe the patent, and that it did so with a specific intent to cause the other to infringe—that is, the accused infringer "knew or should have known his actions would induce actual infringements."[213] To show the requisite intent, both direct and circumstantial evidence of the accused infringer's state of mind may be used.[214] A party accused of inducement may wish to rely upon an opinion of counsel (for example, of noninfringement, invalidity, or unenforceability of the asserted patent) to rebut the claim that it "kn[ew] or should have known [that] its action would cause" another to directly infringe.[215]

When an accused infringer elects to rely on an opinion of counsel, it waives the attorney-client privilege to some extent.[216] The issues of the scope of the waiver (both in terms of the subject matter of the waiver and its temporal scope), and whether that waiver extends to attorney work product (including the work product of trial counsel), have been the subject of much litigation. As discussed below, the evolution of the law on waiver has arisen mostly in the context of the Federal Circuit's willfulness jurisprudence.

1. *The* EchoStar *Decision*

In *In re EchoStar Communications Corp.*,[217] an accused infringer relied on an exculpatory opinion from in-house counsel as a defense to willful infringement.[218] After commencement of the litigation, the accused infringer obtained, but chose not to rely upon, an opinion from outside legal counsel.[219] The district court held that the accused infringer waived the attorney-client privilege and work-product immunity by relying on the advice of its in-house counsel, and that the waiver extended to both in-house and outside opinion counsel. The district court ordered the accused infringer to produce all pre-suit and post-suit communications relating to the opinions it received. In addition, the district court ordered production from the outside opinion counsel of any attorney work product regarding the opinions—even if such work product was not communicated to the accused infringer.

The Federal Circuit affirmed in part the district court's order. The appeals court held that by relying on advice of its in-house counsel, the accused infringer (EchoStar) waived the attorney-client privilege with respect to any communications involving the same subject as the opinion. The waiver included communications with in-house counsel as well as the outside law firm. However, the Federal Circuit reversed that part of the district court's decision that had ordered production of attorney work product that was *not* communicated from the outside opinion counsel to its client.[220]

The Federal Circuit in *EchoStar* identified three categories of work product relevant in addressing the opinion-of-counsel defense:

1. Documents embodying communications between the client and attorney pertaining to the subject matter of the case, such as an opinion letter;
2. Documents analyzing issues but not communicated to the client reflecting an attorney's mental impression with respect to the subject matter of the case; and
3. Documents not communicated between the client and attorney but that discuss communications relating to the subject matter between the client and attorney.[221]

The court further concluded that the second category, uncommunicated work product, was not subject to the waiver because such noncommunicated work product has little or no bearing on the state of mind of the accused infringer.[222] The court affirmed the district court regarding the scope of the waiver of privilege with respect to the first and third categories of work product.

The *EchoStar* decision did not expressly address whether the waiver extended to work product of trial counsel. Nevertheless, in a footnote, the court stated that the waiver extended to advice and work product communicated after the litigation commenced.[223] This statement by the Federal Circuit led to much litigation over whether the scope of the waiver should be extended to the accused infringer's trial counsel.

One district court, applying *EchoStar*, concluded that the waiver extends to trial counsel in respect to privileged and work-product documents that contain advice central and highly material to the advice given by opinion counsel.[224] Other district courts extended the waiver to trial counsel's communications that question or contradict the opinion provided by the counsel that authored the opinion.[225] Still other district courts construed the waiver even more broadly, holding that any communications with trial counsel concerning the subject matter of infringement should be produced.[226]

2. *The* Seagate *Decision*

In August 2007, the Federal Circuit rewrote the law of willful infringement in *In re Seagate*,[227] an en banc decision that reviewed a district court order compelling an accused infringer to produce all communications between it and any counsel, including its trial counsel, on the issues of infringement, invalidity and enforceability of the patents-in-suit. The court's decision was significant in several respects.

First, the court held that proof of willful infringement requires "at least a showing of objective recklessness," which means "an objectively high likelihood that [the infringer's] actions constituted infringement of a valid patent."[228] The court in *Seagate* thus overruled the "affirmative duty of care" standard of proof for willfulness that had governed patent cases since that standard was first announced, in 1983, in *Underwater Devices, Inc. v. Morrison-Knudsen Co.*[229] The court in *Seagate* explained that "[b]ecause we abandon the affirmative duty of due care [standard], we also reemphasize that there is no affirmative obligation to obtain [an] opinion of counsel."[230]

Second, the court held that, as a general rule, where the opinion authoring attorney and trial attorney are different, the waiver of privilege caused by reliance on an opinion-of-counsel defense to willfulness does *not* constitute a waiver of the attorney-client privilege for the client's communications with its trial counsel.[231] The court explained that this rule was not absolute, and that it was possible for district courts in "unique" circumstances (such as when a party or its counsel engages in what the court referred to as "chicanery") to extend the waiver of attorney-client privilege to its trial counsel.[232]

Third, the court held that, absent exceptional circumstances, the waiver resulting from an accused infringer's reliance on an opinion-of-counsel defense to willfulness does not extend to trial counsel's work product. The court explained that "trial counsel's mental processes . . . enjoy the utmost protection from disclosure."[233] As it did with the issue of privilege, the court in *Seagate* left open the possibility that a situation might arise in which the waiver of work-product immunity could be extended to trial counsel. However, as a general rule, there is no waiver of trial counsel work product absent an unusual circumstance, such as when a party or its counsel engages in "chicanery."

Apart from any issue of waiver of work product, the court in *Seagate* reiterated the general standard for discovery of attorney work product. Under this general rule, which is not unique to patent cases, "nonopinion" work product is not discoverable unless the party seeking the discovery makes a showing of substantial need for the materials and undue hardship without it. Furthermore, "opinion work product" (i.e., the mental impressions, thought processes, analyses and conclusions of counsel) is generally not discoverable absent "exceptional circumstances."[234] Thus, the general standards for discovery of attorney work product in patent cases were not altered by the *Seagate* decision.

3. *Post-*Seagate *Decisions*

A number of district courts have had the opportunity to apply the Federal Circuit's decisions in *EchoStar* and *Seagate* in defining the scope of the waiver when the accused infringer wishes to rely upon an advice of counsel defense. Those courts have refused to extend the waiver to trial counsel unless there were "exceptional circumstances."

a. *Waiver Extended to Trial Counsel*

In *Tyco Healthcare Group LP v. E-Z-EM, Inc.*,[235] the district court held that when opinion-authoring counsel was an active member of the accused infringer's trial team, "exceptional circumstances" existed that warranted discovery of trial counsel's privileged communications and work product.

In *Tyco*, the patentee filed suit in 2007 alleging willful infringement. The accused infringer, E-Z-EM, received its first notice of infringement when it was served with the complaint. Several weeks after the lawsuit was filed, an attorney (Scott) with the law firm of Alston & Bird provided E-Z-EM with an opinion letter relating to the subjects of claim construction, invalidity, noninfringement, and unenforceability. E-Z-EM retained Alston & Bird as trial counsel, and Scott was a member of its trial team and participated actively in the case.

In March 2010, E-Z-EM produced the opinion letter intending to rely upon it in defense of the willfulness allegation.[236] Plaintiff filed a motion to compel production of every item on defendant's privilege log, as well as other communications that were not identified on the log.

The district court noted that even under the *Seagate* standard, "trial courts remain free to exercise their discretion in unique circumstances to extend waiver to trial counsel."[237] The court held that by having Scott participate on the trial team, defendant "blurred" the distinction between the distinct functions of trial counsel and opinion counsel. The court further held that if the opinion was prepared in light of trial strategy, the plaintiff had a right to discovery of such information.

The district court thus concluded that this was a case of "unique circumstances" envisioned by *Seagate*, and the court found a broad waiver. In particular, the court held that E-Z-EM waived the attorney-client privilege for all communications on the subjects included in the opinion letter. The court further found that the waived communications included those between (1) the opinion author and the client, (2) the opinion author and the rest of the trial team, and (3) the trial team and the client. The court also concluded that E-Z-EM waived work-product immunity for all attorney work product on the same subject matter included in the opinion letter to the extent that such work product was communicated to the client.[238]

In another case where the opinion coauthor was a member of the defendant's trial team, the district court conditionally permitted a deposition of that trial court. The court, however, restricted the scope of such discovery, limiting it to pre-suit communications with the client.[239]

b. Waiver Not Extended to Trial Counsel

In *Duhn Oil Tool Inc. v. Cooper Cameron Corp.*,[240] defendant asserted an opinion-of-counsel defense to plaintiff's charge of willful infringement. The opinion was on the subject of noninfringement. The authors of the opinion were from a different law firm than trial counsel. The opinion-authoring attorneys were deposed and communications between them and the client were produced. Defendant refused to produce any communications with what it characterized as "trial counsel," citing *Seagate*.

Plaintiff thereafter noticed the deposition of defendant's "in-house counsel" (Vyas) and sought his testimony and documents relating to the opinions received from opinion counsel and additional (allegedly undisclosed) opinions. According to plaintiff, Vyas and defendant's trial counsel were conducting "a separate infringement analysis" (presumably meaning separate from that of opinion counsel), and they were providing advice to the defendant on design-around options. Plaintiff argued that it was entitled "to review 'the full extent of communications and the information Mr. Vyas and [defendant] considered, as well as any other opinions regarding the subject of infringement.'"[241]

Defendant resisted this discovery, asserting that Vyas was actually its "in-house *trial* counsel," and that as such, his communications were privileged and immune from discovery under *Seagate*. Presumably to buttress this assertion, one month *after* plaintiff's motion to compel was filed, Vyas filed an application to appear *pro hac vice* (which the district court judge signed the next day).

The court granted plaintiff's motion to compel. At the outset, the court remarked that Vyas had never before during the three-year history of the litigation been identified as anything other than "in-house counsel."[242] The court further explained that it "is free to exercise its discretion in 'unique circumstance to extend waiver to trial counsel.'" It concluded that "this case presents unique circumstances justifying its finding."[243] The court ordered Vyas's deposition testimony to cover the period in time prior to the date when he filed his *pro hac vice* application. For the time period *after* the *pro hac vice* application was filed, Vyas would be considered "trial counsel" and was not subject to discovery under *Seagate*.

Where there was no issue over the separate identities of trial counsel and opinion counsel, other cases decided post-*Seagate* have limited the scope of the waiver to opinion counsel without implicating trial counsel's privilege or work product. Thus, unless there is something unique or unusual about the circumstances, courts generally will not extend the waiver to postlitigation communications with trial counsel. Furthermore, in circumstances where the opinion was received prior to the initiation of the litigation, courts following *Seagate* have limited the temporal scope of the waiver only to the pre-suit documents and communications on the grounds that any of the post-suit documents or communications were of "marginal value" to the willfulness inquiry.[244]

VII. Privilege Issues Relating to Patentee's State of Mind

A. Piercing Privilege Based on Fraud

Issues of intent in patent cases are not limited to the accused infringer's state of mind. In many patent cases, the accused infringer alleges that the patent-in-suit is unenforceable because the patentee committed inequitable conduct before the PTO. Inequitable conduct involves the alleged violation of the PTO "Rule 56" duty of disclosure, coupled with deceptive intent. An assertion of inequitable conduct places into issue the state of mind of the inventor, prosecuting attorney, and/or in-house personnel who were substantially involved in the prosecution of the suit patent. When inequitable conduct is an issue, the alleged infringer may attempt to "pierce" the patentee's attorney-client privilege under what is commonly referred to as the crime-fraud exception. This exception addresses communications made by the client to his attorney in furtherance of an ongoing or future crime or fraud.[245]

Although they are closely related and often rely upon the same evidence, common law fraud and inequitable conduct are legally distinct concepts.[246] The Federal Circuit has explained that inequitable conduct is a broader, more inclusive concept than is common law fraud.[247] To invoke the crime-fraud exception, a showing of inequitable conduct is insufficient. The party challenging the privilege "must make a *prima facie* showing that the communication was made 'in furtherance of' a crime or [common law] fraud."[248] As one district court explained in denying a motion to pierce a patent-holder's privilege, "[t]he fraud element of the crime-fraud exception must be demonstrated by evidence such that 'the proposed factual basis must strike a prudent person as constituting a reasonable basis to suspect the perpetration or attempted perpetration of a. . . . fraud, and that the communications were in furtherance thereof.'"[249]

To establish a fraud, the party challenging the privilege must show (1) a misrepresentation of a material fact, (2) with intent to deceive, (3) reliance upon the misrepresentation by the party deceived, and (4) resultant injury.[250] Common law fraud includes both affirmative misrepresentations of a material fact, as well as a failure to disclose a material fact.[251]

In establishing the fraud necessary for an accused infringer to attempt to pierce the patentee's privilege in a patent infringement case, the most difficult areas usually involve making the requisite prima facie showings of deceptive intent and detrimental reliance. Rarely is there a smoking gun that unequivocally establishes intent to deceive the PTO.[252] Thus, proof of deceptive intent normally must be inferred from the facts and circumstances surrounding the applicant's conduct.[253] While there must be a factual basis for a finding of deceptive intent,[254] the withholding of a material prior art reference can, in some cases, warrant the inference of intent to deceive the PTO.[255] Evidence of a state of mind reckless as to the consequences of a nondisclosure or misrepresentation to the PTO also can be considered the equivalent of an intent to deceive.[256]

Courts are split on the question of whether, in addition to meeting the common law standard for fraudulent intent, the party seeking to invoke the crime-fraud exception must also establish that the PTO relied on the misrepresentation. Some district courts have held that reliance need not be proven.[257] Other district courts have reached the contrary conclusion.[258] In *Nobelpharma AB v. Implant Innovations, Inc.*, for example, the district court held that "[t]he fact misrepresented must be 'the efficient, inducing, and proximate cause, or the determining ground' of the action taken in reliance thereon."[259] Although it is dicta in that case, the Federal Circuit's decision in *Spalding* also contains language suggesting that proof of reliance is necessary to pierce privilege.[260]

In deciding whether the requirements of the crime-fraud exception have been satisfied in a particular case, the district court may review the disputed documents in camera.[261] In fact, some courts hold that in camera review is required before the court can order the production of documents that would otherwise be privileged.[262] The evidentiary showing that is necessary in order to justify in camera review is less than the showing necessary to actually overcome the privilege.[263] All that is required to justify in camera review is "a factual basis adequate to support a good faith belief by a reasonable person that [the court's] review of the materials may reveal evidence to establish the claim that the crime-fraud exception applies."[264]

B. Patentee's Reliance on Privileged Communications as Waiving Privilege

A patentee that is accused of inequitable conduct may want to rely upon an opinion of the patentee's counsel that the patent owner acted in good faith or did not intend to deceive the PTO. The Federal Circuit apparently has not decided whether such an assertion would result in a waiver of privilege.[265] Applying the reasoning of *Seagate*, at least one district court that has considered this issue concluded that a patentee who relies upon privileged communications to establish a "good faith" defense to inequitable conduct waives the attorney-client privilege as to all other communications relating to the same subject matter.[266] In determining the scope of the waiver, the district court applied the standard set forth by the Federal Circuit in *Fort James Corp. v. Solo Cup Co.*[267] The district court concluded that "the waiver applies not only to otherwise privileged communications between the attorney and client, but also to any of the attorney's documents which reflect the substance of such advice, even if such documents would otherwise be immune from discovery under the work-product doctrine."[268] The court noted that the scope of the waiver did not extend to work product that was not communicated to the client.[269]

If a patentee seeks to use or put into issue privileged materials to support its position, the court may conclude that the patentee has waived the privilege. For example, in *Optimumpath, LLC v. Belkin International, Inc.*,[270] the patentee submitted during prosecution a declaration under 37 C.F.R. § 1.131 to antedate a reference. The declaration itself and some of its attached documents reflected privileged communications. The parties disputed the scope of the waiver, with plaintiff seeking a narrow waiver and defendant seeking a broad waiver. The district court concluded that the privilege was waived, and under the facts of that case determined that the subject matter and temporal scope of the waiver would be relatively narrow.[271]

VIII. Summary

There have been many published decisions on the subject of privilege and immunity in patent cases. Unfortunately, very few of those decisions are from the Federal Circuit, which has exclusive appellate jurisdiction in patent cases. Consequently, it can be difficult in any particular patent case to draw bright-line rules or to know with reasonable certainty how a district court will rule on a particular privilege or work-product issue. Because of this uncertainty, parties who anticipate litigating patent rights would be wise *not* to assume that documents they thought might be privileged will, in fact, be treated that way by the district court judge. As a general rule, parties should be careful not to make potentially embarrassing written admissions or concessions on critical issues such as patent scope, validity, or infringement, as such admissions may be discoverable. Finally, parties should also be cautious in the way they handle and disseminate legal advice, and they would be wise to institute practices to strictly limit the disclosure of such advice and to take measures that protect its confidentiality.

Notes

1. Upjohn Co. v. United States, 449 U.S. 383, 389 (1981).
2. Hickman v. Taylor, 329 U.S. 495, 506 (1947).
3. *In re* Horowitz, 482 F.2d 72, 81 (2d Cir. 1973).
4. *Upjohn Co.*, 449 U.S. at 389.
5. United States v. Schwimmer, 892 F.2d 237, 243 (2d Cir. 1989).
6. Fisher v. United States, 425 U.S. 391, 403 (1976).
7. United States v. United Shoe Mach. Corp., 89 F. Supp. 357, 358–59 (D. Mass. 1950). Although in some instances in patent cases the scope of the attorney-client privilege is governed by the Federal Circuit's standards and not by the law of the regional circuit, *see In re* Spalding Sports Worldwide, Inc., 203 F.3d 800, 804 (Fed. Cir. 2000), there does not appear to be any material difference between the *United Shoe* definition of the test for privilege and the definition applied by the Federal Circuit. *See, e.g.*, Shearing v. Iolab Corp., 975 F.2d 1541, 1546 (Fed. Cir. 1992).
8. *In re* Spalding Sports Worldwide, Inc., 203 F.3d 800, 805 (Fed. Cir. 2000).
9. Carter v. Gibbs, 909 F.2d 1450, 1451 (Fed. Cir. 1990).
10. Fort James Corp. v. Solo Cup Co., 412 F.3d 1340, 1349 (Fed. Cir. 2005); *see also* Detection Sys., Inc. v. Pittway Corp., 96 F.R.D. 152, 156 (W.D.N.Y. 1982) (citations omitted).
11. *Id.* at 154.
12. *See, e.g.*, *In re* EchoStar Commc'ns Corp, 448 F.3d 1294, 1300 (Fed. Cir. 2006); Am. Standard, Inc. v. Pfizer, Inc., 828 F.2d 734, 745 (Fed. Cir. 1987); United States v. (Under Seal), 748 F.2d 871, 874 (4th Cir. 1984); *In re* Grand Jury Subpoena Duces Tecum Dated September 15, 1983, 731 F.2d 1032, 1037 (2d Cir. 1984).
13. *Upjohn Co.*, 449 U.S. at 395.
14. *See, e.g.*, Hickman v. Taylor, 329 U.S. 495, 508 (1947) (attorney-client privilege does not cover information attorney learns from witnesses); Boling v. First Util. Dist. of Knox Cnty., No. 97-CV-832, 1998 U.S. Dist. LEXIS 21157, at *11 (E.D. Tenn. Oct. 5, 1998) (correspondence from counsel to plaintiff that is based on information learned from any person outside the plaintiff's organization is not privileged).
15. *In re* Grand Jury Subpoena, 599 F.2d 504, 511 (2d Cir. 1979) ("Participation of the general counsel does not automatically cloak the investigation with legal garb."); ABB Kent-Taylor, Inc. v. Stallings and Co., Inc., 172 F.R.D. 53, 57 (W.D.N.Y. 1996) ("The mere fact a communication is made directly to an attorney, or an attorney is copied in on a memorandum does not mean that the communication is necessarily privileged.") (citation omitted); *accord* McCook Metals L.L.C. v. Alcoa Inc., 192 F.R.D. 242, 260 (N.D. Ill. 2000); United States Postal Serv. v. Phelps Dodge Ref. Corp., 852 F. Supp. 156, 160 (E.D.N.Y. 1994).

16. Coorstek, Inc. v. Reiber, Civil No. 08-cv-01133, 2010 U.S. Dist. LEXIS 42594, at *20–21 (D. Colo. Apr. 5, 2010).
17. *Id.* at *23 (citing Kovacs v. Hershey Co., 04-cv-01881, 2006 U.S. Dist. LEXIS 77777, at *2 (D. Colo. Oct. 25, 2006)).
18. *Id.* at *23 (quoting Burton v. R.J. Reynolds Tobacco Co., Inc., 170 F.R.D. 481, 484–85 (D. Kan. 1997)).
19. *Hickman*, 329 U.S. at 495.
20. Fed. R. Civ. P. 26(b)(3). While the Federal Rules of Civil Procedure permit discovery "regarding any nonprivileged matter that is relevant to any party's claim or defense," Rule 26(b)(3) affords qualified protection to "documents and tangible things that are prepared in anticipation of litigation or for trial by or for another party or its representative."
21. *Id.*
22. *In re* Pfohl Bros. Landfill Litig., 175 F.R.D. 13, 26 (W.D.N.Y. 1997) (quoting *Hickman*, 329 U.S. at 510–11).
23. *Pfohl*, 175 F.R.D. at 26.
24. *See, e.g.*, Martin v. Bally's Park Place Hotel & Casino, 983 F.2d 1252, 1260 (3d Cir. 1993).
25. *See, e.g.*, Weil Ceramics & Glass, Inc. v. Work, 110 F.R.D. 500, 505 (E.D.N.Y. 1986).
26. United States v. Int'l Bus. Machs. Corp., 71 F.R.D. 376, 378 (S.D.N.Y. 1976).
27. Detection Sys., Inc. v. Pittway Corp., 96 F.R.D. 152, 155 (W.D.N.Y. 1982).
28. *Id.*
29. *In re* Grand Jury Proceedings, 604 F.2d 798, 802–03 (3d Cir. 1979); *see also In re* Pfizer Inc. Sec. Litig., 90 Civ. 1260, 1994 U.S. Dist. LEXIS 7454, at *5 (S.D.N.Y. June 6, 1994).
30. 203 F.3d 800 (Fed. Cir. 2000).
31. *Id.* at 803 n.2.
32. *Id.* at 804.
33. *Id.* at 805 (citations omitted).
34. *Id.* at 806.
35. *Id.* (citing Knogo Corp. v. United States, 213 U.S.P.Q. 936, 941 (Ct. Cl. 1980)). *See also* Carl Zeiss Jena GmbH v. Bio-Rad Labs., Inc., No. 98 Civ. 8012, 2000 U.S. Dist. LEXIS 5825, at *3 (S.D.N.Y. May 3, 2000) (finding *Spalding* "directly on point" and concluding that plaintiff's invention disclosure documents were protected by the attorney-client privilege).
36. Jack Winter, Inc. v. Koratron Co., 50 F.R.D. 225, 228 (N.D. Cal. 1970).
37. *Spalding*, 203 F.3d at 806 n.3 (citing *Jack Winter*, 50 F.R.D. at 228, among other cases).
38. *Id.*
39. *Id.*
40. 227 F.R.D. 382 (W.D. Pa. 2005).
41. *Id.* at 394.
42. *Id.* The district court subsequently determined that the client had waived the privilege.
43. No. 05-C-0575-C, 2006 U.S. Dist. LEXIS 57560 (W.D. Wis. Aug. 14, 2006).
44. *Id.* at *10.
45. No. 97 Civ. 8816, 2000 U.S. Dist. LEXIS 4254 (S.D.N.Y. Mar. 31, 2000).
46. *Id.* at *8–9 (emphasis added) (citations omitted).

47. *Id.* Unfortunately, the district court's opinion does not describe the precise nature of the prosecution documents it considered.
48. 192 F.R.D. 242 (N.D. Ill. 2000).
49. *Id.* at 252–53.
50. *Id.* at 253 (citing Applied Telematics, Inc. v. Sprint Commc'ns Co., No. 94-4603, 1996 U.S. Dist. LEXIS 13782 (E.D. Pa. Sept. 18, 1996)); Sneider v. Kimberly-Clark Corp., 91 F.R.D. 1, 5 (N.D. Ill. 1980).
51. 192 F.R.D. at 253.
52. 263 F.R.D. 40, 45 (D. Me. 2009).
53. 237 F.R.D. 69, 85–86 (S.D.N.Y. 2006).
54. 263 F.R.D. at 45.
55. Case No. 08 C 50078, 2010 U.S. Dist. LEXIS 5284, at *11–12 (N.D. Ill. Jan. 22, 2010).
56. Civil No. 07-cv-0894, 2009 U.S. Dist. LEXIS 111877, at *8 (S.D. Cal. Dec. 1, 2009).
57. Case No. 08-cv-0385, 2009 U.S. Dist. LEXIS 100148, at *10–11 (S.D. Cal. Oct. 27, 2009).
58. 258 F.R.D. 491, 498–99 (D. Utah 2009).
59. McCook Metals L.L.C. v. Alcoa Inc., 192 F.R.D. 242, 255 (N.D. Ill. 2000) (rejecting privilege assertion for technical drawings, sketches, tables, and test results produced from the inventors and sent to in-house patent counsel, on the basis that "[t]he documents themselves contain no request for legal advice, nor is any given, and thus fall outside the ambit of the privilege").
60. *See In re* Spalding Sports Worldwide, Inc., 203 F.3d 800, 805 (Fed. Cir. 2000).
61. *Id.*
62. *See, e.g.*, Softview Computer Prods. Corp. v. Haworth, Inc., No. 97 Civ. 8815, 2000 U.S. Dist. LEXIS 4254, at *29 (S.D.N.Y. Mar. 31, 2000) (transmittal letters, cover sheets, and other documents relating to patent prosecution not privileged); *McCook Metals*, 192 F.R.D. at 253–54 (transmittal letters and cover sheets, and communications from third party, are not privileged).
63. *Spalding*, 203 F.3d at 806.
64. *Id.* at 805 (citing Sharing v. Iolab Corp., 975 F.2d 1541, 1546 (Fed. Cir. 1992) ("The privilege protects a client's confidential communications to an attorney necessary to obtain legal counseling.")).
65. *See, e.g.*, Hickman v. Taylor, 329 U.S. 495, 508 (1947) (attorney-client privilege does not cover information attorney learns from witnesses); *McCook Metals*, 192 F.R.D. at 253–54 (attorney-client privilege does not apply to a summary of patent applications, patents, and invention reports).
66. *See, e.g.*, Itoba Ltd. v. LEP Grp. PLC, 930 F. Supp. 36, 43 (D. Conn. 1996); *In re* Brand Name Prescription Drugs Antitrust Litig., No. 94-C-897, 1995 U.S. Dist. LEXIS 16523, at *13–16 (N.D. Ill. Nov. 3, 1995); AMP, Inc. v. Fujitsu Microelectronics, Inc., 853 F. Supp. 808, 830 (M.D. Pa. 1994), *appeal dismissed*, 47 F.3d 1180 (Fed. Cir. 1995); Baxter Travenol Labs., Inc. v. Abbott Labs., No. 84-C-5103, 1987 U.S. Dist. LEXIS 10300, at *12 (N.D. Ill. June 17, 1987); Duplan Corp. v. Deering Milliken, Inc., 397 F. Supp. 1146, 1167 (D.S.C. 1974).
67. United States v. (Under Seal), 748 F.2d 871, 875 (4th Cir. 1984), *vacated on other grounds*, 757 F.2d 600 (4th Cir. 1985) (since patent examiner is a third party to whom the eventual communication will be disclosed, the communication is not intended to be privileged and therefore is not privileged); P.&B. Marina, L.P. v. Logrande, 136 F.R.D. 50, 56 (E.D.N.Y. 1991), *aff'd*, 983 F.2d 1047 (2d Cir. 1992)

("Drafts of letters or documents to third parties lack the requisite confidentiality to be protected under the attorney-client privilege."

68. *Softview*, 2000 U.S. Dist. LEXIS 4254, at *33.
69. *See, e.g.*, Glaxo, Inc. v. Novopharm Ltd., 148 F.R.D. 535, 540 (E.D.N.C. 1993); *Baxter Travenol Labs.*, 1987 U.S. Dist. LEXIS 10300, at *34–35.
70. 203 F.3d at 806.
71. *Id.*
72. *Id.*
73. *See id.* at 806 ("[A]n attorney cannot evaluate patentability or prepare a competent patent application without knowing the prior art and obtaining relevant technical information from the inventors."); *see also* Martin Marietta Materials, Inc. v. Bedford Reinforced Plastics, Inc., 227 F.R.D. 382, 394 (W.D. Pa. 2005) (prior art search was privileged).
74. *Spalding*, 203 F.3d at 804 (citing *In re* Regents of the Univ. of Cal., 101 F.3d 1386 (Fed. Cir. 1996)). *See also* McCook Metals L.L.C. v. Alcoa Inc., 192 F.R.D. 242, 251 (N.D. Ill. 2000) (applying Seventh Circuit law to whether licensing and contractual documents are privileged).
75. Bulk Lift Int'l Inc. v. Flexcon & Sys., Inc., 122 F.R.D. 482, 491 (W.D. La. 1988), *aff'd*, 122 F.R.D. 493 (1988) (quoting Choat v. Rome Indus., Inc., 462 F. Supp. 728, 732 (N.D. Ga. 1978)); *but see* Hewlett-Packard Co. v. Bausch & Lomb, Inc., 116 F.R.D. 533 (N.D. Cal. 1987).
76. Softview Computer Prods. Corp. v. Haworth, Inc., No. 97 Civ. 8815, 2000 U.S. Dist. LEXIS 4254, at *15–16 (S.D.N.Y. Mar. 31, 2000); Stryker Corp. v. Intermedics Orthopedics, Inc., 145 F.R.D. 298, 302 (E.D.N.Y. 1992) ("This court rejects the theory that litigation is a 'possibility' in every patent application.").
77. Nat'l Union Fire Ins. Co. v. Murray Sheet Metal Co., 967 F.2d 980, 984 (9th Cir. 1992).
78. Bristol-Myers Squibb Co. v. Rhone-Poulenc Rorer, Inc., No. 95 Civ. 8833, 1998 U.S. Dist. LEXIS 12, at *13–14 (S.D.N.Y. Jan. 6, 1998) (holding that patent prosecution is not work product); *Stryker Corp.*, 145 F.R.D. at 304 (same).
79. *Bristol-Myers*, 1998 U.S. Dist. LEXIS 12, at *17.
80. *Id.* at *13–14.
81. *Id. See also* Burlington Indus., Inc. v. Rossville Yarn, Inc., No. 95-CV-0401, 1997 U.S. Dist. LEXIS 10347, at *6 (N.D. Ga. June 2, 1997); *Stryker Corp.*, 145 F.R.D. at 304.
82. *Bristol-Myers*, 1998 U.S. Dist. LEXIS 12, at *14.
83. Hickman v. Taylor, 329 U.S. 495 (1947).
84. *See, e.g.*, Elkay Mfg. Co. v. Ebco Mfg. Co., No. 93-C-5106, 1995 U.S. Dist. LEXIS 473, at *35 (N.D. Ill. Jan 13, 1995) ("[G]iven that there is precedent for extending work-product immunity to *draft* patent applications prepared in anticipation of litigation, it is not unreasonable to extend the benefit of the immunity to the applications themselves.").
85. 143 F.R.D. 494, 500 (S.D.N.Y. 1992).
86. *Id.* at 499.
87. *Id.* at 501.
88. Softview Computer Prods. Corp. v. Haworth, Inc., No. 97 Civ. 8815, 2000 U.S. Dist. LEXIS 4254, at *40 (S.D.N.Y. Mar. 31, 2000) (holding that certain prosecution documents were properly withheld as work product where the patentee alleged that competitors introduced competing model one week after it filed

the patent application, and the patentee showed that it believed those models would infringe its patent once issued. The court held that "the challenged documents . . . reflect that counsel's claim drafting and prosecution of the patent application were informed by Haworth's anticipation of litigation against its competitors once the '798 patent' issued.").

89. United States v. United Shoe Mach. Corp., 89 F. Supp. 357, 358–59 (D. Mass. 1950).
90. 09 Civ. 4373, 2010 U.S. Dist. LEXIS 65871 (S.D.N.Y. June 29, 2010).
91. *Id.* at *16–17.
92. *Id.* at *22 (quoting United States v. Boffa, 513 F. Supp. 517, 523 (D. Del. 1981) and citing United States v. Rivera, 837 F. Supp. 565, 568 n.1 (S.D.N.Y. 1993) ("It is common ground among the parties that the attorney-client privilege attaches to confidential communications made to an individual in the genuine, but mistaken, belief that he is an attorney."))
93. *Id.* at *22 (quoting Fin. Techs. Int'l Inc. v. Smith, 99 Civ. 9351, 2000 U.S. Dist. LEXIS 18220, at *6 (S.D.N.Y. Dec. 19, 2000)).
94. A "registered patent agent" refers to an individual who is licensed to practice before the PTO. 35 U.S.C. § 31; 37 C.F.R. § 10.6(b).
95. E.I. DuPont de Nemours & Co. v. Macdermid, Inc., Civil Action No. 06-3383, 2009 U.S. Dist. LEXIS 85436 (D.N.J. Sept. 17, 2009) (surveying conflicting cases) (unpublished).
96. *See, e.g.*, *id.* at *11–12 (D.N.J. Sept. 17, 2009) (refusing to apply attorney-client privilege to communications with in-house patent agent based on her status as a patent agent since such communications were not in connection with the preparation or prosecution of a patent application and it was not shown that the agent was acting under the control of an attorney); *In re* Rivastigmine Patent Litig., 237 F.R.D. 69, 111–12 (S.D.N.Y. 2006) (declining to extend the attorney-client privilege to communications between clients and U.S. patent agents); Agfa Corp. v. Creo Prods., Inc., No. 00-10836, 2002 U.S. Dist. LEXIS 14269 (D. Mass. Aug. 1, 2002) (concluding that communications to a patent agent are not privileged unless made for the purpose of obtaining legal advice from an attorney); McCook Metals, L.L.C. v. Alcoa, Inc., 192 F.R.D. 242, 256 (N.D. Ill. 2000) (commenting that generally communications from patent agents are not protected by the attorney-client privilege); Santrade, Ltd. v. Gen. Elec. Co., 150 F.R.D. 539, 546 (E.D.N.C. 1993) ("Generally, communications with patent agents, American or foreign, are not subject to privilege in the United States."); Burroughs Wellcome Co. v. Barr Labs., Inc., 143 F.R.D. 611, 616–17 (E.D.N.C. 1992) (same); Detection Sys., Inc. v. Pittway Corp., 96 F.R.D. 152, 155 (W.D.N.Y. 1982) (same); Sneider v. Kimberly-Clark Corp., 91 F.R.D. 1, 5 (N.D. Ill. 1980) ("Notwithstanding the quasi-legal service patent agents render, courts have declined to extend the privilege to the patent agent."); Mead Digital Sys., Inc. v. A.B. Dick Co., 89 F.R.D. 318, 320 (S.D. Ohio 1980) ("There can be no doubt that if Rouse were a domestic patent advisor and had communications to a domestic client through the documents at issue, then no attorney-client privilege could be asserted by the client because Rouse is not a member of the bar of any court."); Duplan Corp. v. Deering Milliken, Inc., 397 F. Supp. 1146, 1169 (D.S.C. 1974) ("The federal courts have refused to extend the attorney-client privilege to encompass *American* patent agents.").
97. *See, e.g.*, Saxholm AS v. Dynal, Inc., 164 F.R.D. 331, 337 (E.D.N.Y. 1996).

98. The weight of authority holds that the attorney-client privilege applies to confidential communications with patent agents acting under the authority and control of counsel. Cargill, Inc. v. Sears Petroleum & Transp. Corp., No. 03-530, 2003 U.S. Dist. LEXIS 27543, at *4–5 (N.D.N.Y. Sept. 17, 2003) (applying attorney-client privilege to nonattorney patent agent when patent agent is acting under instructions of attorney and assisting attorney in providing legal services); Willemijn Houdstermaatschaapij BV v. Apollo Computer Inc., 707 F. Supp. 1429, 1446 (D. Del. 1989) (finding that attorney-client privilege may apply to communications of nonattorney patent agent working at direction, and under supervision, of an attorney); Cuno, Inc. v. Pall Corp., 121 F.R.D. 198, 204 (E.D.N.Y. 1988); *accord* Stryker Corp. v. Intermedics Orthopedics, Inc., 145 F.R.D. 298, 304 (E.D.N.Y. 1992).
99. *See, e.g.*, United States v. Alvarez, 519 F.2d 1036, 1045–46 (3d Cir. 1975) (privilege applies to communications with psychiatrist assisting attorney); United States v. Cote, 456 F.2d 142, 144 (8th Cir. 1972) (privilege applies to communications with accountant assisting attorney).
100. *See, e.g.*, Polyvision Corp. v. Smart Techs. Inc., No. 03-476, 2006 U.S. Dist. LEXIS 12688, at *3 (W.D. Mich. Mar. 7, 2006) (recognizing that attorney-client privilege applies to registered patent agents for limited purpose of presenting and prosecuting patent applications before the PTO); Foseco Int'l Ltd. v. Fireline, Inc., 546 F. Supp. 22, 25 (N.D. Ohio 1982) ("Communications between a patent agent and a client may be privileged, however, where the patent proceeding is before the United States Patent Office and the patent agent is registered with that office. . . ."); *In re* Ampicillin Antitrust Litig., 81 F.R.D. 377, 393 (D.D.C. 1978); Hercules, Inc. v. Exxon Corp., 434 F. Supp. 136, 146 (D. Del. 1977); Vernitron Med. Prods., Inc. v. Baxter Labs., Inc., 186 U.S.P.Q. 324 (D.N.J. 1975).
101. 373 U.S. 379 (1963).
102. *Id.* at 383.
103. *Id.*
104. 81 F.R.D. 377, 393 (D.D.C. 1978).
105. *Id.* at 394.
106. Sperry v. Florida, 373 U.S. 379, 386 (1963).
107. John Labatt Ltd. v. Molson Breweries, 898 F. Supp. 471, 475 (E.D. Mich. 1995).
108. *Id.*
109. *Id.* (internal citations omitted).
110. *See, e.g., In re* Lindsey, 158 F.3d 1263, 1270 (D.C. Cir. 1998).
111. *See, e.g.*, Willemijn Houdstermaatschaapij BV v. Apollo Computer Inc., 707 F. Supp. 1429, 1444 n.21 (D. Del. 1989) ("[V]irtually all *patent attorneys* in Europe have *only* a technical or scientific background and, with rare exceptions, have no legal training and are not members of the bar.").
112. Golden Trade, S.r.L. v. Lee Apparel Co., 143 F.R.D. 514, 518 (S.D.N.Y. 1992).
113. *Id.* at 517 (citing United States v. Goldberger & Dubin, P.C., 935 F.2d 501, 505 (2d Cir. 1991)).
114. *See, e.g.*, Duttle v. Bandler & Kass, 127 F.R.D. 46, 52 (S.D.N.Y. 1989); Burlington Indus. v. Exxon Corp., 65 F.R.D. 26, 40 (D. Md. 1974); *accord* Status Time Corp. v. Sharp Elecs. Corp., 95 F.R.D. 27, 32–33 (S.D.N.Y. 1982).
115. *See, e.g.*, McCook Metals L.L.C. v. Alcoa Inc., 192 F.R.D. 242, 256 (N.D. Ill. 2000).
116. *See, e.g.*, Odone v. Croda Int'l PLC, 950 F. Supp. 10, 12–13 (D.D.C. 1997); *In re* Ampicillin Antitrust Litig., 81 F.R.D. 377, 391 (D.D.C. 1978); Duplan Corp. v. Deering Milliken, Inc., 397 F. Supp. 1146, 1169 (D.S.C. 1975).

117. *Golden Trade*, 143 F.R.D. at 520 (quoting *Duplan Corp.*, 397 F. Supp. at 1170). *See also* VLT Corp. v. Unitrode Corp., 194 F.R.D. 8, 15 (D. Mass. 2000).
118. *See Golden Trade*, 143 F.R.D. at 520 (citing cases).
119. *In re* Rivastigmine Patent Litig., 239 F.R.D. 351, 356 (S.D.N.Y. 2006); Softview Computer Prods. Corp. v. Haworth, Inc., No. 97 Civ. 8815, 2000 U.S. Dist. LEXIS 4254, at *36–37 (S.D.N.Y. Mar. 31, 2000) (quoting Bristol-Myers Squibb Co. v. Rhone-Poulenc Rorer, Inc., No. 95 Civ. 8833, 1998 U.S. Dist. LEXIS 4213, at *2 (S.D.N.Y. Apr. 2, 1998); *see also* Adver. to Women, Inc. v. Gianni Versace S.p.A., No. 98-C-1553, 1999 U.S. Dist. LEXIS 12263 (N.D. Ill. Aug. 4, 1999).
120. *VLT*, 194 F.R.D. at 15.
121. *Id.*
122. *Id.*; *see also* Smithkline Beecham Corp. v. Apotex Corp., 193 F.R.D. 530, 536 n.6 (N.D. Ill. 2000); *Golden Trade*, 143 F.R.D. at 521.
123. *VLT*, 194 F.R.D. at 15. *See also* Bayer AG v. Barr Labs., Inc., No. 92 Civ. 0381, 1994 U.S. Dist. LEXIS 17988 (S.D.N.Y. Dec. 16, 1994); *Golden Trade*, 143 F.R.D. at 521.
124. *VLT*, 194 F.R.D. at 16 (quoting RESTATEMENT (SECOND) OF CONFLICT OF LAWS § 139(2) (1988 Rev.) ("[W]hen the sovereign with the most significant relationship with the communication recognizes a privilege not recognized in the forum state, the communication should be disclosed under the policy of the forum state unless the foreign state's interest overrides.")).
125. Astra Aktiebolag v. Andrx Pharm. Inc., 208 F.R.D. 92, 98 (S.D.N.Y. 2002).
126. *VLT*, 194 F.R.D. at 15 (applying a combination approach).
127. *See In re* Rivastigmine Patent Litig., 237 F.R.D. 69, 75 (S.D.N.Y. 2006) (analyzing privilege claims under the laws of various countries); Saxholm AS v. Dynal, Inc., 164 F.R.D. 331, 337–38 (E.D.N.Y. 1996) ("The plaintiffs here have similarly failed to provide evidence that the attorney-client privilege applies to communications with their foreign patent agents regarding Danish patent applications, and this court accordingly finds that their claims of privilege are not substantiated."); Santrade, Ltd. v. Gen. Elec. Co., 150 F.R.D. 539, 546 (E.D.N.C. 1993) ("The burden, therefore, rests upon Sandvik to show, as to each country, that 'the attorney-client privilege extends to patent attorneys and/or patent agents and that the communications were intended to be confidential and not merely passed on to a patent examiner.'") (quoting Burroughs Wellcome Co. v. Barr Labs., Inc., 143 F.R.D. 611, 617 (E.D.N.C. 1992)).
128. Smithkline Beecham Corp. v. Apotex Corp., 193 F.R.D. 530, 535 (N.D. Ill. 2000) (citing McCook Metals L.L.C. v. Alcoa Inc., 192 F.R.D. 242, 256 (N.D. Ill. 2000)).
129. *McCook Metals*, 192 F.R.D. at 256.
130. *Id.*; *see also Burroughs Wellcome*, 143 F.R.D. at 617 ("The burden rests upon BW Co. to establish that, as to each country, the attorney-client privilege extends to patent attorneys and/or patent agents *and* that the communications were intended to be confidential and not merely passed on to a patent examiner.").
131. *McCook Metals*, 192 F.R.D. at 256.
132. *Id.* at 257; *see also Burroughs Wellcome*, 143 F.R.D. at 616; Baxter Travenol Labs., Inc. v. Abbott Labs., No. 84-C-5103, 1987 U.S. Dist. LEXIS 10300, at *21 (N.D. Ill. June 17, 1987); Foseco Int'l Ltd. v. Fireline, Inc., 546 F. Supp. 22, 25–26 (N.D. Ohio 1982); Mendenhall v. Barber-Greene Co., 531 F. Supp. 951, 954 (N.D. Ill. 1982).
133. Santrade, Ltd. v. Gen. Elec. Corp., 150 F.R.D. 539, 547 (E.D.N.C. 1993) (no privilege for either Japanese patent agent or attorney); *Burroughs Wellcome*, 143 F.R.D. at 623–24 (no privilege for Japanese patent agent); Alpex Computer Corp. v. Nintendo Co., No. 86 Civ. 1749, 1992 U.S. Dist. LEXIS 3129, at *5–7 (S.D.N.Y. Mar.

9, 1992) (no privilege for Japanese patent agent); Detection Sys., Inc. v. Pittway Corp., 96 F.R.D. 152, 156 (W.D.N.Y. 1982) (no privilege for Japanese patent agent).

134. OKI Am., Inc. v. Advanced Micro Devices, Inc., No. C-04-3171, 2006 U.S. Dist LEXIS 66441, at *9–10 (N.D. Cal. Aug. 31, 2006); Murata Mfg. Co. v. Bel Fuse Inc., No. 03-C-2934, 2005 U.S. Dist. LEXIS 37774, at *5–6 (N.D. Ill. Feb. 3, 2005); Knoll Pharm. Co. v. Teva Pharm. USA, Inc., No. 01-C-1646, 2004 U.S. Dist. LEXIS 24057, at *11 (N.D. Ill. Nov. 19, 2004).
135. *See* Eisai Ltd. v. Dr. Reddy's Labs. Inc., 406 F. Supp. 2d 341, 345 (S.D.N.Y. 2005).
136. VLT Corp. v. Unitrode Corp., 194 F.R.D. 8, 17 (D. Mass. 2000) ("[T]he court believes that Japanese law would treat the [document in question] as privileged."). *See also* Murata Mfg. Co. v. Bel Fuse, Inc., 2005 U.S. Dist. LEXIS 37774, at *9 (N.D. Ill. Feb. 3, 2005) (stating that "it seems clear that Japanese law extends the attorney-client privilege to confidential communications involving patent agents or attorneys").
137. 406 F. Supp. 2d 341 (S.D.N.Y. 2005).
138. *Id.* at 343.
139. *Id.*
140. McClarin Plastics, Inc. v. LRV Acquisition Corp., 1999 U.S. App. LEXIS 15491 (Fed. Cir. July 12, 1999) (declining to decide whether communications with French patent agents are or are not privileged) (unpublished decision).
141. 188 F.R.D. 189, 200 (S.D.N.Y. 1999).
142. *See also In re* Rivastigmine Patent Litig., 237 F.R.D. 69, 92 (S.D.N.Y. 2006) (no privilege found where plaintiff failed to present evidence of French law).
143. *See* McCook Metals L.L.C. v. Alcoa, Inc., 192 F.R.D. 242 (N.D. Ill. 2000) (privilege applies for communications between French patent agents and their clients); Duplan Corp. v. Deering Milliken, Inc., 397 F. Supp. 1146, 1170 (D.S.C. 1975); *see also* Baxter Travenol Labs., Inc. v. Abbott Labs., No. 84-C-5103, 1987 U.S. Dist. LEXIS 10300 (N.D. Ill. June 17, 1987) (recognizing privilege for confidential communications between French patent agents and client) (dicta).
144. 397 F. Supp. 1146, 1170 (D.S.C. 1975).
145. *Id.* at 1171.
146. *See* Commissariat a L'Energie Atomique v. Samsung Elec. Co., 245 F.R.D. 177, 182 (D. Del. 2007). Specifically, Article L. 422-11 provides:

    > In all matters and for all services referred to in Article L. 422-1, the industrial property attorney shall observe professional secrecy. Such secrecy extends to all consultations addressed to or destined to his client, to professional correspondences exchanged with his client, a colleague or attorney, to discussion notes, and more generally, to all the documents of the file.

147. *Id.*
148. *Id.*
149. *Id.*
150. *Id.* at 190. This case provides an excellent discussion of the evolution of French law insofar as it relates to privilege in the context of intellectual property matters.
151. *See* Astra Aktiebolag v. Andrx Pharm., Inc., 208 F.R.D. 92, 99–100 (S.D.N.Y. 2002) (client communications with German patent agent privileged); McCook Metals L.L.C. v. Alcoa, Inc., 192 F.R.D. 242 (N.D. Ill. 2000) (privilege applies for communications between German patent agents and clients); Softview Computer

Prods. Corp. v. Haworth, Inc., No. 97 Civ. 8815, 2000 U.S. Dist. LEXIS 4254, at *37 (S.D.N.Y. Mar. 31, 2000) (German law protects communications between a patent agent and his or her clients.); Santrade, Ltd. v. Gen. Elec. Co., 150 F.R.D. 539, 547 (E.D.N.C. 1993) (same); Golden Trade, S.r.L. v. Lee Apparel Co., 143 F.R.D. 514, 524 (S.D.N.Y. 1992) (same).

152. Baxter Travenol Labs., Inc. v. Abbott Labs., No. 84-C-5103, 1987 U.S. Dist. LEXIS 10300, at *22–23 (N.D. Ill. June 17, 1987). In that case, however, it seems clear that the court based its decision on the patentee's failure to present sufficient evidence of German law.
153. *See* 2M Asset Mgmt., LLC. v. Netmass, Inc., No. 06-CV-215, 2007 U.S. Dist. LEXIS 14098, at *10 (E.D. Tex. Feb. 28, 2007); *Astra Aktiebolag*, 208 F.R.D. at 99–100.
154. *See, e.g.*, Smithkline Beecham Corp. v. Apotex Corp., 193 F.R.D. 530, 535 (N.D. Ill. 2000) ("Communications with patent agents have been deemed to be privileged under British law since 1968. At that time, the Civil Evidence Act extended the privilege to communications with patent agents."); *accord In re* Ampicillin Antitrust Litig., 81 F.R.D. 377, 391 (D.D.C. 1978); Duplan Corp. v. Deering Milliken, Inc., 397 F. Supp. 1146, 1169–70 (D.S.C. 1974).
155. 237 F.R.D. 69 (S.D.N.Y. 2006).
156. *Id.* at 109.
157. Mead Digital Sys., Inc. v. A.B. Dick Co., 89 F.R.D. 318, 320–21 (S.D. Ohio 1980).
158. Astra Aktiebolag v. Andrx Pharm. Inc., 208 F.R.D. 92 (S.D.N.Y. 2002) (finding communications between Astra employees, Astra's in-house counsel, and Astra's outside Korean counsel, regarding Korean court procedure, Korean Patent Office procedure, and various issues of trial strategy, privileged).
159. *Id.* at 102.
160. *Id.*
161. *Id.*
162. Law of the People's Republic of China on Lawyers (promulgated by the Standing Comm. Nat'l People's Cong., May 15, 1996, effective Jan. 1, 1997), art. 33.
163. Law of Civil Procedure of the People's Republic of China (promulgated by the fourth session of the seventh Nat'l People's Cong., Apr. 9, 1991). *See also* Gui Hongxia & Li Xiang, *Attorney-Client Privilege: Extended to Foreign Lawyers in China?*, China L. Insight, Apr. 1, 2009, http://www.chinalawinsight.com/2009/04/articles/corporate/attorneyclient-privilege-extended-to-foreign-lawyers-in-china/ (last visited July 15, 2010).
164. Law of the People's Republic of China on Lawyers (promulgated by the Standing Comm. Nat'l People's Cong., May 15, 1996, effective Jan. 1, 1997), art. 45, § 1.
165. *See* Hongxia & Xiang, *supra* note 163.
166. Rule 153, Attorney Client Evidentiary Privilege, Decision of the Administrative Council of 07.12.2006 (CA/D 10/06) (OJ EPO 2007, 8 and Special edition 1/2007), http://www.epo.org/law-practice/legal-texts/html/epc/2010/e/r153.html.
167. Specifically, Rule 153 of the European Patent Convention provides that:

> (1) Where advice is sought from a professional representative in his capacity as such, all communications between the professional representative and his client or any other person, relating to that purpose and falling under Article 2 of the Regulation on discipline for professional representatives, are permanently privileged from disclosure in proceedings before the European Patent Office, unless such privilege is expressly waived by the client.

(2) Such privilege from disclosure shall apply, in particular, to any communication or document relating to:
   (a) the assessment of the patentability of an invention;
   (b) the preparation or prosecution of a European patent application;
   (c) any opinion relating to the validity, scope of protection or infringement of a European patent or a European patent application.

168. *See* Sanofi-Synthelabo v. Apotex Inc., 299 F. Supp. 2d 303, 307–08 (S.D.N.Y. 2004) (finding that communications between Sanofi and its outside European patent attorney were privileged, but ultimately that the privilege had been waived); Solvay, S.A. v. Honeywell Specialty Materials, LLC, No. 06-557-SLR (D. Del. Jan. 16, 2008) (order specifically recognizing the existence of a European patent attorney privilege) (unpublished).
169. *See* 19 U.S.C. § 1337(a)(1)(B)–(D) (2010).
170. *See* 19 U.S.C. § 1337(d) (2010).
171. Some ALJs require a "discovery committee" to be formed and provide that "[n]o motion to compel discovery may be filed unless the subject matter of the motion has first been brought to the Discovery Committee and the Committee has reached an impasse in resolving the matter." *See Certain Silicon Microphone Packages and Products Containing the Same*, 337-TA-695, Order No. 19 (May 21, 2010) (ALJ Robert K. Rogers, Jr.).
172. For exceptions to this general rule, see 19 C.F.R. § 210.24 (2010).
173. 19 C.F.R. § 210.24(b)(2) (2010).
174. A LAWYER'S GUIDE TO SECTION 337 INVESTIGATIONS BEFORE THE U.S. INTERNATIONAL TRADE COMMISSION 117–18 (Tom M. Schaumberg ed., 2010). Schaumberg notes that because extensive prefiling due diligence is required before submitting a complaint to the ITC, questions may arise as to whether communications and work-product conducted precomplaint will be protected by an evidentiary privilege. In recognizing that an evidentiary privilege normally attaches, Schaumberg makes three general observations:

> First, tests conducted specifically for the purpose of determining whether to file a lawsuit, at the request of counsel and not performed for other purposes within the regular course of business, are protected as privileged. Second, the identity of entities whose existence as a possible infringer became known solely through the investigatory efforts of counsel or their agents constitutes protected work product. Third, the rationale for not alleging infringement by certain entities is protected by attorney-client privilege (and likely work product as well).

Id. at 118. Work-product immunity is also extended to tests and data collected for the purpose of determining whether a complaint should be filed. *Id.*

175. *Id.* at 118 (citing Certain Anisotropically Etched One Megabit & Greater DRAMS, Components Thereof, & Prods. Containing Such DRAMS, Inv. No. 337-TA-345, Comm'n Op. at 3 (Sept. 22, 1993)).
176. DONALD KNOX DUVALL ET AL., UNFAIR COMPETITION AND THE ITC: ACTIONS BEFORE THE INTERNATIONAL TRADE COMMISSION UNDER SECTION 337 of THE TARIFF ACT OF 1930 § 4:41, at 227 (2009 ed.) (citing Commercial Food Portioners, Inv. No. 337-TA-339, Order 32 (Dec. 9, 1992)).
177. *See* Schaumberg, *supra* note 174, at 119–22. Schaumberg points to multiple Orders from various ALJs extending the attorney-client privilege to foreign

attorneys or patent agents. *See, e.g.*, Certain Tape Dispensers, Inv. No. 337-TA-354, Notice to All Parties, at 1 (July 19, 1993); Certain Integrated Circuit Telecomm. Chips & Prods. Containing Same, Including Dialing Apparatus, Inv. No. 337-TA-337, Order No. 109, at 3 (Nov. 23, 1992).

178. *Id.* at 122 (quoting Certain Fluidized Bed Combustion Sys., Inv. No. 337-TA-213, Order No. 14, at 1 (June 21, 1985)).
179. 37 C.F.R. § 1.601(l).
180. 37 C.F.R. § 41.150.
181. 37 C.F.R. § 41.150(b)(1)(i) and (2).
182. 37 C.F.R. § 41.150(c)(1). A party may also obtain production of documents "during cross examination of an opponent's witness" or when testimony is compelled.
183. 37 C.F.R. § 41 (2005).
184. 81 U.S.P.Q.2d (BNA) 1342 (BPAI 2005) (nonprecedential). *See generally* Charles Gholz, *When Does Reliance on Attorney Diligence Waive the Attorney-Client Privilege?*, 13 INTELL. PROP. TODAY 4, 24 (2006).
185. *Ginter*, 81 U.S.P.Q.2d (BNA) at 1344–45.
186. *Id.* at 1345.
187. *Id.* at 1346.
188. *Id.*
189. *Id.* at 1346–47.
190. *Id.* at 1347.
191. *Id.*
192. *Id.* at 1348.
193. *Id.*
194. *Id.*
195. Duplan Corp. v. Deering Milliken, Inc., 397 F. Supp. 1146, 1161 (D.S.C. 1974).
196. *See* United States v. Nobles, 422 U.S. 225, 239 (1975).
197. *See, e.g.*, VLT Corp. v. Unitrode Corp., 194 F.R.D. 8, 11 (D. Mass. 2000).
198. FED. R. CIV. P. 26(b)(5) advisory committee's note (2006).
199. *VLT*, 194 F.R.D. at 11.
200. *Id.*
201. S. 2450, 110th Cong. (2008). The act was signed into law on September 19, 2008, and is effective "in all proceedings commenced after September 19, 2008 and, insofar as just and practicable, in all proceedings pending on September 19." FED. R. EVID. 502.
202. FED. R. EVID. 502(a).
203. *Id.* at 502(b).
204. 1:08CV00050, 2010 U.S. Dist. LEXIS 54407 (W.D. Va. June 2, 2010).
205. *Id.*, 2010 U.S. Dist. LEXIS 54407, at *4–6.
206. *See, e.g.*, Alcon Mfg., Ltd. v. Apotex Inc., 1:06-cv-1642, 2008 U.S. Dist. LEXIS 96630, at *11–18 (S.D. Ind. Nov. 26, 2008).
207. *See, e.g.*, *Alcon Mfg.*, 2008 U.S. Dist. LEXIS 96630, at *9–11 (finding that inadvertent production did not waive privilege under the terms of the protective order); United States v. Pepper's Steel & Alloys, Inc., 742 F. Supp. 641, 644–45 (S.D. Fla. 1990) (refusing to order production where the protective order provided that there would be no waiver of any privilege); Eutectic Corp. v. Metco, Inc., 61 F.R.D. 35, 52 (E.D.N.Y. 1973) (same).
208. *VLT*, 194 F.R.D. at 12 n.2 (quoting Harmony Gold USA, Inc. v. FASA Corp., 169 F.R.D. 113, 116 (N.D. Ill. 1996)).

209. Transonic Sys., Inc. v. Non-Invasive Med. Tech., 192 F.R.D. 710, 715 (D. Utah 2000).
210. *See* Amgen, Inc. v. Hoechst Marion Roussel, Inc., 190 F.R.D. 287, 292–93 (D. Mass. 2000) (mistaken production of 200 privileged documents constituting thousands of pages not inadvertent).
211. *Transonic Sys.*, 192 F.R.D. at 715–16; Vakharia v. Swedish Covenant Hosp., No. 90-C-6548, 1993 U.S. Dist. LEXIS 11411 (N.D. Ill. Aug. 16, 1993).
212. One survey, though now somewhat dated, put the figure at over 90 percent. *See* Kimberly A. Moore, *Empirical Statistics on Willful Patent Infringement*, 14 Fed. Cir. B.J. 227, 232 (2005). Although the author is unaware of any more recent empirical data, it would appear likely that the frequency of willfulness allegations has diminished based on the stricter standards for willfulness set forth in the Federal Circuit's en banc decision in *In re* Seagate, 497 F.3d 1360 (Fed. Cir. 2007).
213. DSU Med. Corp. v. JMS Co., 471 F.3d 1293, 1306 (Fed. Cir. 2006) (quoting Manville Sales Corp. v. Paramount Sys., Inc., 917 F.2d 544, 553 (Fed. Cir. 1990)).
214. *Id.*
215. *See, e.g.*, Broadcom Corp. v. Qualcomm Inc., 543 F.3d 683, 699 (Fed. Cir. 2008) (quoting *DSU*, 471 F.3d at 1305)).
216. F & G Scrolling Mouse, L.L.C. v. IBM Corp., 190 F.R.D. 385, 391 (M.D.N.C. 1999).
217. 448 F.3d 1294 (Fed. Cir. 2006).
218. *Id.* at 1297.
219. *Id.*
220. *Id.* at 1303–04.
221. *Id.* at 1302.
222. *Id.* at 1302–04.
223. *Id.* at 1302 n.4.
224. Informatica Corp. v. Bus. Objects Data Integration, Inc., No. C-02-2378, 2006 U.S. Dist. LEXIS 58976 (N.D. Cal. Aug. 9, 2006).
225. Intex Recreation Corp. v. Team Worldwide Corp., 439 F. Supp. 2d 46 (D.D.C. 2006).
226. *See* Convolve, Inc. v. Compaq Computer Corp., 224 F.R.D. 98 (S.D.N.Y. 2004).
227. 497 F.3d 1360 (Fed. Cir. 2007).
228. *Id.* at 1371.
229. 717 F.2d 1380 (1983).
230. *Seagate*, 497 F.3d at 1371.
231. *Id.* at 1373.
232. *Id.* at 1374–75.
233. *Id.* at 1375–76.
234. *Id.* at 1375.
235. 2:07-CV-262, 2010 U.S. Dist. LEXIS 51512 (E.D. Tex. May 24, 2010).
236. *Id.* at *5–7.
237. *Id.* at *9 (quoting *Seagate*, 497 F.3d at 1374–75).
238. *Id.* at *12–13.
239. *See, e.g.*, Newriver, Inc. v. Newkirk Prods., Inc., 1:08-MISC-61, 2008 U.S. Dist. LEXIS 112064, at *7–12 (N.D.N.Y. Dec. 4, 2008) (where coauthor of opinion also served as trial counsel, court permitted the deposition of trial counsel but strictly limited the scope of the waiver only to certain prelitigation communications and not to postlitigation communications or work product).

240. 1:05-cv-01411, 2009 U.S. Dist. LEXIS 100669 (E.D. Cal. Oct. 15, 2009).
241. *Id.* at *5.
242. *Id.* at *41.
243. *Id.*
244. *See, e.g.*, V. Mane Fils, S.A. v. Int'l Flavors & Fragrances Inc., 06-2304, 2009 U.S. Dist. LEXIS 56462, at *14 (D.N.J. July 1, 2009) (refusing request to order production of post-suit documents pertaining to willful infringement); Se-Kure Controls, Inc. v. Diam USA, Inc., No. 06 C 4857, at *8–9 (N.D. Ill. Jan. 17, 2008) (requiring production of communications prior to the filing of the litigation); SPX Corp. v. Bartec USA, LLC, 247 F.R.D. 516, 526–27 (E.D. Mich. 2008) (communications with trial counsel that postdate the filing of the litigation "most likely have bearing on the question of willfulness or [defendant's] reliance upon counsel's advice to shape its accused pre-suit conduct"); Convolve, Inc. v. Compaq Computer Corp., 2007 U.S. Dist. LEXIS 87286, at *13 (S.D.N.Y. Nov. 27, 2007) (following *Seagate* and holding that "there is no basis for taking discovery of in-house counsel's communications after the litigation was commenced").
245. United States v. Zolin, 491 U.S. 554, 563 (1989); Clark v. United States, 289 U.S. 1, 15 (1933); *In re* Antitrust Grand Jury, 805 F.2d 155, 162 (6th Cir. 1986).
246. Nobelpharma AB v. Implant Innovations, Inc., 141 F.3d 1059, 1070–72 (Fed. Cir. 1998).
247. *Id.*
248. *In re* Spalding Sports Worldwide, Inc., 203 F.3d 800, 807 (Fed. Cir. 2000) (citations omitted).
249. Ergo Licensing, LLC v. Carefusion 303, Inc., 263 F.R.D. 40, 49 (D. Me. 2009) (quoting Fuller v. Interview, Inc., No. 07 CIV 5728, 2009 U.S. Dist. LEXIS 93157, at *5 (S.D.N.Y. Sept. 30, 2009)).
250. *Spalding*, 203 F.3d at 807.
251. *See, e.g.*, Restatement (Second) of Torts 551(1).
252. *See* Paragon Podiatry Lab. v. KLM Labs., 984 F.2d 1182, 1189–90 (Fed. Cir. 1993); LaBounty Mfg., Inc. v. United States Int'l Trade Comm'n, 958 F.2d 1066, 1076 (Fed. Cir. 1992).
253. Molins PLC v. Textron, Inc., 48 F.3d 1172, 1180–81 (Fed. Cir. 1995).
254. Hebert v. Lisle Corp., 99 F.3d 1109, 1116 (Fed. Cir. 1996) (citing Kingsdown Med. Consultants v. Hollister, Inc. 863 F.2d 867 (Fed. Cir. 1988)).
255. Baxter Int'l Inc. v. McGaw Inc., 149 F.3d 1321, 1330 (Fed. Cir. 1998) (affirming district court's determination that withholding highly material prior art manifested a culpable state of mind sufficient to warrant a finding of an intent to deceive the PTO).
256. Nobelpharma AB v. Implant Innovations, Inc., 141 F.3d 1059, 1069–70 (Fed. Cir. 1998).
257. Manville Sales Corp. v. Paramount Sys., Inc., No. 86-4157, 1987 U.S. Dist. LEXIS 10400, at *15 (E.D. Pa. Sept. 19, 1987); Synair Corp. v. Am. Indus. Tire, Inc., 645 F. Supp. 1080, 1085 (S.D. Tex. 1986).
258. *See, e.g.*, Domestic Sales Corp. v. Intertherm, Inc., No. S87-81, 1988 U.S. Dist. LEXIS 19362, at *34, *36–37 (N.D. Ind. Mar. 28, 1988); Research Corp. v. Gourmet's Delight Mushroom Co., 560 F. Supp. 811, 820 (E.D. Pa. 1983).
259. 141 F.3d at 1070 (quoting Norton v. Curtiss, 433 F.2d 779, 794 (C.C.P.A. 1970)).
260. *In re* Spalding Sports Worldwide, Inc., 203 F.3d 800, 806–07 (Fed. Cir. 2000).
261. United States v. Zolin, 491 U.S. 554, 565–70 (1989).

262. *In re* Antitrust Grand Jury, 805 F.2d 155, 168–69 (6th Cir. 1986).
263. *Zolin*, 491 U.S. at 570–72.
264. *Id.* at 572 (internal quotes and citation omitted).
265. *See* Brigham & Women's Hosp. Inc. v. Teva Pharms. USA, Inc., No. 08-464, 2010 U.S. Dist. LEXIS 31573, at *14–15 (D. Del. Mar. 31, 2010).
266. *Id.* at *19–20.
267. 412 F.3d 1340, 1349 (Fed. Cir. 2005).
268. 2010 U.S. Dist. LEXIS 31573, at *20.
269. *Id.* at *21 n.8.
270. C 09-1398 CW, 2010 U.S. Dist. LEXIS 65532 (N.D. Cal. June 8, 2010).
271. *Id.* at *10–18.

CHAPTER 18

A Second Look at Privilege and Confidentiality in the Reinsurance Arena*

JOHN W. THORNTON
JANE THORNTON MASTRUCCI
CYNTHIA HARRISON RUIZ

* This chapter is dedicated to the memory of John W. Thornton, Sr., the original author, who passed away Nov. 21, 2003. He was a great lawyer, scholar, and person, and his legacy will live on through the countless colleagues, friends, and family members touched and inspired by his life.

I. Litigation, Reinsurance Policies, and the New Millennium

In recent years, there has been an explosion of litigation directly and indirectly involving reinsurance scenarios. Because of the unique nature of reinsurance agreements, the communications between insurer and reinsurer are more "open" than would otherwise be the case in a traditional contractual scenario. This in turn creates a number of interesting problems relating to confidentiality and the discoverability of communications and information shared with the reinsurer. Before these issues can be considered, however, the unique nature of reinsurance must be briefly explored.

A. Reinsurance: A Brief Primer

A reinsurance contract involves an agreement under which an insurer transfers, or "cedes," a portion of its risk to another insurance company in return for a percentage of the premium.[1] Reinsurance differs from direct insurance in that there is no liability running directly from the reinsurer to the original insured.[2] Rather, a reinsurance contract is a contract of indemnity, and liability does not attach until the reinsured has actually made payment on the underlying claim.[3] Put differently, a reinsurance agreement indemnifies against loss rather than against liability.[4]

The goal of reinsurance is to diversify the risk of loss, which then reduces not only the risk but also the capital reserves that must be held by the ceding company.[5] Moreover, reinsurance serves a number of important corporate and societal interests, such as (1) increasing a carrier's ability to accept new risks and allowing it to accept larger risks that might otherwise exceed its capacity, (2) increasing stability for the ceding company, (3) allowing catastrophic risks to be spread across the industry, and (4) promoting competition amongst insurers.[6] When a reinsurance company transfers a part of its risk, the transaction is termed a "retrocession agreement," with the transferring reinsurer referred to as the "retrocedent" and the reinsurer assuming the risk referred to as the "retrocessionaire."[7]

Reinsurance agreements fall into one of two general categories: "facultative" reinsurance, and "treaty" or "automatic" reinsurance.[8] In facultative reinsurance scenarios, the agreement relates to all or part of a single insurance policy.[9] As a facultative agreement covers all or a part of a particular, identifiable risk, the reinsurer is free to accept or reject each particular risk offered.[10] In contrast, in a treaty or automatic reinsurance scenario, the reinsurance policy concerns a specific group or class of policies issued by the ceding insurer, such as earthquake insurance.[11] As the reinsurer is accepting a type of risk as opposed to a specific identifiable risk, the reinsurer is obligated to accept the class of risks covered by the agreement, including those as yet unwritten.[12] Stated slightly differently, in treaty reinsurance, the ceding company is trying to reduce its risk of loss from either a class of customers or an industry, rather than those relating to a specific policy.[13]

Both facultative and treaty reinsurance agreements can also be further classified as either "proportional reinsurance" or "excess of loss reinsurance." In a proportional, or pro rata, agreement, coverage is typically provided on a pro rata, or percentage, basis for each of the types of coverage placed with the reinsurance company by the underlying insurer. In contrast, in excess of loss scenarios, coverage is not triggered until or unless the loss reaches a certain predetermined threshold.[14]

A reinsurance agreement needs to be distinguished from "assumption" insurance, in which policies already issued by insurance carriers are purchased outright, and the second company then stands in the shoes of the original insurer, with obligations running directly to the insured.[15] In the traditional reinsurance scenario, there is no liability running directly between the reinsurer and the underlying insured. However, in some reinsurance agreements, the parties negotiate what is called a "cut through" clause. When this clause is present, the insured entity can seek coverage directly from the reinsurer.[16] Such an agreement would become quite valuable to an insured if the original insurance carrier were to become insolvent—it would allow the covered entity to avoid the pitfalls posed by insolvency proceedings and instead look to the reinsurer directly for reimbursement of loss. Similarly, if the reinsurance money had already been paid to the cedent prior to bankruptcy, such a "cut through" clause would give the underlying insured priority to the reinsurance proceeds in many jurisdictions.[17]

B. "Follow the Fortunes" Clauses in General

A central tenet of reinsurance law is that the reinsurer must "follow the fortunes" of the ceding company.[18] This means that the reinsurer is responsible for the payment of the loss as determined by the original, underlying policy. The reinsurer may not second-guess a decision made by the ceding company. "Follow the fortunes" clauses or, as John Thornton, the original author of this chapter, liked to call them, "follow the misfortunes" clauses, were originally intended to provide that the reinsurer repay the ceding company for a loss the ceding company was obligated to pay under the terms of its policy, even if it was reformed by the courts. Thus, if the ceding company were obligated to pay its insured, or make a payment on behalf of its insured as a result of the company's liability for loss under the policy of insurance, then the reinsurer in turn would be liable under its contract of reinsurance to the ceding company.

The American Heritage dictionary defines the word "fortune" as "a hypothetical, often personified force or power that favorably or unfavorably governs the events of one's life."[19] Some reinsurers prefer to use the phrase "technical insurance fortunes," meaning only those exposures that are related to, and that flow from, the underwriting of a particular risk. Some prefer to use the term "underwriting fortunes." However, the follow-the-fortunes clause may be construed without resort to such confusing terms. More simply, it can be read as "follow the liability." In more complete, but complex, terms, it can be thought of as "subject in all respects to all the general and special stipulations clauses, etc., of the company's policy."

Until the early 1960s, these clauses were prevalent in the industry. However, developing case law during that period made it apparent that the presence of such clauses in reinsurance contracts was becoming problematic because they were being construed to expose reinsurers on such contracts to direct action lawsuits by third parties in the event of insolvency, even though it was contrary to the generally accepted principle that a person not a party to a contract cannot derive any benefit therefrom. Many reinsurers consequently made herculean efforts to avoid the use of this clause in contracts. However, if the clause could not be eliminated, it was mandated that the following sentence be added to the clause for protection against potential third-party exposure: "Nothing herein shall in any manner create any obligations or establish any rights against the Reinsurer in favor of any third parties or any persons not parties to the agreement."

Another important issue related to the potential exposure that arose for a reinsurer in contracts was excess judgments that were not explicitly considered in follow-the-fortunes clauses. In the landmark case of *Peerless Insurance Co. v. Inland Mutual Insurance Co.*, an insurer who held a $15,000 automobile liability policy reinsured $10,000 of the policy under a reinsurance agreement that included a follow-the-fortunes clause.[20] The insurer affirmatively decided not to settle the case, and a verdict was rendered for $75,000. The insured then brought a negligent failure to settle action against the insurer and settled it for $27,500. The court ruled that the follow-the-fortunes wording rendered the reinsurer liable for two-thirds of the total settlement amount, as that clause expanded the reinsurer's liability to include excess judgments.[21] After this decision was handed down, reinsurers became acutely aware of the fact that if they were unable to delete the follow-the-fortunes clause, they had better specifically exclude those exposures they were not prepared to assume. Moreover, with the surge of bad-faith actions and punitive awards, the *Peerless* decision makes it all the more important to be aware of the ramifications of the follow-the-fortunes clause.

It should be noted that the follow-the-fortunes clause does not prevent the reinsurer from raising the defense that the underlying claim did not fall within the policy coverage.[22] This is true even if the ceding company makes a reasonable, good-faith decision that coverage was owed.[23]

C. Recent Developments in Reinsurance and "Follow the Fortunes" Case Law

A topic that has received a significant amount of attention in recent years is the liability of the reinsurer for the insurer's defense costs incurred in connection with litigating the subject loss. In *Bellefonte Reinsurance Co. v. Aetna Casualty & Surety Co.*, the Second Circuit Court of Appeals held that a follow-the-fortunes clause did not operate to make the reinsurers liable for the insurer's defense costs above and beyond the limits of liability set in the reinsurance certificate; rather, the clause subjected the reinsurer to the direct risks borne by the insurer under the policy.[24] However, this was recently called into question in *TIG Premier Insurance Co. v. Hartford Accident & Indemnity Co.*, which held that there was a genuine issue of material fact relating to the meaning of the policy language pertaining to reimbursement of costs.[25] Expert testimony was offered that the reinsurance industry's standard practice was to assess the reinsurer with the percentage of the defense costs corresponding to the percentage of liability reinsured.[26] Hence, a reinsurer with 20 percent of the underlying obligation would also be responsible for 20 percent of the related defense costs.

In *British International Insurance v. Seguros La Republica*, the court noted that the follow-the-fortunes doctrine has become associated with the duty on the part of the reinsurer to accept without challenge a settlement negotiated by the insurer on the underlying claim.[27] The court also rendered a decision on another topical issue: reimbursement for costs expended by the insurer in a declaratory judgment action.[28] The court held that the fact that one or some reinsurers reimburse the ceding insurer for declaratory judgment expenses does not make the practice so "notorious" that it has become an implied term in a reinsurance contract.[29]

D. The Duty of "Utmost Good Faith"

The duty of utmost good faith, or *uberrima fides*, is considered by many to be the flip side of the follow-the-fortunes doctrine in reinsurance. The origins of the two doctrines are inextricably tied together: the reinsurance carrier must defer to the ceding company as it relates to the claim investigation, attempts at settlement, and most matters relating to the claim itself; however, the ceding company in turn is required to act with the "utmost good faith" in its disclosures to and treatment of the reinsurer. The existence of the duty of utmost good faith dates back to the Supreme Court decision of *Sun Mutual Insurance Co. v.*

Ocean Insurance Co.[30] In that case, the Supreme Court held that the insurance carrier ceding coverage had an absolute duty to disclose all of the underlying facts that had any bearing on issuance of the coverage, and that any failure to do so voided the contract for reinsurance.[31] This doctrine has matured over the years, and is now generally accepted to require disclosure of the information that is material to the decision to underwrite the risk, such as frequency of loss, nature of the business, and existence of excess or other insurance on the risk.[32]

There exists a duty of good faith and fair dealing between the reinsured and the reinsurer in connection with every reinsurance contract.[33] The consequences of a breach of that duty can be severe. In *Reliance Insurance Co. v. Certain Member Cos.*, the reinsurer succeeded in having the reinsurance binder declared void, as both the cedent and its broker breached their duties of utmost good faith relating to disclosure.[34]

E. Recent Example Involving Reinsurance Scenario and Duty of Good Faith

Several of the important issues relating to "bad faith" or, at the very least, breach of the duty of utmost good faith in connection with reinsurance contract litigation are illustrated in the case of *Commercial Union Insurance Co. v. Seven Provinces Insurance*.[35] The landscape in the reinsurance arena has been slowly changing over the years, and reinsurance is gradually transforming itself from a "gentleman's agreement" to a fairly normal insurance contract, fraught with the typical dangers and uncertainties.[36] This case helps to underscore some of the growing pains associated with that transformation.

Knowledge of the underlying facts and circumstances of *Commercial Union* is essential to understanding the legal ramifications of the decision. In the case, a reinsurance arrangement was entered into in the early 1960s between Employers' Surplus Lines Insurance Company (ESLIC) and defendant Seven Provinces Insurance Company. ESLIC wrote a number of different insurance policies for Teledyne, a California-based manufacturing company. In 1963, ESLIC ceded a portion of this risk to Seven Provinces in a facultative reinsurance agreement.

Environmental contamination was discovered at a number of different Teledyne sites in 1982, and the company faced cleanup claims brought by the Environmental Protection Agency (EPA) extending into the millions, along with numerous third-party liability claims. Claims were submitted to Teledyne's insurance carriers, including Commercial Union (CU), ESLIC's successor in interest, and litigation was required to determine CU's obligations to Teledyne under the policies relating to Teledyne's many manufacturing sites. A settlement was eventually reached, in which CU paid Teledyne $2.2 million and Teledyne released CU from all existing and potential future liability relating to environmental claims.

During the settlement negotiations, quite a bit of attention was focused on a single site called the "semiconductor site." The site had been in operation since 1962, and the cleanup costs for this location were estimated at $20.93

million. The insurance agreement between Teledyne and ESLIC, now CU, was a general liability policy covering losses greater than $50,000 and up to $1.95 million, and it was to last for one year. CU determined that $843,000 of the total $2.2 million settlement should be allocated to that site, and its reinsurers were so notified. Losses exceeding $500,000 were reimbursed by a carrier not involved in the suit. The other $450,000 in liability was billed as follows: $225,000—or one half—was billed to Seven Provinces, and $180,000 of CU's remaining half was billed to a pool of treaty reinsurers, which resulted in CU being ultimately responsible for $45,000 of the original loss amount. Suit was ultimately brought by CU to recover the $225,000 from Seven Provinces, along with costs and attorneys' fees.

The first defense raised by Seven Provinces was the "net retention" claim, which was based upon a clause in the original reinsurance agreement. The pertinent clause read as follows:

> Being a reinsurance of and warranted same NETT rate, terms and conditions as and to follow the settlements of the [ESLIC] and that the local office of the said Company retains during the currency of this insurance at least $225,000.00 being 50% of $450,000 excess, $50,000.00 combined single limit subject to reduction by any general excess loss or excess catastrophe reinsurance whether effected by the head office or local office of the Company on the identical subject matter and risk and in identically the same proportion on each separate part thereof, but in the event of the retained line being less than as above, Underwriter's lines to be proportionally reduced.[37]

Seven Provinces argued that this clause required ESLIC, or CU, to retain the entirety of the $225,000 risk, and that their proportionate share of the reinsured risk must be reduced under the language of the agreement since CU reinsured $180,000, or 80 percent, of its $225,000 risk. The court found the language to be ambiguous, and expert testimony was taken from both sides on the issue. After weighing the evidence, the court found that the clause required Seven Provinces' liability to be proportionately reduced only if ESLIC obtained facultative reinsurance on its retained portion, and did not relate to treaty reinsurance; Seven Provinces' liability was not to be reduced by the CU treaty reinsurance pool that was put in place by the head office of the company and which did not amount to reinsurance on the identical subject matter.

Seven Provinces' next challenge related to CU's allocation of $843,000 of the $2.2 million settlement amount to the Teledyne "semiconductor" site for the appropriate coverage year. CU offered testimony showing the rationale behind the allocation decision to illustrate that it was done in good faith, in accordance with their normal allocation procedures relating to hazardous waste claims. Seven Provinces, however, alleged that it was unreasonable or done in bad faith. The court recognized that the interplay between two well-recognized reinsurance doctrines must be considered in this situation:

the follow-the-fortunes doctrine and the "follow the settlements" doctrine. Under the follow-the-fortunes doctrine, Seven Provinces was bound by the reinsured's good-faith determination that the loss was in fact covered by the policy. Under the related follow-the-settlements doctrine, the reinsurer must "abide by a reinsured's good-faith decision to settle, rather than litigate, claims on that policy . . . the reinsurer must go along with however the reinsured settles the claim."[38] To require otherwise would allow the reinsurer to challenge each settlement, attacking one possible choice by the reinsured among a number of reasonable settlement alternatives, which would act as a significant deterrent to settlement. The court found as a matter of law that the allocation was reasonable, and that Seven Provinces had not produced any evidence that it was made in bad faith. Seven Provinces' allegations that the allocation was made so as to maximize reinsurance recovery was not supported by the evidence. Furthermore, the court specifically held that there was no evidence to support the claim that the settlement was an *ex gratia* payment—made as a favor rather than pursuant to a legal obligation—to obtain the release of future claims rather than to compensate for actual damages incurred.

The most interesting analysis came in deciding CU's claim for attorneys' fees and costs for being forced to litigate Seven Provinces' responsibility to pay a valid and outstanding claim. This claim was brought under a Massachusetts statute, and was hence language specific. However, the underlying logic is still quite valuable. The court reviewed the lengthy and somewhat convoluted history behind the presentation of the claim—it was legitimately confused by missing reinsurance certificates and other documentation problems. However, the claim was originally presented in August of 1993. The reinsurance certificate was undisputedly located and in the hands of Seven Provinces as of August 1995. Rather than paying the sum due at that time, Seven Provinces continued to raise other, unrelated issues as barriers to payment while at the same time trying to negotiate some type of compromise on the claim. The court noted that "Seven Provinces' behavior was particularly egregious when seen in the context of the mores of the reinsurance industry, an industry which has operated for centuries on the principle of 'utmost good faith.'"[39] The court went on to note:

> These traditions of trust and mutual reliance came under strain in the 1980s. Because of high interest rates . . . insurers paid less attention to the risks they insured, and the quality of the underwriting began to suffer. At the same time, environmental and asbestos liability began to upset the calculations on which many insurance relationships had been founded. See *Compagnie de Reassurance*, 944 F.Supp at 993. Trade publications are beginning to note the change in tone, speaking of the "death of the handshake." Michael J. Brady and Lawrence O. Monin, *Reinsurance Disputes: Death of the Handshake*, 61 Def. Couns. J. 529 (1994). Seven Provinces' conduct is more in keeping with this new climate.[40]

The court held that Seven Provinces had acted in breach of its duty of utmost good faith, and entered judgment in favor of CU in the amount of $450,000, which was double the amount owed because of a Massachusetts statutory multiplier.

F. How Discovery, Privilege, and Confidentiality Relate to Reinsurance

In the recent past, the majority of reinsurance disputes took the form of arbitration, and reinsurance was a little-discussed topic, especially in actions between a policyholder and an insurance carrier. Simply put, reinsurance and discovery from reinsurers was not a mainstream consideration. However, with the recent growth in large tort actions, such as toxic torts and environmental cleanup cases from contamination, reinsurance has become the subject of more interest at all levels of business and litigation. The issue of the discoverability of reinsurance-related information typically arises in one of two scenarios: (1) a dispute between an insured and an insurer, in which information about reinsurance is sought by the policyholder to bolster some element of the underlying case, or (2) a dispute between the ceding company and the reinsurer relating to the transaction itself, or reinsurance coverage for a particular loss.

The attorney-client and work-product privileges take on a new significance in modern litigation involving large corporate entities with many joint or overlapping issues. For example, communication is essential in a large corporation with numerous far-flung operations, but any communication carries with it the risk of divulgence. Conversations between in-house counsel and corporate employees are protected.[41] However, the following criteria must be met for corporate employee-attorney privilege to attach:

1. The communication would not have been made but for the contemplation of legal services;
2. The employee making the communication did so at the direction of his or her corporate superior;
3. The superior made the request of the employee as part of the corporation's effort to secure legal advice or services;
4. The content of the communication relates to the legal services being rendered, and the subject matter of the communication is within the scope of the employee's duties;
5. The communication is not disseminated beyond those persons who, because of the corporate structure, need to know its contents.[42]

This protects select communication within the corporate entity, but what about between entities? It has been held that if an insured agreed with its excess insurer that it would open its books and records to the excess insurer, then such items, including its attorney reports, were discoverable by the excess insurer.[43] Similarly, if a ceding company voluntarily submits attorney-client privileged information to another reinsurer in the normal course of business negotiations, it waives the privilege as to any reinsurer's requests.[44] However, in a bad-faith action courts have held that the files of an attorney hired by an insurer to investigate claims made by the insured are privileged in a subsequent action brought by that insured against the carrier for bad faith.[45] The application of the doctrine in insurance and reinsurance scenarios is rarely simple or straightforward.

The very nature of the reinsurance relationship makes the issue of discovery sought by a policyholder from a reinsurer especially troublesome. The ceding company has a clearly imposed duty to disclose all pertinent information to the reinsurer; this is the essential element of the duty of utmost good faith, and depending upon the nature of the reinsurance agreement, it could include disclosure of such information as the ceding carrier's attorney's assessment of the risks and merits of the underlying suit, which is clearly privileged. If the courts then decide that the reinsurer must then turn all of that information over to the policyholder, this could put the ceding company at a serious disadvantage. Even more importantly, it could staunch the free flow of information between the ceding and reinsuring carriers, which is an essential element of reinsurance.

II. Discovery of Reinsurance Information by Policyholder in Action against the Insurance Company

A. Discoverability of the Reinsurance Policy Itself

Whether or not reinsurance information is discoverable depends upon what is being sought, along with the posture of the underlying action. Historically, there was some dispute regarding whether or not the reinsurance policy itself was or should be discoverable in litigation between the insured and the insurance company. Some courts have held that Rule 26 of the Federal Rules of Civil Procedure permitted the insured to obtain its insurer's reinsurance agreements as a matter of course because such agreements constituted an "insurance agreement" as defined by Rule 26(a)(1)(2).[46] However, other courts drew a number of distinctions, and allowed exceptions to the basic rule of production.[47] More recently, in *MedMarc Casualty Insurance Co. v. Arrow International, Inc.*, the court decided that a reinsurer had to produce the reinsurance policy in response to a subpoena served by the insured in an underlying declaratory judgment action against the insurer; however, other reinsurance materials were irrelevant, as they had no bearing on the interpretation of an unambiguous policy provision in the primary liability insurance policy.[48] This articulates what has become the general rule: the policy itself may be obtained, but additional information is much more fact-specific.

The prudent practitioner should reference the statutory scheme in the particular state. Many states have specific statutes that mandate disclosure of certain insurance information. For example, the relevant statute in Florida provides:

1. Each insurer which does or may provide liability insurance coverage to pay all or a portion of any claim which might be made shall provide, within 30 days of the written request of the claimant, a statement, under oath, of a corporate officer or the insurer's claims manager or superintendent setting forth the following information with regard to each known policy of insurance, including excess or umbrella insurance:

   a. the name of the insurer
   b. the name of each insured
   c. the limits of the liability coverage
   d. a statement of any policy or coverage defense which such insurer reasonably believes is available to such insurer at the time of filing such statement
   e. a copy of the policy.

   In addition, the insured, or his insurance agent, upon written request of the claimant of the claimant's attorney, shall disclose the name and coverage of each known insurer to the claimant and shall forward such request for information as required by this subsection to all affected insurers. The insurer shall then supply the information required in this subsection to the claimant within 30 days of receipt of such request.
2. The statement required by subsection (1) shall be amended immediately upon discovery of facts calling for an amendment to such statement.[49]

However, in delineating the scope of the chapter, the statute specifically exempts reinsurance from the above mandates.[50] In Florida, reinsurance information is privileged from the viewpoint of the original claimant.[51]

B. Broader Discovery of Other Reinsurance Information

The insured may argue that communications between the reinsured, or ceding insurer, and the reinsurer are relevant to the issue of policy interpretation inasmuch as such communications could reveal admissions from the ceding company interpreting its own policy language to cover the claims at issue.[52] In addition, the insured could contend that the information maintained by the reinsurer with respect to the claims at issue may also be relevant to when the ceding company received notice for each individual claim, which would potentially be reflected in correspondence or notice to the reinsurer, and is also relevant to the issue of whether the ceding company conducted an adequate investigation prior to declining coverage for the claims.[53] The insured may contend that the reinsurance information it seeks may also bear on the issue of whether the ceding company was prejudiced in any fashion by the timing of the insured' s notice of the claims at issue.

There are reported cases that support the position that the reinsurance documents sought by the insured may not be relevant or otherwise subject to production in a declaratory judgment action. For example, in *Leski Inc. v. Federal Insurance Co.*, the court sustained the insurer's objection to the relevancy of documents and information regarding reinsurance in the pending declaratory judgment action as "very tenuous" because the insurer's decision to obtain reinsurance and communicate with its reinsurers is and was based upon "business considerations and not questions of policy interpretation."[54]

Any information regarding reinsurance is, at best, evidence of the undisclosed, unilateral intentions by the insurer, which are not material to the interpretation of an insurance contract between the insurer and the insured.[55] The court in *Rhone-Poulenc v. Home Indemnity Co.* recognized that the issue of reinsurance does not even potentially become relevant until the court makes the specific finding that there is an ambiguity in the policy at issue that requires the consideration of extrinsic evidence.[56] Under this logic, the appropriateness of discovery regarding reinsurance in an action between the insured and the insurer should not even be considered unless and until there has been a finding by the district court that one or more of the provisions of the policies at issue is ambiguous.

It has been clearly held that where the retrocession agreement was unambiguous on its face, parol evidence was inadmissible to explain its terms.[57] Similarly, in *In re Texas Eastern Transmission Corp.*, the court held that there must first be a holding that a policy is ambiguous and therefore subject to the admission of extrinsic evidence of intent before reinsurance information is even arguably relevant.[58] Finding no allegations or evidence of ambiguity in the action before it, the court precluded the disclosure of "any information as to the amount of any reinsurance or the identity of any reinsurer or even the fact of reinsurance."[59] The various states have decided these discovery issues a number of different ways, and the body of case law for each jurisdiction needs to be reviewed prior to proceeding in a state court action. For example, courts in Florida have clearly held that the reinsurance contract is irrelevant to the original claims in an action between an insured and an insurer.[60]

C. Responding to a Third-Party Subpoena for Reinsurance Documents under Rule 45 of the Federal Rules of Civil Procedure

Rule 45 of the Federal Rules of Civil Procedure authorizes the insured's attorney to issue a subpoena directly to the reinsurer, under the auspices of the U.S. district court for the district in which the subpoena seeks to compel the production of documents.[61] The reinsurer is entitled to respond with a motion to quash or modify the subpoena; upon a hearing thereof, even if the court finds that some documents are responsive and should be produced, the court can modify or restrict the subpoena to protect the reinsurer "from significant expense (or burden) resulting from the inspection and copying commanded."[62] Under those circumstances, most courts would likely extend the time for the reinsurer to object and respond to the subpoena rather than quash the subpoena outright.

In reviewing Rule 45, the court may quash or modify a subpoena that requires the "disclosure of privileged or other protected matter to which no exception or waiver applies"[63] or "requires disclosure of a trade secret or other confidential research, development or commercial information."[64] As to this aspect of Rule 45, some courts have recognized a proprietary information or trade secret privilege in connection with certain reinsurance information.[65] The court in *Rhone-Poulenc* supported its decision to preclude the production of reinsurance information on the basis that

> [r]einsurance materials contain confidential business information regarding the pricing and coverage of reinsurance policies, which, if you deal to competitors could damage the insurance carrier's ability to compete in the reinsurance market as well as our present business relationships with reinsurers.[66]

Thus, the reinsurer can object to the production of its reinsurance materials as proprietary business information. However, the court may simply require that the proprietary documents of information with which the reinsurer is concerned be produced subject to in camera review, a confidentiality agreement, or a protective order prohibiting the insured from using the produced documents or information outside the limited scope of the declaratory judgment proceeding.[67]

With respect to the disclosure of documents regarding the ceding company's reserves, most courts have been persuaded that reserve calculations are of tenuous probative value as such calculations assume the likelihood of an adverse verdict and typically such estimates do not entail an evaluation of coverage "based upon a thorough factual and legal consideration."[68] Accordingly, the reinsurer possibly will be able to avoid production of the ceding company's reserve information.[69]

D. Attorney-Client Privilege and the "Common Interest" Rule as Applied to Subpoenas

The strength of the objection that the subpoena requests information and documents protected by the attorney-client privilege and work-product doctrine is somewhat fact-specific. This objection may or may not be available to reinsurers when seeking to prevent the disclosure of information and materials prepared by counsel to the ceding company that happen to end up in the reinsurer's files.[70] However, the attorney-client privilege extends to communications from the ceding company to its reinsurer based on the "community of interest" between the ceding company and its reinsurer.[71] In *Durham Industries v. North River Insurance Co.*, the court held that where the insurer, or ceding company, and the reinsurer share in the risk of potential liability on claims, there is a conformity of interest that serves as a sufficient basis to support the reinsurer's objection to produce materials obtained from the ceding company on the basis of the attorney-client privilege.[72] Thus, the reinsurer may be able to shield documents that reveal attorney-client communications between the ceding company and its coverage counsel from production to the insured in the declaratory judgment action.[73]

More recently, in *Travelers Casualty & Surety Co. v. Excess Insurance Co. Ltd.*, the court strongly reaffirmed the rule that the "common interest" or "joint defense" doctrine would apply to shield communications and notes exchanged in conferences between reinsurers as being protected by the attorney-client privilege.[74] However, as with any privilege, the attorney-client privilege and the work-product privilege can be waived by voluntary disclosure of the information to others.[75] Moreover, while privileges must be recognized, they must be limited to the scope required to effectuate the underlying purpose of the privilege.[76]

It must be remembered that failure to make any objection to this subpoena, even with the intention to negotiate with the insurance counsel, may waive the right to withhold production of the requested materials.[77] However, the simple act of filing one or more objections to the subpoena will shift the burden of securing compliance with the subpoena back on the insured, who must then request that the court order the reinsurer to comply with the terms of the subpoena.[78] Should you take the more extreme measures by responding to the subpoena through an immediate motion for a protective order pursuant to Rule 26(c), you will bear the burden of demonstrating "good cause" entitling you to such an order.[79]

III. Privilege and Confidentiality in Disputes between the Ceding Company and Reinsurer

Disputes with the ceding company can take a number of forms and involve a number of different issues; however, two typical litigation scenarios are most common. In the first, a reinsurer asserts that the underlying claim was poorly handled. For example, it asserts that the follow-the-fortunes doctrine should not apply because the ceding insurer did not give times notice of the claim. In the second common scenario, the reinsurer alleges that coverage should not be afforded because the ceding company did not disclose all of the relevant risk information.

A. Reinsurer's Defense of Late Notice of Claim: Actual Prejudice versus Bad Faith

One potential defense to coverage that a reinsurer can raise is late notice of the underlying claim for which reinsurance is being invoked. The viability of this defense will depend upon the law of the particular state in which the action is brought. However, in a growing number of jurisdictions, either actual prejudice or bad faith needs to be proven to support the viability of this defense. A landmark case in this area is the Second Circuit's *Unigard Security Insurance Co. v. North River Insurance Co.*[80] In *Unigard*, the reinsurer instituted a declaratory judgment action on the issue of whether the ceding insurer's failure to notify it in a timely fashion of the signing of an intercompany agreement (the "Wellington Agreement") that established an asbestos claims facility would support a late-notice defense to claims under the reinsurance policy. Despite the fact that reinsurance agreements are "insurance contracts," the *Unigard* court noted as a preliminary matter that the general rule that any ambiguous policy language will be construed against the insurer does not apply, as reinsurance contracts represent an "arm's length" transaction between two equal, quite sophisticated parties.[81] The canons of construction developed to protect individual purchasers of original insurance policies do not apply in reinsurance scenarios.[82]

In analyzing the viability of the late-notice defense, the *Unigard* court first reaffirmed much of the basic law relating to reinsurance agreements, primary of which is that the reinsurer is not directly liable to the original insured. Rather, reinsurance involves indemnity as opposed to liability, and reinsurers accordingly do not examine risks, receive notice of loss from the original insured, or investigate claims. Rather, the reinsurers are dependent on their ceding insurers for prompt and full disclosure of information concerning pertinent risks to determine whether to associate in the defense of a claim. As a result, the court noted, the relationship between the reinsurer and the ceding company is and must be one of "utmost good faith." It also must be kept in mind that there are two different types of reinsurance agreements. In "facultative reinsurance," the reinsurer is covering a part or all of a single insurance policy; in contrast, in "treaty reinsurance" the reinsurer is covering specified classes of the ceding insurance company's policies.[83] The reinsurance agreement between North River and Unigard was a facultative reinsurance agreement.

The Second Circuit explained the rationale underlying the notice provision to be threefold: (1) to apprise the reinsurer of potential liabilities to enable it to set reserves; (2) to enable the reinsurer to associate in defense and control of the underlying claims; and (3) to assist the reinsurer in determining whether and at what price to renew reinsurance coverage.[84] The court noted that the reinsurance agreement itself provided that "prompt notice shall be given by the [ceding insurer] to the Underwriting Managers on behalf of the Reinsurers of any occurrence or accident which appears likely to involve this reinsurance."[85] The *Unigard* court also noted that "being an insurance company, the [ceding insurer] is held to a high degree of compliance with policy provisions which require prompt notice to the reinsurer."[86]

The court determined that North River did not give adequate notice of the Wellington Agreement to the reinsurer, Unigard. The agreement recited that the Asbestos Claims Facility it established was the sole agent, and that it had exclusive authority and discretion to administer, evaluate, settle, pay, and defend all asbestos-related claims. North River did not give Unigard timely notice of the Wellington Agreement and thus breached the notice clause of the facultative reinsurance certificate in question. The court also clarified its position on requiring a reasonable time after the duty to give notice to the reinsurer has arisen. It held that all that is required is a reasonable possibility of such a happening, based upon an objective assessment of the information available, and that such a possibility may exist even though the ceding company may find "there are some factors that tend to suggest the opposite."[87]

However, the Second Circuit went on to note that Unigard was required to show that it was prejudiced by the lack of notice, though the definition of "prejudice" in the context of reinsurance was quite unclear.[88] Courts have typically examined the loss of the "right of association" that comes from a lack of notice in determining the existence of prejudice. For example, in *Fortress Re, Inc. v. Central National Insurance Co.*, the court held that not only must the reinsurer show that it would have associated if given proper notice, but it also must show that this association would have resulted in a more favorable outcome.[89] An even greater burden was placed on the reinsurer in *Insurance Co. of Pennsylvania v. Associated International Insurance Co.*, when it was required to prove that there was a "substantial likelihood" that it could have defeated the claim or settled it for a smaller sum.[90] Some older cases have placed less of a burden on the reinsurer; however, the trend seems to require a significant showing of "prejudice" in the form of tangible economic injury—loss of the contractual right of association alone is insufficient. The *Unigard* court ultimately held that the reinsurer did not demonstrate sufficient prejudice resulted from the late notice and thus denied the defense to coverage.[91]

However, any "bad faith" on the part of the ceding company to the reinsurer in not giving prompt notice may supplant the requirement of proof of actual prejudice. The duty of good faith requires the ceding insurer to place the reinsurer "in the same [situation] as himself [and] to give to him the same means and opportunity of judging the value of the risks."[92] The Second Circuit therefore queried what "good faith" requires of a ceding insurer in the notice context and held:

> We [thus] think that the proper minimum standard for bad faith should, be gross negligence or recklessness. If a ceding insurer deliberately deceives a reinsurer, that deception is of course bad faith. However, if a ceding insurer has implemented routine practices and control to ensure notification to reinsurers but inadvertence causes a lapse, the insurer has not acted in bad faith. But if a ceding insurer does not implement such practices and controls, then it has willfully disregarded the risk to reinsurers and is guilty of gross negligence. A reinsurer, dependent on its ceding insurer for information, should be able to expect at least this level of protection, and, if a ceding insurer fails to provide it, the reinsurer's late loss notice defense should succeed.[93]

In the recent case *British Insurance Co. of Cayman v. Safety National Casualty*, the Third Circuit held that under New Jersey state law a reinsurer can prevail on a late-notice defense only if it can demonstrate significant prejudice.[94] The court noted that "prejudice in a late notice defense is determined by examining (1) whether substantial rights have been irretrievably lost and (2) the likelihood of success of the insurer in defending against the victim's claim."[95] Similarly, in *Employers Reinsurance Corp. v. NewCap Insurance Co.*, the court noted that untimely notice from the insured to the reinsurer excuses performance only where there is actual prejudice resulting from the late notice.[96] Further, in a reinsurance scenario, it must be shown that the reinsurer's participation in the defense would have altered the result of the trial in order for "substantial prejudice" to be found.[97]

B. "Common Interest" Doctrine as Arises in Litigation between Reinsurer and Ceding Company

The relationship between the "common interest" doctrine and attorney-client privilege is well explained in the matter of *North River Insurance Co. v. Philadelphia Reinsurance Corp.*[98] In the case, North River pursued indemnification from its reinsurer, CIGNA Reinsurance Company (CIGNA Re), for defense costs stemming from asbestos-related excess insurance claims. As part of its discovery efforts, CIGNA Re sought attorney-client communications between North River and the coverage counsel who had represented it in the arbitration dispute that produced the defense costs. CIGNA Re was interested in documents that bore on North River's decision to abandon its appeal of the arbitrator's decision against it. A federal magistrate denied CIGNA Re's discovery request, and the district court upheld the denial.

CIGNA Re first argued that the communications between North River and its counsel were discoverable under what it termed the "common interest" doctrine, which is an exception to the rule relating to attorney-client privilege. The doctrine provides that when multiple parties are represented by the same attorney, communications between the attorney and the parties are not privileged if the parties later sue one other. In a typical litigation claim, for example, counsel may represent both the insured and the insurer in defending the claim, and his communications with either side would be protected as to the rest of the world but not between the insured and insurer.

This argument is not applicable to the relationship between the ceding company and the reinsurer. As the *North River* court noted, the ceding carrier and the reinsurer may have a common interest, but the ceding company's counsel does not have an attorney-client relationship with the reinsurer. Without such a relationship, there is no "common interest" exception to the attorney-client privilege, and communications between the ceding company and its counsel remain protected:

> As a matter of general privilege law, there is no automatic waiver of the attorney-client privilege merely because an insured and its insurers have a "common interest" in the outcome of a particular issue. That waiver may be found only when there has been a dual representation of both parties . . . Thus, although [the federal magistrate judge]

analyzed the issue in a different way, he reached the correct result in finding that the "common interest" doctrine did not require North River to produce its attorney-client documents to CIGNA Re.[99]

CIGNA Re then argued that the "cooperation" clause of the reinsurance certificate waived North River's attorney-client privilege. The cooperation clause, using standard language, provided that North River "shall make available for inspection and place at the disposal of the reinsurer at reasonable times any of its records related to this reinsurance or claims in connection therewith."[100] However, the North River court found that the cooperation clause was not specific enough to provide a blanket waiver of the attorney-client privilege held by the ceding insurer. The court wrote:

> Although a reinsured may contractually be bound to provide its reinsurer with all documents or information in its possession that may be relevant to the underlying claim adjustment and coverage determination, absent more explicit language, it does not through a cooperation clause give up wholesale its right to preserve the confidentiality of any consultation it may have with its attorney concerning the underlying claim and its coverage determination.[101]

CIGNA Re next contended that North River had no reasonable expectation that the attorney-client communications would be confidential because industry custom dictated reinsurers have access to such documents. However, the court concluded that industry custom was not enough to impose a waiver of the attorney-client privilege on North River; rather, only clear and explicit language in the reinsurance certificate could create such a waiver.[102]

CIGNA Re then argued that North River was under a fiduciary obligation of full disclosure. The court quickly rejected this idea because a reinsurer did not have "sufficient influence and control" over the ceding company to create a fiduciary relationship:

> The presence of sufficient influence and control over the affairs of another necessary to give rise to fiduciary responsibilities is absent between reinsured and reinsurer. The reinsurer's "right to associate" gives it adequate means by which to keep informed of events that may give rise to coverage under its agreement, and also provides a sufficient means to protect its own interests. Reinsurance agreements are negotiated at arms-length between equally sophisticated parties. Reinsurers are well aware of the risks inherent in reinsurance obligations and are adequately situated to protect their interests.[103]

Finally, CIGNA Re argued that North River had waived the attorney-client privilege by putting "in issue" the communications with its lawyers. The court rejected this idea as well, stressing that the "in issue" exception to the attorney-client privilege "should be construed narrowly to create an implied waiver of the privilege only when the party puts 'in issue' the contents of an attorney-client communication . . . This will occur only when the party has asserted the claim or defense that he intends to prove by disclosure of an attorney-client communication."[104] Such a defense might include advice of counsel, which sometimes is used in bad-faith cases. The court noted that North River had represented that it had no intention of relying on an attorney-client communication in proving its case. The court dismissed the notion that the ceding company raised the attorney-client privilege merely by "placing the broad question of coverage in issue."[105] It upheld the judge's finding that the privilege applied, and North River could protect its communications with coverage counsel.

The *North River* case clarifies some of the confusing issues involving the relationship between reinsurers and ceding carriers. That relationship is not a fiduciary one, and therefore is not subject to the strict disclosure rules that exist in fiduciary situations.[106] A ceding company can turn to coverage counsel for advice on difficult claims, and can reasonably expect that the advice it receives will be protected from discovery in later disputes with its reinsurers. Under the logic of this case, reinsurers seeking to make the case that a claim is not covered under the ceding company's policy will have to argue that position on the merits, rather than rely on possible "smoking guns" in the files of coverage counsel.

IV. Other Major Issues Involving Privilege and Confidentiality That Arise in Reinsurance Scenarios

A. Arbitration, Privilege, and Reinsurance

Some reinsurers have deleted arbitration clauses from standard contract language, but most reinsurance contracts still mandate arbitration. It must be noted that arbitration can be waived by not asserting the right immediately.[107] One feature of arbitration and other alternative dispute resolution mechanisms often deemed attractive is the heightened level of confidentiality presumed to be available. In the context of reinsurance disputes, confidentiality is often especially critical due to the multifaceted interrelationships so often involved.

Reinsurance contracts often contain a confidentiality provision in the arbitration clause. This inclusion parallels the clear expressions favoring confidentiality in arbitration rules and guidelines promulgated for more general purposes. For example, the Center for Public Resources (CPR), a recognized leader in dispute resolution, has adopted the *Rules for Non-Administered Arbitration*, which provides, in Rule 18, that "the parties, the arbitrators and CPR shall treat the proceedings, any related discovery and the decisions of the Tribunal, as confidential, except in connection with judicial proceedings ancillary to the arbitration."[108] Similarly, the *Code of Ethics for Arbitrators in Commercial Disputes* provides in part that "the arbitrator should keep confidential all matters relating to the arbitration."[109]

Privacy is traditionally one of arbitration's greatest advantages.[110] However, it is unlikely that such a sweeping generalization would apply today. While arbitration participants may genuinely cherish "privacy" in arbitration, to say that "privacy" (or more precisely, "confidentiality") has been "safeguarded" by the courts and "honored by third parties" would be a serious overstatement. When dealing with assertions of confidentiality in situations where discovery rules mandate disclosure, courts are faced with a tension between the confidentiality bargained for in contract and urged by the parties and what is suggested to be the public's "right to every man's evidence."[111] To put it in another way, the disclosure "required by applicable rules of law" can deal a heavy blow to expectations of confidentiality in arbitration.

The reported cases dealing with attempts to intrude upon the confidentiality of the arbitration process most often have involved attempts to depose an arbitrator. Courts routinely have refused to allow a party "to depose an arbitrator for the purpose of impeaching or clarifying his decision."[112] Even when a party tries to undermine the finality of the arbitrator's decision with claims of bias or interest, the questioning of arbitrators, when allowed at all, is conducted under judicial supervision and only in cases where clear evidence of impropriety has been presented.[113]

Courts have rarely analyzed, in confidentiality terms, a third party's request for the discovery of records of arbitration proceedings, perhaps because discovery rules on their face would seem to mandate such disclosure in the absence of an identifiable privilege.[114] In *Milone v. General Motors Corp.*, defendant General Motors, in a products liability action, sought to discover from the plaintiff's insurer documents relating to a no-fault arbitration with the insurer in connection with the accident.[115] The court conducted a traditional privilege inquiry and found that the documents were not prepared in connection with any common interest shared between the insurer and the adversarial plaintiff.[116] Further, since the documents were developed in preparation for the earlier arbitration and not for the pending litigation, no work-product privilege attached.[117] In a similar vein, in an action involving a dispute in the construction industry, a North Carolina court of appeals allowed discovery by a third-party contractor of the transcripts of an arbitration proceeding between a contracting university and a prime contractor on the same job.[118] The recent case of *Security Insurance Co. of Hartford v. Trustmark Insurance Co.* involved a suit between two reinsurers relating to a retrocession agreement.[119] One of the reinsurers requested and was granted production of documents reflecting past disputes relating to that same agreement, despite the fact that arbitration was ongoing relating to some aspects of disputes in the United Kingdom;[120] any confidentiality concerns that might exist relating to documents created for the purposes of arbitration have no bearing on the actual business transaction that was the basis for the dispute being arbitrated.

B. The Impact of Rule 408 of the Federal Rules of Evidence

Federal Rule of Evidence 408, stated broadly, provides that evidence of offering or accepting settlements is not admissible in order to prove liability.[121] It further states that evidence of conduct or statements made in compromise negotiations is likewise not admissible.[122] However, the rule does not require exclusion of evidence that is otherwise discoverable. While FRE 408 explicitly addresses the "admissibility" of settlement discussions, as distinguished from "discoverability," a few courts have extended FRE 408 to apply to the discoverability of settlement proceedings as well.[123] A notable example is *Bottaro v. Hatton Associates*, where the court held that inquiries into a settlement agreement required a "particularized showing of a likelihood that admissible evidence will be generated by the dissemination of the terms of [the agreement]" based on a "strong public policy of favoring settlements."[124]

The *Bottaro* rationale has been explicitly rejected by one court. In *Bennett v. La Pere*, the court explained that it thought that the *Bottaro* decision had misconceived the policy rationale underlying FRE 408.[125] It said that FRE 408 was meant to guard against allowing settlement discussions to "unimpededly creep into evidence at trial."[126] However, after a settlement is obtained, parties no longer have that fear since the matter is postsettlement. Hence, the *Bottaro* court concluded that the concept that discovery should be prevented so as not to discourage negotiations was misconceived. Other courts have held that FRE 408 applies only to the admissibility of settlement discussions, and not to their discoverability.[127]

C. Ethical Considerations in Connection with Privilege and Confidentiality

There are a number of important ethical considerations that come into play when dealing with complex litigation such as that found in insurance and reinsurance scenarios, each of which deserves separate consideration.

1. *Communication with Person Represented by Counsel*

Rule 4.2 of the Model Rules of Professional Conduct specifically addresses communication with a person represented by counsel.[128] The rule provides that a lawyer, in representing a client, shall not communicate with another party regarding the matter if the lawyer knows the party to be represented by another lawyer.[129]

In the comment to this rule, it is specifically noted that the rule does not prohibit communication with a party, or an employer or agent of a party, concerning matters outside the representation.[130] "For example, the existence of a controversy between . . . two organizations does not prohibit a lawyer for either from communicating with nonlawyer representatives of the other regarding a separate matter." Also, "[p]arties to a matter may communicate directly with each other," and "a lawyer having independent justification . . . for communicating with the other party is permitted to do so."[131] Communications authorized by law include, for example, the right of a party to a controversy with a government agency to speak with government officials about that matter.

The comment to the rule states in part:

> In the case of a represented organization, this Rule prohibits communications with a constituent of the organization who supervises, directs

> or regularly consults with the organization's lawyer concerning the matter or has authority to obligate the organization with respect to the matter or whose act or omission in connection with the matter may be imputed to the organization for purposes of civil or criminal liability. Consent of the organization's lawyer is not required for communication with a former constituent. If a constituent of the organization is represented in the matter by his or her own counsel, the consent by that counsel to a communication will be sufficient for purposes of this Rule. Compare Rule 3.4(f). In communicating with a current or former constituent of an organization, a lawyer must not use methods of obtaining evidence that violate the legal rights of the organization. See Rule 4.4.

If an agent or employee of the organization is represented in the matter by his or her own counsel, the consent by that counsel to a communication will be sufficient for purposes of this rule. The rule also covers any person, whether or not a party to a formal proceeding, who is represented by counsel concerning the matter in question.[132]

Rule 4.2 continues the traditional prohibition against communicating with a person known to be represented by another lawyer without that lawyer's consent. The provision is substantially similar to the predecessor Model Code of Professional Responsibility.[133]

a. Purpose of the Rule against Contact

The purpose of Rule 4.2 is to prevent lawyers from taking advantage of uncounseled laypersons and to preserve the integrity of the lawyer-client relationship.[134]

b. Opposing Parties May Speak to Each Other

As the comment to Rule 4.2 states, the parties to a matter may voluntarily speak to each other without their lawyer's consent, and lawyers are not obligated to dissuade their clients from doing so.[135]

c. Can a Lawyer Advise a Client to Communicate with a Represented Party Directly?

A lawyer does not have an obligation to actively dissuade a client from communicating with another party. However, Rule 8.4(a) makes it unethical and improper for a lawyer knowingly to assist or induce another to violate the rules, and, therefore, could be construed to prohibit the lawyer from directing or advising a client to communicate with a represented party.[136]

There are a number of additional specific topics that are directly addressed in the comments to Rule 4.2, which are quite pertinent to this discussion. These include the following:

d. Using a Third Person to Communicate with a Represented Party

Rule 8.4 would also prohibit a lawyer from circumventing Rule 4.2 through the use of a third person.[137] Thus, a lawyer may not advise or permit another to communicate in a manner that would be impermissible if engaged in by the lawyer.[138]

However, the distinction must be drawn between contact that is caused or directed by the lawyer, and contact that occurs independently, and not at the lawyer's behest. In *Hayes v. Commonwealth*, a detective who interviewed an indicted defendant without the prosecutor's knowledge was not considered an "agent" of the prosecutor for purposes of Rule 4.2.[139] However, in *Commonwealth v. Louhisdon*, a district attorney specifically directed a psychiatrist to meet with a represented inmate in order to submit a report to the court, and the court determined this to be in violation of Rule 4.2.[140]

e. Communication Need Not Be Intentional

Communication with the represented party can be an ethical violation even though it was not intentional.[141] Moreover, in *In re Howes*, a prosecutor was found in violation of Rule 4.2 by simply listening to a criminal defendant discuss the case without knowledge of the defense counsel, despite the fact that no questions were asked.[142]

f. Is the Represented Person Subject to the Rule?

There are several conditions that must be met before a Rule 4.2 violation can be established. First, the represented person must be subject to the rule, which applies to any person who is represented by counsel concerning the matter to which the communication relates.[143] The previous language of the rule applied only to "represented parties"; this term is still often used to describe those who fall under the rule.

g. When the Represented Party Is an Organization

When an organization, such as a corporation, is the represented party, certain other persons will be treated as parties as well. The comment to Rule 4.2 has led to a test for determining whether a person such as an employee is a party for purposes of the rule by examining such person's roles in supervision and direction.[144] Stated simply, informal contact is prohibited with any person within the organization "who supervises, directs or regularly consults with the organization's lawyer concerning the matter or has authority to obligate the organization with respect to the matter or whose act or omission in connection with the matter may be imputed to the organization for purposes of civil or criminal liability."[145] For example, in *Palmer v. Pioneer Inn Associates*, the court articulated that "under the managing-speaking test, ex parte interviews are barred for employees holding managerial positions giving the authority to speak for and bind the corporation."[146] Conversely, in *NAACP v. Florida*, the court reasoned that a plaintiff's attorney could interview "rank and file" prison employees, as it was quite "unlikely" that any statements made by those persons could bind the employer, or that their actions could be imputed to the employer.[147]

The distinction drawn by the courts revolves around the status of the employee as an "alter ego" of the corporation, which includes consideration of the relationship between the person and the corporation's lawyers.[148]

However, there have been cases that have gone against this prevailing rule. For example, in *Morrison v. Brandeis University*, plaintiff's attorney was permitted interviews with members of university faculty committee that had passed on plaintiff's eligibility for tenure, even though members might personify defendant university and speak for it with respect to the lawsuit.[149] Moreover, some states rely heavily on the distinction between employees or managers and the individuals in the "litigation control group."[150]

h. Former Employee of a Corporate Party Opponent

The American Bar Association (ABA) Committee on Ethics and Professional Responsibility states that former employees of a corporation may be contacted without consulting the corporation's counsel as they are no longer in positions of authority and, therefore, cannot bind the corporation.[151] The Florida Supreme Court enunciated the rule well when it held that Rule 4.2 was "intended to specifically regulate an attorney's contact with a person represented by counsel and the rule neither contemplates nor prohibits an attorney's ex parte communications with former employees of a defendant-employer."[152]

i. Discussions with Former Corporate Employees: The Confidentiality Problem

The subject matter of the discussion, however, may be protected by the attorney-client privilege.[153] A corporate employee who is a party for purposes of the attorney-client privilege is not necessarily a party for the purposes of Rule 4.2.[154]

j. Witnesses

Rule 4.2 does not preclude a lawyer from interviewing the intended witnesses of another party.[155] However, special rules apply when the witness is also a party to the action, including the special scenarios involving corporate parties.[156]

k. Members of a Class Action

Members of a class action suit are "parties" within the meaning of Rule 4.2.[157]

l. Is the Party Represented?

A second requirement for a Rule 4.2 violation is that the party with whom the lawyer has the "communication" must be represented by counsel.[158]

m. Is the Party Represented in the Matter Being Discussed?

A third requirement for a Rule 4.2 violation is that the party with whom the lawyer is communicating must be represented in connection with the matter being discussed. Thus, a lawyer representing a client against a represented party in one matter may nonetheless communicate with the represented party concerning a wholly unrelated matter for which the client does not have representation so long as the lawyer has an independent justification for doing so.[159] In this context, the client would not be a represented party for the purposes of Rule 4.2. The rule does not prohibit communication with a party, or an employee or agent of a party, concerning matters outside the representation.[160]

In the case of an organization, the "Rule prohibits communications with a constituent of the organization who supervises, directs or regularly consults with the organization's lawyer concerning the matter."[161] It also prohibits communication with anyone who "has authority to obligate the organization with respect to the matter or whose act or omission in connection with the matter may be imputed to the organization for purposes of civil or criminal liability."[162] If an agent or employee of the organization is represented in the matter by his own counsel, the consent by that counsel to a communication will be sufficient for purposes of this rule.[163]

n. Is the Communication Made in Connection with the Representation of a Client?

A Rule 4.2 violation cannot occur unless the lawyer was communicating with the represented party in connection with the representation of a client or on behalf of a client.[164]

o. Consent by Opposing Lawyer

Rule 4.2 permits communications with a represented party when the consent of the party's lawyer is obtained.[165] Further, consent is required regardless of the party's legal sophistication.[166]

p. Direct Settlement Negotiations with Opposing Party

The anticontact prohibition of Rule 4.2 applies to direct settlement negotiations with an opposing party.[167] However, as is reflected in C.W. Wolfram's *Modern Legal Ethics*, some have suggested that an exception to this rule against contact with the opposing party should exist when opposing counsel refuses to convey settlement offers.[168]

q. The Anticontact Rule in Domestic Relations Litigation

The anticontact rule is frequently implicated in domestic-relations litigation.[169]

r. When a Governmental Agency Is the Represented Party

When a governmental agency is the represented party, the comment to Rule 4.2 indicates that communications with government officials are permitted as "authorized by law."[170] Courts interpreting the predecessor to the rule in the Model Code similarly supported broad access to government employees.[171]

s. Prosecutors Communicating with Represented Criminal Defendants

In the context of criminal proceedings, Rule 4.2 prohibits prosecutors and their agents from speaking with a represented criminal defendant without notice to the defendant's lawyer and a reasonable opportunity to be either present or consented.[172] It must further be noted that this prohibition applies even if the defendant initiates the communication.[173]

However, communications with represented criminal suspects prior to the initiation of formal judicial proceedings as part of a noncustodial investigation by government agents or with informants generally are not considered subject to the anticontact rule. The rationale is usually that the rule is coextensive with the accused's Sixth Amendment right to counsel, and that the contact is within the "authorized by law" exception.[174]

t. Federal Prosecutors

In 1988 a sharp debate arose between the American Bar Association and the U.S. Attorney General as to the applicability of Rule 4.2 to federal prosecutors conducting criminal investigations. The Justice Department, in response to the decision in *United States v. Hammad*, which suppressed evidence a prosecutor obtained by violating the anticontact provision of the predecessor Model Code,[175] took the position that federal prosecutors cannot be sanctioned for violating the ethical rule barring contacts with a defendant "in the course of authorized law enforcement activity."[176] The controversial position is based on the Supremacy Clause and on the "authorized by law" exception to the ethical rule.[177]

The American Bar Association responded with a resolution rejecting the Justice Department's position and "oppos[ing] any attempt by the Justice Department unilaterally to exempt its lawyers from the professional conduct rules that apply to all lawyers under applicable rules of the jurisdictions in which they practice."[178]

u. Lawyer Who Violates Rule 4.2 May Be Sanctioned or Disqualified

A lawyer who has violated Rule 4.2 may be disqualified from representing his or her client.[179]

2. *Fairness to Opposing Party and Counsel*

Fairness to opposing party and counsel is specifically addressed in Rule 3.4, which provides:

> A lawyer shall not:
> (a) unlawfully obstruct another's party's access to evidence or unlawfully alter, destroy or conceal a document or other material having potential evidentiary value. A lawyer shall not counsel or assist another person to do any such act;
> (b) falsify evidence, counsel or assist a witness, to testify falsely, or offer an inducement to a witness that is prohibited by law;
> (c) knowingly disobey an obligation under the rules of a tribunal, except for an open refusal based on an assertion that no valid obligation exists;

(d) in pretrial procedure, make a frivolous discovery request or fail to make reasonably diligent effort to comply with a legally proper discovery request by an opposing party;
(e) in trial, allude to any matter that the lawyer does not reasonably believe is relevant or that will not be supported by admissible evidence, assert personal knowledge of facts in issue except when testifying as a witness, or state a personal opinion as to the justness of a cause, the credibility of a witness, the culpability of a civil litigant or the guilt or innocence of an accused; or
(f) request a person other than a client to refrain from voluntarily giving relevant information to another party unless:
  (1) the person is a relative or an employee or other agent of a client; and
  (2) the lawyer reasonably believes that the person's interests will not be adversely affected by refraining from giving such information.

COMMENT

(1) The procedure of the adversary system contemplates that the evidence in a case is to be marshaled competitively by the contending parties. Fair competition in the adversary system is secured by prohibitions against destruction or concealment of evidence, improperly influencing witnesses, obstructive tactics in discovery procedure, and the like.

(2) Documents and other items of evidence are often essential to establish a claim or defense. Subject to evidentiary privileges, the right of an opposing party, including the government, to obtain evidence through discovery or subpoena is an important procedural right. The exercise of that right can be frustrated if relevant material is altered, concealed or destroyed. Applicable law in many jurisdictions makes it an offense to destroy material for purposes of impairing its availability in a pending proceeding or one whose commencement can be foreseen. Falsifying evidence is also generally a criminal offense. Paragraph (a) applies to evidentiary material generally, including computerized information. Applicable law may permit a lawyer to take temporary possession of physical evidence of client crimes for the purpose of conducting a limited examination that will not alter or destroy material characteristics of the evidence. In such a case, applicable law may require the lawyer to turn the evidence over to the police or other prosecuting authority, depending on the circumstances.

(3) With regard to paragraph (b), it is not improper to pay a witness's expenses or to compensate an expert witness on terms permitted by law. The common law rule in most jurisdictions is that

it is improper to pay an occurrence witness any fee for testifying and that it is improper to pay an expert witness a contingent fee.

(4) Paragraph (f) permits a lawyer to advise employees of a client to refrain from giving information to another party, for the employees may identify their interests with those of the client. See also Rule 4.2.[180]

Alteration, destruction, or concealment of evidence is a potential problem area in large, multiparty litigation such as insurance scenarios.[181] Under this rule, procuring the absence of a witness is treated as obstruction of evidence.[182]

3. *Dealing with an Unrepresented Person*

Dealing with an unrepresented person is specifically addressed in Rule 4.3, which provides:

> In dealing on behalf of a client with a person who is not represented by counsel, a lawyer shall not state or imply that the lawyer is disinterested. When the lawyer knows or reasonably should know that the unrepresented person misunderstands the lawyer's role in the matter, the lawyer shall make reasonable efforts to correct the misunderstanding. The lawyer shall not give legal advice to an unrepresented person, other than the advice to secure counsel, if the lawyer knows or reasonably should know that the interests of such a person are or have a reasonably possibility of being in conflict with the interests of the client.
>
> COMMENT
>
> (1) An unrepresented person, particularly one not experienced in dealing with legal matters, might assume that a lawyer is disinterested in loyalties or is a disinterested authority on the law even when the lawyer represents a client. In order to avoid a misunderstanding, a lawyer will typically need to identify the lawyer's client and, where necessary, explain that the client has interests opposed to those of the unrepresented person. For misunderstandings that sometimes arise when a lawyer for an organization deals with an unrepresented constituent, see Rule 1.13(f).[183]
>
> (2) The Rule distinguishes between situations involving unrepresented persons whose interests may be adverse to those of the lawyer's client and those in which the person's interests are not in conflict with the client's. In the former situation, the possibility that the lawyer will compromise the unrepresented person's interest is so great that the Rule prohibits the giving of any advice, apart from the advice to obtain counsel. Whether a lawyer is giving impermissible advice may depend on the experience and sophistication of the unrepresented person, as well

> as the setting in which the behavior and comments occur. This Rule does not prohibit a lawyer from negotiating the terms of a transaction or settling a dispute with an unrepresented person. So long as the lawyer has explained that the lawyer represents an adverse party and is not representing the person, the lawyer may inform the person of the terms on which the lawyer's client will enter into an agreement or settle a matter, prepare documents that require the person's signature and explain the lawyer's own view of the meaning of the document or the lawyer's view of the underlying legal obligations.[184]

Rule 4.3 was amended in 2002 to add the last sentence of the rule, prohibiting an attorney from "giving advice" to an unrepresented person, in an attempt to discourage overreaching in negotiations.[185]

The interplay between rules 4.2 and 4.3 was discussed in *Reynoso v. Greynolds Park Manor Inc.*, which stated that while Rule 4.2 allows attorney contact with former employees, "no inquiry can be made into any matters that are the subject of the attorney-client privilege, and that the requirements of Rule 4.3, entitled 'Dealing With Unrepresented Persons,' must be scrupulously observed."[186]

4. *Respect for Rights of Third Persons*

Respect for the rights of third persons is specifically addressed in Rule 4.4, which provides:

> (a) In representing a client, a lawyer shall not use means that have no substantial purpose other than to embarrass, delay, or burden a third person, or use methods of obtaining evidence that violate the legal rights of such a person.
> (b) A lawyer who receives a document relating to the representation of the lawyer's client and knows or reasonably should know that the document was inadvertently sent shall promptly notify the sender.
>
> COMMENT
>
> (1) Responsibility to a client requires a lawyer to subordinate the interests of others to those of the client, but that responsibility does not imply that a lawyer may disregard the rights of third persons. It is impractical to catalogue all such rights, but they include legal restrictions on methods of obtaining evidence from third persons and unwarranted intrusions into privileged relationships, such as the client-lawyer relationship.
> (2) Paragraph (b) recognizes that lawyers sometimes receive documents that were mistakenly sent or produced by opposing parties or their lawyers. If a lawyer knows or reasonably should

know that such a document was sent inadvertently, then this Rule requires the lawyer to promptly notify the sender in order to permit that person to take protective measures. Whether the lawyer is required to take additional steps, such as returning the original document, is a matter of law beyond the scope of these Rules, as is the question of whether the privileged status of a document has been waived. Similarly, this Rule does not address the legal duties of a lawyer who receives a document that the lawyer knows or reasonably should know may have been wrongfully obtained by the sending person. For purposes of this Rule, "document" includes e-mail or other electronic modes of transmission subject to being read or put into readable form.

(3) Some lawyers may choose to return a document unread, for example, when the lawyer learns before receiving the document that it was inadvertently sent to the wrong address. Where a lawyer is not required by applicable law to do so, the decision to voluntarily return such a document is a matter of professional judgment ordinarily reserved to the lawyer. See Rules 1.2 and 1.4.[187]

Notes

1. *See* Ala. Reassurance Co. v. Sutcher (*In re* Inter-Am. Ins. Co.), 303 Ill. App. 3d 95, 97–98 (Ill. App. Ct. 1st 1999).
2. *See* Travelers Cas. & Sur. Co. v. Certain Underwriters at Lloyd's of London, 96 N.Y.2d 583, 587–88 (2001).
3. *See* Mich. Twp. Participating Plan v. Fed. Ins. Co., 592 N.W.2d 760, 764 (Mich. App. 1999); *see also Travelers*, 96 N.Y.2d at 587–88.
4. *See* Hollipeter v. Stuyvesant Ins. Co., 523 S.W.2d 595, 599 (Mo. Ct. App. 1975).
5. *See* Am. Bankers Ins. Co. v. Nw. Nat'l Ins. Co., 198 F.3d 1332, 1332 n.1 (11th Cir. 1999).
6. *See* Donaldson v. United Cmty. Ins. Co., 741 So. 2d 676, 679 (La. App. 3d Cir. 1999).
7. *See* John Hancock Prop. & Cas. Ins. Co. v. Universale Reinsurance Co., 147 F.R.D. 40, 43 n.2 (S.D.N.Y. 1993).
8. *See* British Ins. Co. of Cayman v. Water St. Ins. Co., Ltd., 93 F. Supp. 2d 506, 509 n.1 (S.D.N.Y. 2000).
9. *See* Unigard Sec. Ins. Co. v. N. River Ins. Co., 4 F.3d 1049, 1053 (2d Cir. 1993).
10. *See* British Ins. Co. of Cayman v. Safety Nat'l Cas., 335 F.3d 205, 211–12 (3d Cir. 2003).
11. *See Unigard*, 4 F.3d at 1053.
12. *See British Ins. Co. of Cayman*, 2003 WL 21536693; N. River Ins. Co. v. Cigna Reinsurance Co., 52 F.3d 1194, 1199 (3d Cir. 1995).
13. *See Travelers*, 760 N.E.2d at 322.
14. *Id.*
15. *See* Merit Life Ins. Co. v. C.I.R., 853 F.2d 1435, 1436 (7th Cir. 1988).
16. *See, e.g.*, Allstate Ins. Co. v. Administratia Asigurarilor de Stat., 875 F. Supp. 1022, 1028 (S.D.N.Y. 1995); Credit Managers Ass'n v. Kennesaw Life & Accident Ins. Co., 809 F.2d 617, 623–24 (9th Cir. 1987).

17. *See* Clark & Co. v. Dep't of Ins. as Receiver of E. Ins. Co., 436 So. 2d 1013, 1015 (Fla. Dist. Ct. App. 1983).
18. *See generally* Travelers Cas. & Sur. Co. v. Gerling Global Reinsurance Corp. of Am., 419 F.3d 181 (2d Cir. Conn. 2005).
19. AMERICAN HERITAGE DICTIONARY OF THE ENGLISH LANGUAGE (Houghton Mifflin Co., 4th ed. 2004), http://dictionary.reference.com/browse/fortune (last visited July 2010).
20. 251 F.2d 696, 697–99 (1958).
21. *Id.* at 704.
22. *See* Am. Ins. Co. v. N. Am. Co. for Prop. & Cas. Ins., 697 F.2d 79, 80–81 (2d Cir. 1982).
23. *See, e.g.*, Christiana Gen. Ins. Corp. v. Great Am. Ins. Co., 979 F.2d 268, 280 (2d Cir. 1992) (finding reinsurer cannot dispute good-faith determinations relating to defense or settlement, but it is not obligated to provider coverage for payments clearly beyond the scope of the policy); *see generally* N. River Ins. Co. v. CIGNA Reinsurance Co., 52 F.3d 1194 (3d Cir. 1995) (finding reinsurer obligated to reimburse for all good-faith payments, but retains the right to question if the underlying liability results from an insured loss); Aetna Cas. & Sur. v. Home Ins. Co., 882 F. Supp. 1328 (S.D.N.Y. 1995) (finding reinsurer not obligated to follow settlement if loss paid is outside scope of coverage; bound by all good-faith determinations of ceding company except as to whether the loss is within the terms of the policy).
24. 903 F.2d 910, 912 (2d Cir. 1990).
25. 35 F. Supp. 2d 348, 351 (S.D.N.Y. 1999).
26. *Id.*
27. 342 F.3d 78., 84–85 (2d Cir. 2003).
28. *Id.*
29. *Id. See also* Emp'rs Reinsurance Corp. v. Mid-Continent Cas. Co., 202 F. Supp. 2d 1221 (D. Kan. 2002) (finding reinsurance agreement provided coverage for declaratory judgment fees and expenses reinsured incurred in connection with underlying action).
30. 107 U.S. 485, 510 (1883).
31. *Id.*
32. *See, e.g.*, Sec. Mut. Cas. Co. v. Affiliated FM Ins. Co., 471 F.2d 238 (8th Cir. 1972); Calvert Fire Ins. Co. v. Unigard Mut. Ins. Co., 526 F. Supp. 623 (D. Neb. 1980), *aff'd*, 676 F.2d 707 (8th Cir. 1982).
33. *See* Sec. Mut. Cas. Co. v. Transp. Indem. Co., 66 Cal. App. 3d 1009, 1014 (1977); *see generally* Nw. Mut. Fire Assoc. v. Union Mut. Fire Ins. Co. of Providence, R.I., 144 F.2d 274 (9th Cir. 1944) (explaining duty is of "utmost good faith"); Mutuelle Generale Francaise Vie v. Life Ins. Co. of Pa., 688 F. Supp. 386 (N.D. Ill. 1988) (describing duty of utmost good faith).
34. 886 F. Supp 1147, 1155 (S.D.N.Y. 1995).
35. 9 F. Supp. 2d 49 (D. Mass. 1998).
36. *Id.* at 69.
37. *Id.* at 53.
38. *Id.* at 66. Under these doctrines, the reinsurer is bound unless there is evidence of gross negligence or recklessness or the settlement was not even arguably within the realm of the reinsurance coverage. *See, e.g.*, N. River Ins. Co. v. CIGNA Reinsurance Co., 52 F.3d 1194 (3d Cir. 1995); Mentor Ins. Co. v. Brannkasse, 996 F.2d 506 (2d Cir. N.Y. 1993).

39. *Id.* at 69.
40. *Id.*
41. *See* Shell Oil Co. v. Par Four P'ship, 638 So. 2d 1050, 1051 (Fla. App. 5th 1994); *see generally* S. Bell Tel. & Tel. Co. v. Deason, 632 So. 2d 1377 (Fla. 1994).
42. Doe *ex rel.* Doe v. Archdiocese of the Catholic Church, 721 So. 2d 428, 429 (Fla. Dist. Ct. App. 3d 1998).
43. Se. Pa. Transit Auth. v. Transit Cas. Co., 55 F.R.D. 553, 557 (E.D. Pa. 1972).
44. N. River Ins. Co. v. Columbia Cas. Co., No. 90 Civ. 2518, 1995 U.S. Dist. LEXIS 9570 (S.D.N.Y. 1995).
45. *See* Aetna Cas. & Sur. Co. v. Superior Court, 153 Cal. App. 3d 467, 479 (1984).
46. *See* Nat'l Union Fire Ins. v. Cont'l Ill. Corp., 116 F.R.D. 78 (N.D. Ill. 1978) (finding reinsurance agreement is an "insurance agreement" for purposes of production in discovery).
47. *See* Rhone-Poulenc Rorer, Inc. v. Home Indem. Co., 139 F.R.D. 609 (E.D. Pa. 1991) (finding Rule 26(b)(2)'s requirement that insurance agreements that would respond to any judgment be produced does not apply to reinsurance agreements unless the insured seeks actual damages against the insurer, rather than just a declaration of policy interpretation).
48. 2003 U.S. Dist. LEXIS 2052, at *10–14 (E.D. Pa. Feb. 4, 2003).
49. Fla. Stat. Ann. § 627.4137 (formerly Fla. Stat. Ann. § 627.7264).
50. *See* Fla. Stat. Ann. § 627.401.
51. *See* McDonough Constr. Corp. v. Pan Am. Sur. Co., 190 So. 2d 617, 620 (Fla. App. 1st 1966).
52. *See generally* Nat'l Union Fire Ins. Co. v. Stouffer Chem., 558 A.2d 1091 (Del. Super. 1989); Potomac Elec. Power v. Cal. Union Ins.; Co., 136 F.R.D. 1 (D.C. 1990).
53. *See* Playtex, Inc. v. Columbia Cas. Co., No. 88C-MR-233, 1993 Del. Super. LEXIS 58, 286 (Feb. 10, 1993; Sept. 20, 1993).
54. 129 F.R.D. 99, 106 (D.N.J. 1989).
55. *See* Rhone-Poulenc Rorer, Inc. v. Home Indem. Co., 139 F.R.D. 609, 611–12 (E.D. Pa. 1991).
56. *Id.*
57. *See* United Equitable Ins. Co. v. Reinsurance Co. of Am., 510 N.E.2d 914, 916 n.3 (Ill. 1st 1987).
58. No. MDL 76D4 (E.D. Pa., July 26, 1989).
59. *Id.*
60. McDonough Constr. Corp. v. Pan Am. Sur. Co., 190 So. 2d 617, 619–20 (Fla. App. 1st 1966).
61. *See* Fed. R. Civ. P. 45(a)(3).
62. Fed. R. Civ. P. 45(c)(3)(A).
63. Fed. R. Civ. P. 45(c)(3)(A)(iii).
64. Fed. R. Civ. P. 45(c)(3)(B)(i).
65. *See* Potomac Elec. Power v. Cal. Union Ins. Co., 136 F.R.D. 1, 3 (D.C. 1990) (holding correspondence regarding underwriting or reinsurance agreements irrelevant and proprietary); Firemans Fund Ins. Co. v. Superior Court, 286 Cal. Rptr. 50, 51 (Cal. App. 1st 1991) (holding that trial court should have conducted an in camera review of claims communications between insurer and reinsurer for sensitive commercial information prior to disclosure to the insured).
66. Rhone-Poulenc Rorer, Inc. v. Home Indem. Co., 139 F.R.D. 609, 612 (E.D. Pa. 1991).

67. *See* Emp'rs Commercial Union Ins. Co. of Am. v. Browning-Ferris Indus., 1993 U.S. Dist. LEXIS 21098, at *13–20 (D. Kan. Apr. 5, 1993).
68. *Rhone-Poulenc*, 139 F.R.D. at 613–14.
69. *See, e.g.*, Union Carbide Corp. v. Travelers Indem. Co., 61 F.R.D. 411, 412–14 (W.D. Pa. 1973).
70. *See* Great Am. Surplus Lines Ins. v. Ace Oil Co., 120 F.R.D. 533, 536–38 (E.D. Cal. 1988) (finding attorney-client privilege may be asserted, and waived, only by the insurer having the attorney-client relationship with counsel).
71. Durham Indus. v. N. River Ins. Co., 1980 U.S. Dist. LEXIS 15154 (S.D.N.Y. Nov. 21, 1980).
72. *Id.*
73. *See also* Int'l Ins. Co. v. Sargent & Lundy, 242 Ill. App. 3d 614, 630–35 (Ill. App. Ct. 1st 1993) (finding communications between an insurer and its reinsurer are privileged and a court should not compel the insurer or the reinsurer to divulge such privileged communications).
74. 197 F.R.D. 601, 606 (S.D. Ohio 2000).
75. *See* Bank of Am., N.A. v. Terra Nova Ins. Co., 212 F.R.D. 166 (S.D.N.Y. 2002).
76. Lintz v. Am. Gen. Fin., Inc., 1999 WL 450197 (D. Kan. 1999).
77. *See* Deal v. Lutheran Hosps. & Homes, 127 F.R.D. 166, 168 (D. Alaska 1989).
78. Fed. R. Civ. P. 45(c)(2)(B).
79. Fed. R. Civ. P. 26(c).
80. 4 F.3d 1049, 1063 (2d Cir. 1993) (applying the law of New York) (also discussed earlier relating to the doctrine of utmost good faith).
81. *Id.* at 1064.
82. *Id.*
83. *Id.* at 1053–54.
84. *Id.* at 1065 (citations omitted).
85. *Id.*
86. *Id.* (citing Christiana Gen. Ins. Co. v. Great Am. Ins. Co., 979 F.2d 268, 278 (2d Cir. 1992)).
87. *Unigard*, 4 F.3d at 1065.
88. *Id.* at 1067.
89. 766 F.2d 163, 166–67 (4th Cir. 1985).
90. 922 F.2d 516, 524 (9th Cir. 1990).
91. 4 F.3d at 1068–69.
92. *Id.* at 1069.
93. *Id.*
94. 335 F.3d 205, 214–15 (3d Cir. N.J. 2003).
95. *Id.* at 212 (citing Baen v. Farmers Mut. Fire Ins., 381 N.J. 187, 712 A.2d 634, 644 (1998)).
96. 295 F. Supp. 2d 1229, 1241 (D. Kan. 2003).
97. *Id.*
98. 797 F. Supp. 363 (D.N.J. 1992).
99. *Id.* at 367–68.
100. *Id.* at 368.
101. *Id.* at 369.
102. *Id.* at 369.
103. *Id.* at 370.
104. *Id.* at 370.

105. *Id.* at 370–71.
106. *Id.* at 369–70.
107. Menorah Ins. Co. v. INX Reinsurance Corp., 72 F.3d 218, 221 (1st Cir. P.R. 1995).
108. Int'l Inst. for Conflict Prevention and Resolution Rules for Non-Administered Arbitration, Rule 18 (Rev. 2007).
109. Am. Arbitration Ass'n Code of Ethics for Arbitrators in Commercial Disputes, Canon VI (B) (Rev. 2004).
110. *See* DOMKE ON COMMERCIAL ARBITRATION § 1:4.
111. *See* Branzburg v. Hayes, 408 U.S. 665, 688 (1972).
112. Sperry Int'l Trade, Inc. v. Gov't of Isr., 602 F. Supp. 1440, 1443 (S.D.N.Y. 1985); *see generally* Wood v. Gen. Teamsters Union, Local 406, 583 F. Supp. 1471 (W.D. Mich. 1984); Brownko Int'l, Inc. v. Ogden Steel Co., 585 F. Supp. 1432 (S.D.N.Y. 1983); Reichman v. Creative Real Estate Consultants, Inc., 476 F. Supp. 1276 (S.D.N.Y. 1979).
113. *See* Andros Compania Maritima, S.A. v. Marc Rich & Co., A.G., 579 F.2d 691, 702 (2d Cir. N.Y. 1978); *see also Sperry*, 602 F. Supp. at 1443.
114. *See* FED. R. CIR. P. 26(b).
115. 84 A.D.2d 921, 446 N.Y.S.2d 650 (1981).
116. *Id.*
117. *Id.*
118. Industrotech Constructors, Inc. v. Duke Univ., 67 N.C. App. 741, 743–45 (1984).
119. 218 F.R.D. 18, 20 (D. Conn. 2003).
120. *Id.* at 22.
121. FED. R. EVID. 408.
122. *Id.*
123. *See generally* Weissman v. Fruchtman, 1986 WL 15669 (S.D.N.Y. 1986).
124. Bottaro v. Hatton Assocs., 96 F.R.D. 158, 160 (E.D.N.Y. 1982).
125. 112 F.R.D. 136, 139–40 (D.R.I. 1986).
126. *Id.* at 140.
127. *See In re* Gen. Motors Corp. v. Engine Interchange Litig., 594 F.2d 1106, 1124 n.20 (7th Cir. 1979); *see also* NAACP Legal Def. & Educ. Fund v. United States Dep't of Justice, 612 F. Supp. 1143, 1146 (D.D.C. 1985).
128. MODEL RULES OF PROF'L CONDUCT R. 4.2 (2009).
129. *Id.*
130. *Id.* at cmt. [4].
131. *Id.*
132. *Id.* at cmt. [2].
133. *See generally* Lewis Kurlantzick, *The Prohibition of Communications with an Adverse Party*, 51 CONN. B.J. 136 (1977); John Leubsdorf, *Communication with Another Lawyer's Client: The Lawyer's Veto and the Client's Interest*, 127 U. PA. L. REV. 683 (1979); Gregory G. Sarno, Annotation, *Communication with Party Represented by Counsel as Ground for Disciplining Attorney*, 26 A.L.R.4th 102 (1983).
134. *See generally* United States v. Batchelor, 484 F. Supp. 812 (E.D. Pa. 1980) ("the profession should not lose sight of the important societal interest at stake in insuring that laypersons not make decisions of major legal implication without the advice of counsel"); Frey v. Dep't of Health & Human Servs., 106 F.R.D. 32 (E.D.N.Y. 1985) (noting courts and commentators have stated that provision is meant to prevent situations in which adverse counsel would take advantage of represented party); Carter v. Kamaras, 430 A.2d 1058 (R.I. 1981) (observing the

rule preserves proper functioning of judicial system); Wright v. Group Health Hosp., 103 Wash. 2d 192 (1984) ("presence of the party's attorney theoretically neutralizes the contact" by opposing party's attorney); ABA Comm. on Ethics & Prof'l Responsibility, Informal Op. 83-1498 (1983) (stating prohibition is necessary to preserve the proper functioning of attorney-client relationship and to shield party from improper approaches); *see also* G.C. Hazard Jr. & W.W. Hodes, The Law of Lawyering 730 (2d ed. 1990) (writing that rule prevents lawyer from taking advantage of layperson to secure admission against interests or achieve unconscionable settlement of dispute); C.W. Wolfram, Modern Legal Ethics § 11.6, at 612–13 (1986) (noting that application of anticontact rule should be guided by its policy objective; unlikely that rule would prevent second lawyer from discussing with another lawyer's client suspected malpractice, excess fees, or possible client dissatisfaction).

135. *See* Lewis v. S.S. Baune, 534 F.2d 1115, 1122 (5th Cir. 1976) ("courts have consistently held that parties have a right to settle or compromise their litigation without the knowledge or consent of their counsel").
136. *See In re* Marietta, 223 Kan. 11, 11–12 (1977) (disciplining lawyer for causing client to communicate with opposing party).
137. *See* Model Rules of Prof'l Conduct R. 8.4 (2009).
138. *See* Schantz v. Eyman, 418 F.2d 11, 14 (9th Cir. 1969) (prosecutor responsible for postindictment questioning of accused by state psychiatrist); Crane v. State Bar, 30 Cal. 3d 117, 123 (1981) (lawyer responsible for letters sent by lawyer's employees on letterhead over lawyer's purported signature); *In re* Burrows, 291 Or. 135, 143–44 (1981) (failure to obtain opposing counsel's consent not excused by delegating task to nonlawyers); *see also* ABA Comm. on Prof'l Ethics, Informal Op. 663 (1963) (lawyer cannot communicate through private investigator).
139. 25 S.W.3d 463, 465–66 (Ky. 2000).
140. 2001 WL 360047, at *3 (Mass. Super. 2001).
141. *See generally* Crane v. State Bar of Cal., 30 Cal. 3d 117 (1981) (noting a negligent failure to prevent employees from contacting represented parties); Carter v. Kamaras, 430 A.2d 1058 (R.I. 1981) (holding it is immaterial whether direct contact is intentional or negligent violation); *In re* McCaffrey, 275 Or. 23 (1976) (holding it is immaterial whether communication is negligent or intentional).
142. 123 N.M. 311, 317 (1997).
143. Model Rules of Prof'l Conduct R. 4.2 cmt. [2].
144. *See* Model Rules of Prof'l Conduct R. 4.2 cmt. [7].
145. *Id.*; *see also* Palmer v. Pioneer Inn Assocs., 257 F.3d 999, 1001 (9th Cir. 2001).
146. *Id.*
147. 122 F. Supp. 2d 1335, 1340 (M.D. Fla. 2000).
148. *In re* FMC Corp., 430 F. Supp. 1108, 1111 (S.D. W. Va. 1977) (denying of motion enjoining party's lawyer from communicating with all salaried employees of defendant without counsel's consent); *see generally* Mills Land & Water Co. v. Golden W. Ref. Corp, 186 Cal. App. 3d 1016 (1986) (noting communication by opposing counsel with current board director improper despite conflict of interest between corporation and director); Fair Auto. Repair, Inc. v. Car-X Serv. Sys., Inc., 128 Ill. App. 3d 763 (1984) (holding prohibition applicable to those in corporate "control" group); Niesig v. Team I, 76 N.Y.2d 363 (1990) (holding rule applies to corporate employees whose acts or omissions in matter at issue

are binding on corporation or imputed to it for liability purposes, or who are implementing advice of corporate counsel); State v. CIBA-GEIGY Corp., 247 N.J. Super. 314 (App. Div. 1991) (adopting *Niesig* rationale wherein corporate criminal defendant is entitled to order barring state from interrogating any of its employees whose acts or omissions state seeks to impute to corporate defendant); Wright v. Grp. Health Hosp., 103 Wash. 2d 192 (1984) ("current . . . employees are parties if they have managerial authority sufficient to give them right to speak for and bind the corporation"); Featherstone v. Schaerrer, 34 P.3d 194 (Utah 2001) (deeming secretary-treasurer of defendant corporation a "represented person" because his statements could bind the company); *see also* ABA Comm. on Ethics & Prof'l Responsibility, Informal Op. 83-1489 (1983) (explaining rationale for rule grounded in notion that certain employees are considered the alter ego of the corporation); ABA Comm. on Ethics & Prof'l Responsibility, Informal Op. 1410 (1978) (officers and employees who can commit corporation are parties); ABA Comm. on Ethics & Prof'l Responsibility, Informal Op. 1377 (1977) (municipal employee with power to commit municipal corporation is a party. *But see* ABA Comm. on Prof'l Ethics & Grievances, Formal Op. 66 (1932) (not improper for attorney to communicate directly with president of adverse corporation concerning name of corporate officer most familiar with subject to be covered by deposition when corporate attorney failed to respond to such request).

149. 125 F.R.D. 14, 18 (D. Mass. 1989).

150. *See generally* Andrews v. Goodyear Tire & Rubber Co., Inc., 191 F.R.D. 59 (D.N.J. 2000) (finding manager of a represented company was not in the litigation control group for the purposes of the anticontact rule, and could be contacted without violation of Rule 4.2). For a general discussion of this complicated topic, see generally Jerome N. Krulewitch, *Ex Parte Communications with Corporate Parties: The Scope of the Limitations on Attorney Communications with One of Adverse Interest*, 82 Nw. U. L. Rev. 1274 (1988); Samuel L. Miller & Angelo J. Calfo, *Ex Parte Contact with Employees and Former Employees of a Corporate Adversary: Is It Ethical?* 42 Bus. Law. 1053 (1987); Lou Stahl, *Ex Parte Interviews with Enterprise Employees: A Post-*Upjohn *Analysis*, 44 Wash. & Lee L. Rev. 1181 (1987) (recommending a functional approach; "any present or former employee who is identified with an enterprise, either for purposes of resolving disputed issues or effective representation of the enterprise, [should be deemed] a party representative for discovery purposes"); Annotation, *Right of Attorney to Conduct Ex Parte Interview with Corporate Party's Non-management Employees*, 50 A.L.R.4th 652 (1985).

151. ABA Comm. on Ethics & Prof'l Responsibility, Formal Op. 91-359 (1991).

152. H.B.A. Mgmt. v. Estate of Schwartz, 693 So. 2d 541, 546 (Fla. 1997).

153. *See* Porter v. Arco Metals Co., Div. of Atl. Richfield Corp., 642 F. Supp. 1116, 1118 (D. Mont. 1986) (finding ex parte contact with former employees proper so long as not concerning a privileged matter).

154. *Id.* (finding interview with former employees of defendant corporation by plaintiff's counsel presented no attorney-client privilege issue unless counsel asked employees to divulge confidential communications); Wright v. Grp. Health Hosp., 103 Wash. 2d 192 (1984) ("policies represented by [Rules 4.2 and 1.6] are different"). *But see* Massa v. Eaton Corp., 109 F.R.D. 312, 314–15 (W.D. Mich. 1985) (finding the predecessor to Rule 4.2 applied to middle- and lower-

level employees because they could be "clients" for purpose of attorney-client privilege if their communication with counsel is needed to advise corporate client); Bobele v. Superior Court, 199 Cal. App. 3d 708, 712 (2d Dist. 1988) (finding under *Upjohn* that prohibition against ex parte contact with represented party extends to all corporate employees). For further discussion, see Stahl, *supra* note 150 (recommending a functional approach: "any present or former employee who is identified with an enterprise, either for purposes of resolving disputed issues or effective presentation of the enterprise, [should be deemed] a party representative for discovery purposes").

155. *See* Devlin v. Rosman, 205 So. 2d 346, 347 (Fla. Dist. Ct. App. 3d 1967) ("attorneys for one party in a pending cause are free to interview the other party's intended witness without the consent or presence of opposing counsel"); ABA Comm. on Prof'l Ethics & Grievances, Formal Op. 117 (1934) (stating communication with witness proper if there is no deception and the lawyer discloses role).

156. *See* ABA Comm. on Prof'l Ethics & Grievances, Formal Op. 187 (1938) (finding anticontact rule is applicable when witness is also a party).

157. *See In re* Fed. Skywalk Comm'n, 97 F.R.D. 370, 376–77 (W.D. Mo. 1983) (holding defendants in contempt because communication with class members violated disciplinary rule); Impervious Paint Indus., Inc. v. Ashland Oil, 508 F. Supp. 720, 722 (W.D. Ky. 1981) (finding plaintiff class members are to be treated as represented by plaintiff's counsel). *But see* Gulf Oil Co. v. Bernard, 452 U.S. 89, 101 (1981) (recognizing that ethics rules against communication with represented parties impose restraints on expression in context of class action).

158. *See* United States v. Jamil, 546 F. Supp. 646, 652 (E.D.N.Y. 1982) (finding person who retains counsel as protection against grand jury investigation is "represented party" for ethical purposes even if adversarial proceedings have not yet begun), *rev'd on other grounds*, 707 F.2d 638 (2d Cir. 1983); Abeles v. State Bar, 9 Cal. 3d 603, 609–10 (1973) (finding "represented" includes party who has counsel of record, regardless of whether such counsel in fact is authorized to act for that party); *see also* ABA Comm. on Prof'l Ethics, Informal Op. 827 (1965) (finding under ABA canons, communication by plaintiff's lawyer with defendant in effort to collect judgment proper where legal relationship between defendant and his lawyer had terminated); ABA Comm. on Prof'l Ethics, Informal Op. 1149 (1970) (finding defense lawyer in suit initiated by insurance company improperly communicated with insured without obtaining consent of insurance company's lawyer, whose representation extended indirectly to insured as well); Monceret v. Bd. of Prof'l Responsibility, 29 S.W.3d 455, 460 (Tenn. 2000) (finding "party" not limited to named plaintiff or defendant; may include witnesses). *But see In re* Boothe, 303 Or. 643, 648 (1987) (finding communication with person no longer represented not improper even though lawyer thought person was represented).

159. *See* United States v. Hammad, 858 F.2d 834, 839 (2d Cir. N.Y. 1988) (finding applicability of anticontact rule should be limited to instances in which the suspect has retained counsel "specifically for representation in conjunction with criminal matter in which he or she is held suspect"); *In re* Conduct of Burrows, 291 Or. 135, 145 (1981) (finding subject matter includes communication with defendant concerning undercover activities disclosed in hope of leniency).

160. Model Rules of Prof'l Conduct R. 4.2 cmt. [4].

161. *Id.* at cmt. [7].

162. *Id.*
163. *Id. But see id.* at R. 3.4(f).
164. *See In re* Complaint as to Conduct of Mettler, 305 Or. 12, 20 (1988) (holding lawyer working as state securities examiner was not acting in the course of representation of client); *see also* ABA Comm. on Ethics & Prof'l Responsibility, Informal Op. 1193 (1971) (finding lawyer conducting investigation for bail bond program was not representing client).
165. *See* State *ex rel.* Neb. State Bar Assoc. v. Hollstein, 202 Neb. 40, 56 (1979) (finding consent to further communication was implied); *In re* Mauch, 107 Wis. 2d 557, 558 (1982) (finding communication proper given ambiguous response from party's lawyer and initiation of contact by party). *But see In re* Murray, 287 Or. 633, 639 (1979) (finding lawyer cannot delegate to client obligation to obtain consent of represented party's lawyer).
166. *See generally* John Leubsdorf, *Communicating with Another Lawyer's Client: The Lawyer's Veto and the Client's Interest*, 127 U. PA. L. REV. 683 (1979) (arguing for client's right to authorize communications).
167. *See* Waller v. Kotzen, 567 F. Supp. 424, 427 (E.D. Pa. 1983) (finding direct settlement negotiations with liability insurance carrier improper); Turner v. State Bar, 36 Cal. 2d 155, 158 (1950) (holding lawyer's communication not excused even though parties independently arrived at settlement terms); *In re* Atwell, 232 Mo. App. 186, 188 (Mo. Ct. App. 1938) (finding it inappropriate when lawyer conducted negotiations and obtained release from opposing party without consulting opposing lawyers); *see also* ABA Comm. on Ethics & Prof'l Responsibility, Informal Op. 1373 (1976) (noting it is improper to mail plea to both opposing lawyer and client); ABA Comm. on Ethics & Prof'l Responsibility, Informal Op. 1348 (1975) (noting it is improper to send copy of settlement offer to opposing party despite belief that lawyer was not relaying offers); ABA Comm. on Prof'l Ethics, Informal Op. 1190 (1971) (noting negotiations with insurance adjuster permitted if lawyer's written consent provided); ABA Comm. on Prof'l Ethics & Grievances, Informal Op. 570 (1962) (noting lawyer's letter to insurance company and insured improper).
168. C.W. WOLFRAM, MODERN LEGAL ETHICS § 11.6 (1986).
169. *See* People v. Selby, 156 Colo. 17, 19 (1964) (reprimanding lawyer for unlawfully and unethically conferring with opposing party in divorce action); *In re* Marietta, 223 Kan. 11, 12 (1977) (censuring lawyer for causing client to communicate with opposing party by preparing release of liability for child support and delivering it to client); Montgomery Cnty. Bar Ass'n v. Haupt, 277 Md. 326, 330–33 (1976) (suspending lawyer for pursuing husband in high-speed car chase and confronting him when representing the wife); Tenn. Bar Assoc. v. Freemon, 50 Tenn. App. 567, 576–77 (Tenn. Ct. App. 1961) (reprimanding lawyer who entrapped opposing party into adultery during divorce proceedings).
170. MODEL RULES OF PROF'L CONDUCT R. 4.2 cmt. [5].
171. *See* Nai Cheng Chen v. Immigration & Naturalization Serv., 537 F.2d 566, 569 (1st Cir. 1976) (questioning of represented alien by immigration officer permitted by immigration rules); N.Y. State Ass'n for Retarded Children v. Carey, 706 F.2d 956, 969 (2d Cir. N.Y. 1983) (finding balance struck in favor of allowing plaintiffs' counsel to interview state mental institution's employees outside presence of defendant's counsel); Vega v. Bloomsburgh, 427 F. Supp. 593, 595 (D. Mass. 1977) (favoring First Amendment interests over state's interest in pro-

hibiting opposing counsel from communicating with state employees likely to be called as witnesses against state); Frey v. Dep't of Health & Human Servs., 106 F.R.D. 32 (E.D.N.Y. 1985) ("stronger reason to construe term 'party' narrowly where the defendant is a government employer"); ABA Comm. on Ethics & Prof'l Responsibility, Informal Op. 83-1496 (1983) (finding government lawyer may conduct authorized inspection of regulated business without prior consent of lawyer for business); ABA Comm. on Prof'l Ethics, Informal Op. 985 (1967) (finding it proper to serve formal offer of judgment directly on opposing party as expressly permitted by statute, provided copy is simultaneously served on lawyer and is not served for improper motive or purpose); *see also* C.W. WOLFRAM, MODERN LEGAL ETHICS § 11.6, at 614–15 (1986) (observing consent requirement particularly inappropriate when adversary is a government agency). *But see* ABA Comm. on Ethics & Prof'l Responsibility, Informal Op. 1377 (1976) (noting opposing counsel may not communicate with municipal employees with power to commit municipality unless authorized by law or with consent of municipality's lawyer).

172. *See* United States v. Thomas, 474 F.2d 110, 112 (10th Cir. N.M. 1973) (finding it immaterial whether government agent knew defendant had counsel); United States v. Four Star, 428 F.2d 1406, 1407 (9th Cir. 1970) (finding prosecutor's use of statement obtained in custodial interrogation by law enforcement agent constituted ethical violation); United States v. Batchelor, 484 F. Supp. 812, 814 (E.D. Pa. 1980) (finding assistant district attorney may not interview defendant without consent of defendant's previously retained counsel). *But see* United States v. Cobbs, 481 F.2d 196, 199 (3d Cir. 1973) (finding custodial interrogation in absence of and without permission of retained or appointed counsel where accused deliberately and voluntarily chose to speak is technically permissible but not commendable).

173. *See* People v. Green, 405 Mich. 273, 290–91 (1979) (finding prohibition applied despite fact that defendant initiated interview and indicated he did not want attorney present); *see generally* Note, *The Prosecutor's Dilemma: Can a Criminal Be Interviewed Outside the Presence of His Attorney?*, 6 J. LEGAL PROF. 347 (1981).

174. *See* United States v. Schwimmer, 882 F.2d 22, 28 (2d Cir. 1989) (finding prosecutor's lawful questioning of convicted criminal defendant before grand jury and outside presence of defendant's counsel was "authorized by law" and did not violate anticontact rule); United States v. Sutton, 801 F.2d 1346, 1366–68 (D.C. Cir. 1986) (finding Sixth Amendment and anticontact rule do not apply to taping that occurred during investigation stage but before initiation of judicial proceedings, such as a formal charge or indictment); United States v. Dobbs, 711 F.2d 84, 85 (8th Cir. 1983) (finding noncustodial interview with government agent prior to initiation of judicial proceedings does not raise ethical issues); United States v. Jamil, 707 F.2d 638, 640–41 (2d Cir. 1983) (finding government investigator who tape recorded suspect in noncustodial setting prior to indictment was not acting as "alter ego" of prosecutor, who was not privy to arrangement); United States v. Kenny, 645 F.2d 1323, 1326–27 (9th Cir. 1981) (finding noncustodial tape recording prior to charge, arrest or indictment does not implicate ethical problems addressed by disciplinary rules); United States v. Lemonakis, 485 F.2d 941, 956 (D.C. Cir. 1973) (finding government instructions to informant provided by prosecutor were not such as to make informant "alter ego" of prosecutor). *But see* United States v. Hammad, 858 F.2d 834, 840 (2d Cir.

1988) (holding informant was alter ego of prosecutor, thus the communication improper).

175. 858 F.2d 834 (2d Cir. 1988), *cert. denied*, 498 U.S. 871 (1990).

176. Memorandum of Richard Thornburgh, *Communication with Persons Represented by Counsel*, June 6, 1989. A thorough analysis of this policy may be found in ABA/BNA LAWYERS' MANUAL ON PROFESSIONAL CONDUCT § 71:301 (2003).

177. *Id.*

178. ABA House of Delegates Report No. 301 (approved Feb. 12–13, 1990). *See generally* Jerry Norton, *Ethics and the Attorney General*, 74 JUDICATURE 203 (1991); Dick Thornburgh, *Ethics and the Attorney General: The Attorney General Responds*, 74 JUDICATURE 290 (1991), ABA/BNA LAWYERS' MANUAL ON PROFESSIONAL CONDUCT § 71:301 (2003); William Glaberson, *Thornburgh Policy Leads to a Sharp Ethics Battle*, N.Y. TIMES, Mar. 1, 1991, at B9.

179. *See* Shelton v. Hess, 599 F. Supp. 905, 909–10 (S.D. Tex. 1984) (disqualifying plaintiff's lawyer for contacts that unfairly prejudiced defendant); *but see* Ceramco Inc. v. Lee Pharms., 510 F.2d 268 (2d Cir. 1975) (finding behavior should not result in disqualification when lawyer called opposing party's corporate employees to secure information to help establish jurisdiction).

180. ANNOTATED MODEL RULES OF PROF'L CONDUCT R. 3.4 (5th ed. 2003). *See also id.* at R. 4.2.

181. *See In re* Zeiger, 692 A.2d 1351, 1353–56 (D.C. 1997) (suspending lawyer for altering medical records and then submitting them to insurance carrier).

182. *See In re* Geisler, 614 N.E.2d 939, 942–44 (Ind. 1993) (suspending lawyer for obstructing prosecutor's access to evidence by helping witness to become unavailable for service and trial); RESTATEMENT (THIRD) OF THE LAW GOVERNING LAWYERS § 116(3) (2000) ("lawyer may not unlawfully induce or assist a prospective witness to evade or ignore process obliging the witness to appear to testify").

183. *See* Rule 1.13(f) for misunderstandings that sometimes arise when a lawyer for an organization deals with an unrepresented constituent.

184. MODEL RULES OF PROF'L CONDUCT R. 4.3, cmts. [1]–[2].

185. *See* Hopkins v. Troutner, 134 Idaho 445, 448 (2000) (allowing plaintiff relief from a settlement agreement because defendant's attorney inappropriately influenced value of settlement without counsel for plaintiff); State *ex rel.* Okla. Bar Ass'n v. Berry, 1998 OK 73, ¶¶10–14 (1998) (suspending lawyer for advising unrepresented party in bankruptcy to convert her bankruptcy claim to be more favorable for his client).

186. 659 So. 2d 1156, 1162 (Fla. Dist. Ct. App. 3d 1995).

187. MODEL RULES OF PROF'L CONDUCT R. 4.4, cmts. [1]–[3]. *See also* R. 1.2, 1.4.

APPENDIX 18-1

Related Topics and Supplemental Authority

Privilege in General

- The privilege between insured and insurer.[1]
- Prosecution's privilege against disclosure of an informer.[2]
- For the rights and duties of the attorney in a criminal prosecution (or civil RICO) when client informs the attorney of intent to present perjured testimony.[3]
- As to testimony by in-house corporate counsel, the test is the client's intent—to reveal or not to reveal—to a third party or to the public.[4]

Work Product and Attorney-Client Privilege

- No attorney-client privilege by attorney or client in connection with the underlying suit or relating to bad faith of the insurer and negligence of the defense attorney.[5]
- Discovery regarding the reinsurer's liability for the primary insurer's failure to compromise or settle.[6]
- Work-product privilege as applying to material prepared for terminated litigation or for claims that did not result in litigation.[7]
- Florida requires the attorney to testify on contemplated or actual civil fraud (including absconding with funds) by his client, dating back to *Kneale v. Williams*.[8]
- Attorney work-product privileges as applicable to documents prepared in anticipation of terminated litigation.[9]
- Inadvertent disclosure of privileged documents does not waive the attorney-client privilege in New Jersey.[10]
- The attorney-client privilege may be asserted as to an existing client or as to one seeking to become a client.[11]
- The statement to an opposing attorney that "strong and valid defenses are available" is at most a legal conclusion, and not a waiver of the

attorney-client privilege; in contrast, selective disclosure of documents to counsel's benefit may be a total waiver.[12]

- The attorney-client privilege and attorney work-product privilege are perverted if used to further illegal activities.[13]
- If the client is deceased, the attorney-client privilege can be waived only by the express consent of the executor, administrator of the estate, or surviving spouse.[14]
- Defendant's notes taken in preparation for consultation with a lawyer were protected.[15]
- Attorney-client privilege is not waived "because a witness changes an answer to a question after consulting with an attorney."[16]
- What to do if conspiratorial intent is disclosed by the client.[17]
- When an independent auditor was hired by an insurer to audit insured's books, the information was considered material prepared for litigation and was privileged.[18]

Disqualification of Law Firm Issues

- Disqualification of the law firm from representing a party in a federal civil suit involving a former client of that firm.[19]

Accountant-Client Privilege and Related Communications

- Privilege for communications in general.[20]
- Statute creating an accountant-client privilege may specifically exclude any information a CPA might have obtained relative to or in connection with the examination, audit, or report of any financial statement, books, or records.[21]
- Conspiracy between a client and an accountant not privileged.[22]
- Accountant-client privilege may be waived.[23]
- Discovery and liability of the independent accountant to the shareholder or investor.[24]
- Preparer of tax returns testimony privileged in federal tax prosecution.[25]
- What to do if the client discloses conspiratorial intent to accountant.[26]

Reinsurance and Insurance Issues

- The covenant of good faith includes the right of the reinsurer and the excess insurer to question the dates of loss used in establishing the underlying coverage in order to determine proper exhaustion of limits or proper reinsurance claim by the ceding company.[27]
- An insurer's duty of good faith constitutes a duty not to withhold unreasonably payment due under a policy.[28]
- Reinsurance and insurance issues generally.[29]

Excess Insurance Issues

- An underlying insurer should honor its duty to an excess insurer to enter into reasonable settlements within the limits of the primary coverage.[30]
- The duty of good faith and fair dealing between the primary carrier and the excess carrier includes a duty to reasonably assign dates of loss so as to result in a fair and appropriate allocation of loss between the underlying and excess carriers.[31]
- There is also a duty placed on the underlying carrier to accept a reasonable settlement offer within the underlying limits to protect the excess carrier.[32] Additionally, if an insurer fails to act in good faith in rejecting a settlement demand that is within the policy limits set by the excess insurer, it will be liable for the entire amount.[33]

Issues of Privilege in Connection with Corporations and Corporate Bankruptcies

- Who can disclose who has possession of various corporate books and records among subsidiaries, branches, and affiliates?[34]
- Who has possession, custody, or control of corporate books or records for purposes of an order to produce?[35]
- The trustee in bankruptcy, or receiver in insolvency, has the power to waive the privilege of communications available to the bankrupt, or insolvent.[36] No testimony in the bankruptcy proceedings is available for use in the criminal proceedings against him.[37]
- Similarly, directors of a corporation have the power to waive the privilege of confidentiality of communications.[38]
- Corporate attorney's privilege in controversy between corporation and officer, director, stockholder.[39]
- Corporation's claim of privilege for agent or employee's communication to the corporate attorney.[40]
- In international trade cases, access to confidential matter as privileged.[41]
- For confidential clerk or stenographer's testimony as privileged.[42]
- For compelling a party to disclose information that is in the hands of an affiliate, subsidiary corporation, or an independent contractor who was not made a party to the suit.[43]
- Individual officer, director, or agent of the corporation or unincorporated association's right to assert personal privilege against self-incrimination with respect to production of corporate books and records.[44]
- Admissibility of computerized private business records.[45]
- Rehabilitator's documents are not public records under the Kentucky Open Records Act.[46] Similarly, in New York, the Liquidation Bureau

of the State Insurance Agency was not an "agency" of the state under the Freedom of Information Act of New York and thus it was not subject to the act's discovery rules.[47]
- Right to privacy and privileged exchange among insurers of medical information concerning applicant or insured.[48]
- Public disclosure of a person's indebtedness as invasion of privacy.[49]
- Oral declarations as invasion of right of privacy.[50]
- Investigations and surveillance, shadowing, or trailing, as invasions of privacy.[51]
- Privileged reports and communications between liability or indemnity insurer and the insured.[52]
- Freedom of Information Act exempts from disclosure personnel and medical files;[53] exempting "confidential source";[54] government attorney exemption.[55]
- For open court refusal by a party to permit introduction of privileged testimony as being prejudicial.[56]

Privilege and Confidentiality Issues in Connection with Electronic Surveillance, Eavesdropping and Wiretapping

- Sound recordings—admissibility into evidence in spite of privileged nature.[57]

Issues Involving Bad Faith in General

- Bad faith on the part of the insurer in failing to pay or in delaying payment of insured's claims versus insured's misrepresentations of bad faith.[58]
- Attorney-client and work-product privileges may be lost by insurers in bad-faith cases.[59]
- A statutory bad-faith claim in Florida should be held in abatement pending the outcome of the underlying contractual dispute.[60]

Related Issues

- Privileged communications between the insurer and its agents and adjusters in actions for libel or slander of its own agents or third party.[61]
- Subpoena duces tecum power and objections.[62]
- Protective orders—are statements of witnesses to be produced?[63]
- Advertisements, brochures, and catalogues by a litigant containing admissions contrary to a position now taken by him.[64]

Notes

1. *See generally* 55 A.L.R.4th 336 (2008); *see also* 85 A.L.R.3d 1161.
2. *See generally* 76 A.L.R.2d 262.
3. *See generally* 64 A.L.R.3d 385.
4. *See generally* Dees v. Scott, 347 So. 2d 475 (Fla. Dist. Ct. App. 1st 1977).
5. *See generally* 4 A.L.R.4th 765 § 5.
6. *See generally* 42 A.L.R.4th 1130.
7. *See generally* 27 A.L.R.4th 568.
8. 158 Fla. 811, 814–17 (1947).
9. *See generally* 41 A.L.R. FED. 123.
10. *See* Trilogy Commc'ns, Inc. v. Excom Realty, Inc., 279 N.J. Super. 442, 444–47 (Law Div. 1994).
11. *See* Dean v. Dean, 607 So. 2d 494, 499 (Fla. Dist. Ct. App. 4th 1992) ("the representation of a client in a court or legal proceeding is not indispensable for the invocation of [attorney-client privilege]").
12. Seattle Nw. Sec. Corp. v. SDG Holding Co., 61 Wash. App. 725, 739–40 (1991).
13. Law Offices of Bernard D. Morley, P. C. v. MacFarlane, 647 P.2d 1215, 1220 (Colo. 1982) (noting that "crime fraud" exception to attorney-client privilege is "subject to the qualification that communications made to an attorney to obtain his advice for the commission of criminal acts are not protected by the privilege").
14. State v. McDermott, 73 Ohio App. 3d 689, 693 (Ohio Ct. App., Lucas County 1991).
15. Lemonik v. E. Airlines, 632 So. 2d 239 (Fla. Dist. Ct. App. 3d 1994).
16. Feltner v. Internationale Nederlanden Bank, N.V., 622 So. 2d 123, 125 (Fla. Dist. Ct. App. 4th 1993).
17. *See generally* 31 A.L.R.4th 458; 64 A.L.R.3d 385.
18. Kent v. Md. Cas. Co., 25 A.D.2d 653, 654 (N.Y. App. Div. 1st 1966).
19. *See generally* 56 A.L.R. FED. 189; Dworkin v. Gen. Motors Corp., 906 F. Supp. 273 (E.D. Pa. 1995).
20. *See generally* 33 A.L.R.4th 539; 36 A.L.R. FED. 686.
21. *See, e.g.*, Rubin v. Katz, 347 F. Supp. 322 (E.D. Pa. 1972) (no privilege for an independent CPA).
22. *See* 33 A.L.R.4th 539 § 3.
23. *See id.* § 5.
24. *See generally* 48 A.L.R.5th 389.
25. *See generally* 36 A.L.R. FED. 686.
26. *See generally* 33 A.L.R.4th 539.
27. Kaiser Found. Hosps. v. N. Star Reinsurance Corp., 90 Cal. App. 3d 786, 792 (2d Dist. 1979).
28. Safeco Ins. Co. v. Kartsone, 510 F. Supp. 856, 859 (C.D. Cal. 1981).
29. *See generally* Robert D. Allen, *Brief Review of Follow-the-Settlements Doctrine in the United States*, 75 DEF. COUNS. J. 276 (July 2008); Paul M. Hummer, *Discovery of Reinsurance Information in Insurance Coverage Litigation*, 68 DEF. COUNS. J. 339 (July 2001); Note, *Work Product Discovery in Insurance Litigation*, 18 IND. L. REV. 547 (1985); APPLEMAN ON INSURANCE §§ 12079. 12085 (2010); Scott O. Reed, *Discovery of Reserve and Reinsurance Information*, 40 FED'N INS. CORP. COUNS. Q. 372 (1990); Charles Silver & Kent Syverud, *The Professional Responsibilities of Insurance Defense Lawyers*, 45 DUKE L.J. 255 (1995).

30. *See generally* Commercial Union Assurance Cos. v. Safeway Stores, 26 Cal. 3d 912 (1980); *Kaiser*, 90 Cal. App. 3d 786; Cont'l Cas. Co. v. U.S. Fid. & Guar. Co., 516 F. Supp. 384 (N.D. Cal. 1981); Peter v. Travelers Ins. Co., 375 F. Supp. 1347 (C.D. Cal. 1974).
31. *See Kaiser*, 90 Cal. App. 3d at 859.
32. *See generally* Nw. Mut. Ins. Co. v. Farmers' Ins. Grp., 76 Cal. App. 3d 1031 (Cal. 4th Dist. 1978).
33. *See* Cont'l Cas. Co. v. U.S. Fid. & Guar. Co., 516 F. Supp. 384, 388–90 (N.D. Cal. 1981).
34. *See generally* 47 A.L.R.3d 676; *see also* FLA. STAT. ANN. § 631.391.
35. *Id.*
36. *See generally* 31 A.L.R.3d 557.
37. *See generally* 22 A.L.R. FED. 643; *see also* 30 A.L.R.4th 1110 § 10.
38. *See generally* 31 A.L.R.3d 522.
39. *See generally* 1 A.L.R.4th 1124; 26 A.L.R.5th 628.
40. *See generally* 26 A.L.R.5th 628.
41 *See* 29 USCA §151 6(a)(b)(2)(B); 73 ALR Fed. 247.
42. *See generally* 26 A.L.R.5th 628 § 15.
43. *See generally* 19 A.L.R.3d 1134; *see also* FLA. STAT. ANN. § 631.391.
44. *See generally* 87 A.L.R. FED. 177.
45. *See generally* 7 A.L.R.4th 8.
46. *See* Ky. Cent. Life Ins. Co. *ex rel.* Stephens v. Park Broad., 913 S.W.2d 330, 335 (Ky. Ct. App. 1996).
47. *See* Consol. Edison Co. v. Ins. Dep't of State, 140 Misc. 2d 969, 975–77 (N.Y. Sup. Ct. 1988). *But see* Allendale Mut. Ins. Co. v. Bull Data Sys., 152 F.R.D. 132, 137–39 (N.D. Ill. 1993) (finding documents relating to reinsurance were discoverable under Rule 26(b)(2)).
48. *See generally* 98 A.L.R.3d 561; 85 A.L.R.3d 1161.
49. *See generally* 33 A.L.R.3d 154.
50. *See generally* 19 A.L.R.3d 1318.
51. *See generally* 13 A.L.R.3d 1025.
52. *See generally* 55 A.L.R.4th 336.
53. *See* 5 U.S.C.A. § 552(b)(6); *see generally* 5 U.S.C.A. § 552.
54. *See* 5 U.S.C.A. § 552(b)(7)(D).
55. *See* 5 U.S.C.A. § 552(b)(5); *see generally* 54 A.L.R. FED. 280.
56. *See generally* 34 A.L.R.3d 775.
57. *See generally* 58 A.L.R.2d 1037.
58. *See generally* 115 A.L.R.5th 589.
59. Tackett v. State Farm Fire & Cas. Ins. Co., 653 A.2d 254, 259–61 (Del. 1995).
60. *See generally* FLA. STAT. ANN. § 624.155. Note "person" under section 624.155 includes third parties, who can also bring suit for bad faith under statute; *see* Auto-Owners Ins. Co. v. Conquest, 658 So. 2d 928, 928 (Fla. 1995). *See also* Doan v. John Hancock Mut. Life Ins. Co., 727 So. 2d 400, 402–04 (Fla. Dist. Ct. App. 3d 1999).
61. *See* 4 COUCH ON INSURANCE § 57:75 (2010).
62. *See generally* 23 A.L.R.2d 862.
63. *See generally* 73 A.L.R.2d 146.
64. *See generally* 44 A.L.R.2d 1027.

APPENDIX 18-2

Federal Rules of Civil Procedure Relating to Privilege

There are a number of Federal Rules of Civil Procedure that shape the privilege and confidentiality issues one may encounter in the course of litigation of primary, excess, umbrella and reinsurer cases. These will be repeated herein for convenience.

Rule 26: General Provisions Governing Discovery; Duty of Disclosure

(a) Required Disclosures.

(1) Initial Disclosure.

(A) *In General.* Except as exempted by Rule 26(a)(1)(B) or as otherwise stipulated or ordered by the court, a party must, without awaiting a discovery request, provide to the other parties:

(i) the name and, if known, the address and telephone number of each individual likely to have discoverable information—along with the subjects of that information—that the disclosing party may use to support its claims or defenses, unless the use would be solely for impeachment;

(ii) a copy—or a description by category and location—of all documents, electronically stored information, and tangible things that the disclosing party has in its possession, custody, or control and may use to support its claims or defenses, unless the use would be solely for impeachment;

(iii) a computation of each category of damages claimed by the disclosing party—who must also make available for inspection and copying as under Rule 34 the documents or other evidentiary material, unless privileged or protected from disclosure, on which each computation is based, including materials bearing on the nature and extent of injuries suffered; and

(iv) for inspection and copying as under Rule 34, any insurance agreement under which an insurance business may be liable to satisfy all or part of a possible judgment in the action or to indemnify or reimburse for payments made to satisfy the judgment.

(B) *Proceedings Exempt from Initial Disclosure.* The following proceedings are exempt from initial disclosure:
   (i) an action for review on an administrative record;
   (ii) a forfeiture action in rem arising from a federal statute;
   (iii) a petition for habeas corpus or any other proceeding to challenge a criminal conviction or sentence;
   (iv) an action brought without an attorney by a person in the custody of the United States, a state, or a state subdivision;
   (v) an action to enforce or quash an administrative summons or subpoena;
   (vi) an action by the United States to recover benefit payments;
   (vii) an action by the United States to collect on a student loan guaranteed by the United States;
   (viii) a proceeding ancillary to a proceeding in another court; and
   (ix) an action to enforce an arbitration award.

(C) *Time for Initial Disclosures—In General.* A party must make the initial disclosures at or within 14 days after the parties' Rule 26(f) conference unless a different time is set by stipulation or court order, or unless a party objects during the conference that initial disclosures are not appropriate in this action and states the objection in the proposed discovery plan. In ruling on the objection, the court must determine what disclosures, if any, are to be made and must set the time for disclosure.

(D) *Time for Initial Disclosures—For Parties Served or Joined Later.* A party that is first served or otherwise joined after the Rule 26(f) conference must make the initial disclosures within 30 days after being served or joined, unless a different time is set by stipulation or court order.

(E) *Basis for Initial Disclosure; Unacceptable Excuses.* A party must make its initial disclosures based on the information then reasonably available to it. A party is not excused from making its disclosures because it has not fully investigated the case or because it challenges the sufficiency of another party's disclosures or because another party has not made its disclosures.

(2) Disclosure of Expert Testimony.

(A) *In General.* In addition to the disclosures required by Rule 26(a)(1), a party must disclose to the other parties the identity of any witness it may use at trial to present evidence under Federal Rule of Evidence 702, 703, or 705.

(B) *Witnesses Who Must Provide a Written Report.* Unless otherwise stipulated or ordered by the court, this disclosure must be accompanied by a written report—prepared and signed by the witness—if the witness is one retained or specially employed to provide expert

testimony in the case or one whose duties as the party's employee regularly involve giving expert testimony. The report must contain:
(i) a complete statement of all opinions the witness will express and the basis and reasons for them;
(ii) the facts or data considered by the witness in forming them;
(iii) any exhibits that will be used to summarize or support them;
(iv) the witness's qualifications, including a list of all publications authored in the previous 10 years;
(v) a list of all other cases in which, during the previous 4 years, the witness testified as an expert at trial or by deposition; and
(vi) a statement of the compensation to be paid for the study and testimony in the case.

(C) *Witnesses Who Do Not Provide a Written Report.* Unless otherwise stipulated or ordered by the court, if the witness is not required to provide a written report, this disclosure must state:
(i) the subject matter on which the witness is expected to present evidence under Federal Rule of Evidence 702, 703, or 705; and
(ii) a summary of the facts and opinions to which the witness is expected to testify.

(D) *Time to Disclose Expert Testimony.* A party must make these disclosures at the times and in the sequence that the court orders. Absent a stipulation or a court order, the disclosures must be made:
(i) at least 90 days before the date set for trial or for the case to be ready for trial; or
(ii) if the evidence is intended solely to contradict or rebut evidence on the same subject matter identified by another party under Rule 26(a)(2)(B) or (C), within 30 days after the other party's disclosure.

(E) *Supplementing the Disclosure.* The parties must supplement these disclosures when required under Rule 26(e).

(3) Pretrial Disclosures.

(A) *In General.* In addition to the disclosures required by Rule 26(a)(1) and (2), a party must provide to the other parties and promptly file the following information about the evidence that it may present at trial other than solely for impeachment:
(i) the name and, if not previously provided, the address and telephone number of each witness—separately identifying those the party expects to present and those it may call if the need arises;
(ii) the designation of those witnesses whose testimony the party expects to present by deposition and, if not taken stenographically, a transcript of the pertinent parts of the deposition; and
(iii) an identification of each document or other exhibit, including summaries of other evidence—separately identifying those items the party expects to offer and those it may offer if the need arises.

(B) *Time for Pretrial Disclosures; Objections.* Unless the court orders otherwise, these disclosures must be made at least 30 days before trial. Within 14 days after they are made, unless the court sets a different time, a party may serve and promptly file a list of the following objections: any objections to the use under Rule 32(a) of a deposition designated by another party under Rule 26(a)(3)(A)(ii); and any objection, together with the grounds for it, that may be made to the admissibility of materials identified under Rule 26(a)(3)(A)(iii). An objection not so made—except for one under Federal Rule of Evidence 402 or 403—is waived unless excused by the court for good cause.

(4) Form of Disclosures. Unless the court orders otherwise, all disclosures under Rule 26(a) must be in writing, signed, and served.

(b) Discovery Scope and Limits.

(1) Scope in General. Unless otherwise limited by court order, the scope of discovery is as follows: Parties may obtain discovery regarding any nonprivileged matter that is relevant to any party's claim or defense—including the existence, description, nature, custody, condition, and location of any documents or other tangible things and the identity and location of persons who know of any discoverable matter. For good cause, the court may order discovery of any matter relevant to the subject matter involved in the action. Relevant information need not be admissible at the trial if the discovery appears reasonably calculated to lead to the discovery of admissible evidence. All discovery is subject to the limitations imposed by Rule 26(b)(2)(C).

(2) Limitations on Frequency and Extent.

(A) *When Permitted.* By order, the court may alter the limits in these rules on the number of depositions and interrogatories or on the length of depositions under Rule 30. By order or local rule, the court may also limit the number of requests under Rule 36.

(B) *Specific Limitations on Electronically Stored Information.* A party need not provide discovery of electronically stored information from sources that the party identifies as not reasonably accessible because of undue burden or cost. On motion to compel discovery or for a protective order, the party from whom discovery is sought must show that the information is not reasonably accessible because of undue burden or cost. If that showing is made, the court may nonetheless order discovery from such sources if the requesting party shows good cause, considering the limitations of Rule 26(b)(2)(C). The court may specify conditions for the discovery.

(C) *When Required.* On motion or on its own, the court must limit the frequency or extent of discovery otherwise allowed by these rules or by local rule if it determines that:

(i) the discovery sought is unreasonably cumulative or duplicative, or can be obtained from some other source that is more convenient, less burdensome, or less expensive;

(ii) the party seeking discovery has had ample opportunity to obtain the information by discovery in the action; or

(iii) the burden or expense of the proposed discovery outweighs its likely benefit, considering the needs of the case, the amount in controversy, the parties' resources, the importance of the issues at stake in the action, and the importance of the discovery in resolving the issues.

(3) Trial Preparation: Materials.

(A) *Documents and Tangible Things.* Ordinarily, a party may not discover documents and tangible things that are prepared in anticipation of litigation or for trial by or for another party or its representative (including the other party's attorney, consultant, surety, indemnitor, insurer, or agent). But, subject to Rule 26(b)(4), those materials may be discovered if:

(i) they are otherwise discoverable under Rule 26(b)(1); and

(ii) the party shows that it has substantial need for the materials to prepare its case and cannot, without undue hardship, obtain their substantial equivalent by other means.

(B) *Protection Against Disclosure.* If the court orders discovery of those materials, it must protect against disclosure of the mental impressions, conclusions, opinions, or legal theories of a party's attorney or other representative concerning the litigation.

(C) *Previous Statement.* Any party or other person may, on request and without the required showing, obtain the person's own previous statement about the action or its subject matter. If the request is refused, the person may move for a court order, and Rule 37(a)(5) applies to the award of expenses. A previous statement is either:

(i) a written statement that the person has signed or otherwise adopted or approved; or

(ii) a contemporaneous stenographic, mechanical, electrical, or other recording—or a transcription of it—that recites substantially verbatim the person's oral statement.

(4) Trial Preparation: Experts.

(A) *Deposition of an Expert Who May Testify.* A party may depose any person who has been identified as an expert whose opinions may be presented at trial. If Rule 26(a)(2)(B) requires a report from the expert, the deposition may be conducted only after the report is provided.

(B) *Trial-Preparation Protection for Draft Reports or Disclosures.* Rules 26(b)(3)(A) and (B) protect drafts of any report or disclosure required under Rule 26(a)(2), regardless of the form in which the draft is recorded.

(C) *Trial-Preparation Protection for Communications Between a Party's Attorney and Expert Witnesses.* Rules 26(b)(3)(A) and (B) protect communications between the party's attorney and any witness required to provide a report under Rule 26(a)(2)(B), regardless

of the form of the communications, except to the extent that the communications:
(i) relate to compensation for the expert's study or testimony;
(ii) identify facts or data that the party's attorney provided and that the expert considered in forming the opinions to be expressed; or
(iii) identify assumptions that the party's attorney provided and that the expert relied on in forming the opinions to be expressed.

(D) *Expert Employed Only for Trial Preparation.* Ordinarily, a party may not, by interrogatories or deposition, discover facts known or opinions held by an expert who has been retained or specially employed by another party in anticipation of litigation or to prepare for trial and who is not expected to be called as a witness at trial. But a party may do so only:
(i) as provided in Rule 35(b); or
(ii) on showing exceptional circumstances under which it is impracticable for the party to obtain facts or opinions on the same subject by other means.

(E) *Payment.* Unless manifest injustice would result, the court must require that the party seeking discovery:
(i) pay the expert a reasonable fee for time spent in responding to discovery under Rule 26(b)(4)(A) or (D); and
(ii) for discovery under (D), also pay the other party a fair portion of the fees and expenses it reasonably incurred in obtaining the expert's facts and opinions.

(5) Claiming Privilege or Protecting Trial-Preparation Materials.

(A) *Information Withheld.* When a party withholds information otherwise discoverable by claiming that the information is privileged or subject to protection as trial-preparation material, the party must:
(i) expressly make the claim; and
(ii) describe the nature of the documents, communications, or tangible things not produced or disclosed—and do so in a manner that, without revealing information itself privileged or protected, will enable other parties to assess the claim.

(B) *Information Produced.* If information produced in discovery is subject to a claim of privilege or of protection as trial-preparation material, the party making the claim may notify any party that received the information of the claim and the basis for it. After being notified, a party must promptly return, sequester, or destroy the specified information and any copies it has; must not use or disclose the information until the claim is resolved; must take reasonable steps to retrieve the information if the party disclosed it before being notified; and may promptly present the information to the court under seal for a determination of the claim. The producing party must preserve the information until the claim is resolved.

(c) Protective Orders.

(1) In General. A party or any person from whom discovery is sought may move for a protective order in the court where the action is pending—or as an alternative on matters relating to a deposition, in the court for the district where the deposition will be taken. The motion must include a certification that the movant has in good faith conferred or attempted to confer with other affected parties in an effort to resolve the dispute without court action. The court may, for good cause, issue an order to protect a party or person from annoyance, embarrassment, oppression, or undue burden or expense, including one or more of the following:

(A) forbidding the disclosure or discovery;

(B) specifying terms, including time and place, for the disclosure or discovery;

(C) prescribing a discovery method other than the one selected by the party seeking discovery;

(D) forbidding inquiry into certain matters, or limiting the scope of disclosure or discovery to certain matters;

(E) designating the persons who may be present while the discovery is conducted;

(F) requiring that a deposition be sealed and opened only on court order;

(G) requiring that a trade secret or other confidential research, development, or commercial information not be revealed or be revealed only in a specified way; and

(H) requiring that the parties simultaneously file specified documents or information in sealed envelopes, to be opened as the court directs.

(2) Ordering Discovery. If a motion for a protective order is wholly or partly denied, the court may, on just terms, order that any party or person provide or permit discovery.

(3) Awarding Expenses. Rule 37(a)(5) applies to the award of expenses.

(d) Timing and Sequence of Discovery.

(1) Timing. A party may not seek discovery from any source before the parties have conferred as required by Rule 26(f), except in a proceeding exempted from initial disclosure under Rule 26(a)(1)(B), or when authorized by these rules, by stipulation, or by court order.

(2) Sequence. Unless, on motion, the court orders otherwise for the parties' and witnesses' convenience and in the interests of justice:

(A) methods of discovery may be used in any sequence; and

(B) discovery by one party does not require any other party to delay its discovery.

(e) Supplementing Disclosures and Responses.

(1) In General. A party who has made a disclosure under Rule 26(a)—or who has responded to an interrogatory, request for production, or request for admission—must supplement or correct its disclosure or response:

(A) in a timely manner if the party learns that in some material respect the disclosure or response is incomplete or incorrect, and if the additional or corrective information has not otherwise been made known to the other parties during the discovery process or in writing; or

(B) as ordered by the court.

(2) Expert Witness. For an expert whose report must be disclosed under Rule 26(a)(2)(B), the party's duty to supplement extends both to information included in the report and to information given during the expert's deposition. Any additions or changes to this information must be disclosed by the time the party's pretrial disclosures under Rule 26(a)(3) are due.

(f) Conference of the Parties; Planning for Discovery.

(1) Conference Timing. Except in a proceeding exempted from initial disclosure under Rule 26(a)(1)(B) or when the court orders otherwise, the parties must confer as soon as practicable—and in any event at least 21 days before a scheduling conference is to be held or a scheduling order is due under Rule 16(b).

(2) Conference Content; Parties' Responsibilities. In conferring, the parties must consider the nature and basis of their claims and defenses and the possibilities for promptly settling or resolving the case; make or arrange for the disclosures required by Rule 26(a)(1); discuss any issues about preserving discoverable information; and develop a proposed discovery plan. The attorneys of record and all unrepresented parties that have appeared in the case are jointly responsible for arranging the conference, for attempting in good faith to agree on the proposed discovery plan, and for submitting to the court within 14 days after the conference a written report outlining the plan. The court may order the parties or attorneys to attend the conference in person.

(3) Discovery Plan. A discovery plan must state the parties' views and proposals on:

(A) what changes should be made in the timing, form, or requirement for disclosures under Rule 26(a), including a statement of when initial disclosures were made or will be made;

(B) the subjects on which discovery may be needed, when discovery should be completed, and whether discovery should be conducted in phases or be limited to or focused on particular issues;

(C) any issues about disclosure or discovery of electronically stored information, including the form or forms in which it should be produced;

(D) any issues about claims of privilege or of protection as trial-preparation materials, including—if the parties agree on a procedure to assert these claims after production—whether to ask the court to include their agreement in an order;

(E) what changes should be made in the limitations on discovery imposed under these rules or by local rule, and what other limitations should be imposed; and

(F) any other orders that the court should issue under Rule 26(c) or under Rule 16(b) and (c).

(4) Expedited Schedule. If necessary to comply with its expedited schedule for Rule 16(b) conferences, a court may by local rule:

(A) require the parties' conference to occur less than 21 days before the scheduling conference is held or a scheduling order is due under Rule 16(b); and

(B) require the written report outlining the discovery plan to be filed less than 14 days after the parties' conference, or excuse the parties from submitting a written report and permit them to report orally on their discovery plan at the Rule 16(b) conference.

(g) Signing Disclosures and Discovery Requests, Responses, and Objections.

(1) Signature Required; Effect of Signature. Every disclosure under Rule 26(a)(1) or (a)(3) and every discovery request, response, or objection must be signed by at least one attorney of record in the attorney's own name—or by the party personally, if unrepresented—and must state the signer's address, e-mail address, and telephone number. By signing, an attorney or party certifies that to the best of the person's knowledge, information, and belief formed after a reasonable inquiry:

(A) with respect to a disclosure, it is complete and correct as of the time it is made; and

(B) with respect to a discovery request, response, or objection, it is:

(i) consistent with these rules and warranted by existing law or by a nonfrivolous argument for extending, modifying, or reversing existing law, or for establishing new law;

(ii) not interposed for any improper purpose, such as to harass, cause unnecessary delay, or needlessly increase the cost of litigation; and

(iii) neither unreasonable nor unduly burdensome or expensive, considering the needs of the case, prior discovery in the case, the amount in controversy, and the importance of the issues at stake in the action.

(2) Failure to Sign. Other parties have no duty to act on an unsigned disclosure, request, response, or objection until it is signed, and the court must strike it unless a signature is promptly supplied after the omission is called to the attorney's or party's attention.

(3) Sanction for Improper Certification. If a certification violates this rule without substantial justification, the court, on motion or on its own, must impose an appropriate sanction on the signer, the party on whose behalf the signer was acting, or both. The sanction may include an order to pay the reasonable expenses, including attorney's fees, caused by the violation.

Rule 30: Depositions upon Oral Examination

[Subparagraph (a) is omitted in its entirety]

(b) Notice of Examination: General Requirements; Method of Recording; Production of Documents and Things; Deposition of Organization; Deposition by Telephone.

(1) A party desiring to take the deposition of any person upon oral examination shall give reasonable notice in writing to every other party to the action. The notice shall state the time and place for taking the deposition and the name and address of each person to be examined, if known, and, if the name is not known, a general description sufficient to identify the person or the particular class or group to which the person belongs. If a subpoena duces tecum is to be served on the person to be examined, the designation of the material to be produced as set forth in the subpoena shall be attached to or included in the notice.

[Subparagraphs (b)(2) through (7) are omitted]

(c) Examination and Cross Examination; Record of Examination; Oath; Objections.

Examination and cross examination of witnesses may proceed as permitted at the trial under the provisions of the Federal Rules of Evidence except Rules 103 and 615. The officer before whom the deposition is to be taken shall put the witness on oath or affirmation and shall personally, or by someone acting under the officer's direction and in the officer's presence, record the testimony of the witness. The testimony shall be taken stenographically or recorded by any other method authorized by subdivision (b)(2) of this rule. All objections made at the time of the examination to the qualification of the officer taking the deposition, to the manner of taking it, to the evidence presented, to the conduct of any party, or to any other aspect of the proceeding shall be noted by the officer upon the record of the deposition; but the examination shall proceed, with the testimony being taken subject to the objections. In lieu of participating in the oral examination, parties may serve written questions in a sealed envelope on the party taking the deposition and the party taking the deposition shall transmit them to the officer, who shall propound them to the witness and record the answers verbatim.

[Subparagraphs (d) through (g) are omitted]

Rule 34: Production of Documents and Things and Entry upon Land for Inspection and Other Purposes

(a) Scope. Any party may serve on any other party a request (1) to produce and permit the party making the request, or someone acting on the requestor's behalf, to inspect and copy any designated documents (including writings, drawings, graphs, Charts, photographs, phonorecords, and other data compilations from which information can be obtained, translated, if necessary, by the respondent through detection devices into reasonable usable form), or to inspect and copy, test, or sample any tangible things which constitute or contain matters within the scope of Rule 26(b) and which are in the possession, custody or control of the party upon whom the request is served; or (2) to permit entry upon designated land or other property in the possession or control of the party upon whom the request if served for the purposes of inspection and measuring, surveying, photographing, testing, or sampling the property or any designated object or operation thereon, with the scope of Rule 26(b).

[Subparagraphs (b) and (c) omitted]

A number of the Federal Rules of Evidence are also quite pertinent, specifically Rules 401, 402, 403, 501, 801, and 803.

Rule 401. Definition of "Relevant Evidence"

"Relevant evidence" means evidence having any tendency to make the existence of any fact that is of consequence to the determination of the action more probable or less probable than it would be without the evidence.

Rule 402. Relevant Evidence Generally Admissible; Irrelevant Evidence Inadmissible

All relevant evidence is admissible, except as otherwise provided by the Constitution of the United States, by Act of Congress, by these rules, or by other rules prescribed by the Supreme Court pursuant to statutory authority. Evidence which is not relevant is not admissible.

Rule 403. Exclusion of Relevant Evidence on Grounds of Prejudice, Confusion, or Waste of Time

Although relevant, evidence may be excluded if its probative value is substantially outweighed by the danger of unfair prejudice, confusion of the issues, or misleading the jury, or by considerations of undue delay, waste of time, or needless presentation of cumulative evidence.

Rule 501: Privileges—General Rule

Except as otherwise required by the Constitution of the United States or provided by Act of Congress or in rules prescribed by the Supreme Court pursuant to statutory authority, the privilege of a witness, person, government, State, or political subdivision thereof shall be governed by the principles of the common law as they may be interpreted by the courts of the United States in the light of reason and experience. However, in civil actions and proceedings, with respect to an element of a claim or defense as to which State law supplies the rule of decision, the privilege of a witness, person, government, State, or political subdivision thereof shall be determined in accordance with State law.

Rule 801: Definitions

Statements Which Are Not Hearsay. A statement is not hearsay if—

Prior Statement by Witness. The declarant testifies at the trial or hearing and is subject to cross-examination concerning the statement, and the statement is (A) inconsistent with the declarant's testimony, and was given under oath subject to the penalty of perjury at a trial, hearing , or other proceeding, or in a deposition, or (B) consistent with the declarant's testimony and is offered to rebut an express or implied charge against the declarant of recent fabrication or improper influence or motive, or (C) one of identification of a person made after perceiving the person; or

Admission by Party-Opponent. The statement is offered against a party and is (A) the party's own statement, in either an individual or a representative capacity, or (B) a statement of which the party has manifested an adoption or belief in its truth, or (C) a statement by a person authorized by the party to make a statement concerning the subject, or (D) a statement by the party's agent or servant concerning a matter within the scope of the agency or employment made during the existence of the relationship, or (E) a statement by a coconspirator of a party during the course and in furtherance of the conspiracy. The contents of the statement shall be considered but are not alone sufficient to establish the declarant's authority under subdivision (C), the agency or employment relationship and scope thereof under subdivision (D), or the existence of the conspiracy and the participation therein of the declarant and the party against whom the statement is offered under subdivision (E).

Rule 803. Hearsay Exceptions; Availability of Declarant Immaterial

(6) Records of Regularly Conducted Activity. A memorandum, report, record, or data compilation, in any form, of acts, events, conditions, opinions, or diagnoses, made at or near the time by, or from information transmitted by, a person with knowledge, if kept in the course of a regularly conducted business activity, and if it was the regular practice of that business activity to make the memorandum, report, record or data compilation, all as shown by the testimony of the custodian or other qualified witness, or by certification that complies with Rule 902(11), Rule 902(12), or a statute permitting certification, unless the source of information or the method or circumstances of preparation indicate lack of trustworthiness. The term "business" as used in this paragraph includes business, institution, association, profession, occupation, and calling of every kind, whether or not conducted for profit.

(8) Public Records and Reports. Records, reports, statements or data compilations, in any form, of public offices or agencies, setting forth (A) the activities of the office or agency, or (B) matters observed pursuant to duty imposed by law as to which matters there was a duty to report, excluding, however, in criminal cases matters observed by police officers and other law enforcement personnel, or (C) in civil actions and proceedings and against the Government in criminal cases, factual findings resulting from an investigation made pursuant to authority granted by law, unless the sources of information or other circumstances indicate lack of trustworthiness.

APPENDIX 18-3

Sample Reinsurance Policy Language

I. Examining Specific Policy Language Considerations

A. Article 1: Business Covered

This Agreement, subject to the terms and conditions herein contained, is to indemnify the reinsured in respect of the net excess liability as herein provided and specified that may occur during the term of this Agreement arising out of any and all binders, policies, and contracts of insurance or reinsurance heretofore or hereafter issued or renewed by the reinsured and classified by the reinsured as Casualty.

B. Article 4: Exclusions

This Agreement does not cover business classified by the reinsured as:

(a) Automobile Liability other than hired car and Auto Nonownership liability when issued with a multiperil policy.
(b) Umbrella business.
(c) Credit Insurance and Financial Guarantee and Insolvency.
(d) Pools, Associations, and Syndicates, as per Clause attached. This exclusion shall not apply to those associations that obtain insurance from the reinsured directly or through a mass marketing arrangement.
(e) Assumed Obligatory Reinsurance.
(f) War Risks.
(g) Nuclear incidents as provided in the Nuclear Incident Exclusion clauses—Liability-Reinsurance, as per attached clause.

C. Article 5: Net Retained Lines

This agreement applies only to that portion of any insurance or reinsurances covered by this Agreement that the Reinsured retains net for its own account, and in calculating the amount of any loss hereunder and also in computing the amount in excess of which this Agreement attaches, only loss or losses in respect of that portion of any insurance or reinsurance that the Reinsured retains net for its own account shall be included. It is understood and agreed that the amount of the Reinsurer's liability hereunder in respect of any loss or losses shall not be increased by reason of the inability of the Reinsured to collect from any other reinsurers, whether specific or general, any amounts that may have become due from them, whether such inability arises from the insolvency of such other reinsurers or otherwise.

D. Article 6: Limit and Retention

No claim shall be made upon the Reinsurer for any loss under this section of the Agreement unless and until the Reinsured shall have first sustained an ultimate net loss in excess of $500,000 in respect of each such loss occurrence. The limit of liability of the Reinsurer in respect of any one such loss occurrence shall be $500,000.

E. Article 7: Ultimate Net Loss ("Arbitration Clause")

The term "ultimate net loss" shall be the sum actually paid or to be paid by the Reinsured in settlement of losses or liability including any Extra-Contractual Obligations after making deduction for all recoveries, all salvages, and all claims upon other reinsurance whether collected or not, and shall include all adjustment expenses arising from the settlement of claims other than the salaries of employees and the office expense of the Reinsured. Nothing in this clause, however, shall be construed to mean that losses are not recoverable from the Reinsurer until the ultimate net loss to the Reinsured has been ascertained.

All salvages, recoveries, or payments recovered or received subsequent to a loss settlement under this Agreement shall be applied as if recovered or received prior to the aforesaid settlement and all necessary adjustments shall be made by the parties hereto.

F. Article 8: Definitions

The Reinsured shall be the sole judge of what constitutes one risk.

The term "loss occurrence" as used herein shall be understood to mean "each and every accident or occurrence or series of accidents or occurrences arising out of any one event."

G. Article 11: Notice of Loss and Loss Settlements

In the event of a loss hereunder, or a happening likely to give rise to a loss hereunder, prompt notice shall be given to the Reinsurer.

The Reinsured shall submit to the Reinsurer promptly an individual notice of each claim or loss that, in the opinion of the Reinsured, involves or is likely to involve the Reinsurer. The Reinsured shall advise the Reinsurer of the amount of gross claims or loss reserve and gross adjustment expense reserve the Reinsured is carrying on each such claim or loss and of any subsequent change(s) in such reserves.

Any loss settlements made by the Reinsured shall be unconditionally binding upon the Reinsurer, and the Reinsurer shall benefit proportionately in all salvages and recoveries.

H. Article 12: Expiration during Loss

If this Agreement should terminate while a loss occurrence is in progress, it is understood and agreed that the Reinsurer is responsible, subject to the other conditions of this Agreement, for its proportion of the entire loss or damage resulting from such loss occurrence.

I. Article 13: Access to Records

The Reinsurer, by its duly appointed representatives, shall have the right at any reasonable time to examine all papers in possession of the Reinsured referring to business affected hereunder.

J. Article 14: Statistics

The Reinsured shall furnish the Reinsurer such quarterly and annual statistics as may be necessary to comply with statutory requirements and in such form as may be mutually agreed upon.

K. Article 15: Errors and Omissions

Any inadvertent delay, omission, or error shall not be held to relieve either party hereto from any liability that would attach to it hereunder if such delay, omission, or error had not been made. Such delay, omission, or error shall be rectified immediately upon discovery.

L. Article 16: Arbitration

As a precedent to any right of action hereunder, if any dispute shall arise between the Reinsured and the Reinsurers with reference to the interpretation of this Agreement or their rights with respect to any transaction involved, whether such dispute arises before or after termination of this Agreement, such dispute upon the written request of either party shall be submitted to three arbitrators, one to be chosen by each party, and the third by the two so chosen. If either Party refuses or neglects to appoint an arbitrator within thirty (30) days after the receipt of written notice from the other party requesting it to do so, the requesting party may appoint two arbitrators. If the two arbitrators fail to agree in the selection of a third arbitrator within thirty (30) days of their appointment, each of them shall name two, of whom the other shall decline one and the decision shall be made by drawing lots. All arbitrators shall be executive officers of insurance or reinsurance companies or underwriters at Lloyd's, London not under control of either party to this Agreement.

The arbitrators shall interpret this Agreement as an honorable engagement and not as merely a legal obligation; they are relived of all judicial formalities and may abstain from following the strict rules of law, and they shall make their award with a view to effecting the general purpose of this Agreement in a reasonable manner rather than in accordance with a literal interpretation of the language.

The decision in writing of any two arbitrators, when filed with the parties hereto, shall be final and binding on both parties. Judgment may be entered upon the final decision of the arbitrators in any court having jurisdiction. Each party shall bear the expense of its own arbitrator and shall jointly and equally bear with the other party the expense of the third arbitrator and of the arbitration. Said arbitration shall take place in Marshall, Michigan, unless some other place is mutually agreed upon by the Reinsured and the Reinsurers.

M. Article 17: Insolvency

In the event of the insolvency of the Reinsured, this reinsurance shall be payable directly to the Reinsured, or to its liquidator, receiver, conservator, or statutory successor on the basis of the insolvency of the Reinsured or because the liquidator, receiver, conservator, or statutory successor of the Reinsured has failed to pay all or a portion of any claim. It is agreed, however, that the liquidator, receiver, conservator, or statutory successor of the Reinsured shall give written notice to the Reinsurers of the pendency of a claim against the Reinsured indicating the policy or bond reinsured which claim would involve a possible liability on the part of the Reinsurers within a reasonable time after such claim is filed in the conservation or liquidation proceeding or in the receivership, and that during the pendency of such claim, the Reinsurers may investigate such claim and interpose, at their own expense, in the proceeding where such claim is to be adjudicated any defense or defenses that they may deem available to the Reinsured or its liquidator, receiver, conservator, or statutory successor. The expense thus incurred by the Reinsurers shall be chargeable subject to the approval of the court, against the Reinsured as part of the expense of conservation or liquidation to the extent of a pro rata share of the benefit that may accrue to the Reinsured solely as a result of the defense undertaken by the Reinsurers.

Where two or more Reinsurers are involved in the same claim, and a majority in interest elect to interpose defense to such claim, the expense shall be apportioned in accordance with the terms of the reinsurance Agreement as though such expense had been incurred by the Reinsured.

The reinsurance shall be payable by the Reinsurers to the Reinsured or to its liquidator, receiver, conservator, or statutory successor, except as provided by Section 315 of the New York Insurance Law or except (a) where the Agreement specifically provides another payee of such reinsurance in the event of the insolvency of the Reinsured, and (b) where the Reinsurers with the consent of the direct insured or insureds have assumed such policy obligations of the Reinsured as direct obligations of the Reinsurers to the payees under such policies and in substitution for the obligations of the Reinsured to such payees.

N. Article 18: Intermediary Clauses

(Intermediary) is hereby recognized as the intermediary through whom all communications relating hereto (including but not limited to notice, statements, premiums, return premiums, commissions, taxes, losses, loss adjustment expense, salvage, and loss settlement) shall be transmitted to both parties. It is understood, as regards remittances due either party hereunder, that payment by the Reinsured to (Intermediary) shall constitute payment to the Reinsured to the extent such payments are actually received by the Reinsured.

O. Article 19: Extra-Contractual Obligations (ECO Clauses)

This Agreement shall protect the Reinsured within the limits hereof, where the ultimate net loss includes any Extra-Contractual Obligations.

"Extra-Contractual Obligations" are defined as those liabilities that are not covered under any other provision of this Agreement and that arise from the handling of any claim on business covered hereunder, such as liabilities arising because of, but not limited to, the following: failure by the Reinsured to settle within the policy limit, by reason of alleged or actual negligence, fraud, or bad faith in rejecting an offer of settlement or in the preparation or prosecution of an appeal consequent upon such action.

The date on which an Extra-Contractual Obligation is incurred by the Reinsured shall be deemed, in all circumstances, to be the date of the original accident, casualty, disaster, or loss occurrence.

However, this Article shall not apply where the loss has been incurred due to fraud of a member of the Board of Directors or a corporate officer of the Reinsured acting individually or collectively or in collusion with any individual or corporation or any other organization or party involved in the presentation, defense, or settlement of any claim covered hereunder.

II. Using Policy Language as a Guide to Discovery

Policy language will often provide a guide, and indicate that certain items will likely be present in the insurer's and insured's underwriting, audit and claim files, as well as in their intermediaries' files. The following provisions (taken from Excess Liability policies) give some examples of such items.

A. Inspection and Audit

Underwriters shall be permitted but not obligated to inspect the Insured's property and operations at any time. Neither the Underwriters' right to make inspections nor the making thereof nor any report thereon shall constitute an undertaking on behalf of or for the benefit of the Insured or others, to determine or warrant that such property or operations are safe.

B. Reporting of Claims

The Insured shall immediately give notice, in writing, to Underwriters' representative, as set forth in Item 5 of the Declarations, of any claim or claim to which this Policy applies that may exceed 25 percent of the applicable amount set forth in the attached Schedule of Underlying Amounts.

C. Assistance and Cooperation

Underwriters shall not be called upon to assume charge of the settlement or defense of any claim made or suit brought or proceeding instituted against the Insured, but Underwriters shall have the right and shall be given the opportunity to associate with the Insured in the defense and control of any claim, suit, or proceeding relative to any Loss either hereunder or within the Underlying Amounts, in which event the Insured and Underwriters shall cooperate in all things in the defense of such claim, suit, or proceeding and the Insured shall make available to Underwriters such information and access to records as Underwriters may require.

D. Service of Suit Clause

It is agreed that in the event of the failure of Underwriters hereon to pay amount claimed to be due hereunder, Underwriters hereon, at the request of the Insured, will submit to the jurisdiction of any court of competent jurisdiction within the United States and will comply with all requirements necessary to give such court jurisdiction and all matters arising hereunder shall be determined in accordance with the law and practice of such court.

It is further agreed that service of process in such suit may be made upon the person(s) or firm named in Item 9 of the Declarations and that in any suit instituted against any one of them upon this Policy, Underwriters will abide by the final decision of such court or of any Appellate court in the event of an appeal. The person(s) or firm named in Item 9 of the Declarations are authorized and directed to accept service of process on behalf of Underwriters in any such suit and/or upon the request of the Insured to give a written undertaking to the Insured that they will enter a general appearance on Underwriters' behalf in the event such a suit shall be instituted.

Further, pursuant to any statute of any state, territory, or district of the United States that makes provision therefore, Underwriters hereon hereby designate the Superintendent, Commissioner, or Director of Insurance or other officer specified for that purpose in the statute, or his or her successor or successors in office, as their true and lawful attorney upon whom may be served any lawful process in any action, suit or proceeding instituted by or on behalf of the insured or any beneficiary hereunder arising out of this Policy of insurance, and hereby designate the person(s) or firm named in Item 9 of the Declarations as the person to whom the said officer is authorized to mail such process or true copy thereof.

E. Insolvency

In the event of the insolvency of the Insured or upon takeover of the Insured's business by any State or Federal Official or Agency, or by any Receiver or Liquidator, acting or appointed for this purpose, this Policy shall be cancelled immediately without the necessity of Underwriters or Underwriters' representative giving notice of such cancellation and as a consequence this Policy will terminate immediately. In the event of such cancellation Underwriters will refund to the Receiver or Liquidator the unearned premium or pro rata of the premium paid hereon, whichever is the lesser. The insolvency of the Insured or the takeover of the Insured's business by any State or Federal Official of Agency or by any Receiver or Liquidator shall not reduce or eliminate the underlying amounts.

III. Consideration of Offset Clauses and Funding Clauses

Examination should also be made of the Offset Clauses and Funding provisions present in the policy language.

A. Offset Clause: One Possible Version

Each party hereto shall have, and may exercise at any time, and from time to time, the right to offset any balance or balances, whether on account of premiums or on account of losses or otherwise, due from such party to the other (or, if more than one, any other party hereto under this Agreement or under any other reinsurance agreement heretofore or hereafter entered into by and between them), and may offset the same against any balance or balances due or to become due to the former from the latter under the same; or any other reinsurance agreement between them; and the party asserting the right of offset shall have and may exercise such right whether the balance or balances due or to become due to such party from the other are on account of premiums or on account of losses or otherwise and regardless of the capacity, whether as assuming insurer or as ceding insurer, in which each party acted under the agreement or, if more than one, the different agreements involved, provided, however, that, in the event of the insolvency of a party hereto, offsets shall be allowed only in accordance with the provisions of the Insurance Law of the State of New York.

B. Offset Clause: Alternative Version

Each party hereto shall have, and may exercise at any time and from time to time, the right to offset any balance or balances, whether on account of premiums or on account of losses or otherwise, due from such party to the other (or, if more than one, any other) party hereto under this Agreement and may offset the same against any balance or balances due or to become due to the former from the latter under the same; and the party asserting the right of offset shall have and may exercise such right whether the balance or balances due or to become due to such party from the other are on account of premiums or on account of losses or otherwise and regardless of the capacity, whether as assuming insurer or as ceding insurer, in which each party acted under the agreement involved, provided, however, that, in the event of the insolvency of a party hereto, offsets shall be allowed only in accordance with the provisions of the Insurance Law of the State of New York.

C. Funding Clause

(This clause is applicable only to those reinsurer(s)who cannot qualify for credit by the state having jurisdiction over the company's loss reserves.)

a. As regards policies or bonds issued by the Company coming within the scope of this Agreement, the Company agrees that, when it shall file with the Insurance Department or set up on its books reserves for losses covered hereunder that it shall be required by law to set up, it will forward to the Reinsurer a statement showing the proportion of such loss reserves that is applicable to the Reinsurer. The Reinsurer hereby agrees that it will apply for and secure delivery to the Company of a clean, irrevocable, and unconditional Letter of Credit, issued by a bank that is acceptable to the regulatory authority or authorities having jurisdiction over the Company's loss reserves in an amount equal to the Reinsurer's proportion of reserves in respect of known outstanding losses that have been reported to the Reinsurer and allocated loss expenses relating thereto as shown in the statement prepared by the Company. Under no circumstances shall any amount relating to reserves in respect of Incurred But Not Reported Losses be included in the amount of the Letter of Credit.

b. The Letter of Credit shall be issued for a period of not less than one year, and shall automatically extend for one year from its date of expiration or any future expiration date unless thirty (30) days prior to any expiration date the issuing bank shall notify the Company by registered mail that the bank elects not to consider the Letter of Credit extended for any additional period. An issuing bank, not a member of the Federal Reserve System or not chartered in New York State, shall provide sixty (60) days notice to the Company prior to any expiration in the event of nonextension.

c. Notwithstanding any other provision of this Agreement, the Company or its successors in interest may draw upon such credit at any time without diminution because of the insolvency of the Company or of the Reinsurer for one or more of the following purposes only:

1. To pay the Reinsurer's share or to reimburse the Company for the Reinsurer's share of any loss reinsured by this Agreement, the payment of which has been agreed by the reinsurer and which has not been otherwise paid;
2. To make refund of any sum that is in excess of the actual amount required to pay the Reinsurer's share of any liability reinsured by this Agreement; or
3. In the event of expiration of the Letter of Credit as provided for above, to establish deposit of the Reinsurer's share of known and reported outstanding losses and allocated expenses relating thereto under this Agreement. Such cash deposit shall be held in an interest bearing account separate from the Company's other assets, and interest thereon shall accrue to the benefit of the Reinsurer.

d. The issuing bank shall have no responsibility whatsoever in connection with the propriety of withdrawals made by the Company or the disposition of funds withdrawn, except to ensure that withdrawals are made only upon the order of properly authorized representatives of the Company.

e. At annual intervals, or more frequently as agreed but never more frequently than quarterly, the Company shall prepare a specific statement, for the sole purpose of amending the Letter of Credit, of the Reinsurer's share of known and reported outstanding losses and allocated expenses relating thereto. If the statement shows that Reinsurer's share of such losses and allocated loss expenses exceeds the balance of credit as of the statement date, the Reinsurer shall, within thirty (30) days after receipt of notice of such excess, secure delivery to the Company of amendment of the Letter of Credit increasing the amount of credit by the amount of such difference. If, however, the statement shows that the Reinsurers share of known and reported outstanding losses plus allocated loss expenses relating thereto is less than the balance of credit as of the statement date, the Company shall, within thirty (30) days after receipt of written request from the Reinsurer, release such excess credit by agreeing to secure an amendment to the Letter of Credit reducing the amount of credit available by the amount of such excess credit.

APPENDIX 18-4

Application Language—Excess Liability Policy

The completion for and submission to Underwriters of this application does not constitute a binder or insurance nor any insurance coverage whatsoever nor do underwriters undertake to offer any terms or coverage.

Application for Excess Liability Policy (London 85)

(Applicants are advised to read the form before completing this application.)

1. Full name of Applicant (including all companies to be insured):

   Notes: (a) Give details of any operations for which coverage is not required; (b) If the companies to be insured are not the Parent Company, please give name of the Parent Company.
2. Description of all Operations.
3. Describe all the products manufactured, handled, distributed, or sold under the following classifications:

Classification	Description	Annual Sales
(a) Aircraft and/or Aerospace Products or any material or substance supplied to or for use by the Aircraft and/or Aerospace Industry		
(b) Pharmaceutical, Chemicals, Petrochemicals, and Nuclear Energy.		
(c) Any other products.		

4. (a) Give details of any insurance the Applicant intends to purchase as respects the Underlying Amounts and details of any insurance that may be in force that would act in the same manner.

   (b) Give details of any nonstandard exclusions contained therein.
5. State loss records during the past ten years specifying:

   (a) Full details of all claims exclusive of expenses (whether insured or not) in excess of $10,000 (enter full amount for first dollar for each case) and specify amounts and date paid and amounts outstanding, showing separately the date of loss and the date claim was first made in writing against the Insured.

(b) In respect to Products Liability, the Aggregate amount, separately by the date of loss and the date the claim was first made in writing against the Insured, of losses (from first dollar) for each year and specify amounts paid and outstanding.

(c) The organization that has evaluated any outstanding amounts and the date of the said evaluation.

6. Has the Applicant ever handled his own losses in any self-insured areas and if so give details of such loss handling.
7. The policy for which this Application is being made does require that the Insured self-insures the Underlying Amounts and as a consequence, give details as to the Applicant's approach to loss handling.

NOTE: Please enclose with this Application the latest Annual Report and Interims. If these are not available or are not published or are not available, Underwriters may not consider this application unless adequate alternative information to Underwriters satisfaction can be supplied.

We know of no other relevant facts that might affect Underwriters' judgment when considering this application.

Dated ________ Signed _______________

CHAPTER 19

The Joint-Defense Privilege: An Illusion or a Magic Wand?

JEFFERY J. CARLSON

I. Introduction

The plaintiff in a toxic tort action often brings suit against several parties, and accordingly the defendants should examine the benefits of entering into a joint-defense or cost-sharing agreement. Besides the obvious cost savings and strategic advantages of undertaking some form of coordinated defense, the joint-defense agreement may also minimize the potential for friction and discord among defendants (which often plays a major role in assisting the plaintiff in establishing its case) and may serve to discourage piecemeal settlements (which helps to finance the plaintiff's action against the remaining defendants). These cost-sharing arrangements may range from the engagement of a single defense counsel for all purposes to the establishment of a defense committee that assigns the lead role on particular projects to a particular defendant or defendants. While the extent to which a joint or coordinated defense is feasible will depend on the facts in each case, it is important to recognize that such arrangements can offer significant benefits and advantages to all parties, and can offer flexibility in the process.

Courts have generally recognized the "joint defense" or "common interest" doctrine in applying the attorney-client privilege and work-product doctrine to multidefendant cases.[1] Under this doctrine, a privilege is not waived upon disclosure to a third party where the third party "shares a common interest with the disclosing party which is adverse to that of the party seeking discovery."[2] However, the determination of a privilege in a toxic tort litigation case, as in any case, is made on a case-by-case basis; therefore, it is important to understand exactly what each privilege seeks to protect before attempting to predict whether a specific communication will be afforded protection.

II. Basic Overview of the Attorney-Client and Work-Product Privileges

A. Attorney-Client Privilege

In federal cases, there is no uniform federal standard defining the attorney-client privilege; therefore, the law of the forum state applies.[3]

The attorney-client privilege exists to protect confidential communications between client and attorney; in effect, to protect the attorney-client relationship. Its purpose is to protect not only the giving of professional advice to those who can act upon it,[4] but also the giving of information to the lawyer to enable him to give sound advice.[5] In general, "the underlying rationale for the attorney-client privilege is to encourage free communication between client and attorney."[6] At the insistence of the client, these communications are permanently protected.[7]

B. Work-Product Privilege

In federal courts, the work-product privilege, unlike the attorney-client privilege, is governed by the uniform federal standard embodied in Federal Rule of Civil Procedure 26(b)(3). Rule 26(b)(3)(A) provides, in part, that:

> [A] party may not discover documents and tangible things that are prepared in anticipation of litigation or for trial by or for another party or its representative (including the other party's attorney, consultant, surety, indemnitor, insurer, or agent). But, subject to Rule 26(b)(4), those materials may be discovered if:
>
> (i) they are otherwise discoverable under Rule 26(b)(1); and
> (ii) the party shows that it has substantial need for the materials to prepare its case and cannot, without undue hardship, obtain their substantial equivalent by other means.[8]

Furthering clarifying the limits of work-product protection, Rule 26(b)(3)(B) provides:

> If the court orders discovery of those materials, it must protect against disclosure of the mental impressions, conclusions, opinions, or legal theories of a party's attorney or other representative concerning the litigation.[9]

The application of the work-product doctrine to specific documents is guided by the seminal case of *Hickman v. Taylor*.[10] In *Hickman*, the Supreme Court undertook the difficult task of reconciling the competing interests of liberalized discovery and the privacy of an attorney's files. The Court recognized that attorneys engaged in the representation of clients must be allowed a certain degree of privacy so as to be able to discharge their duties to their clients responsibly and effectively. To this end, the Supreme Court stated that an attorney's "proper preparation of a client's case demands that he assemble information, sift what he considers to be the relevant from the irrelevant facts, prepare his legal theories and plan his strategy without undue and needless interference."[11]

Since *Hickman*, courts have made a distinction between "ordinary" work product and "opinion" work product. Generally, courts have described "ordinary" work product as those facts and materials gathered by counsel during an investigation of a matter, whereas "opinion" work product consists of the mental impressions and thought process employed by counsel in formulating strategy.[12]

There is a split among the federal courts as to when, if ever, opinion work product may be produced. In the leading case denying all discovery of opinion work product, *Duplan Corp. v. Moulinage et Retorderie de Chavanoz*, the Fourth Circuit reasoned that "no showing of relevance, substantial need or undue hardship should justify compelling disclosure of an attorney's mental impressions, conclusions, opinions or legal theories. This is made clear by the rule's use of the term 'shall' as opposed to 'may.'"[13] However, the same circuit later noted, "[R]ecent decisions which recognize that the protection of opinion work product by Rule 26(b)(3) is not in all cases absolute erode the precedential value of *Duplan*."[14]

Other courts take the position that a party seeking opinion work product must make a showing beyond the substantial need/undue hardship test enunciated in Rule 26(b)(3).[15] Cases requiring a heightened showing, beyond the substantial need/undue hardship test, reason that an ad hoc denial of discovery of all opinion work product ignores the Advisory Committee notes to the 1970 amendment to Rule 26(b)(3), which state that the rule "conform[s] to the holdings of the cases, when viewed in light of their facts. In *Hickman*, the Court stated that 'if there should be a rare situation justifying production of [work product], petitioner's case is not of that type.'"[16] So far, the Supreme Court has declined to decide whether "opinion" work product is absolutely protected from discovery.[17]

III. The Applicability of the Attorney-Client Privilege and the Work-Product Privilege in the Context of a Joint-Defense Arrangement

A. Attorney-Client Privilege

1. Privilege Afforded Communications between Parties to Joint-Defense Agreement and Their Counsel Relating to Joint Defense

Issues involving the attorney-client and work-product privilege naturally arise out of the use of shared counsel. In this respect, the question becomes whether the otherwise applicable privilege is waived as a consequence of disclosure either to a common attorney or to counsel for codefendants.

It is long settled in all American jurisdictions that where two or more parties employ a lawyer as their common counsel, communications to that attorney are confidential and privileged as against all common adversaries.[18]

Where the defendants choose to have their independent counsel work together in a shared defense arrangement, information passed between them is privileged to the extent that it is part of an ongoing and joint effort to set up a common defense strategy. In a joint-defense arrangement, the attorney-client privilege protects communications by a client to his own lawyer, even though the lawyer may subsequently share that information with codefendants.[19]

Similarly, the attorney-client privilege protects information communicated by a client to counsel for codefendants.[20] In *Eisenberg v. Gagnon*, the three defendants were represented by three different law firms, but were undertaking the coordination of a joint defense. A principal of one of the defendants corresponded with the lawyer for another defendant regarding information that one of the other defendants knew and should have disclosed and the trial strategy that the defendant should adopt in connection therewith. The court held that this communication was protected by the attorney-client privilege, reasoning that the shared information was at best viewed as part of an ongoing and joint effort to set up a common defense strategy between a defendant and the attorney responsible for coordinating a common defense position. The court determined that communications to an attorney to establish a common defense strategy are privileged, even though the attorney represents a different client who may have some adverse interests.[21]

Generally, to establish the joint-defense privilege, courts require the parties to demonstrate that the communications: (1) were intended to be kept confidential; (2) were made in the pursuit of a joint legal effort; and (3) were intended to advance a common interest.[22]

It must also be noted that the terms "joint defense privilege" and "common-interest doctrine" have been used interchangeably. On the one hand, it has been stated that:

> Where the third party shares a common interest with the disclosing party which is adverse to the party seeking discovery, any existing privilege is not waived. This is known as the common interest or joint defense doctrine.[23]

Conversely, other courts have distinguished between the two terms; the joint-defense privilege has been described as "protect[ing] communications between two or more parties and their respective counsel if they are engaged in a joint-defense effort."[24] In contrast, the common-interest doctrine "protects communications between a lawyer and two or more clients regarding a matter of common interest."[25] However, review of the cases discussing these terms shows the distinctions are more form than substance; both describe the same concept of maintaining the attorney-client privilege in a joint-defense situation.

A thorough analysis and application of the joint-defense privilege was seen in the Eighth Circuit case *John Morrell & Co. v. Local Union 304A*.[26] In *Morrell*, unions representing workers at plaintiff's meatpacking plant in South Dakota had a judgment entered against them following an illegal strike by the union's members at the plant. On appeal, the union contended the trial court erred in finding that an internal memorandum written by plaintiff's general counsel, which came into the union's possession due to another pending lawsuit, was protected by the attorney-client joint-defense privilege. Prior to the matter at issue, a group of employees at Morrell's Iowa plant brought an action against Morrell and a union involved in the instant appeal regarding the Iowa plant's closing. The union cross-complained against Morrell. Morrell reached a settlement with the workers and entered into a joint-defense agreement with the workers, allowing them access to privileged Morrell documents for use in their case against the union. These privileged documents came into the union's hands when the employees' expert witness inadvertently produced them at his deposition. The union later sought to use these documents in defending the *Morrell v. Local Union 304A* action regarding the illegal strike in South Dakota. The district court barred the use of the documents obtained by the union, citing the attorney-client privilege.

The Eighth Circuit affirmed. The court held that in the previous case (regarding the Iowa plant's closure), "[t]he . . . employees and Morrell shared a joint defense privilege by virtue of being aligned on the same side following their settlement and the international union's cross-claims."[27] In finding the joint-defense privilege applicable, the court reasoned that "when information is exchanged between various co-defendants and their attorneys, . . . this exchange is not made for the purpose of allowing unlimited publication and use, but rather, the exchange is made for the limited purpose of assisting in their common cause."[28] Finding no waiver by the previous inadvertent production of the document, the court found that the joint-defense privilege was a bar to the document's introduction.[29]

a. What Constitutes a Common Interest?

As shown above, with respect to the issue of a "common interest," the Eighth Circuit in *Morell* held that the defendant company shared a joint-defense privilege with formerly adverse employees following settlement, once a third-party union cross-complained against them.[30]

The Ninth Circuit has similarly espoused a broad interpretation of the joint-defense doctrine, and applied the common-interest exception to situations where codefendants have interests that are adverse.[31] In *Hunydee v. United States*, the Ninth Circuit held that the attorney-client privilege applied to a defendant's statements because they concerned a matter of common concern, although the defendant and his codefendant generally had adverse interests and the meeting at issue was not for purposes of a common defense.

In *Hunydee*, a husband and wife were indicted under a single indictment for income tax evasion.[32] They retained separate counsel because of possible conflict of interest. At a preindictment meeting attended by the codefendants and their respective attorneys, the husband stated that he would plead guilty and take the blame.[33] At trial, the wife and her attorney testified as to the husband's comments.[34] The husband objected on attorney-client privilege grounds.[35] The trial court ruled that the conversation was not privileged as it was neither between a client and his attorney nor confidential in character.[36] The Ninth Circuit disagreed.[37]

The court in *Hunydee* held that whether the meeting was called to prepare a trial strategy or defense was not dispositive; it was the nature of the statements that controlled.[38] This court ruled that "where two or more persons who are subject to possible indictment in connection with the same transaction make confidential statements to their attorneys, these statements, even though they are exchanged between attorneys, should be privileged to the extent they concern common issues and are intended to facilitate representation in possible subsequent proceedings."[39]

The statements were privileged because they "apprised the respective attorneys of [defendant's] position at the time and influenced the course of their representation."[40] In light of the foregoing, demonstrating a common interest for the purposes of applying the common-interest doctrine is not an onerous requirement. However, where the joint interest is commercial, rather than legal in nature, the doctrine may not apply.[41]

b. Furtherance of Legal Effort

The common-interest exception requires that the communication at issue be "designed to further that [legal] effort."[42] This includes disclosures that concern the instant litigation; to be protected, they must be made in the course of "formulating a common legal strategy"[43] or otherwise furthering the parties' joint interest in the litigation.[44] In contrast, the providing of a litigation abstract in order to facilitate certain bidders' commercial decision whether to invest in a company has been held to further not a joint defense but rather a commercial transaction, and therefore not subject to the common-interest privilege.[45]

c. Confidentiality

Demonstrating an intent to maintain confidentiality is generally accomplished via a joint-defense agreement and avoiding waiver (see section III.C, *infra*).

2. Limits of Joint-Defense Attorney-Client Privilege

Although information disclosed pursuant to a joint-defense agreement is protected by the attorney-client privilege, the agreement operates more as a shield against waiver of protection for privileged attorney-client communication between one party to the agreement and its particular attorney when it is disclosed to other parties involved in the joint defense. Generally, the joint-defense agreement does not automatically establish a "communal" attorney-client privilege between all parties to a joint-defense agreement and their respective attorneys.[46]

However, the "circumstances of [joint-defense agreement] representation may create an implied attorney-client relationship with co-defendants."[47] If parties to the joint-defense agreement become adverse, one of the parties may seek to disqualify counsel to the other party on the grounds that continued representation violates the "communal" attorney-client privilege between all parties to the joint-defense agreement and their respective attorneys.[48]

The Ninth Circuit has held that counsel for a party to a joint-defense agreement should be disqualified from defending that party in an action adverse to a former party to the agreement based on a implied "communal" attorney-client relationship with the former party.[49] In *United States v. Henke*, the Ninth Circuit held that the obligations set forth in a joint-defense agreement precluded an attorney for one of the parties from using information against a codefendant who had pled out.[50] As part of his plea agreement, the withdrawing party agreed to testify for the government.[51]

The attorney for one of the remaining parties to the joint-defense agreement sought to withdraw as counsel and moved for a mistrial.[52] He claimed that the agreement precluded him from cross-examining the withdrawing party using information obtained during joint-defense meetings.[53] As this impaired his ability to represent his client, he sought to withdraw as counsel.[54]

The district court granted the mistrial but denied the motion to withdraw, asserting that because any privileged information known by current counsel would not be known to new counsel, withdrawal would have no effect.[55] The defense lawyers refused to cross-examine the withdrawing party at the second trial, and both defendants were convicted.

On appeal, the *Henke* court held that the testimony of the withdrawing party created a disqualifying conflict, as the joint-defense agreement prohibited appellants' lawyers from cross-examining the witness.[56] The Ninth Circuit noted that this conflict was created by the implied attorney-client privilege between counsel for the remaining parties to the joint-defense agreement and the withdrawn party.[57] The Ninth Circuit then vacated appellants' convictions, in part on the ground that the trial court should have disqualified counsel for the remaining parties to the agreement.[58]

Even if there is not a "communal" attorney-client privilege to disqualify an attorney representing a client in both (1) a joint defense and (2) a subsequent action adverse to a party to the joint-defense agreement, such an attorney may still be still be disqualified if the attorney cannot show he or she did not obtain any confidential information obtained via participation in the joint defense.[59] However, this would be a rare circumstance, as showing that the parties to a joint-defense agreement shared confidences between their attorneys is a common method to establish a "communal" attorney-client privilege.[60]

B. Work-Product Privilege

It is stated that information shared among defendants participating in a joint-defense arrangement "operates only within narrow confines . . . the principal restriction is that the material in question must have been prepared in anticipation of litigation."[61] The determination of whether documents were prepared in anticipation of litigation is clearly a factual determination.[62] Many courts use the imminence of litigation as a measuring stick for determining whether the documents were actually prepared in anticipation of litigation. The cases are not entirely clear as to how imminent the litigation must be, or whether it must be imminent at all, in order for the privilege to apply. One aspect that is clear in determining the imminence of litigation, and thus whether the documents were prepared "in anticipation of litigation," is that in multiparty situations that arise in the context of toxic tort litigation, the courts usually require some sort of nexus between consultations with lawyers and "representation and possible subsequent proceedings."[63]

A question that will often arise in toxic tort litigation is whether documents that have been afforded the work-product privilege in a previous case continue to be protected by that privilege beyond the termination of the litigation. The split of authority among the courts in this area is clear.[64] Three divergent views have been followed by the courts. Some courts adhere to the view that the work-product privilege applies only if the materials were prepared in anticipation of the present litigation before the court. Thus, documents prepared for one case are freely discoverable in a subsequent case.[65]

This line of cases has been disapproved,[66] and even the strict construction of the *IBM* decision limiting work-product protection only if the materials were prepared in anticipation of the present litigation has been expanded by a subsequent decision. The same court has concluded "that a document was prepared in anticipation of one litigation does not preclude the application of the work-product rule in another litigation."[67]

Some courts have held that "what is needed, if we are to remain faithful to the articulated policies of *Hickman*, is a perpetual protection for work product, one that extends beyond the termination of the litigation for which the documents were prepared."[68]

Finding neither of these extreme options useful, some courts have taken a third, intermediate approach under which the extension of the work-product privilege from one case to a subsequent case depends upon "whether the first action was complete, and upon the relationship between the first and second actions."[69] Following this approach, a substantial body of federal case law supports the conclusion that the work-product privilege extends to subsequent cases only when those cases are related.[70]

C. Waiver

Both the attorney-client and work-product privileges may be deemed waived upon the disclosure of relevant information to third parties, on the theory that disclosure is incompatible with keeping information privileged. However, in the context of a joint-defense arrangement, there should be no waiver where the information is passed to a third party who shares a common interest in the litigation. A substantial amount of case law establishes that attorneys aligned in a joint-defense posture "may exchange privileged communications and attorney work product in order to prepare a common defense without waiving either privilege."[71]

1. Attorney-Client Privilege

As stated, there is no waiver of the attorney-client privilege where the client or client's attorney discloses information to counsel for codefendants when a joint defense has been undertaken.[72] In this scenario, in order to preserve the attorney-client privilege, an attorney must be careful to share only that information that relates to issues presented in the common defense. When such information is shared among joint-defense counsel, it can be inferred that the disclosure was made under the expectation that the communication was confidential and shall remain private. Thus, the information retains its privileged nature because it has remained within the confidential relationship developed and shared by the parties with a common interest in the litigation. It may also be inferred that those parties with common interests on a particular issue against a common adversary share information for the limited and restricted purpose of assisting in asserting their common claims. As such, the transferee is not at all likely to disclose the information to the adversary.[73] In sum, the joint-defense privilege is meant to recognize "the advantages of, and even, the necessity for, an exchange or pooling of information between attorneys representing parties sharing such a common interest in litigation, actual or prospective."[74]

It bears repeating that in order for the applicable joint-defense privileges to remain viable, the information must be shared only among those parties sharing a common interest in the litigation; the privilege *may* be waived where privileged communications are disclosed to third parties. The analysis usually hinges on whether the disclosure was inadvertent or knowing.[75] Three distinct lines of authority have arisen in determining whether a disclosed privileged communication to a third party waives the joint-defense privilege.[76]

The first position taken by the courts on this issue would automatically waive any applicable joint-defense privilege upon *any* disclosure of privileged information. To this end, it has been stated that "[d]isclosure of otherwise privileged material even where disclosure was inadvertent, serves as a waiver of the privilege."[77] A second view would preclude waiver of a joint-defense privilege following the inadvertent production of otherwise privileged material during the course of discovery. This view is grounded on the theory that waiver of a privilege may occur only if the holder of the privilege has knowingly sanctioned the waiver. On this point, it has been stated that "we are taught from first year law school that waiver imports the 'intentional relinquishment or abandonment of a known right' . . . [i]nadvertent production is the antithesis of that concept."[78]

A third position followed by a majority of courts in determining whether waiver of a privilege has taken place through inadvertent production of privileged documents, recognizes the burdens of discovery and realizes that an unintended error in some instances may waive a privilege.[79] Courts following this intermediate approach often take into account a number of factors to determine whether waiver has taken place. Often, the decision regarding whether waiver has taken place turns on the precautions taken by the disclosing party to prevent the disclosure, the number of privileged documents that have been disclosed, the extent of the disclosure, the promptness of measures taken to rectify the disclosure, and whether the interests of justice would be served in finding a waiver of the privilege.[80]

At least one court has taken the position that the determination of inadvertent versus knowing disclosure of privileged material, and the resulting question of waiver, may be avoided by entering into a prediscovery order. It has been suggested that in a document-intensive case, the parties may enter into a prediscovery order stating that unintended disclosure of privileged material will not operate as a waiver of any privilege. Under such facts, the Ninth Circuit concluded that it was "obvious" no such waiver had occurred after the parties had entered into, and the court had approved, such an order.[81]

It has also been held that "the joint defense privilege cannot be waived without the consent of all parties to the defense, except in the situation where one of the joint defendants becomes an adverse party in litigation."[82] For example, the Fifth Circuit in *Wilson P. Abraham Construction Corp. v. Armco Steel Corp.*[83] held that where information is exchanged between codefendants and attorneys in a joint-defense setting, "this exchange is not made for the purpose of allowing unlimited publication and use, but rather, the exchange is made for the limited purpose of assisting in their common cause. In such a situation, an attorney who is the recipient of such information breaches his fiduciary duty if he later, in his representation of another client, is able to use this information to the detriment of one of the co-defendants."[84]

Similarly, it has been held that a subsidiary could not later waive a joint-defense privilege without the consent of its former parent.[85]

Many courts take the position that the joint-defense privilege is waived if the codefendants later litigate against each other.[86] The justification for this rule was discussed in *In re Grand Jury Subpoena Duces Tecum*, wherein the court stated that once the codefendants take action against each other, neither "can reasonably be allowed to deny to the other the use of information which he already has by virtue of the former's known disclosure."[87] Under the joint-defense privilege, communications between codefendants are only privileged as to third parties. Once codefendants reposition themselves so as to take action against each other, there is a restructuring of the parties' rights, so as to make their interests adverse and any information exchanged between them in a previous litigation no longer privileged. This rule can prove to be very damaging in a toxic tort case where a joint defense has been undertaken and one or several codefendants subsequently take action against each other in the form of indemnity claims and the like. For this reason, this waiver rule should always be considered when drafting a joint-defense agreement, and the necessary precautions should be taken in the form of a confidentiality clause. Without this limitation, a joint defense would become impractical as no defendant would be protected against a codefendant trading a waiver in order to obtain a separate settlement.[88]

2. *Work-Product Privilege*

Similarly, the work-product privilege is not considered waived where counsel presenting a joint defense share information relating to their common interests.[89] Again, the scope of the work-product privilege is defined by the purpose of the privilege itself: to promote the adversarial system by safeguarding the fruits of an attorney's trial preparation from the discovery attempts of his opponent.[90] The rationale behind the privilege is that information is to be protected against opposing parties, rather than against all others outside a particular confidential relationship. Thus, communications in the joint-defense scenario will lose their work-product protection only to the extent that the information is either unrelated to the common interests of the parties, or is transferred to someone outside of the confidential relationship, thereby waiving the privilege.

In *D'Ippolito v. Cities Service Co.*,[91] the plaintiff in a private suit raised the work-product privilege to prevent disclosure of an exhibit, but conceded that he had voluntarily disclosed the exhibit to attorneys in the antitrust division of the Department of Justice. Observing that the government was not a party to the lawsuit, the court found that "the disclosure of the document cannot be termed as an interchange of information between counsel on the same side of the litigation."[92] Consequently, the court held the privilege to be waived. This holding illustrates a narrow interpretation of "common interest," which limits it to coparties.

In contrast to *D'Ippolito*, a subsequent case by the same court (the Southern District of New York) held the work-product privilege was not waived by disclosure of trial preparation documents by a private antitrust plaintiff to the government. The court in *G.A.F. Corp. v. Eastman Kodak Co.*[93] found that despite voluntary disclosure of the subject documents to persons not on the same side of the litigation, the privilege remained intact. Rejecting the standard announced by the court in *D'Ippolito*, the court held that waiver would occur, if at all, only if the disclosure "substantially increased" the possibility of an opposing party obtaining the information.[94] Since the disclosure in *G.A.F.* had occurred under a statutory guarantee of confidentiality on the part of the government, the court held the conditions of waiver were not satisfied.

In settling the issue for the Second Circuit, the appellate court declined to adopt a "per se" rule regarding whether all voluntary disclosures to the government operate to waive the protections of the work-product rule.[95] The *Steinhardt* case followed widely publicized allegations of wrongdoing in the market for treasury notes during 1991. Following these allegations, the Securities and Exchange Commission began an informal investigation of Steinhardt Partners and others. As part of the investigation, the SEC's enforcement division requested that Steinhardt's counsel prepare a memorandum addressing various legal issues arising during the investigation. Steinhardt prepared the memo and submitted it to the SEC, requesting that it remain confidential.

Following these events, various civil suits were initiated by private parties against Steinhardt and others, alleging manipulations of the Treasury note markets. During discovery, plaintiffs requested all documents previously produced by Steinhardt to any investigating government agency. Steinhardt identified the memo it had drafted for the SEC, but declined to provide it, citing work-product protection. The district court granted plaintiffs' motion to compel. Steinhardt petitioned the appellate court for a writ of mandamus.

The Second Circuit denied the writ, reasoning that "[o]nce a party allows an adversary to share the otherwise privileged thought processes of counsel, the need for the privilege disappears."[96] The court further held that a client cannot be permitted to pick and choose among third parties for whom the work-product protection is waived and to whom applies.[97] However, the Second Circuit took pains to emphasize that the ruling declined to adopt a per se rule that all voluntary disclosures to the government waive work-product protection, choosing instead to declare that "[c]rafting rules relating to privilege in matters of government investigations must be done on a case-by-case basis."[98]

In still another case, the court in *United States v. AT&T Co.* adopted the *G.A.F.* standard of waiver, reasoning that the purpose of the work-product privilege is to protect information from opponents—not necessarily all other parties. In this light, the court held that "[a] disclosure made in the pursuit of such trial preparation, and not inconsistent with maintaining secrecy against opponents, should be allowed without waiver of the privilege."[99]

The court recognized that the existence of common interests between a transferor and transferee is relevant to deciding whether the disclosure is consistent with the nature of the work-product privilege. However, the court explained that while the *G.A.F.* standard should not be read so broadly as to allow confidential disclosure to *any* person without waiver of the work-product privilege, at the same time the existence of "common interests" should not be interpreted as narrowly limiting the privilege to coparties. The court thus laid down a new standard in defining the boundaries of the work-product privilege: so long as the transferor and the transferee anticipate litigation against a common adversary on the same issue or issues, they have strong common interests in sharing the fruits of their trial preparation efforts.[100]

United States v. AT&T Co. expanded the circle within which information retains its work-product protection. Not only did the court broaden the definition of "common interests," but it also recognized an expansive definition of the type of documents afforded the work-product privilege. The court held that documents can come within this privilege if they were prepared in anticipation of litigation, or for trial by or for another party, or by or for that other party's representative (including that party's attorney, consultant, surety, indemnitor, insurer, or agent).[101] Thus, documents prepared by the attorneys for the intervenor, specifically in anticipation of litigation in a previous case, were protected against discovery in the present case.

D. The Use of a Confidentiality Clause as a Precautionary Measure

Although confidentiality can be inferred from circumstances,[102] it makes better sense to enter into a formal joint-defense agreement. A joint-defense agreement imposes a duty of confidentiality.[103] Even if the agreement was informal, it is still valid.[104]

As a precautionary measure, attorneys participating in a shared joint-defense arrangement should always consider including a confidentiality clause in the joint-defense contract. The inclusion of such a clause may serve to bolster the claim of privilege. When the transfer of information to parties with common interests is conducted under a guarantee of confidentiality, the case against waiver is strengthened.[105] This is so, another court reasoned, because common interests may be seen among parties having the strong incentive "in sharing the fruit of trial preparation efforts."[106] As such, having a signed nondisclosure waiver was described by the court as "a guarantee of confidentiality."[107]

E. The Crime-Fraud Exception

Despite the otherwise rigid protection accorded privileged materials, the immunity granted these documents may be waived by a showing that the documents claimed to be protected under the attorney-client or work-product privileges were prepared in furtherance of a crime or fraud.[108] To this end, it is stated that "[the] privilege serves the purpose of promoting broader public interests in the observance of law and administration of justice. However, it is not an absolute privilege. It applies only where necessary to achieve its purpose and protects only those communications necessary to obtain legal advice."[109]

Generally speaking, documents will lose their privileged nature where the attorney has been used in his professional capacity to facilitate or promote criminal activity.[110] This "crime fraud" exception to the attorney-client and work-product privileges applies even where the attorney is unaware that his advice is sought to further an illegal purpose.[111] As cogently stated by the Sixth Circuit, "[A]ll reasons for the attorney-client privilege are completely eviscerated when a client consults an attorney not for advice on past misconduct, but for legal assistance in carrying out a contemplated or ongoing crime or fraud."[112]

IV. Issues Concerning Insurance Coverage Groups

A. The Privileged Nature of Communications Shared with Insurer

In environmental and toxic tort litigation cases, insurers are usually always involved in one form or another. Sometimes they may be involved as parties to the action, but in many cases they may not be named parties. One question that must be addressed is to what extent the information shared with the insurer is protected by the work-product privilege.

The work-product privilege is not restricted to documents containing the mental impressions of an attorney.[113] The federal rule itself states that the court "must protect against disclosure of the mental impressions, conclusions, opinions, or legal theories of a party's attorney or other representative concerning the litigation."[114] Therefore, any ruling that the work-product privilege is inapplicable to documents containing mental impressions of anyone other than a lawyer is inconsistent with the plain language of the rule. In the context of a criminal case, the Supreme Court has observed that while the rule shelters the mental processes of an attorney, it is not restricted to attorneys. Rather:

> The doctrine is an intensely practical one, grounded in the realities of litigation in our adversary system. One of those realities is that attorneys often must rely on the assistance of investigators and other agents in the compilation of materials and preparation for trial. It is therefore necessary that the doctrine protect materials prepared by agents for the attorney as well as those prepared by the attorney himself.[115]

Accordingly, federal courts have consistently ruled that the work-product doctrine is not inapplicable merely because the material was prepared by or for a party's insurer or agents of the insurer.[116] In *Home Insurance Co. v. Ballenger Corp.*,[117] the defendant sought discovery of a report to the plaintiff insurer's home office made by the plaintiff's regional claims supervisor. The document apparently contained evaluations and opinions of Home's agents as to certain insurance files. The court held that this information was protected by the work-product privilege and thus not discoverable by the defendant.[118]

Material prepared by or for a party's insurer or agents of the insurer have been accorded work-product protection even where the insurer is not a named party in the action. In *Basinger v. Glacier Carriers, Inc.*,[119] defendants served a deposition subpoena upon the assistant claims manager for REMCO Insurance Company, strangers to the litigation, commanding that the claims manager produce for them REMCO's claim file on the motor vehicle accident giving rise to the action. The court noted that if a party to a litigation is partially protected by Rule 26(b)(3) from having to disclose certain information to an opposing party, it would be unjust to require a nonparty to deliver the same kind of information to a party who may subsequently join the nonparty in the litigation. In holding that the files were protected by the work-product privilege, the court observed:

> REMCO's file contains internal memoranda reflecting the mental impressions, conclusions, opinions and theories of its agents regarding the value of a potential claim against [its insured]. Rule 26(b)(3) prohibits their discovery since they concern the litigation.[120]

Federal courts, however, are not in agreement as to whether an insurer's claim file, prepared after an accident that may generate a potential claim, can be protected from discovery under Rule 26(b)(3). Three approaches have been taken by the federal courts in determining whether work-product protection applies. Under one approach, courts deny work-product protection to insurance reports prepared after accidents that may generate a claim. The leading case illustrating this position is *Thomas Organ Co. v. Jadranska Slobodna Plovidba*.[121] *Thomas Organ* was an admiralty matter arising from cargo loss aboard a vessel, wherein the court found that:

> [A] report or statement made by or to a party's agent (other than to any attorney acting in the role of counselor), which has not been requested by nor prepared for an attorney's legal expertise must be conclusively presumed to have been made in the ordinary course of business and thus not within the purview of the limited privilege of . . . Rule 26(b)(3) and (b)(4). . . . An insurance company by the nature of its business is not called into action until one of its insureds has suffered some form of injury and has a potential claim. . . . We do not believe that Rule 26(b)(3) was designed to so insulate insurance companies merely because they always deal with potential claims.[122]

The *Thomas Organ* view has been rejected by many courts and treatise writers as contrary to the intent of Rule 26(b). Courts disagreeing with the restrictive view expressed in *Thomas Organ* have adopted one of two other positions.

A liberal view would greatly expand the protection of the work-product privilege to insurance reports prepared following incidents.[123] However, this has been noted to be a position endorsed only by a minority of courts.[124]

The majority of courts, rejecting the extreme liberal and rigid positions enunciated by the *Fontaine* and *Thomas Organ* courts, respectively, have chosen to employ a case-by-case approach.[125]

Again, to be protected under the work-product privilege, the documents must have been prepared in anticipation of litigation. In *Simon v. G.D. Searle & Co.*,[126] the court held that corporate risk management documents that were prepared by nonlawyer corporate officials were not prepared in anticipation of litigation and thus were not protected from discovery.[127] This inquiry is fact-intensive. It must be shown that in light of the document and the factual situation of the case, it can fairly be said that the document was prepared because of the prospect of litigation. Even though litigation is already a prospect, there is no work-product immunity for documents prepared in the regular course of business that are not for the purposes of litigation.[128]

The court in *State Farm Fire & Casualty Co. v. Perrigan*[129] held that an investigator's report was prepared in the ordinary course of business, and not in anticipation of trial, and thus was discoverable despite the work-product claim. The investigator's report, which was relevant to discover evidence leading to the cause and the motive for a fire, was prepared during the course of performing an investigation approximately nine days after the fire occurred. Moreover, the court noted that the report was prepared while the insurer was in the process of adjusting the claim and before the insurer had decided whether to pay the loss or become involved in litigation. The report was thus held discoverable.

Western National Bank of Denver v. Employers Insurance of Wausau[130] also illustrates a narrow interpretation of when a document is "prepared in anticipation of litigation." In *Western National Bank*, an insured had brought an action against its insurer, alleging bad faith on the part of the insurer for failure to pay a claim. The court held that the insured was entitled to obtain discovery of letters from the law firm retained by the insurer since the test for recovery was whether a reasonable insurer would have denied the claim under similar facts and circumstances. The insured was also allowed to obtain discovery of the law firm's file when the court determined that the file was an investigative file of the insurer prepared in the ordinary course of business, rather than work product.

Some courts have given the "in anticipation of litigation" requirement a broader interpretation. In *Janicker v. George Washington University*,[131] the investigative file of an insurer was held to be work product, immunized from pretrial discovery, as it was prepared in anticipation of claims. These claims, if denied, would have clearly led to suits. Litigation and investigative material generated or produced by counsel after filing of the suit were also deemed to be work product. Similarly, a broad interpretation of the "in anticipation of litigation" requirement is found in *Catino v. Travelers Insurance Co. Inc.*[132] In *Catino*, the plaintiff won a judgment against the defendant's insured, which went unpaid. The insured later assigned his claims against the insurer to the judgment plaintiff, who thereupon filed suit against the insurer for negligence in failing to settle the original action. However, months prior to filing his action against the insurer, the judgment plaintiff sent a demand letter outlining his requirements for settling the case to the insurer. Following the demand letter, the insurer prepared various documents, which were later sought during discovery. The court determined that despite the fact the third-party suit against the insurer had not yet been filed, the documents were clearly work product as they were drafted in anticipation of litigation.[133]

And, an insurer's disclosure of work-product information to its reinsurers did not waive the protection where the insurer intended that the communications would remain confidential and protected from their common adversaries.[134]

B. Privileges Afforded Plaintiffs in Joint Prosecution against Insurer

In some cases, multiple plaintiffs may wish to join in an action against one or more insurers. In this scenario, it can be reasoned that the privileges afforded the plaintiffs in their joint prosecution will be determined in much the same manner as they are for the joint-defense privilege. So long as the plaintiffs have a strong common interest in sharing the fruits of their trial preparation efforts, it would be difficult to argue that privileges attaching to certain confidential documents have been waived. It is settled law that where two or more parties employ a lawyer as their common attorney, their communications to the attorney are confidential and privileged as against a common adversary.[135] This is true whether the parties are defendants or plaintiffs.

As stated, as a general rule there is no waiver of the attorney-client privilege where the client or the client's attorney discloses information to counsel for codefendants after a joint defense has been undertaken.[136] It seems logical that this same general principle will apply where the privilege is asserted by the plaintiffs in a joint prosecution arrangement since the same rationale and justifications apply.[137]

Similarly, the work-product privilege afforded to documents shared among joint defendants would also apply to protect communications shared among plaintiffs in a joint prosecution scenario. Again, so long as the transferor and transferee anticipate litigation against a common adversary on the same issue or issues, they have a strong common interest in sharing the results of their efforts.[138] This logic applies whether the privilege is asserted on the defense side or the plaintiff side. In both situations the disclosure is not inconsistent with maintaining secrecy against opponents.

V. Tips on Drafting Agreements

Although a joint-defense agreement is not required to be in writing,[139] a well-written agreement provides better evidence of the scope of defense protection.[140]

Some suggestions for drafting a joint-defense agreement are as follows:

1. The joint-defense agreement should clearly state the common interest of the parties to the agreement in order to determine the scope of the coverage.
2. The joint-defense agreement should also provide that each party knowingly waives any conflict of interest that may result from its lawyer's receipt of confidential joint-defense information, which the lawyer may not be able to use at trial.
3. Each party should acknowledge that it is represented by its own counsel, and that the other lawyers owe an unqualified duty of loyalty to their clients (the other parties to the agreement) and may take positions adverse to the other parties.
4. The joint-defense agreement should provide that the parties will reasonably cooperate with each other in the defense of the parties' common interests, including the sharing of information protected by the attorney-client privilege to assert joint defenses to the claims in the litigation.

VI. Conclusion

The joint-defense privilege can continue to protect otherwise privileged communication if handled properly. For the attorney-client privilege to apply, the communication between the attorney and client must be for the purpose of giving and receiving legal advice. Similarly, the work-product privilege protects documents containing the thoughts, impressions, and strategy of the attorney or the attorney's agent, prepared in anticipation of litigation. These privileges are often not waived by the communication of such privileged information to coparties, who have aligned themselves in a joint defense.

Notes

1. *See, e.g.*, Wilson P. Abraham Constr. Corp. v. Armco Steel Corp., 559 F.2d 250, 253 (5th Cir. 1977).
2. Allendale Mut. Ins. Co. v. Bull Data Sys., Inc., 152 F.R.D. 132, 140 (N.D. Ill. 1993).
3. United Coal Cos. v. Powell Constr. Co., 839 F.2d 958 (3d Cir. 1988); Samuelson v. Susen, 576 F.2d 546 (3d Cir. 1978); FED. R. EVID. 501.
4. *In re* L.T.V. Sec. Litig., 89 F.R.D. 595 (N.D. Tex. 1981).
5. Upjohn Co. v. United States, 449 U.S. 383 (1981).
6. Fromson v. Anitec Printing Plates, Inc., 152 F.R.D. 2, 3 (D. Mass. 1993).
7. Diversified Indus., Inc. v. Meredith, 572 F.2d 596 (8th Cir. 1977).
8. FED. R. CIV. P. 26(b)(3)(A).
9. FED. R. CIV. P. 26(b)(3)(B).
10. 329 U.S. 495 (1947).
11. *Id.* at 511.
12. *See* Duplan Corp. v. Moulinage et Retorderie de Chavanoz, 509 F.2d 730 (4th Cir. 1974).
13. *Id.* at 734; *accord* Bd. of Trs. v. Coulter Corp., 118 F.R.D. 532 (S.D. Fla. 1987).

14. Charlotte Motor Speedway v. Int'l Ins. Co., 125 F.R.D. 127, 129 (M.D.N.C. 1989) (permitted production of opinion work product for in camera review because activities of counsel were "inextricably interwoven" with subject matter of suit).
15. Holmgren v. State Farm Mut. Auto. Ins. Co., 976 F.2d 573 (9th Cir. 1992); Too Marker Prods. v. Shinhan Art Materials, Inc., 2010 U.S. Dist. LEXIS 108190 (D. Or. Oct. 7, 2010).
16. *Holmgren*, 976 F.2d at 577 (citing *Hickman*, 329 U.S. 495, 511). *Accord In re* Minebea Co., Ltd., 143 F.R.D. 494 (S.D.N.Y. 1992).
17. Upjohn Co. v. United States, 449 U.S. 383, 401 (1981).
18. 2 Jack Weinstein & Margaret Berger, Weinstein's Evidence § 503(b)[06] (1991); John Morrell & Co. v. Local Union 304A, 913 F.2d 544 (8th Cir. 1990), *cert. denied*, 500 U.S. 905 (1991).
19. Waller v. Fin. Corp. of Am., 828 F.2d 579 (9th Cir. 1987); United States v. McPartlin, 595 F.2d 1321 (7th Cir. 1979), *cert. denied*, 444 U.S. 833 (1979); Sedalcek v. Morgan Whitney Trading Grp. , 795 F. Supp 329 (C.D. Cal. 1992).
20. Eisenberg v. Gagnon, 766 F.2d 770 (3d Cir. 1985).
21. *Id.* at 787–88. *See also* Haines v. Liggett Grp., Inc., 975 F.2d 81 (3d Cir. 1992) (tobacco company defendants exchanged information among various attorneys representing them in order to adequately prepare a joint defense); *see also* United States v. Schwimmer, 892 F.2d 237 (2d Cir. 1989) (protecting communications made to an accountant aiding attorneys conducting a joint defense) ; Fresenius Med. Care Holdings v. Roxane Labs. Inc., 2007 U.S. Dist. LEXIS 98216 (S.D. Ohio Mar. 21, 2007) ("the purpose of the [common interest] doctrine is to permit persons with similar legal interests, but represented by different counsel, to enjoy the same ability to communicate confidentially about their common interests with multiple attorneys that each client enjoys separately").
22. *See* United States v. Bay State Ambulance & Hosp. Rental Serv., Inc., 874 F.2d 20 (1st Cir. 1989); United States v. Evans, 113 F.3d 1457 (7th Cir. Ill. 1997).
23. Allendale Mut. Ins. Co. v. Bull Data Sys., Inc., 152 F.R.D. 132, 140 (N.D. Ill. 1993) (citations omitted).
24. *In re* Sealed Case, 29 F.3d 715, 719 n.5 (D.C. Cir. 1994).
25. *Id.* at 719; Boyd v. Comdata Network, Inc., 88 S.W.3d 203 (Tenn. 2002).
26. 913 F.2d 544 (8th Cir. 1990).
27. *Id.* at 555–56.
28. *Id.* (quoting Wilson P. Abraham Constr. Corp. v. Armco Steel Corp., 559 F.2d 250 (5th Cir. 1977)).
29. *Id. See also In re* L.T.V. Sec. Litig., 89 F.R.D. 595 (N.D. Tex. 1981).
30. *Morrell*, 913 F.2d at 555–56.
31. *See, e.g.*, Hunydee v. United States, 355 F.2d 183 (9th Cir. 1965).
32. *Id.* at 184.
33. *Id.*
34. *Id.*
35. *Id.*
36. *Id.*
37. *Id.* at 185.
38. *Id.*
39. *Id.*
40. *Id.*
41. Nidec Corp. v. Victor Co., 249 F.R.D. 575 (N.D. Cal. 2007).

42. United States v. Bergonzi, 216 F.R.D. 487, 495 (N.D. Cal. 2003).
43. *See* Libbey Glass, Inc. v. Oneida Ltd., 197 F.R.D. 342, 348 (N.D. Ohio 1999).
44. *Nidec*, 249 F.R.D. at 578; Lectrolarm Custom Sys., Inc. v. Pelco Sales, Inc., 212 F.R.D. 567, 572 (E.D. Cal. 2002).
45. *Nidec*, 249 F.R.D. at 578.
46. *See, e.g.*, City of Kalamazoo v. Mich. Disposal Serv. Corp., 125 F. Supp. 2d 219 (D. Mich. 2000); Essex Chem. Corp. v. Hartford Accident & Indem. Co., 993 F. Supp. 241 (D.N.J. 1998).
47. *City of Kalamazoo*, 125 F. Supp. 2d at 234.
48. *Id.* at 242–43.
49. *See* United States v. Henke, 222 F.3d 633 (9th Cir. 2000).
50. *Id.* at 638.
51. *Id.* at 637–38.
52. *Id.* at 637.
53. *Id.*
54. *Id.*
55. *Id.*
56. *Id.*
57. *Id.* at 637.
58. *Id.* at 635, 638, 643. *Compare id. with* United States v. Almeida, 341 F.3d 1318 (11th Cir. 2003) (approving cross-examination of a defecting codefendant with joint-defense information, stating withdrawing party waived attorney-client privilege by turning state's evidence).
59. Essex Chem. Corp. v. Hartford Accident & Indem. Co., 993 F. Supp. 241, 252 (D.N.J. 1998).
60. *See* City of Kalamazoo v. Mich. Disposal Serv. Corp., 125 F. Supp. 2d 219, 235 (D. Mich. 2000).
61. Allendale Mut. Ins. Co. v. Bull Data Sys., Inc., 152 F.R.D. 132, 135–36 (N.D. Ill. 1993).
62. *In re* Grand Jury Subpoena, 784 F.2d 857 (8th Cir. 1986).
63. Hunydee v. United States, 355 F.2d 183, 185 (9th Cir. 1965).
64. Doubleday v. Ruh, 149 F.R.D. 601, n.4 (E.D. Cal. 1993).
65. United States v. IBM, 66 F.R.D. 154 (S.D.N.Y. 1974). *See also* Hanover Shoe, Inc. v. United Shoe Mach. Corp., 207 F. Supp. 407 (M.D. Pa. 1962) (materials must be prepared for the case at bar).
66. United States v. Leggett & Platt, 542 F.2d 655, 659 (6th Cir. Ohio 1976).
67. *See, e.g.*, Liberty Envtl. Sys., Inc. v. Cnty. of Westchester, 1997 U.S. Dist. LEXIS 12200, at *21 (S.D.N.Y. August 15, 1997).
68. *In re* Murphy, 560 F.2d 326, 334 (8th Cir. 1977). *See also* Duplan Corp. v. Moulinage et Retorderie de Chavanoz, 487 F.2d 480 (4th Cir. 1973); Panter v. Marshall Field & Co., 80 F.R.D. 718, 724 (N.D. Ill. 1978).
69. Levingston v. Allis-Chalmers Corp., 109 F.R.D. 546 (S.D. Miss. 1985).
70. *Id. See* Republic Gear Co. v. Borg-Warner Corp., 381 F.2d 551 (2d Cir. 1967) (work-product protection applied in subsequent litigation involving third parties intimately involved in the subject matter of previous suit); Leonen v. Johns-Manville, 135 F.R.D. 94, 97 (D.N.J. 1990) ("this Court follows that line of cases which requires a close connection in parties or subject matter between the two matters"). *See also* 8 WRIGHT & MILLER, FEDERAL PRACTICE AND PROCEDURE § 2024 (2d ed. 1994).

71. Schachar v. Am. Acad. of Ophthalmology, Inc., 106 F.R.D. 187, 191 (N.D. Ill. 1985).
72. *Id.* at 191.
73. Cont'l Oil Co. v. United States, 330 F.2d 347 (9th Cir. 1964).
74. *Schachar*, 106 F.R.D. at 192 (quoting Transmirra Prods. Corp. v. Monsanto Chem. Co., 26 F.R.D. 572, 579 (S.D.N.Y. 1960)).
75. *See* 8 Wright & Miller, Federal Practice and Procedure § 2016.2 (2d ed. 1994).
76. FDIC v. Singh, 140 F.R.D. 252 (D. Me. 1992).
77. Wichita Land & Cattle Co. v. Am. Fed. Bank, 148 F.R.D. 456, 457 (D.D.C. 1992).
78. Mendenhall v. Barber-Greene Co., 531 F. Supp. 951, 955 (N.D. Ill. 1982). *See also* Berg Elecs., Inc. v. Molex, Inc., 875 F. Supp. 261 (D. Del. 1995); Redland Soccer Club v. Dep't of the Army, 55 F.3d 827 (3d Cir. 1995) (inadvertent disclosure of documents does not qualify as a voluntary waiver).
79. *See, e.g.*, Amgen Inc. v. Hoechst Marion Roussel, Inc., 190 F.R.D. 287 (D. Mass. 2000) (noting that the judges in that district never adopted the *Mendenhall* rule that waiver must be intentional, the court instead employed a flexible intermediate approach).
80. Edwards v. Whitaker, 868 F. Supp. 226 (M.D. Tenn. 1994).
81. Transamerica Computer Co. v. IBM, 573 F.2d 646 (9th Cir. 1978).
82. Ohio-Sealy Mattress Mfg. Co. v. Kaplan, 90 F.R.D. 21 (N.D. Ill. 1980) (citing *In re* Grand Jury Subpoena Duces Tecum, 406 F. Supp. 381, 393–94 (S.D.N.Y. 1975)); Mackenzie-Childs LLC v. Mackenzie-Childs, 262 F.R.D. 241 (W.D.N.Y. 2009).
83. 559 F.2d 250 (5th Cir. 1977).
84. *Id.* at 253.
85. Medcom Holding Co. v. Baxter Travenol Labs., Inc., 689 F. Supp. 841 (N.D. Ill. 1988).
86. United States v. Moscony, 697 F. Supp. 888 (E.D. Pa. 1988).
87. 406 F. Supp. 381, 394 (S.D.N.Y. 1975).
88. *In re* Sealed Case, 120 F.R.D. 66 (N.D. Ill. 1988).
89. United States v. AT&T Co., 642 F.2d 1285 (D.C. Cir. 1980).
90. *See* Hickman v. Taylor, 329 U.S. 495 (1947).
91. 39 F.R.D. 610 (S.D.N.Y. 1965).
92. *Id.* at 610.
93. 85 F.R.D. 46 (S.D.N.Y. 1979).
94. *Id.* at 72.
95. *In re* Steinhardt Partners, L.P., 9 F.3d 230 (2d Cir. 1993).
96. *Id.* at 235.
97. *Id. But see* Diversified Indus., Inc. v. Meredith, 572 F.2d 596 (8th Cir. 1977) (no waiver of privilege under similar circumstances).
98. *Steinhardt*, 9 F.3d at 236.
99. United States v. AT&T Co., 642 F.2d 1285, 1299 (D.C. Cir. 1980).
100. *Id.* at 1299. *See, e.g., In re* Visa Check/MasterMoney Antitrust Litig., 190 F.R.D. 309, 315 (E.D.N.Y. 2000) (disclosure to government of material did not waive work-product privilege as government's interest and private plaintiff's interest were sufficiently aligned).
101. *Id.* at 1297–98.
102. *See* Eugenia VI Venture Holdings v. Chabra, 2006 U.S. Dist. LEXIS 23421, at *3 (S.D.N.Y. Apr. 25, 2006).

103. *See* United States v. Stepney, 246 F. Supp. 2d 1069, 1076 (N.D. Cal. 2003).
104. *See* Trading Techs. Int'l v. Espeed, 2007 U.S. Dist. LEXIS 32653, at *13 (N.D. Ill. May 1, 2007); Swiss Indus. Co. v. Fres-Co Sys., USA, Inc., No. 91-0699, 1993 U.S. Dist. LEXIS 3576 (E.D. Pa. 1993).
105. *AT&T*, 642 F.2d at 1299–1300.
106. United States v. Gulf Oil Corp., 760 F.2d 292 (Temp. Emer. Ct. App. 1985).
107. *Id. See, e.g.*, Bank Brussels Lambert v. Chase Manhattan Bank, N.A., 1998 U.S. Dist. LEXIS 13611 (S.D.N.Y. 1998) (noting that parties to joint-defense agreement did not waive work product with disclosure to third party, as documents were produced pursuant to confidentiality agreement).
108. *See generally* Fausek v. White, 965 F.2d 126 (6th Cir. 1992).
109. *In re* Antitrust Grand Jury, 805 F.2d 155, 162 (6th Cir. 1986).
110. Loustalet v. Refco, Inc., 154 F.R.D. 243 (C.D. Cal. 1993).
111. *Id.* at 245.
112. *In re* Antitrust Grand Jury, 805 F.2d 155, 162 (6th Cir. 1986).
113. United States v. Nobles, 422 U.S. 225 (1975).
114. FED. R. CIV. P. 26(b)(3).
115. *Nobles*, 422 U.S. at 238–39.
116. *See* R.R. Salvage of Conn., Inc. v. Japan Freight Consolidators (USA), Inc., 97 F.R.D. 37 (E.D.N.Y. 1983), *aff'd*, 779 F.2d 38 (2d Cir. 1985) (correspondence between the defendant and its liability insurance carriers protected).
117. 74 F.R.D. 93 (N.D. Ga. 1977).
118. *Id.*; *compare id. with* Holmgren v. State Farm Mut. Auto. Ins. Co., 976 F.2d 573 (9th Cir. 1992) (finding work-product doctrine applicable, but allowing discovery due to compelling need).
119. 107 F.R.D. 771 (N.D. Pa. 1985).
120. *Id.* at 775.
121. 54 F.R.D. 367 (N.D. Ill. 1972).
122. *Id.* at 372–73.
123. Fontaine v. Sunflower Beef Carrier, 87 F.R.D. 89 (E.D. Mo. 1980).
124. *See, e.g.*, S. D. Warren Co. v. E. Elec. Corp., 201 F.R.D. 280, 283 (D. Me. 2001).
125. *See* Airheart v. Chi. & Nw. Transp. Co., 128 F.R.D. 669 (D.S.D. 1989); Sham v. Hyannis Heritage House Hotel, Inc., 118 F.R.D. 24 (D. Mass. 1987).
126. 816 F.2d 397 (8th Cir. 1987).
127. *See also* Banks v. Wilson, 151 F.R.D. 109 (D. Minn. 1993).
128. *Id.* at 112.
129. 102 F.R.D. 235 (W.D. Va. 1984).
130. 109 F.R.D. 55 (D. Colo. 1985).
131. 94 F.R.D. 648 (D.D.C. 1982).
132. 136 F.R.D. 534 (D. Mass. 1991).
133. *Id.*
134. Minn. Sch. Bd.'s Ass'n Ins. Trust v. Emp'r's Ins. Co. of Wausau, 183 F.R.D. 627 (N.D. Ill. 1999).
135. United Coal Cos. v. Powell Constr. Co., 839 F.2d 958 (3d Cir. 1988).
136. *See* Haines v. Liggett Grp., Inc., 975 F.2d 81 (3d Cir. 1992).
137. *See, e.g.*, Schachar v. Am. Acad. of Ophthalmology, Inc., 106 F.R.D. 187 (N.D. Ill. 1985).
138. *Id.*

139. *See* SIG Swiss Indus. Co. v. Fres-Co. Sys., U.S.A., Inc., 1993 U.S. Dist. LEXIS 3576 (E.D. Pa. 1993).
140. *See, e.g., In re* Grand Jury Subpoena (Newparent), 274 F.3d 563, 569 (2001) (noting lack of specificity that arose from oral joint-defense agreement).

CHAPTER 20

The Scope and Use of the Attorney-Client Privilege in the United States and Its Applicability to Communications in the United States and Abroad

CHRISTOPHER SCOTT D'ANGELO

Although the attorney-client privilege has been described as "one of the most revered of common law privileges,"[1] recent developments have challenged the scope and use of the privilege, particularly concerning government investigations of corporate clients. In a 2005 survey by the National Association of Criminal Defense Lawyers, 87 percent of lawyers surveyed reported that they had experienced recent challenges to the attorney-client privilege.[2] Additionally, 85 percent reported that the Department of Justice and the Securities and Exchange Commission frequently require waiver discussions when negotiating settlements.[3] Reviewing the characteristics of the privilege in the United States will aid clients and practitioners in ensuring that their communications remain as securely shielded by the attorney-client privilege as possible.

I. *What the Privilege Is*

The attorney-client privilege is the oldest confidential communications privilege known to the common law.[4] Though each U.S. jurisdiction retains its own particular privilege test, often codified by statute, most jurisdictions require the same four elements for establishing privilege. There must be (1) a communication (2) between counsel and client (3) made confidentially (4) for the purpose of obtaining or rendering legal advice.[5] Though most jurisdictions have extended the privilege to include a client's confidential communications with a subordinate or outside agent assisting an attorney, the communication must always be confidential and made for the purpose of obtaining or rendering legal advice.[6] The privilege protects these communications to encourage frank discussions between a client and an attorney and to ensure that an attorney is not hindered in providing legal advice and services to a client.[7] The attorney-client privilege rests with the client and survives an individual client's death.[8]

II. *What It Is Not*

Jurisdictions also are similar in what they do not protect under the attorney-client privilege. First, the privilege does not protect facts, including those embedded within otherwise privileged communications.[9] Even facts concerning the attorney-client relationship itself, such as a client's identity, whether such a relationship exists, when an attorney was retained, or the terms of the attorney's engagement, usually are not privileged.[10] Additionally, the attorney-client privilege is applicable only to information sought for the purpose of obtaining legal advice and to communications involving an attorney acting as a legal advisor.[11] Therefore, business advice rendered by an attorney is not privileged.[12] As a practical matter, documents containing both privileged communications and facts or business advice likely are discoverable, but may be redacted before production.

The attorney-client privilege also does not protect information that counsel obtained from third parties during the course of representation.[13] Therefore, "any communications from counsel to the client disclosing information from third parties would not be protected because the underlying communication between counsel and the third party is not protected."[14] Counsel's notes and impressions of third-party conversations may be protected, however, as attorney work product.

III. *Choice of Law*

Because jurisdictions each have their own particular attorney-client privilege laws, choice or conflict of law issues can arise. Federal courts sitting in diversity jurisdiction apply state law concerning the attorney-client privilege.[15] A court determines which state's privilege laws apply by analyzing the forum state's choice or conflict of law principles.[16] States generally look to the state with the greatest interest or most significant relationship to the case generally, or to the privilege issue specifically.[17] Among the factors analyzed are choice of law agreements, the principal locations of the parties involved, the location of the disputed occurrence, the location of the communication, where discovery is occurring, and where any waiver is alleged to have occurred.[18]

If the federal court maintains federal question jurisdiction, federal common law applies to privilege disputes.[19] Where both federal question claims and pendent state law claims are at issue, the federal common law of privilege applies to all claims.[20] In cases involving international privilege disputes, courts have ruled that comity and federal choice of law rules are included within the ambit of federal common law and, therefore, should be referenced and analyzed when deciding such disputes.[21]

Certain courts examining international privilege disputes have adopted a two-tier analysis for determining which jurisdiction's rules should apply.[22] First, if the communication simply "touches base" with the United States, such as by being authored or concerning legal matters in the United States, U.S. federal discovery principles prevail.[23] Second, if the communication relates solely to matters concerning foreign jurisdictions, such as by taking place and involving attorneys or proceedings there, the court analyzes which foreign jurisdiction has the predominant interest, by examining the place where the privileged relationship was entered into or the place in which the relationship was centered at the time of the communication.[24] At least one court, however, has found the first "touching base with the United States" part of the analysis too restrictive, and when faced with a choice of law question, immediately weighed the United States' and the foreign jurisdiction's interests to determine which had the "most direct and compelling interest," taking into account the location of the parties, the substance of the communication, the center of the communicating relationship, the needs of the international system, and whether the application of foreign law would be inconsistent with federal law policies.[25]

IV. Waiver

The attorney-client privilege can be waived in several ways. Most common is when the communication at issue loses its confidential nature. If a privileged communication is shared with third parties, the privilege generally is waived.[26]

Most courts provide for an exception to this rule when parties establish a joint-defense agreement among themselves, allowing for a "community of interest" privilege. The community-of-interest privilege, also known as the joint-defense privilege, protects communications between or among parties with mutual interests and their counsel.[27] To establish the privilege, a party must demonstrate that the communication was made in the course of, and to further, a joint litigation effort.[28] Additionally, because the privilege is not distinct, but rather considered an extension of the attorney-client privilege, the communication still must be made confidentially and for the purpose of obtaining or rendering legal advice.[29]

Though not all jurisdictions require one, the relevant parties should sign a written joint-defense agreement establishing the scope of their shared privilege and, if appropriate, obtain court approval of the agreement.[30] Additionally, because of future disqualification concerns, parties should include a waiver of conflict of interest clause.

Parties must also be wary of inadvertent disclosures of privileged communications as courts are divided concerning whether such disclosures waive the privilege. While certain courts leniently hold that no waiver occurs in such instances, other courts hold that an inadvertent disclosure constitutes a complete waiver of the privilege.[31] Still other jurisdictions decide on a case-by-case basis, weighing the precautions taken to avoid inadvertent disclosure, the time taken to rectify the error, the scope of discovery, the extent of the disclosure, and general considerations of fairness and equity.[32]

Federal Rule of Evidence 502, Attorney-Client Privilege and Work Product; Limitations on Waiver, was enacted in September of 2008 to address the issue of waiver of the attorney-client privilege and work-product doctrine. Although a Federal Rule of Evidence, the rule was enacted by federal legislation and is controlling in both federal and state proceedings.[33] Among other things, FRE 502 states that when disclosure is made in a federal proceeding or to a federal office or agency and waives the attorney-client privilege or work-product protection, the waiver extends to undisclosed communications or information in a federal or state proceeding only if the waiver was intentional, the disclosed and undisclosed materials concern the same subject matter, and "they ought in fairness be considered together."[34] Likewise, FRE 502 also addresses "inadvertent disclosures," stating that when made in a federal proceeding or to a federal office or agency, the disclosure does not operate as a waiver in a federal or state proceeding if the disclosure was inadvertent, the holder of the privilege or protection "took reasonable steps" to prevent disclosure, and the holder promptly took "reasonable steps" to rectify the error.[35]

FRE 502 also addresses the issue of waiver where the disclosure was in a state proceeding. When disclosure is made in a state proceeding and is not subject to a state court order concerning waiver, the disclosure does not operate as a waiver in a federal proceeding if the disclosure would not be a waiver had it been made in a federal proceeding or is not a waiver under the law of the state where the disclosure was made.[36]

Clients can also waive their privilege over communications by placing the communication at issue in litigation. Often this occurs when a client challenges a former attorney's representation or relies on advice of counsel as a defense, or when the case concerns insurance bad-faith claims. Courts generally fall into two categories when analyzing an "at issue waiver." One group holds that if a privileged communication is relevant to the privilege-holder's claim or defense, the privilege is waived.[37] Another group more restrictively holds that a client waives the privilege only if the client relies on the particular communication at issue to support a claim or defense.[38]

Finally, even if a communication is privileged and the privilege has not been waived, litigating parties might argue to the court that the administration of justice nevertheless warrants disclosure of the communication.[39] For example, the former Supreme Court Justice Sandra Day O'Connor has commented in dissent that "a criminal defendant's right to exculpatory evidence or a compelling law enforcement need for information may, where the testimony is not available from other sources, override a client's posthumous interest in confidentiality."[40] Similarly, at least one court has held that where testimony concerning a privileged communication can be obtained only from an attorney, and disclosure of the privileged communications will not prejudice the party, justice requires disclosure of the communication.[41]

V. Corporate Issues

A corporation is a client for purposes of the attorney-client privilege. Therefore, communications between a corporation's employees and its attorney may be as protected as communications between an individual client and his or her attorneys.

In the leading case of *Upjohn Co. v. United States*, which concerned a federal tax issue, the U.S. Supreme Court held that the attorney-client privilege protected communications made by a company's employees to the company's counsel during the attorneys' internal investigation of the company.[42] The Court rejected the "control group test," which posited that the privilege should protect only communications from senior management.[43] Because the corporation was communicating through its lower-level management employees in order to obtain legal advice from its counsel, such communications were privileged.[44] The Court found the following factors important in deciding that the communications at issue were privileged: (1) the communications were made by company employees to company lawyers, each acting in that capacity; (2) the communications concerned matters within the employees' scope of corporate duties; (3) the employees' communications were made to counsel at the direction of corporate superiors; (4) the communications were made to secure for the corporation legal advice from counsel and the employees understood that they were being questioned so that the corporation could obtain legal advice; (5) the communications were confidential and employees understood them to be confidential; (6) the information needed from the investigation could not be obtained from senior management; and (7) the communications were kept confidential by limiting their dissemination.[45]

The holding in *Upjohn Co.*, however, is binding only on federal courts sitting in federal question jurisdiction applying federal common law.[46] While certain states have adopted a privilege test similar to that announced in *Upjohn*

Co., other states continue to analyze the issue under the "control group test" rejected in *Upjohn Co.* Still other states have yet to determine what test should govern this determination. Fifteen states have adopted some variant of the broader test discussed in but not expressly adopted by the Supreme Court in *Upjohn Co.*, also called the "subject matter test," while seven states adopted the "control group test" and 28 states, including Delaware, New York, Pennsylvania, and New Jersey, had not definitively adopted any test.[47]

In fact, the Illinois Supreme Court expressly rejected the test used in *Upjohn Co.*, ruling that the control group test properly protected communications between attorneys and corporate decision makers while also "minimizing the amount of relevant material that is barred from discovery."[48] The court characterized an employee protected under the test as one "whose advisory role to top management in a particular area is such that a decision would not normally be made without his advice or opinion, and whose opinion in fact forms the basis of any final decision by those with actual authority. . . . However, the individuals upon whom he may rely for supplying information are not members of the control group."[49]

VI. Mergers and Dissolutions

Particular privilege concerns can arise when a corporation merges or dissolves. Though stated as dictum, in *Commodity Futures Trading Commission v. Weintraub* the U.S. Supreme Court noted (referring to the parties' agreement) that "when control of a corporation passes to new management, the authority to assert and waive the corporation's attorney-client privilege passes as well."[50] Therefore, "[d]isplaced managers may not assert the privilege over the wishes of current managers, even as to statements that the former might have made to counsel concerning matters within the scope of their corporate duties."[51] In deciding whether a debtor corporation's privilege was held by the bankruptcy trustee or the debtor's directors, the Court ruled that the privilege passed to the trustee because the trustee controlled the corporation's affairs.[52]

Using this language from *Weintraub*, courts have distinguished what it means when "control of a corporation passes to new management." Courts have held that in the case of a merger, if Corporation A acquires Corporation B's business and continues that business, Corporation A also acquires Corporation B's privilege.[53] However, if Corporation A merely purchases some of the assets of Corporation B, no privilege is transferred.[54]

Few courts have addressed whether the attorney-client privilege survives corporate dissolution. Though the attorney-client privilege survives an individual's death, courts have analogized the issue to a corporate merger. For example, where a liquidator assumes control of a dissolved corporation's business, the privilege passes to the liquidator.[55] However, where no entity exists to continue the corporation's business, such as when a liquidator merely oversees distribution of a defunct corporation's assets, the privilege does not transfer, and according to at least one court, the privilege dies with the corporation.[56]

VII. Investigation Issues

Protecting a corporation's privileged communications involves particular concerns. Often, corporate clients and their attorneys must decide whether to share their otherwise privileged communications concerning internal audits and investigations with government investigators.

Though often pressured by the government, expressly or otherwise, to do so to assist an investigation and obtain leniency, sharing such communications risks the confidential nature of those communications, and therefore, may waive the attorney-client privilege. Without such protection, the client's communications may be discoverable to any third party. Moreover, any such waiver may extend to the entire subject matter of the communication, and not merely to the particular document or communication itself.[57]

Efforts by the Department of Justice to pressure corporations to waive the protections of privilege in order to gain credit for government cooperation have exacerbated concerns surrounding this issue. In a June 16, 1999, memorandum, then Deputy Attorney General Eric H. Holder Jr. expressly permitted federal prosecutors to account for a "corporation's timely and voluntary disclosure of wrongdoing and its willingness to cooperate in the investigation of its agents, including, if necessary, the waiver of the corporate attorney-client and work product privileges" when deciding whether to charge a corporation.[58] This policy was reiterated and made mandatory in a 2003 memorandum by then Deputy Attorney General Larry Thompson[59] and a 2005 memorandum by Acting Deputy Attorney General Robert McCallum.[60]

Many criticized the DOJ's pressuring of corporations to disclose privileged information, among them a bipartisan group of 10 former senior Justice Department officials that included former Attorneys General Richard Thornburgh and Griffin Bell and former Solicitor General Theodore Olsen. In September 2006, the group wrote to then Attorney General Alberto Gonzales to protest the government's tactics in investigating corporate wrongdoing.[61] These tactics, they asserted, are "seriously eroding" attorney-client privilege and "undermin[ing], rather than enhanc[ing], compliance with the law" and in fact have discouraged corporate boards and executives from consulting with their lawyers, harmed companies' ability to conduct effective internal investigations.

In December of 2006, in response to the mounting criticism and proposed federal legislation[62] and in what was touted as a significant shift in how the Department of Justice would seek and employ privilege waivers in corporate prosecutions, then Deputy Attorney General Paul J. McNulty issued new guidance limiting federal prosecutors' ability to seek waiver of attorney-client privilege protection to situations "when there is a legitimate need for the privileged information to fulfill their law enforcement obligations."[63] Under the "McNulty Memorandum," prosecutors could request a waiver of privilege protecting purely factual ("Category I") information relating to the alleged underlying corporate misconduct when authorized by the U.S. Attorney, and could consider, for charging decision purposes, the corporation's response to a request for Category I information. Privileged attorney-client communications or nonfactual attorney work product ("Category II") could be sought only in "rare circumstances" where available purely factual information was inadequate. Refusal to produce Category II information could not be a factor in a charging decision, although waiver could still earn a company cooperation credit.

However, the changes made by the McNulty Memorandum did not satisfy the concerns, nor did they effectively reduce the pressures the Department of Justice could and would bring to bear, expressly or impliedly, upon companies to waive the attorney-client privilege in exchange for "cooperation credit," with the obvious corollary. In June 2008, more than 30 former U.S. Attorneys expressed continued concerns and disagreement with the McNulty Memorandum and voiced their support for the Attorney-Client Privilege Protection Act of 2006,[64] which was shortly thereafter reintroduced by Senator Arlen Specter as the Attorney-Client Privilege Protection Act of 2008.

Seeing the handwriting on the wall,[65] and responding to criticism that the Department had promoted an environment that "unfairly eroded" the protections of attorney-client privilege and work-product protection, the Department of Justice abandoned the McNulty Memorandum's framework in August 2008 when Deputy Attorney General Mark Filip issued new guidance for federal prosecutors.[66] Under the "Filip Memorandum," prosecutors must focus on the corporation's willingness to disclose to the government "relevant facts" concerning the alleged misconduct. "[A] corporation should receive the same credit for disclosing facts contained in materials that are not protected by the attorney-client privilege or attorney work product as it would for disclosing identical facts contained in materials that are so protected." Thus, in theory at least, cooperation credit is no longer given based on waiver of privilege protection, and unwillingness to waive privilege is not supposed to factor in bringing charges. In fact, prosecutors are no longer permitted to request privilege waivers.

However, the issuance of the Filip Memorandum did not and still does not quell concern about the erosion of privilege. Indeed, the current DOJ guidelines seem to turn a blind eye to the corporation's continued need to waive privilege protection in order to furnish prosecutors with the "relevant facts" necessary to gain cooperation credit.[67] Moreover, the Filip Memorandum, like those that preceded it, shows a disdain for the attorney-client privilege and work-product protections, and demonstrates a view that having lawyers conduct internal investigations, as opposed to doing so without lawyers and in a manner that would not raise the privilege, is a matter of choice and suggests not only a lack of cooperation but also a desire to be secretive. The DOJ thus continues to ignore the traditional and valuable role lawyers play in such investigations. Further, other agencies, including the SEC and some state regulators, who are not subject to the Filip Memorandum, have also adopted policies encouraging corporations' cooperation with government investigations.[68] Indeed, the American Bar Association has established a task force on the attorney-client privilege to address what it perceives as attempts to erode the privilege, and along with the American Civil Liberties Union, the National Association of Criminal Defense Lawyers, and the U.S. Chamber of Commerce, has challenged the U.S. Sentencing Commission's proposed commentary to section 8.C2.5(g) of the U.S. Sentencing Guidelines, which it believes encourages the waiver of the attorney-client privilege.[69] In the same vein, Senator Specter and other lawmakers reintroduced the Attorney-Client Privilege Protection Act, S. 445, legislation aimed at prohibiting federal agencies from requesting attorney-client privilege and work-product protection waivers, offering rewards for such waiver, or threatening adverse consequences for refusals to waive privilege.[70]

As stated above, FRE 502, Attorney-Client Privilege and Work Product; Limitations on Waiver was enacted in September of 2008. The rule addresses the scope of a waiver of privilege in a federal proceeding or to a federal office or agency, avoiding waiver when an unintentional or inadvertent disclosure occurs, and disclosures in state proceedings.[71] In drafting this rule, the Advisory Committee on Evidence Rules also considered including a provision allowing for "selective waiver" of privilege for a specific limited purpose of responding to a federal government regulatory, investigative, or enforcement authority, but maintaining it for all other purposes. Although, as stated above, the concept has generally been rejected in the courts,[72] it was advanced and included in those proposed amendments. However, the "selective waiver" proposal was deleted during the rule approval process.[73]

Thus, FRE 502 makes no allowance for a waiver specific to responding to a governmental investigation. As stated above, the selective waiver concept has also generally been rejected in the courts.

VIII. Conclusion

Though the attorney-client privilege provides clients and their counsel unique opportunities for candid conversations, attention must be paid to each jurisdiction's unique rules to avoid waving the privilege and to ensure protection.

Notes

1. *In re* Estate of Wood, 818 A.2d 568, 571 (Pa. Super. Ct. 2003) (citing Commonwealth v. Maguigan, 511 A.2d 1327, 1333 (Pa. 1986)).
2. Stephanie A. Martz, *NACDL News: Member Survey: Attorney-Client Privilege Is Under Attack*, 29 Champion 6 (July 2005).
3. *Id. See also infra* section VII, "Investigation Issues."
4. Upjohn Co. v. United States, 449 U.S. 383, 389 (1981).
5. *See, e.g., In re* Teleglobe Commc'ns Corp., 493 F.3d 345, 359 (3d Cir. 2007); John Doe Co. v. United States, 79 F. App'x 476, 477 (2d Cir. 2003); United States v. United Shoe Mach. Corp., 89 F. Supp. 357, 358–59 (D. Mass. 1950) (stating the leading test for determining whether the attorney-client privilege applies).
6. *See, e.g., John Doe Co.*, 79 F. App'x at 477 (holding that district court did not abuse discretion in holding that communications with investigator hired by attorney were not privileged because they were not confidential).

7. *See Upjohn Co.*, 449 U.S. at 389.
8. *See, e.g.*, Swidler & Berlin v. United States, 524 U.S. 399, 405–10 (1998) (holding that attorney's notes from meeting with deceased are privileged).
9. *See Upjohn Co.*, 449 U.S. at 395 ("The privilege only protects disclosure of communications; it does not protect disclosure of the underlying facts by those who communicated with the attorney: 'The protection of the privilege extends only to communications and not to facts.'").
10. *See, e.g.*, *In re* Grand Jury Subpoena Served upon Doe, 781 F.2d 238, 247 (2d Cir. 1986) (en banc) ("We have consistently held that, absent special circumstances, client identity and fee information are not privileged."); Diversified Indus., Inc. v. Meredith, 572 F.2d 596, 603 (8th Cir. 1977) (holding that memorandum of engagement is not privileged).
11. *See* Andritz Sprout-Bauer, Inc. v. Beazer E., Inc., 174 F.R.D. 609, 633 (M.D. Pa. 1997) ("The privilege attaches only if the attorney is acting in the role of legal advisor."); *In re* Estate of Wood, 818 A.2d 568, 571–72 (Pa. Super. Ct. 2003) (holding that information was not privileged because it did not constitute confidential communications made in the context of a legal discussion).
12. *See In re* Ford Motor Co., 110 F.3d 954, 966 (3d Cir. 1997), *abrogated on other grounds*, Mohawk Indus. v. Carpenter, 130 S. Ct. 599 (2009) (holding minutes privileged because "infused" with legal concerns); N. Pacifica, LLC v. City of Pacifica, 274 F. Supp. 2d 1118, 1127–28 (N.D. Cal. 2003) (analyzing communications to determine their primary purpose—business or legal advice).
13. MacQuown v. Dean Witter Reynolds, Inc., 47 Pa. D. & C.3d 21, 24–25 (Pa. Ct. Comm. Pl. 1987) (holding that information counsel obtained from third parties is not privileged).
14. *Id.*
15. Fed. R. Evid. 501.
16. Pritchard-Keang Nam Corp. v. Jaworski, 751 F.2d 277, 281 n.4 (8th Cir. 1984) ("Under the *Erie* doctrine, a federal court must apply the forum's conflict of laws rules."); *In re* Diet Drugs Prods. Liab. Litig., MDL No. 1203, 2004 U.S. Dist. LEXIS 8596, at *6 (E.D. Pa. May 11, 2004) ("Since we are a federal court sitting in Pennsylvania, we will look to its choice of law rule."); Fin. Techs. Int'l, Inc. v. Smith, 99 Civ. 9351 (GEL) (RLE), 2000 U.S. Dist. LEXIS 18220, at *6 (S.D.N.Y. Dec. 19, 2000) ("[T]he choice of law rules of the forum state are controlling.").
17. *See* Urban Outfitters, Inc. v. DPIC Cos., Inc., 203 F.R.D. 376, 379 (N.D. Ill. 2001) (holding that privilege law of the state where discovery is occurring should apply); Fin. Techs. Int'l, Inc., 2000 U.S. Dist. LEXIS 18220, at *6–7.
18. *See Urban Outfitters, Inc.*, 203 F.R.D. at 379; Fin. Techs. Int'l, Inc., 2000 U.S. Dist. LEXIS 18220, at *6–7.
19. Fed. R. Evid. 501.
20. *See* Naquin v. Unocal Corp., Civ. A. No. 01-3124, 2002 U.S. Dist. LEXIS 15722, at *5–6 (E.D. La. Aug. 12, 2002) ("The weight of authority among courts that have confronted this issue in the context of discovery is that the federal law of privilege governs even where the evidence sought might be relevant to pendent state law claims."); *see also* Hancock v. Hobbs, 967 F.2d 462, 466 (11th Cir. 1992) ("Courts that have confronted this issue in the context of the discoverability of evidence have uniformly held that the federal law of privilege governs even where the evidence sought might be relevant to a pendent state claim."); Wm. T. Thompson Co. v. Gen. Nutrition Corp., 671 F.2d 100, 104 (3d Cir. 1982) (applying

rule to accountant-client privilege analysis because the "Senate Report accompanying Rule 501 states that it is also intended that the Federal law of privileges should be applied with respect to pendent State law claims when they arise in a Federal question case" (internal citations omitted)). *See also* FED. R. EVID. 502.

21. *See* Golden Trade, S.r.L. v. Lee Apparel Co., 143 F.R.D. 514, 521 (S.D.N.Y. 1992) (recognizing that courts can rely on applicable choice of law rules under the general rubric of federal common law); *see also* VLT Corp. v. Unitrode Corp., 194 F.R.D. 8, 14–16 (D. Mass. 2000); Duplan Corp. v. Deering Milliken, Inc., 397 F. Supp. 1146, 1169–70 (D.S.C. 1975).
22. *See* Astra Aktiebolag v. Andrx Pharms., Inc., 208 F.R.D. 92, 98 (S.D.N.Y. 2002); *Golden Trade, S.r.L.*, 143 F.R.D. at 520 (S.D.N.Y. 1992) (describing two-tier analysis as the "working standard").
23. *See In re* Philip Servs. Corp. Sec. Litig., 98 Civ. 0835 (MBM) (DF), 2005 U.S. Dist. LEXIS 22998, at *8–9 (S.D.N.Y. Oct. 7, 2005) (holding that opinion letters "touch base" with the United States and applying federal privilege law); *see also Astra Aktiebolag*, 208 F.R.D. at 98; *Golden Trade, S.r.L.*, 143 F.R.D. at 520; *Duplan Corp.*, 397 F. Supp. at 1169–70.
24. *See* Kiobel v. Royal Dutch Petroleum Co., No. 02CIV7618 (KMW) (HBP), 2005 WL 1925656, at *2–3 (S.D.N.Y. Aug. 11, 2005) (examining whether England or Nigeria had more substantial contact with documents); *Astra Aktiebolag*, 208 F.R.D. at 98–99 (analyzing which foreign jurisdiction had predominant interest); *Golden Trade, S.r.L.*, 143 F.R.D. at 521–22 (examining foreign jurisdictions' "predominant interest" in whether communications should remain privileged); *see also Duplan Corp.*, 397 F. Supp. at 1170–71.
25. *See VLT Corp.*, 194 F.R.D. at 15–17 (holding that foreign jurisdictions' privilege laws control); *see also* 2M Asset Mgmt., LLC v. Netmass, Inc., No. 2:06-CV-215, 2007 U.S. Dist. LEXIS 14098, at *9–10 (E.D. Tex. Feb. 28, 2007) (rejecting the argument that if one document touches the United States, then all privilege questions are governed by U.S. law, and recognizing the need to "afford comity and deference to the laws of foreign countries").
26. *See, e.g., In re* Columbia/HCA Healthcare Corp. Billing Practices Litig., 293 F.3d 289, 295–304 (6th Cir. 2002) (discussing various forms of waiver).
27. *See In re* Teleglobe Commc'ns Corp., 493 F.3d 345, 364 (3d Cir. 2007) (defining the community-of-interest privilege and noting that it was formerly known in the criminal context as the "joint defense" privilege).
28. *See* Grand Jury Proceedings v. United States, 156 F.3d 1038, 1042–43 (10th Cir. 1998) (holding that no joint-defense privilege applied where there was no agreement or joint-defense strategy); Haines v. Liggett Grp., Inc., 975 F.2d 81, 94 (3d Cir. 1992) (stating test for joint-defense privilege); United States v. Schwimmer, 892 F.2d 237, 243 (2d Cir. 1989) (holding one party's communications with an accountant hired by another party's attorney were privileged under joint-defense privilege).
29. *See Schwimmer*, 892 F.2d at 243–44.
30. *See* FED. R. EVID. 502(e) ("An agreement on the effect of disclosure of a communication or information covered by the attorney-client privilege or work product protection is binding on the parties to the agreement, but not on other parties unless the agreement is incorporated into a court order.") and 502(d) ("A federal court order that the attorney-client privilege or work product protection is not waived as a result of disclosure in connection with the litigation

pending before the court governs all persons or entities in all state or federal proceedings, whether or not they were parties to the matter before the court, if the order incorporates the agreement of the parties before the court.").

31. *See* Gray v. Bicknell, 86 F.3d 1472, 1483–84 (8th Cir. 1996) (discussing courts' approaches to inadvertent disclosures).
32. *See* Gray, 86 F.3d at 1484; Lois Sportswear, U.S.A., Inc. v. Levi Strauss & Co., 104 F.R.D. 103, 105 (S.D.N.Y. 1985) (holding privilege was not waived through inadvertent disclosure).
33. *See* FED. R. EVID. 502(d), (f).
34. *Id.*
35. *Id.*
36. *Id.*
37. *See* Hearn v. Rhay, 68 F.R.D. 574, 581 (E.D. Wash. 1975) (holding that privilege is waived when (1) the assertion of privilege results from affirmative conduct, such as filing suit; (2) the affirmative act places the privileged information at issue by making it relevant to the case; and (3) application of the privilege will deny the opposing party access to information vital to that party's defense).
38. *See* Glenmede Trust Co. v. Thompson, 56 F.3d 476, 486 (3d Cir. 1995) (holding that defendant waived the attorney-client privilege concerning certain attorney-client communications because defendant raised reliance on the advice of counsel as an affirmative defense).
39. *See* Swidler & Berlin v. United States, 524 U.S. 399, 412 (1998) (O'Connor, J., dissenting).
40. *See Swidler & Berlin*, 524 U.S. at 411 (O'Connor, J., dissenting).
41. *See* Cohen v. Jenkintown Cab Co., 357 A.2d 689, 693–94 (Pa. Super. Ct. 1976) (ordering disclosure because "when it is shown that the interests of the administration of justice can only be frustrated by the exercise of the privilege, the trial judge may require that the communication be disclosed").
42. 449 U.S. 383, 390–96 (1981).
43. *Id.* at 392–93.
44. *Id.* at 394–96.
45. *Id.* at 394–95.
46. *See* FED. R. EVID. 501.
47. The 15 states whose highest courts or legislatures adopted tests based on or similar to the holding in *Upjohn Co.* are Alabama (ALA. R. EVID. 502(a)(2)); Arizona (ARIZ. REV. STAT. § 12-2234); Arkansas (Corteau v. St. Paul Fire & Marine Ins. Co., 821 S.W.2d 45 (Ark. 1991)); California (D.I. Chadbourne, Inc. v. Superior Court, 388 P.2d 700 (Cal. 1964) (en banc)); Colorado (Denver Post Corp. v. Univ. of Colo., 739 P.2d 874 (Colo. 1987)); Florida (S. Bell Tel. & Tel. Co. v. Deason, 632 So. 2d 1377 (Fla. 1994)); Kentucky (KY. R. EVID. 503(a)(2)); Louisiana (LA. CODE EVID. ANN. art. 506(A)(2)); Mississippi (MISS. R. EVID. 502(a)(2)); Nevada (Wardleigh v. Second Judicial Dist. Court, 891 P.2d 1180 (Nev. 1995)); North Dakota (N.D. R. EVID. 502(a)(2)); Oregon (OR. EVID. CODE 503(1)(d)); Texas (TEX. R. CIV. EVID. 503(a)(2)); Utah (UTAH R. EVID. 504(a)(4)); Vermont (Baisley v. Missisquoi Cemetery Ass'n, 708 A.2d 924 (Vt. 1998)). Brian E. Hamilton, *Conflict, Disparity, and Indecision: The Unsettled Corporate Attorney-Client Privilege*, 1997 ANN. SURV. AM. L. 629, 633–40 (1999). The seven states that adopted the "control group test" are Alaska (ALASKA R. EVID. 503(a)(2)); Hawaii (HAW. R. EVID. 503(a)(2)); Illinois (Consol. Coal Co. v. Bucyrus-Erie Co., 432 N.E.2d 250 (Ill. 1982)); Maine (ME.

R. EVID. 502(a)(2)); New Hampshire (N.H. R. EVID. 502(a)(2)); Oklahoma (OKLA. STAT. tit. 12, § 2502(A)(4)); South Dakota (S.D. CODIFIED LAWS § 19-13-2(2)). Notably, lower courts in Delaware, Pennsylvania, and New Jersey have positively cited the *Upjohn Co.* approach, but those states have not definitively adopted the "subject matter" test. *See* Deutsch v. Cogan, 580 A.2d 100, 106 (Del. Ch. 1990) (citing *Upjohn Co.*, in dicta, for the proposition that "the lawyer-client privilege applies even when the client is a corporation, and . . . the corporate lawyer-client privilege [may not] be limited by the application of tests like the 'control group' test"); Amtrak v. Fowler, 788 A.2d 1053, 1056 (Pa. Commw. Ct. 2001) (holding that "entities may claim the privilege for communications between their attorney and their agents or employees who are authorized to act on behalf of the entities"); Wagi v. Silver Ridge Park W., 580 A.2d 1093, 1097 (N.J. Super. Ct. App. Div. 1989) ("The privilege unquestionably extends to corporations which must act through agents, including its officers and employees.").

48. Consol. Coal Co. v. Bucyrus-Erie Co., 432 N.E.2d 250, 257 (Ill. 1982).
49. *Id.* at 258.
50. 471 U.S. 343, 349 (1985).
51. *Id.; see also* Venture Law Grp. v. Superior Court of Santa Clara Cnty., 12 Cal. Rptr. 3d 656, 662 (Cal. Ct. App. 2004) ("Former management of a merged company does not hold the merged company's attorney-client privilege and may not waive the attorney-client privilege post-merger."); Maleski v. Corp. Life Ins. Co., 641 A.2d 1, 3 (Pa. Commw. Ct. 1994) (citing *Weintraub*).
52. *Weintraub*, 471 U.S. at 353.
53. *See* Soverain Software LLC v. Gap, Inc., 340 F. Supp. 2d 760, 763 (E.D. Tex. 2004) (holding that purchasing company was a successor to the business and the privilege that attended that business because it sold the transferee's product, held its patents, and serviced its customers); Bass Pub. Ltd. Co. v. Promus Cos., Inc., 868 F. Supp. 615, 620 (S.D.N.Y. 1994) (holding that postmerger company could waive privilege); Tekni-Plex, Inc. v. Meyner & Landis, 674 N.E.2d 663, 669 (N.Y. 1996) (holding that privilege transferred because business of purchased company remained unchanged, purchaser possessed "all of the rights, privileges, liabilities and obligations" of the purchased company, in addition to its assets, and the purchaser should have "access to any relevant pre-merger legal advice rendered to [the purchased company] that it might need to defend against these liabilities or pursue any of these rights").
54. *See* Zenith Elecs. Corp. v. WH-TV Broad. Corp., 2003 U.S. Dist. LEXIS 13816, at *6 (N.D. Ill. Aug. 7, 2003) (holding that attorney-client privilege was not a property right that could be contractually sold as an asset); *In re* In-Store Adver. Sec. Litig., 163 F.R.D. 452, 458 (S.D.N.Y. 1995) ("[A] transfer of assets, without more, is not sufficient to effect a transfer of the privileges; control of the entity possessing the privileges must also pass for the privileges to pass.") (quoting *In re* Grand Jury Subpoenas 89-3 and 89-4, 734 F. Supp. 1207, 1211 n.3 (E.D. Va. 1990)).
55. *See Maleski*, 641 A.2d at 4 (holding that liquidator may waive dissolved corporation's privilege because the liquidator was functioning as management of the corporation).
56. *See* Lewis v. United States, No. 02-2958 B/An, 2004 U.S. Dist. LEXIS 26680, at *9 (W.D. Tenn. Dec. 7, 2004) ("[C]lient confidentiality does not extend beyond the 'death' of a corporation."); FDIC v. McAtee, 124 F.R.D. 662, 664 (D. Kan. 1988) ("[T]he transfer of assets to the FDIC in its corporate capacity does not transfer

the attorney-client privilege."); FDIC v. Amundson, 682 F. Supp. 981, 987 (D. Minn. 1988) (where FDIC merely acted as receiver and liquidator of bank's assets, FDIC could not assert former attorney-client relationship with bank's attorney for purposes of disqualification).

57. *See* FED. R. EVID. 502 and Committee Letter.
58. Memorandum from the Deputy Attorney General to All Component Heads and United States Attorneys, Bringing Criminal Charges Against Corporations (June 16, 1999), http://www.justice.gov/criminal/fraud/documents/reports/1999/charging-corps.pdf ("One factor the prosecutor may weigh in assessing the adequacy of a corporation's cooperation is the completeness of its disclosure including, if necessary, a waiver of the attorney-client and work product protections, both with respect to its internal investigation and with respect to communications between specific officers, directors, and employees and counsel.").
59. Memorandum from Larry D. Thompson, Deputy Attorney General, to Heads of Department Components and United States Attorneys, Principles of Federal Prosecution of Business Organizations (Jan. 20, 2003), http://www.justice.gov/dag/cftf/corporate_guidelines.htm.
60. Memorandum from Robert D. McCallum, Jr., Acting Deputy Attorney General, to Heads of Department Components, Waiver of Corporate Attorney-Client and Work Product Protection (Oct. 21, 2005), http://lawprofessors.typepad.com/whitecollarcrime_blog/files/AttorneyClientWaiverMemo.pdf.
61. Letter from Griffin R. Bell, et al., to Hon. Alberto Gonzales, Proposed Revisions to Department of Justice Policy Regarding Waiver of the Attorney-Client Privilege and Work Product Doctrine (Sept. 5, 2006), http://lawprofessors.typepad.com/whitecollarcrime_blog/files/thompson_memo_letter_sept_5_2006.pdf.
62. On November 14, 2006, H.R. 3013, the Privilege Protection Act, was passed in the House of Representatives by voice vote without objection. The companion bill in the Senate, S. 186, was then expected to be taken up shortly thereafter.
63. Memorandum from Paul J. McNulty, Deputy Attorney General to Heads of Department Components and United States Attorneys, Principles of Federal Prosecution of Business Organizations (Dec. 12, 2006), http://www.justice.gov/dag/speeches/2006/mcnulty_memo.pdf.
64. Letter from Rebecca A. Betts, former U.S. Attorney for the Southern District of West Virginia, et al., to Senator Patrick Leahy, Chairman, Judiciary Committee (June 20, 2008), http://www.nacdl.org/search.aspx?term=Letter%20from%20Rebecca%20A.%20Betts.
65. *See, e.g.*, Letter from Sen. Arlen Specter to Mark R. Filip, Deputy Attorney General (July 10, 2008), http://federalevidence.com/pdf/Corp_Prosec/Specter_to_Filip_7_10_08.pdf.
66. Memorandum from Mark Filip, Deputy Attorney General, to Heads of Department Components and United States Attorneys, Principles of Federal Prosecution of Business Organizations (Aug. 28, 2008), http://www.justice.gov/dag/readingroom/dag-memo-08282008.pdf, *reprinted in* UNITED STATES ATTORNEYS' MANUAL, §§9-28 *et seq.*, http://www.justice.gov/usao/eousa/foia_reading_room/usam/title9/28mcrm.htm.
67. *See* Press Release, Sen. Arlen Specter, Specter Responds to DOJ's Revisions of Attorney-Client Privilege Guidelines (Aug. 28, 2008), http://www.uslaw.com/library/Corporate_&_Securities_Law/Applause_DOJ_Revises_Attorney

Client_Privilege_Guidelines.php?item=227623 ("[T]here is no change in the benefit to corporations to waive the privilege by giving facts obtained by the corporate attorneys from the individuals in order to escape prosecution or to have a deferred prosecution agreement.").

68. *See* Exchange Act Release No. 44,969, Report of Investigation Pursuant to Section 21(a) of the Securities Exchange Act of 1934 and Commission Statement on the Relationship of Cooperation to Agency Enforcement Decisions (Oct. 23, 2001), www.sec.gov/litigation/investreport/34-44969.htm; Bruce A. Green & David C. Clifton, *Feeling a Chill; Changing Government Policies Are Pressing Corporation and Attorneys to Disclose Protected Information*, A.B.A. J., Dec. 2005, at 63–64; Elkan Abramowitz & Barry A. Bohrer, *White Collar Crime; Waiver of Corporate Attorney-Client and Work Product Protection*, N.Y. L.J., Nov. 1, 2005, at 3.
69. *See* Green, *supra* note 68, at 63; Abramowitz, *supra* note 68.
70. *See* Attorney-Client Privilege Protection Act, S. 445, 111th Cong. (2009); Attorney-Client Privilege Protection Act, H.R. 4326, 111th Cong. (2009).
71. *See supra* notes 33–36 and related text.
72. *See, e.g., In re* Columbia/HCA Healthcare Corp. Billing Practices Litig., 293 F.3d 289, 302–04 (6th Cir. 2002) (holding privilege was waived); Westinghouse Elec. Corp. v. Republic of Philippines, 951 F.2d 1414, 1425–27 (3d Cir. 1991) (distinguishing partial from selective waivers); Weil v. Inv./Indicators, Research, and Mgmt., Inc., 647 F.2d 18, 24–25 (9th Cir. 1981); Velsicol Chem. Corp. v. Parsons, 561 F.2d 671 (7th Cir. 1977); United States v. Doe (*In re* Grand Jury Proceedings), 219 F.3d 175, 183, 186 (2d Cir. 2000) (remanding case to determine whether privilege was waived by disclosure); Diversified Indus., Inc. v. Meredith, 572 F.2d 596, 611 (8th Cir. 1978) (holding that privilege was not waived through disclosure in nonpublic Securities and Exchange Commission investigation); Maruzen Co., Ltd. v. HSBC USA, Inc., 00 Civ. 1079 (RO), 00 Civ. 1512 (RO), 2002 U.S. Dist. LEXIS 13288, at *2–5 (S.D.N.Y. July 23, 2002) (holding that privilege was not waived because communications were disclosed under a confidentiality agreement with the U.S. Attorneys' Office).
73. While some on the Advisory Committee had argued in favor of the selective waiver provision in order to protect against subject matter waiver and to maintain the privilege in other contexts, others argued that such a provision would simply encourage the government to pressure companies more to waive the privilege by arguing that there would be limited detriment to the company outside the government's investigation. Companies rightfully argue that they should not be compelled to waive the privileges due to the far-reaching impact beyond the particular government investigation such as in civil litigation or the ability to conduct effective investigations and counseling in the future (in addition, of course, to the fact that doing so undermines the crucial value of the attorney-client privilege and work-product doctrine to society and parties).

CHAPTER 21

Application of Attorney-Client Privilege and Work-Product Doctrine in Insurance Coverage Litigation

LOUIS SEY ZIMMERMAN

I. Introduction

The relationship between insurance companies and their insureds is complex. Cooperation between an insurance company and its insured on a matter of common interest can easily transition into a coverage dispute. Discovery disputes in insurance coverage cases have led to the development of some specific case law on the application of the attorney-client privilege and work-product doctrine to insurers and their insureds.

In the most common situation, the law seems settled. Where the insurer undertakes to provide a defense for the insured in a lawsuit and the insurer and the insured are represented by the same attorney in that lawsuit, documents related to the lawsuit in the possession of that attorney cannot be shielded from disclosure in the context of a subsequent coverage dispute between the insurer and the insured concerning that case.[1]

There are, however, some differing views on whether those privileges can be asserted in a coverage dispute to protect documents in the possession of an attorney for the insured from disclosure in two other instances: (1) where the documents were prepared by the insured's attorney for use in the underlying lawsuit giving rise to the coverage dispute when the insurer did not provide the insured a defense in that underlying lawsuit, and (2) where the documents were prepared by an attorney who was retained by and represented the insured in a case related to but separate from the particular case giving rise to the coverage controversy.

The court decisions that have examined these two issues have generally discussed them in one of two ways, depending on the nature of the controversy and the type of documents involved. Where the documents are not directly related to any claim or defense raised by a party, the courts will often be asked by a party to determine whether the documents in the possession of the insured's attorney fall within the insurance contract "cooperation clause" exception or the "common interest" exception to the attorney-client and/or work-product privileges. Alternatively, where the documents are directly related to some specific claim or defense the courts will be asked to determine whether the documents meet the "in issue" or "at issue" exceptions to the attorney-client privilege. This chapter reviews both approaches.

II. Cooperation Clause and Common-Interest Exceptions to the Privileges

At this time there appears to be both a majority and a minority view on how these cooperation clause and common-interest exceptions should be applied to the two issues described above. The majority view upholds the privileges in both instances and rejects demands that documents in the possession of the insured's attorney be produced. The minority view rejects the application of the privileges requires production. Since much of the case law has resulted from rejecting what has become the minority view, this discussion is best commenced with a discussion of the minority view.

A. Minority View

The decision of the Illinois Supreme Court in *Waste Management, Inc. v. International Surplus Lines Co.*[2] and its progeny[3] reflect a minority view. In that case the insured sued its insurance company seeking reimbursement of settlement and defense costs incurred in defending and settling a lawsuit (the *Miller* suit) brought against it for environmental liabilities (personal injury and property damage) arising from the alleged migration of toxic wastes from a landfill. The insurer had rejected the insured's claim for reimbursement in part because of the insured's failure to advise it of an even earlier lawsuit (the *Nunn* suit) brought against the insured involving the same landfill. In the *Nunn* suit, the landfill's prior owners had sued the insured asserting that the insured had negligently operated the landfill. The insured handled the *Nunn* suit at its own expense and sought no reimbursement of its costs from the insurer. The Illinois Supreme Court was asked to decide whether the insured's attorney's files concerning both the *Miller* suit (the litigation for which reimbursement of legal expenses was sought from the insurer) and the *Nunn* suit (litigation for which no reimbursement was sought from the insurer) were subject to discovery by the insurance company in the coverage case. The Illinois Supreme Court decided that the insured was required to produce its attorney's files on both the *Miller* and *Nunn* suits.

1. Attorney-Client Privilege Protections

The insured asserted that the requirement that it disclose its defense counsel's files violated its attorney-client privilege. The court rejected that claim of privilege based on its application of the cooperation clause in the insurance policy and the common-interest doctrine.[4]

a. Cooperation Clause

The *Waste Management* court stated that the duties and obligations imposed upon the insurer and insured are defined by the insurance contract, and that the insurance contract's cooperation clause required the insured to fully cooperate with the insurer with respect to any claims for which the insurer might be liable.[5] It stated that the purpose of the cooperation clause was to "protect the insurer's interests and to prevent collusion between the insured and the injured party."[6] The court, focusing on the breadth of the language of the cooperation clause, determined that "it cannot seriously be contended that insureds would not be required to disclose contents of any communications they had with defense counsel representing them on a claim for which the insurers had the ultimate duty to satisfy."[7] It then rejected the attorney-client privilege, stating that the cooperation clause rendered "any expectation of attorney-client privilege under these circumstances unreasonable" because the "element of confidentiality is wanting."[8, 9]

b. Common-Interest Doctrine

In *Waste Management Inc.*, the insurance company also asserted that the attorney-client privilege was unavailable to the insured under the common-interest doctrine. The common-interest doctrine is an exception to the attorney-client privilege. The common-interest doctrine holds that documents in the possession of a lawyer who previously represented two different parties in a matter of common interest are subject to disclosure in a subsequent controversy between those two parties concerning the matter of common interest. The court in *Waste Management Inc.* applied the doctrine to a suit not directly within the scope of the coverage dispute. The court held that the parties had a common interest in the *Miller* suit since the insured was asserting coverage with respect to such claim. It held also that the insured and the insurer had a common interest in defeating the claims against the insured in the *Nunn* suit (the suit for which the insured asserted no coverage claim and sought no reimbursement).[10] The court rejected the assertion that no common interest existed simply because there was no simultaneous representation in the *Nunn* case.[11] The court held that it is the commonality of interests between the insurer and the insured, not just the joint conduct of litigation, that creates the exception to the privilege.[12] The court held that the requirement for simultaneous representation was flexible and that counsel for the insured had in a "limited sense" represented the interests of both the insurer and the insured in both the *Miller* and *Nunn* cases since the insurer could have ultimately been held responsible for payment of any adverse verdict against the insured and the insured might have a contribution claim against the plaintiffs in the *Nunn* case.[13] The fact that the insured was seeking neither attorneys' fees nor settlement costs in the *Nunn* case was not determinative because the obligation to cooperate was not limited to situations where the insured was seeking recovery from the insurer.[14]

Thus the court, in holding that the insured attorney's files in both cases were subject to discovery, had concluded that the common-interest exception was not dependent on the joint representation of the insured and the insurer by a common attorney nor was it limited to just the files related to the case that was subject to the coverage dispute.[15, 16]

2. *Work-Product Protection*

The insured also asserted that the work-product doctrine protected its defense counsel's files.[17] The court acknowledged that the work-product doctrine generally applied to protect disclosure of materials developed to be used against an adversary in the lawsuit where the documents are sought.[18] The court noted that the materials sought to be protected here were developed when the insured and the insurer were not adversaries, making the work-product doctrine inapplicable.[19] It also noted that defense counsel's mental impressions and case assessment in those earlier cases could be "dispositive" of the issues in the coverage case, making disclosure necessary.[20]

B. Majority View

The decision in *Waste Management* has been repeatedly criticized as contrary to the traditional protections afforded attorney-client communications and attorney work product and as creating a new exception to those privileges.[21]

1. *Attorney-Client Privilege Protections*

The majority of courts have rejected both of the underlying justifications in *Waste Management*: the cooperation clause and the common-interest exception.

a. Cooperation Clause

Courts have criticized the *Waste Management* holding on the cooperation clause as improperly implying a contractual waiver of attorney-client privilege where none exists.[22] Other courts have distinguished the decision by noting that Illinois has a more restrictive view of the attorney-client privilege than other states.[23] A reflection of the general disfavor in which the courts have held *Waste Management* can be seen in *Bituminous Casualty Corp. v. Tonka Corp.*,[24] in which the court stated:

> This court finds the reasoning of Illinois Supreme Court to be fundamentally unsound. This court rejects the conclusion that because an insured agrees to cooperate with the insurance company, in the event he is sued or otherwise makes a claim under the policy, that the insured has thereby forever contractually waived the attorney-client privilege. To hold that an insurance policy created a contractual waiver of the attorney-client privilege, even when the insurance company later sues the insured contending the insured's claim is not covered by the policy, would completely eviscerate the attorney-client privilege. Absent a showing that the parties intended the language of the cooperation clauses of the insurance policies at issue here to work a waiver of the attorney-client privilege, the court declines to follow the holding of *Waste Management* to find a contractual waiver of the privilege.[25]

Other courts have held that even very broadly worded cooperation clauses should not be applied to imply duty to provide documents otherwise protected by attorney-client privilege or to constitute a waiver of such privilege.[26]

b. Common-Interest Exception

The courts have generally taken the position that the common-interest exception to the attorney-client privilege should come into play only with respect to documents that were created when two or more clients were represented by the same attorney in the same case and those parties subsequently become adverse to one another over that matter in which they formerly had a common interest.[27] Courts have commonly refused to apply the common-interest exception to the attorney-client privilege in (1) circumstances where the insured and insurer were not represented by the same attorney,[28] (2) circumstances where the case for which documents were sought was not sufficiently related to case underlying the coverage controversy, and (3) cases where there was uncertainty at the time the documents were created whether the insured and the insurer would ultimately be adverse to one another.[29]

2. *Work-Product Protection*

The courts have not favored the broad holding of *Waste Management* that the work-product doctrine does not generally shield documents created by a common attorney at a time when the parties were not adverse. Instead, the courts, particularly federal courts, applying the Federal Rules of Civil Procedure,[30] have tended to focus on whether the documents for which protection is sought were prepared in the "ordinary course of business"[31] as opposed to in "anticipation of litigation"[32] and on whether the requesting party can demonstrate substantial need and the inability to obtain the information otherwise.[33] Even where the attorneys' files might be subject to disclosure under such a test, exceptions are recognized to protect attorney opinions and impressions.[34]

III. The "At Issue" Exception to the Attorney-Client and Work-Product Privileges

While the majority of courts will protect attorney-client privilege documents and work product in coverage dispute, except where there was simultaneous representation in the underlying suit, that protection generally will not extend to documents that are the basis for some claim or defense in the coverage litigation. This is the so-called "at issue" or "in issue" exception to or waiver of privilege.[35] This exception is said to apply when a party (1) by an affirmative act (2) causes information covered by the privilege to become relevant to the case and (3) the opposing party could be deprived of "vital" information that cannot be obtained by any other means should the privilege not be enforced.[36]

An affirmative act is an act by the privilege holder that has a direct bearing on a claim or defense of a party. The court in *Waste Management* found that the filing of a suit in a coverage dispute was a sufficient affirmative act to invoke the exception.[37] Most courts, however, reject the notion that the mere filing of suit in a coverage dispute is by itself a sufficient affirmative act.[38]

Court have discussed how the at-issue exception or waiver might be applied in a variety of different ways. Some courts have required disclosure of documents with a direct bearing on that claim or defense regardless of whether the privilege holder actually intends to use the document.[39] Some courts have found that the claim of privilege could be defeated where the actual conduct of the insured itself or its attorney has been placed at issue and the documents relate to that conduct.[40] And some courts have taken a very restrictive approach and have only permitted disclosure of documents where the privilege holder attempts to prove a claim or defense by specifically disclosing or describing an attorney-client communication.[41]

IV. Conclusion

The weight of judicial precedent supports the conclusion that documents prepared by an insured's attorney when that attorney did not simultaneously represent the insurer and the insured will be protected from disclosure in subsequent coverage litigation upon the insured's assertion of attorney-client privilege and work-product protection. There are "at issue" and "in issue" exceptions, however, which must be investigated before concluding that the privileges apply.

Notes

1. McCormick on Evidence § 91.1, at 413 (6th ed. 2006). It should be pointed out that at least in California, in order for the representation to be considered joint, it must have occurred where there was no reservation of rights by insurer to subsequently contest coverage. Lectrolarm Custom Sys., Inc. v. Pelco Sales, Inc., 212 F.R.D. 567, 571 (E.D. Cal. 2002). *See also* Lamar Adver. of S.D. v. Kay, 267 F.R.D. 568 (D.S.D. 2010) (applying South Dakota law).
2. 579 N.E.2d 322 (Ill. 1991).
3. Among the reported cases, the Illinois cases are in counterpoint to virtually every other reported case. While there continue to be published state court decisions and federal court decisions (applying Illinois law) following *Waste Management*, Illinois remains largely a minority jurisdiction of one on how the cooperation clause and common interest doctrine should be applied in this context. *See, e.g.*, Allianz Ins. Co. v. Guident Corp., 869 N.E.2d 1042 (Ill. App. Ct. 2007).
4. *Waste Mgmt.*, 579 N.E.2d at 328.
5. The cooperation clause in *Waste Management* provided that the insureds shall assist the insurer in pursuing contribution and indemnity claims and that the insureds "shall give all such information and assistance as the insurers may reasonably require." *Id.* at 327–28.
6. *Id.* at 327.
7. *Id.* at 328.
8. *Id.*
9. While the court never discussed expressly why the cooperation clause would invalidate assertion of the attorney-client privilege with respect to documents accumulated by the defense attorney in the *Nunn* case (the case for which the insured sought no reimbursement), it is reasonable to conclude the court thought that the *Nunn* documents, which pertained to operations and conditions at the same landfill, were needed by the insurer and relevant to the coverage issues.
10. *Waste Mgmt.*, 579 N.E.2d at 328.
11. *Id.* Other courts have applied the "common interest" doctrine in a fashion somewhat similar to that in *Waste Management*. In *Independent Petrochemical Corp. v. Aetna Cas. & Sur. Co.*, 654 F. Supp. 1334, 1365 (D.D.C. 1986), the court held that an insured could not withhold on the basis of attorney-client privilege documents that the insured's attorneys recovered, prepared, or compiled in connection with its defense of the toxic tort suits underlying the coverage dispute. It rejected the argument that the existence of the coverage dispute eliminate the common interest. It rejected the argument that the plaintiffs had a reasonable expectation of confidentiality. *See* Carey-Canada, Inc. v. Aetna Cas. & Assurance Co., 118 F.R.D. 250, 251 (D.D.C. 1987) (holding that *Independent Petrochemical* was a very narrow holding in a case where court had decided insured had a duty to defend).
12. *Waste Mgmt.*, 579 N.E.2d at 329–30.
13. *Id.* at 329.
14. *Id.*
15. *Id.*

16. The Illinois Court of Appeals has recently applied *Waste Management* in a case where a former officer of a company was sued by a company for breach of fiduciary duty and breach of contract. The officer objected to the production of certain documents from attorney's files because that attorney had represented him personally as well as the corporation. The court held that the former officer could not reasonably expect the confidentiality of communications between him and the attorney to be protected after the attorney had undertaken to represent both the corporation and the officer concerning the matters in interest. Mueller Indus., Inc., v. Berkman, 2010 Ill. App. LEXIS 235 (2010).
17. *Waste Mgmt.*, 579 N.E.2d at 331.
18. *Id.* at 330. The court made clear that the attorney's files in the instant coverage litigation between the parties would be protected. *Id.* at 331.
19. *Id.* The justification for finding an exception to the work-product privilege where the documents were created when the parties were not adversaries has found some resonance with a few other courts that approached the question from the perspective whether the insured, at the time the documents were created, had a reasonable expectation they would be kept confidential. *See* EDO Corp. v. Newark Ins. Co., 145 F.R.D. 18, 23 (D. Conn. 1992) (noting that the work-product privilege does not apply in subsequent coverage dispute where the materials were prepared where the insured had a duty to cooperate and, when insured and insurer shared common interests); Metro Wastewater Reclamation Dist. v. Cont'l Cas. Co., 142 F.R.D. 471, 476 (D. Colo. 1992) (requiring disclosure of attorney-client communication and attorney-consultant communication).
20. *Waste Mgmt.*, 579 N.E.2d at 331. The New Jersey Superior Court cited the reasoning in *Waste Management* in a restrictive fashion. It held that the files of the insured's attorney can be disclosed but only those portions containing material facts. Mental impressions and legal conclusions would remain privileged. *In re* Envtl. Ins. Declaratory Judgment Actions, 612 A.2d 1338, 1343–44 (N.J. Super. Ct. App. Div. 1992).
21. *See* RML Corp. v. Assurance Co. of Am., 60 Va. Cir. 269, 273–74 (2002); *In re* Imperial Corp. of Am., 167 F.R.D. 447, 452 (S.D. Cal. 1995); N. River Ins. Co. v. Phila. Reinsurance Corp., 797 F. Supp. 363, 367 (D.N.J. 1992); Remington Arms Co. v. Liberty Mut. Ins. Co., 142 F.R.D. 408, 416–17 (D. Del. 1992).
22. *See* cases cited *supra* note 21.
23. *See* Rockwell Int'l Corp. v. L.A. Superior Court, 32 Cal. Rptr. 2d 153, 158 (Cal. Ct. App. 1994) (reasoning that there is no indication that the cooperation clause was intended to waive the privilege); E. Airlines, Inc. v. U.S. Aviation Underwriters, 716 So. 2d 340, 342–43 (Fla. Dist. Ct. App. 1998).
24. Bituminous Cas. Corp. v. Tonka Corp., 140 F.R.D. 381 (D. Minn. 1992).
25. *Id.* at 386.
26. *Remington Arms Co.*, 142 F.R.D. at 416–17; Pittson Co. v. Allianz Ins. Co., 143 F.R.D. 66, 72 (D.N.J. 1992), *rev'd on other grounds*, 124 F.3d 508 (3d Cir. 1997); Fugro-MacLelland Marine Geosciences v. Steadfast Ins. Co., 2009 U.S. Dist. LEXIS 102997 (S.D. Tex. 2008).
27. *Pittson Co.*, 143 F.R.D. at 72.
28. *See, e.g.*, Carey-Canada, Inc. v. Aetna Cas. & Sur. Co., 118 F.R.D. 250, 251 (D.D.C. 1987), *aff'd in part and vacated in part*, 940 F.2d 1548 (D.C. Cir. 1991); Cont'l Cas. Co. v. St. Paul Surplus Lines Ins. Co., 2010 U.S. Dist LEXIS (E.D. Cal. 2010).

29. *See* Vt. Gas Sys., Inc. v. U.S. Fid. & Guar. Co., 151 F.R.D. 268, 277 (D. Vt. 1993); F.P. Woll & Co. v. Valiant Ins. Co., No. 99-0465, 2003 U.S. Dist. LEXIS 3134, at *8–10 (E.D. Pa. 2003).
30. Fed. R. Civ. P. 26(b)(3).
31. Bituminous Cas. Corp. v. Tonka Corp. 140 F.R.D. 381, 388–89 (D. Minn. 1992).
32. The "in anticipation of litigation" standard has not been applied solely to protect documents prepared in anticipation of litigation between the insurer and the insured but also to documents prepared in anticipation of litigation between the insured and the state environmental agency. *Id.*
33. *Remington Arms Co.*, 142 F.R.D. at 418–19.
34. Fed. R. Civ. P. 26(b)(3)(B).
35. *Remington Arms Co.*, 142 F.R.D. at 413 n.4; State v. Hydrite Chem. Co., 582 N.W.2d 411, 418 (Wis. Ct. App. 1998); Koppers Co. v. Aetna Cas. & Sur. Co., 847 F. Supp. 360, 362–63 (W.D. Pa. 1994), *mandamus granted, order vacated without opinion*, 40 F.3d 1240 (3d Cir. 1994); Hearn v. Rhay, 68 F.R.D. 574, 581 (E.D. Wash. 1975). While this chapter largely describes the at-issue waiver as an exception to the attorney-client privilege, certain courts have described it as an implied waiver of the privilege. *Hearn*, 68 F.R.D. at 581.
36. *Id.*; Dedham-Westwood Water Dist. v. Nat'l Union Fire Ins. Co., No. Civ. A. 96-00044, 2000 WL 33419021, at *6 (Mass. 2000); Pittson Co. v. Allianz Ins. Co., 143 F.R.D. 66, 71 (D.N.J. 1992); McElgunn v. CUNA Mut. Grp., 2009 U.S. Dist. LEXIS 46502 (D.S.D. 2009); Lindley v. Life Investors Ins. Co., 2010 U.S. Dist. LEXIS 41798 (W.D. Okla. 2010).
37. *Koppers Co.*, 847 F. Supp. at 363. *See* Edgewater Med. Ctr. v. Rogan, 2010 U.S. Dist. LEXIS 66693 (N.D. Ill. 2010) (citing *Waste Mgmt.*).
38. The courts have generally rejected the idea that a party waives the attorney-client privilege by initiating litigation. *See Hydrite Chem. Co.*, 582 N.W.2d at 418; *Remington Arms Co.*, 142 F.R.D. at 414; Vt. Gas Sys., Inc. v. U.S. Fid. & Guar. Co., 151 F.R.D. 268, 277 (D. Vt. 1993); N. River Ins. Co. v. Phila. Reinsurance Corp., 797 F. Supp. 363, 370–71 (D.N.J. 1992).
39. Metro. Wastewater Reclamation Dist. v. Cont'l Cas. Co., 142 F.R.D. 471, 477 (D. Colo. 1992); *Remington Arms Co.*, 142 F.R.D. at 414; *see Hydrite Chem. Co.*, 582 N.W.2d at 418–19 (The court applied the at-issue doctrine differently with respect to the attorney-client privilege and work-product privilege. With respect to the attorney-client privilege, the party must intend to use the document sought to be protected. With respect to the work-product privilege, opportunity to use the document would not be required.).
40. *Dedham-Westwood Water Dist.*, 2000 WL 33419021, at *3; J.A. Apparel Corp. v. Abboud, 2008 U.S. Dist. LEXIS 1825 (2008).
41. *See Hydrite Chem. Co.*, 582 N.W.2d at 418 (applied to attorney-client privilege documents). Honda Lease Trust v. Middlesex Mut. Assurance Co., 2007 U.S. Dist. LEXIS 72653 (D. Conn. 2007) ("at issue" exception applies only when the contents contains legal advice "integral to outcome of legal claims"). *See also* Emmanouil v. Roggio, 2009 U.S. Dist. LEXIS 29840 (D.N.J. 2009).

CHAPTER 22

Preserving the Attorney-Client Privilege and Work-Production Protections Afforded to Communications with Experts: Be Careful of What You Say and to Whom You Say It

DAVID E. BLAND
GERARDO ALCAZAR

I. Introduction

A regular client calls with a new matter—a series of tort claims allegedly caused by a defect in its most profitable product. The general counsel tells you that this is a "bet the company" situation and to spare no expense in the defense. Even though suit has not yet been filed, you retain several experts as consultants to assist you in the evaluation and defense of these expected suits. You and your client both provide the experts with factual information via e-mail, and you provide the experts with summaries of interviews you and your staff conducted of company witnesses and other third parties. Suits are filed in federal court, and you and your team of experts continue to work on the defense. You provide the experts with summaries of key depositions, summaries of detailed interviews with the company's employees who designed the product, and your detailed outline of the claims and defenses with annotations to the facts already obtained, as well as the areas where further factual and expert inquiry is required. The deadline for your disclosure of experts approaches, and you decide to designate all of the experts you initially hired as testifying experts except one who remains a nontestifying expert. In response to your disclosure, your adversary serves a request for copies of the complete files of all of your testifying experts, as well as the complete files of the nontestifying expert on the grounds that the nontestifying expert provided information relied on by the others. After taking a deep breath, you consider your options. What do you produce?

As we all know, expert testimony has embedded itself as a pivotal component of nearly every lawsuit. There is hardly an action pursued without the guidance or opinion of an expert. As early as 1990, a Rand Corporation study concluded that expert witnesses appeared in 86 percent of California trials, with an average of 3.3 experts per trial.[1] Experts have become a part of daily life for litigators.[2] Accordingly, it is important to be aware of the boundaries regarding what an attorney may communicate to expert witnesses and how those communications relate to the preservation of the attorney-client privilege and the work-product doctrine embodied in Federal Rule of Civil Procedure 26 and its recent amendments.

What can be shared with testifying experts? How about consultants? What rules control? Can confidential client communications be shared with a consultant and remain confidential? How about with your testifying expert? Knowing the answers to these questions is imperative to preserving the attorney-client privilege.

The attorney-client privilege protects communications geared toward giving and receiving legal advice.[3] The privilege exists when the following conditions are met:

> 1) Where legal advice of any kind is sought, 2) from a professional legal advisor in his capacity as such, 3) the communications relating to that purpose, 4) made in confidence, 5) by the client, 6) are at his

insistence permanently protected, 7) from disclosure by himself or by the legal advisor, 8) unless the protection is waived.[4]

"The privilege is based on the two related principles. The first is that loyalty forms an intrinsic part of the relationship between a lawyer and client in our adversary system. . . . The second principle is that the privilege encourages clients to make full disclosures to their lawyers."[5] This privilege is integral not only to the attorney-client relationship but also to the attorney's relationship with consultants hired by the attorney to assist in providing legal advice. An attorney, however, must always be cautious with respect to what information is shared with hired consultants. It is important to keep a broad overarching perspective of the litigation and where it may lead to ensure preservation of privilege.

As discussed in detail in this chapter, Federal Rule of Civil Procedure 26(a)(2) was amended effective December 1, 2010.[6] The amendments are intended to change pre-amendment law as to testifying experts.[7] Therefore, the practitioner is cautioned to note the changes and the likely inapplicability of prior law.

II. Attorney-Client Privilege Is Generally Safe with Your Consulting or Nontestifying Expert

Lawyers involved in litigation typically retain consulting, or nontestifying, experts to evaluate the facts and circumstances of the case and assess the merit of certain arguments or defenses. Such experts provide an array of services that include damage assessments, technical evaluation of products or premises where an event occurred, technical review of prior art in a patent case, and other similar professional work. The questions then are whether the communications among the client, lawyer, and consultant are protected from disclosure, and whether the consultant's work product is likewise protected.

It is generally accepted that a consultant or nontestifying expert may communicate with the client or with the attorney without destroying the attorney-client privilege, if the communications are made on behalf of the client to obtain legal advice.[8] In other words, the privilege extends to communications between agents of the attorney or the client and the client's attorney.[9] The term "agent" has been broadly defined to encompass a range of individuals, from expert consultants to relatives to insurance agents whose presence is necessary to the purpose of the meeting and to the rendering of advice.[10] These protections will typically extend to fact and opinion work product shared with, reviewed by, or prepared by or for a consulting expert as well.[11]

To ensure that such an expert may appropriately assess factual or legal issues in a particular setting, courts have commonly held that confidential communications between a party's counsel and a nontestifying consultant hired to assist the attorney to render legal advice are protected by the attorney-client privilege.[12] While disclosure to a third party who lacks a common legal interest waives the attorney-client privilege,[13] courts protect communications made to an attorney by a consultant so that the attorney may provide sound legal advice to the client.[14] Furthermore, the general rule that a client's disclosure of confidential communications or documents directly to a third party destroys the attorney-client privilege[15] does not apply when the disclosure is made to third parties who assist an attorney in rendering legal advice.[16]

A. Classifying the Nontestifying Expert

How a nontestifying consultant is classified is crucial in determining the extent to which his or her work product may ultimately be discovered. A consultant acting as an arm of the attorney will likely fall within the scope of the attorney-client privilege, rendering the communications among the consultant, the attorney, and the client privileged.[17] On the other hand, a consultant hired, for example, to determine the cause of an event will likely not be deemed to be an arm of the attorney, and the information generated by such a consultant may be discoverable under the dictates for Federal Rule of Civil Procedure 26(b)(4)(B).[18]

Judge Friendly's decision in *United States v. Kovel*[19] lays the foundation for this distinction. In *Kovel*, Judge Friendly identified the need attorneys have to retain consultants to assist them in rendering legal advice.[20] The example Judge Friendly started with was one involving a client who spoke only a foreign language, and the obvious need the attorney had to use an interpreter.[21] Judge Friendly concluded that the attorney-client privilege would never be waived simply because a third-party interpreter was required for the attorney to render legal advice.[22] Following that logic, Judge Friendly observed that attorneys often need other kinds of professionals to assist them in understanding the client's information sufficiently to render legal advice: accountants, engineers, or other professionals.[23] Judge Friendly concluded that, as in the case of the interpreter, the disclosure of privileged information among the lawyer, client, and consultant should not automatically waive the privileged nature of those communications.[24] So long as the purpose in using consultants is to assist the attorney to render legal advice, the attorney-client privilege is not waived because the communications involved a third party.[25]

In re Bieter Co.[26] exemplifies the application of this principle. There, the Eighth Circuit Court of Appeals determined that a consultant for Bieter was operating within the attorney-client privilege.[27] The Eighth Circuit relied heavily on Supreme Court Standard 503(b)(1).[28] That standard, never adopted as part of the Federal Rules of Evidence by Congress, specified that the attorney-client privilege applied "between [client] or his representative and his lawyer or his lawyer's representative."[29] The court also relied on *McCaugherty v. Sifferman*[30] in reaching this decision. The court concluded: "[W]hen applying the attorney-client privilege to a corporation or partnership, it is inappropriate to distinguish between those on the client's payroll and those who are instead, and for whatever reason, employed as independent contractors."[31]

The distinction between a consultant whose work is within the attorney-client privilege and a consultant whose work is not is highlighted in *U.S. Postal Service v. Phelps Dodge Refining Corp.*[32] There, the court acknowledged the *Kovel* theory, but concluded that the expert's "function was not to put information gained from defendants into usable form for their attorneys to render legal advice, but rather, to collect information not obtainable directly from defendants."[33] The court affirmatively held that the consultants were not hired to interpret client confidences, but rather to prepare a remediation plan and to oversee remedial work.[34] The claim in this case was beyond the "outer boundary" of the privilege. The consultants based their opinions on factual and scientific data that they collected, not client confidences:

> Such underlying factual data can never be protected by the attorney-client privilege and neither can the resulting opinions and recommendations. There are few, if any, conceivable circumstances where a scientist or engineer employed to gather data should be considered an agent within the scope of the privilege since the information collected will generally be factual, obtained from sources other than the client.[35]

B. Discovery from Consultants within the Attorney-Client Privilege

Absent waiver, confidential communications offered by and delivered to a consulting expert for the purpose of offering legal advice will be protected. The decision in *Ferko v. NASCAR*[36] provides a good illustration of this. This case involved a discovery dispute between Ferko and International Speedway Corporation (ISC) in which Ferko sought documents pertaining to the American Appraisal Associates' (AAA) review of certain financial statements.[37] ISC's chief counsel, Glenn Padgett, "retained the AAA to investigate and appraise the economic value of sanction agreements for races held at its tracks."[38] Padgett also made available to Ernst & Young LLP, an accounting agency, the documents that AAA prepared and reviewed regarding the statements.[39]

During discovery, Ferko demanded that ISC produce these documents.[40] ISC refused and contended that these records were privileged communications between a client, its attorneys, and the outside consultants. Ferko moved to compel production, and, in response, ISC argued that the attorney-client privilege applied because Padgett "retained the AAA to help him render legal advice regarding anticipated litigation" with separate entity.[41] The court agreed with ISC. It held that an "attorney may, however, divulge client information to accountants or financial professionals in order to represent their client more effectively."[42] So long as an attorney hires a consultant for a specific purpose that relates significantly to the disputed communications or documents at issue, any documents disclosed to such professional and any communications regarding those documents are privileged.[43] In this case, Padgett hired the AAA to advise him on various financial issues,[44] and the AAA helped him translate complicated financial information. It was this translation that enabled Padgett to represent the ISC more effectively.[45] Accordingly, because the purpose for sharing the documents and communications related directly to the documents requested by Ferko, the court held that Ferko could not discover them.[46]

Moreover, the court held that it made no difference that Padgett did not hire the AAA for this particular lawsuit.[47] It was enough that the work done related to a potential lawsuit.[48] The court announced that the purpose for which the consultant was hired need only "relate significantly to the documents and communications at issue in the subsequent litigation."[49] Here, the purpose for which Padgett hired AAA and Ernst & Young related directly to and paralleled the disputed documents and communications requested in Ferko's discovery.[50] Hence, the court found the document and communication to be protected by the attorney-client privilege.[51]

The principle that the attorney-client privilege attaches to third-party consultants also has been applied to representatives of the attorney, such as administrative practitioners not admitted to the bar, and nontestifying experts hired to assist in the rendering of legal advice.[52] Even still, some foresight with respect to what information should and should not be shared with a consulting expert at the outset of litigation is important, as a change in the expert's classification could result in the waiver of this privilege.

C. Discovery from Consultants outside the Attorney-Client Privilege

A consultant hired for the purpose of providing assistance in anticipation of litigation, and not for purpose of rendering legal advice, will not fall under the protection provided by the attorney-client privilege. This consultant's work, however, does not automatically become discoverable. The facts and opinions of such a consultant are protected under Federal Rule of Civil Procedure 26. More specifically, Rule 26(b)(4)(D) provides that discovery of work product created by or shared with a consulting expert is not permitted unless the party seeking discovery can show that "exceptional circumstances" exist.[53]

Historically, the "exceptional circumstances" standard has proven sufficiently rigorous to afford adequate protection to the facts learned and opinions developed by a consulting expert.[54] Rule 26(b)(4)(D), however, is not an "impenetrable fortress."[55] The existence of an "exceptional circumstance" can be shown under a variety of conditions. Typical exceptional circumstances include:

1. The object or condition observed by the consulting expert is no longer observable for the party seeking the deposition;[56]
2. Expert discovery on a contested issue can be replicated, but the costs would be "judicially prohibitive";[57] and
3. The consulting expert provided information considered by a testifying expert informing an opinion, or an opinion resulted from collaboration between both experts.[58]

Bank Brussels Lambert v. Chase Manhattan Bank[59] provides a good representative discussion regarding the discoverability of facts and opinions held by a consultant upon a showing of exceptional circumstances. This case involved a discovery dispute in which Bank Paribas (Suisse) (BPS) sought to compel the production of financial records reviewed by Arthur Andersen & Co.[60] Andersen was retained on December 23, 1991 by AroChem to investigate discrepancies in its inventory and to determine whether the inventory was properly stated in AroChem's financial statements.[61] AroChem became concerned with its reporting practices as they related to its inventory after it was informed that a discrepancy existed in its reported and actual values.[62] Andersen's investigation continued through June 26, 1992,[63] and occupied the time of eight to 15 people consuming approximately 10,000 hours on the project.[64]

In response to the discovery request, Andersen asserted that Rule 26(b)(4)(B) applied, thereby precluding discovery of these facts and opinions because Andersen was hired in anticipation of litigation.[65] BPS put forth various counterarguments, among them that Andersen's facts and opinions were discoverable because "exceptional circumstances" were present.[66] More specifically, BPS argued that the investigation took place at the time when Andersen alone was able to observe and analyze AroChem's financial situation, and it would be impracticable to recreate it.[67] Next, BPS contended that even if AroChem's financial situation could be reproduced, the cost of hiring an expert to reconstruct its situation would be judicially prohibitive.[68]

The court ultimately agreed with BPS and ordered discovery of the facts and opinions held by Andersen regarding its investigation of AroChem's inventory.[69] In its analysis, the court found Andersen to be an expert "in that it brought technical background to bear on AroChem's accounts and records."[70] Moreover, it established that Andersen was hired in anticipation of litigation.[71] The court held that the facts surrounding the decision to hire Andersen reflected that there existed more than a mere possibility of litigation.[72] Lastly, the court affirmatively announced that "exceptional circumstances" were present, which demanded that the facts learned and the opinions held by Andersen be discoverable. Because Andersen's investigation took place two years before the lawsuit was filed and "numerous parties had an opportunity to observe, remove, and copy AroChem's files," the court found that it would be impracticable for BPS to recreate the same financial condition that AroChem was in at the time of Andersen's evaluation.[73] Even though the documents examined by Andersen still existed, the court feared that they had been rearranged or possibly lost or damaged.[74] Furthermore, the court found that even if AroChem's financial situation could be recreated, the costs of reviewing the documents, which took Andersen in excess of 10,000 hours, would be judicially prohibitive.[75]

Courts from various jurisdictions have reached very similar conclusions.[76] Accordingly, when a consultant is hired to interpret financial statements for purposes of rendering legal advice, or merely to determine whether there is a discrepancy between stated and actual numbers regarding inventory, some level of protection is afforded. Although the former communications will not be waived upon a showing of exceptional circumstances, the latter could possibly be waived. For this reason, it is important to consider the circumstances under which the consultant is hired and under what privilege the expert's communications and work product will fall if a motion to compel is brought by the opposing party.

III. The Law as to Testifying Experts

A. Introduction

Prior to 1993, Federal Rule of Civil Procedure 26 required the disclosure of expert opinions by way of interrogatory answers.[77] The amendments effective in 1993 changed the manner by which expert opinions were disclosed: the rule required (1) a report "of all opinions the witness will express and the basis and reasons for them,"[78] (2) disclosure of "the data or other information considered by the witness in forming [the opinions],"[79] and (3) the deposition of the expert.[80] Before 1993, courts were split on the breadth of the information discoverable from testifying experts. Since the 1993 amendments to Rule 26, there is near unanimity of opinion among federal courts that disclosing attorney-client communications to an independent expert witness waives the privilege.[81] State courts have generally followed suit.[82] Several courts, however, have based their decisions on the pre-1993 version of the Federal Rules.[83] Additionally, several states have discovery rules that mirror the pre-1993 federal version of Rule 26.[84]

As noted above, Rule 26 was again amended, effective December 1, 2010. The Advisory Committee comments state the purpose of the amendments:

> This amendment is intended to alter the outcome in cases that have relied on the 1993 formulation in requiring disclosure of all attorney-expert communications and draft reports. The amendments to Rule 26(b)(4) make this change explicit by providing work-product protection against discovery regarding draft reports and disclosures of attorney-expert communications.

B. Attorney-Client Communications

A testifying expert is a witness who is specifically qualified to "assist the trier of fact to understand evidence or to determine a fact in issue."[85] In federal courts, expert testimony is governed by Federal Rules of Evidence 702, 703, and 704, under which expert witnesses are given greater latitude to offer opinions and testify to a wider spectrum of topics than fact witnesses are.[86] Disclosure of privileged information, however, is controlled under Federal Rule of Civil Procedure 26(a)(2)(B).[87] Under the pre-2010 amendment of Rule 26, the vast majority of federal courts required the disclosure of all privileged information considered by a testifying expert.[88] Disclosure requirements changed with the 1993 amendment to the rule, and significantly increased a litigant's ability to obtain expert discovery.[89] The 1970 amendment required the disclosure of all information "relied" upon by the expert. The 1993 amendment required a party to produce all information "considered" by a testifying expert in forming an opinion.[90] Several courts noted that the 1970 amendment was far less inclusive of information than the 1993 amendment.[91]

The change in the text of the rule and the admonition that appears in the Advisory Committee Notes[92] broadened the scope of information that must be disclosed. The decision in *In re Pioneer Hi-Bred International, Inc.*[93] provides the seminal example of how courts across the country have treated the privileged communications that have been shared with testifying experts. *In re Pioneer* involved a suit for breach of contract, patent infringement, and misappropriation of trade secrets.[94] Throughout the discovery process, Monsanto sought information regarding a merger in which Pioneer was involved and shared documents with their testifying expert.[95] Specifically, Monsanto deposed Pioneer's in-house counsel, which Pioneer designated as its representative pursuant to Rule 30(b)(6).[96] During the deposition, Monsanto sought information relating to the analysis of the financial benefits stemming from the merger, to which Pioneer's in-house counsel invoked the attorney-client privilege in some instances.[97]

In response, Monsanto moved to compel Pioneer's in-house counsel to respond to the deposition questions.[98] The district court granted the motion, stating that it was persuaded, "limited to the facts and circumstances presented in this instance, that, if ever privileged, the protection applying to these opinions and communications has been waived by defendant's disclosure of the opinions to expert witnesses."[99] The Federal Circuit agreed[100] and stated:

> [T]he 1993 amendments to Rule 26 of the Federal Rule of Civil Procedure make clear that documents and information disclosed to a testifying expert in connection with his testimony are discoverable by the opposing party, whether or not the expert relies on the document and information in preparing his report. Rule 26(a)(2) requires that the testifying expert's report "contain a complete statement of all opinions to be expressed and the basis and reasons therefore; the data or other information considered by the witness in the opinions." The accompanying Advisory Committee Note explicitly states "[t]he report is to disclose the data and other information considered by the expert. . . . Given this obligation of disclosure, litigants should no longer be able to argue that materials furnished to their experts to be used in forming their opinions—whether or not ultimately relied upon by the expert—are privileged or otherwise protected from disclosure when such persons are testifying or being deposed."[101]

Synthes Spine Co. v. Walden[102] is similarly illustrative. Here, Walden sought the production of all information "considered" by the plaintiff's damage expert, John Stavros, in fashioning his opinions as required by Federal Rule of Civil Procedure 26(a)(2). Walden sought this information irrespective of its privileged status, asserting that disclosure was mandatory under Rule 26(a)(2) and that any privilege had been waived when the information was given to the testifying expert.

The court stated that it was clear from the commentary provided by the advisory committee notes to the 1993 amendment that the term "considered" exceeded the more narrow definition of "relied upon" present in the previous version of the rule.[103] According to the court, "considered" refers to any information furnished to a testifying expert that such expert reviews, reflects upon, reads, or uses in connection with the formulation of his opinions, even if such information is ultimately rejected.[104] Moreover, the court found that "it is equally clear that the disclosure requirements of Rule 26(a)(2)(B) were meant to trump all claims of privilege, mandating production of all information furnished to the testifying expert for consideration in the formulation of her opinions, regardless of privilege."[105] The notes to Rule 26 do not distinguish between types of "privilege," such as the attorney-client or the work product.[106] Hence, a bright-line rule of disclosure is created, which serves important policy considerations, "including the facilitation of effective cross-examination and the resolution of uncertainty as to the discoverability of documentation divulged to a testifying expert."[107]

C. Work Product

The interpretation of the post-1993 Rule 26 as expressed by the courts in *In re Pioneer* and *Synthes* is the nearly unanimous position among courts nationwide with respect to attorney-client privilege.[108] But courts continue to have difficulty coming to an agreement on the extent to which work product shared with a testifying expert is discoverable.[109] The majority of courts agree that work product shared with a testifying expert is discoverable.[110] A minority of cases, however, following the pre-1993 amendment case *Bogosian v. Gulf Oil Corp.*,[111] hold that the 1993 amendment was insufficiently specific to cause waiver with respect to "core" work product protections afforded to the legal conclusions and analysis of lawyers, even when shared with a testifying expert.[112] The 2010 amendment to Rule 26, however, should end application of the majority rule as we know it. Indeed, that is the view expressed in the Committee Notes to Rule 26(a)(2(B): "This amendment is intended to alter the outcome in cases that have relied on the 1993 formulation in requiring disclosure of all attorney-expert communications and draft reports."[113]

1. *Pre-Amendment Majority View*

In the pre-amendment majority view, nothing you disclose to your expert will be protected.

The court's decision in *Regional Airport Authority of Louisville v. LFG, LLC*[114] is revealing of the obstacles one faced in trying to protect from discovery privileged documents disclosed to a testifying expert. This decision represented the majority view among both federal and state jurisdictions. *Regional Airport* involved an action brought by an owner of a contaminated airport property against the prior owner under the Comprehensive Environmental Response, Compensation, and Liability Act (CERCLA)[115] and state law. The Authority purchased a piece of land from LFG for the purpose of expanding the Louisville International Airport. Shortly after the purchase, the Authority discovered the property was more highly contaminated than originally represented prior to purchase.[116]

Extensive discovery ensued.[117] During this time, LFG sought to compel the production of thousands of documents relating to the communications between attorneys for the Authority and employees of outside companies that worked closely with the Authority on the expansion.[118] The district court ordered production of all the documents, which required the disclosure of certain documents that Authority gave its testifying experts.[119] The Sixth Circuit affirmed this decision.[120]

In doing so, the court specifically relied on the language in Rule 26(a)(2) and the 1993 amendments to the rule.[121] In its decision, the court acknowledged that, since the amendment to the rule, two lines of cases have emerged regarding the protection of work-product associated with testifying experts:[122] first, that work product is not discoverable merely because it has been shared with a testifying expert;[123] second, that Rule 26 creates a bright-line rule that requires disclosure of all information provided to testifying experts, including attorney opinion work product.[124] The court, adopting what was considered the majority position, relied on subsection (a)(2) of the rule in holding that the Authority must disclose all information given to its testifying experts, including attorney opinion work product.[125] The court agreed that "a plain reading of subsections (a)(2) and (b) makes clear that (b) applies to the *discovery* of information provided to experts generally, while (a)(2) applies to the disclosure of information provided to testifying experts specifically."[126]

Having determined that subsection (a)(2) mandated disclosure regarding testifying experts, the court then determined the extent of the required disclosure.[127] Here, it focused on the 1993 amendment to the rule and conceded that, from the text alone, the extent of disclosure was ambiguous.[128] But because neither the text of the rule nor the Advisory Committee Notes placed any qualifiers as to the extent of "information" or "materials" given its experts, the court read the rule to require disclosure of all information provided to testifying experts.[129]

The court was clear that subsections (b)(4)[130] and (b)(3)[131] of Rule 26 did not change this analysis.[132] The court deduced that subsection (b)(4) cannot be said to limit subsection (a)(2)'s disclosure requirements.[133] Likewise, the court stated that Rule 26(b)(3) merely placed a limitation on the "discovery of documents and tangible things, otherwise discoverable under subdivision (b)(1),"[134] which articulated a party's general right to discover all relevant materials.[135] Subsection (b)(3) did not place limitations on disclosure requirements of (a)(2), and the court believed it to be axiomatic that a general provision yields to a specific provision when there is no conflict.[136] Therefore, the court held that nothing in Rule 26(a)(2) "displaces or even limits a party's obligation under Rule 26(a)(2) to disclose information provided to its testifying experts."[137]

2. *Pre-Amendment Minority View*

In the pre-amendment minority view, all work product disclosed to your expert will be protected unless, of course, your opponent can show exceptional circumstances exist.

The court's decision in *Krisa v. Equitable Life Assurance Society*[138] is representative of the minority position taken by various courts.[139] Under the minority view, work product produced to an expert was not discoverable unless that party can show "exceptional circumstances."[140] In *Krisa*, Equitable denied Krisa's application for disability benefits under insurance policies issued to Krisa by Equitable.[141] Krisa contended that he was entitled to benefits because a medical condition rendered him "unable to pursue his chosen vocation of a litigation lawyer."[142] On March 10, 1999, Krisa wrote to the court requesting that Equitable be ordered to produce documents generated by or provided to Equitable's experts.[143] Equitable responded and contended that "the documents are outside the scope of permissible discovery of expert witnesses and covered by the work product privilege."[144]

With respect to work product containing communications from Equitable's counsel to the testifying expert witnesses, the court agreed.[145] Much like the approach taken by the court in *Regional Airport*, this court began with a discussion of the significant split among the courts that have addressed whether core attorney work product shared with a party's expert was discoverable.[146] The court acknowledged that several courts have held that the 1993 amendments to Rule 26(a)(2) were "designed to mandate full disclosure of those materials reviewed by an expert witness, regardless of whether they constitute opinion work product."[147] The court added, however, that other courts have rejected the reasoning of these courts based upon their finding that "nothing in any version of subdivisions (b)(3) and (b)(4), or the committee notes . . . suggests core attorney work product was discoverable under subdivision (b)(4)."[148] Accordingly, the protections provided an attorney's mental impressions and opinions by the Supreme Court in *Hickman v. Taylor*[149] were to be preserved. Because contrary language was not present in the rule, the court refused to permit the work-product doctrine to be abridged.[150]

The court sided with the minority position affirmatively set forth in *Bogosian*.[151] The court noted that the marginal value of the policy concerns[152] advanced by the "bright line" rule did not warrant overriding the strong policy against the disclosure of documents consisting of core work product.[153] For example, the court asserted that the "bright line" rule's policy of ensuring effective cross-examination can be equally achieved under the minority position by presenting one's own credible witness.[154] The court stated that:

> The risk of an attorney influencing an expert witness does not go unchecked in the adversarial system, for the reasonableness of an expert can be judged against the knowledge of the expert's field and is always subject to the scrutiny of other experts. Because the law requires expert testimony where the subject matter is outside the common knowledge of the finder of fact, the most effective and dependable manner of discrediting an opponent's expert is the presentation of a credible expert who can dispute, based upon authorities in that expert's field, the conclusions of the other's party.[155]

Lastly, the court stated that the majority's interpretation that Rule 26, which demands the production of all work product that is disclosed to its expert, ignores the language of Rule 26(b)(3).[156] Rule 26(b)(3) requires the production of documents containing work product only when the requesting party shows a necessity and undue hardship to obtain the substantial equivalent of such document by other means.[157] Consequently, the court stated, an interpretation of Rule 26 that mandates production of core work product disclosed to an expert would render the language in Rule 26(b)(3) superfluous.[158]

The position espoused in *Krisa* remains the minority position and its application is progressively shrinking. This may be because of the deep-seated skepticism displayed by some courts that many testifying experts are neither "independent" nor truly knowledgeable, but rather serve simply as conduits for the lawyers to present their own theories in the guise of expert testimony.[159] In deciding to use testifying and nontestifying experts, it is important to understand the degree to which judicial rulings on expert testimony may be influenced by judicial suspicions about the misuse of expert testimony. The court in *Karn v. Ingersoll Rand*[160] was clear on this issue. In *Karn*, the court cited an article that described testifying experts as "saxophones"—"the lawyer plays the tune, manipulating the expert as though the expert was the musical instrument on which the lawyer sounds the desired notes."[161] Similarly, the court in *Manufacturing Administration & Management Systems, Inc. v. ICT Group, Inc.*[162] was unmistakably suspicious when it stated that the attorney-expert relationship "provides fertile ground for improper influence," undermining the "independence" of the expert and mandatory disclosure of all attorney-client interactions reveals such improper influence and "cleanses any canker of corruption."[163]

3. *The 2010 Amendment to Rule 26(a): Finding a Middle Ground?*

On December 1, 2010, three amendments to Rule 26 became effective. The amendments aim to prevent inefficiencies that arise from the current discrepancies in the treatment of written materials created by testifying versus nontestifying experts, and to obviate the need for litigants to retain testifying and nontestifying experts to prepare for trial.[164] The first amendment adds section (b)(4)(B) to Rule 26, and makes all drafts of expert reports protected work product under Rules 26(b)(3)(A) and (B).[165] The second amendment changes the language of Rule 26(a)(2)(B)(ii) from "the data or other information considered by the witness" to "facts or data considered by the witness."[166] This change will likely permit attorneys to communicate freely with experts without fear of creating discoverable written materials adverse to the client's interest.[167] The committee notes state, however, that the disclosure obligation continues to extend to "any materials considered by" an expert, thus leaving the rule open to differing interpretations.[168] The third amendment adds section (b)(4)(C) to Rule 26.[169] This new section provides work-product protection for communications between experts and attorneys, except those that (1) relate to compensation, (2) identify facts or data provided by counsel and considered by the witness, or (3) identify assumptions provided by counsel and relied upon by the witness in forming his or her opinions.[170]

Further, the committee notes to Rule 26 affirmatively state that the changes to Rule 26(a)(2) and 26(b)(4) are intended to be complementary.[171] The notes also express that the new rules are intended to alter Rule 26(a) in those jurisdictions following the majority's bright-line rule.[172] More specifically, the committee notes state that the Rule 26 "amendment is intended to alter the outcome in cases that have relied on the 1993 formulation in requiring disclosure of all attorney-expert communications and draft reports."[173] The notes additionally state that the changes for Rule 26(b)(4) and Rule 26(a)(2)(B)(ii) "rest not on high theory but on the realities of actual experiences."[174] In other words, the committee contends that "routine discovery into attorney-expert communications and draft reports has had undesirable effects" including rising costs and less effective attorney-expert interactions."[175] The changes seek to allow an attorney to communicate freely with an expert without having to engage in time-consuming and wasteful measures to avoid the creation of a draft report.

On at least one occasion, a party has cited to the 2010 amendments to Rule 26(a) as authority for rejecting the majority rule.[176] In *Galvin v. Pepe*, plaintiffs identified an expert and, citing Rule 26(a)(2), provided defendants with a detailed written report of the expert's opinions and the bases and reasons for those opinions.[177] Some time later, defendant deposed the expert and subpoenaed certain documents to be produced at the deposition. The request demanded documents "including any email to a party, an attorney for a party or any non-party, regarding the subject investigation."[178] During the deposition, the expert testified that she received information regarding the case via e-mail and brought hard copies of at least two e-mails exchanged between herself and plaintiff's counsel.[179] Plaintiff's counsel objected to their production on the basis that they included work product.[180]

Pursuant to Rule 26(a)(2)(B), defendant moved to compel production of these and all other similar documents.[181] Plaintiff resisted the motion on the grounds that the e-mails are subject to work-product protection under Rule 26(b)(3)(A), not overcome by substantial need.[182] Plaintiff also asserted that the then proposed 2010 amendments to Rule 26(a) serve as additional authority to reject the majority rule.[183] The court ultimately granted defendant's motion to compel and decided not to make the proposed amendment to Rule 26 immediately applicable to this case.[184] The court found, "Whatever weight the statement of intent might of had on the court interpreting the proposed [Rule 26] in the future . . . it has little bearing on my interpretation of the existing form of Rule 26."[185]

Two recent cases highlight a difference of opinion as to the protections afforded experts who are not required to submit a Rule 26 report.[186] In *Graco, Inc. v. PMC Global, Inc.*,[187] defendant sought production of all communication between Graco's counsel and five employee experts who filed affidavits in support of Graco's motion for an injunction and in opposition to PMC's motion for summary judgment.[188] Graco refused to produce the requested documents, relying on the attorney-client privilege and the work-product doctrine.[189] Graco argued that Rule 26 does not require employee experts to submit a Rule 26 report, and that therefore the protections afforded by the privileges were not waived by using affidavits from the employee experts.[190] The court first concluded that the December 2010 amendments to Rule 26 applied to this dispute because the expert reports were not due until after the amendments' effective date.[191] The court reviewed the Advisory Committee Notes to conclude that the protection of Rule 26(b)(4) is also afforded to experts not required to submit a report.[192] The court also rejected PMC's argument that the work-product privilege had been waived by submitting the employee witness affidavits.[193]

In contrast, the court in *United States v. Sierra Pacific Industries*[194] held that the protections of Rule 26(b)(4) applied only to experts who were required to issue reports under Rule 26 (a)(1)(C)(2). The litigation arose from the "Moonlight Fire" of September 2007. The experts in question were employees of the U.S. Forestry Service and the California Department of Forestry and Fire Protection who investigated the fire and prepared a report documenting their findings as to origin and cause.[195] Sierra sought production of all communications between counsel and these witnesses after they were identified as experts by the government.[196] Noting that the expert reports were due by April 11, 2011, and the depositions were to occur thereafter, the court decided the issue under Rule 26 as amended in December 2010.[197] In a lengthy and detailed opinion, the court rejected the *Graco* concept and chose to apply the pre-amendment law to these experts.[198] The court explained that the protection afforded by Rule 26(b)(4) applied only to experts required to provide a report, and not to employee experts whose disclosure is more limited.[199] Because the government identified these witnesses as expert employees from whom no report was required, the court held that the protections afforded by Rule 26(b)(4) did not apply, and it ordered production of the requested documents as was required before Rule 26 was amended.[200]

The foregoing highlights the difficulty that courts may have in applying these recent rule changes. As of this writing, seven months after the effective date of the amendments, there are only a couple of substantive decisions under the amended Rule 26. Accordingly, it is important to understand the law in the jurisdiction where your case is venued and how those judges have interpreted the 2010 amendments to Rule 26.

IV. The Use of Dual-Role Experts

This section examines the impact that utilizing one expert for a dual consulting-testifying function has on the attorney-client and work-product protections. Additionally, it provides a discussion regarding issues of waiver of attorney-client privilege and work-product protections when the same company provides a consulting and testifying expert to assist in a piece of litigation.

Courts have generally held that "documents having no relation to the [consulting] expert's role as [testifying] expert need not be produced but that any ambiguity as to the role played by the expert when reviewing or generating documents should be resolved in favor of the party seeking discovery."[201] In other words, a privileged document will be preserved if it can be shown that an expert serving in a dual capacity, consulting and testifying, reviewed the document solely in his capacity as a consulting expert. A failure to clearly delineate whether the expert functions as a consulting or testifying expert will result in waiver. This standard, however, is not without dissention, as some courts have totally rejected the idea that an expert can serve as both a consultant and as a testifying expert.[202]

Construction Industry Services Corp. v. Hanover Insurance Co.[203] is an example of a case where the court strictly enforced the principle that documents "considered" by the expert in the production of his or her expert report must be produced. *Hanover* involved various discovery disputes, one of which was whether privileged documents must be produced just because they were reviewed by a testifying expert.[204]

Hanover sought the production of documents created and reviewed by Construction Services' consulting and testifying expert, Liegold.[205] Construction Services made two arguments in support of its claim that the documents were privileged and thus nondiscoverable: that the documents were protected by the attorney-client or work-product privileges and that those privileges had not been waived pursuant to Federal Rule of Civil Procedure 26(a)(2)(B) because the disputed documents related only to Liegold's role as consultant expert.[206]

Specifically, Construction Services argued that Liegold served as its accountant and it was in this capacity that he was consulted regarding the initial decision to bring the lawsuit.[207] The court ultimately sided with Hanover and ordered Construction Services to produce the documents created and reviewed by Liegold.[208] The court felt that Liegold's roles as consultant and as testifying expert were too intertwined and his creation and review of the documents too ambiguous. In so holding, the court discussed the "gray" area of the application of Rule 26 to a consultant-testifying expert.[209] The court noted an earlier decision in *B.C.F. Oil Refinery v. Consolidated Edison*,[210] which held that it "was conceivable that an expert could be retained to testify and in addition, to advise counsel outside of the subject of the testimony. Under such a circumstance it might be possible to claim a . . . privilege if this delineation were clearly made."[211] It also noted the *B.C.F. Oil* court's consideration of *Detweiler*

Trust v. Offenbecher[212] and its conclusion "that documents having no relationship to the expert's role as [a testifying] expert need not be produced but that any ambiguity as to the role played by the expert when reviewing or generating documents should be resolved in favor of the party seeking discovery."[213] Absent a clear distinction between the two roles, the court held, privileged and nonprivileged materials must be produced.[214]

Here, the court was unable to find a clear delineation between Liegold's role as a consulting and testifying expert. As a result of this ambiguity, the court resolved the issue in favor of complete disclosure. This result, the court stated, was mandated by the policies underlying the requirement that a testifying expert disclose all materials that he considered in reaching his opinion, and on the rule that the party seeking to compel the production of the document "should not have to rely on the [resisting party's] representation that the documents were not considered by the expert in forming his opinion."[215]

Other courts have considered whether an expert may act in a dual capacity as a consulting and testifying expert and have dismissed dual roles as an impossibility. *Furniture World v. D.A.V. Thrift Stores, Inc.*[216] is one such case. There, the plaintiff sought discovery of defendant's expert. The defendant contended that its expert was retained as a nontestifying expert consultant with respect to matters involving rebuttal of plaintiff's expert's testimony, and therefore, to seek discovery from its expert, plaintiff had to show "exceptional circumstances."[217] The court disagreed and stated:

> In my view, under the facts and circumstances of this case, a person initially selected to testify as an expert at trial cannot be shielded from questioning by later being also designated as a consultant expert and invoking the work product doctrine. Counsel must choose to designate an expert as either one who will testify at trial or consult with counsel. Having an expert who is both creates an unmanageable situation by requiring a question-by-question analysis of an expert witnesses' deposition testimony to determine whether the work product privilege applies.[218]

The dual designation negates the "exceptional circumstances" requirement. Accordingly, the expert could be deposed as a testifying expert.[219]

Courts similarly have also found an unclear delineation under circumstances where a consulting expert assisted a testifying expert from the same firm in his or her preparation of their opinion.[220] In a situation like this, one court has specifically stated that a litigant is "playing with fire."[221] *U.S. Fidelity & Guaranty Co. v. Braspetro Oil Services*[222] provides a good example of the impact this kind of relationship may have on the attorney-client privilege and the protection afforded work product. In this case, Braspetro furnished its consulting experts with 1.1 million documents, including privileged materials.[223] Braspetro's testifying and nontestifying experts were employed by the same firm and each had equal access to the produced documents.[224] There were no protections or practices in place to keep these documents from being considered by Braspetro's testifying experts.[225] In arguing this motion, Braspetro failed to meet its burden to identify the precise scope of the disclosure of documents to experts, including limitations placed on their use and the type of privilege asserted for those documents.[226]

Consequently, the court held that because experts within the same firm doubled as consulting and testifying experts, and because there was "no evidence supporting Braspetro's base assertion that certain documents were reviewed by the experts solely on a consultative capacity," all of the documents were discoverable.[227] Additionally, Braspetro's failure to present evidence that it tried to limit access to the documents only to the nontestifying expert contributed to this conclusion.[228] Rather, the record indicated "that at least two of the Braspetro's experts, and their staff, had access to the entire universe of defendant's documents for use in connection with the expert's reports and testimony."[229] There were no limitations placed on this access, which ultimately led to the court's finding that all the documents were "considered" by testifying experts and were, therefore, discoverable.[230]

More recently, the court applied the December 2010 amendments to Rule 26 in a case where an expert served in a dual role.[231] In *Sara Lee Corp. v. Kraft Foods, Inc.*, Sara Lee sued Kraft for falsely advertising its hot dogs.[232] Kraft retained an expert to conduct a survey as to one of Kraft's allegedly false ads, and to consult with its counsel on a survey about another allegedly false claim.[233] Sara Lee sought production of all of the expert's files, and Kraft objected to producing the file that related solely to the expert's nontestifying role.[234] The court reviewed the documents in question, and concluded that the expert was, in fact, acting in two roles for Kraft.[235] The court stated:

> Such expert-attorney communications arguably may have been discoverable under the pre-amendment Rule 26, but no more. None of the communications contain facts, data, or assumptions that [the expert] could have considered in assembling his expert report, and thus Defendants had no duty to disclose the communications and Plaintiff no right to discover them.[236]

The court also rejected Sara Lee's argument it had a "substantial need" for the documents because they might be used to impeach the expert as to the survey he did conduct.[237]

V. Testifying to Nontestifying: Redesignating an Expert Witness

Before the 2010 amendment to Rule 26, the law regarding the application of the attorney-client privilege and the work-product concept where a testifying party is redesignated from testifying to nontestifying were in conflict. The adoption of the 2010 amendment, however, should make this issue far less significant because the amendment limits the information that is now discoverable from a testifying expert.[238] Rule 26(b)(4)(C) provides extensive protection for attorney-expert communications irrespective of whether an expert is designated as testifying or nontestifying.[239] But a question still remains as to whether any discovery from a redesignated expert will be allowed. Clearly, nontestifying experts cannot be deposed.[240] But is discovery of portions of their files permitted? Even though the new rule differs from the perspective taken by courts in the past, that perspective may assist the courts in answering this question.

A leading treatise on the attorney-client privilege and the work-product doctrine asserts that "a party is deemed to have waived privilege as to documents provided to its named experts, that party may not avoid production of those documents under Rule 26(b)(4)(A)[241] later by changing the designations of that expert from 'testifying' to 'non-testifying.'"[242] In contrast, a number of courts have held that a party may prevent discovery from a consulting expert after his designation as a testifying expert is withdrawn.[243]

In this context, the underlying purposes of the pre-2010 amendment Rules 26(b)(4)(A) and 26(b)(4)(B) come into conflict. Rule 26(b)(4)(A) permits a party to depose any person who has been identified as an expert, and this provision permits open discovery with respect to privileged and nonprivileged materials considered by a testifying expert because of the necessity to assess the bases for an expert's opinion in preparing effective cross-examination.[244] Rule 26(b)(4)(B) seeks to protect the facts known and the opinions held by a nontestifying expert in the interest of fairness and to promote effective communication among the client, the attorney, and the consulting expert. Accordingly, an important question arises: Where does one provision cease operating and the other begin when a once-testifying expert is later redesignated a nontestifying expert? Some have argued that if an originally designated testifying expert is dropped as a trial witness before Rule 26(a)(2)(B) disclosures are produced, there is no longer the need to know what the expert considered in forming an opinion because the expert will not be testifying. Thus, there is no reason to cross-examine the expert, which then does away with the need to know what information the expert considered. A handful of courts, however, have disagreed with this line of argument and have held that redesignation does not change the fact that the attorney-client privilege is waived when privileged materials are provided to a testifying expert, which consequently makes the materials themselves discoverable.[245]

CP Kelco U.S. Inc. v. Pharmacia[246] provides a good example. Here, Pharmacia retained a testifying expert witness, Schnapf.[247] At Schnapf's deposition, CP Kelco learned that he reviewed documents that had not been produced despite the requirements under Rules 26(a)(2) and 26(b)(4).[248] Pharmacia acknowledged that Schnapf had in fact reviewed these documents but took the position that the documents were privileged.[249]

In response, CP Kelco brought a motion to compel production of these documents and to resume Schnapf's deposition.[250] At the same time this dispute was occurring, the magistrate judge issued a Report and Recommendation, which suggested that certain environmental claims in the case be dismissed.[251]

Subsequently, Pharmacia determined that it no longer required the service of Schnapf as a testifying witness and redesignated him as a nontestifying expert.[252] It asserted that Schnapf was now an expert "as to whom the controlling discovery provision is Federal Rule of Civil Procedure 26(b)(4)(B)."[253] According to Pharmacia, because it had not called Schnapf to the stand, he must be viewed as a nontestifying expert under Rule 26(b)(4)(B), and therefore further discovery pertaining to him, including document discovery, would be inappropriate.[254]

The magistrate judge accepted this argument,[255] basing her decision on the 1993 Advisory Committee Notes to Rule 26.[256] She concluded that attorney-client privilege was waived "when an expert testifies or is deposed."[257] Because Schnapf did not testify and was not deposed, the privilege applied. The district court disagreed.[258] It held that the magistrate judge's ruling was contrary to the law because of its implicit conclusion that a party's knowing waiver of the attorney-client privilege can somehow be "unwaived" by redesignating a testifying expert as a nontestifying expert.[259] "Waiver is a deliberate relinquishment of a right which must otherwise be claimed. Except as in limited circumstances not apposite here,[260] a right that is waived is not available to be picked up again as if it were a handy tool."[261] In the context of an assertion of privilege, the court stated the inviolability of the rule is of fundamental importance:[262] "It would be manifestly unfair to allow a party to use the privilege to shield the information which it had deliberately chosen to use offensively, as Pharmacia did in this instance when it used the allegedly privileged documents to arm its expert for testimony."[263] The court then stated that a privilege cannot be used as both a shield and a sword.[264]

Ultimately, the court did not accept Pharmacia's claim that the parties are free to invoke an already waived privilege simply by changing the designation of an expert from testifying to nontestifying: "It would be a perverse incentive to dilatory discovery practice if, because of the fortuitous timing of a tentative ruling on a partially dispositive motion, the Court were to allow a party to escape disclosure of documents it has shown to a testifying expert."[265]

Rule 26(b)(4)(D) seeks to protect all discovery from nontestifying witnesses absent a showing of exceptional circumstances.[266] The underlying policy of this provision stems from the necessity in litigation today to retain consulting nontestifying experts.[267] Consequently, courts have found it imperative that clients, as well as attorneys, have a level of confidence that privileged information, including attorney-client communications, will be preserved if shared with a consulting expert. Moreover, courts have frequently alluded to the promotion of fairness as a policy concern.[268] As a result, a contrary line of authority, which prohibits discovery of materials considered by a consulting expert once designated as a testifying expert, has risen.[269]

Frequently cited as representing this line of cases are *Callaway Golf Co. v. Dunlop Slazenger Group Americas*[270] and *NetJumper Software, L.L.C. v. Google, Inc.*[271] *Callaway* provides a discussion of authority establishing that a party may not discover information held by a nontestifying expert absent a showing of exceptional circumstances.[272] This case involved a discovery dispute that arose when Callaway advised Dunlop that it was withholding its expert and that it intended to replace him.[273] This information was conveyed a little over a week before the scheduled deposition of Callaway's original expert was to take place. Dunlop objected to the substitution and argued that it had the right to depose Callaway's redesignated expert to inquire into clearly relevant and discoverable information.[274] Relying on Rule 26(b)(4)(B) and case law interpreting the rule, Callaway argued that experts who are initially designated as testifying experts but are later withdrawn may not be deposed absent a showing of exceptional circumstances.[275]

The district court agreed. In its decision, the court first discussed the holdings in *Ross v. Burlington Northern Railroad Co.*[276] and *Dayton-Phoenix Group v. General Motors Corp.*[277] In *Ross*, the plaintiff designated his expert and revealed the subject matter of his testimony.[278] The plaintiff later withdrew the designation. In denying the defendant's motion to compel the expert's testimony the court held, "[S]ince plaintiff changed his mind before any expert testimony was given in this case, the witness never actually acted as a testifying expert."[279] The court in *Dayton-Phoenix* similarly held and relied on the following to support its conclusion:

> The Advisory Committee Notes to Rule 26(b)(4)(B) limit discovery to trial witnesses; the primary purpose of Rule 26(b)(4)(B) is to allow a party to prepare adequately for cross-examination at trial, and its purpose to promote fairness, which would not be accomplished by allowing access to the other's party's trial preparation.[280]

Moreover, absent exceptional circumstance the *Dayton-Phoenix* court refused to allow discovery held by the nontestifying expert.[281]

The court continued with its analysis by examining the holdings in *Mantolete v. Bolger*,[282] *In re Shell Oil Refinery*,[283] and *FMC Corp. v. Vendo Co.*[284] Each of these cases similarly expressed the importance of preserving the underlying policy concerns of Rule 26(b)(4)(B) and the lack of need for an exchange of information regarding nonwitness experts who act as consultants to counsel.[285] Additionally, the court relied on the holdings in *In re Shell Oil Refinery* and *FMC Corp.* for the proposition that exceptional circumstances must be shown to secure discovery from nontestifying experts, irrespective of the fact that the experts produced their reports or expressed opinions.[286] In the end, the court held that Dunlop failed to show that exceptional circumstances existed and, therefore, denied its motion to compel the deposition of Callaway's redesignated expert.

NetJumper Software, L.L.C. v. Google, Inc.[287] is similarly illustrative of the reluctance of certain courts to allow the discovery of the materials considered by a redesignated nontestifying expert absent considerable involvement in litigation. Here, the court distinguished the present facts from those in *CP Kelco* in finding that access to a nontestifying expert was not appropriate absent a showing of exceptional circumstances.[288] NetJumper informed Google that its designated testifying expert was terminated and redesignated as nontestifying expert.[289] Shortly thereafter, Google served the terminated expert with a subpoena duces tecum in an effort to discover the facts considered by the expert.[290] NetJumper objected on the ground that Rule 26(b)(4)(B) controlled and that the expert need not comply with the subpoena absent a showing of exceptional circumstances.[291] Google asserted that Rule 26(b)(4)(A) required the expert to comply regardless of NetJumper's redesignation.[292]

The court sided with NetJumper.[293] In doing so, the court based its decision on the fact that NetJumper's expert had not overly involved himself in the litigation.[294] The expert had not been deposed like the expert in *CP Kelco*, nor had he produced a report like the expert in *House v. Combined*.[295] Because he had not done so, the court felt it inappropriate to designate the expert under Rule 26(b)(4)(B) because the expert "will not testify, has never been deposed and has never produced a report."[296] Accordingly, "to promote fairness by precluding unreasonable access to an opposing party's diligent trial preparation" the court held that the expert was a nontestifying expert subject to the protections of Rule 26(b)(4)(B).[297] The court did add, however, that if the expert's deposition had been taken, access to his testimony would have been permitted.[298]

According to the holding in *NetJumper*, the distinction seems to lie in the level of involvement of the expert in the litigation. The weight of the authority discussed in *Callaway*, however, suggests that the mere reclassification of the expert as nontestifying is more persuasive. For example, in *In re Shell Oil Refinery* the consulting expert set forth his opinions in a preliminary report, which was issued pursuant to a court-ordered deadline, and still his deposition was not permitted to be taken because plaintiff failed to show that exceptional circumstances were present.[299] Similarly, in *FMC Corp.* the consulting experts were withdrawn after their reports and opinions had been provided and again their depositions were not permitted.[300] Accordingly, the level of involvement the expert had in the litigation plays only a minor role, while the expert's classification as testifying or nontestifying is generally the determinative factor. If the expert is designated a nontestifying consultant or expert, exceptional circumstances will likely have to be shown.[301] It is still possible, however, that an expert's involvement by way of producing a report, responding to discovery, or providing testimony may waive some protections.[302]

VI. Conclusion

The first question that you must answer before a consultant is provided with any materials is "Will this expert testify?" If the answer to that question is anything other than an unqualified "no," then you must exercise caution in what is shared with that expert, but substantially less caution because of the 2010 amendments to Rule 26, which became effective on December 1, 2010. Prior to the change in Rule 26, everything in a testifying expert's file, including materials that would otherwise be protected by the attorney-client privilege or the work-product doctrine set forth in Rule 26, was discoverable. The 2010 amendments are intended to abrogate this principle in the federal courts and limit what an expert must disclose. Thus you should consider, in advance of providing anything to the expert, exactly what you want the expert to consider, and whether that information falls into one of the categories of Rule 26(b)(4)(C).

If the role of the expert will be strictly interpretive, and the expert will not testify, it is likely that everything shared among the expert, the attorney, and the client will be protected by the attorney-client privilege. And even if the expert is working outside the protections afforded by the attorney-client privilege, if the expert will not testify, his or her work product should not be discoverable absent a showing of exceptional circumstances under Rule 26.

Notes

1. George Brent Mickum IV & Luther L. Hajek, *Guise, Contrivance, or Artful Dodging?: The Discovery Rules Governing Testifying Employee Experts*, 24 Rev. Litig. 301 (2005) (citing Samuel R. Gross, *Expert Evidence*, 1991 Wis. L. Rev. 1113, 1119).
2. *See* United States v. Nobles, 422 U.S. 225, 238 (1975) ("One of [the] realities [of litigation] is that attorneys often must rely on the assistance of [an expert consultant] in preparation for trial."); *see also* Edward J. Imwinkelried, *The Applicability of the Attorney-Client Privilege to Non-Testifying Experts: Reestablishing the Boundaries Between the Attorney-Client Privilege and the Work Protect Protection*, 68 Wash. U. L.Q. 19 (1990) (stating that by sending the client to an expert without the protection of the privilege, the attorney might well "be stick[ing the client's] head in a noose").
3. Mickum & Hajek, *supra* note 1, at 349 (citing Reed v. Baxter, 134 F.3d 351, 356 (6th Cir. 1998)). *See also* 8 James H. Wigmore, Evidence in Trials at Common Law § 2292, at 554 (James McNaughton rev. ed. 1961 & Supp. 1996).
4. Wigmore, *supra* note 3, at 554.
5. *Reed*, 134 F.3d at 356.
6. *See infra* notes 164–75.
7. *See id.*
8. *See* United States v. Kovel, 296 F.2d 918, 922 (2d Cir. 1961) ("What is vital to the privilege is that the communication be made in confidence for the purpose of obtaining legal advice from the lawyer."); *In re* Grand Jury Subpoenas, 179 F. Supp. 2d 270, 283 (S.D.N.Y. 2001) (citing United States v. Schwimmer, 892 F.2d 237, 243 (2d Cir. 1989), *cert. denied*, 502 U.S. 810 (1991); United States v. El Paso Co., 682 F.2d 530, 541 (5th Cir. 1982); United States v. Judson, 322 F.2d 460 (9th Cir. 1963); *In re* Copper Mkt. Antitrust Litig., 200 F.R.D. 213, 217 (S.D.N.Y. 2001) (citing Sup. Ct. Standard 503(b)); Exp.-Imp. Bank of U.S. v. Asia Pulp & Paper Co., 232 F.R.D. 103, 113 (S.D.N.Y. 2005); Andritz, Sprout-Bauer, Inc. v. Beazer E., Inc., 174 F.R.D. 609, 632 (M.D. Pa. 1997) ("Disclosure to agents retained by counsel to assist him or her in advising the client and handling legal matters does not operate as a waiver. The privilege attaches to agents and representatives of counsel whose services are necessary for effective representation of the client's interests."); United States v. Alvarez, 519 F.2d 1036, 1045–46 (3d Cir. 1975) (use of psychiatrist to assist attorney); United States v. Cote, 456 F.2d 142, 144 (8th Cir. 1972) (use of accountant to assist attorney); *see also* Imwinkelried, *supra* note 2, at 23.

9. *See* Golden Trade v. Lee Ansarel Co., 143 F.R.D. 514, 518 (S.D.N.Y. 1992).
10. Farmaceutisk Laboratorium v. Reid Rowell, Inc., 864 F. Supp. 1274 (N.D. Ga. 1994) (stating that independent consultant was so meaningfully associated with corporation that it could be considered insider for purposes of privilege). *See also, e.g.*, Benedict v. Amaducci, No. 92 Civ 5239 (KMW), 1995 U.S. Dist. LEXIS 573, *3–4 (S.D.N.Y. Jan. 18, 1995) (consultant); Kevlick v. Goldstein, 724 F.2d 844, 849 (1st Cir. 1984) (client's father); Foseco Int'l v. Fireline Inc., 546 F. Supp. 22, 25 (N.D. Ohio 1982) (patent agent); Atmel Corp. v. St. Paul Fire & Marine Co., 409 F. Supp. 2d 1180, 1181–82 (N.D. Cal. 2005) (insurance broker); Harkobusic v. Gen. Am., 31 F.R.D. 264, 265 (W.D. Pa. 1962) (brother-in-law).
11. *See, e.g.*, Martin v. Bally's Park Place Hotel & Casino, 983 F.3d 1252 (3d Cir. 1993) (technical report prepared by a consulting firm was protected from discovery because it was prepared in anticipation of litigation by a party's representative); Sprague v., Dir., Office of Workers' Comp. Programs, 688 F.2d 862, 869–70 (1st Cir. 1982) (opinion letter setting forth expert's medical opinion was protected because it was prepared to advise counsel).
12. *See Kovel*, 296 F.2d 918, 922; *In re Grand Jury Subpoenas*, 179 F. Supp. 2d at 283; *El Paso Co.*, 682 F.2d at 541; *In re Copper Mkt. Antitrust Litig.*, 200 F.R.D. at 217; *Exp.-Imp. Bank of U.S.*, 232 F.R.D. at 113; *Andritz, Sprout-Bauer, Inc.*, 174 F.R.D. at 632; *Alvarez*, 519 F.2d at 1045–46; *Cote*, 456 F.2d at 144.
13. *See* Ferko v. NASCAR, 218 F.R.D. 125, 134 (E.D. Tex. 2003) (citing *In re* Auclair, 961 F.2d 65, 69 (5th Cir. 1992); United States v. Ackert, 169 F.3d 136, 139 (2d Cir. 1999)).
14. *See In re* Alliance Constr. Solutions, Inc. v. Dep't of Corr., 54 P.3d 861, 869 (Colo. 2002).
15. *Ferko*, 218 F.R.D. at 125 (citing *El Paso Co.*, 682 F.2d at 540).
16. *Kovel*, 296 F.2d at 922.
17. *Id.*
18. "A party may, through interrogatories or by deposition, discover facts known, or opinions held by an expert who has been retained or specially employed by another party in anticipation of litigation or preparation for trial and who is not expected to be called as a witness at trial, only as provided in Rule 35(b) or upon a showing of exceptional circumstance under which is impracticable for the party seeking discovery to obtain facts or opinions on the same subject by other means." FED. R. CIV. P. 26(b)(4)(B).
19. 296 F.2d 918 (2d Cir. 1961).
20. *Id.* at 920–21.
21. *Id.* at 921.
22. *Id.* at 922.
23. *Id.*
24. *Id.*
25. *Id.*
26. 16 F.3d 929 (8th Cir. 1994).
27. *Id.* at 939–40.
28. *Reproduced in* 3 J. MCLAUGHLIN, J. WEINSTEIN & M. BERGER, WEINSTEIN'S FEDERAL EVIDENCE ch. 503 (2d ed. 2007).
29. *Id.*
30. 132 F.R.D. 234 (N.D. Cal. 1990).
31. 16 F.3d at 937. For an extensive discussion of the application of *Bieter* to another fact situation, see *Western Resources Inc. v. Union Pacific Railroad Co.*, No.

00-2043-CM, 2002 WL 181494 (D. Kan. Jan. 31, 2002) (concluding that a consultant was within the attorney-client privilege, but that the privilege had been waived by disclosure of the consultant's work product to Western's testifying expert).

32. 852 F. Supp. 156 (E.D.N.Y. 1994).
33. *Id.* at 161.
34. *Id.*
35. *Id.* at 162; *see also* United States v. Bell, No. C94-204342, 1994 WL 665295 (N.D. Cal. Nov. 9, 1994) (wherein the court analyzed an accountant's role under both the attorney-client privilege and the work-product doctrine).
36. 218 F.R.D. 125 (E.D. Tex. 2003).
37. *Id.* at 132.
38. *Id.* at 129.
39. *Id.* at 130.
40. *Id.* at 131–32.
41. *Id.*
42. *Id.* (citing United States v. El Paso Co., 682 F.2d 530, 541 (5th Cir. 1982); United States v. Kovel, 296 F.2d 918, 922 (2d Cir. 1961)).
43. *Id.* at 138–39.
44. *Id.* at 139.
45. *Id.* at 139–40. This was also the case with respect to the documents given to and communications with Ernst & Young. *Id.*
46. *Id.* at 139–40.
47. *Id.* at 139.
48. *See id.* ("An attorney need not hire an accountant or financial professional solely for a particular lawsuit or discovery dispute to gain protection under the attorney-client privilege."). *See also* United States v. Pipkins, 528 F.2d 559, 562 (5th Cir. 1976).
49. *Ferko*, 218 F.R.D. at 139.
50. *Id.*
51. *Id.*
52. *Id.* (citing Edward M. Spiro & Caroline Rule, *"Kovel" Experts Cloaked by Attorney Client Privilege*, N.Y. L.J., Feb. 22, 1994, at S1, S10 (stating that privilege has been applied to "communications with a psychiatrist assisting a lawyer in forming a defense, a bail bondsman, and polygraph operator").
53. *See also, e.g.*, Ariz. R. Civ. P. 26(b)(4)(B); D.C. R. Civ. P. 26(b)(4); Fla. R. Civ. P. 1.280(b)(4)(B); Ill. S. Ct. R. 2001(b)(3); Minn. R. Civ. P. 26.02(d)(2); Ohio R. Civ. P. 26(B)(4); Pa. R. Civ. P. 4003.5(a)(3).
54. Mickum & Hajek, *supra* note 1, at 310 (citing Marine Petroleum Co v. Champlin Petroleum Co., 641 F.2d 984 (D.C. Cir. 1980) (requiring that the information must not be available from other sources); Grindell v. Am. Motors Corp., 108 F.R.D. 94, 95 (W.D.N.Y. 1985) (suggesting the burden is not where the information was discoverable from the retaining party); Crocket v. Va. Folding Box Co., 61 F.R.D. 312, 320–321 (E.D. Va. 1974) (holding that information sought must be material to the cause of action). *See also* Moore U.S.A. Inc. v. Std. Register Co., 206 F.R.D. 72 (W.D.N.Y. 2001); *In re* Shell Oil Refinery, 132 F.R.D. 437, 442 (E.D. La. 1990), *clarified by* 134 F.R.D. 148 (E.D. La. 1990); Hartford Fire Ins. Co. v. Pure Air on the Lake Ltd. P'ship, 154 F.R.D. 202 (N.D. Ind. 1993).
55. *Hartford Fire Ins. Co.*, 154 F.R.D. at 208 (N.D. Ind. 1993) (citing Roesberg v. Johns-Mansville Corp., 85 F.R.D. 292 (E.D. Pa. 1980)).

56. Upon showing exceptional circumstances the opposing party is entitled to know only facts observed by the expert. *See, e.g.*, 800 Front St. Corp. v. Travelers Prop. Cas. Co. of Am., No. CV 06-500 (LDW) (ARL), 2006 U.S. Dist. LEXIS 84160 (E.D.N.Y. Nov. 20, 2006). *See also, e.g.*, Delcastor v. Vail, 108 F.R.D. 405 (D. Colo. 1985) (compelling deposition of consulting expert who investigated a mudslide in part because conditions at the site had changed).
57. *In re* Polymedica Corp., 235 F.R.D. at 33 ("[P]laintiffs have not shown that the cost of discovery are so great as to make it impracticable for them to obtain the information by other means and thus warrant an exception to the Rule."); *see also In re* Agent Orange, 105 F.R.D. 577, 581 (E.D.N.Y. 1985).
58. Long-Term Capital Holdings, No. 01-CV-1290, 2003 WL 21269586 (D. Conn. May 6, 2003); *see also* Herman v. Marine Midland Bank, 207 F.R.D. 26, 30–32 (W.D.N.Y. 2002); Derrickson v. Circuit City Stores, Inc., No. DKC 95-3296, 1999 U.S. Dist. LEXIS 21100, at *18 (D. Md. Mar. 19, 1999); *Hartford Fire Ins. Co.*, 154 F.R.D. at 208; David S. Gray, *Expert Discovery in the Eighth Circuit*, 122 F.R.D. 35, 39 (1988).
59. 175 F.R.D. 34 (S.D.N.Y. 1997).
60. *Bank Brussels*, 175 F.R.D. at 41–42.
61. *Id.* at 38.
62. *Id.*
63. *Id.* at 44.
64. *Id.*
65. *Id.*
66. *Id.*
67. *Id.*
68. *Id.* at 45.
69. *Id.* at 44–45.
70. *Id.* at 42.
71. *Id.* at 43.
72. *Id.*
73. *Id.* at 44–45 (stating also that "one of plaintiff's officers has conceded that it would be more difficult now to reconstruct AroChem's collateral position as of December 1991 than it was for Andersen to reconstruct that collateral position when it conducted its work").
74. *Id.* at 40 ("no one was assigned to watch over the removal and copying of documents").
75. *Id.*
76. *See, e.g.*, Braun v. Lorillard, Inc., 84 F.R.D. 230, 236–37 (7th Cir. 1996) (holding that consultant's facts and opinion regarding asbestos contamination were discoverable because he destroyed the only lung tissue available for purposes of testing).
77. Fed. R. Civ. P. 26 (1987).
78. Fed. R. Civ. P. 26(a)(2)(B)(i) (1993).
79. Fed. R. Civ. P. 26(a)(2)(B)(ii) (1993).
80. Fed. R. Civ. P. 26(b)(4)(a) (1993).
81. For an example of a federal court of appeals decision, see *In re Pioneer Hi-Bred International, Inc.*, 238 F.3d 1370, 1375 (Fed. Cir. 2001) (agreeing with the district court that the attorney-client and work-product protection has been waived by the disclosure of the confidential communications to expert witnesses). For examples of federal district court decisions, *see* Synthes Spine Co., L.P. v. Walden, 232 F.R.D. 460, 463–64 (E.D. Pa. 2005); American Fidelity Assurance Co. v. Boyer, 225

F.R.D. 520, 522 (D.S.C. 2004) ("[I]t is essential during pretrial discovery that the parties be able to discover not only what the opposing expert's opinions are, but also the manner in which they were arrived at, what was considered in doing so, and whether this was done as a result of an objective consideration of the facts, or directed by an attorney advocating a particular position"); *Baxter Diagnostic, Inc. v. AVL Scientific Corp.*, No. CV 91-4178 RG (Ex), 1993 WL 390674, at *1 (C.D. Cal. Aug. 6. 1993); *Vitalo v. Cabot Corp.*, 212 F.R.D. 478, 479 (E.D. Pa. 2002) ("Rule 26(a)(2)(B) . . . vitiates a claim for attorney work product with respect to any information considered by a party's expert, whether or not relied upon by that expert."); and *In re McRae*, 295 B.R. 676, 679 (Bankr. N.D. Fla. 2003) (stating that materials furnished to testifying expert must be disclosed because "plain meaning of Rule 26(a)(2) trumps protections afforded by attorney-client privilege and work product doctrine"). *See also* PAUL RICE, ATTORNEY-CLIENT PRIVILEGE IN THE UNITED STATES § 9:33 (2005) (when an expert witness considers confidential attorney-client communications in developing her testimony, offering of opinions constitutes waiver of the attorney-client privilege for those communications); CHRISTOPHER B. MUELLER & LAIRD C. KIRKPATRICK, MODERN EVIDENCE § 5.10, at 574 (1995) ("Experts hired to testify are generally not viewed as representatives of the client for purposes of the privilege because their communications are subject to disclosure at trial and therefore can not be confidential.").

82. State courts have also held that disclosure of confidential attorney-client communications to a testifying expert will waive the privilege.

California	*See* CAL. EVID. CODE § 912 (a) (2010). *See also* Nat'l Steel Prods. Co. v. Superior Court, 210 Cal. Rptr. 535 (Cal. Ct. App. 1985) (holding that expert report is discoverable when related to the subject matter of the expert's prospective testimony because expert's prospective testimony would disclose a significant portion of privileged communications to the expert).
Colorado	Gall v. Jamison (*In re* Gall), 44 P.3d 233, 234 (Colo. 2002) (reviewing federal authority and holding that privileged material loses its protected status once disclosed to a testifying expert).
Illinois	People v. Wagener, 752 N.E.2d 430, 435 (Ill. 2001) (stating that defendant waived any attorney-client privilege by giving his testifying expert witness the police report containing statements regarding his conversation about his attorney) (citing People v. Knuckles, 650 N.E.2d 974 (Ill. 1995)).
Missouri	*See* MO. SUP. CT. R. 56.01(4) (2010). *See, e.g.*, Tracy v. Danrund, 30 S.W.3d 831, 836 (Mo. 2000) (stating that the Supreme Court of Missouri had adopted a "bright line rule" requiring that "all material given to a testifying expert must, if requested, be disclosed." Additionally, the court stated that attorney-client privilege will be waived when documents containing such information are produced to a testifying expert).
Texas	*See* TEX. R. CIV. P. 192.3(e) (2010). *See also In re* Christus Spohn Hosp. Kleberg, 222 S.W.3d 434, 437–39 (Tex. 2007) (analyzing TEX. R. CIV. P. 192.3(e)(b), which mandates the production of all documents "that have been provided to, [or] reviewed by" a testifying expert. The court also analyzed the rule's similarities to FED. R. CIV. P. 26.).

83. *See* Stephen D. Easton, *Ammunition for the Shoot-Out with Hired Gun's Hired Gun: A Proposal for Full Expert Witness Disclosure*, 32 ARIZ. ST. L.J. 465 (2000) (listing jurisdictions that have retained the pre-1993 versions of the Federal Rules of Civil Procedure 26(a) and 26(b)(4), which include, for example, D.C. R. CIV. P. 26(a), (b)(4); MINN. R. CIV. P. 26.02(a), (d); OHIO R. CIV. P. 26(A), (B)(4); PA. R. CIV. P. 4003.5).
84. A few states have adopted procedural rules or statutes that mirror the 1993 amendments to Federal Rules of Civil Procedure 26(a)(2) and 26(b)(4): *see, e.g.*, COLO. R. CIV. P. 26(a)(2), (b)(4); WASH. R. CIV. P. 26(a), (b)(4). Some jurisdictions appear to have adopted provisions that track some, but not all, of the provisions in the 1993 amendments to Federal Rules of Civil Procedure 26(a)(2) and 26(b)(4). The majority of those jurisdictions allow for the deposition of expert witnesses as in Rule 26(b)(4), but do not require parties to submit expert witness reports as in Rule 26(a)(2). *See, e.g.*, ARIZ. R. CIV. P. 26(a), (b)(4); FLA. R. CIV. P. 1.280(a), (b)(4); MICH. R. CIV. P. 2.302(A), (B)(4); N.J. R. CIV. P. 4:10-2(a), (d); TEX. R. CIV. P. 166b(1), (2)(e); WIS. R. CIV. P. 804.01(1), (2)(d). At least two jurisdictions appear to have adopted some form of the Rule 26(a)(2) requirements for the submission of expert witness reports, but have restricted the allowance of expert witness depositions as in Rule 26(b)(4). *See, e.g.*, NEV. R. CIV. P. 26(b)(5); N.Y. C.P.L.R. § 3101 (McKinney 1998).
85. *See* FED. R. CIV. P. 702.
86. Mickum & Hajek, *supra* note 1, at 310.
87. Rule 26(a)(2)(B) provides:

> *Witnesses Who Must Provide a Written Report.* Unless otherwise stipulated or ordered by the court, this disclosure must be accompanied by a written report—prepared and signed by the witness—if the witness is one retained or specially employed to provide expert testimony in the case or one whose duties as the party's employee regularly involve giving expert testimony. The report must contain:
>
> (i) a complete statement of all opinions the witness will express and the basis and reasons for them;
>
> (ii) the facts or data considered by the witness in forming them;
>
> (iii) any exhibits that will be used to summarize or support them;
>
> (iv) the witness's qualifications, including a list of all publications authored in the previous 10 years;
>
> (v) a list of all other cases in which, during the previous 4 years, the witness testified as an expert at trial or by deposition; and
>
> (vi) a statement of the compensation to be paid for the study and testimony in the case.

88. *See* sources cited *supra* note 55.
89. *See generally* FED. R. CIV. P. 26 advisory committee's note (2010).
90. *See* FED. R. CIV. P. 26(a)(2)(B).
91. *See* FED. R. CIV. P. 26(b)(4) (1993). *See also* Duke Oishi, *A Piece of Mind for Peace of Mind; Federal Discoverability of Opinion Work Product Provided to Expert Witnesses and Its Implications in Hawaii*, 24 U. HAW. L. REV. 859, 868 (2002) (addressing dif-

ferences between pre-1993 expert discovery rules and post-1993 expert discovery rules).

92. "Given this obligation of disclosure, litigant should no longer be able to argue that materials furnished to their experts to be used in forming their opinions—whether or not ultimately relied upon by the expert—are privileged or otherwise protected from disclosure when such persons are testifying or being deposed." FED. R. CIV. P. 26 (a)(2)(B) advisory committee's note (2010).
93. 238 F.3d 1370 (D.C. Cir. 2001).
94. *Id.* at 1372.
95. *Id.*
96. *Id.*
97. *Id.*
98. *Id.* at 1373.
99. *Id.*
100. 238 F.3d at 1372.
101. *Id.* at 1375.
102. 232 F.R.D. 460 (E.D. Pa. 2005).
103. *Id.* ("Prior to 1993, parties were limited both in what they could discover from testifying experts and in how they could obtain this discovery. Expert testimony was only discoverable if 'known' and relied on by the expert.").
104. *Id.* (citing, e.g., Amway Corp. v. P&G, No. 1:98 cv 726, 2001 U.S. Dist. LEXIS 5317, at *1 (W.D. Mich. Apr. 17, 2001) (stating that documents supplied to testifying expert, but not read, reviewed, or considered in forming opinions, were not discoverable under Rule 26(a)(2)(B); Vitalo v. Cabot Corp., 212 F.R.D. 472, 474 (E.D. Pa. 2002) (defining "consider" in Rule 26(a)(2)(B) as reflecting on, reviewing, or using even if ultimately rejected by expert). *See also* Simon Prop. Grp. L.P. v. mySimon, Inc., 194 F.R.D. 644, 647 (S.D. Ind. 2000) (stating there is "no distinction between reviewing a document and considering a document" because such a distinction "could become to easy to dodge"); *In re* Tri-State Outdoor Media Grp., Inc., 283 B.R. 358, 364–65 (M.D. Ga. 2002) ("When an expert has read or reviewed privileged materials before or in connection with formulating their opinion, the expert witness is deemed to have 'considered' the materials to satisfy Rule 26(a)(2)(B).").
105. *Id. See also* Musselman v. Phillips, 176 F.R.D. 194, 202 (D. Md. 1997) (finding that the act of supplying a document to a testifying expert creates a rebuttable presumption that the expert "considered" it, shifting the burden to the party who retained the expert to prove that the document was not considered and therefore does not fall within the mandatory disclosure provision in Rule 26(a)(2)(B)).
106. *Id.*
107. *Id.* (citing *Musselman*, 176 F.R.D. at 198 (outlining policy considerations behind pro-discovery interpretation of Rule 26(a)(2)(B))). *See also* Gall, 44 P.3d at 234 (stating that jury is entitled to know what influenced the expert and opposing counsel must be provided with that information to conduct an adequate cross-examination). *See also* Reg'l Airport Auth. v. LFG, LLC, 460 F.3d 697, 717 (6th Cir. 2006) ("Rule 26 creates a bright-line rule mandating disclosure of all documents . . . given to testifying experts.").
108. Mickum & Hajek, *supra* note 1, at 351 (citing *In re Pioneer Hi-Bred Int'l, Inc.*, 238 F.3d at 1375; *CP Kelco*, 213 F.R.D. at 179; S. Scrap Material Co. v. Fleming, No. 01-2554 Section "M" (3), 2003 U.S. Dist. LEXIS 10815, at *73 (E.D. La.

June 18, 2003); QST Energy, Inc. v. Mervyn's & Target Corp., No. C-00-1699-MJJ (EDL), 2001 U.S. Dist. LEXIS 23266, at *8–10 (N.D. Cal. May 14, 2001) (holding that the right to attorney-client privilege is waived by disclosing confidential communications to experts); *In re Tri-State*, 283 B.R. 358, at 364–65 (holding that testimony at trial of experts on confidential information waives the privilege).

109. B.C.F. Oil Ref. Co. v. Consol. Edison Co., 171 F.R.D. 57, 62 (S.D.N.Y 1997).
110. *See, e.g.*, United States v. Kovel, 296 F.2d 918, 922 (2d Cir. 1961); *In re* Grand Jury Subpoenas, 179 F. Supp. 2d 270, 283 (S.D.N.Y. 2001); United States v. El Paso Co., 682 F.2d 530, 541 (5th Cir. 1982); *In re* Copper Mkt. Antitrust Litig., 200 F.R.D. 213, 217 (S.D.N.Y. 2001); Exp.-Imp. Bank of U.S. v. Asia Pulp & Paper Co., 232 F.R.D. 103, 113 (S.D.N.Y. 2005); Andritz, Sprout-Bauer, Inc. v. Beazer E., Inc., 174 F.R.D. 609, 632 (M.D. Pa. 1997); United States v. Alvarez, 519 F.2d 1036, 1045–46 (3d Cir. 1975) (use of psychiatrist to assist attorney); United States v. Cote, 456 F.2d 142, 144 (8th Cir. 1972). *See also* TV-3, Inc. v. Royal Ins. Co., 194 F.R.D. 585, 589 (S.D. Miss. 2000) (stating that correspondence between expert witnesses and counsel was discoverable, notwithstanding defendant's work-product objection); Simon Prop. Grp. L.P. v. mySimon, Inc., 194 F.R.D. 644, 647 (S.D. Ind. 2000) ("[A]n intentional disclosure of opinion work product to a testifying expert effectively waives the work product privilege.").
111. 738 F.2d 587, 595 (3d Cir. 1984).
112. *See, e.g.*, Krisa v. Equitable Life Assur. Soc'y, 196 F.R.D. 254 (M.D. Pa. 2000); Haworth v. Herman Miller, Inc., 162 F.R.D. 289, 294 (W.D. Mich. 1995); Smith v. Transducer Tech., Inc., No. 1995-28, 2000 U.S. Dist. LEXIS 17212 (D.V.I. Nov. 2, 2000); Ladd Furniture v. Ernst & Young, No. 2:95CV00403, 1998 U.S. Dist. LEXIS 17345, at *45 (M.D.N.C. Aug. 27, 1998) (stating it was "persuaded that it should follow the line of cases in which other courts have found opinion work product to be protected even when it was considered by an expert in forming his opinion"); Helton v. Kincaid, No. CA2004-08-099, 2005 Ohio 2794 (Ohio Ct. App. June 6, 2005).
113. FED. R. CIV. P. 26 advisory committee's note (2010).
114. 460 F.3d 697, 717 (6th Cir. 2006).
115. The Comprehensive Environmental Response, Compensation, and Liability Act (CERCLA), 42 U.S.C. §§ 9601–9675, permits private-party property owners to recover from prior private-party property owners certain costs associated with the cleanup of contamination caused by the prior owners, where the cleanup costs were "necessary." "Necessary" costs means they were incurred in response to a threat to human health or the environment, *see* U.S.C. § 9607(a)(4)(B), and "consistent" with the National Oil and Hazardous Substances Pollution Contingency Plan, *see* 42 U.S.C. § 9607(a).
116. *Reg'l Airport*, 460 F.3d at 700–01.
117. *Id.* at 702.
118. *Id.*
119. *Id.*
120. *Id.* at 713–17.
121. *Id.* at 715.
122. *Id.*
123. *Id.* at 714 (citing Haworth, Inc. v. Herman Miller, Inc., 162 F.R.D. 289, 292–96 (W.D. Mich. 1995); Smith v. Transducer Tech. Inc., 197 F.R.D. 260, 261–62 (D.V.I.

2000); Estate of Moore v. R.J. Reynolds Tobacco Co., 194 F.R.D. 659, 663–64 (S.D. Iowa 2000)).

124. *Id.* (citing *In re* Pioneer Hi-Bred Int'l, Inc., 238 F.3d 1370, 1375 (Fed. Cir. 2001); Karn v. Ingersoll Rand, 168 F.R.D. 633, 637–41 (N.D. Ind. 1996); Gall v. Jamison (*In re* Gall), 44 P.3d 233, 238–39 (Colo. 2002); *cf.* Fid. Nat'l Title Ins. Co. of N.Y. v. Intercounty Nat'l Title Ins. Co., 412 F.3d 745, 751 (7th Cir. 2005)).
125. *Reg'l Airport*, 460 F.3d at 715.
126. *Id.*
127. *Id.* at 716.
128. *Id.*
129. *Id.*
130. Upon exceptional circumstances or as provided in Rule 35(b), "a party may . . . discover facts known or opinions held by an expert who has been retained or specially employed by another party in anticipation of litigation preparation for trial and who is not expected to be called as a witness at trial." *See* FED. R. CIV. P. 26(b)(4)(B).
131. FED. R. CIV. P. 26(b)(3).
132. *Reg'l Airport*, 460 F.3d at 715-16. *See also* Karn v. Ingersoll Rand, 168 F.R.D. 633, 639 (N.D. Ind. 1996) ("New Rule 26 and its supporting commentary reveal that the drafted considered the imperfect alignment between 26(b)(3) and 26(b)(4) under the old Rule, and clearly resolved it by providing that the requirements of (a)(2) 'trump' any assertion of work product privilege.").
133. *Reg'l Airport*, 460 F.3d at 715.
134. Parties may obtain discovery regarding any matter, not privileged, that is relevant to the claim or defense of any party, including the existence, description, nature, custody, condition and location of any books, documents, or other tangible things and the identity and location of persons having knowledge of any discoverable matter. *See* FED. R. CIV. P. 26(b)(1).
135. *Reg'l Airport*, 460 F.3d at 716.
136. *Id.*
137. *Id.*
138. 196 F.R.D. 254 (M.D. Pa. 2000).
139. *See also, e.g.*, Bogosian v. Gulf Oil Corp., 738 F.2d 587, 594 (3d Cir. 1984); Haworth v. Herman Miller, Inc., 162 F.R.D. 289, 295 (W.D. Mich. 1995); Pritchard v. Dow Agro Scis., 263 F.R.D. 277, 293 (W.D. Pa. 2009); Dominguez v. Syntex Labs., Inc., 149 F.R.D. 158, 159 (S.D. Ind. 1993); Smith v. Transducer Tech. Inc., 197 F.R.D. 260, 261–62 (D.V.I. 2000); Estate of Moore v. R.J. Reynolds Tobacco Co., 194 F.R.D. 659, 663–64 (S.D. Iowa 2000). *But see also* Occulto v. Adamar of N.J., 125 F.R.D. 611, 612 (D.N.J. 1989) (balancing policies underlying the work-product doctrine and liberal discovery in a case-specific fashion); All W. Pet Supply Co. v. Hill's Pet Prod. Div., 152 F.R.D. 634, 639 (D. Kan. 1993) (stating that the rule requiring discovery of material *considered* by a testifying expert "does not compel the productions of the documents that transmitted information to the expert, which may well, as here, contain protected work product other than date or information") (emphasis in original).
140. *See, e.g., Krisa*, 196 F.R.D. at 292–94. *See also* FED. R. CIV. P. 26(b)(4)(B).
141. 196 F.R.D. at 255.
142. *Id.*
143. *Id.*

144. *Id.*
145. *Id.* at 260.
146. *Id.* at 258 (citing B.C.F. Oil Ref. Co. v. Consol. Edison Co., 171 F.R.D. 57, 64 (S.D.N.Y 1997)). *See also* Reg'l Airport Auth. v. LFG, LLC, 460 F.3d 697, 714 (6th Cir. 2006).
147. *Krisa*, 196 F.R.D. at 258–59.
148. *Id.* at 259.
149. 329 U.S. 495, 510–11 (1947) ("Historically, a lawyer is an officer of the court and is bound to work for the advancement of justice while faithfully protecting the rightful interest of his client. In performing his various duties, however, it is essential that a lawyer work with a certain degree of privacy, free from unnecessary intrusion by opposing parties and their counsel. Proper preparation of a client's case demands that he assemble information, sift what he considers to be the relevant from the irrelevant facts, prepare his legal theories and plan his strategy without undue and needless interference. That is the historical and the necessary way in which lawyers act within the framework of our system of jurisprudence to promote justice and to protect their client's interests.").
150. *Krisa*, 196 F.R.D. at 259–60.
151. Bogosian v. Gulf Oil Corp., 738 F.2d 587, 595 (3d Cir. 1984).
152. *Krisa*, 196 F.R.D. at 258 (citing Karn v. Ingersoll Rand, 168 F.R.D. 633, 639 (N.D. Ind. 1996)) ("[The bright-line interpretation] makes good sense on several policy grounds: effective cross examination of expert witnesses will be enhanced; the policies underlying the work product doctrine will not be violated; and finally, litigation certainly will be achieved—counsel will know exactly what documents will be subject to disclosure and can react accordingly.").
153. *Id.* at 259.
154. *Id.* at 260.
155. *Id.*
156. *Id.*
157. *Id.*
158. *Id.*
159. *See* Steven S. Anderson & Jonathan M. Palmer, *Work Product Protections for "Dual Purpose" Experts* (Feb. 2005) (unpublished article).
160. 168 F.R.D. 633, 639 (N.D. Ind. 1996).
161. *Id.*
162. 212 F.R.D. 110 (E.D.N.Y. 2002). *See also* Anderson & Palmer, *supra* note 156.
163. *Id.* at 116 ("[A]n attorney controls the information flow to the expert and can, therefore, influence the expert's opinion through his decisions about what to disclose (such as his opinions and mental impressions about the case) and when to do so.").
164. *See generally* FED. R. CIV. P. 26 advisory committee's note (2010).
165. *Id.*
166. *Id.*
167. *Id.* ("The refocus of disclosure on 'facts and data' is meant to limit disclosure to material of a factual nature by excluding theories or mental impressions of counsel. At the same time, the intention is that 'facts or data' be interpreted broadly to require disclosure of any material considered by the expert, from whatever source, that contains factual ingredients. The disclosure obligation extends to any facts or data 'considered' by the expert in forming the opinions to be expressed, not only those relied upon by the expert.").

168. *Id.*
169. *Id.*
170. *Id.* ("The addition of Rule 26(b)(4)(C) is designed to protect counsel's work product and ensure that lawyers may interact with retained experts without fear of exposing those communications to searching discovery. The protection is limited to communications between an expert witness required to provide reports under Rule 26(a)(2)(B) and the attorney for the party on whose behalf the witness will be testifying, including 'preliminary' expert opinions. Protected 'communications' includes those between the party's attorney and assistants of the expert witness.").
171. *Id.*
172. *Id.*
173. *Id.*
174. *Id.*
175. *Id.*
176. Galvin v. Pepe, No. 09-cv-104-PB, 2010 WL 3092640, at *6 (D.N.H. Aug. 5, 2010).
177. *Id.* at *1.
178. *Id.*
179. *Id.*
180. *Id.*
181. *Id.* at *2.
182. *Id.*
183. *Id.* at *6.
184. *Id.* ("The new rules do not apply to cases closed before their effective date and only apply to cases pending on their effective date if their applicability is just and practicable. . . . The proposed rules cannot be construed to apply at this time to govern the outcome of a motion that is currently pending for resolution.").
185. *Id.*
186. Fed. R. Civ. P. 26(a)(1)(B)(2)(C) (2011).
187. No. 08-1304 (FLW), 2011 WL 666056 (D.N.J. Feb. 14, 2011).
188. *Id.* slip op. at *1.
189. *Id.* at *4–5.
190. *Id.* at *5.
191. *Id.* at *7.
192. *Id.* at *10–12.
193. *Id.* at *13.
194. No. CIV S-09-2445 KJM EFB, 2011 WL 2119078 (E.D. Cal. May 26, 2011).
195. *Id.* slip op. at *1.
196. *Id.*
197. *Id.* at *2.
198. *Id.* at *11.
199. *Id.* at *4–7. The court relied heavily on the Advisory Committee reports, especially the May 8, 2009, report, in which the minutes state: "Both the Subcommittee and the Committee concluded that the time has not yet come to extend the protection for attorney expert communications beyond experts required to give an (a)(2)(B) report." *Id.* at *7.
200. *Id.* at *10.
201. *See, e.g.*, B.C.F. Oil Ref., Inc. v. Consol. Edison Co., 171 F.R.D. 57, 61 (S.D.N.Y. 1997).

202. *See, e.g.*, Furniture World, Inc. v. D.A.V. Thrift Stores, Inc., 168 F.R.D. 61 (D.N.M. 1996). *But see* Sara Lee Corp. v. Kraft Foods, Inc., 273 F.R.D. 416, 420–21 (N.D. Ill. 2011) (noting that the 2010 amendments to Rule 26 narrowed the scope of expert discovery, even in the dual expert context).
203. 206 F.R.D. 43 (E.D.N.Y. 2002).
204. *Id.* at 44.
205. *Id.*
206. *Id.*
207. *Id.* at 52.
208. *Id.*
209. *Id.*
210. 171 F.R.D. 57, 61 (S.D.N.Y. 1997).
211. 206 F.R.D. at 54 (quoting *B.C.F. Oil*, 171 F.R.D. at 61).
212. 124 F.R.D. 545 (S.D.N.Y. 1989).
213. 206 F.R.D. at 54.
214. *Id.* (citing *In re* Air Crash, No. 3:98cv2464 (AVC), 2001 U.S. Dist. LEXIS 14334, at *9 (D. Conn. June 4, 2001)).
215. *Id.*
216. 168 F.R.D. 61 (D.N.M. 1996).
217. *Id.* at 62.
218. *Id.* at 63.
219. *Id.*
220. *See, e.g.*, Herman v. Marine Midland Bank, 207 F.R.D. 26, 31 (W.D.N.Y. 2002) (allowing expanded discovery based on the conclusions that there seemed to be a "seamless collaboration" between the consulting and testifying experts).
221. Trigon Ins. Co. v. United States, 204 F.R.D. 277, 280 (E.D. Va. 2001).
222. No. 97 Civ. 6124 (JGK) (THK), 2002 U.S. Dist. LEXIS 111 (S.D.N.Y. Jan. 7, 2002).
223. *Id.* at *11.
224. *Id.*
225. *Id.* at *18–22.
226. *Id.* at *16.
227. *Id.* at *20–21.
228. *Id.* at *21.
229. *Id.* at *21–22.
230. *Id.*
231. Sara Lee Corp. v. Kraft Foods, Inc., 273 F.R.D. 416 (N.D. Ill. 2011).
232. *Id.* at 417.
233. *Id.* at 418.
234. *Id.*
235. *Id.* at 420.
236. *Id.*
237. *Id.* at 421.
238. Fed. R. Civ. P. 26 advisory committee's note (2010).
239. Fed. R. Civ. P. 26(b)(4)(C) (2010).
240. Fed. R. Civ. P. 26(b)(4)(A) ("A party may depose any person who has been identified as an expert whose opinions may be presented at trial. If Rule 26(a)(2)(B) requires a report from the expert, the deposition may be conducted only after the report is provided.").
241. *Id.*

242. James W. Moore, Moore's Federal Practice § 26.80(1)(a) (3d ed. 2007) (Professor Moore cites to *House v. Combined Insurance Co. of America*, 168 F.R.D. 238 (N.D. Iowa 1996), and *CP Kelco U.S. Inc. v. Pharmacia Corp.*, 213 F.R.D. 176 (D. Del. 2003).). *See also* Ferguson v. Michael Foods, Inc., 189 F.R.D. 176 (D. Del. 2003); Rubel v. Eli Lilly & Co., 160 F.R.D. 458, 460 (S.D.N.Y. 1995).
243. *See, e.g.*, Callaway Golf Co. v. Dunlop Slazenger Grp. Ams., Inc., No. A. 01-669 (MPT), 2002 WL 1906628 (D. Del. Aug. 14, 2002); NetJumper Software, L.L.C. v. Google, Inc., No. M19-138, 04-70366CV, 2005 WL 3046271 (S.D.N.Y. Nov. 10, 2005); Ross v. Burlington N. R.R. Co, 136 F.R.D. 638 (N.D. Ill. 1991); *In re* Estate of Manship, 240 F.R.D. 229 (M.D. La. 2006); Green v. Nygard, 143 P.3d 393 (Ariz. 2006).
244. *See, e.g.*, Hoover v. U.S. Dep't of the Interior, 611 F.2d 1132, 1142 (5th Cir. 1980) ("The primary purpose of [Rule 26(b)(4)(B)'s required disclosures about experts to be called at trial] is to permit the opposing party to prepare for an effective cross-examination.").
245. *See* United States v. Kovel, 296 F.2d 918, 922 (2d Cir. 1961); *In re* Grand Jury Subpoenas, 179 F. Supp. 2d 270, 283 (S.D.N.Y. 2001); United States v. El Paso Co., 682 F.2d 530, 541 (5th Cir. 1982); *In re* Copper Mkt. Antitrust Litig., 200 F.R.D. 213, 217 (S.D.N.Y. 2001); Exp.-Imp. Bank of U.S. v. Asia Pulp & Paper Co., 232 F.R.D. 103, 113 (S.D.N.Y. 2005); Andritz, Sprout-Bauer, Inc. v. Beazer E., Inc., 174 F.R.D. 609, 632 (M.D. Pa. 1997); United States v. Alvarez, 519 F.2d 1036, 1045–46 (3d Cir. 1975); United States v. Cote, 456 F.2d 142, 144 (8th Cir. 1972). *See also, e.g.*, Bradley v. Cooper Tire & Rubber Co., No. 07-mc-001-JM, 2007 WL 148764 (D.N.H. Jan. 11, 2007).
246. 213 F.R.D. 176 (D. Del. 2003).
247. *Id.* at 177.
248. *Id.*
249. *Id.*
250. *Id.*
251. *Id.*
252. *Id.*
253. *Id.* at 178.
254. *Id.*
255. *Id.*
256. *Id.* The 1993 Advisory Committee Notes to Rule 26 provide that a litigant may not "argue that materials furnished to their experts to be used in forming their opinions—whether or not ultimately relied upon by the expert—are privileged or otherwise protected from disclosure when such persons are testifying or being deposed."
257. 213 F.R.D. at 179.
258. *Id.*
259. *Id.*
260. *Id.* (Stating in a footnote that "[t]here is authority indicating that disclosure of privileged information can, in certain circumstances, create a limited waiver or be not considered a waiver at all." *Cf. Upjohn*, 449 U.S. at 387).
261. *Id.* (citing United States v. Krasnov, 143 F. Supp. 184, 191 (E.D. Pa. 1956) ("The privilege once waived can not be regained."); Oppenheimer v. United States, 355 U.S. 5 (1951) (discussing the Fifth Amendment privilege against self-incrimination, the Court noted that, having waived the privilege, one cannot

later assert it: "To uphold a claim of privilege in this case would open the way to distortion of facts permitting a witness to select any stopping place in the testimony."). *See also In re* G-I Holdings Inc., 218 F.R.D. 428, 432 (D.N.J. 2003) ("Once a party waives the attorney client privilege, it relinquishes the privilege for all purposes and circumstances thereafter.").

262. *Id.*
263. *Id.* (citing FED. R. CIV. P. 26(b)(4)(A) and advisory committee's note).
264. 213 F.R.D. at 179 (citing United States v. Rylander, 460 U.S. 752, 758, 75 (1983)).
265. *Id.*
266. FED. R. CIV. P. 26(b)(4)(D) provides:

> A party may, through interrogatories or by deposition, discover facts known, or opinions held, by an expert who has been retained or specially employed by another party in anticipation of litigation or preparation for trial and who is not expected to be called as a witness at trial, only as provided in Rule 35(b) or upon a showing of exceptional circumstances under which it is impracticable for the party seeking discovery to obtain facts or opinions on the same subject by other means.

267. *See* United States v. Nobles, 422 U.S. 225, 238 (1975). *See also* Imwinkelried, *supra* note 2, at 23.
268. *See, e.g.*, Emp'r's Reinsurance Corp. v. Clarendon Nat'l Ins. Co., 213 F.R.D. 422, 426 (D. Kan. 2003) (stating that the rule is also designed to promote fairness by preventing access to another party's diligent trial preparation).
269. No. A. 01-669 (MPT), 2002 WL 1906628 (D. Del. Aug. 14, 2002).
270. 2002 WL 1906628, at *1.
271. No. M19-138, 04-70366CV, 2005 WL 3046271 (S.D.N.Y. Nov. 10, 2005).
272. *Callaway*, 2002 WL 1906628, at *1.
273. *Id.*
274. *Id.*
275. *Id.*
276. 136 F.R.D. 638 (N.D. Ill. 1991).
277. No. C-3-95-480, 1997 WL 1764760 (S.D. Ohio Feb. 19, 1997).
278. *Callaway*, 2002 WL 1906628, at *2 (discussing *Ross*, 136 F.R.D. at 638).
279. *Id.*
280. *Id.* (discussing *Dayton-Phx.*, 1997 WL 1764760, at *1).
281. *Id.*
282. 96 F.R.D. 179 (D. Ariz. 1982).
283. 132 F.R.D. 437 (E.D. La. 1990).
284. 196 F. Supp. 2d 1023 (E.D. Cal. 2002).
285. *Callaway*, 2002 WL 1906628, at *2–3.
286. *Id.* at *3.
287. No. M-19-138, 04-70366CV, 2005 WL 3046271 (S.D.N.Y. Nov. 10, 2005).
288. *Id.* at *2.
289. *Id.* at *1.
290. *Id.*
291. *Id.*
292. *Id.*
293. *Id.* at *3.

294. *Id.* at *2–3 (analyzing to the circumstances present in Ross v. Burlington N. R.R. Co., 136 F.R.D. 638 (N.D. Ill. 1991), and Mantolete v. Bolger, 96 F.R.D. 179 (D. Ariz. 1982), among other cases including *Callaway*, 2002 WL 1906628, Durflinger v. Artiles, 727 F.2d 888 (10th Cir. 1984), and Dayton-Phx. Grp. v. Gen. Motors Corp., 1997 WL 1764760 (S.D. Ohio Feb. 19, 1997)).
295. *Id.* at *3.
296. *Id.*
297. *Id.*
298. *Id.*
299. 132 F.R.D. at 440.
300. 196 F. Supp. 2d at 1042–46.
301. Don Zupanec, *Testifying Expert—Redesignation—Deposition*, 22 No. 5 FED. LITIG. 9 (May 2007) ("If a testifying expert has been redesignated a consulting expert, a party seeking to take the person's deposition should assume it will be necessary to satisfy Rule 26(b)(4)(B)'s 'exceptional circumstances' requirement.").
302. *Id.*

TABLE OF CASES

INDEX

Q

R